MOON HANDBOOKS

ARIZONA

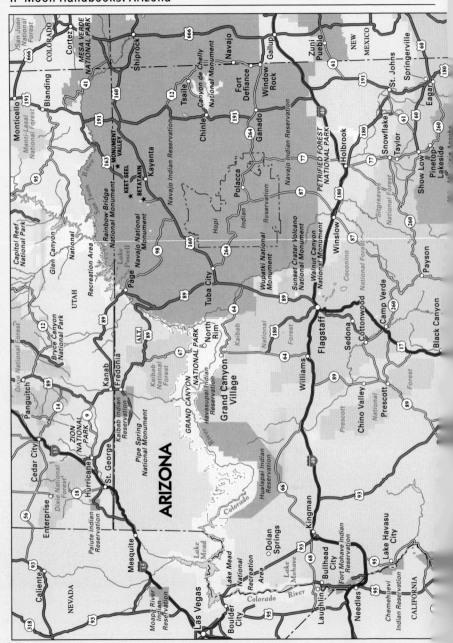

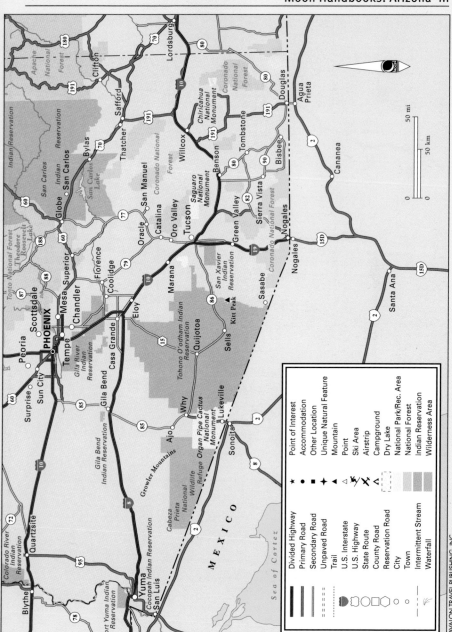

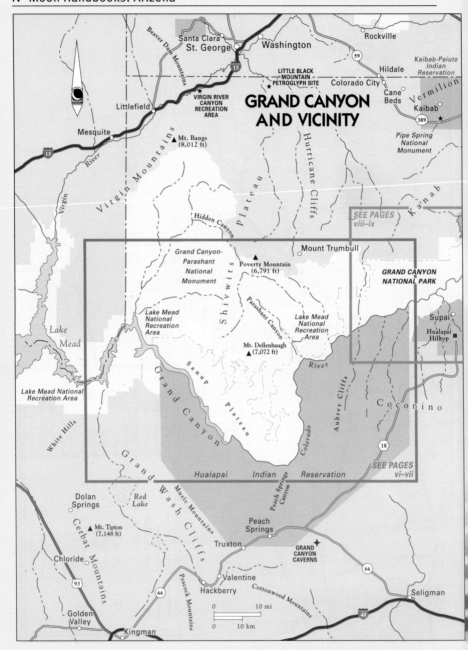

GRAND CANYON AND VICINITY

Rockville

Santa Clara
St. George

Washington

Beaver Dam Mountains

59

Hildale

Kaibab-Paiute Indian Reservation

LITTLE BLACK
MOUNTAIN
PETROGLYPH SITE

Colorado City

Cane Beds

Kaibab

389

Vermilion

VIRGIN RIVER
CANYON
RECREATION
AREA

Littlefield

Pipe Spring
National
Monument

Mesquite

15

Virgin Mountains

▲ Mt. Bangs
(8,012 ft)

Virgin River

Hurricane Cliffs

Plateau

Kanab

Hidden Canyon

SEE PAGES
viii–ix

Mount Trumbull ▲

Grand Canyon-
Parashant
National
Monument

Poverty Mountain
(6,791 ft) ▲

GRAND CANYON
NATIONAL PARK

Shivwits

Parashant Canyon

Supai ●

Hualapai
Hilltop ■

Lake Mead
National
Recreation
Area

Lake Mead
National
Recreation
Area

Lake
Mead

Sanup Plateau

Mt. Dellenbaugh
(7,072 ft) ▲

River

Colorado

Aubrey Cliffs

Coconino

Lake Mead National
Recreation Area

Grand Canyon

White Hills

Grand Wash Cliffs

18

SEE PAGES
vi–vii

Dolan
Springs

Red
Lake

Music Mountains

Hualapai   Indian   Reservation

Peach Springs Canyon

Mt. Tipton
(7,148 ft) ▲

Cerbat Mountains

Peach
Springs

GRAND
CANYON
CAVERNS

Chloride

Truxton

93

66

66

40

Seligman

Valentine

Hackberry

Cottonwood Mountains

Golden
Valley

Peacock Mountains

Kingman

0   10 mi

0   10 km

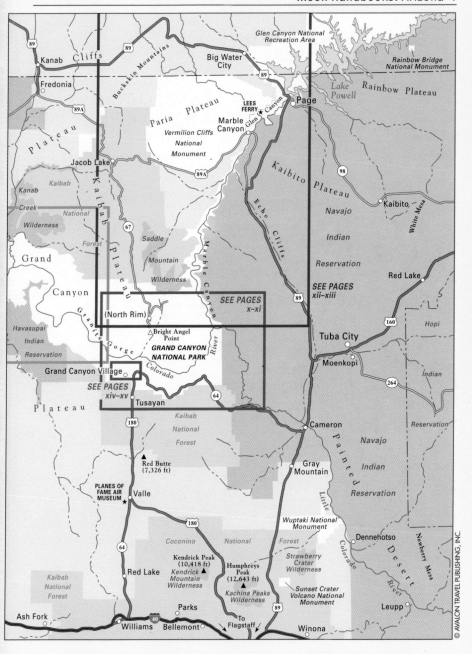

Kanab

Cliffs

89

89

Fredonia

89A

Plateau

Kaibab

Plateau

Jacob Lake

Kaibab

Creek

National

Wilderness

Forest

Kanab

Grand

Canyon

Granite Gorge

Havasupai

Indian

Reservation

Grand Canyon Village

Plateau

SEE PAGES
xiv–xv

Tusayan

Plateau

180

Buckskin Mountains

Paria

Plateau

Vermilion Cliffs
National
Monument

67

Saddle

Mountain

Wilderness

89A

(North Rim)

△Bright Angel
Point

GRAND CANYON
NATIONAL PARK

64

Big Water
City

LEES
FERRY
★

Marble
Canyon

Glen Canyon

Glen Canyon National
Recreation Area

89

Page

Marble

Canyon

River

SEE PAGES
x–xi

Colorado

Kaibab

National

Forest

Red Butte
(7,326 ft)

PLANES OF
FAME AIR
MUSEUM
★

Valle

64

180

Red Lake

Kaibab

National

Forest

Ash Fork

Williams

40

Bellemont

Parks

Coconino

National

Kendrick Peak
(10,418 ft)
Kendrick ▲
Mountain
Wilderness

Humphreys
Peak
(12,643 ft)

Kachina Peaks
Wilderness

To
Flagstaff

89

Winona

Echo

Cliffs

89

Lake
Powell

Rainbow Plateau

Rainbow Bridge
National Monument

98

Kaibito

Plateau

White Mesa

Navajo

Indian

Reservation

Kaibito

Red Lake

160

Tuba City

Moenkopi

264

Cameron

Gray
Mountain

Wuptaki National
Monument

Strawberry
Crater
Wilderness

Forest

Sunset Crater
Volcano National
Monument

Little

Colorado

River

Painted

Desert

Hopi

Indian

Reservation

Navajo

Indian

Reservation

Dennehotso

Newberry Mesa

Leupp

SEE PAGES
xii–xiii

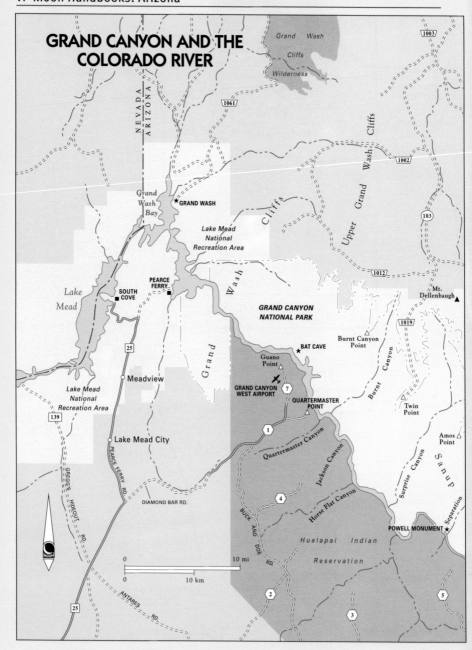

GRAND CANYON AND THE COLORADO RIVER

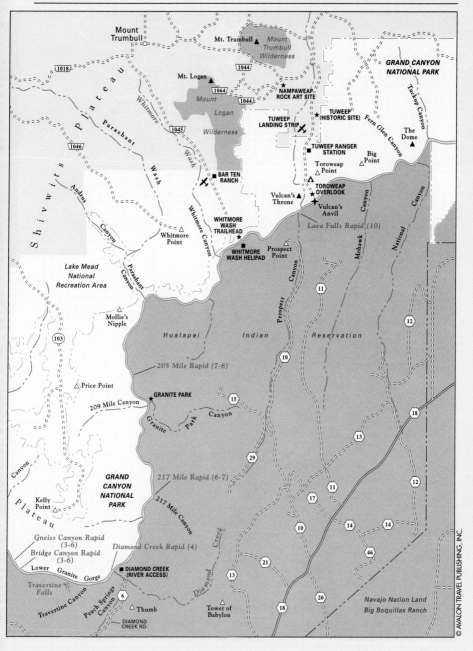

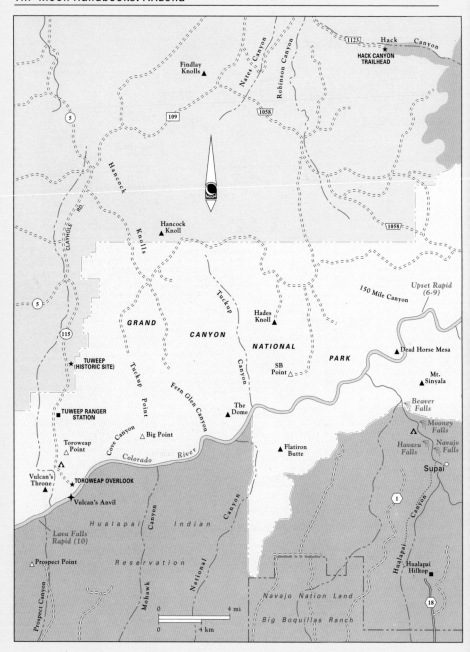

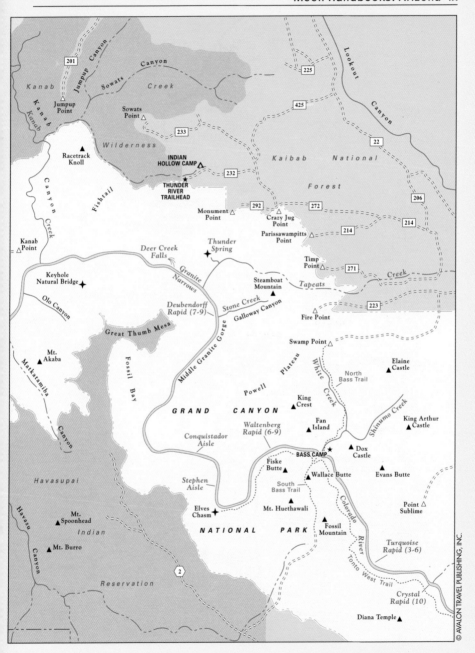

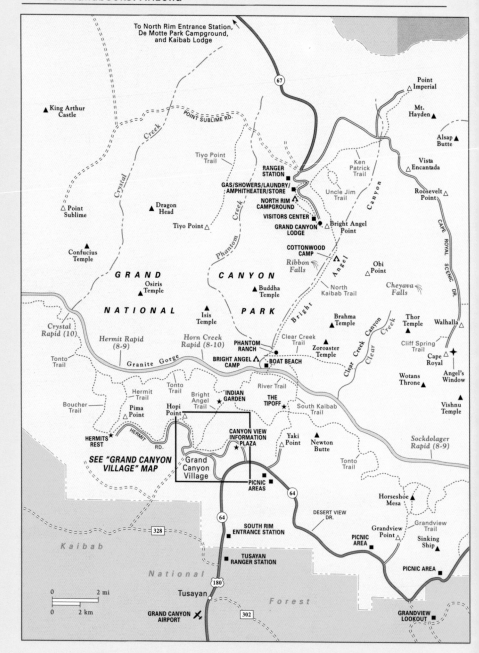

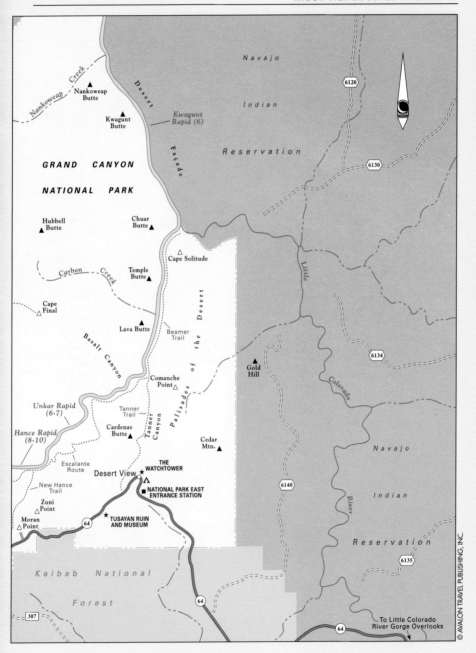

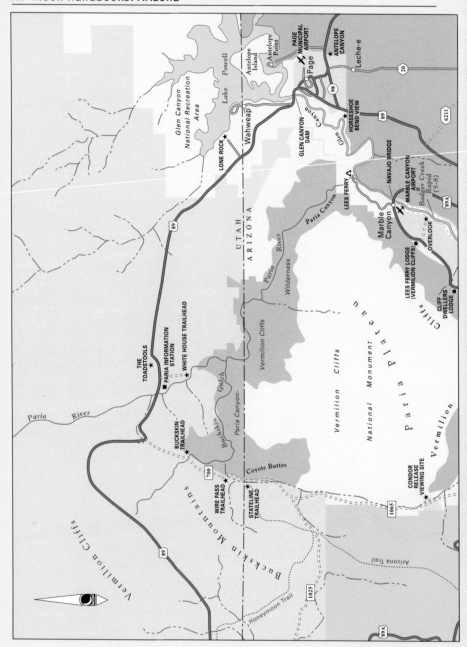

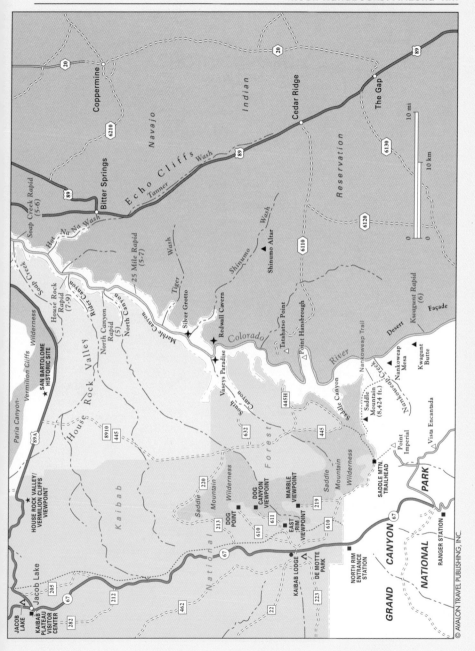

© AVALON TRAVEL PUBLISHING, INC.

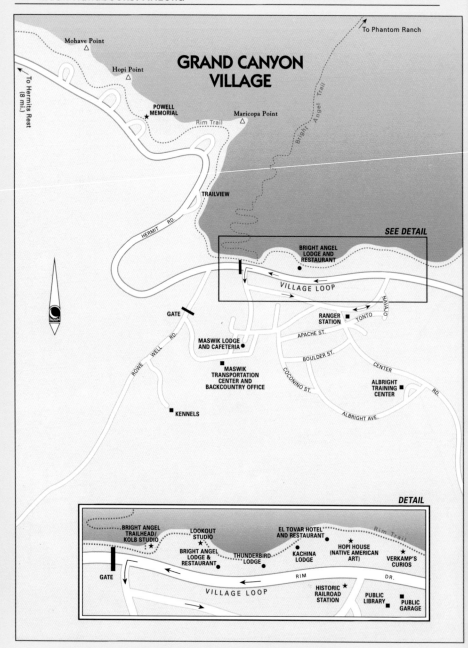

GRAND CANYON VILLAGE

To Phantom Ranch

Mohave Point △

Hopi Point △

To Hermits Rest (8 mi.)

POWELL MEMORIAL ★

Maricopa Point △

Rim Trail

Bright Angel Trail

TRAILVIEW

HERMIT RD.

SEE DETAIL

BRIGHT ANGEL LODGE AND RESTAURANT ●

VILLAGE LOOP

GATE ▬

ROWE WELL RD.

RANGER STATION ■

NAVAJO

TONTO

MASWIK LODGE AND CAFETERIA ●

APACHE ST.

MASWIK TRANSPORTATION CENTER AND BACKCOUNTRY OFFICE ■

BOULDER ST.

COCONINO ST.

CENTER

ALBRIGHT TRAINING CENTER ■

RD.

KENNELS ■

ALBRIGHT AVE.

MOON

DETAIL

BRIGHT ANGEL TRAILHEAD/ KOLB STUDIO ★

LOOKOUT STUDIO ★

EL TOVAR HOTEL AND RESTAURANT ●

Rim Trail

BRIGHT ANGEL LODGE & RESTAURANT ●

THUNDERBIRD LODGE ●

KACHINA LODGE ●

HOPI HOUSE (NATIVE AMERICAN ART) ★

VERKAMP'S CURIOS ★

GATE ▬

VILLAGE LOOP

RIM

DR.

HISTORIC RAILROAD STATION ★

PUBLIC LIBRARY ■

PUBLIC GARAGE ■

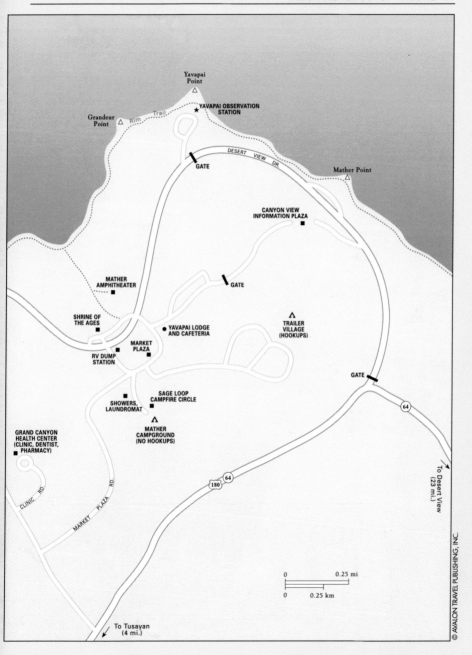

Yavapai
Point

Grandeur
Point

Rim   Trail

YAVAPAI OBSERVATION
STATION

DESERT   VIEW   DR

GATE

Mather Point

CANYON VIEW
INFORMATION PLAZA

GATE

MATHER
AMPHITHEATER

SHRINE OF
THE AGES

YAVAPAI LODGE
AND CAFETERIA

TRAILER
VILLAGE
(HOOKUPS)

MARKET
PLAZA

RV DUMP
STATION

GATE

64

SAGE LOOP
CAMPFIRE CIRCLE

SHOWERS,
LAUNDROMAT

MATHER
CAMPGROUND
(NO HOOKUPS)

GRAND CANYON
HEALTH CENTER
(CLINIC, DENTIST,
PHARMACY)

CLINIC   RD.

MARKET   PLAZA   RD.

180   64

To Desert
View
(23 mi.)

0   0.25 mi

0   0.25 km

To Tusayan
(4 mi.)

© AVALON TRAVEL PUBLISHING, INC.

Monument Valley

MOON HANDBOOKS
ARIZONA

EIGHTH EDITION

BILL WEIR

AVALON
TRAVEL

Moon Handbooks: Arizona
EIGHTH EDITION

Bill Weir

Published by
Avalon Travel Publishing
1400 65th Street, Suite 250
Emeryville, CA 94608, USA
Avalon Travel Publishing is a division of
Avalon Publishing Group, Inc.

Printing History
1st edition—1986
8th edition—April 2002
5 4 3 2

Please send all comments, corrections,
additions, amendments, and critiques to:

Moon Handbooks: Arizona
AVALON TRAVEL PUBLISHING
1400 65TH STREET, SUITE 250
EMERYVILLE, CA 94608, USA
email: atpfeedback@avalonpub.com
website: www.travelmatters.com

ISBN: 1-56691-392-6
ISSN: 1538-120X

Editor: Angelique S. Clarke
Series Manager: Erin Van Rheenen
Copy Editor: Gina Wilson Birtcil
Graphics Coordinator: Susan Mira Snyder
Production: Jacob Goolkasian, Amber Pirker
Map Editors: Naomi Adler Dancis, Olivia Solis
Cartographers: Mike Morgenfeld, Chris Folks, Allen Leech, Suzanne Service
Indexer: Vera Gross

Front cover photo © John Elk III

Distributed by Publishers Group West

Printed in China through Colorcraft Ltd., Hong Kong

ABOUT THE AUTHOR
Bill Weir

© DONALD DEVINE

Back in school, Bill Weir always figured he'd settle down to a career job and live happily ever after. Then he discovered traveling. After graduating with a B.A. degree in physics from Berea College in 1972, Bill found employment as an electronic technician, but the short vacation breaks didn't provide enough time for the trips he dreamed of.

So in 1976 he took off on his trusty bicycle, Bessie, riding across the United States with Bikecentennial '76. The following year he took off on an even longer bicycle trip—from Alaska to Baja California. Then came the ultimate journey—a bicycle cruise around the world. When Bill returned home to Arizona, he set to work researching and writing *Moon Handbooks: Arizona*.

Bill continues to explore Arizona and beyond, always discovering new places and learning more about the old. During 1994, he visited the amazing cultures and landscapes of Tibet and Nepal. Then, in the following year, he dusted off ol' Bessie the Bicycle for the final leg of the round-the-world trip started 19 years ago. Poor Bessie, however, was put out to pasture, so Bill got his new "Bessie Too the Bicycle" and explored more of the Himalayas—riding from Bangladesh to Nepal via Sikkim—and more of Europe, pedaling north from Greece until the road ran out at Nordkapp in the Norwegian arctic. Bill's most recent cycling adventure crossed the "Rooftop of the World" on a ride from Lhasa in Tibet to Katmandu in Nepal, then west across the Himalayan foothills of India and into northern Pakistan, ending in the alpine valley of Swat.

Visit **www.arizonahandbook.com** for the latest updates, web links, photo galleries, and booklists. You'll also find news and photos of Bill's latest cycling and trekking adventures.

Contents

WESTERN GRAND CANYON AND THE ARIZONA STRIP

Abbreviations

4WD—four-wheel drive
a/c—air conditioning
ATV—all-terrain vehicle
AZ—Arizona
B&B—bed and breakfast
BLM—Bureau of Land Management
ca.—circa
CCC—Civilian Conservation Corps
cfs—cubic feet per second
d—double

elev.—elevation
F—Fahrenheit
hp—horsepower
mph—miles per hour
NV—Nevada
RV—recreational vehicle
s—single
U.S.—United States
UT—Utah

Maps

MAP SYMBOLS

═══ Divided Highway	☐ County or Forest Road	⚡ Ski Area
═══ Primary Road	★ Point of Interest	✗ Airfield/Airstrip
─── Secondary Road	• Accommodation	♠ State Park
------- Trail	▾ Restaurant/Bar	⋀ Campground
⊢––⊢ Railroad	▪ Other Location	⫯ Waterfall
⬯ U.S. Interstate	✛ Unique Natural Feature	▲ Mountain
⬯ U.S. Highway	⊙ State Capital	△ Point
◯ State Highway	○ City	⌿ Golf Course
◯ Reservation Road	○ Town	

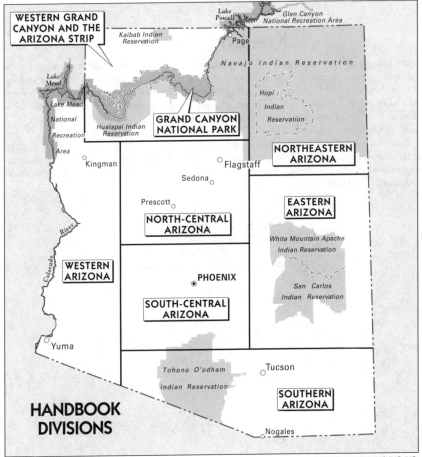

WESTERN GRAND
CANYON AND THE
ARIZONA STRIP

Lake
Powell

Glen Canyon
National Recreation Area

Kaibab Indian
Reservation

Page

Navajo Indian Reservation

Lake
Mead

Hopi

Indian

Lake Mead

National

Reservation

Recreation

GRAND CANYON
NATIONAL PARK

NORTHEASTERN
ARIZONA

Area

Hualapai Indian
Reservation

Kingman

Flagstaff

Sedona

EASTERN
ARIZONA

Prescott

NORTH-CENTRAL
ARIZONA

White Mountain Apache
Indian Reservation

River

WESTERN
ARIZONA

PHOENIX

San Carlos
Indian Reservation

Colorado

SOUTH-CENTRAL
ARIZONA

Yuma

Tohono O'odham

Tucson

Indian Reservation

HANDBOOK
DIVISIONS

SOUTHERN
ARIZONA

Nogales

Keeping Current

Nothing stays the same, it seems. Although this guidebook has been carefully researched, Arizona will continue to grow and change. New sights and services will open while others change hands or close. Your comments and ideas on making *Moon Handbooks: Arizona* more useful to other readers will be highly valued. If you find something new, discontinued, or changed, please let me know so that the information can be included in the next printing or edition. You can reach me directly through www.arizonahandbook.com or c/o Avalon Travel Publishing.

Perhaps a map or worthwhile place to visit has been overlooked; please send an email, postcard, or letter with updates. If you have a question about an order or other business transaction, always contact Avalon Travel Publishing directly—as I may be off at some remote monastery or mountain!

Address your letters to:

Moon Handbooks: Arizona
Avalon Travel Publishing
1400 65th Street, Suite 250
Emeryville, CA 94608 USA
email: atpfeedback@avalonpub.com

Introduction

The Land

Few states feature such spectacular and varied terrain as Arizona. Most of the early travelers who crossed this land kept to the south, traversing the hot desert valleys and plains, and this region forms the popular image of Arizona even today. Yet the northern and eastern parts of the state hold extensive coniferous forests and rushing mountain streams. Volcanic activity, uplift, faulting, and erosion have formed dozens of mountain ranges and canyons. The Grand Canyon, one of the world's greatest natural wonders, rates at the top of most visitors' lists, but many other beautiful and intriguing places remain for you to discover. *Moon Handbooks: Arizona* will help you find them. Wilderness areas, early Spanish sites, Native American reservations, old mining towns, bright city lights—they're all here. This book also provides practical information for every price range, including that of the oft-neglected low-budget traveler.

GEOGRAPHY

Though geologically complex, the land surface of Arizona can be envisioned as tilting slightly downward to the southwest. More than 90 percent of the state's drainage flows into the southwest corner via the Colorado River and its tributaries. By the time the river enters Mexico, it has descended to an elevation of only 70 feet. Mountain ranges rise in nearly every part of Arizona, but they achieve their greatest heights in the north-central and eastern sections. Humphrey's Peak, part of the San Francisco Peaks near Flagstaff, crowns the state at 12,633 feet. Geographers divide Arizona

© BILL WEIR

view down Hack Canyon

into the high Colorado Plateau Province of the north and the Basin and Range Province of the rest of the state. Average elevation statewide is about 4,000 feet. Measuring 335 miles wide and 390 miles long, Arizona is the sixth-largest state in the country.

Colorado Plateau

This giant uplifted landmass in northern Arizona also extends across much of adjacent Utah, Colorado, and New Mexico. Rivers have cut deeply into the plateau, forming the Grand Canyon of the Colorado and other vast gorges. Volcanos have broken through the surface and left hundreds of cinder cones, such as multi-colored Sunset Crater, and larger volcanic complexes, such as the San Francisco Peaks. The most recent burst of volcanic activity in Arizona took place at Sunset Crater and lasted until about 800 years ago. Most elevations on the plateau are between 5,000 and 8,000 feet. Sheer cliffs of the Mogollon (MUGGY-own) Rim drop to the desert, marking the plateau's south boundary. To the west, the plateau ends at Grand Wash Cliffs.

Basin and Range Province

Many ranges of fault-block mountains, formed by the faulting and tilting of the earth's crust, poke through the desert plains of western, central, eastern, and southern Arizona. Several peaks rise above 9,000 feet, creating biological islands inhabited by cool-climate animals and plants. Tucson-area residents, for example, can leave the Sonoran Desert and within an hour reach the cool fir and aspen forests of Mt. Lemmon.

CLIMATE

During any season, some part of Arizona enjoys near-perfect weather. Sunny skies and low humidity prevail over the entire state most of the time. Average winter temperatures range around 50°F in the low desert and 20–40°F in the mountains and high plateaus. Desert dwellers endure average temperatures of 80–100°F in summer, while high-country residents enjoy averages of 70–80°F. Parker, along the Colorado River, attained 127°F on July 7, 1905—the highest reading ever recorded in the state. Even on a normal summer day in the low desert, you can expect highs in the low 100°F. Desert areas can experience swings of 40°F between day and night due to the dry air and the lack of moderating forests.

Precipitation

Rain and snowfall correspond roughly to elevation: The southwest corner receives less than five inches of precipitation annually, while the higher mountains and the Mogollon Rim get about 25 inches. Most falls either in winter as gentle rains and snow, or in summer as widely scattered thundershowers. Winter moisture comes mostly Dec.–March, revitalizing the desert; brilliant wildflower displays appear after a good wet season. Summer afternoon thunderclouds billow in towering formations from about mid-July to mid-September. The storms, though producing heavy rains, tend to be localized in areas fewer than three miles across. Summer thundershowers make up 60–70 percent of the annual precipitation in the low desert and about 45 percent on the Colorado Plateau.

Storm Hazards

Rainwater runs quickly off the rocky desert surfaces and into gullies and canyons. **Flash floods** can form and sweep away anything in their paths, including boulders, cars, and campsites. Take care not to camp or park in potential flash-flood areas. If you come to a section of flooded roadway, a common occurrence on desert roads after storms, just wait until the water goes down—usually within an hour or so. Summer **lightning** causes forest and brush fires, and it poses a danger to hikers foolish enough to climb mountains when storms threaten.

Flora and Fauna

LIFE ZONES

A wide variety of plant and animal life finds homes within Arizona's great range of elevations—more than 12,000 feet. Sensitive and endangered plant species receive protection from a state law that prohibits collecting or destroying most cacti and wildflowers without a permit from the landowner. Cacti need time to grow—a saguaro takes 50 years to mature—and cannot survive large-scale collecting. Some plants, such as the senita cactus and elephant tree, grow only in southern Arizona and Mexico.

Migratory birds often stop by the mountains and wetlands. The colorful parrot-like trogon bird and more than a dozen species of hummingbirds fly up from Mexico to spend their summers in the mountains of southeastern Arizona. Canadian geese and other northern waterfowl settle in for the winter on rivers and lakes in the low desert.

To help simplify and understand the different environments of Arizona, some scientists use the Merriam system of life zones. Because plants rely on rainfall, which is determined largely by elevation, each life zone can be expected to occur within a certain range of elevations. The elevation ranges are not exact—south-facing mountain slopes receive more sun and lose more moisture to evaporation than north-facing slopes at the same level. Canyons and unusual rainfall patterns can also play havoc with classifications. Yet the life zones do provide a general idea of what kind of vegetation and animal life you can expect when traveling through the state.

Lower Sonoran Zone

Arizona's famed desert country of arid plains, barren mountains, and stately saguaro cacti covers about one-third of the state. The southern and western sections under 4,500 feet lie within this zone. The big cities and most of the state's population are here, too. With irrigation, farmers find the land good for growing vegetables, citrus, and cotton. Cacti thrive: you'll see the prickly pear, cholla, and barrel, as well as the giant saguaro—its white blossom is the state flower. Desert shrubs and small trees include the paloverde, ocotillo, creosote, mesquite, and ironwood. Flowering plants tend to bloom after either winter rains (the Sonoran or Mexican type) or summer showers (the Mojave or Californian type).

Most desert animals retreat to dens or burrows during the heat of the day, when ground temperatures can reach 150°F. Look for wildlife in early morning, evening, or at night: kangaroo rats, squirrels, mice, desert cottontail, black-tailed and antelope jackrabbits, spotted and striped skunks, gray and kit foxes, ringtail, javelina, bighorn sheep, coyote, and the extremely shy mountain lion. Common birds include the cactus wren (state bird of Arizona), Gambel's quail, Gila woodpecker, roadrunner, hawks, eagles, owls, and common raven. Sidewinder and western diamondback rattlesnakes are occasionally seen. The rare Gila monster, identified by a bead-like skin with black and yellow patterns, is the only poisonous lizard in the United States; it's slow and nonaggressive but has powerful jaws. Also watch out for poisonous invertebrates, especially the small slender scorpion—its sting is dangerous and can be fatal to children. Spiders and centipedes can also inflict painful bites. Careful campers check for unwanted guests in shoes and other items left outside.

Upper Sonoran Zone

This zone encompasses 4,500- to 6,500-foot elevations in central Arizona and in widely scattered areas throughout the rest of the state. Enough rain falls here to support grasslands or stunted woodlands of juniper, pinyon pine, and oak. Chaparral-type vegetation grows here too, forming a nearly impenetrable thicket of manzanita and other bushes. Many of the animals found in the Lower Sonoran Zone live here as well. You might also see black bear, desert mule deer, white-tailed deer, and the antelope-like pronghorn. Rattlesnakes and other reptiles like this zone best.

INTRODUCTION

STRANGE CREATURES OF THE DESERT

Solpugid (sun spider)

This feisty predator (*Eremobates* spp.) has the largest jaws relative to its size of any animal in the world. Only about two inches long, the solpugid moves fast—its prey has little chance of escaping. The two tiny black eyes atop its head provide poor vision, so this arthropod navigates mostly by waving a pair of sticky arms, called pedipalps, in front. You're not likely to see the hairy, sand-colored beast because it's shy and often hunts at night; dusk is the best time to spot one. They live a solitary life, coming together only to mate. The male excretes seminal fluid on the ground, then transfers it with his pedipalps to the female, who buries her 50–200 eggs in the ground. She stays with the hatchlings, feeding them, until they're ready to fend for themselves. The solpugid doesn't have venom, but shouldn't be handled on account of the powerful jaws. It's beneficial to us because it keeps down populations of ticks, mites, and other harmful arthropods.

Vinegaroon (whip scorpion)

The sharp claws and curved tail of this dark-brown to black arthropod (order Uropygi) resemble those of a scorpion, but the creature lacks any means to inject venom. Instead, for defense, it can aim its whiplike tail with great accuracy and squirt concentrated acetic acid (vinegar) with a small amount of caprylic acid onto a predator. Caprylic acid enables the acetic acid to pass through the hard outer skin of other arthropods. The vinegaroon comes in about 100 species. Two eyes on the front of its head are supplemented by three or four pairs of eyes to the sides. The slender front pair of legs are feelers to navigate and to search out grasshoppers and other prey. Males secrete a sperm sac, which they may transfer to the female. The mother stays with her sac of up to 35 eggs until the offspring hatch, then carries them until they've grown large enough to survive on their own. Vinegaroons are shy and nocturnal, so you'll be lucky to see one. If sprayed, wash or rinse thoroughly with water.

Hercules beetle (rhinoceros or horned beetle)

The Hercules (*Dynastes granti*) has the largest size—as long as three inches—of Arizona's horned beetles.

The male brandishes two splendid black horns, one curving up from his prothorax (section behind the head) and the other downward from his head. The beetle with the biggest horns usually gets the females, though males rarely use the horns to do battle. The beautifully polished head and forewings are gray with brown spots and lines. When threatened, the beetle will squirt a brown substance from its abdomen and fly off with a noisy buzz.

Tarantula

About 30 species of these gentle giants (*Aphonopelma* spp., *Dugesiella* spp.) inhabit Arizona's deserts. Adults have a leg span of 2–4 inches, dense fur on the legs and abdomen, and a light- to dark-brown color. They live in burrows, logs, or under debris, coming out at night to dine on small insects and spiders. Females stay close to home their entire lives—up to 25 years. The males leave their burrows upon reaching sexual maturity at about 10 years, then wander in search of a mate; usually in June through August; this is when you're most likely to see tarantulas. The males die soon after mating; sometimes they're eaten by a female. Females stay with their egg sac for 6–7 weeks until the babies hatch; about a week later the youngsters leave their mother's burrow. Both ends of the spider can be hazardous to predators. The tarantula may rear up on its hind legs and bare its fangs, or stand on its front legs and use the other legs to hurl a cloud of hairs off the abdomen; the hairs may be barbed or poisonous. Enemies include some birds, lizards, snakes, and a wasp—the tarantula hawk—that paralyzes the spider and lays eggs to hatch and feed on the body. Bites, rare in humans, should be allowed to bleed for a few minutes, then cleaned. The irritating hairs can be removed with tape.

tarantula

LOUISE FOOTE

Transition Zone

The sweet-smelling ponderosa pines grow in this zone, at 6,500–8,000 feet, where much of the winter's precipitation comes as snow. Ponderosas cover many parts of the state, but their greatest expanse—the largest in the country—lies along the southern Colorado Plateau, from Williams in north-central Arizona eastward into New Mexico. Gambel oak, junipers, and Douglas fir commonly grow among the ponderosas.

Squirrels and chipmunks rely on the pine cones for food; other animal residents here include desert cottontail, black-tailed jackrabbit, spotted and striped skunks, red fox, coyote, mule deer, white-tailed deer, elk, black bear, and mountain lion. Wild turkey live in the woods, along with the Steller's jay, screech owl, hummingbirds, juncos, and common raven. Most of the snakes—gopher, hognosed, and garter—are harmless, but you might also run across a western diamondback rattler.

Canadian Zone

Douglas firs dominate the cool, wet forests between 8,000 and 9,500 feet, mixed with Engelmann and blue spruce, white and subalpine fir, and quaking aspen. Little sunlight penetrates the dense forests, where the trees function as their own windbreak. Grasses and wildflowers grow in lush meadows amid the forests. You'll find Canadian Zone forests on the Kaibab Plateau of the Grand Canyon's North Rim, the San Francisco Peaks, the White Mountains, and other high peaks. Look and listen for squirrels as they busily gather cones for the long winter. Deer and elk graze in this zone, but rarely higher.

Hudsonian Zone

Strong winds and a growing season of less than 120 days prevent trees from reaching their full size at elevations from 9,500 to 11,500 feet. Forests here receive twice as much snow as their neighbors in the Canadian Zone just below. Often gnarled and twisted, the dominant species are Engelmann and blue spruce, subalpine and corkbark fir, and bristlecone pine. This zone appears in Arizona only atop the highest mountains.

On a bright summer day, the trees, grasses, and tiny flowering alpine plants buzz with insects, rodents, and visiting birds. Come winter, most animals move to lower and more protected areas.

Alpine Zone

In Arizona, only the San Francisco Peaks exhibit this zone, which lies above about 11,500 feet, the upper limit of tree growth. Freezing temperatures and snow can blast the mountain slopes even in midsummer. About 80 species of plants, many also present in the North American Arctic, manage to survive on the Peaks despite the rocky soil, wind, and cold. One species of groundsel and a buttercup appear only here. Seasonal visitors include a dwarf shrew and three species of birds, the Lincoln and white-crowned sparrows and the water pipit.

OLD-GROWTH FORESTS

Only five percent of Arizona's old-growth forest remains. It survives in remote canyons and on a few mountains, some under federal protection. Scientists find the old-growth forests an amazingly complex interaction of life and decay. Hundreds of species of fungi, insects, birds, animals, and plants feed or protect one other in ways still being discovered. We've also learned about forest management from these old systems. Checks and balances in these forests limit damage of insect and mistletoe infestations, an advantage that managed forests of uniformly aged trees don't share. Fires in the old growths burn cool and close to the ground and do little harm, because the shade from mature trees prevents excessive growth of brush and thickets of small trees; also, the branches of mature trees lie above the reach of most fires. Natural fires move through every 5–7 years, clearing the underbrush and fertilizing the soil with ash. Even in death, a large tree can stand 50 years, providing a home for generations of birds and insects. Foresters once removed these old snags as fire hazards, but now we know that many birds depend on them.

RATTLESNAKES

Arizona is home to 11 species of rattlesnake (*Crotalus* spp.). They range in length from less than two to about five feet. All feed on small rodents and can live more that 20 years in the wild. Eggs stay within the mother's body until hatched. The newborn snakes need no maternal care; they have poison and the ability to strike just minutes after birth. Babies stay where they were born for the first 7–10 days until they shed their skin and gain their first rattle. These tiny rattlesnakes can be aggressive and deadly—they cannot make a rattle sound, are difficult to see, and haven't developed the ability to regulate how much venom they inject. A new rattle appears each time a snake sheds its skin—as often as three times a year for a rapidly growing youngster. The number of rattles doesn't accurately indicate the snake's age; the snakes grow at varying rates, and the rattles can break off over the reptile's lifetime.

Rattlesnakes belong in the backcountry—we can share their space by being watchful and respectful. They come out only when the air temperature is a comfortable 65–85°F, typically in the daytime during spring and autumn, and at night during summer. Like other creatures, rattlesnakes display different temperaments. Mojave rattlesnakes have a fiercer reputation than other species and may even pursue an intruder. Rattlers in the Grand Canyon and other parts of the Colorado Plateau seem relatively docile.

On rare occasions a snake might strike without warning, but more often it will just rattle or ignore you completely. They tend to be very defensive, however, and will strike if someone steps on them or gets too close. If you find yourself uncomfortably near a rattlesnake, the best advice is to back off slowly; a quick movement could provoke a strike. Snakes can blend in re-markably well with the colors and patterns of their surroundings, so hikers must be alert to see them. More than once the author has been asked by someone coming from behind, "Hey, did you see that rattlesnake beside the trail?" "Rattlesnake?"

Who Gets Bitten?

According to Steven Curry, Associate Medical Director of the Samaritan Regional Poison Control Center in Phoenix, "The majority [of snakebite victims] are inebriated men, frequently unemployed, and almost universally tattooed." An estimated 80 percent of snakebite victims had been "messing around" with snakes.

Treatment

The only effective treatment for rattlesnake bites is an antivenin injection, available at a hospital. Identification of the species will help in the selection of the best antivenin. To give first aid: calm and reassure the victim, remove jewelry before swelling begins, avoid movement of the affected part, keep the limb lower than the heart, wash with cold water to reduce infection risk, and get the person to a hospital as soon as possible. Despite what actors in the movies do, don't give any alcohol or drugs. Also, don't apply ice packs, make incisions, or use a tourniquet, as these may do more harm than good. Venom has a variety of effects, including damage to muscle tissue and the dangerous lowering of blood pressure that can damage major organs. On a happier note, many strikes are "dry bites" with no venom injected; these are more likely in brief, surprise encounters—yet another incentive not to tease snakes.

BOB RACE

western diamondback rattlesnake

History

PREHISTORIC PEOPLES

Paleo-Indians

Arizona's first people discovered this land more than 15,000 years ago. Spears in hand, tribespeople hunted bison, camel, horse, antelope, and mammoth. Smaller game and wild plant foods completed their diet. About 9000 B.C., when the climate grew drier and grasslands turned to desert, most of the large animals died off or left. Overhunting may have hastened their extinction.

Desert Culture Tradition

The early tribes survived these changes by relying on seeds, berries, and nuts collected from wild plants and by hunting smaller game such as pronghorn, deer, mountain sheep, and jackrabbit. Having acquired a precise knowledge of the land, the small bands of related families moved in seasonal migrations timed to coincide with the ripening of plants in each area. They traveled light, probably carrying baskets, animal skins, traps, snares, and stone tools. Most likely they sought shelter in caves or built small brush huts. Some Arizona tribes continued a similar nomadic lifestyle until the late 1800s.

Emergence of Distinct Cultures

Between 2000 and 500 B.C., cultivation skills came to the uplands of Arizona from Mexico. Groups planted corn and squash in the spring, continued their seasonal migration in search of wild food, then returned to harvest the fields in autumn. Agriculture became more important after about 500 B.C., when beans were introduced; the combination of beans, corn, and squash gave the people a nutritious, high-protein diet. The earliest pottery, for cooking beans and storing other foods and water, was developed at about the same time.

From about 100 B.C. to A.D. 500, as they devoted more time to farming, the tribes began building villages of partly underground pithouses near their fields. Regional farming cultures appeared: the Hohokam of the southern deserts, the Mogollon of the eastern uplands, and the ancestral Puebloans (Anasazi) of the Colorado Plateau in the north.

Growth and the Great Pueblos

Villages grew larger and more widespread as populations increased from A.D. 500 to 1100. Aboveground pueblo dwellings began to replace the old-style pithouses. Trade among the Southwest cultures and with those in Mexico brought new ideas for crafts, farming, and building, along with valued items such as copper bells, parrots (prized for their feathers), and seashells and turquoise for jewelry. Cotton cultivation and weaving skills also developed.

Major towns appeared between A.D. 900 and 1100, possibly serving as trade centers. Complex religious ceremonies, probably similar to those of the present-day Hopi, took place in kivas (ceremonial rooms) and village plazas in the uplands. Ball courts and platform mounds, most often found in the southern deserts, likely served both religious and secular purposes. Desert dwellers also dug elaborate irrigation networks in the valleys of the Salt and Gila Rivers.

Decline and Consolidation

People began to pack up and abandon, one by one, whole villages and regions throughout Arizona between 1100 and the arrival of the Spanish in 1540. Archaeologists attempt to explain the migrations with theories of drought, soil erosion, warfare, disease, and aggression of Apache and Navajo newcomers. Refugees swelled the populations of the remaining villages during this period; eventually, most of these places emptied too.

Some ancestral Puebloans survived to become the modern Hopi in northeastern Arizona, but the Mogollon seem to have disappeared completely. Pima, likely descendents of the Hohokam, have legends of conflicts among the Hohokam that brought an end that civilization.

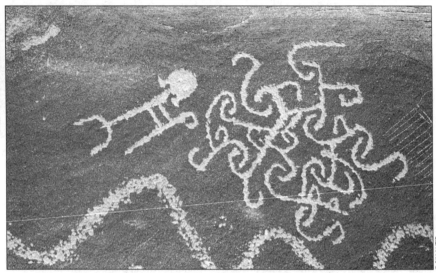

© BILL WEIR

petroglyphs at Inscription Point, north of Wupatki National Monument

The Athabaskan Migration

From western Canada, small bands of Athabaskan-speaking people slowly migrated to the Southwest. They arrived about 1300 to 1600 and established territories in the eastern half of present-day Arizona and adjacent New Mexico. Never a unified group, they followed a nomadic life of hunting, gathering, and raiding neighboring tribes. Some of the Athabaskans, later classified as Navajo on the Colorado Plateau and Apache farther south and east, learned agriculture and weaving from their pueblo neighbors.

SPANISH EXPLORATION AND RULE

The Conquistadors

Estévan, a Moorish slave of the viceroy of Mexico, became the first non-Native American to enter what is now Arizona. He arrived from the south in an advance party of Fray Marcos de Niza's 1539 expedition, sent by the viceroy to search for the supposedly treasure-laden Seven Cities of Cíbola.

The first of these "cities" that the party entered, a large Zuni pueblo in present-day New Mexico, proved disastrous for the explorers—they met their deaths at the hands of the villagers. Upon hearing the news, Fray Marcos dared view the pueblo only from a distance. Though he returned to Mexico empty-handed, his glowing accounts of a city of stone encouraged a new expedition led by Francisco Vásquez de Coronado.

Coronado departed from Mexico City in 1540 with 336 soldiers, almost 1,000 Native American allies, and 1,500 horses and mules. Instead of gold, the expedition found only houses of mud inhabited by hostile people. Despite hardships, Coronado explored the region for two years, traveling as far north as Kansas. A detachment led by García López de Cárdenas visited the Hopi mesas and the Grand Canyon rim. Another officer of the expedition, Hernando de Alarcón, explored the mouth of the Colorado River in hopes of finding a water route to resupply Coronado. He found the task impossible.

Missions and Presidios

Nearly 100 years passed after Coronado's failed quest before the Spanish reentered Arizona. A few explorers and prospectors made brief visits, but Franciscan missionaries came to stay. They opened three missions near the Hopi villages and had some success in gaining converts, despite strong objections from traditional Hopi.

When pueblo villages in neighboring New Mexico revolted against the Spanish in 1680, the traditional Hopi joined in, killing the friars and many of their followers. Missionary efforts then shifted to southern Arizona, where the tireless Jesuit priest, Eusebio Francisco Kino, explored the new land and built missions from 1691 to 1711. Harsh treatment by later missionaries and land abuses by settlers caused the Pima tribes to revolt in 1751. The Spanish then instituted reforms, meanwhile building a presidio at Tubac to prevent another outbreak. Similar harsh treatment by Spaniards at two missions on the lower Colorado River caused a revolt there in 1781; no attempt was made to reestablish them.

Arizonac

A fantastic silver strike during the Spanish era in 1736 drew thousands to an arroyo known by local Native Americans as Arizonac, where sheets of native silver weighing 25–50 pounds each were said to cover the ground. The exact location of this extraordinary find is uncertain, but it probably lay west of present-day Nogales. The boom soon ended, but a book published in 1850 in Spain recounted the amazing story. An American mine speculator picked up the tale and used it to publicize and sell mining shares. The name Arizonac, shortened to Arizona, became so well known that politicians later chose it for the entire territory. Or at least that's one theory of how Arizona got its name.

Mexican Takeover

This land had always existed on the far fringes of civilization, so politics and the Mexican fight for independence had little effect on Arizona. When three centuries of Spanish rule came to an end with Mexican independence in 1821, almost nothing changed. In the presidios, a new flag and an oath of loyalty to Mexico marked the transition. Isolation and hostile Apache continued to discourage settlement. Mission work declined as the Mexican government expelled many of the Spanish friars.

ARRIVAL OF THE ANGLOS

Mountain Men

Early in the 19th century, adventurous traders and trappers left the comforts of civilization in the eastern states to seek new lives in the West. In 1825, Sylvester Pattie and his son made the first known journey by Anglos to what is now Arizona. The younger Pattie later set down his adventures in *The Personal Narrative of James Ohio Pattie* (see Suggested Reading). Although occasionally suffering attacks by hostile tribes, the Patties and later mountain men coexisted more or less peacefully with the Mexicans and Native Americans. When U.S. Army explorers and surveyors first visited Arizona in the 1840s and 1850s, they relied on mountain men to show them trails and water holes.

Arizona Enters the United States

Anglo traders did an increasingly large business in the Southwest after Mexican independence—their supply route from Missouri was far shorter and more profitable than the Mexicans' long haul from Mexico City. Arizona was of little importance in the Mexican War of 1847–48, which was ignited by American desire for Texas and California, disputes over Mexico's debts, and Mexican indifference to a political solution. The 1848 Treaty of Guadalupe Hidalgo ceded to the United States not only Texas and California, but everything in between—including Arizona and New Mexico. As part of the vast New Mexican Territory, created by Congress in 1850, Arizona remained a backwater. The Gadsden Purchase added what's now southernmost Arizona in 1854.

New Trails

Most early visitors regarded Arizona as nothing but a place to cross on the way to California. The safest routes lay within the lands of the Gadsden Purchase, where Capt. Philip Cooke built a wagon road during the Mexican War. Many '49ers, headed for gold strikes in California, used Cooke's road, better known as the Gila Trail. Hostile tribes and difficult mountain crossings discouraged travel farther north, even after Lt. Edward Beale opened a rough wagon road across northern Arizona in 1857. Steamboat service on the lower Colorado River, beginning in 1852, brought cheaper and safer transportation to western Arizona.

Americans Settle In

As the California Gold Rush died down in the mid-1850s, prospectors turned eastward to Arizona. They made their first big find, a placer gold deposit, near the confluence of the Colorado River and Sacramento Wash in 1857. More strikes followed. For the first time, large numbers of people came to Arizona to seek their fortunes. Farmers and ranchers established themselves, cashing in on the market provided by the new mining camps and army posts.

Native American Troubles and the Civil War

Mountain men and government surveyors initially maintained good relations with local tribes, but this peace ended only a few years after first contact. Conflicts between White people and tribespeople over economic, religious, and political rights, and over land and water, led to loss of land and autonomy for the Native Americans. Both sides committed atrocities as each sought to drive out the other. Army forts provided a base for troops attempting to subdue the tribes as well as a refuge for travelers and settlers.

Most Arizonans sided with the Confederacy during the Civil War, but quickly switched when large numbers of federal troops arrived. The Battle of Picacho Pass, on April 15, 1862, was the most significant conflict of the Civil War this far west. Confederate forces killed Lt. James Barrett, leader of the Union detachment, and two privates. Aware that Union reinforcements

President Taft signs the 1912 Valentine's Day gift to the Arizonans.

would soon arrive, the Confederates retreated back down the Butterfield Road to Tucson and on toward Texas.

TERRITORIAL YEARS

Despite the wars and uncertainties of the early 1860s, Arizona emerged for the first time as a separate entity on February 24, 1863, when President Lincoln signed a bill establishing the Arizona Territory. Formerly, as part of New Mexico, Arizona had lacked both federal representation and law and order. In 1864, Gov. John Goodwin and other appointed officials laid out Arizona's first capital at Prescott.

Continuing Troubles

Control of hostile tribes, especially the Apache and Navajo, proved to be the new territory's most serious problem. Although Arizona's Native Americans failed to drive out the newcomers, they did succeed in holding back development. Not until the great Apache leader Geronimo surrendered for the last time in 1886 did White residents of the territory feel safe.

Frontier Days End

The arrival of the railroads in the 1870s and 1880s and concurrent discoveries of rich copper deposits brought increasing prosperity. Ranching, farming, and logging grew in importance. By 1890 Arizona no longer needed most of its army forts. Only Fort Huachuca in southeastern Arizona survived as an active military post from the Indian wars to the present.

Mormon Settlement

Mormons in Utah, seeking new freedoms and opportunities, migrated south into Arizona. They first established Littlefield in the extreme northwest corner of Arizona in 1864. A flood washed out the community in 1867, but determined settlers rebuilt in 1877. Mormons developed other parts of the Arizona Strip in the far north and operated Lees Ferry across the Colorado River, just upstream from the Grand Canyon. From Lees Ferry, settlers headed as far south as St. David on the San Pedro River in

Cochise County. Some settlements had to be abandoned due to land ownership problems, poor soil, or irrigation difficulties. Mormon towns prospering today include Springerville (founded 1871), Joseph City (1876), Mesa (1878), and Show Low (1890).

STATEHOOD AND MODERN ARIZONA

After years of political wrangling, Pres. William H. Taft signed a proclamation admitting Arizona as

STATE SYMBOLS

The seal portrays Arizona at statehood in 1912. It contains the Latin motto *Ditat Deus,* "God Enriches." On the left, a quartz mill and a miner with pick and shovel symbolize the state's mining industry. Fields of cotton and citrus grow in fields on the right, irrigated by the reservoir and mountain watershed beyond. Cattle graze in the lower right. A rising sun represents Arizona's sunny climate.

the state seal

The central star has a copper color, identifying Arizona as the United State's greatest copper producer. The red and yellow rays form a sunset, as this is a western state, and have the colors of the Spanish flags brought to this land by Coronado in 1540; their number 13 commemorates the original American colonies. The solid-blue field of the lower half of the flag further links the state with the union, as this color is also in the American flag.

the state flag

the 48th state on Valentine's Day, February 14, 1912. Citizens turned out for parades and wild celebrations. In Phoenix, Governor-elect George W.P. Hunt led a triumphant procession to the Capitol. He had arrived in the territory in 1881 as an unemployed miner, then worked his way up to become a successful merchant, banker, territorial representative, and president of Arizona's Constitutional Convention. Hunt's support of labor, good roads, and other liberal causes won him seven terms in the governor's office.

Arizona lived up to its nickname, the Copper State, riding the good times when copper prices were high, as during WW I and the Roaring '20s, then suffering during economic depressions. Water, that all-important resource for farms and cities, also preoccupied citizens. New dams across the Gila, Salt, and Verde Rivers of central Arizona ensured the state's growth.

Claims on the Colorado River, however, led to a long-running feud with California and other thirsty states. Arizona pressed for its water rights from the early 1920s until 1944, even calling out the National Guard at one point to halt construction of Parker Dam, designed to supply water to Los Angeles. Wartime priorities finally forced the Arizona Legislature to make peace and join the other river states in the Colorado River Compact.

WW II and the Postwar Boom

The pace of life quickened considerably during WW II, when Arizona devoted much of its land and resources to the war effort. The good flying weather convinced the Army Air Corps to build training bases here. Arizona deserts proved ideal for General Patton and other army officers to prepare their troops for coming battles. Aeronautical and other defense industries built factories, helping state manufacturing income to jump from $17 million in 1940 to $85 million just five years later. Several massive POW camps housed captured Germans and Italians. Japanese-Americans also endured internment; in fact, authorities herded so many Japanese into the Poston camp south of Parker that for a time it ranked as Arizona's third-largest city.

The war, and the air-conditioning that made low-desert summers bearable, changed the state forever. Many of the workers and armed forces people who passed through during the hectic war years returned to settle in Arizona. Even some of the German POWs, it's said, liked Arizona so well that they made their homes here. Much of the industry and many military bases remained as well. Retired people took a new interest in the state's sunny skies and warm winters. Whole towns, such as Sun City, rose just for the older set. Arizona has continued to grow and diversify, yet it retains its natural beauty and Old West heritage.

THE FABULOUS FIVE

In 1998, women swept into all five top executive spots in Arizona's state government. Crowned the "Fabulous Five" by local newspapers, Jane Dee Hull won the governor's race, Betsey Bayless took Secretary of State, Janet Napolitano became Attorney General, Carol Springer the Treasurer, and Lisa Graham Keegan the Superintendent of Public Instruction. Never before had a state elected women to even the top two executive offices, let alone to all five! "This was not a backlash against men," stated Napolitano, "This was about qualified women running for office and winning."

Women had earned important posts in Arizona government since the early days, when Sharlot Hall had accepted the appointment of Territorial Historian in 1909. The challenges of Arizona politics during early statehood in 1915 didn't deter Rachel Allen Berry, who took her seat in the Arizona House of Representatives, and Frances Willard Munds, who became an Arizona State Senator. Both women were among the first in the nation to hold such posts. Women have gone to the top in the judicial branch too. Sandra Day O'Connor, after rising to Arizona Senate Majority Leader, took on the job of Maricopa County Superior Court Judge, then served as an Arizona Court of Appeals Judge before becoming the first woman to be appointed to the U.S. Supreme Court (in 1981).

The People

TRIBES OF NORTHERN ARIZONA

Havasupai

Long before the first White people arrived, this tribe farmed the fertile Havasu Canyon floor during the summer, then moved to the plateau after the harvest to gather abundant wild foods and firewood during winter. Spanish missionary Francisco Garcés visited the Havasupai in 1776, finding them a happy and industrious people. Though a peaceful group, they suffered the usual fate of American tribes—confinement to a tiny reservation while White people grabbed their lands. The Havasupai protested, but it wasn't until 1975 that the tribe's winter homelands were returned. Their reservation now spans 188,077 acres; most of the 500–600 tribal members on the reservation live in Supai village.

Supai lies 35 air miles northwest of Grand Canyon Village in Havasu Canyon, a major Grand Canyon tributary. The waterfalls, travertine pools, and greenery of the remote canyon have earned it fame as a Shangri-La.

Hualapai

The "Pine-tree People" once occupied a large area of northwestern Arizona. In language and culture, they're closely tied to the Havasupai and Yavapai tribes. Early White visitors enjoyed friendly relations with the Hualapai, but land seizures and murders by the newcomers led to warfare. Army troops defeated the Hualapai and herded them south onto the Colorado River Reservation, where many died. Survivors fled back to their traditional lands, part of which later became the Hualapai Indian Reservation. About half of the 1,500 tribal members live on the 993,000-acre reservation, which includes much of the lower Grand Canyon's South Rim. Highlights for visitors include the spectacular viewpoints from the rim of the lowermost Grand Canyon, a drive into the Grand Canyon along Diamond Creek, and rafting trips on the Colorado River.

Peach Springs, a small town 54 miles northeast of Kingman on AZ 66, is the only one on the reservation. The road that descends to the Colorado River in the Grand Canyon begins here.

Paiute

A small band of Paiute lives on the Kaibab-Paiute Reservation, west of Fredonia in far northern Arizona. In earlier times they used this area as a winter home and spent summers in the forests of the Kaibab Plateau to the east. About 250 Paiute, who speak a Uto-Aztecan language, live on the reservation. The tribe arrived sometime after A.D. 1300, though members believe themselves related to the ancestral Puebloans who had once lived on this land. The adjacent Pipe Spring National Monument preserves pioneer and tribal ways of life.

Navajo

The semi-nomadic Navajo, relatives of the Athabaskans of western Canada, wandered into the area east of the Grand Canyon between A.D. 1300 and 1600. This adaptable tribe learned agriculture, weaving, pottery, and other skills from its Pueblo neighbors and became skilled horsemen and sheepherders with livestock obtained from the Spanish.

The Navajo habit of raiding neighboring tribes—this time, White people—almost caused the tribe's downfall. In 1863–64, the U.S. Army rounded up all the Navajo it could find and forced the survivors to make "The Long Walk" from Fort Defiance in eastern Arizona to a bleak camp at Fort Sumner in eastern New Mexico. This attempt at forced domestication failed dismally, and the Navajo were released four years later to return to their homeland. The colorful velveteen blouses and long, flowing skirts worn by some Navajo women date back in style to this period; they were what U.S. Army wives were then wearing!

Hopi

Legends and long-abandoned pueblos indicate that the tribe has lived here for more than a

Hopi woman preparing fry bread

Curious tourists overwhelm the tribe at times, but the Hopi welcome visitors who respect local culture and regulations. Highlights of a visit on the reservation include a trip to Walpi, a traditional stone village that seems to grow out of its spectacular ridge-top setting on First Mesa; the museum at the Cultural Center on Second Mesa; and the kachina and other dances performed on many weekends. (Only some dances are open to the public.)

TRIBES OF WESTERN ARIZONA

Six tribes now live along the lower Colorado River between the Grand Canyon and the Gulf of California. The three Yuman-speaking tribes—Mohave, Quechan, and Cocopah—have occupied this land since prehistoric times. Uto-Aztecan-speaking Chemehuevi, followed by some Hopi and Navajo of northeastern Arizona, later joined them.

Mohave

Northernmost of the Yuman tribes, the Mohave formerly lived in loosely organized bands, uniting only for warfare or defense. They farmed the bottomlands, hunted, and gathered wild foods. Crafts included finely made baskets, pottery, and beadwork. Ceremonial dances and long funeral wakes played important roles in Mohave social life. Even today, the Mohave and Quechan cremate their dead—a rare practice among Native Americans.

Mohave live on the Fort Mohave Reservation near Needles, California, and in a larger group on the Colorado River Reservation near Parker, Arizona. You can learn more about the tribe and view their crafts at the tribal museum just south of Parker.

Chemehuevi

This group of Paiute once roamed the eastern Mohave Desert as hunting and gathering nomads. They settled in the Chemehuevi Valley of the Colorado River in the early 1800s, taking up the agricultural practices of their Mohave neighbors. The U.S. government granted the Chemehuevi a reservation in 1907, but Lake

thousand years. Old Oraibi, a Hopi village dating from at least A.D. 1150, is thought to be the oldest continuously inhabited settlement in the United States, and some Hopi identify even older village sites as the homes of their ancestors, whom they call *Hisatsinom.*

Spanish explorers entered the region in the 1500s, looking for gold and treasure, but they had to leave empty-handed. Desiring to save Hopi souls, Spanish friars arrived about 1630 and had some success until traditional Hopi leaders, fearing the loss of their own culture, joined with the New Mexico Pueblo tribes in a revolt against the Spanish in 1680. Hopi killed any foreigner unable to escape, massacred many of their own people who were Christians, and tore down the mission buildings. During the 1800s, American frontiersmen arrived seeking mineral wealth and fertile lands, but they met with disappointment. So the Hopi continued to farm in relative peace, raising crops of corn, squash, and beans.

Havasu inundated much of their farmland in 1938. The tribe now lives on the Chemehuevi Reservation opposite Lake Havasu City and on the Colorado River Reservation.

Quechan

Formerly known as the Yuma, the tribe now prefers the name Quechan. In the 19th century, Quechan territory included much of the lower Colorado and about 25 miles of the Gila River Valley. The federal government trimmed their land considerably during the late 19th and early 20th centuries. Today the tribe lives in California on the Quechan Indian Reservation opposite Yuma, Arizona. You can visit their museum in a historic building of former Camp Yuma.

Cocopah

Before the arrival of White people, the Cocopah lived downstream from the Quechan in the Colorado River delta, once one of the most fertile areas of the Southwest. Like other Colorado River tribes, though, the people suffered greatly from European-introduced diseases. Today the Cocopah live on three tiny reservations south of Yuma and in Mexican villages in Sonora and Baja California.

TRIBES OF CENTRAL ARIZONA

Pima and Maricopa

The Pima followed the prehistoric Hohokam, with whom they had much in common and are probably related. Living along the valleys of the Gila and Salt Rivers, the Pima used the farming methods of their predecessors but had many difficulties when White people built dams upstream early in the 20th century. Today the Pima farm, raise cattle, work in small industries, and create traditional handicrafts.

Maricopa tribespeople, who originally lived along the Colorado River, migrated up the Gila River to escape their aggressive Mohave and Yuma neighbors. Pima and Maricopa now share the Salt River Indian Reservation (east of Scottsdale) and Gila River Indian Reservation (southeast of Phoenix). You'll find tribal museums on each of the reservations.

Yavapai

The tribe shares cultural traits with the Hualapai and Havasupai to the north. Yavapai, along with Tonto Apache, received the Rio Verde Reservation in 1873, but the federal government took it away two years later, ordering the displaced Native Americans to proceed to the San Carlos Reservation, 150 miles away. In the cold February of 1875, they started the two-week journey on foot; of the 1,451 who began the trek, at least 90 died from exposure, were killed by infighting, or escaped.

Early in the 20th century, some Yavapai and Apache received permission to return to their Verde River homelands. What were once thousands of Native Americans occupying millions of acres now number less than 1,000 people on a few remnants of their former lands on the Camp Verde, Prescott, and Fort McDowell Reservations.

Apache

While most Apache in Arizona live in the eastern part of the state (see below), some make their homes on several small reservations in north-central Arizona and with the Mohave on Fort McDowell Reservation northeast of Phoenix.

TRIBES OF EASTERN ARIZONA

Apache

Groups are thought to have migrated from western Canada to the Southwest via the Great Plains, reaching Arizona in about the 16th century. Close relatives of the Navajo, the Apache share a similar language and customs. The early Apache lived a nomadic life—the men hunted game while the women gathered wild plant foods. They had few material possessions and probably lived in small conical huts covered with animal skins. Cultivation of corn, beans, and squash, learned from either the Pueblo or Navajo tribes, later supplemented hunting and gathering.

Horses obtained from the Spanish gave the Apache great mobility, and by the mid-18th century their raiding routes stretched from the Hopi mesas in the north to central Sonora in Mexico. Their predatory habits did not endear them to

INTRODUCTION

APACHE SCOUTS

Why did Apache with the U.S. Army fight other Apache? Western Apache bands in central Arizona felt little tribal identity with eastern (Chiricahua) bands of southeastern Arizona and adjacent New Mexico and Mexico. Apache rivalries made it easy for the army to recruit.

As warriors, the Apache scouts took naturally to soldiering. They already knew their own methods of fighting, so they needed little formal training. Scouts enjoyed the prestige of having weapons and the freedom to travel, unlike their reservation-bound brethren. They realized that cooperation with the army and government officials provided a better alternative than risking deportation, which was inflicted on the Navajo and the Chiricahua Apache.

Pay provided another inducement—scouts received the equivalent of a regular soldier's pay and they could claim horses, mules, and equipment captured from renegade Apache. They also sought to pick up knowledge from the Anglo soldiers and share with their own society.

Apache could enlist for terms of three, six, or 12 months. They formed units of 250 men commanded by regular army officers and Apache noncommissioned officers.

their neighbors—in fact, the name Apache may have come from a Zuni word for "enemy."

The Apache vigorously defended their lands from encroaching settlers, and soon earned a reputation as the fiercest tribe in the Southwest. Though nothing could stop men hungry for gold and land, the Apache certainly tried. Apache resistance slowed the development of Arizona towns and industries until late in the 19th century.

Two large reservations provide homes for most tribal members. The White Mountain Apache Reservation spreads across a very scenic region of forests and lakes northeast of Phoenix. To the south, across the Salt and Black Rivers, the San Carlos Apache Reservation has both forest and desert country, including the large San Carlos Lake. Each tribe has a good cultural center/museum and offers visitors extensive outdoor recreation activities.

TRIBES OF SOUTHERN ARIZONA

Tohono O'odham

The first White people couldn't believe that humans lived in such wild and parched desert, yet the Tohono O'odham (tah-HO-no AH-tomb) have thrived here for centuries. Close relatives of the Pima, the Tohono O'odham once occupied a vast section of the Sonoran Desert of southern Arizona and northern Mexico. Neighboring tribes called these desert dwellers Papago ("Bean People"), but the tribe prefers the more dignified term Tohono O'odham, meaning "Desert People Who Have Emerged from the Earth." The Tohono O'odham believe that their tribe, like the plants and animals, belongs to the earth.

Originally, the Tohono O'odham maintained both winter and summer villages, staying near reliable springs in the winter, then moving to fields watered by summer thunderstorms. They gathered mesquite beans, agave, cactus fruit, acorns, and other plant foods and hunted rodents, rabbits, deer, and pronghorn. Their farms yielded native tepary beans, corn, and squash.

After the 1854 Gadsden Treaty split their land between Mexico and the United States, the Mexican Tohono O'odham population gradually withered away, absorbed into Mexican culture. Some families migrated into Arizona. Today only about 200 Tohono O'odham remain south of the border. In 1874, the U.S. government began setting aside land for the tribe in the 71,095-acre San Xavier Reservation. Tohono O'odham land now totals about 2.8 million acres—roughly the size of Connecticut. The second-largest reservation in the country, it stretches across much of southern Arizona and is home to more than 8,000 people.

The old ways have largely disappeared because of contact with modern technology. Today most Tohono O'odham, like everyone else in Arizona, live in standard houses and farm, ranch, or work for wages. Skilled basketmakers continue their ancient tradition, however. You'll see the attractive Tohono O'odham crafts in gift shops and in the visitor center at Kitt Peak.

Early Spanish missionaries gained many converts—the Roman Catholic Church has the largest following on the reservation, though Protestant churches have believers as well. Almost all villages have a small chapel.

Most Tohono O'odham are friendly, but the tribe has shown little interest in tourism. The vast reservation has hardly any visitor facilities and not a single motel, tourist office, or tribal museum. Two attractions, in addition to the desert scenery, make a visit worthwhile: the world-famous Kitt Peak Observatory and the Tohono O'odham All-Indian Rodeo and Fair.

On the Road

Recreation

OUTDOOR ACTIVITIES

Hiking

You'll get the best feel for Arizona's canyons and mountains by visiting them on foot. The Grand Canyon offers the most challenging and extensive hiking in the state—a lifetime is too short to see everything here. Countless canyons, especially in the Colorado Plateau of northern Arizona, also offer exceptionally scenic hiking opportunities. The state's many mountains can keep a hiker well entertained, too. You can climb most summits on a day hike.

Whitewater

The Colorado River through the Grand Canyon has it all—big-water rapids, contemplative smooth water, gorgeous canyons, and an amazing tour of the earth's geology. The 280 river miles from Lees Ferry to the end of the Grand Canyon at Lake Mead requires a big commitment in time and gear, so you'll want to plan carefully. You can go either on your own—if suitably equipped and experienced—or with a river company. A trip all the way through typically takes 14 days by oar-powered rafts or dories, but motorized rigs can do it in eight.

The Salt River in central Arizona has exciting rapids, too, though on a much smaller scale. It takes 3–5 days to run the Salt's 51 miles of whitewater between the US 60 bridge north of Globe and the AZ 288 bridge near Roosevelt Lake. One-day trips on the upper part of this section

Grand Canyon Railway

© BILL WEIR

ARIZONA HIGHLIGHTS

- **The Grand Canyon:** The world's most magnificent chasm features views, hiking, mule trips, and river rafting.
- **Indian Country:** Experience new cultures among spectacular landscapes.
- **San Francisco Volcanic Field:** A land of beautiful volcanoes, prehistoric pueblos, and great hiking surrounds the San Francisco Peaks.
- **Flagstaff:** This university town in the mountains features a wide diversity of culture, science, and recreation.
- **Sedona:** The Red Rock Country's magical setting inspires visitors and offers great outdoor adventures.
- **Western Arizona:** The original London Bridge distinguishes Arizona's "West Coast."
- **Phoenix:** The desert capital pulses with political, business, and cultural energy.
- **Coronado Trail:** A wildly scenic drive leads through eastern Arizona's forested mountains.
- **Tucson:** The "Old Pueblo" displays a sense of history alongside a vibrant cultural life.
- **Southeastern Arizona:** This region, famous for its bird life on "sky islands," has a lengthy history—from early Spanish missions to the latest astronomical discoveries.

shops sell publications on bicycle touring. As when hiking, always carry rain and wind gear and plenty of water. Also don't forget to wear a bicycling helmet.

Start with short rides if you're new to bicycle touring, then work up to longer cross-country trips. By learning to maintain and repair your steed, you'll seldom have trouble on the road. An extra-low gear of 30 inches or less will take the strain out of long mountain grades. The performance of mountain bikes for touring can be improved by using road tires (no knobs) and handlebar extensions (for a variety of riding positions).

Mountain bikes, with their shocks, fat tires, and rugged construction, come into their own in the backcountry. The national forests offer some fine riding on roads and trails. County parks surrounding Phoenix are popular for their desert scenery. Some other parks around the state offer riding possibilities, too. For a real adventure you can try the wide-open spaces of the Arizona Strip, though you'll probably need a 4WD vehicle to carry water here. The main limitations for cyclists are that they cannot ride in designated wilderness areas or off-road on National Park Service lands.

Skiing

Sunrise Ski Area on the White Mountain Apache Reservation in eastern Arizona features the state's best downhill action with many runs and lifts. The Snowbowl, farther north in the San Francisco Peaks, also offers great skiing. Williams, to the west, has a small downhill area on Bill Williams Mountain. Mount Lemmon Ski Valley near Tucson is the country's southernmost ski area.

Cross-country skiers can take to groomed trails near Flagstaff, Grandview Lookout area (near the Grand Canyon's South Rim), Williams, Forest Lakes (Mogollon Rim), and Sunrise Ski Area. The Grand Canyon's North Rim area offers almost limitless backcountry skiing.

Four Wheeling

Back roads offer superb scenery in almost every part of Arizona. You'll experience the desert, hill,

are very popular. See "Salt River Canyon Wilderness" in the South-Central Arizona chapter.

Other river trips have fine scenery without such big rapids. They include Glen Canyon of the Colorado River between Glen Canyon Dam and Lees Ferry, Black Canyon of the Colorado River below Hoover Dam, sections of the lower Colorado River, the Verde River in central Arizona, the Gila River in eastern Arizona, and the Virgin River in the state's northwest corner.

Bicycling

To be fully alive to the land, skies, sounds, plants, and birds of Arizona, tour on a bicycle. Gliding across the desert or topping out on a mountain pass are experiences beyond words. Some effort, a lightweight touring or mountain bicycle, and awareness of your surroundings are all that's required. Bookstores and bicycle

THE ARIZONA TRAIL

The inspiration for a trail across the entire state from Mexico to Utah came to Flagstaff teacher and hiker Dale Shewalter in the mid-1980s. Now his vision nears completion, thanks to government agencies and volunteers who have worked hard to make the 790-mile trail a reality.

The trail offers great hiking and riding opportunities, whether you're looking for a day's outing or a major adventure. It traverses some of the state's most scenic, historic, and biologically diverse areas and is open to hikers, cyclists, and equestrians—but not to motorized vehicles. In winter, cross-country skiers and snowshoers can take to the snow on some sections. Cyclists will need to find alternate routes where needed in order to bypass the Grand Canyon and other wilderness areas that are closed to them.

The first hikers have already completed the entire length, though they've had to do some bushwhacking and difficult navigation through the remaining gaps in the route. If you want to travel the whole distance, a spring departure works well because you can enjoy the cooler weather of the desert sections in the state's south and central regions, then hit ideal summer weather atop the plateaus in the north. You can follow progress of the trail—and find out how you can volunteer—by contacting the **Arizona Trail Association,** P.O. Box 36736, Phoenix, AZ 85067-6736; 602/252-4794; www.aztrail.org. Books include *On the Arizona Trail; A Guide for Hikers, Cyclists, & Equestrians* by Kelly Tighe and Susan Moran (Pruett Publishing), with detailed descriptions, maps, and lists of agencies that manage the lands along the way.

At the south end, the trail begins on the Mexican border in Coronado National Memorial, winds north to Montezuma Pass, then climbs into the Huachuca Mountains and Miller Peak Wilderness via the Crest Trail. The route drops down to the Parker Canyon Lake area and runs through the Canelo Hills to Patagonia. It continues north through the Santa Rita, Rincon, Santa Catalina, and Superstition Mountains before descending to Roosevelt Lake near Tonto National Monument. The trail crosses Roosevelt Dam, then winds up into the Mazatzal Mountains in the heart of Arizona.

The sheer cliffs of the Mogollon Rim mark the next major climb; then the trail crosses East Clear Creek, Anderson Mesa, and upper Walnut Canyon. Here the trail heads for the mountains again, this time to volcanic Mt. Elden and the San Francisco Peaks—Arizona's highest. The Arizona Trail skirts the Peaks before turning northwest toward Grandview Lookout and the South Rim of the Grand Canyon. After crossing this great chasm, the trail follows the 50-mile Kaibab Plateau Trail along the Canyon's east rim with views across Marble Canyon and beyond. The trail crosses AZ 89A about two miles east of Jacob Lake, then continues north 12 miles through the forest to the Utah border and trail's end.

Cyclists can take forest roads around most of the wilderness areas, but they will have to do some highway stretches, too, most notably around the Grand Canyon via Navajo Bridge near Lees Ferry.

plateau, and alpine countryside of the state close at hand. Forest Service and BLM offices provide maps and current road conditions for their areas. Weather reports can warn you of possible flash flood and heavy snowfall hazards that sometimes strand even the most capable vehicles and drivers. Books and literature explain how to enjoy the remote areas in safety. **Arizona State Association of 4 Wheel Drive Clubs, Inc.,** (P.O. Box 23904, Tempe, AZ 85285), 602/258-4294, can direct you to clubs in the state; the website www .asa4wdc.org has links, photos, and articles.

The Great Western Trail, about 50 percent complete, follows existing back roads between the Mexican border and Canada via Arizona, Utah, Wyoming, Montana, and Idaho. The 800-mile Arizona segment crosses roughly through the middle of the state. Some segments may require 4WD. You can contact the Great Western Trail Association at P.O. Box 2365, Prescott, AZ 86302; www.gwt.org. Arizona State Parks (see below) also has information on the Arizona section. New maps may show the trail too, such as the *Arizona Road & Recreation Atlas* by Benchmark Maps.

PARKS
National Parks and Monuments
Grand Canyon National Park takes first place as the most popular federal parkland in Arizona, but you'll find many other National Park Service managed scenic, historic, and recreation lands within the state as well.

With Grand Canyon National Park charging a stiff $20 and Petrified Forest National Park running $10 for a seven-day entry, you may be best off buying the $50 **National Parks Pass,** which will get you and others in your vehicle into these or any other national park, monument, or historic site in the United States for 12 months. A Golden Eagle hologram for the pass costs an extra $15 and covers entrance fees to U.S. Fish and Wildlife, U.S. Forest Service, and Bureau of Land Management areas, but it's of little use in Arizona. Seniors age 62 and older who are U.S. citizens can take advantage of the $10 **Golden Age Pass,** good for a lifetime; it ad-

ditionally gives a discount at many campgrounds on federal lands. Individuals who receive government benefits because of permanent disabilities should look into the lifetime **Golden Access Pass.** Drop by any National Park Service fee station or regional office to obtain these cards.

Arizona State Parks
You can choose from three types of state parks—recreation areas, historic sites, and conservation areas—all offering a high-quality experience. Most of the recreation areas and a few of the other types have campgrounds, where you're likely to find electric hookups and showers. Historical reenactments, nature programs, and other interpretive programs will add to your enjoyment. All of the parks feature wheelchair access. Arizona State Parks publishes books and pamphlets on history and outdoor recreation in Arizona.

Day-use admission fees to recreation parks cost $4–10 per vehicle, up to four persons, and $1 per person for each additional passenger and for cyclists or walk-ins. Historical and conservation parks charge $2–6 for adults (age 14 and up) and $1–2.50 children (ages 7–13). If you're camping, the nightly fees *per vehicle* run $8–12 no hookups or $15–20 with electricity. Day-use permits are $15 for a 5-visit pass (any park except Kartchner), $35 per year (not valid weekends at Colorado River parks or Kartchner), or $65 per year for unlimited use (includes entry to Kartchner but not cave tours) for the holder and up to three others in the same vehicle. Group and long-term rates can be arranged, too.

For details on facilities, events, and publications, you can contact the individual parks, the main state office, or the website. Volunteers are often needed in various aspects of park operations; you could be a campground host, work in interpretive services, assist in archaeology documentation, collect oral histories, or help maintain trails.

The main office of Arizona State Parks is at 1300 W. Washington, Phoenix, AZ 85007. It's open Mon.–Fri. 8 A.M.–5 P.M. and has an information desk and gift shop. Call 602/542-4174, 800/285-3703 (Arizona outside the

Phoenix area); fax is 602/542-4188. On the Web, visit www.pr.state.az.us. Staff answer a **Wildflower Hotline** 602/542-4988 during office hours in spring.

State Trust Lands

Although not specifically intended for recreation, these lands have some backcountry areas that you may wish to explore. To do so, purchase a 12-month Recreation Permit for $15/person or $20/family. (Licensed fishermen and hunters pursuing their activities are exempt but need a permit if camping.) Permits can be obtained by mail or in person in Phoenix (602/542-4631), Tucson (520/628-5480), and Flagstaff (928/774-1425).

KEEPING THE "WILD" IN WILDERNESS— KNOW BEFORE YOU GO

Arizona offers many wilderness areas, yet we need to take extra care with this fragile and precious resource as more people seek relief from the confusion and stress of urban life. All of the designated wilderness areas are closed to mechanized vehicles—including mountain bikes—to protect the environment and enhance the experience of solitude. Hikers need to obtain permits to camp in backcountry areas in the National Park System and certain wilderness areas of the Bureau of Land Management. You're normally free to visit designated wilderness areas on national forests and most Bureau of Land Management lands anytime without a permit.

Some of the most spectacular and memorable hiking and camping await the prepared outdoors enthusiast, but because Arizona's deserts and canyons are very different from most other parts of the country, even expert hikers can get into trouble. If you're new to these outdoors, read up on hiking conditions and talk to rangers and local hikers. Backpacking stores and the Internet are good sources of information. Start with easy trips, then work up gradually.

Hypothermia

Your greatest danger outdoors is one that can sneak up and kill with very little warning. Hypothermia, a lowering of the body's temperature below 95°F, causes disorientation, uncontrollable shivering, slurred speech, and drowsiness. The victim may not even realize what's wrong. Unless corrective action is taken immediately, hypothermia can lead to death. That's why hikers should travel with companions and always carry wind and rain protection; close-fitting raingear works better than ponchos.

Remember that temperatures can plummet rapidly in Arizona's dry climate—a drop of 40°F between day and night is common. Be especially careful at high elevations, where sum-

GIARDIA

It can be tough to resist: You're hiking in a beautiful area by the banks of a crystal clear stream. The water in your canteen tastes stale, hot, and plastic; the nearby stream looks so inviting that you can't resist a cautious sip. It tastes delicious, clean, and cold, and for the rest of your hike you refresh yourself with water straight from the stream.

Days pass and you forget about drinking untreated water. Suddenly one evening after your meal you become terribly sick to your stomach. You develop an awful case of cramps and feel diarrhea beginning to set in. Food poisoning?

Well, it could be the effects of *Giardia*, a protozoan that has become common in even the remotest of mountain streams. *Giardia* is carried in animal or human waste that is deposited or washed into natural waters. When ingested, it begins to reproduce, causing a sickness that can become very serious and may not be cured without medical attention.

You can take precautions against *Giardia* with a variety of chemical purifying and filtering methods or by boiling water before drinking it. Directions for chemical and filtering methods need to be followed carefully to be effective against the protozoan in its cyst stage of life, when it encases itself in a hard shell. The most effective way to eliminate such threats is to boil all suspect water for a few minutes.

mer sunshine can quickly change into freezing rain or a blizzard.

If cold and tired, don't waste time. Seek shelter and build a fire; change into dry clothes and drink warm liquids. A victim not fully conscious should be warmed by skin-to-skin contact with another person in a sleeping bag. Try to keep the victim awake and drinking warm liquids.

Coping with Heat

We can take cues from desert wildlife on how best to live in a potentially hostile landscape. In summer, the early morning and evening have the most pleasant temperatures to be out and about. Photographers know that these times offer the best light for photography, too. When captivated by the grand scenery, it's easy to forget to drink enough water, but you'll be glad you did drink enough at the end of the day! For maximum efficiency, the body also needs food when hiking—snacks will increase your endurance.

Suggestions for backcountry travel and camping include these wilderness guidelines:

• Before heading into the backcountry, check with a knowledgeable person about weather, water sources, fire danger, trail conditions, and regulations.

• Tell a reliable person where you're going and when you expect to return.

• Travel in small groups for the best experience; group size may also be regulated.

• Try not to camp on meadows, as the grass is easily trampled and killed.

• Avoid digging tent trenches or cutting vegetation.

• Use a campstove to prevent marring the land.

• Camp at least 300 feet away from springs, creeks, and trails. State law prohibits camping within a quarter mile of a sole water source so that wildlife and stock won't be scared away.

• Wash away from streams and lakes.

• Don't drink untreated water in the wilderness,

Arizona's Native American lands are among the country's most beautiful. Highlights include the Navajo's Monument Valley, the Hopi's ancient stone villages, the Havasupai's waterfalls and travertine pools, the Hualapai's western Grand Canyon viewpoints, and fishing and camping in the cool forests of the White Mountain Apache.

no matter how clean the water appears. It may contain the parasitic protozoan *Giardia lamblia,* which causes the unpleasant disease giardiasis. Boiling your water for several minutes will kill giardia as well as other bacterial or viral pathogens. Filtering and iodine treatments usually work, too, although they're not as reliable as boiling.

• Bring a trowel for personal sanitation and dig 4–6 inches deep. In desert areas it's best to bag and carry out toilet paper because the stuff lasts for years and years in a dry climate; backcountry visitors in the Grand Canyon and Paria Canyon *must* pack it out.

• Carry plenty of feed for horses and mules.

• Leave dogs at home; they foul campsites and disturb wildlife and other hikers. If you do bring one, please keep it under physical control at all times. They're not allowed in the backcountry of national parks.

• Take home all your trash, so animals can't dig it up and scatter it.

• Help preserve Native American and historic ruins.

• A survival kit and small flashlight can make the difference if you're caught in a storm or are out longer than expected. A pocket-sized container can hold what you need for the three essentials: *fire building* (matches in waterproof container and candle), *shelter* (space blanket, knife, and rope), and *signaling* (mirror and whistle).

• If lost, *realize it,* then find shelter and stay in one place. If you're sure of a way to civilization and plan to walk out, leave a note of your departure time and planned route.

VISITING NATIVE AMERICAN LANDS

Meeting Arizona's tribespeople offers the opportunity to learn about other cultures. Their lands represent 27 percent of the state, and include some beautiful mountain, canyon, and desert country. Tribes in Arizona, from north to south,

SHOPPING FOR NATIVE AMERICAN ARTS AND CRAFTS

The strength of the Navajo and Hopi cultures appears in their excellent arts and crafts. Trading posts and Native American crafts shops on and off the reservations offer large selections. You'll also have the opportunity to buy directly from the maker. Navajo sell from roadside stands, most numerous on the highways to Grand Canyon National Park. Hopi usually sell directly from their village homes. To learn about Native American art, visit the Heard Museum in Phoenix or the Museum of Northern Arizona in Flagstaff. Books—available in trading posts, bookstores, and libraries—describe crafts and what to look for when buying; see Suggested Reading for more information.

The best work commands high prices but can be a fine memento of a visit to Native American lands. Tribespeople know what their crafts are worth, so bargaining is not normally done. Competition, especially among Navajo at their roadside stands, can make for some very low prices, however. Discounts often mark the end of the tourist season in September and October.

The Navajo have long earned fame for silver jewelry and woven rugs; you'll also see their stonework, pottery, basketry, and sand paintings. Craftsmen learned to work silver from Mexicans in the 19th century, then gradually developed distinctive Navajo styles, such as the squash-blossom necklace with its horseshoe-shaped pendant. Silversmiths also turn out bracelets, rings, concha belts, buckles, and bolo ties. The Navajo are especially fond of turquoise, which appears in much of their work. Navajo once wove fine blankets using sheep obtained from the Spanish and weaving skills learned from pueblo Indians, but factory-made blankets in the late 19th century nearly ended the market for hand-woven ones. At the suggestion of trader Lorenzo Hubbell, weavers switched to a heavier cloth for use as rugs, which became extremely popular. Rugs have evolved into more than a dozen regional styles and may be made from hand-spun and dyed yarn or less expensive commercial yarn. Navajo once used sand-paintings only in ceremonies but now also produce the distinctive designs and colors for the tourist trade.

The Hopi carve exotic kachina dolls from cottonwood and create jewelry, pottery, and basketry.

---

are Paiute, Navajo, Hopi, Havasupai, Hualapai, Yavapai, Apache, Mohave, Chemehuevi, Cocopah, Yaqui, Pima, and Tohono O'odham. See descriptions in the individual travel sections for tribal museums, dances, crafts, recreation, food, and accommodations.

On any of the 23 reservations, keep in mind that you're a guest on private land. Many residents prefer not to be disturbed. You'll generally need permits or permission to camp, hike, or leave the main roads. Usually a small charge applies for these activities. All fishing and hunting on Native American lands require tribal permits, though you won't need Arizona state licenses. Sometimes parts of a reservation are closed to outsiders. Native Americans prefer *not* to be treated as anthropological subjects, so it's important to ask permission before taking photos. The Hopi generally forbid photography, sketching, and recording—so don't even think of pulling a camera out on their reservation!

Highlights for visitors on Native American lands include the canyons and Monument Valley of the Navajo, ancient stone villages of the Hopi, waterfalls and travertine pools of the Havasupai, western Grand Canyon viewpoints and the road into the Grand Canyon of the Hualapai, and fishing and camping in the cool forests of the White Mountain Apache. You can learn about tribal beliefs and see arts and crafts at museums on lands of the Navajo, Hopi, Apache, Mohave, Pima/Maricopa (Salt River and Gila River Reservations), Quechan, and Cocopah. Three other museums of Native American culture—the Heard in Phoenix, the Museum of Northern Arizona in Flagstaff, and the Amerind Foundation near Benson—provide excellent introductions to Arizona's tribes and their artistry. You'll find at least one motel and campground

The kachina dolls originally followed simple designs and served to educate children about Hopi religion. With the rise of interest from outsiders, the Hopi began to carve more elaborate and realistic figures from the diverse Hopi pantheon. The dolls include clowns (painted with black and white stripes and often holding watermelon slices), animal-like forms, solemn masked figures, and fearsome ogres. Much thought and symbolism go into a Hopi carving, so even though its price is high, the doll will be good value. (Some Navajo have cashed in on the kachina-doll trade, but the Hopi may tell you that the Navajo don't really know about the kachina religion; Navajo dolls tend to have more fur, fiercer features, and lower prices.) Hopi silversmiths use traditional symbols for their inlay work, made from two sheets of silver, one with a design cut out, sandwiched together. This style, now a Hopi trademark, is seen in earrings, bracelets, rings, bolo ties, and belt buckles. The Hopi also turn out beautiful pottery and baskets, as they have for many centuries.

Artists of both tribes create attractive paintings, prints, and sculpture with Native American motifs.

© BILL WEIR

Navajo roadside jewelry stall

on lands of the Navajo, Hopi, White Mountain Apache, and San Carlos Apache.

Tribes in western, central, eastern, and southern Arizona have gotten into the casino business. This book mentions those facilities, but the author does not recommend gambling—whether Native American, private, or state.

VISITING MEXICO

Arizona has always had a close relationship with Mexico. About 16 percent of Arizona's population is of Spanish descent, and Spanish and Mexican influences are apparent in the state's architecture, food, language, and music.

You may easily visit Mexico via any of the six state border crossings. Most people in the border towns understand English, and shopkeepers happily accept U.S. dollars. Nogales, close to Tucson, offers the best shopping and receives the most

visitors. In all the border towns except Sonoita, you can park on the U.S. side and stroll across to the shops and restaurants in Mexico. Sonoita lies two miles beyond the boundary, and you'll probably want to drive there.

Permits

United States and Canadian citizens may visit border towns for as long as 72 hours without any formalities; just announce your nationality when returning to the U.S. side. Bring proof of citizenship—passport, voter-registration card and a photo ID, or birth or naturalization certificate (original or official copy only) and a photo ID. Another possibility is to fill out an Affidavit of Citizenship form, have it notarized, and bring a photo ID; this should be done before coming to the border. Travelers from other countries should ask for regulations about entering and returning *before* crossing over.

Longer stays or travel to the interior require visitors to carry a tourist card, easily obtainable by U.S. and Canadian citizens at the border with proof of citizenship—a driver's license alone won't work—and usually good for 90 days.

Motorists may drive to the border towns and to Baja California without a permit. To go farther, vehicle permits are necessary; trailers and motorbikes require permits too. To obtain permits, you need to show proof of ownership—title, bill of sale, or registration—and pay a fee. Drivers visiting only Sonora and entering and exiting via Nogales can obtain a free permit. If the vehicle belongs to someone else, check requirements first with a Mexican consulate.

Most U.S. insurance policies are worthless in Mexico. Unless you have Mexican insurance, the police there might throw you in jail after an accident, even if it wasn't your fault. Buy Mexican insurance, available by the day or longer, in border towns or in cities of southern Arizona.

Information

Tourist offices on the Arizona side (Yuma, Nogales, and Douglas) know about neighboring towns in Mexico. With luck, you might be able to find a tourist office in the Mexican towns, too. In Arizona, Mexico has a consulate in Phoenix, Tucson, Nogales, and Douglas. On the Internet, visit www.mexonline.com for tourist information.

Events

Arizona offers a full schedule of rodeos, parades, art festivals, historic celebrations, gem and mineral shows, and sports events. Activities tend to shift between desert communities in winter and those in the cool mountains in summer. Stop at a visitor center to see what's coming up. These also provide the statewide *Calendar of Events,* published by the Arizona Office of Tourism, or you can get it on the Web at www.arizonaguide.com.

Major Holidays

Even though not always mentioned in the text, many museums and other tourist attractions close on such holidays as Thanksgiving, Christmas, and New Year's Day; call ahead to check. Most places stay open on Easter, as it's observed mainly in churches.

Major American holidays include
- **New Year's Day:** January 1
- **Martin Luther King, Jr.'s Birthday:** January 15; usually observed the third Monday in January
- **Presidents' Day:** third Monday in February; honors Washington and Lincoln
- **Easter Sunday:** late March or early April
- **Cinco de Mayo:** May 5; a Mexican festival celebrated in many Southwest communities
- **Memorial Day:** last Monday in May
- **Independence Day:** July 4
- **Labor Day:** first Monday in September
- **Columbus Day:** second Monday in October
- **Veterans Day:** November 11
- **Thanksgiving Day:** fourth Thursday in November
- **Christmas Day:** December 25

Accommodations and Food

ACCOMMODATIONS

Price Categories

This book has been written to assist travelers of all budgets. You'll rarely need to spend more than $35 for a room except at the Grand Canyon and at peak travel times elsewhere, when camping will be a good option. If you have the funds to pamper yourself, top-notch resorts will do just that. And you'll have plenty of mid-range accommodations almost everywhere. Prices quoted in this book are peak season rates and generally do not include taxes, which average about 10 percent; guest ranches and resorts may add an additional service charge of about 15 percent.

Motels and Hotels

The busiest tourist seasons are winter and spring in the central and southern desert country (Phoenix, Yuma, Tucson), and summer in the high country (Grand Canyon National Park, Flagstaff, Prescott, Payson, Pinetop-Lakeside). Lodging reservations come in handy at these times. Rates fluctuate dramatically with the seasons at the more expensive places, where off-season prices can be great value. Economy motels offer some great deals, too, when business is slow.

You'll find the major hotel and motel chains well represented in Arizona. Some of the state's historic hotels offer the elegance and romance of the old days. Outstanding historic places, worth a visit to the lobby even if you're not staying there, include El Tovar at the Grand Canyon, Hassayampa Inn in Prescott, Copper Queen Hotel in Bisbee, and the Gadsden Hotel in Douglas.

Bed and Breakfasts

These private houses or small inns make rooms available to travelers in the European tradition. The degree of luxury varies, but the hosts offer a personal touch not found in motels.

You'll find B&Bs in many parts of the state—in cities, in resort towns, and on ranches. Usually they don't advertise; some are listed in these pages or with local chambers of commerce. Always call ahead for reservations.

Bed and breakfast agencies will help match you to the best place without charge. *Mi Casa Su Casa* (Spanish for "My house [is] your house"), P.O. Box 950, Tempe, AZ 85280; 480/990-0682, 800/456-0682, www.azres.com handles reservations for about 65 B&Bs in the Phoenix area and hundreds of others throughout the Southwest. Prices range $50–275 d, with most in the $75–125 d range; singles usually get $5–10 off. Arizona Trails Reservation Service, P.O. Box 18998, Fountain Hills, AZ 85269, 480/837-4284, 888/799-4284, www.arizonatrails.com, offers listings statewide. Rates range $65–450 d; singles may get about $10 off.

Hostels

Hostelling International (HI) and **independent** hostels offer clean and friendly accommodations for people of all ages. Hostels generally consist of dormitory rooms (usually separate men's and women's) and perhaps some rooms for families plus a kitchen and a common room. Besides being good places for low-budget travelers, they enable you to meet visitors from other countries. Arizona currently has one HI hostel in Phoenix and independents in Tuba City (Navajo Nation), Flagstaff, Williams, Sedona, Tucson, and Bisbee. Visitors should be prepared to bring or rent bed linens and to pitch in to take care of the hostel. Rates run about $15 per night. Some hostels will accept phone reservations made with a credit card.

In Arizona, Metcalf House, 1026 N. Ninth St., Phoenix, AZ 85006; 602/254-9803, sells membership cards good at any member hostel in the world, or you can contact the national office at Hostelling International, 733 15th St. NW, Suite 840, Washington, D.C. 20005; 202/783-6161; www.hiayh.org.

Hostel directories can come in handy. For news and listings online, check out www.hostels.com. Hostelling International has an annual guide, usually available free at their hostels, but it covers

MOTEL AND HOTEL CHAINS

By Stephen Metzger

If you've been on the road at all in the United States in the last few years, you've noticed the amazing proliferation of chain lodging—from Motel 6s to Super 8s to all the Inns (Holiday, Ramada, Comfort, Days . . .). Even many of the ol' Best Westerns have been upgraded and remarketed in recent years; the familiar yellow-crown signs that once rose comfortably into the low skylines of twilight have been replaced by modern deep-blue signs with stylized red crowns and electronic marquees advertising sports bars and exercise rooms. Most of these lodges offer competitive rates; clean, quiet rooms; and a known quantity in terms of price, amenities, and general quality. Unfortunately, they've also helped further the depersonalization of small-town America; the colorful little mom-and-pop places can't compete.

Following is a list of some of the common hotel and motel chains and what you can expect them to provide. In general, you can count on a swimming pool, laundry, television with a movie channel, free local phone calls, free morning coffee, and a choice of smoking or no-smoking rooms; most places have a few handicapped-accessible rooms too. Many offer discounts to members of various groups and clubs: the American Automobile Association, American Association of Retired Persons, military employees, and others. Always ask.

Refer to this information when you come across a listing for one of the chains described below.

Best Western, 800/528-1234; www.bestwestern.com. Best Westerns are individually owned and range considerably in size and appearance—from roadside motels to downtown high-rises. They all must meet strict standards, however, and you are generally assured of quality and comfort. I stay at them frequently, as I know they'll be clean and quiet and the service dependable and friendly. Most have pools; many have restaurants on the premises.

Days Inn, 800/DAYS INN (800/329-7466); www.daysinn.com. Consistently comfortable and clean, though without much personality. Most have pools; no restaurants.

Holiday Inn, 800/HOLIDAY (800/465-4329); www.holiday-inn.com. Generally the most upscale of the lodges listed here. Each has a restaurant, lounge, pool, and meeting rooms.

Holiday Inn Express (same telephone and Internet) is a scaled-down version of Holiday Inns. These lodges offer continental breakfasts, and most have pools.

Motel 6, 800/4-MOTEL-6 (800/466-8356); www.motel6.com. Cookie cutter, but comfortable and less expensive than the other chains. Each may have a small pool and bathrooms with shower stall but no tub. This chain is extremely popular, and rooms fill up quickly. Often times the No Vacancy sign goes up well before nightfall.

Ramada Inn, 800/2-RAMADA (800/272-6232); www.ramada.com. Ranging from urban high-rises to smaller-town motels, Ramadas all offer restaurants, lounges, and meeting rooms and are reliably comfortable and clean.

Super 8, 800/800-8000; www.super8.com. These are consistently clean, quiet, and inexpensive.

A Word about Hotel Rates

The more I travel the more I realize how capricious hotel rates are, how the rate you get depends on so many variables: whether you phone in your reservation or walk in off the street; whether it's 2:00 in the afternoon or 10:00 at night; whether you asked for a "discount" or not. Keep in mind hotels, and to some degree motels, have widely fluctuating rates, and that above all they don't want empty rooms. True story: I pulled into Fort Collins, Colorado, one afternoon and walked into the lobby of a major hotel chain. Since it was packed with group-ers, and waiting 10 minutes at the counter got me no closer to a clerk, I walked outside to a pay phone and called the front desk. "Rates are $79 a night," I was told, "but sorry, no rooms available tonight." So I walked next door, where I was told there was one room available, a smoking room. Nope, wouldn't do. So I walked back to the lobby of the first hotel, worked my way to the counter, and asked for a room. "Yes, we do have a room, Sir. For $69."

"Do you offer any corporate discounts?" I asked.

"Let's see ... Yes, we can give you a room for $59." Now, this is backward from how it usually works (though it does go to show how arbitrary it can all be). Often you can get a better rate by phone, even if you're calling from just outside the door, as they figure you're not committed yet, and they *want* you. Once you're in the door they figure you're less likely to go somewhere else.

Another true story: One night in Raton, New Mexico, I stopped for the night at dusk at a small independent motel. A man in front of me was talking with the desk clerk.

"How much for a room?"

"Do you qualify for any discounts?" the woman asked.

Shrugging and giving her a blank look, he said, "What do you mean?"

"Triple A, corporate, AARP, you know ... "

"Uh, I guess not ... "

"Sixty-four dollars for a single."

He said he'd take it, filled out the registration form, and left with his key.

My turn: "Do you have a nonsmoking single available for this evening?"

"Do you qualify for any discounts?"

"Yes, I do."

"Fifty-four dollars for a single."

"I'll take it."

Is there a lesson here? If there is it's that, like I said, rates are not as fixed as you might think. Some things to keep in mind: The later in the day the better your chance of getting a cut rate. The owners want their rooms full, and, if it looks as if they might not be, they'll offer incentives, in the form of a few bucks off the "standard" rate. (Of course, you also risk not finding a vacancy, and that risk might not be worth it to you.) Also, *ask* about discounts. Most hotels offer at least American Automobile Association, American Association of Retired Persons, and corporate discounts, and you might qualify. Finally, in the case of chain and franchise lodging, I've had better luck phoning the hotel directly than calling the 800 number and talking to an operator who might be booking a room in a town 3,000 miles away from the switchboard.

Bottom line: Phone around, and talk like you do it all the time. You might be surprised at the results.

Stephen Metzger is the author of Moon Handbooks to Colorado, New Mexico, and Santa Fe–Taos.

---

only HI places. The *Hostel Handbook* lists both HI and independents; get it from Jim Williams (722 St. Nicholas Ave., New York, NY 10031; www.hostelhandbook.com). *Hostels U.S.A.* provides a comprehensive guide to HI and the independents along with detailed descriptions of the atmosphere at each place. It's published by Globe Pequot Press (888/249-7586; www.globe-pequot.com) and sold in bookstores. All three publications cover the U.S. and Canada.

Guest Ranches

These ranches feature horseback riding, miles of open country, ex-

For a truly "Western" experience, try one of Arizona's guest ranches: in addition to enjoying miles of open country and excellent food, guests participate in roping and riding instruction, hayrides, cookouts, square dancing, and even working cattle. Twenty-first century activities include tennis and swimming.

cellent food, and an informal Western atmosphere. Activities may include tennis, swimming, roping and riding instruction, hayrides, cookouts, square dancing, and even working cattle.

Wickenburg and Tucson are the major guest ranch centers, with other ranches scattered about, mainly in the southern half of the state. Rates typically run more than $100 per person per day and include all meals and some activities. Most visitors come in winter to enjoy the desert at its best; some guest ranches close in summer. On the Web, you'll find a handy directory at www.guestranches.com.

Campgrounds

The best parts of Arizona lie outdoors, where you can choose among hundreds of campgrounds on federal, state, Native American, or private lands. Federal government sites, the most common, are offered by the Forest Service, National Park Service, and Bureau of Land Management; campgrounds commonly feature tables, toilets, and drinking water, with fees ranging from free to $15 per night; only a few have showers. Many state campgrounds include showers and hookups; they're good values at rates of $8–12 per vehicle per night, or $15–20 with hookups. Some Native American reservations, most notably the Havasupai, Navajo, and White Mountain Apache, offer primitive campgrounds. Commercial campgrounds provide the most frills, often including showers, Laundromats, hookups, stores, game rooms, and perhaps a swimming pool. Rates start about $15 per night; tents may or may not be accepted. Families should be aware that many of Arizona's RV parks cater to retired people and may not welcome children. Unless otherwise stated, all campgrounds mentioned in these pages do accept families.

Other types of camping are also possible. You're welcome to camp almost anywhere in the national forests and on most BLM lands; this dispersed style of camping costs nothing and for seasoned campers provides the best outdoor experience. Since there are no facilities, it's up to you to leave the forest or desert in its natural state. Be very careful with fire—try to use a campstove rather than leave a fire scar. Sometimes high fire danger in early summer causes the Forest Service to prohibit campfires or even to close sections of forest. The seven national forests in Arizona cover vast expanses of mountain, plateau, and desert country from the state's far north to the far south. Stop at a Forest Service office for maps and information on camping, hiking, fishing, and back-road travel. The Bureau of Land Management looks after much of the Arizona Strip, western Arizona, and a few areas elsewhere.

FOOD

South-of-the-border food attracts a large following—you're rarely far from a Mexican restaurant! Southwestern cuisine—flavored with Mexican spices and traditions—has also become very popular. Western-style restaurants dish out cowboy food—beef, beans, and biscuits. You can sample Indian fry bread and the Navajo taco—beef, beans, lettuce, and tomatoes, and cheese on fry bread—on or off the reservations. Chinese have operated restaurants since territorial days and still do a good business across the state. Larger cities offer a cosmopolitan array of ethnic and fine-dining restaurants.

Price ranges accompanying the dining descriptions in this guide refer to the prices of dinner entrees (per person). Only the sales tax is added to your bill; you're expected to leave a tip of at least 15 percent for table service.

Transportation

BY CAR

Most people choose cars as the most convenient and economical way to get around; you can easily rent them in any sizable town in Arizona. Four-wheel-drive vehicles will be handy if you plan extensive travel on back roads. Phoenix and Tucson offer the largest selection as well as RV and possibly 4WD rentals. Nearby Las Vegas and Albuquerque can be convenient for car rentals too. It's worth shopping around not only for the best deal from each agency, but also at different cities as taxes form a large part of the rental cost.

Public transportation serves the cities and some towns but very few scenic, historic, and recreational areas. Unless you'll be taking tours, you really need your own wheels.

Look for road maps in visitor centers, gift shops, and bookstores. For greater detail, check out the Arizona atlases; the one by Benchmark Maps is especially easy to read. The AAA *Indian Country* map provides superb coverage of the Four Corners region, including the Grand

Canyon and Navajo and Hopi reservations; the map is free at AAA offices for members and for sale in stores.

Driveaways

These are autos scheduled for delivery to another city. If the auto's destination is a place you intend to visit, a driveaway can be like getting a free car rental. You have to be at least 21 years old and pay a refundable deposit of $75–150. There will be time and mileage limits. Ask for an economy car if you want the lowest driving costs. In a large city—Phoenix or Tucson in Arizona—look in the Yellow Pages under "Automobile Transporters and Driveaways."

Hitchhiking

Opinions and experiences vary on hitching. It can be a great way to meet people, despite the dangers and long waits. Offer to buy lunch or help with gas money to repay the driver. Often you can arrange rides with fellow travelers at hostels. The ride boards at Northern Arizona University (Flagstaff), Arizona State University (Tempe, near Phoenix), and the University of Arizona (Tucson), list rides available and desired. Highway police tolerate hitchhiking as long as it doesn't create a hazard or take place on an interstate or freeway. Police do routinely check IDs, however. Women should be especially cautious when hitchhiking.

BUS AND SHUTTLE SERVICES

By Bus

Greyhound offers frequent service on its transcontinental bus routes across northern and southern Arizona and between Flagstaff and Phoenix; call 800/231-2222 or visit the Web at www.greyhound.com. The company often offers special deals on bus passes and "one-way anywhere" tickets. Overseas residents may buy a Greyhound Ameripass at additional discounts outside North America.

Sedona Phoenix Shuttle serves Sedona, Cottonwood, Camp Verde, and Phoenix/Sky Harbor; call 928/282-2066 (Sedona) or 800/448-7988; www.sedona-phoenix-shuttle.com.

Navajo Transit System traverses the Navajo and Hopi Reservations in northeastern Arizona; 928/729-4002. **White Mountain Passenger Line** heads to the pines at Payson, Show Low, and other eastern Arizona destinations from Phoenix; 928/537-4539 (main office in Show Low). **Golden State** connects Tucson with the southeastern towns of Nogales, Sierra Vista, Bisbee, and Douglas; its sister company, **Crucero,** serves destinations in Mexico from Tucson and Nogales; for either company, visit the Greyhound station in Tucson or call 520/623-1675. Some bus companies give small discounts for round-trips.

Local bus services run at Grand Canyon National Park (South Rim), Phoenix, and Tucson. Service in other towns is usually too infrequent for travelers. Always have exact change ready when taking local buses.

By Train

Amtrak runs two luxury train lines across Arizona. Both connect Los Angeles with New Orleans, Chicago, and other destinations to the east. On the northern route, the Southwest Chief runs daily in each direction with stops in Arizona at Kingman, Williams, Flagstaff, and Winslow. On the southern route, the Sunset Limited stops in Yuma, Tucson, and Benson, but it runs only three times per week in each direction. Shuttle buses from Phoenix connect with both trains.

Amtrak usually charges more than buses but has far roomier seating, as well as parlor cars and sleepers; 800/872-7245 (800/USA-RAIL); www.amtrak.com. Fares depend upon availability—advance planning or off-season travel will get you the lowest prices. "Explore America" fares and rail-flight programs offer some interesting possibilities. Travel agents outside North America sell USA Railpasses (not for U.S. or Canadian citizens).

By Air

More than a dozen major airlines fly to Phoenix and Tucson. Fares and schedules tend to change frequently—a travel agent can help you find the best flights, or you can do it

M

DRIVING TIPS

Summer heat puts an extra strain on both car and driver. Make sure the cooling system, engine oil, transmission fluid, fan belts, and tires are in top condition. Carry several gallons of water in case of breakdown or radiator trouble. Never leave children or pets in a parked car during warm weather—temperatures inside can cause fatal heatstroke in just minutes. Radiator caps must not be opened when the engine is hot, because the escaping steam can cause severe burns.

At times the desert has *too much water*—late-summer storms frequently flood low spots in the road. Wait for the water to go down, until you can see bottom, before crossing. If the car begins to hydroplane after a rainstorm, it's best to remove your foot from the accelerator, avoid braking, and keep the steering straight until the tires grip the road again. Drive in the "footsteps" of the car ahead, if you can.

Dust storms also tend to be short-lived but can completely block visibility. Treat them like dense fog: pull completely off the road and stop, turning off your lights so as not to confuse other drivers.

Radio stations carry frequent updates when weather hazards exist. With a VHF radio (between 162.4 and 162.55 MHz), you can pick up continuous weather forecasts in many areas.

If stranded in the backcountry, whether on the desert or in the mountains, stay with the vehicle unless you're *positive* of the way out; then leave a note detailing your route and departure time. Airplanes can easily spot a car—leave your hood and trunk up

© BILL WEIR

A hole in the radiator knocks out Larry Lipchinsky's car.

yourself on the Internet. Big-city newspapers usually run advertisements of discount fares and tours in their Sunday travel sections. Phoenix offers the most connections and generally the lowest fares. Sometimes you can get good deals to Tucson; if not, there's a shuttle bus service between the two cities. You'll have the best chance of getting low fares by planning a week or more ahead and staying over a Saturday night (any night with Southwest Airlines); round-trip fares will almost always be a much better value than one-ways, though changes may be costly.

Phoenix serves as the hub for nearly all flights within the state. Destinations from Phoenix's Sky Harbor Airport (PHX) include Page (PGA), Flagstaff (FLG), Prescott (PRC), Kingman

(IGM), Bullhead City (IFP), Lake Havasu City (HII), Yuma (YUM), Tucson (TUS), and Sierra Vista (FHU). The cost per mile of these short hops is high but you'll often enjoy excellent views.

America West, 800/235-9292, www.ameri cawest.com, uses the Phoenix airport as a hub and claims to have the most Arizona flights, including many within the state; it also flies from Tucson, but all flights go via Phoenix. **Southwest Airlines** offers many flights from Phoenix and some direct connections out of Tucson. Southwest has long been a leader in low-cost fares, and since its flights don't appear on flight reservation computers, it's worth contacting them directly; call 800/IFLY-SWA (800/435-9792) or look them up on the Web at www.southwest.com.

and tie a piece of cloth to the antenna—but a person trying to walk out is difficult to see. If you're stranded, emergency supplies can definitely help: blankets or sleeping bags, raingear, gloves, first-aid kit, tools, jumper cables, motor oil, shovel, rope, traction mats or chains, flashlight, flares, fire extinguisher, maps, water, food, and a can opener.

School crossings and buses require extra care. You must stop if someone is using a crosswalk. Crossings in use by school children have a 15 mph posted speed; police have ticketed drivers going 20 mph in them! When you see a school bus stopped with red lights flashing and a stop sign arm extended, you must stop in *both* directions until the lights and arm are turned off, unless there is a *physical* barrier dividing the roadway and you're traveling in the opposite direction.

Unless posted otherwise, speed limits are 15 mph when you're approaching a school crossing, 25 mph in business and residential districts, and 55 mph on open highways and city freeways. Although it's tempting to let loose on long, empty highways, they haven't all been designed for extreme speeds—a speeding car could top a small rise and suddenly find itself bearing down on a flock of sheep crossing the road. Deer, elk, and other stray animals can pose a danger too, especially at night.

Right turns on red are permissible after a complete stop. Left turns from a two-way street onto another two-way street, may require extra vigilance. Most intersections feature a four-tiered light with a green right-of-way arrow. After the turning arrow goes to red, the green circle light then comes on: you can still turn left, but you no longer have the right-of-way. These types of accidents are common, so be wary.

Reversible lanes in Phoenix and some other cities have signs designating the lane for certain hours for "Through Traffic," "Do Not Use," and "Other times 2 way left."

Seat belts must be worn by all front-seat passengers. Child safety seats are now required for all children under five years old, regardless of weight.

Arizona has very strict laws against driving under the influence of drugs or drink. Penalties for the first offense include mandatory jail term, fine, license suspension, and screening, education, and/or treatment.

The *Arizona Driver License Manual* contains a good review of driving knowledge and road rules. It's available free in most large towns at the state Motor Vehicle Division office.

TOURS

See your travel agent or travel websites for the latest on package tours to Arizona. Within the state, local operators offer everything from city tours to rafting trips through the Grand Canyon. Gray Line offers the largest selection of bus excursions, ranging from half a day to three days; tours leave from Flagstaff, Phoenix, and Tucson. Smaller companies offer back-road trips to scenic spots inaccessible to regular vehicles; you'll find them in Page, Monument Valley, Canyon de Chelly, Sedona, Yuma Phoenix, and Tucson. Flightseeing trips provide a birds-eye view of the Grand Canyon, Sedona's Red Rock Country, and other spectacular areas. The "Tours and Transportation" sections in each chapter list operators; also consult local chambers of commerce and visitor centers.

Elderhostel

This nonprofit organization offers educational adventures for people 55 and over (spouses can be under 55). Many of the programs take place in Arizona, exploring archaeology, history, cultures, crafts, nature, and other topics. Participants join small groups for short-term studies and stay in simple accommodations, which helps keep costs low. For a catalog, contact Elderhostel, 11 Avenue de Lafayette, Boston, MA 02111; 617/426-7788 or toll-free 877/426-8056; www.elderhostel.org.

Information and Services

Arizona Office of Tourism

This office, 1110 W. Washington Street, Suite 155, Phoenix, AZ 85007, 602/364-3700 or toll-free at 888/520-3434, fax 602/240-5475, provides information on every region of the state. You can find most of the literature at other tourist offices, but this office has the best selection. It's open Mon.–Fri. 8 A.M.–5 P.M. Surf to the excellent website, www.arizon-aguide.com, for travel tips, event listings, and links to many chamber of commerce sites. Painted Cliffs Welcome Center provides information at I-40 Exit 359 near the New Mexico border, daily 8 A.M.–5 P.M.

Medical Services

In emergencies, dial 911 or use the emergency number listed on most telephones. Hospital emergency rooms offer the quickest help. When heading for any of Arizona's emergency rooms, keep in mind that patients may be treated according to severity of condition.

Foreign Currency Exchange

You can change foreign currency in Phoenix, but anywhere else in the state may involve extra delay and expense. ATM machines found in nearly every town provide cash at good rates. Traveler's checks in U.S. dollars can easily be cashed at most businesses.

Postal and Telephone Services

Normal post office hours are Mon.–Fri. 8:30 A.M.–4:30 P.M. and sometimes Saturday 8:30 A.M.–noon. You can get a variety of postal information at 800/275-8777 or on the Web at www.usps.gov.

Most of Arizona uses the 928 **area code** except for the Phoenix area and the southeastern part of the state. Phoenix has a 602 area code, but Glendale and other cities to the west use 623, while Tempe, Scottsdale, Mesa, and other places to the east have 480. Tucson, Florence, and the rest of southeastern Arizona are in the 520 code. Use these when dialing 1+ or 0+ numbers *inside* as well as outside Arizona. To obtain a local number from Information, dial 1-411; for a number in other places or for another state, dial 1, the area code, then 555-1212. Many airlines, auto rental firms, and motel chains have toll-free 800, 866, 877, or 888 numbers; if you don't have the number, just dial 800/555-1212.

Pre-paid telephone cards provide much lower costs for long-distance calls than plunking in coins or using a telephone company billing card; discount stores often have the lowest prices for the pre-paid cards.

Measurements

If you ask a rancher how many kilometers to the next town, all you'll receive is a blank stare. Most Arizonans are completely unfamiliar with the metric system, so visitors need to know the Olde English system:

one inch = 2.54 centimeters
foot = 0.305 meter
mile = 1.609 kilometers
square mile = 2.590 square kilometers
acre = 0.405 hectare
ounce = 0.028 kilogram
pound (lb.) = 0.454 kilogram
quart = 0.946 liter
U.S. gallon = 3.785 liters
To figure Celsius temperatures (°C), subtract 32 from Fahrenheit (°F) and divide by 1.8.

Time

Travelers in Arizona should remember that the state is on Mountain Standard Time all year, except for the Navajo Reservation, which goes on daylight saving time—add one hour April–Oct.—to conform with its Utah and New Mexico sections. Note that the Hopi Reservation, completely within Arizona and surrounded by the Navajo, stays on standard time year-round along with the rest of the state. In summer, Arizona runs on the same time as California and Nevada, and one hour behind Utah, Colorado, and New Mexico. In winter, Arizona is one hour ahead of California and Nevada, on the same time as Utah, Colorado, and New Mexico.

Electricity

Electric current in the United States is 110–120 volts, 60-cycle; appliances manufactured for use in other countries may need a transformer, as well as a plug adapter for the flat two-pin style of the U.S. plug.

VIRTUAL ARIZONA

Although a virtual visit to Arizona cannot replace the real thing, you'll find an enormous amount of helpful information on the Internet's **World Wide Web.** Thousands of websites interlink to cover everything from the Grand Canyon's environmental issues to Scottsdale restaurant reviews. Up-to-the-minute weather and news reports lie at your fingertips 24 hours a day. Email links let you write to many of the tourist offices and other people who can provide additional information. The websites will save you time and money by quickly providing information that you would otherwise have to write or call for. Nearly all public libraries offer free use of Internet computers. If you're new to the online world, library staff or a friend can get you started.

Web "surfing" will have choppy waves at times, however, due to out-of-date sites and missing links. Also, don't expect to find every topic covered in *Moon Handbooks: Arizona*! Note that you'll often see Internet addresses beginning with an "http://" but most Web browsers need only the part of the address that follows, which usually begins with "www."

Where to Start

Drop by the **author's website,** www.arizonahandbook.com for the latest updates, Internet links, and photo galleries; it's an extension of this book and a way to put in your "two cents" worth.

The **Yahoo** site will take you almost anywhere in Arizona with its well-organized offerings. Enter www.yahoo.com and select Regional U.S. States, then Arizona. From there you can select "cities" or such topics as arts, community and culture, government, news, recreation and sports, and travel. Other search engines work well, too.

The **Arizona Office of Tourism** site, www.arizonaguide.com, leads you to many corners of the state in its online guide. **Arizona Web Hub** at www.azwebhub.com also has an extensive listing by subject. **AZ Tourist Online** at www.aztourist.com describes the travel scene with stories, news, dining reviews, and event listings. Although based in the Phoenix area, the **Arizona Republic** site, www.azcentral.com, has excellent statewide coverage of news, weather, sports, business, entertainment, and travel. *Arizona Highways* at www.arizonahighways.com offers some of the same beautiful photos, travel information, hike descriptions, and entertaining stories found in its magazine pages. You'll find lots of hiking and other outdoor information at the **Great Outdoor Recreation Pages,** www.gorp.com/gorp/location/az/az.htm. If you're interested in learning about the desert, check **Desert USA** at www.desertusa.com for information on places to visit and the plants and animals you might meet there. **Adventure in Hiking,** at www.swlink.net/~ttidyman/hiking/index.htm, features trails, hiking news, links, clubs, and Grand Canyon information.

Outstanding Local Sites

Grand Canyon National Park has so many things to see and do that it's well worth visiting the official site, www.nps.gov/grca. In north-central Arizona, the **Flagstaff Chamber of Commerce** at www.flagstaff.az.us will fill you in on the sights and services there. **Sedona-Oak Creek Chamber of Commerce** at www.visitsedona.com takes you to the magical Red Rock Country south of Flagstaff. In south-central Arizona, the **Phoenix area** site www.azfamily.com presents regional news, sports, restaurant reviews, and entertainment listings. Farther south, **Metropolitan Tucson Convention & Visitors Bureau** at www.visittucson.org has the latest on travel in and around the "Old Pueblo."

Grand Canyon National Park

Note: See color maps of the Grand Canyon National Park at the front of the book.

Two mighty but opposing forces—uplifting of the massive Colorado Plateau and vigorous downcutting by the Colorado River—created the awe-inspiring Grand Canyon and its many tributaries. Neither pictures nor words can fully describe the sight. You have to experience the Canyon by traveling along the rim, descending into the depths, riding the waves of the Colorado River, and watching the continuous show of colors and patterns as the sun moves across the sky.

The Canyon's grandeur stretches for 277 miles across northern Arizona; it's as much as 18 miles wide—10 miles on average—and one mile deep. Roads provide access to developed areas and viewpoints on both rims. Trails allow hikers and mule riders to descend the precipitous cliffs to the Colorado River. Yet most of the park remains as remote as ever, rarely visited by humans.

Getting Started

Most people head first to the South Rim, entering at either the South Entrance Station near Grand Canyon Village or the East Entrance Station near Desert View. A 25-mile scenic drive along the rim connects these entrances.

The South Rim features great views, a full range of accommodations and restaurants, and easy access—it's just 58 miles north of I-40 from Williams. Roads and most facilities stay open all year. Attractions include views from Yavapai Observation Station and other points near Grand Canyon Village and the scenic drives of Hermits Road to Hermit's Rest (8 miles) and Desert View Drive to Desert View (25 miles). Some remarkable architecture lines the South Rim, including a series of unique stone structures designed by Mary Colter. The South Rim also features most of the Canyon's easily accessible viewpoints and trails. It's not surprising, then, that large crowds of visitors, especially in summer, are the main drawback of this part of the Canyon. Park staff have big plans to relieve the congestion by adding more shuttles, bike paths, and foot trails; see the Special Topic "Shuttling Out to the South Rim," in this chapter.

The park collects an admission fee of $20 per private vehicle ($10 per pedestrian or bicyclist) that's good for seven days at the south and east entrances of the South Rim and at the main entrance of the North Rim. You'll get a park brochure and a copy of *The Guide* newspaper, which lists programs and sightseeing suggestions. Once you're in the park, visitor centers, exhibits, programs, and day hiking are free. Budget travelers can save money by stocking up on gas, groceries, and camping supplies at Flagstaff, Williams, or other towns away from the Canyon; prices at Tusayan and within the park can run substantially higher.

Only about one in 10 visitors makes it to the North Rim, but that visitor is rewarded with pristine forests, rolling meadows, splendid wildflower displays, and superb panoramas. Viewpoints here are about 1,500 feet higher than those at the South Rim and provide a dramatically different perspective of the Canyon. The North Rim area offers lodging, dining, and camping facilities similar to the South Rim's, though on a smaller scale. Unless you ski in (backcountry permit required), the North Rim's high country is open only from mid-May to late October, depending on the arrival of the first big winter storm. Although the rims stand just 10 miles apart, motorists on the South Rim must drive 215 miles and about five hours via Cameron and Jacob Lake to get here.

Adventurous travelers on the North Rim willing to tackle 61 miles of dirt road (each way; impassable when wet) can head west and south to **Toroweap Overlook.** This perch sits a dizzying 3,000 feet directly above the Colorado River—one of the Canyon's most spectacular viewpoints. Don't expect any facilities other than the road and outhouses. Bring all supplies, including water. Low elevations of 4,500–5,000 feet allow access most of the year; you can check road conditions with a ranger, 928/638-7888.

GRAND CANYON HIGHLIGHTS

Dramatic Views: Many easily accessible viewpoints line both rims of the Grand Canyon.

Amazing Hiking: Trails on the rims and into the depths draw people of all abilities.

Mule Trips: You can descend into the Canyon just as the first tourists did, letting the animals do most of the work.

Grand Canyon Railway: Passenger trains once again steam into the Grand Canyon depot on a nostalgic ride from Williams.

Kaibab Plateau: Alpine meadows and forests with summer wildflowers lie just back from the North Rim.

Toroweap: Dizzying views of the Colorado River from cliffs nearly 3,000 feet high lie at the end of a long, unpaved road on the North Rim.

River Running: The mighty Colorado River will sweep you through the heart of the Grand Canyon on one of the world's greatest adventures.

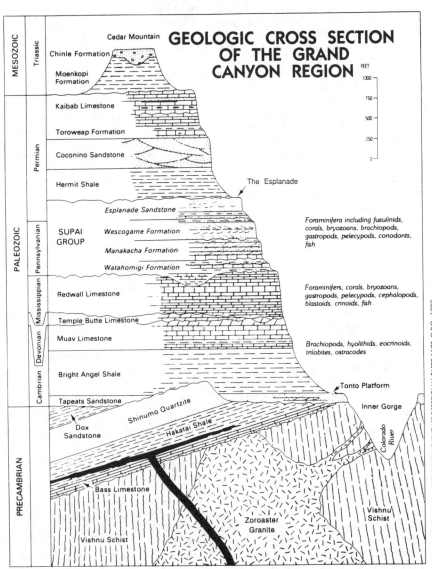

GEOLOGIC CROSS SECTION OF THE GRAND CANYON REGION

MESOZOIC	Triassic		Cedar Mountain
			Chinle Formation
			Moenkopi Formation

FEET
1000
750
500
250
0

Kaibab Limestone

Toroweap Formation

Coconino Sandstone

Hermit Shale

The Esplanade

SUPAI GROUP

Esplanade Sandstone

Wescogame Formation

Manakacha Formation

Watahomigi Formation

Foraminifera including fusulinids, corals, bryozoans, brachiopods, gastropods, pelecypods, conodonts, fish

Redwall Limestone

Foraminifers, corals, bryozoans, gastropods, pelecypods, cephalopods, blastoids, crinoids, fish

Temple Butte Limestone

Muav Limestone

Brachiopods, hyolithids, eocrinoids, trilobites, ostracodes

Bright Angel Shale

Tonto Platform

Tapeats Sandstone

Inner Gorge

Shinumo Quartzite

Hakatai Shale

Dox Sandstone

Colorado River

Bass Limestone

Zoroaster Granite

Vishnu Schist

Vishnu Schist

PALEOZOIC — Permian — Pennsylvanian — Mississippian — Devonian — Cambrian

PRECAMBRIAN

Park Practicalities

The Grand Canyon offers too much to see in one day—you'll probably wish to spend the night in the area. In Grand Canyon Village you can stay right on the rim at Bright Angel Lodge, Thunderbird Lodge, Kachina Lodge, or El Tovar Hotel. Other lodges lie back in the woods. The town of Tusayan, just outside the park nine miles south of Grand Canyon Village, provides additional places to stay. And farther south, the towns of Flagstaff and Williams offer a large selection of accommodations at lower prices; also, the little community of Valle on the way has two motels. One can usually find a place to stay anytime, but advance reservations will give the best choice of rooms. If planning a late arrival, you might consider either a reservation or staying in one of the towns surrounding the park.

You can obtain a copy of *The Guide* newspaper before your arrival by writing to the park at P.O. Box 129, Grand Canyon, AZ 86023. The **automated switchboard,** 928/638-7888, connects to all park offices and offers recorded information, including the latest weather forecast. **Hearing-impaired** people can use the TDD number for park information, 928/638-7804.

CANYON ROCKS

With 94 types of rock discovered in the Grand Canyon, how can you remember even the major formations? All you have to do is keep in mind, "Know the canyon history. See rocks made by time very slowly." From top to bottom,

Know	Kaibab Limestone
the	Toroweap Formation
canyon	Coconino Sandstone
history.	Hermit Shale
See	Supai Group
rocks	Redwall Limestone
made	Muav Limestone
by	Bright Angel Shale
time	Tapeats Sandstone
very slowly.	Vishnu Schist

Internet sites can help you plan your trip too. The National Park Service site, www.nps.gov/grca, contains news, visiting tips, hiking possibilities, and river-running information. The Grand Canyon Chamber of Commerce site, www.thecanyon.com, offers listings of accommodations, restaurants, and other services near the park.

An unfortunate note: Theft has become a problem at the Canyon—be sure to keep valuables hidden or keep them with you. Park rangers patrol the park, serving as law enforcement officers and firefighters; see them if you have difficulties.

THE LAND

This is a land of time. Massive cliffs reveal limestone composed of animals who lived in long-departed seas, sandstone formed of ancient desert sand dunes, and shale made of silt from now-vanished rivers and shores. Volcanic eruptions deposited layers of ash, cinders, and lava. Deeper into the Canyon lie the roots of mountain ranges, whose peaks towered over a primitive land two billion years ago. Time continues to flow in the Canyon with the cycles of the plants and animals that live here, and with the erosive forces of water and wind ever widening and deepening the chasm.

Forming of the Grand Canyon

Geologists have a difficult time pinpointing the age of the Grand Canyon itself, though it is far younger than even the most recent rock layers—those on the rim, which are about 250 million years old. These lay near sea level 70 million years ago, when the earth's crust began a slow uplift. Some time after that the ancestral Colorado River settled on its present course and began to carve the Canyon. The big question is when! Too much of the geologic record is missing to provide a conclusive answer yet. Studies of river deposits have led to conflicting theories of the birth of the Grand Canyon: any time between 5 and 70 million years ago. Even the direction of the ancestral Colorado is in dispute—some geologists think that the Little Colorado and upper Colorado once drained northward; a look at a map of Marble Canyon supports this view because the tributaries suggest a tilt of the land to the north. Or perhaps the Colorado River followed its present course but in the opposite direction, later to be reversed by tilting of the Colorado Plateau. Other theories claim that the Colorado and Little Colorado flowed southward either into a giant lake or into the Rio Grande to the Gulf of Mexico. A second, younger river could have carved the lower Grand Canyon and eventually captured the upper river near the present junction of the Colorado and Little Colorado Rivers. Or perhaps the lake had filled to overflowing from other sources, then broken through and carved the Little Colorado and Colorado Rivers in a catastrophic flood about 5 million years ago. Still other geologists stick with John Wesley Powell's theory that the Colorado has always followed its present course after the uplift began about 70 million years ago. The problem with this idea is that no river deposits older than 5 million years have been found near the lower end of the Grand Canyon.

No matter how the Grand Canyon did form, gradual uplift continued, giving the waters a steeper gradient and thus greater power. Today, the South Rim reaches elevations of 7,000–7,500 feet, while the North Rim towers about 1,500 feet higher. The Colorado River drops through the Canyon at an average gradient of 7.8 feet per mile, 25 times that of the lower Mississippi.

CLIMATE

In the Grand Canyon, as on a mountainside, temperatures change with elevation, but with added canyon peculiarities. In winter, the sun's low angle allows only a few hours of sunlight a day to reach the Inner Gorge, creating a cooling effect. The situation reverses during the summer, when the sun's high angle turns the Canyon into an oven. At night, temperatures often drop lower than you'd expect, when cold, dense air on the rims pours over the edge into the depths.

The Seasons

In one day, a hiker can travel from the cold fir and aspen forests of the North Rim to the hot cactus country of the Canyon bottom—a climate change equal to that between Canada and Mexico. In the Inner Gorge (elev. 2,480 feet at Phantom Ranch), summer temperatures soar, with average highs over 100°F; the thermometer commonly tops 115° in early July. Spring and autumn offer pleasantly warm weather and are the best times to visit. Winter down by the river can be fine too; even in January, days warm up to the 50s or low 60s and it rarely freezes. Only 9.4 inches of precipitation makes it to the bottom in an average year; snow and rain often evaporate completely while falling through the mile of warm Canyon air.

The South Rim enjoys pleasant weather most of the year. Summer highs reach the mid-80s, cooling during winter to highs in the upper 30s

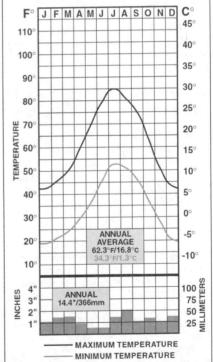

and lower 40s. Winter campers need warm sleeping bags to combat frosty nights when temperatures plunge into the teens. Yearly precipitation at the South Rim's Grand Canyon Village (elev. 6,950 feet) is 14.4 inches, with snow accumulations seldom exceeding 2 feet.

Although averaging only 1,500 feet higher, the North Rim in the Bright Angel Point area really gets socked in by winter storms. Snow piles up to depths of 6–10 feet in an average season, and the National Park Service doesn't even try to keep the roads open there from early November to mid-May. Summers can be a joy in the cool, fresh air; highs then run in the 60s and 70s. Bright Angel Ranger Station (elev. 8,400 feet) on the North Rim receives 25.6 inches of annual precipitation.

Most moisture falls during the winter and late summer (mid-July to mid-September). Summer rains often arrive in spectacular afternoon thunderstorms, soaking one spot in the Canyon and leaving another bone dry only a short distance away. The storms put on a great show from the rim viewpoints, but you should take cover if lightning gets close (less than seven seconds between the flash and the thunder) and especially if the hair on your head stands on end or if you smell ozone. As in mountain areas, the Grand Canyon's weather can change rapidly. Always carry water and raingear when heading down a trail.

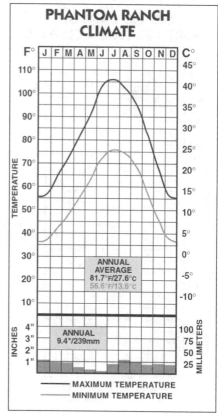

FLORA AND FAUNA

The seemingly endless variations of elevation, exposure, and moisture allow for an astonishing range of plant and animal communities. The Canyon also acts as a barrier to many nonflying creatures who live on just one side of the Colorado River or only in the Inner Gorge. Some mammals, such as Abert's (on the South Rim) and Kaibab (on the North Rim) squirrels, spotted skunk, cliff chipmunk, and common pocket gopher, evolved into separate subspecies on each rim.

Spruce-Fir Forest

You'll find dense forests of spruce and fir and groves of quaking aspen on the Kaibab Plateau of the North Rim, mostly above 8,200 feet. Common trees include Engelmann and blue spruce, Douglas fir (not a true fir), white and subalpine fir, aspen, and mountain ash. Lush meadows, dotted with wildflowers in summer, spread out in shallow valleys at the higher elevations.

Animals of the spruce-fir forest include mule deer, mountain lion, porcupine, red and Kaibab squirrels, Uinta chipmunk, long-tailed vole, and northern pocket gopher. Birds you might see include turkey, great horned owl, saw-whet owl, broad-tailed hummingbird, hairy woodpecker, hermit thrush, Clark's nutcracker, Steller's jay, and mountain bluebird.

Ponderosa Pine Forest

Stands of tall ponderosas grow between elevations

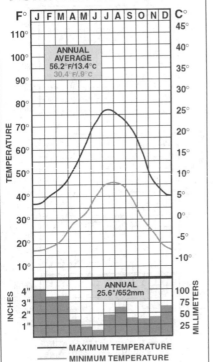

GRAND CANYON NORTH RIM AREA CLIMATE

ANNUAL AVERAGE 56.2°F/13.4°C 30.4°F/.9°C

ANNUAL 25.6"/652mm

MAXIMUM TEMPERATURE
MINIMUM TEMPERATURE

Pinyon-Juniper Woodland

These smaller trees abound in drier and more exposed places between elevations of 4,000 and 8,000 feet. Their neighbors commonly include broadleaf yucca, cliffrose, rabbit brush, Mormon tea, sagebrush, fernbrush, serviceberry, and Apache plume.

Mule deer, mountain lion, coyote, gray fox, desert cottontail, Stephen's woodrat, pinyon mouse, rock squirrel, cliff chipmunk, lizards, and snakes (including rattlesnakes) make their homes here. Birds include mourning dove, plain titmouse, Bewick's wren, black-throated gray warbler, and pinyon and scrub jays.

Desert Scrub

Except near permanent water, the low-desert country below 4,500 feet cannot support trees. Instead, you'll find such hardy plants as black-brush, Utah agave, narrowleaf yucca, various cacti, desert thorn, Mormon tea, four-wing salt-bush, and snakeweed.

Animals include bighorn sheep, black-tailed jackrabbit, spotted skunk, desert woodrat, antelope ground squirrel, and canyon mouse. Most reptiles hole up during the day, though lizards seem to tolerate higher temperatures than snakes. Chuckwalla, spiny and collared lizards, common king snake, whipsnake, and the Grand Canyon rattlesnake live in this part of the Canyon. The shy Grand Canyon or pink rattlesnake, a subspecies of the western rattlesnake, lives nowhere else. Birds of the desert scrub have to either look elsewhere for nesting trees or choose a spot in cliffs or on the ground. Species you might see include common raven, turkey vulture, golden eagle, red-tailed hawk, rock and canyon wrens, and black-throated sparrow. You'll probably hear the song of the water-loving canyon wren without ever seeing him; he sings in an unforgettable descending scale.

Riparian Woodlands

Until 1963, seasonal floods of the Colorado River ripped away most vegetation below the high-water mark. Then, when the Glen Canyon Dam was completed upstream, tamarisk (an exotic species originally from the Arabian

of 7,000 and 8,000 feet on both rims. Mature forests tend to be open, allowing in sunlight for Gambel oak, New Mexican locust, mountain mahogany, greenleaf manzanita, cliffrose, wildflowers, and grasses.

Animals and birds found here include most of those resident in the spruce-fir forests. The Abert's squirrel, though common in the Southwest, lives within the park only on the South Rim. This squirrel has tufted ears and a body and tail that are mostly gray with white undersides. The shy Kaibab squirrel, easily identified by an all-white tail and tufted ears, lives only on the North Rim. It probably evolved from Abert's squirrels that crossed the Colorado River long ago, perhaps during the Pleistocene epoch.

deserts) speeded up its takeover of formerly barren beaches. Native cattail, coyote willow, and arrowweed now thrive too. Seeps and springs support luxuriant plant growth and supply water for desert wildlife.

Beaver, river otter, ringtail cat, raccoon, deer mouse, spotted sandpiper, blue grosbeak, Lucy's warbler, Woodhouse's toad, and the tree lizard make their homes near the streams. Fremont cottonwood trees in the tributaries provide welcome shade for overheated hikers. The cold, clear waters that flow from Glen Canyon Dam have upset breeding patterns of the seven native fish species; they now spawn in warmer waters at the mouths of the Little Colorado River and Havasu Creek. Rainbow trout and 10 other species have been introduced.

HISTORY
The First Peoples

Native Americans knew of this land and its canyons centuries before white people arrived. At least 4,000 years ago, a hunting and gathering society stalked the plateaus and canyons of northern Arizona, leaving behind stone spear points and some small split-twig figures resembling deer or sheep. Preserved in caves in the Grand Canyon, these figurines date from approximately 2000 B.C.

The Ancestral Puebloans Arrive

Ancestors of today's Pueblo tribes came to the Grand Canyon area in about A.D. 500. Like their predecessors, they hunted deer, bighorn sheep, jackrabbits, and other animals, while gathering such wild plant foods as pinyon nuts and agave. The ancestral Puebloans also fashioned fine baskets and sandals. At their peak, between 1050 and 1150, they grew crops, crafted pottery, and lived in aboveground masonry villages. Toward the end of this period, drought hit the region. By 1150 nearly all the ancestral Puebloans had departed from the Grand Canyon, leaving more than 2,000 sites behind. It's likely that their migrations eventually took them to the Hopi mesas.

Archaeologists have used the term Anasazi for this culture, but the Navajo word means "ancient enemies"—not a phrase that modern-day Pueblo tribes care to use in reference to their ancestors! So this book uses the more respectful phrase "ancestral Puebloans."

Other Tribes Come to the Canyon

While the ancestral Puebloans kept mostly to the east half of the Grand Canyon (east of today's Grand Canyon Village), another group of hunter-gatherers and farmers, the Cohonina, lived downstream between A.D. 600 and 1150. They adopted many of the agricultural and building techniques and crafts of their neighbors to the east. In 1300, the Cerbat, probable ancestors of the modern Havasupai and Hualapai, migrated onto the Grand Canyon's South Rim from the west. They lived in caves or brush shelters and ranged as far upstream as the Little Colorado River in search of game and wild plant foods. The Cerbat also planted crops in areas of fertile soil or permanent springs. It's possible that the Cerbat had cultural ties with the earlier Cohonina.

Paiute living north of the Grand Canyon made seasonal trips to the North Rim, occasionally clashing with the Cerbat. The Paiute lived in brush shelters and relied almost entirely on hunting and gathering. They spent their summers in high country such as the Kaibab Plateau, then moved to lower elevations for the winter. Hopi knew of the Grand Canyon too; they came on religious pilgrimages to collect salt.

Spanish Explorers

In 1540, when Francisco Vásquez de Coronado led an expedition in search of the Seven Cities of Cíbola, Hopi villagers told a detachment of soldiers about a great canyon to the west. Hopi guides later took a party of Coronado's men, led by García López de Cárdenas, to the South Rim but kept secret the routes into the depths. The immensity of the Grand Canyon impressed the Spaniards, who failed in their attempt to find a way to the river. Franciscan priest Francisco Tomás Garcés, looking for souls to save, visited the Havasupai and Hualapai in 1776 and was well received. Historians credit Garcés with naming the Río Colorado ("Red River").

Americans Explore The Grand Canyon

James Ohio Pattie and other American fur trappers probably found the Grand Canyon in the late 1820s, but they provided only sketchy accounts of their visits. Lieutenant Joseph Ives led the first real exploration of the Colorado River. He chugged 350 miles by steamboat upstream from the river's mouth in 1857–58 before crashing into a rock in Black Canyon. The party then continued overland to the Diamond Creek area in the western Grand Canyon. Ives thought the region worthless and doubted that people would come again.

Most of the Canyon remained a dark and forbidding unknown until Major John Wesley Powell bravely led a boat expedition through the chasm in 1869. On this trip and on a second journey in 1871–72, he and his men made detailed drawings and took notes on geology, flora and fauna, and prehistoric ruins. Powell recorded his experiences in *Canyons of the Colorado,* now published as *The Exploration of the Colorado River and Its Canyons.*

Miners and Tourists

After about 1880, prospectors entered the Grand Canyon to search for copper, asbestos, silver, and lead deposits. Their trails, many following old Indian routes, are still used by modern hikers.

In 1883, stagecoaches began bringing tourists to the Canyon at Diamond Creek, where J.H. Farlee opened a four-room hotel the following year. Prospectors Peter Berry and Ralph and Niles Cameron built the Grandview Hotel in 1895 at Grandview Point and led tourists down a trail to Horseshoe Mesa. Other prospectors, such as John Hance and William Bass, also found guiding visitors more profitable than mining. Tourism began on a large scale soon after the railroad reached the South Rim in 1901. The Fred Harvey Company bought Bright Angel Lodge, built the deluxe El Tovar Hotel, and took over from the smaller operators.

The Park Is Born

As the Canyon became better known, President Theodore Roosevelt and others pushed for greater federal protection. First a forest reserve in 1893, the Grand Canyon became a national monument in 1908 and a national park in 1919. The park's size doubled in 1975 when legislation extended the boundaries west to Grand Wash and northeast to Lees Ferry. Grand Canyon National Park now includes 1,892 square miles and receives about five million visitors annually.

South Rim Sights

GRAND CANYON VILLAGE AREA

Parking may be your first thought upon arrival! Maps in the literature given out at the entrance stations show parking areas in Grand Canyon Village. Once you've found a spot, the free Village Shuttle will take you around. Cycling is another option, though it's restricted to roads and bike paths. Walking, especially on the very scenic Rim Trail, is the most enjoyable way of seeing the sights here.

Eventually parking for Grand Canyon Village will be moved south to Tusayan, where buses or a light-rail will convey visitors to Canyon View Information Plaza and beyond.

Canyon View Information Plaza

This new visitor center complex, a short stroll south of Mather Point, opened in late 2000 and has replaced the old visitor center. Because it's designed as part of the public transport system, there's no parking here. You can take the Village Shuttle or walk via the Rim Trail. The Village Shuttle stops on the west side of the Plaza and the Kaibab Trail Shuttle on the east side. Despite the name, there's no view here! You have to walk over to Mather Point to see the Canyon.

Large outdoor panels have maps, sightseeing destinations, hiking possibilities, lodging, campgrounds, and other helpful information to get you started on your visit to the park. You can also check listings of ranger-guided rim walks, Canyon hikes, talks, family activities, photography workshops, campfire programs, and evening presentations. Step inside the Visitor Center for the information desk and some exhibits. Kids 4–14 can sign up to learn skills in the Junior Ranger Program; it's also available at Yavapai Observation Station and Tusayan Museum. The Visitor Center is open daily 8 A.M.–6 P.M. and the outdoor lights stay on until 9 P.M. Call 928/638-7888 to reach the automated switchboard with recordings of scheduled programs and offices or surf over to the Website www.nps.gov/grca. (People with hearing impairments can call the TDD, 928/638-7804.)

South across the Plaza, you'll find Books & More. This spacious new bookstore of the Grand Canyon Association features a great selection of Canyon-related books (including ones for kids), posters, topo maps, videos, slides, and postcards.

Mather Point

The panorama here is the first view of the Grand Canyon for many visitors. Walk north from the Canyon View Information Plaza or walk east on the Rim Trail from Grand Canyon Village. You may be able to park here, but finding a space takes some luck. Below Mather Point (elev. 7,120 feet) lie Pipe Creek Canyon, the Inner Gorge of the Colorado River, and countless buttes, temples, and points eroded from the rims. Stephen Mather served as the first director of the National Park Service and was in office when the Grand Canyon joined the national park system on February 26, 1919.

Rim Trail

People of all ages enjoy a walk along this easy trail, which offers views from many different vantage points. The four-mile section from Mather Point past the El Tovar Hotel to Maricopa Point is paved and nearly level. Another paved section, between Mather Point and the first viewpoints on Desert View Drive, should be open in 2002. The Rim Trail continues west 6.7 miles from Maricopa Point as a dirt path to Hermit's

© ROBERT M. BUTTERFIELD AND GRAND CANYON NATIONAL PARK (NEG #6725)

A cloud inversion "fills" the Grand Canyon at Mather Point.

GRAND CANYON

SHUTTLING OUT TO THE SOUTH RIM

The park already provides public transit to ease vehicle congestion in the popular Grand Canyon Village area. In the future, the inadequate spaces here will be replaced by new parking areas in Tusayan, just outside the park. Visitors will be able to park and quickly check out a menu of sightseeing options before hopping on a bus or light rail shuttle to the Canyon View Information Plaza near Mather Point, already open with its new visitor center and bookstore. Lodge and campground guests will be able to drive into Grand Canyon Village on a new road, but once in the park, everyone will walk, cycle, or use shuttles.

Cyclists, walkers, and eventually equestrians will have a new Greenway trail network totaling about 73 miles on both rims. The first sections—connecting Canyon View Information Plaza with Grand Canyon Village and Tusayan—should open in summer 2002. Eventually the Greenway system will go all the way to Desert View and have a spur trail to Yaki Point.

The Desert View Drive will continue to be open to motorists for at least the near future, though private vehicles may not be able to go all the way out to some overlooks. (South Kaibab Trailhead and Yaki Point are already on a shuttle-only route.)

The **Heritage Education Campus**, planned for central Grand Canyon Village, will have exhibits on natural and cultural aspects of the park, current issues, and Native American cultures.

People unable to take shuttle buses may request an **accessibility permit** that allows a private vehicle to travel on the shuttle-only routes. Accessible shuttle buses can be arranged by calling at least two days ahead at 928/638-0591.

Rest, at the end of Hermit Road. Shuttle buses stop at both ends of the trail and at many places along the way.

Pick up biology and geology brochures for the trail at the Visitor Center, at Yavapai Observation Station, or outside Verkamp's Curios (near El Tovar Hotel). Start anywhere you like, as there are no keyed trail numbers. Pinyon pine, juniper, cliff rose, and smaller plants grow on exposed areas of the rim; ponderosa pines stick to more protected areas farther back or below the rim.

Yavapai Observation Station

Set on the brink of the Canyon, this overlook makes a great spot to take in the panorama or watch sunrises and sunsets. Panels identify the many buttes, temples, points, and tributary canyons seen through the windows. A few geology exhibits are on display too. It's open daily 8 A.M.–5 P.M., with extended summer hours. Grand Canyon Association sells books, maps, videos, slides, and postcards. Parking is difficult here—the Village Shuttle or a walk along the Rim Trail are the best ways to come.

Hopi House

Designed by Mary Colter to resemble a pueblo, this unusual building opened in 1905. She patterned it after structures in the Hopi village of Old Oraibi with a stone and adobe exterior, thatched ceilings, and corner fireplaces. Hopi not only helped in the construction, but lived inside on the upper floors, worked as craftsmen, displayed their work, and performed nightly dances. Today Hopi House has an outstanding collection of Native American art and crafts for sale on two floors. It's near the Canyon rim just east of El Tovar.

Verkamp's Curios

Just east past Hopi House, this venerable institution is also worth a look for Native American crafts and Canyon souvenirs. John Verkamp found business too slow during his first attempt at a curio shop out of a tent in 1898, but he returned in 1905 and built on the present site. The family continues to run the business.

Lookout Studio

The inspiration and materials of this Mary Colter building came from the Grand Canyon itself. Early visitors, after the 1914 completion, could relax by the fireplace in the lounge, purchase souvenirs and postcards in the art room, or gaze into the Canyon depths with a high-power telescope. It's open today with a gift shop and viewing platform. The studio stands on the Canyon's edge, just west of Bright Angel Lodge.

Kolb Studio

Perched on the rim near Lookout Studio and the Bright Angel Trailhead, this building began in 1904 as a photo studio of the Kolb brothers. Emery Kolb expanded and operated it until his death in 1976 at the age of 95. Canyon visitors could watch movies taken by the Kolbs on an early river-running expedition along with movies and stills of other Canyon subjects. The Grand Canyon Association now has a bookstore inside where you can still see some of the Kolb photography on computer screens. The auditorium where Emery showed his movies now hosts visiting art exhibitions.

WEST OF GRAND CANYON VILLAGE

Hermit Road

The Santa Fe Railroad built this eight-mile-long road from Grand Canyon Village to Hermit's Rest in 1912. Stops along the way allow visitors to walk to the rim and enjoy the views. Highlights include a great overlook of the Bright Angel Trail from Trailview, the copper and uranium Orphan Mine from Maricopa Point, some of the best views and a large historic marker at Powell Memorial, the Colorado River from Hopi and Mohave Points, the 3,000-foot sheer drop of the Abyss, and, from Pima Point, views of Granite Rapid and foundations of an old hotel below. Your map will help identify Canyon features: Bright Angel Trail switchbacking down to the grove of trees at Indian Garden; Plateau Point at the end of a short trail from Indian Garden; long, straight Bright Angel Canyon on the far side of the river; the many majestic temples rising to the north and east; and the rapids of the Colorado River.

Hermit's Rest—with restrooms, gift shop, and drinking water—marks the westernmost viewpoint and end of the drive. Mary Colter designed the imaginative stone building and its Great Fire-

place according to what she thought a hermit might like. A free shuttle bus runs the length of the drive except in winter, when you can take your own vehicle. Bicyclists enjoy this drive too, and they aren't affected by the shuttle-season ban on cars. Because Hermit Road is so narrow, cyclists need to pull off and dismount when large vehicles wish to pass.

If you've walked to Hermit's Rest on the Rim Trail, you'll probably want to rest too. Louis Boucher, the Hermit, came to the Canyon in 1891 and stayed 21 years; he lived at Dripping Springs and constructed the Boucher Trail to his mining claims in Boucher Canyon.

Hermit Trail, built by the Fred Harvey Company after Louis Boucher departed, begins just beyond Hermit's Rest at the end of a gravel road. It descends to the Tonto Trail, then continues down to the river at Hermit Rapids. Visitors who took this trail between 1912 and 1930 could stay at a tourist camp partway down on the Tonto Platform; only foundations remain today. A branch in the upper trail goes to Dripping Springs and Boucher Canyon.

EAST OF GRAND CANYON VILLAGE

Desert View Drive

Outstanding overlooks line this 25-mile drive between Grand Canyon Village and Desert View. Each has its own character and is worth a stop, but many people consider the aptly named Grandview Point one of the best. It's 12 miles east of Grand Canyon Village (13 miles before Desert View), then 0.8 mile north. Sweeping panoramas take in much of the Grand Canyon from this commanding site above Horseshoe Mesa. The vastness and intricacies of the Canyon show themselves especially well here.

Other major viewpoints on Desert View Drive include Yaki Point, Moran Point, Lipan Point, and Desert View. At Lipan, by looking both up- and down-canyon, you can see the entire geologic sequence of the Canyon.

Tusayan Ruin

Prehistoric ancestral Puebloans built this village

MARY COLTER, ARCHITECT OF THE SOUTHWEST

In an early 20th-century world dominated by male architects, Mary Colter (1869–1958) succeeded in designing many of the Grand Canyon National Park's most notable structures. After her father died in 1886, her mother gave Colter permission to attend the California School of Design in San Francisco to learn skills to support the remaining members of the family. Upon graduation, Colter moved to St. Paul, Minnesota, and began teaching mechanical drawing. She later applied for work with the Fred Harvey Company and, in 1901, ob-

Mary Colter shows blueprints to Mrs. Ickes, wife of the Secretary of the Interior, in 1935.

© GRAND CANYON NATIONAL PARK (NEG# 16940)

tained a contract to decorate the Indian Building—a new museum and sales gallery of Native American crafts between the Alvarado Hotel and the railroad depot in Albuquerque. Her association with the Fred Harvey Company eventually spanned more than 40 years.

Colter's keen interest and research in Native American architecture led to a remarkable series of buildings along the Grand Canyon's South Rim, beginning with the Hopi House that opened in 1905. She used Southwestern themes and simple designs with careful attention to detail—interiors had to have just the right colors and furnishings, for example. So much thought went into the design of the buildings that each tells a story about its history or setting. Colter gave the stone Lookout Studio, perched on the Canyon rim, a jagged roof to blend into the scenery; it opened in 1914. In the same year she completed Hermit's Rest at the end of Hermit Road; its Great Fireplace and cozy interior seem much like a place that a hermit prospector would inhabit. She had workmen smear soot on the new fireplace to enhance the

in A.D. 1185–1190, according to tree-ring dating. Perhaps 30 people lived here, contending with poor soil, little rainfall, and scarce drinking water. After staying 35–40 years, they moved on. Archaeologists who excavated the site in 1930 named it Tusayan, a Spanish term for Hopi territory.

A small museum introduces the ancestral Puebloans with artifacts and illustrations of dwellings. An exhibit about archaic cultures has some split-twig figures dating as far back as 4,000 years; other exhibits introduce modern tribes of the region. Outside, a short, self-guided trail leads around the plaza and ruins of living quarters, storage rooms, and two kivas. A leaflet (pick

one up at the trailhead) and interpretive signs describe how the ancestral Puebloans farmed and obtained some of their wild foods. You can also take a free guided 45-minute tour, check *The Guide* for times. Related books can be purchased.

The museum is open daily 9 A.M.–5 P.M., except in winter when it may close some days, but the trail stays open then, weather permitting. It's on Desert View Drive, 22 miles east of Grand Canyon Village and three miles west of Desert View, 928/638-2305.

Desert View

This overlook presents a stunning view at the east end of Desert View Drive. Although the atmosphere and to give the building a "lived-in look." Colter's work also extended to the bottom of the Grand Canyon, where in 1922 she designed the stone lodge and four cabins of Phantom Ranch. In 1932 she finished the Desert View Watchtower using a variety of prehistoric and modern Native American themes; it's the most intriguing of her buildings. After settling on a watchtower patterned after those of the Four Corners region, Colter wrote, "First and most important was to design a building that would . . . create no discordant note against the time eroded walls of this promontory." She not only designed the 1935 Bright Angel Lodge, intended to provide accommodations for tourists with moderate incomes, but she also incorporated into it the 1890s Buckey O'Neill Cabin and Red Horse Station. Without her interest in these historic structures, they would have been torn down. She also designed the unusual geologic fireplace in the lodge's History Room.

La Posada Hotel, which opened in 1930 beside the railroad tracks in downtown Winslow, might be her most exotic commission—a fantasy of arches, halls, and gardens in a Spanish Colonial Revival style. La Posada nearly suffered demolition, the fate of the Alvarado Hotel, but it has been saved and restored; Winslow visitors are welcome to tour the public areas. Train travelers at Union Station in Los Angeles, built in 1939, can admire an interior design that brings a Southwestern style into the geometry of Art Deco. Colter enjoyed her professional life—she never married and was reportedly rarely at home. Only in recent times has the public taken note of Colter's work. Perhaps her position as "house architect" on a relatively small number of major buildings, some in remote areas, led to her relative obscurity. That's changed now, with books, exhibits, and documentaries out on her life. Five Colter structures have become National Historic Landmarks.

© GRAND CANYON NATIONAL PARK (NEG# 8307)

Hopi artist Fred Kabotie worked with Mary Colter on the Desert View Watchtower's interior artwork.

surrounding pinyon pines and junipers suggest a lower elevation, this is the highest viewpoint on the South Rim at an elevation of 7,500 feet. Far to the east lies the multi-hued Painted Desert that gave the viewpoint its name. Below, to the north, the Colorado River comes out of Marble Canyon, then curves west through the Grand Canyon.

The strange-looking Desert View Watchtower, designed by Mary Colter, incorporates design elements from both prehistoric and modern tribes of the Four Corners region. The Fred Harvey Company built the 70-foot structure in 1932, using stone around a steel frame. The interior contains reproductions of Hopi paintings and petroglyphs; stairs lead to several levels inside and to an outdoor terrace. You enter the watchtower through a room shaped like a Navajo hogan with a traditional log ceiling.

Desert View has a small information center/bookstore, gift shop, snack bar, general store, service station, and campground. There is a $10 fee for the campsites, which have drinking water but no hookups; they're open mid-May to the end of October, weather permitting; no reservations taken.

GRAND CANYON

GRAND CANYON

Vicinity of Desert View

Highway AZ 64 continues east 33 miles from Desert View to Cameron and US 89. On the way you'll pass two impressive overlooks of the **Little Colorado River**—signed Scenic View—on the Navajo Reservation. The sheer 800-foot cliffs of the Little Colorado create a spectacular sight. The first overlook, 16.5 miles from Desert View, requires a half-mile walk out to the best viewpoints. The second overlook, 5.2 miles farther east, offers a large market of Native American jewelry, pottery, and other crafts with just a short walk to the views.

Cape Solitude, directly above the confluence of the Little Colorado and Colorado Rivers, lives up to its name and features amazing views of both canyons. The jeep road has been closed to vehicles, but adventurous drivers with 4WD can take back roads on the Navajo Reservation (tribal permit needed) to the park boundary, then walk the last 6.7 miles. When the Little Colorado isn't in flood, you'll see turquoise-blue waters from mineral-rich springs in its canyon. Hikers can reach Blue Springs on a very rough route, estimated at 1.5 miles one way and an elevation change of 2,100 feet; it's on the Navajo Reservation (tribal permit required) and approached on 4WD roads from Desert View via Cedar Mountain or from the Kaibab National Forest farther east. The Little Colorado offers a challenging hiking route between Cameron and the Colorado River; conditions constantly change, and it should be avoided when in flood. Hiking books describe some of these routes. Ask around at Desert View, Tusayan Ruins, and the Backcountry Office to find a ranger knowledgeable in these areas. See **Cameron** (Northeastern Arizona chapter) for details on obtaining Navajo tribal permits to explore this remote country east of the Grand Canyon.

KAIBAB NATIONAL FOREST (TUSAYAN RANGER DISTRICT)

Grandview Lookout

Some of the prettiest country of the Tusayan Ranger District surrounds the lookout. You can climb the 80-foot steel tower, built by the Civilian Conservation Corps in 1936, for a panorama of the region. The tower is easily reached from the Desert View Drive, two miles east of the Grandview Point turnoff; turn south at the sign for "Arizona Trail" between Mileposts 252 and 253 and proceed 1.3 miles on a dirt road. You can also drive east 15 miles on unpaved Forest Road 302 from the south edge of Tusayan.

Cross-country ski loops begin one-third of a mile north of Grandview Lookout; the Forest Service grooms trails here in the snow season, beginning about late December.

The historic **Hull Cabin** and outbuildings, two miles from the lookout by bumpy dirt road, once belonged to a sheep ranch. You're welcome to visit the grounds. The Kaibab Forest Map (Tusayan District) shows the way in.

Hikers have several options at the trailhead beside Grandview Lookout. **Vishnu Trail** makes a 2.2-mile loop with a spur trail to Grand Canyon viewpoints. The trail heads northeast from the tower, then loops back on the Arizona Trail. Whether you're setting out on a months-long expedition or just a short stroll, the **Arizona Trail** offers some scenic hiking and mountain biking. The first mile southeast from the trailhead has interpretive signs about mistletoe. Altogether, the Arizona Trail runs 24.2 miles one way between the lookout and the south boundary of the Tusayan Ranger District. The Coconino Rim Trail segment follows the top of 500-foot cliffs southeast of Grandview Lookout; it's 12 miles one way to Russell Tank with views of the Painted Desert, moderate grades, and some switchbacks. The 12.2-mile, mostly level Russell Wash segment farther south crosses the transition from ponderosa forest in the north to pinyon pine and juniper in the south and parallels the old Moqui Stage route (1893–1901) from near Russell Tank past the station site, reached by a quarter-mile-long trail, to the south forest boundary. Forest roads intersect the Arizona Trail allowing a variety of loops for mountain bikers.

Tusayan Bike Trails

Three interconnected loops for mountain bikers

begin from a trailhead on the west side of AZ 64 between Moqui Lodge and Tusayan. Trail 1 is three miles (it takes about half an hour); Trail 2 goes eight miles (just over an hour); and Trail 3 runs nine miles (about an hour and a half).

Red Butte Trail

Few hikers know about this mountain south of Tusayan, despite the good trail and fine views. It's a remnant of the red-colored Moenkopi Formation, protected from erosion by a thick lava cap. The hike is 2.4 miles round-trip and takes about 1.5 hours to the summit (7,326 ft.), an 866-foot elevation gain. You can visit the lookout tower for the best 360-degree panorama. The large meadows just to the north once hosted Grand Canyon's original airport; a bit farther north stands the green tower of a uranium mine, currently inactive due to low ore prices. A long stretch of the North Rim rises farther to the north, Grandview Lookout can just be seen on the wooded ridge to the northeast, and the San Francisco Peaks and Volcanic Field lie to the south. From Tusayan, head south nine miles on AZ 64 to between Mileposts 226 and 227, then turn east 4.3 miles on Forest Roads 305, 340, and 340A. From the south, you can take AZ 64 to Milepost 224, then turn east 2.7 miles via Forest Roads 320, 340, and 340A to the trailhead. As on all trails in the Southwest, keep an eye out for rattlesnakes.

VALLE

Highways US 180 from Flagstaff and AZ 64 from Williams meet at this road junction 28 miles south of Grand Canyon Village. The tiny community has an excellent aviation museum, a simple theme park based on the cartoon Flintstones, two motels, a campground, convenience stores, gift shops, and a gas station. The desolate high-desert spot isn't a place to linger, except for the museum. The motels are poor value compared with those in Flagstaff or Williams, and the restaurants lack a smoke-free area. The campground at the theme park is exposed to winds, and the café here also fails to provide a non-smoking area.

Planes of Fame Air Museum

Outstanding aircraft of the past, along with some oddities and replicas, reside beside Valle's airport on the south side of town. During the Korean War, General Douglas MacArthur flew aboard the Lockheed Constellation C-121A named "Bataan," which has been beautifully restored and opened for tours. The 1928 Ford Trimotor, said to have been a personal aircraft of Henry Ford, still flies; it's a type of plane used in early tourist flights over the Grand Canyon. You'll see replicas of a few famous WW I aircraft. World War II highlights include a Fuji Ohka 11 piloted suicide rocket, a Messerschmitt Bf 109G Gustav fighter plane, and an early P-51A Mustang. Newer fighters represent the dawn of the jet age. Some homebuilts and other light aircraft, a Link Trainer Model C-3 ("the sweat box"), and a timeline of women in aviation round out the collection. The museum, open daily 9 A.M.–6 P.M. (to 5 P.M. in winter) except Thanksgiving and Christmas, is part of the Planes of Fame Air Museum based in Chino, California; some planes rotate between the two collections. The website www.planesoffame.org has information on both, or call 928/635-1000 for information. Admission is adults $5, children 5–12 $2, and "Bataan" tours cost an extra $3.

Around the last weekend in June, the museum sponsors the **High Country Warbirds Air Display** with flybys of vintage aircraft and ground displays.

Flintstones Bedrock City

Fans of the cartoon series *The Flintstones* may enjoy walking around this life-size town. It has the houses of Fred and Barney and their families, businesses, dinosaur statues (one is a kid's slide), a little ride through a "volcano," and a theater where the cartoons play. The park, 928/635-2600, is open year-round but the volcano ride and theater don't run in winter; admission is $5 for ages two and up. There's also a campground here (see Accommodations for details).

South Rim Practicalities

SOUTH RIM ACCOMMODATIONS

The Grand Canyon offers too much to see in one day. In Grand Canyon Village you can stay right on the rim at Bright Angel Lodge, Thunderbird Lodge, Kachina Lodge, or El Tovar Hotel. Other lodges lie back in the woods. The town of Tusayan, just outside the park nine miles south of Grand Canyon Village, provides additional places to stay. One can usually find a room anytime, but reservations from six up to 23 months in advance will give you the best choice. If planning a late arrival, you might consider either a reservation or staying in one of the gateway towns surrounding the park.

Grand Canyon Village

Grand Canyon National Park Lodges operates all the lodges here, as well as Phantom Ranch at the bottom of the Canyon, Moqui Lodge just outside the South Entrance Station, and the lodge and cabins at the North Rim's Bright Angel Point. All the lodges have non-smoking rooms and totally smoke-free public areas. Make reservations at 14001 E. Iliff Ave., Suite 600, Aurora, CO 80014; 303/297-2757 (advance reservations) or 928/638-2631 (same-day reservations), or fax 303/297-3175; www.grandcanyonlodges.com.

One of the grand old hotels of the West, **El Tovar** has offered the Canyon's finest accommodations and food since 1905. This national historic landmark offers rooms—no two alike—with modern conveniences, yet it retains an old-fashioned lodge ambience; guests enjoy a restaurant, lounge, and concierge service. Four suites have Canyon views. Room rates run $118 d for a standard double up to $176 d for a deluxe and $201–286 for a suite.

Kachina and **Thunderbird** Lodges, on the rim between El Tovar and Bright Angel Lodge, offer modern rooms for $116 d back side or $126 d canyon side.

Historic 1935 **Bright Angel Lodge** sits on the rim a short distance from the Bright Angel trailhead. Hikers and other visitors gather in the lobby, patio, restaurant, and lounge of this popular place. Rates for historic cabins run $76 d, rim cabins $98 d, and rim cabins with fireplace $118 d. Rooms in the lodge cost $48 with sink only, $54 with toilet, $66 d with toilet and shower or tub; other facilities are down the hall. The Buckey O'Neill Suite dates from the early 1890s and is one of the oldest structures in the park; it costs $236 d. The Bright Angel History Room displays memorabilia from early tourist days and a "geological fireplace" in which Canyon rocks have been laid, floor to ceiling, in the proper stratigraphic sequence. The transportation desk in the lobby organizes scheduled bus service, bus and air tours, mule trips, and Phantom Ranch accommodations. The lodge also features two restaurants, an ice cream fountain, lounge, and a gift shop.

Maswik Lodge, two blocks south of Bright Angel Lodge, has a cafeteria and cozy cabins for $64 d (closed in winter) and modern rooms for $76 d in the south section, $119 d in the north section. **Yavapai Lodge,** one mile east of Bright Angel Lodge, then one-third mile south near Market Plaza, offers modern rooms for $89 d in the west section and $103 d in the east section; there's also a cafeteria here; the lodge closes for part of the winter.

Tusayan

Motels, restaurants, a campground, an IMAX Theater, and other tourist services line AZ 64 in this compact town, nine miles south of Grand Canyon Village. They're all well signed. Prices run on the high side for accommodations, though they drop a bit in winter or any time business is slow. You're unlikely to find any rooms under $50.

$50–100: Seven Mile Lodge, 928/638-2291, offers basic rooms at $68 d in summer, less in winter; no reservations taken.

VISITING GRAND CANYON NATIONAL PARK ON A SHOESTRING

The steep prices charged for park admission and services may seem daunting, yet the Grand Canyon can easily be seen for little more than a song. Getting a small group together will slice costs on the entry, camping, and lodging. A $50 National Parks Pass will give unlimited entry to the park and all other National Park Service areas in the country for 12 months, a much better deal than forking out $20 every seven days to visit the Grand Canyon. You can camp free in the Kaibab National Forest that adjoins both the South and North Rims, though you'll need your own wheels to do this. Backpackers and cyclists can stay in cheap walk-in campgrounds at both rims. The cafeterias at Yavapai and Maswik Lodges in Grand Canyon Village offer good deals, or you can fix your own meals. And the best things—the views, sunsets, day-hikes, and interpretive programs—are free.

$100–150: Red Feather Lodge/Rodeway Inn, 928/638-2414, 800/538-2345, or 800/228-2000 (Rodeway reservations), has standard rooms at $79–119 d in the older motel-style annex and deluxe rooms at $99–129 d in the new building with lower rates off-season; guests can enjoy an outdoor pool and hot tub, fitness room, and adjacent restaurant.

Grand Canyon Quality Inn & Suites, 928/638-2673, 800/228-5151, features a restaurant, the Wintergarten Lounge, and an 18-foot hot tub in a huge atrium; there's also an outdoor pool and hot tub and a gift shop. Standard rooms are $118–128 d and suites go for $188 d from April to October 15, less off-season.

Best Western Grand Canyon Squire Inn, 928/638-2681, 800/622-6966, offers three restaurants, lounge, sports bar, outdoor pool, hot tub, sauna, exercise room, tennis courts, bowling alley, beauty salon, and gift shop. Rooms cost $135 d standard, $150 d deluxe, and the few suites are $175–225 d; www.grandcanyonsquire.com.

Holiday Inn Express, 928/638-3000, 888/538-5353, or 800/HOLIDAY, includes a continental breakfast with its rooms, which run $139 d in summer. A nearby building offers suites with one bedroom at about $148 d and two bedrooms for about $250.

The Grand Hotel, 928/638-3333, 888/634-7263, presents a dinner theater with Native American programs and cowboy songs, a restaurant, and an indoor pool and hot tub on the south side of town; rooms go for $139 d ($149 with a balcony) in summer; www.gcanyon.com/grand.htm.

Valle

You'll pass through this little town, 28 miles south of Grand Canyon Village, if coming on the direct routes from Williams or Flagstaff. **Grand Canyon Motel** ($79 d) and the nearby **Grand Canyon Inn** ($49–69 d) are under the same management, 928/635-9203, 800/635-9203. Both may close mid-winter. The inn has a smoky restaurant, summer pool, and a gift shop.

SOUTH RIM CAMPGROUNDS
Grand Canyon Village

Campgrounds tend to be crowded in the warmer months and it's strongly recommended to have a reservation from mid-March to October; otherwise, try to arrive before noon to look for a site. Rangers enforce the "No Camping Outside Designated Sites" policy with stiff fines. Backpackers inside the Canyon or in backcountry areas atop the rim need a permit from the Backcountry Office. RVs have a dump station near the road to the campgrounds.

Mather Campground, 928/638-7851, in Grand Canyon Village accepts both tenters and RVers; it's open year-round with drinking water but no hookups for $15 per night, $7.50 with a Golden Age or Access pass. Make reservations for family and group sites at 800/365-2267 (365-CAMP) or on the Internet at http://reservations.nps.gov. Backpackers and bicyclists can camp in a walk-in area for $4 per person, no reservations needed; it has space even when the campground is signed "FULL." Coin-operated showers and Laundromat and ice sales are nearby. You can attend campfire programs during the warmer months.

Trailer Village, just east of Mather Campground, has RV sites for $24 with hookups all year. Reservations are highly recommended from the week before Easter to the end of October; you can make them with Grand Canyon National Park Lodges, 14001 E. Iliff Ave., Suite 600, Aurora, CO 80014, 303/297-2757 (advance reservations) or 928/638-2631 (same-day reservations), fax 303/297-3175, www.grandcanyonlodges.com. Coin-operated showers and laundry lie within walking distance.

Desert View

This campground, near the East Entrance Station (25 miles east of Grand Canyon Village), has sites in a pinyon-juniper forest with drinking water but no hookups. It's open mid-May to October, weather permitting, for $10; no reservations taken.

Tusayan

Grand Canyon Camper Village, 928/638-2887, offers sites for tents ($18) and RVs ($22–26 including hookups) with coin showers and a playground. Tepee tents ($20) are available during the warmer months. Reservations can be made only for the hookup sites, though spaces are usually available. The campground may close in winter.

Ten X Campground in the ponderosa pines of the Kaibab National Forest has drinking water but no hookups or showers; it's open

May–Sept. for $10 per vehicle and usually has room. Amphitheater programs take place many nights. From Tusayan, go south two miles (between Mileposts 233 and 234), then turn east a quarter mile. **Charley Tank Group Site** nearby can be reserved; 928/638-2443 (Tusayan Ranger Station).

Dispersed camping in the Kaibab National Forest south of the park is another possibility—just practice no-trace camping, carry your own drinking water and a shovel, and stay at least a quarter mile from the nearest paved road and from any surface water. Check with the ranger station, on the right one mile north of Tusayan, to learn whether campfires are permitted; staff can also suggest areas for dispersed camping. The Kaibab Forest map (Williams and Tusayan Districts) shows the back roads.

Valle

Flintstones Bedrock City campsites in Valle, 28 miles south of Grand Canyon Village on AZ 64, 928/635-2600, cost $12 for tents or RVs ($16 w/hookups). It has coin showers, a store, snack bar (smoky), and theme park. The campground is open year-round.

SOUTH RIM FOOD

Grand Canyon Village Area

El Tovar Hotel, 928/638-2526 ext. 6432, offers elegant continental and American dining daily for breakfast, lunch, and dinner at moderate to expensive prices; you'll need to make reservations for dinner.

Bright Angel Lodge features two moderately priced restaurants, the **Bright Angel Restaurant,** 928/638-2526 ext. 6189, serving breakfast, lunch, and dinner daily, and the **Arizona Room,** 928/638-2526 ext. 6296, offering Southwestern fare nightly for dinner. The Arizona Room closes Jan.–February. Neither restaurant takes reservations but you can often get in for dinner without much waiting by arriving before sunset.

Maswik Lodge, two blocks south of Bright Angel Lodge, and **Yavapai Lodge,** one mile east of Bright Angel Lodge, then one-third mile south near Market Plaza, both have large cafeterias open daily for breakfast, lunch, and dinner at relatively low prices.

The **general store** in Market Plaza has a supermarket and a deli counter with tables. You can also buy groceries at general stores in Desert View and Tusayan. **Bright Angel Fountain** serves ice cream and other snacks on the Canyon rim behind Bright Angel Lodge; it's closed in the winter.

Tusayan

The spacious atrium and greenery in the **Grand Canyon Quality Inn & Suites'** restaurant, 928/638-2673, provide an enjoyable setting. Diners have a choice of ala carte or buffets daily for breakfast, lunch, and dinner. The large selection of salads and fruit in the buffets will appeal to vegetarians; non-veggies will appreciate steak and seafood on the menu as well as a variety of meat dishes in the buffet. **Canyon Star** at the Grand Hotel, 928/638-3333, features a dinner theater with Native American programs and cowboy songs as well as breakfast, lunch, and dinner daily; buffet options for breakfast, lunch, and dinner run in summer and early autumn. **Café Tusayan,** 928/638-2150, serves American favorites daily for breakfast, lunch, and dinner next to the Red Feather Lodge. The **Grand Canyon Squire Inn's** Coronado Room offers fine dining of steak, barbecued ribs, prime rib, seafood, pasta, and some Mexican items nightly for dinner; the Canyon Room serves ala carte meals (year-round) and buffets (summer only) daily for breakfast and lunch; 928/638-2681. **The Steakhouse,** 928/638-2780, serves up steak, chicken, shrimp, and even a few veggie options; it's open daily for lunch (summer only) and dinner. **We Cook Pizza & Pasta,** 928/638-2278, offers pizza, pasta, calzones, and sandwiches daily for lunch and dinner. **Pizza Hut** and **Taco Bell** can be found in the Grand Canyon IMAX Theater complex. **McDonald's** is nearby across the highway.

SOUTH RIM SERVICES
Entertainment

Rangers present **evening programs** and **campfire talks;** see *The Guide* listings for times and places, check the panels outside the Visitor Center, or call 928/638-7888 for the day's topics. Chamber music comes to the Grand Canyon in September during the **Grand Canyon Music Festival,** held at Shrine of the Ages auditorium on the South Rim. The **Grand Canyon IMAX Theatre,** 928/638-2468/2203, in Tusayan projects an impressive movie, *The Grand Canyon—The Hidden Secrets,* on a 70-foot screen with six-track stereo sound. The spectacular photography of the 34-minute presentation portrays prehistoric tribes, explorers, wildlife, river-running, and flying. Showings take place every day on the half hour 8:30 A.M.–8:30 P.M. March–October, then 10:30 A.M.–6:30 P.M. in winter. Admission is $9.50 adults, $6.50 children 3–11. You'll also find fast-food restaurants, gift shops, ATM, and tourist information here.

Shopping

Grand Canyon Association has excellent selections of regional books, children's books, topo maps, posters, and videos in its shops at Canyon View Information Plaza, Kolb Studio, Yavapai Observation Station, Tusayan Ruin, and Desert View; www.grandcanyon.org. **General stores,** at Market Plaza in Grand Canyon Village, at Tusayan, and at Desert View, sell groceries, camping and hiking supplies, clothing, books, maps, souvenirs, and offer one of the best selections of camera film. The Market Plaza store is the largest and has a deli. There's a gift shop almost everywhere you turn in the developed areas of the South Rim! El Tovar, other lodges, most motels, helicopter terminals, and the airport have them. **Hopi House,** the pueblo replica just east of El Tovar, has an impressive array of Native American crafts and art from the Southwest; it's worth a visit to see both the architecture—interior and exterior—and the high-quality merchandise. A bit farther east is **Verkamp's Curio** with Native American crafts and other souvenirs. **Lookout Studio,** on the rim's edge near Bright Angel Lodge, features curios and books in a picturesque stone building. Other places to shop in the park include Hermit's Rest and Desert View Lookout Tower, at opposite ends of the South Rim drives.

Other Services

Backpackers can stow their bags with staff in the Bright Angel Lodge lobby. The **post office,** near the general store in Market Plaza, 928/638-2512, is open Mon.–Fri. 9 A.M.–4 P.M. and Saturday 11 A.M.–3 P.M.; stamp machines in the lobby are available after hours. **Bank One** next door has a 24-hour ATM; it cannot change foreign currency or cash out-of-town checks. The **general store** in Tusayan also includes a post office and an ATM, and there's another ATM at the IMAX Theater across the highway. **Western Union,** 928/638-2608, does wire transfers at Canyon Food Mart in Tusayan. **Print film processing** is offered at the general stores and several places in Tusayan. **Grand Canyon Garage,** 928/638-2225 (638-2631 ext. 6502 after hours), fixes ailing cars and provides 24-hour emergency service. **Grand Canyon Clinic,** 928/638-2551, offers medical services, open in summer Mon.–Fri. 8 A.M.–8 P.M. and Sat. noon–6 P.M. (shorter hours in winter); for a dentist, call 928/638-2395. For an ambulance or other emergency, dial 911.

National Park Service staff provide wheelchairs, the *Accessibility Guide,* and other services for visitors with special needs; ask at the entrance stations, visitor centers, or write ahead to the park, Box 129, Grand Canyon, AZ 86023.

The **Pet Kennel,** 928/638-0534, houses the furry companions who won't be welcome in the park lodges or permitted on the inner-canyon trails; reservations are suggested. Leashed pets may walk the rim trails in developed areas and may be able to stay in some of the motels in Tusayan. Service animals may be allowed below the rim—check in first at the Backcountry Information Center. You'll find a coin-operated **Laundromat** and **showers**—a welcome sight to any traveler who's been a long time on the road or trail—near Mather Campground.

Theft has become a problem at the Canyon— be sure to keep valuables hidden or carry them with you. Park rangers patrol the park, serving as law enforcement officers and firefighters; see them if you have difficulties.

SOUTH RIM INFORMATION
Visitor Center

Canyon View Information Center, just south of Mather Point, provides on its outdoor panels an overview of things to see and do in the park; step inside the Visitor Center for the information desk; it's open daily 8 A.M.–6 P.M. with extended hours in summer. At the entrance stations, you'll receive a copy of *The Guide* newspaper with the latest visitor information including sightseeing, hiking, programs, places to stay and eat, and other visitor services. You can contact the park at Box 129, Grand Canyon, AZ 86023 or on the Web at www.nps.gov/grca.

The **automated switchboard,** 928/638-7888, has a **weather forecast** and other recordings, and it connects to all park offices if you're patient. The **Hearing-impaired** can use the TDD number for park information, 928/638-7804.

Tusayan's tourist information counter offers local and regional information daily 9 A.M.–5 P.M. beside the IMAX Theater's ticket office.

Planes of Fame Air Museum in Valle also has Arizona tourist information.

Backcountry Information Center

For trail information and backcountry camping permits, drop by this office in the Maswik Transportation Center, open daily 8 A.M.–noon and 1–5 P.M.; 928/638-7875. Call between 1 and 5 P.M. to speak with someone in person. Day-hikers don't need a permit.

Kaibab National Forest

Though often ignored in the shadow of Grand Canyon National Park, the Kaibab offers hiking, mountain biking, and both developed and primitive camping. Stop by the **Tusayan Ranger Station** for handouts on hiking and biking trails, scenic drives, and other attractions. The Kaibab National Forest map for the Tusayan District shows the trails and back roads. Staff can also provide directions for hiking the Red Butte Trail, the prominent butte 12 miles south of Tusayan, as well as the Arizona Trail just south of the park. In winter, cross-country skiers can glide along loops near the Grandview Lookout. The station, open Mon.–Fri. 8 A.M.–4:30 P.M., is in the Tusayan Administrative Site, across and 0.2 mile south of Moqui Lodge just outside the South Entrance Station. Contact the Tusayan District, 928/638-2443, at Box 3088, Tusayan, AZ 86023; www.fs.fed.us/r3/kai.

Internet Sites

A "virtual tour" can give you ideas of things to do on your visit. The National Park Service site contains news, visiting tips, hiking information, and river-running opportunities at www.nps.gov/grca. The "Unofficial Grand Canyon National Park Home Page" is also a good source at www.kaibab.org. Grand Canyon Chamber of Commerce offers an introduction to the park with listings of services and links to surrounding towns at www.thecanyon.com.

Grand Canyon Community Library

This small collection resides in an old schoolhouse tucked behind the garage and general office for the lodges in Grand Canyon Village. It's open daily 1–6 P.M. with general and Southwestern reading, periodicals, and Internet computers; 928/638-2718.

SOUTH RIM TOURS

Most of the lodges in the park, along with Moqui Lodge just outside, and the airport have a transportation desk where you can arrange tours.

Mule Rides

Sure-footed mules have carried prospectors and tourists in and out of the Canyon for more than a century. These large animals, a crossbreed of female horses and male donkeys, depart daily year-round on day and overnight trips. Although easier than hiking, a mule ride should still be considered strenuous—you need to be able to sit in the saddle for long hours and control your mount. These trips are definitely not for those afraid of heights or large animals.

Day trips proceed down the Bright Angel Trail to Indian Garden and out to Plateau Point, a spectacular overlook directly above the river; the 12-mile, seven-hour round-trip costs about $118 per person. On the overnight trip you follow the Bright Angel Trail all the way to the river, cross a suspension bridge to Phantom Ranch, spend the night in a cabin, then come out the next day via the South Kaibab Trail. This costs $335 for one person, $599 for two, and $276 for each additional person; meals are included. Three-day, two-night trips offered mid-November to March 31 cost $457 for one, $774 for two, and $339 for each additional person. Mules will also carry hikers' overnight gear to Phantom Ranch, $53 each way (30-pound limit). All these rates include tax.

Enforced requirements for riders include good health, weight under 200 pounds (91 kg), fluency in English, height at least four feet seven inches (138 cm), and ability to mount and dismount without assistance. No pregnant women are allowed. A broad-rimmed hat, tied under the chin, long pants, a long-sleeved shirt, and sturdy shoes (no open-toed footwear) are necessary. Don't bring bags, purses, canteen, or backpacks, but you can carry a camera or binoculars. A bota (water carrier), which ties on the saddle horn, is supplied.

Reservations should be made 9–12 months in advance for summer and holidays. Also be sure to claim your reservation at least one hour before departure. Without a reservation, there's a chance of getting on via the waiting list, especially off-season; register in person between 6 and 10 A.M. the day before you want to go.

For information and reservations less than two days in advance, see the Bright Angel transportation desk, 928/638-3283. To make reservations more than two days in advance, contact Grand Canyon National Park Lodges at 14001 E. Iliff Ave., Suite 600, Aurora, CO 80014, 303/297-2757, www.grandcanyonlodges.com.

Trail Rides

Apache Stables, 928/638-2891 (stables) or 928/638-2424 (Moqui Lodge), offers mule and horse rides through the Kaibab National Forest for one hour ($30.50), two hours ($55.50), and all the way to the South Rim and back in four hours ($95.50) from the stables near Moqui Lodge, one mile north of Tusayan. Campfire trips ($40.50) ride out and take a wagon back, or you can take the wagon both ways ($12.50); bring your own food. Riding season runs spring to autumn depending on the weather. Reservations are recommended two weeks ahead in summer or two days the rest of the year—though last-minute openings are possible; www.apachestables.com.

Bus Tours

Fred Harvey Transportation Co., 928/638-3283, will show you the sights of the South Rim and narrate the Canyon's history, geology, wildlife, and architecture. Hermit's Rest Tour visits viewpoints on Hermit Road (two hours, $15.25). Desert View Tour travels along Desert View Drive (just under four hours, $27.25). Begin or end the day with sunrise or sunset tours (hour and a half, $11.75 each, May–Oct. only). Children under 16 go free. You can purchase the Desert View Tour and any other excursion at $32.50 and take the tours on separate days if you wish.

Railroad Express drives you to Williams early in the morning to catch the train ride back to Grand Canyon Village, $40 adult, $20 children 16 and under. A river raft excursion runs the smooth-flowing Colorado River in Glen Canyon from the dam to Lees Ferry; at stops on the drive to the dam you'll see highlights along Desert View Drive and the Navajo Nation (12 hours, $101 adult, $53 age 12 and under, April to early November). Tours in the park leave daily (twice a day in summer for the Hermit's Rest and Desert View tours). Lodge transportation desks have tickets. Reservations recommended; contact Box 699, Grand Canyon, AZ 86023; www.grand canyonlodges.com.

Jeep Tours

Grand Canyon Jeep Tours & Safaris, 928/638-5337, 800/320-5337, in Tusayan visits back-country historic and scenic spots in the Kaibab National Forest and the Grand Canyon. The two-hour Canyon Pines Tour departs mid-day for $48 adult ($35 age 12 and under). The three-hour Grand Sunset Tour goes late in the afternoon—a good time to spot wildlife—and includes a stop to watch the sunset for $53 ($40 age 12 and under). The Indian Cave Paintings Tour visits a site with petroglyphs and pictographs in the Kaibab National Forest at $35 adult ($25 age 12 and younger). Tours run March–Oct.; www.grandcanyonjeeptours.com.

Grand Canyon Field Institute

Small groups explore the Grand Canyon with day hikes, backpacking, river-running trips, van tours, and classroom instruction. You can pick up a schedule at the Grand Canyon Association bookstores in the park or write the institute at Box 399, Grand Canyon, AZ 86023, 928/638-2485, www.grandcanyon.org/fieldinstitute.

Air Tours

Flights over the Canyon provide breathtaking views and a look at some of the park's more remote areas. About 40 scenic flight companies operate helicopters or fixed-wing aircraft here, mostly out of Las Vegas. The 50,000-plus flights a year sometimes detract from the wilderness experience of backcountry users—Tusayan's airport is the third busiest in the state. However, restrictions on flight routes and elevations help minimize the noise.

Scenic flights depart all year from Tusayan Airport. Helicopters fly near rim-level and offer the novelty of their takeoffs and landings, but they cost more. Fixed wing aircraft fly about 1,000 feet higher and provide more air time for your dollar; they also offer better children's discounts. Most fixed-wing aircraft leave from the main terminal, while Grand Canyon Airlines and the helicopter companies fly from separate terminals nearby.

Grand Canyon Airlines, 928/638-2407, 800/528-2413, started flying here in 1927 with Ford Trimotors. Today the company uses high-wing, twin-engine planes on a 45- to 55-minute loop over the South Rim, Little Colorado River, and back over the North Rim ($75 adult, $45 children under 12). Planes leave from just north of the main terminal; www.grandcanyonairlines.com.

Air Grand Canyon, 928/638-2686, 800/247-4726, flies high-wing Cessnas on: a 30- to 40-minute flight over the eastern Canyon ($79 adult, $57 children 12 and under); a 50- to 60-minute loop over the eastern Canyon and North Rim ($95 adult, $52 children 12 and under); a 90- to 100-minute grand tour of the Grand and Marble Canyons to Lake Powell ($186 adult, $100 children 12 and under), a three-hour trip to Monument Valley and Lake Powell ($260 adult, $240 children 12 and under; add $35 for a ground tour), and an all-day excursion with a flight to Page, smooth-water river trip to Lees Ferry, then by road back to the Grand Canyon ($260 adult, $240 children 12 and under). A full-day combination flying and rafting tour to the lower Grand Canyon can be arranged with two days notice ($635 per person); www.air grandcanyon.com.

AirStar Airlines, 928/638-2139, 800/962-3869, takes off in high-wing Cessnas on a 50-minute tour to the eastern Grand Canyon and over the North Rim ($81 adult, $61 children under 15); www.airstar.com.

Papillon Grand Canyon Helicopters, 928/638-2419, 800/528-2418, flies across the Canyon to the North Rim (25–30 minutes, $104 adult, $85 children 2–11) and over the eastern Grand Canyon and North Rim (45–50 minutes, $164 adult, $132 children 2–11). You can also arrange to land at Supai village in Havasu Canyon and visit the waterfalls on day and overnight excursions. Helicopters fly from a site across the street and north of the main terminal; there's a gift shop and photo lab here; www.papillon.com.

AirStar Helicopters, 928/638-2622, 800/962-3869, will take you across the Canyon to the North Rim and back (25–30 minutes, $99), around the eastern Grand Canyon (40–45 minutes, $145), and over both the eastern and North Rim areas (50–55 minutes; $165) from the hill just east of the main terminal; www.airstar.com.

Kenai Helicopters, 928/638-2764, 800/541-4537, heads across the Canyon to the North Rim (25–30 minutes, $105 adult, $99 children 2–12) and over the eastern Grand Canyon and North Rim (40–45 minutes, $164 adult, $154 children) from the hill just east of the main terminal; www.flykenai.com.

SOUTH RIM TRANSPORTATION
Shuttle Services
The park offers free shuttle services to reduce traffic congestion. You can get the schedules in *The Guide* newspaper, free at entrance stations and information desks. Hermit Road and the Yaki Point/S. Kaibab Trailhead road are closed to private vehicles when the shuttles are running, but handicapped people can obtain a permit at the Visitor Center to drive their own vehicles.

Village Shuttle connects Canyon View Information Plaza, Yavapai Observation Station, campgrounds, lodges, shops, and offices of Grand Canyon Village; buses operate daily year-round about every 10–15 minutes from early morning to late at night. The route takes about 50 minutes round-trip.

Hermit's Rest Shuttle leaves from the West Rim Interchange near Bright Angel Lodge and goes to Hermit's Rest with stops at overlooks along the way; it operates daily every 10–30 minutes from an hour before sunrise to an hour after sunset. The trip out and back takes 90 minutes if you don't get off. Shuttles may not run in winter, in which case you can take your own vehicle.

The Kaibab Trail Shuttle connects Canyon View Information Plaza with the South Kaibab Trailhead and Yaki Point from one hour before sunrise to one hour after sunset about every 30 minutes.

Eco Shuttle, 928/638-0821, serves Bright Angel Lodge and other places in Grand Canyon Village from Tusayan and the airport April–Oct. for a small charge; charter tours can be arranged too; you can also check with the lodge transportation desks.

Trans-Canyon Shuttle, 928/638-2820, offers daily round-trip van service to the North Rim from May to Oct., $60 one way, $100 round-trip; or contact any lodge transportation desk.

Auto Rentals and Taxi

Enterprise Rent-a-Car, 928/638-2871, 800/736-8222, is at the Tusayan airport. For a taxi, call **Fred Harvey Transportation Dispatch** at 928/638-2822.

Train

Passenger trains rolled into the railroad station at the Grand Canyon from 1901 to 1968. Twenty-one years later, steam locomotives of the **Grand Canyon Railway** began a new service pulling vintage railway cars from downtown Williams to the historic 1909 log depot in Grand Canyon Village.

Trains run daily except December 24th and 25th out of Williams. Steam engines lead the way in summer, then diesels are used the rest of the year. See the Williams section for the many options and entertainment provided; 800/THE-TRAIN; www.thetrain.com. Transportation Services desks in the lodges have a tour that combines a bus to Williams with the train back to the Grand Canyon.

Air

The airport just southwest of Tusayan has both north and south entrances from AZ 64. The main terminal offers scheduled flights, fixed-wing scenic tours, a Harveycar Excursions desk (ground tours), and a gift shop.

Scenic Airlines flies large F-27 and some smaller aircraft from Las Vegas at least twice a day year-round. Fares run $139 one way, $227 round-trip; tour packages are offered out of Las Vegas; 928/638-2617 (Grand Canyon), 702/638-3300 (Las Vegas), or 800/634-6801; www.scenic.com.

Air Vegas Airlines offers both scheduled and tour flights four or five times daily all year in small twin-engine turbo prop planes. Tickets are $139 one way, $278 round-trip, or you can sign up for one of the many tours out of Las Vegas; 928/638-9351 (Grand Canyon), 702/736-3599 (Las Vegas), or 800/255-7474; www.airvegas.com.

North Rim Sights

The North Rim offers an experience very different from that of the South Rim. Elevations 1,000–1,500 feet higher result in lower temperatures and nearly 60 percent more precipitation. Rain and snowmelt have cut deeply into the North Rim so that it is now about twice as far back from the Colorado River as the South Rim. Dramatic vistas from the north inspired early explorers to choose names like Point Sublime, Cape Royal, Angel's Window, and Point Imperial.

Even away from the viewpoints, the North Rim displays great beauty. Spruce, fir, pine, and aspen forests thrive in the cool air. Wildflowers bloom in blazes of color in the meadows and along the roadsides.

You'll find visitor facilities and major trailheads near Bright Angel Point, a 45-mile drive south on AZ 67 from Jacob Lake in the far north of Arizona. The road to Bright Angel Point opens in mid-May, then closes after the first big winter storm, anytime from early October to the end of November.

In winter, a deep blanket of snow covers the Kaibab Plateau's rolling meadow and forest country. The snow cover typically reaches a depth of 4–10 feet, and during the winter of 1994–95 it was more than 19 feet deep. Cross-country skiers and snowshoers find the conditions ideal. The park itself has no facilities open on the North Rim in winter; you can camp here, however, with a permit from the Backcountry Information Center.

BRIGHT ANGEL POINT AND VICINITY

Bright Angel Point

You'll get a North Rim edition of *The Guide* at the entrance station on the drive in. Park at the end of the highway, near Grand Canyon Lodge, and follow the paved foot trail to the tip of Bright

Angel Point, an easy half-mile round-trip walk. Shells and other fossils can be spotted in the outcrop of Kaibab limestone on your right, just after a stone bridge. Roaring Springs Canyon on the left and Transept Canyon on the right join the long Bright Angel Canyon below. John Wesley Powell's 1869 expedition camped at the mouth of this canyon and gave the name Bright Angel Creek to its crystal-clear waters. Listen for Roaring Springs far below on the left and you'll see where the springs shoot out of the cliff. A pumping station at the base supplies drinking water to both North and South rims. Roaring Springs makes a good day-hike or mule-ride destination via the North Kaibab Trail. (See the "Corridor Trails of the Inner Canyon" section later in this chapter.) The volcanic summits on the horizon to the south are, from left to right, O'Leary, San Francisco Peaks, Kendrick, and Sitgreaves. Red Butte, on the right and closer, preserves a remnant of Moenkopi Formation under a lava cap.

Transept Trail

This easy level trail winds along The Transept's rim between Grand Canyon Lodge and the campground, 1.5 miles one way. You can enter the mouth of this canyon, which usually has only a small flow, from the North Kaibab Trail; it's best attempted on an overnight trip, when you can stay at nearby Cottonwood Campground.

Cape Royal Scenic Drive

The paved Cape Royal Road, which begins three miles north of the lodge, leads to some of the North Rim's most spectacular viewpoints. Follow it 5.3 miles, then turn left 2.7 miles for **Point Imperial** (elev. 8,803 feet), which offers picnic tables and the highest vantage point from either rim. Views encompass impressive geology in the park's eastern section. You'll see Nankoweap Creek below, Vermilion Cliffs on the horizon to the north, rounded Navajo Mountain on the horizon in Utah to the northeast, the Painted Desert far to the east, and the Little Colorado River Canyon to the southeast.

Hikers can descend to Nankoweap Creek and the Colorado River on the difficult Nankoweap Trail. (See the "Inner Canyon Hiking" section

© BILL WEIR

Mt. Hayden, from Point Imperial

later in the book.) You can hike to Saddle Mountain Trailhead on a four-mile trail through the forest from Point Imperial; it begins on the far side of the road loop from the overlook. You can also drive there on Forest Service roads from De Motte Park.

Cape Royal Road continues beyond the Point Imperial turnoff past **Vista Encantadora** (with picnic tables), **Roosevelt Point, Walhalla Overlook,** and other viewpoints to a parking area and a few picnic tables at the end of the road, just before Cape Royal. Total driving distance from Grand Canyon Lodge is 23 miles one way. A paved level trail continues south 0.3 mile from the parking lot to Cape Royal. Trailside signs identify plants growing on this high, arid ridge. On the way you'll see **Angel's Window,** a massive natural arch, which you can walk out on via a short side trail. **Cape Royal** (elev. 7,865 feet) features a fantastic panorama; it's the southernmost viewpoint of the North Rim in this part

SILENCE IN THE CANYON

Wilderness can provide a refuge from the ever busier worlds that we create. Just being out in the canyons turns out to be a delightful experience. Part of this delight seems to come from the space and the silence, which then reflects back on our own minds. "Preserving the power of presence," as Jack Turner terms it in his book, *The Abstract Wild*, is far more complex than just looking after the biodiversity. Rather than believing that presence is something that we can add on to make the wilderness whole, he states that "the loss of aura and presence is the main reason we are losing so much of the natural world." Turner thinks that by viewing wilderness as amusement and resource, we lose sight of the magic and sacred nature of it.

In the Grand Canyon, this value of presence or silence has come under assault from a steady stream of aircraft circling over the heart of the Canyon. No local topic has become as heated or difficult to resolve. Pilots and passengers enjoy flying so much that they refuse to consider a ban on flights, yet proponents of presence will not be satisfied until the skies over the park become silent. Congress first addressed the noise problem in 1987, banning nonemergency flights below the rims and requiring the designation of flight-free zones. The current compromise of restricted flight paths reduces the noise over some parts of the park, but it comes far short of the tranquility that early tourists to the park must have experienced. Only public opinion, expressed to representatives in Congress and to the Grand Canyon National Park administration, will determine how much natural silence the Canyon will offer to future visitors.

of the Grand Canyon. Signs point out Freya Castle to the southeast, Vishnu Temple and the distant San Francisco Peaks to the south, and a branch of Clear Creek Canyon and flat-topped Wotans Throne to the southwest.

Cliff Spring Trail

Hikers enjoy pretty scenery on this trail, which takes you into a forested ravine, past a small prehistoric ruin, and under an overhang to the spring in half a mile one way. The canyon walls open up impressively as you near the spring. It's possible to continue on a rougher trail another half mile for more canyon views. Cliff Spring Trail begins from Angel's Window Overlook, a small pullout on a curve of Cape Royal Road, 1.1 miles past Walhalla Overlook and 0.6 mile before road's end.

Cape Final

An easy two-mile (each way) hike brings you east of Cape Royal Road to a unique perspective from the Kaibab Plateau above Unkar Creek Canyon. The trailhead at a small unpaved parking area on the east side of the road can be difficult to spot—it may or may not be signed. Drive 5.5 miles past Roosevelt Point to the parking spot, which is one mile before Walhalla Overlook and 2.7 miles before road's end at Cape Royal. Other scenic vistas on the North Rim can be reached on back-road hikes on the Walhalla Plateau; consult a ranger for suggestions.

Walhalla Ruins

Ancestral Puebloans, known by archaeologists as Kayenta Anasazi, farmed more than 300 sites on the plateau, most of them near the rim where warm air currents extended the growing season. The villagers probably occupied the pueblo at Walhalla (elev. 8,000 feet) in summer and wintered at Unkar Delta (visible from Walhalla Overlook); they departed from the Grand Canyon about A.D. 1150. A 100-yard walk across the road from Walhalla Overlook leads to this site.

Widforss Trail

Gently rolling terrain, fine Canyon views, and a variety of forest types attract hikers to the Widforss Trail. From the edge of a meadow, the trail climbs a bit, skirts the head of The Transept, then leads through ponderosa pines to an overlook near Widforss Point. The trail and point honor Swedish artist Gunnar Widforss, who painted the national parks of the West between 1921 and 1934.

Haunted Canyon lies below at trail's end, flanked by The Colonnade on the right and Manu Temple, Buddha Temple, and Schellbach Butte on the left; beyond lie countless more temples, towers, canyons, and the cliffs of the South Rim.

Widforss Trail is 10 miles round-trip and takes about six hours to hike. Many people enjoy going just part way. You'll often see mule deer along the trail. From Grand Canyon Lodge, go 2.7 miles north on the highway, then turn left and go one mile on a dirt road; the turnoff is 0.3 mile south of the Cape Royal Road junction.

Ken Patrick Trail

This trail, 10 miles one way, offers forest scenery and views across the headwaters of Nankoweap Creek. From Point Imperial, the Ken Patrick winds about three miles along the rim to Cape Royal Road, then continues seven miles through forest to the North Kaibab trailhead, with an elevation drop of 560 feet. Allow six hours for the entire hike, one way.

You can start either from trailheads near the south end of the Point Imperial parking area, on Cape Royal Road one mile east of the Point Imperial junction, or from the upper end of the North Kaibab trailhead parking area, two miles north of Grand Canyon Lodge.

Ken Patrick worked as a ranger on the North Rim for several seasons in the early 1970s. He was shot and killed by escaped convicts while on duty at California's Point Reyes National Seashore in 1973.

Uncle Jim Trail

The first mile follows the Ken Patrick Trail—from the North Kaibab trailhead—then turns southeast to make a loop around Uncle Jim Point. Allow three hours for the five-mile round-trip. Views from the point include Roaring Springs Canyon and North Kaibab Trail. James "Uncle Jim" Owens served as the Grand Canyon Game Reserve's first warden from 1906 until establishment of the national park.

THE WESTERN KAIBAB PLATEAU

Kanab Creek Wilderness

Kanab Creek has the largest canyon system in the Grand Canyon's North Rim, with headwaters 100 miles north on the Paunsaugunt Plateau in Utah. The wilderness area protects 77,100 acres along the Kanab and its tributaries. Springs in Kanab Canyon nourish large cottonwood trees and lush growths of desert willow, tamarisk, maidenhair fern, and grass. From Hack Canyon, a popular entry point on the west, hikers can descend 21 miles down Kanab Creek to the Colorado River; allow three days each way. You'll need a Grand Canyon backcountry permit to camp below the junction with Jumpup Canyon. Hack Canyon and a bit of the wilderness lie on BLM land; the office in Kanab, Utah, has information on trailhead access and hiking. The trailhead is also worthwhile as a scenic drive if you don't mind the bumpy road; see the Hack Canyon entry in the Arizona Strip section. Other trailheads lie on the Kaibab National Forest; contact the Fredonia or Kaibab Plateau Visitor Center offices for road and trail information. The easy to moderate, 17-mile **Ranger Trail** wraps around the base of Jumpup Point in the heart of the wilderness. You can reach it on the west side via the easy, 21.5-mile **Snake Gulch-Kanab Creek Trail #59**, as well as from Kanab or Hack Canyons. On the east side, Jumpup Cabin Trailhead and the difficult, six-mile **Jumpup-Nail Trail #8** provide access.

Jumpup Point

An amazing canyon panorama greets the rare visitor who ventures out along the rough road on this long point in the western Kaibab Plateau. Five miles before the end of the point, the vast Jumpup Canyon first appears on the left, along with its tributaries Sowats Canyon and Indian Hollow. Much of this canyon country belongs to the Kanab Creek Wilderness, which almost completely surrounds Jumpup Point. Although there's no trail access to the canyons from here, Ranger Trail can be seen far below, where it's joined by Jumpup-Nail Trail, which descends from Sowats

Point across to the east. You might spot a bighorn sheep on one of the precarious ledges. At road's end, a short walk reveals more views. Lower Kanab Canyon and the Grand Canyon seem almost lost in the vastness. Kanab Canyon and the broad Hack Canyon lie to the west. Mt. Trumbull stands as the highest of the volcanoes across Kanab Canyon. The summit of Mt. Logan, identified by its cliff profile, is just to the left and farther back. Vermilion Cliffs and other high points of Utah lie to the northwest and north.

Sparse pinyon pine, juniper, sage, and cactus of the high desert cover the point at an elevation of 5,650 feet. The Kaibab National Forest map (North Kaibab District) shows the ways in. From Jacob Lake, go south 0.3 mile on AZ 67, turn west on Forest Road 461, and take Forest Roads 462, 22, 423, 235, 423, then 201 to its end. Forest Road 22 provides access from either the east edge of Fredonia (US 89A between Mileposts 607 and 608) or DeMotte Park (0.8 mile south of the North Rim Store on AZ 67), then you'll follow Forest Roads 423, 235, 423, and 201. A high-clearance vehicle will be needed for the rocky sections of the last 10 miles of road. Mountain bikers enjoy this ride too.

Sowats Point

This viewpoint of Jumpup Canyon lies east across from Jumpup Point at an elevation of 6,200 feet. **Jumpup-Nail Trail #8** descends into the depths here, six miles and a drop of 2,000 feet—steep in places—to Ranger Trail #41 in Kanab Creek Wilderness. You can start on the same roads as those to Jumpup Point, but take Forest Roads 425 and 233 off Forest Road 22. High-clearance vehicles will be needed for the last several miles.

Indian Hollow and Thunder River Trailhead

A tiny campground with an outhouse and tables is 0.4 mile before the end of Forest Road 232 at

An amazing canyon panorama greets the rare visitor who ventures out along the rough road at Jumpup Point in the western Kaibab Plateau. Much of this canyon country belongs to the Kanab Creek Wilderness. You might spot a bighorn sheep on one of the precarious ledges.

an elevation of 6,300 feet. Ponderosa pine start to thin out closer to the rim, where pinyon pine, juniper, and Gambel oak predominate. At the rim, a short walk from road's end, you'll have a view of the Deer Creek drainage of the Grand Canyon. Great Thumb Mesa lies directly across to the south. The full length of the Powell Plateau presents itself to the southeast. Down canyon, Mt. Sinyala stands near the mouth of Havasu Canyon.

Thunder River Trail drops steeply from the rim for the first few hundred yards, then contours west half a mile to a break in the cliffs, a good day-hike destination. (See the "Inner Canyon Hiking" section for a description of the hike to Thunder River and Deer Creek Falls.) Forest Road 22 provides access either from the east edge of Fredonia (US 89A between Mileposts 607 and 608) or from DeMotte Park (0.8 mile south of the North Rim Store on AZ 67), then you'll follow Forest Roads 425 and 232 to the end of 232. Cautiously driven cars might be able to make it; check with Kaibab National Forest staff.

Crazy Jug Point

This point features great views and good access roads at an elevation of 7,500 feet. Pinyon pine, cliff rose, and some ponderosa grow here. A walk of a few hundred feet from the parking area leads to the overlook. The Colorado River comes out from behind the Powell Plateau, wraps around Great Thumb Mesa, then winds far downstream. Dark, forested volcanoes of Mt. Trumbull and the rest of the Uinkaret Mountains rise to the west. Directly below are Crazy Jug Canyon, Tapeats Amphitheater, and other parts of the Tapeats Creek drainage. The lineup of Fence, Locust, North Timp, Timp, and Fire Points marks the Kaibab Plateau to the southeast; all of these points can be reached by road for a variety of perspectives of this part of the Grand Canyon. Directions for Crazy Jug Point are the same as those for Indian Hollow except that you continue south on Forest Roads 425 and 292B, following signs. Cars can do this trip in dry weather.

Monument Point and Bill Hall Trailhead

Bill Hall Trail climbs west up along the rim nearly a mile before plunging steeply to the Thunder River Trail. The ridge just above the trail has a sweeping panorama up Tapeats Canyon and down the Grand Canyon. Near the trailhead area (elev. 7,050 feet), you'll see effects of the Bridger Burn of 1996. This fire affected 54,000 acres—a large portion of the western Kaibab Plateau—but pinyon pine, juniper, and lots of cliff rose and wildflowers grow here. Follow directions for Crazy Jug Point until the junction half a mile before the point, then keep straight 1.7 miles on Forest Road 292A; it's okay for cars in dry weather.

Timp, North Timp, and Parissawampitts Point

Walk about one-third mile out on Timp Point from the parking area for the best panoramas and to see Thunder River emerge from the north wall of Tapeats Canyon and drop in two large cascades amidst lush cottonwoods. You can also spot the trail that climbs from Thunder River to the top of cliffs and over into Surprise Valley. Binoculars give the best view. Nearby North Timp and Parissawampitts Points also provide good perspectives.

Rainbow Rim Trail #10 follows the convoluted rim between Timp and Parissawampitts for 18 miles one way. Mountain bikers can make many pleasant loops on this trail and on forest roads in the area. Forest Road 250 connects roads to these points, though you'll need a high-clearance vehicle or mountain bike for it. Cars can reach Timp Point (elev. 7,600 feet) in good weather by turning off AZ 67 at DeMotte Park (0.8 mile south of the North Rim Store on AZ 67), then following Forest Roads 22, 270, 222, 206, and 271. Forest Road 271A branches to North Timp Point from 271. Parissawampitts Point may also be okay for cars; take Forest Roads 22, 270, 222, 206, then 214 to its end.

Fire Point

The panorama here takes in Tapeats Amphitheater, Steamboat Mountain, and Powell Plateau (you can spot the trail to its top); Great Thumb Mesa lies across the river. Walk 100 feet out on the rocks for an even better look. A fine stand of ponderosa pine grows on the point. Carefully driven cars can negotiate the roads in good weather.

Turn west two miles on Forest Road 22 from AZ 67 in De Motte Park (0.8 mile south of the North Rim Country Store), head south two miles on Forest Road 270, then turn west 13 miles on Forest Road 223 to its end. The last mile is within Grand Canyon National Park and will probably be closed to vehicles.

Point Sublime

This well-named overlook and picnic area, southeast of Fire Point and west of Bright Angel Point, lies at the end of a 17-mile dirt road negotiable by high-clearance vehicles, mountain bicycles, on horseback, or on foot. Point Sublime extends far into the Grand Canyon for awesome views. You can scan a great length of both North and South Rims and spot a section of Colorado River. The South Rim can be traced from below Bass Canyon upcanyon nearly to Desert View. Binoculars help you to see parts of the Tonto, Hermit, and South Kaibab Trails along with Grand Canyon Village and Hermit's Rest. On the North Rim, the Powell Plateau lies to the northwest, Confucius and Mencius Temples to the southeast, and Tiyo Point and Cape Royal to the east, truly sublime. Closer in, cliffs drop into the Tuna Creek drainage. Point Sublime makes a great place to camp, but you'll need a backcountry permit to do so.

The route is bumpy and not always passable; check at the North Rim Backcountry Office or the North Rim Visitor Center. You can enter from the Kaibab National Forest by turning west two miles on Forest Road 22 from the AZ 67 turnoff in De Motte Park (0.8 mile south of the North Rim Country Store), heading south two miles on Forest Road 270, turning west six miles on Forest Road 223, then south 1.5 miles on Forest Roads 268 and 268B to the park boundary, where the road becomes rougher and less well signed on the last 15 miles to Point Sublime. Keep left at the junction 0.2 mile inside the park (the right fork goes to Swamp Point), then keep right past the junctions for Kanabownits Lookout and the road to AZ 67. The Kaibab National Forest map (North Kaibab District) is essential for navigating these back roads. A second way in begins near Bright Angel Point—go north 2.7 miles on AZ 67 from Grand Canyon Lodge, then turn left on the unpaved Point Sublime Road (high-clearance vehicle needed) past the Widforss and Tiyo Point trailheads to Point Sublime.

Tiyo Point has been closed to vehicles, but you can hike in or go by horseback. Turn south 6.3 miles from Point Sublime Road at a large meadow, 4.2 miles in from AZ 67.

THE EASTERN KAIBAB PLATEAU

Saddle Mountain Wilderness

This 40,610-acre wilderness includes part of the densely forested Kaibab Plateau, along with sheer cliffs and narrow canyons. Mountain lions, bears, and mule deer roam the area. North Canyon Wash is noted for its pure strain of native Apache trout. Saddle Mountain (elev. 8,424 feet) stands northeast of the Bright Angel Point area on the Grand Canyon's North Rim. (You can see Saddle Mountain from Point Imperial.) Nankoweap, South Canyon, and North Canyon trails cross the wilderness from the Kaibab Plateau to House Rock Valley.

East Rim Viewpoint

Expansive vistas across the Marble Canyon area greet visitors at this overlook on the east edge of the Kaibab Plateau. The site (elev. 8,800 feet) lies on Kaibab National Forest land several miles north of Grand Canyon National Park. Cars and small RVs can easily travel the gravel roads in good weather. East Rim Viewpoint features great sunrises and sunsets; colors reflect off the distant Vermilion Cliffs and Painted Desert. The Forest Service offers some outhouses but no other facilities. Camping may be restricted at the viewpoint, but good places for primitive camping lie

in the conifer and aspen forests nearby; no camping permit or fee is required. From AZ 67 in De Motte Park (0.8 mile south of the North Rim Country Store), turn east about four miles on Forest Road 611. Another fine panorama lies farther north at the end of Forest Road 611, 6.9 miles from AZ 67 (keep right at the fork 6.5 miles in; this last 0.4 mile is too rough for cars); walk a few hundred feet beyond road's end for the views. Still farther north, **Dog Point** also features a fine view; head east 1.2 miles on Forest Road 611 from AZ 67, then turn left (north) 7.2 miles on Forest Road 610 to its end; keep right at the fork 6.4 miles in.

Hikers can follow some of the Kaibab Plateau/Arizona Trail #101 along the rim or descend into North Canyon in the Saddle Mountain Wilderness from East Rim Overlook. East Rim Trail #7 descends from a trailhead 300 feet north of the overlook, and North Canyon Trail #4 descends from the rim two miles south. Together, these three trails make a loop of about six miles into the valley below. North Canyon Trail #4 continues down North Canyon to House Rock Valley, a total of seven miles one way.

Marble Viewpoint

This overlook, southeast of East Rim Viewpoint, provides another perspective. From AZ 67 in De Motte Park (0.8 mile south of the North Rim Country Store), turn east 1.3 miles on Forest Road 611, right 6.7 miles on 610, then left 4.6 miles on 219 to its end.

Saddle Mountain Trailhead

The drive out Forest Road 610 is worthwhile for the spectacular views of Marble Canyon, Nankoweap, and House Rock Valley areas. From the trailhead (elev. 8,800 feet), Nankoweap Trail #57 drops several hundred feet to the best viewpoints; this trail continues to the Nankoweap Trailhead (three miles) and on to Road 8910/445G (5–6 miles) in House Rock Valley. From the AZ 67 turnoff in De Motte Park, 0.8 mile south of the North Rim Country Store, head east 1.3 miles on 611, then turn right 12 miles on 610 to the trailhead. Cautiously driven cars should be able to do this in dry weather. A trail to Point

Imperial begins on the right 0.2 mile before Saddle Mountain Trailhead; it follows a former fire road about four miles through the forest. The national park border is just south of 611, so do not camp here without a backcountry permit. The Kaibab National Forest has many spots suitable for dispersed camping.

Although not shown on the Kaibab Forest map, the road continues 1.4 miles past Saddle Mountain Trailhead to another great viewpoint of Marble Canyon, House Rock Valley, and far beyond. Use a high-clearance vehicle or hike in.

House Rock Valley

Rolling hills of grasslands and pinyon-juniper woodlands of this valley separate cliffs of the Kaibab Plateau above and Marble Canyon below. Viewpoints provide intimate and detailed views of Marble Canyon. The turnoff for House Rock Buffalo Ranch Road (Road 8910/445) from AZ 89A is between Mileposts 559 and 560, 20 miles east of Jacob Lake and 21.5 miles west of Marble Canyon Lodge. About 90 **buffalo** roam freely across 67,000 acres of the valley; you're most likely to see them in summer, least likely during hunting season in autumn.

For **Buck Farm Overlook,** head south 23.5 miles from US 89A to a fork; take the left fork east two miles, then turn left three miles on Forest Road 445H to its end.

Triple Alcoves Overlook features a different panorama; go 2.5 miles south on Forest Road 445 from the 445-445H junction, then hike east a half mile on an old jeep road to the overlook. Signs mark the trailhead. House Rock Buffalo Ranch Road provides nearly year-round access to these and other viewpoints as well as to Saddle Mountain Wilderness.

The very scenic Forest Roads 213 and 220 connect the Kaibab Plateau with House Rock Valley. You'll need a high-clearance vehicle for the steep and winding sections. Turnoff from AZ 67 is between Mileposts 601 and 602, about three miles north of the North Rim Country Store. Forest Road 213 crosses the Arizona Trail 2.6 miles in. Seven miles in from AZ 67, Forest Road 213 begins the descent on short switchbacks. It skirts the north edge of

Saddle Mountain Wilderness before ending after 8.6 miles at the East Side Game Road (Forest Road 220). Turn right 8.2 miles to continue down to House Rock Valley, following Tater Canyon part of the way to a T-junction with Road 8910/445, 17 miles south of US 89A. Turn left here for US 89A or turn right for Buffalo Ranch, Saddle Mountain trailheads, and Marble Canyon overlooks.

TOROWEAP

This remote area of the North Rim lies between Kanab Canyon to the east and the Pine Mountains (Uinkaret Mountains) to the west. An overlook (elev. 4,552 feet) provides awesome Canyon views from sheer cliffs nearly 3,000 feet high above the river. Toroweap, also known as Tuweap or Tuweep, lies 140 road miles west of the developed North Rim area of Bright Angel Point. The views, many hiking possibilities, and solitude

© BILL WEIR

view up Colorado River from Toroweap Overlook

GRAND CANYON

GRAND CANYON

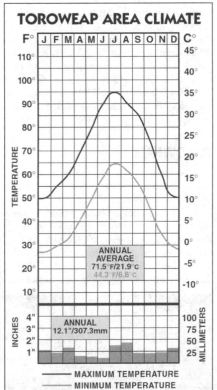

TOROWEAP AREA CLIMATE

ANNUAL
AVERAGE
71.5°F/21.9°C
44.3°F/6.8°C

ANNUAL
12.1"/307.3mm

—— MAXIMUM TEMPERATURE
—— MINIMUM TEMPERATURE

reward visitors who make it here. No park entry or campground fee was charged here at press time, though user fees may be forthcoming. Obtain hiking information, backcountry permits, and emergency help at the Tuweep Ranger Station, open all year though the ranger does take a few days off now and then. There's an emergency phone here and possibly emergency water. If you'll need a backcountry permit, it's safer to obtain it beforehand, though you could try for a last-minute permit here or at Pipe Spring National Monument.

Pinyon pine, juniper, cactus, and small flowering plants cover the plateau. Watch for rattlesnakes. Hikers can enjoy many easy rambles near the rim, a difficult descent to the river near Lava Falls, a scramble up Vulcan's Throne, or multi-day trips on the Tuckup Trail.

Toroweap Overlook

The views begin at road's end, where sheer cliffs drop to the Colorado River. **Mount Sinyala,** a butte 25 miles east of the overlook, marks the mouth of Havasu Canyon. Most of the Havasupai who live on the reservation dwell in Supai village, nine miles up Havasu Canyon. The **Hualapai Indian Reservation** lies directly across the Colorado River from the overlook. **Vulcan's Anvil,** also known as Vulcan's Forge or Thor's Hammer, rises in the middle of the river directly below. This 50-foot-high lava neck is all that remains of an extinct lava vent.

Lava Falls, visible 1.5 miles downstream, roars with a vengeance. You can see it from a point just one-eighth mile to the right from the overlook. Debris from Prospect Canyon on the South Rim forms the rapids, perhaps the roughest water in the Grand Canyon. Water flowing between 12,000 and 20,000 cubic feet per second drops abruptly, then explodes into foam and spray. River-runners commonly rate these rapids a 10-plus on a scale of 1–10. Lava Falls Route is a steep and very strenuous hike that leads down to the rapids from a nearby trailhead; see "Inner Canyon Hiking" below.

Saddle Horse Canyon Trail

The trailhead for this easy hike lies beside the main road 5.7 miles south of the ranger station. The path heads east to a Colorado River overlook, then north with views of wonderfully weathered rock near Saddle Horse Canyon; it's about 1.6 miles round-trip.

Esplanade Loop Trail

This 2.9-mile hiking trail begins at the campground, 5.4 miles south of the ranger station.

Vulcan's Throne

Vulcan's Throne, the 600-foot-high rounded cinder cone west of the overlook, is one of the youngest volcanoes in the area. The hike to the top (no trail) is about 1.5 miles round-trip with a 500-foot elevation gain; it's most easily reached by road via normally dry Toroweap Lake. Between 30,000 and 1.2 million years ago, eruptions of red-hot lava built about 60 volcanic cones here, even forming dams across the Colorado River. One of the dams towered nearly 2,000 feet, but the river washed it away long ago.

More adventurous hikes in the area include the Lava Falls Route and Tuckup Trail (see "Inner Canyon Hiking" below).

Toroweap Campground

The small campground has a great setting backed by low cliffs and overlooking small canyons; it's 5.4 miles past the ranger station and 0.9 mile before the overlook at the end of the road. The overlook itself is planned to become a day-use area. There's no water, no camping charge, no reservations accepted, and no permit needed for the established sites; an eight-person, two-vehicle limit per site applies. If all campsites are full, you must obtain the expensive backcountry permit for other areas in the park or simply drive north and find an undeveloped spot on BLM land. Bring lots of water, extra food, and camping gear.

Getting There

Three roads lead in to the area. The most popular one begins at AZ 389, nine miles west of Fredonia; turn south 40 miles on Road 109 at the sign for "Toroweap 61," continue straight seven miles on Road 5, and straight 14 miles on Road 115. These dirt roads are usually in good condition when dry but have washboard sections. Watch for livestock and take it slow through washes and cattleguards. The last few miles are slow and rocky, but careful drivers should make it through fine. The Tuweep Ranger Station is on the left 6.3 miles before the overlook. Beyond the ranger station, Toroweap Point (summit elev. 6,393 feet) towers on the left; dumpy Vulcan's Throne (summit elev. 5,102 feet) sits on the right.

You can also drive to Toroweap on a 90-mile dirt road from St. George (Roads 1069 and 5 for 76 miles, then right 14 miles on Road 115) or a 58-mile road from Colorado City (Road 5 for 44 miles, then continue straight 14 miles on Road 115). Avoid driving these roads after heavy rain or snow, especially the route from Colorado City. Snows usually block the road from St. George between October and May. Water, food, and gas are not available in this country. Bring a map—the BLM's Arizona Strip one is best—as signs may be missing at some junctions.

North Rim Practicalities

The road from Jacob Lake to the North Rim may be open earlier in the spring and later in the fall than the Grand Canyon Lodge, restaurants, gas station, and campground. A sign at Jacob Lake near the turnoff for the North Rim lists the services available. If you're looking for a room in summer, be sure to make reservations as far in advance as possible, as every lodge on the Kaibab Plateau will be full! Alternatives are to stay to the west in Fredonia or Kanab, or to the east in the lodges along US 89A or in Page. In autumn, you have a chance of getting in on short notice. During winter and spring, when the North Rim is closed, Jacob Lake Inn stays open and should have plenty of rooms.

BRIGHT ANGEL POINT

Accommodations and Campgrounds

Grand Canyon Lodge, overlooking Transept Canyon near Bright Angel Point, offers the only accommodations within the park on the North Rim. Lodging comes in five types: Rim Cabins with a view from the porch, $109 d; Western Cabins, $99 d; two-bedroom Pioneer Cabins, $94 for one to four persons; Frontier Cabins, $80 d; and modern motel rooms, $87 d. The season runs mid-May to mid-October, when reservations and a deposit are highly recommended. Call 303/297-2757 for advance reservations, 928/638-2611 for same-day reservations, or fax 303/297-3175; the lodges can also be reached at 14001 E. Iliff Ave., Suite 600, Aurora, CO 80014; www.grandcanyonnorthrim.com.

North Rim Campground, 1.5 miles north and west of Grand Canyon Lodge, provides drinking water but no hookups. It's open mid-May to mid- or late October at $15 per night, $7.50 with Golden Age or Access passes; reservations are required. Four rim sites have views—and winds—at a higher cost. Backpackers and bicyclists can camp at a walk-in area for $4 per person; a "FULL" sign at the campground means that all drive-in spaces are taken but spaces will be available for walk-ins. Coin-operated showers, a Laundromat, store, and ice are available nearby. Reservations for family and group sites can be made one day to three months in advance at 800/365-2267 (365-CAMP); http://reservations.nps.gov.

Food and Services
Grand Canyon Lodge, 928/638-2611, serves moderately priced breakfasts, lunches, and dinners in a huge rustic dining room with Canyon views; open daily mid-May to mid-October. You'll need reservations for dinner. A cafeteria style **snack bar,** also part of the lodge, offers faster service and lower prices but no atmosphere; it's open for breakfast, lunch, and dinner. The **Saloon** in the lodge serves gourmet coffees as well as more potent beverages.

You'll also find a **post office** and **gift shop** in Grand Canyon Lodge. A **service station** is near the campground, along with a small **general store/snack bar** offering camping supplies, groceries, and cooked food.

Information
The **North Rim Visitor Center,** 928/638-7864, near the lodge has an information desk, book sales, and a few exhibits; it's open daily 8 A.M.–6 P.M.; signs list times of nature walks, talks, and children's programs. Kids 4–14 can take part in Junior Ranger activities.

Obtain overnight camping permits and trail information from the **Backcountry Information Center** (Box 129, Grand Canyon, AZ 86023) on the South Rim or at the ranger station on the North Rim. The North Rim ranger station, 928/638-7868, is open daily 8 A.M.–noon and 1–5 P.M. from May 15 to Oc-

tober 15, weather permitting. The turnoff from the highway is a quarter mile north of the campground turnoff; walk around to the window on the side of the building. The park's automated switchboard, 928/638-7888, has recorded **weather forecasts** and other information and will connect you to any office. Or visit the website www.nps.gov/grca.

Mule Rides, Tours, and Transportation
Mule rides take you along the rim and into the Canyon. One-hour rim rides cost $20 (minimum age seven), half-day trips down the North Kaibab Trail to the tunnel are $45 (minimum age eight), and full-day rides to Roaring Springs are $95 including lunch (minimum age 12). Requirements for riders are similar to those for South Rim trips, including proper riding attire (long pants and wide-brimmed hat), good health, weight under 200 pounds/91 kilograms for the full-day (220 pounds/100 kilograms for the shorter rides), and fluency in English. Reservations with the mule rides desk in the Grand Canyon Lodge lobby are a good idea; call 928/638-9875 at the lodge or 435/679-8665 (residence).

A **Hiker Shuttle** goes to the North Kaibab trailhead early in the morning from Grand Canyon Lodge; make advance reservations at the lodge's front desk. **Trans-Canyon Shuttle,** 928/638-2820, offers daily round-trip van service between the South and North Rims from May to Oct., $60 one way, $100 round-trip.

NORTH OF THE PARK
Accommodations, Campgrounds, and Services
Kaibab Lodge, 928/638-2389 in season, then 928/526-0924, 800/525-0924 the rest of the year, lies 18.5 miles north of Bright Angel Point and 26 miles south of Jacob Lake at the edge of a large meadow just west of AZ 67. Guests stay in cabins ($80 d to $130 for four people) and dine at the restaurant (breakfast and dinner daily) during the mid-May to late October season; www.canyoneers.com. Across the highway, **North**

Rim Country Store sells groceries, camping and auto supplies, and gas and diesel.

De Motte Park Campground, just south of Kaibab Lodge, is open early June to late September with drinking water and interpretive programs but no showers or hookups; $12 per night. Try to arrive before noon for the best chance of getting a space—no reservations are taken.

Jacob Lake Inn, 45 miles north of the North Rim at the junction of AZ 67 and US 89A, 928/643-7232, stays open all year with basic motel rooms ($90–92 d to $98–105 four persons), cabins (April to November only, $72–118), restaurant (American food daily for breakfast, lunch, and dinner), grocery store, Native American crafts shop, and service station; www .jacoblake.com.

Jacob Lake Campground, 928/643-7770, has sites in the ponderosa pines with drinking water but no hookups or showers from mid-May to mid-October for $12 per night; there's usually room. Campers can enjoy summer interpretive programs and nearby hiking trails. Head west 0.1 mile on US 89A from AZ 67, then turn right at the sign. Only groups can reserve sites with Recreation Resource Management at 928/204-1698; www.camprrm.com.

Kaibab Camper Village, 928/643-7804, 800/525-0924 (reservations), overlooks tiny Jacob Lake just 0.3 mile south on AZ 67 from US 89A, then west 0.7 mile; it's open May 15–Oct. 15 with coin showers. Tent spaces and dry RV sites run $12 and sites with hookups cost $22. Tent sites are usually available, though RVers should make reservations or arrive by noon.

Allen's Outfitters, 435/644-8150, 435/689-1979, offers trail rides of one and two hours in the forest, half- and full-day trips to overlooks, and pack trips from about mid-May to early September at their stables 0.3 mile south on AZ 67 from US 89A and year-round in Kanab.

Information

Staff at the Forest Service's **Kaibab Plateau Visitor Center,** 928/643-7298, in Jacob Lake provide information on the many viewpoints, trails, campgrounds, and historic sites in the Kaibab National Forest along the North Rim; they also issue backcountry permits for most areas of Grand Canyon National Park. Exhibits include a 3-D model of the Grand Canyon and wildlife displays. You can purchase books and maps. It's open daily 8 A.M.–5 P.M. from about mid-May to mid-October and possibly later in the year with a shorter schedule; www.fs.fed.us/r3/kai.

Inner Canyon Hiking

The wonders of the Canyon reveal themselves best to those who enter its depths. Just remember that the Inner Canyon is a wilderness area, subject to temperature extremes, flash floods, rockslides, and other natural hazards. You can have a successful trip in the Canyon only by taking enough food, water, and other essential supplies.

Always carry—and drink—water. All too often people will walk merrily down a trail without a canteen, and then suffer terribly on the climb out. Only the Bright Angel and North Kaibab trails have sources of treated water. In summer, carry one quart or liter of water for each hour of hiking; half a quart per hour should be enough in the cooler months. Electrolyte-replacement drinks may be helpful too.

Canyon trails offer little shade—you'll probably need a hat, sunglasses, and sunscreen. Footgear should have good traction for the steep trails; lightweight boots work well. During winter and early spring, instep crampons—metal plates with small spikes—greatly improve footing on icy trails at the higher elevations. Rain gear will keep you dry during rainstorms; ponchos, on the other hand, provide poor protection against wind-driven rain. Be careful when rock-scrambling—soft and fractured rocks dominate in the Canyon. Don't swim in the Colorado River—its cold waters and swift currents are simply too dangerous.

FUN ON THE TRAIL CHECKLIST

- In summer, it's well worthwhile to hit the trail at first light, before 7 A.M. at the latest—or start after 4 P.M.; a lightweight flashlight provides the option of hiking after dark.
- Water and sun protection will come in handy even on short hikes, as the grand scenery will try to draw you in farther than you'd planned!
- Keep your body humming with frequent water and food (carbohydrate) breaks. All water and no food can lead to water intoxication—a dangerous condition caused by low electrolytes.
- Rangers recommend one gallon of water for an eight-hour hike in hot weather.
- Drinking water *before* you get thirsty will prevent the 10–20 percent loss of efficiency caused by even slight dehydration.
- If it's hot, try soaking your clothing in water for refreshing coolness.
- An easy pace allows the body to function more efficiently and feel better.

- Kicking back and putting your legs up for a five-to-seven-minute break once or twice an hour will refresh your leg muscles.
- It's best to ignore that temptation to try a rim-to-river-to-rim hike unless you're sure you can do it AND the weather is cool.
- The Canyon Rule is to allow one-third of the time and energy on the descent and the rest for the climb back up.
- Wind and rain can cause hypothermia even in summer, so raingear can save the day year-round.
- Traveling light increases the fun; food and water should be the heaviest items. You might be able to replace a heavy tent with a tarp and ground sheet, a heavy sleeping bag with a lightweight blanket, and the Walkman with sounds of the Canyon.
- Rangers will be happy to advise you on your trip plans and possible difficulties that may lie ahead.

Zones

Backcountry areas of the Grand Canyon have been divided into zones to give hikers an idea of what conditions to expect.

Corridor Zone trails receive regular maintenance and have signs, emergency phones, toilets, and easy trailhead access. They're the best choice for first-time visitors because someone will likely be around in case of difficulty. Drinking water is available at some places along the way, but ask before relying on them. You should still carry water because water sources may be hours apart. Camping is permitted only in established campgrounds.

Threshold Zone areas receive less maintenance and have fewer signs; you'll need to know where water sources are and purify before drinking. The more heavily used areas have designated camping sites. Most trailheads are reached by dirt roads.

Primitive Zone hiking requires route finding and Canyon experience because you'll see only the occasional sign. The long distances between water make this zone best in autumn through spring. Trails and routes receive no maintenance—you could encounter difficult or hazardous conditions. Some trailheads require a 4WD vehicle.

Wild Zone routes should be tackled only by highly experienced Canyon hikers who can find their way on indistinct or non-existent routes. Water may be unavailable or scarce, so this zone is best suited for the cooler months.

Information and Permits

Rangers are the best source of up-to-the-minute information for trails and permit procedures. On the South Rim, the **Backcountry Information Center** at Maswik Transportation Center is open daily 8 A.M.–noon and 1–5 P.M. all year. Staff answer the **Backcountry Information Line,** 928/638-7875, Mon.–Fri. 1–5 P.M. The Backcountry Information Center at the North Rim Ranger Station is open daily 8 A.M.–noon and 1–5 P.M. May 15–Oct. 15, weather permitting. Bookstores in the park sell hiking guides and topo maps. Also see Suggested Reading at the back of this book for additional titles.

You'll need a permit for all overnight camping trips in the backcountry, but not for day hikes or stays at Phantom Ranch. Permits can be requested in person or by mail through the Backcountry Information Center, Grand Canyon National Park, P.O. Box 129, Grand Canyon, AZ 86023 or by fax at 928/638-2125. Ask for the *Backcountry Trip Planner,* which includes regulations, a map, and a permit request form, or obtain the information over the Internet at www.nps.gov/grca. Permits will be sent through the mail.

Each permit costs a nonrefundable $10 plus $5 per person per night. If you plan on doing a lot of trips, the 12-month Frequent Hiker membership of $25 will let you purchase permits for just the $5 per person per night fee. The Park Service limits the number of campers in each section of the Canyon to provide visitors with a quality wilderness experience and to protect the land from overuse. Try to submit your choices early, especially for holidays and the popular months of March to May. Requests are not accepted more than four months in advance, starting with the first day of the month of that four-month period. Small groups (fewer than six people) have a greater chance of getting a permit, because the backcountry has only a few spots for larger ones; 11 is the maximum group size.

Permits can sometimes be obtained from rangers on duty at Tuweep, Meadview, and Lees Ferry Ranger Stations. However, these rangers are often hard to find because patrol duties have priority. Two other options in the Arizona Strip area are Pipe Spring National Monument and Kaibab Plateau Visitor Center, which can issue last-minute permits for some areas if space is available. Do not depend on obtaining a permit on a walk-in basis.

If you arrive without a permit, show up at the Backcountry Information Center by 8 A.M. to find out what's available or to get on a waiting list. If you're flexible and have extra days, there's a good chance of getting into the Canyon.

Other Areas

Not all of the Grand Canyon lies within the park. The Havasupai Indian Reservation contains Havasu Canyon, famous for its waterfalls, travertine pools, and blue-green waters. The Hualapai have the only road access to the bottom of the Grand Canyon via Diamond Creek and some spectacular rim viewpoints. The Arizona Strip has trailheads and amazing views from the North Rim; these places—some very remote—lie on lands of the Kaibab National Forest, Bureau of Land Management, and Lake Mead National Recreation Area.

CORRIDOR TRAILS OF THE INNER CANYON

Park Service rangers usually recommend that first-time visitors try one of the trails in the Corridor Zone to get the feel of Canyon hiking. These trails are wide and well signed. Rangers and other hikers will be close by in case of problems.

Camping along Corridor trails is restricted to established sites at Indian Garden, Bright Angel, and Cottonwood. Mice and other small varmints at these campgrounds have voracious appetites for campers' food—keep yours in the steel boxes provided or risk losing it.

Bright Angel Trail

Havasupai used this route from the South Rim to reach their fields and the spring at Indian Garden. Prospectors widened the trail in 1890, later extending it to the Colorado River. Now it's the best-graded and most popular trail into the Canyon.

The trailhead lies just west of Bright Angel Lodge in Grand Canyon Village. Resthouses one and a half miles and three miles below the rim contain emergency telephones and usually offer water from May 1 to September 30. Pipeline breaks commonly occur, so it's best to check that water is available by asking at the Visitor Center or Backcountry Information Center. One-way distances from the top are 4.6 miles to Indian Garden (campground, water, and ranger station), 7.7 miles to the Colorado River, and 9.3 miles to Bright Angel Creek (campground, water, ranger station, and Phantom Ranch). Allow 4–5 hours for the descent to the river and 8–10 hours coming out (elevation change 4,500 feet).

Plateau Point makes a good all-day hike. Perched 1,300 feet directly above the swirling

ARIZONA TRAIL: THE GRAND CANYON SECTION

This part of the Arizona Trail presents one of the biggest challenges for trail users. Besides the deep descent into the chasm and long climb out the other side, hikers must plan ahead to obtain the required backcountry permit or to make a reservation at Phantom Ranch. The rim-to-rim distance is just too great to hike and enjoy in one day. If you don't get a permit or reservation ahead of time, you can show up at the Backcountry Office for a camping permit or at the Bright Angel Lodge Transportation Desk for a Phantom Ranch bed and hope that space is available. Obtaining a last-minute permit or reservation may delay transcanyon hikers for several days.

Bicyclists face a long detour. Not even the most experienced mountain biker will be permitted to ride down any of the trails into the Canyon because of dangers to the cyclist and other trail users.

Also, the Park Service won't allow cyclists to carry their bikes across the Canyon on pack frames, because a wide load could knock hikers off the trail. So cyclists will have to follow the same route as cars—adding more than 200 miles to the route. Cyclists planning to camp on the Navajo Nation should obtain permission from the local landowner first.

The Arizona Trail reaches Grandview Lookout Tower from the south. (This area has some good day hiking, too; see "Grandview Lookout and Vicinity".) The Arizona Trail will eventually follow the multi-use Greenway Trail along the rim west to Tusayan, then north to Grand Canyon Village to join the 9.3-mile Bright Angel Trail. You could also hike the short distance from Grandview Lookout to Grandview Trailhead, then take the Grandview, Tonto, and either South Kaibab or Bright Angel Trails

© BILL WEIR

Hikers Yvonne Arntzen and Greg Jones, two of the first people to hike all of the Arizona Trail from Mexico to Utah, Grandview Lookout

Colorado River, you'll enjoy a 360-degree panorama of the Canyon. To reach Plateau Point, take the Bright Angel Trail to Indian Garden, then follow the signs. This strenuous day hike is 12.2 miles round-trip from the rim with elevation change of 3,080 feet.

River Trail

This short, 1.7-mile trail parallels the river in the twisted rocks of the Inner Gorge, connecting the bottoms of the Bright Angel and South Kaibab trails. There's little elevation change. Two suspension bridges cross the river to Bright Angel Creek.

South Kaibab Trail

Hikers enjoy sweeping views up and down the Canyon on this trail. From the trailhead near Yaki Point, 4.5 miles east of Grand Canyon Village,

the South Kaibab drops steeply, following Cedar Ridge toward the river and Bright Angel Creek (6.4 miles one way). There's an emergency telephone at the Tipoff, 4.4 miles below the rim, where the trail begins to descend into the Inner Gorge.

Lack of shade and water and the steep grade make this trail especially difficult in summer. Allow 3–5 hours for the descent and 6–8 hours coming out (elev. change 4,800 feet). Cedar Ridge, partway down, is a good day hike destination—three miles round-trip and an elevation change of 1,160 feet. Strong hikers enjoy continuing down to the nearly level Tonto Trail (4.4 miles from the rim), turning left 4.1 miles on the Tonto to Indian Garden, then heading 4.6 miles up the Bright Angel Trail. The park's shuttles connect the trailheads for this 13.1-mile hike. Only very strong hikers can make it all the way from rim to down to the Colorado River. From the Colorado, North Kaibab Trail climbs 14 miles to the top of the North Rim. The next part of the route—approximately 13 miles one way and still under construction at press time—follows AZ 67 north for about 0.75 mile, turns west for about 1.5 miles on the road past the Widforss Trailhead, follows a utility corridor northeast and crosses AZ 67 again to pick up the utility corridor east of the highway, turns north to the park's North Entrance station, then heads to the northeast and meets with the trailhead on Forest Road 610.

An alternative route, not officially the Arizona Trail, begins at the North Kaibab Trailhead and goes north 9.9 miles on the Ken Patrick Trail to Point Imperial, then continues north four miles on a former road to the Saddle Mountain Trailhead near the end of FR 610 in the Kaibab National Forest. From the Saddle Mountain Trailhead, you can hike west 7.5 miles along the park boundary on FR 610 to the trailhead for Kaibab Plateau/Arizona Trail 101.

To drive to this trailhead, take the AZ 67 turnoff in De Motte Park, 0.8 mile south of the North Rim Country Store, and head east 1.3 miles on 611, then turn right 4.8 miles on 610 to the trailhead, marked by log fences and an outhouse. The Arizona Trail goes north seven miles from here to East Rim View and on to AZ 89A. Arizona Trail ends on the Utah border at Stateline Trailhead, which has a small campground; it's reached by turning 19 miles north on unpaved House Rock Valley Road from US 89A (between Mileposts 565 and 566) or south 11 miles on House Rock Valley Road from US 89 in Utah (between Mileposts 25 and 26). The North Kaibab Ranger District office, 928/643-7395, has handouts and advice for this part of the Arizona Trail at 430 S. Main St. in Fredonia, open Mon.–Fri. 8 A.M.–5 P.M., or write Box 248, Fredonia, AZ 86022; www.fs.fed.us/r3/kai. You can also stop by the Kaibab Plateau Visitor Center at Jacob Lake, 928/643-7298, open daily 8 A.M.–5 P.M. from about mid-May to mid-October and possibly later in the year with a shorter schedule.

GRAND CANYON

river and back in one day. During summer, however, this is grueling and dangerous for *anyone* and isn't recommended.

North Kaibab Trail

Few other Canyon trails compare in the number of interesting side trips and variety of scenery. Hikers on this trail start in the cool forests of the North Rim, descend through the woods into Roaring Springs Canyon, then follow rushing Bright Angel Creek all the way to the Colorado River. Look for the trailhead at the lower end of the parking lot, two miles north of Grand Canyon Lodge. Snows close the road from some time in October or November until mid-May, but you can reach the lower end of the North Kaibab at Bright Angel Campground year-round on trails from the South Rim. A long section of trail between the rim and Roaring Springs has been cut into sheer cliffs; waterfalls cascade over the rock face in spring and after rains. A picnic area near Roaring Springs makes a good destination for day hikers; it's 9.4 miles

round-trip from the North Rim and has an elevation change of 3,160 feet. Water is available May–September.

Cottonwood Campground, 6.8 miles below the rim, is a good stopping point for the night or a base for day trips—it has a ranger station and, from May to September, water; winter campers must obtain and purify water from the creek. **Ribbon Falls** pours into a miniature paradise of travertine and lush greenery, nestled in a side canyon 1.5 miles from Cottonwood Campground. **The Transept,** a canyon just upstream and across the creek, offers good exploring too.

From Cottonwood Campground, the North Kaibab Trail continues downstream along Bright Angel Creek, entering the dark contorted schists and other rocks of the ancient Vishnu Group. Near the bottom you'll walk through Phantom Ranch, then Bright Angel Campground. Most people can descend the 14.2-mile North Kaibab in 8–9 hours of steady hiking (elev. change 5,700 feet). Climbing out requires 10–12 hours and is best attempted over two days. Anglers are often successful in pulling rainbow trout from Bright Angel Creek, especially in winter.

Phantom Ranch

Rustic buildings along Bright Angel Creek at the bottom of the Canyon offer dormitory beds ($23), cabins ($65 d, $12 each extra person), meals (breakfast $13, box lunch $8, stew dinner $18, steak dinner $29), drinks, snacks, and souvenirs. You must make reservations for meals and accommodations with transportation desks in the lodges or contact Grand Canyon National Park Lodges, 14001 E. Iliff Ave., Suite 600, Aurora, CO 80014, 303/297-2757 in advance or 928/638-3283 if four days or less in advance, www.grandcanyonlodges.com. Reservations can be difficult to get; make them up to 23 months in advance. If you'd rather have your gear carried by someone else, mules are available for $53 in or out with a weight limit of 30 pounds. Mules will carry you, too (see **Mule Rides** in "South Rim Tours").

THRESHOLD, PRIMITIVE, AND WILD ZONES OF THE INNER CANYON (SOUTH RIM)

Trails and routes in these zones lead to some beautiful corners of the park, offering solitude and new Canyon perspectives. Hikers here must be self-reliant—know where water sources are, how to use map and compass, and how to handle emergencies. Most trails follow prehistoric Indian routes or game trails that miners improved in the late 1800s. Conditions vary widely; some trails are in excellent condition, while others are dangerous or require careful map reading. Hermit and Grandview get some maintenance, and other trails may receive attention if they become impassable. Hermit Trail, Hermit and Granite Rapids, Horseshoe Mesa, and parts of the Tonto Trail have designated camping areas, which you're required to use.

The Canyon offers thousands of possible routes for the experienced hiker. Harvey Butchart, master of Canyon off-trail hiking, describes many routes in his books (see Suggested Reading in the Resources section of this book). Staff at the Backcountry Information Center will suggest interesting routes as well, and they'll give you an idea of current conditions. You'll no doubt come up with route ideas of your own while hiking through the Canyon and studying maps.

Just keep in mind that much of the Canyon's exposed rock is soft or fractured—a handhold or foothold can easily break off. The Colorado River presents a major barrier, as the water is too cold, wide, and full of treacherous currents to swim.

The following trails and routes are listed from west to east.

Tonto Trail

Canyon views change continually along this 92-mile trail as it contours along the Tonto Platform, winding in and out of countless canyons and sometimes revealing spectacular panoramas from the edge of the Inner Gorge. The Tonto connects most of the trails below the South Rim between the mouth of Red Canyon at Hance Rapids and Garnet Canyon far downstream. Average elevation on the gently rolling trail is 3,000 feet. You might lose the trail occasionally, but with attention to rock cairns and the map, you'll soon find it again. The sun bears down relentlessly in summer, when it's best to hike elsewhere.

South Bass Trail

William Bass learned about this route from the Havasupai in the 1880s, then used it to start a small tourist operation. Bass also built a trail up to the North Rim, crossing the river by boat and later by a cage suspended from a cable. No crossing exists today.

The South Bass Trail is generally in good condition and easy to follow. It drops to the Esplanade, a broad terrace, then down to the river. You'll need a high-clearance vehicle to reach the trailhead, four miles north of Pasture Wash Ranger Station; ask at the Backcountry Information Center for directions. Hiking the nine-mile trail to the river takes about five hours down and nine hours up, with an elevation change of 4,400 feet. No reliable water is available before the river.

prospector and tourist guide William Bass, with dog Shep, circa 1899

GRAND CANYON

Boucher Trail

Louis Boucher, the Hermit, came to the Canyon in 1891 and mined copper along the creek that bears his name until 1912. Steep terrain and rockslides can make the trail difficult—it's best for experienced hikers with light packs.

Take Hermit and Dripping Springs trails to Boucher Trail, which contours along the base of the Hermit Shale, high above the west side of Hermit Canyon with excellent views. You'll reach Tonto Trail just before Boucher Creek. The route down the creek to Boucher Rapids on the Colorado River is an easy 1.5 miles. From the Hermit trailhead at the end of Hermit Road, it's 11 miles to Boucher Creek; allow 7–8 hours down and 9–10 hours coming up, with an elevation change of 3,800 feet. The Boucher, Tonto, and Hermit Trails make a fine three- or four-day loop hike. Boucher and Hermit Creeks have water year-round.

Hermit Trail

Although named for Boucher, the trail was actually built for tourists by the Santa Fe Railroad in 1912. Visitors took this route to Hermit Camp, which operated until 1930. Most of Hermit Trail is in good condition; the few places covered by rockslides can be easily crossed. The trail begins just beyond Hermit's Rest, at the end of Hermit Road. Water is available at Santa Maria Spring (two miles one way) and Hermit Creek (seven miles one way). Hermit Rapids on the Colorado River is an easy 1.5-mile walk down the bed of Hermit Creek; a sign on the Tonto Trail points the way down to Hermit Creek. The elevation change from rim to river is 4,300 feet, so allow 5–6 hours going down and 8–10 hours climbing out.

Hermit Trail also connects with Waldron, Dripping Springs, and Tonto Trails. Day-hikers can head to Dripping Springs, a six-mile round-trip hike requiring 4–6 hours with an elevation change of 800 feet. Descend the Hermit Trail 1.5 miles, then turn left 1.5 miles on Dripping Springs Trail. Carry water for the entire trip, as the springs offer only a tiny flow. The 22.5-mile Hermit Loop hike, which follows the Hermit, Tonto, and Bright Angel Trails, is quite popular. You can find water on this loop year-round at Monument Creek and Indian Garden. Hikers can easily walk down the bed of Monument Creek to Granite Rapids, 1.5 miles one way.

Grandview Trail

Day-hikers frequently use this steep but scenic trail to Horseshoe Mesa. The trailhead lies at Grandview Point on Desert View Drive. Miners improved an old Indian route in 1892 so they could bring out high-grade copper ore from Horseshoe Mesa. Mining ceased in 1907, but mine shafts, machinery, and ruins of buildings remain. Three trails descend Horseshoe Mesa to the Tonto Trail. Bring water, as the springs are either unreliable or difficult to reach. Allow two hours down and three up for the six-mile round-trip hike to Horseshoe Mesa, with an elevation change of 2,600 feet.

New Hance Trail

John Hance, one of the first prospectors to take up the tourist business, built this trail down Red Canyon in 1895. The unsigned trailhead lies about one mile southwest of the Moran Point turnoff on Desert View Drive; obtain directions from a ranger. Suited for more experienced hikers, the trail—with poor footing in places—descends steeply to the river at Hance Rapids. Most of the trail is easy to follow, especially when you're descending. No reliable water is available before the river. The eight-mile trail takes about six hours to descend and eight to 10 hours to ascend, with an elevation change of 4,400 feet.

Escalante Route

The Tonto Trail's upper end gives out at Hance Rapids, but you can continue upstream to Tanner Rapids and the Tanner Trail. Cairns mark the 15-mile Escalante Route. Expect rough terrain and a difficult time finding the route in some sections. The Colorado River, easily accessible only at the ends of the route, provides the only reliable source of water. The route is somewhat easier to hike in the downstream direction, Tanner to Hance.

Tanner Trail

Seth Tanner improved this Indian trail in the 1880s to reach his copper and silver mines along the Colorado River. Although in good condition and easy to follow, the Tanner Trail is long—10 miles one way—and dry, and best attempted in the cooler months. Hikers often cache water partway down for the return trip.

The trailhead lies about 100 yards back down the road from Lipan Point, off Desert View Drive. Allow 6–8 hours for the descent and 8–10 hours for the return, with an elevation change of 4,700 feet.

Beamer Trail

This slim path begins at Tanner Canyon Rapids (lower end of Tanner Trail) and follows the river four miles upstream to Palisades Creek, then climbs to a high terrace for the remaining five miles to the Little Colorado River confluence. No camping is allowed within a half mile of the confluence.

THRESHOLD, PRIMITIVE, AND WILD ZONES OF THE INNER CANYON (NORTH RIM)

Whitmore Wash Trail

Although little known or used, this three-quarter-mile-long trail offers the park's easiest hike from trailhead to river. The trick is in reaching the trailhead! You'll need a high-clearance 4WD vehicle and lots of time. Follow County 5 and other dirt roads on the Arizona Strip from Toroweap, Fredonia, Colorado City, or St. George to the four-way intersection at Mt.

Trumbull Schoolhouse, turn south 1.8 miles on BLM Road 257, then bear left 21.7 miles on BLM Road 1045 its end. The last 7.5 miles are rough, as the road crosses lava flows from Mt. Emma. This lava acts as a ramp for the road to descend deep into the Grand Canyon. The trail appears to drop off the rim where the road ends, but that's not the real trailhead. Instead, climb up above the barbed-wire fence to the trail.

You'll drop about 850 feet as the trail switchbacks, then skirts the base of a massive cliff of columnar basalt before ending on a sandy beach. Remnants of ancient lava dams can be seen on both sides of the river. A small trail near the bottom leads a half mile downstream to Whitmore Rapids and lower Whitmore Canyon, which you can explore for about a half mile upstream.

Lava Falls Route

The Colorado River explodes in a fury of foam and waves at Lava Falls, reached by this short but steep route from the Toroweap area. Cairns mark the way down a lunarlike landscape of volcanic lava. Barrel cacti thrive on the dark, twisted rock. Although the route is only 1.5 miles one way, it's considered difficult because of steep grades and poor footing. It is not a developed or maintained trail. Summer temperatures get *extremely* hot; elevation at the river is only 1,700 feet. Summer hikers should start at dawn and carry plenty of water.

From Toroweap Overlook, backtrack on the road 2.8 miles and look for a dirt track on the left (3.5 miles south of Tuweep Ranger Station); follow it 2.5 miles across normally dry Toroweap Lake and around the west side of Vulcan's Throne. The route is too rough for cars and impassable for any vehicle when the lake contains water. At road's end, the route descends to a hill of red cinders about two-thirds of the way down; the last part of the descent follows a steep gully. Lava Falls lies 0.3 mile downstream. Camping is allowed along the river with a permit. Allow two hours going down and 3–6 hours coming out, with an elevation change of 2,500 feet.

Tuckup Trail

Experienced Canyon hikers looking for solitude and expansive vistas can try this faint trail. It follows the Esplanade of the North Rim for more than 70 miles between the Toroweap Point area and Hundred and Fifty Mile Canyon. Back roads lead to trailheads near these two areas and to upper Tuckup Canyon, about the halfway point on the trail.

The trailhead lies just east of the Toroweap Overlook road, 4.7 miles south of the ranger station and 1.6 miles north of the overlook. You can wander off on a variety of jaunts in this remote area. Hikers have followed the Tuckup Trail from Toroweap Point to Cottonwood Canyon, descended Cottonwood and Tuckup canyons to the Colorado River (rope needed), hiked the shore downstream to Lava Falls Route, and climbed back up to Toroweap in a week or so of travel. Springs of varying reliability may provide water along the Tuckup Trail. Talk with rangers knowledgeable about the area for trailhead, spring, and hiking conditions.

Thunder River and Bill Hall Trails

Thunder River blasts out of a cave in the Muav Limestone, cascades a half mile, then enters Tapeats Creek. It's not only the world's shortest river but suffers the humiliation of being a tributary to a creek!

Deer Creek Falls, another area attraction, plummets more than 100 feet onto the banks of the Colorado River. Cottonwood trees, willows, and other cool greenery grace the banks of Thunder River and both creeks. Trails are generally good and easy to follow, though spring runoff and rains can make Tapeats Creek too high to cross safely.

Two trails descend from the North Rim: the **Thunder River Trail** from the end of Forest Road 232 (just past Indian Hollow Campground) and the **Bill Hall Trail** from the east side of Monument Point at the end of Forest Road 292A. The Bill Hall Trail saves five miles of walking but the steep grade can be slippery and hard on the knees.

Reach the trailheads by turning west on Forest Road 22 from AZ 67 in De Motte Park, 0.8 mile south of the North Rim Store and 17.5 miles north of Bright Angel Point; consult a Kaibab National Forest map (North Kaibab Ranger District). It's about 35 miles of dirt road and an hour and a half from AZ 67 to either trailhead. Cars can negotiate the roads in good weather, but winter snows bury this high country from about mid-November to mid-May. Thunder River and Bill Hall Trails both drop to the Esplanade, where they meet. The Esplanade could be used for dry camping, and you may wish to cache some water here for the climb back out. Thunder River Trail then switchbacks down to Surprise Valley, a giant piece of the rim that long ago slumped thousands of feet to its present position. The valley turns into an oven in summer and lacks water; it's about eight miles from the Bill Hall Trailhead.

In another two miles, **Thunder River Trail** goes east across Surprise Valley, drops to Thunder River, and follows it to Tapeats Creek. Except at high water, Tapeats Creek can be followed 2.5 miles upstream to its source in a cave. The Colorado River is a 2.5-mile hike downstream from the junction of Thunder River and Tapeats Creek. If the creek runs too deep to cross, you can stay on a west-side trail all the way to the Colorado. Upper Tapeats Campsite is just below the Thunder River–Tapeats Creek confluence; Lower Tapeats Campsite lies downstream on the Colorado River. Good fishing attracts anglers to Tapeats Creek and perhaps has for a long time—prehistoric Cohonina left ruins here. The trek from Bill Hall trailhead at Monument Point to Tapeats Rapids is about 12.5 miles one way, with an elevation change of 5,250 feet. Figure seven hours to reach the upper campsite on Tapeats Creek and nine hours to hike all the way to Tapeats Rapids; return times are nearly double. Thunder River, 9.5 miles from the Bill Hall trailhead, is the first source of water.

The wonders of the Canyon reveal themselves best to those who enter its depths. Just remember that the Inner Canyon is a wilderness area, subject to temperature extremes, flash floods, rockslides, and other natural hazards. Come prepared with ample food, water, and supplies.

Deer Creek Trail, marked by a large cairn in Surprise Valley, splits off to the west and drops about 1.5 miles to Deer Creek (Dutton) Spring, another cave system from which a waterfall gushes. You can hike up to the falls for a closer look or take the path that goes higher and behind the falls. The creekside trail winds down one mile past some remarkable Tapeats narrows, then drops to the base of Deer Creek Falls at the river. Watch out for poison ivy here. Campsites lie along Deer Creek between Deer Creek Springs and the head of the narrows. Distance from the Bill Hall Trailhead to the Colorado River is about 11 miles one way with a descent of 5,400 feet; Deer Creek Springs, 9.5 miles in, is the first water source. Allow about seven hours to reach Deer Creek and 45 minutes more to descend to the Colorado River, then almost double that to return.

North Bass Trail

This long and faint trail drops from Swamp Point on the North Rim to Muav Saddle, where there's a 1925 Park Service cabin. The trail makes a sharp left toward Muav Springs, drops steeply to White Creek in Muav Canyon, follows a long bypass to a safe descent through the Redwall Limestone, winds down White Creek to Shinumo Creek, continues to Bass Camp, then cuts over a ridge to the left and drops down to a fine beach on the Colorado River. The trail reaches the Colorado about 0.3 mile below where the South Bass Trail comes down on the other side. No crossing exists today, though people occasionally hitch rides to the far shore with river-rafters. A waterfall blocks travel down Shinumo Creek just before the river, which is why the trail climbs over the ridge. The Muav and Shinumo drainages create their own canyon worlds—you're not really exposed to the Grand Canyon until you reach the ridge above the Colorado River near trail's end.

Once at the Colorado River via the main trail, you can loop back to Bass Camp on another trail; it begins at the downstream end of the beach and crosses over to lower Shinumo Creek, which you can then follow upstream back to Bass Camp and the North Bass Trail. Many routes off the North Bass Trail invite exploration, such as the Redwall Narrows of White Creek above the trail junction, Shinumo Creek drainage above White Creek, and Burro Canyon.

Muav Saddle Springs offers water just off the trail. White Creek has intermittent water above and below the Redwall. Shinumo Creek's abundant flow supports some small trout. Shinumo can be difficult to cross in spring and after summer storms; at other times you can hop across on rocks. Allow 3–4 days for the 28-mile round-trip to the river, with an elevation change of 5,300 feet; the trail is best suited for experienced hikers.

With a high-clearance vehicle you can reach the trailhead at Swamp Point from AZ 67 in De-Motte Park via Forest Roads 22, 270, 223, 268, 268B, and Swamp Point Road. You'll need the current Kaibab Forest map, as old ones may not show these roads correctly. The drive from De-Motte Park to Swamp Point takes nearly two hours due to the roughness of Swamp Point Road.

Powell Plateau Trail

A good trail from Swamp Point connects this isolated "island" that lies within the vast reaches of the Grand Canyon. Once part of the North Rim, the plateau has been completely severed from the rim by erosion, except for the Muav Saddle connection. The trail is about 1.5 miles one way; you drop 800 feet to Muav Saddle on the North Bass Trail, then continue straight across the saddle and up another set of switchbacks to a ponderosa pine forest on the Powell Plateau. Here the trail fades out. Many places on the seven-mile-long plateau offer outstanding views. Travel is cross-country, so you'll need a map and compass; expect to do some bushwhacking.

The easiest viewpoint to reach lies to the northwest; just follow the north edge of the plateau (no trail) to a large rock cairn about one mile from

where the trail from Swamp Point tops out on the plateau. You can camp on the Powell Plateau with a backcountry permit; all water must be carried in from the trailhead or Muav Saddle Springs. See **North Bass Trail** for directions to Swamp Point.

Clear Creek Trail

This trail, in very good condition and easy to follow, is the North Rim's version of the Tonto Trail. It begins 0.3 mile north of Phantom Ranch and climbs 1,500 feet to the Tonto Platform, which it follows—winding in and out of canyons—until dropping at the last possible place into Clear Creek, nine miles from Phantom Ranch. Carry water—there's no source before Clear Creek—and be prepared for very hot weather in summer. The best camping sites lie scattered among the cottonwood trees where the trail meets the creek.

Day-hikers enjoy the first mile or so of Clear Creek Trail for its scenic views of the river and Inner Gorge. Strong hikers can walk all the way to Clear Creek and back in a long day. Better still is a trip of several days.

The route to **Cheyava Falls,** the highest waterfall in the Canyon, takes 6–8 hours round-trip up the long northeast fork of Clear Creek. Cheyava Falls puts on an impressive show only in spring and after heavy rains. Other arms of the creek offer good hiking as well. The canyon that branches east about a half mile downstream from the end of Clear Creek Trail cuts through a narrow canyon of quartzite. You can also walk along Clear Creek to the Colorado River, a 5–7 hour round-trip hike through contorted granite and schist, a dark, easily split metamorphic rock with closely spaced bands of mica. The 10-foot-high waterfall a half mile from the river is bypassed by clambering around to the right.

Nankoweap Trail

Thrilling ledges on the Nankoweap Trail discourage hikers afraid of heights. But if you don't mind tiptoeing on the brink of sheer cliffs, this trail will open up a large section of the park for your exploration. The trailhead lies at Saddle Mountain Saddle, 2.4 crow-flying miles northeast of Point Imperial. You can't drive to the trail-head, however; it must be approached on foot, either three miles one way from House Rock Buffalo Ranch Road (south from US 89A), or three miles one way from near the end of Forest Road 610 (east off AZ 67). Both access roads are dirt, passable by cars, but House Rock Buffalo Ranch Road lies at a lower elevation and is less likely to be snowed in.

The Nankoweap Trail drops several hundred feet, then contours along a ledge all the way to Tilted Mesa before descending to Nankoweap Creek. Some care in route finding is needed between Tilted Mesa and the creek. Nankoweap Creek, 10 miles from the trailhead, is the first source of water; you may want to cache water partway down to drink on your return. The remaining four miles to the river is easy. Allow 3–4 days for a round-trip journey, with an elevation change of 4,800 feet.

Running the Colorado River

Running the Colorado River through the Grand Canyon provides the excitement of roaring rapids and the tranquility of gliding in silent passages. It rates as one of the world's greatest adventures! A journey through the Canyon by river with some side hikes might be the single best way to see and appreciate the grandeur and beauty here. Many beautifully sculptured side canyons, some with lush vegetation, can be easily reached only from the river. Just being at the bottom of the Canyon is a delight, whether you're riding atop the waves, strolling between the convoluted walls of an unnamed side canyon, or enjoying life at camp.

Within the Grand Canyon, the Colorado River flows 277 miles, drops 2,200 feet, and thunders through 70 major rapids. Although explorers of the 19th century feared this section of the river, rendering it in dark and gloomy drawings, boating the Canyon has become a safe and enjoyable experience. It opens some of the grandest and most remote corners of the Canyon. River parties stop frequently to explore the twisting side canyons, old mining camps, and prehistoric ruins along the way.

A river trip through the Grand Canyon requires a large commitment in time, whitewater experience, equipment, expense, and permit procedures. About one-third of river-runners do it themselves with a noncommercial river trip permit from the park. The easier option, taken by most people, simply involves setting aside the time for the trip and paying a river company to handle the many details.

YOUR OPTIONS

Boats

Both oar-powered and motor-powered craft run the river. Motor-powered rafts can zip through the entire Canyon in six days, or zoom from Lees Ferry to Phantom Ranch in two days. The oar-powered boat trips take half again as much time but provide a quieter and more natural experience. On these smaller boats, passengers have the advantage of being able to talk easily with the crew and one another. Whether in a little or a big rig, you can be assured that the crew will work hard to provide a safe and enjoyable trip.

All but two of the tour companies use rafts of various sizes; the exceptions are Grand Canyon Dories and Grand Canyon Expeditions, which employ sturdy, hard-shelled dories with upturned ends. The dories ride high in the water as they dance through the waves. They're small—16–18 feet long—with one person at the oars and just four passengers. Only the most skilled boaters can handle dories because, unlike rafts, they can't bounce off rocks without damage.

Small rafts typically measure 18 feet and carry four or five passengers plus one crew member to do the rowing. Some companies provide a paddleboat option—not a Mississippi-type paddle wheeler, but a small raft in which everyone has a paddle! The guide sits at the stern to steer and give instructions, but it's up to the passengers to succeed in running each rapid.

The motor-powered rigs can be 30 feet long or more and have pontoon outriggers for extra stability. A small outboard motor near the stern provides steering and speed. Some people dislike the use of motors in a wilderness, but these boats do allow more people to run the Colorado than would be possible if everyone went in non-motorized rigs.

Routes

Most tours put in at Lees Ferry, just upstream from the park, and end downstream at Diamond Creek or Pearce (also spelled Pierce) Ferry on Lake Mead. You can also travel just half the distance by joining or leaving the rafts at Phantom Ranch, which requires a hike or mule trip to get in or out. You can leave or join a tour in the lower section of river via a helicopter ride from or to Hualapai land near Whitmore Wash, at Mile 187 below Lava Falls. If you'd like just a taste of river-running, try a one-day smooth-water trip from Glen Canyon Dam to Lees Ferry, just above Grand Canyon National Park, with **Wilderness River Adventures,** based in Page. Or you can visit the lowermost part of the Grand Canyon and run a few rapids on a one-day trip with **Hualapai River Runners,** based in Peach Springs.

A typical commercial oar trip takes 12–16 days from Lees Ferry to Diamond Creek, covering 226 miles. The upper half takes 5–6 days from Lees Ferry to Phantom Ranch, 87.5 miles; the lower half requires eight or nine days from Phantom Ranch to Diamond Creek, 138.5 miles. Continuing to Pearce Ferry on Lake Mead adds just a day or two. Equivalent motorized trips typically run eight days from Lees Ferry to Diamond Creek or Pearce Ferry with 3–4 days from Lees Ferry to Phantom Ranch and 4–5 days from Phantom Ranch to Diamond Creek or Pearce Ferry.

Those preferring shorter trips can end a trip or begin a two- or three-day run in the lowermost Grand Canyon at Whitmore Wash. Although a trail from the North Rim ends here, river parties use helicopters between the river (on Hualapai land) and the Bar 10 guest ranch, where small planes shuttle people to Las Vegas or other destinations.

Other combinations are available too. Extra days may be added to some trips for hiking or layovers, especially early or late in the season. Expect to pay about $250 per day; discounts may be available for groups, children under 14, early booking, and off-season journeys.

If you have children in tow, check for minimum age requirements. Sometimes these are left up to the passenger; at other times operators require minimum ages of 8 to 16 years. Most trips depart from Flagstaff, Page, St. George, or Las Vegas. Meals, camping gear, waterproof bags, and land transportation are usually included in the price. Experienced kayakers can tag along with many tours, paying a lower rate.

Seasons

The river-running season normally lasts April–October, with only nonmotorized craft departing mid-September to mid-December. When you choose to go makes a big difference in the river experience. Most people go during summer because that's when they take their vacations. The Canyon gets very hot then, but a splash of river water will always be cooling. Hiking at this time is limited to shady side canyons with water. Spring—April to early June—offers many advantages. The redbud trees and many plants bloom in beautiful colors, hiking weather will be near perfect, days get long, trip operators often add a couple of extra days for long hikes or layovers, and it's much easier to get a reservation for a trip. The downside is the possibility of cold weather, even sleet, which the author woke up to on one April morning in the upper Canyon! Some boaters think that early June offers the best weather for a boat trip, though hiking can get hot then. Autumn brings shorter days, along with cooler temperatures. The Canyon quiets after mid-September, when all the motorized rigs have left the river. Heavy-duty rain gear with sweaters underneath can keep spring and autumn boaters warm during cool spells.

Rafting the Lower Grand Canyon

This last section, beginning at Diamond Creek, offers beautiful Canyon scenery and some rapids. You can get on a trip here much more easily than in the upper Canyon, either with Hualapai River Runners or on your own. The Park Service gives free permits for up to two private parties (16 people maximum in each) per day. River-runners will need to pay for a Hualapai permit to use the Diamond Creek Road access or to camp on the south shore. The lower canyon bakes in summer, so spring, autumn, or even winter offer better weather for exploring side canyons.

Boating into the Lower Grand Canyon from Lake Mead

Boats—but not personal watercraft—may go up as far as Separation Canyon (Mile 240 on the river) from Lake Mead National Recreation Area without a permit. Primitive camping is allowed on the Park's shore in this section without permits, though high lake levels can flood all the spots; you'll need a backcountry permit from the Park Service to camp inland. A permit for the Hualapai is required to camp on their lands (the south shore). Boats must have a toilet. South Cove offers the closest paved boat ramp, reached by the paved road via Dolan Springs from US 93. Pearce Ferry nearby is closer with a primitive boat ramp and camping, but the last four miles in are unpaved.

Canoeing the Lower Grand Canyon

Canoes in the Grand Canyon? Yes, indeed, in the last 40 miles within the park. You'll need a powerboat to carry the canoes from Lake Mead to Separation Canyon. Most of the south shore on this trip belongs to the Hualapai, so obtain tribal permits if you plan to camp or hike on their land.

Private River Trips

Step One is to read Grand Canyon National Park's regulations and procedures! Obtain them from the River Trips Office, Box 129, Grand Canyon, AZ 86023, 928/638-7884, 800/959-9164 (call Mon.–Fri. 8 A.M.–5 P.M. to reach someone in person), or online at www.nps.gov/grca. Step Two—getting the permit—will be the hard part. Unfortunately, you'll be at the end of a very long line. So many groups have applied that the waiting list extends for more than 12 years! Cancellations do occur during this lengthy wait, so flexible and lucky groups might get on sooner, even the same year. The River Permits Office has worked out a system for applications that's as fair as possible to everyone during this waiting period. To get on the waiting list, carefully follow the instructions for an initial application ($100 fee at press time) and annual renewals (no charge), all of which you must submit within specified date ranges.

RIVER COMPANIES

The following companies offer a wide variety of trips through the Canyon, ranging from one- or two-day introductions to adventurous 19-day expeditions. Write Grand Canyon National Park for the latest list of companies (Box 129, Grand Canyon, AZ 86023), ask at the visitor center, or check listings on the Internet at www.nps.gov/grca. The Internet works best because you get not only a list, but also links to the companies, which have colorful and informative sites. If possible, make reservations (with deposit) six months to a year in advance. It's possible to get on a trip with short notice, especially if there are just a few in your group and you're going early or late in the season. **Rivers and Oceans,** 928/526-4575, 800/473-4576, specializes in river trips and will supply information about companies, make reservations, and let you know about last-minute openings at 12620 N. Copeland Lane, Flagstaff, AZ 86004; www.rivers-oceans.com.

All of the companies put in at Lees Ferry except for Wilderness River Adventure's day trips, which start from Glen Canyon Dam, and Hualapai River Runners trips, which begin at Diamond Creek in the lower Grand Canyon. Prices will be lower if you start or leave from Phantom Ranch or Whitmore Wash.

Arizona Raft Adventures, 928/526-8200, 800/786-7238, goes to Diamond Creek on 12- to 15-day oar ($2,550–2,870) and eight- or 10-day motorized trips ($1,840–2,170), most with the option of ending or starting at Phantom Ranch. It offers paddle raft trips too, either in combination with oar-powered rafts or all by themselves. Contact 4050 E. Huntington Dr., Flagstaff, AZ 86004; www.azraft.com.

Arizona River Runners, 602/867-4866, 800/477-7238, offers a 13-day oar trip to Diamond Creek ($2,520) with an option to end or start at Phantom Ranch and an eight-day motorized run to Pearce Ferry ($1,745) which you can leave or join at Whitmore Wash. Contact Box 47788, Phoenix, AZ 85068; www.raftarizona.com.

Canyon Explorations/Expeditions, 928/774-4559, 800/654-0723, uses oar boats on runs to Diamond Creek of 13–16 days ($2,565–3,165); a paddle raft and inflatable kayaks come along on selected trips too. Some departures have a Phantom Ranch exit/entry option. Contact Box 310, Flagstaff, AZ 86002; www.canyonexplorations.com.

Canyoneers, 928/526-0924, 800/525-0924, runs motorized rafts to Pearce Ferry in seven days for $1,725 ($1,525 in April) with the option of ending/starting at Phantom Ranch. Contact Box 2997, Flagstaff, AZ 86003; www.canyoneers.com.

Colorado River & Trail Expeditions, 801/261-1789, 800/253-7328, goes to Pearce Ferry in 12 days by oar-powered raft ($2,550) and 8–9 days in motorized rafts ($1,850); a paddleboat goes along on the oar trips. You can leave or join at Phantom Ranch on both trips. Contact Box 57575, Salt Lake City, UT 84157; www.crateinc.com.

Diamond River Adventures, 928/645-8866, 800/343-3121, offers 12-day oar trips ($2,397) and eight-day motorized trips ($1,812) to Diamond Creek with options of leaving or joining at Phantom Ranch; an excursion just to Whitmore Wash from Lees Ferry takes 10 days by oar ($2,365) and seven days by motor ($1,725). Contact Box 1316, Page, AZ 86040; www.diamondriver.com.

Grand Canyon Dories, 209/736-0805, 800/877-3679, features dories on 16-day trips ($3,953) to Pearce Ferry; 19-day trips also run in spring and autumn ($4,026). You can join or leave the trip at Phantom Ranch or Whitmore Wash. Contact Box 216, Altaville, CA 95221; www.oars.com.

Grand Canyon Expeditions, 435/644-2691, 800/544-2691, runs dories on 14-day trips to Pearce Ferry ($2,705); motorized rafts do this run in eight days ($1,933). All trips go straight through without any passenger exchanges. Contact Box O, Kanab, UT 84741; www.gcex.com.

Hatch River Expeditions, 435/789-3813, 800/433-8966, runs motorized rafts to Whitmore Wash in six and a half days for $1,625 with the option to leave or join at Phantom Ranch. Contact Box 1200, Vernal, UT 84078.

High Desert Adventures, 435/673-1733, 800/673-1733, offers oar rafts to Pearce Ferry in 14 days ($3,115) with an exchange option at Phantom Ranch, and motorized rafts to Pearce Ferry ($2,135) in eight days without passenger exchanges. Contact Box 40, St. George, UT 84771; www.boathda.com.

Hualapai River Runners, 928/769-2219, 800/255-9550, travels just the lower Grand Canyon on motorized rafts, putting in at Diamond Creek and coming out by helicopter to Grand Canyon West on a one-day run for $250. Overnight trips to Lake Mead can be chartered. Contact Box 246, Peach Springs, AZ 86434; www.river-runners.com.

Moki Mac River Expeditions, 801/268-6667, 800/284-7280, heads down to Pearce Ferry in 14-day oar trips ($2,795), with an option to end or begin from Phantom Ranch, and eight-day motorized rafts ($1,855) without a passenger exchange. Contact Box 71242, Salt Lake City, UT 84171; www.mokimac.com.

O.A.R.S., 209/736-4677, 800/346-6277, offers oar rafts to Diamond Creek in 13 days for $3,368 and 14- to 17-day runs all the way to Pearce Ferry for $3,579–3956 with options to leave or join at Phantom Ranch (and Whitmore Wash, for the Pearce Ferry trips). Contact Box 67, Angels Camp, CA 95222; www.oars.com.

Outdoors Unlimited, 928/526-2852, 800/637-7238, goes to Pearce Ferry on oar rafts in 13 days ($2,690) with an option to leave or join at Phantom Ranch; a paddle raft comes along too, and some trips are all paddle rafts. Contact 6900 Townsend Winona Rd., Flagstaff, AZ 86004; www.outdoorsunlimited.com.

Tour West, 801/225-0755, 800/453-9107, runs oar rafts to Whitmore Wash in 12 days ($2,363) without any passenger exchanges; paddle rafts can be added on request. Motorized rafts go to Whitmore Wash in six days ($1,695), then another three days to Pearce Ferry ($2,095 from Lees Ferry or $830–885 from Whitmore Wash). Contact Box 333, Orem, UT 84059; www.twriver.com.

Western River Expeditions, 801/942-6669, 800/453-7450, motorized rafts go to Pearce Ferry in eight days ($1,740 April, $1,930 May–Sept.) with a passenger exchange at Whitmore Wash. Contact 7258 Racquet Club Dr., Salt Lake City, UT 84121; www.westernriver.com.

Wilderness River Adventures, 928/645-3296, 800/992-8022, heads for Whitmore Wash on 12-day oar trips at $2,655 with a Phantom Ranch end or start option. Motorized trips take eight days to Whitmore Wash for $2,094 and can be joined or left at Phantom Ranch. The company also offers a day trip from Glen Canyon Dam to Lees Ferry, a scenic ride on smooth water. Contact Box 717, Page, AZ 86040; www.river adventures.com.

DOWN THE COLORADO THROUGH THE GRAND CANYON

This miniguide of river-running highlights contains just a sampling of the sights along the river. Even so, it would be impossible to fit them all into a single trip. Experienced river guides know far more places, including some "secret" ones they may share with you. Weather, schedules, and where other river parties have will affect which places your group will decide to take in. Rapids with ratings of five stopped or more on the 1–10 scale are listed in parentheses. (The 1–10 scale is unique to the Colorado River; other rivers are rated on a 1–6 scale.)

The place descriptions come from the author's experience on two river trips and advice from river guides and National Park Service staff. Geologic information is mostly from the out-of-print book *River Runner's Guide to the Canyons of the Green and Colorado Rivers: With Emphasis on Geologic* *Features, Vol. III* by George C. Simmons and David L. Gaskill (Northland Publishing, 1969).

Mile 0: Lees Ferry
This historic site on the Colorado River, once the only easily accessible crossing for hundreds of miles upstream or down, now marks the beginning of river voyages into the Grand Canyon. Most boaters have only one thing on their minds here—getting on the river and embarking on their adventure. Yet it's worthwhile to come early or at another time to explore Lonely Dell Ranch, other historic buildings, and remnants of past mining attempts at Lees Ferry. Spencer Trail beckons hikers from the rim of the Canyon and the far more gentle Cathedral Wash route offers a walk to the river below. The Paria Canyon hike, one of the finest in the region, ends here after 4–6 days of twisting through its wonderful sandstone walls from a trailhead north across the Utah border. Some people come just to relax or fish by the cold, clear, trout-filled river. See the **Lees Ferry** section later in this book for details on the area, including lodging, camping, and restaurant information.

You're now at an elevation of 3,116 feet. A descent of 1,936 vertical feet lies ahead as you plummet deep within the Grand Canyon through more than a dozen geologic formations before meeting the Canyon's last riffles near Separation Canyon, where the Colorado River joins Lake Mead. Note how the types of rock affect the river and thus your ride—wide and smooth through the soft shales, then narrower and bumpier in the sandstone, limestone, granite, and schist—but be ready for surprises where tributaries have dumped huge piles of rocks into the river!

Rock layers visible near Lees Ferry formed during the Triassic and Jurassic Periods, roughly 240–140 million years ago, when the dinosaurs first appeared and walked this land. Rocks of this age actually once lay atop the older layers seen on the much higher rims of the Grand Canyon, but there they've been reduced by erosion to just a few remnants such as Cedar Mountain, visible from Desert View. Dramatic folding and faulting downstream have raised the Colorado Plateau

GRAND CANYON

thousands of feet, whose increasingly older rock layers you'll soon plunge into. The sights mentioned below follow the convention of "river right" and "river left" facing downstream.

Mile 0.8: Kaibab Formation
Look on the left for the emergence of the Kaibab Formation, the cream-colored, weather-resistant limestone that caps much of the Grand Canyon rims. Scientists have found fossils of marine invertebrates and some fish. You've now crossed a major geologic time boundary into the Permian Period (290–240 million years ago) of the Paleozoic era.

Mile 1: Paria Riffle
The Colorado gets some of its namesake reddish color here if the Paria River (on the right) is flowing. Major John Wesley Powell and his men saw the sheer, polished walls from here down to the Little Colorado confluence and named this section Marble Canyon, although no marble is actually present.

Mile 2: Toroweap Formation
This silty limestone, formed near the ancient sea's edge, was also deposited during the Permian Period. The Toroweap has thinner beds and less chert than the Kaibab.

Mile 4: Coconino Sandstone
Tilted crossbedding, reptile tracks, and even imprints of raindrops indicate windblown deposits—ancient sand dunes built up during the middle of the Permian Period. By comparing the angles of the crossbedding with those of modern sand dunes, geologists have concluded that winds had blown the sand from the north.

Mile 4.5: Navajo Bridge
The bridge, recently built beside the 1929 original, connects the Canyon rims 470 feet above the river. In 1937, river runner Buzz Holmstrum stopped near here to get supplies at what looked on his map like the nearby Marble Canyon store. He did make it up and down the cliff somehow and then went on to make the first intentional solo run through the Grand Canyon.

Mile 7: Hermit Shale
Fossils of ferns, other plants, and even some insects have been collected from this soft reddish shale. The rock formed in a vast river floodplain in the early part of the Permian Period.

Mile 8: Badger Creek Rapid (5–8)
River-runners rate this, your first of many exciting rapids, at 5–8, depending on flow. The outwash from ephemeral streams of Badger Canyon on the right and Jackass Canyon on the left creates the rapid. A rough three-mile trail connects the river to US 89A via Jackass Canyon; Navajo sometimes come down this way to fish. Hikers can scramble up Badger Canyon for about a mile. Badger and nearby Soap Creek got their names when 19th-century Mormon explorer Jacob Hamblin shot a badger, took it back to camp, stewed it overnight, and then found that the alkaline water had turned the fat in his breakfast into soap!

Mile 11.2: Soap Creek Rapid (5–6)
Soap Creek comes in from the right. This rapid marks the beginning of a series of tragic sites for the 1889 Stanton-Brown survey, which came to study a proposed railroad route through the Grand Canyon. Despite having portaged the rapid, Frank M. Brown, the organizer of the Denver, Colorado Canyon, and Pacific Railroad Company, drowned below here. Five days later, two other members drowned before the group abandoned its work and climbed out of the Canyon. The following year, Robert B. Stanton and a team returned equipped with lifejackets and better gear to complete the survey.

The Supai Group exposed here comprises four formations that contain fossils of plants deposited in ancient deltas. Tracks of primitive reptiles have been found in the upper half of the group. First, you'll see reddish-brown sandstone from the early part of the Permian Period (about 280 million years ago) with thinner layers of ripple-marked siltstone and shale. The rock commonly weathers into ledges. Below are rocks of the Pennsylvanian Period (330–290 million years ago)—crossbedded sandstone in the middle part of the group, then thin-bedded sandstone with much interbedded siltstone and mudstone in the lower part.

Mile 12: Salt Water Wash
A rough route on the left climbs about four miles to US 89A; lots of boulders in the lower half make for slow going.

Mile 16.9: House Rock Rapid (7–9)
Rider Canyon comes in from the right. Robert B. Stanton used this difficult canyon route during his second expedition in 1890 to carry out an injured photographer who had fallen from a 20-foot cliff.

Mile 20.5: North Canyon Rapid (5)
You've now entered the "Roaring 20s"—a lively section of rapids in Marble Canyon. North Canyon, on the right, offers beautiful hiking.

Pete heading into the "Roaring 20's"

It's less than a mile to where cliffs block the way; you may see pools and small waterfalls.

Mile 21.2: 21 Mile Rapid (5)

Mile 23: Redwall Limestone
Perhaps the most distinct layer in the Grand Canyon, the Redwall forms long, unbroken cliffs. Here it makes up much of the impressive walls of Marble Canyon. The Redwall challenges skills of trailbuilders and hikers who attempt rim-to-river routes. The upper Redwall contains many caves; sometimes you'll even see matching caves on both sides of the river. The namesake color comes not from the limestone itself, but from staining by the Hermit Shale above. Fossils of nautiloids (straight and spiraled), corals, brachiopods, crinoids, and sponges show that the limestone was deposited on the floor of a shallow sea in the Mississippian Period (360–330 million years ago).

Mile 23.3: 23 Mile Rapid (4–6)

Mile 24.2: 24 Mile Rapid (6–8)

Mile 24.5: 24^1/$_2$ Mile Rapid (5–6)

Mile 24.9: 25 Mile Rapid (5–7)
It's also known as Hansbrough-Richards Rapid in memory of two members of the trouble-plagued Stanton-Brown railroad survey expedition of 1889. They drowned when their boat capsized just after they lined it through the rapid.

Mile 25.3: Cave Springs Rapid (5–6)

Mile 26.6: Tiger Wash Rapid (4–5)
Tiger Wash is on the left.

Mile 29.2: Silver Grotto and Shinumo Wash
In warm weather, boaters clamber up into the narrow canyon of lower Shinumo Wash on the left and swim through several icy pools to Silver Grotto. You can also see Silver Grotto from above by pulling over on the left at Mile 30.1 and hiking back upstream on the Fence Fault Route. Shinumo Altar rises from the south side of Shinumo

© BILL WEIR

M

GRAND CANYON

© BILL WEIR

Redwall Cavern

1889 and 1890 Brown-Stanton railroad expeditions, who used the cave to store gear when the demoralized first expedition walked out South Canyon. Archaeologists value the cave for the split-twig figurines left behind thousands of years ago and for more recent pottery and granaries left by the ancestral Puebloans. The Park Service has closed it to the public.

Mile 31.9: Vasey's Paradise
Springs transform the right shore into a beautiful oasis of flowers, maidenhair fern, mosses, and poison ivy. The Park Service recommends that visitors don't enter the vegetated area because of endangered Kanab ambersnails, found only here and at one spot in southern Utah. George W. Vasey worked as a botanist with Major Powell on an 1868 expedition to what's now the state of Colorado.

Mile 33: Redwall Cavern
Major Powell thought that this giant alcove on the left could serve as a theater seating 50,000 people, but he allowed that "at high water the floor is covered with a raging flood." Today it's a popular stop, though camping isn't permitted.

Mile 34.8: Nautiloid Canyon
On the left, stop to see large fossils embedded in the floor of the canyon. They are chambered shells of an animal related to squid.

Mile 35: Muav Limestone and The Bridge of Sighs
The contact between the Redwall and the underlying Muav (at river level) can be difficult to see; at some places a small slope or a bench marks the line. The Muav was deposited in a sea about 535 million years ago during the Cambrian Period and has very few fossils. The Bridge of Sighs, a natural arch, appears high on the right.

Mile 43: Point Hansbrough and Anasazi Bridge
A log bridge high on the right survives from a prehistoric trail of ancestral Puebloans. The river begins a big loop to the right around the point. The second Stanton expedition found the skeleton of Peter Hansbrough here six months after he had drowned at 25 Mile Rapid.

Wash; the name comes from the Paiute word for the former inhabitants (ancestral Puebloans).

Mile 30: Redwall Dam Site
This spot is remarkable for what you *don't* see. Recognized as one of a series of potential dam sites by government surveys in the 1920s, it was later proposed by the Bureau of Reclamation as the site for a dam that would have raised the water 222 feet in a lake stretching nearly to Lees Ferry.

Mile 31.6: South Canyon
South Canyon, on the right, provides hikers with a route from the rim.

Mile 31.8: Stanton's Cave
High up (150 feet) and to the right in the Redwall you'll see a large cave entrance. The name honors Robert B. Stanton, chief engineer of the

GRAND CANYON

Mile 43.7: President Harding Rapid

A U.S. Geological Survey expedition, led by Claude Birdseye, came through in 1923 to make the first detailed maps of the Canyon and to survey potential dam sites. The expedition carried the first radio receiver into the Canyon. Having heard earlier on the radio of the president's death, the group stopped here for a day in observance of the president's funeral. Eminence Break Trail on the left beside the rapid climbs out to the rim; you'll enjoy great panoramas on the way up. You can reach the upper trailhead (difficult to find) by road (difficult to navigate); see **Tatahatso Point** in the Western Navajo Country section.

Mile 46.6: Triple Alcoves

The alcoves appear on the right.

Mile 47: Saddle Canyon

Hike up this canyon on the right one mile, past redbud trees flowering in the spring in shady recesses, to pools and a little waterfall.

Mile 50: Bright Angel Shale

This purple and green shale formed in the sea during the Cambrian Period about 550 million years ago.

Mile 51.9: Little Nankoweap Creek

Like many tributaries, this canyon on the right becomes prettier as you head upstream; cliffs eventually block the way. Redbud trees and pools add to the beauty.

Mile 52.2: Nankoweap Area

Nankoweap Rapid (3) offers a long ride, but hiking in the area draws more attention. The Nankoweap and Little Nankoweap form a large delta with many places to camp and explore. A short, steep hike leads to an impressive row of granaries constructed by ancestral Puebloans. Between 900 and 1150, they built many structures on the section of river between here and Unkar Delta (Mile 72.5). Hikers could spend days exploring Nankoweap Canyon and its tributaries or even hike out to the North Rim on the Nankoweap Trail. Most river runners

prefer shorter explorations in the area. A good loop day trip begins by hiking up the Nankoweap about two miles, turning south up the first major draw and going down the other side to Kwagunt Creek, and then following Kwagunt back to the river, where you can either meet the other boaters in your party or hike up the Colorado back to Nankoweap. Bring plenty of water and a sun hat for this spring or autumn trek.

Mile 56: Kwagunt Rapid (6)

You can explore Kwagunt Creek on the right on foot.

Mile 60: Tapeats Sandstone

The brown, medium- to coarse-grained sandstone formed about 570 million years ago during the Cambrian Period.

Mile 61.4: Little Colorado River

This major tributary of the Colorado flows from the left in two colors. During spring snowmelt or summer storms in the mountains of eastern Arizona, the Little Colorado carries a heavy load of brown silt. In dry periods, the only flow comes from mineral-laden Blue Spring, 12.5 miles upstream. Salts and calcium carbonate turn the water a beautiful aquamarine, but it's not recommended for drinking. Endangered fish hang out near the confluence, so no fishing or camping is permitted here.

You can hike up the Little Colorado nearly a mile to see Ben Beamer's stone-slab cabin on the south bank. Beamer came here in 1889 to prospect and do a bit of farming; he likely "borrowed" stones from ruins left by ancestral Puebloans to build his cabin. Beamer's Trail still connects the confluence with Tanner Rapid downstream and the Tanner Trail to the South Rim.

Back on the Colorado River, you'll spot some salt deposits along the left bank in the next three miles. Hopi once made long pilgrimages from their villages to collect this salt. The salt mines remain sacred to the Hopi, so Park Service rangers prohibit others from visiting them. Instead, wait until Mile 119.8, where you can stop and take a close look at a salt deposit.

Mile 63.4: The Great Unconformity
About 250 million years have been lost from the geologic record at this unconformity between the Tapeats Sandstone above and the Unkar Group of the Precambrian Period below. The Unkar contains five formations of about 1,250 to 825 million years ago. From the oldest (lowermost), they are the Bass Limestone, Hakatai Shale, Shinumo Quartzite, Dox Sandstone, and the Cardenas Lavas. You'll also hear the term "Grand Canyon Supergroup," which includes the Unkar Group and three formations of roughly the same age that occur in the Colorado River's tributaries but not at river level: Nankoweap Formation (Nankoweap and Basalt Canyons); Chuar Group (Nankoweap, Carbon, and Lava Canyons); and Sixtymile Formation (Nankoweap Butte and upper Sixtymile Canyon). Faulting has tilted these formations and caused large offsets between one side of the Canyon and the other.

Mile 64.7: Carbon Creek
For a look at the complex geology in this part of the Canyon, you can hike up Carbon Creek (on the right), cut south over a pass, and then descend Lava Canyon to the river, where you should arrange to be picked up. The pass has especially fine views of the Unkar Group and lava flows. On the way down Lava Canyon, look for a trail to the left that passes a dry fall.

Mile 65.6: Lava Canyon (Chuar) Rapid (3–5)
Lava Canyon is on the right, Palisades Creek on the left. A park naturalist found a moonshine still in Lava Canyon in 1928, but you'd be safer to carry your own liquid refreshment on hikes here.

Mile 68.5: Tanner Canyon
Hikers descend from the South Rim on the Tanner Trail to the beach and the small rapid at the river. The Beamer Trail goes upstream to the Little Colorado. The Escalante Route winds downstream to connect with the Tonto and New Hance (Red Canyon) Trails.

Mile 71: Cardenas Creek
You can scramble south up the ridge for a wonderful panorama of the Canyon and a look at a stone structure left by ancestral Puebloans; it may have been a watchtower. Spanish explorer García López de Cárdenas, arriving on the South Rim in 1540, was the first White man to see the Grand Canyon; his group tried but failed to reach the river.

Mile 72.5: Unkar Rapid (6–7)
Ancestral Puebloans once farmed the Unkar delta on the right. You can stop to look at stone foundations of their village.

Mile 75.5: Nevills Rapid (6)
Norm Nevills led the first commercial river trip through the Grand Canyon in 1938.

Mile 76.8: Hance Rapid (8–10)
Rock gardens in the river present a real challenge, especially to the hard-shelled dories. Red Canyon on the left is the start of the long Tonto Trail that heads downstream and the Hance (Red Canyon) Trail that climbs to the South Rim. John Hance arrived at the Grand Canyon in 1883, built the first lodge on the South Rim two years later, made trails, did some mining, and guided tourists. All the while he entertained his tour guests with amazing yarns, such as the tale about the Canyon filling with clouds, when he just strapped on his snowshoes and walked across. On stretches where trails parallel the river, the difference in time between foot and boat travel is amazing. A lazy day on the river with just an oar-powered boat can cover as much distance as several hard days on the trail.

Mile 77: Upper Granite Gorge
Another Great Unconformity marks the boundary between the Unkar Group and rocks even more ancient, perhaps 1.7 billion years old, formed in the early part of the Precambrian Period. Unimaginable extremes of time, pressure, and heat have folded, twisted, and crystallized these rocks, which probably once lay beneath a mountain range. Despite the gorge's name, you'll find mostly gneiss (a coarse-grained metamorphic rock with bands of visibly different

minerals) and schist (a dark, easily split, meta-morphic rock with closely spaced bands of mica). Pink pegmatite (a coarse-grained igneous rock) was injected into these rocks. You'll see milky quartz, too. The Upper Granite Gorge extends about 48 miles downstream. The Canyon's character changes dramatically as the dark walls close in, constrict the river, and speed up the water's flow.

Mile 78.7: Sockdolager Rapid (8–9)
Major Powell's second expedition used a slang word meaning "knockout blow" for this one. Powell's men weren't able to portage their frail craft here, so they ran the rapid with the loud roar of the waves reverberating off the Canyon walls.

Mile 81.5: Grapevine Rapid (8)
Grapevine Creek comes in from the left, Vishnu Creek from the right. Many of the rock "temples" and canyons below the North Rim bear names of Eastern gods and philosophers. The Hindu god Vishnu preserves the world. Geologist Clarence Dutton started the "heroic nomenclature" for Grand Canyon features.

Mile 83.5: 83 Mile Rapid (3–5)

Mile 84: Clear Creek Canyon
You wouldn't think such a small stream and canyon could drain a large area of the North Rim. It's worth making the short hike of about half a mile up to a small waterfall. You could also climb around the waterfall and continue far upstream. Clear Creek Trail connects the creek with the North Kaibab Trail near Phantom Ranch.

Mile 84.6: Zoroaster Rapid (5–8)
Zoroaster Creek on the right descends from the south side of Zoroaster Temple. About 700 B.C., the Persian philosopher Zoroaster founded what became a major religion of that region.

Mile 85: 85 Mile Rapid (2–6)

Mile 87.5: Kaibab Bridge
The South Kaibab Trail from the South Rim crosses the river here on its way to Phantom

Ranch after a very scenic descent of 6.8 miles to Bright Angel Camp via Cedar Ridge. The bridge warns you that a touch of civilization lies just ahead. River trips put in at the beach on the right past the bridge to exchange passengers leaving or joining at this point. You can wander over to Phantom Ranch to use a telephone, mail your postcards via mule train, buy snacks or souvenirs at the store, or ogle at a flush toilet, which you won't have seen for days.

If you have time for a hike, try part of the North Kaibab or climb the Clear Creek Trail for views. Or leave the crowds and head up Phantom Creek to lush greenery and small waterfalls; walk about one mile up the North Kaibab Trail until you see the creek on the other side of Bright Angel Creek, which you'll have to ford.

Mile 87.8: Bright Angel Rapid and Bright Angel Bridge
Major Powell named the swift and clear-flowing Bright Angel Creek to honor the forces of good, after earlier naming the muddy Dirty Devil River upstream in Utah. Much of the Bright Angel's flow comes from Roaring Springs, which blasts out of caves in the Redwall Limestone below the North Rim. Hikers can reach the North Rim on the 14.2-mile North Kaibab Trail.

Mile 89: Pipe Springs Rapid (4–5)
The Bright Angel Trail turns up Pipe Creek Canyon on its well-graded, 7.8-mile-long ascent to the South Rim.

Mile 90.2: Horn Creek Rapid (8–10)
Horn Creek comes in on the left. Two boulders near midstream give the rapid its name.

Mile 93.5: Granite Rapid (9)
Monument Creek on the left offers an easy walk up to the Tonto Trail.

Mile 95: Hermit Rapid (8–9)
Hermit Creek on the left also provides a scenic walk up the Tonto Trail. Louis Boucher, the Hermit, mined copper and guided tourists in the area during his stay from 1891 to 1912. He

wore a white beard, rode a white mule, and told only "white lies."

Mile 96.8: Boucher Rapid (3–5)
The route along Boucher Creek on the left is an easy walk to the Tonto and Boucher Trails.

Mile 98.2: Crystal Rapid (10)
This fierce rapid has weakened the knees of many a river-runner scouting it from the shore. Places in the Grand Canyon may stay nearly unchanged for more than a century, only to be turned topsy-turvy by a single storm. That happened here in 1966, when a massive flood tore through Crystal Creek (on the right), washing many huge boulders into the Colorado and forcing the river into the left wall. Now boaters must pick out a route that stays clear of the rocks, the wall, and giant, boat-flipping holes. If you're camping near here, Crystal Creek offers a pleasant stroll up its relatively open canyon.

Mile 99.2: Tuna Creek Rapid (6)

Mile 101.3: Sapphire Rapid (7)

One of a series of rapids here called "The Jewels." Sapphire Canyon is on the left.

Mile 102: Turquoise Rapid (3–6)
Turquoise Canyon is on the left.

Mile 103.9: 104 Mile Rapid (5–7)

Mile 104.6: Ruby Rapid (6–7)
Ruby Canyon is on the left.

Mile 106: Serpentine Rapid (6–8)
Serpentine Canyon is on the left. Serpentine (an ornamental stone) and asbestos (sought by Hance, Bass, and other prospectors) occur in the Canyon where molten volcanic rock subjected the Bass Limestone to intense heat.

Mile 107.8: Bass Rapid (3–6)
Bass Canyon on the left and the South Bass Trail, just upstream of the rapid, provide access to the Tonto Trail and South Rim. William Bass arrived in the 1880s, did some prospecting, raised a family, and ran a tourist operation until he left the area in 1923. He built tourist camps and

the boat-flipping Crystal Rapid

© BILL WEIR

Shinumo Creek

constructed trails to both South and North Rims. Boats, and in 1908 a cableway with a cage big enough for horses, connected his trails. The Park Service cut the cable in 1968, so there's no crossing today. A metal boat, the *Ross Wheeler,* lies on the left bank just above the rapid, where it was abandoned about 1914.

Mile 108.2: Beach and Trailhead for Bass's Camp
From this popular campsite on the right, a trail climbs high over a ridge (blazing with yellow brittlebush in spring), drops to Shinumo Creek, and then winds upstream to Bass's Camp. You'll discover relics of his camp and small farm along the swift, sparkling creek. Cottonwood trees shade the banks. Be sure to carry lots of water and a sun hat for this hike of two miles each way. The North Bass Trail continues another 12 miles upcanyon to the pine-forested North Rim.

Mile 108.7: Shinumo Rapid
Boats can pull in at lower Shinumo Creek on the right so that you can take a short walk to a pool and waterfall. The waterfall blocks hikers from continuing upstream to Bass's Camp.

Mile 112.2: Waltenberg Rapid (6–9)
John Waltenberg worked with William Bass in developing copper and asbestos mines in the area during the early 20th century.

Mile 112.6: $112^{1}/_{2}$ Mile Rapid (1–6)

Mile 113.1: Rancid Tuna Rapid (6)
One can only assume that this rapid was named by an unlucky early boating expedition that discovered the terrible truth about its food situation here.

Mile 114.4: Garnet Canyon
The Tonto Trail ends its 92-mile meandering at this canyon on the left.

Mile 116.5: Elves Chasm
Royal Arch Creek creates this beauty spot on the left with a waterfall, greenery and flowers, and extensive travertine deposits.

Mile 116.9: Stephen Aisle
This straight section of Canyon runs about two miles. The Upper Granite Gorge ends at a fault

where the river cuts into Tapeats Sandstone. From here until the start of the Middle Granite Gorge at Mile 126.6, you'll be seeing stretches of Tapeats Sandstone, Precambrian gneiss, and Bright Angel Shale.

Mile 119.8: Salt Deposits
Look on the right for alcoves filled with salty stalactites, stalagmites, and columns. It's possible to stop here or walk back from the Blacktail Canyon camp 0.3 mile farther.

Mile 120.1: Blacktail Canyon and Conquistador Aisle
Blacktail Canyon on the right offers a short hike into Tapeats Sandstone narrows. Conquistador Aisle, another two-mile straight section of canyon, lies downstream.

Mile 121.7: 122 Mile Rapid (4–6) and Bright Angel Shale

Mile 122.8: Forster Rapid (6)
Forster Canyon is on the left.

Mile 125: Fossil Rapid (6–7)
Fossil Canyon is on the left.

Mile 126.6: Middle Granite Gorge
Schist and quartzite make up most of the low walls of this narrow, 3.9-mile gorge. Sheet-like dikes of igneous pegmatite (coarse-grained rock) and amphibolite (dark rock composed mostly of the mineral hornblende) have cut into the older rocks. You'll see salt deposits on the left.

Mile 129: Specter Rapid (5–8)
Specter Chasm is on the left.

Mile 130.5: Bedrock Rapid (8) and Unkar Group
Bedrock Canyon and the "Doll's House" are on the right. Middle Granite Gorge ends just below, where the river cuts into the Unkar Group. Bass Limestone, with its igneous intrusions, dominates the next five miles.

Mile 131.7: Deubendorff Rapid (7–9), Galloway Canyon, and Stone Creek
Galloway Canyon, on the right just above the rapid, and Stone Creek, on the right just below, invite exploration. Galloway is dry, but Stone Creek features pools, waterfalls, greenery, flowers, and a magical narrows. Stone Creek makes a great spot for a layover day. The whole walk up offers pretty scenery, so just tramp as far as the spirit moves you. Look for a bypass trail on your right around the first high waterfall about one mile up; another mile of climbing will take you to the short narrows that end in a waterfall.

In 1909, Julius Stone earned the distinction of being the first to boat through the Grand Canyon for the fun of it. A president of a gold-dredging company, he had met pioneering boatman Nathaniel Galloway in Glen Canyon and hired him to supervise construction of four wooden, flat-bottomed boats. Galloway had devised not only superior riverboat designs but also a better way of rowing them in the rapids. He found that it made no sense to row blindly into the dangerous rapids when one could simply turn the boat around, face the rapids, and pull upstream to give more time and control to make a safe descent. The new boats, $16^1/2$ feet long and four feet wide, featured sealed compartments and lightweight construction. Stone and four companions, including Galloway and helper Seymour Deubendorff, pushed off from Green River, Wyoming, and reached Needles, California, just over two months later. Galloway became the first to make two complete transits of the canyons, and his rowing technique endures today. Deubendorff capsized here, much to his embarrassment at the time.

Mile 133.7: Tapeats Rapid (5–8), Tapeats Creek, and Thunder River
Two sets of voluminous springs feed crystal-clear Tapeats Creek, on the right just above the rapid. Thunder Spring rates as one of the Grand Canyon's top hiking destinations—you're not likely to be disappointed! Trails run up both sides of Tapeats Creek from the Colorado. In spring, when the creek can be too high and

swift to ford easily, it's best to get off the boats on the downriver side of the creek. In 2.5 miles you'll reach Thunder River, which suffers the indignity of both being short and serving as a tributary to a creek.

A trail climbs steeply half a mile to good vantage points of Thunder Spring as it blasts out of a cave system in the Muav Limestone. Large Fremont cottonwood trees provide shade. In spring or autumn, you can continue 1.5 miles up the trail past Thunder Spring and down into the gently sloping Surprise Valley, renowned for its ovenlike heat in summer. A cairn marks the junction of the Thunder River Trail to the North Rim, but continue west 1.5 miles on the Deer Creek Trail, which drops to Deer Creek (Dutton) Spring, another cave system gushing a waterfall. You can hike up to the falls for a closer look or take the path that goes higher and behind the falls. The creekside trail winds down one mile past the remarkably narrow and twisting Tapeats narrows, then drops to the base of Deer Creek Falls at the river. Watch out for poison ivy here. If it's too hot to hike or you can't arrange to be met by boats, Deer Creek makes a great stop on its own.

climbing a ladder at the mouth of Olo Canyon
© BILL WEIR

Mile 134.7: 135 Mile Rapid (5) (Helicopter Eddy)

Mile 135.4: Granite Narrows
The Colorado constricts to just 76 feet in the Granite Narrows, its smallest width in the Grand Canyon.

Mile 136.2: Deer Creek Falls
See the Mile 133.7: Tapeats Creek/Thunder River entry above for hiking details on the Deer Creek Trail (on the right).

Mile 136.6: Unconformable contact of Precambrian rocks and overlying Tapeats Sandstone Tapeats predominates for the next 3.5 miles; you'll also see some Precambrian quartzite and spring-deposited travertine.

Mile 137.7: 137^1/$_2$ Mile (Doris) Rapid (5–7)
Doris, wife of Norm Nevills, took a swim here

after getting washed overboard on one of the early commercial river trips in 1940.

Mile 139: Fishtail Rapid (5–7)
Fishtail Canyon is on the right.

Mile 140.1: Conformable contact (no gap in the geologic record) between the underlying Tapeats Sandstone and Bright Angel Shale
The river cuts through Bright Angel Shale for the next seven miles.

Mile 143.5: Kanab Rapid and Kanab Canyon
A major canyon system with many tributaries of its own, Kanab Creek on the right extends far north into Utah past the town of Kanab to the Paunsaugunt Plateau, 100 miles from the Grand Canyon. Kanab means "willows" in Paiute. Major Powell ended his second river expedition here in 1872 and walked out Kanab Canyon. Whis-

pering Falls makes a good hiking destination; walk up about four miles from the river and turn right into the first tributary.

Mile 145.6: Olo Canyon

The overhanging cliff to the left with a waterfall doesn't look promising for hikers, but some groups will send a rock climber on a bypass just downriver to put in a cable ladder at the pour-off. Two other steep sections a little farther upstream can be rigged with ropes to aid hikers. The climb is worthwhile to view the water-sculpted canyon full of pools. Upstream, the canyon widens a bit, and vegetation finds soil to take root. Olo is Havasupai for "little horse."

Mile 147.1: Conformable Contact between the Bright Angel Shale and overlying Muav Limestone

The river flows through the Muav for the next 18.6 miles.

Mile 147.9: Matkatamiba Canyon

"Matkat" on the left presents a beautiful show of rock sculpture and pools similar to those in Olo Canyon. Agile hikers should be able to make it up Matkat without ropes. As in Olo, you can hike a long way in, limited mainly by the time you have. Matkatamiba is a Native American family name.

Mile 149.7: Upset Rapid (6–9) and 150 Mile Canyon

The 1923 Birdseye (U.S. Geological Survey) River Expedition had made it this far when the head boatman, Emery Kolb, performed the group's first flip. On the right is 150 Mile Canyon.

Mile 156.8: Havasu Canyon

The turquoise-blue waters and Shangri-La reputation of this canyon on the left put it at the top of many river-runners' favorite hikes. Trees, grass, and flowers fill the canyon floor. Havasupai live in their secluded Supai village about nine miles upcanyon; *havasu* means "blue water" and *pai* means "people." Everyone wants to visit Havasu Canyon, yet there's no beach to land boats. So boaters have to tie up in the canyon mouth—an

amazingly complex network of interconnected ropes at times.

The trail upstream crosses the creek many times, but has little elevation gain to Beaver Falls, four miles away, the most popular destination for river-runners. Here you can swim in large pools enclosed by travertine terraces. Fleet-of-foot hikers can continue two more miles to see 196-foot Mooney Falls, the most impressive in Havasu Canyon. No camping is allowed in the lower canyon, so boaters are limited to day trips. For a longer visit, it's best to hike in from the top at another time to visit Supai Village and the other waterfalls; see the **Havasupai Indian Reservation** section later in this book.

Mile 165.7: Contact of Muav Limestone and the underlying Bright Angel Shale

The river flows through Bright Angel Shale for the next 10.2 miles.

Mile 166.5: National Canyon

The canyon on the left, sometimes with a small stream, is an easy one-mile walk; you'll need a rope to go farther.

Mile 168: Fern Glen Rapid (3) and Fern Glen Canyon

A worthwhile hike of about half a mile through the canyon on the right takes you to seeps that support expanses of maidenhair fern.

Mile 175.9: Contact of Bright Angel Shale and the underlying Tapeats

The river flows through Tapeats for the next 3.2 miles.

Mile 178: Vulcan's Anvil

The Anvil, a remnant of a lava vent, rises in the middle of the river. The Anvil marks the beginning of a long stretch of volcanic features in the Grand Canyon. A series of eruptions took place over the last million years, burying the countryside under lava and cinders and even filling the Grand Canyon with massive lava dams. Much of the basaltic lava formed columnar jointing. The fractures developed as the basalt cooled; cooler spots commonly formed three radial fracture

ENDANGERED FISH OF THE COLORADO RIVER

Colorado pikeminnow *(Ptychocheilus lucius)*

Native only to the Colorado and its tributaries, this species is the largest minnow in North America. It has been reported as weighing up to 100 pounds and measuring six feet long. Loss of habitat due to dam construction has greatly curtailed its size and range. Fishermen often confuse the smaller more common roundtail chub *(Gila robusta)* with the Colorado pikeminnow; the chub is distinguished by a smaller mouth extending back only to the front of the eye.

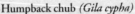

Humpback chub *(Gila cypha)*

Scientists first described this fish only in 1946 and now know little about its life. The small fish usually weighs in under two pounds and under 13 inches. Today the humpback chub hangs on the verge of extinction: it has retreated to a few small areas of the Colorado River where the water still runs warm, muddy and swift. The bonytail chub *(Gila robusta elegans)* has a similar size and shape, but without a hump; its numbers are also rapidly declining.

Humpback or Razorback sucker *(Xyrauchen texanus)*

This large sucker grows to weights of 10–16 pounds and lengths of about three feet. Its numbers have been slowly decreasing, especially above the Grand Canyon. They require warm, fast-flowing water to reproduce. Mating is done as a bizarre ritual in the spring. When the female has selected a suitable spawning site, two male fish press against the sides of her body. The female begins to shake her body until the eggs and males' spermatozoa are expelled simultaneously. One female can spawn three times, but she uses a different pair of males each time.

LOUISE FOOTE

GRAND CANYON

planes (120 degrees apart) that grew outward and intersected other fracture planes to create the columnar joints—usually hexagons. The faster the basalt cooled, the more fractures occurred, so you'll sometimes see cross-sections of fanlike columns near the surface branching out from larger "trunks" below.

Toroweap Overlook stands high above on the North Rim with some classic Canyon views. Lava Falls Route connects the river and the Toroweap area, though it's probably best to come by road at another time to explore this region; see **Toroweap** earlier in this book.

Mile 179.1: Crossing the Toroweap Fault
The downstream side of the fault has dropped 580 feet, so you go from Tapeats Sandstone to the younger Muav Limestone without seeing the intervening Bright Angel Shale; look for the fault on the left (the right side is covered by lava). From here to the head of the Lower Granite Gorge at Mile 215.1, you'll be in one of these three formations or some Precambrian rocks at river level.

Mile 179.3: Lava Falls Rapid (10)
Boaters may discuss whether Crystal or Lava Falls is the more difficult, but there's no denying that both are BIG and receive lots of respect. After a lengthy scout of the rapid from shore, you're in the boats and into the wild waves for an exhilarating ride.

Mile 183: Plugged Channel
An old river channel on the right is filled with lava.

Mile 187: Whitmore Wash
When lava filled the mouth of Whitmore Wash on the right, the stream cut a new channel farther downriver. You can easily hike about a half mile up this new canyon. Whitmore Trail climbs from river to rim in only three-quarters of a mile—the shortest access trail within Grand Canyon National Park—but you're still a very long and bumpy road from the nearest town. Some river parties do a passenger exchange here, not by trail, but by helicopter using a pad on Hualapai land across the river. The helicopter flies to the North Rim's

Bar 10 guest ranch, where a day of activities is usually included; small planes then take departing guests to Las Vegas or other destinations.

Mile 205.5: 205 Mile (Kolb) Rapid (7–8)
205 Mile Creek is on the left.

Mile 208.5: Granite Park
The large beach on the left makes an attractive campsite. Nearby canyons invite exploration. The river splits around a large, low island just downstream.

Mile 212.2: Little Bastard Rapid (1–7)

Mile 214.3: Shady Ledges (below 214 Mile Creek)
The lower Canyon can get mighty hot even in spring and autumn. These ledges on the right provide a shady lunch spot.

Mile 215.1: Entering Lower Granite Gorge
The Tapeats Sandstone makes an unconformable contact with the underlying Precambrian granite.

Mile 217.4: 217 Mile Rapid (6–7)
217 Mile Canyon is on the left.

Mile 225.6: Diamond Creek Rapid (4) and Diamond Creek
The name comes from the distinctive 3,512-foot peak that you see long before reaching the creek; the summit is only 400 feet higher in elevation than Lees Ferry. This left side of the Colorado River belongs to the Hualapai, who maintain a 21-mile unpaved road from here to Peach Springs on old Route 66. If you were to stay on the Colorado, there's only one day's river-running remaining, and then a long stretch of lake to Pearce Ferry, the next road access. Still, this last section offers great beauty, well worth seeing if you can do it. You can also start river trips here; contact the Hualapai River Runner's office in Peach Springs.

Mile 229: Travertine Rapid (3) and Travertine Canyon
A bit of steep scrambling (a rope is handy) up some travertine on the left will take you into a large cavelike room with a refreshing waterfall.

Mile 230.6: Travertine Falls
A waterfall near the river splashes thousands of sparkling drops off large travertine deposits on the left.

Mile 230.8: 231 Mile Rapid (4–7)

Mile 232.2: 232 Mile Rapid (4–7)

Mile 233.5: 234 Mile Rapid (4–6)

Mile 235.3: Bridge Canyon Rapid (3–6)
Bridge Canyon, with a spring and a natural bridge, is on the left.

Mile 236: Gneiss Canyon Rapid (3–6)
Gneiss Canyon is on the left.

Mile 237.2: 237 Mile Rapid (3–6)

Mile 239.6: Separation Canyon
On August 28, 1869, during Major Powell's first river expedition, the hardships of the unknown, the rapids, and dwindling food supplies brought three of the crew to the breaking point; they decided to hike out here through this canyon on the right. Rapids roared just downstream, and what lay beyond, Powell and the men could only guess. When they separated here, each group assumed the other to be embracing the greater danger. Powell and his remaining party safely negotiated the last rapids and left the Grand Canyon at noon on the following day. The three who climbed out never made it home. Powell later personally investigated and concluded that the men met their deaths at the hands of Shivwits tribesmen.

Today there's not much more than riffles where rapids once terrified Powell's men. You're on Lake Mead now, though the Colorado still provides a current and the Canyon still reveals magnificent views. Most groups start motoring out or arrange to be met by motorboats somewhere below Separation, even if they've been rowing so far.

Mile 259.3: End of the Lower Granite Gorge
Exposures of Tapeats Sandstone and Bright Angel Shale appear at lake level, though they're likely to be covered by silt. In pre-dam days, scattered exposures of Precambrian rocks reportedly extended all the way to the end of the Grand Canyon.

Mile 266.3: Bat Cave and Guano Point
U.S. Guano sank a lot of money into the mining of a deposit of bat guano (dung used as fertilizer) in a cave during the late 1950s. Cables suspended from the towers once carried the guano from Bat Cave high on the north side across the Canyon to Guano Point high on the Hualapai Plateau. The Park Service prohibits entry to the cave because it disturbs the bats. You can visit Guano Point by road or air for spectacular views and a close look at one of the towers; see **Grand Canyon West** in the Hualapai Indian Reservation section in the following chapter.

Mile 277.7: Grand Wash Fault and End of the Grand Canyon
The Canyon abruptly ends at Grand Wash Fault because rock layers on the west side lie several thousand feet lower—the Colorado never had a chance to carve a canyon in them. You're now on the vast expanse of water in Lake Mead National Recreation Area.

Mile 280: Pearce Ferry
Takeout and the road home.

Western Grand Canyon and the Arizona Strip

Havasupai Indian Reservation

Note: See color maps of Western Grand Canyon and the Arizona Strip at the front of the book.

VISITING HAVASU CANYON

The towering cliffs of Havasu Canyon enclose a land of blue-green waters, breathtaking waterfalls, and lush vegetation. Havasu Creek rushes through the canyon past the village of Supai before beginning its wild cascade down to the Colorado River. The canyon and its creek, about 35 air miles northwest of Grand Canyon Village, belong to the Havasupai (*havasu* means "blue water," and *pai* means "people").

Havasupai lived here long before the first White people arrived. The tribe farmed the fertile

canyon floor each summer, then moved to the plateau after harvest to gather abundant wild foods and firewoodduring winter. Spanish missionary Francisco Tomás Garcés visited the Havasupai in 1776 and thought them a peaceful and industrious tribe. However, as was often the case, White settlers grabbed tribal lands over the following years. The Havasupai protested, and the tribe's winter homelands were finally returned in 1975. The Havasupai Reservation now spans 188,077 acres and houses 500–600 members, most of whom live in Supai village.

Coyotes Buttes north of Page

© BILL WEIR

WESTERN GRAND CANYON AND THE ARIZONA STRIP HIGHLIGHTS

Havasu Canyon: Waterfalls and travertine pools in this beautiful canyon create a "Shangri-La" setting.

Diamond Creek: You can drive along this creek to the bottom of the Grand Canyon on an unpaved road on the Hualapai Indian Reservation.

Grand Canyon West: Spectacular panoramas take in the lower Grand Canyon from remote viewpoints.

Arizona Strip: Adventurous travelers who love wilderness and solitude seek out the canyons and mountains of this vast area.

Pipe Spring National Monument: You can experience life on a ranch straight out of the Old West.

Paria Canyon and Coyote Buttes: Exquisitely sculptured rock awaits hikers in the Paria Canyon-Vermilion Cliffs Wilderness.

ARIZONA STRIP

Getting There

The tribe wisely decided against allowing road construction in the canyon, so most residents and tourists enter by mule, horse, or on foot. Helicopters provide another option, though the noisy machines seem out of place here.

The eight-mile trail from Hualapai Hilltop to Supai is the usual way in. From Seligman on I-40, take AZ 66 northwest for 28 miles (to between Mileposts 110 and 111), then turn right and go 63 miles on signed Indian 18, paved all the way to Hualapai Hilltop. If coming from the west, take AZ 66 northeast out of Kingman for 60 miles, then turn left and drive the 63 miles. Fill up with gas before leaving AZ 66, as no water, supplies, or stores are available after the turnoff. The road to Hualapai Hilltop climbs into forests of ponderosa pine that give way to pinyon and juniper, then desert grasslands close to the rim. Parking areas and stables mark road's end. Various dirt-road shortcuts to Hualapai Hilltop suffer from poor signing and rough surfaces.

Hiking In

You *must* obtain reservations to camp or to stay in the lodge. From Hualapai Hilltop (elev. 5,200 feet), the trail descends at a moderate grade into Hualapai Canyon for the first 1.5 miles, then levels off slightly for the remaining 6.5 miles to Supai village (elev. 3,200 feet). About 1.5 miles before the village, the trail joins the sparkling waters of Havasu Canyon. Avoid the heat of the day in summer when

temperatures soar past 100°F, and always carry drinking water. All visitors must pay a $20 entrance fee on arrival at Supai. The tribe asks you to leave pets, alcohol, and firearms at home. To preserve the canyon floor, no fires or charcoal are allowed, so campers need to bring stoves if they plan to cook.

Riding In

If you'd rather ride than walk, local families will take you and your gear on horses or mules from the parking lot at Hualapai Hilltop to Supai ($70 one-way or $120 roundtrip) or all the way to the campground ($75 each way), 2.75 miles farther. One animal can carry about four backpacks. Try to get an early start from Hualapai Hilltop, especially in the warmer months; a small surcharge is added for departures after 10 A.M. A sightseeing ride from Supai to the falls and back can be arranged with the lodge. You should make reservations at least six weeks in advance and pay a 50 percent deposit. Campers make arrangements through Havasupai Tourist Enterprise; lodge guests through the lodge. Also call two weeks before arrival to make sure your animal is available. Visitors may bring their own horses if they take along feed and pay a $20 trail fee.

Sights

The famous waterfalls of the canyon begin 1.5 miles downstream from Supai—three cascades plunge over cliffs of Redwall Limestone in a space of just two miles. You'll first come to 75-foot-high **Navajo Falls** which has several widely spaced branches. It's named after a 19th-century Havasupai tribal chief kidnapped by Navajo as an infant and raised as a Navajo. Not until he grew to manhood did he learn of his true origin and return to the Havasupai.

A bit farther, spectacular **Havasu Falls** drops 100 feet into a beautiful turquoise-colored pool rimmed by travertine deposits. Clear, inviting waters make this a perfect spot for swimming or picnicking.

Awe-inspiring **Mooney Falls** plummets 196 feet into a colorful pool one mile beyond Havasu Falls. The Havasupai named this most sacred of waterfalls Mother of the Waters. The present name is that of a prospector who died here in 1880. When assistants lowered Daniel Mooney down the cliffs next to the falls, the rope jammed and Mooney hung helpless as the rope frayed and broke. He fell to his death on the rocks below, and 10 months passed before his companions could build a wooden ladder down the falls to reach and bury the travertine-encrusted body. A rough trail descends beside the falls along the same route hacked through the travertine by miners in those months after Mooney's death. You'll pass through two tunnels and then ease down with the aid of chains and iron stakes. At the bottom—as soon as your knees stop shaking—you can enjoy a picnic or swim in the large pool. Miners extracting silver, lead, zinc, and vanadium drilled the holes that you see high on the canyon walls.

Beaver Falls, two miles downstream from Mooney, makes a good day-hike from the campground or Supai village. You'll pass countless inviting travertine pools and small cascades, of which Beaver Falls is the largest. The trail, rough in places, crosses the creek three times, climbs high up a cliff, then descends and crosses a fourth time below Beaver Falls. The trail continues downstream along Havasu

The Arizona Strip appeals to those who love wilderness and solitude. Nine designated wilderness areas totaling nearly 400,000 acres protect some of its more scenic sections. Travelers can wander along the canyons, back roads, and trails here without meeting another soul.

Creek four more miles to the Colorado River. Travel fast and light if going to the river, as camping is prohibited below Mooney Falls. Photographing the falls can be a challenge; the best time to snap them in full sunlight is in May, June, and July.

Havasu Campground

Most visitors prefer to camp, listening to the sounds of the canyon and enjoying the brilliant display of stars in the nighttime sky. Havasu Campground begins a quarter mile below Havasu Falls (or 10.75 miles from Hualapai Hilltop) and provides spring water, picnic tables, litter barrels, and pit toilets. It's recommended that campers treat or filter the spring water. Most people don't realize that the campground extends three-quarters of a mile along Havasu Creek to the brink of Mooney Falls. You'll enjoy more solitude if you walk to the far end. Theft is a serious problem in the campground, so don't leave valuables in your tents or lying around.

To camp, you must have reservations and pay $10 per person per night. Camping outside the established campground is prohibited. Call 928/448-2141 or write Havasupai Tourist Enterprise, P.O. Box 160, Supai, AZ 86435; www.havasupaitribe.com. Try to make reservations far ahead, especially for holidays, weekends, and all of April, May, June, and July. The tribe now accepts Visa and Master Card.

Accommodations and Food

The modern **Havasupai Lodge,** 928/448-2111, in Supai village offers rooms with air-conditioning, two double beds, and private bath for $75 s, $80 d. Obtain the required reservations—recommended two–three months in advance; P.O. Box 159, Supai, AZ 86435.

A café nearby serves breakfast, lunch, and dinner daily 6 A.M.–7 P.M. (8 A.M.–5 P.M. in

the steep descent to the base of Mooney Falls

winter) Try the Indian taco—red beans, beef, cheese, onion, and lettuce on Indian fry bread. Ice cream prices are high, though not so bad when you consider what it takes to bring the frozen dessert to such a remote area. A store across the street, open daily, sells meat, groceries, and cold drinks.

Services

Send your postcard home via pack train—with a postmark to prove it! The **post office** is open weekdays 9 A.M.–4 P.M. next to the store. A **health clinic** in Supai provides emergency medical care.

VISITING THE HUALAPAI INDIAN RESERVATION

The Hualapai (Pine Tree People) once occupied a large area of northwestern Arizona. In language and culture, they're closely tied to the Havasupai and Yavapai tribes. Though the Hualapai were friendly to early white visitors,

land seizures and murders by the newcomers led to warfare. In 1869 the tribe surrendered to the U.S. Army and were held at Camp Beale Springs (present-day Kingman) and other locations before being forced south onto the Colorado River Reservation in 1874. Many died there due to the oppressive climate, hard labor, and lack of food. Survivors escaped the following year and fled back to their traditional lands, only to find the best areas already been taken by white people. In 1883, the government gave the Hualapai a 993,000-acre reservation, now housing about half the tribe's 1,500 members. Much of the lower Grand Canyon's South Rim belongs to the Hualapai. Highlights for visitors include the drive into the Grand Canyon at Diamond Creek, Colorado River trips, and spectacular viewpoints from the rim of the lowermost Grand Canyon. Respect the privacy of the tribal residents and obtain permits for sightseeing or other activities off the main highway.

Peach Springs

This community, 54 miles northeast of Kingman on AZ 66, is the only town on the reservation. Peach Springs offers neither charm nor anything to see, but it does have lodging and offices where you can obtain required permits for back-road drives and outdoor recreation. **Hualapai Lodge,** 928/769-2230, 888/255-9550, has comfortable rooms ($75 d, less in winter) and a restaurant that serves breakfast, lunch, and dinner daily.

The lodge's front desk sells permits to drive into the Grand Canyon via Diamond Creek Road, detailed below. Grand Canyon West permits, also described below, can be obtained when you arrive there. For other areas, you'll need to contact the tribe's Wildlife office, across the highway from the lodge and several doors to the west; open Mon.–Fri. 8 A.M.–4:30 P.M.; 928/769-2227. **Hualapai Office of Tourism,** 888/255-9550, has a desk open daily 9 am.–5 P.M. in the lobby of Hualapai Lodge, where you can arrange rafting trips through the lower Grand Canyon and get information about visits to Grand Canyon West; contact P.O. Box 359, Peach Springs, AZ 86434; www.hualapai

tours.com. After hours, ask at the front desk. A grocery store and post office lie across the highway and a few doors west. Craft vendors may set up in the park across from the lodge.

Grand Canyon Caverns Inn, 13 miles southeast on AZ 66, 928/422-3223, offers accommodations ($45 s, $50 d, lower rates in winter), an RV park for self-contained vehicles ($6.50), pool, and snack bar.

Frontier Motel, nine miles southwest in Truxton on AZ 66, 928/769-2277, has motel rooms ($35 s, $40 d), an RV park ($20 w/hookups; self-contained only), and a smoky café.

Diamond Creek Road

This scenic 21-mile gravel road winds north from Peach Springs to the Colorado River at Diamond Creek, providing the only road access to the river within the Grand Canyon. You'll see fine canyon views, though not as spectacular as those in the developed areas of Grand Canyon National Park. Except for river-runners, who use the road to take out or put in boats, few people visit this spot. Yet the very first organized groups of tourists to the Canyon arrived at Diamond Creek in 1883. A hotel built here and used in 1884–89 was the first in the Grand Canyon.

If the weather has been dry for several days, cars with good ground clearance can traverse the road. Summer rains in July and August may wash out sections and require use of a truck. A camping area near the Colorado River has some picnic tables and an outhouse or two. Hikers can explore Diamond Creek and other canyons. Before turning down Diamond Creek Road, you must stop at the Hualapai Lodge front desk to obtain permits; hikers may also need to visit the Wildlife office for a hiking permit. Staff at either place can advise on road conditions. Sightseeing permits cost $5 per day per person (ages 6 and over). Camping is $10 per day per person and includes the sightseeing fee. Fishing is an extra $8 per day

Spectacular Havasu Falls drops 100 feet into a beautiful turquoise-colored pool rimmed by travertine deposits. Clear, inviting waters make this a perfect spot for swimming or picnicking.

per person. Diamond Creek Road turns off AZ 66 opposite the Hualapai Lodge.

River-Running

Hualapai River Runners, 928/769-2219, 888/255-9550, will take you on a one-day motorized-raft trip down the lower Grand Canyon from Diamond Creek, lift you out by helicopter to the rim at Grand Canyon West, then return you by road to Peach Springs, $250. Overnight trips to Lake Mead can be chartered. This is the only company to offer a day trip within the Grand Canyon. Rates during the March–Oct. season cover food, waterproof bag for personal gear, and transportation from Peach Springs. Contact the office at Hualapai Lodge or write P.O. Box 246, Peach Springs, AZ 86434; www.river-runners.com.

Grand Canyon West

The Hualapai tribe offers a 4.5-mile tour along the rim of the western Grand Canyon to Guano Point, where visitors enjoy a great panorama of this little-visited part of the Canyon. The Colorado River, placid now that it has met the waters of Lake Mead, lies nearly 4,000 feet directly below. Sheer, terraced cliffs rise even higher on the North Rim than where you're standing. The Canyon remains grand to the end, as you'll see. The Grand Wash Cliffs, which lie just out of sight downstream, mark the west end of both the Grand Canyon and the Colorado Plateau. One of the steel towers and some of its machinery once used in a guano mining operation still stand on the point, and another tower is visible below. When in use, a tram carried guano from a bat cave located across the river. The tour also makes a short stop at an overlook of Eagle Point, an exceptionally long and narrow neck of land extending out into the Canyon.

Cost for the bus tour and a barbecue lunch at Guano Point runs $35 adult, $22 children 3–12; the lunch contains enough vegetables to satisfy most vegetarians too. Tours depart frequently during the day year-round and last about two hours; the first is at 10 A.M. and the last about 3 P.M.; no reservations are needed. Tickets, Quartermaster Point permits, and a gift shop are in the terminal building at the Grand Canyon West airport. It's a good idea to call ahead and allow plenty of time, because this is such a long drive out. Contact the Hualapai Office of Tourism for information (see Peach Springs, above).

While at Grand Canyon West, you can also enjoy a visit on your own to **Quartermaster Point,** another outstanding panorama of the Grand Canyon farther upstream. A quarter-mile trail from road's end leads down to the best views at the top of sheer cliffs. Quartermaster Canyon lies to your right, and Burnt Canyon is across the river. Twin Point stands above Burnt Canyon. Farther upcanyon, Kelly Point extends even farther out from the North Rim. (Both of these points can be visited via back roads; see "The Arizona Strip" section.) You can also picnic at Quartermaster Point; the spot has a few tables and an outhouse. First, obtain a permit from the Grand Canyon West Terminal, $10 per person (free if you also take a tour). The turnoff is 1.1 miles before the Grand Canyon West Terminal, then 2.3 miles in at the sign to the rim.

Getting to Grand Canyon West is an adventure too. Allow at least two hours for any of the driving routes. Four roads allow loop possibilities, or you can fly from Las Vegas. Buck and Doe Road stays within the reservation all the way. This dirt road is passable by cars when

the weather has been dry, but it can be rough—ask about road conditions before you leave. When it's wet, even 4WD vehicles should avoid it. Buck and Doe turns north from AZ 66 between Mileposts 100 and 101, several miles west of Peach Springs; follow it to the end, then turn right 4.3 miles on paved Diamond Bar Road. Antares Road, also dirt but likely to be better graded, turns north off AZ 66 farther west from Peach Springs, between Mileposts 74 and 75; take it 33 miles, turn right seven miles on Pearce Ferry Road (paved), then go right 21 miles on Diamond Bar Road. The first 14.4 miles on Diamond Bar Road is dirt but very scenic; you pass Joshua trees and enter a canyon through the Grand Wash Cliffs. Another back-road route involves heading north 40 miles on Stockton Hill Road from Kingman, then right 7.1 miles on Pearce Ferry Road and right 21 miles on Diamond Bar Road. The best road in approaches from the west; take US 93 from Kingman or Las Vegas to paved Pearce Ferry Road, near Milepost 42, follow it 29 miles east, then turn right 21 miles on Diamond Bar Road.

Several fixed wing and helicopter companies offer tours from Las Vegas; check with operators there for the many options. Helicopters also fly from Grand Canyon West into the Canyon and land either near the river or on a bench part way down on Hualapai land. Some flights allow passengers to get out and be picked up later in the day for the flight back to the top.

The Arizona Strip

Lonely and vast, the Arizona Strip lies north and west of the Colorado River. This land of forests, desert grasslands, mountains, and canyons covers 14,000 square miles, yet supports only 3,200 people. The Grand Canyon presents a formidable barrier between these citizens and the rest of the state; all highway traffic has to follow a circuitous route around the mighty chasm. To cover 140 miles as the crow flies, residents of Moccasin in the Arizona Strip must drive 357 miles to the Mohave County seat at Kingman, detouring through Utah and Nevada before reentering Arizona at Hoover Dam.

Historically, the Strip has far more in common with Utah; Mormon pioneers first settled this region. Today, the Strip appeals to those who love wilderness and solitude. In addition to Grand Canyon National Park and Glen Canyon National Recreation Area, nine designated wilderness areas totaling nearly 400,000 acres protect some of the most scenic sections. Much of this land has also been included in the Grand Canyon-Parashant National Monument, which exceeds one million acres. Travelers can wander along the canyons, back roads, and trails here without meeting another soul. Many viewpoints provide spectacular panoramas of the Grand Canyon, and you'll never have to joust with tour-bus crowds or search for a parking spot. Other attractions include fishing and boating on Lake Powell, historic Lees Ferry (15 river miles below Lake Powell), and Pipe Spring National Monument, an early Mormon ranch.

Several tiny communities in the Arizona Strip offer food and accommodations; more extensive facilities lie just outside in Mesquite across the Nevada border to the west, in St. George and Kanab across the Utah border to the north, and in Page across the Colorado River to the east.

History

Few pioneers took an interest in the prairie here—the ground proved nearly impossible to plow and lacked water for irrigation. Deter-

near the mouth of Kanab Creek

THE EXPLORATION OF THE COLORADO RIVER AND ITS CANYONS

ARIZONA STRIP

mined Mormons began ranching in the 1860s despite the constant isolation and occasional Navajo raids. They built Winsor Castle, a fortified ranch, in 1870 as a base for a large church-owned cattle herd. Mormons also founded the towns of Fredonia, Short Creek (now Colorado City), and Littlefield.

Some of these settlers had fled Utah to escape federal laws prohibiting polygamy. About 3,000 members of a polygamous, excommunicated Mormon sect still live in Colorado City and neighboring Hildale, Utah. (Note the huge size of "family" houses here!) Federal and state officials raided Colorado City several times, most recently in 1953, when 27 arrests were made—those charged received one year of probation. Up until the recent trial

THE DESERT TORTOISE

(Gopherus agassizii)

A threatened species, the desert tortoise survives the harsh climate of western Arizona by burrowing underground for about 95 percent of its lifetime. Here it escapes the 140°F surface temperatures in summer and the freezes of winter. It also seeks out catchment basins, where it will lie waiting when the rare rains seem likely. A tortoise's bladder can store a cup of liquid for later use, and they've been known to expel the bladder's contents at intruders. Wastes are excreted in a nearly dry form. Tortoises can withstand dehydration, then increase their weight 43 percent by drinking after a storm. Growth and sexual maturity depend much on availability of food and moisture. Several growth rings may appear each year. The female reaches maturity when about 7–8 inches long (mid-carapace), perhaps at 15 years of age. Mating peaks in late summer/early autumn, though egg laying won't take place until May–June, when tortoises lay two or three batches of 2–9 eggs. Babies emerge 3–4 months later. Oddly, experiments have shown that eggs incubated at 79–87°F turn out to be all males, at 88–91°F all females.

The tortoise's diet includes grasses, herbs, flowers, and new cactus growth. Males may fight each other for territory until one flees or gets flipped onto its back. If the defeated rival cannot right itself, it will die in the sun. Because the tortoise needs sand or gravel to burrow, you're most likely to see them in washes and canyon bottoms. Life span may be 70 years or more. The male has a longer protruding plate (used in jousting matches) under its neck; he may be as much as 14 inches long and weigh up to 20 pounds. The female is a bit smaller. Laws forbid disturbing or collecting a wild tortoise, but habitat loss and "kidnappers" have left their future in doubt. The western box turtle *(Terrapene ornata),* sometimes confused with the desert tortoise, is much smaller at about five inches long and has distinctive light and dark striping on its shell.

BOB RACE

the desert tortoise

and conviction of Tom Green for polygamy, government policy has seemed mostly "live and let live."

Information

For hiking and access information for public lands on the Arizona Strip and into Utah, contact the **Interagency Visitor Center,** 435/688-3246, at 345 E. Riverside Dr., St. George, UT 84790; open Mon.–Fri. 7:45 A.M.–5 P.M. (best times for reaching someone with first-hand travel experience) and Saturdays and holidays 9 A.M.–5 P.M.; www.az.blm.gov. Take I-15 Bluff Street Exit 6 and turn southeast one-third mile on Riverside Dr.; the office is on your left. This is also the home of the Arizona Strip Interpre-

tive Association (ASIA), which has a good bookshop here.

The BLM's **Kanab Resource Area** office, 318 N. 100 East (Kanab, UT 84741), 435/644-4600, takes care of the Paria Canyon area and Grand Staircase-Escalante National Monument; open Mon.–Fri. 7:45 A.M.–4:30 P.M.; www.ut.blm.gov.

The U.S. Forest Service manages Saddle Mountain Wilderness and most of the Kanab Creek Wilderness from the **North Kaibab Ranger District** office, 928/643-7395, at 430 S. Main St. in Fredonia (P.O. Box 248, Fredonia, AZ 86022); open Mon.–Fri. 8 A.M.–5 P.M.; www.fs.fed.us/r3/kai.

The BLM's *Arizona Strip District* map shows topography, roads with numbers, and land ownership at a 1:168,960 scale. The St. George Interagency office, Kanab Resource Area office, and most regional bookstores have the map; you can also order it online from the Interagency Internet address. The more detailed USGS 1:100,000- and 1:24,000-scale topo maps will be handy for hikers.

Exploring the Arizona Strip

Paved highways lead to the Virgin River gorge in the northwest corner, Pipe Spring National Monument in the north, the Grand Canyon's North Rim farther east, and Lees Ferry at the east edge. Elsewhere, high-clearance 4WD vehicles are recommended in this remote and rugged land. Cautiously driven 2WD vehicles can negotiate roads to the Trumbull and Toroweap areas in dry weather from St. George, Colorado City, and Fredonia. Parts of these roads are so smooth that one can drive at high speeds, often too fast to spot that washout or rough cattle guard! Drivers of 2WD vehicles need to take extra care not to become stuck on steep, sandy, or washed-out roads.

Mountain bikers can do exciting trips in the mountains and out to Grand Canyon viewpoints. Marked trails for cyclists include the Dutchman Trail, an "easy" nine-mile loop near Little Black Mountain (south of St. George) and the "more difficult" 8.5-mile Sunshine Loop southeast of St. George. The Arizona Trail farther east is another cycling destination.

All visitors must respect the remote location, lack of water, and absence of facilities here. Be sure to carry camping gear, extra food and water, tools, and a first-aid kit in case of breakdown. Distances can be great—make sure you have enough gas. Some roads shown on maps will be very difficult, hazardous, or completely closed; learn of current conditions from the BLM or Forest Service. Major junctions have signs and most roads also have a number, which helps with navigation. Some critical intersections lack signs, however, so it's highly recommended to have the BLM's Arizona Strip District map and to make frequent reference to it. Leave an itinerary with a reliable person in case you don't emerge on time. Some people live seasonally on the Arizona Strip, but you cannot count on being able to find any-

one in case of trouble. Ranchers run cattle on the strip, so gates should be left as you found them. Drivers need to keep an eye out for endangered desert tortoises that might wander across the road in the Mohave Desert, west of the Grand Wash Cliffs and the Virgin Mountains.

WILDERNESS AND SCENIC AREAS ON THE WESTERN ARIZONA STRIP

Virgin River Canyon Recreation Area

Picnic areas and campsites overlook the Virgin River at this scenic spot just south of I-15 Cedar Pocket Exit 18. It's open year-round with water but no showers or hookups; the gate closes at 9 P.M. Expect hot weather in summer at this 2,260-foot elevation. Campsites cost $8, picnic areas $2; groups can reserve day-use and camping areas with the BLM's Arizona Strip office in St. George, Utah; 435/688-3200. A one-fifth-mile nature trail leads to hilltop views, where interpretive signs explain the unusual geology of the canyon at this transition between the Colorado Plateau and the Basin and Range Province; trailhead parking is on the left where the picnic and campground roads divide. Other trails drop from the picnic and camping areas to the river.

River-Running on the Virgin

Experienced whitewater boaters prepared for changing conditions can tackle the Virgin River. A minimum of about 1,000 cubic feet per second (cfs) is needed, which doesn't occur every year; spring, and especially May, offers the best chance of sufficient flow. No permits are needed. The Interagency Visitor Center in St. George can advise on river travel and possibly on local boat rentals and shuttle services. River-runners can put in at the Man of War Road bridge in Bloomington, just south of St. George. Take-out can be at the last I-15 bridge or farther down on slow water near the Arizona town of Beaver Dam.

Littlefield and Beaver Dam

These two farming communities lie near the Virgin River on opposite sides of I-15 in Arizona's extreme northwest corner. Turn north 0.6 mile

ARIZONA STRIP

from Beaver Dam Exit 8 for **Hamilton Ranch,** a historic hotel on old Highway 91 once used as a movie star retreat; call for rates. The restaurant serves breakfast, lunch, and dinner daily (summer dinners are by reservation); 928/347-5111; www.hamiltonranchgolf.com. Golfers have an 18-hole course. A gas station/grocery store is nearby. Mesquite, Nevada, offers motels, restaurants, supermarkets, and glitter just eight miles west on I-15.

Beaver Dam Mountains Wilderness

This 19,600-acre wilderness includes alluvial plains and the rugged mountains of extreme northwestern Arizona and part of adjacent Utah. Desert bighorn sheep, desert tortoises, raptors, the endangered woundfin minnow, Joshua trees, and several rare plant species live here. There are no trails, but hikers enjoy traveling cross-country through the beautiful Joshua tree forest or exploring canyons. Unpaved BLM Road 1005, 10 miles long, follows a corridor through the wilderness, providing easy access. The east end begins at I-15 Cedar Pocket Exit 18, opposite the Virgin River Recreation Area, 20 miles southwest of St. George. The west end (unsigned) turns off between Mileposts 14 and 15 of Hwy. 91, 5.5 miles north of I-15 Beaver Dam Exit 8.

Paiute Wilderness

This 84,700-acre wilderness lies south of I-15 and the Virgin River in the northwest corner of Arizona. The jagged Virgin Mountains contain a wide variety of plant and animal life, from desert country at 2,400 feet to pine and fir forests surrounding 8,012-foot Mt. Bangs.

Several hiking trails wind through the rugged terrain. Cougar Spring Trailhead at the wilderness boundary provides the easiest route to the summit. Follow an old road up one mile through the wilderness to a saddle, then turn left one more mile up another old road toward the top. When the road ends, you'll need to bushwhack through some chaparral (look for cairns and wear long pants) and rock scramble the last quarter mile to the top; the climb takes about four and a half hours roundtrip. Despite the high elevations, only a few pines grow on the upper slopes;

© BILL WEIR

Beaver Dam Mountains

you'll see mostly manzanita, jojoba, Gambel oak, and some hedgehog and prickly pear cactus. Surrounding ridges have forests, however.

Other hiking options from Cougar Spring Trailhead area include the ridge north of Mt. Bangs and the Sullivan Trail. The 15-mile Sullivan Trail crosses the wilderness from Cougar Spring Trailhead or Black Rock Road to the Virgin River via Atkin Spring and Sullivan Canyon; expect some rough and poorly defined sections. The lower trailhead lies 1.5 miles downstream and across the Virgin River from Virgin River Campground, near I-15, 20 miles southwest of St. George; check the depth of the Virgin River carefully and turn back if it's too high to cross safely.

Hikers have a choice of approaching Cougar Spring Trailhead from the east via Black Rock Road (#1004), a pretty route through ponderosa pines on Black Mountain (good camping and a few picnic tables); from the south via Lime Kiln Canyon (#242) and other roads; or from the west on the very steep Elbow Canyon Road (#299; best driven downhill). From Mesquite, Nevada, turn south 0.9 mile on Riverside Road (just east of Oasis Casino), then turn left onto Lime Kiln Canyon Road #242 (just after crossing the Virgin River bridge). After 0.9 mile you'll see the road to Elbow Canyon on the left, but keep straight 16 miles for Lime Kiln Canyon, cross over a pass and descend past some pretty red sandstone outcrops, then turn left 22 miles on BLM Road 1041 to Cougar Spring Trailhead.

From St. George, take the I-15 Bloomington Exit 4, head east 1.8 miles (becomes Brigham Road), turn south 3.8 miles on River Road to the Arizona border and continue south another 20 miles on Quail Hill Road (#1069), turn right 25 miles on Black Rock Road (#1004), then right 0.5 mile to the trailhead.

If coming from Toroweap, take County 5 to Mt. Trumbull Schoolhouse, turn north 40 miles on County 5, then left 25 miles on Black Rock Road (#1004) and right 0.5 mile to the trailhead. If you're feeling adventurous and have a high-clearance 4WD vehicle, Elbow Canyon Road (#299) is an option—head west from the trailhead, climb a bit to a pass, then plummet down the rough road to the desert plains below.

Loose rock makes this drive much easier going downhill. Mesquite is about 18 miles from the trailhead. Lots of other very scenic roads head toward the Virgin Mountains too; see the Arizona Strip District Map.

Little Black Mountain Petroglyph Site

Impressive groups of rock art, most believed to have ceremonial or calendar functions, cover boulders at the base of this mesa just south into Arizona from St. George. Archaeologists have discovered more than 500 individual designs. A short trail winds past the petroglyphs, where signs describe some of their features. From St. George, take the I-15 Bloomington Exit 4 and head east 1.8 miles (becomes Brigham Rd.), then turn south 3.8 miles on River Road to the Arizona border and continue south 0.4 mile on unpaved Quail Hill Road (#1069). Turn east 4.5 miles to a T-junction (there's a gate on the way), then left into the parking area, which has a picnic table and outhouse.

Cottonwood Point Wilderness

The 6,860-acre wilderness contains part of the multicolored 1,000-foot-high Vermilion Cliffs, jagged pinnacles, and wooded canyons. Springs and seeps in the main canyon east of Cottonwood Point support a world of greenery surrounded by desert. The wilderness lies on the Utah border near Colorado City, west of Fredonia. Dirt roads from AZ 389 and Colorado City provide access; check with the BLM for trailhead directions.

Grand Wash Cliffs Wilderness

Grand Wash Cliffs mark the west edge of the Colorado Plateau and the end of the Grand Canyon. The wilderness protects 36,300 acres along a 12-mile section of the cliffs in an extremely remote portion of Arizona. Desert bighorn sheep and raptors live in the high country; desert tortoises forage lower down. **Grand Wash Bench Trail,** a 10-mile gated road, follows a bench between the upper (1,800 feet high) and lower (1,600 feet high) cliffs; trailheads are on the north and south wilderness boundaries.

Hikers can also head out cross-country to the cliffs from BLM Road 1061 along the west boundary of the wilderness.

An exceptionally scenic 4WD road through Hidden Canyon crosses the Grand Wash Cliffs north of the wilderness. To reach the east end of this drive, follow Parashant Road (#103) southwest 16.6 miles from County 5 (turnoff is 11.5 miles north of Mt. Trumbull Schoolhouse and 46 miles south of St. George), then turn right on BLM Road 1003 at the sign for Hidden Canyon. Small canyon cliffs appear four miles in, then become higher and higher as the road winds downstream along the canyon floor, repeatedly crisscrossing the normally dry streambed. Juniper and pinyon pine on the Shivwits Plateau in the upper canyon give way to Joshua trees in the desert country below. After about 20 miles, you leave the canyons. BLM Road 1061 turns south for the west face of the Grand Wash Cliffs Wilderness and you can continue on BLM Road 1003 for Grand Wash Bay of Lake Mead. Other roads turn north to the Virgin Mountains. Numerous sandy washes require a high-clearance 4WD vehicle for Hidden Canyon and for most roads in the Grand Wash Cliffs area.

Mount Dellenbaugh

This small volcano atop the Shivwits Plateau offers a great panorama of the Arizona Strip. Vast forests of juniper and pinyon and ponderosa pine spread across the plateau. A long line of cliffs marks the Grand Canyon to the south. Beyond rise the Hualapai Mountains near Kingman. You can see other mountain ranges in Arizona, Nevada, and Utah as well. Frederick Dellenbaugh served as artist and assistant topographer on Major John Wesley Powell's second river expedition through the Grand Canyon in 1871–72.

From Mt. Trumbull Schoolhouse, go north 11.5 miles on County 5, then turn southwest 42 miles on Parashant Road (#103), following signs. Note that this road is *not* the one into Parashant Canyon. From St. George, Utah, it's 46 miles to the junction, then 42 miles to Mt. Dellenbaugh. The last five miles can be negotiated only when dry; high-clearance vehicles are recommended. The trailhead lies just past the BLM's

Shivwits Ranger Station; follow an old jeep road, now closed to motor vehicles. The trail is an easy four miles roundtrip, climbing 900 feet to the 7,072-foot summit.

Twin Point

Beautiful views from this overlook take in the lower Grand Canyon, Surprise Canyon, Burnt Canyon, and Sanup Plateau. Follow Parashant Road 103 south 37 miles, keep straight where the road to Mt. Dellenbaugh turns left, and continue south another 14 miles. You'll pass Parashant Field Station on the left two miles beyond the Mt. Dellenbaugh turnoff. Ponderosa pine gives way to juniper and pinyon pine as you near the point. At a fork three miles past the field station, you can detour right one mile to an overlook of upper Burnt Canyon, perhaps named for the colorful yellow and red rock layers. The main road continues south 2.7 miles, then skirts the west rim of Burnt Canyon, offering many fine views. Just before the road ends, it forks left for Twin Point and right for a trailhead to Sanup Plateau. Ranchers run cattle down this trail for winter grazing. Twin Point offers plenty of places to camp, and no permit is needed.

Kelly Point

Located east of Twin Point, this point extends much farther south than any other on the North Rim. Road conditions have so deteriorated that the route is now extremely rough, rocky, and slow—figure 5 m.p.h. on the last 20 miles. Getting here can be more an expedition than a casual sightseeing jaunt—Twin Point has similar views without the hardships for you and your vehicle. If you're determined and well prepared, follow Parashant Road (#103) past Mt. Dellenbaugh and continue south to road's end.

Whitmore Point

Spectacular views of the Grand Canyon, Parashant Canyon, Mt. Logan, and the Uinkaret Mountains greet those who head out to this 5,500-foot-high perch. Volcanoes and massive lava flows between here and the Toroweap area to the east can be seen clearly. There are plenty of good places to camp, with no permit needed.

From Mt. Trumbull Schoolhouse, head west then south 22.2 miles on BLM Road 1063. Some junctions feature signs, but you'll need to refer frequently to a map. At 9.9 miles in, a jeep road to the right heads down Trail Canyon to Parashant Canyon, a good area for adventurous hikers. Continue straight (south) for Whitmore Point. As with most roads on the Arizona Strip, conditions get rougher as you move closer to the Grand Canyon; a high-clearance vehicle is necessary. Whitmore Point and other areas north of the western Grand Canyon are the responsibility of the Lake Mead National Recreation Area; the agency could improve its road maintenance and signing efforts, as you'll see.

Whitmore Wash Road

Lava flows from Mt. Emma in the Uinkaret Mountains enable you to drive a high-clearance, 4WD vehicle deep into the Grand Canyon, though the last part of the drive is very rough. A short trail at road's end leads down to the Colorado River. See **Whitmore Wash Trail** for directions and hiking information.

Bar 10 Ranch, 435/628-4010, 800/582-4139, lies along this road 80 miles from St. George and about nine miles before the rim. It offers miles of open country, cowboy-style meals, and an informal Western atmosphere. Activities include horseback riding, pack trips, hiking, scenic flights, river trips, ATV tours, and entertainment. Many visitors spend a day here when shuttling in or out from a river trip by helicopter and flying by small plane to Las Vegas or other destinations. You can also drive (high-clearance vehicles recommended) or fly in. Make the required reservations with Bar 10, which stays open all year, at P.O. Box 910088, St. George, UT 84791, www.bar10.com.

Mt. Trumbull School

Homesteaders arrived in this remote valley about 1917 to farm and raise livestock. Population peaked at 200–250 in the 1930s, when a drier climate forced residents to switch their livelihood from crops to cattle and sheep. People gradually drifted away until the last full-time resident departed in 1984. Abandoned houses stand empty, along with some houses that are inhabited seasonally. No trespassing is allowed on private lands, but you can get some good photos from the main roads. Dedicated teachers taught at the remote one-room schoolhouse from 1922 until the bell rang for its last class in 1968. The school recently burned, but volunteers have rebuilt it; photo and document exhibits that show what life was like here. Donations are appreciated.

Mount Trumbull Wilderness

Forests cover the basalt-rock slopes of Mt. Trumbull (8,028 feet), the centerpiece of this 7,900-acre wilderness. Oak, pinyon pine, and juniper woodlands grow on the lower slopes; ponderosa pine, Gambel oak, and some aspen cover the higher and more protected areas. Kaibab squirrels, introduced in the early 1970s, flourish in the forests. You might see or hear a turkey, too. The 5.4-mile roundtrip climb to the summit makes an enjoyable forest ramble with some views through the trees. From the marked trailhead at an elevation of 6,500 feet on the southwest side of Mt. Trumbull, the wide path climbs around to the south side, with some good views across Toroweap Valley, the Grand Canyon, and the San Francisco Peaks. The trail then turns north and becomes faint, but cairns show the way to the summit, marked by a survey tower and some viewpoints. You can reach the trailhead by County Road 5 from Toroweap, Fredonia, Colorado City, or St. George; you'll know that you're close when ponderosa pines appear. The buildings and trailers across the field belong to a BLM site; if staff are in, they may be able to help with local information.

Mormon pioneers built a steam-powered sawmill just west of the trailhead in 1870 to supply timbers for the St. George Temple. A historic marker tells about the sawmill operation and you can explore the site for the scant remnants. Water from Nixon Spring, higher on the slopes, once supplied the sawmill. A faucet near the road between the historic site and trailhead usually has water from the spring—a handy resource for travelers in this arid land. Mount Trumbull and nearby Mt. Logan lie northwest of the Toroweap area of the Grand Canyon. John Wesley Powell named both peaks after U.S. senators.

Mount Logan Wilderness

Scenic features of this 14,600-acre volcanic region include Mt. Logan (7,866 feet), other parts of the Uinkaret Mountains, and a large natural amphitheater known as Hell's Hole. Geology, forests, and wildlife resemble those of Mt. Trumbull, a short distance to the northeast. A road climbs the east side of Mt. Logan to within a half mile of the summit; the rest of the way is an easy walk—just continue north along the side of the ridge. On top you can peer into the vast depths of Hell's Hole, a steep canyon of red and white rock. The sweeping panorama takes in much of the Arizona Strip and beyond to mountains in Nevada and Utah. Trees block views to the south.

From County 5, just southeast of the Mt. Trumbull trailhead, turn southwest 4.2 miles on BLM Road 1044, then right 2.2 miles on BLM Road 1064 until it becomes rough and steep at its end. Many fine spots in the ponderosa pines suitable for camping line the roads in.

A rough 4WD road follows a corridor through the wilderness, from which hikers can turn south onto the old Slide Mountain Road (closed to vehicles) or enter Hell's Hole from below. You'll need to follow a map closely as none of these destinations will be signed; roads also branch off to other unsigned areas, adding to the navigational challenge. Loose rock and erosion of the corridor road require a high-clearance 4WD; it's slow going, but the road continues all the way down to the Whitmore Wash Road (#1045), one mile north of the Bar 10 Ranch.

Nampaweap Rock Art Site

Archaic, ancestral Puebloan, and Paiute tribes have pecked thousands of glyphs into boulders near Mt. Trumbull. Nampaweap means "foot canyon" in Paiute, perhaps referring to it being on a travel corridor dating back to prehistoric times. From the Mt. Trumbull Trailhead, go east 3.5 miles on County Road 5 (or west 3.7 miles from the junction with Toroweap Rd.), turn south 1.1 miles on BLM Road 1028 toward the private Arkansas Ranch, turn east into the parking area,

© BILL WEIR

Nampaweap Rock Art Site

and then walk three-quarters of a mile to the head of a small canyon. The rock art is on the canyon's north side.

Kanab Point

A great expanse of canyon falls away below your feet from this perch overlooking the confluence of the Kanab and Grand Canyons. Few people know about this lonely spot, yet it's one of the best Grand Canyon viewpoints. The drive out takes some care with navigation as not all the junctions may be signed. You'll need the BLM's Arizona Strip Field Office Visitor Map, a high-clearance vehicle, and dry weather. The turnoff on County 109 is 34 miles north of Toroweap and 34 miles southwest of Fredonia. Head east on BLM Road 1058, keep right at a fork 7.5 miles in, turn right on a fork 10.1 miles in (the wider left fork goes to an uranium mine), turn left at a T-junction 16.4 miles in and continue 0.8 mile to the national park boundary; you'll reach Kanab Point in another 4.0 miles, for a total of 21.2 miles one way from County 109. At the rim, the best panoramas of the Grand Canyon are 0.2 mile to the right and the best ones of Kanab Canyon lie 0.3 mile to the left.

Hack Canyon

This tributary of Kanab Canyon offers both great scenery—you'll feel like you're in the Grand Canyon—and access to the Kanab Creek Wilderness. The road gets rough in the last few miles where 4WD will be handy. The turnoff from County 109 is 4.7 miles north of the Kanab Point junction, or 38 miles north of Toroweap and 30 miles southwest of Fredonia. Head east on BLM Road 1123 and you'll see the headwall of Hack Canyon on the left after 1.1 miles. The road drops in and follows the normally dry canyon bottom with ever higher and grander walls on each side. You'll reach the wilderness boundary and road's end at 9.7 miles from County 109. A trail continues into the wilderness toward Kanab Canyon, five miles one way, where you could turn downstream another 10.5 miles to the mouth of Jumpup Canyon or 16 miles to the Colorado River; a backcountry permit is needed to camp below Jumpup Canyon. Black Willow Spring, a short distance down the trail on your right in Hack Canyon, is a rare source of water here.

PIPE SPRING NATIONAL MONUMENT

Excellent exhibits in Winsor Castle, an early Mormon ranch southwest of Fredonia, provide a look into frontier life. The abundant spring water here first attracted prehistoric Basket Maker and Pueblo tribes, who settled nearby more than 1,000 years ago, then moved on. Paiute, who

Arizona's first telegraph office opened in 1871 at what is today Pipe Spring National Monument. Deemed "a memorial of Western pioneer life" by President Harding in 1923, Pipe Spring still shows evidence of its frontier spirit— the National Park Service maintains the ranch much as it was in the 1870s, complete with weaving, quilting, butterchurning, and cheesemaking activities.

believe they're related to these people, arrived more recently and now live on the surrounding Kaibab-Paiute Indian Reservation; in earlier times, they spent summers on the Kaibab Plateau and winters near Pipe Spring.

Mormons found the spring in 1858 and began ranching five years later, despite Navajo raiders who occasionally stole stock and were suspected of having killed two Mormon men who pursued them. Raids ended after 1870 when Mormons and Navajo signed a treaty. Mormon leader Brigham Young then decided to move the church's southern Utah cattle herd to Pipe Spring. A pair of two-story stone houses went up with walls connecting the ends to form a protected courtyard; workers added gun ports just in case, but the settlement was never attacked.

The structure became known as Winsor Castle—the ranch superintendent, Anson P. Winsor, possessed a regal bearing and was thought to be related to the English royal family. Winsor built up a sizable herd of cattle and horses and oversaw farming and the ranch dairy.

A telegraph office—the first in Arizona—opened in 1871, bringing the rest of the world closer. Eventually, so many newlyweds passed through after marriage in the St. George Temple that the route became known as the Honeymoon Trail. In the 1880s, the Mormon Church came under increasing assault from the U.S. government, primarily over the practice of polygamy. Fearing the feds would soon seize church property, the church sold Winsor Castle to a non-Mormon in 1895.

President Harding proclaimed Pipe Spring a national monument in 1923 "as a memorial of Western pioneer life." Today, National Park Service staff keep the frontier spirit alive by maintaining the ranch much as it was in the 1870s. Activities such as gardening, weaving, spinning,

the parlor in Winsor Castle

quilt-making, cheese-making, and butter-churning still take place, albeit on a smaller scale. You can also see a traditional Paiute shelter *(wickiup)* and demonstrations of Paiute food and crafts. At times a cowboy or a Paiute speaker tells of life on the Arizona Strip. Short guided tours of Winsor Castle relate how people lived here in the early days, and you can explore the outbuildings and gardens on your own. The half-mile-loop Rim Trail climbs the small ridge behind the ranch to a viewpoint, where signs describe the history and geology of the area. Paiute guides offer a walking tour to a nearby rock art site for a fee; call ahead to the tribal office, 928/643-7245, open weekdays.

Visitor Center

Historic exhibits are open daily 8 A.M.–5 P.M. year-round with extended hours in summer; $3 per person admission (16 and under free); 928/643-7105; www.nps.gov/pisp. A short

video, photo exhibits, and historic artifacts introduce the monument. Demonstrations, talks, and walks take place mainly in summer. Produce from the garden is oftentimes given away. A gift shop has a good selection of regional books, maps, and Southwestern Native American arts and crafts. Hikers may be able to obtain last-minute backcountry permits for the Grand Canyon National Park, a useful service for some North Rim destinations. Pipe Spring National Monument lies north off AZ 389, 14 miles southwest of Fredonia.

The Paiute tribe operates a **campground** one quarter mile northeast of the monument. It has showers and is open all year at a bargain-priced $5 tent or $10 RV with hookups; non-campers can use the showers for $3; 928/643-7245 (tribal office). There's a gas station/convenience store at the highway turnoff. Colorado City and Fredonia also offer gas and grocery stores. The nearest restaurants and motels are in Fredonia, but Kanab has more extensive services, including supermarkets.

FREDONIA TO MARBLE CANYON ON US 89A
Fredonia

Though just a tiny town, Fredonia (pop. 1,220) is the largest community on the Arizona Strip. Mormon polygamists, seeking refuge from federal agents, settled here in 1885. They first called the place Hardscrabble but later chose the name Fredonia, perhaps a contraction of the words "freedom" and "doña" (Spanish for wife).

The town's modest places to stay, listed north to south, lie along Main St. (US 89A). **Grand Canyon Motel,** 175 S. Main St., 928/643-7646, offers a choice of motel rooms at $32.50–38 d and hotel rooms at $27.50–32.50 with no extra charge for tax or kitchenettes. **Ship Rock Motel,** 337 S. Main St., 928/643-7355, is $30–37 d; it closes in winter. **Blue Sage Motel and RV,** across the highway at 330 S. Main St., 928/643-7125, runs $35–45 d, $15 RV with hookups; the motel closes in winter. **Crazy Jug Motel,** 465 S. Main St., 928/643-7752; costs $35–45 d. The town of Kanab, seven miles north, offers a much larger selection of accommodations (including a hostel), restaurants, shopping, and recreation.

For Mexican and American food, dine at **Nedra's Cafe,** 165 N. Main St., 928/643-7591, open daily for breakfast, lunch, and dinner in summer, then closed Mon. the rest of the year. **Crazy Jug Restaurant,** next to the motel at 465 S. Main St., 928/643-7712, has American food daily for breakfast, lunch and dinner. A couple of convenience stores offer groceries in town.

The **post office** is downtown at 85 N. Main Street. A **city park** offers picnic tables and playground on 2nd East; turn east three blocks on Brown or Hortt from Main Street. The **public library,** 130 N. Main St., 928/643-7137, has reading and Internet computers downtown; closed Sunday.

Fredonia is building a **welcome center** at the north end of town to offer information about local services and area attractions; 928/643-7241 (town office).

Folks at the **North Kaibab Ranger District** office, 430 S. Main St. (P.O. Box 248, Fredonia, AZ 86022), 928/643-7395, will tell you about hiking, Grand Canyon viewpoints, and the back roads of the national forest north of the Grand Canyon. The Kaibab National Forest map (North Kaibab Ranger District) sold here is a must for exploring the Kaibab Plateau. Hours run Mon.–Fri. 8 A.M.–5 P.M. and you can pick up information at other times inside the vestibule; www.fs.fed.us/r3/kai.

Jacob Lake

High in the pine forests at an elevation of 7,925 feet, this tiny village is on US 89A at the AZ 67 turnoff for the Grand Canyon North Rim. The nearby lake honors Mormon missionary and explorer Jacob Hamblin. A **1910 forest cabin** that overlooks the lake has been restored and opened to visitors; from US 89A, head south 0.3 mile on AZ 67, turn right 0.6 mile, then go south 0.2 mile on Forest Road 282; check hours at the Kaibab Plateau Visitor Center. **Jacob Lake Lookout** offers views of plateaus and mountains in Utah to the north; it's one mile south on AZ 67, between Mileposts 580 and 581, from US 89A. **Dry Park Lookout** features great views from a

125-foot tower southwest of Jacob Lake. These and other lookouts, all shown on the Kaibab National Forest map, welcome visitors when they're staffed.

Jacob Lake Inn, 928/643-7232, stays open all year with basic motel rooms ($90–92 d to $98–105 four persons), cabins (April to November only, $72–118), restaurant (American food daily for breakfast, lunch, and dinner), grocery store, Native American crafts shop, and service station; www.jacoblake.com.

Jacob Lake Campground, 928/643-7770, offers sites in the ponderosa pines with drinking water but no hookups or showers from mid-May to mid-Oct. at $12 per night; there's usually room. Campers can enjoy summer interpretive programs and nearby hiking trails. Groups (only) can reserve sites with Recreation Resource Management at 928/204-1698. It's on the north side of US 89A just west of the AZ 67 turnoff.

Jacob Lake Picnic Area is on the left 0.1 mile south on AZ 67.

Kaibab Camper Village overlooks the lake just 0.3 mile south on AZ 67 from US 89A, then west 0.7 mile; it's open May 15–Oct. 15 and has coin showers and a modem jack. Tent spaces and dry RV sites run $12 and sites with hookups cost $22; 928/643-7804, 800/525-0924 (reservations). Tent sites are usually available, though RVers should make reservations or arrive by noon.

Allen's Outfitters offers trail rides of one and two hours in the forest, half- and full-day trips to overlooks, and pack trips from about mid-May to early September at its stables 0.3 mile south on AZ 67 and year-round in Kanab; 435/644-8150, 435/689-1370.

Staff at the Forest Service's **Kaibab Plateau Visitor Center,** 928/643-7298, in Jacob Lake provide information on the many viewpoints, trails, campgrounds, and historic sites in the Kaibab National Forest along the North Rim; they also issue backcountry permits for most areas of Grand Canyon National Park. Exhibits include a 3-D model of the Grand Canyon and wildlife displays. You can purchase books and maps. It's open daily 8 A.M.–5 P.M. from about mid-May to mid-Oct. and possibly later in the year with a shorter schedule; www.fs.fed.us/r3/kai.

Vermilion Cliffs

These sheer cliffs, a striking red, appear to burst into flames at sunrise and sunset. The cliffs dominate the northern horizon for many miles; a hilltop pullout 11 miles east of Jacob Lake on US 89A offers the best view. John Wesley Powell described them as "a long bank of purple cliffs plowed from the horizon high into the heavens."

San Bartolome Historic Site

Markers tell the story of the Dominguez-Escalante Expedition, which camped near here in 1776. Returning from a failed attempt to reach Monterey, California, the group struggled to find a route through the forbidding terrain to Santa Fe. The site is signed on the north side of US 89A between Mileposts 557 and 558, about midway between Marble Canyon and Jacob Lake.

Cliff Dweller's Lodge

About 1890, White traders built an unusual trading post underneath a giant boulder. You can still see the old buildings beside the modern establishment. The lodge, 928/355-2228, 800/433-2543, offers rooms ($60 d and $72 d, less in winter), restaurant (American food for breakfast, lunch, and dinner), small store, and a gas station. It's on US 89A, nine miles west of Marble Canyon and 32 miles east of Jacob Lake.

Lee's Ferry Anglers Guides & Fly Shop, 928/355-2261, 800/962-9755, has guides and supplies for fishermen; www.leesferry.com.

Lees Ferry Lodge (Vermilion Cliffs)

The lodge, 928/355-2231, has motel rooms ($45 s, $50 d) and a smoky restaurant (American food for breakfast, lunch, and dinner daily). It's on US 89A, three miles west of Marble Canyon and 38 miles east of Jacob Lake; www.leesferrylodge.com.

Badger Canyon-Marble Canyon Overlook

A dirt road leads to the edge of precipitous cliffs where these two canyons meet. The cold waters of

the heart of Marble Canyon

THE EXPLORATION OF THE COLORADO RIVER AND IT'S CANYONS

the Colorado glide below. You may see river runners bouncing through Badger Creek Rapid or camped on the shore. Jackass Canyon meets Marble Canyon on the opposite side. There's no sign for the turnoff on US 89A, but it's on the left just 0.1 mile southwest (toward Jacob Lake) from Lees Ferry Lodge. Go through a gate and continue two miles to road's end. On the way you'll have views of Badger Canyon. Endangered cacti live here, so keep to the existing road and pullouts when driving or camping.

Marble Canyon Lodge

Major John Wesley Powell named the nearby section of Colorado River canyon for its smooth, marblelike appearance. The lodge, 928/355-2225, 800/726-1789, is on US 89A at the turnoff for Lees Ferry. You can stay in motel rooms ($54 s, $64–70 d), a cottage ($86 with four beds), and two-bedroom apartments ($134). Other amenities are a smoky restaurant (American food for breakfast, lunch, and dinner daily), store (Native American crafts, regional books, and supplies for camping, river-running, and fishing), post office, Laundromat, coin showers, gas station, convenience store, and paved airstrip.

Marble Canyon Outfitters, 928/355-2245, 800/533-7339, offers guided trips and a shop for fishermen; www.leesferryflyfishing.com.

LEES FERRY

The Colorado River cuts one gorge after another as it crosses the high plateaus of southern Utah and northern Arizona. Settlers and travelers found the river a dangerous and difficult barrier until well into the 20th century. A break in the cliffs above Marble Canyon provided one of the few places where a road could be built to the water's edge. Until 1929, when Navajo Bridge finally spanned the canyon, vehicles and passengers had to cross by ferry. Zane Grey expressed his thoughts about this crossing—Lees Ferry—in *The Last of the Plainsmen* (1908):

> *I saw the constricted rapids, where the Colorado took its plunge into the box-like head of the Grand Canyon of Arizona; and the deep, reverberating boom of the river, at flood height, was a fearful thing to hear. I could not repress a shudder at the thought of crossing above that rapid.*

The Dominguez-Escalante Expedition tried to cross at what's now known as Lees Ferry in 1776, but without success. The river proved too cold and wide to swim safely, and winds frustrated attempts to raft across. The Spaniards traveled 40 miles upriver into present-day Utah before finding a safe ford.

About 100 years later, Mormon leaders determined the Lees Ferry crossing to be the most convenient route for expanding Mormon settlements from Utah into Arizona. Jacob Hamblin led a failed rafting attempt in 1860, but he returned four years later and made it safely across.

Although Hamblin first recognized the value of this crossing, it now bears the name of John D. Lee, a colorful character who gained notoriety in the 1857 Mountain Meadows Massacre. One account of this unfortunate chain of events relates that Paiute, allied to the Mormons, attacked an unfriendly wagon train; Lee and fellow Mormons then joined in the fighting until all but the small children, too young to tell the story, lay dead.

When a federal investigation some years later uncovered Mormon complicity in the slaughter, the Mormon Church leaders, seeking to move Lee out of sight, asked him to start a regular ferry service on the Colorado River. This he did in 1872. One of Lee's wives remarked on seeing the isolated spot, "Oh, what a lonely dell," and thus Lonely Dell became the name of their ranch. Lee managed to succeed with the ferry service despite boat accidents and sometimes hostile Navajo, but eventually his past caught up with him. In 1877, authorities took Lee back to Mountain Meadows, where a firing squad and casket awaited.

Miners and farmers came to try their luck along the Colorado River and its tributaries. Charles Spencer, manager of the American Placer Company, brought in sluicing machinery, an amalgamator, and drilling equipment. In 1910 his company tried using mule trains to pack coal from Warm Creek Canyon, 15 miles upstream. When the mules proved inadequate, company financiers shipped a 92-foot-long steamboat in sections from San Francisco. The boat, the *Charles H. Spencer,* performed poorly, burning almost its entire load of coal in just one roundtrip, and was used only five times. The boiler, decking, and hull can still be seen at low water on the shore upstream from Lees Ferry Fort (see below). Although Spencer's efforts to extract fine gold particles proved futile, he persisted in his prospecting here as late as 1965 and made an unsuccessful attempt to develop a rhenium mine.

The ferry service continued after Lee's departure, though fatal accidents occurred from time to time. The last run took place in June 1928, while the bridge was going up six miles downstream. The ferry operator lost control in strong currents and the boat capsized; all three people aboard and a Model-T were lost. Fifty-five years

ARIZONA STRIP

NAVAJO BRIDGE—THE OLD AND THE NEW

Anew, wider bridge for traffic has replaced the old Navajo Bridge across Marble Canyon. The old bridge, admired for its design and beauty, has been preserved as a pedestrian path just upstream from the new one. Now you can enjoy a walk 470 feet above the water on the old bridge's 834-foot length. (Do not throw anything off the bridge, as even a small object can pick up lethal velocity from such a height and hurt boaters below.) A 1930s stone shelter built by the Civilian Conservation Corps and a new visitor center stand just west of the bridges. Indoor and outdoor exhibits illustrate the history and construction details of both structures. You'll find local travel information for the Grand Canyon and Glen Canyon National Recreation Area and a large selection of books, maps, videos, music (Native American and Southwest), and posters in the Navajo Bridge Interpretive Center; it's open daily 8 A.M.–5 P.M. from mid-April to mid-November. Navajo sell crafts on the old bridge's east end. Both ends of the old bridge have parking.

of ferryboating had come to an end. Navajo Bridge opened in January 1929, an event hailed by the Flagstaff *Coconino Sun* as the "Biggest News in Southwest History."

Today, the Lees Ferry area and the canyon upstream belong to the Glen Canyon National Recreation Area. Grand Canyon National Park begins just downstream. Rangers of the National Park Service administer both areas.

Lonely Dell Ranch and Lees Ferry

You can tour old buildings, mining machinery, the ferry site, and trails in these two historic districts. A self-guided tour booklet, available on site as well as at the Carl Hayden Visitor Center at Glen Canyon Dam, identifies historic features and traces their backgrounds. A log cabin thought to have been built by Lee, root cellar, blacksmith shop, ranch house, orchards, and cemetery survive at Lonely Dell Ranch, a short distance up the Paria River.

Historic buildings on the Colorado River include Lees Ferry Fort (built in 1874 to protect settlers from possible Indian attack, but used as a trading post and residence), a small stone post office (in use 1913–23), and structures occupied by the American Placer Company and the U.S. Geological Survey. A trail along the Colorado leads about one mile upstream to the main ferry site, now marked by ruins of ferrymen's stone houses. On the way you'll pass the partially submerged wreck of Spencer's steamboat.

A paved road to Lees Ferry turns north from US 89A just west of Navajo Bridge. Follow the road in 5.1 miles and turn left 0.2 mile for Lonely Dell Ranch Historic District or continue 0.7 mile on the main road to its end for Lees Ferry Historic District. The **ranger station** offers boating, fishing, and hiking information and sells some books and maps but is open irregular hours; it's on the left 0.4 mile after the campground turnoff; 928/355-2234.

Entry fees for Glen Canyon National Recreation Area, which can be paid at a self-service station half a mile in from US 89A, cost $10 per vehicle or $3 per cyclist or hiker for seven days; admission is free if you have a National Parks Pass, Golden Eagle, Golden Age, or Golden Access card.

Spencer Trail

Energetic hikers climb this unmaintained trail for fine views of Marble Canyon from the rim 1,500 feet above the river. The ingeniously planned route switchbacks up sheer ledges above Lees Ferry. It's a moderately difficult hike to the top, three miles roundtrip; you should carry water. From Lees Ferry parking lot at the end of the road, follow the path through the historic district to the sign, then take the trail leading to the cliffs.

Cathedral Wash Route

This 2.5-mile roundtrip hike follows a narrow canyon to Cathedral Rapid and back. Park at the second pullout, overlooking the wash, on the road to Lees Ferry, 1.4 miles in from US 89A and three miles before the campground.

Boating and Fishing

Rainbow trout flourish in the cold, clear waters released from Lake Powell through Glen Canyon Dam. Special fishing regulations apply here and are posted. Anglers should be able to identify and must return to the river any of the endangered native fish—the Colorado pikeminnow, bonytail chub, humpback chub, and razorback sucker. There's a fish-cleaning station and parking area on the left just before the launch areas. At road's end, you'll reach a paved upriver launch site used by boaters headed toward Glen Canyon Dam; Grand Canyon river-running groups use the unpaved downriver launch area. Powerboats can travel 14.5 miles up Glen Canyon almost to the dam. The Park Service recommends a boat with a minimum 10-hp motor to negotiate the swift currents. Boating below Lees Ferry is prohibited without a permit from Grand Canyon National Park.

Campground

The $10 sites at Lees Ferry Campground have drinking water but no hookups or showers; there's usually space available. Campers can use showers and laundry facilities beside Marble Canyon Lodge. From US 89A, take Lees Ferry Road in 4.4 miles and turn left at the sign. A dump station is on the right on the main road, 0.4 mile past the campground turnoff. The National Park Service allows boat camping on the Colorado River above Lees Ferry only at the plentiful developed campsites. These sites lack piped water but are free. Remember to purify river water before drinking and pack out what you pack in.

PARIA CANYON—VERMILION CLIFFS WILDERNESS

The wild and twisting canyons of the Paria River and its tributaries offer a memorable adventure for experienced hikers. Silt-laden waters have sculpted the colorful canyon walls, revealing 200 million years of geologic history. You enter the 2,000-foot-deep gorge of the Paria in southern Utah, then hike 38 miles downstream to Lees Ferry in Arizona, where the Paria empties into the Colorado River. Besides the canyons, this 110,000-acre wilderness area protects colorful cliffs, giant natural amphitheaters, sandstone arches, and parts of the Paria Plateau. On top of the plateau, wonderful swirling patterns in sandstone hills, known as the "Coyote Buttes," enthrall visitors. The 1,000-foot-high, rosy-hued Vermilion Cliffs meet the mouth of Paria Canyon at Lees Ferry. The river's name, sometimes spelled Pahreah, is Paiute for "muddy water."

History

Ancient petroglyphs and campsites indicate that ancestral Puebloan people traveled the Paria more than 700 years ago. They hunted mule deer and bighorn sheep while using the broad lower end of the canyon to grow corn, beans, and squash.

The Dominguez-Escalante Expedition, the first White people to see the Paria, stopped at its mouth in 1776. After John Lee began his Colorado River ferry service in 1872, he and others farmed the lower Paria Canyon. Though outlaws used it and prospectors came in search of gold, uranium, and other minerals, much of the Paria Canyon remained little visited.

In the late 1960s, the Bureau of Land Management (BLM) organized a small expedition whose research led to protection of the canyon as a primitive area. The Arizona Wilderness Act in 1984 designated Paria Canyon a wilderness, together with parts of the Paria Plateau and Vermilion Cliffs. In 2000, the Arizona portion of the wilderness and surrounding lands became the 294,000-acre Vermilion Cliffs National Monument.

Hiking

You can hike Paria Canyon in four days, though it's better to have five or six because there are many river crossings, and you'll want to take side trips up some of the tributary canyons. The hike is considered moderately difficult. Hikers should have enough backpacking experience to be self-sufficient, as help may lie days away. Flash floods can race through the canyon, especially from July to September. Rangers will advise if they think danger exists, but they no longer close the canyon when storms threaten. The upper end

the Narrows inside Paria Canyon

You can draw good drinking water from springs along the way—see the BLM's book noted below. It's best not to use river water because of possible chemical pollution from farms and ranches upstream. Normally the river flows only ankle deep, but can rise to waist-deep levels in the spring or after rainy spells. During thunderstorms, the river can roar up to 20 feet deep in the Paria Narrows, so heed weather warnings. Floods usually subside within 12 hours. Quicksand, most prevalent after flooding, is more a nuisance than a danger—rarely more than knee deep. Many hikers carry a walking stick for probing the opaque waters before crossing. Conditions can change dramatically after a flood, especially in the narrow sections of Paria, Buckskin, and Wire Pass canyons, so it's best to get the latest advice from BLM staff.

Permits and Information

Backpackers need to apply in advance for a permit that costs $5/person or dog per day. Dayhikers simply pay $5/person or dog at any of the trailheads for a pass that's good for all three canyons—Paria, Buckskin, and Wire Pass. Backpacking permits, Coyote Buttes permits, weather forecasts, and up-to-date information are available from BLM staff at the Paria Information Station, which is in Utah, 30 miles northwest of Page on US 89 near Milepost 21, on the south side of the highway just east of the Paria River. The station is open daily 8:30 A.M.–4:15P.M. (Daylight Savings Time!) about mid-March to mid-Nov. and intermittently the rest of the year. Hikers can get drinking water at a faucet in front and see the current weather forecast. You can check Paria and Coyote Buttes dates by phone and obtain permits by mail by writing **Arizona Strip Interpretive Association,** 345 E. Riverside Dr., St. George, UT 84790; 435/688-3246. Information and permits are also available from the Kanab Area Office, 318 N. 100 East, Kanab, Utah 84741, 435/644-4600, open Mon.–Fri. 7:45 A.M.–4:30 P.M. year-round. An interactive website shows available dates and gives reservation procedures at https://www.az.blm.gov/paria. The BLM's *Hiker's Guide to Paria Canyon* book ($8) has detailed maps and information.

contains narrow passages, particularly between Miles 4.2 and 9.0. Rangers suggest all hikers obtain up-to-date weather information. For safety in case of flood, one should register at White House, Buckskin, Wire Pass, or Lees Ferry Trailheads when entering or exiting the canyons.

All visitors need to take special care to minimize impact on this beautiful canyon. Check the BLM "Visitor Use Regulations" before you go. Rules include no campfires in the Paria and its tributaries, a pack-in/pack-out policy (including toilet paper!), and a latrine location at least 100 feet away from river and campsites. Hiking parties may not exceed 10 people.

The best times to travel along the Paria are mid-March to June and late September to November. May, especially Memorial Day weekend, is the most popular time. Winter hikers often complain of painfully cold feet. Wear shoes suitable for frequent wading; light fabric and leather boots or jungle boots work better than heavy leather hiking boots.

Trailheads and Shuttle Services

Most hikers start from White House Trailhead, which lies two miles south of Paria Information Station on a dirt road near an old homestead site called White House Ruins, of which only rubble remains. You may camp here (pit toilets and picnic tables) for a $5 fee (up to five persons). The exit trailhead is at Lonely Dell Ranch near Lees Ferry, 44 miles southwest of Page via US 89 and 89A; vehicles can be left at the 14-day parking area.

The hike requires a 150-mile roundtrip car shuttle. You can make arrangements for someone else to do it for you, using either your car, or theirs. Staff at the Arizona Strip Interpretive Association, Paria Information Center, or BLM Kanab Resource District can supply you with a list of shuttle services.

Wrather Canyon Arch

One of Arizona's largest natural arches lies about one mile up this side canyon off Paria Canyon. The massive structure has a 200-foot span. Veer right (southwest) at Mile 20.6 on the Paria hike. The mouth of Wrather Canyon, which is easily missed, and other points along the Paria are unsigned; you need to follow your map. No camping is allowed in this canyon.

Buckskin Gulch

This amazing Paria tributary—said to be the world's longest slot canyon—features convoluted walls hundreds of feet high, yet narrows to as little as four feet in width. In some places the walls block out so much light that you'll think you're walking in a cave. Be *very* careful to avoid times of flash floods. Hiking can be strenuous, with rough terrain, deep pools of water, and log and rock jams that sometimes require the use of ropes.

You can descend into Buckskin from two trailheads, Buckskin and Wire Pass, both approached by a dirt road passable for cars in dry weather. The hike from Buckskin trailhead to the Paria River is 16.3 miles one-way and takes 6–8 or more hours. From Wire Pass Trailhead it's 1.7 miles to Buckskin Gulch, then 11.8 miles to the Paria. You can climb out to a safe camping place

on a hazardous route—extremely hazardous if you're not an experienced climber—about halfway down Buckskin Gulch; this way out should not be counted on as an escape route. Carry enough water to last until you reach the mouth of Buckskin Gulch.

Wire Pass and upper Buckskin Canyons make a great day-hike loop—you can follow Buckskin 4.5 miles from its trailhead to the confluence of Wire Pass Canyon, then turn 1.7 miles up Wire Pass; you could then walk, do a car shuttle, or hitch the four miles by road back to Buckskin Trailhead. Only the last mile of Buckskin enters narrows on this loop, but all of this country has pretty scenery. Wire Pass Canyon, which is even narrower in spots than Buckskin, may have some ledges. Look for petroglyphs on the right at the lower end of Wire Pass. Try to allow time for exploration into the narrows below the confluence.

To reach these trailheads, go 4.9 miles west on US 89 from Paria Information Station to the unsigned House Rock Road (Road 700) between Mileposts 25 and 26, then turn south 4.5 miles to Buckskin or another 4 miles for Wire Pass. The Arizona border is just 1.2 miles farther, where you'll find the north end of the Arizona Trail at Stateline Trailhead; a tiny campground (no water) is here too. House Rock Road, signed in Arizona as Road 1065, continues 20 miles south to US 89A between Mileposts 565 and 566, near where the highway begins its climb to the Kaibab Plateau. California condor information panels 2.9 miles before US 89A tell of the birds' release site atop the Vermilion Cliffs nearby; an observer may be stationed here who will answer questions and let you take a look through a telescope.

Coyote Buttes

The secret is out on this colorful swirling sandstone atop the Paria Plateau! You've probably seen photos of these wonderful features, but not directions on how to reach them. The buttes lie mostly in Arizona south of Wire Pass Canyon and have been divided into Coyote North and Coyote South. The famous "Wave" is in the north, so this region is the most popular. Once you get the required permit, BLM staff will give you a map and directions to the Wave, but you're then on your own, as the wilderness lacks signs. Even if you get permits by mail, it's worth dropping by the Paria Information Station for directions. The Wave is about six miles roundtrip and takes half a day, though there's more to see in the area. Photographers will find a wide-angle lens handy to take in the sweep of the curved rock. Both north and south areas have countless beauty spots to discover, so it's worth making a full day of it and carrying food and lots of water.

The BLM issues the required permits for Coyote Buttes, which are day-use only; there's a $5/person fee, and permit procedures are the same as for the Paria River. Permits sell out far ahead in spring and autumn—the best times to visit—and on weekends. If you don't have a permit but your schedule is flexible, try for a walk-in permit—check the procedure with BLM staff or on the website.

Only a small number of people may visit each area per day because the Navajo Sandstone rock here is so fragile. It can break if climbed on—causing damage to both the scenery and hikers' bones—so it's important to stay on existing hiking routes and wear soft-soled footwear. Hikers need to carry water and keep an eye out for rattlesnakes. Lightning storms occur most often in late summer but can appear at any time of year.

Trailhead access is off House Rock Road. You can reach Coyote North from Wire Pass Trailhead or the more difficult Notch Access, about two miles south of Wire Pass Trailhead. Coyote South requires 4WD for Paw Hole Access, 2.6 miles in, and Cottonwood Cove Access farther back; deep sand may make these areas impassable during summer. You could walk in to Paw Hole but it would be a tough slog. BLM staff can advise on road conditions.

The Wave

The Toadstools

An easy hike of about a mile roundtrip leads to these fanciful rock formations. From the Paria Information Station, drive east 1.5 miles on US 89 and look for the unsigned parking on the north side where power lines turn away from the highway between Mileposts 19 and 20. Go through the pedestrian gate and follow footprints up the valley to red and white balanced rocks; more can be seen if you continue around to the left. No permits or fees are required.

Page

Until 1957, only sand and desert vegetation lay atop Manson Mesa in far northern Arizona, where Page now sits. In that year the U.S. Bureau of Reclamation decided to build a giant reservoir in Glen Canyon on the Colorado River. Glen Canyon Dam became one of the largest construction projects ever undertaken: the 710-foot-high structure created a lake covering 250 square miles with a shoreline of nearly 2,000 miles.

The town of Page, named by the Bureau of Reclamation for one of its commissioners, was born when workers set up prefabricated metal buildings for barracks, dining hall, and offices. Trailers rolled in, one serving as a bank, another as a school. Newly planted grass and trees brought a touch of green to the desert. The remote spot (elev. 4,300 ft.) gradually turned into a modern town with schools, businesses, and churches. Though small (pop. 9,500), it's the largest community close to Lake Powell and offers travelers a variety of places to stay and eat.

With the Arizona Strip to the west, Glen Canyon National Recreation Area to the north, and the Navajo Reservation to the east and south, Page makes a useful base for visiting all of these areas. The town overlooks Lake Powell and Glen Canyon Dam. Wahweap Resort and Marina's extensive services lie just six miles away.

SIGHTS AND HIKES

Powell Museum

This collection honors scientist and explorer John Wesley Powell. In 1869 Powell led the first expedition down the Green and Colorado River canyons, then ran the rivers a second time in 1871–72. It was he who named the most splendid section the Grand Canyon.

Old drawings and photographs illustrate Powell's life and voyages. Fossil and mineral displays interpret the thick geologic sections revealed by the canyons of the Colorado River system. Other exhibits contain pottery, baskets, weapons, and tools of Southwestern tribes, as well as memorabilia of early river runners, Page's early days, and Glen Canyon Dam. You can ask to see related videos and purchase regional books as well. Staff offer travel info and can book Lake Powell boat tours, all-day and half-day float trips, Antelope Canyon tours, and scenic flights.

In summer (June–Aug.), the museum is open Mon.–Fri. 8:30 A.M.–5:30 P.M.; spring and autumn hours are Mon.–Fri. 9 A.M.–5 P.M.; it's closed mid-December to mid-February. Admission is $1 adult, $.50 children kindergarten–8th grade. The museum is in downtown Page at the corner of 6 N. Lake Powell Blvd. and N. Navajo Dr., 928/645-9496, 888/597-6873, www.powellmuseum.org.

Navajo Village

Navajo offer cultural programs about their beliefs and traditional skills from April to October at this living museum on the edge of town. **An Evening with the Navajo** begins with demonstrations of cooking, weaving, and silversmithing. Your hosts will also explain features of the sweat lodge and the two types of hogans here. You'll enjoy a dinner of traditional foods, watch song and dance performances, and listen to campfire stories. The four-hour evening presentations cost $50 adults and $35 children 6–13 plus tax. You can also sign up for a shorter evening program or take a guided tour of the exhibits during the day. Call 928/660-0304 for information or check the Web at www.navajovillage.net. The Page/Lake Powell Chamber of Commerce and Powell Museum also sell tickets.

The Best Dam View

An excellent panorama of Glen Canyon Dam and the Colorado River can be enjoyed just west of town. It's reached via Scenic View Road behind Denny's Restaurant off US 89; turn west at the junction of US 89 and N. Lake Powell Blvd. or west beside the Glen Canyon N.R.A. headquarters building and turn at the sign for "scenic overlook." A short trail leads down to the best viewpoint.

ARIZONA STRIP

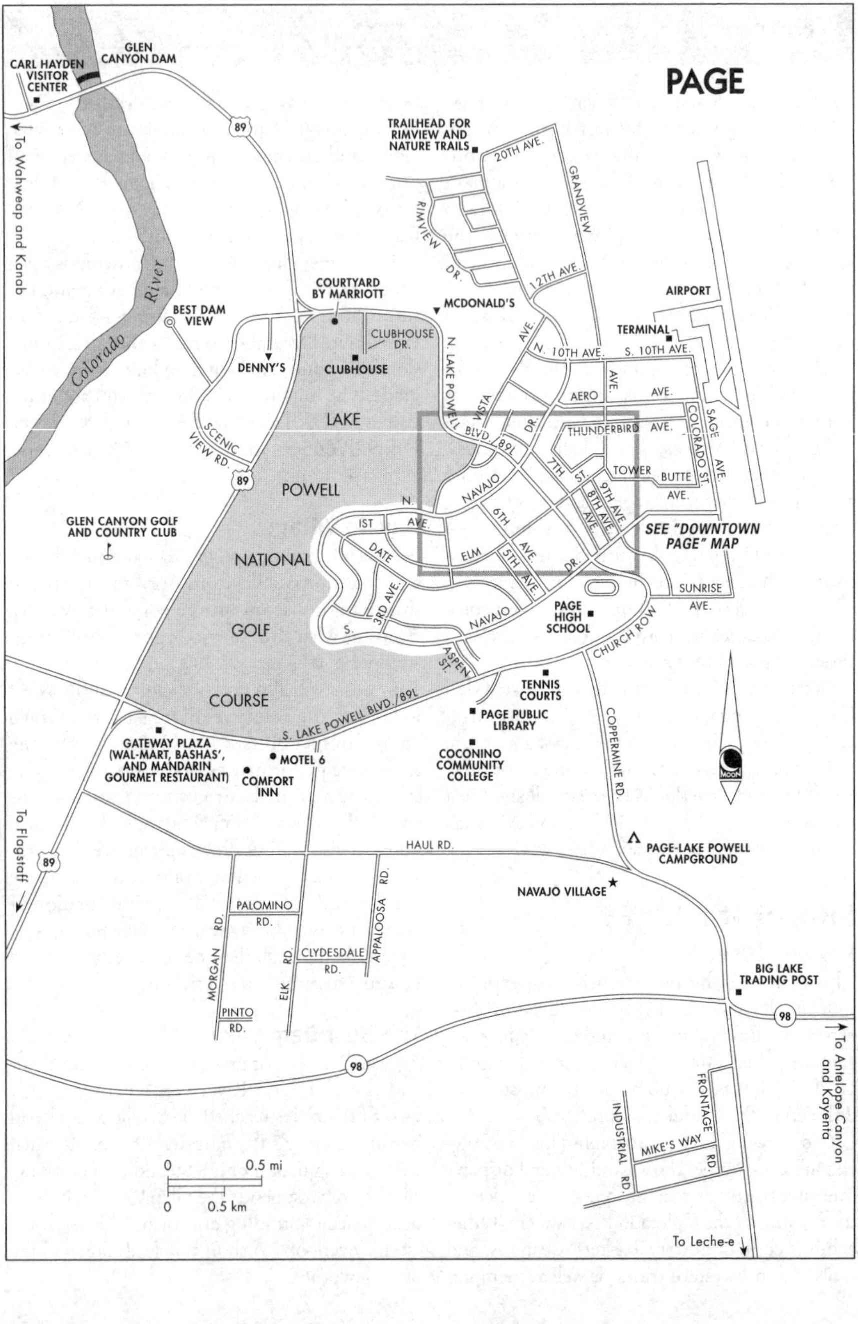

PAGE

CARL HAYDEN VISITOR CENTER

GLEN CANYON DAM

89

To Wahweap and Kanab

Colorado River

GLEN CANYON GOLF AND COUNTRY CLUB

TRAILHEAD FOR RIMVIEW AND NATURE TRAILS

20TH AVE.

GRANDVIEW

12TH AVE.

RIMVIEW DR.

MCDONALD'S

AIRPORT

TERMINAL

N. 10TH AVE.

S. 10TH AVE.

AERO

AVE.

SAGE AVE.

THUNDERBIRD

AVE.

COLORADO ST.

TOWER

BUTTE

AVE.

SEE "DOWNTOWN PAGE" MAP

BEST DAM VIEW

COURTYARD BY MARRIOTT

CLUBHOUSE DR.

DENNY'S

CLUBHOUSE

SCENIC VIEW RD.

89

LAKE

POWELL

NATIONAL

GOLF

COURSE

N. LAKE POWELL BLVD. /89L

VISTA

AVE.

7TH ST.

9TH AVE.

8TH AVE.

N.

NAVAJO

1ST

AVE.

DATE

6TH AVE.

ELM

5TH AVE.

DR.

SUNRISE AVE.

S.

3RD AVE.

NAVAJO

ASPEN ST.

PAGE HIGH SCHOOL

CHURCH ROW

COPPERMINE RD.

MOON

GATEWAY PLAZA (WAL-MART, BASHAS', AND MANDARIN GOURMET RESTAURANT)

MOTEL 6

COMFORT INN

S. LAKE POWELL BLVD. /89L

TENNIS COURTS

PAGE PUBLIC LIBRARY

COCONINO COMMUNITY COLLEGE

To Flagstaff

89

HAUL RD.

PAGE-LAKE POWELL CAMPGROUND

NAVAJO VILLAGE

PALOMINO RD.

MORGAN RD.

CLYDESDALE RD.

APPALOOSA RD.

ELK RD.

PINTO RD.

98

BIG LAKE TRADING POST

98

To Antelope Canyon and Kayenta

INDUSTRIAL RD.

MIKE'S WAY

FRONTAGE RD.

To Leche-e

0   0.5 mi

0   0.5 km

ARIZONA STRIP

© AVALON TRAVEL PUBLISHING, INC.

Rimview Trail

An eight-mile trail for walkers, joggers, and cyclists encircles Page with many views of the surrounding desert and Lake Powell. The unpaved route generally follows the edge of the mesa and has some sandy and rocky sections that will challenge novice bike riders. If you find yourself more than 30 vertical feet below the mesa rim, you're off the trail. You can pick up a map from the chamber office. A popular starting point is at the short nature trail loop near Lake View School at N. Navajo Dr. and 20th Ave. in the northern part of town.

Antelope Canyon

You'll see photos around town of the beautifully convoluted red rock in this canyon, so narrow in places that you have to squeeze through. Sunshine reflects off the smooth Navajo Sandstone to create extraordinary light and colors that entrance visitors. Light beams reach the floor of upper Antelope only at midday from May to August. Photographers, not wishing to spoil the effect of light and shadow in the dark interior with a flash, bring a tripod to help capture the infinite shapes and patterns.

Antelope Canyon has a wider upper section known as "Corkscrew" that's exceptionally user-friendly—it's an easy walk on the sandy floor all the way through. The narrower lower section has ladders and a bit of scrambling. The shallow wash in between that you see from the highway gives no hint of the marvels up or downstream. Both sections can easily be reached from Page by driving south on Coppermine Road or east on AZ 98 to the junction at Big Lake Trading Post, then continuing east one mile on AZ 98 toward the power plant. Turn right into the parking area for the upper canyon, or stay on AZ 98 just 0.15 mile farther and then turn left half a mile on paved Antelope Point Road for the lower canyon. You'll pay $5 for a tribal entry permit—good for both sections—plus shuttle or entry fees. Sightseers can tour either section easily in an hour; photographers will probably wish to spend more time. The upper section has a $12.50 shuttle charge for the 3.5-mile drive to the trailhead and a one-hour visit; no walk-ins or private drive-ins are permitted. The shuttle cost increases to $17.50 for a two-hour visit, $22.50 for 3–4 hours, and $32.50 for all day. The lower canyon can be visited on self-guided walks of $12.50 plus the $5 entry fee. Children pay less. You can also take a guided excursion from Page that costs little more and may be more convenient.

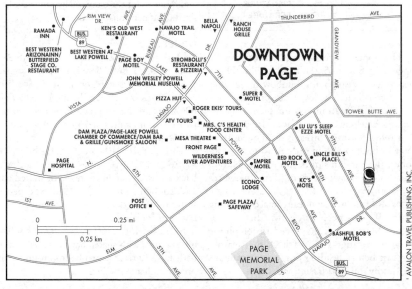

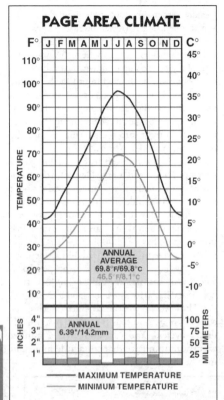

PAGE AREA CLIMATE

ANNUAL
AVERAGE
69.8°F/69.8°C
46.5°F/8.1°C

ANNUAL
6.39"/14.2mm

—— MAXIMUM TEMPERATURE
—— MINIMUM TEMPERATURE

The upper canyon ticket booth is usually open daily 8 A.M.–5 P.M. from April to October; you can also obtain Rainbow Bridge hiking permits here. The lower canyon closes by 4 P.M. For information and off-season access, call the Antelope Canyon Navajo Tribal Park at 928/698-2808; the office is 4 miles south of Page in Leche-e. From early April to late October, the canyon hours run on the Navajo Reservation's daylight saving time (when it's 4 P.M. in Page, it's 5 P.M. at Antelope). Late starts also run the risk of canyon access closing early if business is slow. In winter (Nov.–March) you may need to telephone ahead to arrange a visit. Check the weather forecast before heading out, as slot canyons are deadly during a flash flood.

Horseshoe Bend View

The Colorado River makes a sharp bend below this spectacular viewpoint. Look for the parking area just west of US 89, 0.2 mile south of Milepost 545; it's 2.5 miles south of Page's Gateway Plaza. A three-quarter-mile trail (one way) leads from the parking over a sandy ridge to the overlook. Photographers will find a wide-angle lens handy to take in the whole scene. Mornings have good light for pictures; afternoons can be dramatic if the sky is filled with clouds.

PRACTICALITIES
Accommodations

Nearly all Page motels lie on or near Lake Powell Blvd./Hwy 89L, a 3.25-mile loop that branches off the main highway. Page is a busy place in summer, however, and a call ahead is a good idea if you don't want to chase around town looking for vacancies. Expect to pay top dollar for views of the lake. The summer rates listed here drop in winter (Nov.–March).

The Eighth Ave. places lie in Page's "historic district," a quiet residential area two blocks off Lake Powell Boulevard. These apartments date back to 1958–59 when they housed supervisors and foremen for the dam; today some have been fixed up as pensions and motels.

Under $50

Lu Lu's Sleep EZZe Motel, 105 Eighth Ave., 928/608-0273, 800/553-6211, features some of the most luxurious rooms on this street, $43–59 d.

Red Rock Motel, 114 Eighth Ave., 928/645-0062, has private baths and some kitchens plus two-bedroom suites at $39 s, $49 d and up; www.redrockmotel.com.

Uncle Bill's Place, 117 Eighth Ave., 928/645-1224, provides a quiet garden in back and a choice of rooms with shared bath and kitchen ($30 s, $36–39 d) and private suites ($59–69 d and up); www.canyon-country.com/unclebill.

KC's Motel, 126 Eighth Ave., 928/645-2947, offers rooms with shared bath at $36 d, private bath for $39 d, and two-bedroom units with private bath at $59–79 d.

Bashful Bob's Motel around the corner at 750 S. Navajo Dr., 928/645-3919, offers mostly two-bedroom apartments, all with kitchens, $39–45 d; www.page.az.net/bashfulbobsmotel.

Navajo Trail Motel has rooms at two downtown locations and on the southern outskirts; contact the office for all three places at 800 Bureau downtown, where rooms are $35 s, $39 d; 928/645-9508. The nearby motel at 630 Vista, behind Glen Canyon Steak House, costs $39 s, $44 d; the third unit is at 524 Haul Road, where rooms go for $35 s, $39 d.

$50–100
Courtyard by Marriott, 600 Clubhouse Dr., 928/645-5000, 800/321-2211, offers views, a restaurant, a pool, hot tub, exercise room, and adjacent 18-hole golf course, $94–109 d.

Best Western ArizonaInn, 716 Rim View Dr. and N. Lake Powell Blvd., 928/645-2466, 800/826-2718, provides fine views, swimming pool, adjacent restaurant, and continental breakfast, $89 d.

Best Western at Lake Powell, 208 N. Lake Powell Blvd., 928/645-5988, 800/528-1234, has mountain views, a pool, hot tub, and exercise room, $79–99 d.

Page Boy Motel, 150 N. Lake Powell Blvd., 928/645-2416, offers a swimming pool, $45–49 d.

Empire Motel, 107 S. Lake Powell Blvd., 928/645-2406, 800/551-9005, features a swimming pool, $49 s, $54 d.

Econo Lodge, 121 S. Lake Powell Blvd., 928/645-2488, 800/553-2666, has a pool, $60 d.

Super 8 Motel, is at 75 S. Seventh Ave., 928/645-2858, 800/800-8000, $60 d.

Holiday Inn Express, 751 S. Navajo Dr., 928/645-9000, 800/HOLIDAY, offers two-bedded rooms, pool, hot tub, and continental breakfast, $79 d.

South from downtown, you'll find the **Motel 6,** 637 S. Lake Powell Blvd., 928/645-5888, 800/4MOTEL6, with a pool, $64–72 s, $70–78 d.

Next door, **Comfort Inn,** 649 S. Lake Powell Blvd., 928/645-5858, 800/228-5150, offers a pool, $70 s, $75 d.

Lake Powell Days Inn & Suites, 961 Hwy. 89, 928/645-2800, 877/525-3769, lies on the south edge of town beside US 89 with a pool and hot tub, $69–94 d.

Canyon Colors Bed & Breakfast, 928/645-5979, 800/536-2530, has a pool, patio, and fireplaces, $70–90 d; www.canyon-country.com/colors.

Sunrise View Bed & Breakfast, 928/608-4763, offers a shaded backyard and views of lake and mountains, $85–95 d; www.canyon-country.com/sunrise.

$100–150
Quality Inn, 287 N. Lake Powell Blvd., 928/645-8851, 800/808-6682, features a swimming pool, restaurant, and great views over Lake Powell, $104–114 d.

Campgrounds
Page-Lake Powell Campground, 928/645-3374, offers sites for tents ($17) and RVs ($20–26 w/hookups) with an indoor pool and hot tub, store, laundry, and showers; non-guests may use the showers or dump station for a small fee; the campground is 0.7 mile southeast of downtown on Coppermine Road. Other campgrounds, an RV park, and motels are in the Wahweap area (see "Wahweap" under "Glen Canyon National Recreation Area").

Food and Entertainment
Ken's Old West, 718 Vista Ave., 928/645-5160, serves up Western dinners and music nightly; the menu includes steaks, prime rib, chicken, and seafood; closed Sun.–Mon. in winter. **Dam Bar & Grille,** 644 N. Navajo Dr. in the Dam Plaza, 928/645-2161, fixes steak, barbecue, seafood, pasta, and sandwiches daily for dinner; it also has a sports bar. The adjacent **Gunsmoke Saloon** features country bands and a variety of other music Wed.–Saturday.

Ranch House Grille, 819 N. Navajo Dr., 928/645-1420, is a handy place for breakfast and does lunch too; it's open daily. **Family Tree Restaurant,** in the Quality Inn at 287 N. Lake Powell Blvd., 928/645-8851, offers a varied menu daily for breakfast and dinner; in summer, you can choose a breakfast buffet and a Friday seafood buffet dinner. **Butterfield Stage Co. Restaurant,** 704 Rim View Dr. next to Best Western Arizona-Inn, 928/645-2467, serves American food daily for breakfast, lunch, and dinner; dinner choices include steak, prime rib, and seafood. **Pepper's Restaurant** at the Courtyard by Marriott on 600 Clubhouse Dr., 928/645-1247, offers American and continental cuisine with a Southwestern touch and is open daily for breakfast (also a buffet), lunch (buffet summer weekdays), and dinner. **Denny's,** 669 Scenic View Dr. (turn west at the US 89-N. Lake Powell Blvd. junction), 928/645-3999, is open 24 hours and serves popular American fare for breakfast, lunch, and dinner.

Bella Napoli, 810 N. Navajo Dr., 928/645-2706, offers fine Italian cuisine daily for dinner in summer and Mon.–Sat. for dinner the rest of the year; closed late Dec. to mid-February. **Strombolli's Restaurant & Pizzeria,** 711 N. Navajo Dr., 928/645-2605, provides diners have a choice of indoor seating or the outdoor deck—a popular gathering spot for boaters in the summer; it's open daily for lunch and dinner except closed Dec.–March. **Pizza Hut,** 6 S. Lake Powell Blvd. in Dam Square, 928/645-2455, serves pizza, spaghetti, and other Italian fare daily for lunch and dinner.

For Chinese cuisine, try **Mandarin Gourmet Restaurant** in Gateway Plaza, 928/645-5516, open daily for lunch and dinner.

You can buy **groceries** at Safeway (Page Plaza at corner of S. Lake Powell Blvd. and Elm St.), Bashas' (Gateway Plaza), or at Mrs. C's Health Food Center (34 S. Lake Powell Blvd.). Catch movies at **Mesa Theatre,** 42 S. Lake Powell Blvd., 928/645-9565.

Events

In March, Fishermen test their skills in the Bullfrog Open bass tournament. On July 4th, there's a parade followed by fireworks that light the sky over Glen Canyon Dam. Mr. Burfel's Softball Tournament plays in September. Lake Powell Stampede, over Labor Day weekend in September, presents a rodeo, parade, arts and crafts, and entertainment. In October, Air Affaire takes off over Page with airplane acrobatics and para-

chutists. Bullfrog's Festival of Lights Parade takes place on the Saturday after Thanksgiving. In December, the Here Comes Santa Parade marks the holiday season in Page. Wahweap Festival of Lights Parade on Lake Powell glides by on the first Saturday.

For more information on any Lake Powell event, ask at the marina where it's held. To learn about other events, contact Page/Lake Powell Chamber of Commerce, 928/645-2741.

Shopping, Services, and Recreation

Blair's Dinnebito Trading Post, 626 N. Navajo Dr., 928/645-3008, 800/644-3008, has the feel of an old-style trading post; if you're interested in its history, staff will show you old Native American works and mementos of the family's trading business in the exhibit rooms upstairs; www.blairstradingpost.com.

The **post office** is at 44 Sixth Ave.; 928/645-2571. **Page Hospital,** 928/645-2424, stands at the corner of 501 N. Navajo Dr. and Vista Avenue. In **emergencies**—police, fire, medical—dial 911.

City of Page Memorial Park, off S. Navajo Dr., offers tables, playground, and greenery in the middle of town.

Play **tennis** at the courts on S. Lake Powell Blvd. (Church Row). **Lake Powell National Golf Course,** 928/645-2023, offers an 18-hole championship golf course that wraps around the west side of the mesa; turn in on Clubhouse Dr. adjacent to the Courtyard by Marriott. **Glen Canyon Golf and Country Club,** 928/645-2715, has a 9-hole golf course west across US 89 from the 18-hole course. Both stay open all year. **Twin Finn Diving Center,** 811 Vista Ave., 928/645-3114, offers a variety of diving and snorkeling activities, classes, and rentals; you can also rent both touring and sit-on-top kayaks; www.twinfinn.com.

Information

The **Page/Lake Powell Chamber of Commerce,** 644 N. Navajo Dr. in the Dam Plaza (Box 727, Page, AZ 86040), 928/645-2741, 888/261-7243, offers information about area sights and services and books lake and river tours, Antelope Canyon tours, and scenic flights; open Sun. 9 A.M.–6 P.M. and Mon.–Sat. 8 A.M.–8 P.M. from May 16 to October 16, then Mon.–Fri. 9 A.M.–5 P.M. the rest of the year; www.pagelakepowellchamber.org.

The semi-circular **Page Public Library,** 479 S. Lake Powell Blvd., 928/645-4270, rises impressively from the mesa rim with fine views; it has an Arizona/Native American collection and Internet computers; hours run Mon.–Thurs. 10 A.M.–8 P.M. and Fri.–Sat. 10 A.M.–5 P.M. **Front Page,** 928/645-5333, has regional titles, general reading, and office supplies at 48 S. Lake Powell Boulevard.

Tours

You can obtain information and make reservations for many area tours through the Page/Lake Powell Chamber of Commerce or Powell Museum. Staff can tell you of additional tour operators, not listed here, that offer kayaking, cycling, or hiking trips.

Overland Canyon Tours, 18 N. Lake Powell Blvd., 928/608-4072, heads to upper Antelope Canyon; a six-hour photographic tour visits "Canyon X," a relatively unknown and uncrowded slot canyon. **Roger Ekis' Antelope Canyon Tours,** 22 S. Lake Powell Blvd., 928/645-9102, 435/675-9109, goes to both upper and lower Antelope Canyon except in winter; www.antelopecanyon.com. **Grand Circle Adventures,** 48 S. Lake Powell Blvd. in Front Page, 928/645-5594, 800/835-8859, will take you to upper Antelope year-round. **Lake Powell Jeep Tours,** 104 S. Lake Powell Blvd., 928/645-5501, 866/645-5501, offers regular and photographers' tours to upper Antelope year-round; www.jeeptour.com.

ATV Tours, 26 S. Lake Powell Blvd., 928/645-9557, 800/962-9706, takes visitors on guided ATV tours year-round in the Page and Kaibab Plateau areas; beginners receive instruction; www.atvtours.net.

Wilderness River Adventures, 50 S. Lake Powell Blvd., 928/645-3279, 800/528-6154, offers raft trips down the Colorado River from just below Glen Canyon Dam to Lees Ferry, traveling over 15 miles of smooth-flowing water through the beautiful canyon of Navajo Sandstone. You'll stop to inspect some fine petroglyphs, and you're likely to see condors, blue herons, ducks, and other birds. Half-day trips leave once or twice daily March–Oct., weather permitting; the cost is $55 adults, $47 children 12 and under. All-day trips have more time on the water and include a lunch buffet; they run May 15 to Sept. 15 and cost $77 adults, $69 children 12 and under.

Classic Helicopter Tours, 928/645-5356, takes to the air with a variety of tours: 10 minutes for Tower Butte ($39), 15 minutes for Tower Butte & Antelope Creek ($59), about 30 minutes for Rainbow Bridge ($95), and 50 to 55 minutes to Rainbow Bridge and Escalante ($160); there's a four-person minimum; www.helicoptours.com. **Boat tours** to Rainbow Bridge and other destinations leave from nearby Wahweap Marina; see below.

Transport

Great Lakes Aviation operates daily scheduled flights south to Phoenix and northeast to Moab and Denver; make reservations with United Airlines, 800/241-6522, or visit www.greatlakesav.com.

Wahweap Lodge operates **Page Shuttle,** 928/645-2433, frequently to Page and the airport. Most area motels also provide transportation for guests to and from the airport. **R&S Pickup & Delivery,** 928/645-0069, runs a shuttle van to area cities. **Avis,** 928/645-2024, 800/331-1212, rents cars at the airport.

Glen Canyon National Recreation Area

This vast recreation area covers 1.25 million acres, most of which spreads northeast into Utah. Lake Powell is the centerpiece, surrounded by beautiful canyon country. Just a handful of roads approach the lake, so you'll need to go by boat or on foot to truly explore this unique land of water and rock. The recreation area also includes a beautiful remnant of Glen Canyon in a 15-mile section of the Colorado River from Glen Canyon Dam to Lees Ferry. As big as the lake is, it comprises only 13 percent of the vast Glen Canyon National Recreation Area—there's much more to discover!

Rainbow Bridge National Monument—50 miles uplake from the dam—holds the world's largest natural bridge; it's easily reached on boat tours from Wahweap or Bullfrog or by your own boat. You can also hike in on a spectacular trail; see below. The Carl Hayden Visitor Center has information on Rainbow Bridge.

Entry Fees

Visits to most areas now cost $10 per vehicle or $3 per cyclist or hiker for seven days—free if you have a National Parks Pass, Golden Eagle, Golden Age, or Golden Access card; an annual pass to the recreation area is $20. Motorized boats are an extra $10, then $4 for each additional one on same trailer; an annual boat pass runs $20. Admission to the Carl Hayden Visitor Center is still free.

Climate

Summer, when temperatures rise into the 90s and 100s F, is the busiest season for swimming, boating, and waterskiing. Visits during the rest of the year can be enjoyable, too, though more conducive to sightseeing, fishing, and hiking. Spring and autumn are the best times to enjoy the backcountry. Winter temperatures drop to highs in the 40s and 50s, with freezing nights and the possibility of snow. Lake surface temperatures range from a comfortable 80°F in August to a chilly 45°F in January. Chinook winds can blow day and night from February to May. Thunder-storms in late summer bring strong, gusting winds with widely scattered rain showers. Annual precipitation averages about seven inches.

Geology, Flora, and Fauna

Deposits of ancient deserts, oceans, and rivers formed the colorful rock layers that you see rising above the lake's surface. Uplift of the Colorado Plateau, beginning about 60 million years ago, started a cycle of erosion that has carved canyons and created delicately balanced rocks and graceful natural arches and bridges.

The desert comes right to the edge of the water, because fluctuating lake levels prevent plant growth along the shore. Common plants of this high-desert country include prickly pear and hedge-hog cacti, rabbitbrush, sand sagebrush, blackbrush, cliffrose, mariposa and sego lilies, globemallow, Indian paintbrush, evening primrose, penstemon, and Indian rice grass. Pinyon pine and juniper trees grow on the high plateaus. Springs and permanent streams support sandbar willow, tamarisk, cattail, willow, and cottonwood. Look for hanging gardens of maidenhair fern, columbine, and other water-loving plants in small alcoves, often high on the sandstone walls. The Park Service recommends not walking on or swimming near these delicate plant communities.

Most animals are secretive and nocturnal; you're most likely to see them in early morning or in the evening. Local mammals include desert bighorn sheep, pronghorns, mule deer, mountain lions, coyotes, red and gray foxes, ringtail cats, spotted and striped skunks, bobcats, badgers, river otters, beavers, prairie dogs, Ord kangaroo rats, black-tailed jackrabbits, several species of squirrels and chipmunks, and many species of mice and bats. Types of lizards you might spot sunning on a rock include collared, side-blotched, desert horned, and chuckwalla. Snake species include the common kingsnake, gopher snake, striped whipsnake, western rattlesnake, and western diamondback rattlesnake.

Birds stopping by on their migratory routes include American avocet, Canada goose, and teal.

Others, such as blue heron, snowy egret, and bald eagle, come for the winter. Birds in residence all year are American merganser, mallard, canyon wren, pinyon jay, common raven, red-tailed and Swainson's hawks, great horned and long-eared owls, peregrine and prairie falcons, and the golden eagle. The giant California condors, recently released in the area, have been spotted in Glen Canyon downstream of the dam.

Recreation at Lake Powell

Boating: If you don't have your own craft, Wahweap and other marinas will rent you a boat for fishing, skiing, or houseboating. Boat tours visit Rainbow Bridge and other destinations from Wahweap, Bullfrog, and Halls Crossing Marinas. Sailboats find the steadiest breezes in Wahweap, Padre, Halls, and Bullfrog Bays, where spring winds average 15–20 knots. Kayaks and canoes can be used in the more protected areas. All boaters need to be alert for approaching storms that can bring wind gusts up to 60 mph. Waves on open expanses of the lake are sometimes steeper than ocean waves and can exceed six feet from trough to crest. Marinas and bookstores sell Lake Powell navigation maps. Carbon monoxide poisoning of boaters has been in the news—pick up safety literature or visit www.nps.gov/glca for advice on how to avoid this invisible killer.

Fishing: You'll need an Arizona fishing license for the southern five miles of Lake Powell and a Utah license for the rest. Get licenses and information from marinas on the water or from sporting goods stores in Page. Anglers can catch bass (largemouth, smallmouth, and striped), walleye, channel catfish, black crappie, carp, and bluegill. Wahweap has a swimming beach (no lifeguards), and boaters can find their own remote spots.

Hiking: Hikers can choose between easy day trips or long wilderness backpack treks. The canyons of the Escalante in Utah rate among America's premier hiking areas. Other good areas within or adjacent to Glen Canyon N.R.A. include Rainbow Bridge National Monument, Paria Canyon, Dark Canyon, and Grand Gulch. You'll find descriptions of these last two places as well as Escalante in *Moon Handbooks: Utah*. Na-tional Park Service staff at the Carl Hayden Visitor Center and the Bullfrog Visitor Center can suggest trips and supply trail descriptions. Several guidebooks to Lake Powell offer detailed hiking, camping, and boating information. Most of the canyon country near Lake Powell remains wild and little explored—hiking possibilities are limitless. Be sure to carry plenty of water.

Mountain Biking: Cyclists can head out on many back roads. The visitor center has a list of possibilities.

Scuba: Divers can visit the canyon cliffs and rock sculptures beneath the surface. Visibility runs 30–40 feet in late Aug.–Nov., the best season, and there's less boat traffic then. In other seasons, visibility can drop to 10–20 feet.

Packing It Out

Much of the revenue from the fees has gone toward improving water quality and cleaning up the shore. Visitors can help by packing out all trash. Also, anyone camping within one-quarter mile of the lake must have a container (not plastic bags) for solid human wastes unless a toilet is available on the beach or on your own boat. Camps also need to be within 200 yards of a toilet, even at the primitive camping areas, such as Lone Rock Upper Bullfrog, Stanton Creek, Farley Canyon and Dirty Devil River. Eight "restrooms/pump-outs/dump stations," shown on maps, are located along the lake between Warm Creek Bay (13 miles from the dam) and Forgotten Canyon (106 miles from the dam).

LAKE POWELL

Of all the artificial lakes in the United States, only Lake Mead, farther downstream, has a greater water-storage capacity. Lake Powell boasts a shoreline of 1,960 miles and holds enough water to cover the state of Pennsylvania a foot deep. Bays and coves offer nearly limitless opportunities for exploration by boaters. Only the southern part extends into Arizona—Glen Canyon Dam, Wahweap Resort and Marina, Antelope and Navajo Canyons, and the lower parts of Labyrinth, Face, and West Canyons.

© BILL WEIR

Glen Canyon Dam from the Colorado River

ARIZONA STRIP

Lake Powell's surface elevation fluctuates an average of 20–30 feet through the year (fluctuation has reached nearly 100 feet), peaking in July; it reaches 3,700 feet when full. The Carl Hayden Visitor Center, perched beside the dam, offers tours of the dam, related exhibits, and an information desk for the Glen Canyon National Recreation Area.

GLEN CANYON DAM

Construction workers labored from 1956 to 1964 to build this giant concrete structure. It stands 710 feet high above bedrock, the top measuring 1,560 feet across. Thickness ranges from 300 feet at the base to just 25 feet at the top. As part of the Upper Colorado River Storage Project, the dam provides water storage (its main purpose), hydroelectricity, flood control, and recreation on Lake Powell. Eight giant turbine generators churn out a total of 1,150,000 kilowatts at 13,800 volts. Vertigo victims shouldn't look down when driving across Glen Canyon Bridge, just downstream of the dam. The cold

green waters of the Colorado River emerge 700 feet below.

Conservationists deplore the loss of remote and beautiful Glen Canyon, buried today beneath Lake Powell, and call for the removal of the dam. That's very unlikely in the near future, so for now, only words, pictures, and memories remind us of Glen Canyon's lost wonders.

Carl Hayden Visitor Center and Dam Tours

Photos, paintings, and video programs in the visitor center present various features of the Glen Canyon National Recreation Area, including Lake Powell and the construction of the dam. A giant relief map helps you visualize the rugged terrain surrounding the lake; look closely and you'll spot Rainbow Bridge. Guided one-hour tours visit the top of the dam, tunnels, the generating room, and the transformer platform; they depart daily every 30 or 60 minutes from Memorial Day to Labor Day with the first tour at 8:30 A.M. and the last at 4:30 P.M.; tours run less frequently the rest of the year—call for times. No purses or bags may be taken on the tours nor are there storage lockers. Senator Carl Hayden, a major backer of water development in the West, served as an Arizona member of Congress from 1912 to 1969, a record 57 consecutive years.

Staff operate an information desk where you can find out about boating, fishing, camping, and hiking in the immense Glen Canyon National Recreation Area, or you can write P.O. Box 1507, Page, AZ 86040, 928/608-6404, www.nps.gov/glca. The Glen Canyon Natural History Association sells a variety of books on the recreation area and its environs. A gift shop in the visitor center building sells souvenirs, snacks, and postcards; www.pagelakepowell.com.

The Carl Hayden Visitor Center is open daily 8 A.M.–7 P.M. in summer and 8 A.M.–5 P.M. the rest of the year. Tours, exhibits, and movies are free. In summer, you can attend an evening program most nights at nearby Wahweap Campground amphitheater.

MARINAS

The **National Park Service** provides public boat ramps and ranger offices at most of the marinas. Rangers know current boating and back-road conditions, primitive camping areas, and good places to explore. **Lake Powell Resorts & Marinas** operates marina services, boat rentals, boat tours, accommodations, RV parks, and restaurants; for information and reservations (strongly recommended in summer) write P.O. Box 56909, Phoenix, AZ 85079, call 800/528-6154, 602/278-8888 in greater Phoenix, or fax 602/331-5258, www.visitlakepowell.com. To make reservations seven days or fewer in advance, contact each marina or resort directly. All the marinas stay open year-round; you can avoid crowds and peak prices by arriving in autumn, winter, or spring. Private or chartered aircraft can fly to Page Airport, Bullfrog's small airstrip, and Halls Crossing's large airstrip.

Wahweap

The name means Bitter Water in the Ute language. Wahweap Lodge and Marina, Lake Powell's largest, offers complete boaters' services and rentals, deluxe accommodations, an RV park, and fine dining. Wahweap lies seven miles northwest of Page; turn right on Lake Shore Dr. about 0.7 mile past the visitor center. Fee stations on the way in collect the entry charge for Glen Canyon National Recreation Area.

Wahweap Lodge offers swimming pools and several types of rooms—many with lake views—at $150 d ($160 d lake view) April–Oct. and $105 d ($112 d lake view) in winter. The lodge's fine-dining restaurant, the Rainbow Room, features a panoramic view for its daily breakfast, lunch, and dinner; in summer there's live entertainment and dancing. The nearby Navajo Room serves buffets for breakfast and lunch in summer. A café serves pizza, subs, and salads daily in summer. Just off the lobby lie a boat tour desk and a large gift shop (books, Native American crafts, and souvenirs). Contact Lake Powell Resorts & Marinas for reservations at P.O. Box 56909, Phoenix, AZ 85079, 800/528-6154, 602/278-8888 in greater Phoenix, fax 602/331-5258; www.visitlakepowell.com. You can also reach Wahweap Lodge & Marina at P.O. Box 1597, Page, AZ 86040; 928/645-2433.

An **RV park** with coin showers and laundry costs $28 with hookups ($20 in winter). **Wahweap Campground** is operated first-come, first-served by the concessionaire from mid-March to Oct.; the $15 sites have drinking water but no showers or hookups. Evening **interpretive programs** take place here most days in the summer. Campers may use the pay showers and laundry at the RV park. Turnoffs for the RV park, campground, a free picnic area, and a fish-cleaning station lie between Wahweap Lodge and Stateline, 1.3 miles northwest of the lodge. Beyond the Stateline area, you'll come to the picturesque **Coves Day-Use Area,** set on low white bluffs overlooking the lake and a few beaches. You'll find public boat ramps just past the lodge and at Stateline. You can obtain maps and brochures from the **Wahweap Ranger Station** (usually unstaffed) near the picnic area and at Carl Hayden Visitor Center.

Primitive camping—outhouses but no drinking water—costs $6 per vehicle at **Lone Rock** in Utah, six miles northwest of Wahweap off US

89. Boaters may also camp along the lakeshore, but not within one mile of developed areas.

The marina offers seven **lake tours,** ranging from an hour-long paddle-wheel cruise around Wahweap Bay ($11 adults, $8 children 2–12) to an all-day trip to Rainbow Bridge, 50 miles away ($106 adults, $69 children 2–12). Half-day trips to Rainbow Bridge cost $80 adults, $55 children 2–12. The other tours are a 90-minute Antelope Canyon cruise ($27 adults, $21 children 2–12), two-and-a-half-hour Canyon Explorer/Navajo Tapestry tour ($43 adults, $31 children 2–12), and 2.5-hour dinner cruise ($60 adults, $59 children 2–12). **Boat rentals** at Stateline include kayak, personal watercraft, fishing, runabout, patio, and a variety of houseboats. You can rent fishing gear and waterskis, too.

Dangling Rope

This floating marina lies 42 miles uplake from Glen Canyon Dam. The only access is by boat. Services include a ranger station, store, minor boat repairs, gas dock, and sanitary pump-out station. A dangling rope left behind in a nearby canyon, perhaps by uranium prospectors, prompted the name. The Rainbow Bridge dock lies 10 miles farther uplake in Bridge Canyon, a tributary of Forbidding Canyon.

San Juan

You can hand-launch boats at **Clay Hills Crossing** at the upper end of the San Juan Arm. An unpaved road that requires a high-clearance vehicle branches 11 miles southwest from UT 276 to the lake; don't attempt the road after rains. River-runners on the San Juan often take out here, but no facilities are provided. Boat access to the lake is sometimes blocked at low water by a bar of sediment dropped by the San Juan River as it enters Lake Powell. During times of low lake levels, a waterfall pours off the bar, which can be portaged on a long and sloppy hike. At high water the bar is covered.

Halls Crossing-Bullfrog Ferry

The *John Atlantic Burr* and *Charles Hall* ferries can accommodate vehicles of all sizes as well as passengers for the short 20-minute crossing be-

tween these marinas. Halls Crossing and Bullfrog Marinas lie on opposite sides of Lake Powell about 95 lake miles from Glen Canyon Dam, roughly midway up the length of the lake. Highway UT 276 connects both marinas with UT 95. No reservations are needed and you can pick up a schedule at either marina.

Halls Crossing

In 1880, Charles Hall built the ferry used by the Hole-in-the-Rock pioneers who crossed the Colorado River to settle in southeastern Utah. The approach roads were so bad, however, that in 1881 Hall moved the ferry 35 miles upstream to present-day Halls Crossing. Business remained slow, and Hall quit running the ferry in 1884.

Arriving at Halls Crossing by road, you first pass a small store offering **three-bedroom units** ($180 up to six persons April to late Sept., $125 off season), an **RV park** ($28 with hookups in summer, $20 off season), and gas pumps. The store may close in winter, but services are still available—ask at the trailer office next door. Coin-operated showers and laundry at the RV park are also open to the public. The separate campground just beyond and to the left offers sites with good views of the lake, drinking water, and restrooms for $12. A half mile farther down the main road are the boat ramp and **Halls Crossing Marina.** The marina features a larger store with groceries and fishing and boating supplies, tours to Rainbow Bridge, a boat rental office, a gas dock, slips, and storage. The ranger station is here too and may be open with recreation exhibits even if not staffed. Rangers are often out on patrol; look for their vehicles in the area if the office is closed.

Contact Lake Powell Resorts & Marinas for accommodations, boat rental, and tour reservations at P.O. Box 56909, Phoenix, AZ 85079, 800/528-6154, 602/278-8888 in greater Phoenix, fax 602/331-5258; www.visitlake powell.com. You can also reach the marina at P.O. Box 5101, Lake Powell, UT 84533, 435/684-7000.

Stabilized ancestral Puebloan ruins at **Defiance House** in Forgotten Canyon make a good boating destination 12 miles uplake; a sign marks the beginning of the trail to the ruins.

Bullfrog

Before the days of Lake Powell, Bullfrog Rapids offered boaters a fast and bumpy ride. Today, Bullfrog Marina rivals Wahweap in its extensive visitor facilities. When arriving, you'll come first to the **visitor center** on the right, open daily 8 A.M.–5 P.M. April to Oct.; 435/684-7400. The **clinic** is here too; it's open mid-May to mid-October 9:30 A.M.–6 P.M.; 435/684-2288. Next you'll see a large **campground** on the left; the $18 charge includes drinking water and restrooms. Continue on the main road to a junction, where a service station offers repairs and supplies. Continue straight at the junction for a picnic area and the boat ramp, or turn right at the service station for Defiance House Lodge and Restaurant, Trailer Village, Bullfrog Painted Hills RV Park, and Bullfrog Marina.

Defiance House Lodge offers luxury accommodations for $115 d ($125 d with a lake view) April–Sept. and $81 d ($88 d with a lake view) in winter and the **Anasazi Restaurant** (open daily for breakfast, lunch, and dinner). The front desk at the lodge also offers boat tours and handles **three-bedroom units** and an **RV park,** both nearby with the same rates as at Halls Crossing. Showers, laundry, and post office are at **Trailer Village.** The RV park also has showers. Ask rangers for directions to primitive camping areas at Upper Bullfrog and Stanton Creek near Bullfrog Bay; these cost $6 per vehicle.

All-day **Rainbow Bridge tours** stop on request to pick up passengers at Halls Crossing Marina; call for dates. The cost is $106 adults, $69 children 2–12. **Canyon Explorer/Navajo Tapestry tours** spend two and a half hours in nearby canyons from both marinas at $43 adults, $31 children 2–12. **Escalante Canyon excursions** visit this canyon on half-day trips from both marinas for $80 adults, $55 children 2–12. **Bullfrog Resort & Marina** offers boat rentals, gas dock, slips, storage, and a store. Contact Lake Powell Resorts & Marinas for accommodations, boat rental, and tour reservations at P.O. Box 56909, Phoenix, AZ 85079; 800/528-6154,

602/278-8888 in greater Phoenix, fax 602/331-5258; www.visitlakepowell.com. Contact Bullfrog Resort & Marina at P.O. Box 4055-Bullfrog, Lake Powell, UT 84531, 435/684-3000.

Hite

In 1883, Cass Hite came to Glen Canyon in search of gold. He found a few nuggets at a place later named Hite City, setting off a small gold rush. Hite and some of his relatives operated a small store and post office, the only services available for many miles.

Travelers wishing to cross the Colorado River here faced the difficult task of swimming their animals across. Arthur Chaffin put through the first road and opened a ferry service in 1946. The Chaffin Ferry served uranium prospectors and adventurous motorists until the lake backed up to the spot in 1964. A steel bridge now spans the Colorado River far upstream; Cass Hite's store and the ferry site lie underwater about five miles downlake from Hite Marina.

The uppermost marina on Lake Powell, Hite lies 141 lake miles from Glen Canyon Dam. From here boats can continue uplake to the mouth of Dark Canyon in Cataract Canyon at low water or into Canyonlands National Park at high water. Hite tends to be quieter than the other marinas and is favored by anglers. The turnoff for the marina from UT 95 lies between Hanksville and Blanding. On the way in, you'll find a small **store** with gas pumps, **three-bedroom units** (same rates as at Halls Crossing), and a small **campground** (no drinking water, $6). Primitive camping is also available nearby off UT 95 at Dirty Devil, Farley Canyon, White Canyon, Blue Notch, and other locations for $6. **Hite Marina,** at the end of the access road, features boat rentals (fishing, ski, and houseboat), slips, storage, gas dock, and a small store. Hikers can make arrangements with the marina for drop-offs and pick-ups at Dark Canyon. A **ranger station,** 435/684-2457, is occasionally open.

Contact Lake Powell Resorts & Marinas for accommodations and boat rentals at P.O. Box 56909, Phoenix, AZ 85079; 800/528-6154, 602/278-8888 in greater Phoenix, fax 602/331-5258; www.visitlakepowell.com. Reach Hite

ARIZONA STRIP

Marina at P.O. Box 501-Hite, Lake Powell, UT 84533, 435/684-2278.

RAINBOW BRIDGE NATIONAL MONUMENT

Rainbow Bridge forms a graceful span 290 feet high and 275 feet wide; the Capitol building in Washington, D.C., would fit neatly underneath. The easiest way to Rainbow Bridge is by boat tour on Lake Powell from Wahweap, Bullfrog, or Halls Crossing Marinas.

The more adventurous can hike to the bridge from the Cha Canyon Trailhead (just north across the Arizona-Utah border on the east side of Navajo Mountain) or from the Rainbow Lodge ruins (just south of the Arizona-Utah border on the west side of Navajo Mountain). Rugged trails from each point wind through highly scenic canyons, meet in Bridge Canyon, then continue two miles to the bridge. The hike on either trail, or a loop with both (a car shuttle is needed), is 26–28 miles roundtrip. Hikers must be experienced and self-sufficient, as these trails cross a wilderness. Because the trails are unmaintained and poorly marked, hikers should consult a Navajo Mountain (Utah) 15-minute topo map or the newer 7.5-minute Navajo Begay and Chaiyahi Flat maps.

No camping is allowed at Rainbow Bridge and no supplies are available. You may camp a half mile east of the bridge at Echo camp. The Dangling Rope Marina and National Park Service ranger station are 10 miles away, by water only. The best times to go are April to early June, September, and October. Winter cold and snow discourage visitors, and summer is hot and can bring hazardous flash floods. The National Park Service offers "Hiking to Rainbow Bridge" trail notes; write Glen Canyon N.R.A., P.O. Box 1507, Page, AZ 86040; 928/608-6404; www.nps.gov/rabr.

The National Park Service cannot issue hiking permits to Rainbow Bridge. Obtain the required tribal hiking permit ($5 for one person, $10 group of 2–10, $20 group of 11 or more) and camping permit ($2 per person per night) from the Cameron Visitor Center/Ranger Station at

© BILL WEIR

Rainbow Bridge

P.O. Box 459, Cameron, AZ 86020; 928/679-2303, fax 928/679-2330; or from the Navajo Parks and Recreation Department, P.O. Box 9000, Window Rock, AZ 86515; 928/871-6647, 928/871-6635. Both offices are open Mon.–Fri. about 8 A.M.–5 P.M.; the Cameron office may extend its hours to daily 7 A.M.–6 P.M. from Memorial Day to Labor Day weekends. Allow six weeks for permit processing. In the Page area, permits area available at the upper Antelope Canyon ticket booth (usually open daily 8 A.M.–5 P.M. from April to October) and the Antelope Canyon Navajo Tribal Park office, 928/698-2808, four miles south of Page in Leche-e.

The only road access to the Navajo Mountain area is Indian Route 16 from AZ 98, between Page and Kayenta. To reach the east trailhead, drive north 32 miles on Indian Route 16 past Inscription House Trading Post to a road fork, and then turn right six miles to Navajo Mountain Trading Post. Continue on the main road 6.5 miles (go straight at the four-way junction) to an earthen dam. Drive straight across the dam, take the left fork after a half-mile, and then go 1.6 miles to Cha Canyon Trailhead at the end of the road.

You can reach the west trailhead by driving north 32 miles on Indian Rt. 16 to the road fork, then turning left about six miles to the Rainbow Lodge ruins. Always lock vehicles and remove valuables at trailheads. Because Navajo Mountain is sacred to the Navajo, you probably won't get permission to climb it; check with the Navajo Parks Department in Window Rock.

ARIZONA STRIP

Northeastern Arizona

Ancient cultural traditions of Native Americans— ways of life that have survived to the present— make this region a special place. The hardworking Hopi have lived here longest. Ruins, occupied by their ancestors as long ago as 1,500 years, lie scattered over much of northeastern Arizona and adjacent states. The once warlike and greatly feared Navajo came relatively late, perhaps 500–700 years ago. Today, Hopi and Navajo welcome visitors who respect tribal customs and laws. Here you'll have an opportunity to glimpse unique ways of life in a land of rare beauty.

THE LAND

Multihued desert hills, broad mesas, soaring buttes, vast treeless plains, and massive mountains give an impression of boundless space. The Colorado Plateau, which averages 4,500–7,000 feet in elevation, covers all of northeastern Arizona. Several pine-forested ranges rise above the desert near Arizona's borders with Utah and New Mexico. Navajo Mountain, just across the border in Utah, is the highest peak in the area at 10,388 feet. Nearby you'll find Rainbow Bridge, the world's highest natural stone span over water. You can reach the bridge by boat on Lake Powell or by a spectacular 26- to 28-mile

Sky Village

COURTESY OF AISLINN RACE

roundtrip hike. The beautiful canyons in Navajo and Canyon de Chelly National Monuments also offer excellent scenery and hiking.

Climate

Expect warm to hot summers and moderate to cold winters. Spring and autumn are the ideal times to visit, especially for hiking, though winds in March and April can kick up dust and sand. Afternoon thunderstorms frequently build up from early July to early September. Showers usually pass quickly, but flash floods pose a danger in low-lying areas.

HISTORY

Indian Reservations

In 1878 the federal government began ceding to the Navajo land that has since grown into a giant reservation spreading from northeastern Arizona into adjacent New Mexico and Utah. The Navajo Nation, with more than 200,000 members, ranks as the largest Native American tribe in the country. In 1882 the federal government also recognized the Hopi's age-old land rights and began setting aside land for them. Approximately 10,000 Hopi live today on a reservation completely surrounded by Navajo land. Government officials have redrawn the reservation boundaries of the Navajo and Hopi many times, never to the satisfaction of all parties. In 1978, congressional and court decisions settled a major land dispute between the two tribes in favor of the Hopi. The victorious Hopi regained part of the territory previously designated for joint use but largely settled by Navajo. To the Hopi this was long-overdue justice, while the Navajo called it The Second Long Walk. The Navajo and Hopi Indian Relocation Commissioners faced the daunting task of resettling hundreds of families in their respective reservations.

NATIVE AMERICAN CULTURES

Non–Native Americans have always had difficulty understanding Arizona's tribes, perhaps because these Native American cultures emphasize very different spiritual values. The Hopi and Navajo exist in accord with nature, not against it, adapting to the climate, plants, and animals of the land. Yet when visiting Native American villages, outsiders often see only the material side of the culture—the houses, livestock, dress, pottery, and other crafts. The visitor has to look deeper to gain even a small insight into Native American ways.

Hopi and Navajo differ greatly in their lifestyles. The Hopi usually live in compact villages, even if this means a long commute to fields or jobs. The Navajo spread their houses and hogans across the countryside, often far from the nearest neighbor.

Ceremonies

Religion forms a vital part of both Hopi and Navajo cultures. The Hopi have an elaborate, almost year-round schedule of dances in their village plazas and kivas (ceremonial rooms). Some, such as those in the kivas, are closed to outsiders, but others may be open to the public. Nearly all Hopi dances serve as prayers for rain and fertile crops. The elaborate and brilliant masks, the ankle bells, the drums and chanting—all invite the attention of the kachinas (supernatural spirits) who bring rain. Men perform

---

NORTHEASTERN ARIZONA HIGHLIGHTS

Navajo and Hopi lands: Visitors can experience the cultures of these two dynamic, yet very different, Native American peoples.

Navajo National Monument: You can see two large prehistoric cliff dwellings that have been amazingly well preserved.

Monument Valley: Towering buttes and pinnacles create an enchanting landscape.

Canyon de Chelly National Monument: Exceptionally beautiful canyons preserve both prehistoric cliff dwellings and traditional Navajo life.

Hopi Country: Centuries-old villages seem to grow out of the mesa tops, where you may be fortunate enough to watch dancers perform religious ceremonies.

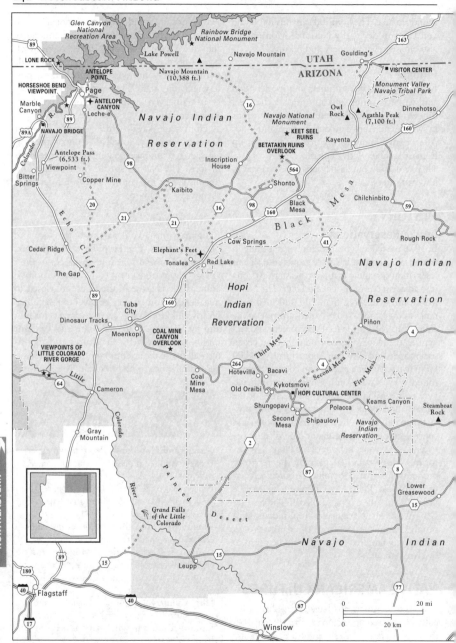

Glen Canyon
National
Recreation Area

Rainbow Bridge
National Monument

Lake Powell

Navajo Mountain

UTAH

Goulding's

163

LONE ROCK

VISITOR CENTER

89

ANTELOPE
POINT

Navajo Mountain
(10,388 ft.)

ARIZONA

Monument Valley
Navajo Tribal Park

HORSESHOE BEND
VIEWPOINT

Page

ANTELOPE
CANYON

Owl
Rock

Agathla Peak
(7,100 ft.)

Dinnehotso

Marble
Canyon

Leche-e

89

Navajo Indian

Navajo National
Monument

160

89A

NAVAJO BRIDGE

Reservation

KEET SEEL
RUINS

Kayenta

Antelope Pass
(6,533 ft.)

98

BETATAKIN RUINS
OVERLOOK

Viewpoint

Inscription
House

Bitter
Springs

Copper Mine

564

Shonto

Chilchinbito

20

Kaibito

16

98

160

Black
Mesa

59

21

21

M
e
s
a

Cedar Ridge

Black

Rough Rock

Cow Springs

41

Navajo Indian

Elephant's Feet

The Gap

Tonalea

Red Lake

Reservation

89

Hopi

Piñon

4

Tuba
City

Indian

Dinosaur Tracks

160

Revervation

Third Mesa

Moenkopi

COAL MINE
CANYON
OVERLOOK

Second Mesa

4

VIEWPOINTS OF
LITTLE COLORADO
RIVER GORGE

264

Hotevilla

Bacavi

First Mesa

Coal
Mine
Mesa

Old Oraibi

Kykotsmovi

Keams Canyon

Steamboat
Rock

64

Cameron

HOPI CULTURAL CENTER

Shungopavi

Polacca

Navajo
Indian
Reservation

8

Gray
Mountain

Second
Mesa

Shipaulovi

2

Lower
Greasewood

87

15

Grand Falls
of the Little
Colorado

P
a
i
n
t
e
d

D
e
s
e
r
t

Navajo

Indian

89

15

15

180

Leupp

77

40

Flagstaff

40

87

0   20 mi

17

Winslow

0   20 km

NORTHEASTERN

© AVALON TRAVEL PUBLISHING, INC.

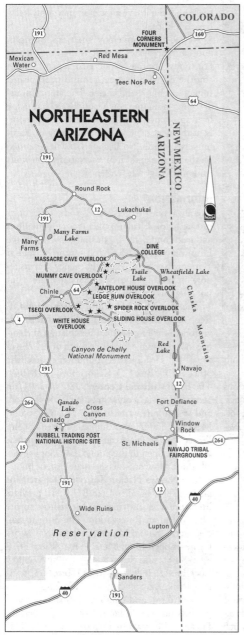

these dances and while they're dancing they *are* kachinas. At the end of the line of dancers, you might see boys who are learning the ritual; dance steps must be performed precisely. When watching, remember that this is a religious service. Dress respectfully, keep clear of the performers, be quiet, and don't ask questions. Hopi ceremonies generally take place on the weekends; call or ask at the Hopi Cultural Center or the Hopi Tribe Cultural Preservation Office.

Most Navajo ceremonies deal with healing. If someone is sick, the family calls in a healer who uses sand paintings, chants, and dancing to effect a cure. These events, often held late at night, aren't publicized. If you're driving at night and see large bonfires outside a house, it's likely there's a healing ceremony going on, but don't go over unless invited.

Visiting the Hopi and Navajo

Learning about Native American cultures can reward visitors with new insights. It's easy to visit Navajo and Hopi lands; the tribes ask guests to follow only a few simple rules.

Hordes of eager photographers besieged Hopi villages from the late 1800s to the early 1900s, when the Hopi cried "No more!" And that's the way it is now—photography, recording, and sketching by visitors are *strictly* forbidden in all Hopi villages. Even the sight of a camera will upset some tribal members. The Navajo are more easygoing about photos, but you should always ask first; expect to pay a posing fee unless attending a public performance.

Reservation land, though held in trust by the government, is private property; obtain permission before leaving the roadways or designated recreational areas. Don't remove anything—a few feathers tied to a bush may make a tempting souvenir, but they're of great religious importance to the person who put them there. Normal good

Hopi method of dressing the hair, 1890's

manners, respect, and observance of posted regulations will make your visit pleasurable for both you and your hosts.

You might enjoy tuning in local radio stations to hear favorite tunes and languages of the tribes. Hopi Radio KUYI at 88.1 FM has a large following for its traditional and contemporary Native American and other styles of music.

NORTHEASTERN ARIZONA PRACTICALITIES

Accommodations and Food

Because of the distances involved, visitors usually stay overnight on or near the reservations. Most towns have a motel or two that can quickly fill up in the summer tourist season, when reservations come in very handy. Motel prices run on the high side because there's so little competition. Accommodations in towns just outside the reservations—in Flagstaff, Winslow, Holbrook, Page, or Gallup—are generally a much better value. Campgrounds are likely to have

space and you'll save a lot of money; only a few have hookups.

Navajo and Hopi enjoy American, Mexican, and Chinese dishes as well as the ever-present fast foods. Try the Navajo taco, a giant tortilla smothered with lettuce, ground beef, beans, tomatoes, chilies, and cheese. The Hopi Cultural Center restaurant on Second Mesa has many local specialties, but chances are the Hopi family at the next table will be munching on hamburgers and fries. No alcohol is sold or permitted on the Navajo and Hopi reservations; you won't find much nightlife, either.

Information

Not always easy to get! Motels and trading posts can be helpful; tribal police know regulations and road conditions. Try the museums run by the Hopi on Second Mesa and by the Navajo at Window Rock and Tsaile. Local newspapers report on politics, sports, and social events, but not religious ceremonies.

The **Hopi Tribe Cultural Preservation Office,** 928/734-2244, provides information for visitors to the Hopi Indian Reservation at its office in Kykotsmovi, one mile south of AZ 264 in the Tribal Headquarters building; contact the office at P.O. Box 123, Kykotsmovi, AZ 86039. The **Hopi Cultural Center,** 928/734-2401, on Second Mesa has a museum, motel, campground, and restaurant; write to P.O. Box 67, Second Mesa, AZ 86043; www.hopiculturalcenter.com. People at either place can tell you about upcoming dances open to the public. The Hopi generally don't allow outsiders to hike, fish, or hunt.

The **Navajo Nation Tourism Department** office, 928/871-7371 or 928/871-7941, provides literature and information for visitors to the Navajo Indian Reservation. The information desk in the Navajo Museum, Library & Visitor's Center is open Mon. 8 A.M.–5 P.M., Tues.–Fri. 8 A.M.–8 P.M., and Sat. 9 A.M.–5 P.M. in Window Rock on AZ 264; write to P.O. Box 663, Window Rock, AZ 86515; www.navajo.org.

For hiking and camping information and permits on Navajo lands, contact the **Navajo Parks & Recreation Department,** 928/871-6647, 928/871-6635, near the museum and zoo in Window Rock, open Mon.–Fri. 8 A.M.–5 P.M.; P.O. Box 9000, Window Rock, AZ 86515; www.navajonationparks.org. Or, in the western Navajo Nation, which contains most of the open backcountry areas, contact the Cameron Visitor Center at the US 89-AZ 64 junction in Cameron, 928/679-2303; it's open Mon.–Fri. 8 A.M.–5 P.M. and may be extended to daily 8 A.M.–6 P.M. from Memorial Day to Labor Day weekends; write P.O. Box 459, Cameron, AZ 86020. Backcountry permits cost only $5 per person per entry and $5 per person per night for camping; allow two weeks for processing.

Fishing and hunting on the Navajo Reservation require tribal permits from **Navajo Fish and Wildlife,** 928/871-6451, 928/871-6452, open Mon.–Fri. 8 A.M.–5 P.M.; P.O. Box 1480, Window Rock, AZ 86515; www.navajofishandwildlife.org. Of the 12 lakes stocked with fish on the reservation, the most popular are the trout lakes Wheatfields and Tsaile in eastern Arizona and Whiskey nearby in New Mexico. State game and fish agencies have no jurisdiction; you need only tribal permits.

> *Native American reservation land is private property; obtain permission before leaving the roadways or designated recreational areas. And don't remove anything—a few feathers tied to a bush may make a tempting souvenir, but they're likely of great religious importance to the person who put them there.*

What Time Is It?

This must be the question most frequently asked by reservation visitors! While the Navajo Nation and most of the United States go on daylight saving time from early April to late October, the rest of Arizona stays on Mountain Standard Time. Keep in mind the time difference on Navajo land during daylight saving time or you'll always be one hour late; an easy way to remember is that the reservation follows the same time as its New Mexico and Utah sections. The Hopi, who rarely agree with the Navajo on anything, choose to stay on Mountain Standard Time.

Getting Around

Your own transportation is by far the most convenient, but tours of Navajo country do leave from major centers. **Navajo Transit System,** offers bus service across the Navajo and Hopi reservations Mon.–Fri. and a Saturday service from Window Rock and Fort Defiance to Gallup; no buses run on Sunday and holidays; 928/729-4002. One route connects Fort Defiance and Window Rock in the east with Tuba City in the west, once daily in each direction. Buses also head north from Window Rock and Fort Defiance to Kayenta via Chinle. Other routes connect Fort Defiance and Window Rock with the New Mexico towns of Gallup, Crownpoint, Shiprock, and Farmington.

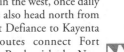

Western Navajo Country

CAMERON

Cameron Trading Post, built in 1916 overlooking the Little Colorado River, commemorates Ralph Cameron, Arizona's last territorial delegate before statehood. The trading post's strategic location near the Grand Canyon makes it a popular stopping point. Facilities include a motel ($89–159 d, less in winter), RV park across the highway ($15 with hookups, no tents, no showers), restaurant, grocery store, Native American crafts shop, post office, and service station. The excellent restaurant, featuring American with some Mexican and Navajo food, is open daily for breakfast, lunch, and dinner—try the Navajo taco in meat or vegetarian versions. The separate gallery in a stone building in front contains museum-quality Native American crafts and art for sale, well worth a look. The trading post is on the west side of US 89, one mile north of the junction with AZ 64 and 54 miles north of Flagstaff; 928/679-2231, 800/338-7385; www.cameron tradingpost.com.

Drop in at the **visitor center/ranger station,** at the US 89-AZ 64 junction, for information about the Navajo Reservation; you can buy tribal hiking and camping permits here, too. The center is open Mon.–Fri. 8 A.M.–5 P.M.; write to P.O. Box 459, Cameron, AZ 86020, 928/679-2303, fax 928/679-2330. **Navajo Arts & Crafts Enterprise** next door offers a good selection of Native American crafts. An **RV park** across US 89 is open all year with sites for tents ($8.50) and RVs ($14.50 with hookups) as well as showers ($2) and laundry; check in at the Chevron station; 928/679-2532. Nearby, the **Trading Post** sells Native American crafts, and **Simpson's Market** has groceries.

Vicinity of Cameron

You'll see the colorful hills of the **Painted Desert** from roads to the north and east of Cameron. To the west, the high, sheer walls of the **Little Colorado River Canyon** make an impressive sight. Viewpoints are 9 and 14 miles west of Cameron on AZ 64, about halfway to Desert View in Grand Canyon National Park. You'll also have a chance to shop for Navajo jewelry at the many roadside stands in the Cameron area on US 89 and AZ 64.

Gray Mountain Trading Post, 10 miles south of Cameron on US 89, has the **Anasazi Inn** and a gas station/convenience store on the east side of the highway and a restaurant (lacks a smoke-free area) and an Native American crafts shop on the west side. The inn has a pool; rates run $70–90 d; 928/679-2214.

Backcountry Areas

Experienced hikers can explore remote and beautiful areas in the western Navajo lands. The visitor center/ranger station in Cameron sells the required permits and has some information; hiking guidebooks have more detailed descriptions. Navajo permits can also be obtained from staff at the Navajo Parks and Recreation office in Window Rock. If you'll be camping in Grand Canyon National Park, permits will also be needed from the Backcountry Information Center there.

Navigating the unsigned back roads to many of the trailheads may require as much map reading skill as does hiking the routes. When it's not in flood, you can follow the Little Colorado River all the way from Cameron down to the Colorado River in the Grand Canyon, though deep pools, quicksand, and flash floods can make the way difficult. The Little Colorado Canyon can also be entered via the Blue Springs Trail, Hopi Trail Crossing, and Hopi Salt Trail, all very challenging and only for knowledgeable canyon hikers. Marble Canyon has difficult rim-to-river routes at Eminence Break, Shinumo Wash, Salt Water Wash, and Jackass Canyon. Rainbow Bridge rates as one of the best hiking destinations on the Colorado Plateau; see "Rainbow Bridge National Monument."

Tatahatso Point

Spectacular views of Marble Canyon greet adventurous drivers who negotiate the confusing network of roads out to the rim. The name

© BILL WEIR

Point Hansbrough encircled by the Colorado River as viewed from Tatahatso Point

comes from the Navajo *dida'a hotsa'a,* meaning "the edge or top of it is big." The rare visitor experiences the precipitous edge, the vastness, and the solitude here. From Cedar Ridge on US 89, the route is about 20 miles to the Point Hansbrough overlook or 25 miles all the way to the end of the road on Tatahatso Point. High-clearance vehicles must be used, and you'll need 4WD if you drive all the way to the end of the point. The trip should be done only in dry weather with good visibility (to see the landmarks); topo maps will be useful. Bring water, food, and camping gear in case of a breakdown, and leave your plans with a reliable person. Although you can drive out in an hour or so, staying overnight will allow you to see the changing colors and patterns in Marble Canyon and on the plateaus all around. *Arizona Highways* did an illustrated article on Tatahatso Point in the July 1998 issue, though the directions seem suspect: "HOW far is it to the stock pond, Sam?"

First obtain a Navajo permit, most easily done at the visitor center/ranger station in Cameron,

then drive to Cedar Ridge on US 89, 40 miles north of Cameron, and turn west on an unpaved road marked by a cairn 0.2 mile north of Milepost 505. This is Indian Route 6110, a wide and bumpy gravel road. Soon the dark, forested Kaibab Plateau comes into view ahead to the west, then Shinumo Altar to the northwest. It's a good idea to look back occasionally for landmarks to help with navigation on the return drive. The route generally heads west, passing several miles south of Shinumo Altar, then at a point southwest of Shinumo, it curves northwest toward Tatahatso Point. Don't panic if you lose the way, as there's more than one way across the plateau—rather, be amazed if you don't make a wrong turn! The author counted one (1) sign on the entire drive! Just try not to disturb anyone at the widely scattered ranches out here.

Keep right on 6110 where the road forks after 6.8 miles. After another 0.6 mile, take the left fork (a small earthen dam is on the left here). After 0.8 mile take the right fork, then a left fork after 0.3 mile; there's a little outcrop of white rocks to the south. Take a right fork after 1.6 miles, then a left fork after 0.2 mile, then right at the next two forks just 0.1 mile apart; Shinumo Altar is almost due north and the San Francisco Peaks rise to the south. The route continues west or slightly northwest 2.7 miles past several crossroads, then takes a right fork 0.3 mile down to a watering hole for local livestock. In another 0.3 mile take the right fork, then keep straight on the left fork 0.7 mile farther. After 1.3 miles, take the right fork, then keep straight on the left fork 0.2 mile farther. In half a mile the road veers to the northwest; there's an earthen ridge to the left in another 0.6 mile. Keep straight on the left fork 0.4 mile past the ridge. Marble Canyon reveals itself to the left after 0.7 mile; the road curves north in another 0.8 mile, then comes to a fork 0.3 mile farther. Turn left here and at the next fork, and you'll have arrived at a cairn marking the end of the road just 0.2 mile farther! The Colorado River makes a 180-degree bend around Point Hansbrough below your feet. President Harding Rapid lies directly below, though only the lower part can be seen. The little side canyon here and cliffs off to your right mark the Eminence Break Fault. Experienced canyon hikers can descend a rough trail from here to President Harding Rapid.

This is the best viewpoint, but you can drive or hike out onto Tatahatso Point for additional views. A rough, steep section of rocky road at the fault requires 4WD—don't descend it unless you're sure that you can make it back up! Although just a short walk below the viewpoint, this rough spot is reached by retracing 0.2 mile back to the main road and continuing around and down to the left in 1.7 miles. Once past the rocks, it's an easy three-mile drive across the point, covered in sage, cholla, and Mormon tea, to an old tramway site at road's end. There's a good view downstream to Buck Farm Canyon. One could hike cross-country about 1.5 miles to the southwest corner of Point Tatahatso or drive half a mile north along the rim to the northwest corner of the point and a view upriver.

TUBA CITY

This administrative and trade center for the western Navajo has nothing to do with tubas and is hardly a city. The town (pop. 7,612, elev. 4,936 feet) commemorates Chief Tuba of the Hopi tribe. The business district isn't much to look at, but the area north of Tuba Trading Post has some fine stone buildings in an oasis of green lawns and shade trees. The springs nearby attracted Mormons who founded a settlement in 1877. They could not gain clear title to the land, however, and the U.S. Indian Agency took it over in 1903. Besides the U.S. government offices, the town has a hospital, schools, and a bank.

Sights Nearby

Dinosaur tracks left by several different species lie preserved in sandstone 5.5 miles west of Tuba City off US 160, about midway between the Tuba City junction and US 89. The turnoff is on the north side of the highway between Mileposts 316 and 317, marked by signs for dinosaur tracks and Moenave. Navajo sell jewelry from stalls here. A guide will probably offer his services, but you can find the several pathway sites on your own—look for the stone-lined paths to them.

Elephant's Feet, a pair of distinctive sandstone pillars, stand near Red Lake, 23 miles northeast of Tuba City on US 160 near Milepost 345.

White Mesa Natural Bridge can be viewed from a distance on a seriously corrugated back road north of Red Lake. Turn north off US 160 between Mileposts 349 and 350 through an oval tunnel under the railroad tracks, continue north 3.7 miles on Indian Route 16, then turn left and go about 5.5 miles on Indian Route 6270; you'll see the huge arch off to the left. Surrounding private ranches prevent a closer approach. The AAA *Indian Country* map shows the roads but not the arch.

Accommodations and Camping

Under $50: Greyhills Inn provides one of the few inexpensive places to stay on the Navajo Nation; students of Greyhills High School operate the motel and youth hostel as part of a training program. Rates are $47 s plus $5 for each additional person; people with hostel cards can stay in shared rooms for $16. The bath is down the hall. Guests have use of a kitchen and

TV lounge. It's open 24 hours. You can make reservations by phone or mail with the Hotel Management Program, Greyhills High School, P.O. Box 160, Tuba City, AZ 86045, 928/283-4450, 928/283-6271, ext. 141/142. From the junction of US 160 and AZ 264, go east a half mile on US 160 to just past the pedestrian overpass, turn left 0.2 mile, turn right, then make the first left into the parking lot.

$50–100: Quality Inn, 928/283-4545, 800/644-8383, sits in the center of town behind Tuba Trading Post, one mile north of the highway junction; $81 s, $86 d (less in winter). The **RV park** here has some trees, showers, and laundry for $20 RV w/hookups and $12 for tents. **Diné Inn Motel,** 928/283-6107, offers basic rooms—all non-smoking—on US 160 east of the AZ 264 junction; $65 s, $70 d.

Food

Hogan Restaurant, 928/283-5260, is next to the Quality Inn and serves Mexican-American food daily for breakfast, lunch, and dinner and has a fruit and salad bar. A half block farther east, **Kate's Cafe,** 928/283-6773, serves American and pasta dishes daily for breakfast, lunch, and dinner. Fast food places line the road into town.

The Truck Stop Cafe, at the US 160-AZ 264 junction, 928/283-4975, has American food daily for breakfast, lunch, and dinner.

Toh Nanees Dizi Shopping Center, a half mile east on US 160, offers two restaurants, a Bashas' supermarket and deli, a movie theater, and shops. **Szechuan Restaurant,** 928/283-5807, at the shopping center serves Chinese cuisine daily for lunch and dinner; there's often a lunch buffet on weekdays. **Pizza Edge,** 928/283-5938, is also at the shopping center and serves pizza, calzone, subs, sandwiches, and ice cream Mon.–Sat. for lunch and dinner.

Shopping

The unusually shaped **Tuba Trading Post** in the center of town offers Native American arts and crafts. It dates to 1870 and had the two-story octagon added in 1920. **Van Trading Co.,** 1.5 miles west of town on US 160, sells Native American crafts, groceries, and most everything else.

Northern Navajo Country

NAVAJO NATIONAL MONUMENT

Navajo National Monument preserves three spectacular prehistoric cliff dwellings, last occupied about 700 years ago. The ancestral Puebloan people who once lived here probably have descendants in present-day Hopi villages. Of the three sites, Betatakin is the most accessible; you can see it from a viewpoint near the visitor center. Rangers lead groups into Betatakin during summer.

Keet Seel, a 16-mile roundtrip hike to the northeast, is the largest cliff dwelling in Arizona. Inscription House, to the west, is the smallest of the three ruins and is closed to the public; it should not be confused with Inscription House Trading Post, which lies some distance away.

You can reach the monument's headquarters and visitor center by following US 160 northeast 52 miles from Tuba City—or southwest 22 miles from Kayenta—then turning north nine miles on AZ 564 at Black Mesa Junction. Tsegi Overlook, on the right just after you enter the monument, has a fine panorama of canyons.

Visitor Center

The ancestral Puebloan people left many questions behind when they abandoned this area. You can learn what is known about these people and ponder the mysteries at the visitor center. Exhibits of prehistoric pottery and other artifacts attempt to piece together what life was like for them. An excellent 25-minute movie on the ancestral Puebloan people is shown on request. A bulletin board lists campfire programs and ranger-led walks. Navajo often demonstrate their art and crafts in or near the visitor center. You can peek into an old-style Navajo forked-stick hogan and see a sweathouse and wagon behind the center. Rangers answer questions and sell books and maps. A gift shop offers Navajo crafts and Hopi, Navajo, and Zuni jewelry. There's a **picnic area** across the parking area.

The visitor center is open daily 8 A.M.–5 P.M., except Thanksgiving, Christmas, and New Year's Day. Contact monument staff at HC 71, Box 3, Tonalea, AZ 86044, 928/672-2700, www.nps.gov/nava.

Sandal Trail

This easy paved trail begins behind the visitor center and winds through a pinyon-juniper woodland to Betatakin Point Overlook, which has a good view of Betatakin across the canyon. The trail is one mile roundtrip and drops 160 feet to the viewpoint. Signs along the way identify native plants and describe how Native Americans used them.

Aspen Trail branches off to the left 400 feet down Sandal Trail, then drops 300 feet with some steps into the head of Betatakin Canyon, 0.8 mile roundtrip. The trail offers pretty scenery along the way and a view of the quaking aspen, Douglas fir, water birch, and redosier redwood trees on the canyon floor below; there's no ruin view or access from this trail.

Visiting Betatakin

Betatakin—Navajo for Ledge House—lies tucked in a natural alcove that measures 452 feet high, 370 feet across, and 135 feet deep. It contains 135 rooms and one kiva. Inhabitants built and abandoned the entire village within two generations, between A.D. 1260 and 1300.

You may hike here only with park rangers, who lead one four-hour tour a day from Memorial Day to Labor Day weekends. Groups are limited to 25 people, first come, first served, so be early. Starting at the trailhead (one mile from the visitor center), the five-mile roundtrip trail is primitive and drops 700 feet, which you have to climb on the way back, and winds around to a viewpoint of the cliff dwelling. At press time, you couldn't enter the ruins due to rockfall danger. Thin air—the trailhead elevation is 7,300 feet—can make the hike very tir-

© BILL WEIR

Betatakin Ruins

ing. People with heart, respiratory, or mobility problems shouldn't attempt it.

Visiting Keet Seel

This isolated cliff dwelling is one of the best preserved in the Southwest. Keet Seel—Navajo for Broken Pottery—has 160 rooms and four kivas. The ruins look as though they were abandoned just a few years back, not seven long centuries ago. The site, 8.5 miles by trail from the visitor center, is open from Memorial Day to Labor Day weekends. A permit is required, and there's a limit of 20 people per day. Visitors should make reservations two months ahead with Navajo National Monument, HC 71, Box 3, Tonalea, AZ 86044, 928/672-2700. To pick up your permit, you must attend a scheduled trail orientation in the morning or the afternoon before. (Remember that you're in daylight saving time.)

The trail descends from Tsegi Point to the canyon bottom, travels downstream a short distance, then heads upstream into Keet Seel Canyon. You may have to do some wading. Carry water, as livestock pollute the streams. Visitors may not enter the site without a ranger, stationed nearby. Backpackers can stay in a primitive campground (free, one-night limit) near Keet Seel. Strong hikers can do the roundtrip in a day, though spending a night here makes for an easier, more relaxing visit.

Services

A free **campground** in a pinyon-juniper woodland lies near the visitor center; you can stay year-round but water is on only from about mid-May to mid-October. Campfire programs run many nights in summer. There's nearly always room; no reservations taken. Expect cold and likelihood of snow from November to mid-March. **Anasazi Inn** ($79–99 d, less in winter) and its café (open daily for breakfast, lunch, and dinner) lie 18 miles away on the road to Kayenta; 928/697-3793. Kayenta, 11 miles farther, offers three motels, a basic RV park, and several restaurants.

Black Mesa Shopping Center, nine miles south of the visitor center at the junction of AZ 564 and US 160, has the closest grocery store and service station. The road south from here goes to the coal mines of the Peabody Coal Company, a major employer of the Navajo.

Shonto

This Navajo settlement sits in a small canyon southwest of Navajo National Monument. A trading post offers groceries and Navajo crafts. The shaded park in front is a good spot for a picnic. A chapter house and Bureau of Indian Affairs (BIA) boarding school lie nearby. Shonto is 10 miles from the visitor center on a sandy road not recommended for cars (except during the school year, when it's kept graded), or 33 miles via US 160 on paved roads.

KAYENTA

The "Gateway to Monument Valley" has a population of 7,549 in a bleak, windswept valley (elev. 5,660 feet). Its name is loosely derived from the Navajo word *Teehindeeh,* meaning "boghole," as there were once shallow lakes here. Kayenta makes a handy stop for travelers, with three good motels, a basic RV park, several restaurants, and shopping.

Accommodations and Camping

$50–100: Hampton Inn, 928/697-3170, 800/426-7866, offers spacious rooms at $91–99 s, $98–106 d in summer along with a restaurant, gift shop, and outdoor pool on US 160 west of the Kayenta turnoff. **Best Western Wetherill Inn,** 928/697-3231, 800/528-1234, lies in the center of town on US 163, one mile north of US 160. Its name honors John Wetherill, an early trader and rancher in the region who discovered Betatakin, Mesa Verde, and other major ancestral Puebloan sites. Rooms cost $98 d in summer, less off-season. Guests can enjoy an indoor pool and a gift shop. **Roland's Navajoland Tours,** 928/697-3524, 800/368-2785, offers bed and breakfast rooms on US 163, half a mile north of the US 160 junction, for $50–75 d, less in winter; you can also arrange Monument Valley tours here.

$100–150: Holiday Inn, on US 160 at the turnoff for Kayenta, 928/697-3221,

800/HOLIDAY, offers rooms for $129 d in summer, as well as a restaurant, gift shop, tours, and an outdoor pool.

The **Coin-Op Laundry** in town offers basic RV spaces for $10 with hookups; tent campers are welcome too, though campgrounds at Monument Valley or Navajo Natl. Monument are far more scenic. Showers are also available to noncampers for $2.75; 928/697-3738.

Food

Hampton Inn's **Reuben Heflin Restaurant,** 928/697-3170, serves American and Navajo food daily for lunch and dinner. Holiday Inn's **Wagon Wheel Restaurant** serves up good Navajo tacos and American fare daily for breakfast, lunch, and dinner; there's also a breakfast buffet in season and a salad bar. **Amigo Cafe** prepares Mexican and American food Mon.–Sat. for breakfast, lunch, and dinner. You'll find it 0.2 mile in on US 163 between the Kayenta turnoff and town; 928/697-8448. **Golden Sands Cafe** near the Wetherill Inn offers American food daily for breakfast, lunch, and dinner; 928/697-3684.

For pizza, calzones, and subs, try **Pizza Edge,** open Mon.–Sat. for lunch and dinner in the Teehindeeh Shopping Center; 928/697-8427. Also near the shopping center, **Blue Coffee Pot Cafe,** 928/697-3396, prepares Mexican and American food Mon.–Fri. for breakfast, lunch, and dinner. **McDonalds** and **Burger King** also lie near the shopping center; Burger King has exhibits on WW II Navajo Code Talkers. Buy groceries at Bashas' supermarket and deli in the shopping center or at the Kayenta Trading Post behind the Wetherill Inn.

Shopping and Services

Kayenta Visitor Center, 928/697-3572, in front of the shopping center, sells Navajo arts and crafts and provides local information. **Navajo Cultural Center** to the west has traditional forked-stick and octagonal hogans, sweathouse, and shade house; a weaver demonstrates her craft here during the warmer months. **Navajo Nation Arts & Crafts Showroom,** just east of the highway junction past Thriftway gas station, has a good selection. The motels have Native American arts and crafts, too.

Tours in 4WD vehicles to Monument Valley and the surrounding country can be arranged at the motels and the Kayenta Visitor Center, or you can wait until you arrive at Monument Valley, where Navajos offer a variety of driving, horseback riding, and hiking tours.

MONUMENT VALLEY

Towering buttes, jagged pinnacles, and rippled sand dunes make this an otherworldly landscape. Changing colors and shifting shadows add to the feeling of enchantment. Most of the natural monuments are remnants of sandstone eroded by wind and water. Agathla Peak and some lesser summits, roots of ancient volcanoes, rise in the southern part of the valley; their dark rock contrasts with the pale yellow sandstone of the other formations. The desert valley lies at an elevation of 5,564 feet; annual rainfall averages about 8.5 inches.

In 1863–64, when Kit Carson was ravaging Canyon de Chelly and rounding up Navajo, Chief Hoskinini led his people to the safety and freedom of Monument Valley. Merrick Butte and Mitchell Mesa commemorate two miners who discovered rich silver deposits on their first trip to the valley in 1880. On their second trip both were killed, reportedly by Paiutes. Hollywood movies made the splendor of Monument Valley known to the outside world. *Stagecoach,* filmed here by John Ford in 1938, began a long series of movies, television shows, and commercials shot in the valley that continues to this day; warriors from John Wayne to Susan Sarandon have ridden across these sands.

The Navajo have preserved the valley as a tribal park with a visitor center, scenic drive, and campground. The **visitor center,** 435/727-5872, has an information desk, a few exhibits, and booths where you can sign up for tours; it's open 7 A.M.–7 P.M. in summer and 8 A.M.–5 P.M. the rest of the year; closed Thanksgiving Day afternoon and Christmas; www.navajonation parks .org. Entry to the drive closes half an hour before the visitor center and you must be out before dark. Navajos sell crafts and food from little shops near the highway turnoff. Visitors pay a $3 per person fee (free ages seven and under) collected on the entrance road. From Kayenta, head 24 miles north on US 163 and turn right 3.5 miles.

Monument Valley Drive

A 17-mile, self-guided scenic drive begins at the visitor center and loops through the heart of the valley. Overlooks along the way provide sweeping vistas. The dirt road is normally okay if you drive cautiously, but don't attempt it with RVs over 27 feet or extremely low-clearance vehicles. Avoid stopping and becoming stuck in the loose sand that sometimes blows across the road. Allow one and a half hours for the drive. No hiking or driving is permitted off the signed route. Only the visitor center and campground have water, so you'll probably like to bring some along.

Valley Tours

Navajo guides in the visitor center offer tours year-round. The shortest trips last an hour and a half and cover places on the self-guided route. Longer trips of two and a half or three and a half hours visit hogans, cliff dwellings, and petroglyphs in areas beyond the self-guided drive. Horseback rides from stables near the visitor center can easily be arranged for one and a half hours to all day; overnight trips are available too. If you'd like to hike in Monument Valley, you must hire a guide at the visitor center; hiking tours can last from a few hours to a day or more.

Reservations aren't required on the tours. If you'd like to do overnight trips, it's best to call ahead and bring your own food and camping gear. **Totem Pole Tours,** 435/727-3313, 800/345-8687, offers driving trips, photography tours, trail rides, and hiking including cookouts and overnights. **Homeland Tours,** 435/727-3245, 800/388-5613, can take you on a variety of backroad drives, trailrides, or hikes. **Roland's Navajoland Tours,** 928/697-3524, 800/368-2785, offers a variety of backcountry drives, photography tours, hiking trips, and a bed and breakfast (in Kayenta). **Sacred Monument Tours,** 435/727-3218, leads jeep, horse-

back, hiking, and photography tours; www.monumentvalley.net. **Monument Valley Horseback Trailrides,** 435/683-2327, will take you out for an hour or more—up to five days.

Accommodations and Food

Sites at **Mitten View Campground** near the visitor center have great views though tent campers often have to contend with pesky winds in this exposed location. The cost is $10, with coin-operated showers from early April to mid-October. No hookups are available, but there's a fill and dump station. Off-season the rate drops to $5 and you can use restrooms next to the visitor center. Goulding's Lodge offers the nearest motel, store, and telephone. You'll also find motels at Kayenta in Arizona and at Mexican Hat and Bluff in Utah.

Country of Many Hogan Bed & Breakfast, 928/283-4125, near Monument Valley offers accommodations in hogans with traditional food at $145 d in summer (less in winter) with a continental breakfast. Dinner, camping, sweat lodge, horseback rides, hiking tours, and driving trips can be arranged at extra cost; http://navajoland.com/cmh.

Goulding's Lodge and Trading Post

In 1924, Harry Goulding and his wife, Mike, opened a trading post at this scenic spot, just north of the Arizona-Utah border and 1.5 miles west of the US 163 Monument Valley turnoff. **Goulding's Museum,** in the old trading post building, displays prehistoric and modern Native American artifacts, movie photos, period rooms, and Goulding family memorabilia. It's open daily (on request in winter) and donations are appreciated. Nearby, a shack built for John Wayne in *She Wore a Yellow Ribbon* has exhibits from the movie.

Motel rooms go for $155 d June 1–Oct. 15, dropping to $62 d midwinter; a stiff 17 percent tax is added. Guests enjoy views and an indoor pool. The Stagecoach Restaurant's menu offers such American favorites as steak, chicken, pork, fish, sandwiches, and a salad bar. Local specialties include Navajo tacos, both beef and vegetarian, and there are a few pasta and stir-fry items. The Stagecoach is open daily for breakfast, lunch, and dinner.

The large gift shop sells high-quality Native American work plus souvenirs and books. A multimedia show, *Earth Spirit,* portrays the region. The nearby gas station has a fast-food counter and there's a convenience store across the road. An airstrip also lies nearby. Monument Valley tours operate year-round at $25.50 for two and a half hours, $30.50 for three and a half hours, and $60.50 full day with lunch; children under 8 pay less. For accommodation and tour information, contact P.O. Box 360001, Monument Valley, UT 84536; 435/727-3231, 800/874-0902; www.gouldings.com.

Goulding's Monument Valley Campground, 435/727-3235, 800/874-0902, offers a spectacular canyon setting one mile west of the lodge turnoff. Tent ($15) and RV ($24 with full hookups) campers have an indoor pool, showers, laundry, and convenience store/gift shop. It's open March 15–Oct. 31. The Seventh-Day Adventist Church founded the nearby hospital and mission.

FOUR CORNERS MONUMENT

An inlaid concrete slab marks the place where Utah, Colorado, New Mexico, and Arizona meet. This is the only spot in the United States where you can put your finger on four states at once. It's said that more than 2,000 people a day stop at the marker in the summer. Average stay? Seven to 10 minutes. On the other hand, five national parks and 18 national monuments lie within a 150-mile radius of this point. Navajo, and occasionally Ute and Pueblo, set up dozens of craft and refreshment booths here in summer. Navajo Parks and Recreation collects a small fee during the tourist season.

Eastern Navajo Country

CANYON DE CHELLY NATIONAL MONUMENT

You'll find prehistoric cliff dwellings and traditional Navajo life preserved in spectacular canyons here. The main canyons are 26-mile-long Canyon de Chelly (pronounced *d'SHAY*) and adjoining 35-mile-long Canyon del Muerto. Sheer sandstone walls rise as high as 1,000 feet, giving the canyons a fortress-like appearance. Rim elevations range from 5,500 feet at the visitor center to 7,000 feet at the end of the scenic drives. Allow at least a full day to see some of the monument's 83,840 acres. April to October is the best time to visit. Winter brings cold weather and a chance of snow. Afternoon thunderstorms arrive almost daily in late summer, creating thousands of waterfalls that cascade over the rims, stopping when the skies clear.

The small, spread-out town of Chinle, just west of Canyon de Chelly National Monument, takes its name from a Navajo word meaning "Water Outlet"—the Rio de Chelly emerges from its canyon here. Chinle offers motels, several restaurants, a supermarket, shops, post office, Laundromat, and service stations.

The First Peoples

Nomadic tribes roamed these canyons more than 2,000 years ago, collecting wild foods and hunting game. Little remains of these early visitors, who must have found welcome shelter from the elements in the natural rock overhangs of the canyons. The ancestral Puebloan people made their first appearance about A.D. 1, living in alcoves during the winter and brush shelters in summer. By A.D. 500 they had begun cultivating permanent fields of corn, squash, and beans and fashioning pottery. Villagers lived at that time in year-round pithouses, partly underground structures roofed with sticks and mud.

Around A.D. 700 the population began to build above-ground cliff houses of stone. These pueblos (Spanish for "villages") also contained underground ceremonial rooms, known as kivas, used for social and religious purposes. Most of the cliff houses now visible in Canyon de Chelly date from A.D. 1100–1300, when an estimated 1,000 people occupied the many small villages. At the end of this period the ancestral Puebloan people migrated from these canyons and from other large population centers. Archaeologists speculate that possible causes include floods, drought, overpopulation, and soil erosion.

It's likely that some ancestral Puebloan people moved to the Hopi mesas, as Hopi religion, traditions, and farming practices have many similarities with those of the Canyon de Chelly cliff dwellers. During the next 400 years, Hopi farmers sometimes used the canyons during the growing season, but they returned to the mesas after each harvest.

The Navajo Arrive

First entering Canyon de Chelly about A.D. 1700, the Navajo found it an ideal base for raiding nearby Native American and Spanish settlements. In 1805 the Spanish launched a punitive expedition; soldiers reported killing 115 Navajo, including 90 warriors. The Navajo identified the dead as mostly women, children, and old men. The site of the killing became known as Massacre Cave. During the Mexican era, raids took place in both directions; the Navajo sought food and livestock, while Mexicans kidnapped women and children to serve as slaves.

Contact with Americans also went badly— settlers encroached on Navajo land and soldiers proved deceitful. Conflict came to an end in the winter of 1863–64, when Colonel Kit Carson led detachments of the U.S. Cavalry into the canyons. The army destroyed the tribe's livestock, fruit trees, and food stores and captured or killed nearly every Navajo it could find. The starving survivors had no choice but to surrender and be herded onto a desolate reservation in eastern New Mexico. After this infamous "Long Walk," and four miserable years there, they were permitted to return to their beloved canyons in 1868.

Today, Navajo continue farming and grazing sheep on the canyon floors. You can see their distinctive round hogans next to the fields. More

© BILL WEIR

White House Ruin, Canyon de Chelly

than 50 families live in the canyons, but most find it convenient to spend winters on the canyon rims, returning to their fields after the spring floods have subsided.

Visitor Center

Exhibits reveal Native American history from the Archaic period (before A.D. 1) to the present, with many fine artifacts. A 22-minute video, *Canyon Voices,* provides additional insights into the peoples who have lived here, as do regional books available for purchase. You can step into a Navajo hogan next to the visitor center. A bulletin board lists scheduled talks, campfire programs, and hikes. Rangers are happy to answer your questions. The visitor center is open daily 8 A.M.–6 P.M. from about May 1 to September 30, and daily 8 A.M.–5 P.M. the rest of the year; contact P.O. Box 588, Chinle, AZ 86503, 928/674-5500, www.nps.gov/cach.

NORTHEASTERN

Sights

Canyons de Chelly and del Muerto each feature a paved scenic rim drive with viewpoints along the edges, or you can travel inside the canyons by 4WD vehicle, horseback, or foot. Except on the White House Ruin Trail, you may enter the canyons only with an authorized Navajo guide or monument ranger. This rule is strictly enforced to protect the ruins and the privacy of families living in the canyons. All land belongs to the Navajo people; the National Park Service administers policies only within monument boundaries.

Vehicle break-ins have become a major problem at overlooks, especially at the top of White House Ruin Trail. Sneak thieves search out cash, cameras, camcorders, computers, and other valuables, which you'll want to keep stored out of sight.

Hiking

If you have a guide, you can hike almost anywhere. Navajos will usually be waiting near the visitor center to accompany you on canyon trips; they can suggest routes depending on your interests and time available. Rangers at the visitor center can help make arrangements and issue the necessary permit. Comfortable walking shoes, water, insect repellent, and a hat will come in handy. Expect to do some wading. In fact, under the hot summer sun with red rocks all around, you may insist on it—the cool water and the shade of the trees are irresistible. Autumn can bring especially good hiking weather, with comfortable temperatures and the spectacle of cottonwoods turning to gold.

Guides charge $15 per hour for up to 15 people. Overnight trips are possible with additional charges for the guide and landowner, but costs can be very high.

Guides sometimes lead scheduled half-day hikes in the lower canyon from late May to the end of September. Meet the guides at the visitor center, and check departure time the day before—hikes leave promptly. Also, it's a good idea to make reservations the day before, as group size is limited.

Canyon Driving Tours

Tours leave Thunderbird Lodge daily at 9 A.M. and 2 P.M. during the busy season and visit both canyons. In winter, you should call ahead to make sure trips are scheduled; there's a minimum of six passengers. The trips, very popular with visitors, run half day ($39 adults, $30 children 12 and under) and full day ($63.50 per person—all ages—including lunch). You'll enjoy unobstructed views from the back of an open truck that stops frequently for photography and viewing of ruins. Half-day trips typically head up Canyon del Muerto to Antelope House Ruin and up Canyon de Chelly to White House Ruin. Full-day excursions can go much farther up each canyon—as far as Mummy Cave in Canyon del Muerto and Spider Rock in Canyon de Chelly.

De Chelly Tours offers private jeep and hiking trips, from three hours to all day or overnight starting at $125 per vehicle for three hours; 928/674-3772.

You can also take your own 4WD vehicles into the canyons with a guide and permit arranged at the visitor center; cost is $15 per hour with a three-hour minimum for up to five vehicles.

Horseback Riding

Justin's Horse Rentals, 928/674-5678, is at the entrance to the canyons opposite the Thunderbird Lodge/Cottonwood Campground turnoff. Rides, available all year, cost $10 per hour for each rider and $15 per hour for the guide (one per group). You can arrange trips of two hours to several days; contact P.O. Box 881, Chinle, AZ 86503.

Tohtsonii Ranch, 928/755-6209, offers four-hour guided horse rides down the Bat Trail in the Spider Rock area and all-day trips that continue to the mouth of the canyon at $10 per hour per person plus $15 per hour for the guide; overnight trips can be arranged too. The ranch is 1.6 miles down a dirt road off the South Rim Drive of Canyon de Chelly (keep straight where the drive turns left for Spider Rock Overlook); contact P.O. Box 434, Chinle, AZ 86503.

You can also ride your own horse by arranging board and feed at one of the stables near the park and by hiring an authorized Navajo guide, preferably from one of the horse concessions.

Accommodations and Camping

Under $50: Many Farms Inn, 17 miles north of Chinle on the way to Monument Valley and Four Corners, 928/781-6362, offers rooms with two beds at $30 (1–4 people, shared baths) in a school training program. Guests can use the coffee room, TV lounge, and laundry. From the junction of US 191 and Indian Route 59, go north 0.7 mile on US 191, turn left 0.7 mile at the Many Farms High School sign, then right 0.3 mile.

$100–150: Thunderbird Lodge, 928/674-5841/5842 or 800/679-2473, has an attractive setting amidst lawns and shade trees a half mile south of the visitor center. The cafeteria, large gift shop, and tours here are a big hit with many visitors. The lodge began as a trading post for the Navajo in 1902, then expanded to accommodate tourists as they began arriving in sizable numbers. Rates from April 1 to November 15 start at $97 s, $101 d, less in winter; www.tbirdlodge.com. **Holiday Inn,** 928/674-5000, 800/465-4329 (HOLIDAY), is at the Chinle entrance to the monument; guests enjoy a restaurant, gift shop, and outdoor pool; rates are $99–109 d in season. **Best Western Canyon de Chelly Inn,** 928/674-5875, 800/327-0354, lies 2.5 miles west of the visitor center and offers a restaurant, indoor pool, and gift shop; rates run $109 d from May 2 to October 31, less off season.

Cottonwood Campground, between the visitor center and Thunderbird Lodge, offers pleasant sites with many large cottonwood trees. It's free and open all year, with water available only from April to October; no showers or hookups are available, though there is a dump station. Rangers present campfire programs from late May to the end of September. The campground usually has space; reservations are accepted only for group sites. Cottonwood trees also shade a **picnic area** near the campground; water is available except in winter.

You can escape the crowds at **Spider Rock Campground,** a primitive, privately owned place in a pinyon-juniper woodland; it's eight miles from the visitor center and half a mile before the Spider Rock turnoff on the South Rim Drive; there's a fee with extra charges for water, solar showers, and local tours.

Food

Thunderbird Lodge features a good cafeteria open daily 6:30 A.M.–9 P.M. (8 P.M. in winter). **Holiday Inn's** dining room features the most extensive menu and attractive decor in the area; for dinner you can choose from steaks, ribs, lamb, trout, shrimp, Southwestern, and pasta dishes. In high season, there's a breakfast buffet and a salad bar; the restaurant is open daily for breakfast, lunch, and dinner. **Canyon de Chelly Inn's** Junction Restaurant has American and some Navajo dishes daily for breakfast, lunch, and dinner.

Pizza Edge serves up pizza, calzones, and sandwiches Mon.–Sat. for lunch and dinner in the **Tseyi Shopping Center,** on US 191 just north of the junction with Indian Route 7. **Bashas'** supermarket and deli, **Taco Bell,** and **Burger King** are in the shopping center too; **A&W** is across the highway. **Church's Chicken** is several blocks east of the junction on Route 7.

Shopping and Services

Navajo Nation Arts & Crafts Showroom sits opposite the Canyon de Chelly turnoff from US 191. The three lodges also display Native American work in their gift shops. The **post office** is in Tseyi Shopping Center.

SOUTH RIM DRIVE OF CANYON DE CHELLY

All pullouts and turns are on the left. Distances include mileage between turnoffs and overlooks. Allow at least two hours for the drive. Parked vehicles should be locked and valuables removed. Binoculars come in handy at the viewpoints.

Mile 0: Visitor Center. The nearby canyon walls stand only about 30 feet high where the Rio de Chelly enters Chinle Wash.

Mile 2.0: Tunnel Canyon Overlook. The canyon is about 275 feet deep here. Guides sometimes lead short hikes down the trail in this side canyon. Don't go hiking without a ranger or Navajo guide.

Mile 2.3: Tsegi Overlook. You'll see a Navajo hogan and farm below. Tsegi is the Navajo word for "rock canyon," which the Spanish pronounced "de chegui." American usage changed it to "de chelly" (d'SHAY).

Mile 3.7: Junction Overlook. Here Canyon del Muerto, across the valley, joins Canyon de Chelly. Canyon depth is about 400 feet. Look for two cliff dwellings of ancestral Puebloan people. First Ruin is located in the cliff at the far side of the canyon. The pueblo has 10 rooms and two kivas, and dates from the late 11th to late 13th centuries. Junction Ruin lies straight across, where the two canyons join. It has 15 rooms and one kiva. These dwellings, like most others in the monument, face south to catch the sun's warmth in winter.

Mile 5.9: White House Overlook. Canyon walls rise about 550 feet at this point. White House Ruin, on the far side, is one of the largest in the monument. The name comes from the original white plaster on the walls in the upper section. Parts of 60 rooms and four kivas remain in the upper and lower sections; there may have been 80 rooms before floodwaters carried away some of the lower section. As many as 12 ancestral Puebloan families may have lived in this village about A.D. 1060–1275.

From the overlook, **White House Ruin Trail** begins about 500 feet to the right. Many trails connect the rim with the canyon bottom, but few are as easy as this one. The Navajo often used it to move sheep. Allow two hours for the 2.5-mile roundtrip; bring water but no pets. This is the only hike in the canyon permitted without a guide, but you must stay on the trail. You can buy a pamphlet describing the trail at the visitor center.

Mile 12.0: Sliding House Overlook. These ruins, perched on a narrow ledge across the canyon, are well named. The people who constructed the village on this sloping ledge tried to brace rooms with retaining walls. Natural de-

pressions at the overlook collect water and are still sometimes used by the Navajo.

Mile 19.6: Face Rock Overlook. Small cliff dwellings sit high on the rock face opposite the viewpoint. Though the rooms look impossible to reach, the ancestral Puebloan people cleverly chipped handholds and toeholds into the rock.

Mile 20.6: Spider Rock Overlook. The South Rim Drive ends where rock walls plummet 1,000 feet from the rim to the canyon floor. Spider Rock, the highest of the twin spires, rises 800 feet from the bottom of Canyon de Chelly. One story relates how newly arrived Navajo found an old woman in the canyon who taught them how to weave. She's now known as Spider Woman, a Navajo deity who makes her home atop Spider Rock.

You can see tiny cliff dwellings in the canyon walls if you look hard enough. Monument Canyon comes in around to the right. Black Rock Butte (7,622 feet high), on the horizon, is the weathered heart of an extinct volcano.

© BILL WEIR

Antelope House Ruin

NORTH RIM DRIVE OF CANYON DEL MUERTO

All turnoffs are on the right. Distances include mileage between turnoffs and overlooks. Allow at least two hours for the drive. Parked vehicles should be locked and valuables removed. Binoculars come in handy at the viewpoints.

Mile 0: Visitor Center. Cross the nearby Rio de Chelly bridge and continue northeast on Indian Route 64.

Mile 5.9: Ledge Ruin Overlook. The ruin, set in an opening 100 feet above the canyon floor, dates from A.D. 1050 to 1275 and has 29 rooms, including two kivas, in a two-story structure. Walk south a short way to another overlook and a view downcanyon; a solitary kiva is visible high in the cliff face. A toe-and-handhold trail connects it with other rooms in a separate alcove to the west.

Mile 10.0: Antelope House Overlook. Keep right at the fork on the a quarter-mile walk to the viewpoint. Antelope House Ruin had 91 rooms and a four-story building. The village layout is clear—from the overlook you gaze almost straight down on it. The round outlines are kivas. The square rooms were for living or storage. Floods have damaged some of the rooms, perhaps while the ancestral Puebloan people still lived there. Residents abandoned the site about 1260. Its name comes from paintings of antelope, some believed to be the work of a Navajo artist in the 1830s.

The Tomb of the Weaver sits across from Antelope House in a small alcove 50 feet above the canyon floor. Here, in the 1920s, archaeologists found the elaborate burial site of an old man. The well-preserved body had been wrapped in a blanket made from what appeared to be golden eagle feathers. A cotton blanket was enclosed;

> *Spider Rock rises 800 feet from the bottom of Canyon de Chelly. One story relates how newly arrived Navajo found an old woman in the canyon who taught them how to weave. She's now known as Spider Woman, a Navajo deity who makes her home atop Spider Rock.*

these were covered with cotton yarn topped with a spindle whorl.

Look for Navajo Fortress, the sandstone butte across the canyon, from a viewpoint a short walk east from Antelope House Overlook. When danger threatened, the Navajo climbed up the east side using log poles as ladders. They pulled in the uppermost logs and pelted attackers with a hail of rocks. Navajo used this natural fortress from the time of the Spanish until the Kit Carson campaign.

Mile 18.7: Mummy Cave Overlook. Archaeologists in the late 1800s named this large cliff dwelling for two mummies found in the talus slope below. Canyon del Muerto (Spanish for Canyon of the Dead) reportedly also took its name from this find. Mummy Cave Ruin sits within two separate overhangs several hundred feet above the canyon floor. The largest section is on the east (to the left), with 50 rooms and three kivas; the west cave contains 20 rooms. Between these sections is a ledge with seven rooms, including a three-story tower of unknown purpose. The tower dates from about A.D. 1284 and is thought to have been built by ancestral Puebloan people from Mesa Verde in Colorado.

Mile 20.6: Massacre Cave Overlook. The North Rim Drive ends here. In 1805, Antonio de Narbona led an expedition of Spanish soldiers and allied Native Americans to these canyons. A group of fleeing Navajo managed to scale the nearly 1,000 feet to this overhang. Narbona's troops, however, ascended the rim overlooking the cave and fired down. Narbona's account listed 115 Navajo killed and 33 taken captive.

From Yucca Cave Overlook nearby, you can see a cave with at least four rooms and a kiva. A small cave to the left was used for food storage; a toe-and-handhold trail connected the two alcoves.

EAST OF CANYON DE CHELLY NATIONAL MONUMENT

Diné College (Tsaile Campus)

Recognizing the need for college education, the Navajo in 1957 established a scholarship fund financed by royalties from oil. Students had to leave the reservation to receive a college education, but the cultural gap between the Navajo and the outside world proved too great, and many students dropped out. So in 1969 the tribe created Navajo Community College, later renamed Diné College. ("Diné" is the name Navajo prefer when speaking of themselves.) Students used temporary facilities at Many Farms, Arizona, until 1973, when campuses opened at Tsaile and at Shiprock, New Mexico. Students can choose from many Navajo and Native American studies courses—crafts, language, politics, music, dance, herbology, and holistic healing. The colleges offer vocational training and adult education too. The website www.dinecollege.edu lists programs, visitor information, museum exhibits, and college-published books.

The unusual campus layout resulted from Navajo elders and healers working together with conventional architects. Because important Navajo activities take place within a circle, the campus grounds and many of the buildings took on that shape. If you know your way around a hogan, you'll find it easy getting around campus: the library is tucked in where the medicine bundle is kept during a ceremony, the cooking area (dining hall) lies in the center, sleeping (dormitories) is centered in the west, the teaching area (classrooms) occupies the south, and the recreation area (student union and gym) is in the north. The central campus entrance, marked by the glass-walled Ned A. Hatathli Center, faces east to the rising sun.

The **Hatathli Museum** claims to be the "first *true* Native American museum." Managed entirely by tribespeople, the collection occupies the third and fourth floors of the hogan-shaped Hatathli Center. Exhibits display art and interpret the cultures of prehistoric peoples as well as Navajo and other modern tribes. The museum and adjacent sales gallery are open Mon.–Fri. 8:30 A.M.–4:30 P.M.; 928/724-6654. A donation is requested. Ned

Hatathli was the first Navajo manager of the tribal Arts and Crafts guild and a Tribal Council member.

Diné College Press publishes and sells books on the Navajo and related topics on the first floor of the Hatathli Center. Visitors are welcome in the college cafeteria (on the right) and library (on the left) as you walk west behind the Hatathli Center. The Tsaile campus lies 23 miles east of the Canyon de Chelly Visitor Center and 54 miles north of Window Rock.

Wheatfields Lake

This large mountain lake lies surrounded by a ponderosa forest at an elevation of 7,300 feet, 10 miles south of Tsaile and 44 miles north of Window Rock on Indian Route 12. Visitors enjoy camping and trout fishing at this pretty spot. The rugged Chuska Mountains rise to the east. Campground charges run $2 per person for ages 13 and over; bring water. You'll need Navajo fishing and boat permits, as on all tribal waters. In winter, snow and ice often make driving here unsafe.

Navajo, New Mexico

Trees from the extensive woodlands that surround the town of Navajo supply the town's large sawmill. A supermarket sells groceries and tribal fishing permits. Nearby **Red Lake,** named for the color of its aquatic vegetation, has fishing. Navajo is 17 miles north of Window Rock on Route 12, on the way to Wheatfields Lake, Tsaile, and Canyon de Chelly. **Assayi Lake,** 11 miles northeast in New Mexico at Bowl Canyon Recreation Area, has trout fishing and camping, $10 day use or $15 overnight; it's not suitable for RVs. Whiskey Lake is farther east, also on dirt roads, and offers trout fishing.

WINDOW ROCK

In the early 1930s, "The Rock With a Hole in It" so impressed Commissioner of Indian Affairs John Collier that he chose the site for a Navajo administration center. An octagonal Navajo Council House, representing a great ceremonial hogan, went up, and Window Rock became the capital of the Navajo Nation. Tribal Council delegates meet here to decide on reservation policies and regulations.

Window Rock is a small (area pop. about

8,000) but growing town at an elevation of 6,750 feet. Besides the Council Chambers and offices, the town contains a museum, small zoo, two parks, a motel, and a shopping center. Window Rock's downtown is the shopping center at the junction of AZ 264 and Indian Route 12.

Window Rock hosts the Navajo Nation Fair, said to be the world's largest Native American fair, on the first weekend after Labor Day in September. The five-day festival offers a mixture of traditional and modern attractions, including singing and dancing, a parade, agricultural shows, food, crafts, concerts, rodeo, and the crowning of Miss Navajo. Write for a brochure from the Navajo Nation Fair office, P.O. Box 2370, Window Rock, AZ 86515, 928/871-6478, 928/871-6702; www.navajonationparks.org.

Navajo Museum, Library, and Visitor Center
The entrance of this impressive building opens to the east, like the traditional log hogan in front.

© BILL WEIR

Window Rock

Massive wood pillars soar to the central skylight high above. Museum galleries, 928/871-7941, present excellent historical and art exhibits from the permanent collection and visiting shows. The library, across the lobby, has many books on Native American subjects, as well as general reading; 928/871-6376, 928/871-6526. A gift shop off the lobby offers Native American arts and crafts.

Staff at the information desk in the lobby answer questions and provide Navajo and Arizona travel literature; 928/871-7941, 928/871-7371 (tourism office); navajo.org. The desk, museum, library, and gift shop all stay open Mon. 8 A.M.–5 P.M., Tues.–Fri. 8 A.M.–8 P.M., and Sat. 9 A.M.–5 P.M. There's also an indoor theater and large outdoor amphitheater. It's on the north side of AZ 264 in Tse Bonito Tribal Park, a half mile east of Window Rock Shopping Center. The park also offers some shaded picnic tables. The Navajo camped here in 1864 on The Long Walk to eastern New Mexico.

Navajo Nation Zoological and Botanical Park
Set beneath towering sandstone pinnacles known as The Haystacks, the zoo offers a close look at animals of the Southwest. Once past the rattlesnakes and other small creatures of the orientation building near the entrance, you'll wander by golden eagles, hawks, elk, coyotes, black bears, mountain lions, wolves, bobcats, and other life. Domestic breeds include the Navajo churro sheep, which has a double fleece and often four horns. Prairie dogs, free of restricting cages, run almost everywhere. Visit daily 8 A.M.–5 P.M.; free admission; 928/871-6573. You'll find it just northeast of the museum and library building.

Window Rock Tribal Park
This beautiful spot shaded by juniper trees lies at the foot of Window Rock. The "window" is a great hole, averaging 47 feet across, in a sandstone ridge. Loose stones just below the hole mark the site of a prehistoric pueblo. You're not allowed to climb up to the hole, though a trail around to the left passes through wonderfully sculptured hills. The park has picnic tables, water, and restrooms for day-use only. The Navajo Nation Veterans Memorial here honors warriors from all eras of war and

peace. Head north about a half mile on Indian Route 12 from AZ 264, turn right at the sign and head a half mile in, passing the Council Chambers on your left just before the park.

Navajo Nation Council Chambers

The Council meets at least four times a year within the circular walls here. At other times twelve standing committees of the Council carry out legislative work. Colorful murals depict Navajo history. If not in use, the chambers can be visited Mon.–Fri. 8 A.M.–5 P.M. For more information, call the Speaker's Office at 928/871-7160.

Accommodations and Camping

$50–100: Navajo Nation Inn, 928/871-4108, 800/662-6189, features Navajo-style rooms at $62–67 d and has a restaurant; it's on AZ 264, just east of the shopping center. **Days Inn,** 928/871-5690, 800/325-2525, offers an indoor pool and spa 3.4 miles west in St. Michaels at 392 W. Hwy. 264; rates are $65 s, $75 d.

Window Rock lacks campgrounds; Wheat-fields Lake, 44 miles north, and Assayi in New Mexico (17 miles north to Navajo, then 11 miles northeast) are the closest options.

Food

The **Navajo Nation Inn** dining room serves a varied menu of American, Navajo, and Mexican food daily for breakfast, lunch, and dinner, but closes at 6 P.M. on weekends. **Hong Kong Restaurant,** 928/871-5622, has Chinese favorites Mon.–Fri. for lunch and dinner in the Window Rock Shopping Center. The shopping center also has **Taco Bell Express, Pizza Hut Express,** and a supermarket. **Bashas'** supermarket and deli lies just west on AZ 264; **McDonald's** and **Church's Chicken** are also nearby. A quartet of fast-food places, **Party Time Pizza, Kentucky Fried Chicken, Blakes Lotaburger,** and **Subway,** are in New Mexico one mile to the east.

Shopping and Services

Navajo Arts & Crafts Enterprise, 928/871-4095, sells Navajo paintings, rugs, jewelry, jewelry-making supplies, and crafts by other Southwest tribes near the junction of AZ 264

and Indian Route 12. The **post office** is on a hill behind the Navajo Nation Inn.

Information

The **Navajo Nation Tourism Department,** 928/871-7941, 928/871-7371, has literature and information for visitors in the lobby of the Navajo Museum, Library & Visitor's Center; it's open Mon. 8 A.M.–5 P.M., Tues.–Fri. 8 A.M.–8 P.M., and Sat. 9 A.M.–5 P.M.; navajo.org.

For hiking and camping information and permits on Navajo lands, contact the **Navajo Parks and Recreation Department,** next door to the Zoological and Botanical Park, open Mon.–Fri. 8 A.M.–5 P.M.; P.O. Box 9000, Window Rock, AZ 86515, 928/871-6647, 928/871-6635; www.navajonationparks.org. Fishing and hunting on the Navajo Nation require tribal permits from **Navajo Fish and Wildlife,** located behind the Motor Pool; open Mon.–Fri. 8 A.M.–5 P.M.; P.O. Box 1480, Window Rock, AZ 86515, 928/871-6451, 928/871-6452; www.navajofishand wildlife.org. Arizona Game and Fish has no jurisdiction over the reservation—you need only tribal permits.

Transportation

Navajo Transit System connects Window Rock with many communities on the Navajo and Hopi Reservations; 928/729-4002.

VICINITY OF WINDOW ROCK

Fort Defiance

Permanent springs in a nearby canyon attracted the Navajo, who named the area Tsehotsoi, "Meadow between the Rocks." Colonel Edwin Vose Sumner had another name in mind in September 1851, when, in defiance of the Navajo, he established a fort on an overlooking hillside. Though the Navajo nearly overran Fort Defiance in 1860, the army successfully repelled a series of attacks before abandoning it during the Civil War. In 1863–64, Colonel Kit Carson headquartered at the fort while rounding up and moving the Navajo. After the Navajo returned, destitute, in 1868, the first Navajo Agency offices issued them sheep and supplies here. The first

© BILL WEIR

Navajo woman weaving, Hubbell Trading Post

The original mission building has been restored as a **historical museum** with a chapel, missionary room, displays of Native American culture, and information on the life of the early missionaries. A gift shop sells regional books, cards, and posters; admission is free. It's open daily 9 A.M.–5 P.M. from Memorial Day to Labor Day; groups can visit at other times by appointment; 928/871-4171. St. Michael Mission is 2.9 miles west of Window Rock Shopping Center on AZ 264, then 0.2 mile south at the sign.

GANADO

The Spanish called this place Pueblo Colorado ("Colored House") after a nearby ruin left by ancestral Puebloan people. The name later changed to Ganado to honor one of the great Navajo chiefs, Ganado Mucho, or Big Water Clansman, a signer of the treaty of June 1868 that returned the Navajo lands. A Presbyterian mission founded here in 1901 provided the Navajo with a school and hospital. The school grew into the two-year College of Ganado, whose buildings are now used as a hospital. Hubbell Trading Post, Arizona's most famous, comes straight of the Old West. Ganado is on AZ 264, 30 miles west of Window Rock, 44 miles east of Keams Canyon, and 36 miles south of Chinle.

There are no accommodations in the area, but you can find bargain-priced cafeteria meals at the **Sage Cafe** on the old college campus. It's open Mon.–Fri. for breakfast, lunch, and dinner. Turn north into the hospital and follow the signs to a two-story building at the north end of an open park; a playground and some picnic tables lie next to the café. A small **museum** off the Sage Cafe's food line displays many old photos of the Navajo and has historic exhibits of the school and hospital; ask one of the café attendants to open it. **Ramon's Restaurant** nearby has American and Mexican food; turn north one block on the street opposite the junction of AZ 264 and US 191. The Conoco station at the highway junction has a little café open Mon.–Fri. for breakfast and lunch; a grocery store nearby is open daily.

school on the reservation opened in 1869, and the first regular medical service arrived in 1880. The old fort is gone now, but the town remains an administrative center with a hospital, schools, and Bureau of Indian Affairs offices.

St. Michael Mission

In 1898, Franciscan friars established a mission to serve the Navajo. St. Michael School, opened by the Sisters of the Blessed Sacrament in 1902, lies a short distance away. The mission's large stone church dates from 1937, when it replaced an earlier adobe structure; it's usually open during the day. The chapel behind the parking area has a circular shape, earthen floor, and a 16-foot woodcarving. The German artist who made the carving called it "The Redemption of Humanity" or "American Pieta"; it shows a dead Native American being lowered from a teepee tarp to a woman in mourning with two attendants, like the body of Jesus being lowered from the cross.

HUBBELL TRADING POST NATIONAL HISTORIC SITE

John Lorenzo Hubbell began trading in 1876, a difficult time for the Navajo, who were still recovering from their traumatic internment at Fort Sumner. Born in New Mexico, Hubbell had already learned some Navajo culture and language by the time he set up shop. Money rarely exchanged hands during transactions; Navajo brought in blankets or jewelry and received credit. They would then select desired items, such as coffee, flour, sugar, cloth, and harnesses. If they had credit left after buying supplies, Navajo generally preferred silver or turquoise to money. Those bringing wool or sheep to the trading post usually received cash, however.

Hubbell distinguished himself by his honesty and appreciation of the Navajo. His insistence on excellence in weaving and silverwork led to better prices for Navajo craftspeople. The trading post helped bridge the Anglo and Native American cultures, as Navajo often called on Hubbell to explain government programs and to write letters to officials explaining their concerns.

Visitor Center, Hubbell's House, and Trading Post

Weavers (usually women) often demonstrate their skills in the visitor center, which also has an excellent bookstore with many titles about Native American history, art, and culture. Guides offer free scheduled tours of Hubbell's house and you can take a self-guided tour of the grounds and barn. The house contains superb rugs, paintings, baskets, and other crafts collected by Hubbell before his death in 1930 and by the Hubbell family thereafter.

The trading post still operates much as it always has, offering high-quality crafts or most anything else. Canned and yard goods jam the shelves, glass cases display pocket knives and other small items, horse collars and harnesses still hang from the ceiling, and Navajo still drop in with items for trade. Check out the Native American baskets and other old artifacts on the ceilings and walls of the jewelry and rug rooms. A tree-shaded picnic area lies next to the visitor center. The National Historic Site, 928/755-3475, is open daily 8 A.M.–6 P.M. from June to September, daily 8 A.M.–5 P.M. the rest of the year, and closed Thanksgiving, Christmas, and New Year's Day; www.nps.gov/hutr. Major art auctions of works by Navajo and Hopi artists take place in April and August. It's on the south side of AZ 264, one mile west of Ganado.

Hopi Country

For centuries the Hopi people have made their homes in villages atop three narrow mesas, fingerlike extensions running south from Black Mesa. Early European visitors dubbed these extensions—from east to west—First Mesa, Second Mesa, and Third Mesa. Arizona 264 skirts First Mesa and crosses over Second and Third Mesas on the way to Tuba City from Window Rock.

The mesas have provided the Hopi with water from reliable springs and protection from enemies, as the 600-foot cliffs discourage assailants. Hardworking farmers, the Hopi are usually peaceable and independent. They keep in close touch with nature and have developed a rich ceremonial life, seeking to maintain balance and harmony with their surroundings and one another. Villages remain largely autonomous even today. The Hopi Tribal Council serves mainly as a liaison between villages and agencies of the federal and state governments.

Visiting Hopi Villages

The Hopi tend to be very private people, though they do welcome visitors to their lands. Policies may vary from village to village and are often posted. All villages *strictly* prohibit such disturbing activities as photography, sketching, and recording. To give residents their privacy, try to visit only between 8 A.M. and 5 P.M. and keep to the main streets and plazas. Walpi asks that visitors enter only with an authorized Hopi guide.

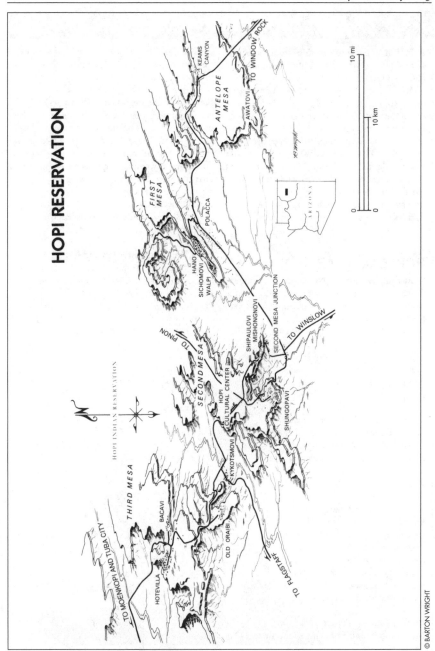

HOPI RESERVATION

NORTHEASTERN

HOPI KACHINAS AND CALENDAR

Kachinas appear to the Hopi from the winter solstice on December 21 until mid-July. They dance and sing in unison, symbolizing the harmony of good thought and deed, harmony required for rain to fall and for a balanced life. The rest of the year the kachinas remain in their home in the San Francisco Peaks.

A kachina can take three forms: a powerful unseen spirit, a dancer filled with the spirit, or a wooden figure representing the spirit. Kachina dancers are always male, even when the spirit is female. The men may present gifts of kachina figures to women and children during the dances. Each village sponsors its own ceremonies.

HOPI CALENDAR

Wuwuchim and Soyala (November to December)
These months symbolize the time of creation of the world. The villages tend to be quiet, as Hopi spend time in silence, prayer, and meditation.

Wuwuchim, a tribal initiation ceremony, marks the start of the ceremonial calendar year. Young men are initiated into adulthood, joining one of four ceremonial societies. The society a man joins depends on his sponsor. Upon acceptance, the initiate receives instruction in Hopi creation beliefs. He's presented with a new name, and his childhood name is never used again.

Only the Shungopavi village performs the entire Wuwuchim ceremony, and not every year. Other villages engage in parts of the Wuwuchim.

The Soyala Kachina appears from the west in the winter solstice ceremony, marking the beginning of the kachina season. As the days get longer, the Hopi begin planning the upcoming planting season; fertility is a major concern in the ceremony.

Buffalo Dances (January)
Men, women, and children perform these social dances in the plazas. They deal with fertility, especially the need for winter moisture in the form of snow.

Powamuya, the Bean Dance (February)
Bean sprouts are grown in a kiva as part of a 16-day ceremony. On the final day, kachina dancers form a long parade through the village. Children of about 10 years are initiated into kachina societies during the Powamuya. Ogre kachinas appear on First and Second mesas.

Kiva Dances (March)
A second set of nighttime kiva dances consists of Anktioni or "repeat dances."

Plaza Dances (April, May, and June)
The kachina dancers perform in all-day ceremonies lasting from sunrise to sunset, with breaks between dances. The group—and the people watching—concentrate in a community prayer calling on the spirits to bring rain for the growing crops.

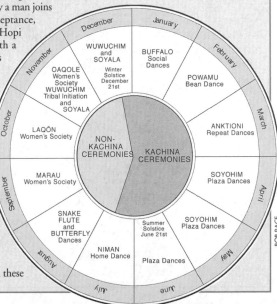

Niman, the "Home Dance" (July)

At the summer solstice on June 21, the plaza dances end and preparations begin for the Going Home Ceremony. In a 16-day rite, the last of the season, kachina dancers present the first green corn ears, then dance for rain to hasten growth of the remaining crops. Their spiritual work done, the kachinas return to their mountain home.

Snake, Flute, and Butterfly Dances (August)

The Snake and Flute ceremonies, held in alternate years, represent the clan groups who perform them in the interests of a good harvest and prosperity. The Snake Dance, usually closed to non-Hopi, takes place in even-numbered years at Shungopavi and Hotevilla and in odd-numbered years at Mishongnovi. The snakes,

often poisonous rattlers, act as messengers to the spirits.

The Flute Ceremony takes place in odd-numbered years at Shungopavi and Walpi.

The Butterfly Dance, a social dance performed mainly by children, takes place in all villages. It also celebrates the harvest.

Women's Society Dances (September, October, and Early November)

Held in the plazas, these ceremonies celebrate the harvest with wishes for health and prosperity. Chaos reigns during the Basket Dances; female dancers throw out baskets and other valuables to the audience, who engage in a mad free-for-all to grab the prizes. They mark the end of the ceremonial year.

The best time to visit a village is during a ceremony open to the public. Some ceremonies have been placed off limits because of visitors' lack of respect. Please remember that these are important religious rituals and you are a guest. Check with the village having a dance to make sure that visitors are welcome. If so, residents will expect visitors and you'll be allowed to experience Hopi culture. Dances take place in plazas many weekends. For information, try calling the Second Mesa Cultural Center, 928/734-2401, or the Hopi Tribe's Cultural Preservation Office, 928/734-2244; www.hopionline.com. The village names given below have their old spellings, seen on most maps and signs, along with Hopi spellings in parentheses.

KEAMS CANYON

This easternmost community on the Hopi Reservation is not a Hopi village, but an administrative town with various U.S. government agencies. The settlement lies at the mouth of a scenic wooded canyon named after Thomas Keam, who built a trading post here in 1875. From the town, the canyon winds northeast for about eight miles; the first three-mile stretch has a road. Kit Carson

engraved his name on Inscription Rock, on the left about two miles in from AZ 264. You'll pass a picturesque Catholic church, then some pleasant picnic spots on the way in.

Practicalities

The motel and campground once here have closed. **Keams Canyon Shopping Center,** on AZ 264 just west of the Keams Canyon turnoff, features McGee's Indian Art Gallery, a grocery store, an ice cream parlor, and a café serving American, Mexican, and Native American food. The café, 928/738-2296, is open Mon.–Fri. for breakfast, lunch, and dinner, and Sat. for breakfast and lunch. A service station is next door. The gallery, 928/738-2295, has a fine selection of Native American arts and crafts and an informative website, www.hopiart.com. Turn north into Keams Canyon for the **post office** (to the right).

Awatovi

Beginning as a small village in the 12th century, Awatovi (ah-WAHT-o-vee) had become an important Hopi town by 1540, when Spanish explorers from Coronado's expedition arrived.

Franciscan friars in 1629 built a large church and friary using Hopi labor. Their mission lasted 51 years until 1680, when, fearing that their culture would be destroyed by Christianity, Hopi villagers joined their New Mexico Pueblo neighbors in successfully overthrowing Spanish rule, wrecking the Awatovi church, and killing most of the priests.

Spaniards re-established the mission in 1700, but other Hopi villages became so angered by this continued alien influence that they banded together and promptly destroyed Awatovi. Of the 800 inhabitants, almost all the men were massacred and the women and children removed to other Hopi villages. Spanish troops retaliated a year later with little effect. Further missionary efforts among the Hopi proved futile. Only ghosts live at Awatovi today—it was never resettled. The ruin sprawls across 23 acres on the southwest tip of Antelope Mesa, with piles of rubble as high as 30 feet. The site is currently closed to the public.

FIRST MESA
Polacca
With an increasing population, some Hopi have built houses in settlements below the mesas, as at Polacca (po-LAH-kah). Still, if you ask residents of Polacca where they're from, they'll likely name one of the three villages on the mesa above. Polacca stretches for about a mile along the highway, but offers little of interest. Thrilling views, however, lie atop First Mesa, reached by a paved road that climbs steeply for 1.3 miles to Sichomovi on the crest. If you have a trailer or large vehicle, you must park it in Polacca or at parking areas 0.6 mile and one mile up. A shuttle may be started in the future, in which case all visitors will park below.

Hano (Hanoki)
The first village you reach *looks* Hopi but is really a settlement of the Tewa, a Pueblo tribe from the Rio Grande region to the east. Fleeing from the Spanish after an unsuccessful revolt in 1696, a number of Tewa sought refuge with the Hopi. Hopi leaders agreed, on the condition that the Tewa act as guardians of the access path to the mesa. Despite living close to the

Hopi for so long, the Tewa have retained their own language and ceremonies. Hano's fascinating history is detailed in *A Tewa Indian Community in Arizona* by Edward P. Dozier (see **Suggested Reading**).

Sichomovi (Sitsomovi)
To the visitor, Hano and the Hopi village of Sichomovi (see-CHO-mo-vee) appear as one, but residents know exactly where the dividing line is. Sichomovi is considered a branch of Walpi, the village at the tip of the mesa.

Walpi (Waalpi)
One of the most inspiring places in Arizona, Walpi (WAHL-pee) stands surrounded by sky and distant horizons. Ancient houses of yellow stone appear to grow from the mesa itself. Coming from Sichomovi, you'll watch the mesa narrow to just 15 feet before widening again at Walpi.

Visitors may enter this traditional village only with an authorized Hopi guide; Walpi is small and its occupants sensitive. Walking tours of about 60 minutes leave daily from Ponsi Hall in Sichomovi 9 A.M.–5 P.M. in summer and 9:30 A.M.–4 P.M. the rest of the year. The tour cost is $8 adult and $5 youth 6–17; 928/737-2262 (Ponsi Hall) or 928/737-2670 (Community Development office). Tours may not run on weekends, so it's best to call ahead before making a special trip out.

Unlike most other Hopi villages, Walpi lacks electricity and running water. Residents have to walk back toward Sichomovi to get water or to wash. Look for bowl-shaped depressions once used to collect rainwater. Precipitous foot trails and ruins of old defenses and buildings cling to the mesa slopes far below. Inhabited since the 13th century, Walpi is well known for its ceremonial dances and crafts, although most First Mesa dances were closed to the public at press time. Kachina dolls carved by the men and pottery created by the women are sold in the village; signs indicate which houses sell crafts. With sweeping panoramas at every turn and a determined hold on traditions, Walpi is probably the most rewarding of all the Hopi villages.

SECOND MESA
Second Mesa (Junction)

Highways AZ 264 and AZ 87 meet at the foot of Second Mesa, seven miles west of Polacca and 60 miles north of Winslow. **LKD's Diner,** 928/737-2717, serves Hopi tacos and tostadas, Mexican food, and burgers Mon.–Sat. for lunch and dinner. **Hopi Fine Arts-Alph Secakuku** gallery sells arts and crafts. You'll also find a grocery store and a post office here. **Honani Crafts Gallery** and a service station lie a half mile west at the turnoff for Shipaulovi and Mishongnovi villages.

Shipaulovi (Supawlavi) and Mishongnovi (Musangnuvi)

These villages are close neighbors on an eastern projection of Second Mesa. Dances often take place; ask at the Cultural Center for dates. You reach Shipaulovi (shih-PAW-lo-vee) and Mishongnovi (mih-SHONG-no-vee) by a short paved road that climbs steeply from AZ 264, a half mile west of the intersection with AZ 87, or by a mesa-top road (also paved, but not to be confused with the Pinon-Hard Rock Road) 0.3 mile east of the Cultural Center. Mishongnovi is east of Shipaulovi, at the end of the mesa.

Shungopavi (Songoopavi)

Shungopavi (shong-O-po-vee or shih-MO-pah-vee) is the largest (pop. 742) of the three Second Mesa villages. Dances performed include the Butterfly Dance (a social dance) and the Snake Dance (late August in even-numbered years), though most have been closed to the public. **Dawa's Art and Crafts** on the road into the village sells locally made work. More galleries lie between the village turnoff and the Cultural Center. Shungopavi is 0.8 mile south off AZ 264, midway between the junction with AZ 87 and the Cultural Center.

HOPI CULTURAL CENTER

Proclaiming itself "At the Center of the Universe," this excellent pueblo-style museum/ motel/restaurant/gift shop complex is popular with both visitors and local Hopi. The Hopi Cultural Center is situated on the west side of Second Mesa just before the road plunges down on the way to Third Mesa. For a shortcut to Chinle and Canyon de Chelly, turn north off AZ 264 beside the Cultural Center to Pinon Trading Post, proceed 26 miles (mostly rough and only partly paved), then east 42 miles on paved roads.

The museum displays good exhibits of Hopi culture and crafts with many historic photos. It's open all year Mon.–Fri. 8 A.M.–5 P.M.; from late March to late Oct. it's also open Sat.–Sun. 9 A.M.–3 P.M. There's a small gift shop just inside the entrance. Admission runs $3 adults, $1 children 13 and under; 928/734-6650; www.hopi culturalcenter.com. (To learn more of Hopi mythology and customs, dig into off-reservation sources such as the Special Collections at Northern Arizona University or the Museum of Northern Arizona libraries, both in Flagstaff.)

The modern motel's nonsmoking rooms run $90 s, ($95 s Fri.–Sat.) and $5 each additional person; rates drop $30 in winter. Reservations are recommended; contact P.O. Box 67, Second Mesa, AZ 86043, 928/734-2401. You'll find a free camping and picnic area next door, between the Cultural Center and the Hopi Arts & Crafts shop. No water or hookups are offered, but you can use the restrooms in the Cultural Center.

The restaurant prepares good American and Hopi dishes. This is your big chance to try *paatupsuki* (pinto bean and hominy soup), or maybe some *noqkwivi* (traditional stew of Hopi corn and lamb), or a breakfast of blue pancakes made of Hopi corn. Not to be outdone by Navajo neighbors, the restaurant serves a Hopi taco (with beef) and a Hopi tostada (vegetarian). It's open daily for breakfast, lunch, and dinner.

Hopi Arts & Crafts (Silvercrafts Cooperative Guild), a short walk across the camping area, offers a variety of traditional work; 928/734-2463; closed Sunday. A small exhibit has examples of early Hopi silver jewelry.

You may also see artwork for sale in a gallery at the Hopi Cultural Center and displayed by vendors on tables outside. Iskasopu Gallery (on the left one mile to the east), Hopi Silver Arts and Crafts (on the right 1.1 miles east), and Tsakur-shovi (on the left 1.5 miles east) all offer good selections. Joseph and Janice Day at Tsakurshovi are a treasure trove of information about visiting and shopping in the Hopi lands.

Guides offer backcountry trips to petroglyph sites; ask at the motel desk.

THIRD MESA
Kykotsmovi (Kiqötsmovi)

The name means Mound of Ruined Houses. Hopi from Old Oraibi (o-RYE-bee) founded this settlement near a spring at the base of Third Mesa. Peach trees add greenery to the town. Kykotsmovi (kee-KEUTS-mo-vee), also known as New Oraibi, has offices of the Hopi Tribal Council.

The **Hopi Tribe Cultural Preservation Office,** 928/734-2244, provides information for visitors to the Hopi Indian Reservation at its office in Kykotsmovi, one mile south of AZ 264 in the Tribal Headquarters building; contact staff at P.O. Box 123, Kykotsmovi, AZ 86039. The **Kykotsmovi Village Store** in town sells groceries and fixes pizza, subs, and snacks in the back. **Sockyma's** is a good source of souvenirs.

You can stop for a picnic along AZ 264 at Oraibi Wash, 0.8 mile east of the Kykotsmovi turnoff, or the Pumpkin Seed Hill overlook 1.2 miles west on the climb to Old Oraibi; both of these lie just north of the highway. Indian Route 2, leading south from Kykotsmovi to Leupp (pronounced loop), is paved and is the shortest way to Flagstaff.

Old Oraibi (Orayvi)

This dusty pueblo perched on the edge of Third Mesa dates from A.D. 1150 and is probably the oldest continuously inhabited community in the United States.

The 20th century was difficult for this ancient village. In 1900 it ranked as one of the largest Hopi settlements, with a population of more than 800, but dissension caused many to leave. The first major dispute occurred in 1906 between two chiefs, You-ke-oma and

Tawa-quap-tewa. Instead of letting fly with bullets and arrows, the leaders staged a "push-of-war" contest. A line was cut into the mesa and the two groups stood on either side. They pushed against each other as hard as they could until Tawa-quap-tewa's group crossed the line and won. You-ke-oma, the loser, left with his faction to establish Hotevilla four miles away. This event was recorded a quarter mile north of Oraibi with the line and inscription: "Well, it have to be done this way now, that when you pass this LINE it will be DONE, Sept. 8, 1906." A bear paw cut in the rock is the symbol of Tawa-quap-tewa and his Bear Clan, while a skull represents You-ke-oma and his Skeleton Clan. Other residents split off to join New Oraibi at the foot of the mesa.

A ruin near Old Oraibi on the south end of the mesa is all that remains of a church built in 1901 by the Mennonite minister, H.R. Voth. Most villagers disliked having it so close to their homes and were no doubt relieved when lightning destroyed the church in 1942. It's closed to the public but you can see the ruin from the village.

Old Oraibi lies two miles west of Kykotsmovi. Avoid driving through the village and stirring up dust; park outside—or next to Hamana So-o's Arts & Crafts shop—and walk. Hopi arts and crafts are available there, at the **Calnimptewa Gallery** east of the turnoff for Old Oraibi, and at **Monongya Gallery** west of the Old Oraibi turnoff.

Hotevilla (Hot'vela)

Hotevilla (HOAT-vih-lah) is known for its dances, basketry, and other crafts.

Founded in 1906 after the split from Old Oraibi, Hotevilla got off to a shaky start. Federal officials demanded that the group move back to Old Oraibi so their children could attend school there. Twenty-five men agreed to return with their families, despite continued bad feelings. About 53 others refused to leave Hotevilla and were jailed for 90 days while their children were forcibly removed to a Keams Canyon boarding school. That winter the women and infants fended for themselves, with little food and inadequate shelter. In the following year the men returned, building better houses and planting crops. Exasperated authorities continued to haul You-ke-oma off to jail for his lack of cooperation and refusal to send village children to school. In 1912, government officials invited the chief to Washington for a meeting with President Taft, but the meeting didn't soften You-ke-oma's stance.

The turnoff for Hotevilla is 3.7 miles northwest of Old Oraibi and 46 miles southeast of Tuba City.

Bacavi (Paaqavi)

The You-ke-oma loyalists who returned to Old Oraibi under federal pressure continued to clash with the people of Tawa-quap-tewa. At one point, when two of the returning women died in quick succession, cries of witchcraft went up. Finally, in November 1909, tensions became unbearable. Members of the unwelcome group packed their bags once more and settled at a new site called Bacavi (BAH-kah-vee) Spring. The name means "jointed reed," after a plant found at the spring. Bacavi lies on the opposite side of the highway from Hotevilla.

Coal Mine Canyon

This scenic little canyon is 31 miles northwest of Bacavi and 15 miles southeast of Tuba City on AZ 264. Look for a windmill and the Coal Mine Mesa Rodeo Ground on the north side of the highway (no signs) between Mileposts 337 and 338, and turn in across the cattle guard. Hopi have long obtained coal from the seam just below the rim. Hoodoos rise out among the white and red cliffs below the overlook. Take care near the rim as the rock layers are very brittle.

Moenkopi (Munqapi)

This Hopi village lies two miles southeast of Tuba City. Chief Tuba of Oraibi, 48 miles southeast, founded Moenkopi ("The Place of Running Water") in the 1870s. Mormons constructed a woolen mill in 1879 with plans to use local labor, but the Hopi disliked working with machinery and the project failed. Moenkopi has two sections—only the upper village participates in the Hopi Tribal Council; the more conservative lower village does not. Water from springs irrigates fields, an advantage not enjoyed by other Hopi villages.

NORTHEASTERN

North-Central Arizona

The high country surrounding Flagstaff offers dramatic and remarkably diverse landscapes. Cool forests, which cover much of the region, provide a delightful respite from the desert. Highways wind through many scenic and historic areas, yet backcountry travelers can explore on trails or forest roads all day without ever crossing a paved road. Anglers enjoy the many lakes on the Colorado Plateau and the streams below it. In winter, skiers zip down the runs on the San Francisco Peaks near Flagstaff and the shorter runs on Bill Williams Mountain near Williams. Cross-country skiers can strike out on their own or glide along groomed trails near the San Francisco Peaks, at Mormon Lake, or near Williams.

THE LAND

Flagstaff (elev. 7,000 feet) lies atop the Colorado Plateau, a giant uplifted landmass extending into Utah, Colorado, and New Mexico. As the land rose, vigorous rivers cut deeply through the rock layers, revealing beautiful forms and colors in countless canyons. Sheer cliffs of the

Red Rock Crossing, Sedona

© BILL WEIR

Mogollon Rim mark the south edge of the Colorado Plateau.

While rivers cut down, volcanoes shot up. For the last million years, large and small volcanoes sprouted in the San Francisco Volcanic Field around Flagstaff. The most striking include the San Francisco Peaks, of which Humphrey's Peak at 12,633 feet is Arizona's tallest mountain. Sunset Crater, the state's most beautiful volcano, is the youngster of the bunch, last erupting about 800 years ago—just yesterday, geologically speaking.

Climate

Expect a cool, invigorating mountain climate in most of the Flagstaff area. Spring, summer, and autumn bring pleasant weather to this high country, where temperatures generally peak in the 70s and 80s F. From early July into September, thunderstorm clouds billow into the air, letting loose scattered downpours.

Snow and sun battle it out in winter, when temperatures vary greatly—from the bitter cold of storms to the warmth of bright Arizona sunshine. In Flagstaff, average winter lows reach the teens, warming to highs in the lower 40s. The winter visitor should be prepared for anything from sub-zero weather to warm, spring-like temperatures. Skiers enjoy the snow, though not many people brave the higher elevations for camping or backpacking. Annual precipitation, arriving mostly in summer and winter, varies between 10 and 30 inches, depending on elevation and rain shadows.

Flora and Fauna

The great range in elevation, together with a varied topography, provide many different habitats. Tiny alpine plants hug the ground against strong winds and extreme cold on the highest slopes of the San Francisco Peaks, where no trees can survive. At lower elevations, dense groves of aspen, fir, and pine thrive on the mountainsides and in protected canyons. Squirrels busy themselves storing away food for the long winters here, while larger animals just visit for the summer.

Vast forests of ponderosa pine and Gambel oak cover much of the Colorado Plateau. Elk, mule deer, a few black bears, coyotes, and smaller animals make these forests their home. Some of the many birds you'll likely see include the ubiquitous common raven, noisy Steller's jay, and feisty hummingbird. Drier parts of the Flagstaff area support woodlands of juniper, pinyon pine, oak, and Arizona cypress. Herds of pronghorn, a graceful, antelope-like creature, roam the arid grasslands north of the San Francisco Volcanic Field.

HISTORY
Native Americans

Archaeologists have dated prehistoric sites along the Little Colorado River as far back as 15,000 B.C., when now-extinct species of bison, camel, antelope, and horse roamed the land. Although some tribes engaged in agriculture between 2,000 and 500 B.C., they maintained a seasonal migration pattern of hunting and gathering.

NORTH-CENTRAL ARIZONA HIGHLIGHTS

- **Flagstaff:** This lively university town offers history, science, entertainment, and many travelers' facilities.
- **San Francisco Volcanic Field:** Arizona's highest summit and hundreds of other volcanoes rise in scenic splendor.
- **Walnut Canyon National Monument:** Prehistoric cliff dwellings lie tucked in alcoves of this pretty canyon.
- **Meteor Crater:** You can see what a meteorite can do at the world's best preserved impact crater.
- **Sedona:** The Red Rock Country's magical energy entices visitors.
- **Prescott:** Arizona's first capital displays history and charm.

These nomadic groups planted corn, squash, and beans in the spring, continued their travels, then returned to harvest the fields in autumn.

From about A.D. 200 to 500, as the tribes devoted more time to farming, they built clusters of pithouses near their fields. Regional ancestral Puebloan cultures then began to form, classified by scientists as the Anasazi of the Colorado Plateau, the Mogollon of the eastern Arizona uplands, and the Hohokam of the desert to the south. A fourth culture, the Sinagua, evolved near present-day Flagstaff between A.D. 900 and 1000 as a blend of the three other groups. The Sinagua (Spanish name "without water") could live here despite the area's dry volcanic soil.

As these societies developed further, the people started to build pueblos above ground. Villages, usually situated on hilltops or in cliff overhangs, went up in widely scattered locations over north-central Arizona. By about A.D. 1100 the population reached its peak. Most inhabitants then migrated, abandoning villages and even whole areas. Archaeologists attempt to explain these departures with theories of drought, soil erosion, disease, and raids by the newly arrived Apache. By the 1500s, when Spanish explorers arrived in northern Arizona, the Pueblo tribes had retreated to northeastern Arizona and adjacent New Mexico. Thousands of empty villages remain in the Flagstaff area, some protected in the four national monuments of Wupatki, Walnut Canyon, Tuzigoot, and Montezuma Castle-Montezuma Well. You might also discover ruins while hiking in the backcountry.

Americans Settle In

Beginning in the 1820s, mountain men such as Antoine Leroux became expert trappers and guides in this little-known region between Santa Fe and California. They and other early travelers sent out glowing reports of the climate, water, and scenery of the region, but hostile Apache, Navajo, Yavapai, and Paiute discouraged settlement. As a result, development in the Flagstaff area started later than in southern and central Arizona. Captain Lorenzo Sitgreaves brought a surveying expedition across northern Arizona

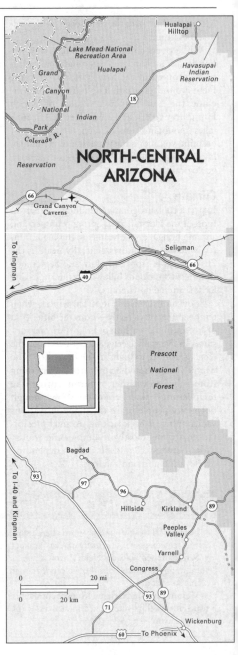

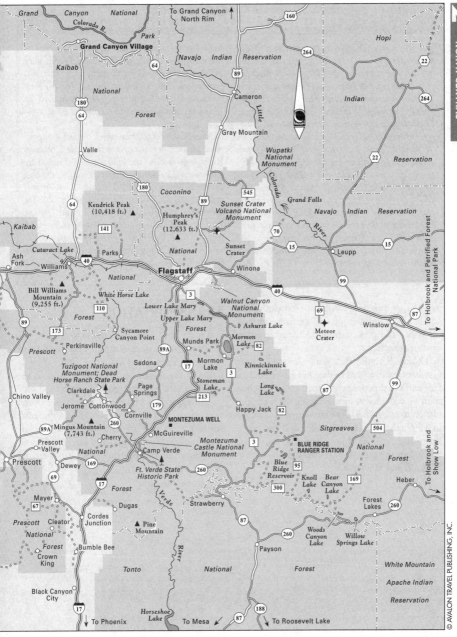

THE MARVELLOUS COUNTRY

In the early 1870s, former Tucson judge Samuel Cozzens traveled east to stir up prospective settlers with a large, well-illustrated book titled *The Marvellous Country; or, Three Years in Arizona and New Mexico, the Apache's Home*. The subtitle expanded upon this theme: *Comprising a Description of this Wonderful Country, Its Immense Mineral Wealth, Its Magnificent Mountain Scenery, the Ruins of Ancient Towns and Cities Found Therein, With a Complete History of the Apache Tribe, and a Description of the Author's Guide Cochise, the Great Apache War Chief, the Whole Interspersed with Strange Events and Adventures*. Cozzens's book sold well in New England and he gave many talks to eager audiences. With each retelling, his descriptions of Arizona's climate, forests, water, and mineral wealth grew and improved. By 1875, the Arizona Colonization Company, with Cozzens as president, was established in Boston. In February 1876, a group of about 50 men, each with 300 pounds of tools and clothing, set off for Arizona under the auspices of the company. In May a second group embarked for the "marvellous country."

After 90 days of arduous travel, the first group arrived at their destination on the Little Colorado River only to find the land already claimed by Mormons. The group continued west to the San Francisco Peaks and started to build a settlement, dubbed Agassiz. But finding no land suitable for farming or mining, they gave up and left for Prescott and California even before the second group arrived. The second group gave up, too, but not before stripping a pine tree and flying a flag from it to celebrate July 4th.

in 1851, prompting Lieutenant Edward Beale and others to build rough wagon roads, but hostile tribes and poor farming land continued to discourage settlers.

Thomas Forsythe McMillan, who arrived from California with a herd of sheep in 1876, became Flagstaff's first permanent settler. Other ranchers soon moved into the area, bringing the total population to 67 in 1880. The coming of the railroad in 1882, thriving lumber mills, and success in sheep and cattle ranching opened up the region and led to the growth of railroad towns such as Flagstaff and Williams.

TRANSPORTATION

You really need your own vehicle to visit the national monuments and most of the scenic and recreation areas. Tours make brief stops at highlights of the region but tend to be rushed; see "Tours" in the Flagstaff section. Greyhound provides frequent bus service across northern Arizona via Flagstaff and between Flagstaff and Phoenix. Amtrak runs daily trains across northern Arizona in each direction between Los Angeles and Albuquerque and beyond. A regional airline serves Flagstaff.

Flagstaff

Surrounded by pine forest in the center of northern Arizona, Flagstaff (pop. 63,000) has long served as an important stop for ranchers, Native Americans, and travelers. The older, downtown part of Flagstaff still offers a bit of that frontier feeling, expressed by its many historic buildings. Other parts of this small city may seem like endless lines of motels, restaurants, bars, and service stations, but even here one can find reminders of old Route 66 that once linked Flagstaff with the rest of America.

Downtown is an enjoyable place to stroll, to admire the architecture, and perhaps to sample some of the unique restaurants and shops. Many of the old structures have plaques describing their history. To visit the distant past, when the land rose up, volcanoes erupted, and the early tribes arrived, drop by the Museum of Northern Arizona. To learn about the pioneers of 100 years ago, head over to the Pioneer Historical Museum and the Riordan Mansion State Historic Park. To see the current art scene, swing by the Art Barn and University Art Galleries. For a trip out of this world, visit Lowell Observatory, where astronomers discovered Pluto, or the U.S. Geological Survey, where astrogeologists map celestial bodies.

For the great outdoors, head for the hills—Arizona's highest mountains begin at the northern outskirts of town. In summer, the mountains, hills, and meadows offer pleasant forest walks and challenging climbs. Winter snows transform the countryside into some of the state's best downhill and cross-country skiing areas. As a local guidebook, *Coconino County, the Wonderland of America,* put it in 1916, Flagstaff "offers you the advantages of any city of twice its size; it has, free for the taking, the healthiest and most invigorating of climates; its surrounding scenic beauties will fill one season, May–Nov., full to overflowing with enjoyment the life of any tourist, vacationist, camper or out doors man or woman who will but come to commune with nature."

© BILL WEIR

bull riding at the Prescott Frontier Days Rodeo

NORTH-CENTRAL

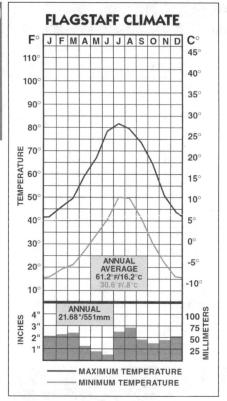

FLAGSTAFF CLIMATE

ANNUAL AVERAGE
61.2°F/16.2°C
30.6°F/.8°C

ANNUAL
21.68"/551mm

— MAXIMUM TEMPERATURE
— MINIMUM TEMPERATURE

SIGHTS

Flagstaff has many free parking spaces along the streets, by the Visitor Center, and in a few lots; these generally have a two-hour limit. A free all-day lot lies off Beaver Street; turn south from Route 66, then right just after the railroad tracks; RVs can park in an adjacent lot by crossing the railroad tracks on Beaver Street, turning right on Phoenix Avenue, then right into the parking area.

Museum of Northern Arizona

This active museum features excellent displays of the geology, archaeology, anthropology, cultures, and fine art of the Colorado Plateau. A timeline of Native Americans illustrates their stages of development during prehistoric times

with beautiful archaeological findings. A prehistoric kiva mural comes from an excavation of Awatovi on Hopi lands. Contemporary Native American exhibits illustrate the traditions of northern Arizona tribes and their basketry, pottery, weaving, kachina dolls, and ceremonies. Art galleries display changing exhibits of Native American and Southwestern works. The museum's attractive building has walls of dark volcanic stone and tile roofs; it encloses courtyards filled with native flora.

Popular museum-sponsored shows take place during the summer, exhibiting excellent arts and crafts: The Hispanic Festival runs the weekend before Memorial Day; the Hopi Marketplace runs on the weekend nearest July Fourth; Navajo Marketplace is on the first weekend in August; Zuni Marketplace is held in late August or early September, and the Festival of Pai Arts is in late September. Enduring Creations, a changing sales exhibition of the finest Native American, Hispanic, and Western artwork, runs through the summer. The museum shop sells high-quality Native American work, including Navajo blankets, jewelry (by Navajo, Hopi, and Zuni), Hopi kachina dolls and pottery by several tribes. A bookstore stocks an excellent selection of books and posters related to the region. Rio de Flag Nature Trail makes a half-mile loop in the little canyon behind the museum; borrow the trail booklet—both adult and children's versions available—from the ticket desk. You can use the museum's library—one of the most extensive for Southwest topics—across the highway in the Research Center; it's open Mon.–Fri. 9 A.M.–5 P.M.

A visit to the Museum of Northern Arizona is highly recommended for anyone planning to buy Native American crafts, to visit the reservations of northern Arizona, or to better understand the natural history of the area surrounding the Grand Canyon.

Set beside a little canyon in a pine forest, the museum is open daily 9 A.M.–5 P.M.; admission is $5 adults, $4 seniors, $3 students with I.D., $2 ages 7–17; 928/774-5213; www.musnaz.org. From downtown Flagstaff, head three miles northwest on US 180; the museum is on the left.

FLAGSTAFF'S FLAGPOLES

It's obvious that Flagstaff was named for a flagpole. The question is, which one? The first group of settlers to arrive from Boston claimed to have erected a flagpole in April or May of 1876, before the July 4th celebration held by the second Boston group later that year. The stripped pine tree left by the second group at their Antelope Spring camp may have been the pole that served as the town's namesake. Later travelers referred to the spot as the spring by the flag staff. As the first sheep ranchers settled nearby, the area became known as Flag Staff, then finally Flagstaff.

However some early settlers regarded a tall tree, trimmed of all branches, at the foot of McMillan Mesa as *the* flagstaff. Others disputed this idea, stating that Lieutenant Edward Beale had delimbed the tree in the 1850s or that it was the work of a later railroad-surveying party. No record actually exists of a flag ever flying from the tree.

At any rate, citizens gathered in the spring of 1881 and chose the name "Flagstaff" for the settlement.

Scenic Sky Ride

Arizona Snowbowl's chairlift will take you to 11,500 feet on the San Francisco Peaks for great panoramas. It's open daily 10 A.M.–4 P.M. in summer (June 21–Labor Day weekend), then Fri.–Sun. from Labor Day to mid-October, weather permitting; 928/779-1951. A restaurant serves lunch. The ride costs $9 adult, $6.50 seniors 65–69 (free age 70+), $5 kids 8–12. To reach the Snowbowl, drive northwest seven miles from downtown on US 180, then turn right at the sign and drive seven miles on a paved road.

Pioneer Museum

After completion in 1908, this venerable stone building served 30 years as the Coconino County Hospital for the Indigent. Townspeople also knew it as the "poor farm"—because stronger patients grew vegetables in the yard.

Today the building houses permanent and changing exhibits that illustrate many aspects of life in Flagstaff's pioneering days. Old photos and artifacts tell the stories of ranchers, timber men, scientists, explorers, and families. A giant stuffed bear greets visitors on the second floor; slip by the beast to see a restored hospital room and more galleries. Exhibits here may include memorabilia of Percival Lowell and his observatory and the camera gear and photos of Emery Kolb, who came to the Grand Canyon in 1902, set up a photo studio with his brother Ellsworth, and continued showing movies and stills until 1976.

Outside, you can peer into the restored 1908 Ben Doney Cabin, moved here from a site east of town. A working blacksmith shop, often in use in summer, and old farm machinery lie behind the museum. By the road stands a powerful 1929 steam locomotive used by the logging industry, with a log car and caboose. On the first weekend in June, the Wool Festival features shearing and other skills, and the Independence Day Festival demonstrates traditional crafts on the weekend nearest July Fourth. Playthings of the Past marks the winter holiday season. Pioneer Historical Museum, 928/774-6272, is open Mon.–Sat. 9 A.M.–5 P.M.; www.infomagic.net/~ahsnad. The Northern Division of the Arizona Historical Society takes care of the museum and a donation is requested. There's a small gift shop. From downtown, the museum lies on the right just past Sechrist School, about two miles northwest on US 180.

The Art Barn

Regional artists and art patrons have banded together to operate this large sales gallery. Here you'll find a great selection of works by both Native American and Anglo artisans, including paintings, sketches, photographs, pottery, jewelry, kachina dolls, Navajo rugs, sand paintings, rock art (petroglyph reproductions), and books. You can also purchase old pawn jewelry. The Art Barn has its own bronze foundry and a frame shop. Prices are right, too, since there's no distributor markup or big advertising budget. The Art Barn is open Tues.–Sat. 10 A.M.–5 P.M.;

NORTH-CENTRAL

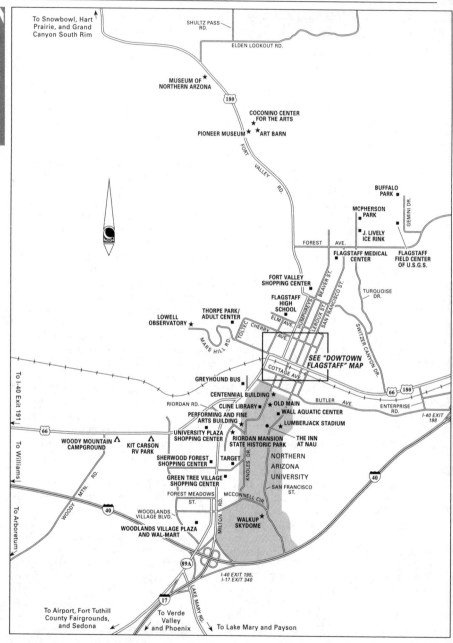

To Snowbowl, Hart Prairie, and Grand Canyon South Rim

SHULTZ PASS RD.

ELDEN LOOKOUT RD.

MUSEUM OF NORTHERN ARIZONA ★

180

COCONINO CENTER FOR THE ARTS ★

PIONEER MUSEUM ★ ★ ART BARN

FORT VALLEY RD.

BUFFALO PARK ■

GEMINI DR.

MCPHERSON PARK ■

■ J. LIVELY ICE RINK

FOREST AVE.

FLAGSTAFF MEDICAL CENTER ■

FLAGSTAFF FIELD CENTER OF U.S.G.S.

FORT VALLEY SHOPPING CENTER ■

TURQUOISE DR.

FLAGSTAFF HIGH SCHOOL ■

HUMPHREYS ST.
LEROUX ST.
BEAVER ST.
SAN FRANCISCO ST.
SWITZER CANYON DR.

THORPE PARK/ ADULT CENTER ■

ELM AVE.

LOWELL OBSERVATORY ★

CHERRY AVE.

TOLTEC

MARS HILL RD.

SEE "DOWTOWN FLAGSTAFF" MAP

COTTAGE AVE.

66   180

GREYHOUND BUS ■

CENTENNIAL BUILDING ★

RIORDAN RD.

BUTLER AVE.

ENTERPRISE RD.

CLINE LIBRARY ■   ★ OLD MAIN

★ WALL AQUATIC CENTER

PERFORMING AND FINE ARTS BUILDING ★

● LUMBERJACK STADIUM

To I-40 Exit 191

UNIVERSITY PLAZA SHOPPING CENTER ★

RIORDAN MANSION STATE HISTORIC PARK ★

THE INN AT NAU ★

66

WOODY MOUNTAIN CAMPGROUND ⋀

KIT CARSON RV PARK ⋀

NORTHERN

To Williams

SHERWOOD FOREST SHOPPING CENTER ■

TARGET ■

ARIZONA

WOODY MTN. RD.

GREEN TREE VILLAGE SHOPPING CENTER ■

UNIVERSITY

FOREST MEADOWS ST.

● SAN FRANCISCO ST.

KNOLES DR.

40

MCCONNELL CIR.

40

WOODLANDS VILLAGE BLVD.

MILTON RD.

WALKUP SKYDOME ★

WOODLANDS VILLAGE PLAZA AND WAL-MART ■

To Arboretum

89A

I-40 EXIT 195, I-17 EXIT 340

LAKE MARY RD.

17

To Airport, Fort Tuthill County Fairgrounds, and Sedona

To Verde Valley and Phoenix

To Lake Mary and Payson

I-40 EXIT 198

MOON

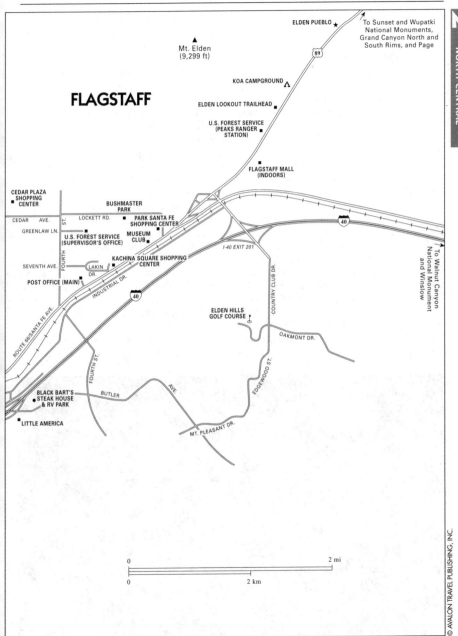

FLAGSTAFF

ELDEN PUEBLO

To Sunset and Wupatki
National Monuments,
Grand Canyon North and
South Rims, and Page

89

Mt. Elden
(9,299 ft)

KOA CAMPGROUND

ELDEN LOOKOUT TRAILHEAD

U.S. FOREST SERVICE
(PEAKS RANGER
STATION)

FLAGSTAFF MALL
(INDOORS)

CEDAR PLAZA
SHOPPING
CENTER

BUSHMASTER
PARK

CEDAR   AVE.   LOCKETT RD.

GREENLAW LN.

PARK SANTA FE
SHOPPING CENTER

U.S. FOREST SERVICE
(SUPERVISOR'S OFFICE)

MUSEUM
CLUB

40

I-40 EXIT 201

KACHINA SQUARE SHOPPING
CENTER

SEVENTH AVE.   LAKIN
DR.

POST OFFICE (MAIN)

To Walnut Canyon
National Monument
and Winslow

40

ELDEN HILLS
GOLF COURSE

COUNTRY CLUB DR.

OAKMONT DR.

BLACK BART'S
STEAK HOUSE
& RV PARK

BUTLER

EDGEWOOD ST.

LITTLE AMERICA

MT. PLEASANT DR.

0   2 mi

0   2 km

928/774-0822. It's conveniently located behind the Pioneer Museum.

Lowell Observatory

Percival Lowell (1855-1916) founded the observatory in 1894, using his personal fortune to fund a search for signs of intelligent life on Mars. The observatory's early contributions to astronomy included spectrographic photographs by V.M. Slipher that resulted in the discovery of the expanding universe, and Clyde Tombaugh's 1930 discovery of Pluto. Research continues with telescopes here, at Anderson Mesa 12 miles southeast of town, and at other locations.

In the Steele Visitor Center, you can explore the field of astronomy with interactive exhibits and see many examples of instruments used by astronomers over the years. Informative 90-minute tours begin with a multimedia program illustrating the history and work of the observatory; you'll then visit the 1896 24-inch Clark refractor telescope used to study Mars and the expanding universe and to map the Moon for lunar expeditions. The tour continues to the Rotunda, designed as a library by

Lowell's wife but completed only in 1916—the year of Lowell's death. Inside you can see the spectrograph used in the discovery of the expanding universe and other historical exhibits, such as the Pluto photographic plates, with the same view Tombaugh enjoyed at the instant he found Pluto. The final stop on the tour visits the specially designed telescope used to discover Pluto. You're free to join and leave the tours as you wish and explore the grounds on your own, but guests can see interiors only with the tour guide. A solar viewing program takes place daily if the clouds cooperate; call for the time.

The visitor center is open daily 9 A.M.–5 P.M. April–Oct. and noon–5 P.M. the rest of the year, except closed Mon.–Tues. in January and February. A bookstore has good reading along with posters and videos. Admission is $4 adults, $3.50 seniors and university students, and $2 ages 5–17. The entry fee includes the guided tours, which depart at 10 A.M., 1 P.M., and 3 P.M. April–Oct., but only at 1 P.M. and 3 P.M. Nov.–March.

At night, the visitor center reopens for Sky Tonight Programs and viewing through the his-

Pine Country Rodeo Parade

© BILL WEIR

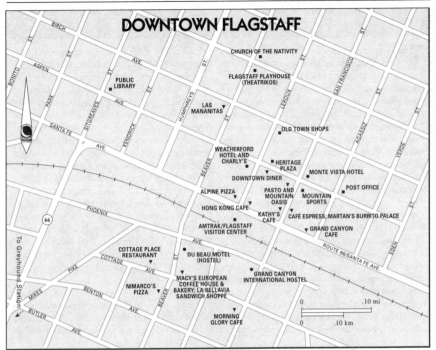

DOWNTOWN FLAGSTAFF

CHURCH OF THE NATIVITY

FLAGSTAFF PLAYHOUSE
(THEATRIKOS)

PUBLIC
LIBRARY

LAS
MANANITAS

OLD TOWN SHOPS

WEATHERFORD
HOTEL AND
CHARLY'S

HERITAGE
PLAZA

MONTE VISTA HOTEL

DOWNTOWN DINER

ALPINE PIZZA

PASTO AND
MOUNTAIN
OASIS

MOUNTAIN
SPORTS

POST OFFICE

HONG KONG CAFE

KATHY'S
CAFE

CAFÉ ESPRESS; MARTAN'S BURRITO PALACE

AMTRAK/FLAGSTAFF
VISITOR CENTER

GRAND CANYON
CAFE

ROUTE 66/SANTA FE AVE.

COTTAGE PLACE
RESTAURANT

DU BEAU MOTEL
(HOSTEL)

GRAND CANYON
INTERNATIONAL HOSTEL

NIMARCO'S
PIZZA

MACY'S EUROPEAN
COFFEE HOUSE &
BAKERY; LA BELLAVIA
SANDWICH SHOPPE

MORNING
GLORY CAFE

To Greyhound Station

0   .10 mi

0   .10 km

toric Clark telescope, weather permitting; these run Mon.–Sat. in summer, then decrease to only Sat. in midwinter; call to check days and times. The cost is the same as for a daytime visit.

The observatory schedules many special events through the year, so it's worth calling or looking at the website to check times and see what's coming up; 928/774-2096 (recording); www.lowell.edu. The observatory sits atop Mars Hill, one mile from downtown, and is well signed; head west on Route 66 and continue straight on Santa Fe Avenue where the highway curves left. In winter the steep road up Mars Hill requires caution and often snow chains.

Earth and Planetary Geologic Studies

Many of the scientists at the Flagstaff Field Center of the U.S. Geological Survey study and map Earth's moon, the planets, and other solid bodies of our solar system using data collected from space missions. They also investigate

Earth's landforms such as volcanoes and sand dunes, formed by the same processes as those on extraterrestrial bodies. The Apollo astronauts received geologic training and tested their equipment here, and were later guided while on the Moon by geologists from this center. Other scientists at the center investigate and monitor many of Earth's geologic processes. Hydrologists monitor stream flows and geologists study rock layers, faults, and volcanoes. Geologic mapping helps define our landscape and what lies beneath it.

You're welcome to visit the Field Center and browse among exhibits throughout the buildings' hallways. Begin by picking up a self-guided tour brochure in the lobby of Buildings 3, 4, or 6. Giant maps and spectacular color images from spacecraft cover the walls in the hallways. Images include shots of Jupiter and Saturn and their moons, remote-sensing products showing the Earth's features, and views sent back by spacecraft landing on Mars and Venus. The

PLANET X

The ancients recorded five bright star-like wandering bodies. Later generations figured out that these—and Earth as well—are planets. While conducting star surveys in 1781, William Herschel discovered a seventh planet, now known as Uranus, which had been plotted on sky charts at least two dozen times as a star. Astronomers used these positions to plot the planet's orbit, but Uranus was not moving according to Newton's mechanics. In the early 1820s it was moving too slowly, but by the end of that decade it was moving too fast.

British astronomer John Couch Adams and French astronomer Urbain Leverrier, working independently, performed laborious calculations based on the assumption that the gravitational pull of an undiscovered eighth planet was affecting Uranus' movement. Both men's predicted positions for the new planet were very close and a short telescopic search soon revealed the "new" planet, which was named Neptune.

Neptune had also been plotted as a star on several charts before its 1846 discovery. Again, the planet did not seem to be following a perfect orbit.

Several astronomers started calculations to find a ninth planet, which they dubbed "Planet X." Percival Lowell spent years figuring a position for Planet X but did not have suitable telescopes to search the sky for it. Since his main interest lay in finding signs of life on Mars, his instruments were powerful, but did not show wide-angle views, and they were so slow photographically that some exposures required guidance hour after hour—night after night in some cases—for a single photograph.

Lowell died before a suitable telescope could be built, and the sky search for Planet X did not begin again for more than a decade. Harvard president A. Lawrence Lowell (Percival's brother) donated money to build a small but wide-angled and photographically fast telescope. This instrument exposed plates 14 inches by 17 inches covering a field 12 by 14 degrees and required less than an hour of exposure.

Each plate showed between 40,000 and one million stars. Since the distant planet was too far away to be recognizable as one by any telescope, only its motion against the background of stars as

Pluto, pictured with its small moon Charon, remains the only planet in our solar system that has not been visited by a spacecraft.

it circled the Sun would reveal it as a planet. Thus, each plate would be duplicated several days later and then each star image would be compared from plate to plate until one of the "stars" was found to have moved a distance appropriate for a planet that far from the Sun.

Twenty-two-year-old Kansas farm boy and astronomy student Clyde Tombaugh set to work exposing the plates by night and using a blink comparator by day to conduct the search. The blink comparator would flash a view of part of one plate through a microscope eyepiece, then flash a view of the corresponding section of a second plate. If an object had moved, it would appear in the eyepiece as if it were jumping back and forth. That sounds easy, but Tombaugh examined hundreds of thousands of star images during a search of about nine months before finding one that moved an appropriate distance.

He also found some asteroids and variable stars in the process.

Although Tombaugh discovered Pluto on February 18, 1930, using plates made on January 23 and January 29, Lowell Observatory cautiously waited to announce the new planet, studying its motion in the meantime to verify that it was truly the long-sought Planet X. The announcement was made on March 13, 1930—the 75th anniversary of Lowell's birth.

Many people wanted to name the new planet for Percival Lowell; others favored Clyde Tombaugh. An English schoolgirl sent in the winning suggestion "Pluto" in honor of the Greek god of the underworld, brother of Jupiter and Neptune. The planet's astronomical symbol became "P" with an "L" bottom stem. This abbreviation for Pluto also represented Percival Lowell's initials and honored his contribution.

geology of the Moon and most solid-surfaced planets and their satellites has been mapped in surprising detail. Even cloud-covered Venus gave up some of her secrets through radar images with computer-generated color. Building 4 displays additional planetary exhibits, while the hallways of Building 3 show maps and photos of geologic and hydrologic studies here on Earth. Building 6, the Eugene M. Shoemaker Center for Astrogeology, should be open by late 2002. You'll be able to step into the lobby to see the exhibit area with the stories of Shoemaker, Apollo astronauts, and others who have contributed to our knowledge of the Moon and beyond. Models and dioramas will show spacecraft. Building 6 will also feature "A Walk Through the Solar System," as well as a specialized library open to the public for reference use.

You may visit Mon.–Fri. 8 A.M.–4:30 P.M. Remember that the people working here are normally too busy to show visitors around. Also, don't enter offices or labs unless invited. To arrange tours for scientific or educational groups, call or write in advance to the U.S. Geological Survey, 2255 N. Gemini Dr., Flagstaff, AZ 86001; 928/556-7000. The Flagstaff Field Center's website, wwwflag.wr.usgs.gov, features some of the work done and products available. The Center lies atop McMillan Mesa off Forest Avenue/Cedar Avenue, 1.5 miles northeast of downtown. Nearby Buffalo Park is a good place to go for a walk or hike.

Riordan Mansion State Historic Park

The Riordan brothers, Timothy and Michael, arrived in Flagstaff during the mid-1880s and eventually took over the Arizona Lumber & Timber Company. Both became involved with the social, business, and political life of early Flagstaff. In 1904, they built a grand mansion just south of downtown. A "Rendezvous Room" connected the wings occupied by each brother's family. The architect Charles Whittlesey, who also designed El Tovar Hotel on the rim of the Grand Canyon, used a similar rustic style of logs and stonework for the mansion exterior. The brothers christened their joint home *Kinlichi,* Navajo for "Red House."

Tours of 50–60 minutes visit Timothy's side of the house and reveal how the wealthy lived in Flagstaff during the early 1900s. Guides offer history and comment on the furnishings and architectural features. Only the Riordans have lived here, and all the rooms still display their original furniture, most done in American Craftsman style. The wing occupied by Michael's family has recently opened to the public as well, with exhibits that you can see on your own. You can compare the two sides of the house, which mirror each other.

The park is open daily 8:30 A.M.–5 P.M. from May to October; tours depart on the hour with the first one at 9 A.M. and the last at 4 P.M. During the rest of the year, hours are 10:30 A.M.–5 P.M. daily with the first tour at 11 A.M. and the last at 4 P.M. There's no charge to see the exhibits in the visitor center or to take the self-guided tour of the grounds. Fees to go inside the mansion are $5 adults, $2.50 ages 7–13; 928/779-4395. It's best to phone in advance for tour reservations. A video shown on request has interior views. Standard wheelchairs can access the lower floor. Picnic tables are near the parking area. You'll find this piece of historic Flagstaff between S. Milton Road and Northern Arizona University, about a half mile south of downtown; turn east on Riordan Road toward NAU from S. Milton, then turn right at the sign, opposite Ardrey Auditorium.

Northern Arizona University (NAU)

Flagstaff's character and population owe much to this school, just south of downtown. The university began in 1899 as Northern Arizona Normal School, housed in a vacant reformatory building. Four young women received their diplomas and teaching certificates two years later.

In 1925 the school began offering a four-year Bachelor of Education degree and took the name Northern Arizona State Teachers College. The program broadened over the years to include other degrees, a program in forestry, and graduate studies. In 1966 the institution became a university. NAU's sprawling campus now covers 686 acres, supplemented by the School of Forestry's 4,000-acre laboratory forest. The High Altitude Training Center's programs attract athletic teams from around the world to improve their performance in the thin mountain air.

The 1893 Old Main building, on McMullen Circle in the northern part of campus, houses changing exhibits of the **Old Main Art Gallery** on the first floor and a permanent collection of fine art and furniture in the **Marguerite Hettel Weiss Gallery** on the second floor. Be ready for almost anything in the **Richard E. Beasley Gallery** upstairs in the Fine and Performing Arts Building, south on Knoles Drive, where 30-day shows feature contemporary art. Call 928/523-3471 or check www.nau.edu to find what's showing at the galleries; they're open Mon.–Sat. except between shows.

Northern Arizona University (NAU) Observatory, 928/523-7170, built by the U.S. Air Force as an atmospheric research observatory in the early 1950s, is still used today for research, but it primarily serves as an educational tool for university students and the general public. Volunteers, mostly astronomy club members, hold an open house most clear Friday nights at 7:30 P.M. with special open nights for astronomical events such as eclipses and occultations. It's off S. San Francisco Street adjacent to a high-rise dormitory and practice field.

Wall Aquatic Center, 928/523-4508, contains a large indoor swimming pool on Franklin Avenue between S. Beaver and S. San Francisco Sts.; it's open to the public. Call or check the Web for the schedule.

To learn about NAU services and events, call or visit the University Union Information Desk, 928/523-4636, or call the switchboard, 928/523-9011; www.nau.edu. **NAU Downtown** also offers information, event tickets, and parking permits in Heritage Square at Aspen Avenue and Leroux Street; 928/523-1628. A free shuttle bus makes a loop around the northern and southern parts of the main campus. Ask someone for the location of the stop nearest you. The service runs about every 15 minutes Mon.–Thurs. 7:35 A.M.–11 P.M. and Friday 7:35 A.M.–5 P.M. during the main school terms. To park on campus, pick up a visitor's permit from NAU Downtown (see above) or from the **Parking Services/Visitor Information** office, 928/523-3591, in the Centennial Building at the southwest corner of

Dupont Avenue and S. Beaver Street; it's open Mon.–Fri. 7:30 A.M.–5 P.M. (4:30 P.M. in summer). After hours you can obtain a parking permit from the police office at Lumberjack Stadium off S. San Francisco Street.

The Arboretum

Plant enthusiasts here do research on native and non-native flora that thrive in the cool climate of the Flagstaff area. More than 700 species of plants and trees grow on the 200-acre grounds, despite the short 75-day average growing season. At 7,150 feet elevation, the arboretum is the highest botanical garden in the U.S. doing horticultural research. You'll get a good introduction to the flora of the Colorado Plateau here. Northern Arizona residents can gain a wealth of landscaping and gardening information.

Tours of 45–60 minutes, which begin at 11 A.M. and 1 P.M., introduce ongoing projects and take you through the solar greenhouse and outdoor gardens. You'll see endangered species that the staff works to propagate. Exhibits, which you can also visit on your own, include gardens of native and adapted plants, wildflowers, herbs, and vegetables. The constructed wetlands area uses native plants to treat wastewater, which gets recycled for watering other plants. A nature trail through the ponderosa pine forest has a 0.6-mile inner loop and a one-mile outer loop. The visitor center has exhibits, including mounted specimens of many local species. A gift shop offers books, cards, a bird list, Extension Bulletins (gardening and tree advice), seeds, and gardening supplies. You can purchase plants at the Summer Plant Sale and Garden Fair on the third weekend of June and through the season, then again at the Holiday Plant Sale on the first Saturday in December.

Annual events include the two plant sales and an Open House on the second Saturday in July. The Arboretum is open daily 9 A.M.–5 P.M. from April 1 to Dec. 15; admission is $4 adults, $3 age 6–12; 928/774-1441; www.thearb.org. No pets permitted. Summer (June–Sept.) is the best time to visit. Picnic tables are available. From S. Milton Road in Flagstaff, head west 1.9 miles on Route 66, then turn south four miles on Woody Mountain Road.

Elden Pueblo

The resourceful Sinagua tribe lived at this site below Mt. Elden about A.D. 1150. Some of the pueblo, including a large community room, has been excavated. A leaflet explains and illustrates features of the ruin, open during daylight hours; there's no admission charge. It's on the northeast edge of town; head north on US 89 past the Flagstaff Mall and the Peaks Ranger Station to the signed turn on the left, just before the Camp Townsend-Winona Road.

RECREATION
City Parks

Drop in one of these for a picnic under the pines, a playground for the kids, or a game of tennis or basketball. You can reach Flagstaff Parks & Recreation at 211 W. Aspen Ave.; 928/779-7690. **Thorpe Park** lies just west of downtown at 245 N. Thorpe Road; the adjacent Adult Center, 928/774-1068, hosts many community activities and clubs. From downtown, head west on Route 66 and keep straight where the highway curves left, continue west on Santa Fe Avenue about 5 blocks, then turn right one block on Toltec Street. **McPherson Park** and the adjacent ice skating rink at **Jay Lively Activity Center,** 928/774-1051, lie northeast of downtown at 1650 N. Turquoise Dr.; you can head north on San Francisco Street from downtown, turn right on Forest Avenue, then left on Turquoise Drive. Over on the east side of town, **Bushmaster Park** is at Lockett Road and Alta Vista Drive (turn south from Lockett Road at the sign); there's also a skate park here for skateboards, rollerskates, and rollerblades.

Flagstaff Urban Trail System

You don't have to go far for a hike, as this trail network goes right through town. It connects the Mt. Elden trails with the Arizona Trail, Walnut Canyon National Monument, and other areas surrounding Flagstaff. Mountain bikers, hikers, joggers, and cross-country skiers use the trails, which currently total about 20 miles. The City Planning Office in the Flagstaff City Hall at 211 W. Aspen has maps.

Horseback Riding

The Flagstaff area is great horse country. If you don't have your own steed, local riding stables can provide one; reservations are advised.

The Flying Heart Barn, 928/526-2788, offers hour-long, half-day, and full-day rides year-round on and near the San Francisco Peaks; head 3.5 miles north on US 89 from I-40 Exit 201. **MacDonalds Ranch,** US 180 and Snowbowl Rd., 928/774-4481, rides below the Peaks on one- and two-hour trips and hayrides between Memorial Day and Labor Day weekends.

Cross-country skiers will enjoy the rolling meadow and forest country of Hart Prairie and Wing Mountain, two undeveloped skiing areas near the San Francisco Peaks—they're ideal for ski touring.

Downhill Skiing

Arizona Snowbowl, on the San Francisco Peaks, has some of Arizona's best downhill action. Four chair lifts and a tow rope service 30 runs/trails ranging from novice to expert. From the top of Agassiz Chairlift, it's two miles and 2,300 feet down. With sufficient snow, the Snowbowl is open for skiing daily 9 A.M.–4 P.M. from mid-December to Easter. Lift tickets cost $33 ($27 afternoons on weekends and holidays; $20 afternoons on weekdays) for adults; $18 ($13 afternoons) for ages 8–12; $13 seniors 65–69; and free for kids seven and younger and for seniors over 70. Call 928/779-1951 for recorded information about lifts, rentals, and instruction and for weather and road conditions; www.arizonasnowbowl.com.

Hart Prairie Lodge (elev. 9,200 feet) offers a ski school, rentals, repairs and a restaurant. **Ski Lift Lodge,** on US 180 opposite the Snow Bowl Road turnoff, 928/774-0729, 800/472-3599, has rooms and a restaurant. To reach the Snowbowl, drive northwest seven miles from downtown on US 180 to the sign, then turn right seven miles on a paved road, which sometimes requires chains and/or 4WD.

Cross-Country Skiing

Flagstaff Nordic Center, 928/779-1951, offers more than 40 km of groomed trails ranging

from beginner to advanced near Hart Prairie and the San Francisco Peaks. A five-km marked trail leads to the Hochderrfer Hills (maximum elevation 9,200 feet). The center provides ski lessons, a beginner package, a snowshoe-only trail, equipment rentals and sales, and a snack bar. Races, clinics, and moonlight tours highlight the calendar. It's open daily from about mid-November until mid-April, as weather permits. Trail passes run $10, free for kids seven and under and seniors 70 and over; snowshoers pay $5; www.arizonasnowbowl.com. Take US 180 northwest 16 miles from downtown to near Milepost 232.

Cross-country skiers also head to Hart Prairie and Wing Mountain, two undeveloped skiing areas near the San Francisco Peaks. The rolling meadow and forest country is ideal for ski touring. Reach Hart Prairie by driving 9.5 miles northwest of town on US 180, then turning right on the south end of Forest Road 151 and continuing as far as the road is clear. Parking on US 180 is prohibited, but there are some signed parking areas just off it. For Wing Mountain, continue on US 180 just past Hart Prairie Road, then turn left onto Forest Road 222B. For road and skiing conditions near the Peaks, call the Forest Service's Peaks Ranger Station at 928/526-0866.

The groomed trails of Mormon Lake also attract cross-country skiers. **Mormon Lake Ski Center,** in the village of Mormon Lake, has 20 km of groomed diagonal and skating trails ranging from easy to challenging. It's open daily, snow permitting, with a trail fee of $5 per adult or $15 per family, rentals, and instruction; 928/354-2240 (toll call from Flagstaff). Drive 20 miles southeast on Lake Mary Road, then turn right eight miles on Mormon Lake Loop Road. **Mormon Lake Lodge** has rooms, cabins, and a café/steakhouse; 928/774-0462 (Flagstaff) or 928/354-2227 (local). For Mormon Lake road and ski conditions, call the Forest Service's Mormon Lake Ranger Station at 928/556-7474.

Climbing

Vertical Relief Climbing Center, 928/556-9909, 877/265-5984, has indoor walls up to 40 feet high to challenge all ages and abilities. Staff also offer instruction, a store, and local climbing information. The center is open daily at 205 S. San Francisco St.; www.verticalrelief.com.

ACCOMMODATIONS

Accommodation costs fluctuate greatly with the number of visitors, the season, and the day of the week; summer weekends are the most expensive. Rates listed below apply in summer but go higher on holiday or special-event periods. Off-season, prices can drop substantially, especially at the more expensive establishments. Winter rates may rise a bit during the ski season and weekends, depending on demand.

Although hostels offer the cheapest places for solo travelers, a party of two or more can often do better in a motel. Drive along East Route 66 to look for the bargain places; the "strip" extends three miles. Most motels post prices except on summer weekends, when no bargains exist. The low-priced places usually have satisfactory rooms, but always check them first to make sure they're clean.

Bed and Breakfasts

Birch Tree Inn Bed & Breakfast, 824 W. Birch Ave. 928/774-1042, 888/774-1042, offers comfortable rooms, some with private bath, and a hot tub in a 1917 house for $59–99 s and $69–119 d; www.birchtreeinn.com.

Dierker House Bed & Breakfast, 423 W. Cherry Ave., 928/774-3249, has rooms with shared bath in a 1914 house decorated in antiques; rates start at $60 d with tax.

The Tree House Bed & Breakfast, 615 W. Cherry Ave., 928/214-8664, 888/251-9390, features suites with private bath on the second floor of a 1915 house surrounded by large cottonwoods; a hot tub is outdoors; rates are $105 d.

Lynn's Inn, 614 W. Santa Fe Ave., 928/226-1488, 800/530-9947, has beautifully restored early 20th-century furnishings in a ca. 1905 house; rooms and suite have private bath and run $85 d ($95 d rooms and $105 d suite Fri.–Sat.).

The Inn at 410, 928/774-0088, 800/774-2008, offers distinctive guest suites in a 1907 residence, a restored Craftsman-style bungalow at 410 N. Leroux St.; all have private bath, most have fireplaces, and some a Jacuzzi tub; rates run $135–190 d; www.inn410.com.

Jeanette's Bed & Breakfast, 928/527-1912, 800/752-1912, is furnished with early 20th-century antiques in a Princess Ann-style house at 3380 E. Lockett Road; each room has private bath at rates of $99–145 d including a gourmet breakfast; www.jeanettesbb.com.

Lake Mary Bed & Breakfast, 928/779-7054, 888/241-9550, lies out in the country, three miles southeast of town on Lake Mary Road, with many hiking, biking, and horse riding opportunities. The house was built in Jerome in the 1930s, then moved here and added to; the four guest rooms all have private bath and go for $80 d, $110 four people.

The Sled Dog Inn, 928/525-6212, 800/754-0664, is in the woods six miles south of town at 10155 Mountainaire Road (I-17 Exit 333). You can go dog sledding in winter. Rooms have private bath and range from $110 d for a regular room to $185 d for a two-bed suite; www.sleddoginn.com.

Hostels

For a lively backpacker scene with an international crowd, head south across the tracks to the Grand Canyon or Du Beau hostels. Each offers free pickup at the Greyhound station, discounts for car rentals, and tours to the Grand Canyon and Sedona. Guests have use of a kitchen, common room, and Internet computers (small fee); both hostels are under the same management and on the Internet at www.grandcanyonhostel.com. There's no need for a hostel card or passport. Call ahead, if possible, to make the recommended reservations with a credit card; summer is the busiest time.

Grand Canyon International Hostel, 19 S. San Francisco St., 928/779-9421, 888/442-2696, offers dorm beds at $14 ($16 in summer) and double rooms at $28–31 d ($32–35 d in summer) including tax and breakfast.

The **Du Beau International Hostel,** nearby at 19 W. Phoenix Ave., 928/774-6731, 800/398-7112, has dorm spaces at $14 ($16 in summer) and motel rooms for $29–31 d ($32–35 d in summer) including tax and breakfast.

Historic Downtown Hotels

Both of Flagstaff's hotels here are registered historic landmarks. The **Weatherford Hotel,** 23 N. Leroux St., 928/774-2731, is named for J.W. Weatherford, who came to Flagstaff in 1887 from Texas and stayed 47 years. He built the hotel, quite elegant in its day, in 1897. Zane Grey wrote *Call of the Canyon* while staying here, describing the hotel as it was in 1918. Weatherford's other projects included an opera house and the Weatherford Road (now a hiking trail) in the San Francisco Peaks. Rooms in this historic hotel cost $35–45 d ($55–65 d in summer), but expect some noise from the nightclub. **Charly's,** the hotel's restaurant and pub, serves food and brew downstairs. Musicians often perform foot-tapping bluegrass, jazz, blues, folk, or rock 'n' roll Friday and Saturday nights. Upstairs, the Zane Grey Bar has live music on special occasions.

Hotel Monte Vista, 100 N. San Francisco St., 928/779-6971, 800/545-3068, dates to 1927 and has seen a lot of history. This was Flagstaff's grand hotel where movie stars stayed to film in nearby locations. You can stay in rooms named for those guests, such as the John Wayne, Jane Russell, and Gary Cooper suites. The Monte Vista still has many businesses under its roof, including Hennessy's (breakfast, lunch, and dinner daily), a lounge, the Old Post Office Salon & Spa, and Gadfly's Gifts. Rooms with shared bath cost $50 d but are rarely available, rooms with private bath run $60–150 d and suites are $90–150 d; www.hotelmontevista.com.

Motels Under $50: Downtown

Townhouse Motel, 122 W. Route 66, 928/774-5081, offers a very central, though noisy, location for $27 d ($30–32 d Fri.–Sat.).

Motels Under $50: South and West of Downtown

Family Inn, 121 S. Milton Rd., 928/774-8820, costs $30 d ($32 d and up Fri.–Sat.). **Arizonan Motel,** 910 S. Milton Rd., 928/774-7171, is near NAU, $29 s, $32 d ($36 d Fri.–Sat.). **Autolodge,** 1313 S. Milton Rd., 928/774-6621, is a good value in this part of town at $35 d ($39 d Fri.–Sat.). **Hidden Village Motel,** 822 W. Route 66, 928/774-1443, has an indoor pool at $35–38 s, 40 d ($48 d Fri.–Sat.).

Motels Under $50: East of Downtown

"Budget Row" features the best selection in town of bargain places. You can try:

Snowbowl Motel, 618 E. Route 66, 928/773-4818, is basic at $25 s, $30 d ($27 s, $32 d Fri.–Sat.). **Whispering Winds Motel,** 922 E. Route 66, 928/774-7391, has mostly kitchenettes from $30 s, $35 d ($40 s, $45 d Fri.–Sat.). **Relax Inn Motel,** 1500 E. Route 66, 928/779-4469, runs $25 s, $30 d ($30 s, $35 d Fri.–Sat.). **Western Hills Motel,** 1580 E. Route 66, 928/774-6633, has a pool and the Asian Gourmet Restaurant, $30 s, $35 d ($40 s, $45 d Fri.–Sat.). **Chalet Lodge,** 1990 E. Route 66, 928/774-2779, costs $25 s, $29 d ($29 s, $35 d Fri.–Sat.). **Wonderland Motel,** 2000 E. Route 66, 928/779-6119, is $26 s, $28 d ($35 d Fri.–Sat.). **Twilite Motel,** 2010 E. Route 66, 928/774-3364, runs $28 s, $32 d ($32 s, $35 d Fri.–Sat.). **66 Motel,** 2100 E. Route 66, 928/774-6403, has some kitchenettes from $22 s, $25 d ($32 d Fri.–Sat.). **Royal Inn,** 2140 E. Route 66, 928/774-7308, costs $28 d ($35 d Fri.–Sat.). **Pinecrest Motel,** 2818 E. Route 66, 928/526-1950, has some kitchenettes from $25 s, $35 d ($30 s, $40 d Fri.–Sat.). **Carousel Inn,** 2918 E. Route 66, 928/526-3595, charges $22–38 d ($35–60 d Fri.–Sat.). **Geronimo Inn,** 3100 E. Route 66, 928/527-3377, runs about $30 s, $40 d ($36 s, $46 d Fri.–Sat.).

Motels Under $50: Butler Avenue Area (I-40 Exit 198)

Motel 6, 2440 E. Lucky Lane, 928/774-8756, 800/4MOTEL6, has a pool at $30 s, $36 d ($34 s, $40 d Fri.–Sat.).

Motels and Hotels $50–100: South and West of Downtown

The Inn at NAU, 928/523-1616, puts you in the heart of campus with large rooms and fine dining; students operate the facilities under the School of Hotel and Restaurant Management at a cost of $79 d ($99 d Fri.–Sat.) including breakfast; there's no tax; www.hrm.nau.edu. **University TraveLodge,** 801 W. Route 66, 928/774-3381, 888/259-4404, features a Jacuzzi, hot tub, sauna, and family suites at $70 d ($80 d Fri.–Sat.). **Economy Inn,** 224 S. Mikes Pike, 928/774-8888, is near NAU and runs $35–45 d ($49–69 d Fri.–Sat.). **Highland Country Inn,** 223 S. Milton Rd., 928/774-5041, 877/470-6626, sits near NAU and goes for $32–49 d ($32–69 d Fri.–Sat.). **Canyon Inn,** 500 S. Milton Rd., 928/774-7301, has a location near NAU, $30 s, $37 d ($90 s, $100 d Fri.–Sat.). **Crystal Inn,** 602 W. Route 66, 928/774-4581, 800/654-4667, features an indoor pool and a hot tub near NAU, $45–55 d ($50–70 d Fri.–Sat.). **Saga Budget Host,** 820 W. Route 66, 928/779-3631, 800/BUD-HOST, has a pool for $35–39 s, $49–59 d ($49 s, $59–69 d Fri.–Sat.). **Days Inn,** 1000 W. Route 66, 928/774-5221, 800/329-7466, offers a pool, $50–99 d ($59–119 d Fri.–Sat.). **Budget Inn,** 913 S. Milton Rd., 928/774-5038, offers a pool and hot tub near NAU, $49 d ($89 d Fri.–Sat.). **Comfort Inn,** 914 S. Milton Rd., 928/774-7326, 800/221-2222, has a pool near NAU, $69 d ($94–99 d Fri.–Sat.). **Quality Inn,** 2000 S. Milton Rd., 928/774-8771, 800/228-5151, offers a pool for $69–89 d ($79–120 d Fri.–Sat.). **Fairfield Inn by Marriott,** 2005 S. Milton Rd., 928/773-1300, 800/574-6395, or 800/228-2800, has a pool at $59–65 d ($75–79 d Fri.–Sat.). **Motel 6 Woodlands Village,** 2745 S. Woodlands Village Blvd., 928/779-3757, 800/4MOTEL6, has a pool, $40 s, $46 d ($52 s, $58 d Fri.–Sat.). **Sleep Inn,** 2765 S. Woodlands Village Blvd., 928/556-3000, features an indoor pool and hot tub at $75–80 d, $85–90 d for a mini-suite; add $5 on weekends. **Econo Lodge West,** 2355 S. Beulah Blvd., 928/774-2225, 800/490-6562, or 800/553-2666, has a pool and two hot tubs at $60–80 d ($70–90 d Fri.–Sat.). **Ramada Ltd.**

West, 2755 S. Woodlands Village Blvd., 928/773-1111, 877/703-0291, or 800/2-RA-MADA, offers mini-suites with microwaves and refrigerators plus a pool, sauna, and exercise room at $50–80 d ($70–100 d Fri.–Sat.).

Motels and Hotels $50–100: North of Downtown

Ski Lift Lodge, on US 180 opposite the Snow Bowl Road turnoff, 928/774-0729, 800/472-3599, is open year-round and has a restaurant and winter ski packages, $75 d ($85 d Fri.–Sat.).

Motels and Hotels $50–100: East of Downtown

Inn Suites, 1008 E. Route 66, 928/774-7356, 800/898-9124, features a pool and rooms with microwave and refrigerator (the most expensive rooms also have a Jacuzzi tub and kitchenette), $70–130 d ($90–150 d Fri.–Sat.). **King's House Motel (Best Western),** 1560 E. Route 66, 928/774-7186, 800/528-1234, offers a pool at $69 d ($79 d Fri.–Sat.). **Flagstaff Motel,** 2204 E. Route 66, 928/774-0280, runs $27 s, $29 d ($49 s, $59 d Fri.–Sat.). **Rodeway Inn,** 2650 E. Route 66, 928/526-2200, 800/228-2000, costs $30–60 d ($50–70 d Fri.–Sat.). **Pony Soldier Motel (Best Western),** 3030 E. Route 66, 928/526-2388, 800/356-4143, includes an indoor pool, hot tub, and restaurant at $69–89 d ($79–99 Fri.–Sat.). **Howard Johnson Inn,** 3300 E. Route 66, 928/526-1826, 800/437-7137, has the Crown Railroad Restaurant, $39 d ($50 Fri.–Sat.). **Hampton Inn,** 3501 E. Lockett Rd., 928/526-1885, 800/HAMPTON, offers an indoor pool and hot tub for $69 d ($75–79 d Fri.–Sat.). **Days Inn East,** 3601 E. Lockett Rd., 928/527-1477, 800/446-6900, has an indoor pool and hot tub at $80 d ($100 d Fri.–Sat.). **Super 8,** 3725 N. Kaspar Ave., 928/526-0818, 888/324-9131, costs $49 s, $54 d ($54 s, $59 d Fri.–Sat.).

Motels and Hotels $50–100: Butler Avenue Area (I-40 Exit 198)

Motel 6 Butler Avenue, 2010 E. Butler Ave., 928/774-1801, 800/4MOTEL6, has a pool for $38 s, $44 d ($52 s, $58 d Fri.–Sat.). **Continental**

Inn & Suites, 2200 E. Butler Ave., 928/779-6944, features an indoor pool and hot tub in an atrium and a game room at $35 s, $59 d ($35 s, $69 d Fri.–Sat.), fireplace suites run $89 d ($99 Fri.–Sat.). **Super 8,** 2285 E. Butler Ave., 928/774-1821, 800/800-8000, has a pool and sauna at $45 s, $52 d ($79–89 d Fri.–Sat.). **Holiday Inn,** 2320 E. Lucky Lane, 928/526-1150, 800/465-4329, has an indoor/outdoor pool and a hot tub at $99 d every day. **Econo Lodge Lucky Lane,** 2480 E. Lucky Lane, 928/774-7701, 888/349-2523, includes an indoor pool and hot tub for $60 d ($79–99 d Fri.–Sat.). **Aspen Country Inn,** 2500 E. Lucky Lane, 928/226-7111, offers a pool at $35 s, $45 d ($40 s, $50 d Fri.–Sat.). **Red Roof Inn,** 2520 E. Lucky Lane, 928/779-5121, 800/545-5525, includes a pool and hot tub at $48–58 d ($67–80 d Fri.–Sat.).

Motels and Hotels $100–150 and up: Downtown

Comfi Cottages of Flagstaff, 928/774-0731, 888/774-0731, have kitchens and provide a full breakfast at various locations, $110–145 d or $220–250 for up to 6–8 guests; www.comfi cottages.com.

Motels and Hotels $100–150 and up: South and West of Downtown

Radisson Woodlands Hotel, 1175 W. Route 66, 928/773-8888, 800/333-3333, offers a pool, indoor and outdoor hot tubs, sauna, and exercise room at $109–149 d every day. **Embassy Suites Hotel,** 706 S. Milton Rd., 928/774-4333, 800/EMBASSY, has a pool and hot tub near NAU for $119–129 s, $129–139 d ($129–139 s, $139–159 d Fri.–Sat.). **Hampton Inn & Suites,** 2400 S. Beulah Blvd., 928/913-0900, 800/HAMPTON, features an indoor pool and hot tub at $99 d ($101–129 d Fri.–Sat.), Jacuzzi rooms cost $109–139. **AmeriSuites,** 2455 S. Beulah Blvd., 928/774-8042, 800/833-1516, includes an indoor pool, hot tub and rooms with microwave and refrigerator for $99–149 d ($129–149 d Fri.–Sat.). **Arizona Mountain Inn,** 4200 Lake Mary Rd., 928/774-8959, 800/239-5236, nestles in the pines about three miles southeast of downtown; rooms (including breakfast) and rustic cabins are $80 d ($110 d Fri.–Sat.); www.arizona mountaininn.com.

Motels and Hotels $100–150 and up: East of Downtown

Residence Inn by Marriott, 3440 N. Country Club Dr., 928/526-5555, 800/331-3131, has kitchens in all units and fireplaces in some and includes a pool, hot tub, and nearby golf at $99–170 d studio or $170–209 two-bedroom every day. **Mountain Country Management & Realty,** 2380 N. Oakmont Dr. (office), 928/526-4287, 800/424-7748, has furnished condos of 1–3 bedrooms in the Continental Country Club area, $110–200 per day or you can arrange weekly or monthly stays.

Motels and Hotels $100–150 and up: Butler Avenue Area (I-40 Exit 198)

Little America, 2515 E. Butler Ave., 928/779-2741, 800/352-4386, offers a pool, restaurants, and coffee shop for $119–129 d rooms and $150–275 d suites every day. **Ramada Limited,** 2350 E. Lucky Lane, 928/779-3614, 800/2RAMADA, has a pool at $69–95 d suites ($125–150 d suites Fri.–Sat.).

Campgrounds

You really need your own vehicle to camp. The following places nestle in ponderosa pines; all have showers except as noted. **Fort Tuthill County Campground,** 928/774-3464, is open May 1–Sept. 30 with $9 dry sites for tents or RVs and $13 sites with water and sewer (no electricity) plus a $5 reservation fee; the restroom/shower building may be closed during renovation but porta-johns will be available; there's a quarter-mile nature trail and the five-mile Soldiers Trail. The campground is five miles south of downtown off I-17 Exit 337.

Black Bart's RV Park, 928/774-1912, is open all year, $20 tent (three-night limit) and $22 RV with hookups; there's a steak house on the premises. It's two miles east of downtown near I-40 Butler Ave. Exit 198.

Flagstaff KOA, 5803 N. Hwy. 89, 928/526-9926, 800/KOA-FLAG, is open all year, $21 tent or RV no hookups, $25 with water and electricity, $27 with full hookups, and $36 for a "kamping kabin"; it's five miles northeast of downtown on Route 66/US 89, 1.1 miles north from I-40 Exit 201.

Greer's Pine Shadows, 7101 N. Hwy. 89, 928/526-4977, is an adult RV park for self-contained rigs (no restrooms or showers) open mid-April to mid-October. Sites cost $19 with hookups; it's 1.8 miles north of I-40.

J&H RV Park, 7901 N. Hwy. 89, 928/526-1829, has sites for RVs only from early April to late October in an adult-oriented atmosphere three miles north of I-40 Exit 201. Rates are $23.50–29 with hookups; there's also a hot tub.

Kit Carson RV Park, 2101 W. Route 66, 928/774-6993, is open year-round, $27 RV with hookups. You'll find it two miles west of downtown; take I-40 Exits 191 or 195.

Woody Mountain Campground, 2727 W. Route 66, 928/774-7727, is a half mile farther west and open mid-March to October; rates are $17 tents or $23 RVs with hookups.

Munds Park RV Resort, 928/286-1309, offers sites 17 miles south of Flagstaff near I-17 Exit 322; it's open April 1–Oct. 31. Rates are $19 tent, $19–23.50 RV with hookups.

Ponderosa Forest RV Park & Campground, 928/635-0456, 888/635-0456, has year-round sites in the woods for tents ($13) and RVs ($19 with hookups) with a nearby store. It's north of I-40 Parks Exit 178, 17 miles west of Flagstaff and about halfway to Williams.

The closest established campgrounds on the Coconino National Forest lie southeast off Lake Mary Road; see "South Of Flagstaff: Lake And Rim Country" below. More campgrounds line Oak Creek Canyon farther south. North of Flagstaff, Bonito Campground has sites next to Sunset Crater Volcano National Monument and Little Elden Springs Horse Camp is close to Mt. Elden; see "North of Flagstaff." All of the Forest Service campgrounds near Flagstaff close in winter, but some of those in Oak Creek Canyon stay open all year. For more information, contact the Peaks Ranger Station, 5075 N. Hwy. 89, Flagstaff, AZ 86004; 928/526-0866; www.fs.fed.us/r3/coconino.

Dispersed camping on Forest Service lands surrounding town provides another option. The ponderosa pine forests offer lots of room but no facilities—just be sure you're well out of the city and not on private or state land. The Coconino National Forest map shows Forest Service land and the back roads. Carry water and be *very* careful with fire; in dry weather the Forest Service often prohibits fires in the woods and may even close some areas.

FOOD

Flagstaff, for its size, offers an amazing number of places to eat. But then, it has a lot of hungry tourists and students to feed. Most restaurants cater to the eat-and-run crowd. You'll find the well-known chains and fast-food places on the main roads, but with a little effort you can discover some unique restaurants and cafés. Come downtown for local atmosphere—old-fashioned home-style eateries abound.

You'll enjoy Flagstaff's clean mountain air while dining because of the city's nonsmoking ordinance. A few places, such as Granny's Closet and Fiddlers on S. Milton, have separate smoking and nonsmoking sections; bars that serve food may be all smoking.

Downtown (north of the tracks)

Chez Marc Bistro, 503 N. Humphreys St., 928/774-1343, offers fine country French cuisine with indoor and outdoor seating at a historic 1911 residence; it's open Thurs.–Sun in summer for lunch and daily year-round for dinner. Most dinner entrees run about $30 and reservations are recommended.

Charly's Pub and Grill, in the old Weatherford Hotel at 23 N. Leroux St., 928/779-1919, serves good American food daily for lunch and dinner. **Downtown Diner,** 7 E. Aspen Ave., 928/774-3492, dishes out American food daily for breakfast and lunch and Mon.–Sat. for dinner, but don't expect much in the way of decor. **Mountain Oasis,** 11 E. Aspen Ave., 928/214-9270, has a tasty mix of Mediterranean, Southwestern, and international flavors with many vegetarian options; open Sat.–Sun. for breakfast and daily for lunch and dinner. **Pasto,** 19 E. Aspen Ave., 928/779-1937, serves Italian food, including vegetarian and wheat-free options, in a casual fine-dining atmosphere with seating indoors and in a courtyard; open nightly for dinner. **Alpine Pizza,** 7 N. Leroux St., 928/779-4109, is open daily for lunch and dinner.

Café Espress, 16 N. San Francisco St., 928/774-0541, serves homemade natural foods, including many vegetarian items, plus coffees from the espresso bar and baked goodies from the oven; it's open daily for breakfast and lunch, and Wed.–Sat. for dinner. **Kathy's,** 7 N. San Francisco St., 928/774-1951, is a cozy café with American standbys and a few exotic items such as Aussie burgers and Navajo tacos; it's open daily for breakfast and lunch. The historic Monte Vista Hotel offers **Hennessey's,** 104 N. San Francisco St., 928/779-3211, open daily with American food for breakfast, lunch, and dinner.

You'll find good Mexican food at bargain prices in **Martan's Burrito Palace,** 10 N. San Francisco St., 928/773-4701, open Mon.–Sat. for breakfast and lunch. **Las Mananitas,** 103 W. Birch and Beaver St., 928/226-7144, offers Mexican dining Mon.-Sat. for lunch and dinner. **Kachina Downtown,** 522 E. Route 66, 928/779-1944, presents Mexican food in a pleasant setting daily for breakfast, lunch, and dinner.

If you're looking for inexpensive Chinese-American food and don't care about the decor, try the **Grand Canyon Cafe,** 110 E. Route 66, 928/774-2252, or the **Hong Kong Cafe,** at 6 E. Route 66, 928/774-9801; both are open Mon.–Sat. for breakfast, lunch, and dinner.

Downtown (south of the tracks)

Macy's European Coffee House and Bakery, 14 S. Beaver St., 928/774-2243, offers a big selection of fresh-roasted coffee and a menu of pasta dishes, sandwiches, soups, salads, quiches, and home-baked goodies daily for breakfast, lunch, and dinner. **La Bellavia Sandwich Shoppe,** 18 S. Beaver St., 928/774-8301, is a little café open daily for breakfast and lunch. **Beaver Street Brewery/Whistle Stop Cafe,** 11 S. Beaver St., 928/779-0079, serves pizza, sandwiches, salads, and fondues along with a selection of local brews daily for lunch and dinner; there's a beer garden outside. **Ni-Marco's Pizza,** 101 S. Beaver St., 928/779-2691, is open daily. **Cottage Place,** 126 W. Cottage Ave., 928/774-8431, serves American and continental specialties in a romantic setting; open Tues.–Sun. for dinner in a 1909 bungalow; reservations are recommended.

Thai food devotees enjoy the **Dara Thai Restaurant,** 14 S. San Francisco St., 928/774-0047, open Mon.–Sat. for lunch and dinner. **Pesto Brothers,** 34 S. San Francisco St., 928/913-0775, offers a café and deli with antipasto, salads, pasta, fish, and meat dishes; open Mon.–Sat. for lunch and Tues.–Sat. for dinner. **Morning Glory Cafe,** 115 S. San Francisco St., 928/774-3705, features a mostly vegetarian menu of home-made food including blue corn tamales, chicken pozolé, and a variety of salads and soups for lunch. It's open Mon.–Fri. for lunch and Sat. for breakfast. **Cafe Olé,** 119 S. San Francisco St., 928/774-8272, specializes in homemade Mexican dishes; it's open Tues.–Sat. for lunch and dinner. **Aladdin's,** 211 S. San Francisco St., 928/213-0033, serves tasty Middle Eastern, Greek, and International specialties (takeout too) open Mon.–Sat. for lunch and daily for dinner. **El Charro,** 409 S. San Francisco St., 928/779-0552, is a popular Mexican café open Mon.–Sat. for lunch and dinner.

Northern Arizona University

The Garden Terrace Dining Room, 928/523-1616, at The Inn at NAU prepares a breakfast buffet daily, fine lunches Mon.–Fri., and dinners Tues.–Friday. The Friday dinners often feature a magnificent seven-course set menu; reservations are required. In summer, the dining room serves only breakfast and lunch. The Inn is off S. San Francisco Street.

University Union, in the north-central campus, offers a variety of fast-food eateries. **University Dining** is a large cafeteria in the central campus. **North Union** has fast-food establishments on the north edge of campus. **South Campus Dining** offers cafeteria fare and the **South Campus Student Union** contains **The Peaks,** serving food ready to go.

Other Areas

American Cuisine: Galaxy Diner, 931 W. Route 66, 928/774-2466, features '50s music and movie-star decor with American classics such as sandwiches, platters, milkshakes, sodas, and sumptuous deserts; breakfasts are especially good and are served all day; open daily for breakfast, lunch, and dinner. **Woodlands Cafe,** 1175 W. Route 66, 928/773-9118, serves American food daily for breakfast, lunch, and dinner in a Southwestern atmosphere at Radisson Woodlands Ho **Granny's Closet,** 218 S. Milton Rd. (just south of the railroad underpass), 928/774-8331, fixes steak and other meat dishes, seafood, and Italian cuisine; open daily for lunch and dinner. **Mike and Ronda's,** 21 S. Milton Rd., 928/774-7008, pulls in the crowds with generous servings of low-priced American café fare, open daily for breakfast and lunch. A second location at Park Santa Fe Shopping Center, 3518 E. Route 66, 928/526-8138, is open daily for breakfast and lunch and Tues.–Sat. for dinner. Breakfasts are very popular.

Fiddlers Restaurant, 702 S. Milton Rd., 928/774-6689, serves up ranch-style steaks, chicken, shrimp, and sandwiches daily for dinner. **Casa del Panzon,** 801 S. Milton Rd., 928/556-0093, prepares Southwestern dishes with a choice of meat, seafood, and vegetarian; open daily except Mon. for lunch and dinner. **Furr's Family Dining,** 1200 S. Milton Rd., 928/779-4104, offers buffets daily for lunch and dinner. **Souper!Salad!,** 1300 S. Milton Rd., 928/774-8030, is open daily for lunch and dinner with a buffet of soups and salads. **Buster's,** 1800 S. Milton Rd., 928/774-5155, features seafood and an oyster bar along with steak, ribs, chicken, veal, and sandwiches in Green Tree Village; open daily for lunch and dinner. The two **Sizzlers** offer

good deals on meat and fish entrees plus a big salad bar at 2105 S. Milton Rd., 928/779-3267, and at 3540 E. Route 66, 928/526-3391. **Red Lobster,** 2500 S. Beulah Blvd. in the Woodlands Village area, 928/556-9604, has the nautical decor of a Maine lobster house for fish, shrimp, crab, and of course lobster, along with steak and chicken; it's open daily for lunch and dinner. A model train circles the dining areas of **The Crown Railroad Cafe,** which does popular American standbys, including a choice of 66 omelets, at 2700 S. Woodlands Village Blvd. near Wal-Mart, 928/774-6775, and at 3300 E. Route 66, 928/522-9237.

Little America's Western Gold Dining Room, 2515 E. Butler Ave., 928/779-7900, serves a big brunch on Sunday, a buffet lunch Mon.–Fri., and dinner nightly; the coffee shop is open daily for breakfast, lunch, and dinner. Also in the Butler Avenue area and just off I-40 Exit 198 are the **Country Host Restaurant** and **Kettle Restaurant,** both open daily for breakfast, lunch, and dinner.

Black Bart's Steak House, 2760 E. Butler Ave. near I-40 Exit 198, 928/779-3142, serves up steak, seafood, and other American fare; it's open nightly for dinner with singing waiters and waitresses to entertain you. Many locals say you'll find the best steaks in town at **Lupo's Horsemen Lodge,** 928/526-2655, which fixes steak, ribs, chicken, trout, and seafood; it's open for dinner nightly except Sunday (and Mon. in winter) on US 89, 3.6 miles north from I-40 Exit 201.

Jackson's Grill at the Springs, 928/213-9332, has an idyllic setting in a meadow just south of town. The extensive menu includes steak, ribs, chicken, seafood, brick oven pizza, and salads, plus there's a choice of more than 100 wines. You have a choice of seating in the main dining room, deck, patio, café, or lounge. Head south on AZ 89A or I-17 to the Fort Tuthill/Airport Exit 337, then continue half a mile south on AZ 89A.

Italian Cuisine: Mamma Luisa, 2710 N. Steves Blvd., 928/526-6809, has excellent Italian cuisine nightly for dinner at Kachina Square off E. Route 66; reservations are advised. The Olive Garden Italian Restaurant, 2550 Beulah

Blvd. in the Woodlands Village area, 928/779-3000, serves pasta, seafood, meats from the grill, and breadstick-style pizzas; there's a children's menu too; it's open daily for lunch and dinner. The nearby **Fazoli's,** 2675 S. Beulah Blvd., 928/214-8220, offers "Italian food . . . fast" in an informal setting for pastas, pizza, and salads at; open daily for lunch and dinner. **Dan's Italian Kitchen,** 1850 N. Fort Valley Rd. (US 180), 928/779-9349, is a small place open Mon.–Sat. for lunch and dinner on the route to the Grand Canyon.

Mexican Cuisine: Flagstaff's large Mexican-American population provides the town with some tasty food. In addition to the Mexican eateries listed under downtown, try **Jalapeño Lou's,** 3050 E. Route 66, 928/526-1533, which specializes in New Mexico cuisine and will please chili lovers; open nightly for dinner. In the southern part of town there's **Chili's Grill & Bar,** 1500 S. Milton Rd., 928/774-4546, open daily for lunch and dinner.

Asian Cuisines: Delhi Palace, 2700 S. Woodlands Village Blvd. near Wal-Mart, 928/556-0019, offers fine north Indian food daily for lunch (buffet available) and dinner. It's the restaurant where you're most likely to spot the author!

Sakura Restaurant, 1175 W. Route 66, 928/773-9118, prepares Japanese teppanyaki and sushi Mon.–Sat. for lunch and nightly for dinner in the Radisson Woodlands Ho

Chinese dining is always close at hand in Flagstaff. The following restaurants serve lunch and dinner daily except as noted. South of downtown, you can choose from **Hunan West** (closed Monday) in University Plaza off S. Milton Rd., 928/779-2229; **August Moon,** 1300 S. Milton Rd., 928/774-5280; and **Szechuan,** 1451 S. Milton Rd., 928/774-8039. In east Flagstaff, **Asian Gourmet,** 1580 E. Route 66, 928/773-7771, has an exceptionally long vegetarian menu as well as good selections of meat and seafood dishes in the Western Hills Motel; the dining room décor is an odd mix of cowboy and Chinese, but the food is authentic! Farther east, you'll find **China Star,** 1802 E. Route 66, 928/8880,

with buffets and ala carte; **Hunan East,** 2028 N. Fourth St., 928/526-1009; **Golden Dragon Bowl,** 2730 Lakin Dr. across from Kachina Square, 928/527-3238; and **Mandarin Gardens,** Park Santa Fe Shopping Center at 3518 E. Route 66, 928/526-5033.

Groceries

Nearly every shopping center has a supermarket, and you can find **Fry's** and **Albertsons** at the corner of E. Route 66 and Switzer Canyon Drive. **Farmer's Market** specializes in fresh produce, often at bargain prices; it's at 1901 N. Fourth St., just off E. Route 66; 928/774-4500. **New Frontiers,** 1000 S. Milton Rd., 928/774-5747, sells natural foods and offers deli dining and take-out.

ENTERTAINMENT AND EVENTS

The free weekly paper *Flagstaff Live!* details the local music scene, movies, arts, restaurants, events, sports, and hikes.

Sports and NAU Culture

Northern Arizona University presents theater, opera, dance, concerts, and a variety of sports events. For information and tickets, contact NAU Central Ticket Office, University Union, 928/523-5661, or NAU Downtown, Heritage Square at Aspen Ave. and Leroux St., 928/523-1628. During the summer, three professional teams hold training camps on NAU's campus: the **Arizona Cardinals** (football), the **Phoenix Suns** (basketball), and the **Phoenix Mercury** (women's basketball). Call the Flagstaff Visitor Center for fan information.

Nightlife

The **Museum Club,** 3404 E. Route 66, 928/526-9434, began in 1931 as a museum and trading post with such taxidermy oddities as a two-headed calf and a one-eyed lamb along with more conventional animals, Native American artifacts, and a rifle collection. Curious motorists sputtering down early Route 66 dropped in to see the thousands of exhibits inside this huge log structure. Five years later another entrepreneur converted it into a nightclub to attract the growing crowds of motorists as well as local folk looking for some good music and dancing. Aspiring recording artists traveling cross-country stopped by to perform for appreciative audiences. The Museum Club continues the tradition of fine country music while introducing additional music styles popular with the younger crowd. It's also known as the "The Zoo" because stuffed animals still gaze down from the walls. *Car and Driver* magazine named it one of the top 10 roadhouses in the nation. Wandering through the rustic interior, you'll find photos and news clippings on the walls, a dance floor, and a magnificent late-19th century bar. Something's happening nightly in the Museum Club; call or check www.museumclub.com.

You'll find most of the other nightlife downtown, where venues include **Charly's,** 23 N. Leroux St., 928/779-1919; **Flagstaff Brewing Co.,** 16 E. Route 66, 928/773-1442; **The Alley,** 22 E. Route 66, 928/774-7929; **Mogollon Brewing Co.,** 15 N. Agassiz St., 928/773-8950; and **Monte Visa Lounge,** 100 N. San Francisco St., 928/774-2403.

Events

People in Flagstaff put on a variety of festivals, fairs, shows, and concerts during the year. The Flagstaff Visitor Center will tell you what's happening; 928/774-9541, 800/842-7293; www.flagstaff.az.us. Major annual events include **Flagstaff Winterfest** in February, featuring over 100 events such as skiing competitions, sled-dog races, snow games, and entertainment. In May, residents celebrate **Cinco de Mayo** with a parade and arts and crafts fair. June activities include **The Great Fiesta del Barrio & Fajita Cook-off** on the second Saturday and **Pine Country Rodeo and Parade** on the third weekend. Flagstaff's **Fabulous Fourth Festivities** commemorate the 4th of July and Flagstaff's founding with a parade, the Fair of Life arts and crafts show, a gem show, historic walks, horse racing, a pioneer festival, barbecue, and fireworks. Also in July, **Arizona Highland Celtic Festival** celebrates the people of Brittany, Cornwall, Ireland, Isle of Man, Scotland, and Wales with

dancing, athletic demonstrations and, of course, bagpiping. **Summerfest** on the first weekend in August features top Southwestern artists for an arts and crafts show. Heritage Square downtown hosts ongoing summer events. Also, from May to September, the Museum of Northern Arizona's **Heritage Program** features Hispanic and Native American marketplaces, entertainment, artists' demonstrations, and Enduring Creations, a sales exhibit. **Coconino County Fair** runs over Labor Day weekend in September as does an arts and crafts show. The **Festival of Science** presents talks, demonstrations, and open houses during a ten-day period in late September. The **Northern Lights Holiday Parade** and **Holiday Lights Festival** in December round out the year's activities.

SHOPPING AND SERVICES
Art Galleries and Native American Crafts

Shops in downtown Flagstaff display a wealth of regional arts and crafts. Native American artists create much of the distinctive work. You'll see paintings, jewelry, Navajo rugs, Hopi kachina dolls, pottery, and baskets. The **Museum of Northern Arizona's** gift shop and the **Art Barn,** both northwest of town on US 180, feature excellent selections of Native American arts and crafts.

Bookstores

Barnes & Noble Booksellers, 701 S. Milton Rd., 928/226-8227, offers a spacious store with a café. **NAU Bookstore,** 928/523-4041, includes many regional and general publications on the east side of campus. **Northland Publishing,** 2900 N. Fort Valley Rd./US 180, 928/774-5251, produces outstanding regional and children's books plus some cookbooks and posters; the sales room often has discounted titles and is open Mon.–Fri. 8 A.M.–5 P.M.; www.northland pub.com. The **Museum of Northern Arizona,** 3101 N. Fort Valley Rd./US 180, 928/774-5213, sells excellent books on Southwestern Native American cultures, archaeology, and natural history; it's three miles northwest of downtown.

Waldenbooks, in the Flagstaff Mall, 928/526-5196, stocks good regional and general reading selections. **Crystal Magic,** 5 N. San Francisco St., 928/779-2528, features spiritual and New Age titles downtown.

For used books, including many regional titles, drop by **Bookman's Used Books,** 1520 S. Riordan Ranch St., 928/774-0005; it offers 250,000 used books and some new ones as well as music, videos, and games. A few doors south, **Hastings,** 928/779-1880, sells discounted new books, music, and videos. **Dragon's Plunder,** 217 S. San Francisco St. and Butler Ave., 928/774-1708, has about 80,000 used books. **Starlight Books,** 15 N. Leroux St., 928/774-6813, has a smaller selection of mostly used books and specializes in modern first editions, rare and antique books, and does out-of-print orders.

Outdoor Equipment and Rentals

Babbitt's Backcountry Outfitters, 12 E. Aspen Ave., 928/774-4775, carries an extensive selection of backpacking, climbing, and cross-country ski gear downtown. **Peace Surplus,** 14 W. Route 66, 928/779-4521, offers hiking, camping, winter sports, and fishing gear downtown; www.peacesurplus.com. **Mountain Sports,** 1800 S. Milton Rd., 928/779-5156, has mountain bikes as well as hiking, camping, and winter sports gear south of downtown.

Photo Equipment and Supplies

Wal-Mart and supermarkets carry print and a bit of slide film. **P.R. Camera Repair,** 111 E. Aspen Ave., 928/779-5263 offers service.

Postal Services

The main **post office,** 928/714-9302, is at 2400 N. Postal Blvd. off E. Route 66; General Delivery mail can be sent to you with a zip code of 86004. There's a downtown branch at 104 N. Agassiz St.; 928/779-3589, and another in the NAU Bookstore basement.

Medical Services

If you need medical attention, it's cheaper to go directly to a doctor's office or clinic than to the hospital. You'll find many offices along N. Beaver Street. **Concentra Medical Centers,** 120 W. Fine (west of Beaver), 928/773-9695, welcomes walk-in patients daily. **Walk-in Medical Care,** near the Flagstaff Mall at 4215 N. Hwy. 89, 928/527-1920, provides similar services. **Flagstaff Medical Center,** 1200 N. Beaver St., 928/779-3366 is the local hospital. In **emergencies**—police, fire, and medical—dial 911.

INFORMATION

Visitor Center

The very helpful **Flagstaff Chamber of Commerce's Visitor Center** staff can answer your questions and tell you what's happening. The office, downtown in the Amtrak depot (1 E. Route 66, Flagstaff, AZ 86001), is open daily 8 A.M.–5 P.M. Literature in the lobby may be available after hours; 928/774-9541, 800/842-7293; fax 928/556-1308; email visitor@flagstaff.az.us.; www.flagstaff.az.us. Other useful websites include www.flagguide.com and www.flaglive.com.

Coconino National Forest

The **U.S. Forest Service** provides information and maps about camping, hiking, and road conditions in the Coconino National Forest surrounding Flagstaff. The **Supervisor's Office,** 928/527-3600, is at 2323 E. Greenlaw Lane (Flagstaff, AZ 86004) behind Knoles Village Shopping Center; it's open Mon.–Fri. 7:30 A.M.–4:30 P.M. Staff have information sheets on recreation in all of the districts on the Coconino Forest. You can buy any of the National Forest maps for Arizona here or choose from a small selection of books. On the Web, visit the forest at www.fs.fed.us/r3/coconino.

For more detailed information on the Mt. Elden, Humphrey's Peak, and O'Leary Peak areas north of Flagstaff, contact the **Peaks Ranger Station,** 5075 N. Hwy. 89 (Flagstaff, AZ 86004), 928/526-0866; it's open Mon.–Fri. 7:30 A.M.–4:30 P.M. For the lake and forest country south of town, check with the **Mor-**

mon **Lake Ranger District** office, 4373 S. Lake Mary Rd. (Flagstaff, AZ 86001), 928/774-1182; it's open Mon.–Fri. 7:30 A.M.–4:30 P.M. and Saturday during summer. Each of these two offices has information for both areas, so you can often get everything that you need with one visit.

Arizona Game and Fish Department

This office provides fishing and hunting licenses and information at 3500 S. Lake Mary Rd. (Flagstaff, AZ 86001); it's open Mon.–Fri. 8 A.M.–5 P.M.; 928/774-5045; www.azgfd.com.

Libraries

Looking for a good place to read up on Arizona or to keep dry on a rainy day? The **Flagstaff City Library's** attractive ski-lodge architecture makes it an especially enjoyable spot downtown at the corner of 300 W. Aspen Ave. and Sitgreaves St.; 928/779-7670. Hours are Mon.–Thurs. 10 A.M.–9 P.M., Friday 10 A.M.–7 P.M., Saturday 10 A.M.–6 P.M., and Sunday 11 A.M.–6 P.M.; www.flagstaffpubliclibrary.org. Many good regional books enrich the Arizona Collection. Art exhibits by local artists and photographers change monthly.

NAU's **Cline Library,** 928/523-2171, carries many books and periodicals. It's also far easier to find an available Internet computer here than at the city library. Hikers can plan trips and copy maps in the Government Documents section. The library is open daily during regular school sessions and Mon.–Fri. between terms. Upstairs, the **Special Collections and Archives Department,** 928/523-5551, contains an outstanding array of Arizona-related publications and photos; changing exhibits appear in the entranceway. It's open Mon.–Fri. 8 A.M.–6 P.M. (5 P.M. in summer). The library website, www.nau.edu/library, has the entire card catalog online, encyclopedias, plus a searchable database of about 7,000 images from Special Collections.

The **Museum of Northern Arizona,** 928/774-5211, ext. 256, has an excellent regional library in the Research Center across the highway from the museum; it's normally open Mon.–Fri. 9 A.M.–5 P.M.

TRANSPORTATION

Tours

Local taxi companies (see below) can arrange Flagstaff and northern Arizona tours. Other local tour operators have brochures at the Visitor Center.

Car Rental and Taxi

A rental car allows more extensive sightseeing than public transportation and costs less if several people get together. Rates fluctuate with supply and demand, competition, and the mood of the operators; call around for the best deals. See the Yellow Pages for agencies; you'll find offices in town and at the airport. For a taxi, call **Sun Taxi,** 928/774-7400; **Arizona Taxi,** 928/779-1111; or **A Friendly Cab,** 928/774-4444.

Local Bus

Mountain Line, 928/779-6624 (TDD number is 928/779-6635), serves most of the city with three routes Mon.–Fri. and two routes on Saturday. Pick up a schedule at the Flagstaff Visitor Center, public library, or at one of the Safeway stores in town.

Long-Distance Bus

Greyhound, 399 S. Malpais Lane, 928/774-4573, 800/231-2222, offers daily departures south to Phoenix and Sky Harbor Airport, east along I-40 to Winslow and Holbrook and west to Williams and Kingman. Services also continue to Tucson, Los Angeles, Las Vegas, Albuquerque, and other destinations. The station lies just south of downtown off S. Milton Road; it's open 24 hours; www.greyhound.com.

Train

Amtrak, 1 E. Route 66, 928/774-8679, 800/872-7245, offers service on the Southwest Chief every evening for Los Angeles ($64–114 one way), and every morning for Albuquerque ($59–106 one way) and on to Chicago or Orlando. The price depends on availability—book ahead or travel off-season for the lowest rates; roundtrip tickets are double but there are also special All Aboard America and fly/train fares; www.amtrak.com.

Air

America West, 800/235-9292, flies about six times daily to Phoenix for a stiff $195 each way, but a roundtrip with a 21-day advance purchase and a Saturday overnight costs little more; www.americawest.com. Pulliam Field, Flagstaff's airport, lies five miles south of town; take I-17 Exit 337. **Greyhound** offers ground transport to Sky Harbor Airport in Phoenix at much lower costs; see "Long-Distance Bus" above.

East of Flagstaff

WALNUT CANYON NATIONAL MONUMENT

Sinagua made this pretty canyon their home more than 800 years ago. Ledges eroded out of the limestone cliffs provided shelter from rain and snow—the inhabitants merely had to build walls under the ready-made roofs. Good farmland, wild plant foods, and forests filled with game lay close by. Clear waters of Walnut Creek flowed seasonally in the canyon bottom.

After occupying Walnut Canyon from A.D. 1125 to 1250, the people moved on. Some Hopi clans trace their ancestors back to this site. More than 300 Sinagua cliff dwellings remain; you can see and enter some along a loop trail constructed by the National Park Service. Another loop trail on the rim passes a pithouse site and a small pueblo.

Visitor Center

A small museum displays pottery and other artifacts of the Sinagua Culture. Exhibits show how the people farmed and how they used wild plants for baskets, sandals, mats, soap, food, and medicine. A map illustrates trading routes to other indigenous cultures. Rangers will answer questions about the archaeology and natural history of Walnut Canyon. During the summer, they offer interpretive programs; call ahead for times and to make reservations for the hikes. Ranger-led trips include the Ledges Hike to cliff dwellings off the main trail and the Ranger Cabin Hike to a 1904 Forest Service that once served as a visitor center for Walnut Canyon. A bookstore sells a wide selection of books, maps, and videos related to the monument and region.

The self-guided 0.9-mile **Island Trail** begins behind the visitor center and winds past 25 cliff dwellings. You can get a feeling of what it was like to live here. The paved path descends 185 feet with 240 steps, which you'll have to climb on the way out; allow 45–60 minutes. Because of the high elevation (6,690 feet), the trail isn't recommended for people with mobility, respiratory, or cardiovascular problems. The easy **Rim Trail** visits two scenic viewpoints, a pithouse site, and a small pueblo, and signs describe the varied plants and wildlife found here. Allow 20–30 minutes for the three-quarter-mile loop, which is paved, level, and wheelchair accessible. Pets cannot go on trails.

Vegetation changes dramatically from the pinyon and juniper forests near the rim to the tall Douglas firs clinging to the canyon ledges. Black walnut and several other kinds of deciduous trees grow at the bottom. Rock layers will be familiar to Grand Canyon visitors. The lower 100 feet of Walnut Canyon belongs to the Coconino Sandstone, 265-million-year-old sand dunes that have turned to stone. The upper 300-foot layer of rock is Kaibab Limestone, formed in a sea about 255 million years ago.

Walnut Canyon National Monument remains open all year except Christmas, though snows can close the trails for short periods. The visitor center is open daily 9 A.M.–5 P.M. and hours may be extended in summer. Island Trail closes one hour before the visitor center does. The entrance fee is $3 per person age 17 and over. Vehicles pulling cars and large trailers may have trouble negotiating the turnaround loop at the visitor center. You'll find picnic areas near the visitor center and on the drive in. From Flagstaff, head east seven miles on I-40 to Walnut Canyon Exit 204, then turn south three miles on a paved road; 928/526-3367; www.nps.gov/waca.

Arizona Trail near Walnut Canyon

Hikers and mountain bikers enjoy forests, canyon scenery, and views of the San Francisco Peaks along this section of trail. A sign 2.5 miles in on the Walnut Canyon National Monument road points the way to a trailhead 1.7 miles to the west along a graded dirt road. From here the path heads southwest, crossing a side canyon of Walnut and paralleling the rim before dropping down into upper Walnut Canyon just west of Fisher Point in about six miles. A branch of Flagstaff's Urban Trail System joins here. In another mile you'll reach the junction for Sandy's Canyon Trail, which climbs the canyon to a trailhead near Lake Mary Road in three-quarters of a mile. The Arizona Trail curves to the southeast and continues four miles to Marshall Lake. Mountain bikers may need to walk the steep sections at the side canyon and at the descent into Walnut Canyon. The monument visitor center may have a map.

GRAND FALLS OF THE LITTLE COLORADO RIVER

In the spring, a thundering torrent of muddy brown water plunges 185 feet into the canyon of the Little Colorado River about 30 miles northeast of Flagstaff. The best time to see the spectacle is during March and April; in other months the river may dry up and yield nothing but an unimpressive trickle. High-clearance vehicles will be required for the dirt access roads, which should be avoided if muddy.

A lava flow from Merriam Crater, the large cinder cone 10 miles southwest, created the falls about 100,000 years ago. The tongue of lava filled the canyon, forcing the river out of its gorge, around the dam, and back over the rim into the original channel.

Grand Falls lies on the southwest corner of the Navajo Indian Reservation. From Flagstaff, take US 89 north 1.8 miles past Flagstaff Mall, turn right eight miles on the Camp Townsend-Winona Road, then turn left onto Leupp Road. Follow Leupp Road northeast 13 miles, then turn north 10 miles on unpaved Indian Route 70 or turn north 10 miles on unpaved Indian Route 6910 between Mileposts 5 and 6, seven miles farther east; the overlook is a half mile west on a rocky road from the main road (if you come to the Little Colorado River ford, you've gone 0.4 mile too far). The AAA Indian Country map will help in navigation, as the unpaved roads may not be signed. You'll see hues of the Painted Desert as the road descends to the river.

Other approaches: I-40 Winona Exit 211 (seven miles east of Flagstaff)—drive two miles on the Townsend-Winona Road, then right on Leupp Road to the Grand Falls turnoffs; I-40 Exit 245 (46 miles east of Flagstaff)—take AZ 99 to Leupp, then Leupp Road to the Grand Falls turnoffs. From Kykotsmovi, on the Hopi Indian Reservation, take paved Indian Route 2 southwest 49 miles to Leupp, then Leupp Road to the Grand Falls turnoffs.

The overlook has picnic tables; admission is free, though the Navajo Tribe asks you to help keep the area clean and leash your dogs so they won't disturb livestock. Also, don't go out in the streambed—mud makes the rocks very slippery and the strong currents have carried people over the falls to their deaths.

METEOR CRATER

A museum perched on the edge of Meteor Crater offers exhibits on meteorites, impact crater geology, space exploration, and astronomy. Paintings and a video portray meteors and the drama of Meteor Crater's formation. You can look closely at a hefty 1,450-pound meteorite found nearby and see examples of other types of meteorites. Shattercones and shock metamorphism show what happens when rocks undergo powerful compression forces. Maps and photos illustrate additional impact craters on earth and other bodies of the solar system. Space exhibits and videos tell the story of

SUDDEN IMPACT

About 50,000 years ago, a blinding flash of light in the sky preceded an explosion on earth equivalent to 20 million tons of TNT. A meteor of nickel-iron speeding along at around 40,000 miles an hour had smashed onto a plain east of where Flagstaff is today. The chunk of extraterrestrial rock, roughly 150 feet across and weighing several hundred thousand pounds, struck the earth with such force that fragments were buried 3,000 feet underground. About 80 percent of the meteor vaporized upon impact, then precipitated back to earth. Shock waves killed every living thing in the area. Perhaps five percent of the meteor had worn away by the atmosphere on entry and another five percent was blasted out to rain down as fragments. An estimated 10 percent lies buried underground.

When the crater was first discovered in 1871, scientists thought it to be of volcanic origin. Philadelphia mining engineer Daniel Barringer, convinced that it was an impact crater, devoted the last 26 years of his life to finding the buried meteor. When drill holes in the crater floor missed the nickel-iron, he took a closer look at the rock layers and realized that the meteor had struck at an angle. He then started drilling on the southeast rim, where cores showed meteorite fragments, but a hard material jammed the drill bit at a depth of 1,376 feet as Barringer's money ran out. Despite the failure to recover a rich mass of metal, his geologic studies added to the world's knowledge of impact structures. By 1929, the year of Barringer's death, the scientific community had finally come around to believing the crater to be of meteoric origin, the first one on earth to be proved as such. Apollo astronauts learned about crater geology here, and they practiced travel on the lunarlike surface.

Though larger impact craters exist on our planet, none are so well preserved or spectacular. The giant pit measures 560 feet deep, 4,100 feet across, and 2.4 miles in circumference—enough room for 20 football fields.

© METEOR CRATER, ARIZONA

exploration to the moon, Mars, and beyond. An Astronaut Hall of Fame, Apollo test capsule, and video program bring back memories of America's first manned ventures into space. At a viewing window, you can hear a recorded lecture on Meteor Crater's origin and history. Step out to the rim overlooks for views of the crater and surrounding countryside; telescopes and sight tubes help you see and identify features of the crater. In a courtyard around in front, the American Astronaut Wall of Fame honors those who have flown into space.

Staff at the privately owned Meteor Crater offer guided walks of about an hour along a short section of the rim trail, weather permitting, at no extra charge; you'll need good walking shoes (no sandals or open-toed shoes), hat, sunscreen, and perhaps some water. The visitor center offers rock and gift shops and a snack bar. No pets are permitted, but you may be able to leave your caged animal in shade near the entrance.

Meteor Crater is open daily 6 A.M.–6 P.M. in summer (mid-May to mid-September) and 8 A.M.–5 P.M. the rest of the year; 928/289-2362; www.meteorcrater.com. Admission is $10 adults, $9 ages 60 and over, and $5 children 6–17. The site is 40 miles east of downtown Flagstaff or 20 miles west of Winslow; take I-40 Meteor Crater Exit 233, then head south 5.5 miles on a paved road.

Meteor Crater RV Park offers year-round camping for tents ($17) and RVs ($17–19) with showers, laundry, and a convenience store/gas station. It's just off the I-40 exit for Meteor Crater; 928/289-4002.

North of Flagstaff

Peaceful today, this 3,000-square-mile area of volcanic peaks, cinder cones, and lava flows presents some impressive landscapes and geology. The majestic San Francisco Peaks, highest of all Arizona mountains, soar 5,000 feet above the surrounding plateau. Eruptions beginning between 1.4 million and 400,000 years ago created this giant stratovolcano, which may have stood 16,000 feet. The center later collapsed, perhaps in a violent Mount St. Helens-style blast, forming a caldera. During Pleistocene ice ages, glaciers then carved deep valleys on its slopes. Hundreds of small cinder cones, of which Sunset Crater is the youngest, surround the Peaks. There's no reason to assume the San Francisco Volcanic Field is finished, either. The area has experienced volcanic activity, with periods of calm, during its long history (but no eruptions in the past 700 years).

Tribes of northern Arizona regard the San Francisco Peaks as a sacred place. The Hopi believe the Peaks are the winter home of their kachina spirits and the source of clouds that bring rain for crops. The Peaks also occupy a prominent place in Navajo legends and ceremonies, representing one of the cardinal directions.

In 1984, the federal government set aside 18,963 acres of this venerable volcano for the Kachina Peaks Wilderness, selecting the name because of the importance of the site to the Hopi people. The Forest Service maintains a network of trails in the wilderness, and any of the peaks and hills make a good day-hike destination. Cyclists may not ride here, even on the former roads, because of the wilderness designation. Foresters at the **Peaks Ranger Station,** 5075 N. Hwy. 89 (Flagstaff, AZ 86004), 928/526-0866, offer maps and hiking information for this region. The book *Flagstaff Hikes* by Richard and Sherry Mangum lists many possibilities in the San Francisco Peaks area.

SUNSET CRATER VOLCANO NATIONAL MONUMENT

Sunset Crater, a beautiful black cinder cone tinged with yellows and oranges, rises 1,000 feet above jagged lava flows about 15 miles northeast of Flagstaff. Although more than 700 years have passed since the last eruptions, the landscape still presents a lunar-like appearance, with trees and plants struggling to grow.

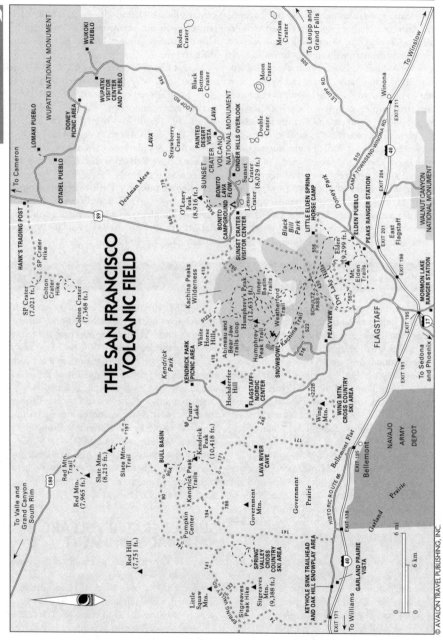

THE SAN FRANCISCO VOLCANIC FIELD

To Valle and Grand Canyon South Rim

To Cameron

HANK'S TRADING POST

SP CRATER HIKE

SP Crater (7,021 ft.)

Colton Crater Hike

Colton Crater (7,368 ft.)

Red Mtn. Trail

Red Mtn. (7,965 ft.)

Slate Mtn. (8,215 ft.)

Slate Mtn. Trail

Red Hill (7,751 ft.)

Kendrick Park

Kendrick Park

KENDRICK PARK PICNIC AREA

Crater Lake

Kendrick Peak (10,418 ft.)

Kendrick Peak Trails

BULL BASIN

Pumpkin Center

Government Mtn.

LAVA RIVER CAVE

Government Prairie

Wing Mtn.

FLAGSTAFF NORDIC CENTER

FLAGSTAFF NORDIC CENTER

Hochderffer Hill

Abineau and Bear Jaw Trails Loop

White Horse Hills

Kachina Peaks Wilderness

Humphrey's Peak (12,633 ft.)

Humphrey's Peak Trail

Inner Basin Trails

Weatherford Trail

Kachina Trail

SNOWBOWL

PEAKVIEW

SCHULTZ PASS

Dry Lake Hills

Mt. Elden Trails

Mt. Elden (9,299 ft.)

Elden

Black Bill Park

Doney Park

LITTLE ELDEN SPRING HORSE CAMP

PEAKS RANGER STATION

ELDEN PUEBLO

East Flagstaff

WALNUT CANYON NATIONAL MONUMENT

FLAGSTAFF

To Sedona and Phoenix

MORMON LAKE RANGER STATION

To Williams

GARLAND PRAIRIE VISTA

KEYHOLE SINK TRAILHEAD AND OAK HILL SNOWPLAY AREA

SPRING VALLEY CROSS COUNTRY SKI AREA

WING MTN. CROSS COUNTRY SKI AREA

Sitgreaves Peak Hike

Sitgreaves Mtn. (9,388 ft.)

Little Squaw Mtn.

Bellemont

NAVAJO ARMY DEPOT

Garland Prairie

Prairie

HISTORIC ROUTE 66

Deadman Mesa

LAVA

Strawberry Crater

PAINTED DESERT VISTA

LAVA

SUNSET CRATER VOLCANO NATIONAL MONUMENT

CINDER HILLS OVERLOOK

Sunset Crater (8,029 ft.)

O'Leary Peak (8,916 ft.)

BONITO CAMPGROUND

BONITO LAVA FLOW

SUNSET CRATER VISITOR CENTER

Lenox Crater

WUPATKI NATIONAL MONUMENT

LOMAKI PUEBLO

CITADEL PUEBLO

WUPATKI VISITOR CENTER AND PUEBLO

DONEY PICNIC AREA

WUKOKI PUEBLO

Roden Crater

Black Bottom Crater

Moon Crater

Double Crater

Merriam Crater

LOOP RD.

To Leupp and Grand Falls

To Winslow

Winona

CAMP TOWNSEND-WINONA RD.

LEUPP RD.

Navajo Army Depot

0   6 mi

0   6 km

© AVALON TRAVEL PUBLISHING, INC.

Eruptions beginning in A.D. 1064 or 1065 sent indigenous people fleeing for safety. By 1110 activity had subsided enough to allow them to settle in the Wupatki Basin, 20 miles northeast of Sunset Crater. You can visit the remains of their communities and see a museum in Wupatki National Monument, reached via the Sunset Crater-Wupatki Loop Road, one of the prettiest scenic drives in Arizona. Lava flows and smaller ash eruptions continued from Sunset Crater possibly as recently as 1280.

In the late 1920s, some Hollywood filmmakers thought Sunset Crater would make a great movie set. They planned to use dynamite to simulate an avalanche, but local citizens put a stop to their plans. Sunset Crater became a national monument in 1930.

Visitor center exhibits illustrate the forces deep within the Earth and their fury during volcanic eruptions. You can watch a seismograph as it tracks the earth's movements. Film clips of Hawaiian volcanic eruptions show how Sunset Crater may have looked during its periods of activity. Rangers give varied programs, mainly during the summer, on geology, seismology, birds, and other topics. Check the bulletin board at the visitor center or call for times and places.

Lenox Crater (elev. 7,240 feet), one mile east of the visitor center at the first pullout on the left, provides a close look at a cinder cone with a crater. It's a short, steep climb, requiring 30–45 minutes to the rim and back; elevation change is 280 feet.

The self-guided **Lava Flow Trail,** which begins 1.5 miles east of the visitor center, loops across the Bonito Lava Flow at the base of Sunset Crater; allow 30–60 minutes for the one-mile walk, less for the paved quarter-mile inner loop that's wheelchair accessible. A trail leaflet, available at the start of the trail and at the visitor center, explains geologic features and ecology.

At Sunset Crater's Lava Flow Trail (wheelchair accessible), you'll see fumaroles (gas vents), lava bubbles, squeeze-ups, and lava tubes that seem to have cooled only yesterday.

You'll see fumaroles (gas vents), lava bubbles, squeeze-ups, and lava tubes that seem to have cooled only yesterday.

Before rangers prohibited climbing on Sunset Crater in 1973, hikers wore a deep gash in the soft cinder slopes. Most of the damage has been repaired, though you can still see faint scars.

Bonito Campground, across the road from the visitor center, is open from mid-May to mid-September; it costs $12 a site and offers drinking water and restrooms but no showers; groups can reserve sites; 928/527-1474 (campground) or 928/526-0866 (Peaks Ranger Station). Campfire programs run on summer evenings. Dispersed camping is allowed in other areas of the national forest such as along Forest Roads 420, 552, and 418 west of US 89; Forest Road 776 (can be dusty from ATVs) south of Sunset Crater; and Forest Road 150 (hot in summer) south of the road through Wupatki. Visitor center staff can make suggestions and sell you the Coconino Forest map.

You'll find **picnic areas** near the visitor center, at the Lava Flow Trail, and at Painted Desert Vista between Sunset Crater and Wupatki National Monuments. The visitor center is open daily 9 A.M.–5 P.M. except Christmas with extended hours in summer; the road and trails stay open all day; 928/526-0502; www.nps.gov/sucr. The admission fee of $3 per person age 17 and up includes entry to Wupatki National Monument. You can reach the visitor center by driving north 12 miles from the Flagstaff Mall on US 89, then turning east two miles on a signed road. This very scenic drive, known as the Loop Road, continues past Sunset Crater, drops down to pinyon-juniper country with views of the Painted Desert, crosses Wupatki National Monument, then rejoins US 89 26 miles north of Flagstaff; the drive is 36 miles one way and takes about an hour plus stops.

O'Leary Peak

Weather permitting, the summit of this 8,965-foot lava-dome volcano provides outstanding views into Sunset Crater. Forest Road 545A begins about a quarter mile west of Sunset Crater visitor center and climbs 5.5 miles to the fire lookout tower at the top. A gate about a quarter mile in blocks motor vehicles. You can hike or mountain bike up the scenic road and get a good workout. The summit provides the best view of the colors of Sunset Crater and the Painted Desert beyond in late afternoon; the San Francisco Peaks are best in the morning.

WUPATKI NATIONAL MONUMENT

Prehistoric farmers, identified as the Sinagua Culture by archaeologists, settled in small groups near the San Francisco Peaks in about A.D. 600. They lived in partly underground pithouses and tilled the soil in those few areas with sufficient moisture to support corn and other crops. The eruption of Sunset Crater in A.D. 1064 or 1065 forced many to flee, but it also improved the farming potential: volcanic ash, blown by winds over a large area, acted as a water-conserving mulch.

After about 1110, people returned and were joined by ancestral Puebloan people from northeastern Arizona. They settled 20 miles northeast of Sunset Crater in Wupatki Basin, which became the center of a group of cosmopolitan villages. A mix of cultural traits can be seen at Wupatki, including Kayenta Anasazi, Sinagua, Cohonina, and Hohokam. Large, multistoried pueblos replaced the brush shelters and pithouses of former times. Some villages seem defensively built; competition for scarce resources may have created friction or fostered cooperation.

During the 1200s, people began to leave the area. Archaeologists think the inhabitants migrated southward to the Verde Valley, eastward to Homolovi on the Little Colorado River, and northeastward to the Hopi mesas and Zuni villages. Hopi oral histories trace at least eight clans to the Wupatki area.

Seven of the best-preserved pueblos have road and trail access; all other sites and the monument's backcountry remain closed to visitors except for the seasonal ranger-guided hikes to Crack-in-Rock. Please stay on designated trails. The pueblos are open daily from sunrise to sunset, and the road is open 24 hours.

Wupatki Visitor Center

You'll see pottery, tools, jewelry, and other artifacts of early cultures on exhibit here. A Wupatki room reconstruction shows how the interior of a typical living chamber might have looked. You'll also learn a little about the present-day Navajo and Hopi tribes who live near the monument. You can buy books, posters, maps, and videos related to the region. Rangers may offer 15–minute orientation talks and provide demonstrations of prehistoric and modern crafts and activities at Wupatki Pueblo.

Wupatki Visitor Center, 928/679-2365, is open daily 9 A.M.–5 P.M. with extended hours in summer; closed Dec. 25th; www.nps.gov/wupa. From Flagstaff, you can drive 12 miles north on US 89, then turn right and go 21 miles via Sunset Crater Volcano National Monument on the scenic Loop Road. Or take the northern turnoff from US 89 for the Loop Road, 26 miles north of Flagstaff, and head east 14 miles. The nearest motels and restaurants are in Flagstaff and Gray Mountain. Hank's Trading Post offers groceries and snacks 1.2 miles north of the US 89-Wupatki junction. See Bonito Campground in the Sunset Crater section above for area camping possibilities.

Doney Picnic Area sits between cinder cones about four miles northwest of the visitor center on the loop road. **Doney Mountain Trail** climbs gradually to a saddle in the Little Doney Craters, from which you can turn left to a lower overlook or right to a higher one, each about 0.4 mile one way from the picnic area. Both forks pass small dwellings, probably used by the prehistoric people as field houses while tending nearby gardens. You'll enjoy a panorama of the Wupatki Basin, Painted Desert, and San Francisco Peaks. Interpretive signs explain area ecology and the exploits of prospector Ben Doney.

Wupatki Pueblo

Wupatki Pueblo

At its peak, Wupatki contained nearly 100 rooms and towered multiple stories. The Hopi name refers to "something long that has been cut or divided." A self-guided trail, beginning behind the visitor center, explains many of the features of Wupatki; pick up a trail brochure at the start.

A community room, where village meetings and ceremonies may have taken place, lies to one side of Wupatki. The ballcourt at the far end of the village may have been used for games or religious functions. It's one of several found in northern Arizona, probably introduced by the Hohokam Culture of the southern deserts. Archaeologists reconstructed the masonry ballcourt from wall remnants; the rest of Wupatki Pueblo is stabilized. A blowhole, 100 feet east of the ballcourt, may have had religious importance. A system of underground cracks connects to this natural surface opening; air blows out, rushes in, or does nothing at all, depending on atmospheric pressure. Researchers once tried to enter the system but couldn't get through the narrow passageways.

Wukoki Pueblo

Two–three families lived in this small pueblo, the best-preserved structure in the park, for perhaps three generations. You can step inside the rooms, one of which towers three stories and still has pieces of wood beam embedded in the walls. From the Wupatki visitor center, drive a quarter mile toward Sunset Crater, then turn left 2.5 miles on a paved road.

Citadel Pueblo

This fortress-like pueblo, perched atop a small volcanic butte nine miles northwest of the Wupatki Visitor Center, stood one or two stories high and contained about 30 rooms. From the top, look for some of the more than 10 other residences nearby (most of these are not open to visits). On the path to the Citadel, you'll pass the pueblo of **Nalakihu,** Hopi for "House Standing Outside the Village." Nalakihu consisted of two stories with 13 or 14 rooms. You can visit both sites on a short self-guided trail.

Lomaki Pueblo

Lomaki, Hopi for "Beautiful House," sits along

a small box canyon. Tree-ring dating of roof timbers indicates the occupants lived here from about A.D. 1190 to 1240. The small two-story pueblo contained nine rooms. A quarter-mile trail from the parking area also passes small dwellings beside Box Canyon. The turnoff for Lomaki lies northwest of Wupatki Visitor Center, 0.3 mile beyond Citadel on the opposite side of the road.

Crack-in-Rock Pueblo

Rangers lead overnight backpack trips to this area during April and October. Crack-in-Rock stands atop an easily defended mesa with sweeping views of the Little Colorado River and distant hills. You will see petroglyphs carved around the base of the mesa and on two nearby mesas, as well as many other pueblo sites. The 14-mile roundtrip hike is moderately difficult and costs $30. Call or write for information at least two months in advance; Wupatki National Monument, 928/679-2365, HC 33, Box 444A #14, Flagstaff, AZ 86004.

MOUNT ELDEN TRAIL SYSTEM

To reach the summit of Mt. Elden, a 9,299-foot peak on the north edge of Flagstaff, you can hike any of several good trails or drive up a rough road. Wildflowers, a variety of forests, and panoramic views reward those who ascend even part way. A fire-lookout tower marks the summit. Climb the tower, if it's open, for the best views. On a clear day you'll see much of north-central Arizona: Oak Creek Canyon and Mormon Lake to the south; the Painted Desert to the east; Humphrey's Peak, Sunset Crater, and other volcanoes to the north; and Bill Williams Mountain to the west. Flagstaff lies directly below. An eruption of thick, sticky lava created Mt. Elden.

The hiking season runs from May to October, a bit longer for the drier eastern slope. You'll need to carry water. To avoid the hair-raising experience of afternoon thunderstorms, set out early when hiking during July and August, the peak storm months. Allow at least half a day for a hike to the summit and back; elevation change

is 1,300–2,400 feet, depending on the trailhead. Horseback riders and mountain bicyclists can use most of the trail system. Contact the Peaks Ranger Station for current trail information; 928/526-0866. The distances given below are one-way. Hikes are described clockwise, beginning on the east side.

Elden Lookout Trail #4

This 2.9-mile trail seems easy at first, but then it becomes a steep and strenuous climb up the rocky east slope of Mt. Elden to the lookout tower, gaining 2,400 feet in elevation. To reach the Mt. Elden Trailhead (elev. 6,900 feet), head east from downtown Flagstaff on Route 66, which becomes US 89, or take I-40 Exit 201 toward Page; the trailhead is on the left side of US 89 a half mile north of the Flagstaff Mall. The grades and loose surface of this trail make it too hazardous for horse travel or mountain biking; neither is allowed.

Fatman's Loop Trail #25

The moderate two-mile loop has a few short steep sections. You'll pass volcanic rock formations (one that hikers have to squeeze through) and diverse plant life; elevation gain is 600 feet. Views take in parts of east Flagstaff and beyond. The loop begins from the lower part of Mt. Elden Lookout Trail; it's closed to horses.

Pipeline Trail #42

This easy 3.1-mile trail follows a gas pipeline right-of-way between the lower parts of Mt. Elden Lookout and Oldham Trails. You can see old lava flows on the south side of Mt. Elden and in the Elden Environmental Study Area. The Forest Service set aside the study area in the mid-1970s for school and environmental groups. Ponderosa pine and Gambel oak dominate the forest at the trail's 7,100- to 7,200-foot elevations.

Oldham Trail #1

Mt. Elden's longest trail at 5.5 miles, it begins at the north end of Buffalo Park (elev. 7,000 feet) in Flagstaff and climbs gradually past boulder fields and cliffs on the west side of Mt. Elden. You cross Elden Lookout Road several times as the

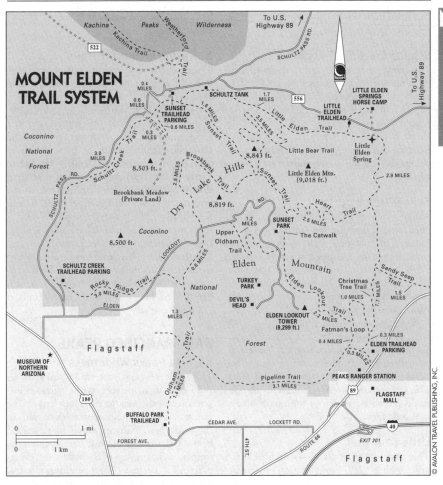

MOUNT ELDEN
TRAIL SYSTEM

© AVALON TRAVEL PUBLISHING, INC.

trail winds higher through forest and meadows to Oldham Park and on to Sunset Trail near the summit. The trail is moderately difficult and has an elevation gain of 2,000 feet.

Rocky Ridge Trail #153

Ponderosa pine, Gambel oak, alligator juniper, cliffrose, and yucca line this western approach to Mt. Elden. The easy three-mile trail begins from Schultz Creek Trailhead and connects with the Oldham and Brookbank Trails. Schultz Creek Trailhead lies a short way off Schultz Pass Road

about 0.8 mile in from US 180. Elevation change is only about 100 feet.

Brookbank Trail #2

This moderate 2.5-mile trail climbs north through a forested drainage to the edge of Brookbank Meadow, owned by the Navajo Tribe, then curves east to eventually meet Sunset Trail at a low saddle. Elevation gain is 1,000 feet. The trailhead (elev. 7,800 feet) can be reached by hiking the Rocky Ridge or Oldham Trails or by driving a half mile in on Schultz

Pass Road from US 180, then turning 2.5 miles up Elden Lookout Road.

Schultz Creek Trail #152

This gentle 3.6-mile trail parallels an intermittent creek flowing between Sunset (elev. 8,000 feet) and Schultz Creek (elev. 7,200 feet) Trailheads. Sunset Trailhead is at Schultz Pass, 5.6 miles up Schultz Pass Road from US 180, and Schultz Creek Trailhead is a short way off Schultz Pass Road about 0.8 mile in from US 180. Motorcycles use this trail and it's also popular with mountain bikers.

Sunset Trail #23

Alpine meadows and forests on the north side offer some of the most pleasant hiking on Mt. Elden. The four-mile trail climbs gradually through pine, fir, and aspen to Sunset Park and on to the summit; elevation gain is 1,300 feet. The Radio Fire of 1977 left scars visible on the east slope below. You can view the San Francisco Peaks, Sunset Crater, and Painted Desert.

Begin from the Sunset Trailhead (elev. 8,000 feet), just west of Schultz Tank at Schultz Pass. To reach the trailhead, follow US 180 northwest three miles from downtown Flagstaff to Schultz Pass Road, then turn right 5.6 miles. This and the following Mt. Elden trails are open to people on horseback or mountain bike as well as on foot.

Little Bear Trail

This trail—steep in places—switchbacks 3.5 miles with a 1,000-foot elevation change between Little Elden Trail and Sunset Trail. See the map for the trailhead options.

Heart Trail #103

In a strenuous 2.5 miles, the trail switchbacks along a steep, rocky ridge within the area devastated by the 5,000-acre Radio Fire of June 1977. It connects Sandy Seep and Little Elden Trails with Sunset Trail at the saddle between Mt. Elden and Little Elden Mountain; elevation change is 1,300 feet. Local mountain bike enthusiasts have dubbed it "expert only." Experienced horseback riders can use the trail too. Seemingly desolate at

first glance, the land is actually full of new growth and new life.

Northside Connector Trails

Three easy trails on the north side of Mt. Elden link with other trails to form a complete loop around the peak. They offer a variety of views and terrain—from the cool fir and pine forest of the north slope around the buttress of Little Elden Mountain, past the lower reaches of the Radio Fire area, and into dry ponderosa pine and Gambel oak of the east flank of Mt. Elden. **Little Elden Trail** curves around the north side of Mt. Elden from Schultz Tank to the bottom of Heart Trail in five miles. **Sandy Seep Trail #129** has a trailhead on US 89, 1.5 miles north of the Peaks Ranger Station; from there it goes west 1.5 miles to the Christmas Tree Trail, then a bit farther to Heart and Little Elden Trails. **Christmas Tree Trail** connects the north end of Fatman's Loop with Sandy Seep, Heart, and Little Elden Trails in 1.7 miles one way.

SAN FRANCISCO PEAKS
Kachina Peaks Wilderness

This wilderness area protects 18,960 acres on the Peaks. Its name reflects the religious importance of the area to the Hopi Tribe. The Forest Service maintains a network of trails in the wilderness, many of which are described below. Cyclists may not ride here, even on the former roads, because of the wilderness designation. For current hiking conditions, maps, and other trails, call the Peaks Ranger Station at 928/526-0866.

Lamar Haines Memorial Wildlife Area

A small pond fed by two springs attracts birds and other wildlife. Ludwig Veit, for whom the springs are named, homesteaded here in 1892. Petroglyphs decorate nearby volcanic rocks. From the parking area, near Milepost 4.5 on the paved Snowbowl Road, walk through the gate and turn right 0.7 mile on an abandoned road. Lamar Haines (1927–86) was active in education and conservation in the Flagstaff area.

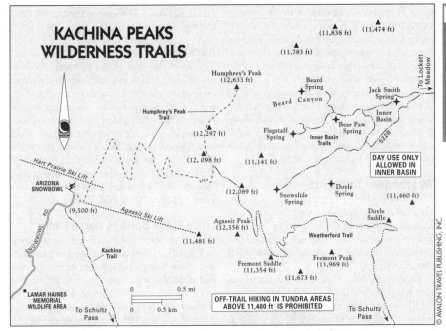

KACHINA PEAKS
WILDERNESS TRAILS

(11,838 ft)   (11,474 ft)

(11,783 ft)

Humphrey's Peak
(12,663 ft)

Beard
Spring

Jack Smith
Spring

To Lockett
Meadow

Beard   Canyon

Humphrey's Peak
Trail

Bear Paw
Spring

Inner
Basin

(12,297 ft)

Flagstaff
Spring

Inner Basin
Trails

(12, 098 ft)

(11,141 ft)

DAY USE ONLY
ALLOWED IN
INNER BASIN

ARIZONA
SNOWBOWL

Hart Prairie Ski Lift

(12,089 ft)

Snowslide
Spring

Doyle
Spring

(11,460 ft)

(9,500 ft)

Agassiz Ski Lift

Doyle
Saddle

SNOWBOWL RD.

Kachina
Trail

Agassiz Peak
(12,356 ft)

(11,481 ft)

Weatherford Trail

(11,673 ft)

Fremont Saddle
(11,354 ft)

Fremont Peak
(11,969 ft)

LAMAR HAINES
MEMORIAL
WILDLIFE AREA

To Schultz
Pass

0   0.5 mi

0   0.5 km

OFF-TRAIL HIKING IN TUNDRA AREAS
ABOVE 11,400 ft IS PROHIBITED

To Schultz
Pass

© AVALON TRAVEL PUBLISHING, INC.

Scenic Sky Ride

Hop on this chairlift at the Arizona Snowbowl for the most leisurely way to the heights. You'll be swept from 9,500 to 11,500 feet and treated to some fantastic views. The Sky Ride operates daily 10 A.M.–4 P.M. from June 21 through Labor Day, then Fri.–Sun. until mid-October, weather permitting; 928/779-1951. A restaurant serves lunch. To reach the Snowbowl, drive northwest seven miles from downtown on US 180 to the turnoff, then turn right seven miles on a paved road.

You can't hike from the upper chairlift station, though. The Forest Service closed Agassiz Peak to protect the fragile alpine vegetation, including *Senecio franciscanus,* found only on the San Francisco Peaks. Hikers headed for Humphrey's Peak must take the Humphrey's Peak or Weatherford Trails, described below.

Humphrey's Peak Trail #151

The alpine world on the roof of Arizona makes a challenging day-hike destination. Get an early start, as the strenuous nine-mile roundtrip usually requires about eight hours to reach the summit and return. To protect fragile alpine tundra, the Forest Service asks hikers to stay on the designated trails above 11,400 feet. Also, don't build campfires or set up camps here.

Snow blocks the way much of the year, so the hiking season usually runs only from late June to September. Come prepared for bad weather with good rain and wind gear. Snow and fierce winds can arrive any month of the year; getting caught in a storm near the top with just a T-shirt and shorts could be deadly. Lightning frequently zaps the Peaks, especially during July and August, so you'll need to be prepared to turn back if storms threaten. In winter, winds and sub-zero cold can be extremely dangerous—only the most experienced groups should attempt a climb then. Carry plenty of water; you'll need more when hiking at these high elevations.

The trail begins from the Snowbowl (elev. 9,300 feet), contours under the Hart Prairie chairlift, then switchbacks up the mountain. You'll hike through dense forests of Engelmann spruce, corkbark fir, and quaking aspen. Near 11,400 feet, stunted Engelmann spruce and bristlecone pine cling precariously to the slopes. Higher still, only tiny alpine plants survive the fierce winds and long winters. At the saddle (elev. 11,800 feet), turn left for Humphrey's Peak and follow the trail along the ridge. On a clear day you can see a lot of northern Arizona and some of southern Utah from the 12,633-foot summit.

Weatherford Trail #102

J.W. Weatherford completed this road into the Peaks in 1926, using only hand labor and animals. Cars could then sputter up to Doyle and Fremont Saddles. The toll road had few customers in the Depression years and fell into disrepair.

Today, only hikers and those on horseback may travel the Weatherford Road. Mechanized vehicles—including mountain bikes—are prohibited. You'll reach Doyle Saddle (elev. 10,800 feet), which is marked "Fremont Saddle" on older maps, after 5.3 miles. Here you'll enjoy views of the Inner Basin, summits, and surrounding countryside. Although it's possible to reach the summit of Humphrey's Peak on the Weatherford Trail, the long 19.4-mile roundtrip discourages most climbers. Energetic hikers who've arranged a car shuttle can continue on the Weatherford Trail another 3.4 miles to its end at the junction with Humphrey's Trail, decide whether to make the side trip to the summit of Humphrey's Peak, about two miles roundtrip from here, then descend 3.5 miles on Humphrey's Peak Trail to the Snowbowl. Carry water and foul-weather gear.

The Weatherford Trail's gentle grade and excellent views make it a good choice for a family outing. Begin from the trailhead (elev. 8,000 feet) at Schultz Pass, just west of Schultz Tank. To reach the trailhead, follow US 180 northwest three miles from downtown Flagstaff, then turn right 5.6 miles on Schultz Pass Road.

For an easier hike, you can drive 2.4 miles up the Snowbowl Road and turn right four miles on Forest Road 522 to its end (elev. 8,800 feet); the trail is just beyond.

Kachina Trail #150

This moderate trail on the southern slopes of Humphrey's Peak is five miles one way. It's most easily done downhill by using a car shuttle to meet you at the lower end. From the upper trailhead, on the south end of the lower Snowbowl parking lot (elev. 9,300 feet), the Kachina winds east through spruce, fir, aspen, and ponderosa pine to meet the lower end of the Weatherford Trail, which has two trailheads—one near Schultz Pass (elev. 8,000 feet) and one at the end of Forest Road 522 (elev. 8,800 feet). Carry water.

Little Elden Springs Horse Camp

One of the closest National Forest campgrounds to Flagstaff, it offers pull-through campsites, picnic tables, vault toilets, water, hitching posts, and ample room for horse trailers from late May to mid or late October. Sites are $12 and can be reserved at 877/444-6777; www.reserveusa.com. Anyone may stay here, but users should be prepared to camp among horses. Head north 4.1 miles on US 89 from the Flagstaff Mall, turn west two miles on Forest Road 556, then north 0.3 mile at the sign.

Inner Basin Hiking

The San Francisco Peaks surround a giant U-shaped valley known as the Inner Basin. Aspen, fir, spruce, and wildflowers thrive here. You can reach Lockett Meadow, at the Inner Basin entrance, by car from the northeast. Park here and continue on foot. Roads (gated) and trails extend as far as 3.5 miles up the Inner Basin; all offer wonderful hiking. Elevations range from 8,600 feet at Lockett Meadow to about 11,000 feet at Snowslide Spring. No one should hike above Snowslide because of the danger to tundra vegetation. The many springs in the Inner Basin supply some of Flagstaff's water, but most are covered and locked; it's safest to carry your own water. Aspen put on a magnificent golden show in late September and early October. You may camp near Lockett Meadow, but not in the Inner Basin just beyond because it is protected as a watershed.

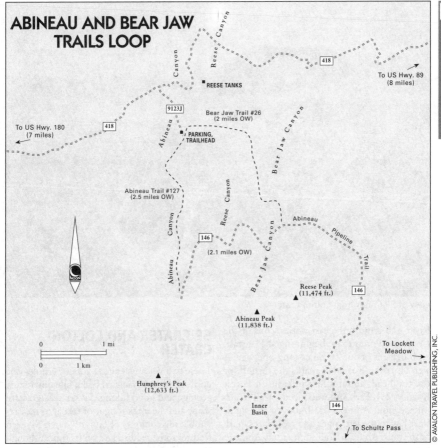

ABINEAU AND BEAR JAW
TRAILS LOOP

To US Hwy. 89
(8 miles)

REESE TANKS

9123J

Bear Jaw Trail #26
(2 miles OW)

To US Hwy. 180
(7 miles)   418

PARKING,
TRAILHEAD

Abineau Trail #127
(2.5 miles OW)

Reese Canyon

Abineau

Pipeline

Trail

146

(2.1 miles OW)

Reese Peak
(11,474 ft.)   146

Abineau Peak
(11,838 ft.)

0   1 mi

0   1 km

To Lockett
Meadow

Humphrey's Peak
(12,633 ft.)

Inner
Basin   146

To Schultz Pass

© AVALON TRAVEL PUBLISHING, INC.

From the Flagstaff Mall, drive north 12 miles on US 89 and turn left (west) onto Forest Road 420, opposite the Sunset Crater turnoff; look for the sign that says "Forest Access." Drive 0.25 mile on Forest Road 420, then turn right on Forest Road 522 and follow it about 3.5 miles to Lockett Meadow. The road is very narrow in places and may be difficult for low-clearance vehicles, large RVs, and vehicles pulling trailers.

Abineau and Bear Jaw Trails

These two trails climb about halfway up the north side of the San Francisco Peaks. On either path you'll enjoy cool forests of pine, fir, and aspen. Wildflowers grow in rocky alpine meadows near the top of Abineau Trail. Both trails start near Reese Tanks. Abineau Pipeline Trail, a dirt road closed to vehicles, connects the upper ends. With this road, Abineau and Bear Jaw make a good 6.5-mile hiking loop. Abineau is probably the prettier of the two, a good choice if you don't want to do the whole loop.

The trailhead lies on the opposite side of the Peaks from Flagstaff. Either take US 180, Forest Road 151 (second turnoff), and Forest Road 418 around the west side of the Peaks, or follow US 89, Forest Road 420, and Forest

© BILL WEIR

view of SP Crater from Colton Crater

Road 418 around the east slopes; consult the Coconino Forest map. Beginning at Flagstaff, each drive is about 26 miles long one way. A sign on Forest Road 418 marks the turnoff for the trailhead, about a half mile in on Forest Road 9123J. Park and walk up the trail to a T intersection: Abineau Trail goes to the right, Bear Jaw to the left. Signs and tree blazes mark both trails. Abineau Trail soon enters Abineau Canyon—actually more of a valley—and stays in it all the way to Abineau Pipeline Trail, 2.5 miles away. You can retrace your steps or turn left 2.1 miles on the pipeline trail and keep a sharp eye out for the upper end of Bear Jaw Trail, marked with a sign.

Bear Jaw Trail, two miles one way, doesn't follow a valley at all—you have to be very careful to look for signs and tree blazes. Take special care near the bottom when following a road, because the trail later turns left away from the road; this turn is easy to miss. Allow 4–5 hours for the complete loop. You'll begin at 8,500 feet at the trailhead and reach 10,500 feet at the upper end of Abineau Trail. Carry water and raingear.

SP CRATER AND COLTON CRATER

These two volcanic craters, about 14 miles due north of the San Francisco Peaks, offer interesting geology and good hiking. SP Crater's graceful shape and the black tongue of lava at its base resemble the contours of Sunset Crater. SP even features some reddish lava on its rim. Although Sunset Crater is closed to climbing, you can still hike up SP Crater. The near-perfect symmetry of this cinder cone has earned it photos in many geology textbooks.

Actually "SP" isn't the real name of this little volcano. Most likely prudish mapmakers were redfaced when they heard what local cowboys called it. The cowboys saw the black spatter on the rim of the bowl-shaped crater and the leaking lava flow below, and figured the thing "looks just like a shit pot." The name stuck.

Climbing SP Crater

The climb is moderately difficult; you ascend 800 feet to the rim. Any time of the year is all right for a hike as long as the weather is good. The Coconino Forest map or the 15-minute SP MTN topo map help in navigating the dirt roads, none of which are signed. From Flagstaff, drive 27 miles north on US 89 to Hank's Trading Post (Milepost 446). Or, from the Wupatki National Monument turnoff, go north 1.2 miles to the trading post. Turn left (west) 6.5 miles on the unsigned dirt road just south of the trading post. You can pick out SP, straight ahead, among the other volcanoes by its height and symmetry. Keep left where the road forks a half mile in. Six miles in—with SP Crater on your right and a large black water tank on your left—keep right at the fork, then look for a vehicle track on the right 100 yards farther. Take this track for a half mile and park. People four-wheeling beyond this point have made deep ruts on the slope.

Follow the track on foot to the grassy ridgetop—SP Crater adjoins it on the right—then start up the black-cinder slope of SP itself. There's no real trail—it's one step up and two steps back on the loose sliding cinders. Perseverance will get you onto the rim for a close look at lava formations and a panoramic view of the San Francisco Volcanic Field. Walking around the rim is rewarding, but descending into the 360-foot-deep crater is hazardous. The thick, blocky lava flow from SP's base extends 4.3 miles north and is about 70,000 years old.

Climbing Colton Crater

If you'd like to see another volcano or prefer an easier hike, visit nearby Colton Crater. Colton lies two miles due south of SP; take the other (left) fork near the black water tank on the road in, then go south two miles to an intersection with a road from the right. Park near here and head up the gentle slope to the rim, ascending about 300 feet. A gigantic explosion blew out the center of this volcano when hot basaltic magma met water-saturated rocks. Rock layers can be seen clearly. A baby red cinder cone, only 500 feet across, sits at the bottom of Colton Crater. It's an easy walk to the crater floor, actually 260 feet lower than the elevation outside the crater. Or you can walk around the rim through juniper and pinyon trees,

climbing about 600 feet higher than the lowest part of the rim.

OTHER GOOD HIKING AREAS
Strawberry Crater Wilderness

Extrusions of slow-moving basaltic andesite formed this crater 50,000 to 100,000 years ago. Strawberry Crater's jagged features contrast with the much younger cinder cones nearby. Because the San Francisco Peaks form a rain shadow over this area, the crater receives only about seven inches of annual precipitation. Sparse vegetation of juniper, pinyon pine, cliffrose, and a few ponderosa pines cover the gently rolling terrain of cinders and lava. The 10,140-acre wilderness offers good cross-country hiking and a challenging climb to the crater summit. Prehistoric ruins lie within the area as well; artifacts must not be removed.

Strawberry Crater is northeast of Flagstaff between Sunset Crater Volcano and Wupatki National Monuments. The wilderness boundary lies just north of the Painted Desert Vista area on the road between the monuments, but it would be a long hike to reach the crater from here. You can drive much closer by going north about 16 miles from the Flagstaff Mall on US 89 to the bottom of a long grade, turning east 3.4 miles on Forest Road 546, then continuing 1.1 miles east on Forest Road 779 to a set of power lines near the wilderness boundary. An unmarked trail contours left around the crater to the inner basin, then follows a ridge to the summit, about two miles roundtrip with a 500-foot elevation gain. You'll have a great panorama of the surrounding volcanoes and lava flows. Help preserve Strawberry Crater by not hiking on the steeper slopes; they're fragile and easily damaged.

Slate Mountain

A well-graded trail provides good views in all directions. Kendrick Peak is to the south, the San Francisco Peaks to the southeast, and Red Mountain—with its distinctive red gash—just to the north. Trail markers label many trees and plants. Flowers line the way from spring through fall.

Early settlers mistook the fine-grained, light-gray rock of this mountain for slate. Geologists say it's rhyolite, a volcanic rock. Hiking time is about three hours for the five-mile roundtrip; you'll ascend 850 feet. The 8,215-foot summit is a pleasant spot for a picnic. Hiking season runs from May to October; carry water. To reach the trailhead, drive northwest 27 miles from Flagstaff on US 180, then turn west two miles on Forest Road 191, between Mileposts 242 and 243 on US 180. A sign marks the trailhead.

Red Mountain

Ever wanted to walk into the heart of a volcano? Then try Red Mountain. Unusual erosion has dissected the cinder cone from the summit straight down to its base. Walk through a little canyon between towers of black cinders to enter the volcano. A ladder helps you get up a six-foot-high stone wall, the only real climb. Ranchers built the wall for a stock pond, but cinders filled it in.

Beyond the dam you'll enter a magical land of towering pinnacles and narrow canyons. This is a great place to explore; children will love it. Trees offer shade for a picnic. Most of Red Mountain is soft volcanic tuff. Look for the rocks and minerals extruding from it: blocks and bombs of lava; small crystals of plagioclase feldspar, transparent, with striations; black, glassy pyroxene and hornblende; and volcanic dust, cinders, and lapilli (large cinders). A lava flow covers part of Red Mountain's southwest side about 100 feet below the summit. To reach the top (elev. 7,965 feet), take the trail back out of the crater and climb the gentle cinder slopes on the southeast side. You'll ascend about 1,000 feet.

Red Mountain is easy to reach; drive 33 miles northwest from Flagstaff on US 180—or 42 miles southeast from Grand Canyon National Park—to Milepost 247, then turn west 0.3 mile on a dirt road to the parking. Red Mountain lies 1.25 miles in on an easy trail with a 300-foot elevation gain.

Kendrick Peak Wilderness

Although the San Francisco Peaks are higher,

Kendrick Peak might well provide the better view—you get not only a splendid panorama of northern Arizona, but a view of the Peaks themselves. The Painted Desert, Hopi mesas, and far-distant Navajo Mountain lie to the northeast; the north rim of the Grand Canyon juts up to the north; Sitgreaves and Bill Williams mountains poke up to the west; Oak Creek Canyon and the Mazatzals lie to the south; and the magnificent San Francisco Peaks, surrounded by many smaller volcanoes, rise directly to the east. Three trails, ranging in length 8–11 miles roundtrip, lead to Kendrick's 10,418-foot summit and fire-lookout tower. Hiking season lasts from late June to September; longer on the southern Kendrick Trail. Carry water. The 15,000-acre Pumpkin Fire in 2000 burned much of the forest on Kendrick, including parts of the Pumpkin Trail and most of the Bull Basin Trail; check with the Williams Ranger District office, 928/635-5600, for current trail conditions and possible new trailheads.

Kendrick Trail #22: This shortest trail, eight miles roundtrip, is the one most used and was the least affected by the fire. Because it climbs the sunny southern slopes, you'll find it more likely to be open early or late in the season. A lookout cabin, equipped with a wood stove and three bare bunk beds, stands on the ridge a quarter mile below the summit. Hikers may use this little cabin, which has withstood the elements since 1912. To reach the trailhead, take I-40 Bellemont Exit 185 (10 miles west of Flagstaff), follow the frontage road one mile west, drive 12.5 miles north on Forest Road 171, then turn right one mile on a road signed Kendrick Trail. Alternatively, you can head northwest 14 miles on US 180 from Flagstaff, turn left three miles on Forest Road 245, turn right 3.1 miles on Forest Road 171, then right one mile at the sign for Kendrick Trail.

Pumpkin Trail #39: The longest approach (11 miles roundtrip) starts west of Kendrick Peak. Hiking Pumpkin Trail allows you to use the one-mile Connector Trail and part of Bull Basin Trail to make a loop. Schedule a full day. To reach the trailhead, follow directions for Kendrick Trail #22, but continue on Forest Road 171 another four miles, then turn right one mile at the sign for Pumpkin Trail.

Bull Basin Trail #40: This nine-mile-roundtrip route from the north can be a little difficult to follow. Much of the forest here burned and fallen or hazardous trees still blocked the trail at press time. To reach the trailhead, continue 2.5 miles on Forest Road 171 past the Pumpkin Trail turnoff, turn right 1.5 miles on Forest Road 144, then turn right and proceed six miles on Forest Road 90.

Lava River Cave

This well-preserved cave is about four miles south of Kendrick Peak. Red-hot lava broke through the ground near the San Francisco Peaks about 100,000 years ago, then moved westward across Hart and Government Prairies, reaching a thickness of more than 100 feet in places. As the outer layers of the smoking mass cooled, some of the fiery interior burst through a weak spot in the surface, partly draining the lava flow. This underground river of fire eventually cooled, too.

Today, a collapsed ceiling reveals the passageway. No one knows the total length of this lava-tube cave, but about 0.7 mile is easily explored. The interior remains cool year-round, so a jacket or sweater is recommended. Keep an eye out for the ice that's often present just inside the entrance. Bring at least two flashlights to explore the cave, as it wouldn't be fun trying to feel your way out after your one-and-only light died.

The walls and ceiling form an amazingly symmetrical tunnel. The former lava river on the floor still displays all the ripple marks, cracks, and squeeze-ups of its last hours. There's only one main passageway, though a small loop branches off to the right about one-third of the way through and then rejoins the main channel. The main channel is large, with plenty of headroom, except for a section about two-thirds of the way through where you'll have to stoop.

To reach Lava River Cave, follow the previous directions to Kendrick Peak, but travel only 7.5 miles north on Forest Road 171, then turn right 0.3 mile on Forest Road 171B and walk another 0.2 mile. Alternatively from Flagstaff, you can head northwest 14 miles on US 180, turn left three miles on Forest Road 245, turn left one mile on Forest Road 171, then left on Forest Road 171B. The Coconino and Kaibab (Williams and Tusayan Districts) forest maps show the roads and cave, but may not identify the cave. A large ring of stones indicates the cave entrance.

Sitgreaves Mountain

Great views and beautiful forests make the 9,388-foot Sitgreaves summit an attractive destination. Reddish cinder cones, forested mountains, and vast grasslands stretch to the distant horizon.

Allow about four hours to hike the four miles to the top and back. Carry water. Hiking season for this northern approach lasts from about May to October. The route follows a valley from the trailhead to the summit ridge, then turns right up the ridge to the highest point. No established trails or signs exist on Sitgreaves but none are needed—just stay in the valley until you reach the ridge. Be sure to descend via the same valley, unless you want a much longer hike! Walking is a bit easier if you keep to the right when going up—not so many fallen trees. Beautiful groves of aspen find this cool, moist, sheltered area to their liking.

Sitgreaves Mountain lies about seven miles north of I-40, about two-thirds of the way from Flagstaff to Williams. To find the trailhead you'll need either the Coconino or Kaibab (Williams and Tusayan districts) forest map. Take I-40 Pittman Valley Exit 171, go north seven miles on Forest Road 74 to its end, turn right and drive three miles on Forest Road 141 (Spring Valley Road), then look *really hard* on the right for a small road. The turnoff is very easy to miss and probably won't be signed. Map designations for the turnoff are T.23N., R.3E., sec. 13. You can drive your car in about one mile. When the road gives out, continue walking in the same direction up the valley.

West of Flagstaff

WILLIAMS

Small and friendly, Williams (pop. 2,800) proudly proclaims itself "Gateway to the Grand Canyon." Arizona 64, on the east edge of town, is the shortest route—58 miles—between I-40 and the famous park. Williams, nestled among pine-forested hills and expansive meadows at an elevation of 6,780 feet, offers a better choice of accommodations and restaurants at lower prices than those at the Grand Canyon. Travelers also enjoy the old architecture downtown, Route 66 nostalgia, and staged gunfights. The popular Grand Canyon Railway puffs its way north to the Grand Canyon daily from the old station downtown. Even if you're not riding the rails, it's worth taking a look at the historic train, the museum, and morning Wild West show. Most travelers, in a hurry to get someplace else, miss the pretty country surrounding Williams—splendid Sycamore Canyon, small fishing lakes, high volcanoes, forest drives, and hiking trails. Route 66 fans can drive segments of the old highway east of Williams and mountain bike two loops on old alignments west of town; the Visitor Information Center and the Forest Service office have brochures with maps.

History

Charles Rodgers, the first white settler here, started a cattle operation in 1878. The railroad and lumber town founded several years later took its name from Bill Williams Mountain just to the south. The mountain in turn honored mountain man Bill Williams, who roamed the West from 1825 until his death at the hands of Utes in 1849. He earned reputations as a skilled marksman, trapper, trader, and guide—and, some say, as an accomplished horse thief, preacher of profane sermons, and prodigious drinker. An 8.5-foot statue of "Old Bill" stands in Monument Park at the west end of downtown.

Today the Bill Williams Mountain Men perpetuate his adventurous spirit. The group dons buckskin clothing and fur hats, stages a 180-mile horseback ride from Williams to Phoenix most years, and works to keep the history of the mountain men alive. The Buckskinners, a family-oriented group, puts on frontier-era garb for black-powder shoots.

A more recent period of Western history came to an end at Williams in October 1984, when I-40 bypassed the last section of old US Route 66. A sentimental ceremony, complete with songwriter Bobby Troup of "Route 66" fame, marked the transition. The famous highway from Chicago to Los Angeles carried many families to a new life in Arizona and California. Its replacement, I-40, now travels an unbroken 2,400-mile path from Durham, North Carolina, to Barstow, California. Local businesses suffered when traffic bypassed Williams, but I-40 signs attempt to lure Grand Canyon visitors through downtown even though the real exit for the park is just east of town!

Grand Canyon Railway

Passenger trains first steamed out of Williams to the Grand Canyon's scenic splendor in 1901, replacing an expensive and arduous stage ride. Railroad service ended with the last passenger train carrying just three customers in 1968, but it started anew after a 21-year hiatus. Once again, Canyon visitors can enjoy a relaxing ride through the forests and ranching country of northern Arizona to the historic log depot in Grand Canyon Village, just steps away from the rim. Grand Canyon Railway runs steam locomotives from Memorial Day weekend through September, then vintage diesels the rest of the year. (If the train is too long for the steam engine to pull by itself, a diesel will be slipped in, too.) Trains run roundtrip daily except December 24 and 25 from the 1908 Williams Depot downtown; the depot is half a mile south from I-40 Exit 163 on Grand Canyon Blvd., or it can be reached via either of the other two I-40 Williams exits to downtown. Wheelchair users can access the depot and some of the train.

Before the ride starts, you can take in the Grand Canyon Railway Museum (open daily

7:30 A.M.–5 P.M.), outdoor train exhibits, and a Wild West show; all these are free and open to the public. The depot also has a gift shop. The restaurant Max and Thelma's serves meals.

Once underway, strolling musicians and Wild West characters on board entertain. Passengers on the return trip can expect a little excitement during a staged horseback chase and train robbery before "the law" catches up with the outlaws.

The restored 1923 Harriman coaches have reversible seats; roundtrip fare is $60 adults and $27 children ages 2–16. Passengers can also go Club Class (same as coach but with a bar and coffee, juice and pastries provided in the morning) for $82, First Class (reclining chairs and continental breakfast plus appetizers and champagne or sparkling cider on the afternoon journey) for $120, Deluxe Observation Class (First Class with dome views; ages 11 and up only) for $142, and the Luxury Parlor Car (First Class with seating in overstuffed divans and an open-air rear platform) for $153; children get discounts on all of these. One-way fares are available too. If you have a national park pass, let reservations staff know so that you won't be charged for park admission. The Grand Canyon Railway also offers packages with train tickets, a room at the Fray Marcos Hotel, and some meals, with options for Grand Canyon tours and accommodations; 800/843-8724 (800-THE-TRAIN); www.thetrain.com.

Recommended check-in is 8 A.M. or earlier, in time to have breakfast, see the museum and Wild West show, and board the train for its 9:30 A.M. departure. The train arrives at Grand Canyon, across the street from El Tovar Hotel and canyon rim, about 11:45 A.M. Boarding time for the return trip is 3 P.M. for a 3:15 P.M. departure and 5:30 P.M. return to Williams. South Rim tours within this time period are available at extra cost when you make reservations. The three hours at the Grand Canyon is enough for only a quick look, so you may wish to arrange to stay and ride back another day.

Recreation

Mountain Ranch Stables, behind the Quality Inn, 928/635-0706, offers a variety of trail rides from half an hour to overnight during the April–Oct. season; it's just south of I-40 Pittman Valley Exit 171, six miles east of Williams. **Stable in the Pines,** beside the Circle Pines KOA, 928/635-1930, has summer horseback riding; it's three miles east at I-40 Exit 167, then east 0.4 mile on the north frontage road. Play golf in the pines at the 18-hole **Elephant Rocks Golf Course,** 928/635-4936, during the roughly mid-March to mid-Nov. season. Go west on Railroad Avenue across I-40 (or take I-40 Exit 161 and head north) and drive a mile and a half.

Downhill-ski in winter at the small **Williams Ski Area,** four miles south of town on Bill Williams Mountain, 928/635-9330. It offers a 2,000-foot poma lift (600 vertical feet), 700-foot rope tow for the beginners' slope, lessons, snack bar, rental shop, and ski shop. Full-day weekend lift tickets cost $25 for adults and $20 for children and seniors; rates are lower for weekdays and half days. Cross-country skiers have marked trails. The ski season lasts from about mid-December to the end of March; turn south 2.2 miles on Fourth Street, then right at the sign.

Spring Valley Cross-Country Ski Trail has three loop possibilities of six and a half to eight miles each, rated easy to moderate; the season at the 7,480-foot-plus elevations runs winter to early spring. Spring Valley is 14 miles east on I-40 to Parks Exit 178, then north six miles on Forest Road 141; Forest Service offices have a ski trail map. Undeveloped cross-country ski areas include Sevier Flat and Barney Flat on the way to Williams Ski Area and the White Horse Lake area.

Oak Hill Snowplay Area is eight miles east of town on I-40 to the Pittman Valley Road/Deer Farm Exit 171, then east 2.4 miles on Route 66 on the north side of I-40. Only inner tubes and flexible materials may be used. Separate runs accommodate tubers and skiers.

Motels and Hotels

Business Route I-40, between Exits 161 and 165, divides downtown into one-way streets—Route 66 eastbound and Railroad Avenue westbound. Grand Canyon Blvd. meets these streets in the center of downtown from I-40 Exit 163. Most of the town's motels and restaurants lie along Rt.

66, formerly known as Bill Williams Avenue. Downtown offers the most atmosphere and the convenience of being able to walk to many places. The older places can be bargains with prices as low as the $20s in summer and teens in winter, though it's a good idea to check the rooms first. Don't believe the old sign that still advertises rooms "from $3.50" on the 1892 Grand Canyon Hotel on Rt. 66—the hotel has been closed awhile! The following summer rates will fluctuate depending on how busy the town is.

Under $50: From west to east, you can check out **Budget Host Inn,** 620 W. Route 66, 928/635-4415, 800/745-4415, $40–60 s, $45–69 d. **Westerner Motel,** 530 W. Route 66, 928/635-4312, 800/385-8608, $48 d. **9 Arizona,** 315 W. Route 66, 928/635-4552, $25–35 d. **Arizona Welcome Inn & Suites,** 750 N. Grand Canyon Blvd. off I-40 Exit 163, 928/635-9127, 888/895-0997, $45–59 d, $69–130 d suites. **Route 66 Inn,** 128 E. Route 66, 928/635-4791, 888/786-6956, $40 s, $40–48 d. **American Inn,** 134 E. Route 66, 928/635-4591, $28–48 d. **The Downtowner Motel,** 201 E. Route 66, 928/635-4041, $35 s, $40 d. **Grand Motel/Gateway Motel,** 219 and 234 E. Route 66, 928/635-4601, $40–50 d. **Courtesy Inn,** 344 E. Route 66, 928/635-2619, $45 d.

$50–100: Also from west to east, try **Days Inn,** 2488 W. Route 66 near I-40 Exit 161, 928/635-4051, 800/329-7466, $62–120 d. **Norris Motel,** 1001 W. Route 66, 928/635-2202, 800/341-8000, offers a pool and hot tub, $55 s, $55–59 d. **Super 8,** 911 W. Route 66, 928/635-4045, 800/800-8000, $59–69 d. **Motel 6,** 831 W. Route 66, 928/635-9000, 800/466-8356, $46 s, $52 d ($56 s, $62 d Fri.–Sat.). **Motel 6,** 710 W. Route 66, 928/635-4464, 800/466-8356, $42 s, $48 d ($52 s, $58 d Fri.–Sat.). **Highlander Motel,** 533 W. Route 66, 928/635-2541, 800/800-8288, $48 s, $52 d. **Mountain Country Lodge,** 437 W. Route 66, 928/635-4341, 800/973-6210, $69 d. **Howard Johnson Express Inn,** 511 N. Grand Canyon Blvd. off I-40 Exit 163, 928/635-9561, 800/720-6614, has an indoor pool and hot tub at $35–59 s, $49–89 d. **Holiday Inn,** 950 N. Grand Canyon Blvd. near I-40 Exit 163, 928/635-4114, 800/HOLI-

DAY, features a restaurant, indoor pool, hot tub, and sauna at $89–119 d or $119–159 d for a suite. **Fairfield Inn by Marriott,** 1029 N. Grand Canyon Blvd. north of I-40 Exit 163, 928/635-9888, 800/228-2800, has a pool and hot tub for $79 d. **Econo Lodge,** 302 E. Route 66, 928/635-4085, 800/553-2666, $55–65 d. **TraveLodge,** 430 E. Route 66, 928/635-2651, 800/578-7878, $50–59 d. **El Rancho Motel,** 617 E. Route 66, 928/635-2552, 800/228-2370, is $57–63 s, $63–73 d. **Mountain Side Inn,** 642 E. Route 66, 928/635-4431, 800/462-9381, has a steak house, pool, and hot tub for $86 d. **Super 8,** 2001 E. Route 66 near I-40 Exit 165, 928/635-4700, 800/800-8000, $50–60 s, $55–65 d. **Quality Inn Mountain Ranch,** seven miles east, just south of I-40 Exit 171, 928/635-2693, 800/228-5151, features a meadow and forest setting, two restaurants, pool, tennis, and summer horseback riding, $89 d.

$100–150: **Best Western Inn of Williams,** 2600 W. Route 66 near I-40 Exit 161, 928/635-4400, 800/635-4445, offers a pool and hot tub at $99–109 d, $119 d for a suite. **Fray Marcos Hotel,** downtown at Grand Canyon Railway Depot, 928/635-4010, 800/843-8724, has a pub and a nearby restaurant, $119 d.

Bed and Breakfasts

For a real sense of history, it would be hard to beat the **Red Garter Bed and Bakery,** 137 W. Railroad Ave., 928/635-1484, 800/328-1484, a restored 1897 Victorian Romanesque building. The upstairs rooms of the former brothel all have private bath and include the Parlor ($75 d), Madam's Room ($90 d), Big Bertha's Room ($110 d), and Best Gal's Room ($110 d). Guests awaken to fresh-baked pastries for breakfast in the downstairs bakery, once a rowdy saloon. The establishment at one time had a Chinese chop house and opium den out back. Innkeeper John Holst has photos of the building, saloonkeeper, madam, and customers of the old days. It closes mid-Dec. to mid-Feb.; www.redgarter.com.

Sheridan House Inn, 460 E. Sheridan, 928/635-9441, 888/635-9345, features suites with a gourmet breakfast, casual dinner, private bath, and many extras. Suites go for $135–195 d; www.grandcanyonbbinn.com.

Canyon Country Inn, 442 W. Route 66, 928/635-2349, 877/405-3280, offers homey rooms with private bath and continental breakfast downtown for $77.50 d, $120 family.

Terry Ranch Bed & Breakfast, 701 Quarterhorse off Rodeo Drive, 928/635-4171, 800/210-5908, is a Country Victorian log house with a veranda and rocking chairs; rooms have private bath, $110–155 d; www.terryranchbnb.com.

Campgrounds

Railside RV Ranch, 877 Rodeo Rd., 928/635-4077, 888/635-4077, is the closest campground to downtown; it has showers and a store, but lacks shade trees. Rates run $16 tents (just a few sites available) and $19–23 RVs with hookups. From I-40 Exit 165, take the business route west toward town, then turn right on Rodeo Road; or from downtown, go north on Grand Canyon Blvd., right on Edison Avenue, left on Airport Road, then right on Rodeo Road.

Red Lake Campground and Hostel, 10 miles north on AZ 64 from I-40 Exit 165, 928/635-4753, is open all year with coin-operated showers, limited cooking facilities, a store, and tour booking. Rates are $12–14 tents and $18 RVs with hookups; the hostel facilities cost $11 per person or $33 d for a private room.

Circle Pines KOA, 928/635-2626, 800/562-9379, is open year-round in the ponderosa pines; head three miles east to I-40 Exit 167, then go east 0.4 mile on the north frontage road. Rates are $18 tents, $24–27 RVs with hookups, $35 "kamping kabins"; amenities include volleyball, badminton, basketball, game room, and an indoor pool and hot tub. In summer, there's a snack bar and you can take in evening movies, van tours to the Grand Canyon, and horseback riding.

Grand Canyon KOA, 928/635-2307, 800/562-5771, lies five miles north of Williams on AZ 64 (I-40 Exit 165) on the way to the Grand Canyon; it offers tent ($18.50) and RV ($25–29 with hookups) sites and cabins ($36–42) with indoor pool, hot tub, store, game room, laundry, and showers from March to October.

Ponderosa Forest RV Park & Campground, 928/635-0456, 888/635-0456, has year-round sites in the woods for tents ($13) and RVs ($19 with hookups) with showers and a nearby store. It's north of I-40 Parks Exit 178, 14 miles east of Williams and about halfway to Flagstaff.

The Forest Service maintains four campgrounds, all on small fishing lakes (trout and catfish) with drinking water, interpretive programs, and camp hosts, but no showers. They're open from early May to about mid-October at elevations of 6,600–7,100 feet. Kaibab, Dogtown, and White Horse Lake may stay open off-season without drinking water, fee, or camp host. Dispersed camping is allowed throughout most of the forest except within half a mile of developed campgrounds, one-quarter mile of surface water, or where signed "No Camping." Boaters can use motors up to eight hp on Cataract and Kaibab lakes, but only electric motors are allowed on the other lakes.

Cataract Campground lies two miles northwest of town; head west on Railroad Avenue across I-40 to Country Club Drive (or take I-40 Exit 161 and go north), then turn right one mile immediately after going under railroad tracks and look for the entrance on the left. Sites cost $10.

Kaibab Campground is four miles northeast of town; drive east on Route 66 across I-40 (or turn north from I-40 Exit 165), go north two miles on AZ 64, then left one mile at the sign. Sites are $12.

Dogtown Campground and several trails lie 7.5 miles southeast of town; drive 3.5 miles south on Fourth Street (South Rd./Perkinsville Rd.), turn left three miles on Forest Road 140, then left 1.2 miles at the sign. Campsites go for $12.

White Horse Lake Campground lies 19 miles southeast near Sycamore Canyon; go eight miles south on Fourth Street, turn left on Forest Road 110, and follow signs. Sites are $12. A trail goes around the lake. Winter visitors to the White Horse Lake area enjoy ice fishing, cross-country skiing, and snowmobiling.

Food

Max and Thelma's, next to the depot, 928/635-8970, serves American food daily for breakfast, lunch, and dinner, including steak, barbecue, seafood, and pasta. The restaurant has South-western and railroad décor. It's named after the couple who brought the Grand Canyon Rail-way back to life.

Rod's Steak House, 301 E. Route 66, 928/635-2671, is a Western-style restaurant serving good steak, seafood, and sandwiches daily for lunch and dinner. **Miss Kitty's Steakhouse and Saloon,** 642 E. Route 66, 928/635-9161, serves up cowboy steak, ribs, seafood, and sandwiches in a spacious hall; musicians perform most evenings. Miss Kitty's is open daily for breakfast (buffet available) and dinner.

For Route 66 atmosphere, you can't beat **Cruisers Cafe 66,** 233 W. Route 66, 928/635-2445, with meat and vegetarian fajitas, steak, chicken, ribs, seafood, and pasta dishes, and sandwiches; it's open Sat.–Sun. for lunch (summer only) and daily for dinner.

The **Red Garter Bakery,** 137 W. Railroad Ave., 928/635-1484, is open mornings and evenings for baked goodies. **Grand Canyon Coffee & Cafe,** 125 W. Route 66, 928/635-1255, fixes coffees, sandwiches, and cakes daily for breakfast and lunch and Mon.–Sat. for dinner. For good American café food—and non-smoking despite the name!—try **Old Smokeys,** 624 W. Route 66, 928/635-1915, open daily for breakfast and lunch. **Pine Country Restaurant,** 107 N. Grand Canyon Blvd., 928/635-9718, is another café and serves breakfast, lunch, and dinner daily.

Pancho McGillicuddy's Mexican Cantina, 141 W. Railroad Ave., 928/635-4150, serves Mexican cuisine and a few American items daily for lunch (summer only) and dinner in the 1893 Cabinet Saloon building. Musicians perform daily on summer evenings and some weekends off season. **Rosa's Cantina,** 411 N. Grand Canyon Blvd., 928/635-0708, offers traditional Mexican food daily (may close Mon.) for lunch and dinner.

Pizza Factory, 214 W. Route 66, 928/635-3009, turns out pizza, pasta, calzones, and sandwiches and has a small salad bar. It's open daily for lunch and dinner.

Safeway supermarket is at 637 W. Route 66.

Events

Downtown rings to the sound of gunfire as cowboys stage shootouts every morning year-round at the train depot; gunfights also break out on the streets every evening during summer. Working cowboys show their skills in the **Summer Rodeo Series** on Fri. and Sat. nights. **Bill Williams Rendezvous** on Memorial Day weekend attracts the Buckskinners and Mountain Men to town for a black powder shoot, Saturday parade, street dance, and arts and crafts. **Festival in the Pines** on the last weekend of June is a juried arts and crafts show with food and entertainment. Townsfolk celebrate **July 4th** with a parade and fireworks. Working cowboys show what they've learned in the **Cowpuncher's Reunion Rodeo** on the first weekend in August. Top rodeo cowboys compete in the **PRCA Rodeo** on Labor Day weekend. **Old Route 66 "Cruisin' the Loop" Day** brings back the classic cars and memories of the '50s on the second weekend of October. **Mountain Village Holiday** runs from Thanksgiving to New Year's Day with arts and crafts and, on the second Saturday in December, a parade of lights.

Information

The **Visitor Information Center,** 200 W. Railroad Ave. (Williams, AZ 86046), 928/635-4061, 800/863-0546, has staff from both the Williams-Grand Canyon Chamber of Commerce and the Kaibab National Forest to help you explore and enjoy the region. The office serves so many travelers headed for the Grand Canyon that it stocks brochures and sells maps and books for that area too, as well as the rest of Arizona. It's open daily 8 A.M.–5 P.M. (to 6:30 P.M. in summer) in the heart of downtown in a 1901 passenger train depot; www.visitwilliams.com and www.thegrandcanyon.com. The *Williams Guidebook* by Richard and Sherry Mangum covers local history, walks, hikes, mountain bike trips, and scenic drives.

Kaibab National Forest staff can tell you about backcountry drives, hiking, camping, fishing, and road conditions in the Williams area. Stop by the Visitor Information Center downtown at 200 W. Railroad Avenue or visit the **Williams Ranger District** office, 928/635-2633, open

Mon.–Fri. 7:30 A.M.–4 P.M. The office is 1.5 miles west from downtown at 742 S. Clover Road (Williams, AZ 86046); head west on Railroad Avenue and turn left at the sign before I-40 onto the frontage road; www.fs.fed.us/r3/kai.

The **public library,** 113 S. First St. (just south of Route 66), 928/635-2263, is open Tues.–Saturday.

Tours and Transportation

To tour the Grand Canyon, try **Grand Canyon Van Tours** (summer only) at Circle Pines KOA, 928/635-2626 or **Marvelous Marv's Tours,** 928/635-4948, 800/655-4948; www.marvelousmarv.com.

Canyon Dreams, 135 W. Route 66, 928/635-9434, 888/731-4680, has a tiny backpacking shop and offers day and overnight hiking tours in the Grand Canyon; www.canyondreams.com.

Greyhound, 1050 Grand Canyon Blvd., 928/635-0870, 800/231-2222, offers several east- and westbound departures daily from the stop at the Chevron station just north of I-40 Exit 163. **Amtrak** trains stop at Williams Junction, three miles east of town; 800/872-7245 or www.amtrak.com; the Fray Marcos Hotel offers a shuttle.

VICINITY OF WILLIAMS

Grand Canyon Deer Farm

Visitors enjoy walking among tame deer and hand feeding them at this well-run petting zoo. Llamas, miniature donkeys, pronghorn, wallabies, and talking birds get the attention, too. The farm also has a buffalo, reindeer, exotic goats, a potbellied pig, and other familiar creatures. Peacocks strut across the grounds. The Deer Farm is open daily year-round except Thanksgiving and Christmas; the hours are 8 A.M.–7 P.M. in June–Aug., 9 A.M.–6 P.M. in March–May and Sept.–Oct, and 10 A.M.–5 P.M. Nov.–Feb. (weather permitting). Admission is $5.50 adults, $4.50 seniors 62 and over, $3 children 3–13; 928/635-4073, 800/926-3337. It's on Deer Farm Road, eight miles east of Williams off I-40 Pittman Valley/Deer Farm

Exit 171. Or from Flagstaff, head west 24 miles on I-40 to Exit 171.

Get Your Bikes on Route 66!

Abandoned sections of historic Route 66 have become two mountain bike trails west of Williams. You can ride loops on both by following the unpaved 1922 and partly paved 1932 alignments. Devil Dog Bicycle Tour makes a five-mile loop in ponderosa pines south of I-40 Devil Dog Exit 157; it can be done in 30 minutes. Ash Fork Hill Bicycle Tour is a six-mile loop farther west in pinyon-juniper woodlands and takes about an hour; the ride begins just north of I-40 Welch Exit 151. Stop by the Visitor Information Center or Forest Service office in Williams for a brochure with maps.

Bill Williams Mountain

You can reach the summit of this 9,256-foot peak by any of three hiking trails or by road. Pine, oak, and juniper trees cover the lower slopes, and dense forests of aspen, fir, and spruce grow in protected valleys and at higher elevations. On a clear day, you'll enjoy views of the Grand Canyon to the north, San Francisco Peaks and many smaller volcanoes to the east, Sycamore Canyon and parts of the Verde Valley to the south, and vast rangelands to the west. If it's open, climb up the Forest Service lookout tower at the top for the best views. Hiking season lasts from about June to September; you should always carry water. With a car shuttle, you can go up one trail and down another, or hike a trail just in one direction.

The eight-mile roundtrip **Bill Williams Mountain Trail** climbs the north face of the mountain. You'll reach the road about a half mile from the summit; either continue on the trail across the road or turn up the road itself. The trailhead (elev. 6,900 feet) is near the Williams Ranger District office, 1.5 miles west of town; from I-40, take Exit 161 toward Williams, then turn right (west) 0.7 mile on the frontage road.

The nine-mile roundtrip **Benham Trail** climbs the south and east slopes, crossing the road to the lookout tower several times. To reach the

Benham Trailhead (elev. 7,265 feet) from Williams, go south 3.5 miles on Fourth Street, then turn right about 0.3 mile on Benham Ranch Road. The gentler grade of this trail makes it good for horseback riders as well as hikers; the trailhead has a corral.

The **Bixler Saddle Trail** starts at Bixler Saddle on the west side of Bill Williams Mountain and climbs past majestic rock formations and good viewpoints. It joins the Bill Williams Mountain Trail fairly close to the top, five miles roundtrip; the summit is another half mile or so. For the trailhead, take I-40 west from Williams to Devil Dog Road Exit 157, head south on Forest Road 108 about a mile, then turn left 3.6 miles on Forest Road 45/Bixler Saddle Road to its end. The last bit may require a high-clearance vehicle. The Kaibab National Forest map (Williams District) will help to navigate the forest roads.

You can also drive up with a high-clearance vehicle; from Williams head 4.7 miles south on Fourth Street, then turn right seven miles on Forest Road 111. The road closes in winter.

Keyhole Sink Trail

A pleasant stroll, also marked for cross-country skiers, leads through ponderosa pines to a seasonal pool in a little box canyon. Aspen, wildflowers, and lush grass thrive here; you're likely to see some birds, too. Prehistoric people left petroglyphs, estimated to be 1,000 years old, on the dark basaltic rock. The easy walk is about 1.2 miles roundtrip with little elevation gain. To reach the trailhead, drive east on I-40 from Williams to Pittman Valley Exit 171, exit north, then head east 2.4 miles on Historic Route 66; parking is on the right at Oak Hill Snowplay Area, which features picnic tables, a warming shed, and toilets. The trailhead is north across the road. Coming from Flagstaff, you can take I-40 Parks Road Exit 178, turn north, then west 4.3 miles on Route 66; you'll pass **Garland Prairie Vista Picnic Area** 1.1 miles before reaching Oak Hill Snowplay Area.

Dogtown Trails

Dogtown Lake (elev. 7,100 feet) offers a campground, picnic area, and good hiking. **Dogtown**

Lake Trail makes a pleasant 1.8-mile stroll around the lake from the picnic area. **Davenport Hill Trail** begins near the boat ramp on the east side of the lake, follows Dogtown Wash, climbs to a bench, then switchbacks to the 7,805-foot summit. You'll pass through ponderosa pine, Douglas fir, white fir, and aspen forests with some good views. The trail is five miles roundtrip and has an elevation gain of 700 feet. **Ponderosa Nature Trail** is an easy, level, three-quarter-mile loop that branches off the Davenport Hill Trail; a brochure describes the forest environment at stops along the way. Dogtown Lake, named for the prairie dogs common in the Williams area, is 7.5 miles southeast of town; drive 3.5 miles south on Fourth Street (South Rd./Perkinsville Rd.), turn left three miles on Forest Road 140, then left 1.2 miles at the sign.

Sycamore Canyon Point

Sycamore Canyon remains wild and rugged, without any roads or facilities. Elk, deer, black bears, and other animals find food and shelter on the canyon's rim and within its depths. Hikers and horseback riders can use a network of trails. Sycamore Canyon Point, 23 miles southeast of Williams, offers a breathtaking panorama. From town, drive eight miles south on Fourth Street (South Rd./Perkinsville Rd.), then turn left on Forest Road 110 and travel to its end, approximately 15 miles farther. The last five miles are single lane and may be signed "Not For Low-Clearance Vehicles," but careful drivers may make it. Road signs may direct you left on Forest Roads 109 and 12, then back to 110, but you should be able to get through staying on 110. No trails enter the canyon from this side, though you can spot a path going down the opposite side.

Sycamore Rim Trail

This 11-mile loop overlooks parts of upper Sycamore Canyon and travels past seasonal waterfalls, lumber mill and railroad sites, lily ponds (good swimming), and pretty forest country. Stone cairns mark the trail, shown on both the Kaibab and Coconino Forest maps. Trailheads lie southeast of Williams near the junction of Forest Routes 13 and 56, at the end of Forest

Road 56, at Pomeroy Tanks off Forest Road 109, and at Sycamore Falls off Forest Road 109; see the Kaibab or Coconino Forest maps. If you're in the mood for only a short hike, walk 0.3 mile south from the end of Forest Road 56 to an overlook of Sycamore Canyon. The Visitor Information Center downtown at 200 W. Railroad Avenue and the Williams Ranger District office have a map and trail description.

Sycamore Falls

You can easily reach two waterfalls near White Horse Lake. The spectacle, however, occurs only during spring runoff and after heavy rains. From White Horse Lake, turn right two miles (north) on Forest Road 109 to the Sycamore Falls Trailhead, about two miles south of the junction with Forest Road 13. A small waterfall is visible in a canyon just to the right, but walk ahead and a bit to the left to see a larger one, 80–100 feet high.

Perkinsville Road

Beginning as Fourth Street in downtown Williams, Perkinsville Road heads south through the pine forests of the Mogollon Rim, drops down to the high-desert lands of the Verde Valley, crosses the Verde River at historic Perkinsville Ranch, then climbs rugged hills to the old mining town of Jerome. The first 25 miles is paved, followed by 27 miles of dirt. Though dusty and bumpy in spots, the route is usually okay in dry weather. No vehicle should attempt the unpaved section after winter snowstorms or heavy summer rains. Allow three hours for a one-way drive, more if you'd like to stop to admire the views. Stock up on gas and water before heading down this lonely road. The Prescott National Forest map covers the entire route.

ASH FORK

Declaring itself the "Flagstone Capital of the USA," Ash Fork occupies high-desert grasslands 19 miles west of Williams and 50 miles north of Prescott. Its location at the junction of I-40 and AZ 89 makes this small community a handy stopping place for travelers. The town grew up around a railroad siding built near Ash Creek in

1882, where passengers and freight transferred to stagecoaches or wagons for Prescott and Phoenix. Ash Fork (pop. 650) now serves as a highway stop and center for livestock raising and sandstone quarrying.

Accommodations

As in Williams, most of the businesses lie along two parallel one-way streets—Lewis Avenue for westbound traffic and Park Avenue for eastbound. Take I-40 Exits 144 or 146. **Ashfork Inn,** west of downtown near I-40 Exit 144, 928/637-2514, is the best choice; $22 s, $29 d.

Ash Fork KOA includes a pool, store, and laundry at 783 Old Route 66, 928/637-2521; rates run $16.50 tents, $19.50–21.50 RV with hookups, and $27 d for cabins. **Cauthen's Hillside RV Park** is on the south frontage road near I-40 Exit 144, 928/637-2300; rates are $7 tents or RVs without hookups, $14 with hookups. Both campgrounds stay open all year and have showers.

Food

Ruby's 8th Street Deli, 823 Park Ave., 928/637-0066, serves up Mexican food, pizza, and subs. **Picadilly Pizza & Subs** is next to the Chevron station, just south of the west I-40 Exit 144. A park on Lewis Avenue has picnic tables.

SELIGMAN

Another old railroad town, Seligman (pop. 900) now relies more on ranching and tourists. The first residents arrived in 1886 and called the place Prescott Junction, because a rail line branched south to Prescott. Though the Prescott line was later abandoned, the town survived. The present name honors brothers who owned the Hash Knife Cattle Company. Modern travelers on I-40 can take Exits 121 or 123 for the motels and restaurants in town or head northwest on old Route 66. This former transcontinental highway is a longer route to Kingman than I-40, but it offers a change of pace and a glimpse of America's motoring past. It also provides access to the Havasupai and Hualapai reservations (see "Western Grand Canyon and The Arizona Strip"). You'll also find food and lodging at the Grand Canyon Caverns Inn northwest of Seligman, Hualapai Lodge in Peach Springs, and Frontier Motel in Truxton. There's also a 17.5-mile segment of Route 66 east of town that turns southeast just east of downtown; if approaching Seligman from Ash Fork, you can drive it by turning off I-40 at Crookton Road, Exit 139.

Accommodations

Nearly all businesses lie along Route 66: **Stagecoach 66 Motel,** 639 E. Route 66, 928/422-3470, $30 s, $34 d; **Deluxe Inn,** 203 E. Route 66, 928/422-3244, $28 s, $31 d; **Canyon Lodge,** 114 E. Route 66, 928/422-3255, $37 s, $40 d; **Romney Motel,** 122 W. Route 66, 928/422-7666, $35 d; and **Historic Route 66 Motel,** 500 W. Route 66, 928/422-3204, $47 s, $57 d.

Food

Get your malts, sodas, fast food, and maybe a joke or two at the colorful **Delgadillo's Snow Cap,** 301 E. Route 66, 928/422-3291. **Countryside Cafe,** at the Stagecoach Motel just east of town, 928/422-3470, serves breakfast, lunch, and dinner daily. **Patty's Home Cookin',** 223 E. Route 66, 928/422-0014, has Thai-American food daily for breakfast and lunch and Mon.–Sat. for dinner. Patty's also offers a couple of bed & breakfast rooms and a small grocery. The **Copper Cart Restaurant,** 103 W. Route 66, 928/422-3241, offers a varied American menu daily for breakfast, lunch, and dinner. The steak house and café on the west end of downtown lack smoke-free sections. A small park downtown has picnic tables.

GRAND CANYON CAVERNS

Vast underground chambers and some pretty cave formations attract travelers on old Route 66. The caverns lie 25 miles northwest of Seligman, then one mile off the highway. A giant dinosaur stands guard in front. On 45-minute guided tours, you descend 21 stories by elevator to the caverns and walk about a quarter mile with some steps and inclines. Tours operate daily 8 A.M.–6 P.M. from Memorial Day to October 16, then 9 A.M.–5 P.M. in winter (closed Christmas Day); admission is $9.50 adults, $6.75 children 4–12. A gift shop at the entrance has some cave exhibits and photos from the early days, when visitors were lowered 150 feet at the end of a rope.

Grand Canyon Caverns Inn offers year-round accommodations near the turnoff on Route 66; rates are $45 s, $50 d, lower in winter. Self-contained RVs only may park in a campground with drinking water but no showers or hookups for $6.50. The cavern restaurant is open about the same hours as the tours. For information on cave tours or motel reservations, call 928/422-3223.

South of Flagstaff: Lake and Rim Country

More than a dozen mountain lakes dot the pine-forested plateau country southeast of Flagstaff. Anglers, picnickers, hikers, and campers enjoy the quiet waters, rolling hills, and scenic canyons of the region. Animal life flourishes—you might spot elk, deer, turkey, maybe even bear. Abert's squirrels with long tufted ears scamper through the trees. The best times to see wildlife are early and late in the day. Rim-country temperatures remain comfortably cool even in midsummer, and showers fall almost daily on July and August afternoons.

Most of the campgrounds on the Coconino National Forest provide drinking water and stay open from about May to September or October, depending on weather. Campsites often fill up during the peak summer months; you'll find less crowded conditions early and late in the season, or at any time away from developed sites. Dispersed camping is available almost anywhere in any season within the national forests, though you're asked to avoid camping on meadows or within a quarter mile of springs, streams, stock tanks, or lakes. Only fee campgrounds offer trash collection; everywhere else you need to pack it out. Boats are limited to those with electric motors on the smaller lakes and eight-hp gas motors on the larger ones; no restrictions apply on Upper Lake Mary.

MORMON LAKE RANGER DISTRICT

Two offices provide information about recreation and road conditions for this area. South of town, you can stop at the **Mormon Lake Ranger District** office, 4373 S. Lake Mary Rd. (Flagstaff, AZ 86001), 928/774-1182, about one mile from Hwy. 89A; books and forest and topo maps are sold. It's open Mon.–Fri. 7:30 A.M.–4:30 P.M. and Saturdays (call for hours) during summer. **Peaks Ranger Station** at 5075 N. Hwy. 89 (Flagstaff, AZ 86004) on the northeast side of town, 928/526-0866, is open Mon.–Fri. 7:30 A.M.–4:30 P.M. Online, check www.fs.fed.us/r3/coconino.

Canyon Vista Campground

The Forest Service campground closest to Flagstaff is also the newest. Follow Lake Mary Road for just over five miles, then turn left after crossing a cattle guard. Sites lie in a ponderosa pine forest, have drinking water, and cost $10.

Lower and Upper Lake Mary

Beginning just eight miles from Flagstaff, these long, narrow reservoirs offer fishing, boating, and birdwatching. Walnut Creek, dammed to form these lakes, once continued down through Walnut Canyon past the many Sinagua ruins there. The Riordan brothers, who built the first reservoir early in the 20th century to supply water to their sawmill, named the lake for a daughter.

Lower Lake Mary varies greatly in size, depending on rainfall and water needs. **Lower Lake Mary Boating and Picnicking Area,** near the dam, offers tables, grills, ramadas, and a place to hand-launch boats; it's between Mileposts 337 and 338. Anglers catch mostly northern pike.

Water-skiers zip across Upper Lake Mary in summer—it's one of the few lakes in this part of Arizona long and deep enough for the sport. Fishermen pull catfish, northern pike, walleye, sunfish, and bluegill from the waters. **Lake Mary Boat Landing** features picnic tables, grills, ramadas, and a paved boat ramp; it's on Lake Mary Road 0.8 mile upstream from the dam, between Mileposts 334 and 335. **The Narrows Picnic Area,** on Lake Mary Road 1.5 miles farther uplake, features a fishing area with wheelchair access, tables, grills, ramadas, and a paved boat ramp; it's between Mileposts 331 and 332.

Lakeview Campground provides camping near the lakes. It lies across the road from the Narrows of Upper Lake Mary, 14 miles southeast of Flagstaff at Milepost 331; the $10 fee includes drinking water. Some sites are too small for trailers.

Lake Mary Road (Forest Hwy. 3) parallels the shores of both lakes. From downtown Flagstaff, head south on Milton Road, turn right on Forest Meadows Street before the I-40 junction, turn left on Beulah Blvd. (Hwy. 89A), then follow signs for Lake Mary Road. If you're driving north on I-17, take Exit 339 just before the I-40 junction.

Sandy's Canyon Trail

This easy 1.5-mile roundtrip trail features canyon, forest, and mountain views, with the option to continue on the Arizona Trail. Local rock climbers tackle the cliffs visible from the first few hundred feet of the trail. The path follows the rim of Walnut Canyon a short way, drops down Sandy's Canyon, then follows the floor of Walnut Canyon to a junction with the Arizona Trail in about three-quarters of a mile. Here you can turn southeast about four miles to Marshall Lake or north one mile to Fisher Point, then continue toward the trailhead near Walnut Canyon National Monument, another six miles. Another trail near Fisher Point branches northwest toward Flagstaff and its Urban Trail System. Sandy's Canyon Trailhead is reached 5.5 miles down Lake Mary Road from AZ 89A, then left 0.2 mile just past the second cattle guard. During winter you can park off the road near the locked gate and walk to the trailhead.

Marshall Lake

This small trout lake and its primitive boat ramp lie north of Upper Lake Mary. Head nine miles down Lake Mary Road from Flagstaff to the signed Marshall Lake turnoff, between Upper and Lower Lake Mary, then turn left three miles to the lake.

Ashurst Lake

Anglers pursue rainbow trout while windsurfers slice through the water on this small lake. Two campgrounds, both with water and a $10 fee, sit beside the lake—**Ashurst Campground** on the west shore and **Forked Pine** on the east. On the way in you'll pass the **Ashurst Dispersed Camping Area,** which offers a campground host, toilets, and dumpsters but no water or fee. There's a boat ramp near the entrance to Ashurst Campground. From Flagstaff, travel southeast 18 miles on Lake Mary Road, then turn left four miles on paved Forest Road 82E (between Mileposts 326 and 327). **Coconino Reservoir,** one mile south of Ashurst Lake on a dirt road, also has a good reputation for rainbow trout.

Pine Grove Campground

Entrance to this large campground lies opposite the turnoff for Ashurst Lake, 18 miles southeast of Flagstaff; turn west 0.8 mile on Forest Road 651 from Lake Mary Road. The camping area has drinking water, paved roads, and a $12 fee. Some sites can be reserved through 877/444-6777; www.reserve.usa. Although not on a lake, Pine Grove is within a few miles of Upper Lake Mary and Ashurst and Mormon lakes.

Mormon Lake

Mormon settlers arrived on the shores of this lake in 1878 and started a dairy farm. Although Mormon is the largest natural lake in Arizona, the average depth is only 10 feet. The water level fluctuates; when it's low the lake is not much more than a marsh. Occasionally it dries up completely. Still, at times, anglers reel in sizable bullhead catfish and northern pike. Boats must be hand-carried to the water.

Lake Mary Road parallels the east shore and has a scenic viewpoint. You'll need to turn onto Mormon Lake Loop Road (Forest Road 90), which circles around the west side of the lake, to reach the lodges, camping, and hiking areas; the north turnoff is between Mileposts 323 and 324; south turnoff is between Mileposts 317 and 318. **Dairy Springs** and **Double Springs** campgrounds on this loop road both have drinking water and a $10 fee. **Dairy Springs Group** area can be reserved by calling 877/444-6777; www.reserve.usa. From Flagstaff, head southeast 20 miles on Lake Mary Road, then turn right four miles on Mormon Lake Loop Road to the Dairy Springs turnoff, or go two miles farther to the turnoff for Double Springs.

Lakeview Trail (two miles roundtrip) climbs a small hill from Double Springs Campground. For a longer trip, start near Dairy Springs Campground and hike 1,500 feet above Mormon Lake on the six-mile-roundtrip **Mormon Mountain Trail;** you'll enjoy pretty forest country, though trees block views at the top. **Ledges Trail,** an easy one-mile-roundtrip hike from Dairy Springs Campground, runs out to a ledge overlooking the lake.

Cabins of **Montezuma Lodge,** 928/354-2220, spread across 16 acres in the woods a quarter mile beyond Dairy Springs Campground; they're open from mid-May to mid-October and cost $90–135 for up to four persons; www.arizonamountainresort.com. **Mormon Lake Lodge,** on the loop road at the south end of the lake, serves as a recreational center for many visitors. The lodge offers a variety of rooms and cabins ($40–145 for as many as seven persons), an RV park (open May 15–Oct. 31 with fees of $24 RV with hookups, $9 RV or $6 tent no hookups, and $3 for showers), a smoky café/steakhouse (open daily in summer with breakfast, lunch, and dinner), dinner theater on summer Thursdays, a saloon, grocery store with fishing and hunting supplies, and a gas station; 928/774-0462 (Flagstaff) or 928/354-2227 (local). Mountain bikes can be rented at the store. **High Mountain Stables,** 928/354-2359, has trail and wagon rides near the lodge from early May to mid-October. Across the road, **Mormon Lake Ski Touring Center** offers trails, rentals, and lessons for cross-country skiers; contact the lodge for information as well as snowmobile rentals. A small **post office** is wedged between the lodge and store. **Munds Park,** 11 miles west of the Mormon Lake Loop Road via unpaved Forest Road 240, has a motel, RV park, restaurants, and a service station; it's at I-17 Exit 322, 18 miles south of Flagstaff.

Kinnikinick Lake

Rainbow and brown trout, with the occasional catfish, swim in this reservoir. Ponderosa and juniper trees and grasslands cover the gentle terrain around it. You're more likely to find solitude here because the area lies off paved roads. Kinnikinick Lake has a campground with an $8 fee but there's no drinking water. Sites are open year-round, with a camp host present May–Sept.; there's usually room even on summer weekends. Fishermen can use the gravel boat ramp and motors up to eight horsepower. From Flagstaff, go southeast 25 miles on Lake Mary Road to just past Mormon Lake (between Mileposts 318 and 319), then turn left 4.7 miles on Forest Road 125, then right 4.4 miles on Forest Road 82, following signs. Though unpaved, these forest roads are usually okay for cars. Be warned that Forest Road 82 from here south to Long Lake is extremely rough and rocky, requiring high-clearance vehicles, dry weather, and lots of time; it's not recommended.

LONG VALLEY–BLUE RIDGE RANGER DISTRICT

The cool ponderosa pine forests atop the Mogollon Rim here offer many opportunities for camping, fishing, hiking, and back-road travel. In winter, pullouts along AZ 87 and Forest Hwy. 3 will be plowed for people to play in the snow. The region centers on Clints Well, the junction of AZ 87 between Payson and Winslow and Forest Hwy. 3 from Flagstaff. **Happy Jack Information Center,** a half mile south of this junction at Milepost 290 on AZ 87, 928/477-2172, provides recreation information and sells topo maps, forest maps, and regional books. It's open daily 9 A.M.–5:30 P.M. (with half an hour off for lunch)

from May to Oct.; the rest of the year it's usually open Thurs.–Tues. 8 A.M.–4:30 P.M. and closed a half hour for lunch; mailing address is P.O. Box 19664, Happy Jack, AZ 86024 or visit on the Web at www.fs.fed.us/r3/coconino.

Foresters provide similar information at the **Blue Ridge Ranger Station,** 928/477-2255, open Mon.–Fri. 7:30 A.M.–4 P.M.; HC 31, Box 300, Happy Jack, AZ 86024. From Clints Well, go northeast 10.5 miles on AZ 87 to the office on the right. From Winslow, head 43 miles southwest on AZ 87.

Stoneman Lake

Geologists have not decided whether the circular depression that holds this unusual lake is an old volcanic crater or a sinkhole. Anglers agree that its waters are a hot spot for yellow perch; record catches have been landed here. Pike and sunfish also thrive. The lake has a picnic area and boat ramp but no campground. To reach Stoneman, either take the I-17 Stoneman Lake Exit 306 (34 miles south of Flagstaff) and go east nine miles on mostly unpaved Forest Road 213, or head south on Lake Mary Road eight miles past Mormon Lake, then turn west seven miles on Forest Road 213.

West Clear Creek Wilderness (East Half)

The transparent waters of this year-round creek wind below pretty canyon walls on the way to the Verde River. Of the many canyons in the Mogollon Rim, west Clear Creek has the greatest length—40 miles. Cross-bedded patterns of ancient sand dunes in Coconino Sandstone show clearly on the sheer cliffs. The creek offers excellent hiking, swimming, and fishing, though it may be difficult to entice the trout onto a hook.

Several trails into the canyon provide a choice of day hikes or overnight trips. Adventurous hikers could spend a week traveling downstream to Bull Pen Ranch or Clear Creek Campground. Or you can day-hike to the upper reaches of West Clear Creek and along the tributaries of Willow and Clover creeks; **Maxwell Trail** provides the easiest access to this area.

The warmer months are best for a visit to this canyon. There isn't much of a trail, so you'll be wading and swimming much of the time. In spring, snowmelt can raise the stream level too high for hiking, as can very heavy rains in any season. Water is always available from the creek; purify first. Hikers should remember that trails out can be difficult to spot. Exceptions include the **Tramway Trail,** marked by a steel cable across the creek, and a trail near the power lines—two sets of high-tension lines shown on the Coconino Forest map.

A hike between these points makes a good overnight backpacking trip, but you'll have to cross a deep pool about 150 feet long hemmed in by cliffs, where a small inflatable boat will come in handy. The pool is about 0.7 mile upstream of the power lines. Many more deep pools, including one a quarter mile long, must be crossed if you're going downstream from the powerlines. Allow plenty of time for a trek all the way through the canyon, as the rugged terrain and pools make for extremely slow going. Flotation vests are recommended for such trips because inflatable boats, tubes, and air mattresses are

rainbow trout (Salmo gairdneri)

easily punctured. It's easy to forget to drink water in the cool depths, but one does need to drink a lot because of the exertions.

To reach the Tramway trailhead (Forest Trail 32), go 21 miles south of Mormon Lake on Lake Mary Road, then turn west eight miles on dirt Forest Roads 81 and 81E; keep straight past the turnoff for Maxwell Trail, go about 1.5 miles, then turn left at the fork. Tramway descends steeply in less than a mile to the canyon floor. At the power lines downstream, a rough trail connects the creek with Forest Road 142A on the south rim. This trailhead is about 18 miles southwest of Clints Well via AZ 87 and Forest Roads 142 and 142A. Roads to the trailheads may be too rough for cars after heavy rains.

The lower section of West Clear Creek has some good day-hike possibilities; see "Beaver Creek Ranger District" below.

Clints Well

Natural springs here, a rarity in the region, have long been a stopping place for travelers. They were named for Clint Wingfield, an early pioneer. Lake Mary Road (Forest Hwy. 3) meets AZ 87 at Clints Well; turn left for Winslow, right for Payson and Mesa. The small Clints Well Campground near the end of Lake Mary Road is free but lacks water. **Happy Jack Information Center,** the smoky **Long Valley Cafe,** a grocery store, and a service station are a half mile south on AZ 87. **Happy Jack Lodge & RV Park,** two miles north of the junction on Lake Mary Road, 928/477-2805, 800/430-0385, is open year-round, weather permitting. It has cabins with kitchens ($65 d), suites ($110 d), RV sites ($21 with hookups, showers, laundry, and dump station), tent sites ($15), a small store, and a steakhouse (open Tues.–Sat. for breakfast, lunch, and dinner, and on Sun. for breakfast and lunch).

Kehl Springs

Great views at the edge of the Mogollon Rim lie just a short walk away from this small campground; no fee or water. Aspen and oak trees put on a colorful display in autumn. From Clints Well, go southwest 3.3 miles on AZ 87, then turn left on Forest Road 147 to the Rim Road (see the Coconino Forest Map). These roads tend to be rough and dusty, but they should be okay for passenger vehicles in good weather.

Blue Ridge Reservoir

Hemmed in by the canyon walls of East Clear Creek, this skinny lake offers good trout fishing—best in spring and autumn—and great scenery. Trails lead to the water's edge, but steep terrain makes fishing easier from a boat. The popular **Rock Crossing Campground** nearby offers good views; it's open with water and a $5 fee from Memorial Day to Labor Day weekends. From Clints Well, head northeast five miles on AZ 87, turn right three miles on Forest

BOB RACE

Road 751 to the campground, then another three miles to the dam.

The smaller **Blue Ridge Campground** is open during the same season with the same fee; trailers are limited to 16 feet. From Clints Well, go northeast nine miles on AZ 87, then turn right one mile on Forest Road 138. Sections of **Moqui Group Area,** on Forest Road 138 before Blue Ridge Campground, can be reserved through Happy Jack Information Center. Anglers use Blue Ridge Campground as a base for Blue Ridge Reservoir, East Clear Creek, and Long Lake.

Long Lake

Catfish and northern pike are the fish most commonly pulled from this two-mile-long lake, but the waters harbor trout, bass, walleye, and panfish as well. You can camp in the area and use the primitive boat ramp; outhouses are the only facilities. Soldier Annex Lake and Soldier Lake lie to the west; electric motors only.

Turn northwest three miles on Forest Road 211 from AZ 87 near Blue Ridge Ranger Station, then head north 12 miles on Forest Road 82 to Long Lake. Or, from Forest Hwy. 3, head eight miles east on Forest Road 211, then turn north 12 miles on Forest Road 82. The turnoff for Soldier Annex Lake is a mile farther north, then left half a mile. The Coconino Forest map shows Forest Road 82 continuing another 12 miles to Kinnikinick Lake, but this section is extremely rough and makes for slow going.

East Clear Creek Hiking

This canyon offers pleasant scenery, where deep, clear pools invite swimming or solitary fishing. Beavers, shy and nocturnal, live and work along the stream. Watch out for snakes—most are harmless, but rattlesnakes live here, too. A rough trail follows the canyon, crossing the creek in many places. Crossings shouldn't be more than knee deep, though spring snowmelt or heavy rains can raise the creek too high for hiking. Long pants will protect your legs from bramble patches. Water is always available, though be sure to purify it. East Clear Creek flows northeast and joins the Little Colorado River near Winslow; it has no connection

with West Clear Creek, which flows in the opposite direction.

Macks Crossing, only two miles from AZ 87, provides the easiest access. From Clints Well, go 15 miles northeast (4.5 miles past Blue Ridge Ranger Station) on AZ 87 and turn right on Enchanted Lane (shown as Forest Road 137 on the Coconino Forest map). After a short distance, turn right 0.7 mile on Green Ridge Road, then turn right again on Juniper, which leads to Forest Road 137. The narrow rocky road descends one mile across a cliff face—no guardrails—to the creek. Park at the top or at several places on the way down. Near the creek and on the other side, the road is too rough for cars. From Macks Crossing, a good overnight loop hike (15 miles) heads upstream on East Clear Creek to Kinder Crossing Trail, takes this trail to Forest Road 137, and follows the forest road back to Macks Crossing. The section of road requires only 2–3 hours of easy walking—less than a third of the time needed for hiking in the creek.

Kinder Crossing Trail has a west trailhead on Forest Road 95, about 4.5 miles south of Blue Ridge Ranger Station. The trail (#19) is marked by tree blazes down to the creek, then by stone cairns and tree blazes for a half mile downstream along the creek before climbing the other side of the canyon to Forest Road 137. Both the topo and Coconino Forest maps may incorrectly show the trail as simply crossing the creek and climbing the opposite side, instead of following the creek a half mile.

Horse Crossing Trail #20 (see Coconino Forest map) also descends into the canyon from both sides. Kinder Crossing and Horse Crossing trailheads should be distinct and signed. Horse Crossing Trail can be very difficult to spot while walking along the creek; pay careful attention to your topo map and tree blazes.

Other Hikes

The **Arizona Trail** crosses the district on its journey between Mexico and Utah. **Cabin Loop Trail** connects three historic guard stations—Pinchot, General Springs, and Buck Springs—in a 28-mile trail network. Happy Jack Information Center has handouts on these and other trails.

Knoll Lake

A rocky island in the middle gives this lake its name. Knoll Lake is in Leonard Canyon, several miles north of the Mogollon Rim. There's a campground on a hill near the lake; sites have water and an $8 fee during the Memorial Day to Labor Day season. A road and hiking trail lead down to the boat ramp. Anglers come mostly to seek out rainbow trout. Getting here involves about 28 miles of dirt road from either AZ 87 or Woods Canyon Lake off AZ 260.

BLACK MESA RANGER DISTRICT

Foresters of the Black Mesa Ranger District of the Apache-Sitgreaves National Forest provide information and maps on recreation in the Mogollon Rim country from Chevelon Canyon to Black Canyon Lakes, including the very popular Rim Lakes Recreation Area. The **Mogollon Rim Visitors Center** has a handy location right on the rim at Al Fulton Point, opposite the Forest Road 300 turnoff from AZ 260; it's open daily 9 A.M.–4:30 P.M. from Memorial Day to Labor Day with an information desk, a few exhibits, and map sales. Step out on the back porch for a great panorama from the rim across wooded ridges extending all the way to Four Peaks near Phoenix. The first quarter mile of Forest Road 171 east of the visitor information center has **picnic areas**—all with views; continue along the road for some designated dispersed camping sites. The visitor information center is six miles west of Forest Lakes between Mileposts 282 and 283. From Payson, head 32 miles east on AZ 260 to just past where the highway tops out on the Mogollon Rim.

You can also stop by the **Black Mesa Ranger Station,** 2748 Hwy. 260, 928/535-4481, for recreation information on the Rim Country; it's open Mon.–Fri. 8 A.M.–4:30 P.M. year-round, two miles east of Heber on the south side of the highway between Mileposts 307 and 308; or write P.O. Box 968, Overgaard, AZ 85933; www.fs.fed.us/r3/asnf.

Both offices have a pamphlet for the self-guided *Black Canyon . . . Journey Through Time Auto Tour,* that describes prehistoric and historic sites

along a 15.3-mile length of Forest Road 86 southwest of Heber.

A large part of the Rim Lakes Recreation Area has been set aside as a wildlife habitat area. Hikers, backpackers, cyclists, and equestrians are welcome here, but not motorized vehicles. The Mogollon Rim offers a great opportunity for seeing elk, deer, and other animals, especially in early morning and again in the evening. Take care not to be near the edge of the rim during summer thunderstorms, most likely in July and August, because it's said to be the second most lightning-struck place in the world.

Campgrounds fill on weekends from about the third week of June to Labor Day; you'll need to make a reservation or arrive by Friday morning to secure a spot. Groups can reserve sites at Woods Canyon, Spillway, Canyon Point, and Gentry campgrounds. Designated dispersed camping sites also help to accommodate the throngs of summer visitors. These areas are free but lack water or facilities; look for them along sections of Forest Roads 237, 300, 169, 171, 195, 9350, and 9354. The forest roads east of Forest Lakes tend to be the least crowded for dispersed camping. Some people like autumn best—September and October generally have good weather and fishing, solitude, and colors of aspen turning to gold. Spring can be a fine time to visit as well.

ATVs may travel numbered forest roads only. Both vehicles and operators must be licensed for highway use.

Chevelon Crossing

This small campground overlooks Chevelon Creek many miles downstream from Woods Canyon Lake. The sites remain open most of the year (elev. 6,200 feet) with no water or fee. Parking is tight and small vehicles will fit best. Try fishing in the large pools upstream, which harbor rainbow trout. Three routes lead to this remote campground. Forest Road 504 is the usual way in; turn off AZ 260 one mile west of Heber. You could also take AZ 99 south from Winslow and turn left on Forest Road 504, or take Forest Road 169 north from Forest Road 300 (the Rim Road; closed in winter) west of Woods Canyon Lake.

Chevelon Canyon Lake

This long, skinny reservoir lies 12 miles upstream from Chevelon Crossing via Forest Roads 169 and 169B. See the Apache-Sitgreaves Forest map for other ways of getting here. The lake offers trophy fishing for rainbow and brown trout; anglers must use artificial lures and observe size and catch limits. With 208 surface acres, this is one of the larger lakes on the Mogollon Rim. There's a primitive campground (elev. 6,400 feet, no water or fee) near the north shore.

Bear Canyon Lake

Anglers enjoy fishing with artificial lures or bait on this trout lake. The shore is steep and tree-covered, so it's easier to use boats for fishing, though you'll have to lug them to the water. There's a campground (no water or fee) near the north end. From Woods Canyon Lake, travel west 10 miles on Forest Road 300 (the Rim Road), then turn north and drive 2.5 miles on Forest Road 89.

Woods Canyon Lake

This popular lake was one of the first of seven created on the rim. Camp at either Aspen Campground ($12) or Spillway Campground ($14) near the lakeshore; both have drinking water and a season of about May to mid-September. Call 877/444-6777, www.reserveusa.com, to reserve a site. A store that stays open into autumn has groceries, boat rentals, and motors (only electrics are permitted here). On summer weekends, staff lead walks and offer evening programs. **Rocky Point Picnic Area** on the south side of the lake is open for day use only, $5. **Woods Canyon Nature Trail** makes a half-mile loop here. From AZ 260, near the edge of the Mogollon Rim, turn northwest five miles on paved Forest Roads 300 and 105.

Wells Springs Trailhead and Snowplay Area

A large parking area, just 0.1 mile in from AZ 260 on Forest Road 300, provides access to General Crook Trail 611, Rim Lakes Vista Trail, and the 235 Road Bike Trail. In winter,

it's plowed so visitors can enjoy the snow (no sleds or tubing).

Rim Lakes Vista Trail

This easy trail follows the rim for three miles with some fine views between Rim and Mogollon Campgrounds, both off Forest Road 300; elevation is 7,500 feet. **Military Sinkhole Trail** drops west and south 2.25 miles from Rim Lakes Vista Trail to Two-Sixty Trailhead and the Highline National Recreation Trail; you'll find the upper trailhead 1.9 miles in from AZ 260 on Forest Road 300, and the Two-Sixty Trailhead 27 miles east of Payson just off AZ 260.

Mountain Bicycle Trails

Cyclists enjoy **Willow Springs Loop,** an 8.1-mile series of forest roads in a wildlife habitat area signed for nonmotorized use. It's northeast of Willow Springs Lake; from AZ 260, go a half mile north on Forest Road 237 to the trailhead at the junction with Forest Road 236. The **235 Road Bike Trail,** west of Willow Springs Lake, heads north about four miles (one way) into the wildlife habitat area. Both trails are at an elevation of about 7,600 feet.

Rim Road — Forest Road 300

This scenic road follows the Mogollon Rim between AZ 260 and AZ 87 for 51 miles. Most of it is dirt, passable by cautiously driven cars. Allow 3–4 hours one way. Slow speeds are necessary because of hazardous washboard sections. Attractions include rim views, pretty forest scenes, wildlife sightings, and effects of the Dude Fire. The eastern section lies within the Rim Lake Recreation Area, where one must use designated campsites. Dispersed camping is allowed along the western part of the drive, which is in the Coconino National Forest.

Willow Springs Lake

Anglers catch mostly rainbow trout in this U-shaped lake. There's a boat ramp but no campground. You can camp in designated dispersed areas nearby or at **Sinkhole Campground,** which has water and a $8 fee from mid-May to late October. From AZ 260, about one mile east of Forest Road 300 (Rim Road) junction and four miles west of Canyon Point Campground, turn in a half mile on Forest Road 149 to Sinkhole Campground, then continue 3.5 miles to Willow Springs Lake. **Rim, Crook,** and **Mogollon Campgrounds** lie along Forest Road 300, beginning 0.8 mile in from AZ 260; all are open mid-May to late October with water and a $8 fee.

Canyon Point Campground

This large, easily accessible campground has drinking water, showers, a dump station, and some quad sites from mid-May to late September; call 877/444-6777, www.reserveusa.com, to reserve a site. Sites without hookups cost $14. Loop A has electric hookups at $16. Naturalists offer walks, children's programs, and evening presentations on summer weekends. **Sinkhole Trail** begins from Loop B and leads to a sinkhole, one mile roundtrip. Canyon Point Campground lies just off AZ 260, five miles east of the Forest Road 300 (Rim Road) junction.

Forest Lakes

Summer visitors at **Forest Lakes Touring Center,** 928/535-4047, can rent fishing boats with trolling motors for $28 per day and canoes for $18 per day (including paddles and life jackets). In winter, the center provides cross-country skiers with approximately 30 miles of marked and groomed trails and skating lanes atop the Mogollon Rim; trail passes cost $8. You can also arrange rentals, lessons, and tours. Year-round cabins run $68–85 d Fri.–Sat. and holidays, $60–75 d Sun.–Thursday. There's an RV park here, but it offers overnights only during off-season, Oct.–April. Forest Lakes Touring Center is in the village of Forest Lakes on AZ 260 near Milepost 288, six miles east of the Forest Road 300 (Rim Road) turnoff or 36 miles east of Payson.

A nearby store sells groceries, camping gear, and fishing supplies. Heber, 15 miles east, and Overgaard just beyond, have a few motels and cafés.

Black Canyon Lake

This small trout lake doesn't have a campground,

but **Black Canyon Rim** and **Gentry** campgrounds lie within a few miles. Black Canyon Rim has water and an $8 fee from mid-May to late September. Gentry has no water or fee, but sites can be reserved for families or groups at 800/280-2267. Both stay open all year when not blocked by snow. From Canyon Point Campground, go east 4.5 miles on AZ 260, turn right 2.5 miles on Forest Road 300, then turn left three miles on Forest Road 86 to Black Canyon Lake.

Heber and Overgaard

These small towns stretch out along AZ 260. Both have cafés, stores, and a few RV parks. Heber offers the **Best Western Sawmill Inn,** 1877 Hwy. 260, 928/535-5053, 800/372-9564, with a hot tub and exercise room at $58 d Sun.–Thurs. and $65 d Fri.–Sat.; and **Canyon View Motel,** 1842 Hwy. 260, 928/535-4598 at $40 s, $45 d (add $5 Fri.–Sat.).

The restaurant **Inn at the Ponderosa,** 2281 Hwy. 260 in Overgaard, 928/535-4230, serves fine American and Italian cuisine Fri.–Sun. for dinner only. **Black Mesa Ranger Station,** described at the beginning of this section, is also in Overgaard.

Buffalo Museum of America

A large collection of art and memorabilia celebrates this magnificent animal. Inside you'll see an amazing variety of many examples of pop art, paintings, and sculpture that depict the buffalo. Besides life-sized stuffed figures of adults and calves, there's a buffalo prop from the movie "Dances With Wolves"—producers had to replicate the violent buffalo hunts without harming a single animal. Old photos and illustrations depict the colorful life of Buffalo Bill, along with the gloves and Sharps rifle that he used. Plains Indian exhibits display elaborate ceremonial costumes.

The museum's Wild West Theater shows western classics in the afternoons and newer westerns Fri.–Sat. evenings. The museum, formerly in Scottsdale, is now just east of Overgaard at 2269 Hwy. 260, 928/535-4141. It's open in summer Sun.–Thurs. 10 A.M.–6 P.M.

and Fri.–Sat. 10 A.M.–10 P.M.; call for winter hours. Admission runs $5 adult, $3 age 8–17. Look for it in a group of large western-style buildings of the Bison Ranch development on the south side of the highway near Overgaard. Bison Ranch, 928/535-6990, also has trail and carriage rides, dining, shopping, and cabin rentals; www.bisonranch.net.

The Country Below the Rim

PAYSON

Payson (elev. 5,000 feet) stand at almost the exact center of Arizona. The sheer cliffs of the Mogollon Rim tower 2,000 feet above to the north. Forested mountains lie in all directions and provide many opportunities for outdoor recreation. Hikers can explore the Mazatzal Wilderness to the southwest, Hellsgate Wilderness to the east, and Sierra Ancha and Salome Wildernesses to the southeast. Trout-filled streams and stocked reservoirs lure anglers to the water. Hunters come in season to bag elk, deer, turkey, and other game. Although Payson itself (pop. 10,000) boasts only a few sights, the town makes a good base for exploring the surrounding countryside.

History

It wasn't the cool climate and beautiful scenery that attracted Payson's first settlers, but the glitter of gold. Miners set up camp in 1881, though ranching and lumbering soon reigned as the most rewarding occupations. A fort provided protection against Apache raids in the precarious early years.

The town's name honors Senator Louis Edwin Payson, who had nothing to do with the community and never came here. Frank C. Hise, former postmaster, assigned the name to repay a political favor.

Novelist Zane Grey fell in love with the canyons, towering forests, and expansive views of the Rim Country. He built a lodge at the foot of the Rim in 1920, then stayed often over the next nine years, enjoying the wilderness while working on novels about the American West. His hunting expeditions secured both ideas for stories and trophies for his walls. The devastating Dude Fire burned the cabin in 1990, but you can see exhibits about his life and books at the two museums in Payson.

Rim Country Museum

Visiting and permanent exhibits take you back to the days of the earliest peoples of the region, then to the Apache conflicts, timber and mining operations, agriculture, and pioneer entertainment. A blacksmith shop and a 1908 kitchen portray aspects of life in early Payson. The display on Zane Grey, who produced 131 novels, has some of his books and personal belongings. The museum complex includes Payson's original 1907 forest ranger's station (part of the interior has been restored as a forest ranger office), the 1930s forest ranger's residence (now the Museum Store and ticket office), a replica of the two-story Herron Hotel (the main exhibit hall), and the upper section of the Mt. Ord Firetower. Early fire-fighting equipment and Payson's first fire truck are on display, too. The Museum Store has books on local and Arizona history as well as gift items. Open Wed.–Sun. noon–4 P.M.; admission runs $3 adults, $2.50 seniors, and $2 students 12–17; 928/474-3483. Picnic tables are outside; the adjacent Green Valley Park has a playground and lake (electric motors okay). From AZ 87, turn west one mile on Main St. (at the chamber of commerce), right on Green Valley Parkway, then the next left into the parking lot.

Zane Grey Museum

The prolific novelist Zane Grey led a colorful and adventurous life, well told by the museum's displays. A 28-minute video recounts the story of his career and family. Photos illustrate his interest in baseball, which got him through college on a scholarship, Arizona travels, and fishing trips. You'll see posters and stills from his movie business, Zane Grey Productions, which produced seven films in 1919-22, and some of the 130 other movies based on his books that were made by other producers. Grey's books on display include many editions in many languages. A gift shop sells books and souvenirs. Open daily in summer 10 A.M.–3 P.M. (check winter hours); $2 adults, $1 students; 928/474-6243. It's at 503 W. Main St. between the chamber office and the Rim Country Museum.

Accommodations

You can choose from motels in town, secluded cabins in the surrounding forests, or campgrounds and RV parks. Make reservations for the weekend rush in summer, when you'll have to pay the highest prices. Summer rates are listed here; winter visits will be less expensive.

Under $50: Star Valley Motel, four miles east of Payson, 928/474-5182, has the basics for $30 s, $35 d ($40 s, $45 d Fri.–Sat.).

$50–100: Driving in from the south, you'll pass **Paysonglo Lodge,** 1005 S. Beeline Hwy., 928/474-2382, 800/772-9766, $62 d ($79 Fri.–Sat.); **Rim Country Inn,** 101 W. Phoenix and S. Beeline Hwy., 928/474-4526, 800/482-5719, $45 d ($69 d Fri.–Sat.); **Trails End Motel,** 811 S. Beeline Hwy., 928/474-2283, $49 d, $59 d ($69 d Fri.–Sat.); **Budget Inn & Suites,** 302 S. Beeline Hwy., 928/474-2201, $44–89 d; and **Holiday Inn Express** 206 S. Beeline Hwy., 928/472-7484, 800/HOLIDAY, $65 d ($99 d Fri.–Sat.). North of downtown, you can stay at the **Inn of Payson,** 801 N. Beeline Hwy., 928/474-3241, 800/247-9477, $59–69 d ($79–89 d Fri.–Sat.). Heading east on Hwy. 260 from the Beeline Highway are two of Payson's top-end places: **Majestic Mountain Inn,** 602 E. Hwy. 260, 928/474-0185, 800/408-2442, $62–99 d ($99–140 d Fri.–Sat.); and **Payson Pueblo Inn,** 809 E. Hwy. 260, 928/474-5241, 800/888-9828, $49–54 d ($98–139 d Fri.–Sat.).

Three little settlements east of Payson near AZ 260 offer places to stay in the pines. **Ye Ole Country Inn** lies 16 miles east and north in Tonto Village, 928/478-4426, $49 d ($69 d

Fri.–Sat.). **Kohl's Ranch Lodge,** 17 miles east of Payson, 928/478-4211, 800/331-5645, features very comfortable lodging, an impressive A-frame lobby, restaurant, pool, and horse stables; studios run $105 d ($85 Oct.–April) or $125 d with fireplace ($105 April–Oct.); cabins cost $230–295 ($200–270 Oct.–April). **Christopher Creek Lodge,** 23 miles east of Payson in the resort village of Christopher Creek, 928/478-4300, offers motel rooms at $42 d ($53 d Thurs.–Sat.) and cabins for $90–110 d. Nearby you'll find **Creekside Cabins,** 928/478-4557, with a restaurant, $100 d; and **Grey Hackle Lodge,** 928/478-4392, $60–170 d. **Mountain Meadows Cabins** lie east of Christopher Creek, then two miles east down Colcord Road, 928/478-4415, $90–130 d.

Forest Service Campgrounds

The Payson Ranger District office, 928/474-7900, of the Tonto National Forest provides recreation information on their lands. Reservations for individual sites at Houston Mesa and the horse camp and for all of the district's group areas can be made with National Recreation Reservation Service at 877/444-6777; www .reserveusa.com.

Houston Mesa Campground is about 1.5 miles north of town and open year-round; take AZ 87 north, then turn right 0.2 mile on Houston Mesa Road; the main campground is on the left with coin showers, a half-mile interpretive trail, summer weekend interpretive programs, and a dump station; $12. **Houston Mesa Horse Camp** across the road is just for people with horses; $10. There are also two group reservation areas and a trailhead for Houston Mesa Trail.

Ponderosa Campground lies 12 miles east of Payson on the south side of AZ 260; it's open year-round with water and a dump station; sites cost $11; there's also a group campground across the highway. **Lower Tonto Creek Campground** is 15 miles east of Payson, then just north on Forest Road 289; it's open with water April–Oct.; $8. **Upper Tonto Creek Campground** is a smaller place one mile farther up Forest Road 289 with the same season and fee.

Horton Picnic Area is beyond; no charge. **Christopher Creek Campground** lies 19 miles east of Payson on the south side of AZ 260; sites have water April–Oct.; $11. **Christopher Creek Picnic Area** (no charge) and a group reservation area are nearby.

East Verde River Complex offers primitive camping in a series of recreation areas that begins about five miles in on Houston Mesa Road/Forest Road 199; none have water or fee. **Flowing Springs Recreation Site,** also part of the East Verde River Complex, is the only one with a toilet; head about five miles north of Payson on AZ 87, then turn right 0.8 mile on Forest Road 272. Many areas of the Tonto National Forest can be used for dispersed camping (no facilities or fee); for example, you can look for a spot off Control and Houston Mesa Rds. below the Rim and off Forest Road 300 atop the Rim.

Oxbow Estates RV Park, three miles south on the Beeline Highway, has both tent and RV camping with showers; 928/474-2042; $20 tent, $24 RV with hookups. **Lamplighter RV Resort** caters to seniors, 3.5 miles east on AZ 260; 928/474-5048; $25 RV with hookups.

Food

Dinner reservations will come in handy on Friday and Saturday at many restaurants. **Mogollon Grille,** 202 W. Main St., 928/474-5501, prepares prime rib, steak, ribs, chicken, fish, and a few pasta and Mexican dishes for dinner, plus a Sunday brunch and light lunches; closed Monday.

Home-style cooking is featured at **Beeline Cafe,** 815 S. Beeline Hwy., 928/474-9960; and **Country Kitchen,** 210 E. Hwy. 260, 928/474-1332; both are open daily for breakfast, lunch, and dinner.

For Italian-American dining, try **Mario's** at 600 E. Hwy. 260, 928/474-5429. Pick up pizza at **R&R Pizza,** 213 E. Hwy. 260 near Safeway, 928/474-6789, closed Sunday; **Pizza Factory,** 238 E. Hwy. 260, 928/474-1895; or **Pizza Hut,** 113 S. Beeline Hwy., 928/474-1100

Sesame Inn, 203 Hwy. 260 (near Safeway), 928/472-6888, serves good Chinese food, including Mandarin, Hunan, and Szechwan styles.

Wok Express, 136 E. Hwy 260 (near Bashas'), 928/474-0688, is a simpler place with Cantonese and Mandarin cuisine.

Dine Mexican at **El Rancho,** 200 S. Beeline Hwy., 928/474-3111; **Chema's,** 430 S. Beeline Hwy., 928/472-6906; or **La Casa Pequeña,** 911 S. Beeline Hwy., 928/474-6329.

Zane Grey Steakhouse & Saloon, 17 miles east of Payson at Kohl's Ranch Resort, serves Western-style breakfasts, lunches, and dinners daily; 928/478-4211. **Christopher Creek Landmark Restaurant & Saloon,** 23 miles east on AZ 260 in Christopher Creek, has a large patio in back overlooking the creek; open daily with American food for breakfast, lunch, and dinner; 928/478-4472.

For groceries visit **Bashas'** on the north side of Hwy. 260 or **Safeway** on the south side of Hwy. 260 near the intersection with the Beeline Highway.

Entertainment and Events

Sawmill Theatres, 201 W. Main St., 928/474-3918, plays current flicks.

Music concerts and art festivals enliven the town during the warmer months; the chamber and newpaper listings tell what's on. Some annual events: The **PRCA Spring Rodeo** rides in May. Pine has an **arts & crafts festival** on Memorial Day weekend. **June Bug Blues Festival** and **Rim Country Classic Car Show** play on the same weekend in early June. **Square Dance Festival** shakes in June. Early in June, **Strawberry Festival,** in the town of Strawberry, makes merry with entertainment and arts and crafts. Pine usually celebrates **July Fourth** on the weekend before, while Payson's entertainment and fireworks take place on the fourth. The world's oldest **Continuous Rodeo** (since 1884), dance, and parade arrive on the third weekend of August. **Rim Country Western Heritage Festival** brings in cowboy poets and Western artisans on Labor Day weekend. Pine also has an **arts & crafts festival** on Labor Day Weekend. **Northern Gila County Fair** in Pine showcases local produce and crafts in mid-September. The **Old-time Fiddlers' Contest** plays on the last weekend of September. **Tonto Apache Tribal Recognition Days,** on the first weekend of October, presents a rodeo, pow wow, carnival, and sports tournaments. **Swiss Village Christmas Lighting** adds a glow on the Friday after Thanksgiving. Pine has their **Tree Lighting** on the first of December.

Recreation

You'll find a swimming pool, tennis courts, ball fields, and picnic grounds in **Rumsey Park** on N. McLane Road; from the junction of Beeline and Hwy. 260, go west on Overland or Longhorn Roads, then turn right a half mile on McLane; 928/474-2774 (Taylor Pool) or 928/474-5242 (Parks & Recreation). **Green Valley Park,** one mile west on Main Street, features a fishing lake, picnic areas, playground, and the Rim Country Museum.

Play golf on the 18-hole **Payson Golf Course,** 1504 W. Country Club; 928/474-2273. Trail rides are offered during summer at **Kohl's Ranch Lodge,** 17 miles east on AZ 260, 928/478-4211; and **OK Corral,** 14 miles north on AZ 87 near Pine, 928/476-4303; www.okcorrals.com. For camping, fishing, and hunting supplies, visit **Wal-Mart** at 400 E. Hwy. 260; 928/474-0029. **Mazatzal Casino** has gambling and a restaurant half a mile south of Payson on the Beeline Highway; 928/474-6044, 800/777-7529.

Information and Services

The **Rim Country Regional Chamber of Commerce** occupies the northwest corner of Beeline Hwy. and Main St. (P.O. Box 1380, Payson, AZ 85547); it's open Mon.–Fri. 8 A.M.–5 P.M. and Sat.–Sun. 10 A.M.–2 P.M.; 928/474-4515, 800/672-9766 (800/6PAYSON); www.rim countrychamber.com.

The **Payson Ranger District** office of the U.S. Forest Service, 928/474-7900, has outdoor recreation information for the surrounding forests, Mogollon Rim, Mazatzals, and other scenic areas; you can purchase books and maps; it's open Mon.–Fri. 7:45 A.M.–4:30 P.M., also some Saturdays in summer; it's one mile east of town (1009 E. Hwy. 260, Payson, AZ 85541); www.fs.fed.us/r3/tonto.

Payson Public Library, at press time, was planning to move to a new location at 328 N.

McLane Rd. in Rumsey Park; 928/474-5242 (town hall). **Leaves of Autumn Books** carries mainly used books at 518 W. Main; 928/474-3654. **Jackalope** has new and used books at 234 E. Hwy. 260; 928/474-7081.

The **post office** is at 100 W. Frontier St.; 928/474-2972. **Payson Regional Medical Center** is at 807 S. Ponderosa St.; 928/474-3222.

Transportation

White Mountain Passenger Lines, 902 N. Beeline Hwy. (Maytag Equip.), 928/474-5450, runs buses south to Mesa and Phoenix and northeast to Heber, Snowflake, and Show Low; services are once daily in each direction Mon.–Sat.; the main office, 928/537-4539, is in Show Low.

VICINITY OF PAYSON

Shoofly Village

A quarter-mile interpretive trail winds through scant ruins of this prehistoric settlement northeast of town. Occupied 1000-1250, it had a stone wall encircling courtyards, plazas, and about 80 rooms. Part of the trail has been paved for easy access. A pleasant picnic area and a trailhead for Horse Camp Loop lie nearby. From AZ 87 on the north edge of Payson, turn northeast three miles on Houston Mesa Road (keep right at the fork about two miles in), then turn right at the sign to a parking area. After turning onto Houston Mesa Road, you'll pass Houston Mesa Campground and Horsecamp in 0.2 mile, then Houston Mesa Trailhead one mile in from AZ 87.

Tonto Natural Bridge State Park

Deposits left by mineral springs have created the world's largest natural travertine bridge—and it's still growing! The springs flow as they have for many thousands of years, making the massive arch even larger and watering lush vegetation. You might not even realize you're standing on top when you arrive—the bridge measures 400 feet in width, 183 feet high, and spans a canyon 150 feet wide. Graceful travertine formations underneath look like those inside a limestone cave. A small waterfall cascades over the top of the arch, forming jewel-like droplets of water that sparkle in the sun and create pretty rainbows.

Visitors can admire both sides of the bridge from viewpoints at the top and from trails in the canyon. Wheelchair users can reach three of the viewpoints. On **Waterfall Trail**, you can descend steps part way down the canyon to a spring-fed waterfall for a close-up look at travertine formations and some caves; the trail is only 400 feet long one-way. **Gowan Loop Trail** drops 200 feet in elevation to an observation platform at the lower end of the bridge, where you can admire the waterfall and explore the inside of the bridge's vast tunnel-like interior; the trail continues across Pine Creek and ascends the far canyon wall, then loops back across the top of the bridge in about half a mile. Adventurous hikers can rock scramble over huge boulders on a route through the bridge; most easily done in the upstream direction between Gowan Loop and Pine Creek Trails; high water may occasionally prevent access. **Pine Creek Trail** descends to the creek above the bridge; markers along the boulder-strewn creekbed show the way down to the bridge; rim to bridge is about half a mile. For safety and preservation of the environment, park staff ask that you don't enter caves, climb on moss, cliffs, or under the waterfall; there's no swimming or wading inside the bridge. Pets cannot go on the trails, but they're okay on a leash atop the bridge.

Picnic areas in this pretty forested valley make fine spots for lunch; groups can reserve day-use ramadas. There's no camping and there are no rooms for rent, though groups may be able to reserve the historic lodge for overnights. Staff offer interpretive programs and lodge tours some days; call for the schedule. A gift shop in the lodge sells books on the region. The park is open daily 8 A.M.–7 P.M. from Memorial to Labor Day weekends, 9 A.M.–5 P.M. Nov.–March, and 8 A.M.–6 P.M. the rest of the year; closed Christmas; admission is $5/vehicle (up to four persons), $1 each additional person, walk-ins, or cyclists; 928/476-4202. From Payson, go 11 miles north on AZ 87, then turn left three miles on a paved road at the sign. The last 1.5 miles are steep and winding; it's recommended that vehicles and trailers over 16 feet use the parking lot at the top of the grade.

Pine

This small community lies 15 miles north of Payson. **Pine-Strawberry Museum** has good pioneer exhibits in a former LDS church (1917) beside the Community Center; open Sun. 1–4 P.M. and Mon.–Sat. 10 A.M.–4 P.M. from May 15 to Oct. 15, then Mon.–Sat. 10 A.M.–2 P.M. the rest of the year. **Timberline Restaurant & Motel,** 3618 N. Hwy. 87, 928/476-0988, serves up American meals daily for breakfast, lunch and dinner; the rooms start at $45 d. The **Alden Manor Inn,** 3270 N. Hwy. 87 (on the south side of Pine), 928/476-2150, serves breakfast Fri.–Sun., then lunch and dinner daily; cabins cost $100 d and $150 d. The **post office** lies across from the museum. Pine has a few trailer parks that may accept overnighters. Pine-Strawberry Arts & Crafts Guild sponsors **arts and craft festivals** in Pine on the weekends of Memorial Day, July Fourth, and Labor Day.

Strawberry

This tiny village sits just below the Mogollon Rim, 19 miles north of Payson. Wild strawberries used to grow here but nowadays they're hard to find. Turn west 1.5 miles on Fossil Springs Road at Strawberry Lodge to see Arizona's oldest **schoolhouse**. Pioneers built the one-room log structure in 1885. You can view the restored interior and photos of pioneers. Open summer weekends and holidays 10 A.M.–4 P.M., other times by appointment; ask at Strawberry Lodge. The road continues west and turns to dirt, descends a long grade to Fossil Creek (good hiking), passes an access road to Childs on the Verde River, then joins AZ 260 near Camp Verde. This very scenic drive can be hard going for cars; see **Beaver Creek Ranger District.** A much easier route to Camp Verde involves going north eight miles on AZ 87 up onto the Rim, then turning left on the paved General Crook Trail (AZ 260).

Rooms in **Strawberry Lodge** cost $45–57 d; the more expensive ones feature fireplaces and balconies; a restaurant serves breakfast, lunch, and dinner daily but lacks a smoke-free area;

928/476-3333. **Strawberry Hill Cabins** run $85 d ($115 d Fri.–Sat.); 928/476-4252. **Strawberry Motel** rooms are $49–59 d room, $99 d suite; check in at Strawberry Market; 928/476-3040. **Windmill Corner Inn** charges $58 d ($88 d Fri.–Sat.); 928/476-3064. **Giuseppe's** serves Italian cuisine, steaks, seafood, and pizza; it's open Fri.–Sun. for lunch and Wed.–Sun. for dinner; 928/476-3355. The **Strawberry Festival** in June has entertainment, crafts, and strawberries.

Tonto Creek Hatchery

Rainbow, brook, and sometimes Apache trout grow up at this hatchery just below the Mogollon Rim. Visitors can take the interpretive walk, learn about the life history of trout, peer into the incubator and production rooms, and view fingerlings and catchable trout in outdoor raceways. A show pond has large fish, which you can feed. Trout in the raceways shouldn't be touched or fed because of the danger of spreading diseases. Open daily 8 A.M.–4 P.M.; 928/478-4200. From Payson, head east 17 miles on AZ 260 to Kohl's Ranch Lodge, then turn north four miles on Forest Road 289 at the sign.

Highline National Recreation Area

Highline Trail weaves in and out for 51 miles beneath the cliffs of the Mogollon Rim. Settlers built the trail in the 1800s to link their ranches and homesteads. Today hikers, horseback riders, and mountain bicyclists use the many interconnecting trails for a wide variety of journeys.

Pine Trailhead, at the west end, lies 15 miles north of Payson just off AZ 87. Two-Sixty Trailhead marks the east end, 27 miles east of Payson just off AZ 260. You can also reach the Highline from four other trailheads, from trails descending the Mogollon Rim above, and from valleys below. You can see effects of the Dude Fire of July 1990 on the central section. The Tonto National Forest *Highline Trails Guide* offers a map and brief trail descriptions; pick it up at Forest Service offices or the Payson Chamber of Commerce.

Mazatzal Wilderness

Native Americans knew this vast country of desert and mountains as Mazatzal, "Land of the Deer." The name still fits, as only scattered ruins tell of the tribes, pioneers, and miners who tried to live here. The wilderness covers over 252,500 acres beginning eight miles west of Payson and extending 30 miles south. Climate zones range from the Lower Sonoran Desert, with saguaro and palo verde (2,200-4,000 feet); up through the dry grasslands, oaks, pinyons, and junipers of the Upper Sonoran Desert (4,000-7,000 feet); to the Transition Zone, with ponderosa pines and a few pockets of firs on the upper slopes (7,000-7,900 feet). You might meet deer, javelina, black bear, or even a mountain lion. Hikers in this big country should be self-sufficient with maps, compass, and water; you can't rely on springs and streams in the summer.

Spring and autumn are the best times for a visit; summer is okay if you're prepared for possible 100°F-plus temperatures and late-season thunderstorms; winter can be fine at the lower elevations, but severe snowstorms sometimes hit the high country. No permits are needed to hike or ride horseback in the wilderness.

Of the 14 trailheads, the Barnhardt is the most popular. From just south of the Rye Creek bridge, 14.5 miles south of Payson on AZ 87, go west 4.8 miles on Forest Road 419 to the end of the road. You then have a choice of three trails. A popular 19-mile, two-day backpack loop encircles Mazatzal Peak via the **Barnhardt, Mazatzal Divide,** and **Y Bar Basin** (Shake Tree) Trails. For detailed hiking information see the Forest Service people at Payson, 928/474-7900, or Phoenix, 602/225-5200. They'll provide free hiking trail literature and sell you a Mazatzal Wilderness topo map.

YOUNG

Remote and off the tourist track, Young is one of Arizona's last cow towns. To get here you must drive largely unpaved roads. From the Mogollon Rim in the north, take AZ 260 to near Milepost 284, about 33 miles east of Payson, then turn south 24 miles on Forest Road 512; the first 20 miles are dirt road. From the south near Roosevelt Lake, take AZ 88 from Roosevelt or

Globe to the junction with AZ 288, then turn north 47 miles; the last 34 miles are dirt. The roads to Young are best avoided after winter snows or heavy rains.

In the late 1800s one of Arizona's bloodiest and most savage feuds took place in Pleasant Valley, between Young and the Rim. The trouble started when the Tewksbury clan gave protection to a band of sheep brought into the area in 1887. Cattle owners led by the Graham clan couldn't stand "woollies" and attacked, killing a Navajo sheepherder and destroying or driving away the animals. The Tewksburys retaliated, and the war was on. The fighting didn't end until every Graham had been killed. All efforts by the law to restore order failed; at least 30 people died during five years of terror. History buffs can visit many of the battle sites near Young. The cemetery near Young Baptist Church, a half mile east of Moon's Saloon, contains marked graves belonging to five members of the Graham clan: Harry Middleton, Al Rose, Charles Blevin, William Graham, and John Graham.

Historians still debate details of the feud. Accounts of the tragedy are given in *A Little War of Our Own* by Don Dedera, *Arizona's Dark and Bloody Ground* by Earle Forrest, and *Globe, Arizona* by Clara Woody and Milton Schwartz. Zane Grey dramatized the events in his novel *To the Last Man.* Grey obtained his material during hunting trips in Pleasant Valley.

Today, a very independent breed of people inhabits Young. These folks, many retired, don't like authority or development. Even the Forest Service—Young's largest employer—represents too much government for some of them.

On the Road in Young

Young social life revolves around the **Antlers Cafe** (closed Mon.), 928/462-3265, which serves inexpensive breakfasts, lunches, and dinners daily, though don't count on a nonsmoking section. **Sugar Babes,** closed Tues.–Wed., serves lunch.

Valley View Cabins, 928/462-3422, offers rentals with kitchens for $35 d. **Pleasant Valley Inn,** 928/462-3593, has fridges and microwaves in the rooms at $55 s, $67 d. **Pleasant Valley Days**

lets loose with a parade, entertainment, equestrian events, and arts and crafts in late July. The **post office** is in the northeastern part of town. **Pleasant Valley Medical Center,** 928/462-3435, provides limited services on some days. There's also a grocery store and gas station in town.

For fishing, hiking, and camping information, contact the Tonto National Forest's **Pleasant Valley Ranger District** office in Young (P.O. Box 450, Young, AZ 85554); www.fs.fed.us/r3/tonto. It's open Mon.–Fri. (and Saturday in summer) 7:45-11:45 A.M. and 12:30–4:30 P.M.; 928/462-4300; a sign marks the turnoff. As there's no visitor center in Young, staff can offer information about the town and surrounding area.

VICINITY OF YOUNG

North of Young

The unfortunate Navajo sheepherder who fell as the first victim of the Pleasant Valley War is buried north of Young. A white cross, pile of stones, and sign mark the spot; from the main road (Forest Road 512), four miles north of Young and 20 miles south of AZ 260, turn west nearly one mile on Forest Road 200.

Alderwood Campground (elev. 5,200 feet; no water or fee) is beside Haigler Creek six miles in on Forest Road 200 from Forest Road 512, then west half a mile on Forest Road 200A. **Haigler Canyon Recreation Site** (elev. 5,250 feet; no water or fee) has camping and fishing (trout April–Aug.); it's nine miles in on Forest Road 200 from Forest Road 512; you can also approach it from the north via AZ 260 and Forest Roads 291 and 200.

Valentine Ridge Campground (elev. 6,600 feet; no water or fee) lies 18 miles north of Young or six miles south of AZ 260 via Forest Road 512, then two miles east on Forest Road 188. **Colcord Ridge Recreation Site** (no water or fee) is just east on Forest Road 33 from Forest Road 512, about three miles south of AZ 260 or 21 miles north of Young. **Airplane Flat Campground** (elev. 6,600 feet; no water or fee) is about four miles farther in on Forest Road 33. **Upper Canyon Creek Recreation Site** (elev. 6,600 feet; no water or fee) and **Canyon Creek Hatchery** lie just below the Rim; follow Forest Road 33 in five miles. The fish hatchery features a self-guided tour, open daily 8 A.M.–4 P.M. Anglers can fish in Canyon Creek for rainbow and brown trout; check local fishing regulations.

Colcord Lookout (elev. 7,513 feet) offers a sweeping panorama of the Young area and the Mogollon Rim; the tower is open about May to October; turn west three miles on Forest Road 291 from Forest Road 512 (opposite the Forest Road 33 turnoff).

South of Young

Groups can contact the Pleasant Valley Ranger District office to reserve **Reynolds Creek Group Site** (elev. 5,200 feet), 19 miles south of Young, for day or overnight use. It's a good base for exploring the Salome and the Sierra Ancha Wilderness Areas and a worthy spot in itself for enjoying the pretty creek and wildlife; there's a fee but no potable water.

Workman Creek Waterfalls plunge 200 feet in a spot south of Young; to get there, go south 21 miles on AZ 288, then turn left 3.2 miles on Forest Road 487 at the sign for "Workman Creek Recreation Area, Sierra Ancha Wilderness"; the turnoff is between Mileposts 284 and 285. A gate 2.6 miles in is closed Dec. 15–March 31. The last quarter mile may be too rough for cars. On the way to the falls, you'll pass primitive campsites at **Creeksite, Cascade,** and **Falls Recreation Sites;** no water or fee. This pretty canyon supports dense stands of Douglas fir and white fir, as well as smaller numbers of Arizona sycamore and the relatively rare Arizona maple.

Forest Road 487 continues 3.7 miles past the falls through pine forests, aspen groves, and meadows to the lookout tower atop Aztec Peak (7,748 feet); you can get here with a high-clearance vehicle, mountain bike, or on foot. The tower, when open, provides great panoramas of the Sierra Anchas, Roosevelt Lake, Four Peaks, the Mazatzals, and many other features of central Arizona. **Abbey's Way Trail #151** also climbs to the top of Aztec Peak (800 feet in two miles one-way); the trailhead is on the left 0.6 mile past the falls. **Parker Creek Trail #160** is on the

right side of the road one mile past the falls; it goes southwest 3.4 miles to AZ 288, dropping 2,100 feet. The **Rim Trail #139** begins a short way down Parker Creek Trail and curves east and north 7.6 miles to Edwards Spring with good views. Most of the hike lies within the Sierra Ancha Wilderness. It makes an easy outing, with only a 500-foot elevation gain. **Coon Creek Trail #254** also branches off Parker Creek Trail for a 4.4-mile, 2,400-foot descent south along Coon Creek to a trailhead at the end of Forest Road 189. **Moody Point Trail #140** begins on the right 2.2 miles past the falls on Forest Road 487; it connects with the Rim Trail and continues east all the way across the Sierra Ancha Wilderness to Cherry Creek (which may be too high to cross when it's in flood) and Forest Road 203; this challenging trail is 8.6 miles long and drops 4,200 feet. You can find many places for dispersed camping along Forest Road 487 above the falls, but only the established recreation areas can be used below the falls.

Hikers can cool off in the **"tubs,"** natural pools in Workman Creek; from the Workman Creek bridge on AZ 288, follow the trail downstream 250 yards.

Rose Creek Campground (elev. 5,400 feet) enjoys a beautiful forest setting beside a creek 23 miles south of Young; no drinking water or fee. The turnoff from AZ 288 is between Mileposts 282 and 283.

Wilderness Areas

The 20,850-acre **Sierra Ancha Wilderness** lies 15 miles south of Young and 36 miles north of Globe. Lack of good roads and rugged terrain discourage most visitors—box canyons and sheer cliffs make travel difficult. Elevations range from 3,200 to 7,800 feet. Spring-fed creeks in the eastern portion of the wilderness have carved several short but deep box canyons, including Pueblo, Cold Springs, and Devil's Chasm. Prehistoric Salado built cliff dwellings in these canyons, then departed.

Forest Road 203 (Cherry Creek Rd.) loops around the east side of the Sierra Anchas, providing views into the spectacular canyons. You need a 4WD vehicle for this trip; the northern part of the road is particularly rough. Allow 3.5 hours for the drive.

Forest Road 487, described above, and other roads off AZ 288 provide access to trailheads in the high country of the west side. For hiking information and a wilderness map, contact the Forest Service in Young, 928/462-4300, or in Phoenix, 602/225-5200.

Salome Wilderness, between Young and Roosevelt Lake, protects 18,530 acres of the Salome and lower Workman Creek watersheds. Perennial waters hold trout and a rich riparian habitat for wildlife. The upper end and the higher slopes (elev. 6,543 feet) support pinyon pine and juniper and some Douglas fir and ponderosa pine; the 5.3-mile **Hell's Hole Trail #284** begins at AZ 288 at the Reynold's Trailhead, 19 miles south of Young, and ends at Hell's Hole on Workman Creek in the upper part of the canyon. The lower end of the wilderness (elev. 2,500 feet) has some saguaro, ocotillo, and chaparral vegetation; the two-mile-long **Jug Trail #61** connects Forest Road 60, north of Roosevelt Lake, with the lower end of Salome Creek.

Hellsgate Wilderness, between Young and Payson, preserves 36,780 acres of the watersheds of Tonto, Haigler, Marsh, and Houston Creeks. Sheer cliffs rising above the confluence of Tonto and Haigler Creeks form Hell's Gate; there's good fishing here but only the most adventurous anglers make it in on the steep, difficult **Hellsgate Trail #37,** which descends into Hell's Gate from both rims. The north trailhead is reached from Payson via AZ 260 and Forest Roads 405A and 893, then it's a six-mile hike to the creeks. Hikers with 4WD vehicles can drive to the south trailhead via Forest Roads 129 and 133; from there it's a 2.5-mile hike in. The trail can get very hot in summer; carry plenty of water.

Sedona and the Red Rock Country

Drifting clouds, towering pinnacles, and sheer canyon walls create a magical setting for the Red Rock Country surrounding Sedona. Monoliths of vivid red sandstone stand as if cast adrift from the Mogollon Rim. Oak Creek, which carved much of this landscape, glides gracefully through Sedona.

Early Days to Modern Times
The prehistoric Hohokam and Sinagua tribes tilled the soil along Oak Creek for corn, beans, and squash long before white people came. American settlers first arrived in the late 1800s to farm and run cattle in the valley. The town dates from 1902, when Theodore Schnebly opened a post office, naming it "Sedona" for his wife. In the same year, Schnebly also built a wagon road up the rim to haul vegetables and fruit to Flagstaff and lumber back to Sedona; the journey took about 11 hours each way.

From a tiny agricultural community 40 years ago, Sedona has developed into a major art center, resort, and spiritual retreat. The present area population of more than 16,000

© BILL WEIR

Loy Canyon Trail

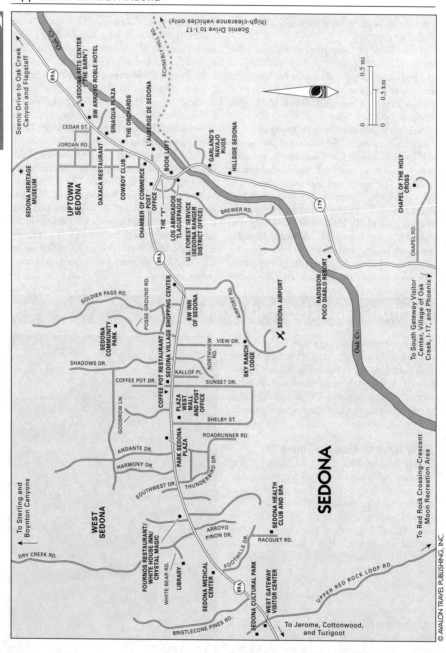

Scenic Drive to I-17
(high-clearance vehicles only)

Scenic Drive to Oak Creek
Canyon and Flagstaff

SEDONA ARTS CENTER
("THE BARN")

BW ARROYO ROBLE HOTEL

SINAGUA PLAZA

THE ORCHARDS

L'AUBERGE DE SEDONA

CEDAR ST.

JORDAN RD.

SCHNEBLY HILL RD.

GARLAND'S
NAVAJO
RUGS

HILLSIDE SEDONA

SEDONA HERITAGE MUSEUM

OAXACA RESTAURANT

COWBOY CLUB

BOOK LOFT

UPTOWN
SEDONA

CHAMBER OF COMMERCE
POST OFFICE

THE "Y"

LOS ABRIGADOS
TLAQUEPAQUE

U.S. FOREST SERVICE
(SEDONA RANGER
DISTRICT OFFICE)

BREWER RD.

179

CHAPEL OF THE HOLY
CROSS

CHAPEL RD.

SOLDIER PASS RD.

POSSE GROUND RD.

89A

SEDONA VILLAGE SHOPPING CENTER

BW INN
OF SEDONA

AIRPORT RD.

SEDONA AIRPORT

RADISSON
POCO DIABLO RESORT

To South Gateway Visitor
Center, Village of Oak
Creek, I-17, and Phoenix

SEDONA
COMMUNITY
PARK

SHADOWS DR.

COFFEE POT DR.

COFFEE POT RESTAURANT

NORTHVIEW
RD.

VIEW DR.

SKY RANCH
LODGE

Oak Cr.

To Sterling and
Boynton Canyons

GOODROW LN.

PLAZA
WEST
MALL
AND POST
OFFICE

KALLOF PL.

SUNSET DR.

SHELBY ST.

PARK SEDONA
PLAZA

ROADRUNNER RD.

ANDANTE DR.

HARMONY DR.

SEDONA

SOUTHWEST DR.

THUNDERBIRD DR.

WEST
SEDONA

SEDONA HEALTH
CLUB AND SPA

FOURNOS RESTAURANT/
WHITE HOUSE INN/
CRYSTAL MAGIC

ARROYO
PINON DR.

RACQUET RD.

DRY CREEK RD.

WHITE BEAR RD.

LIBRARY

FOOTHILLS DR.

To Red Rock Crossing-Crescent
Moon Recreation Area

SEDONA MEDICAL
CENTER

SEDONA CULTURAL PARK

WEST GATEWAY
VISITOR CENTER

89A

UPPER RED ROCK LOOP RD.

BRISTLECONE PINES RD.

To Jerome, Cottonwood,
and Tuzigoot

0   0.5 mi

0   0.5 km

© AVALON TRAVEL PUBLISHING, INC.

includes many retired people, artists, and nature lovers.

Planning a Visit

Sunny skies and pleasant temperatures prevail here. At an elevation of 4,500 feet, Sedona avoids the extremes of both low desert and high mountains. The community centers around the AZ 89A-AZ 179 junction, referred to as the "Y," 28 miles south of Flagstaff. Uptown Sedona lies north of the Y on AZ 89A, which continues on through Oak Creek Canyon. West Sedona stretches out west of the Y along AZ 89A, which goes to Cottonwood. AZ 179 branches off at the Y and goes south to the Village of Oak Creek and on to I-17.

In addition to the surrounding scenery, Sedona's attractions include outstanding art galleries, elegant restaurants, and luxurious resorts. Fountains and tree-shaded courtyards grace **Tlaquepaque** (t'lah-kay-PAH-kay), a recreated village famed for its art galleries, crafts shops, and fine restaurants. It's named for a suburb of Guadalajara, Mexico.

Hikers head for wilderness areas surrounding Sedona to explore the West Fork of Oak Creek, Wilson Mountain, Munds Mountain, Pumphouse Wash, and hundreds of other areas.

Vortexes

New age people believe strong spiritual energies concentrate here in vortexes, or psychic-energy points. In the early 1980s, Page Bryant and her otherworldly guide, Albion, identified seven vortexes in the Sedona area. Prominent among them are Bell Rock and Airport Mesa, emanating "electric energy" to invigorate and inspire visitors, and Red Rock Crossing/Cathedral Rock, bearer of calming "magnetic energy." You may see altars or medicine wheels made of rocks at the sites.

If you'd like to learn more about these energy fields, drop by some of the town's many spiritual and New Age bookstores and gift shops. Some tour operators offer vortex experiences.

SIGHTS

Sedona Arts Center

Galleries showcase both emerging and well-

known artists on the north edge of town at N. Hwy. 89A and Art Barn Road, 928/282-3865; www.sedonaartscenter.com. Exhibits are open daily 10 A.M.–4 P.M. and are free. Shows change every one or two months. A gift shop sells work by local artists. The Center also offers classes and workshops.

Sedona Heritage Museum

Exhibits in the house and apple-packing shed of the 1930 Jordan farmstead take you back to the pioneering days of Sedona. The Cowboy Room showcases early ranchers and their gear. Movie-makers came to the Red Rock Country as early as the 1920s, and you'll learn about their films in the Movie History Room. Other sections of the museum illustrate work of the U.S. Forest Service and home life. An apple-sorting machine, which still runs, old vehicles, and other equipment lie in the nearby shed. Call 928/282-7038 for hours, but the museum is normally open daily 11 A.M. to 3 P.M., when the last tour begins; $3 age 12 and up; www.sedonamuseum.org. To get to the museum, take Jordan Road north 0.6 mile from AZ 89A, then turn left into parking after crossing a bridge. A short trail leads to the buildings; handicapped people have parking next to the museum.

Airport Saddle Loop Trails

Airport Mesa, on of Sedona's vortex sites, offers great views and some short hikes right in the middle of Sedona. These short trails begin from the trailhead on the left, halfway up Airport Road. A 600-foot trail to Overlook Point climbs 105 feet. It connects with Coconino and Yavapai loops, which total 0.7 mile for all the segments. A map at the trailhead shows the trails. From the Y, head west one mile on Hwy. 89A, then turn left a half mile up Airport Road. If you continue by road to the top of Airport Mesa, there's a fine viewpoint on the right.

Chapel of the Holy Cross

The chapel's unusual architecture incorporates a giant cross and presents a striking sight atop a sandstone ridge. There's a commanding view

NORTH-CENTRAL

VICINITY OF SEDONA

To Flagstaff (Woody Mtn. Rd.)

To Flagstaff

231

89A

PUMPHOUSE WASH

OAK CREEK VISTA

PUMPHOUSE WASH BRIDGE

West Fork Of Oak Creek Hike

PINE FLAT CAMPGROUND

Canyon

CALL OF THE CANYON PARKING AREA

CAVE SPRINGS CAMPGROUND

17

East Pocket Knob (7,196 ft.)

East Pocket Trail

Oak Creek

BOOTLEGGER CAMPGROUND

BANJO BILL PICNIC AREA

Red Rock Secret Mountain Wilderness

BEAR SIGN CANYON

HALFWAY PICNIC AREA

SLIDE ROCK STATE PARK

Secret Canyon Trail

VULTEE ARCH

Vultee Arch Trail

Sterling Pass Trail

MANZANITA CAMPGROUND

MUNDS PARK INTERCHANGE

Sterling Canyon

N. Wilson Mtn. Trail

ENCINOCO PICNIC AREA

Long Canyon

Wilson Mtn. (6,960 ft.)

Boynton Canyon

Devil's Bridge Trail

INDIAN GARDENS

EXIT 320

RAINBOW TROUT FARM

Wilson Mtn. Trail

152C

152

DEVIL'S BRIDGE

SCHNEBLY HILL VISTA

HILL ROAD

To Palatki, Honanki, Loy Canyon, and Sycamore Pass

DRY CREEK ROAD

Capitol Butte (6,354 ft.)

GRASSHOPPER POINT

SCHNEBLY (HIGH-CLEARANCE VEHICLES ONLY)

MIDGLEY BRIDGE

WEST SEDONA

SEDONA

To Phoenix

153 (CLOSED IN WINTER)

To Cornville and Cottonwood

89A

216

SEDONA AIRPORT

Munds

Munds Mountain (6,825 ft.)

Mountain

Wilderness

RED ROCK LOOP ROAD

Oak Creek

CHAPEL OF THE HOLY CROSS

RED ROCK CROSSING-CRESCENT MOON RECREATION AREA

179

TRAILHEAD

0   3 mi

RED ROCK STATE PARK

BELL ROCK PATHWAY

0   3 km

© AVALON TRAVEL PUBLISHING, INC.

© BILL WEIR

Sedona on a Red Rock Biplane tour

south toward Bell Rock. A gift shop is downstairs. You're welcome to visit daily 9 A.M.–5 P.M.; donations welcome. Drive three miles south on AZ 179 from AZ 89A, then turn left three-quarters of a mile on Chapel Road.

ACCOMMODATIONS

Confirm your reservations if coming to Sedona for the weekend during the March–Nov. peak season, when the popular places can fill up fast. Rates listed here apply to the main season, though prices can go higher on holidays and lower in the heat of summer. Categories are based on weekend double occupancy. Prices drop 10 percent or so in winter. Travelers on a low budget may wish to check prices in the Camp Verde and Cottonwood areas to the south and Flagstaff to the north.

Sedona-Oak Creek Chamber of Commerce, 928/282-7722, can supply up-to-date information about places to stay. Rooms can be booked through **Sedona Central Reservations,** 928/282-

1518, 800/445-4128; or **Outwest Tours,** 928/649-9424; www.toursoutwest.com.

Bed and Breakfasts

A Touch of Sedona Bed and Breakfast in uptown Sedona at 595 Jordan Rd., 928/282-6462, 800/600-6462, offers rooms, one with a fireplace, for $109–159 d; www.touchsedona.com. **Apple Orchard Inn,** 656 Jordan Rd., 928/282-5328, 800/663-6968, has a different Old West theme for each room. Some rooms have fireplaces and most have patios and jetted tubs; $135–230 d; www.appleorchardbb.com.

Casa Sedona, in west Sedona at 55 Hozoni Dr., 928/282-2938, 800/525-3756, features rooms with a fireplace; most have a hot tub. Another shared hot tub is out in the garden. Rates run $175–255 d; www.casasedona.com. Also in west Sedona, **Lantern Light Inn Bed & Breakfast,** 3085 W. Hwy. 89A, 928/282-3419, 877/275-4973, offers rooms with an elegant country French decor; $115–325 d; www.lanternlightinn.com.

A Territorial House Traditional Southwest Bed and Breakfast, in west Sedona at 65 Piki Dr., 928/204-2737, 800/801-2737, offers Western hospitality with a common room, hot tub, bicycles, and video library. Rooms run $115–185 d; the two-bedroom suite is $250 d; www.territorialhousebb.com. **Boots & Saddles Bed & Breakfast,** in west Sedona at 2900 Hopi Dr., 928/282-1944, 800/201-1944, offers many rooms with a fireplace, hot tub, and patio or balcony; $135–225 d; www.sedona-bed-breakfast.com. **Stoneflower Bed & Breakfast,** 90 Chavez Ranch Rd., 928/282-2977, 800/338-2334, has a scenic setting near Red Rock Crossing and an outdoor Jacuzzi; $95 d; www.stoneflower.com.

Almost a mile from the Y junction, **The Inn on Oak Creek,** 556 Hwy. 179, 928/282-7896, 800/499-7896, offers rooms with fireplaces and whirlpool tubs for $170–260 d; some rooms have private decks overlooking Oak Creek; www.sedona-inn.com. Farther south in the Village of Oak Creek, **The Penrose B&B,** 250 Red Rock Butte Dr., 928/284-3030, 888/678-3030, has great views of the Red Rock Country from the rooms, each of which has a porch or balcony; $140–190; www.thepenrose.com. **The Graham Bed & Breakfast Inn,** 150 Canyon Circle Dr. in the Village of Oak Creek, 928/284-1425, 800/228-1425, offers standard rooms, most with fireplaces and all with hot tub tubs for $169–569 d, plus casitas at $389–439 d; guests have use of a pool, hot tub, and bicycles; www.sedonasfinest.com. **Canyon Villa Bed and Breakfast Inn,** 125 Canyon Circle Dr. in the Village of Oak Creek, 928/284-1226, 800/453-1166, has a pool, and some rooms have a fireplace; $160–279 d; www.canyonvilla.com. Many other bed and breakfasts can be found in the Sedona area; contact the chamber of commerce for a full listing.

Hostel Sedona

This small place has dorm beds ($15) and couple's rooms ($30 s, $35 d), along with a kitchen and common room, tucked in a lane near the Y; you'll need to call ahead for availability, 928/282-2772. To get there, turn south on Brewer Road, then left on Soldiers Wash Drive just after Ranger Road.

Motels and Inns $50–100

Star Motel, in uptown Sedona at 295 Jordan Rd., 928/282-3641, offers rooms and two kitchenettes; $45 d ($55 d Fri.–Sat.). **Iris Garden Inn,** 390 Jordan Rd., 928/282-2552, 800/321-8988, has a garden, patio, and hot tub; rooms are $59–125 d ($74–125 d Fri.–Sat.), and a cabin goes for $90 d. **A Touch of the Southwest Motel & Suites,** 410 Jordan Rd., 928/282-4747, 800/309-7883, offers mostly suites with kitchens; $70–135 d. **Rose Tree Inn,** 376 Cedar St., 928/282-2065, 888/282-2065, includes some kitchens, some fireplaces, video and book libraries, VCRs, and a hot tub; $85–135 d. **La Vista Motel,** on the north end of town at 500 N. Hwy. 89A, 928/282-7301, 800/896-7301, has some kitchenettes; $49 d ($59 d Fri.–Sat.).

Sedona Motel, 218 Hwy. 179, 928/282-7187, is one block south of AZ 89A; $64–74 d ($74–95 d Fri.–Sat.). A half mile south from Hwy. 89A, **Comfort Inn,** 725 Hwy. 179, 928/282-3132, 800/228-5150, offers a pool and hot tub; $75–85 d ($85–99 d Fri.–Sat.). **King's Ransom Quality Inn,** 771 Hwy. 179 (0.7 mile south from Hwy. 89A), 928/282-7151, 800/846-6164, has a restaurant, pool, and hot tub; $69–119 d ($69–159 d Fri.–Sat.).

Holiday Inn Express, 6176 Hwy. 179, 928/284-0711, 800/465-4329, has a pool and hot tub in the Village of Oak Creek; rooms run $69–109 d ($89–159 d Fri.–Sat.), suites are $98–119 d ($119–159 d Fri.–Sat.). **Desert Quail Inn,** in the Village of Oak Creek at 6626 Hwy. 179, 928/284-1433, 800/385-0927, offers a pool; some rooms have fireplaces for $69–160 d.

Cedars Resort on Oak Creek, 20 W. Hwy. 89A, 928/282-7010, 800/874-2072, has a pool, hot tub, and creek access; the more expensive rooms have views, $76–109 d ($88–119 d Fri.–Sat.). **Sky Ranch Lodge,** atop Airport Mesa on Airport Rd., 928/282-6400, 888/708-6400, offers a pool and some views, kitchenettes, and fireplaces; $75–179 d rooms, $179 d cottages.

Hampton Inn, 1800 W. Hwy. 89A, 928/282-4700, 800/426-7866, provides a pool, hot tub, microwaves, and refrigerators; $89–149 d. ($59–89 d Dec.–Feb.). **Sugar Loaf Lodge,** 1870 W. Hwy. 89A, 928/282-9451, 877/282-0632, has a pool and hot tub along with some of the lowest rates in town; $45 d ($55 d Fri.–Sat.). **Super 8 Motel,** 2545 W. Hwy. 89A, 928/282-1533, 800/858-7245, includes a restaurant and pool; $79 d ($86 d Fri.–Sat.). **White House Inn,** 2986 W. Hwy. 89A, 928/282-6680, is low priced and has some kitchenettes; $42 s, $46 d ($52 s, $58 d Fri.–Sat.). **Days Inn,** 2991 W. Hwy. 89A, 928/282-9166, 800/329-7466, offers a pool and hot tub; rooms are $66–85 ($75–120 d Fri.–Sat.), suites run $75–99 d ($99–139 d Fri.–Sat.).

Lo Lo Mai Springs, 928/634-4700, has cabins—all with kitchens—along Oak Creek southwest of town. The 26-acre grounds have shade trees, a pool, hot tub, and volleyball and basketball courts; $50 d and up; www.lolomai.com. Head west 10 miles on Hwy. 89A, turn left on Page Springs Road, then left at the sign.

Hotels $100–150

Los Abrigados Lodge, 280 N. Hwy. 89A, 928/282-7125, 800/542-8484, has a pool and some fireplaces. Standard rooms go for $109 d, deluxe studios with a view and fireplace are $129 d, and suites run $149 d. The lodge is managed by, but is in a different location from, Los Abrigados resort off Hwy. 179.

Guests of **Best Western Arroyo Roble Hotel,** 400 N. Hwy. 89A, 928/282-4001, 800/773-3662, have the use of its health club with indoor and outdoor pools and hot tubs, a sauna, exercise room, and tennis; $109–179 d hotel rooms, $250–299 d creekside villas.

Bell Rock Inn & Suites in the Village of Oak Creek at 6246 Hwy. 179, 928/282-4161, 800/881-7625, features two pools, two hot tubs, a restaurant, and a sports lounge; $100 d rooms, $140 d studio suites. Also in the Village of Oak Creek, **Kokopelli Inn,** 6465 Hwy. 179, 928/284-1100, 888/733-5656, has a pool, $99 d ($130 d Fri.–Sat.).

Best Western Inn of Sedona, 1200 W. Hwy. 89A, opposite the Airport Road turnoff, 928/282-3072, 800/292-6344, offers terraced rooms—most with views—along with a pool and hot tub; $110–135 d ($135–155 d with fireplace). **Southwest Inn at Sedona,** 3250 W. Hwy. 89A, 928/282-3344, 800/483-7422, features fireplaces, a pool, hot tub, and concierge services; $139–189 d rooms, $219–239 d suites.

Resorts in Sedona

The French country inn **L'Auberge de Sedona,** 301 L'Auberge Lane (off N. Hwy. 89A, one-quarter mile north of the Y), 928/282-1661, 800/272-6777, provides a romantic getaway in a wooded setting beside Oak Creek. You have a choice of cottages ($330–430 d), lodge rooms and suites ($240–295 d), and, on the hill, the Orchards rooms and suites ($185–250 d); www.lauberge.com. Guests have a pool and hot tub. The three dining-room options include L'Auberge Restaurant, which serves some of the finest food in Arizona.

Los Abrigados, 160 Portal Lane next to Tlaquepaque (turn south one block on Hwy. 179 from the Y), 928/282-1777, 800/521-3131, offers exercise equipment, a sauna, pools, whirlpools, tennis courts, 18-hole miniature golf, and the Sedona Spa, which provides treatment and fitness programs; www.ilxresorts.com. The resort's restaurants serve grilled and Italian food. Rates run $225–395 d for suites and $775 or $1,500 for a two-bedroom house.

Radisson Poco Diablo Resort ("Little Devil"), near Oak Creek (from the Y, head two miles south on Hwy. 179), 928/282-7333, 800/333-3333, features a nine-hole executive golf course, tennis center, fitness center, pools, hot tubs, and a restaurant; www.radisson.com/sedonaaz. Kids are welcome, too. Rooms, some with fireplaces and whirlpools, range $99–299 d.

Resorts Northwest of Sedona

The **Enchantment Resort,** 928/282-2900, 800/826-4180, lies in a truly enchanting setting at the mouth of Boynton Canyon. Guests can take advantage of the fitness center, pools, tennis courts, children's camp, and restaurants—all amid splendid canyon scenery. The Southwestern-style rooms, suites, and casitas all have private decks;

suites and casitas also have fireplaces and kitchens. Rates run $195–745 d; you can choose from several packages; www.enchantment resort.com. A destination spa, Mii amo, on the resort grounds provides many types of therapies and activities along with rooms, suites, and a restaurant; its Native American name means "journey" or "passage." From the Y, head west 3.1 miles on W. Hwy. 89A, then turn right five miles on Dry Creek Road, following signs on paved roads.

Resorts in Oak Creek Canyon

Resorts nestled along Oak Creek north of town feature spectacular surroundings as well as natural swimming holes in summer. Distances given are from the north edge of Sedona.

Red Rock Lodge, just north of town at 901 N. Hwy. 89A, 928/282-3591, has a fireplace or hot tub in some rooms; $49–175 d; a two-bedroom house costs $175.

Briar Patch Inn, 2.6 miles north at 3190 N. Hwy. 89A, 928/282-2342, 888/809-3030, features cabins, some with kitchens, in a natural environment (no phones); $159–295 d; www .briarpatchinn.com.

Oak Creek Terrace Resort, four miles north at 4548 N. Hwy. 89A, 928/282-3562, 800/224-2229, has motel rooms, bungalows, and a cabin. Some units include kitchenettes, fireplaces, or hot tubs; rates run $72–210 d; www.oakcreek terrace.com.

Slide Rock Lodge, 928/282-3531, lies six miles north at 6401 N. Hwy. 89A and only half a mile from Slide Rock State Park. Rooms, some with fireplaces, are $69–99 d; www.sliderock lodge.com.

Garland's Oak Creek Lodge, 7.7 miles north at 8067 N. Hwy. 89A, 928/282-3343, offers log cabins, some with fireplaces. Rates of $178–208 d (two-night minimum), include breakfast, afternoon tea, and dinner; www.gar landslodge.com. The lodge closes mid-November to late March or early April.

Junipine Resort, eight miles north at 8351 N. Hwy. 89A, 928/282-3375, 800/742-7463, features a kitchen and two fireplaces in each unit; some also have hot tubs. The resort's Knotty Pine Cafe serves Southwestern and continental cuisine. Rates are $170–310 d ($210–345 d Fri.–Sat.), depending on your choice of one or two bedrooms, hot tub, and view; www.junipine.com.

Forest Houses Resort, 8.9 miles north at 9275 N. Hwy. 89A, 928/282-2999, offers houses, each with a kitchen and either a fireplace or wood-burning stove, but no TVs. Rates run $80–140 d; there's a four-night minimum stay in summer, two nights other times, and it's closed January 1 to mid-March.

Don Hoel's Cabins lies 9.1 miles north at 9440 N. Hwy. 89A, 928/282-3560, 800/292-4635. Some of the rustic cabins—no two alike—have kitchens and all are non-smoking; rates are $90–185 d; www.hoels.com. Hoel's Indian Shop, across the highway and north a bit, offers Native American work.

Forest Service Campgrounds

You'll find the prettiest places in Oak Creek Canyon off AZ 89A. You can make reservations for some sites at Cave Springs and Pine Flat at 877/444-6777, www.reserveusa.com. Otherwise you'll need to arrive by Friday morning or even Thursday to find a weekend spot at any of the campgrounds. All have a $15 fee, plus $7 for a second vehicle. None provide hookups, but Cave Springs offers coin showers. Trailers and large RVs (up to 36 feet) should head for Cave Springs or Pine Flat Campgrounds.

Manzanita Campground, 5.6 miles north of Sedona on the right, is open year-round and is often the first to fill up. **Bootlegger Campground,** 8.4 miles north of town on the left, is small—only ten sites—and lacks drinking water, but some people prefer it; it closes Nov. to mid-April. **Cave Springs Campground,** 11.1 miles north, lies west across the creek and has the most secluded setting; it also closes Nov. to mid-April. **Pine Flat Campground,** one mile farther, has loops on both sides of the highway; it closes mid-Nov. to March.

Chavez Group Campground lies at the south edge of town off AZ 179, just beyond Radisson Poco Diablo Resort. Sites are available by reservation only at 877/444-6777, www.re serveusa.com.

Oak Creek Canyon and much of the Red Rock Country are restricted to established campground use. Backpackers can camp in wilderness areas if they go at least one mile in from the boundary. The Forest Service in Sedona, 928/282-4119, can advise on both established and dispersed camping; www.fs.fed.us/r3/coconino.

RV Parks

Hawkeye RV Park, 40 Art Barn Rd. in uptown Sedona, 928/282-2222, offers year-round sites with showers, laundry, and access to Oak Creek for tenters ($17) and RVers ($22.50 w/water & elect., $27.50 full hookups); the campground may close soon, so it's a good idea to call ahead. The other RV parks in town stay open year-round, but don't accept tents. **Rancho Sedona RV Park,** 928/282-7255, 888/641-4261, offers shaded sites with showers and laundry along Oak Creek. Rates run $27 for electricity and water, $32.50 with full hookups, $35 for the adult quiet area, and $52 for full-service sites close to the creek. The centrally located park is a half mile south on Hwy. 179 from Hwy. 89A, left on Schnebly Hill Road, then left on Bear Wallow Lane.

Lo Lo Mai Springs, 928/634-4700, has tent sites ($20 s, $25 d), RV sites ($28), and cabins ($50 d and up) along Oak Creek southwest of town. The 26-acre grounds have shade trees, showers, a pool, hot tub, and volleyball and basketball courts. To get there, head west 10 miles on Hwy. 89A, turn left on Page Springs Road, then left at the sign; www.lolomai.com.

The nearby Verde Valley offers additional places to camp year-round; see the Camp Verde and Cottonwood listings.

FOOD
Resort Dining: American and Continental

You can enjoy some of Arizona's finest dining in Sedona. Reservations are recommended at the more expensive places. Price ranges refer to dinner entrees (per person); lunches usually cost less.

L'Auberge de Sedona, 301 L'Auberge Lane (off N. Hwy. 89A, one quarter mile north of the

Y), 928/282-1667, prepares French cuisine in an elegant setting. Open daily for breakfast (brunch on Sunday, $30–35), lunch ($16–21 entrée or $30 prix fixe), and dinner ($32–39 entrée or $65 prix fixe).

The Orchards Bar & Grill at L'Auberge de Sedona, 254 N. Hwy. 89A, 928/282-7200, prepares creative regional American fare—chicken, ribs, fish, pasta, pizza, and sandwiches—using fresh ingredients, $13–21. It's open daily for breakfast, lunch, and dinner. Atmosphere is casual.

Steak & Sticks, at Los Abrigados, 160 Portal Lane, 928/204-7849 (STIX), features steaks, lamb, chicken, and fish, $22–28. It also offers Sedona's only billiard club. Open daily for breakfast and dinner.

T. Carl's, at Radisson Poco Diablo Resort, two miles south on Hwy. 179 from Hwy. 89A, 928/282-7333, ext. 235, offers an extensive menu of Southwestern and continental dishes daily for breakfast (buffet available on Sat.–Sun. $11), lunch, and dinner, $15–23. The restaurant is named after the husband of Sedona Schnebly.

Yavapai Restaurant at the Enchantment Resort, 525 Boynton Canyon, off Dry Creek Rd., 928/282-2900, serves fine American and Southwest cuisine. You can dine inside or out on the terrace and enjoy beautiful canyon views. Open daily for breakfast (brunch on Sunday $28.50), lunch, and dinner ($22–40; reservations required).

Garland's Oak Creek Lodge, 7.5 miles north of Sedona on Hwy. 89A, 928/282-3343, prepares memorable American regional cuisine for breakfast and dinner during the April to mid-November season, $29–35; reservations required.

Knotty Pine Cafe, in the Junipine Resort, 7.9 miles north of Sedona on Hwy. 89A, 928/282-7406, serves Southwestern and continental fare daily for breakfast, lunch, and dinner (may close some days in winter), $10–18.

Additional Dining: American and Continental

Rosebuds, in the Sinagua Plaza, 320 N. Hwy. 89A, 928/282-3022, offers steak, prime rib, seafood, pasta, $18–22. It's open daily for lunch and dinner and has great views.

Cowboy Club, in uptown Sedona at 241 N. Hwy. 89A, 928/282-4200, features "high desert cuisine" of Western-style steak, ribs, chicken, and fish ($14–33) for dinner, as well as lighter fare for lunch; it's open daily.

René at Tlaquepaque, in Tlaquepaque, 0.3 mile south on Hwy. 179 from Hwy. 89A, 928/282-9225, serves outstanding American and continental cuisine in a French Provincial atmosphere, $19–33. It's open for lunch and dinner daily.

Shugrue's Hillside Grill, in the Hillside Sedona at 671 Hwy. 179, 928/282-5300, prepares seafood along with choices of pasta and meat dishes daily for lunch and dinner, $19–48;

The **Sedona Airport Restaurant,** atop Airport Mesa, 928/282-3576, offers creative dining while you watch the planes come and go, $9–17. It's open daily for breakfast, lunch, and dinner. To get there, take Airport Road from W. Hwy. 89A.

Prime Cut, 2250 W. Hwy. 89A, 928/282-2943, fixes steak, seafood, and pasta among other specialties, $9–45. It's open for Sunday brunch and nightly for dinner.

Casa Rincon, 2620 W. Hwy. 89A, 928/282-4849, features Southwest and Spanish cuisine for lunch and dinner daily except Monday, $12–25. Bands perform Fri.–Saturday.

Fournos, 3000 W. Hwy. 89A, 928/282-3331, offers Greek and Italian cuisine along with a variety of other continental and Mediterranean styles, $15–18. It's open Thurs.–Sat. for dinner.

Rainbow's End Steakhouse & Saloon, 3235 W. Hwy. 89A, 928/282-1593, serves steak, ribs, prime rib, chicken, and Mexican food, $8–25. It's open daily for lunch and dinner; bands play Fri.–Sat. nights.

American Cafes

Hitching Post Restaurant & Bakery, in uptown Sedona at 269 N. Hwy. 89A, 928/282-7761, is a handy café open daily for breakfast, lunch, and dinner, $7.50–15.

Heartline Cafe, 1610 W. Hwy. 89A, 928/282-0785, serves American fare "with a twist," $14–30; open Fri.–Mon. for lunch and nightly for dinner.

Denny's, 1950 W. Hwy. 89A in the Bashas' Shopping Center, 928/282-5481, offers American favorites daily for breakfast, lunch, and dinner, $6–9.

Coffee Pot Restaurant, 2050 W. Hwy. 89A, 928/282-6626, cooks up 101 omelets; kids go for #101 with peanut butter, jelly, and banana. It's open daily for breakfast (served all day) and lunch, $7–11, and with indoor and patio dining.

Desert Flour Bakery & Bistro, in the Village of Oak Creek at Castle Rock Plaza, 6446 Hwy. 179, 928/284-4633, makes specialty breads, baked goodies, sandwiches, and salads; open daily for breakfast and lunch, under $6. The bakery also has branches at the Pink Jeep Plaza in Uptown Sedona and at the corner of W. Hwy. 89A and Dry Creek Rd. in West Sedona.

Italian

The Hideaway, in the Country Square shopping center on Hwy. 179 (0.2 mile south of Hwy. 89A), 928/282-4204, overlooks Oak Creek and serves sandwiches for lunch and fine Italian food for dinner, $8.50–11; it's open daily.

Joey Bistro in Los Abrigados Resort, 160 Portal Lane (0.2 mile south on Hwy. 179 from Hwy. 89A), 928/204-5639, offers tempting Italian pasta, meat, and seafood dishes, $9–18; open daily for dinner.

Dahl and DiLuca Ristorante Italiano, 2321 W. Hwy. 89A, 928/282-5219, features a chef from Rome who prepares traditional Italian cuisine as well as seafood, chicken, and steaks, $10–27; open nightly for dinner, with indoor and patio dining.

Pago's Pizzeria & Italian Cuisine, at Castle Rock Plaza in the Village of Oak Creek, 928/284-1939, fixes chicken, veal, seafood, pasta, pizza, and subs, $10–15; open daily for lunch and dinner.

Mexican

El Rincon Restaurante Mexicano at Tlaquepaque, 928/282-4648, serves excellent Mexican/Navajo-inspired food, $8.50–14; it's open with indoor and patio seating Tues.–Sun. for lunch and dinner.

Javelina Cantina, 671 Hwy. 179 in Hillside Sedona, 928/203-9514, prepares a variety of old standbys and new specialties, $5–19; open daily for lunch and dinner.

The Oaxaca Restaurante, 231 N. Hwy. 89A, 928/282-4179, offers Mexican and some gringo favorites daily for breakfast, lunch, and dinner, $9–22. The Fiesta Deck has outdoor dining with views.

Wild Toucan, 6376 Hwy. 179 in Village of Oak Creek, 928/284-1604, cooks American and Mexican food daily for lunch and dinner, $10–21.

Asian

India Palace, 1910 W. Hwy. 89A in Bashas' Shopping Center, 928/204-2300, prepares their food with wonderful spices in a north India style, $7–15; it's open daily for lunch (with a buffet option) and dinner.

Also in Bashas' Shopping Center, Lotus Garden, 928/282-3118, serves Chinese cuisine, $7–17; open daily for lunch (buffet available) and dinner.

Mandarin House, 6486 Hwy. 179 in Village of Oak Creek, 928/284-9088, offers Mandarin and Szechuan Chinese food, $7–25; open daily except Monday for lunch and dinner.

Thai Spices, Natural Cuisine of Thailand, 2986 W. Hwy. 89A, 928/282-0599, cooks flavorful fresh Thai food with many vegetarian items, $6–12.50; open Mon.–Sat. for lunch and dinner.

Takashi Japanese Restaurant, 465 Jordan Rd., 928/282-2334, serves a variety of Japanese styles and sushi, $15–21; open Tues.–Sat. for lunch and Tues.–Sun. for dinner.

Sasaki Japanese Restaurant, 65 Bell Rock Blvd. in the Village of Oak Creek, 928/284-1757, features a large menu, $13.50–45; open daily for dinner.

RECREATION AND ENTERTAINMENT

Outdoor Recreation

In town, you'll find picnic tables, a playground, and ball fields at The Posse Ground, on Posse Ground Road, 0.3 mile north of Hwy. 89A. The Sedona Health Club & Spa offers tennis courts, a year-round pool, Jacuzzis, fitness room, aerobics room, and snack bar on Racquet Road, 928/282-

4197; go 3.8 miles west on Hwy. 89A from the Y, head south on Foothills Drive, then right on Racquet Road.

Radisson Poco Diablo Resort, two miles south of town on Hwy. 179, 928/282-7333, features tennis courts (call and ask for the tennis shop to make reservations) and a nine-hole golf course. Oak Creek Country Club, in the Village of Oak Creek, 928/284-1660, offers an 18-hole golf course; from the Y, head south 6.5 miles on Hwy. 179, right on Bell Rock Road, then it's half a mile on the right. Sedona Golf Resort, 35 Ridge Trail Dr., 928/284-9355, also has an 18-hole course open to the public in the Village of Oak Creek; head about 7 miles south on Hwy. 179, then turn right on Ridge Trail Drive. Canyon Mesa Country Club, 500 Jacks Canyon Rd., 928/284-0036, offers a nine-hole course in the Village of Oak Creek; take Hwy. 179 south 6.75 miles from the Y, then turn left about half a mile on Jacks Canyon Road. Verde Santa Fe Golf Course, 928/634-5454, is an 18-hole course, 15 miles west of town on Hwy. 89A toward Cottonwood.

Anglers can pull rainbow trout from Oak Creek. Rainbow Trout Farm, three miles north of Sedona in Oak Creek Canyon, 928/282-5799, offers easier fishing for a fee, though you must pay for what you catch. Equipment is available and no license is needed. It's open daily.

Trail Horse Adventures offers a wide variety of trail rides and pack trips year-round in the Red Rock Country around Sedona. The stables are five miles southwest of town off lower Red Rock Loop Road; call 928/282-7252, 800/723-3538 (SADDLEUP) for directions and reservations; www.trailhorseadventures.com.

Entertainment

Sedona Cultural Park, 928/282-0747, 800/780-2787, hosts a variety of performances and events in a large outdoor amphitheater on the west side of town. From the Y, head west 4.2 miles on AZ 89A then turn right opposite the Upper Red Rock Loop Road; www.sedonaculturalpark.org. Sedona SuperVue Theater, 6601 Hwy. 179 (behind the factory stores in the Village of Oak

The Blazin' M Cowboys put on a great show.

© BILL WEIR

Creek on Hwy. 179), 928/284-3214, presents a giant screen movie, "Sedona, the Spirit of Wonder," a fine introduction to the area with some great aerial photography. Another film is usually shown, too; check handouts at tourist offices or motels or visit the website at www.supervue.com.

Current movies play at the six-screen **Harkins,** 2081 W. Hwy. 89A, 928/282-0222. To get the latest on Sedona's music, events, and nightlife, check the weekly *Red Rock News* and monthly *Red Rock Review* newspapers.

Events

Schedules may vary from what's listed here. Sedona-Oak Creek Canyon Chamber of Commerce, 928/282-7722, 800/288-7336, is your best source for the latest information; sedonachamber.com. Spring starts off with the **Sedona International Film Festival** usually on the first weekend in March; www.sedonafilm festival.com. Sedona goes green for the **St. Patrick's Day Parade** on March 17 or the nearest Saturday. **Chamber Music Sedona** attracts musicians from all over the world for tens days in May; concerts also take place over the Sept.–April season; www.chambermusicsedona.org. Sedona's best chefs offer samples of their food and wine in **Sedona Taste** on the first Sunday in June. Actors present the Bard's plays in **Shakespeare Sedona** in July; www.shakespearesedona.com. Fireworks light the sky on the **Fourth of July.**

In September, look for **Fiesta del Tlaquepaque** (mariachi bands, Mexican dances, food, arts, and crafts on the 2nd Sat.; www.tlaq.com), **Pops Concert in the Park,** and **Jazz on the Rocks Festival** (3rd weekend; www.sedonajazz.com).

Los Abrigados sponsors a **Sculpture Walk.** Also in October, the **Sedona Arts Festival** presents entertainment, arts and crafts, and food, usually on the 2nd weekend.

In November, Los Abrigados shows off more than a million lights in the **Red Rock Fantasy of Lights;** it starts the day after Thanksgiving and runs into early January.

The year winds up with the **Festival of Lights,** when more than 5,000 candle-lit luminarias brighten Tlaquepaque. It's usually held on the second Saturday; www.tlaq.com.

SHOPPING
Art Galleries

As an art center, what Sedona lacks in size, it makes up for in quality. Its 40 art galleries display an impressive range of original art. Southwestern themes run through much of the work, in colors, forms, Indian motifs, and cowboy legends.

Most of the art galleries lie along the first half mile of Hwy. 179 south of the Y; others can be found in uptown Sedona along the first half mile of Hwy. 89A north of the Y. **Tlaquepaque,** 0.3 mile south on Hwy. 179 from Hwy. 89A, 928/282-4838, makes a good starting point for a trip into Sedona's art world; www.tlaq.com. Fountains, sycamore-shaded courtyards, and Spanish-colonial architecture create a delightful atmosphere. Even nonshoppers will enjoy exploring the many shops and galleries here. **Gar-**

land's **Navajo Rugs,** a bit farther south at 411 Hwy. 170, 928/282-4070, has an especially fine selection. A couple blocks farther, **Hillside Sedona,** 671 Hwy., 928/282-4500, offers galleries and restaurants in an attractive shopping area decorated with sculpture. In uptown Sedona, **Sinagua Plaza** offers galleries and dining.

Bookstores and Gift Shops

The Worm Books & Music, 207 N. Hwy. 89A; 928/282-3471, carries an excellent selection of regional, new age, and general reading, plus topo maps and audio tapes. **The Book Loft,** 175 Hwy. 179; 928/282-5173, sells mostly used books along with new regional and children's titles.

The Center for the New Age, 341 Hwy. 179, 928/282-2085, offers books, local event information, vortex tours, astrological reports, aura photos, and other services and treatments; it's open daily. Other sources for new age books and services include **The Eye of the Vortex,** 1405 W. Hwy. 89A, 928/282-5614; **Crystal Magic,** 2978 W. Hwy. 89A, 928/282-1622; **The Hub of the Now Age,** 164 Coffee Pot Dr. (Bashas' Shopping Center), 928/282-3856; and **Golden Word Book Centre,** 3150 W. Hwy. 89A, 928/282-2688.

Outdoor Gear

Sedona Sports, Creekside Plaza at 151 Hwy. 179, 928/282-1317, has outdoor recreation gear, maps, and rents mountain bikes and fishing poles. **Canyon Outfitters,** 2701 W. Hwy. 89A, 928/282-5293, carries a large selection of supplies for hiking, backpacking, and climbing. **Mountain Bike Heaven,** 1695 W. Hwy. 89A, 928/282-1312, sells and rents mountain bikes and offers parts and repairs.

Factory Outlets

Prime Outlets at Sedona, 6601 Hwy. 179 in the Village of Oak Creek, 928/284-2150, 888/545-7227, features brand-name bargains and a giant-screen movie theater.

INFORMATION AND SERVICES

Gateway Visitor Information Centers

Whatever highway you take into Sedona, you'll pass at least one Gateway Visitor Center with recreation and at least some tourist information! All of these sell the Red Rock Pass required for most visits to the Coconino National Forest near Sedona.

Both chamber and Forest Service people staff the information desk of **Uptown Gateway,** which is home to the **Sedona-Oak Creek Canyon Chamber of Commerce.** The office has a good supply of literature and information on sights, services, and upcoming events. It's open Sunday 9 A.M.–3 P.M. and Mon.–Sat. 8:30 A.M.–5 P.M. (9 A.M.–5 P.M. Nov.–March). It's at the corner of N. Hwy. 89A and Forest Rd., a block north of the Y (P.O. Box 478, Sedona, AZ 86339); 928/282-7722, 800/288-7336; www.visitsedona.com.

If you're coming on AZ 179 from I-17, the **South Gateway,** will be on your left in the Tequa Plaza as you enter the Village of Oak Creek. It's set back a block from the highway and is open daily 8:30 A.M.–5 P.M.

West Gateway will be convenient if you're driving AZ 89A from Cottonwood. Turn left at the light for the Sedona Cultural Center as you enter Sedona. It's open the same hours as the Uptown Gateway.

Oak Creek Vista serves as the **North Gateway,** well worth a stop for the view if you're coming on AZ 89A from Flagstaff. This is the smallest visitor center in the national forest. It's open daily 8 A.M.–5 P.M. except when blocked by snow. You can purchase books and maps. Oak Creek Vista is about 12 miles south of Flagstaff and 15 miles north of Sedona.

Oak Creek Visitor Center, under the trees at the south end of Indian Gardens, 3.5 miles north of Sedona, 928/203-0624, and is open daily 8 A.M.–4:30 P.M. You can obtain recreation information, fishing licenses, maps, and some books.

Coconino National Forest

The **Sedona Ranger District** office of the U.S. Forest Service, 250 Brewer Road (take the street opposite the post office near the Y on W. Hwy. 89A), 928/282-4119, supplies information on camping, hiking, Native American ruins, and road conditions in the national forest surrounding Sedona. The office sells maps and books, and staff can suggest back-road drives. It's open Mon.–Fri. 8 A.M.–4:30 P.M. You can write to Sedona Ranger District, P.O. Box 300, Sedona, AZ 86339 or check the website www.fs.fed.us/r3/coconino.

Other Information Sources

Sedona Public Library, 928/282-7714, is open Mon. 3–9 P.M., Tues. and Thurs.–Sat. 9:30 A.M.–5 P.M., and Wed. 9:30 A.M.–9 P.M.; users.sedona.net/~library. To get there, head west 3.1 miles from the Y on Hwy. 89A, turn right on Dry Creek Road, then make the first left on White Bear Road.

The *Sedona Red Rock News* comes out twice a week and publishes the free *Red Rock Country Visitors' Guide* every month with things to do. The free *Red Rock Review* also comes out monthly and lists activities and events.

Services

The main **post office,** 928/282-3511, is on Hwy. 89A just west of the Y; another is at 2081 W. Hwy. 89A in West Sedona. **Sedona Medical Center** is on the edge of town at 3700 W. Hwy. 89A; 928/204-3000. The nearest hospital is the **Verde Valley Medical Center** at 202 S. Willard in Cottonwood, 19 miles southwest of Sedona; 928/634-2251. For **emergencies** (fire, police, ambulance) call 911.

TOURS AND TRANSPORTATION

Ground Tours

Sedona Trolley provides two 55-minute tours of town and the surrounding area. The chamber office has schedules; 928/282-5400, 928/282-6826.

Many companies offer jeep trips into Sedona's rugged and spectacular backcountry. You have a choice of relatively gentle rides or serious four-wheeling, though drivers take it slow and easy even on the roughest roads. **Pink Jeep Tours,** 204 N. Hwy. 89A, 928/282-5000, 800/873-3662, has been taking visitors around

for more than 40 years. Their various scenic, prehistoric-ruin, and rock-art trips cost $32–60 for 1.5–2.5 hours; www.pinkjeep.com. **Sedona Adventures,** 276 N. Hwy. 89A, 928/282-3500, 800/888-9494, offers 4WD touring with a choice of backcountry rides and hiking; the cost runs $38–40 for a two-hour ride and $45–55 for 2.5-hour trips; www.sedonaadventures.com. **A Day in the West,** 928/282-4320, 800/973-3662, offers a variety of scenic trips from a 1.5-hour back-road tour for $32 to the 4.5-hour Western Experience that combines a Jeep tour, horseback ride, and cookout for $95; www.adayinthewest.com. **Sedona Red Rock Jeep Tours,** 270 N. Hwy. 89A, 928/282-6826, 800/848-7728, offers 1.5 to 3-hour scenic trips for $36–68 and 3 to 7-hour archaeology tours for $75–159; www.redrockjeep.com.

Earth Wisdom Jeep Tours, 293 N. Hwy. 89A, 928/282-4714, 800/482-4714, presents

© BILL WEIR

The challenging Broken Arrow Trail, navigated by Pink Jeep Tours, thrills riders with its steep grades and red rock scenery.

trips centered around Indian lore and vortexes. You can go by Jeep, by Jeep and horseback, or on foot on excursions of 2–4 hours that cost $42–88; www.sacredsites.com/earth wisdom.html. **Spirit Steps Tours,** 928/282-4562, 800/728-4562, has a spiritual emphasis on vortex trips (3–4.5 hours; $20/hour/person) and Native American ruin excursions (3–8 hours; $20/person); drumming ceremonies and Jerome excursions are offered too; www.spiritsteps.org.

Air Tours

For aerial views, head to one of the flightseeing services at Sedona Airport. **Red Rock Bi-Plane Tours,** 928/204-5939, 888/866-7433, offers exciting rides in an open cockpit and less expensive rides in a Cessna; a 10-minute flight runs $36 for the bi-plane ($25 Cessna) and a 45–minute bi-plane tour is $139 ($75 Cessna); www.sedonaairtours.com. **AeroVista,** 928/282-7768, 866/594-5365, flies high-wing Cessnas over the Sedona area (15–45 minutes; $35–69); www.aerovista.com.

Arizona Helicopter Adventures, 928/282-0904, 800/282-5141; www.azheli.com, offers tours of the Sedona area (12–35 minutes; $48–128) and a 2.5-hour ride all the way to the Grand Canyon for $595. **Skydance Helicopters,** 928/282-1651, 800/882-1651, offers five different tours of 10–40 minutes at $40–160 and a 2.5-hour Grand Canyon excursion for $625; www.skydancehelicopters.com.

Fly high in a balloon with **AeroZona Balloon Company,** 928/282-1499; **Sky High Balloon Adventures,** 928/204-1395, 800/551-7597; **Northern Light Balloon Expeditions,** 928/282-2274, 800/230-6222; or **Red Rock Balloon Adventures,** 928/284-0040, 800/258-3754.

Transportation

For a taxi, call **Bob's Taxi Service,** 928/282-1234. Rental cars are available at the airport and in town.

The **Sedona-Phoenix Shuttle,** 928/282-2066, 800/448-7988 (Arizona only), travels about eight times daily south to Camp Verde, Cottonwood, and Sky Harbor Airport ($35 one-way, $60 roundtrip). The shuttle leaves from Bell Rock Inn in the Village of Oak Creek and from Super 8 Motel on W. Hwy. 89A in Sedona; www.sedona-phoenix-shuttle.com. **Ace Xpress Shuttle Service,** 928/639-3357 (Cottonwood) or 800/336-2239, provides door-to-door service from Sedona and the Verde Valley to Sky Harbor Airport ($47 one-way, $78 roundtrip).

Exploring the Red Rock Country Around Sedona

Gorgeous scenery of rock and forest surrounds Sedona on all sides. The scenic drive up Oak Creek Canyon north of town is one of the best in the state. Back roads branch off from Sedona in many directions, but most of these are rough and require a high-clearance vehicle. Hikers have the most options. Two wilderness areas of pinnacles, mesas, and canyons begin at the edge of town—Munds Mountain Wilderness has 18,150 acres to the southeast and Red Rock/Secret Mountain Wilderness protects 43,950 acres to the northwest. Sedona's famous red rocks belong to the Schnebly Hill Formation, composed of ancient coastal deposits.

Red Rock Passes

Most of this land lies in the Sedona Ranger District of the Coconino National Forest. To improve and maintain roads and trails, the Forest Service requires visitors to purchase a Red Rock Pass to park anywhere in the forest near Sedona, except at one of the concession-operated day-use areas or campgrounds, all of which have separate fees. You don't need a pass if you stop and stay close and within sight of your vehicle to admire the scenery. The passes are available at gateway visitor information centers, from vending machines on some back roads, from the Forest Service, and from some local shops and resorts. You can purchase daily ($5), weekly ($15), and annual passes ($20 or $40). The $40 annual pass includes five entries for day use at the concession-operated Grasshopper Point, Banjo Bill, Call of the Canyon, or Crescent Moon areas; it saves you $5. Golden Age and Golden Access cardholders get a 50 percent discount on passes. You can find out more about the passes at www.redrockcountry.org. The two state parks near Sedona have separate admissions and are not part of the Red Rock Pass program.

Hiking

Rugged canyons, delicate natural arches, and solitude await those who venture into the backcountry, much of which has changed little from prehistoric times. Hiking possibilities are virtually limitless—you can venture out on easy day-hikes or chart a week-long trek across the wilderness. The Sedona Ranger District has 80–90 trails with plans to double that number. Vehicle break-ins have been a problem at trailheads, so you'll want to remove all valuables.

Spring and autumn offer the most pleasant temperatures, but hiking is possible all year. Summer visitors can avoid 100°F-plus desert temperatures by starting early or heading for the high country; winter hikers keep to the desert and canyon areas when snow blocks trails in the ponderosa pine forests above.

For information on backcountry travel, contact the U.S Forest Service office in Sedona at 250 Brewer Road, 928/282-4119, or one of the gateway visitor information centers. The Coconino Forest map shows back roads and many trails. Also, consult *Sedona Hikes,* by Richard and Sherry Mangum.

Mountain Biking

Cyclists cannot ride in the wilderness areas, but many trails are open to them elsewhere. The Forest Service offers handouts on places to ride and sells maps. Popular areas include Brins Mesa northwest of town, Little Horse Trail (can be a loop with the Broken Arrow Trail) southeast of town, Mystic Trail (from Little Horse Trailhead, then north), Deadman's Pass Trail in Boynton Canyon, and Bell Rock Pathway off AZ 179 between Sedona and the Village of Oak Creek.

Cathedral Bike Loop follows mostly unpaved roads in a 6.5-mile loop via Red Rock Crossing (no bridge) and Red Rock State Park (entry fee required), which has a map handout. Most Sedona cycling is rated beginner to intermediate.

NORTH OF SEDONA: OAK CREEK CANYON

Take AZ 89A north from Sedona for a beautiful scenic drive past dramatic rock features, dense forests, and the sparkling creek. Picnic areas, hiking trails, and campgrounds along the way invite travelers to stop. Grasshopper Point and Slide Rock State Park offer natural swimming holes in Oak Creek. Secluded lodges and cabins provide accommodations (see "Resorts in Oak Creek Canyon" above). At the head of the canyon, 13 miles from Sedona, the highway climbs 700 feet in 2.3 miles of sharp switchbacks to Oak Creek Vista, a scenic viewpoint overlooking Oak Creek Canyon and Pumphouse Wash. The highway continues on to I-17 and Flagstaff, where you could also start the drive. In autumn (mid-October to mid-November), multicolored leaves add to the rich hues of the sculptured canyon walls.

The beauty of Oak Creek Canyon attracts large crowds on summer weekends, when the highway becomes very crowded, parking can be impossible at popular stops, and campgrounds fill to the brim. Weekdays and off-season travel will be much easier, but if you can come only on a weekend, it's still worth doing. An early start will put you ahead of the pack and score a parking spot.

Wilson Mountain Trail #10

Energetic hikers will enjoy this climb from the bottom of Oak Creek Canyon to the top of Wilson Mountain. A stiff 2,300-foot ascent is followed by a long, level stretch extending to the north edge of the flat-topped mountain. Total trail length is nine miles roundtrip, or six miles if you turn around where the trail levels off on the summit plateau.

Two very different trails, South Wilson and North Wilson, start from the bottom (elev. 4,600 feet), meet part way up on First Bench, then continue as one trail to the top. South Wilson Trail begins at the north end of Midgley Bridge, 1.3 miles north of Sedona, and switchbacks through Arizona cypress, juniper, pinyon pine, agave, yucca, and other sun-loving plants. Higher up, manzanita, scrub live oak, and other chaparral-zone plants become more common. North Wilson Trail, on the other hand, climbs steeply through a cool canyon filled with tall ponderosa pine and Douglas fir; look for the trailhead on AZ 89A just north of the Encinoso Picnic Area, 4.6 miles north of town.

A stone cairn marks the junction of the trails at First Bench. This large level area dates from long ago, when a piece of Wilson Mountain's summit slid part way down the mountain. More climbing takes you to the rim of Wilson Mountain; keep right where the trail forks and follow the path north to some spectacular viewpoints. From the northernmost overlook, you can see tiny Vultee Arch far below across Sterling Canyon. Beyond, on the horizon, stand the San Francisco Peaks. Small meadows and forests of ponderosa pine and Gambel oak cover the large expanse of Wilson's summit. Carry 2–3 quarts of water on this hike.

Wilson Canyon and Mountain get their names from Richard Wilson, a bear hunter who lost a battle with a grizzly in June 1885. Wilson's bear gun was undergoing repairs on the day he spotted grizzly tracks in Oak Creek Canyon, but he set out after the bear anyway, toting a smaller rifle. Nine days later, horsemen found Wilson's badly mauled body up what's now Wilson Canyon. You can hike about 1.5 miles up the canyon from Midgley Bridge. The Huckaby Trail goes down the canyon from Midgley Bridge, crosses Oak Creek, follows an old wagon road through the valley, then connects with lower Schnebly Hill Road.

Grasshopper Point

This natural swimming hole in Oak Creek lies on the right 1.8 miles north of town. A $5 parking fee is charged at the gate. Bring your own drinking water and perhaps a picnic. Hikers can follow Huckaby Trail downstream to the lower Schnebly Hill Road or go upstream on Allens Bend Trail

and connect with Casner Canyon Trail, which climbs to upper Schnebly Hill Road.

Rainbow Trout Farm

Anglers will find the easiest fishing for rainbow trout on the right across Oak Creek, three miles north of Sedona; 928/282-5799. Equipment is available and no license is needed, but you must pay for what you catch; open daily.

Indian Gardens and Oak Creek Visitor Center

An historic marker tells the history of this spot, 3.5 miles north of town. Oak Creek Visitor Center, tucked under trees on the left, offers recreation information, fishing licenses, maps, and some books. To the north, a store and deli has tables in the patio in back. Garland's Indian Jewelry offers a large selection of Native American work.

Encinoso Picnic Area

Tables with drinking water on the left, 4.6 miles from town, offer a rest from travels. You can stop by year-round; a Red Rock Pass is needed to park.

Manzanita Campground

Turn right down the hillside to the sites beside Oak Creek, 5.6 miles north of town. It's open all year with water and a $15 fee. **Sterling Pass Trail #146** begins north of the campground on the other side of the highway and climbs the west rim, with a 1,000-foot elevation gain to the pass; you could continue down the other side to Vultee Arch, adding two miles to the roundtrip.

Sterling Pass Trail #46

A hike to Sterling Pass (elev. 5,960 feet) from Oak Creek Canyon provides fine views; you can continue down the other side to Vultee Arch. Begin from the west side of AZ 89A, 5.6 miles north of Sedona; the trailhead (elev. 4,840 feet) lies a short way south of Slide Rock Lodge and 300 feet north of Manzanita Campground. The trail ascends through a small canyon to the pass, then drops into Sterling Canyon to join Vultee Arch Trail; it's 3.3 miles roundtrip to the pass or 5.3 miles roundtrip to Vultee Arch.

This approach to the arch avoids the bumpy drive on Forest Road 152.

Slide Rock State Park

Natural chutes and swimming holes at this park in Oak Creek Canyon are a great way to cool off in summer. It's on the left, 6.4 miles north of Sedona. Other attractions on the 43 acres include a short trail along cliffs above the creek, picnic spots, and an historic apple orchard. On the walk to the swim area, you'll see the orchard, farm machinery, old tourist cabins, packing shed, and farmhouse. Some people like to wear jeans for sliding down the rock chutes, as the ride can be hard on the seat. Pets and glass containers may not go to the swim area. Slide Rock Market serves snacks daily, then weekends in winter. Birds like the area, too, and the park has a checklist. The parking lot fills nearly every day from Memorial Day to Labor Day, and you may have to wait for a spot. For safety, Oak Creek water is tested every day and the report is posted; you can also check the Water Quality Hotline, 602/542-0202 (Phoenix). Occasionally bacteria levels go too high and the swim area may close for the day. Slide Rock State Park, 928/282-3034, is open all year for day use only; $5 per vehicle (up to four people), $1 for each additional passenger and for walk-ins or cyclists.

Halfway Picnic Area

Tables, 7.3 miles north of town on the left, lie on a shelf above Oak Creek. Open all year; you'll need a Red Rock Pass.

Banjo Bill Picnic Area

Located 7.7 miles north of town on the left, the area has water and a $5 parking fee; it's closed in winter.

Bootlegger Campground

Though lacking water and close to the highway, this spot is a favorite of some campers. It lies on a shelf above the creek on the left, 8.4 miles north of town. The season runs April 15–Oct. 31.

A.B. Young Trail #100

This well-graded but strenuous trail climbs out of

Oak Creek Canyon to East Pocket Mesa, north of Wilson Mountain. The trail makes more than 30 switchbacks to reach the ponderosa pine-forested rim, a 1,600-foot climb and 3.2-mile roundtrip. From the rim, the trail climbs gently to East Pocket Knob Lookout Tower, another 0.8 mile and 400 feet higher. You can enjoy excellent views of Oak Creek Canyon on the way up, from the rim, and atop the lookout tower (open during the fire season in summer).

The trailhead (elev. 5,200 feet) lies across Oak Creek behind Bootlegger Campground, just north of Milepost 383 on AZ 89A, 8.4 miles north of Sedona. Wade or hop stones across the creek—though don't cross if it's flooded—to a dirt road paralleling the bank, then look for a sign to the well-used trail climbing the slope. After leaving the woodlands along Oak Creek, the trail ascends through chaparral. Allow 3–4 hours and carry 1–2 quarts of water. Cattle ranchers built this trail in the 1880s to bring herds to pasture. The Civilian Conservation Corps under A.B. Young improved it in the 1930s.

Call of the Canyon Picnic Area and West Fork Trail #108

Sheer canyon walls, luxuriant vegetation, and a beautiful clear stream make West Fork, a major tributary of Oak Creek, an idyllic spot. An easy, almost level trail extends about three miles upstream through the narrow canyon. West Fork inspired Novelist Zane Grey's book *Call of the Canyon*. Because of the quantity and diversity of plant and animal species here, the lower six miles of the canyon has been designated a Research Natural Area. The stream, which you'll cross many times, usually only flows ankle deep; you have the option of wading or stepping across on stones. Carry water and plenty of film. Because the Natural Area receives heavy use, one shouldn't build fires or camp here.

Turn left 10 miles north of Sedona, between Mileposts 384 and 385, for the picnic area and trailhead parking, which costs $5. Try to arrive early as there's often a wait for parking by midday. The tables are in an old apple orchard planted by the Thomas family who homesteaded here in the 1880s; bring your own water. After crossing Oak

Creek on a bridge, you'll pass the ruins of Mayhews Lodge, built in the early 1900s and burned in 1980, before turning up West Fork. Only the lower end of the canyon features a trail; in other areas you must walk in the streambed or clamber over boulders. The twisting canyon forms many overhangs, reflected in pools of the tranquil stream. Beyond the three-mile point, the canyon narrows and you'll have to start wading.

Although most visitors come for a leisurely day-hike, strong hikers can travel the entire 14-mile length of West Fork canyon in one day. It helps to get an early start and arrange a car shuttle. Those making the full trip should start at the upstream trailhead, where Forest Road 231 (Woody Mountain Road) crosses West Fork. Woody Mountain Road begins as a turnoff from Rt. 66, about two miles west of Flagstaff. The first six miles from the upper trailhead are usually dry, but this stretch is followed by a series of deep pools that may require swimming. Avoid hiking in the canyon after heavy rains or if storms threaten. The rough terrain, fallen trees, and deep pools make backpacking difficult, so most people do the trip as a long day-hike.

From the picnic area you can follow a trail to another trailhead—**Thomas Point Trail #142.** This strenuous trail rises about 900 feet in one mile of hiking to the rim on the east side of the canyon and offers great scenery.

Cave Springs Forest Campground, 11.1 miles up the canyon and to the left, may be the prettiest of the Oak Creek campgrounds. The sites are secluded in the forest and well away from the highway. You can look inside the small cave, where a spring supplies the campground's water. The season runs April 15–Oct. 31 and there's a $15 fee. Campers have a store and coin showers. Some sites can be reserved at 877/444-6777; www.reserveusa.com.

Pineflat Campground is 12.1 miles from Sedona on both sides of the highway. Ponderosa pines, Douglas fir, oaks, and sycamores provide shade. The season runs April 1–Nov 15 with water and a $15 fee. You can also reserve some sites at 877/444-6777; www.reserveusa.com.

Hikers can get a workout and some views on the climb to the east rim on **Cookstove Trail #143.** It's 1.5 miles roundtrip and a 1,000-foot climb. The trailhead is on the east side of the highway just north of the campground.

Oak Creek Vista and North Gateway Visitor Center

On your right at the top of the climb out of Oak Creek Canyon, this overlook has splendid views down the length of the canyon. Pumphouse Wash lies directly below. A little visitor center, sponsored by the Arizona Natural History Association, is open daily, weather permitting, with recreation information on the Coconino National Forest and sales of books and maps. Native Americans display jewelry and other crafts for sale nearby. Oak Creek Vista is 15.3 miles from Sedona. Parking here is free and you don't need a Red Rock Pass.

EAST OF SEDONA
Schnebly Hill Road

You'll enjoy some of the best views in the area along this bumpy back road that descends the Mogollon Rim east of town. It's the most spectacular approach to Sedona, but is too rocky for cars—high clearance vehicles are needed. If you'd rather have someone else do the driving, sign up for a tour with one of the companies in uptown Sedona.

Take I-17 Exit 320 for the descent or, from Sedona, turn off AZ 179 at the sign a half mile south of the Y (Hwy. 89A junction); the drive is about 12 miles one-way and is closed in winter. Allow plenty of time for the many curves and views. Schnebly Hill Vista features a spectacular panorama at about the halfway point. The National Forest office in Sedona, 928/282-4119, can advise on road conditions.

SOUTH OF SEDONA
Bell Rock Pathway

This easy 3.7-mile (one-way) trail passes along the base of Bell Rock and connects with Courthouse Butte Loop, a six-mile hike around the butte, and other trails; elevation change is 200 feet. It's easy to moderate for hikers and cyclists. Both trailheads lie just east of AZ 179. The north trailhead, also used to reach the Little Horse Trail, is near Milepost 310, just south of the Back O'Beyond/Indian Cliffs junction. The south trailhead is just north of the Village of Oak Creek.

WEST OF SEDONA

Crescent Moon Ranch/ Red Rock Crossing

Photographers and moviemakers have long admired this spot for its beautiful view of Cathedral Rock reflected in the waters of Oak Creek. Visitors also come for a swim in the creek or a picnic in the splendid surroundings. Buildings and a working waterwheel of Crescent Moon Ranch add some history. Open daily with a $5 parking fee. From the Y in Sedona, head west 4.2 miles on AZ 89A, turn left 1.8 miles on Upper Red Rock Loop Road, then left 0.9 mile on Chavez Ranch Road.

Red Rock State Park

Visitors come to enjoy nature and to picnic in this beautiful section of Oak Creek southwest of Sedona. Birdwatching is good, with 150 species identified; ask for a list. Short hiking trails wind through the valley and nearby hills. Smoke Trail, a 0.4-mile loop from the visitor center, follows the shore of Oak Creek. Eagles Nest Trail crosses the creek to a scenic overlook, 1.8 miles roundtrip. Rangers offer nature walks, bird walks, moonlight walks (April–Oct.), and First Sunday programs; check for times. The House of Apache Fire across the valley has distinctive architecture and stonework; construction started in 1947 and never really finished, though the house served as a retreat center in the early 1970s. You can go up to the house only on ranger-led walks. Drop in at the visitor center to see exhibits on natural communities of plants and animals; staff answer questions, tell of upcoming events, and sell books. To protect the fragile riparian area, no swimming, wading, or pets are allowed; some areas may be closed to protect wildlife. Mountain bikers can do a 6.5-mile Cathedral Bike Loop from the park on mostly unpaved roads, some closed to motorists; there's a ford at Red Rock Crossing. A handout available at the park shows the way.

The park is open daily all year for day use only; $5 per vehicle, $1 per person on foot, bicycle, or horseback. From Sedona, head west 5.5 miles on AZ 89A from the Y, turn left (south) three miles on Lower Red Rock Loop Road, then turn right 0.8 mile into the park to the visitor center, 928/282-6907. You can also drive via Upper Red Rock Loop Road—two miles of pavement followed by 1.2 miles of bumpy dirt road. On this route you will see a turnoff to the famous **Red Rock Crossing—Crescent Moon Recreation Area,** a favorite of landscape photographers and the site of many scenes in old Western movies; there's a parking fee.

Page Springs Hatchery

Meet the trout on a self-guided tour. They hatch at Sterling Springs, near the head of Oak Creek Canyon, then come here when they're three inches long. After a stay of 8–9 months, the trout reach a length of 8–10 inches and are ready to be released. A show pond contains large specimens. Warm-water fish, including threatened and endangered species, live in separate pools. The visitor center has exhibits on native fish of Oak Creek, sport fish, and fisheries management. The hatchery is open daily 7 A.M.–3:45 P.M.; 928/634-4805. From the Y, head southwest 11 miles on AZ 89A, then turn left 3.2 miles on Page Springs Road.

Devil's Bridge Trail #120

From the trailhead (elev. 4,600 feet), a well-graded path climbs steadily through juniper, pinyon pine, Arizona cypress, and manzanita to the base of a long natural arch. You can't see the bridge until you're almost there, but when you arrive, the majestic sweep of the arch and fine views of distant canyons and mountains reward your effort. To reach the top of the arch, continue toward the base of the cliff to the left of where the trail passes under the overhanging cliff. The 1.8-mile roundtrip hike gains 400 feet in elevation. A smaller trail forks off to the right about 330 feet before the bridge, climbing steeply to the top of the arch.

Devil's Bridge lies northwest of Sedona on the other side of a ridge. From the Y in Sedona, head west 3.1 miles on AZ 89A, turn right two miles on paved Dry Creek Road (Forest Road 152C), then turn right and go 1.3 miles on the bumpy dirt Forest Road 152. Cautiously driven cars may be able to negotiate this road in dry weather; check with the Forest Service. The trailhead turnoff is signed; parking is limited at the trailhead. The first part of the trail follows an abandoned road.

Vultee Arch Trail #22

This hike follows Sterling Canyon upstream to a small natural bridge visible in the sandstone to the north. Though the canyon is dry most of the year, Arizona cypress, sycamore, ponderosa pine, and other trees and plants find it to their liking. From the trailhead (elev. 4,800 feet), you'll climb 400 feet on the 3.2-mile roundtrip trail. Carry water, especially on hot days. The arch and a bronze plaque at the end of the trail commemorate aircraft designer Gerard Vultee and his wife Sylvia, who died when their plane hit East Pocket Mesa during a snowstorm on January 29, 1938. The trailhead for Vultee Arch lies at the end of Forest Road 152; follow the directions for Devil's Bridge Trail, then continue three miles past that turnoff to road's end.

Palatki and Honanki Ruins

Prehistoric Sinagua built these cliff dwellings, the largest pueblos in the Sedona Red Rocks area, more than 700 years ago. Later, these early architects moved on, possibly to Tuzigoot and other sites along the Verde River and Oak Creek. Great care must be taken not to touch the fragile rock art or ruins. Palatki and Honanki ruins are open for entry daily 9:30 A.M.–4 P.M.; you'll need a Red Rock Pass. There's a visitor center/bookshop at Palatki, 928/282-3854, where you can get information and drinking water.

Palatki (Hopi for "Red House") has two pueblos, dated to 1150–1300, that once housed 30–50 people. Look on the alcove walls for pictographs that possibly represent clans. Red Cliffs, on a separate trail to the west, contains much more rock art and there's often a volunteer here to explain the different styles and time periods of the artwork. Pictographs and a few petroglyphs at the site have been attributed to the Archaic period (3,000–8,000 years ago), Southern Sinagua (A.D. 900–1300), Yavapai or Apache (1583–1875), and Anglo pioneers.

Honanki (Hopi for "Bear House"), below Loy Butte, once had as many as 72 rooms, built between 1130 and 1280. You'll find rock art here too.

The sites can be reached via Red Canyon Road (Forest Road 525), an unsigned turn five miles west of the traffic light at Upper Red Rock Loop, or from Dry Creek Road/Boynton Pass Road (Forest Road 152C), off AZ 89A in west Sedona. The roads make a scenic loop with AZ 89A, though they are mostly unpaved and best avoided in wet weather. Red Canyon Road is the smoother of the two: From the Y in Sedona, head west 9.2 miles on AZ 89A to a group of mailboxes between Mileposts 364 and 365, turn right (north) five miles on Red Canyon Road, then continue north 1.6 miles on Forest Road 795 to its end at Palatki. The rougher but more scenic route follows AZ 89A west 3.2 miles from the Y, turns right (north) about six miles on Dry Creek Road (Forest Road 152C), which curves west to Forest Road 525, where you turn right, then right again on Forest Road 795 to Palatki. For Honanki, return to the junction of Forest Roads 525 and 795, then follow Forest Road 525 northwest four miles. The gateway visitor information centers and the Forest Service office in Sedona, 928/282-4119, have a handout on the ruins and sell the Coconino Forest map.

Sycamore Canyon Wilderness

Imagine Oak Creek Canyon without the highway, resorts, campgrounds, and Sedona. That's Sycamore Canyon, a twisting slash in the earth 21 miles long and as wide as seven miles. As the crow flies, Sycamore Canyon lies about 15 miles west of Oak Creek Canyon. A wilderness designation protects the canyon, so only hikers and horseback riders may descend to its depths. Several trails wind down to Sycamore Creek, mostly from the east side, but not a single road. Motorists can enjoy the sweeping view from Sycamore Point on the west rim, approached from Williams.

Sycamore Canyon Wilderness is under the jurisdiction of three different national forests: Coconino, Kaibab, and Prescott. The gateway visitor information centers and the Forest Service office in Sedona, 928/282-4119, are your best sources of information for trail conditions, trailhead access, and water sources.

BEAVER CREEK RANGER DISTRICT

Heading southeast of Sedona, you'll eventually leave the famous Red Rock Country, but not the spectacular scenery. The pine-forested Mogollon Rim and its narrow canyons harbor many beautiful spots. The Verde River, just south of the Mogollon Rim, cuts a broader canyon and can be explored by road, raft, or kayak. The gateway visitor information centers and the Forest Service office in Sedona, 928/282-4119, can tell you about recreation in this district.

V-Bar-V Ranch Petroglyph Site

Thirteen panels hold more than one thousand petroglyphs near Beaver Creek. Archaeologists think that the Sinagua created them during the end of their stay in the region. A volunteer at the site will point out and explain some of the symbols on the cliff face. You can visit only Fri.–Mon. 9:30 A.M.–4 P.M. and gates close at 3:30 P.M.; bring a Red Rock Pass to get in. From Sedona, head south 15 miles on AZ 179 to the I-17 overpass (Exit 298) and continue straight on paved Forest Road 618 another 2.4 miles; turn right at the sign just past the Beaver Creek bridge. An easy one-third-mile walk takes you to the rock art.

Wet Beaver Creek Wilderness

Sycamore, cottonwood, ash, alder, Arizona walnut, and wildflowers grow along the pretty creek

here. Yet, a short way from the water, the prickly pear cactus, agave, Utah juniper, and pinyon pine of the high desert take over. You might see mule or white-tailed deer, ringtail cat, coyote, javelina, Gambel's quail, red-tailed hawk, bald eagle, and great blue heron. Keep an eye out for rattlesnakes and poison ivy. Verde trout, some brown and rainbow, and suckers live in the creek, though most people find fishing conditions poor. Hikers enjoy trails along the lower creek, climbs to the Mogollon Rim, and difficult routes through the upper canyons. The many swimming holes in Wet Beaver Creek offer cool comfort in summer. Hiking in the lower canyon can be pleasant year-round. To reach these 6,700 acres of rugged wilderness, take I-17 Sedona Exit 298, turn southeast two miles on Forest Road 618, then left a quarter mile at the sign to **Bell Trail #13.** Elevations range from 3,820 feet at the trailhead to 6,500 feet atop the Mogollon Rim.

The first two miles of trail follow an old jeep road into the canyon, where the way narrows to a footpath. **Apache Maid Trail #15** begins at this point, climbing steeply out of the canyon to the north, then continuing at a moderate grade to Forest Road 620 near Apache Maid Mountain. This route is 9.5 miles one way and gains 2,380 feet in elevation. The Bell Trail continues upstream another mile past pretty pools to Bell Crossing, where it crosses the creek and climbs out to the east to Roundup Basin and Forest Road 214 near Five Mile Pass; you'll cover 10.8 miles one-way and gain 2,450 feet in elevation.

The Crack, a deep pool 150 feet upstream from Bell Crossing, makes a good turnaround point for a leisurely day-hike. Please don't camp here, as the area gets heavy use.

Adventurous hikers can continue upstream if they're willing to swim through many deep pools of cold, clear water; bring some flotation devices, especially if toting a camera or pack. Experienced hikers can also enter the upper canyon via Waldroup, Jacks, or Brady canyons. These routes involve some brush and descents on small cliff faces. Beaver Creek and unpalatable stock tanks are the only sources of water, so it's best to bring your own. Topo maps are a must for off-trail travel and the sometimes-faint trails on the Mogollon Rim.

West Clear Creek Wilderness (West Half)

This 13,600-acre wilderness offers some of the most awe-inspiring canyon country of the Mogollon Rim. West Clear Creek, the longest of the rim's streams, winds 30 miles and cuts canyons as deep as 2,000 feet. Deep pools in the middle section and only a few access points make most of the wilderness difficult to visit. The lower end of the canyon, however, can easily be explored on **West Clear Creek Trail #17.**

From I-17, take any of the Camp Verde exits and drive through town, continue east five miles on the General Crook Trail (AZ 260), turn left (north) two miles on Forest Road 618, then right (east) four miles on Forest Road 215 to the east end of Bull Pen dispersed camping area (elev. 3,700 feet). The first six miles is an easy walk along the creek, past fishing spots and swimming holes. You'll have to cross the creek several times, which can be difficult or impossible during high water. After six miles, the trail turns northwest and climbs steeply two miles to Forest Road 214A (elev. 5,780 feet).

Blodgett Basin Trail #31 can be combined with West Clear Creek Trail and 2.5 miles of forest roads (214A and 214) to make a 12.7-mile loop. The trailhead is a bit easier to reach than the one for West Clear Creek Trail. From the General Crook Trail, turn north four miles on Forest Road 618, then east 4.3 miles on Forest Road 214 to the trailhead (elev. 5,280 feet). Blodgett Basin Trail drops steadily in 2.5 miles to West Clear Creek Trail, about a half mile in from Bull Pen. To make the loop, turn up West Clear Creek Trail to its end at Forest Road 214A, follow the road west 1.2 miles to Forest Road 214, then turn left and walk 1.3 miles to the Blodgett Basin Trailhead.

The east half of West Clear Creek Wilderness provides excellent hiking adventures, too. The Long Valley-Blue Ridge Ranger District of the Coconino National Forest manages this land; see "Long Valley-Blue Ridge Ranger District," above.

Fossil Springs Wilderness

Springs northwest of Strawberry gush forth more than a million gallons of heavily mineralized water per hour. The water, emerging at a constant 72° F, supports a lush riparian environment. This 11,550-acre wilderness protects the scenic beauty and abundant wildlife of Fossil Creek and some of its tributaries. Elevations range from 4,300 feet at the springs to 6,800 feet on the Mogollon Rim.

Few trails enter the canyons, so much of the hiking in the wilderness is cross-country. Three trails lead to Fossil Springs. You can descend on Fossil Springs Trail #18 from the south rim, dropping 1,280 feet in 3.1 miles on a rough wagon road; the trailhead is 4.7 miles from Strawberry via Fossil Springs Road (Forest Road 708), then right 0.75 mile on Forest Road 784.

A hike from Irving Trailhead offers the gentle way in—Flume Road Trail #154 leads a half-mile to the Flume Road, then follows the road up-canyon 3.5 miles to the springs. Elevation gain is 440 feet. Flume Road, between the springs and Irving Power Plant, is open for hikers and bicyclists but closed to public motor vehicles; cyclists must park before the wilderness boundary, just before the springs. The power plant has produced electricity at this remote location since 1916; both it and the flume are listed on the National Register of Historic Places. The Irving and nearby Childs plants are to be destroyed and removed by Dec. 2004, though local historical groups are trying to preserve these venerable structures. The Irving Trailhead is at the bottom of a long, white-knuckle descent on Fossil Springs Road, 9.7 miles from Strawberry. Nervous drivers may prefer to approach from Camp Verde by heading east seven miles on AZ 260, then turning right 16.5 miles on Fossil Springs Road.

Mail Trail #84 descends from the north rim, dropping 1,300 feet in 3.1 miles; trailhead is 13 miles east on AZ 260 from the West Clear Creek bridge, then right on Forest Road 9247B to Mail Trail Tank #2 (high-clearance vehicle needed).

Verde Hot Springs

Two pools, one warm and one hot, lie on the west bank of the Verde River in the Tonto

National Forest. They attract hot-springs enthusiasts willing to make the drive and hike to this remote spot. A resort once operated here, but only the baths and piles of rubble remain; yellow stains on the cliffs above the river mark past thermal activity. Visitors irregularly clean the baths, so it's best to use caution before jumping in. It has evolved as a clothing-optional site.

You can approach the trailhead on unpaved Fossil Springs Road (Forest Road 708) either from Strawberry, north of Payson, or from Camp Verde. This road may be passable by cautiously driven cars, though people with a fear of heights will feel more comfortable coming from Camp Verde. From AZ 87 in Strawberry, you can head west 12.5 miles on Fossil Springs Road past the schoolhouse, descend into Fossil Creek Canyon, go past the Irving Power Plant area and Fossil Creek bridge, then turn left 6.5 miles at the sign for Childs Power Plant and the Verde River. From Camp Verde, take Main Street/AZ 260 east seven miles, turn right 14 miles on Fossil Springs Road, then

right 6.5 miles to the Verde River. On the last 6.5 miles, you'll climb high into the hills, pass a turnoff for Stehr's Lake and a scenic 4WD route to Ike's Backbone, then descend to Childs Dispersed Recreation Area on the riverbank at road's end; the last quarter mile may be too rough for cars.

There's an outhouse and primitive camping at this heavily used site. Lovers of solitude will do better to camp elsewhere. A five-day stay limit applies. Because it's a family area, no nudity is permitted here. Nearby Childs Power Plant is closed to the public, but a one-mile trail heads upriver past the power plant's outflow channels and climbs to the road that goes upriver. When the road descends to river level, look for a place to ford the Verde River, then follow the trail downriver a few hundred yards to the hot springs. Don't count on finding signs for the last part of the hike.

All these roads in the Fossil Creek and Verde River areas lead through magnificent scenery, worthwhile drives even if you don't come for the hot springs.

Along the Verde River

Below the cream- and red-colored cliffs of the Mogollon Rim, the Verde River brings life to a broad desert valley. Spanish explorers named the river *verde* ("green") for the luxuriant growth that lines its banks. The waters come from narrow canyons of Oak Creek, Wet and Dry Beaver creeks, West Clear Creek, Sycamore Creek, and other streams.

Prehistoric tribes camped in the area, finding a great variety of wild plant food and game between the 3,000-foot elevation of the lower valley and the rim country 4,000 feet higher. From about A.D. 600–700, Native American groups began cultivating the Verde Valley, taking advantage of the fine climate, fertile land, and abundant water. Trade and contacts with the Hohokam culture to the south also aided development of the region. Hohokam people probably migrated into the Verde Valley too, though archaeologists can't determine whether early farm-

ing communities were actually Hohokam or simply influenced by their culture. Verde inhabitants learned to grow cotton, weave cloth, make pottery, and build ball courts.

The Sinagua people arrived from what is now the Flagstaff area between A.D. 1125 and 1200, gradually absorbing the local cultures. Villages then started to consolidate. Large, multistoried pueblos replaced the small pithouses of earlier times. Two of these pueblos, Montezuma Castle and Tuzigoot, have become national monuments. Archaeologists don't know why, but the Verde Valley population departed by 1425. The elaborate Hohokam culture, based in the Gila and Salt River Valleys to the south, also disappeared about this time. Perhaps some of the Sinagua migrated northeast, eventually joining the Hopi and Zuni pueblos.

Early Spanish explorers, arriving a century and a half later, found small bands of nomadic

Tonto Apache and Yavapai roaming the valley. In language and culture, the Tonto Apache are related to the Apache and Navajo tribes to the east, while the Yavapai share cultural traits with the Hualapai and Havasupai to the northwest.

Anglos and Mexicans poured into the valley during a gold rush at the Hassayampa River and Lynx Creek in 1863. Farmers and ranchers followed, taking for themselves the best agricultural land along the Verde. The displaced tribes attacked the settlements but failed to drive off the newcomers. Soon the army arrived, building Camp Lincoln, later christened Fort Verde. General George Crook eventually subdued local tribes through clever campaigning and the enlistment of Apache scouts.

Tonto Apache and Yavapai received the Rio Verde Reservation in 1873, but the federal government took it away two years later, ordering the displaced tribes to proceed to the San Carlos Reservation, 150 miles away. In the cold February of 1875, they started the two-week journey on foot; of the 1,451 who began the trek, at least 90 died from exposure, were killed by infighting, or escaped.

Early in the 20th century, some Apache and Yavapai received permission to return to their Verde River homelands. What were once thousands of Native Americans occupying millions of acres now number less than 1,000 people on a few remnants of their former lands on the Camp Verde, Prescott, and Fort McDowell reservations.

Meanwhile, Anglo farmers in the Verde Valley prospered. Cottonwood, founded in 1879, became the valley's main trading center. Copper mining succeeded on a large scale at Jerome, which sprang to life high on a mountainside in 1882. Mine company officials built a giant smelter below Jerome in 1910 and laid out the town of Clarkdale. Depletion of the ore bodies in the early 1950s, however, forced many residents of Jerome and Clarkdale to seek jobs elsewhere. Today the Verde Valley thrives due to industry, farming, and popularity with tourists and retirees.

THE BALD EAGLE

(Haliaeetus leucocephalus)

Like many humans, the bald eagle prefers fast food and a home near waterways. Fish make up over half its diet, supplemented with small mammals, birds, and some carrion.

The Second Continental Congress designated this bird as a national symbol in 1782 and Congress gave it official protection in 1940, but by the early 1970s biologists could find only seven pairs in Arizona. Populations have come back now that DDT has been eliminated and nesting sites protected.

Southern bald eagles live in central and northwest areas of Arizona and nest in the central part. Eagles may be either year-round residents or winter visitors who nest elsewhere, most often in the Pacific Northwest. Their yellow eyes have vision thought to be eight times sharper than ours. White feathers cover the head and tail of adults, with brown over the rest of the body. Youngsters have dark-brown feathers with some white on the underside, so they are sometimes mistaken for golden eagles, Arizona's only other eagle species. Both sexes look alike except for size; adult males weigh 8–9 pounds, while females weigh 10–14. They hold their wings—which span up to 7.5 feet—horizontally when soaring, unlike the uptilted wings of vultures and golden eagles.

Breeding pairs look for a tall tree or cliff site with good visibility, protection from wind, and a nearby source of fish; nests average 6–8 feet across. Resident eagles breed in January and February, so that the young won't be subject to heat stress. The mother lays two or three white eggs, which hatch in about 35 days. Both parents attend to the incubation and feeding of the eaglets. After 11 weeks the babies can fly, then after several more weeks they can live on their own. Because raising eaglets is such delicate business—frightened parents can break eggs or stay away from the nest too long—known breeding areas are closed to the public December 1–June 30. It's best to view with binoculars from a quarter of a mile away or more. Good places to sight bald eagles include the Verde and Salt Rivers, Lake Pleasant, Bartlett Lake, the Coolidge area, and Alamo Lake.

CAMP VERDE

Early in 1865, 19 men set out from Prescott to start a farming settlement in the Verde Valley. They knew the mining camps around Arizona's new capital at Prescott would pay well for fresh food. The eager farmers chose land where West Clear Creek joins the Verde, about five miles downstream from the modern town of Camp Verde. After the farmers had planted fields, dug an irrigation system, and built a fort, raiding tribes destroyed much of the crops and livestock. Army troops marched in and built Camp Lincoln, one mile north of the present townsite. Because some people thought that too many place names commemorated the former president, the army later changed the post's name to Camp Verde.

Native American hostilities kept the cavalry and infantry busy during the late 1860s and early 1870s. The infantry built a road, later known as the General Crook Trail, west to Fort Whipple (near Prescott) and east along the Mogollon Rim to Fort Apache. In 1871 the post moved one mile south to its current location, where more than 20 buildings lined up beside a parade field. An 1882 battle at Big Dry Wash marked the last large engagement between soldiers and Native Americans in Arizona. Having served its purpose, Fort Verde closed in 1891.

Today exhibits and the four surviving fort buildings at Fort Verde State Historic Park give a feeling of what life was like for the enlisted men, officers, and women who lived here. Other attractions near town include the multistoried cliff dwelling of Montezuma Castle, the unusual lake at Montezuma Well, wilderness areas, and the Verde River.

Fort Verde State Historic Park

Like most forts of the period, Fort Verde served as a supply post and staging area for army patrols. It never had a protective wall, nor did Native Americans ever attack it. Today, a 12-acre park preserves the administration building, commanding officer's house, bachelors' quarters, doctor's quarters, and old parade ground.

Begin your visit at the adobe administration building, used by General George Crook during

Montezuma Castle

© BILL WEIR

the winter campaign of 1872–73 that largely ended Native American raids in the region. Exhibits recall the soldiers and their families, Apache army scouts, settlers, and prospectors who came through here more than 100 years ago. You'll see old photos, maps, letters, rifles, uniforms, saddles, and Native American artifacts. The three adobe buildings of Officers' Row have been restored and furnished as they were in the 1880s. Cavalry, infantry, and Indian scout reenactments take place during Fort Verde Days on the second weekend in October and a few other times during the year.

Fort Verde State Historic Park, 928/567-3275, is open daily 8 A.M.–5 P.M.; $2 adults, $1 ages 7–13. A gift shop sells history books. From Main Street in downtown Camp Verde (two miles east of I-17 Exit 287), turn east one block on Hollamon Street.

Montezuma Castle National Monument

This towering cliff dwelling so impressed early

visitors that they mistakenly believed followers of the famous Aztec ruler had built it. Actually, this pueblo had been neither a castle nor part of Montezuma's empire. Sinagua built it in the 12th and 13th centuries, toward the end of their stay in the Verde Valley. The five-story stone and mortar structure contains 20 rooms, once occupied by about 35 people. It's tucked back under a cliff 100 feet above Beaver Creek. The overhang shielded the village from rain, snow, and the hot summer sun but allowed the winter sun's low-angle rays to warm the dwellings. The ruins are well preserved, but too fragile to be entered, so you must view them from below. An even larger pueblo, Castle A, once stood against the base of the cliff; it had six stories and about 45 rooms, but little remains today. A level, paved one-third-mile trail loops below Montezuma Castle to the foundations of this second ruin.

The visitor center has exhibits of Sinagua artifacts and their everyday life, as well as of the plants, animals, and geology of the Verde Valley. Related books, videos, and maps are sold. Giant Arizona sycamore trees shade a picnic area beside the river. Montezuma Castle National Monument is open daily 8 A.M.–5 P.M., extended to 8 A.M.–7 P.M. in summer (Memorial Day–Labor Day); $3 per person (free under 17); 928/567-3322; www.nps.gov/moca. Take I-17 Exit 289 and follow signs two miles; from Camp Verde, drive north three miles on Montezuma Castle Road, then turn right two miles at the sign.

Montezuma Well

This natural sinkhole, 11 miles northeast of Montezuma Castle, attracts visitors both for its scenic beauty as a desert oasis and for its prehistoric ruins. The Sinagua built pueblos here between A.D. 1125 and 1400, using lake water to irrigate their crops. Parts of their villages and irrigation canals can still be seen. The sinkhole measures 470 feet across and is only partly filled by a 55-foot-deep lake. Signs describe some of the plants and animals that dwell in the clear water. You may see turtles swimming in the lake but no fish, as the carbon dioxide level is too high for them. A one-third-mile, self-guiding loop trail climbs to the rim, where a short trail winds down to the lake and to ruins sheltered in a cave. The main trail continues along the rim past a pueblo site and a large rectangular structure, which may have been a kiva, before beginning its descent to an ancient irrigation ditch. A short side trail to the left leads to the outlet where the lake drains into the ditch as it has since Sinagua times. Modern farmers continue to use the water, which flows at 1,100 gallons per minute. The main trail returns you to the parking area.

On the drive in, a tree-shaded picnic area and a prehistoric canal segment are down the road to the right a half mile before Montezuma Well. In another quarter mile on the main road, you can stop on the left to see a pithouse exhibit. Timbers that once held up the walls and roof have long since rotted away, but distinct outlines remain of the supporting poles, walls, entrance, and fire pit.

Montezuma's Well is part of Montezuma Castle National Monument and is open during the same hours, but there's no admission charge here. From Camp Verde or Montezuma Castle, take I-17 north to Exit 293 and follow signs five miles; another approach begins at I-17 Sedona Exit 298, turns east, then south three miles on a gravel road.

Accommodations

B's B&B, 94 Coppinger St., 928/567-1988, offers bed and breakfast with views and private baths in a home near Fort Verde State Park: $50 s, 60 d. Hacienda de la Mariposa, 3875 Stagecoach Rd., 928/567-1490, 888/520-9095, is a bed & breakfast resort with large rooms in a Santa Fe-style building. The pretty setting on five acres along Beaver Creek is only a mile from Montezuma Castle; seasonal rates run $155–195 d; www.lamariposa-az.com.

Three motels lie off AZ 260 (Finnie Flat Rd.) just east of I-17 Exit 287: Super 8 Motel, 928/567-2622, 800/800-8000, offering an indoor pool and hot tub, $52 s, $57 d and up; Microtel Inn & Suites, 928/567-3700, 888/771-7171, with an outdoor pool and hot tub, $45–49 s, $49–54 d, $69–74 suite; and Comfort Inn, 928/567-9000, 800/228-5150, which also has an outdoor pool and hot tub, $50 d and up.

Cliff Castle Lodge and Casino, three miles from downtown on Middle Verde Road near I-17 Exit 289 and the turnoff for Montezuma Castle, 928/567-6611, 800/524-6343, features luxury accommodations, restaurants, a casino, tours, trail rides, pool, and hot tub; $59 s, $69 d; add $5 on weekends. The lodge, along with The Gathering Restaurant and tour offices, is below the hilltop casino; www.cliffcastle.com. **Beaver Creek Golf Resort,** 928/567-4475, lies north in the community of Lake Montezuma near Montezuma Well; take I-17 Exit 293 and follow signs three miles, $60–65 d; golf packages may be available too.

Campgrounds

These normally stay open all year in the Verde Valley's mild climate. **Trails End RV Park,** 983 Finnie Flats Rd., 928/567-0100, is between downtown and I-17 Exit 289; RV sites cost $22 with hookups and there are showers and laundry. **Rancho Verde RV Park,** 1488 W. Horseshoe Bend, 928/567-7037, has showers and laundry; it's two miles west on AZ 260 from I-17 Exit 289, then right about a mile on Horseshoe Bend; RV sites with hookups cost $16. **Zane Grey RV Park** (adult) lies on the left seven miles southeast on Main St./AZ 260, just beyond the West Clear Creek bridge, 928/567-4320, 800/235-0608; $20 RV with hookups, showers, and laundry.

Two campgrounds on national forest land have drinking water all year and a $10 fee, but no showers or hookups. **Clear Creek Campground** is six miles southeast on Main St./AZ 260, then left just before West Clear Creek bridge. **Beaver Creek Campground** lies to the northeast; take I-17 north to Sedona Exit 298, then turn southeast 2.3 miles on Forest Road 618; or you can turn north on Forest Road 618 from AZ 260 at a junction west of the West Clear Creek bridge.

Food

Ming House, 238 S. Main St. downtown in Fort Verde Plaza, 928/567-9488, serves Chinese food daily for lunch and dinner and offers buffets. **Vito's Pizza,** 238 S. Main St. (behind the

Ming House), 928/567-6300, is open daily for lunch and dinner. **Rio Verde Restaurant,** on the south edge of town at 77 South Access Rd., 928/567-9966, cooks up Mexican and some American food daily for lunch and dinner. **Sister's and Co. Café** in the Outpost Mall on Finnie Flats Rd., 928/567-0351, serves standard American fare daily for breakfast, lunch, and dinner. **Basha's** supermarket is also in the Outpost Mall. Other cafés in town may lack a smoke-free section.

The Gathering Restaurant in Cliff Castle Lodge, three miles north of town on Montezuma Castle Hwy., 928/567-6611, serves breakfast and lunch daily. The casino on the hill above the lodge has several places to eat, but they suffer from smoke-laden air and slot-machine noise. **The Ranch House,** beside Beaver Creek Golf Course at Lake Montezuma (near Montezuma Well), 928/567-4492, has a large menu. Dinner specialties include steak, prime rib, and seafood plus country favorites such as mesquite-cooked barbecue. It's open daily for breakfast, lunch, and dinner.

La Fonda Mexican Restaurant, 928/567-3500, lies about four miles outside town on Finnie Flats Road (AZ 260) toward Cottonwood; go west two miles past I-17, then turn right and drive 0.1 mile on Horseshoe Bend Drive. It's open Mon.–Sat. for lunch and dinner.

Events

Southwest Days in late April celebrates with mule races, other equestrian events, art, crafts, and food. **Armed Forces Day,** on the third weekend of May, commemorates the "History of the Soldier" through all eras of American history with encampments and drills at Fort Verde State Historic Park. The July 4th **Independence Day Celebration** has family activities and fireworks. **Verde Valley Pow Wow,** sponsored by Cliff Castle Casino in July, presents Native American dance and drumming performances. The **Cornfest** marks the beginning of the harvest season on the Saturday of the fourth weekend in July with lots of corn and other food, entertainment, arts, and crafts. **Fort Verde Days,** on the second weekend in October, brings back the old days with cavalry parades and drills, a barbecue, roping events, arts and crafts shows, games, and a dance.

Recreation

Play **golf** at Beaver Creek's 18-hole course at Lake Montezuma (near Montezuma Well); 928/567-4487.

Information and Services

The **Camp Verde Chamber of Commerce,** 928/567-9294, will help you with area sights and services, including Forest Service recreation opportunities; open Mon.–Fri. 8 A.M.–4 P.M. and sometimes on Saturday in summer. It's downtown at 385 S. Main and Hollamon Sts. (P.O. Box 3520, Camp Verde, AZ 86322); www.campverde.org.

The **Verde Ranger District** office of the Prescott National Forest, 928/567-4121, provides information on running the Verde River, wilderness areas, camping, hiking, and road conditions for the lands south and west of town; you can purchase books and maps. It's open Mon.–Fri. 8 A.M.–4:30 P.M.; www.fs.fed.us/r3/prescott. Head southeast one mile from downtown on Main St./AZ 260 and turn left at the sign (P.O. Box 670, Camp Verde, AZ 86322).

The **post office** lies just west of downtown on Finnie Flats Road.

Native Visions, at the Lodge at Cliff Castle, 928/567-3035, offers van tours to Montezuma Castle, Montezuma Well, and Tuzigoot as well as horseback rides through nearby hills.

VICINITY OF CAMP VERDE (VERDE RANGER DISTRICT)

Beasley Flat

Visitors enjoy pretty scenery, a picnic area, nature trail, and river access on the bank of the Verde River at Beasley Flat. The nature trail extends half a mile along the riverbank in the recreation area with viewpoints and river access trails; the lower section has a paved loop. From downtown Camp Verde, head south on Main Street about half a mile, turn right 8.5 miles on Salt Mine Road/Forest Road 574, then left two miles on unpaved Forest Road 529. Fishermen can also access the river six miles in on Salt Mine Road. From I-17, you can take Exit 285 and go east 1.8 miles toward Camp Verde, turn right 0.5 mile on Oasis Road, right 7.4 miles on Salt Mine Road/Forest Road 574, then left two miles on unpaved Forest Road 529. No camping or motorized boats are permitted. Prescott National Forest offices have a map handout.

River Running on the Verde

Experienced boaters in kayaks or rafts can venture downriver from Camp Verde to Sheep Bridge near Horseshoe Reservoir, 59 miles away. People are just beginning to discover this wild and scenic stretch of river. You're likely to see wildlife and well-preserved prehistoric ruins along the way. An area of shoreline is closed Dec.–April to protect a bald eagle nesting site. The main river-running season lasts from January to early April during spring runoff, but inflatable kayaks can sometimes negotiate the shallow waters off-season. The ice-cold water in winter and spring necessitates use of full or partial wetsuits. With time for rest stops and scouting rapids, rafts typically average two miles per hour.

The wildest water flows between Beasley Flat and Childs. Canoeists often experience trouble negotiating the rapids here, winding up with smashed boats. Unless you really know what you're doing, it's best to avoid the potentially dangerous conditions below Beasley Flat.

Shuttle services may be available—ask at the Camp Verde Chamber of Commerce. The Forest Service offers a *River Runners Guide to the Verde River;* contact the Verde Ranger District or the Tonto National Forest office at 2324 E. McDowell Rd. in Phoenix; 602/225-5200.

Mild to Wild, 800/567-6745, offers rafting trips of one, two, and four days on the Verde from February to late April if conditions permit. Wetsuits and camping gear may be rented. The company also offers trips on the Salt River in Arizona and on rivers in the state of Colorado. Its main office is at 1111 Camino del Rio, Durango, CO 81301; www.mild2wildrafting.com.

Cedar Bench Wilderness

Three trails cross the 16,000-acre wilderness,

which extends along the Verde Rim as high as 6,678 feet and drops to a section of the Verde River at 2,800 feet in a remote area south of Camp Verde. Backcountry travelers can reach trailheads at the lower elevations off Forest Road 574 near Beasley Flat and from the rim via Dugas Road from I-17 Exit 268. Utah and alligator juniper, which the pioneers mistakenly called "cedars," grow at the higher elevations and in some canyons along with pinyon pine and Gambel oak. Chaparral covers much of the lower slopes. Topo maps are Horner Mountain, Tule Mesa, and Arnold Mesa. The Prescott, Tonto, and Coconino Forest maps show the back roads. The Verde Ranger District office near Camp Verde provides road conditions and trail descriptions.

Pine Mountain Wilderness

Pine Mountain (6,814 feet) crowns part of the Verde Rim south of Cedar Bench Wilderness and Camp Verde. The 20,100-acre Pine Mountain Wilderness offers solitude and natural beauty far from towns and highways. Forests of majestic ponderosa pine, pinyon pine and juniper woodlands, and chaparral cover the rough terrain. The rugged eastern side drops to an elevation of 3,800 feet in the Verde Valley. You might see mule or white-tailed deer, javelina, bear, or mountain lion.

To reach the trailhead, take I-17 Exit 268 (Dugas Rd.)—18 miles south of Camp Verde and six miles north of Cordes Junction—then head southeast 18 miles on dirt Forest Road 68 to Salt Flat, a quarter mile before Nelson Place, an abandoned homestead. This road is best attempted in cars only in good weather.

A 9.6-mile roundtrip loop to the top of Pine Mountain consists of Nelson Trail #159, Pine Mountain Trail #14, Verde Rim Trail #161, and Willow Springs Trail #12. Allow six hours for the trip, and carry water. Elevation gain is about 1,600 feet. Other loop hikes in the area can be done too. Consult the Prescott, Tonto, or Coconino forest maps and the 7.5-minute Tule Mesa topo map. The Verde Ranger District office near Camp Verde can advise on road and trail conditions.

COTTONWOOD

Named for the trees along the Verde River, Cottonwood provides a handy base for visiting the old mining town of Jerome, prehistoric Tuzigoot ruins, wildlife areas, and the other attractions of the Verde Valley. The town is 14 miles northwest of Camp Verde, 17 miles southwest of Sedona, and 41 miles northeast across Mingus Mountain from Prescott.

Cottonwood has two downtowns—a new section along AZ 89A and the original "Old Town," now bypassed by the highway. Clarkdale, just two miles northwest of Cottonwood, displays many old houses and businesses dating from its construction as a smelter town beginning in 1912; tourist offices may have a *Tour Historic Clarkdale* brochure. Although many residents lost their jobs when the smelter shut down in 1952, others were glad to be rid of its heavy black smoke. A newer industry, the Phoenix Cement Company, supplied cement used in building Glen Canyon Dam on the Colorado River.

Verde Canyon Railroad

Travelers embark at the Clarkdale station for a leisurely journey upstream into the beautiful Verde River Canyon. A guide narrates the history and points out some of the historic ranches, wildlife, and geologic features. Bald eagles can sometimes be seen nesting in spring; golden eagles, hawks, and blue herons may be sighted, too. The ride lasts about four hours roundtrip, with turnaround at the historic railway buildings in Perkinsville. Vintage diesel engines pull comfortable, climate-controlled cars. If the weather's fine, you can stroll out to the open cars for the best panoramas. A café/grill at the station serves lunch, which you can have on the picnic tables outside or take on the train. A few snack items can be purchased on board; first-class includes hot and cold hors d'oeuvres. A small railroad museum in the station exhibits historic photos and artifacts; free. A gift shop sells souvenirs.

Tickets for coach class cost $40 adults, $40 seniors 65 and older, and $21 children under 12; first-class has plush, more spacious seating at $55 (all ages). Trains run 2–6 days a week depending on season—spring and autumn have the most departures. Special excursions include the Starlight Tours, which run on Saturday evenings near the full moon in the warmer months. Check schedules and make recommended reservations at 300 N. Broadway, Clarkdale, AZ 86324; 928/639-0010, 800/293-7245; www.verdecanyonrr.com. Wheelchair users have access to the station and train. From Cottonwood, head north on Main St., which becomes Broadway; if coming from Jerome, follow signs for Clarkdale and the railroad.

Tuzigoot National Monument

Sinagua built and lived in this hilltop pueblo from A.D. 1125 to 1400. Tuzigoot (TOO-zee-goot) stood two stories and contained about 77 ground-floor and perhaps 15 second-story rooms. At its peak in the late 1300s, the pueblo housed 225 people. The large size of the ruin may be the result of a drought in the 1200s, which forced many dry-land farmers to resettle at Tuzigoot and other villages near the Verde River. Most rooms lacked doorways—a ladder through a hatchway in the roof permitted entry. The original roofs, now gone, were pine and sycamore beams covered by willow branches and sealed with mud. While excavating the site in 1933–34, University of Arizona researchers found a wide variety of artifacts, including grave offerings for 408 burials.

A visitor center next to the ruins displays some of the archaeological finds, including stone axes and tools, projectile points, pottery, turquoise and shell jewelry, and religious objects. Other exhibits illustrate what's known about Sinagua agriculture, weaving, building techniques, and burials. A room replica shows how a living area at Tuzigoot might have looked. Outside, a quarter-mile trail loops through the maze of ruins. You can climb up to a second-story lookout at the summit for a panorama.

The Apache name Tuzigoot originally referred to nearby Peck's Lake and meant Crooked Water; people liked the word because it had a nice ring to it, so they gave the name to this site. Tuzigoot National Monument, 928/634-5564, is open daily 8 A.M.–5 P.M., extended to 8 A.M.–7 P.M. in summer (Memorial Day to Labor Day); $3 per person admission, free for ages under 17; www.nps.gov/tuzi. Take Broadway, the old road running between Cottonwood and Clarkdale, then turn east and drive 1.3 miles on Tuzigoot Road to the ruins.

Dead Horse Ranch State Park

Visitors enjoy picnicking, camping, hiking, and fishing year-round along the Verde River. The park, 928/634-5283, offers day-use areas, campgrounds with showers, a group reservation area, equestrian facilities, a trail network, a fishing lagoon, and a playground. About 40 miles of trails inside and adjacent to the park attract hikers, mountain bikers, and equestrians. The Verde Valley Birding Festival takes place here on the last weekend in April; contact the park, chamber, or visit www.birdyverde.org. Birders enjoy sightings year-round, especially along the Verde River Greenway Trail near the river in the park and from a viewing platform at Tavasci Marsh, 1.5 miles northwest of the park. Mountain bikers and hikers can make a seven-mile loop on Raptor Hill, Thumper, and Lime Kiln Trails; wagons once followed Lime Kiln Trail on an old route between Sedona and Jerome. This intermediate ride, which connects with other trails, takes about 1.5 hours on a mountain bike or 3.5 hours on foot. The river and a lagoon harbor trout in winter in addition to year-round largemouth bass, catfish, and bluegill; fly fishermen use a riverside trail upstream from the River Day Use Area.

The campground has loops for both tenters and RVers. Equestrians can arrange to camp with their horses (ask in advance). On spring and autumn weekends all sites may fill and it's best to arrive early; you can call to check availability, but family sites are first-come, first served. A dump station is just inside the park entrance. Day use costs $4 per vehicle, campsites for tents or RVs run $10 ($15 with water and electric hookups). From Main St. in Cottonwood, turn north on 10th St. and follow signs 0.9 mile.

Clemenceau Heritage Museum

The Verde Historical Society operates this museum, 928/634-2868, in the Clemenceau School

Building, built in 1923–24. The imaginative displays include permanent and rotating exhibits on local history, a model train room (illustrates seven historic Verde Valley lines), and a vintage classroom. The 1921 Bank of Clemenceau has been recently moved and restored at its new site beside the museum. A gift shop sells books and souvenirs. The museum sponsors a "Crafts American Style" art show on the second Saturday of February and a "Zeke Taylor Bar-B-Que" on the second Saturday of November. Open Wed. 9 A.M.–noon and Fri.–Sun. 11 A.M.–3 P.M. except major holidays; donations welcome. It's on the corner of Willard St. and Mingus Avenue.

Accommodations

Under $50: Little Daisy Motel, 34 S. Main St., 928/634-7865, starts at $48 d ($52 d kitchenettes). **Pines Motel,** 920 S. Camino Real, 928/634-9975, 800/483-9618, runs $36 s, $49 d ($39 s, $55 d weekends). **View Motel,** 818 S. Main/AZ 89A, 928/634-7581, offers a pool and hot tub from $36 s, $40 d ($48 s, $50 d for kitchenettes). **Sundial Motel,** 1034 N. Main St., 928/634-8031, is a restored 1932 establishment in Old Town Cottonwood with daily rates of $40 d ($45 d for a kitchenette) and weekly rates of $175 d ($185 d kitchenette).

$50–100: Willow Tree Inn, 1089 S. Hwy. 260 (near the junction with AZ 89A), 928/634-3678, runs $48 s, $58 d. **Quality Inn,** 301 W. Hwy. 89A, 928/634-4207, 800/228-5151, offers a restaurant, pool, and hot tub; $65–69 d ($69–79 d weekends). The **Best Western Cottonwood Inn,** 993 S. Main St. (on the corner of AZ 89A and AZ 260), 928/634-5575, 800/350-0025, also features a restaurant, swimming pool, and hot tub; $79–89 d.

Flying Eagle Country Bed & Breakfast, 2700 Windmill Lane, 928/634-0211, has fine views of the Verde Valley from a hillside above Clarkdale; amenities include a hot tub and full breakfast for $85 and $95 d.

Campgrounds

Dead Horse Ranch State Park, described above, and RV parks offer year-round camping with showers. **Turquoise Triangle RV Park,** 2501 E.

Hwy. 89A (1.5 blocks east of the junction with AZ 260), 928/634-5294, 888/994-7275, has RV sites for $22 with hookups. **Rio Verde RV Park,** 3420 E. Hwy. 89A (one mile east from the junction with AZ 260), 928/634-5990, costs $15 for a tent, $25 for an RV with hookups.

Food

Country Kitchen Restaurant, 991 S. Main St. (at the junction of AZ 89A and AZ 260), 928/634-3696, offers a varied menu and pleasant atmosphere at the Cottonwood Inn; it's open daily for breakfast, lunch, and dinner. **Sizzler,** across the street at 1041 Hwy. 260, 928/634-3605, has steak, seafood, and a big salad bar, open daily for lunch and dinner. **Famous Sam's Restaurant & Sports Bar,** 3360 E. Hwy. 89A (one mile east from the junction with AZ 260), 928/634-2271, features steak, seafood, prime rib, and a good salad bar overlooking the Verde River; it's open daily for lunch and dinner.

Rosalie's Bluewaters Inn, 517 N. 12th and Main Sts., 928/634-8702, serves American food including prime rib, steak, and seafood; open Tues.–Sun. for breakfast, lunch, and dinner. **Hobo Joe's,** 660 E. Mingus, 928/634-2651, serves American food for breakfast and lunch daily. **Georgie's Café,** 634 S. Main St. (Verde Valley Plaza at the junction of AZ 89A and Cottonwood St.), 928/639-0751, is open daily for breakfast (the house specialty) and lunch, and Tues.–Sat. for dinner. **Bluegrass Café,** 315 S. Main St., 928/639-3620, prepares steak, chicken, seafood, pasta, fajitas, and sandwiches daily except Mon. for lunch and dinner.

Artwork decorates **Old Town Café,** 1025 N. Main in Old Town Cottonwood, 928/634-5980, which has an espresso bar, pastries, soups, and sandwiches open Tues.–Sat. for breakfast and lunch.

Golden Dragon, 1675 E. Cottonwood St. (Sawmill Square Shopping Center), 928/634-0588, features Mandarin and Szechwan cuisine daily for lunch and dinner. **Ming House,** 888 S. Main St., 928/639-2885, prepares Cantonese and Mandarin food daily for lunch and dinner.

Gabriela's, 1425 E. Hwy. 89A (just east of the junction with AZ 260), 928/649-3949, prepares Mexican cuisine Mon.–Sat. for lunch and dinner. **Guero's,** 1695 E. Cottonwood St. (Sawmill Square Shopping Center), 928/634-6470, serves Mexican and American food; open Mon.–Sat. for lunch and dinner. **Su Casa,** 1000 S. Main St. in Clarkdale, 928/634-2771, is a south-of-the-border café with a good selection of burritos and vegetarian items; it's open weekends for breakfast and daily for lunch and dinner.

You can buy groceries at **Fry's** in the Wal-Mart Shopping Center, at **Safeway** in the Sawmill Square Shopping Center, or at **Bashas'** in Verde Valley Plaza. **Mount Hope Foods Naturally** is at 853 S. Main Street.

Entertainment and Events

Blazin' M Ranch, 928/634-0334, 800/937-8643, serves up a chuckwagon supper followed by a Western stage show with cowboy songs and humor. Other attractions include the photo studio, shooting gallery, petting zoo, and sarsaparilla bar. It's open Wed.–Sat. at 5 P.M. for outdoor activities, 6:30 P.M. for dinner of barbecue beef or chicken or a vegetarian option, then the show at 7:30 P.M.; closed January and August. Dinner and show cost $20 adults, $10 lil' wranglers 10 and under. Reservations are recommended, especially for a vegetarian dinner; www.blazinm.com. Take 10th St. past the Dead Horse Ranch State Park entrance, then turn left at the sign.

Major annual events include the **Verde Valley Gem and Mineral Show** in late March, **Verde Valley Birding Festival** on the last weekend in April (see www.birdyverde.org), **Antique Auto, Cycle & Aeroplane Show** and **Cinco de Mayo Sizzlin' Salsa Sunday** on the first weekend in May, **Verde Valley Fair** in early May, **Fourth of July Celebration, Verde River Days** (environmental programs) on the last Saturday in September, and a **Christmas Parade** in early December.

Information and Services

People at the **Cottonwood Chamber of Commerce,** 928/634-7593, will tell you about the sights, events, and facilities in the area. The office is in an adobe-style building conveniently located at the intersection of AZ 89A and AZ 260 (1010 S. Main St., Cottonwood, AZ 86326). It's open daily except holidays 9 A.M.–5 P.M.; chamber.verdevalley.com. Cottonwood's **public library,** 100 S. Sixth St., 928/634-7559, is open Monday–Saturday.

The **post office** is at 700 E. Mingus Avenue. **Verde Valley Medical Center,** 269 S. Candy Lane, 928/634-2251, provides medical services; a regional physician directory is at www.verdevalleymedicalcenter.com. A **swimming pool,** 928/634-7468, open in summer, and **tennis courts** are at Garrison Park, near the corner of E. Mingus Avenue and Sixth Street. **Verde Santa Fe Golf Course,** five miles northeast of town on Hwy. 89A, 928/634-5454, has 18 holes.

Tours and Transportation

Walking Tours of Old Town Cottonwood, 928/634-9468, take you to historic sites and relate stories of notable characters; call for days and times of the tours, which run year-round; www.oldtown.org. The **Sedona-Phoenix Shuttle,** 928/282-2066, 800/448-7988, operates about eight times daily between Sedona and Phoenix Sky Harbor Airport with stops at Cottonwood and Camp Verde. **Ace Xpress Shuttle Service,** 928/639-3357, 800/336-2239, provides door-to-door service from the Verde Valley to Sky Harbor Airport ($47 one-way, $78 roundtrip).

JEROME

Jerome, clinging to the slopes of Cleopatra Hill above the Verde Valley, might be Arizona's most unusual town in both its layout and history. For more than 70 years the town's booming mines produced copper, gold, and silver. Most residents departed after 1953 when the mines closed, but Jerome has come back to life with museums, art galleries, antique shops, and restaurants. Old-fashioned buildings—some restored, others abandoned but still standing—add to the atmosphere. Walking Jerome's winding streets is like touring a museum of early 20th-century American architecture.

Expansive views across the Verde Valley take in Sedona's Red Rock Country, Sycamore Canyon, the Mogollon Rim, and the distant San Francisco Peaks. Three very different museums will introduce you to the human and mining history of the area.

History

Prehistoric tribes came to dig brilliant blue azurite and other copper minerals for use as paint and jewelry. Spanish explorers, shown the diggings by Native American guides, failed to see any worth in the place. In 1876, several American prospectors staked claims to the rich copper deposits, but they lacked the resources to develop them. Eugene Jerome, a wealthy lawyer and financier, smelled a profit and offered financial backing to those who would mine the ore. A surveyor laying out the townsite named it in honor of the Jerome family, though Eugene himself never visited the area.

From the time the United Verde Copper Company began operating in 1882, the town's economy went on a wild roller-coaster ride dependent on copper prices. Mines closed for brief periods, then reopened. So many saloons, gambling dens, and brothels thrived in Jerome that a New York newspaper called it the "wickedest town in the West." Fires roared through the frame houses and businesses three times between 1897 and 1899, yet Jerome rose again each time, eventually becoming Arizona's fifth-largest city. Underground blasting and fault slippage shook the earth so much that some buildings keeled over and banks refused to take the average Jerome house or business as collateral. The town's famous sliding jail took off across the street and down the hillside, where it still lies today.

The community enjoyed its greatest prosperity during the Roaring '20s, when the population hit 15,000. The stock market crash and ensuing Depression spelled disaster for the copper industry; mines and smelter shut down and the population plummeted to less than 5,000. World War II brought Jerome's last period of prosperity before the mines shut down for good in 1953.

Many people thought Jerome would become a ghost town when the population shrank to only 50 souls. But, beginning in the late 1960s, artists, shop owners, tourists, retirees, and others rediscovered Jerome's unique character and setting.

Jerome State Historic Park

The Douglas Mansion, built in 1916 by James "Rawhide Jimmy" Douglas, tops a hill overlooking the Little Daisy Mine. Today, the old adobe-brick mansion brims with Jerome mining lore.

A video presentation portrays the many changes Jerome has seen. An assay office, the Douglas library, old photos, mining tools, smelter models, and mineral displays show different aspects of the effort expended to extract metals from the earth. Upstairs, a three-dimensional model illustrates Jerome's mineshafts, underground work areas, and geologic features.

Outside, you'll see a giant stamp mill and the more primitive *arrastre* (drag-stone mill) and Chilean wheels once used to pulverize ore. Signs at viewpoints identify some of Jerome's historic buildings.

Jerome State Historic Park, 928/634-5381, is open daily 8 A.M.–5 P.M.; $3 adults, $2 ages 7–13. A small picnic area beside the mansion offers expansive views of the Verde Valley. Turn off AZ 89A at Milepost 345 at the lower end of Jerome (eight miles west of Cottonwood), then follow the paved road one mile.

Jerome Historical Society Mine Museum

Exhibits in an 1899 building that once housed a fashion salon now illustrate Jerome's development with paintings, photos, stock certificates, mining tools, and ore samples. A gift shop sells books about Jerome's fascinating history. The museum, 928/634-5477, is open daily 9 A.M.–4:30 P.M.; admission is $1 adults, free for children under 12. Look for the two large half-wheels downtown at the corner of Main Street (AZ 89A) and Jerome Avenue.

Gold King Mine & Ghost Town

If you're fascinated by old machinery, or if you've ever wanted to poke around a ghost town, this

Poisonous fumes belch from the smokestacks of the Jerome Smelter in about 1900. The main stack was 160 feet tall and 22 feet in diameter. Miners' houses cling to the hillside in the background.

©JEROME STATE HISTORIC PARK

collection should satisfy your curiosity. The mine and the town of Haynes came to life here in 1890–1914, when miners dug a 1,200-foot-deep shaft to extract a modest amount of gold and silver. Among the hoists, pumps, engines, and ore cars, look for the prospect tunnel, a blacksmith shop, a 1930s gas station, and an assay office. A small petting zoo attracts the kids. You can watch an antique sawmill in operation daily. An impressive collection of historic vehicles, some restored, crowds the lanes. Many are Studebakers, including a 1902 electric that still runs. An antique truck and equipment show takes place here in June; there's also a VW bus show in September.

Enter through the gift shop, which sells mining memorabilia and other souvenirs. The ghost town, 928/634-0053, is open daily 9 A.M.–5 P.M. Admission is $4 adults, $3 seniors 62–74, $2 children 6–12; you get in free if under 6 or over 74. From the upper switchback on AZ 89A in downtown Jerome, turn northwest and drive one mile on Perkinsville Road. On the way you'll pass a large open-pit mine on the left, where Jerome's smelter stood at the beginning of the 20th century.

Perkinsville Road

This scenic back road drops from Jerome to the Verde River at the historic Perkinsville Ranch, then climbs into the ponderosa pine forests of the Mogollon Rim and on to downtown Williams. The first 27 miles are dirt, followed by 25 of pavement. Cars may be able to negotiate the road—bumpy and dusty in places—in dry weather. All vehicles should avoid the route after winter snowstorms or heavy summer rains. Allow at least three hours for a one-way drive, or more to stop for views, hikes, or a picnic. Stock up on gas and supplies, as none are available along the way. Turn northwest onto Perkinsville Road at the upper switchback in Jerome.

Accommodations

Modern motels have yet to hit town, but Jerome does offer character and great views at its hotels and bed and breakfasts. Reservations should be made for weekends. **Jerome Grand Hotel,** 928/634-8200, 888/817-6788, features a commanding panorama, comfortable lodging, and fine dining in the upper part of town. After opening in 1927 as the United Verde Hospital, then closing in 1950, the building lay dormant until an extensive renovation converted it to the hotel in 1996. All rooms have private bath and run $85 d for a standard, $110 d for a balcony, $140 d for connecting rooms, and $195 d for a suite; www.jeromegrandhotel.net. It's at the top of narrow Hill Street, which turns up opposite Jerome Palace's Haunted Hamburger.

The 1898 **Connor Hotel,** 164 Main St., 928/634-5006, 800/523-3554, is the only original Jerome hotel still in business. Rooms all have private bath and go for $75–125 d; www.connor hotel.com.

The Surgeon's House, at the base of Hill St., 928/639-1452, 800/639-1452, has bed and breakfast rooms, all with private bath, for $100–150 d. The circa 1899 **Inn at Jerome,** 309 Main St., 928/634-5094, 800/634-5094, features Victorian-style rooms—two with private bath—at $55–85 d including breakfast; www.innatjerome.com. **Cottage Inn,** 747 East Ave., 928/634-0701, dates from 1904 and has 1940s decor; rates are $70 d with breakfast. **Ghost City Inn,** 541 Main St., 928/634-4678, 888/634-4678, occupies an 1898 Victorian boardinghouse filled with antiques; two of the rooms have private bath and there's a hot tub; rates are $85–125 d; www.ghostcityinn .com. Cottonwood has a good selection of modern motels eight miles south.

Campgrounds

Besides **Dead Horse Ranch State Park** and the RV parks in Cottonwood below town, you can head seven miles up AZ 89A to the cool forest of Mingus Mountain. At the 7,023-foot pass, turn right a half mile on a paved road for **Potato Patch,** which offers pull-thru RV sites with electricity and water in B Loop for $15, and non-hookup sites farther back in the forest at Loop A for $10; the season runs May to September. On the way in, you'll pass a trailhead on the left for the Woodchute Wilderness.

The turnoff for **Mingus Mountain Campground** is on the other side of the highway at the pass; head in three miles on unpaved Forest Road 104; sites are open about May to September with a $6 fee but no drinking water. Groups can reserve **Playground,** 2.5 miles in on Forest Road 104, at 877/444-6777; reserveusa.com.

Food

The Asylum at Jerome Grand Hotel (head up Hill St. opposite the Haunted Hamburger), 928/639-3197, prepares New American cuisine daily for lunch and dinner; bands entertain some weekends.

Jerome Palace's Haunted Hamburger, on the upper side of town at 410 N. Clark St. (AZ 89A), 928/634-0554, features steak, prime rib, pasta, and sandwiches. You can dine indoors or on the patio, which has great views; open daily for lunch and dinner.

Jerome Brewery, 111 Main St., 928/639-8477, offers several of their brews plus a long list of tasty appetizers, pizzas, gourmet sandwiches, and salads; open daily for lunch and dinner. The 1899 **English Kitchen,** 119 Jerome Ave., 928/634-2132, is the oldest restaurant in Arizona. It serves breakfast and lunch daily except Monday; there's a patio but no smoke-free section.

Jerome Grill, 309 Main St., 928/634-5094, serves American and Southwestern food daily for breakfast and lunch. **Flatiron Cafe,** at the fork in the lower part of town where AZ 89A divides, 928/634-2733, serves breakfast, sandwiches, baked goods, fancy coffees, salads, and other refreshments. It's open daily in the morning and afternoon, except may close Tues. and Wed.; there's a patio across Main Street. Next door on Main, **A Pizza Heaven,** 928/649-1843, serves pizza, salad, and baked goods for lunch and dinner, but is open only Fri.–Sunday.

Entertainment and Events

For entertainment, locals hang out in the Spirit Room of the **Connor Hotel** and at **Paul & Jerry's Saloon,** both on upper Main Street.

Arts festivals take place occasionally. The Gold King Mine & Ghost town has its **Antique Truck and Equipment Show** on the first weekend of May. The **Jerome Home Tour** visits historic houses and buildings not normally open to the public; it's held on the third weekend of May.

Shopping

Shops up and down Main St. and Hull Avenue display a wide variety of artwork, crafts, antiques, jewelry, and clothing. The **Old Mingus Art Center** houses galleries in former school buildings at the lower end of town. Of these, **Anderson/Mandette Studio,** 928/634-3438, has by far the largest collection on display. It's open daily 11 A.M.–6 P.M.; www.anderson-mandette.com.

Information and Services

The small **chamber of commerce** office, 310 Hull Ave. (Drawer K, Jerome, AZ 86331), 928/634-2900, has information on sights and services in town. Open daily 11 A.M.–3 P.M., depending on staffing. It's near the sliding jail just past the large parking lots on the uphill section of AZ 89A; jerome.chamber.com. The **Jerome Public Library,** at 111 Jerome Ave. 928/639-0574, is open daily, though hours may be short. The **post office** is at 120 Main Street.

VICINITY OF JEROME
Mingus Mountain

The high country seven miles southwest of Jerome offers many hikes and back-road drives. Besides the two developed campgrounds (see Jerome campgrounds above), campers can also find many undeveloped places. Winter visitors enjoy **Summit Snowplay** at the 7,023-foot pass on AZ 89A between Jerome and Prescott. Inner tubes and plastic dishes can be used, but no sleds. The site has paved parking, toilets, and a $5/vehicle fee. In summer it's the **Summit Picnic Area** (no fee). The Prescott National Forest offices near Camp Verde and in Prescott have information sheets on campgrounds and hiking trails.

Woodchute Wilderness

This small, 5,700-acre wilderness protects the gentle slopes of Woodchute Mountain (7,834 feet), about 10 miles west of Jerome. Woodchute Trail heads north to the summit from a trailhead near Potato Patch Campground.

Prescott and Vicinity

That's *Prescutt,* pardner. The mile-high town rests in a mountain basin ringed by the pine-forested Bradshaws, towering Thumb Butte, the jumbled mass of Granite Mountain, boulder-strewn Granite Dells, and the vast grasslands of Chino and Lonesome Valleys. Downtown, the Doric-columned courthouse sits in a spacious grassy plaza surrounded by tall elm trees. The equestrian statue in front of the courthouse commemorates the spirit of William "Buckey" O'Neill, newspaperman, sheriff, mayor, adventurer, and Spanish-American War hero. Buckey led a company of Theodore Roosevelt's Rough Riders in Cuba, where an enemy bullet cut him down.

The Palace and a few other bars on Montezuma Street opposite the courthouse carry on the tradition of "Whiskey Row," where more than 20 saloons roared full-blast day and night in the late 1800s and early 1900s. The Sharlot Hall Museum, two blocks west, preserves Prescott's past with early buildings and excellent historical collections. On the other side of downtown, the Smoki (SMOKE-eye) Museum displays a wealth of artifacts from Native American cultures. About 100 Yavapai live in the Prescott area, mostly on a 1,400-acre reservation just north of town.

Though small, Prescott (pop. 34,000) contains several art galleries, an active artists' community, two colleges, and an aeronautical university. Just outside town the visitor will discover the area's beautiful forests, fishing lakes, mountains, and ghost towns.

History

Unlike most Western towns, which haphazardly boomed into existence, Prescott sprang from a plan. Soon after Congress carved the territory of Arizona from New Mexico Territory

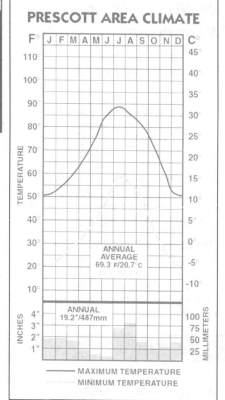

PRESCOTT AREA CLIMATE

ANNUAL
AVERAGE
69.3 F/20.7°C

ANNUAL
19.2"/487mm

MAXIMUM TEMPERATURE
MINIMUM TEMPERATURE

felled trees to build the Capitol and Governor's Mansion.

Early citizens named the settlement after William Hickling Prescott, a historian noted for his writings about Mexico. Unlike towns to the south, with their adobe buildings and strong Spanish-Mexican flavor, Prescott derived its character from the settlers of New England and the Midwest. Vast forests provided timber for log cabins and later frame buildings.

In 1867 the Legislature had a change of heart and moved the capital down to Tucson. Prescott's future looked bleak, as Apache attacks and high transportation costs threatened further mining and agricultural development. However, improved mining techniques and the gold strikes of the 1870s brought the region back to life. Even the Legislature returned, in 1877, before moving to Phoenix for good in 1889. By then Prescott was a thriving city that no longer needed the politicians. Mining, ranching, and trade prospered.

Even a disastrous fire in 1900, which wiped out much of Prescott's business district—including Whiskey Row—couldn't destroy community spirit. Undaunted, the saloonkeepers moved their salvaged stock across the street and continued to serve libations as the fires blazed. Within days the townsfolk began rebuilding, creating the downtown you see today. Agriculture and a bit of mining continue in the Prescott area, but it's the character of the place that charms most people. You'll find it in the many historic buildings lining Prescott's tree-shaded streets, the clean pine-scented air, and the agreeable four-season climate.

SIGHTS

Sharlot Hall Museum

Nine buildings make up this superb historical museum at 415 W. Gurley St. (two blocks west of the plaza), 928/445-3122. It's open Sunday 1–5 P.M. and Mon.–Sat. 10 A.M.–5 P.M. (until 4 P.M. Nov.–March); a donation of $4 adult, $3 seniors 65 and up, or $5 family is welcomed. The museum hosts living history programs, lectures, festivals, and theater productions; ask for

in 1863, Governor John Goodwin and a party of appointed officials set off from Washington on a tour of the area. Their arduous three-month journey took them to the rich mineral districts of central Arizona, a promising new region relatively free of the Confederate sympathizers who lived in the southern towns of Tucson and Tubac.

Goodwin and his party first set up a temporary capital at Fort Whipple in Chino Valley. Then, to be closer to mining activities and timbered land, both the government and the fort moved 17 miles south to a site along Granite Creek. Fort Whipple served as the center for campaigns against Tonto Apache and Yavapai during the 1860s and 1870s. Sentries stood on alert for Native American attacks as workers

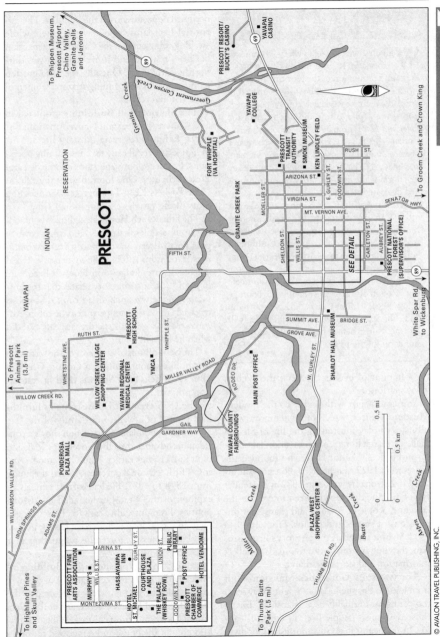

To Phippen Museum, Prescott Airport, Chino Valley, Granite Dells and Jerome

PRESCOTT RESORT/ BUCKY'S CASINO

YAVAPAI CASINO

YAVAPAI COLLEGE

FORT WHIPPLE (VA HOSPITAL)

PRESCOTT TRANSIT AUTHORITY

SMOKI MUSEUM

KEN LINDLEY FIELD

RUSH ST.

ARIZONA ST.

E. GURLEY ST.

GOODWIN ST.

VIRGINA ST.

MOELLER ST.

SENATOR HWY.

MT. VERNON AVE.

GRANITE CREEK PARK

SHELDON ST.

WILLIS ST.

CARLETON ST.

AUBREY ST.

PRESCOTT NATIONAL FOREST (SUPERVISOR'S OFFICE)

SEE DETAIL

FIFTH ST.

Granite Creek

Government Canyon Creek

PRESCOTT

YAVAPAI

INDIAN

RESERVATION

To Groom Creek and Crown King

89

89

69

To Prescott Animal Park (3.5 mi)

WHETSTINE AVE.

RUTH ST.

WILLOW CREEK VILLAGE SHOPPING CENTER

PRESCOTT HIGH SCHOOL

YAVAPAI REGIONAL MEDICAL CENTER

YMCA

WILLOW CREEK RD.

WHIPPLE ST.

MILLER VALLEY ROAD

RODEO DR.

SUMMIT AVE.

GROVE AVE.

BRIDGE ST.

W. GURLEY ST.

SHARLOT HALL MUSEUM

MAIN POST OFFICE

White Spar Rd. to Wickenburg

0.5 mi

0.5 km

GAIL

GARDNER WAY

YAVAPAI COUNTY FAIRGROUNDS

PONDEROSA PLAZA MALL

WILLIAMSON VALLEY RD.

IRON SPRINGS RD.

ADAMS ST.

To Highland Pines and Skull Valley

PLAZA WEST SHOPPING CENTER

THUMB BUTTE RD.

To Thumb Butte Park (.5 mi)

Miller Creek

Butte Creek

Aker Creek

PRESCOTT FINE ARTS ASSOCIATION

MURPHY'S

MARINA ST.

GURLEY ST.

UNION ST.

PUBLIC LIBRARY

HOTEL VENDOME

WILLIS ST.

HASSAYAMPA INN

ST. MICHAEL

HOTEL

COURTHOUSE AND PLAZA

THE PALACE (WHISKEY ROW)

GOODWIN ST.

POST OFFICE

PRESCOTT CHAMBER OF COMMERCE

MONTEZUMA ST.

© AVALON TRAVEL PUBLISHING, INC.

BUCKEY O'NEILL

William Owen O'Neill (1860–98) came to Arizona in 1879, lured by Gov. John C. Frémont's promotion of the territory. After first visiting Tombstone and Phoenix, he arrived in Prescott, where he worked as court reporter, editor of the *Miner,* editor and publisher of the *Hoof and Horn,* probate judge, school superintendent, sheriff, tax assessor, author, onyx quarry operator, militia commander, volunteer fireman, and mayor. O'Neill got his nickname Buckey for "bucking the tiger" in faro, whose game cards had tigers on their backs.

When the Spanish-American War broke out in 1898, this popular figure petitioned Governor McCord for permission to raise "one thousand Arizona cowboys" to fight in Cuba. Although only 170 men came from Arizona, recruits from other western states and territories joined the group. Newspapers christened the volunteers the "Rough Riders." Displaying his courage below Kettle Hill in Cuba, Buckey reportedly said, "the Spanish bullet is not molded that will kill me"—just before being fatally shot by a sniper on July 1, 1898.

the calendar of events or check the Web at www.sharlot.org.

You could start with a visit to the modern **Museum Center,** which offers temporary exhibits, a display illustrating the life of Sharlot Hall, a research library, a conservation laboratory, and offices. Sharlot Hall, who founded the museum in 1927, was herself a pioneer—she arrived in Arizona by wagon in 1882 at the tender age of 12. She developed a keen interest in the land and people of Arizona and shared her impressions in stories and poems. From 1909 to 1911 Sharlot served as the territory's first historian, traveling Arizona's primitive roads to collect information and stories firsthand.

The two-story **Governor's Mansion,** built from logs on this site in 1864, might today seem too primitive to qualify as a "mansion," but in those days most people lived in tents or lean-tos. In the beginning, Governor John Goodwin and Territorial Secretary Richard McCormick

occupied opposite ends of the building. The territorial Legislature may have met here while awaiting completion of the Capitol. The mansion has been restored and furnished as it was during the early years. Outside, the **rose garden** commemorates outstanding Arizona women of the territorial years.

The **Sharlot Hall Building,** completed in 1934, houses pioneer and Native American displays. Exhibits re-create military life at Fort Whipple and recall early ranches, mining operations, frontier saloons and stores, home life, and Prescott heroes. One room houses the exhibit "The Baskets Keep Talking: The Continuing Story of the Yavapai-Prescott Indian Tribe."

The little **Ranch House** has a display of branding irons, saddles, harnesses, and other cowboy gear. **Fort Misery,** one of Prescott's earliest buildings, dates from 1863 to 1864 when it served as a general store. Judge John Howard lived here in the 1890s, and one story relates that the hospitable judge was such a bad cook that guests received "misery" at suppertime. The cabin, Arizona's oldest wooden structure, appears as it did when he lived in it.

The **Schoolhouse** is a replica of the territory's first public school, built near Granite Creek in 1867. A **Blacksmith Shop** is used in restoration projects.

The 1875 **Frémont House** contains furnishings typical of a well-to-do family of the late 1870s. Its wood-plank construction shows a considerable advance over the Governor's Mansion built just 11 years earlier. John C. Frémont, Arizona's fifth territorial governor, rented the house from 1878 to 1881. He had earned fame as an explorer of the West, but he failed in Arizona politics. Frémont didn't care for Prescott's climate and spent long periods back East or in Tucson. Public pressure forced his resignation after three years in office.

Exhibits in the **Transportation Building** include Sharlot Hall's 1927 Star auto, a stagecoach, wagons, sleighs, and bicycles. A gift shop in the 1877 **Bashford House** offers crafts and a selection of books on Arizona history. William Bashford bought the house and remodeled it during the 1880s in an ornate late Victorian style.

© SHARLOT HALL MUSEUM

historian Sharlot Hall in the Governor's Mansion

Smoki Museum

From a split-twig figure of 4,000 years ago to the beautiful baskets and pottery of modern tribes, this collection preserves a wide variety of Southwest Native American artifacts. Much of the pottery and many of the stone tools come from prehistoric pithouses excavated in nearby Chino Valley. Paintings and sketches by Kate Cory illustrate Native American life; she lived with the Hopi from 1905 to 1912 and helped design the stone museum building, which opened in 1935. Finely crafted baskets show the skills of Apache, Yavapai, Hualapai, and Havasupai tribes. Some Hopi kachinas are on display too. Former Senator Barry Goldwater, who belonged to the Smoki, donated many of the museum's items. Kids have a touch table and can try their hand at grinding corn. Guest artist and lecture programs occasionally take place.

The collection, 928/445-1230, is open Sunday 1–4 P.M. and Mon.–Sat. 10 A.M.–4 P.M. from April 1 to October 31, then Sat.–Sun. 10 A.M.–4 P.M. the rest of the year. Groups may also visit by appointment. Researchers can arrange to use the library. A gift shop offers books along with jewelry and other arts and crafts made by Native American and Latin American artisans. Admission is $4 adults, $3 seniors over 65, $2 students, and free for children 12 and under; www.smoki.com. The pueblo-style museum building is at 147 N. Arizona St., one block north of E. Gurley Street.

Anglo members of the community organized the Smoki "tribe" in 1921 to raise funds for the annual Frontier Days Rodeo by performing Native American dances. The presentations became very elaborate with a cast and crew in the hundreds. Although criticized for this by some Native American groups, the Smoki took a serious interest in Native American rituals, dance, and artifacts. The Smoki danced last in 1990. In 1991 the museum incorporated as its own nonprofit organization.

Phippen Museum

Paintings, sketches, and the occasional bronze by outstanding artists celebrate Western heritage and art. Promising new artists receive attention as well. The main exhibit changes every three months and there's also a permanent display devoted to George Phippen (1915–66), a well-known Western artist who helped found Cowboy Artists of America and served as its first president. You can watch videos on request and use the small library. Special events take place on Memorial Day weekend, in autumn, and during the Thanksgiving-Christmas holiday season. A museum store sells artwork, jewelry, crafts, and cards.

The museum, 4701 N. Hwy. 89, 928/778-1385, is in a ranch-style building six miles north of Prescott. It's open in summer Mon.–Sat. 10 A.M.–4 P.M. and Sunday 1–4 P.M. with possible extended evening hours; call for the schedule the rest of the year when the museum may close some days and have shorter hours. Admission runs $3 adults, $2 seniors and students, free for children 12 and under; www.phippenmuseum.org.

Heritage Park Zoo

Meet denizens of the Southwest, exotic creatures, and farm animals at this small but growing zoo. Celebrities include Abbey the mountain lion, Shikar the Bengal tiger, Inca the black jaguar, and Shash the friendly black bear. Others that you'll meet include ring-tailed lemur, llamas, coatimundi, Mexican wolf, pronghorn, and collared peccary. Birds and reptiles are represented too, and the tarantulas have their own "grotto."

The zoo is about six miles north of downtown on Heritage Park Road, just south off Willow Creek Road, 928/778-4242. It also offers a picnic area, playground, and gift shop. Zoo by Moonlight takes place on full-moon nights May to September. Groups can arrange tours. Open daily 9 A.M.–5 P.M. May–Oct. and daily 10 A.M.–4 P.M. Nov.–April; admission is $5 adults, $4 seniors over 65, $2 children 3–12; www.prescottzoo.org.

Fort Whipple

This army fort dates from 1863 and honors Brigadier General Amiel Weeks Whipple, who served with the Army Corps of Topographical Engineers until his death in the Civil War. The

Little Jessie miners at McCabe, northwest of Mayer in the Bradshaw Mountains, ca. 1880.

©SHARLOT HALL MUSEUM

post played a major role during the Indian wars and was maintained until 1912. Ten years later it took on its present role as a Veterans Administration hospital. Many of the military buildings, including the barracks and officers' quarters, date from around 1900. You're welcome to visit the hospital grounds, though there's no museum or visitor center. Fort Whipple lies on the northeast edge of town off AZ 89.

ACCOMMODATIONS

Prescott offers a fine selection of places to stay, though few have rooms under $50 in summer. Try to secure reservations for weekends during the warmer months, when desert dwellers come here to escape the heat. Book far in advance for Frontier Days, held around July Fourth, and expect to pay more. The following summer rates usually drop in winter. Categories are based on the cost of weekend double occupancy.

Historic Hotels Downtown

$50–100: Hotel St. Michael, 205 W. Gurley St. (at Montezuma), 928/776-1999, 800/678-3757, opened as the Hotel Burke in 1891, then was rebuilt after the great fire wiped out Whiskey Row in 1900. Rooms, all with private bath, go for $49–79 d and suites are $89 d; add $10 to all prices on weekends. The building also holds a coffeehouse and specialty shops.

$100–200: Hassayampa Inn, 122 E. Gurley St., 928/778-9434, 800/322-1927, ranked as the town's premier grand hotel in 1927 and remains near the top today. The plush lobby features a painted ceiling, old piano, and other antiques. All rooms have private baths; rates run $120–130 d, $170–185 d for a suite. The hotel's Peacock Room offers elegant dining. **Hotel Vendome,** 230 S. Cortez St., 928/776-0900, 888/468-3583, is a smaller place built in 1917. It offers attractively restored rooms with private baths for $79 d room, $119 double suite (up to 4 persons); add $40 to rates on weekends.

Motels

Under $50: Senator Inn, 1117 E. Gurley St., 928/445-1440, costs only $32 s, $37 d ($45 s, $49 d Fri.–Sat.).

$50–100: Those near downtown and Yavapai College include the **Wheel Inn Motel,** 333 S. Montezuma St., 928/778-7346, 800/717-0902, $45 d ($59 d Fri.–Sat.); **Motel 6,** 1111 E. Sheldon St., 928/776-0160, 800/466-8356, $40 s, $46 d ($46 s, $52 d Fri.–Sat.); and **Super 8 Motel,** 1105 E. Sheldon St., 928/776-1282, 800/800-8000, $50 s, $55 d ($58 s, $63 d Fri.–Sat.). Heading south on AZ 89 from downtown you'll see **Prescott Sierra Inn,** 809 White Spar Rd., 928/445-1250, 800/513-2014, $39–55 d ($49–69 d Fri.–Sat.), some rooms have a kitchen; and **Comfort Inn,** 1290 White Spar Rd., 928/778-5770, 800/889-9774, $60–70 d ($89 and up Fri.–Sat.). East from downtown on AZ 89, you'll find **Apache Motel,** 1130 E. Gurley St., 928/445-1422, $30 s, $40 d ($60 s or d Fri.–Sat.); **Colony Inn,** 1225 E. Gurley St., 928/445-7057, 800/350-3782, $45 d ($65 d Fri.–Sat.); and **Best Western Prescottonian Motel,** 1317 E. Gurley St., 928/445-3096, 800/528-1234, $80 d ($89 d Fri.–Sat.).

$100–200: At **Prescott Resort Conference Center & Casino,** 1500 Hwy. 69 (on top of the hill), 928/776-1666, 800/967-4637, guests enjoy an indoor pool, Jacuzzi, sauna, fitness room, racquetball, and tennis. The resort has great views, especially from the suites; rates run $165 d room and $185 d suite; www.prescottresort.com. **Forest Villas Hotel,** 3645 Lee Circle (four miles east of downtown off AZ 69), 928/717-1200, 800/223-3449, offers views, an outdoor pool, and a hot tub; rates for rooms and suites run $95–208 d ($109–208 d Fri.–Sat.); www.forestvillas.com.

Prescott Valley Motels

This fast-growing suburb of Prescott, a 10-mile drive east on AZ 69, has a **Days Inn,** 7875 E. Hwy. 69, 928/772-8600, 800/329-7466, $59 s, $69 d ($69 s, $79 d Fri.–Sat.); **Motel 6,** 8383 E. Hwy. 69, 928/772-2200, 800/466-8356, $46 s, $52 d ($77 s or d Fri.–Sat.); and **Prescott Valley Motel,** 8390 E. Hwy. 69, 928/772-9412, $40 s, $45 d ($55 s, $65 d Fri.–Sat.).

Inns and Bed & Breakfasts

Dolls & Roses Bed and Breakfast, 109 N. Pleasant St., 928/778-2642, 800/924-0883, occupies an 1883 Victorian house; rates run $89–99 d room, $109 d suite. **Pleasant Street Inn,** 142 S. Pleasant St. (at Goodwin), 928/445-4774, 877/226-7128, offers bed and breakfast with a variety of rooms and suites in an English Traditional style; $95–130 d. **Marks House Bed and Breakfast Inn,** 203 E. Union St., 928/778-4632, 800/370-6275, is an 1894 Victorian house with antique decor and feather beds; rates run $85–135 d. **Prescott Country Inn Bed and Breakfast,** 503 S. Montezuma St., 928/445-7991, 888/757-0015, provides rooms, suites, and cottages with country decor for $39–99 d ($69–129 d Fri.–Sat.); www.cableone.net/cottages. **Prescott Pines Inn,** on the south edge of town at 901 White Spar Rd. (S. AZ 89), 928/445-7270, 800/541-5374, offers "country Victorian" rooms for $65–109 d and a three-bedroom chalet for $269; breakfast is extra; www.prescottpinesinn.com.

Near Watson Lake, **Log Cabin Bed and Breakfast,** 928/778-0442, 888/778-0442, is a modern log cabin with decks, hot tub, and full breakfast for $85–125 d; www.prescottlogcabin.com. In the hills five miles east of town, **Lynx Creek Farm Bed and Breakfast,** 928/778-9573, 888/778-9573, features an organic orchard and garden as well as farm animals. Rates for rooms and cabins run $85–200 d; www.vacationlodges.com. **Juniper Well Ranch,** 928/442-3415, is surrounded by the Prescott National Forest 12 miles out Iron Springs Road; each log cabin, adobe, and ranch house has a kitchen and views for $105 d with discounts for longer stays; juniperwellranch.com.

Forest Service Campgrounds

The Prescott National Forest, 928/771-4700, has established **dispersed campsites** in the Prescott Basin area near town. Each site has a marker, fire ring, and place to camp, but no water, toilets, or fees. Pick up a map from the Forest Service or check the website www.fs.fed.us/r3/prescott for the locations. Dispersed camping isn't permitted elsewhere within the Prescott Basin boundary.

White Spar Campground, 2.5 miles south of downtown on AZ 89, has drinking water but no showers or hookups; $10. One loop stays open in winter, when water may or may not be available. **Indian Creek Campground** lies four miles south on AZ 89, then left 0.7 mile on Forest Road 97; it's open mid-May to the end of September; $6 (no water). **Lower Wolf Creek Campground** south of town is open mid-May to mid-November; $6 (no water); take Senator Highway (Forest Road 52) south 7.5 miles, then turn west one mile on Forest Road 97. Or from AZ 89, four miles south of Prescott, turn east five miles on Forest Road 97. Groups can reserve **Upper Wolf Creek Campground,** 877/444-6777; reserveusa.com.

You and your horse can stay at **Groom Creek Horsecamp,** which offers water, family sites ($10), and a group reservation area (contact the Bradshaw Ranger District). It's open May 1–Oct. 31. To get there, go 6.5 miles south from town on Senator Highway (Forest Road 52). It's near a trailhead for the popular **Groom Creek Loop Trail #307,** which makes an 8.7-mile loop through ponderosa pine forests to Spruce Mountain.

Southeast of Prescott, **Lynx Lake** and nearby **Hilltop Campgrounds** sit above a pretty lake containing trout and catfish. Lynx sites are open April 1–Nov. 15, while Hilltop is open May 1–Sept. 30; both have drinking water and a $10 fee. Picnickers may use tables at a vista point on the north end of the lake and near the boat ramp at the south end; $2. To reach Lynx Lake, head east four miles on AZ 69 from town, then turn south 2.5 miles on Walker Road/Lynx Lake Road; Hilltop Campground is one mile farther. Lynx Lake Store, 928/778-0720, rents rowboats, paddleboats, canoes, and kayaks at the north end of the lake; closed Mondays in winter.

Yavapai Campground lies northwest of town near the base of Granite Mountain; it's open all year with water and a $10 fee. From W. Gurley Street, turn northwest and drive 4.3 miles on Grove Avenue, Miller Valley Road, and Iron Springs Road, then turn north and proceed 3.5 miles on Forest Road 374. Groups can reserve **Granite Group Camp** at 877/444-6777; www.reserveusa.com.

Powell Springs Campground, in ponderosa pines near the village of Cherry, stays open all year and has spring water (no charge). From the turnoff on AZ 169 (25 miles east of Prescott and 5.5 miles west of I-17 Exit 278), turn north 4.5 miles on Forest Road 372 (Cherry Rd.); see a highway or forest map. Forest Road 372 is a winding, gravel road with good scenery. You can also drive in from the Verde Valley; take I-17 Exit 287, go northwest 2.8 miles, then turn left (south) and drive 12.6 miles on Cherry Road to Powell Springs Campground.

Other Campgrounds

Watson Lake Park, four miles north of town on AZ 89, 928/771-5841, overlooks Granite Dells. The season runs Memorial Day to Labor Day, but the campground is open only on Fri. and Sat. nights; $10 tents or RVs. Showers are available to campers. Day-use parking is free. **Point of Rocks RV Campground,** just north of Watson Lake Park, 928/445-9018, is open all year with RV sites for $18 with hookups (no tents). **Willow Lake RV and Camping Resort,** 928/445-6311, 800/940-2845, features a swimming pool, fishing, store, and showers for $14 tent, $20 RV with hookups; it's five miles north of town off Willow Creek Road.

FOOD

American and Continental (Downtown)

Murphy's, 201 N. Cortez St., 928/445-4044,

serves sandwiches, steak, prime rib, seafood, and other dishes in an old mercantile building dating from 1890. Dim lighting, antiques, and greenery add to the romantic setting. It's open daily for lunch and dinner.

Zuma's Woodfire Café, 124 N. Montezuma St., 928/541-1400, has an attractive Mediterranean decor and patio for gourmet pasta, pizza, sandwiches, and salads; open daily for lunch and dinner.

The **Peacock Room,** in the Hassayampa Inn at 122 E. Gurley St., 928/778-9434, offers a luxurious old-fashioned atmosphere for its varied menu of American and continental specialties. It's open daily for breakfast, lunch, and dinner.

Plaza Café, 106 W. Gurley St., 928/445-3234, offers breakfasts, sandwiches, salads, and rice bowls; it's open daily for breakfast and lunch across from the plaza.

Prescott Brewing Company, 130 W. Gurley St., 928/771-2795, crafts its own beers and serves up a varied menu of tasty snacks, steak, fish, salads, and vegetarian items; it's open daily for lunch and dinner across from the plaza.

Caffe St. Michael, on Whiskey Row at 205 W. Gurley St. (at Montezuma), 928/776-1999, is a San Francisco-style coffee house offering espresso, sandwiches, salads, and pastries daily.

Gurley Street Grille, 230 W. Gurley St., 928/445-3388, serves upscale burgers, pasta, pizza, and sandwiches; it's open daily for lunch and dinner.

The **Palace's** dining room in the heart of Whiskey Row at 120 S. Montezuma St., 928/541-1996, is an historic setting for steak, prime rib, seafood, and pasta dinners and for sandwich and salad lunches. It's open daily. The separate bar area has a magnificent 1880's Brunswick bar that patrons carried across to safety in the plaza during the fire of 1900. Country and cowboy bands play Fri.–Sat. nights and dinner theaters take place every other Monday; www.historicpalace.com.

Prescott Natural Foods Market, 330 W. Gurley St., 928/778-5875, has a deli (take out or eat in) and grocery open daily.

Agostino's Italian Cucina, 107 S. Cortez St., 928/778-6818, serves seafood, meat, and pasta dishes in both southern and northern Italian styles for dinner Tues.–Sat. across from the plaza.

Chef Linda Rose presides over the fine dining at **The Rose Restaurant,** 234 S. Cortez St., 928/777-8308. Diners have both indoor and outdoor seating at the early 20th-century Victorian cottage. Open Wed.–Sun. for dinner only.

American and Continental (Other Areas)

Thumb Butte Dining Room on the hill at the Prescott Resort, 1500 Hwy. 69, 928/776-1666, ext. 693, offers views and fine dining daily for breakfast, lunch, and dinner and features a Sunday brunch buffet. The dinner menu includes steak, prime rib, seafood, pasta, veal, and pizza.

Red Lobster, 1821 E. Hwy. 69 (Frontier Village Center), 928/778-2717, specializes in seafood, with some steak and chicken items; it's open daily for lunch and dinner.

Juniper House, 810 White Spar Rd., 928/445-3250, is a family restaurant open daily for breakfast and lunch.

Papa's Italian Restaurant, 1124 White Spar Rd., 928/776-4880, prepares northern Italian cuisine. It's open Mon.–Fri. for lunch and Sat. for dinner.

The menu at **Pine Cone Inn,** 1245 White Spar Rd., 928/445-2970, lists steak, seafood, and other American favorites; it's open Sunday for breakfast, lunch, and dinner, then Tues.–Sat. for dinner only. Musicians provide dinner music Tues.–Sunday.

New Frontiers Natural Foods Market, 1112 Iron Springs Rd., 928/445-7370, features healthful foods and a deli open daily for dine in or take out.

Denny's, 1316 Iron Springs Rd. in Ponderosa Plaza, 928/778-1230, offers 24-hour service for breakfast, lunch, and dinner.

Dry Gulch Steak House, 1630 Adams St., two blocks west of Ponderosa Plaza off Iron Springs Rd., 928/778-9693, serves up steak and seafood Tues.–Sun. for dinner.

Latin American

El Charro, 120 N. Montezuma St., 928/445-

7130, is a Mexican café open daily for lunch and dinner.

Chico's Tecate Grill, 200 E. Gurley and Marina Sts., 928/541-1035, serves such favorites as arroz con pollo, grilled quesadilla asada, a burrito especial, and combination platters daily for lunch and dinner.

Machu Picchu, 111 Grove Ave., 928/717-8242, prepares Peruvian cuisine with beef, chicken, seafood, and vegetarian options, Mon.–Sat. for lunch and dinner.

Asian

Thai House Cafe, 230 N. Cortez St., 928/777-0041, cooks flavorful meat and tofu dishes Mon.–Sat. for lunch and dinner.

Chi's Cuisine, 114 N. Cortez St., 928/778-5390, is a little downtown café with Chinese and Thai food; there's often a buffet. It's open Mon.–Sat. for lunch and dinner.

China Jade Restaurant, 1781 E. Hwy. 69 (Frontier Village Center), 928/445-4072, prepares Szechuan, Cantonese, and American cuisines; it's open Tues.–Sun. for lunch and dinner.

Fujiyama, 1781 E. Hwy. 69 (Frontier Village Center), 928/776-8659, offers Japanese food with a sushi bar; it serves lunch and dinner daily except Monday and the last Sunday of the month.

Taj Mahal Restaurant, 1781 E. Hwy. 69 (Frontier Village Center), 928/445-5752, features north Indian dining daily for lunch and dinner. Staff offer buffets daily for lunch and some days for dinner.

Canton Cafe, 1102 Willow Creek Rd., 928/445-0070, offers Cantonese dining Mon.–Fri. for lunch and Mon.–Sat. for dinner.

ENTERTAINMENT AND EVENTS

Entertainment

The **Prescott Fine Arts Association,** 208 N. Marina St., 928/445-3286, sponsors an art gallery and gift shop plus a program of plays, musicals, concerts, and family theater. The gallery and gift shop are open Wed.–Sat. 11 A.M.–4 P.M. and Sunday noon–4 P.M.; the box office is open Mon.–Sat. 11 A.M.–4 P.M.; www.pfaa.net.

Yavapai College, 1100 E. Sheldon St., 928/776-2033, 877/928/4253, presents a variety of plays, concerts, and other events in Performance Hall, on the left as you enter the campus. **Yavapai College Art Gallery,** in the same building, 928/776-2031, puts on exhibits by college, community, and national artists. The gallery is open Mon.–Sat. 10 A.M.–3 P.M. with new shows appearing about every six weeks. You'll find listings of performances and art shows at www.yavapai.cc.az.us.

The Palace and other bars along Whiskey Row (Montezuma St.) sometimes have live bands. The **Pine Cone Inn,** 1245 White Spar Rd., 928/445-2970, offers more sedate live dinner music Tues.–Sunday.

You'll find two casinos on the east edge of town off Hwy. 69, a few hundred feet past the Hwy. 89 junction. **Bucky's Casino** sits on the hill in the Prescott Resort, 1500 Hwy. 69, 928/776-5695. The **Yavapai Casino** is across the highway at 1501 Hwy. 69, 928/445-5767. Both are open 24 hours and have recorded information at 800/SLOTS-44.

Events

There's something happening every summer night on the **Courthouse Plaza**—could be a concert, dance, or speech. **Softball** fans can catch a game in summer—Prescott bills itself as the Softball Capital of the World; 928/445-5291 (Parks and Recreation), 928/777-2489 (recording); www.cityofprescott.net/recreation.htm. Local newspapers list what's going on in town. Major annual events are listed below.

Horses race May to September at **Yavapai Downs,** 10401 Hwy. 89A, 928/445-7820. From Prescott, head north on AZ 89, then turn right 8.5 miles on AZ 89A; in Prescott Valley, turn north on Glassford Hill Road, then right on AZ 89A; www.yavapaidownsatpv.com.

On Memorial Day weekend, **Phippen Museum Fine Art Show & Sale** brings about 150 artists to the Courthouse Plaza for a juried fine arts show. **Prescott Off Street Festival** has arts and crafts nearby on the same weekend.

June is a busy month in Prescott. On the first weekend of the month, the **Sharlot Hall**

Folk Arts Fair celebrates pioneer skills with costumed participants demonstrating blacksmithing, woodworking, spinning, weaving, churning, and cowboy cooking. **Prescott Days** in the middle of the month features a parade, carnival, horse racing, car show, games, entertainment, and dancing. Down-home musicians pick and sing during the **Bluegrass Festival.** Late in the month, **Young's Farm Garlic Festival,** 928/632-7272, features a garlic barbecue and other food, Western music, crafts, pony rides, and hayrides east in Dewey at the junction of AZ 69 and AZ 169.

July's **Frontier Days,** held during the July Fourth holiday, draws spectators from all over Arizona and beyond for the "World's Oldest Rodeo," a huge parade, western art show, entertainment, dances, and fireworks. Cowboys have pitted themselves against livestock in the rodeo since 1888. Events begin in late June and last nearly a week; the parade runs about two hours and is held on a Saturday; www.worldsoldestrodeo.com. In mid-July, Sharlot Hall Museum hosts the **Indian Art Market.**

In August, the **Antique Auto Show** rolls into Prescott; and the **Arizona Cowboy Poets Gathering** brings the stories and songs of the range to town on the third weekend.

In September, look for the **Faire on the Square Arts & Crafts Show;** the Phippen Museum's **Autumn Art Auction** fund-raiser with dinner and entertainment; and the **Yavapai County Fair.**

The first weekend of October sees both the **Fallfest in the Park Arts & Crafts Show** and the **Folk Music Festival.**

The year winds up with the Phippen Museum's **Holiday Show and Sale** from mid-November to Christmas; and the **Arizona's Christmas City** events. They begin with the **Courthouse Christmas Lighting** and **Christmas Parade** on the first Saturday in December, followed by the **Acker Musical Showcase** on the following Friday evening, and a **Light Parade** the week after.

RECREATION

The **YMCA,** 750 Whipple St., 928/445-7221,

has two year-round indoor pools, one mainly for lap swimming and the other with a 150-foot water slide. Or swim at the indoor **Yavapai College pool,** 928/776-2175; turn north onto the campus from 1100 E. Sheldon St. and look for the pool in the main cluster of buildings at the end of the drive on the left. Prescott Valley's **Mountain Valley Splash,** 8600 E. Nace, 928/775-3165, has a summertime swimming pool with a small water slide 10 minutes east of town. Play **tennis** at Yavapai College, at Prescott High School (on Ruth St.), or next to Ken Lindley Field (E. Gurley and Arizona Sts.).

Twenty-three miles to the north, **Summit Snowplay** offers fun in the snow at the 7,023-foot pass on AZ 89A between Prescott and Jerome. Inner tubes and plastic dishes can be used, but no sleds. The site has paved parking, toilets, and a $5/vehicle fee. In summer it's available as the **Summit Picnic Area** (no fee).

Golfers play on the 36-hole course at **Antelope Hills Golf Course** next to the airport, eight miles north of town on AZ 89, 928/776-7888, 800/972-6818. The town of Dewey, 14 miles east on AZ 69, offers two 18-hole golf courses: **Prescott Golf & Country Club,** 928/772-8984, 800/717-7274; and **Quailwood Greens Golf Course,** 928/772-0130.

Granite Mountain Stables, 928/771-9551, offers hourly, all day, and overnight rides year-round; it's northwest of town off Williamson Valley Road.

SHOPPING

The vast **Frontier Village Center** offers several restaurants and many stores one-half mile east on AZ 69. Other shopping centers lie northwest and west of downtown. Antiques enthusiasts will find shops in the two blocks of N. Cortez St. north of Courthouse Plaza.

The **Worm Bookstore,** 128 S. Montezuma St., 928/445-0361, offers both new and used books, including many regional titles; topo and other maps are sold too.

Granite Mountain Outfitters, 320 W. Gurley St., 928/776-4949, offers outdoor equipment and supplies, as does **Popular Outdoor**

Outfitters, 1841 E. Hwy. 69 (Frontier Village Center), 928/445-2430.

INFORMATION AND SERVICES

The **Prescott Chamber of Commerce** is at 117 W. Goodwin St. opposite the plaza (P.O. Box 1147, Prescott, AZ 86302), 928/445-2000, 800/266-7534; fax 928/445-0068; www.prescott.org. It's open Mon.–Fri. 9 A.M.–5 P.M., Saturday 9 A.M.–3 P.M., and Sunday 10 A.M.–2 P.M.

The Prescott National Forest's **Prescott Office,** 344 S. Cortez St. (Prescott, AZ 86303), 928/771-4700, has recreation information for the area, including the Bradshaw District; it's open Mon.–Fri. 8 A.M.–4:30 P.M.; www.fs.fed.us/r3/prescott.

Prescott's excellent **public library,** 215 E. Goodwin St., 928/445-8110, includes a Southwest collection; it's open Sun. 1–5 P.M., Mon. 9 A.M.–5:30 P.M., Tues.–Thurs. 9 A.M.–9 P.M., and Fri.–Sat. 9 A.M.–5:30 P.M.; www.prescott lib.lib.az.us. **Yavapai College** also has a fine library, open daily during school terms, Mon.–Fri. in summer. To get there, turn north onto the campus from 1100 E. Sheldon St., 928/776-2260 (circulation) or 928/776-2261 (reference); www.yavapai.cc.az.us.

The main **post office** is at 442 Miller Valley Rd.; the downtown branch sits on the corner of Goodwin and Cortez, across from the Courthouse Plaza. **Yavapai Regional Medical Center,** 1003 Willow Creek Rd., 928/445-2700, provides hospital services.

TOURS AND TRANSPORTATION

On **Prescott Historical Tours,** 928/445-4567, Melissa Ruffner dresses in a Victorian costume when she leads visitors around the original Prescott town site; you'll need to make a reservation. Check with the chamber office for local tour and outdoor adventure companies.

Buses of the **Prescott Transit Authority,** 820 E. Sheldon St., 928/445-5470, 800/445-7978, head for Phoenix's Greyhound bus station and to Sky Harbor Airport about every hour during the day. **Shuttle U,** 1505 W. Gurley St., 928/772-

6114, 800/304-6114, also will take you to Sky Harbor Airport; it goes about 11 times daily. For a taxi, call **Ace** at 928/445-5510. You can rent cars at the airport and in town.

VICINITY OF PRESCOTT

Granite Dells

With giant boulders that have weathered into delicately balanced forms and fanciful shapes, the scenic Dells are a good place for a picnic or hike. Rock climbers like to tackle the challenging granite formations. Ruins and artifacts indicate that Native Americans used to live here. From the 1920s to the '50s, Granite Dells Resort attracted crowds of vacationers; a large dance pavilion of that era still stands. Watson Lake Park (camping and day use) lies at the south edge of the Dells, four miles north of town on AZ 89.

Thumb Butte Trail

This popular loop hike begins just west of town and climbs Thumb Butte Saddle (6,300 feet) for good views of Prescott and the surrounding countryside. The trail winds through a valley of dense ponderosa pine, then crosses windswept ridges where pinyon, juniper, oak, and prickly pear grow. A spur trail leads to a vista point with a panorama of the city, Granite Dells, Chino Valley, and countless mountains, including the distant San Francisco Peaks.

Reaching the fractured granite summit of Thumb Butte takes some effort and skill; the last 200-foot ascent is best left to rock climbers. The trail itself is a moderately easy outing, 1.7 miles roundtrip with an elevation gain of 600 feet; allow 2.5 hours. Signs identify many of the plants along the way and explain the forest ecosystem. Hiking season runs year-round except after winter snowstorms.

From downtown, head west 3.5 miles on Gurley Street and Thumb Butte Road to Thumb Butte Park; the trailhead is on the left side of the road (there's a small parking fee). Picnic tables are nearby.

Granite Mountain Wilderness

On a day trip, hikers can explore the rugged Granite Mountain Wilderness and enjoy fine views from an overlook at an elevation of 7,185 feet. Rock climbers come to challenge the granite cliffs, which offer a nearly complete range of difficulties. Five trails allow many hiking combinations, but only **Granite Mountain Trail #261** climbs to the top. This trail ascends gently 1.3 miles to a trail junction at Blair Pass, then turns right and switchbacks 1.3 miles to a saddle on Granite Mountain; from here the trail turns southeast, climbing another mile to a viewpoint. Ponderosa pines grow at the trailhead and on top of Granite Mountain, though much of the trail passes through manzanita, mountain mahogany, pinyon, agave, and other plants of the chaparral.

Average hiking time for the 7.5-mile roundtrip hike is six hours. It's a moderately difficult trip with an elevation gain of 1,500 feet; carry water. It's open all year except when blocked by snow. Forest Service offices sell a Granite Mountain Wilderness map; you can also use the Iron Springs and Jerome Canyon 7.5-minute topos. From W. Gurley Street in Prescott, drive northwest 4.3 miles on Grove Avenue, Miller Valley Road, and Iron Springs Road, then turn right and travel five miles on Forest Road 374 past the campground and lake turnoffs.

Chino Valley Ranger District

This section of the Prescott National Forest lies northwest of town beyond Granite Basin Wilderness. It lacks developed sites, but it does have hiking trails, two wilderness areas, and good opportunities to spot wildlife. Except in hunting season, you're likely to have this country to yourself. Granite Knob (6,632 feet) dominates **Apache Creek Wilderness.** Pinyon pine, juniper, and chaparral cover most of the land with some ponderosa pine in the southwest corner.

Juniper Mesa Wilderness has cliffs on the south side of the mesa and some canyons on the north. Ponderosa pine, Arizona white oak, and alligator juniper grow in the canyons and on ridgetops, while pinyon pine, juniper, and chaparral cover the south slope; elevations run 5,650–7,050 feet. Prescott National Forest offices sell a map that covers both wilderness areas. Chino Ranger District office, 735 Hwy. 89 N

in Chino Valley (P.O. Box 485, Chino Valley, AZ 86323), 928/636-2302, is open Mon.–Fri. 8 A.M.–4:30 P.M.

Other Hikes and Sights

Dozens of trails wind through the rugged Bradshaw Mountains south of Prescott and in the Mingus Mountains north of town. Forest Service staff provide trail descriptions, maps, and back-road information.

Spruce Mountain has views, a lookout tower, and a picnic area at its 7,700-foot summit. From Prescott, turn south 5.5 miles on Mt. Vernon Avenue/Senator Highway/Forest Road 52, then turn left four miles up Forest Road 52A (not suited for RVs or trailers). **Groom Creek Trail #307** makes an 8.7-mile loop between here and Groom Creek Horsecamp.

Probably the most unusual trail is the 1,200-foot **Groom Creek School Nature Trail,** built by the Sunrise Lions Club of Prescott especially for blind people. Trail pamphlets—available at the Prescott office in both Braille and print—explain natural features and processes. The trail lies just past the village of Groom Creek, six miles south of town on Mt. Vernon Avenue/Senator Highway/Forest Road 52.

An 1880s **charcoal kiln,** made of fitted granite blocks, once served precious-metal smelters in the Walker area. From Prescott, head east four miles on AZ 69, turn south 6.5 miles on Walker Road/Lynx Lake Road/Forest Road 197 to Walker, turn left on Big Bug Mesa Road (Forest Road 670) just north of Walker Fire Station, and follow signs 0.8 mile to parking—then it's a three-minute walk to the kiln.

Stagecoach passengers in the 19th century stopped at **Palace Station** on their way between Prescott and Peck's Mine. The station lies 11 miles south of Prescott on Mt. Vernon Avenue/Senator Highway/Forest Road 52; you'll need a high-clearance vehicle. The rustic structure is now used as a residence and isn't open to the public, but you can view the exterior.

Crown King and Vicinity

Old mines, ghost towns, and wilderness surround this rustic village 55 miles southeast of Prescott.

Prospectors discovered gold at the Crown King Mine in the 1870s, but mine owners had to wait until the late 1880s before the ore could be processed profitably. A branch line of the Prescott and Eastern Railroad reached the site in 1904. Legal battles closed mine operations in the early 1900s, and today the mining camp attracts retired people and serves as an escape from summer heat. The Crown King Saloon dates back to 1898, when it was built at Oro Belle camp, five miles southwest. Pack mules later hauled the structure piece by piece to Crown King.

Rough roads discourage the average tourist, but the region can be explored with maps, determination, and a high-clearance vehicle. The easiest way in is from Cleator on Forest Road 259, reached from the I-17 Bumble Bee or Cordes Exits. You'll follow the twisting path of the old railroad on the drive up; cautiously driven passenger vehicles can make it okay. With a high-clearance vehicle, you approach Crown King on the very scenic Senator Highway (Forest Road 52) across the rugged Bradshaws from Prescott. Another route follows Pine Flat Road (Forest Road 177) from Mayer into the Bradshaws, then turns south on the Senator Highway. The Prescott National Forest map, sold at Forest Service offices, shows back roads and most trails.

Bradshaw Mountain Guest Ranch, 928/632-4477, offers rooms ($80–140 d), suites ($80 d), and cabins ($110–140 d) on the left as you turn into Crown King; guests enjoy the gardens, barbecue pits, and continental breakfast delivered to their doors; www.crownking.com. You can also stay near Crown King at **Bear Creek Cabins,** 928/632-5035, $80 up to four persons; and **Cedar Roost,** 928/632-5564, $60–95 d (add $10 Fri.–Sat.).

For atmosphere and great American food, try **The Mill,** 928/632-7133, open Sun. for breakfast, lunch, and dinner, and Fri.–Sat. for lunch and dinner. The huge Gladiator Stamp Mill, built in 1893 and moved here from a site two miles away, now forms the centerpiece of the restaurant along with other materials salvaged from old buildings. Take the road opposite the turnoff for Crown King from the main road. In Crown King, you can eat at the saloon or at a restaurant across the street, both open daily. The general store sells groceries and has a post office. The staff at Crown King Work Center, up the hill from town, can tell you about trails and roads; they're mostly local people who know the area well. *Arizona Ghost Towns and Mining Camps* by Philip Varney contains good information on this historic and very scenic part of Arizona.

Horsethief Basin Recreation Area, seven miles to the southeast, offers camping in the Prescott National Forest. The usual season for Kentuck Springs and Hazlett Hollow Campgrounds (elev. 6,000 feet) is May–Oct.; Hazlett Hollow has water and a $6 fee. On the way you'll pass near 3.5-acre **Horsethief Lake,** a reservoir used for boating (electric motors okay) and fishing; no swimming or camping. **Turney Gulch Campground** is a group area with water; make the required reservations at 877/444-6777, reserveusa.com. **Castle Creek Wilderness,** east of the campgrounds, has very steep and rocky terrain with vegetation ranging from chaparral to ponderosa pine.

Bloody Basin Road

Drivers with high-clearance vehicles can leave the crowds behind on this 60-mile scenic back road through the Tonto National Forest, connecting I-17 Bloody Basin/Crown King Exit 259 with Carefree and Cave Creek north of Phoenix. You'll enjoy views of the Mazatzals, rugged high-desert hill country, and wooded canyons. In Bloody Basin, 26 miles from I-17, a very bumpy side road goes southeast 12 miles to the Verde River and Sheep Bridge, where hikers can head into the Mazatzal Wilderness. Primitive camping is possible almost anywhere in Tonto National Forest, or you can stop at Seven Springs, CCC, or Cave Creek campgrounds near the south end of the drive.

ARCOSANTI

This unique experiment of visionary Italian architect Paolo Soleri is slowly rising in the high-desert country between Flagstaff and Phoenix. Here Soleri and his apprentices seek to correct many of the world's urban problems through revolutionary architecture. He calls his joining of architecture and ecology "arcology." A former student of Frank Lloyd Wright, Soleri has designed Arcosanti to make the best use of energy and land while providing a human-scale environment for its residents. The town will grow vertically, leaving surrounding land in its natural state by using pedestrian walkways and elevators instead of the sprawl and freeways found in most urban areas. Arcosanti's strangely shaped buildings make efficient use of the sun's energy. The south-facing apses, for example, allow winter sunlight to enter for warmth yet shade the interior during summer. Greenhouses will provide both food and heating, while using only a fraction of the water normally needed for agriculture.

Construction began in 1970 and progresses slowly as funds come in. The current population of 70–85 can rise considerably during summer when the number of workshoppers increases. Soleri typically spends three days of a week here and the rest at Cosanti, the facility he designed in Scottsdale. Currently in the first of three phases, Arcosanti will house about 7,000 people upon completion, yet it will take up only five percent as much land as a conventional town. Soleri envisions three-dimensional cities that will foster community spirit—now lost in many urban areas. Instead of long commutes, residents will take an elevator and short walks between home, work, and shopping; they will have more time to enjoy life and to socialize with neighbors.

The public is welcome to visit this project, the first of its kind. A visitor center is open daily 9 A.M.–5 P.M. all year except major holidays. To see the rest of the site you'll need to sign up for a guided tour. The 50-minute tours depart on the hour, with the first at 10 A.M. and the last at 4 P.M.; guides explain Soleri's methods and goals while taking you through some of the buildings; $8 adults, free for 12 and under. The visitor center features a model of Arcosanti, architectural exhibits, and books by and about Soleri. His famous Cosanti bronze and clay windbells sold here make attractive gifts and help finance the project. A café and bakery serve snacks and meals. The Visitors Trail leads across a small canyon to a viewpoint of the project. Arcosanti regularly schedules concerts, usually preceded by dinner and often followed by a light and sound show projected onto the mesa across the canyon. Seminars and workshops allow interested people to participate in construction. For information on seminars, workshops, and other events, write Arcosanti, HC 74, Box 4136, Mayer, AZ 86333, or call 928/632-7135; www.arcosanti.org.

Guest rooms cost $20 s, $25 d ($30 d with private bath), and $75 for the Sky Suite, which has two bedrooms and a kitchen. Reservations and an arrival between 9 A.M. and 5 P.M. are needed; 928/632-6217. Arcosanti lies 34 miles southeast of Prescott and 65 miles north of Phoenix. It's easy to reach from I-17; take Cordes Junction Exit 262A, then follow signs 2.5 miles on a dirt road.

Other Accommodations Nearby

Near the interchange you'll find the **Lights On Motel & RV Park;** 928/632-5186, 928/772-2501; $31 s, $39 d, $20 RV with hookups. The small town of Mayer, 10 miles northwest on AZ 69 (26 miles southeast of Prescott) has **Teskey's Motel,** 928/632-9696, at $31 s, $36 d including tax; a café serves breakfast, lunch, and dinner daily.

Western Arizona

Few landlocked states can boast more than 1,000 miles of shoreline! The Colorado River, after its wild run through the Grand Canyon, begins a new life in the western part of the state. Tamed by massive dams and irrigation projects, the Colorado here flows placidly toward the Gulf of California. The deep blue waters of the river and lakes form Arizona's west boundary, separating the state from Nevada and California. Boaters enjoy this watery paradise, breezing along the surface or seeking quiet backwaters for fishing.

But once you step away from the life-giving waters, you're in desert country, the real desert, where legends abound—of Native American tribes, hardy prospectors, determined pioneer families, even a U.S. Army camel corps.

THE LAND

Many small ranges of rocky hills break up the monotonous desert plains of western Arizona, much of which lies at elevations under 2,000 feet. The valley of the Colorado River, home to most of the human inhabitants of western Arizona, drops from about 1,220 feet at the west boundary of the Grand Canyon to just 70 feet at the Mexican border.

A few mountain ranges in the north rise high enough to support forests of oak, pinyon and ponderosa pine, and even some fir and aspen. The Hualapai Mountains, easily reached by road from Kingman, stand as the highest and most notable of these "biological islands."

Hualapai Mountains

© BILL WEIR

Hualapai Peak (8,417 feet) crowns the range. Old mines and ghost towns dot the mineral-rich Cerbat and Black Mountains, also in the north. The Kofa and Castle Dome Mountains in the south make up the Kofa National Wildlife Refuge, home of desert bighorn sheep, mule deer, desert tortoise, Gambel's quail, and rare native palm trees.

Along the Colorado River, the three national wildlife refuges of Havasu, Cibola, and Imperial protect plants, animals, and migratory and native birds.

Climate

The sun shines down from azure skies nearly every day; few places in the United States receive more sunshine than western Arizona. In winter, thousands of "snowbirds" descend on the desert from northern climes to enjoy the sun and fresh air. Winter nights can be frosty, but daytime temperatures usually warm to the 60s or 70s F. Spring and autumn often bring perfect weather—wildflowers, too, in the early spring.

By May the snowbirds have returned to their nesting grounds, and Arizona towns along the Colorado River often make the news as the hottest spots in the country. Parker holds the Arizona record—127°F on one sizzling day in 1905. Yet despite average highs that exceed 100°F from June to September, many visitors do come in summer to play in the water, cooling off by boating, water skiing, swimming, and tubing.

So western Arizona actually has two seasons: a winter that attracts many retirees and others who enjoy fishing, exploring ghost towns, prospecting, and hiking in the desert; and a summer of active water sports. Annual rainfall ranges from about 10 inches in the high country to less than three inches in the south near Yuma.

Flora and Fauna

For most of the year, plant and animal life in the desert appears very sparse. Actually it's there—a great variety of plants, reptiles, amphibians, mammals, and birds—just awaiting the right conditions to emerge. With good winter or summer rains, dormant seeds spring to life, quickly bloom,

WESTERN ARIZONA HIGHLIGHTS

- **Colorado River Recreation:** The river and its lakes provide year-round recreation in the desert.
- **Lake Mead National Recreation Area:** Hoover Dam, two huge lakes, a section of river, and the surrounding desert have many places to explore.
- **London Bridge:** A symbol of early 19th-century England now spans a channel in Lake Havasu.
- **Swansea:** This remote ghost town is the best preserved in the region.
- **Yuma:** At a crossing of the Colorado River used since prehistoric times, this small city has a dramatic history and a wonderful winter climate.

and produce new seeds; seemingly dead sticks sprout leaves and flowers. Cactus and other succulents rapidly absorb precious rain for the long dry spells ahead.

Most animals, large and small, hide out during the day in caves, burrows, or bushes. The small pocket mice and kangaroo rats do not even require drinking water; they feed mainly on seeds and manufacture their own water. Larger animals include western spotted skunk, kit and gray fox, badger, ringtail cat, bobcat, mountain lion, mule deer, and desert bighorn sheep. Early morning and evening afford your best chance of seeing desert critters; binoculars come in handy.

Birds flock to the wetlands along the Colorado River in great numbers, especially in spring and autumn. Canada geese and many species of ducks winter here. Nesters include the great blue heron, green heron, great egret, least bittern, white-winged dove, and Yuma clapper rail.

HISTORY
Native Americans

Groups lived along the shores of the lower Colorado River long before the first white people arrived. Frequent wars between the tribes, lasting into the mid-19th century, forced the Maricopa to migrate up the Gila River to what is no

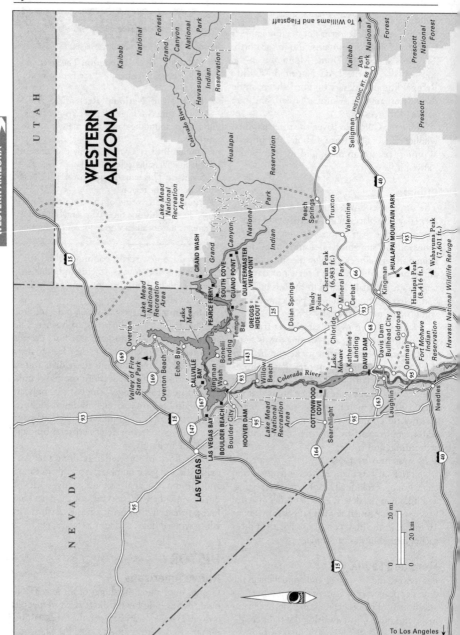

WESTERN ARIZONA

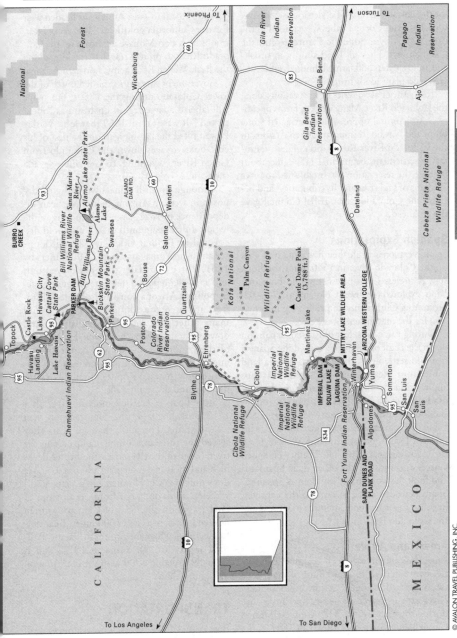

south-central Arizona. The victorious Mohave, Quechan, and Cocopa tribes were joined in the early 1800s by a nomadic Paiute group, the Chemehuevi. They all lived simply in brush-and-mud shelters and farmed, hunted, and gathered wild plant foods from the desert.

Today they have a series of reservations along the Colorado River. Many work at farms or casinos. Agricultural opportunities attracted some Hopi and Navajo from northeastern Arizona to the Colorado River Reservation. Their voluntary resettlement, begun in 1945, came about because the reservation was established to serve "Indians of said river and its tributaries" and because the Colorado River Tribal Council gave the go-ahead.

Spanish Explorations

Spanish explorers made their first tentative forays up the Colorado River in 1540, but they didn't stay. A tireless Jesuit priest, Eusebio Francisco Kino, explored the lower Colorado in 1700–02, promoting Christianity and collecting information for the mapmakers of the day.

During the 1760s, fear of Russian expansion down the coast of California caused the Spanish to build settlements there and to open a land route from Mexico. In 1780, Spanish troops and missionaries built two missions on the Colorado River, La Purísima Concepción (opposite today's Yuma) and nearby San Pedro y San Pablo de Bicuner. Abuses by these foreigners infuriated local Quechan Indians, who revolted the following year. They killed Father Francisco Garcés and most of the other male Spaniards and took the women and children as prisoners. Spanish troops came to ransom the captives, but they made no more attempts to settle along the Colorado River.

Americans Arrive

Rugged mountain men such as James Ohio Pattie, who later wrote an account of his travels (see Suggested Reading), explored the Colorado River area in search of beaver and adventure during the early 1800s. The Army established Camp Yuma (later Fort Yuma) in 1851 at the river crossing of the Southern Overland Trail (Cooke's Road) to assist Americans headed west for the California goldfields. Ten years later, troops built Fort Mohave upstream on the Colorado River to protect travelers trekking along the Beale Wagon Road across northern Arizona.

Government surveyors explored much of the lower Colorado during the 1850s, but maps still labeled a large region upstream as "unexplored." It wasn't until 1869 that John Wesley Powell filled the last big gap on the first of his epic boat voyages down the Colorado from Green River, Wyoming, to Callville, Nevada (now under Lake Mead).

Although Spanish miners worked gold deposits in western Arizona before Mexican independence in 1821, large-scale mining in the region didn't begin until the 1860s. Gold discovered in 1858 at Gila City, 20 miles upstream from Yuma, attracted 1,200 miners by 1861. Three years later the gold played out, and a traveler reported that "the promising metropolis of Arizona consisted of three chimneys and a coyote." Prospectors later found many other gold and silver deposits up and down western Arizona, hastening development of the region. Lead-zinc and copper mines opened too. Most of the old workings lie abandoned now, marked by piles of tailings, foundations, and decaying walls.

Steamboats plied the Colorado River after 1852, providing faster and safer transport than wagon trains. For more than 50 years they served the forts and mining camps along the river. Some of the riverboats stood three decks high and measured more than 140 feet long, yet drew only two feet of water. These giant stern-wheelers took on cargo from ocean ships at Port Isabel on the Gulf of California, then headed upstream as far as 600 miles. Boat traffic declined when the Southern Pacific Railroad went through Yuma in 1877, and it virtually ended in 1909 with the construction of Laguna Dam.

TRANSPORTATION

Boat cruises and raft trips show visitors some of the scenery in Lake Mead National Recreation

Area. Other boat tours go through the scenic Topock Gorge between Lake Havasu City and Bullhead City or in the Martinez Lake/Imperial Wildlife Refuge area farther downstream. Your own car (or boat) allows you to explore the quiet and scenic backcountry of western Arizona.

Greyhound buses and Amtrak trains serve Kingman on routes across northern Arizona, and Yuma on southern Arizona routes. Greyhound also connects Kingman and Laughlin with Las Vegas and Phoenix.

Regional airports in Kingman, Bullhead City, Lake Havasu City, Blythe (California), and Yuma offer connections to Phoenix or southern California.

The Northwest Corner

KINGMAN

Kingman lies in high-desert country at an elevation of 3,345 feet surrounded by the Cerbat, Hualapai, and Black mountain ranges. Lewis Kingman came through the area in 1880 while surveying a right-of-way for the Atlantic and Pacific Railroad between Albuquerque, New Mexico, and Needles, California. The railroad camp that later bore his name grew into a major mining, ranching, and transportation center for northwestern Arizona. A county election in 1886 required the county seat to move from Mineral Park to Kingman, but residents of Mineral Park balked at turning over county records. Kingmanites, according to one story, then sneaked over to Mineral Park in the dead of night to snatch the records and bring them to Kingman, where they've stayed ever since.

Kingman (area population 37,000) lies in the heart of the longest remaining stretch of Route 66—one of the historic predecessors of today's transcontinental highways. Area businesses promote the Route 66 theme, and there's a new museum on the highway in the Powerhouse Visitor Center. Numerous motels and restaurants serve motorists on their way across the country on I-40 or US 93. Other visitors use the town as a base to explore regional attractions such as Hoover Dam and Lake Mead National Recreation Area, ghost towns and old town sites such as Oatman and Chloride, the cool forests of Hualapai Mountain Park, London Bridge in Lake Havasu City, and the glittering casinos of Laughlin.

Historic Sights

A map available at the town's visitor center or the Mohave Museum provides a brief rundown on many of the old buildings in the historic downtown area. You can tour the early 20th-century Bonelli House or stay in the historic Brunswick Hotel, which also has a good restaurant. A few doors down from the Brunswick, Hotel Beale dates from 1899 and was the boyhood home of actor Andy Devine. It currently awaits restoration. The huge steam locomotive across from Powerhouse Visitor Center ran from 1929 to the mid-1950s, when the era of steam ended for the Santa Fe Railroad.

Mohave Museum of History and Arts

The museum's varied collection offers a good introduction to the history of northwestern Arizona. Dioramas, murals, and many artifacts show development from prehistoric times to the present. A ranching video tells about life on the range, past and present, in Mohave County. The Hualapai Native American Room contains a full-size wickiup brush shelter, pottery, baskets, and other crafts.

Other sights include paintings, sculpture, and crafts in the art gallery, photos showing construction of Hoover Dam, carved turquoise mined in the Kingman area, portraits of U.S. presidents with their first ladies, and a special exhibit on local-boy-turned-movie-star Andy Devine. The museum even features a pipe organ, used in concerts here. Outdoor exhibits display ranching and mining machinery plus a 1923 railroad caboose. History buffs can dig into the museum's library. A gift shop sells regional books

KINGMAN

To Airport and Peach Springs

To Seligman and Flagstaff

66

40

BUS STATION

EXIT 53

TOWNSEND ST.

To Haulapai Mountain Park

0.5 mi

0.5 km

0

0

AVENUE

AIRWAY

BEVERLY AVE.

RUTHERFORD ST.

BLM KINGMAN RESOURCE AREA OFFICE

AIRFIELD AVE.

ANDY DEVINE AVE.

PORTOFINO RISTORANTE ITALIANO

HARRISON ST.

BURBANK ST.

CENTENNIAL PARK

MOHAVE COUNTY FAIRGROUNDS

AVE.

MOTOR AVE.

FAIRGROUNDS BLVD.

HUALAPAI MOUNTAIN ROAD

To Northern Ave.

MOHAVE COUNTY DISTRICT LIBRARY

STOCKTON HILL RD.

CLUB AVE.

ARIZONA ST.

MAIN POST OFFICE

66

EXIT 52

KINGMAN REGIONAL MEDICAL CENTER

DETROIT AVE.

CAPPELLO'S

GATES AVE.

WESTERN AVE.

COUNTRY CLUB DR.

GOLF DR.

OAK ST.

93

ANDY DEVINE AVE.

GREENWAY DR.

CERBAT CLIFFS GOLF COURSE

WAGON TRACKS

N 7TH ST.

N 5TH ST.

PARK ST.

SEE DETAIL

To I-40 Exit 44 and Oatman

BONELLI HOUSE

COURTHOUSE

POST OFFICE

EL PALACIO

AMTRAK TRAIN

N. 4TH ST.

N. 3RD ST.

OAK ST.

N. 2ND ST.

HOTEL BRUNSWICK

BEALE ST.

SWIMMING POOL

GRANDVIEW AVE.

66

METCALFE CITY PARK

MOHAVE MUSEUM OF HISTORY AND ARTS

LOCOMOTIVE PARK

ANDY DEVINE AVE.

POWERHOUSE VISITOR CENTER

66

LEAD ST.

SILVER

GOLD

SPRING

To Bullhead City, Hoover Dam, and Las Vegas

93

To Needles (CA) and Lake Havasu City

40

and Native American crafts. The museum, 928/753-3195, is open Mon.–Fri. 9 A.M.–5 P.M. and Sat.–Sun. 1–5 P.M., closed major holidays; admission is $2 ages 13 and up, free for children 12 and under with adult. You'll find it at 400 W. Beale; take I-40 Exit 48 and go east 0.3 mile on Beale Street.

Route 66 Museum

Head upstairs in the Powerhouse Visitor Center to experience the history of travel on the 35th Parallel. The story begins with early trade routes and the Beale Wagon Road, which allowed pioneers to cross the land in "prairie schooners" such as the one on display. An old Chevrolet truck and quotations from John Steinbeck's *Grapes of Wrath* recount the tough times along Route 66 during the Great Depression of the 1930s. Storefronts, murals, and a 1950 Studebaker Champion car illustrate the good times of the post-World War II era. Photo exhibits and personal accounts bring the past to life. A small theater shows videos on request. Open daily 9 A.M.–6 P.M. (5 P.M. in winter); $3 ages 13 and up; 928/753-9889.

Bonelli House

This historic house reflects the lifestyle and taste of a prominent Kingman family early in the 20th century. The Bonellis built it of native stone in 1915 using both American and European designs. Thick walls insulate the interior from the temperature extremes of Kingman's desert climate. A member of the Bonelli family lived here until 1973, when the city of Kingman bought the house for restoration as a bicentennial project. It's at 430 E. Spring St. (at N. 5th St.), 928/753-1413. Open Thurs.–Mon. 1–4 P.M. except major holidays; donation requested.

Wagon Tracks

Wagons creaking down the hill into Kingman from the 1870s to the early 1900s carved deep ruts in the soft volcanic bedrock. Wagon masters used the evenly spaced holes beside the road for braking or leverage with long poles. Another road bypassed this spot in 1912, leaving the old road in its original condition.

The site lies near a pretty canyon just a short drive from town. From the Mohave Museum of History and Arts, take Grandview Avenue north 0.4 mile, then turn right and drive 0.6 mile on Lead Street, which becomes White Cliffs Road. Look for a wooden footbridge on the right; follow the path across to the old wagon road.

Accommodations

Most of Kingman's motels and restaurants line W. Beale Street (US 93) and E. Andy Devine Avenue (Route 66/AZ 66) between I-40 Exits 48 and 53. Travelers have a choice of older, well-kept motels, newer "economy" places, high-standard chains, and one historic hotel. Competition keeps prices low—often at bargain levels. Summer rates, quoted below, tend to be higher; reservations are recommended for weekends, especially during an event. See **Hualapai Mountain Park** below for cabins available there.

Historic Hotel: The historic 1909 **Hotel Brunswick,** downtown at 315 E. Andy Devine, 928/718-1800, has been beautifully restored. Rooms start at $25 d for a small one with bath down the hall and cost $50 d with bath or $75–110 d for a suite; www.hotel-brunswick.com. Hubbs Café (closed Sunday) offers French cuisine for dinner.

Under $50: Motels just off I-40 Exit 48 on the way to Las Vegas are **Budget Inn Motel,** 1239 W. Beale, 928/753-2773, $25–30 d; **Economy Inn,** 1225 W. Beale, 928/753-3881, $30–45 d; and **Frontier Motel,** 1250 W. Beale, 928/753-6171; $20 s, $25 d.

Another long string of under $50 motels lies between I-40 Exits 48 and 53. These include **Motel 6 West,** 424 W. Beale, 928/753-9222, 800/466-8356, $45 d; **Arizona Inn,** 411 W. Beale, 928/753-5521, $35 d; **Arcadia Lodge,** 909 E. Andy Devine, 928/753-1925, $26 s, $31 d; **Ramblin' Rose Motel,** 1001 E. Andy Devine, 928/753-5541, $29 s, $32 d; **El Trovatore Motel,** 1440 E. Andy Devine, 928/753-4050, $24 s, $28 d; **Hill Top Motel,** 1901 E. Andy Devine, 928/753-2198, $32–39 s, $32–42 d; **Imperial Motel,** 1911 E. Andy Devine, 928/753-2176, $30 s, $33 d; **Orchard Inn,** 1967 E. Andy Devine, 928/753-5511, $25–35 d; **High Desert Inn,**

Hotel Beale lobby in downtown Kingman

© BILL WEIR

2803 E. Andy Devine, 928/753-2935, $25 s, $28 d; **Route 66 Motel,** 2939 E. Andy Devine, 928/753-5586, $24 s, $26 d; **Mohave Inn,** 3016 E. Andy Devine, 928/753-9555, $27 d; **Best Value Inn,** 3100 E. Andy Devine, 928/753-6262, 888/315-2378, $30 s, $33 d; and **Lido Motel,** 3133 E. Andy Devine, 928/753-4515, $23 s, $24 d. Continuing east of I-40 Exit 53 are **1st Value Inn,** 3270 E. Andy Devine, 928/757-7122, $27 d; **Silver Queen,** 3285 E. Andy Devine, 928/757-4315, $30 d; **Motel 6 East,** 3351 E. Andy Devine, 928/757-7151, 800/466-8356, $33 d; **Days Inn East,** 3381 E. Andy Devine, 928/757-7337; or 800/329-7666, $35 d; **Super 8,** 3401 E. Andy Devine, 928/757-4808, 800/800-8000, $40 s, $45–50 d; and **Travel Inn,** 3421 E. Andy Devine, 928/757-7878, $30–35 s, $40–45 d.

$50–100: Motels between I-40 Exits 48 and 53 include **Quality Inn,** 1400 E. Andy Devine, 928/753-4747, 800/869-3252, $60 d; **Best Western Wayfarer's Inn,** 2815 E. Andy Devine, 928/753-6271, 800/548-5695, $68 s, $76 d; **Best Western Kings Inn & Suites,** 2930 E. Andy Devine, 928/753-6101, 800/750-6101, $60–92 s, $66–92 d; **Days Inn West,** 3023 E. Andy Devine, 928/753-7500, 800/329-7466,

$55–99 d; and **Comfort Inn,** 3129 E. Andy Devine, 928/718-1717, 800/228-5150, $54–64 d. Just east of I-40 Exit 53 is a **Travelodge,** 3275 E. Andy Devine, 928/757-1188, 800/578-7878, $50–60 d.

Campgrounds

All of the following campgrounds stay open year-round. The **Kingman KOA,** 928/757-4397, 800/562-3991, offers a pool, showers, game room, store, and miniature golf; $18 tent or RV no hookups, $22–24 RV with hookups, $37 kamping kabin. To get there, take I-40 Exit 52, go north half a mile on Stockton Hill Road, turn right one mile on Airway Ave., then left on Roosevelt to the campground. **Zuni Village RV Park,** 2840 Airway Ave. near I-40 Exit 53, 928/692-6202, has a pool and showers, $16.50 RV with hookups. **Circle S Campground,** 2360 Airway near I-40 Exit 53, 928/757-3235, costs $12 tent, $14 RV with hookups.

Fort Beale RV Park, 300 Metcalfe Rd. near I-40 Exit 48, 928/753-3355, features a pool, showers, and views; $20 RV with hookups. **Canyon West RV,** two miles west of downtown off Andy

Devine, 928/753-9378, offers tent and RV sites with a shower; $16 with hookups. **Highway 66 RV Park** lies northeast 16 miles down Route 66 at Valle Vista (near Milepost 71 on the way to Peach Springs), 928/757-8878; $15 with hookups, self-contained RVs only.

Blake Ranch RV Park is 18 miles east of Kingman on Blake Ranch Road, just off I-40 Exit 66, 928/757-3336; $17 tent, $18–20 RV with hookups, and has showers. **Adobe RV Park** is one of several to the west in Golden Valley off AZ 68, 928/565-3010; $14.50 RV with hookups. **Hualapai Mountain Park,** 14 miles southeast of town, offers tent and RV sites in cool pine forests; see Vicinity of Kingman below.

Food

Hubbs Café in the **Hotel Brunswick** downtown at 315 E. Andy Devine, 928/718-1800, serves excellent French food for dinner; closed Sunday. The Route 66 era lives on downtown at **Memory Lane Soda Fountain and Deli,** in the Powerhouse at 120 W. Andy Devine, 928/718-2020. **Mr. D'z Route 66 Diner,** 105 E. Andy Devine, 928/718-0066, also has great atmosphere and features a more extensive menu including breakfasts.

Other places for American food include **Calico's Restaurant,** 418 W. Beale, 928/753-5005; **City Cafe,** 1929 E. Andy Devine and Stockton Hill/Hualapai Mountain Rds., 928/753-3550; **Dambar Steakhouse,** 1960 E. Andy Devine and Stockton Hill/Hualapai Mountain Rds., 928/753-3523; and **Golden Corral,** 3157 Stockton Hill Rd. just south of I-40 Exit 52, 928/753-1505.

For 24-hour restaurants, drop into **Country Pride** in Travel Centers of America, 946 W. Beale just northwest of I-40 Exit 48, 928/753-7600; **Cookery** in Flying J Travel Plaza, 3300 E. Andy Devine just east of I-40 Exit 53, 928/757-7311; or **Denny's,** 3255 E. Andy Devine, 928/757-2028.

Portofino Ristorante Italiano (recently moved to 2215 Hualapai Mountain Rd. on the left, 0.4 mile south of Andy Devine), 928/753-0542; and **Cappello's,** 1921 Club Ave. (just east

off Stockton Hill), 928/718-3300, prepare fine Italian pasta and meat dishes. **Pizza Hut,** 928/757-3292, is east of I-40 Exit 53 at 3395 E. Andy Devine.

For Mexican food, try **El Palacio,** downtown at 401 E. Andy Devine; 928/718-0018.

Dine Chinese at **House of Chan,** 960 W. Beale, just northwest of I-40 Exit 48, 928/753-3232, which offers a lunch buffet; **Uncle King's Restaurant,** 3370 Stockton Hill, 928/757-3207; or **Golden China Restaurant,** 4135 Stockton Hill, 928/757-5265.

Popular chain and fast-food places lie near all three I-40 exits.

Entertainment and Events

Catch films at **The Movies,** 4055 Stockton Hill Rd.; 928/757-7985.

Staff at the Powerhouse Visitor Center provide information on local happenings. The Kingman Area Chamber of Commerce has an online calendar at www.kingmanchamber.org. Classic and antique cars highlight the **Route 66 Fun Run Road Rally** in early May. Artists and craftspeople display their work at the **Festival of the Arts** on Mothers' Day weekend in May.

Take in the exhibits and entertainment of the **Mohave County Fair** in mid September. Kingmanites and visitors celebrate **Andy Devine Days** with a parade, PRCA rodeo, and other festivities in late September or early October. The **Kingman Air & Auto Show** takes off in October. See handmade crafts in the **Kingman Cancer Care Arts and Crafts Fair,** second weekend in November. The **Caroling Festival and Christmas Parade** brighten winter in mid-December.

Recreation

Metcalfe City Park offers shade trees, picnic tables, and a playground at W. Beale and Grandview Ave., diagonally opposite the Mohave Museum of History and Arts. You'll find **swimming pools** downtown at the corner of Grandview Ave. and Gold St., 928/753-8155, and in Centennial Park at 3333 N. Harrison, 928/757-7910. **Centennial Park** also features tennis and racquetball courts, ball fields, and picnicking.

Cerbat Cliffs Golf Course has 18 holes at 1001 E. Gates, west off Stockton Hill Rd., 928/753-6593. **Valle Vista** offers an 18-hole course at 9686 N. Concho Dr., 17 miles northeast on AZ 66, 928/757-8744.

Information and Services

Staff at the **Powerhouse Visitor Center,** downtown at 120 W. Andy Devine (P.O. Box 1150, Kingman, AZ 86402), 928/753-6106, 866/427-7866, can help you explore this corner of Arizona. The large building dates from 1907 and was one of Arizona's first reinforced concrete structures. It also houses a Route 66 museum, photo exhibits, movie theater, soda fountain, model train store, and gift shop.

It's open daily 9 A.M.–6 P.M. (5 P.M. in winter); www.arizona guide.com/cities/kingman or www.kingmanchamber.org

Find out about recreation areas and the backcountry near Kingman at the Powerhouse Visitor Center or the **BLM Kingman Field Office,** 2475 Beverly Ave. (Kingman, AZ 86401), 928/692-4400; it's open Mon.–Fri. 7:30 A.M.–4:30 P.M.; http:// kingman.az.blm.gov.

The main **post office** is at 1901 Johnson and Stockton Hill Rd., 928/753-2480, though the downtown branch at 209 N. Fourth St. can be more convenient. **Kingman Regional Medical Center** is at 3269 Stockton Hill Rd., just north from I-40 Exit 52; 928/757-2101.

Transportation

Buses run by **Greyhound** stop at the tiny station behind McDonald's at 3264 E. Andy Devine, just east of I-40 Exit 53; 928/757-8400. **Amtrak** offers daily passenger train service west to Los Angeles and east to Williams, Flagstaff, Albuquerque, and beyond. The terminal is downtown at the corner of Fourth Street and Andy Devine; 800/872-7245. **America West Express** flies to Phoenix from the airport northeast of

Check out Lake Havasu City in October: there's the Relics and Rods Run to the Sun event, featuring one of the country's largest gatherings of antique and classic autos; the London Bridge Square Dance Jamboree; or rev-up for Bike-toberfest.

town; 800/235-9292. For a taxi call **Kingman Cab** at 928/753-3624.

VICINITY OF KINGMAN

Hualapai Mountain Park

The Hualapai, whose name means "pine tree folk," lived in these mountains until the military relocated the tribe northward in the 1870s. Now a county park, the mountains are easily reached on the 14-mile paved Hualapai Mountain Road that runs southeast from Kingman.

The park offers dense forests, scenic views, hiking trails, picnicking, camping, and rustic cabins. Elevations range from 5,000 to 8,417 feet, attracting wildlife rarely seen elsewhere in northwestern Arizona. Groves of manzanita, scrub and Gambel oak, pinyon and ponderosa pine, white fir, and aspen grow on the slopes. Mule deer, elk, mountain lion, fox, and raccoon roam the forests. The park office maintains checklists of plants and animals found here. Hiking trails wind through the mountains to the summit of Aspen Peak and overlooks on Hayden Peak.

Campsites have drinking water (except in winter) but no showers, $8. A small RV area offers hookups for $15. Cabins, built for a Civilian Conservation Corps camp in the 1930s, contain kitchens and bathrooms; $25–65. You can visit the park any time of year, though winter snows sometimes require the use of chains or 4WD. For information and reservations at the cabins, contact the Mohave County Parks Department, P.O. Box 605, Bullhead City, AZ 86430; 928/754-7273, 877/757-0915; open Mon.–Fri. 8 A.M.–4 P.M. The Hualapai Ranger Station near the park entrance is open daily 7 A.M.–3 P.M.; 928/757-3859; www.huala paimountainpark.com.

The nearby **Hualapai Mountain Lodge,** in the village of Pine Lake, 928/757-3545, offers a motel, RV park, restaurant, and store. Some of

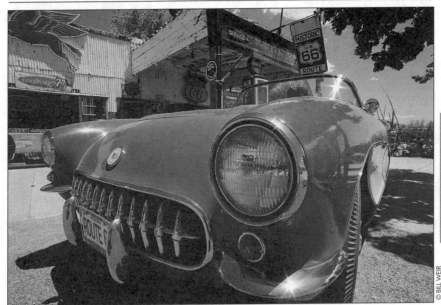

© BILL WEIR

A '57 Corvette stands ready to cruise at the Old Route 66 Visitor Center.

the well-preserved buildings here once belonged to the Civilian Conservation Corps camp. The motel ($75 d, $110 suite) and restaurant are open Tues.–Sun. year-round. The restaurant serves breakfast (Sat.–Sun. only), lunch, and dinner; closed Monday. RVs can park for $20 with hookups. From Kingman, drive to the Hualapai Mountain Park, then continue on the paved road 0.75 mile past the ranger station. **Pine Lake Inn Bed & Breakfast,** 928/757-1884, is 0.75 mile farther and overlooks the lake; open year-round; $95 d.

The Bureau of Land Management's **Wild Cow Springs Campground** ($5, no water) nestles in a secluded valley of ponderosa pine and Gambel oak at an elevation of 6,200 feet, but you'll need a high-clearance vehicle; the season normally runs May to October. From Hualapai Mountain Park, continue just past the turn for Hualapai Mountain Lodge, then turn right four miles at the sign on rough unpaved road.

With 4WD, you can continue high on the ridge 13.5 miles past the campground to the trailhead for Wabayuma Peak in **Wabayuma**

Peak Wilderness Area. The trail begins at 6,047 feet and climbs to the summit and great views at 7,601 feet in three miles one-way; use the 7.5-minute Wabayuma topo map. The rough 4WD road continues south, then west to Yucca at I-40 Exit 25. The drive is slow, taking at least three hours one way from Wild Cow Springs Campground to I-40, but you'll have great panoramas of the Hualapai Mountains and beyond. The amazing range of vegetation on this drive includes ponderosa pine forests, pinyon pine and juniper woodlands, chaparral atop the ridges, then saguaro, ocotillo, yucca, and Joshua trees in the desert below. You'll see mill ruins at an abandoned mine on the descent.

Burro Creek Recreation Site

If you're driving between Kingman and Wickenburg or Phoenix, you'll pass this picturesque spot. A perennial stream flows through a scenic canyon area (elev. 1,960 feet), feeding deep blue pools and lush greenery in the desert. Open all year, it's a great place to take a break from the long drive on US 93. Visitors enjoy camping, picnicking, birding, swimming, hiking, four-wheeling, and rockhounding for agates and Apache tears. A cactus garden and interpretive signs introduce life of the desert. Hikers can head up the creekbed if the water isn't too high—the creek extends some 40 miles upstream and goes through the heart of Burro Creek Wilderness; downstream is private land. Day use is free. The campground has drinking water, flush toilets, and a dump station, but no showers; $10 per night. For information and group campsite ($30) reservations, contact the Kingman Field Office of the BLM at 2475 Beverly Ave., Kingman, AZ 86401; 928/692-4400; http://kingman.az.blm.gov. Head southeast 65 miles from Kingman on I-40 and US 93, or northwest 63 miles from Wickenburg, then turn west 1.3 miles at the sign. An overlook on the west side of the highway near the bridge provides a fine panorama of the area.

Old Route 66 Visitor Center

For a trip into America's motoring past, turn off onto Route 66 between Kingman and Seligman. On the north side of the road 24 miles northeast of Kingman, you'll see the Old Route 66 Visitor Center surrounded by colorful collection of Route 66 memorabilia. A '57 Corvette and other vintage cars and trucks stand outside. Old gas pumps have unbelievable prices but have long since gone dry. Signs from long ago cover the walls inside and outside the building. The Visitor Center is open daily and sells Route 66 memorabilia; there's no charge for stopping and looking around.

Cerbat

Gold and silver deposits in the Cerbat Mountains, north of present-day Kingman, attracted miners in the late 1860s. They founded the town of Cerbat and worked such mines as the Esmeralda, Golden Gem, and Vanderbilt. Cerbat became the Mohave County seat in 1871 but lost the honor two years later to nearby Mineral Park. By 1912 the Cerbat post office had closed. The Golden Gem mill and headframe still stand, structures that rarely survive in other ghost towns. You'll also see stone foundations and ruins of other buildings.

banana yucca in bloom atop the Cerbat Mountains

© BILL WEIR

The turnoff for Cerbat lies nine miles northwest of Kingman on US 93, near Milepost 62; head east 0.8 mile on a dirt road, turn left and drive a half mile, then turn right and travel another two miles to the site. Keep left when passing a ranch, then a group of modern buildings just outside old Cerbat. The last bit may be too rough for cars.

Mineral Park

During most of the 1870s and 1880s, Mineral Park reigned as the county seat and most important town in the area, losing those distinctions in 1886 to Kingman. By 1912 Mineral Park had lost its post office. Some tattered houses, a headframe, mill foundations, and scattered mine shafts survive from the old days. The huge piles of tailings to the south belong to a copper and molybdenum mine that operated from 1961 to 1982. It still contains the world's largest known turquoise deposit, which is mined along with decorative rock. Cyprus Mineral Park Corp. currently runs a solvent extraction electrowinning operation for copper. The signed turnoff for Mineral Park lies 14 miles northwest of Kingman on US 93, between Mileposts 58 and 59. Turn east 4.4 miles on a paved road, then left 0.3 mile at the Mineral Park Historical Mining District interpretive sign to the site.

Chloride

This friendly town lies 20 miles northwest of Kingman on US 93; turn east three miles on a paved road at the sign between Mileposts 52 and 53.

After discovering silver chloride ore here in the early 1860s, prospectors founded the town—the oldest mining camp in northwestern Arizona. Hualapai made life precarious during Chloride's first years until army troops subdued the tribe. Several buildings survive from the town's lengthy mining period, which lasted into the 1940s. A few hundred people, including many retirees and artists, now live here.

Historic structures include old miners' shacks, the post office, Old Tennessee Saloon, jail, bank, and railroad depot; the cemetery is to the right at the sign as you enter town. It's fun to wander around the historic buildings and check out some of the antique and crafts shops.

Artist Roy Purcell painted giant, brightly colored murals in 1966 and 1975 on cliffs two miles southeast of town. He titled his work "The Journey—Images from an Inward Search for Self." You can also spot prehistoric petroglyphs near the murals. From Chloride, take Tennessee Avenue (the main road into town) past the post office and Tennessee Mine, then follow signs; the road may be too rough for low-slung cars. It's possible to continue up the road, which becomes rocky and steep, with a high-clearance 4WD vehicle to a seasonal waterfall in another half mile or all the way up past old mines to the Big Wash Road in the Cerbat Mountains; some of this land is private.

Sheps Miners Inn, on Second St. downtown, 928/565-4251, 877/565-4251, offers rooms with private bath and individual entrances at $45–55

d; www.shepsminersinn.com. **Chloride Western RV Park,** on the left as you enter town, 928/565-4492, is open year-round with tent sites ($7), RV sites ($7 without hookups, $12.50 with), showers, a laundry, and a rec. room.

The town's dismal dining scene offers only smoky cafés, either the Shep's Mining Camp Café, Western Corner Café & Saloon, or the Old Tennessee Saloon. Better to bring your own food or order take-out and dine in the park on Second Street across from Shep's.

Try to visit on the first or third Saturdays of each month when the **Immortal Gunfighters** shoot it out at high noon in the Old West set "Cyanide Springs" across from Shep's. Old-time vaudeville shows by the Chloride Vaudeville Troupe perform on the same days (may close July–August). Townspeople dress up in old-fashioned clothing on **Old Miners' Day,** the last Saturday (and following Sunday) in June, for a street dance, games, vaudeville shows, shootouts, and mine tours. Smaller events include a St. Patrick's Day celebration in March and all-town yard sales in May and October. The post office and a small grocery are downtown on Tennessee Avenue.

Chloride Chamber of Commerce is downtown in a historic house on Tennessee Ave. (P.O. Box 268, Chloride, AZ 86431), 928/565-2204; it's usually open daily 9 A.M.–5 P.M.; www.chloridearizona.com. Across the street, Mineshaft Market & Variety offers Arizona tourist information and a few photo exhibits in the back. A room-reservation service, across from the Tennessee Saloon, arranges lodgings and national parks in the Southwest, 928/565-9777, 800/578-3379; www.freerooms.com.

The Cerbat Mountains

Unpaved Big Wash Road twists up to the crest of the Cerbat Mountains, where visitors can enjoy expansive views, picnicking, camping, and hiking among pinyon pine and chaparral. The road begins near Milepost 51 on US 93, 1.5 miles north of the Chloride junction. It's graded but too steep and winding for RVs or trailers.

Packsaddle Recreation Area lies nine miles in, and the **Windy Point Recreation Area** entrance is 1.5 miles beyond that. Both areas have sites

© BILL WEIR

Fast Fanny's Place, Oatman

with picnic tables and vault toilets but no water; a $4 camping fee applies at Windy Point, which has a particularly scenic setting among boulders and great views to the west.

Cherum Peak Trail climbs to near the 6,983-foot summit of the peak, second highest in the Cerbats, then it's a short rock scramble up the last 200 feet to the top. This five-mile roundtrip hike takes about 3.5 hours. The trailhead (elev. about 6,000 feet) is on the left, two miles past Windy Point. (Beyond this point, the road begins a steep, rough 4WD descent toward Chloride.) Mountain bikes are permitted on the Cherum Peak Trail, but loose soil and steep grades would make it a difficult proposition. The trail passes through pinyon pine and large areas of chaparral, which contains shrub live oak, manzanita, Wrights's silktassel, broom snakeweed, skunkbush, New Mexican locust, Gambel oak, and desert ceanothus. Many wildflowers bloom in early summer. See the 7.5-minute Chloride topo map and the handouts available from the BLM Kingman Field Office; 928/692-4400.

Oatman

The weather-beaten gold-mining town of Oatman nestles in the western foothills of the Black Mountains, 28 miles southwest of Kingman. Elephant's Tooth, the gleaming white quartz pinnacle east of town, beckoned prospectors, who knew that gold and silver often run with quartz. Gold mining began in 1904, attracting hordes of miners and businesspeople. Citizens named the community for the Oatman family, victims of an 1851 Mohave attack.

Oatman prospered, attracting many new businesses, seven hotels, 20 saloons, and even a stock exchange. Area mines produced nearly two million ounces of gold before panning out in the 1930s. The town, which once boasted more than 12,000 citizens, began to fade away, and might have disappeared altogether had it not become a travelers' stop on Route 66. Oatman lost its highway traffic in 1952, when engineers rerouted the road to the south. A few hundred citizens hang on today, relying largely on the growing tourist business stemming from the designation of Old Route 66 as a National Backcountry Byway between Kingman and Golden Shores (north of I-40 Topock Exit 1). The mountain curves on this very scenic section of road challenged early motorists. Today it's paved and an easy drive, though not for one in a hurry. Between Kingman and Oatman you'll cross 3,550-foot Sitgreaves Pass; pullouts on each side allow a stop for the views. Near Oatman, you'll pass the Addwest Gold Road Mine, which has a long history and now offers underground tours.

Two other roads connect Oatman with the outside world. From Bullhead City and Needles, you can take paved Boundary Cone Road east from AZ 95. The unpaved but more scenic Silver Creek Road turns off Bullhead Parkway east of Bullhead City and joins the Oatman Highway between Oatman and the Addwest Gold Road Mine; cautiously driven cars can usually negotiate it.

Many of the town's old buildings survive, and some are now gift shops. The **Oatman Hotel,** a two-story adobe structure built in 1902, contains historic exhibits. In March 1939, newlyweds Clark Gable and Carole Lombard spent part of their honeymoon in the hotel. Gable liked to visit Oatman, a place where he could get away from the hectic pace of Hollywood and enjoy poker with the miners. The hotel rents basic rooms for $35 d and the Lombard-Gable honeymoon room for $55; 928/768-4408. Small rock shops, gift shops, the public library, and the post office also lie along Main Street. The old jail has recently opened as a museum. Pick up a self-guiding tour sheet at one of the local shops to learn more about Oatman history. You're almost sure to meet the town's wild burros, who wander the streets looking for handouts. Shops sell burro feed (people food is bad for the animals), but be careful—the critters bite.

Shootouts, usually just for fun, take place daily on Main Street. Hilarity reigns in January as

> *Oatman, complete with wild burros, certainly won't disappoint. Enjoy daily shootouts (just for fun), or attend an annual event: January hosts a Bed Pan Parade; the Sidewalk Egg Fry makes for a fun Fourth of July; and Labor Day weekend's Gold Camp Days features, among other events, a burro biscuit-tossing contest.*

costumed participants march in the Bed Pan Parade and compete in the Bed Race. Around the Fourth of July, competitors warm up for the **Oatman Sidewalk Egg Fry.** Oatman celebrates **Gold Camp Days** on Labor Day weekend with shootouts, a burro biscuit tossing contest, costume parade, and dancing.

The **Oatman Hotel** serves food and drink, but don't expect luxuries such as a non-smoking area. Live bands play at the hotel on weekend evenings and sometimes on other days. RVs can park at **Blackstone RV Park,** about 12 miles west of town at 3299 E. Boundary Cone Rd., 928/768-3303, for $15 w/hookups; no tents.

Vicinity of Oatman

At **Gold Road Mine,** 928/768-1600, you can tour the underground passages where the gold boom started! A guide gives you a hard hat and transports you in a "getman" or other vehicle up to the original entrance. On an easy one-hour walk you'll enter the workings and learn how miners did their job; $12, $6 age 12 and under. An ore-processing tour, on the surface, takes you to the machinery that converts the ore to gold; it lasts about an hour and costs $10. Longer tours, stagecoach rides (October to mid-April), and trail rides can be arranged by reservation; www.goldroadmine.com. Head east 2.5 miles from Oatman on Route 66 up into the Black Mountains.

Mohave and Milltown Railroad Trails follow a seven-mile section of the old railway bed, beginning about five miles southwest of Oatman. Separate trails and trailheads accommodate both off-highway vehicles/equestrians and hikers/bikers. The BLM Kingman Field Office has a map and description.

Dinosphere

This odd structure, looking like a cross between a

giant golf ball and a spaceship, stands near Yucca (I-40 Exit 25) between Kingman and the California state line. It has three levels and measures 40 feet in diameter. Lake Havasu Estates built it in 1976 as a restaurant and cocktail lounge for a land development. The company went bankrupt, however, and the white sphere now is a private house. (It's not open to the public.)

BULLHEAD CITY

This community of more than 27,000 residents parallels AZ 95 and the Colorado River for about 10 miles. Gamblers, anglers, and boaters enjoy the river setting. Although gold miners worked prospects nearby, this remote site lay deserted until the 1940s, when construction workers arrived to build Davis Dam upstream. With completion of the dam in 1953, everyone thought the construction camp called Bullhead City would disappear. Instead it became a center for outdoor recreation.

In addition to the Colorado River at the town's doorstep, Lake Mohave's 240 square miles of deep blue water beckon six miles north. The "bullhead" rock formation that gave the place its name nearly did disappear—only the "horns" now poke out of the lake.

Bullhead City lies 35 miles west of Kingman via AZ 68, and 25 miles north of Needles, California, on AZ 95. The bright lights of gambling casinos in sister city Laughlin glow from across the river in Nevada. South of town, the Colorado River enters Havasu National Wildlife Refuge; see North of Lake Havasu City, below.

Colorado River Historical Society Museum

Exhibits commemorate local Native Americans, steamboating on the Colorado River, mining, ranching, and dam construction. Photographs and maps show the growth of the Bullhead City/Laughlin area from early beginnings to modern times. It's open Tues.–Sun. 10 A.M.–4 P.M.; closed Mon. and July–Aug.; donations welcome. Head north one-third mile on AZ 95 from the Laughlin Bridge junction, then turn left; 928/754-3399.

Accommodations and Campgrounds

You have a choice of more than a dozen motels and about a dozen RV parks in Bullhead City, or you can stay across the river at the casinos in Laughlin. Try to make reservations for motels, casinos, and RV parks, especially if you're arriving on a weekend. You can save money at many places by visiting Sun.–Thurs., when casino rates may drop into the $20s.

Campgrounds and RV parks stay open year-round; most RV parks prefer that guests stay a week or longer. **Davis Camp Park,** maintained by Mohave County, offers beach sites for tents and RVs ($10 no hookups, $13–16 with hookups), a picnic area, boat ramps, and showers. Day use is $4, or $7 if pulling a boat trailer. The park is just off AZ 95 0.8 mile north of the Laughlin Bridge junction; 928/754-7250, 877/757-0915; www.daviscamp.com. You'll also find a motel, RV park, and campground six miles north of Bullhead City at Katherine Landing; see Lake Mohave below.

Food

For Italian dining, try **Antonucci's Ristorante,** 1751 Hwy. 95, 928/763-8118, open Mon.–Sat. for lunch and dinner. Enjoy Chinese cuisine at **China Szechuan,** 1890 Hwy. 95, 928/763-2610; or **China Panda,** 2164 Hwy. 95, 928/763-8899; both are open daily for lunch and dinner. Mexican cuisine is prepared at **El Encanto,** in the north part of town at 125 Long Ave. and Seventh St., 928/754-5100; **El Palacio,** 1884 Hwy. 95, 928/763-2494; and on the water at **Iguana's Mexican River Cantina,** 2247 Clearwater Dr., 928/763-9109; all are open daily for lunch and dinner. Casinos on the Nevada side feature enticing menus and prices.

Events

Silvery Colorado Gem & Mineral Show gleams in March. **Laughlin River Stampede Rodeo** gallops in April. In May, you can enjoy food and games—but no burro—at the **Burro Barbecue** in Bullhead Community Park. In June, Nevadans celebrate **Laughlin River Days** with a boat race. **Fireworks** light up the skies on July Fourth in Laughlin. Boats at Lake Mohave

Resort (Katherine Landing) stage a **Parade of Lights** in December.

Recreation

Bullhead Community Park, just north of the chamber of commerce, is a pleasant spot for a picnic overlooking the Colorado River; there's also a playground and boat ramp.

One of the best fishing areas along the Colorado River lies right in front of Bullhead City. The cold swift waters from Davis Dam harbor large rainbow trout, channel catfish, and, during late spring and early summer, giant striped bass weighing 20 pounds and more.

Golfers can play on the nine-hole **Chaparral Country Club** course, 1260 E. Mohave Dr., five miles south of town, 928/758-6330; the nine-hole **Riverview Golf Course,** 2000 E. Ramar Rd., three miles south on AZ 95, then 1.5 miles east on Ramar, 928/763-1818; or the 18-hole **Desert Lakes Golf Course,** 10 miles south on AZ 95, then east on Joy Lane, 928/768-1000.

Information and Services

The **Bullhead Area Chamber of Commerce** is on the south side of Bullhead Community Park at 1251 Hwy. 95, Bullhead City, AZ 86429; 928/754-4121; www.bullheadcity.com. It's open year-round Mon.–Fri. 8 A.M.–5 P.M. The **public library** is open Mon.–Sat. at 1170 E. Hancock Rd. in south Bullhead City; 928/758-0714. **Hastings Books,** 1985 Hwy. 95, 928/763-0025, offers regional and general-interest titles.

The downtown **post office** is at 990 Hwy. 95; 928/758-5711; the main one is at 1882 Lakeside Drive. **Western Arizona Regional Medical Center** is at 2735 Silver Creek Rd.; 928/763-2273.

Transportation

Greyhound buses no longer stop in Bullhead City, but they do serve Laughlin at the Horizon Outlet Center, 1955 S. Casino Dr. (across from the Flamingo); 702/298-1934.

Air Laughlin, 866/359-2386, flies to Phoenix and California destinations from Bullhead City's airport; www.airlaughlin.com. The airport is just north of Bullhead City (turn east at the Laughlin Bridge junction) and has car rentals, charter flights, and a snack bar.

Laughlin, Nevada

The casinos on the Nevada side of the river try to attract your business with bright lights, entertainment, and food-and-lodging deals. Laughlin's casinos have a more casual—some say more friendly—atmosphere than the bigger gambling centers of Las Vegas and Reno. Besides the games of chance, you can check out the movies, live shows, hotel rooms, swimming pools, and dining bargains offered by many casinos.

Standard rooms at the casinos typically run $19–25 Sun.–Thurs., $35–55 Fri.–Sat., $45–145 on holiday weekends; advance reservations help to secure lower prices. Buffets cost very little, but they often have long lines. Many locals prefer to patronize the town's fine-dining restaurants, which have better service and still offer good prices.

Horizon Outlet Center, 1955 S. Casino Dr., 702/298-3003, offers shopping and a nine-plex movie theater. Riverside Casino, 702/298-2535, 928/763-7070 or 800/227-3849, features **Don Laughlin's Classic Car Collection** and a six-plex movie theater at the north end of the strip; www.riversideresort.com.

The **Laughlin Visitor Center,** 1555 Casino Dr. (P.O. Box 502, Laughlin, NV 89029), 702/298-3321, 800/452-8445, is on your right as you enter the strip from Bullhead City; it's open daily 8 A.M.–4:30 P.M. Staff will provide you with information on local accommodations, events, and entertainment. They can also help with local and statewide lodging reservations; courtesy phones are available to contact local and Las Vegas establishments directly; www.visitlaughlin.com.

The **Laughlin Chamber of Commerce,** next door at 1585 Casino Dr. (P.O. Box 77777, Laughlin, NV 89028), 702/298-2214, 800/227-5245, will also answer your questions about casinos and events on the Nevada side. It's open Mon.–Fri. 8:30 A.M.–4:30 P.M.

London Bridge Jet Boat Tours, 702/298-5498, 888/505-3545, offers excursions to Lake Havasu City via Topock Gorge from the Pioneer Hotel; $52 adult, $47 seniors 65+, $32 children 3–12; no tours Dec.–Jan.; www.jetboattour.com.

From Bullhead City you can reach Laughlin by driving across the Colorado River bridge just north of town or by taking the eight-mile route via Davis Dam farther north. Riverside Casino offers a passenger ferry that leaves from the shore north of downtown Bullhead City. Shuttle buses connect the casinos.

Lake Mead National Recreation Area and Vicinity

The Colorado River forms two long lakes as it winds more than 144 miles through Lake Mead National Recreation Area. From Grand Canyon National Park, the blue waters flow around the extreme northwest corner of Arizona past black volcanic rocks, stark hillsides, and white sandy beaches. Striking desert scenery and inviting waters make the area a paradise for boaters, anglers, water-skiers, swimmers, and scuba divers. Visitors often sight bighorn sheep on the canyon cliffs and wild burros in the more level areas. Adventurous hikers can explore the hills and canyons of the wild, seldom-visited country inland.

To get the most from a visit to Lake Mohave and Lake Mead, you really need a boat; roads approach the waterline at only a few scattered points. If you don't have your own, marinas offer rentals, from humble fishing craft to luxurious houseboats. Boat tours take in some of the scenery of Lake Mead from Boulder Beach and Hoover Dam. You can also glide through Black Canyon below Hoover Dam on raft tours. Back roads wind through many areas; ask for the maps that show the "Approved Backcountry Roads" of the areas you plan to visit. All vehicles in the recreation area must stay on these roads or on designated highways. The National Park Service provides boat ramps, developed campgrounds ($10 per night; water, but no showers or hookups), and ranger stations at most developed areas. Park Service people and volunteers also staff the Alan Bible Visitor Center at the turnoff for Boulder Beach, four miles west of Hoover Dam.

The boating and camping season lasts all year at the lakes. Most people come in summer, and though it's hot, swimmers and water skiers best appreciate the water then. Spring and autumn bring pleasant temperatures both on land and on water. In winter, you wouldn't want to hop in without a wetsuit, though topside temperatures are usually pleasant during the day. Unless you have a valid pass for national parks, entry for five days costs $5/vehicle plus a Lake Use Fee of $10/first vessel and $5/each additional vessel. Annual passes are $20/vehicle for entry, $20/first vessel, and $10/each additional vessel.

Fishing

Both Lake Mohave and Lake Mead offer excellent fishing year-round, for trout, largemouth and striped bass, channel catfish, crappie, and bluegill. Lake Mohave's upper reaches are especially good for rainbow trout. Both lakes offer hot fishing for striped bass—some specimens top 50 pounds. Most marinas sell licenses and tackle. Marinas and ranger stations can advise you on the fishing regulations and the best spots to fish. Shore anglers need a license only from the state they're in. If you fish from a boat, you'll need a license from one state and a special-use stamp from the other.

LAKE MOHAVE

Heading upstream from Bullhead City, you first arrive at Lake Mohave. Squeezed between hills and canyon walls, the lake is like a calmer version of the Colorado River. Though 67 miles long, Mohave spans but four miles at its widest point. **Davis Dam,** completed in 1953, holds back the waters; visitors can park at an overlook on the dam.

Katherine Landing

Also known as Katy's Gulch to some folks, Katherine Landing lies six miles north of Bullhead City. A **ranger station/information center** near the entrance is open daily 8 A.M.–4

P.M. all year; 928/754-3272. Katherine Landing offers a public swimming beach, boat ramp, and campground ($10). **Lake Mohave Resort,** 928/754-3245, 800/752-9669, provides a motel ($80–90 d, $100–110 d with kitchenette; less in winter), house rental ($200), RV park ($18), restaurant (daily for breakfast, lunch, and dinner), marina with boat rentals (fishing boats, ski boats, patio boats, and houseboats), and store; www.sevencrown.com. Showers, laundry, fish-cleaning station, and dump station are also available. The ranger station provides information on hikes and back-road drives in the area.

For an easy walk with some history, you can hike to **Katherine Mine,** about one mile roundtrip. Drive out of Katherine Landing and turn left 0.7 mile on the road just past the ranger station and campground, park on the right opposite the turnoff for Telephone Cove, then walk up the wash. You'll see the white tailings all along the way and, where the wash opens up, the foundations and tanks of the mill on your right. The mine produced less than two million dollars of gold and silver between 1900 and 1940, but the mill, built in 1925, continued to process ore from area mines until shut down by the War Production Board in 1943.

Cottonwood Cove

This developed area lies about halfway upstream on the main body of water on the Nevada side. If driving, turn off US 95 at Searchlight and go east 14 miles on NV 164. Cottonwood Cove has a motel ($90–95 d, less in winter), RV park ($17–20), campground ($10), restaurant (daily for breakfast, lunch, and dinner), marina (fishing, ski, personal watercraft, patio, and houseboat rentals), a boat ramp, and a public swimming beach. Call **Cottonwood Cove Marina** at 702/297-1464, 800/255-5561 (houseboat rentals); www.foreverresorts.com.

Eldorado Canyon

Northward, the lake narrows at Eldorado Canyon, becoming more riverlike. Trout and trout anglers frequent the cold river currents upstream. A paved road (NV 165) approaches Eldorado Canyon from the Nevada side; no facilities.

Willow Beach Harbor

About a dozen river miles before Hoover Dam you'll reach Willow Beach Harbor on the Arizona shore—only a four-mile paved detour from US 93. Facilities include a store, dock dock, fuel dock, boat ramp, and rentals of ski boats, fishing boats, and patio boats. The "Wall of Fame" in the store features photos of anglers and their trophy trout catches; 928/767-4747; www.foreverresorts.com. No overnight accommodations or camping are available in the area. A ranger station at Willow Beach is open irregularly as staff are often in the field; 928/767-4000.

Willow Beach National Fish Hatchery, a half mile upstream by road, 928/767-3456, raises large numbers of rainbow trout for stocking the Colorado and Lake Mohave. Hatchery staff also study and propagate the endangered razorback sucker, bonytail chub, humpback chub, and Colorado pikeminnow, all of which are native to the Colorado River. You're welcome to visit the raceways outside daily 7 A.M.–5 P.M.

Black Canyon River Running

A popular float trip for canoes, kayaks, and rafts begins below Hoover Dam, following the swift Colorado beneath the sheer 1,500-foot cliffs of Black Canyon to Willow Beach (12 miles) or Eldorado Canyon (25 miles). A sauna cave and hot springs make enjoyable stops.

Boats can also continue across Lake Mohave to Cottonwood Cove (50 miles) or Katherine Landing (72 miles); this section below Eldorado Canyon isn't recommended for nonmotorized boats from April through October because of the prevailing southerly winds. Obtain permission to launch your boat below Hoover Dam from the Bureau of Reclamation (write Attn.: Canoe Launch Permits), P.O. Box 60400, Boulder City, NV 89006; 702/293-8204; www.hooverdam.usbr.gov. Call daily 8 A.M.–4 P.M. Nevada time. The launch charge is $5 per person. You must follow regulations carefully; you can write for equipment requirements, trip description, maps, and a list of

The visitor center has a great view of Hoover Dam and Black Canyon.

© ANDREW PERNICK/BUREAU OF RECLAMATION

boat rental companies. Reservations can be made as much as six months in advance and as little as the day before.

Black Canyon Raft Tours runs this trip daily Feb. 1–Nov. 30 to Willow Beach for $65 adults and $40 children 5–12. Price includes three hours on the river, lunch, and transportation from the tour office at 1297 Nevada Hwy. (Hwy. 93) in Boulder City; 702/293-3776, 800/696-7238; www.rafts.com. Pickup from Las Vegas hotels can be arranged at extra cost. The rafts are wheelchair accessible.

Arizona Hot Springs Hike

This six-mile-roundtrip hike follows a canyon through layers of volcanic rock to hot springs near the Colorado River, downstream from Hoover Dam. The highly mineralized spring water surfaces in a side canyon at temperatures ranging from 113° to 142° F.

Allow five hours for the hike down and back, plus more time to soak in the hot springs. You'll descend 800 feet to the river. Rangers warn that the water may contain dangerous amoebas; avoid trouble by keeping your head out of the water. Hiking isn't recommended in summer, when

temperatures can reach hazardous levels. As for any desert hike of this length, bring plenty of water and wear a sun hat. Also, be alert for rattlesnakes and flash floods; don't hike if thunderstorms threaten. Check trail conditions with a ranger before departing—the route may be difficult to follow in spots.

From Hoover Dam, drive 4.2 miles southeast on US 93 to a dirt parking area on the right, at the head of White Rock Canyon. Follow the canyon on foot down to the Colorado River, then walk a quarter mile downstream along the river to the side canyon with the hot springs. Climb a 20-foot ladder to reach the best springs.

HOOVER DAM

When completed in 1935, this immense concrete structure ranked as one of the world's greatest engineering feats. It remains impressive today, especially when you contemplate the mind-boggling statistics: the dam contains 3.25 million cubic yards of concrete, rises 726 feet above bedrock, and produces more than four billion kilowatt-hours of energy per year.

With all these numbers coming at you, it's

easy to miss the beauty of the dam. Look for the graceful curves, the sculptures of the Winged Figures of the Republic, the art deco embellishments, and the terrazzo floor designs. There's a lot to see outside on the dam, in the impressive visitor center, and on tours of the dam.

Visitor Center

The large visitor center on the Nevada side of the dam, 702/294-3523, offers historic exhibits, a viewing platform, multimedia presentation, and dam tours. It's open daily 8:30 A.M.–6 P.M. except Thanksgiving and Christmas; admission is free with tours, otherwise $4 ages seven and up. The easiest parking lies across the road from the visitor center and up the hill a bit. This parking structure—for cars only—will be appreciated in hot weather and for its convenient location; it costs $5. Several lots across on the Arizona side have free parking; RVs and vehicles with trailers can park at the lots designated for oversize vehicles.

Take the escalator or elevator from the parking structure down to the ticket office, theater, and exhibit hall on the lower level. Tours start here. A multimedia program in the theater illustrates construction of the dam; last show is at 5 P.M. Head up one floor to visit the main exhibit gallery and learn about the people who built the dam and how they did it. You can listen to recorded narrations of their experiences. Exhibits also illustrate the plants, wildlife, and other aspects of the region. Continue upstairs to the third level for a viewing platform overlooking the dam and Black Canyon.

The website www.usbr.gov/lc/hooverdam has tour information, a virtual tour of the dam, and details on the operations here.

Tours

"Traditional" guided tours (wheelchair accessible) run about 35 minutes and leave frequently, with the last one at 5:45 p.m. In a half-mile walk they visit the Nevada Power Wing with its eight turbine generators, head outside to the tailraces for a view of the face of the dam from below, then enter a former diversion tunnel that now contains a 30-

foot-diameter penstock pipe. The cost is $10 adults, $8 seniors 62 and up, and $3 children 7–16; no reservations needed. The Hard Hat Tours take visitors on a far more extensive exploration of the dam's innards, making 8–10 stops compared with just three on the regular tours; you're issued a hard hat (which you keep) for the 60-minute walk that covers 1–11/2 miles. These tours are offered between 9:30 a.m. and 4:30 p.m. and cost $25; no wheelchairs or guide dogs. A shorter Hard Hat Tour may be available too. Reservations are recommended for Hard Hat Tours.

Practicalities

The High Scaler Café in the parking structure and Hoover Dam Snacketeria overlooking the reservoir offer fast food and gift shops. Another snackbar/gift shop is on the Arizona side. **Boat tours,** 702/293-6180, leave from a dock beside the dam on the Nevada side for hour-long cruises to Kingman Wash, $14 adult, less for children 2–11.

Boulder City, Nevada

Originally built for construction workers of Hoover Dam in the 1930s, the town has an attractive downtown and a good selection of motels and restaurants. It's about eight miles from Hoover Dam; take the business route turnoff, then continue to the museum and services downtown.

Boulder City/Hoover Dam Museum, 1305 Arizona St. (just east off the business route), 702/294-1988, is in the restored 1933 Boulder Dam Hotel. Exhibits tell the story of the dam's construction, Boulder City, and how early residents and workers lived. You'll also find interactive exhibits, a documentary video, and a gift shop. The museum is open Mon.–Sat. 10 A.M.–5 P.M. and Sunday noon–5 P.M.; admission is $2 adult, $1 children, students, and seniors.

The **Boulder Dam Hotel,** 702/293-3510, also has restored rooms ($109 d w/breakfast), the Boulder Dam Hotel Café (American food daily for breakfast, lunch, and dinner), an art gallery, and other shops. The Boulder City Chamber of Commerce,

WINGED FIGURES OF THE REPUBLIC

A statue stands guard on each side of the flag at Hoover Dam. Norwegian-born Oskar J.W. Hansen gave them eagle wings to represent America's construction skills, daring, and readiness to defend its institutions. He explained that the figures express "the immutable calm of intellectual resolution, and the enormous power of trained physical strength, equally enthroned in placid triumph of scientific accomplishment."

Hansen also likened the feat of building the dam to construction of the great pyramids of Egypt. The two figures rest on black igneous rock and rise 30 feet; more than four tons of bronze went into their $5/8$-inch-thick shells. The terrazzo floor surrounding the base contains an inlaid star chart that future civilizations can use to determine the date that President Franklin D. Roosevelt dedicated the dam—September 30, 1935.

© BILL WEIR

one of the two guardians of Hoover Dam

702/293-2034, is in the hotel too; its hours run Mon.–Fri. 9 A.M.–5 P.M.; or online at www.bouldercity.com.

LAKE MEAD

Lake Mead, held back by Hoover Dam, is the largest artificial lake in the United States. The reservoir holds the equivalent of two years' flow of the Colorado River. Its shape is a rough "Y"; one arm of Lake Mead reaches north up the Virgin River, while the longer east arm stretches up the Colorado River into the Grand Canyon. Boaters enjoy lots of room on the 110-mile-long lake. Countless little beaches and coves provide hideaways for camping and swimming. Largemouth black bass, striped bass, trout, channel catfish, bluegill, and crappie swim in the waters.

Alan Bible Visitor Center

Four miles west of Hoover Dam on US 93, near the NV 166 turnoff for Boulder Beach, the Alan Bible Visitor Center, 601 Nevada Hwy. (Boulder City, NV 89005), 702/293-8990, offers National Park Service exhibits introducing Lake Mead National Recreation Area's fishing, boating, wildlife-watching, and desert recreation opportunities; www.nps.gov/lame.

Inside, exhibits illustrate the region's geology, wildlife, plants, and cultural history. A video pro-

gram is shown on request. Staff provide handouts and information on backcountry camping, roads, and trails. You can ask for the interpretive program schedule. A botanical garden surrounding the visitor center displays and identifies plant communities found throughout the recreation area. Books on lake history, geology, plants, and wildlife are for sale, as are nautical charts and topo maps. The visitor center is open daily 8:30 A.M.–4:30 P.M. (except Thanksgiving, Christmas, and New Year's Day).

Historic Railway Trail

A section of railway bed used during construction of Hoover Dam has become a trail with excellent views of Lake Mead. The trailhead and parking are just down the hill from the Alan Bible Visitor Center. You can follow the path 2.7 miles one-way through five tunnels—cool in summer—toward Hoover Dam; eventually the trail will continue down to the dam. The tunnels had been cut oversize to accommodate the huge penstock pipes and other equipment. In the opposite direction from the trailhead, you can hike 3.6 miles to Boulder City via the old railroad grade.

Boulder Basin

Upstream of Hoover Dam, the lake opens into

the broad Boulder Basin. You'll find campgrounds and marinas at Boulder Beach, Las Vegas Bay, and Callville Bay. **Boulder Beach,** two miles by car along Lakeshore Scenic Drive (NV 166) from Alan Bible Visitor Center, offers good swimming with picnic sites. On the way you'll pass a boat ramp at Hemenway Harbor. **Boulder Beach Campground** ($10) lies on the south side of the beach. RVers can stay just south of Boulder Beach Campground in **Lakeshore Trailer Village,** 268 Lakeshore Scenic Dr., 702/293-2540; $18 with hookups and showers, no tent camping.

Lake Mead Lodge, 322 Lakeshore Scenic Dr., 702/293-2074, 800/752-9669, lies on the north side of Boulder Beach and features lake views; $70–80 d, less in midwinter; www.sevencrown.com.

Lake Mead Resort Marina, half a mile farther north, 702/293-3484, 800/752-9669, has a restaurant (daily for breakfast, lunch, and dinner), store, and boat rentals (fishing, ski, patio, and personal watercraft).

A triple-decked sternwheeler, the **_Desert Princess,_** 702/293-6180, leaves from a dock about half a mile past the marina for a scenic 90-minute trip on the lake to Hoover Dam. The excursions run three or four times a day; $19 for a sightseeing cruise, $28.50 for a breakfast cruise, $39.50 for a dinner cruise, and $51 for a dinner/dance cruise. Children 2–11 travel at reduced rates except on the dinner/dance cruise; www.lakemeadcruises.com.

You're welcome to drop in at the **Lake Mead Fish Hatchery,** 702/486-6738, just off Lakeshore Scenic Drive between Boulder Beach and Las Vegas Bay, to see the trout and exhibits. The Nevada Division of Wildlife raises trout here and sends most of them to Lake Mohave; others go to Lake Mead and scattered locations around southern Nevada. The hatchery is open daily 8 A.M.–4 P.M.

About 10 miles from Alan Bible Visitor Center on Lakeshore Scenic Drive, **Las Vegas Bay** has a campground ($10), restaurant (open daily for breakfast, lunch, and dinner), store, and marina (fishing-, ski-, and patio-boat rentals); 702/565-9111. To the east off Northshore Scenic

Drive, **Callville Bay Resort & Marina** provides an RV park (about $17 with hookups and tax), snack bar, and a marina with boat rentals (ski, patio, personal watercraft, and houseboats); 702/565-8958, 800/255-5561 (houseboat reservations); www.foreverresorts.com. Two campgrounds in the area cost $10; pay showers are available at the resort.

Kingman Wash

This undeveloped cove lies on the Arizona shore, east across the lake from Boulder Beach. Lava-capped cliffs of white and orange volcanic rock overlook the scenic spot. People come to fish from the shore or launch boats from a primitive ramp. Kingman and other washes provide hikers easy access into the colorful hills. From Hoover Dam, head 2.5 miles into Arizona on US 93 (about midway between Mileposts 2 and 3), then turn left 3.5 miles on a bumpy gravel road; there's no sign on the highway and the turnoff is easy to miss.

Virgin Basin

Traveling upstream by boat from Boulder Basin you pass through six-mile-long Boulder Canyon, also called the Narrows, before emerging into Virgin Basin, the largest and most dramatic part of Lake Mead. Rock formations with names such as Napoleon's Tomb, the Haystacks, and the Temple are scenic landmarks. Many narrow coves snake back into the mountains.

Two resorts lie along the giant Overton Arm, which branches north into the Virgin River. **Echo Bay Resort,** 702/394-4000, 800/752-9669, features a motel ($85–115 d), RV park ($18 with hookups and showers), restaurant (daily for breakfast, lunch, and dinner), and boat rentals (fishing, ski, patio, personal watercraft, and houseboats); www.sevencrown.com. The Echo Bay area also has a campground ($10); campers can use the RV park's showers.

Farther north, **Overton Beach Resort,** 702/394-4040, offers an RV park ($18 with hookups; showers cost extra and are open to the public), snack bar, store, and a marina with boat rentals (fishing, ski, patio, and personal watercraft).

Valley of Fire State Park, about five miles west of Overton Beach, 702/397-2088, is noted for its impressive rock formations of 150-million-year-old red Jurassic sandstone. The park is open year-round, with visitor center exhibits (open daily 8:30 A.M.–4:30 P.M.), two campgrounds ($12 with showers), picnic areas, and hiking trails. Entry fee is $5 per vehicle, $1 for pedestrians and bicyclists.

See Native American artifacts from Pueblo Grande de Nevada in the **Lost City Museum,** 702/397-2193, open daily 8:30 A.M.–4:30 P.M. on a hill at the south edge of Overton, 11 miles north of Overton Beach; $2 ages 18 and over. Built on an actual Virgin Anasazi site, the museum includes a reconstructed pithouse and pueblo, pottery, jewelry, stone tools and other artifacts and historic exhibits. Civilian Conservation Corps workers in the 1930s excavated artifacts from many prehistoric sites, some now lost beneath Lake Mead. This adobe museum was built to house them.

Temple Bar Resort, 928/767-3211, 800/752-9669 (reservations), is Arizona's only development on Lake Mead. It offers fishing cabins ($55 d), a motel ($75–95 d, $90–105 d with kitchenette), an RV park ($18 with hookups), a restaurant (daily for breakfast, lunch, and dinner), and a marina with boat rentals (fishing, ski, patio, and personal watercraft); www.sevencrown.com. There's also a campground ($10) here. From Hoover Dam, go southeast 19 miles on US 93, then turn left 28 miles on paved Temple Bar Road.

Bonelli Landing is a primitive campground/parking area on the Arizona shore farther west; take the dirt road off the route to Temple Bar.

Gregg Basin

Upstream, the lake narrows in Virgin Canyon before opening into Gregg Basin, the uppermost large open-water area of Lake Mead. The basin has no campgrounds or resorts; facilities are limited to a picnic area and paved boat ramp at South Cove on the Arizona side. By car, you reach South Cove by heading south 41 miles on US 93 from Hoover Dam, then turning left 45 miles on paved Pearce Ferry Road. You'll pass through **Dolan Springs** (a small motel, RV parks, restaurants, and stores) and an area with Joshua trees up to 25 feet tall. The tree looks like a strange cactus but belongs to the lily family.

Pearce Ferry, accessible by dirt road off the road to South Cove, offers primitive boat ramps and campsites at the upper end of Lake Mead. Grand Canyon National Park begins just upstream.

Grand Wash Bay extends north into Nevada above Iceberg Canyon; no facilities. You'll need a high-clearance 4WD vehicle and a good map to reach this lonely spot, as much of the road follows sandy washes. Check road conditions and weather forecasts before attempting this route.

West-Central Arizona

LAKE HAVASU CITY

In 1958, upon spotting Lake Havasu from the air, the late Robert McCulloch decided to build a town along its shores. The planned community came to life on the east shore 19 miles south of I-40 and 73 miles north of I-10, both major cross-country routes. Factories provided employment for the town's residents. Still, Lake Havasu City might have become just another ho-hum town if not for a brainstorm by McCulloch and town planner C.V. Wood. They decided to buy London Bridge!

Back in England, the 136-year-old bridge was slowly sinking into the Thames. No longer able to handle busy city traffic, the famous London landmark was put up for sale in 1967. McCulloch snapped it up for $2,460,000, then spent seven million dollars to have the 10,276 granite blocks shipped to Long Beach, California, trucked to Lake Havasu City, and painstakingly reassembled. After three years of construction, the bridge stood in its new home. The Lord Mayor of London graciously came over in October 1971 to preside at the bridge dedication. London Bridge may be one of the stranger sights on the Arizona desert, but it certainly put Lake Havasu City on the map.

More has been added since—an English Village complete with shops, galleries, pub, a double-decker bus, and even bright-red British telephone booths. Nearby London Bridge Resort adds more English atmosphere.

At first, the bridge spanned only dry land. Workers later dug a water channel underneath, cutting off Pittsburgh Point. Now you walk or drive across London Bridge to reach the hotels, campground, RV parks, beaches, marina, and other facilities on the new island, still known as Pittsburgh Point.

As in other Colorado River towns, fun on the water draws many visitors. Lake Havasu, 45 miles long and three miles wide, offers great boating, water-skiing, and sailing. Boat rentals, boat tours, swimming beaches, tennis, and golf courses lie

London Bridge

© BILL WEIR

close at hand. You can stroll along the shoreline at English Village or seek out an adventure to the east in the Mohave Mountains, topped by Crossman Peak (5,100 feet). The present population of Lake Havasu City is more than 42,000.

Lake Havasu State Park— Windsor Beach

This park occupies about two miles of shoreline north of London Bridge. Visitors enjoy the swimming beaches, picnicking, boating, fishing, hiking, and camping. Boaters can use the three launch ramps (one just for personal watercraft).

You can stroll along Mojave Sunset Trail, about 1.5 miles one way, through desert and riparian habitats from near the contact station in the north to Windsor 4 day-use area in the south. Halfway along the trail, a botanical garden (also accessible from the park road) demonstrates native and exotic plant landscaping. The park offers interpretive programs some evenings Oct.–March at the main campground. A fish-cleaning station is provided for anglers. Day use costs $7/vehicle. Campsites run $12/vehicle and accommodate both tents and RVs; facilities include showers and a dump station, but no hookups. Groups can reserve a day-use area, but no other reservations are taken. Windsor Beach is 1.5 miles north of London Bridge off London Bridge Road, or turn west off AZ 95 on Industrial Blvd.; 928/855-2784.

Lake Havasu Museum of History

This new and growing collection introduces the region with a video and offers exhibits on the Chemehuevi tribe, mining and riverboating, Parker Dam, London Bridge, and the development of Lake Havasu City. Displays also illustrate local flora and wildlife. The museum store sells souvenirs. Call for hours, 928/854-4938. It's conveniently located at 320 London Bridge Road next to the Lake Havasu Tourism Bureau on the west frontage road of AZ 95.

Accommodations

You can choose from about two dozen motels and resorts. The tourist office in English Village (beside London Bridge) and the Visitor Bureau on London Bridge Road will help find the best place for you. Rates go up on Friday and Saturday at most locales and still higher during major holidays or events. The categories are based on weekend double occupancy rates.

Under $50: These include: **Lakeview Motel,** 440 London Bridge Rd., 928/855-3605, $40 d ($45 d Fri.–Sat.); **E-Z 8 Motel,** 41 S. Acoma Blvd., 928/855-4023, $35 s, $40 d ($40 s, $45 d Fri.–Sat.); and **Havasu Motel** (all kitchenettes), 2035 W. Acoma Blvd., 928/855-2311, $37 d.

$50–100: Places north of English Village include **Bridgeview Motel,** 101 London Bridge Rd., 928/855-5559, $40 d ($60 d Fri.–Sat.); **Holiday Inn,** 245 London Bridge Rd., 928/855-4071, 800/465-4329, $63–73 d ($83–93 d Fri.–Sat.); **Super 8 Motel,** 305 London Bridge Rd., 928/855-8844, 800/800-8000, $36 s, $46 d ($46 s, $56 d Fri.–Sat.); **Howard Johnson Express Inn & Suites,** 335 London Bridge Rd., 928/453-4656, 800/446-4656, $75–120 d ($85–130 d Fri.–Sat.); **Windsor Inn,** 451 London Bridge Rd., 928/855-4135, 800/245-4135, $39 d ($59 d Fri.–Sat.); and **Havasu Travelodge,** 480 London Bridge Rd.,

928/680-9202, 800/578-7878, $60–90 d ($80–111 d Fri.–Sat.).

In other areas of town, try: **Sandman Inn,** 1700 McCulloch Blvd., 928/855-7841, 800/835-2410, $45 d ($50 d Fri.–Sat.); **Days Inn,** 2190 Birch Sq., 928/855-4157, 800/982-3622, $59 d ($69 d Fri.–Sat.); **Ramada Inn at Lake Havasu,** 271 S. Lake Havasu Ave., 928/855-1111, 800/2RAMADA, $70 d ($90 d Fri.–Sat.); and **Sands Vacation Resort,** 2040 Mesquite Ave., 928/855-1388, 800/521-0360, $69.50 d ($89.50 d Fri.–Sat.).

London Bridge Resort, close to London Bridge and the water at 1477 Queen's Bay Rd., features a nine-hole executive golf course, tennis, swimming pools, boat slips, restaurant, and elegant decor. It's worth stepping inside the lobby to see the world's only replica of the ornate Gold State Coach. The original, built in 1762, has carried all British monarchs since George III to coronation ceremonies at Westminster Abbey. All of the rooms have converted to time-share, but some may be available for rent; to see what's available call 928/855-0888, 800/624-7939, $69–169 d ($89–189 d Fri.–Sat.); www.london bridgeresort.com.

$100–150: Across the bridge on the island, you can choose from **Island Inn,** 1300 McCulloch Blvd., 928/680-0606, 800/243-9955, $60–110 d ($90–120 d Fri.–Sat.); and **Nautical Inn Resort & Conference Center,** 1000 McCulloch Blvd., 928/855-2141, 800/892-2141, $110–250 d ($120–290 d Fri.–Sat.). In the Main Street District, you can stay at **Best Western Lake Place Inn,** 31 Wings Loop and Swanson Ave., 928/855-2146, 800/258-8558, $70 d ($110 d Fri.–Sat.). **Acoma Condominiums,** 89 N. Acoma Blvd., 928/854-8082, 800/851-8082, cost $100–150 d.

Campgrounds

Pleasant camping is available in the two nearby state parks; see **Lake Havasu State Park** above and **Cattail Cove State Park** below. Boaters can choose among hundreds of BLM and state park campgrounds, accessible by water only, on the Arizona coast south of town; they have fees but no drinking water.

A half mile beyond London Bridge on the island, **Crazy Horse Campground,** 1534 Beachcomber Blvd., 928/855-4033, offers tent camping ($24) and RV sites ($24 with hookups) with showers, a dump station, swimming beach, pool, spa, store, boat ramp, and docks; the showers and dump station are also open to the public for a fee. **Islander RV Resort,** 751 Beachcomber Blvd. (just past Nautical Inn), 928/680-2000, provides RV sites ($30–42 with hookups), a swimming beach, pools, a boat ramp, docks, and children's activities. At the far end of the island, **Beachcomber Resort,** 601 Beachcomber Blvd., 928/855-2322, has RV sites ($34 with hookups), a swimming beach, pools, a rec. hall, boat ramp, and docks.

London Bridge RV Park, 3405 London Bridge Rd. (4.5 miles north of English Village), 928/764-3700, is open Oct.–April with a pool, and showers; RV spaces cost $25 with hookups. The nearby **Havasu Falls RV Park,** 3493 N. Hwy. 95, 928/764-0050, 877/843-3255, overlooks Lake Havasu with RV sites ($31 with hookups, less in summer), showers, and a pool.

Havasu Landing Resort, 760/858-4593, 800/307-3610, directly across the lake from Lake Havasu City and connected by a boat shuttle from English Village, offers a casino, restaurant (open daily for lunch and dinner), swimming beach, and campground ($9–10 tents, $18–20 RV with hookups; higher holidays). **Park Moabi,** 760/326-3831 (park office) or 760/326-4777 (marina), on the California side near the I-40 Colorado River bridge, charges a $6 day-use fee and offers spaces for tents ($12) and RVs ($18–20 with hookups) along with showers, a boat ramp, marina with rentals, and store.

Undeveloped BLM lands used for dispersed camping include **Craggy Wash** north of town past the airport on AZ 95 (turn in near Milepost 190 and continue past state trust land) and south of town at **Standard Wash,** which is an off-highway-vehicle area, between Mileposts 172 and 171 on AZ 95.

Food

Bridgewater Café in London Bridge Resort, 928/855-0888, serves American cuisine daily for breakfast, lunch, and dinner. The dinner menu includes steak, prime rib, seafood, and pasta. **City of London Arms Pub,** in English Village, 928/855-8782, features a microbrewery in addition to their continental and traditional British food; open daily for lunch and dinner. For seafood and steak, try **Captain's Table,** in the Nautical Inn at 1000 McCulloch Blvd., 928/855-2141; it's open daily for breakfast, lunch, and dinner.

Shugrue's, in Island Mall, just across London Bridge, 928/453-1400, offers bridge views along with a menu of meat, seafood, and international foods; it's open daily for lunch and dinner. **Barley Brothers Brewery & Grill,** also in Island Mall with a great view of the bridge, 928/505-7837, provides diners with a good selection of sandwiches, pizza, pasta, and grilled meats along with brews. **Makai Café,** on the lower level of Island Mall, 928/505-2233, serves breakfasts and light lunches; closed Monday. Or try **Krystal's Fine Dining,** 460 El Camino Way, 928/453-2999, for dinners of steak, chicken, and seafood. **Max & Ma's,** 90 Swanson Ave., 928/855-2524, has a long and varied menu for breakfast, lunch, and dinner.

For pizza and other Italian dishes, you can try **Papa Leone's Pizza,** at English Village, 928/453-5200; **Nicolino's Italian Restaurant,** 86 S. Smoketree Blvd., 928/855-3484, open for dinner Mon.–Sat.; and more than half a dozen other places.

Dine Chinese at **London Bridge Chinese Restaurant,** 1971 McCulloch Blvd., 928/453-5002; or **Lo's Restaurant,** 357 S. Lake Havasu Ave., 928/855-4800, which also has a sushi bar and some Thai items. For Mexican food try **Chico's Tacos,** 1641 McCulloch Blvd. in Bashas' Plaza, 928/680-7010; or **Taco Hacienda,** 2200 Mesquite Ave., 928/855-8932.

Safeway and **Bashas'** supermarkets lie off McCulloch Blvd. just east of London Bridge and AZ 95.

Entertainment and Events

For movies, drop in at the 10-screen **Movies Havasu,** 180 Swanson Ave.; 928/453-7900.

Sailing or powerboat races are held on many weekends throughout the year. Lake Havasu City honors winter visitors with the **Winterfest**

Jamboree, a day of entertainment in February. **Winterblast Fireworks Display** goes off on Presidents' Day in February at an annual convention of pyrotechnic professionals. Chili and live entertainment mark the **Chili Cookoff,** also on Presidents' Day weekend in February. The **Blue Water Invitational Boat Regatta** takes place in March. Classic motor vehicles roll into town in March for the **Havasu Happening.** The **Havasu Art Guild Juried Spring Show** in April features work of regional artists. **Hava-Salsa Challenge** also spices up April.

Anglers compete for the best catches in the **Lake Havasu Striper Derby** in May or June. **Fireworks** light up the sky on July Fourth.

Personal watercraft racers compete in the **Skat-Trak World Finals** in the second week of October. One of the country's largest gatherings of antique and classic autos converges for a parade and show in **Relics and Rods Run to the Sun** in the third week of October. **London Bridge Square Dance Jamboree** swings under the bridge in October. **London Bridge Days** in the fourth week of October celebrates the dedication of the famous structure with a "Grande Parade," contests, games, live entertainment, and food. Motorcyclists convene in October for the **Bike-toberfest.**

The **Gem and Mineral Show** sparkles in November. Radio-controlled model airplanes take off in the **London Bridge Seaplane Classic,** also in November. The **Festival of Lights** brightens the holiday season from late November to early January with entertainment and more than a million lights. Watercraft promote holiday cheer in a **Boat Parade of Lights** on the first Saturday of December.

Check with the tourism bureau for dates and details or visit www.golakehavasu.com.

Recreation

For swimming and picnicking, cross London Bridge and turn left at the sign to **London Bridge Beach;** free. **Rotary Park Beach,** south of the English Village area, offers beaches, covered picnic tables, and ball fields; you can drive there (west end of Smoketree Blvd.) or take the shoreline footpath from London Bridge. The **Recreation Aquatic Center** at 100 Park Ave. (on Hwy. 95 just southeast of Swanson Ave.), 928/453-2687, features an indoor wave pool, 257-foot water slide, hot tub, children's pool, and adjacent gymnasium. **Lake Havasu State Park—Windsor Beach** offers beaches, picnic areas, hiking, camping, and boat ramps 1.5 miles north of London Bridge on the mainland (see description above).

London Bridge Racquet & Fitness Center has tennis and racquetball courts at 1425 McCulloch Blvd. in Island Fashion Mall, on the right just after crossing the bridge; 928/855-6274. **London Bridge Golf Club,** 2400 Club House Dr. (off S. Acoma Blvd.), 928/855-2719, features two 18-hole courses. **Havasu Island Golf Course,** 1040 McCulloch Blvd. (across London Bridge), 928/855-5585, offers an executive 18-hole course near the Nautical Inn. **Bridgewater Links,** 928/855-4777, has a nine-hole executive course adjacent to London Bridge Resort.

Many places in town rent water sports equipment; ask the tourist office for a list. **Fun Center,** on the water next to English Village, 928/453-4386, offers parasailing and rents pedal boats, mini-boats, and personal watercraft. **Club Nautical Sports Center,** at the Nautical Inn on the island, 928/855-2141, offers rentals of kayaks, paddleboats, pontoon boats, ski boats, and personal watercraft, plus water-ski and parasail rides.

You can rent fishing boats, patio boats, and houseboats from **Sandpoint Marina,** 14 miles south of Lake Havasu City (take the Cattail Cove turnoff), 928/855-0549; and from **Havasu Springs Resort,** 20 miles south of town, 928/667-3361. **Park Moabi,** in California near the I-40 Colorado River bridge, 760/326-4777, also has a boat ramp and marina with rentals.

Anglers discovered Lake Havasu long before any developer. Fishing was good—and still is—for largemouth bass, channel catfish, bluegill, green sunfish, and black crappie. Saltwater striped bass, introduced in the early '60s, have thrived. Weighing up to 60 pounds, this landlocked fish is now the hottest thing in the lake. The stripers feed in spring and summer below Davis Dam, eating threadfin shad and other fish churned up by water flowing from the turbines. During fall and winter, the bass return to the lake and are sought out by thousands of eager anglers. Pick up a local fishing booklet for tips on striper techniques.

Information and Services

The **English Village Information Center** is open daily 9 A.M.–4 P.M. (to 5 P.M. Tues.–Sat. in winter) in English Village; 928/855-5655. An adjacent parking lot just off London Bridge Road has a $3 charge but may let you park free if you're just dropping in for the Information Center. **Lake Havasu Tourism Bureau**, 928/453-3444, 800/242-8278, also has helpful staff and literature several blocks north. It's open Mon.–Fri. 8 A.M.–5 P.M. The address is 314 London Bridge Rd. (Lake Havasu City, AZ 86403), though the entrance is on the AZ 95 west frontage road; www.golakehavasu.com. The commercial website www.coloradoriverinfo.com also has regional information.

The **BLM Lake Havasu Field Office,** 2610 Sweetwater Ave. (Lake Havasu City, AZ 86406), 928/505-1200, is at the south end of town near AZ 95 and S. Acoma Boulevard. It's open Mon.–Fri. 7:45 A.M.–4:30 P.M. and offers recreation information and wildlife exhibits; http://lakehavasu.az.blm.gov.

Arizona State Parks has a regional office on the south side of town in the Lake Havasu Water Safety Center, 1801 Hwy. 95; 928/855-7851; open Mon.–Fri. 8 A.M.–4 P.M.

The **public library,** 1770 McCulloch Blvd., 928/453-0718, is open Mon.–Sat. 9 A.M.–5 P.M. (to 8 P.M. on Tues. and Thurs.). **Hastings Books,** 1755 McCulloch Blvd., 928/680-7272, offers new and used books and periodicals.

The main **post office** is on the corner of 1750 McCulloch and Capri Boulevards; 928/855-2361. **Havasu Regional Medical Center** is at 101 Civic Center Lane; 928/855-8185.

Tours

Several boat tours leave from the shore at English Village. They depart most frequently in the cooler months; in summer only the Dixie Belle runs daily. **Dixie Belle Cruises,** 928/453-6776, will take you out in a paddlewheel replica on a nar-

rated one-hour tour around the island; $13 adults, $7 children 4–12. The same company runs the small Kon Tiki boat to Copper Canyon, located on the California side in the southern part of the lake, on one-hour tours for $12 adult, $7 children 12 and under. The Kon Tiki also heads north to spectacular Topock Gorge on 2.5-hour excursions at $25 adult, $15 children. **Bluewater Jetboat Tours** in English Village, 928/855-7171, 888/855-7171, offers 2.5-hour trips most days upstream into Topock Gorge; $35 adults, $32 senior, $17.50 ages 10–16; pontoon and ski boats can be rented; www.coloradoriverjetboattours.com.

Outback Off-Road Adventures, 928/680-6151, offers 4WD adventures into the Mohave Mountains east of town with a narration about the area's Native Americans, gold mine history, plants, and wildlife; www.outbackadventures.com.

Transportation

K-T Services buses run daily to Las Vegas via Needles, California, and Laughlin and to Phoenix via Parker and Wickenburg; they leave from behind the Shell/Busy "B," four miles north of downtown at 3201 N. Hwy. 95; 928/764-4010. **America West Express** flies to Phoenix; 800/235-9292; www.americawest.com. The airport lies off AZ 95 about five miles north of town.

NORTH OF LAKE HAVASU CITY

Topock Gorge by Canoe or Kayak

This is a perfect one-day outing on the cool waters of the Colorado River above Lake Havasu. The usual put-in point is Park Moabi, California, or Topock, Arizona, where I-40 crosses the river. Swift currents speed canoeists and kayakers down the river without rapids or serious turbulence. Take-out is at Castle Rock on the upper end of Lake Havasu, about seven hours and 17 river miles later. Topock Gorge is part of the Havasu National Wildlife Refuge, where you can spot hundreds of bird species. Look for swallows' nests of mud that cling to the cliffs; herons, ducks, geese, long-billed prospectors, and red-winged blackbirds also visit the canyon. If you're lucky, you may spot a desert bighorn sheep on the steep slopes.

Prehistoric petroglyphs cover Picture Rock, a huge dark mass about halfway between Devil's Elbow and Blankenship Bend. The sandy beaches are ideal for a walk or picnic, but no fires or camping are permitted.

Summer temperatures can get uncomfortable, but a hop in the river will cool you off. Bring a hat and sunscreen to protect yourself from the Arizona sun. Other kinds of boats can make the trip—rafts require more time, and powerboat skippers should watch for sandbars. Topo maps (1:24,000 scale) for the area include Topock, Ariz.-Calif.; and Castle Rock, Calif.-Arizona.

Jerkwater Canoe & Kayak Co., 928/768-7753, 800/421-7803, offers rentals, shuttle service, meals, and bed and breakfast out of Golden Shores, north of I-40 Topock Exit 1. Another office is at Boulder City. Staff can set you up for any section of the Colorado between Hoover Dam and Yuma; www.jerkwater.com. **Bob's Canoe Trips** offers rentals and canoe transport; 928/855-4406. **WACKO**, 928/855-6414, rents canoes and kayaks, provides shuttle services, and offers guided trips; www.azwacko.com. Many other canoe and kayak trips are possible; for example, you can start at Needles for a two-day trip or at Bullhead City for a three- or four-day excursion.

Havasu National Wildlife Refuge

The marshes, open water, and adjacent desert of the refuge support many types of birds and animals. In winter, you'll see large numbers of Canada and snow geese, many species of ducks, and other waterfowl. The refuge includes Topock Marsh, north of I-40, and Topock Gorge, which extends southward from I-40 to just north of Lake Havasu City. Most of the more than 44,371 acres lies in Arizona and includes a designated wilderness area south of I-40.

Boating, fishing, and other water sports are permitted except where signed. No camping is allowed along the shore except at Five Mile Landing. You may camp in Havasu Wilderness with a permit, but you must be more than one mile from the river. For a map, bird list, and regulations, contact the Havasu National

Wildlife Refuge office, 317 Mesquite Ave. (P.O. Box 3009, Needles, CA 92363), 760/326-3853; open Mon.–Fri. 7:30 A.M.–4 P.M. (7 A.M.–3:30 P.M. in winter).

Five Mile Landing, 928/768-2350, has a private campground ($7 dry camping for tent or RV) and marina (fishing-boat rentals, slips, and boat ramp) on the east side of Topock Marsh off AZ 95, five miles north of I-40 Exit 1 and 35 miles south of Bullhead City.

SOUTH OF LAKE HAVASU CITY

Cattail Cove State Park

On Lake Havasu 15 miles south of downtown, Cattail Cove State Park, 928/855-1223, offers a swimming beach, boat ramp, picnicking, camping, and hiking. (The turnoff is between Mileposts 167 and 168 of AZ 95.) Visitors can learn about the area in the cactus garden and at year-round interpretive programs. Anglers can use a fish-cleaning station. Day use runs $7/vehicle. The campground provides water and electric hookups, showers, and a dump station at a cost of $17/vehicle. Sites are all first-come, first-served, and tend to fill Jan.–March and on some summer weekends.

Whytes Trail begins just south of the boat ramp, then winds along the shore to the BLM Whytes Retreat boat camp, 1.5 miles one way. **McKinney Loop Trail** follows an inland route through low desert hills to Whytes Trail and Whytes Retreat, 2.5 miles one way; the trailhead is just a couple of hundred feet inland from Whytes Trailhead.

Lake Havasu Boat Campgrounds

Boaters can choose from many state or BLM water-access campgrounds south of Lake Havasu City. Arizona State Parks maintains those between Cattail Cove and Red Rock Cove to the north with a fee of $10 per site. The BLM offers boat camps south of Cattail Cove and north along the coast between Red Rock Cove and near Lake Havasu City; these cost $2/person. Most boat camps have tables, grills, and outhouses, though none of the sites has drinking water.

Sandpoint Marina & RV Park

Take the Cattail Cove State Park turnoff from AZ 95, then turn right at the sign for this lakeside resort. Amenities include sites for tents or RVs ($27.50 with hookups; shore sites are $35), a store, marina (fishing-boat, patio-boat, and houseboat rentals), café (open daily except Tues. for breakfast and lunch, and Thurs.–Sat. for dinner), and snowbird activities; 928/855-0549; www.lakehavasu.com/sandpoint.

Bill Williams River National Wildlife Refuge

Six thousand acres in the lower 12 miles of Bill Williams River, south of Lake Havasu City, contain the largest surviving cottonwood-willow woodland of the lower Colorado. Birders flock to the refuge and see many species year-round— 328 at last count. Good places for birding include the marsh behind the refuge office and areas two, 3.5, and seven miles up the refuge road. A half-mile-roundtrip interpretive trail leads to the water from the office; there's a trail leaflet. You can also hand launch non-motorized craft behind the office and explore the estuary on a canoe trail that's described in a brochure available at the office. Staff run a program to propagate razorback sucker and bonytail chubs, endangered fish native to the Colorado River. The office, 60911 Hwy. 95 (Parker, AZ 85344), 928/667-4144, is 0.8 mile south of the Bill Williams River across from a pumping station. It's open Mon.–Fri. 8 A.M.–4 P.M. with wildlife exhibits, literature, and an observation deck.

A scenic road provides access into the refuge. The turnoff from AZ 95 is 0.3 mile south of the Bill Williams River bridge and one-half mile north of the visitor center; it's marked only by a sign with a binocular symbol. The first 3.5 miles, usually passable by cars, winds over desert hills with good views of the riparian vegetation below and canyon walls above. Drivers with high-clearance 4WD vehicles (only!) can continue upstream another 3.5 miles across many fords and sections of riverbed, and return the same way or take Mineral Wash Road and Shea Road about 25 miles to Parker or Swansea ghost town. Reservoir re-leases upstream may close the 4WD road in the refuge at times due to flooding.

Havasu Springs Resort

This full-service resort is on Lake Havasu near Parker Dam, 20 miles south of Lake Havasu City, 928/667-3361; www.havasusprings.com. Guests can choose from three motels ($90–105 d summer, $38–42 d winter), apartments ($155–185 summer, $60–75 winter), and an RV park ($26). Amenities include a restaurant (lunch and dinner daily, breakfast on weekends), nine-hole golf course, swimming beaches, a pool, tennis, boat rentals (fishing, pontoon, houseboat), a boat ramp, docks, and a store.

Parker Dam

The world's deepest dam lies about 15 miles upriver from its namesake, the town of Parker. During construction, workers had to dig down 235 feet through the sand and gravel of the riverbed before hitting the bedrock needed to secure the foundation.Only the top third of the dam is visible. Lake Havasu, the reservoir behind the dam, has a storage capacity of 211 billion gallons. Pumps transfer one billion gallons a day into the Colorado River Aqueduct for southern California destinations. You can park at both ends of the dam.

PARKER AND THE PARKER STRIP

From 1871 to 1908, Parker was nothing but a post office on the Colorado River Indian Reservation. When the railroad came through, the town began to expand, becoming a trading center for the reservation and nearby mining operations. Mining later declined, but agriculture and tourism thrived with the construction of two dams upstream.

Headgate Rock Dam, finished in 1941 just upstream from Parker, forms Lake Moovalya, which provides water for the irrigation of reservation farmlands. In 1938 workers completed Parker Dam, which created Lake Havasu, supplying water and electrical power to southern California. Resorts and parks line Lake Moovalya and both shores of the river, drawing visitors year-round. Better known as the Parker Strip, this 11-mile stretch of scenic waterway begins several miles north of Parker and extends north to Parker Dam. Despite summer temperatures that are among the nation's highest, many people enjoy the excellent boating and water-skiing from Easter through Labor Day. In September, the scene calms and the temperature cools. Winter visitors, many retired, enjoy fishing, hunting, hiking, rockhounding, and exploring ghost towns. You can learn more about local history in the **Parker Area Historical Society Museum** downtown at 1214 California Ave., but it's open only short hours a few days a week; ask at the chamber office.

Accommodations in Parker

Rates go up at most places on summer weekends, especially if it's a holiday or if a special event is going on. The motels in town lie on or just off California Avenue, Parker's main street.

Under $50: If crossing the bridge from California, you'll first come to **Motel 6,** 604 California Ave., 928/669-2133, 800/4MOTEL6; $35 s, $40 d ($50 s, $60 d Fri.–Sat.). The nearby **Stardust Motel,** 700 California Ave., 928/669-2278, has a pool; $35 s, $39 d ($45 d, $55 d Fri.–Sat.). **El Rancho Parker Motel,** 709 California Ave., 928/669-2231, also has a pool; $32 s, $35 d. **Budget Inn Motel** is one block off California at 912 Agency Rd., 928/669-2566; $35 s, $45 d ($45 s, $55 d Fri.–Sat.). On the way to Quartzsite, **Kofa Inn,** 1700 California Ave., 928/669-2101, has a pool; $41 d.

$50–100: Best Western Parker Inn, 1012 Geronimo Ave. at Riverside Dr., 928/669-6060, 888/889-6808, offers high standards and a pool two blocks off California on the way to the Parker Strip; $59 s, $64 d ($64–100 s, $74–100 d Fri.–Sat.).

The huge **Bluewater Resort Hotel & Casino** features luxury accommodations, restaurants, indoor pools and falls, exercise center, mini golf, movie theater, arcade games, boat slips, and a casino. The complex overlooks the Colorado River 1.4 miles north of downtown Parker at 11300 Resort Dr., 928/669-7000, 888/243-3360; www.bluewaterfun.com. You can reach the casino at 928/669-7777, 800/747-8777.

Rooms cost $39 d ($114 d Fri.–Sat.) and suites run $199 d ($249 d Fri.–Sat.).

Campgrounds in Parker

Lazy D Mobile Park, 1800 15th St., 928/669-8797, offers RV sites ($16 with hookups) and showers at the southwest corner of town. **Wheeler In Family Resort,** 760/665-8487, is on the California shore—follow the highway across the Colorado River bridge, then turn left. Tent or RV sites with hookups cost $18–27.50 depending on the site; guests can use the showers, boat ramp, dock, putting green, and store.

Accommodations on the Parker Strip

Both the Arizona and California shores have resorts, RV parks, campgrounds, day-use areas, restaurants, and marinas. You'll also enjoy good views of the river and rugged mountains. Parker Dam Road in California and AZ 95/Business 95 make a 32-mile loop using the bridge at Parker and the road atop Parker Dam to connect the ends. For the Arizona side, head north 4.4 miles on AZ 95 from downtown Parker, then turn in on Riverside Drive, signed as "Business AZ 95." If coming from the north, turn in on the business route near Buckskin Mountain State Park, a few miles south of Parker Dam.

$50–100: Arizona Shores Resort Motel, 5.5 miles north of Parker at 9388 Riverside Dr., 928/667-2685, has all kitchenettes and a water-skiing school; $115 d in summer, $65 d in winter. **J.T.'s on the Keys Motel** is a small place at 8982 Riverside Dr. 928/667-4336, $83 d ($99 d Fri.–Sat.) in summer, $45–70 d in winter.

Branson's Resort, 7.5 miles north of Parker at 7804 Riverside Dr., 928/667-3346, offers rooms with kitchenettes for $79 d ($91 d Fri.–Sat.) in summer, $50 d in winter; house trailers run $91–250 depending on size and day. Facilities include a boat ramp, docks, and store. **Castle Rock Shores,** off AZ 95, 12 miles north of town between the two state parks, 928/667-2344, 800/701-1277, rents park models (manufactured houses) for $70–110 in summer depending on size and day; in winter, the units are rented by the month; there's a little golf course and a marina.

About two miles south of Parker Dam at Holiday Harbor, **Harbour Inn,** 4749 Riverside Dr. (AZ 95), 928/667-2931, offers motel rooms in summer at $55 d ($75 d Fri.–Sat.) or $49 d ($55 d Fri.–Sat.) the rest of the year.

Camping on the Parker Strip

Branson's Resort, 7.5 miles north of Parker at 7804 Riverside Dr., 928/667-3346, offers RV sites ($21–32 with hookups depending on location), a boat ramp, docks, and store.

La Paz County Park, 7350 Riverside Dr., 928/667-2069, covers a long section of riverbank about eight miles north of Parker. The park offers picnicking, tent and RV camping, showers, tennis, a swimming beach, a boat ramp, and a dump station. Fees run $2 per person (12 years and over) for day use, $10/vehicle dry camping, $12/vehicle near the river, and $15 for an RV site with hookups. The 18-hole **Emerald Canyon Golf Course** lies across the street; 928/667-3366.

Roadrunner, 7000 Riverside Dr., 928/667-4252, features the largest floating restaurant/bar on the river and a small RV park ($25 tent or RV with hookups). The restaurant is open daily for breakfast (except winter weekdays), lunch, and dinner; there's a game room too.

Red Rock Resort, 6400 Riverside Dr., 928/667-3116, has sites for tents ($25 summer, $15 winter) and RVs with hookups ($35 summer, $20 winter). Facilities include showers, a boat ramp, beach, and game room.

Fox's Pierpoint Landing, 6350 Riverside Dr., 928/667-3444, has the oldest floating restaurant/bar on the river; the restaurant is open Fri.–Sunday. RV sites cost $30 with hookups; guests have showers and a rec. room; no tents.

Buckskin Mountain State Park, 11 miles north of Parker off AZ 95, 928/667-3231, sits on a bend in the river backed by low cliffs. Trees provide welcome shade in summer. Visitors enjoy use of the picnic area, swimming beach, boat ramp, playground, volleyball court, basketball court, horseshoe pit, and hiking trails. Day use costs $6/vehicle. Campsites go for $17/vehicle with showers and water and electric hookups. Some sites also have sewer hookups, and a dump

station is available. Cabana sites by the river have a covered table and electricity; $20. All camping is first come, first served; try to arrive early on summer weekends. You can join interpretive programs and hikes Jan.–April, then in summer, full-moon hikes. An interpretive garden near the ranger station identifies plants of the desert; old mining relics lie nearby. A concession, closed in winter, runs a café, store, gas dock, and inner-tube sales/rental; 928/667-3231. The one-third-mile (roundtrip) **Lightning Bolt Trail** climbs to an overlook from near the ranger station. Also start here for the interpretive **Buckskin Trail** that first follows a bridge over the highway, then winds into scenic hills on a one-mile loop; a spur trail halfway leads half a mile farther into the hills to some mines; another trail branches off the mine trail and follows a ridge to an overlook at Interruption Point, adding about a mile roundtrip.

River Island State Park, a part of Buckskin Mountain State Park, is 1.5 miles north on AZ 95, 928/667-3386. It offers picnicking, camping, a swimming beach, boat ramp, volleyball court, horseshoe pit, hiking, a reservable group ramada, and an amphitheater. Interpretive programs run some days Jan.–April. Day use costs $6/vehicle. Campsites with showers are $12/vehicle; some hookup sites are planned. Try to arrive early for summer weekends. **Wedge Hill Trail** climbs to an overlook in about half a mile roundtrip; a trail leaflet tells of wildlife habitats.

Castle Rock Shores, off AZ 95 between the two state parks, 928/667-2344, 800/701-1277, offers tent and RV camping for $15 ($20 Thurs.–Sat.); add $4 for electricity. Facilities include a small golf course and a marina.

Accommodations and Camping on the California Side of the Parker Strip

River Shore Resort, seven miles from Parker, 760/665-2572, has motel units, some with kitchens, for $50–80 d. **Big Bend Resort,** 12 miles from Parker, 760/663-3755 offers motel units ($65 d) and park models ($140–180 d), all with kitchens, plus RV sites ($31 w/hookups), and tent spots ($18.50). **River Lodge Resort,** 14 miles from Parker, 760/663-4934, 800/577-4837, has one-bedroom park models ($80 d;

morning on the Colorado River, Buckskin Mountain State Park

© BILL WEIR

$95 d Fri.–Sat.), RV sites ($15–25 depending on location and day), and tent sites ($12.50); www.riverlodge-resort.com. **Black Meadow Landing** on Lake Havasu above Parker Dam, 25 miles from Parker, 760/663-4901, 800/742-8278, features motel rooms ($54.50 d; $76 d Fri.–Sat.), cabins ($58 d; $87 d Fri.–Sat.), park models ($90 d; $105 d Fri.–Sat.), RV sites ($20–35 w/hookups), and tent sites ($15); the resort also offers a restaurant (Thurs.–Mon. for breakfast, lunch, and dinner), store, and marina; www.blackmeadowlanding.com.

The Bureau of Land Management oversees two campgrounds, several day-use areas, and two off-highway-vehicle areas along the California side of the river. **Empire Landing,** eight miles from Parker, offers a beach, picnicking, and camping (cold showers); day use is $3, camping costs $10 per vehicle. Other BLM recreation sites include **Crossroads** ($4 camping, free day use on the river one mile south of Empire Landing, no water); **Rock House Boating Facility** (boat launch and day-use area just south of Empire Landing); **Bullfrog** (day-use beach and picnic area two miles north of Empire Landing); and **Quail Hollow** (day-use picnic and wildlife interpretive area, four miles north of Empire Landing).

Food

Look for American fare at **Coffee Ern's,** 1720 California Ave., 928/669-8145, open 24 hours; **Grandma's Kitchen,** 1000 Hopi Ave., 928/669-2660, open Fri.–Tues. for breakfast and lunch; and the **Early Bird Café,** 904 California Ave., 928/669-5355, with breakfast and lunch daily.

El Sarape, 1200 California Ave., 928/669-0110, serves Mexican food daily for lunch and dinner. **Señor Manny's** is another south-of-the-border choice at 213 Riverside Dr., 928/669-9237; it may close Sun. or Monday. **Jalapeño's,** 621 Riverside Dr., 928/669-2309, offers Mexican lunches and dinners daily. **Ruperto's Mexican Food,** 800 Riverside Dr., 928/669-8420, is a little café with a drive-through and long hours; open daily for breakfast, lunch, and dinner.

For pizza try **Pizza Hut,** centrally located at 1004 California Ave., 928/669-8888, open daily for lunch (buffet available most days) and dinner; **La Piazza,** 801 11th St. (across the tracks from Dairy Queen), 928/669-2441, open daily for lunch and dinner; or **Toby's Pizza,** 1317 Joshua Ave. in Joshua Street Mall, 928/669-9388, open Mon.–Fri. for lunch and dinner.

Entertainment and Events

Annual events include the **Parker 400 and 200** off-road-vehicle races in January; **International Water Ski Race** in March; **Another Dam Race** by road cyclists in February or March; **La Paz County Fair** in March; and **Enduro Aquasports Weekend** races in late March.

The **River Happening Classic Car Show** occurs on Mother's Day weekend in May. There's a **Great Western Tube Float** in June; **fireworks** on July 4th; **Indian Day Celebration** in late September or early October; **Parker Rodeo and Parade** in mid-October; **Parker Mini-Boat Enduro** in November; **Christmas Lighted Boat Parade** on the Saturday after Thanksgiving; and **All Indian Rodeo** in December.

Recreation

Cool off in Parker's public **swimming pool,** 1317 Ninth St.; 928/669-5678. Play golf at the 18-hole **Emerald Canyon Golf Course,** across the road from La Paz County Park, eight miles north of Parker, 928/667-3366928/667-3366, or at **Havasu Spring's** nine-hole course, 16 miles north of Parker, 928/667-3361.

Marinas along the Parker Strip rent boats. Anglers head for the river below Headgate Rock Dam for largemouth and smallmouth bass, striped bass, catfish, crappie, and bluegill. Boaters and water-skiers discourage some anglers from Lake Moovalya, but the fish are there. You need tribal fishing permits for lower Lake Moovalya and the Colorado River downstream. Tubers enjoy leisurely trips downriver; a popular ride is the seven-mile, three-hour float from Parker to Big River Park on the California side. **River Parasail** winches riders out into the sky from a boat; 928/667-4837.

Information and Services

The **Parker Area Chamber of Commerce** staff will help you find what you're looking for. The office is open Mon.–Fri. 8 A.M.–5 P.M. (also Sat. 10 A.M.–2 P.M. from Oct. to March) at 1217 Cali-

fornia Ave. (Parker, AZ 85344); 928/669-2174; www.coloradoriverinfo.com/parker. The **public library,** corner of 1001 Navajo Ave. and Agency Rd., 928/669-2622, is open Mon.–Fri. 9 A.M.–7 P.M. and Sat. 9 A.M.–2 P.M.

The main **post office** is at the corner of 1500 California Ave. and 15th St.; 928/669-8179. **La Paz Regional Hospital** is on the south side of town at 1200 Mohave Rd.; 928/669-9201.

Transportation

K-T Services buses go once daily north to Las Vegas via Lake Havasu City, Needles, and Laughlin, and southeast to Phoenix via Wickenburg from the Hole in the Wall restaurant, 612 California Ave.; 928/669-9755.

VICINITY OF PARKER

Colorado River Indian Reservation

Established in 1865, this 268,691-acre reservation lies mostly in Arizona. Inhabitants include Mohave, Chemehuevi, Hopi, and Navajo people. Don't expect any picturesque villages—the 6,000-plus inhabitants live in modern houses and work at farms and jobs like everyone else along the Colorado River.

To learn about the tribes and others who've passed this way, visit the **Colorado River Indian Tribes (CRIT) Museum** two miles southwest of Parker. You'll see models of traditional shelters and a large collection of fine baskets and other crafts. Old photos and artifacts illustrate early reservation life and the Japanese relocation camps. A library houses an extensive collection of books, manuscripts, photographs, and tapes relating to various tribes. Beadwork and other Native American crafts are sold in the gift shop. To reach the museum, 928/669-9211, ext. 1335, head southwest from downtown Parker about two miles on Agency Road, or take California Avenue to the south edge of Parker, then turn right 1.8 miles on Mohave Road. Hours are Mon.–Fri. 8 A.M.–noon and 1–5 P.M.; donations welcome.

Poston Memorial Monument marks the area where 17,867 people of Japanese ancestry had to endure confinement in the harsh desert during the hysteria of World War II. Plaques on the monument and a kiosk tell the story of these people who lived in three camps from May 1942 to November 1945. Farmlands have replaced the tar-paper barracks, but an adobe auditorium at Camp I can be seen to the west from the highway; these sites all lie on private land. The memorial stands on the east side of the Parker-Ehrenberg road 13 miles south of the CRIT Museum; look for the broken column just south of Poston.

Quartzsite

Like swallows returning to Capistrano, thousands of snowbirds flock to this tiny desert town every winter. From an estimated 2,000 to 3,000 summer residents, the area population jumps to about one million during the gem and mineral shows from mid-January to mid-February.

Charles Tyson settled here in 1856 and built a fort to fend off Native American attacks. Tyson's Well soon became an important stage stop on the run from Ehrenburg to Prescott. Later it took the name Quartzite, after the rock, but the post office added an "s" for "Quartzsite."

Tyson's Well Stage Station, built in 1866–67, now houses pioneer and mining artifacts, photos, and mineral specimens. An assay office lies out back with more exhibits. The museum is on the south side of the business route one block west of the AZ 95 junction (look for a historical marker sign), 928/927-5229. It's open Wed.–Sun. 10 A.M.–4 P.M. from November to March; admission is by donation.

Hadji Ali rests under a pyramid-shaped marker in the local cemetery; turn north at the sign from the business route in the west part of town. Ali served as one of several camel drivers imported by the U.S. Army from the Middle East with about 80 camels in 1856–57. The army hoped the large, hardy beasts would improve transportation and communication in the Southwest deserts. Although the camels showed promise, the army abandoned the experiment during the Civil War. Most of the camels wandered off into the desert, terrorizing stock and wild animals for many years. While the other camel drivers, homesick for their native lands, sailed home, Hadji Ali, whose name soldiers

changed to "Hi Jolly," stayed in Arizona and took up prospecting.

Quartzsite lies 35 miles south of Parker and 20 miles east of Blythe, California, at the junction of I-10 and US 95/AZ 95. A few motels and restaurants and many RV parks serve passing motorists and the winter community. Most RVers, however, prefer the open freedom of the desert and head for La Posa Long-Term Visitor Area just south of town. La Posa has four sections, with vault toilets and a dump station. During the main Sept. 15–April 15 season, visitors pay a $125 fee for long-term use or $25 for a 14-day permit. Off-season, the fee is $5 per night or you can purchase a $50 recreation pass, good for the entire off-season and some other BLM areas. You can camp free (14-day limit) year-round in undeveloped areas such as Mile Markers 99 and 112 on US 95. The Bureau of Land Management Yuma District office, 928/317-3200, can advise you on these recreation areas.

Most restaurants, a post office, and a motel or two lie on the west side of town along the I-10 business route. You'll find many RV parks scattered around town. The giant Quartzsite gem and mineral shows and swap meets take place from November to mid-February. People buy and sell rocks, minerals, gems, lapidary supplies, crafts, antiques, and other treasures. Smaller swap meets are held from October to March.

The Quartzsite Chamber of Commerce (P.O. Box 85, Quartzsite, AZ 85346), 928/927-5600, provides visitor information in a trailer one block north of the four-way stop at the west end of Business I-10, just off I-10 Exit 17; www.quartzsitechamber.com. In season, October to mid-March, the office is open Mon.–Fri. 9 A.M.–noon and 1–4 P.M.; summer hours run Tues.–Thurs. 10 A.M.–noon and 1–3 P.M.

Alamo Lake State Park

This Alamo, Spanish for "cottonwood," lies far from the one where Davy Crockett and his friends fought it out with the Mexicans. The remote desert lake, at an elevation of 1,200 feet, lies on the Bill Williams River. When Alamo Lake began to fill in the mid-'60s, cottonwood, mesquite, and paloverde trees were flooded, becoming homes for small fish. Hungry largemouth bass and channel catfish fed on the small bluegill, sunfish, and tilapia. Anglers then moved in to hook the bass, crappie, and catfish.

The park offers picnic tables, campgrounds with showers and hookups, a group reservation area, boat ramps, and a dump station; costs per vehicle run $4 day use, $8 undeveloped camping sites (chemical toilets), $10 no hookups, and $17 with hookups; 928/669-2088. January to early May is the busiest season with autumn the next most popular, but the park always has room; groups can reserve a camping area. A store provides groceries, fishing supplies, and rental fishing boats year-round: 928/925-0133. Fishing draws the most visitors. You can also hike or go bird-watching in the surrounding desert, though there are no designated trails; the ranger station has a bird list.

To get here, drive to Wenden on US 60 (60 miles southeast of Parker or 108 miles northwest of Phoenix), then go 35 miles north on a paved road. You'll first come to Cholla Road in the park; turn right for a choice of undeveloped and developed sites, fish-cleaning station, and paved boat ramp; this area offers closest access to the upper lake and is less likely to be crowded. Continue 1.5 miles on the main road to the ranger station; turn right for a day-use area, developed campgrounds, the store, fish-cleaning station, and paved boat ramp. Bill Williams Over-look near the dam provides a great overview of the lake and surrounding desert; continue straight 1.3 miles at the sign near the ranger station.

Swansea

Of the ghost towns near Parker, Swansea is the best preserved, with ruins of a large brick smelter, mine, and more than a dozen buildings. The Clara Consolidated Gold and Copper Mining Co. built the smelter in the early 1900s to process its ore locally instead of sending the stuff to such faraway places as Swansea, Wales. Clara Consolidated closed the smelter in 1912, but other companies continued mining until 1924.

You should use a high-clearance vehicle to navigate the dirt roads to the site. From Bouse, 27 miles southeast of Parker, take the road north across the railroad tracks and go 13 miles to Midway (keep left at a fork three miles from Bouse). Take the left fork at Midway, crossing under power lines after 0.4 mile, and go northwest 5.7 miles to a road junction (Four Corners), then turn right and drive 7.2 miles to Swansea. In this last section you'll cross a pipeline twice, pass through very scenic desert hills, and see a natural arch. From Parker, take Shea Road at the south edge of town and continue east to the Four Corners junction and on to Swansea. Obtain local advice and good maps such as the Swansea 15-minute topo map; BLM and tourist offices may have a brochure on Swansea.

The Southwest Corner

YUMA

Yuma's rich historical background and sunny, subtropical climate make it an attractive destination. In winter, an estimated 80,000 snowbirds more than double the town's normal population of 65,000, filling the many trailer parks in town, along the river, and out on the desert. Boaters and anglers can explore countless lakes and quiet backwaters on the Colorado River. Date palms, citrus trees, and vegetables grow on irrigated farmlands around Yuma. The Mexican border towns of Algodones (8.5 miles southwest) and San Luis (25 miles south) offer colorful shopping.

Yuma's Beginnings

The long recorded history of Yuma begins in 1540, nearly 70 years before the founding of Jamestown, Virginia. Captain Hernando de Alarcón, the first white person to visit the area, led a Spanish naval expedition along the west coast of Mexico and then a short way up the Colorado River. He hoped to meet and resupply Francisco Vásquez de Coronado's expedition to the fabled Seven Cities of Cíbola farther east, but the two groups never met.

While searching for a land route between Mexico and California, later Spanish explorers discovered that the best crossing on the lower Colorado River lay just below the mouth of the Gila River. Soldiers and missionaries built a fort and missions here, across from present-day Yuma, but angry Quechan destroyed the settlements during a violent uprising in 1781, ending Spanish domination of Yuma Crossing.

Although small bands of American mountain men started drifting through in the early 1800s, little attention was paid to the area until the Mexican War. Kit Carson passed this way in 1829 with a group of trappers, returning in 1846 to guide Colonel Stephen Kearny and 100 soldiers endeavoring to secure former Mexican lands between Santa Fe and San Diego. Colonel Philip Cooke followed with the Mormon Battalion and

supply wagons, blazing the first transcontinental road across the Southwest. Crowds of '49ers, seeking gold in the Sierra Nevada of California, pushed westward along Cooke's Road a few years later.

In 1851 the army built Camp Yuma atop a hill on the California side to protect Yuma Crossing from attacks by local tribes. Nearby mining successes, the coming of steamboats, and road improvements encouraged the founding of Colorado City in 1854. Residents changed the name to Arizona City in 1858, then rebuilt on higher ground after a disastrous 1862 flood. They adopted the present name of Yuma in 1873. Yuma Territorial Prison, the town's first major construction project, went up in 1876. Laguna Dam ended the riverboat era in 1909, but it guaranteed water for the fertile desert valleys.

Modern Yuma

Today Yuma is one of Arizona's most important cities and the center of a rich agricultural area. The military has a big presence, too. You'll probably see aircraft speeding overhead from the Marine Corps Air Station on the southeast edge of town. Army combat vehicles, weapon systems, and other gear roar across the desert during tests at Yuma Proving Grounds, 26 miles north.

You can explore downtown Yuma on foot. The Yuma Convention and Visitors Bureau makes a good starting point for a visit to shops and galleries on Main Street. To reach the Century House Museum, follow the row of small shops signed "224 Main Street" west, then cross Madison Avenue. A riverside park lies at the north end of Madison. To visit the Yuma Quartermaster Depot, you could follow the Riverside Trail downstream from either the prison or the riverside park, or walk west on 1st Street (not Avenue) from Madison past Yuma City Hall and turn right on 4th Avenue.

Yuma Territorial Prison State Historic Park

You can explore the old prison here and learn about its colorful history. Photos show the faces

YUMA TERRITORIAL PRISON

In 1875 the Territorial Legislature was set to award $25,000 to Phoenix for construction of a major prison. But Yuma's representatives, Jose Maria Redondo and R.B. Kelly, did some fast talking and won the project for their hometown.

The righteous citizens of the territory were fed up with murders, robberies, and other lawless acts on the frontier, and they wanted bad characters behind bars. The niceties of reform and rehabilitation didn't concern them. Yuma, surrounded by hostile deserts and the treacherous currents of the Colorado and Gila Rivers, seemed the ideal spot for a prison.

All prisoners endured searing 120°F summer temperatures, and recalcitrant inmates faced confinement in a Dark Cell. Prisoners themselves built the stone and adobe walls, as money and labor were scarce.

Most of Yuma's convicts were locked away for acts of robbery. Other crimes of the time that could get people to Yuma included seduction, polygamy, adultery, and obstructing a railroad. No executions took place here, though some prisoners died trying to escape.

Despite its notoriety today, Yuma in the late 19th century had a reputation as a model prison. It provided benefits and services unknown at other "pens" of the age; prisoners enjoyed a library, workshop, school, and hospital. Some critics even called it a "country club."

During the 33 years of prison operation, 29 women and about 3,000 men paced the yard and gazed between iron bars. The prison withstood the toughest outlaws of frontier Arizona's wildest years until it outgrew its site and closed in 1909. The remaining 40 prisoners marched in shackles down Prison Hill to a train waiting to take them to a new cage in Florence. High school students in Yuma attended classes at the prison from 1910 to 1914, and even today the Yuma High School sports teams call themselves the Yuma Criminals.

WESTERN ARIZONA

© BILL WEIR

Though advanced for its time, the prison offered few comforts.

of men and women once imprisoned here and of those who guarded them. Stories tell of inmates, guards, riots, and escape attempts. A model shows how the prison originally looked. Outside, you can wander through the cellblocks, climb the main watchtower, and visit the prison graveyard. Staff offer a video program on request and lead wintertime walking tours. Old West reenactors bring piston-packing action on Sundays from October to April and join the Gathering of the Gunfighters on the second weekend of January.

Picnic tables are available on the grounds and in a small park off Prison Hill Road. A gift shop sells souvenirs. For additional information about the history of the prison, consult the well illus-

trated *Prison Centennial 1876–1976* by Cliff Trafzer and Steve George.

Yuma Territorial Prison, 928/783-4771, is open daily 8 A.M.–5 P.M.; admission is $3 adults, $2 ages 7–13. There's a $1 discount if you visit both state parks in Yuma on the same day. Take Prison Hill Road off Giss Parkway near I-8 Exit 1. You can also walk **Riverside Trail** along the shore of the Colorado between here and Yuma Crossing State Historic Park, 0.9 mile one way.

Yuma Crossing State Historic Park

Exhibits in the historic setting of the Yuma Quartermaster Depot give a sense of the importance that the place had for past travelers. After 1865, when the army designated the site as a depot, it supplied military posts in the Southwest during the Indian wars. Ships carried cargo to Port Isabel, near the mouth of the Colorado River, where dockworkers transferred goods to river steamers for the trip to Yuma. The oldest buildings have been restored to their mid-1870s appearance, when the depot was at its peak. In the years after, the railroad arrived and greatly reduced waterfront business. The supply depot closed in 1883 and the Signal Corps telegraph office shut down in 1891, but the U.S Weather Service operated here until 1949. Except for the stone-block reservoir, all structures have adobe walls, because adobe was the only material that early builders had in abundance.

A 30-minute video in the visitor center illustrates the changes and conflicts brought by Native Americans, Spanish missions, mountain men, the '49ers, and pioneers. A 1909 Model-T Ford rests on a section of plank road once used to cross nearby sand dunes; it represents the last link of the Ocean-to-Ocean Highway to San Diego that passed through here. Old photos and documents also help to tell the story of Yuma Crossing.

You can peer into the restored rooms of the Commanding Officer's Quarters, built in the late 1850s and possibly the oldest Anglo house in Arizona. The telegraph office in the 1872 quartermaster depot looks ready for business. A surviving storehouse holds a "Transportation Through Time" collection of wagons, a Butterfield

YUMA AREA CLIMATE

| | J F M A M J J A S O N D | |
|F°| |C°|
110°		45°
100°		40°
90°		35°
80°		30°
70°		25°
60°		20°
50°		15°
40°		10°
30°	ANNUAL AVERAGE 86.8°F/30.4°C	5°
20°	57.9°F/14.2°C	0°
10°		-5°
		-10°

TEMPERATURE

| | | |
|INCHES| |MILLIMETERS|
4"		100
3"	ANNUAL 3.3"/83mm	75
2"		50
1"		25

——— MAXIMUM TEMPERATURE
——— MINIMUM TEMPERATURE

stagecoach replica, and relics of steamboats and barges. The 1931 Model-A truck comes from a time when dust-bowl victims passed this way hoping for a new life in California. A 1907 Southern Pacific steam locomotive and a passenger car sit outside. On weekends during winter, members of the Yuma Weavers & Spinners demonstrate their skills in the corral house.

The park is at 201 N. 4th Ave., just before the Colorado River bridge, 928/329-0471. It's open daily 10 A.M.–5 P.M. Admission is $3 adults, $2 ages 7–13. Picnic tables lie around the site.

Century House Museum

The influential businessman E.F. Sanguinetti once lived in the Century House, built in the 1870s and today one of Yuma's oldest buildings. Exhibits inside relate the history of Yuma Crossing—the lives of Native Americans, explorers, missionaries, soldiers, miners, riverboat captains, and early settlers. Period rooms and a changing gallery provide additional perspectives. The garden out back harbors flaming bougainvillea and chattering parakeets, colorful parrots, and peacocks.

Century House is downtown at 240 S. Madison Ave., one block west of Main St., 928/782-1841. It's open year-round Tues.–Sat. 10 A.M.–4 P.M.; donations welcome. **Adobe Annex,** next to Century House and open the same hours, offers local crafts and an excellent selection of books on regional history, tribes, and gold mining. The **Garden Café** serves breakfast and lunch from mid-October to the end of May on a patio adjacent to the museum gardens.

Yuma Valley Railway

All aboard for an excursion on a levee of the Colorado River! On weekends from October to May, a 1952 diesel-electric locomotive pulls a 1922 Pullman coach on the 34-mile, 3.5-hour roundtrip. A crewmember will tell you about the farms, canals, Cocopah lands, and birds that you'll see on the way. Tickets cost $13 adults, $12 seniors 55 and older, and $7 ages 4–16. Steak dinners are sometimes offered. The station is behind the city hall at 1st Street and 2nd Avenue; 928/783-3456.

© BILL WEIR

an engineer at the controls of a 1952 Davenport-Beshler locomotive of the Yuma Valley Railroad

Quechan Indian Museum (Fort Yuma)

On the hill just across the Colorado River from Yuma, the museum building dates from 1855 and the days of Camp Yuma. Renamed Fort Yuma in 1861, the site now belongs to the Quechan, who have a museum and tribal offices here. Museum exhibits illustrate the arrival of the Spanish missionary Father Francisco Garcés, the Quechan Revolt, history of Fort Yuma, and Quechan life. Artifacts include clay figurines, flutes, gourd rattles, headdresses, bows and arrows, and war clubs. No photos allowed.

To reach the museum, 760/572-0661, take 4th Avenue or I-8 across the river to Winterhaven, turn right on S24, and follow the signs. It's open daily 8 A.M.–noon and 1–5 P.M. Arizona time. Admission is just $1, free for children under 12. The nearby 1922 St. Thomas

Mission occupies the site of Concepción Mission, where Quechan murdered Father Garcés in 1781.

Accommodations

Yuma, midway between Phoenix and San Diego, is a convenient travelers' stop. Most of the two dozen or so motels in town lie along Business I-8 (old US 80) on 4th Avenue and 32nd Street. Nearly all have pools, which you can appreciate most of the year. Rates tend to peak in late winter/early spring (Jan.–March) and drop in summer. Approximate peak rates are listed below.

Under $50: Choices in this category include **Yuma Inn Motel,** 260 S. 4th Ave., 928/782-4592, $40–60 d; **RegaLodge Motel,** 344 S. 4th Ave., 928/782-4571, $23 s, $27 d; **Travelodge 4th Avenue,** 2050 S. 4th Ave., 928/782-3831, 800/578-7878, $42–82 d; **El Rancho Motel,** 2201 S. 4th Ave., 928/783-4481, $42 d; **Corcovado Motel,** 2607 S. 4th Ave., 928/344-2988, $48 d; and **Royal Motor Inn,** 2941 S. 4th Ave., 928/344-0550, 800/729-0550, $40 d.

$50–100: The 1917 **Hotel Lee,** 390 S. Main St. downtown, 928/783-6336, offers rooms, some with shower and toilet, at $40–55 d. In the future, staff plan to offer bed and breakfast at a higher rate. You can make reservations for high tea on weekends and for historical tours of Yuma and vicinity.

Other options are **Best Western Coronado,** 233 S. 4th Ave., 928/783-4453, 800/528-1234, $72–99 d; **Super 8 Motel,** 1688 S. Riley Ave. (at 16th St.), 928/782-2000, 800/800-8000, $70–75 d; **Comfort Inn,** 1691 S. Riley Ave. (at 16th St.), 928/782-1200, 800/228-5150, $81–86 d; **Motel 6 Yuma Downtown,** 1640 S. Arizona Ave., 928/782-6561, 800/4MOTEL6, $42–46 s, $52 d; **Motel 6 Yuma East,** 1445 E. 16th St. near I-8, 928/782-9521, 800-4MOTEL6, $46 s, $52 d; **Yuma Best Western Innsuites,** 1450 Castle Dome Ave. off I-8 16th St. Exit, 928/783-8341, 800/842-4242, $89 d; **La Fuente Inn,** 1513 E. 16th St., 928/329-1814, 800/841-1814, $88–99 d; **Hacienda Motel,** 2150 S. 4th Ave., 928/782-4316, $46 s, $57 d; **Yuma Cabana,** 2151 S. 4th Ave., 928/783-8311, 800/874-0811, $44 s, $50 d; **Torch Lite Lodge,** 2501 S. 4th Ave., 928/344-1600, $55 d; **Palms Inn,** 2655 S. 4th Ave., 928/344-0082, $55 d; **Interstate 8 Inn,** 2730 S. 4th Ave., 928/726-6110, 800/821-7465, $57 d; **Desert Grove,** 3500 S. 4th Ave., 928/726-1400, $65 d; **Airport Travelodge,** 711 E. 32nd St., 928/726-4721, 800/835-1132, $89–99 d or **Ramada Chilton Inn,** 300 E. 32nd St., 928/344-1050, 800/672-6232, $79–99 d.

$100–150: Choices include **Shilo Inn** 1550 Castle Dome Ave. off I-8 16th St. Exit, 928/782-9511, 800/222-2244, $101; **Radisson Suites,** 2600 S. 4th Ave., 928/726-4830, 800/333-3333, $99–139 d; and **Holiday Inn Express,** 3181 S. 4th Ave., 928/344-1420, 800/HOLIDAY, $99–109 d.

Campgrounds

The 80 or so RV parks in and around Yuma cater mostly to retired people. Only a few parks welcome families with children, and usually only in the slow season (summer and autumn)—parks will take what they can get then! Similarly, very few places will consider renting tent spaces and then only off-season. Ask the Yuma County Chamber of Commerce for the latest listing of RV parks. Some of the best camping—and the places to go for tenting—lie upstream on the Colorado River, see "North of Yuma" below.

Dateland, 65 miles east on I-8 (Exit 67), 928/454-2772, offers RV sites ($16 with hookups), showers, and an American-Mexican café famed for its date milkshakes (open daily for breakfast, lunch, and dinner; you can buy dates, too). Nearby **Oasis RV Park,** 928/454-2229, has a more secluded setting with camping for tents ($14) and RVs ($20 with hookups). Amenities include showers, a pool, and good hiking in the nearby Aztec Hills. To get to the park, continue past Dateland to road's end, turn left two miles, then right at the sign to the entrance.

Food

For American food, try **Brownie's Restaurant,** 1145 S. 4th Ave., 928/783-7911, open daily for breakfast, lunch, and dinner; **Red Lobster,** 1601 S. 4th Ave., 928/782-4000, with a nautical setting for lunch and dinner daily; **Chester's Chuckwagon,** 2256 S. 4th Ave., 928/782-

4152, for breakfast (all day), lunch, and dinner; **Hunter Steakhouse,** 2355 S. 4th Ave., 928/782-3637, lunch and dinner daily; **Home Town Buffet,** 2595 S. 4th Ave., 928/317-1303, daily for breakfast, lunch, and dinner; or **The Crossing,** 2690 S. 4th Ave., 928/726-5551, daily for lunch and dinner.

The varied menu at **Yuma Landing Restaurant,** near downtown at 195 S. 4th Ave., 928/782-7427, includes steak, seafood, and pasta; it's open daily for breakfast, lunch, and dinner. **Julieanna's Patio Café,** 1951 W. 25th St., 928/317-1961, features seafood, prime rib, lamb, and pasta in a garden setting; open Mon.–Fri. for lunch and Mon.–Sat. for dinner. **Chateau Basque,** 4340 E. Hwy. 80, 928/341-9776, offers steak, lamb, pork tenderloin, and seafood flavors from the Basque region of Spain; the food is served family style, nightly except Monday. **Britain's Farms Chuckwagon & Steakhouse,** 4330 Riverside Dr. 928/782-4699, fixes Western-style dinners with entertainment some nights during the cooler months; call for reservations.

Bella Vita serves pizza and Italian cuisine in a little café at 2755 S. 4th Ave.; 928/344-3989. **Domino's** offers pizza daily at its three Yuma locations: 741 S. 4th Ave., 928/782-7561; 710 E. 32nd St., 928/344-0555; and 1701 S. Ave. B, 928/783-3030. Other pizza places, also open daily for lunch and dinner, include **Village Inn Pizza Parlor,** 41 E. 16th St., 928/783-8353; and **Rocky's New York Style Pizzeria,** 2601 S. 4th Ave., 928/344-4260.

Good places for Mexican dining include **Mi Rancho,** with locations at 188 S. 4th Ave., 928/783-2116, and at 2701 S. 4th Ave., 928/344-6903, both open daily for breakfast (some days), lunch, and dinner; **El Charro,** 601 W. Eighth St., 928/783-9790, with lunch and dinner daily; **Chretin's,** 485 S. 15th Ave., 928/782-1291, open Mon.–Sat. for lunch and dinner; and **Latin Quarter Cafe,** 2255 South 4th Ave., 928/343-2977, daily for breakfast, lunch, and dinner.

For Chinese and American, try **Gene's,** 771 S. 4th Ave., 928/783-0080, open daily except Mon. and Sat. for lunch and daily except Mon. for

dinner. You'll also find Chinese cuisine at **Tai San,** 2100 S. 4th Ave., 928/329-1672; and **Mandarin Palace,** 350 E. 32nd St., 928/344-2805; both are open daily for lunch and dinner. **Papa-San Rice Bowl** offers tasty Japanese fast food at 2770 S. 4th Ave., 928/726-1788, daily for lunch and dinner.

You'll find supermarkets and many other restaurants along S. 4th Avenue and E. 32nd Street (Business I-8).

Entertainment

For the latest information on dining, night spots, concerts, plays, art exhibits, sports, and other local events, see *Que Pasa,* a magazine supplement to the Thursday *Yuma Daily Sun,* and the free weekly *The Sun Visitor* (winter only). Or call the **Cultural Council of Yuma,** 928/783-2423, to learn what's happening in theater, ballet, etc.

Take in local color downtown at **Lute's Casino,** 221 S. Main St., 928/782-2192, a popular spot to play dominoes, pinball, and pool. The snack bar serves up burgers and tacos. Unfortunately, Lute's doesn't have a smoke-free area.

Catch movies at **Plaza Theatres,** 1560 S. 4th Ave., 928/782-9292, or at **Mandarin Cinemas,** 3142 S. Arizona Ave., 928/782-7409.

Both local tribes have casinos. The Quechan offer **Paradise Casino,** across the river; 888/777-4946. Cocopah run **Cocopah Casino & Bingo,** south of town at the junction of US 95 and 15th St.; 928/726-8066.

Events

January: Southwest Antique Show, All State Picnic (a big snowbird jamboree), and American Indian & Western Art Show

February: Silver Spur Rodeo and Parade, Yuma Square Dance Festival, and Yuma Crossing Day (pioneer crafts demonstrations, Native American dances, art exhibits, and a big-name band).

March: Air Show at the Marine Corps Air Station, Midnight at the Oasis Festival (classic car show), and Quechan Pow Wow.

April: Yuma County Fair, Yuma Birding and Nature Festival (presentations and tours;

www.yumabirding.org), Mi Vida Custom Car Show, and Spring Fling Block Party downtown.

May: Cinco de Mayo Fiesta on Main Street Plaza.

July: July Fourth Celebration.

September: Hispanic Heritage Fiesta Night.

October: Oktoberfest, Over-the-Line Tournament (bat and ball game), and YRMC Western Dance & Barbecue.

November: Quilt & Antique Show, Colorado River Crossing Balloon Festival, and Día de los Muertos.

December: AKC All Breed Dog Show, Nutcracker Ballet, and Christmas Arts & Crafts Festival.

Recreation

Yuma Conservation Garden, on 32nd St. one block east of Pacific Avenue (just west of the county fairgrounds), 928/317-1935, has a Sonoran Desert interpretive trail, duck pond, and old farm machinery; call for hours as it's open only a few days a week in the cooler months.

In summer, you can cool off in one of the public **swimming pools:** Carver, corner Fifth St. and 13th Ave.; Kennedy, corner 24th St. and Kennedy Lane; or **Marcus,** corner Fifth St. and Fifth Ave.; 928/783-1284 (Yuma Parks and Recreation). Play **tennis** at **Desert Sun Courts,** 35th St. and Ave. A (near the Convention Center); 928/344-3800. For a round of **golf,** try the 18-hole courses at **Arroyo Dunes,** 32nd St. and Ave. A, 928/726-8350; **Desert Hills Municipal,** 1245 Desert Hills Dr., 928/344-4653; and **Mesa del Sol,** 12213 Calle del Cid, 928/342-1283. You'll find shooting and archery ranges at **Adair Park,** 16 miles northeast of Yuma off US 95; 928/726-0022 (Sprague's Sports).

Anglers on the Colorado River and nearby lakes catch largemouth black bass, striped bass, channel catfish, tilapia, bluegill, and crappie. Check fishing regulations with **Arizona Game and Fish,** 928/342-0091; or **Quechan Indian Fish and Game** in California, 760/572-0544. The Visitors Bureau offers fishing information.

Information

The **Yuma Convention & Visitors Bureau** is downtown at the corner of Giss Parkway and Maiden Lane, just off I-8 Exit 1 (377 S. Main St., Yuma, AZ 85364), 928/783-0071, 800/293-0071, www.visityuma.com. In the cooler months of October to April, it's open Sun. 10 A.M.–1 P.M., MON.–FRI. 9 a.m.–6 P.M., and Sat. 9 A.M.–4 P.M.; in summer (May–Sept.) the office closes at 2 P.M. Saturday and is closed all day Sunday.

The Visitors Bureau publishes a very informative visitors guide with descriptions of sights and listings of practicalities. The free weekly paper *The Sun Visitor* tells what going on in town, including snowbird activities. It's published in winter by the *Yuma Daily Sun,* Yuma's main paper.

The **Kofa National Wildlife Refuge** office of the U.S. Fish and Wildlife Service, 356 W. 1st St. (Yuma, AZ 85364), 928/783-7861, has Kofa information downtown near the river; open Mon.–Fri. 8 A.M.–4:30 P.M.

Staff at the **Bureau of Land Management** Yuma District office, 2555 E. Gila Ridge Rd. (Yuma, AZ 85365), 928/317-3200, yuma.az.blm.gov, can advise on camping and other recreation in various areas of the region; open Mon.–Fri. 7:45 A.M.–4:30 P.M.

Arizona Game and Fish, 9140 E. 28th St. (Yuma, AZ 85365), 928/342-0091, offers information, licenses, and watercraft registration; it's open Mon.–Fri. 8 A.M.–5 P.M.; www.azgfd.com.

The large and attractive **Yuma Main Library,** 350 Third Ave., 928/782-1871, is open Mon.–Thurs. 9 A.M.–9 P.M. and Sat. 9 A.M.–5 P.M.; call for the six branch locations and their hours; www.yumalibrary.org. Books of regional interest can be purchased at **Barnes & Noble,** 819 W. 32nd St., 928/317-1466, and across the street at **Hastings,** 501 W. Catalina Dr., 928/344-4614.

Services

The main **post office** is at 2222 S. 4th Ave., 928/783-2124. The **Yuma Regional Medical Center** occupies 2400 S. Ave. A, 928/344-2000. **Schuman Insurance Agency,** 670 E. 32nd St. #11, 928/726-0300, offers auto insurance and information for drives into Mexico, as does **Farm Bureau Insurance,** 1000 W. 16th St.,

928/782-1638. **Big Five Sporting Goods,** 505 W. Catalina Dr., 928/726-2884, sells hiking and camping gear.

Tours

Yuma Desalting Plant, 928/343-8100 (Bureau of Reclamation), offers tours in the world's largest reverse osmosis desalting plant, Mon.–Fri. 7:30 A.M.–4:15 P.M. by appointment only. To get there take Eighth Street west five miles, then turn right at the sign. The plant supplies Mexico with its share of Colorado River water; before the treatment began, the water flowing into Mexico had picked up so much salt that crops died.

Skim across the Colorado River by jetboat with **Yuma River Tours.** The popular five-hour tour in the Imperial Wildlife Refuge takes in the region's beauty and rich mining history; $49 including lunch, half price children 12 and under. Trips go year-round (10-person minimum); shorter and longer trips can also be arranged. Boats leave from Fisher's Landing on Martinez Lake, 32 miles north of Yuma. The office is in the Durashield Building at 1920 Arizona Ave., between 19th and 20th Sts.; 928/783-4400.

The paddlewheel *Colorado King I* will take you out on the river for a narrated three-hour tour. Cruises cost $35 ($25 ages 12 and under) with lunch, $42 ($25 ages 12 and under) with dinner; sightseeing only is $27 adults, $20 age 12 and under. Trips leave October to May from Fisher's Landing on Martinez Lake. The office is in Yuma at 1636 S. 4th Ave.; 928/782-2412.

The **Yuma Convention & Visitors Bureau,** 928/783-0071, organizes tours to local points of interest during the winter; participants provide their own transportation. Bureau staff can also advise on tour operators in the area.

Transportation

Greyhound, 928/783-4403, travels several times a day to Phoenix, Tucson, Los Angeles, San Diego, and other destinations from the bus station at 170 E. 17th Place (off 16th Street behind Staples, three blocks east of 4th Avenue).

Amtrak trains run three times a week in each direction between Los Angeles and points east. The eastbound trains split, with the Sunset Limited continuing to Orlando, Florida, and the Texas Eagle going to Chicago; fares depend upon availability (go off-peak or plan ahead for lower prices). Roundtrips are double one-ways, but you may do best with an "all-aboard" fare, flyride, or other special deal; children and seniors get discounts. The depot is at 281 Gila St.; 800/872-7245 (USA-RAIL); www.amtrak.com.

Yuma International Airport is conveniently located on the south side of town, off 32nd Street. The airport includes a travel agency, restaurant, and car rentals. **America West,** 800/235-9292, www.americawest.com., offers daily service to Phoenix. **United Express,** 800/241-6522, www.ual.com, will take you west to Los Angeles. Both airlines offer many onward connections. Fares vary widely depending on seat availability and competition. **TourWest Travel,** downtown at 333 S. Main St., 928/343-4848, sells both air and Amtrak tickets.

NORTH OF YUMA

Upstream of Yuma, the Colorado River's cool waters support lush greenery along the riverbanks. Backwater lakes, created by silting, provide additional areas to explore. Rugged desert mountains, such as the Trigo Mountains Wilderness, furnish a scenic backdrop. A rich historical legacy recalls the riverboats and mining towns of the late 19th and early 20th centuries. Parks and wildlife refuges help keep the area in its natural state, though dams have raised the water level and greatly changed the ecology.

Mittry Lake Wildlife Area and Betty's Kitchen

This natural area offers fishing, boating, picnicking, primitive camping, and wildlife viewing. Laguna Dam, finished in 1909 and the oldest of nine dams along the Colorado River within Arizona, holds back the waters. From Yuma, head east 5.5 miles on US 95, then turn north 9.3 miles on Ave. 7E (pavement ends one-half mile before the lake). Turn left at the signed fork for Betty's Kitchen, a day-use area ($5/vehicle) with picnic tables, a fishing pier, and an easy half-mile loop interpretive trail that's wheelchair accessible. Take the right fork for additional places to fish, including a barrier-free fishing pier after one mile and a boat ramp just beyond. Primitive camping places also line this side of the lake; no water or fee. A 10-day per year stay limit applies. No jet skis or waterskiing allowed. The BLM can answer questions on the area; 928/317-3200. At 6.3 miles from the fork, the road meets the paved Imperial Dam Road, where you can turn left for Imperial Dam Recreation Area or right to Yuma Proving Grounds and US 95.

Yuma Proving Grounds (YPG)

Driving north on US 95, you can't miss seeing the big guns at the entrance to this facility. The army tests equipment here on the YPG's 1,300 square miles of desert, a greater area than the state of Rhode Island and one of the world's largest military installations. Turn in at the guns (between Mileposts 44 and 45 on US 95) and continue one mile to see an outdoor display of armament on the left. You can also visit the **YPG Heritage Center,** 928/328-3394, a museum on the main post with many photos, tank models, and artifacts from WW II to the present. To get there, continue 4.4 miles west past the outdoor display, turn right into the base proper, and continue one block; the museum is in Building 2 on the left. It's open Mon.–Thurs. 10 A.M.–3 P.M. The Golden Knights parachute team practices landings on Cox Field in front of the Heritage Center Jan.–Feb.; call the base's public-affairs office at 928/328-6533 for times. You can learn about work done here at www.yuma.army.mil.

Imperial Dam Recreation Area

On the California shore of the Colorado River, 20 miles north Yuma, this recreation area offers desert walks, fishing, boating, and camping. Cross the river to Winterhaven, California, then turn north on Imperial County Road S-24 and follow signs. The **Imperial Dam Long-Term Visitor Area** includes the sites of Quail Hill, Kripple Kreek, Skunk Hollow, Beehive Mesa, and Coyote Ridge, serving self-contained vehicles only (the sites lack improvements). A $125 season pass or a $25 14-day pass is required for any stay during the Sept. 15–April 15 season. At other times, camping is $5 per night or you can purchase a 12-month $50 recreation pass; there's a 14-day limit during the off season.

South Mesa Recreation Site, also within the Imperial Dam visitor area, offers water, restrooms, and outside showers; the same seasons and fees apply. **Squaw Lake Campground,** at the end of the road, offers water, restrooms, outside showers, paved parking, and two boat ramps; $5 per night or the $50 recreation pass year-round. An easy two-mile nature trail winds through river vegetation and desert hills from the north end of the parking lot. Contact the Bureau of Land Management Yuma District office for information on these and other recreation areas; 928/317-3200. **Hidden Shores RV Village** is nearby on the Arizona side, close to Imperial Dam; 928/783-1448. Tent or RV dry camping is $18 and with hookups it's $26; showers are coin operated. A restaurant serves breakfast and lunch Thurs.–Mon. and dinner Fri.–Saturday during the cooler months; in summer it opens Fri.–Sat. for breakfast, lunch, and dinner, and Sun. for breakfast and lunch. Other amenities include a store, car and boat gas, fishing supplies, and boat ramps.

Martinez Lake

Martinez Lake is on the Arizona side farther upstream, about 35 miles north of Yuma; go north 24 miles on US 95, then turn left (between Mileposts 46 and 47) and drive 11 miles on Martinez Lake Road. Keep straight near road's end for **Fisher's Landing.** The campground here, 928/539-9495, offers tent sites ($3 per person) and RV sites ($15 with hookups) with coin showers (available to visitors, too). **The Other Place,** 928/782-7049, serves breakfast, lunch, and dinner daily; there's also a saloon. Other services here include a store, post office, boat ramp, and marina (boat gas and fishing supplies). Yuma River Tours boats and the *Colorado King I* dock nearby.

Turn right just before Fisher's Landing for **Martinez Lake Resort,** 928/783-9589, 800/876-7004, which rents rustic cabins ($65 summer, $50 in winter) and trailers ($87.50 summer, $67.50 winter). RV sites cost $22 with hookups. A restaurant and cantina are open daily. The marina rents fishing boats, pontoon boats, canoes, and kayaks, and has boat gas, fishing and picnic supplies, a boat ramp, canoe shuttle service, and a fishing guide service.

Imperial National Wildlife Refuge

Plants and animals of the Colorado River have received protection within this long, narrow refuge since 1941. Birds are quite conspicuous, especially migratory waterfowl in winter. The 30-mile-long refuge includes the river, backwater lakes, ponds, marshland, river-bottom land, and desert. Fishing, boating, and birding are popular activities, though some areas are signed against entry. No camping is permitted in the refuge, but water-skiers can use two sections of it. Fisher's Landing and Martinez Lake Resort offer camping, a motel, restaurants, and marinas just downstream.

The refuge is about 40 miles north of Yuma; head north 24 miles on US 95, turn left 10 miles on Martinez Lake Road (between Mileposts 46 and 47), then right four miles on a gravel road at the sign. The visitor center is on the north side of Martinez Lake, 928/783-3371; open Mon.–Fri. 7:30 A.M.–4 P.M., also Sat.–Sun. 9 A.M.–4 P.M. from Nov. 15 to March 31. The refuge mailing address is P.O. Box 72217, Yuma, AZ 85365. The visitor center has maps and information on the refuge. A nearby observation tower provides a panorama. Meer's Point, half a mile away, has picnic tables and a boat launch.

Four lookout points and a nature trail lie off Red Cloud Mine Road, which turns north one mile before the visitor center. The first lookout point turns off 0.7 mile in; the last turns off 3.6 miles in. (Caution is needed with a car as this road can be rough.) **Painted Desert Nature Trail** makes a one-mile loop up a winding wash, over a ridge, and down another wash with pretty scenery; a trail leaflet is at the trailhead, 2.3 miles in on Red Cloud Mine Road. Spring wildflowers bloom in profusion here after a wet winter.

Picacho State Recreation Area

This recreation area lies on the California side of the river opposite Imperial Wildlife Refuge. The 7,000-acre park has a campground with solar showers ($7), boat campgrounds, two boat ramps, store, and hiking. At its peak in 1904, the gold mining town of Picacho had 2,500 people. You can explore remnants of the Picacho mill and railroad grade, though the townsite lies underwater. From Yuma, cross the river to Winterhaven, California, then turn north on Imperial County Road S-24 and follow signs 25 miles; most of the way is gravel road, normally passable by cars. Contact the recreation area at P.O. Box 848, Winterhaven, CA 92283, 760/393-3052.

Cibola National Wildlife Refuge

Cibola lies along the Colorado River just upstream from Imperial Refuge. In winter, the refuge hosts 16 duck species, three goose species, an occasional swan, and sandhill cranes. Visitors come to see about 700–1,000 sandhill cranes and roughly 20,000 geese, including 80–85 percent of the Canada geese that winter in Arizona. Best viewing runs from mid-November to early February. You can call the refuge for a recording of current bird counts.

The visitor center, 928/857-3253, has an exhibit room and wildlife leaflets; it's open Mon.–Fri. 8 A.M.–4:30 P.M. From the center, Canada Goose Drive makes a four-mile loop that offers great opportunities to see wintering waterfowl.

You're welcome to hike, boat, or fish on the refuge, but camping is prohibited. (Private and BLM camping areas lie along the river near the refuge.) Fishermen catch largemouth bass, flathead catfish, and channel catfish in Cibola Lake (open March 15 to Labor Day) and river channels (open year-round). Power boaters and water-skiers must stay in the river's main channel.

You can easily reach the refuge headquarters on paved roads from the California side; take the I-10 Neighbours Blvd. Exit (two miles west of Blythe, California), proceed south 14 miles on Neighbours Blvd. through irrigated fields to Farmers Bridge over the Colorado River, then continue four miles farther to the headquarters in Arizona. Drivers with high-clearance vehicles can follow a 32.5-mile backcountry route across the desert on East Cibola Road, between AZ 95 at Milepost 82 and the River Road-Baseline Road junction (four-way stop) 1.2 miles north of the visitor center; signs warn of "Primitive Road," but it's normally passable except after storms.

For a map and more information, write to Cibola National Wildlife Refuge, Rt. 2, Box 138, Cibola, AZ 85328.

Kofa National Wildlife Refuge

Desert bighorn sheep, desert mule deer, coyote, bobcat, fox, cottontail, and other creatures live in the dry, rugged Castle Dome and Kofa Mountain Ranges. Gambel's quail scurry into the brush, while falcons and golden eagles soar above. Rare stands of native palm grow in Palm Canyon.

Gold, discovered in 1896, led to development of the King of Arizona Mine, from which the Kofa Mountains took their name. Some mining claims remain today, and they'll be signed against trespassers. Castle Dome, in the range just south of the Kofas, serves as a landmark visible in Yuma. Several roads penetrate the scenic mountains and canyons, but most tend to be rough, suited best to 4WD high-clearance vehicles. Visitors must carry water and all supplies. The refuge covers 665,400 acres, of which 82 percent has official wilderness designation. Hikers can explore this rugged country more extensively.

A short hike up **Palm Canyon** reveals tall California fan palms *(Washingtonia filifera)* tucked into a narrow side canyon, lit by sun only at midday. To reach the trailhead, go north 62 miles on US 95 from Yuma (or south 18 miles from Quartzsite) and turn east 7.2 miles on Palm Canyon Road; the turnoff is between Mileposts 85 and 86. Cars can negotiate this gravel road. At road's end, follow the trail into Palm Canyon for about a half mile and look for towering palms in the cleft on the north side of the main canyon. Take care if climbing up to the palms, as you'll cross sheer cliffs and contend with loose rock.

The trail pretty much ends here, though it's possible to rock-scramble another half mile up the main canyon to a large "palmless" natural amphitheater. Allow one hour from the trailhead up to the viewpoint in the main canyon and back, or three hours to go all the way to the amphitheater and back. Other areas of the Kofas are better for long hikes; ask a refuge employee for suggestions. For information on the Kofa Refuge, visit the Kofa National Wildlife Refuge office in Yuma at 356 W. 1st St. (Yuma, AZ 85364); 928/783-7861.

New Water Mountains Wilderness

These rugged 24,600 acres adjoin the north edge of Kofa National Wildlife Refuge. Black Mesa (3,639 feet) in the northwest rises 1,200 feet above the Ranegras Plain. Rock spires, cliffs, and canyons offer scenic vistas for the adventurous hikers who make it here. Bighorn sheep can sometimes be spotted. Gold Nugget Road, seven miles east of Quartzsite, provides access to the northwest section of the wilderness from I-10 Exit 26. Ramsey Mine Road reaches the north-central part from US 60.

SOUTH AND WEST OF YUMA

Cocopah Indian Museum

The Cocopah number about 800 members on three pieces of reservation in the Yuma area; they also live in towns in the U.S. and villages in Mexico. The museum, 928/627-1992, is in the tribal headquarters, a large building with a tribal emblem, on the west reservation. To get there from Yuma, take US 95 south 13 miles to Somerton, continue one mile past town, turn right one mile on Ave. G, turn left about two miles on 15th Street, turn right after crossing railroad tracks, then make the next right, following signs for "West Cocopah Indian Reservation" and "Tribal Headquarters."

The museum's small collection contains dioramas that portray traditional Cocopah life. Other exhibits illustrate musical instruments, beadwork, games, hunting, pottery, and military service; no photos permitted. The museum is open Mon.–Fri. 9 A.M.–4 P.M.; donations are welcome. A gift shop sells crafts (mostly beadwork) and snacks.

Mexico

Algodones and San Luis shopping attract many visitors, who simply park on the U.S. side and walk across the border. More than a dozen shops lie within a few blocks of the crossings. Many local craftspeople work with leather; you can see them turning out belts, bags, and saddles in some shops. Other crafts come from all over Mexico—including clothing, blankets, pottery, carved onyx chess sets, glassware, and musical instruments.

Algodones (population 20,000) in Baja California, just 8.5 miles away, offers the most convenient shopping to Yuma. Take I-8 6.5 miles west into California, then turn south two miles at the Algodones Road/Andrade Exit. Park in the large lot on the right just before the border. Shops and restaurants lie a short stroll across the border; a tourist office is on the right just after you cross.

Farmers founded San Luis Rio Colorado in 1906. The current population of about 150,000 makes it the largest city along the Arizona-Mexico border. A spacious park with welcome greenery and flowers marks the downtown area. Bus lines run to places such as Tijuana, Mexicali, Ensenada, San Felipe, Santa Rosalía, Hermosillo, Mazatlán, Guadalajara, and Mexico City. White sandy beaches, fishing, and swimming on the Gulf of California draw sun lovers. El Golfo de Santa Clara, a small fishing village 70 miles south, and the larger town of San Felipe 125 miles southwest, are both approached by paved roads.

U.S. citizens may visit Algodones, San Luis, El Golfo, San Felipe, and Mexicali without formalities for as long as 72 hours. You'll need a tourist card for longer stays or more distant destinations; obtain cards at the border or from a Mexican consulate or Mexican tourist office. To obtain a card, show proof of citizenship—passport, birth or naturalization certificate, voting registration card, or notarized affidavit of citizenship. A permit for your vehicle is required unless you're headed for border areas or Baja

California; obtain it at the border by showing proof of ownership. You can buy Mexican insurance in Yuma.

Sand Dunes

Though not typical of the Sonoran Desert, barren sand dunes lie 17 miles west of Yuma. Movie producers have used this "Great American Sahara" for films ranging from *Beau Geste* to *Star Wars*. People at the Yuma Convention & Visitors Bureau can tell you about recent or current filming.

Rest areas on I-8 in the middle of the dunes provide a place to stop and park, but you cannot go out onto the dunes from here. To do so, take the I-8 Gray's Well Exit (just east of the rest areas), then follow the south frontage road west into the dunes. Dune-buggy drivers like to play here; you'll see a parking area for them at the beginning of the frontage road. Continue 3.2 miles to the site of Gray's Well (you've gone too far if the pavement ends) to see a surviving segment of the **plank road** on the left. From 1914 to 1927, motorists crossed the dunes on a seven-mile road made of these moveable planks until engineers figured out how to build a conventional road through the dunes.

The BLM's **Midway Campground** lies along the frontage road and has vault toilets but no water. Campers should stay near the south frontage road; the Mexican border is less than a mile south of I-8 and not safe for overnight visits (only white posts mark the border). To stay at Midway Campground or to use other facilities in the Imperial Sand Dunes, you'll need a permit ($10 for seven days or $30 for the season); contact the BLM's El Centro Field Office for details, 760/337-4400.

WESTERN ARIZONA

South-Central Arizona

Nowhere else in Arizona do you find such a contrast between city and wilderness as in the south-central part of the state. More than half the state's population lives in the urban sprawl surrounding Phoenix. Yet just beyond you'll find craggy mountains, vast woodlands, and seemingly endless desert. People today tend to keep close to the rivers, which provide water to nourish crops and cities. But a different kind of thirst—for gold and silver—once lured many pioneers into the rugged mountains of south-central Arizona. Most of the towns they founded have faded into memory, but a few survive on income from tourism, copper, or other resources.

The Land

The mountains in this region aren't particularly high—most summit elevations range from 3,000 to 8,000 feet. But what they lack in size they make up for in challenging terrain—off-trail travel can be very difficult. The major ranges, all with good hiking and wilderness, lie north and east of Phoenix. These include the Bradshaw, Mazatzal, Sierra Ancha, Superstition, and Pinal Mountains. South and west from Phoenix you'll find a very different sort of country—the often harsh desert most people associate with Arizona. In this region,

Superstition Mountains from Lost Dutchman State Park

small craggy ranges break through plains of rock and sand, springs and streams rarely flow, and only hardy desert plants and wildlife survive.

Climate

Because most of south-central Arizona lies below 4,500 feet, temperatures stay on the warm side. In winter you'll enjoy springlike weather while people in the north are digging out from snowstorms. Spring and autumn also bring fine weather; in the high country, these are good seasons to be outdoors. In summer (May–Sept.), the sun turns the desert into a giant oven; highs commonly top 100°F! Drink plenty of liquids and wear a hat when venturing out into the summer heat.

Annual rainfall varies from about five inches in the lowest desert to more than 20 inches in the highest mountains. Most moisture arrives in two seasons: gentle rains arrive between December and March, and spectacular thunderstorms occur during July and August. The summer storms can kick up huge clouds of dust, cause flash floods, and start lightning-ignited brush fires.

Flora and Fauna

Cacti feel right at home across much of the region. You'll see lots of prickly pear, cholla, barrel cactus, and giant saguaro. Small plants and low trees also thrive. Rainfall prompts spectacular floral displays in early spring and sometimes in summer. Learn more about desert flora at the Desert Botanical Garden in Phoenix and the Boyce Thompson Arboretum near Superior.

Most animals hole up during the day, though lizards seem to enjoy sitting on hot rocks. In the larger mountain ranges you might meet mountain lion, black bear, bighorn sheep, javelina, pronghorn, or deer. Always watch where you put hands and feet in the desert so as not to disturb rattlesnakes, Gila monsters, scorpions, or poisonous spiders.

Prehistoric Tribes

Nomadic groups roamed across the region in seasonal cycles for thousands of years before learning to cultivate the land. Around 200–300 B.C., a tribe we know as the Hohokam settled in the Gila and Salt River Valleys. Industrious agriculturalists, the Hohokam dug more than 300 miles of irrigation canals in the Salt River Valley alone. The larger canals measured more than 15 feet wide and 10 feet deep. Using water from the canals, the Hohokam grew hardy, drought-resistant corn—the staple of their diet— as well as beans and squash. They also hunted game and gathered wild plants.

For most of their history the Hohokam lived in pithouses built of brush and mud over shallow pits. Later, some built square adobe houses. Larger towns had houses by the hundreds and ball courts—large walled fields likely made for games played with rubber balls. The Hohokam made pottery, clay figurines, stone bowls, shell jewelry, paint palettes, and cotton cloth. Much mystery surrounds the origin and demise of the Hohokam; their civilization disappeared around A.D. 1450.

SOUTH-CENTRAL ARIZONA HIGHLIGHTS

- **Phoenix:** This political and economic powerhouse offers many museums, parks, events, and entertainment venues in the heart of the "Valley of the Sun."
- **Tempe:** Home of dynamic Arizona State University, Tempe also boasts an exceptionally attractive downtown.
- **Scottsdale:** Visitors enjoy exceptional cultural activities, resorts, shopping, and atmosphere.
- **Mesa:** Arizona's third-largest city features a rich history—with museums to prove it—and the Mormons' Arizona Temple.
- **The Apache Trail:** This spectacular scenic drive winds along reservoirs of the Salt River between the Valley of the Sun and Theodore Roosevelt Lake.
- **Casa Grande Ruins National Monument:** Arizona's most enigmatic prehistoric building rises four stories high from an earthen platform.
- **Wickenburg:** Cowboys and visitors ride the range among picturesque desert hills near this Old West town.

Getting There and Around

Phoenix Sky Harbor Airport, just east of downtown, has by far the best flight connections in Arizona. You also have a good choice of rental cars and long-distance bus connections from the city. Amtrak trains no longer serve Phoenix, but Amtrak shuttle buses connect the city with the train routes across northern and southern Arizona.

Phoenix

Though you'll rarely see the name on a map, you'll frequently hear people call the greater Phoenix area the "Valley of the Sun," a name that accurately reflects the area's pleasant winters and its average of 300 sunny days per year.

Hub of the sprawling Valley, Phoenix has a larger population, bigger businesses, and greater clout than any other city in Arizona. Here state laws are made and big corporate deals signed. A Western sense of informality and leisure slows the pace a bit, making for a relaxed style quickly picked up by the hordes of newcomers flocking to the city. Phoenix is the sixth-largest city in the country and one of the fastest growing. The city proper holds more than 1.3 million residents, while a similar number inhabit the surrounding area. Many retired people live in the Valley of the Sun, and whole towns are planned just for them.

Cultural and sports activities pack the calendar in the cooler months. The Valley's dozens of museums include not only the usual repertoire—those detailing history, archaeology, religion, science, and art—but a few others focusing on more unusual topics as well. The Heard Museum (Southwest cultures) rates as the best local museum and makes a good choice if you have time to see only one Phoenix museum. Many stadiums, including two large ones downtown, host major- and minor-league sports action, including baseball teams visiting for spring training.

The Landscape

Desert mountains form the skyline of the Valley. Some, like Squaw Peak, poke up in the middle

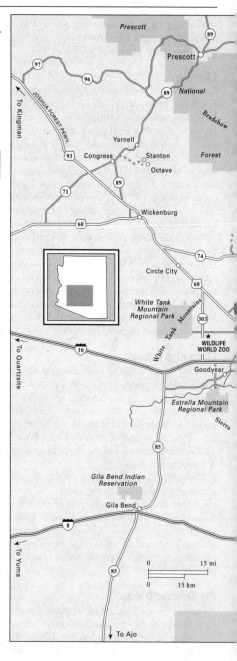

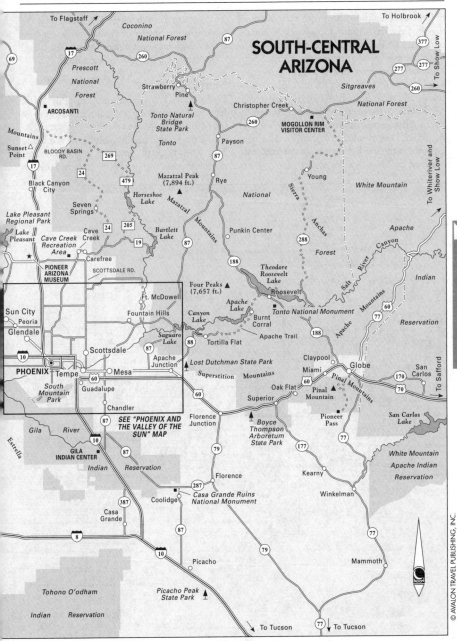

SOUTH-CENTRAL

of Phoenix, rewarding hikers with a panorama of the city from the summit. Camelback Mountain stands as a Phoenix landmark northeast of downtown. South of downtown, the bulky South Mountains comprise the world's largest city park, offering nearly 15,000 acres for hiking, horseback riding, and picnicking. Farther out, you'll see the McDowells to the northeast, the Superstitions to the east, the Sierra Estrellas to the southwest, and the White Tank Mountains to the west. The highest peaks in the area lie northeast in the Mazatzals, crowned by 7,894-foot Mazatzal Peak.

The most famous range of all has to be the Superstitions. Stories of Jacob Waltz's lost gold mine, which may exist somewhere in these jagged mountains, still excite the imagination.

Sunny Skies

Phoenix lies at an elevation of roughly 1,100 feet. You can expect average summer highs to go over 100°F, dropping to the 70s or 80s at night. The Valley comes into its own from October to May, when flocks of snowbirds migrate from the northern states and provinces. Even in midwin-

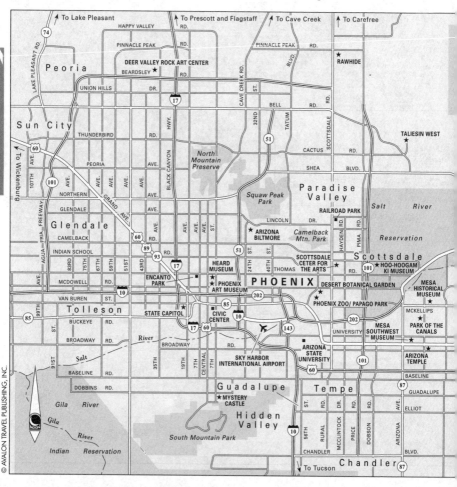

ter, daytime temperatures range in the 60s or low 70s—and you don't have to shovel sunshine! Average rainfall is only 7.45 inches a year.

HISTORY
Why Phoenix?

It's the water. Hohokam tamed the Salt River as early as 300 B.C., channeling its waters through intricate networks of canals to fields of beans, corn, squash, and cotton. The Hohokam may have had the most sophisticated ancient culture

ever developed north of Mexico. They introduced cotton and weaving to the Southwest, and their cities featured ball courts and multistory adobe buildings.

The Hohokam tilled the soil here for at least 1,700 years. At their peak, around A.D. 1100, their settlements contained a population of between 50,000 and 100,000. Then around A.D. 1450 this sophisticated culture came to an end. Pima, likely descendents of the Hohokam, later settled here and described their predecessors as Hohokam—a word meaning "all used up" or "departed." Today you can see Hohokam artifacts and one of their culture's most impressive ruins at Pueblo Grande Museum.

PHOENIX AND THE VALLEY OF THE SUN

Americans Arrive

Spanish and early American explorers overlooked the area. It wasn't until after the Civil War that stories of gold in Prescott and other parts of central Arizona attracted streams of fortune hunters into this wild land. Pinal and Tonto Apache discouraged outsiders, but in September 1865, the army arrived to build Camp McDowell. Ranching and businesses soon followed.

Jack Swilling, a former Confederate soldier-turned-prospector, first took advantage of the Valley's farming potential. In 1867, he formed a company with $400, eight mules, and 16 unemployed miners to dig out the Hohokam canals. By the summer of 1868 he harvested his first crops of wheat and barley. Swilling's success attracted 30 more farmers the following year; soon the beginnings of a town appeared.

Darrel Duppa, one of the early settlers, predicted a new city would rise from the ruins of the Hohokam civilization, just as the mythical phoenix arose from its own ashes. Surveyors laid out Phoenix in 1870, marking off lots selling for $20–140 apiece. Wood was scarce, so early settlers built with adobe. The results looked, according to some accounts, much like an ancient Hohokam village.

Phoenix Comes of Age

With increasing prosperity and a nearby railroad line, residents built ornate Victorian houses, planted trees, put in sidewalks, and opened an

SOUTH-CENTRAL

icehouse. Soon Phoenix resembled a town transplanted from the Midwest.

By 1889 Phoenix had enough energy and political muscle to wrest the state capital from Prescott. Not even 20 years old, Phoenix had established itself as the business, political, and agricultural center of the territory. Roosevelt Dam, dedicated by Theodore Roosevelt in 1911, ensured water for continued growth. With the glamorous West now safe, Easterners flocked to dude ranches where they could dress like cowboys, ride the range, and eat mesquite-grilled steaks.

World War II brought new industry and an increased military presence. Growth has been frantic ever since, helped by the development of air-conditioning, which makes the desert summer bearable. Though major manufacturing and service industries now dominate the Phoenix economy, agriculture remains important. Area farmers raise crops of citrus, cotton, melons, sugar beets, and vegetables.

GETTING AROUND

Downtown Phoenix sits in the heart of the Valley. Here you'll find the State Capitol, Phoenix Civic Plaza, Heritage and Science Park, America West Arena, Bank One Ballpark, and many offices. Streets running east-west in the downtown take the names of U.S. presidents—Van Buren, Monroe, Adams, Washington, Jefferson, and others; Washington Street divides city addresses between north and south. A newer downtown, or "midtown," extends one mile north on Central Avenue. Along this strip you'll find the central library, Art Museum, Little Theatre, Heard Museum, and still more office buildings. The Camelback Corridor in northeast Phoenix between 24th and 44th Streets also holds many corporate offices, along with some of the city's best restaurants and shopping.

Central Avenue neatly divides both downtown and midtown into west and east halves. Parallel roads west of Central are numbered as Avenues, those east as Streets. (Grand Avenue, however, angles northwest from downtown across this grid on its way to Wickenburg.) In finding

Valley addresses, it helps to remember that odd-numbered addresses line the south and east sides of the roads.

A little planning and phone-checking will save a lot of time, as distances can be great and traffic slow. New freeways help a lot, but traffic gets very thick during rush hour. Smoke from industry and the many cars has created a serious air pollution problem, something not historically associated with the blue skies of Arizona.

In addition to the metered street parking downtown, you'll find many indoor and outdoor parking lots. Usually it's easy to find a space, but if a special event is taking place costs will soar and you may have to do some hunting.

Valley Metro, 602/253-5000, will get you around the Valley with an extensive and low-cost bus service. It's best, however, if you're not in much of a hurry. **Downtown Area Shuttle (DASH),** 602/257-0338, loops around the central area. The Downtown Transit Center is on Van Buren St. between First and Central Avenues.

DOWNTOWN PHOENIX

In recent years, downtown has become a "happening place," with new museums, restaurants, entertainment venues, stadiums, and shopping centers. If you haven't been here in a while, you'll notice big changes. The Greater Phoenix Convention & Visitors Bureau provides much helpful information at 50 N. Second St.; it's open Mon.–Fri. 8 A.M.–5 P.M.; 602/254-6500, 877/225-5749; you can park at 15-minute meters in front or in nearby lots.

Arizona Center, at Third and Van Buren Sts., offers an oasis of palms, waterfalls, and pools with dozens of restaurants and specialty shops, a 24-screen movie theater, and some night spots. Two blocks south you'll find the oldest and the newest in Phoenix—Heritage Square, Phoenix Museum of History, and Arizona Science Center. Two blocks farther south and you'll be at the huge Bank One Ballpark with its retractable roof. Turn west two blocks and you'll reach America West Arena, another major sports center. Other attractions in the heart of downtown include Symphony Hall, Herberger Theater, and the Orpheum Theater—a 1929 Spanish Baroque Revival building restored to its original elegance. Look west down Washington St. and you'll see the gleaming copper dome of the old state capitol, where much of Arizona's past history has taken place.

Arizona State Capitol

The old state capitol, with its winged figure of victory and shiny copper dome, rose in 1900, a dozen years before statehood. The Arizona Legislature outgrew this structure in 1960 and moved into adjacent new quarters. The old capitol is now a museum, carefully restored to look as it did when Arizona became a state in 1912. You'll see a lifelike statue of then-governor George W.P. Hunt sitting behind his desk. The Senate and House chambers and other rooms contain period furnishings, historical photos, tales of frontier days, a silver service set from the battleship USS *Arizona,* a scale model of the same ship, and other memorabilia.

The capitol is at 1700 W. Washington St., 602/542-4675. It's open Mon.–Fri. 8 A.M.–5 P.M., except on state holidays; admission is free. Guided tours leave at 10 A.M. and 2 P.M. (groups of 12 or more must schedule tours in advance), or you can take a self-guided tour whenever the building is open. When the legislature is in session, early Jan. to April or early May, exhibits stay open to 8 P.M. on Thurs. and on Sat. they're open 10 A.M.–3 P.M. To dig deeper into the state's past, drop into the research library, Room 300, where you'll see the 1930s' murals *Pageant of Arizona Progress* by Jay Datus. A gift shop on the first floor sells books and souvenirs.

Free parking is available in front (east side) of the capitol at Wesley Bolin Memorial Plaza; turn in from Adams Street. The Plaza features many commemorative markers and an anchor and signal mast from the USS *Arizona.*

For more information, check out the capitol's website at azcapitol.lib.az.us, or, to see what the legislature is up to, www.azleg.state.az.us.

Arizona Mining and Mineral Museum

Many Arizona pioneers came in search of gold, silver, or copper. In this museum you'll see examples of these and many other minerals. Specimens of copper minerals—azurite, malachite, chrysocolla, cuprite, and chalcanthite—sparkle in brilliant hues. A fluorescent light makes otherwise undistinguished-looking minerals glow in bright colors. Lapidary exhibits display the art of gem cutting and polishing, while old mining tools, lamps, assay kits, photos, and models reveal how miners worked. Fossils illustrate the evolution of life from cyanobacteria more than a billion years old, to the dinosaurs, to more recent organisms.

The **Rose Mofford Collection,** an eclectic assemblage of mementoes from Arizona's first woman governor, is in a separate gallery.

The museum staff can tell you of upcoming rock and mineral shows—most are held during the winter—and put you in touch with local rock shops and clubs. A gift shop sells specimens, gold pans, handcrafted jewelry, and an excellent selection of rockhounding books.

Look for the museum's unusual Moorish architecture at 1502 W. Washington St. (at 15th Ave.); 602/255-3791. Hours are Mon.–Fri. 8 A.M.–5 P.M., Saturday 11 A.M.–4 P.M.; closed Sunday and state holidays. Admission is free, and parking is available behind the museum. Visit on the Web at www.admmr.state.az.us.

Arizona Hall of Fame

The classic/eclectic-style building now housing the Arizona Hall of Fame opened as Phoenix's Carnegie Public Library in 1908. Inside, rotating historical exhibits join the permanent Arizona Women's Hall of Fame in honoring individuals who have made outstanding contributions to the state. The hall is at 1101 W. Washington St.; 602/255-2110. Hours are Mon.–Fri. 8 A.M.–5 P.M., except state holidays. Admission is free, and parking is available across the street beside the 1893 Victorian Evans House. For handicap access, park behind the Hall of Fame (enter from Jefferson St.).

Phoenix Police Museum

Exhibits at this small museum relate the challenges and stories of men and women who have served over the years. You'll learn of Phoenix's first marshal, Henry Garfias, and his difficult job of dealing with lawless elements in the 1880s. Police equipment shows the many changes in communications and transportation over the decades. A memorial room honors those who have lost their lives or suffered injuries while answering the call of duty. The museum is downtown at 101 S. Central Ave. (southeast corner of Central Ave. and Jefferson St.); 602/534-7278. It's open Mon., Wed., and Fri. 9 A.M.–3 P.M., except holidays. Admission is free; look for nearby metered parking.

Museo Chicano

Vibrant art of Latin America focusing on Chicano and Mexican culture fills the galleries here. Each exhibit changes several times a year. A gift shop offers colorful art and crafts, including prints, posters, cards, jewelry, books, and videos. The museum is downtown at 147 E. Adams St.; 602/257-5536. It's open Tues.–Sat. 10 A.M.–4 P.M. Admission is $2 adults, $1 students and seniors.

Arizona Center

Shade trees, fountains, and waterfalls provide a pleasant respite from busy city life at this large shopping, dining, and entertainment complex on Van Buren St. between Third and Fifth Sts.; www.arizonacenter.com. A variety of restaurants—many with both indoor and outdoor seating—offer seafood, Mexican, Italian, or Southwestern cuisine. An AMC 24-screen movie theater, 602/956-4262, and several nightspots provide entertainment. Parking is available just to the north in the same block; enter from Fillmore or Fifth Streets. Businesses will validate your parking stub.

St. Mary's Basilica

Catholic residents built an adobe church here in 1881 and finished the present basilica in 1914. The interior contains beautiful art and symbolism in a peaceful setting. The basilica is on E. Monroe St. between Third and Fourth Sts.; 602/252-7651. Open Mon.– Fri. 10 A.M.–2 p.m and during liturgies; free admission. You can purchase a *An Historical Guide to the Sacred Art of St. Mary's Basilica* next door at the church office, on the corner of Third and Monroe Streets.

Heritage and Science Park

Museums and historic buildings in this park downtown at Fifth and Monroe Streets reflect Phoenix's past, present, and future. Some of the houses on Heritage Square are the only ones remaining on the original townsite. You'll find a small museum inside historic houses here and two large museums nearby in the park—Phoenix Museum of History and the Arizona Science Center. For information, contact the individual museum or the office in the Duplex, all listed below. Two garages offer parking—on the northwest corner of the park (enter from Fifth or Monroe Sts.) and south across Washington Street (RVs and tall vehicles must park here); bring your ticket into a museum for validation.

Heritage Square

The Victorian-style, 1895 **Rosson House** stands tall on the north side of Heritage Square. Meticulous restoration has returned the structure—once one of Phoenix's most elegant houses—to its original grand appearance. Today you can tour the house and learn about its construction and former residents. Hours are Sunday noon–3:30 P.M. and Wed.–Sat. 10 A.M.–3:30 P.M. (call ahead to check hours in August). Admission is $4 adults, $3 seniors, $1 children 6–12. Buy tickets at the Burgess Carriage House; 602/262-5070, 602/262-5071. Tours start at the front gate.

The Burgess Carriage House next door was constructed in a colonial Williamsburg style rarely seen this far west. Originally located at Second and Taylor, this was the first of two structures moved to Heritage Square. A second Carriage House (ca. 1900) at the site is now an education center. The Lath Pavilion dates from 1980 but is typical of early Phoenix architecture.

The other buildings on Heritage Square also represent early Phoenix. The Duplex (1923) now contains offices; you can drop into the city office on the left for more information about the historic buildings; 602/262-5071, 602/262-5029 (recording), www.ci.phoenix.az.us/parks/heritage.html. The Stevens House (1901) holds the

Arizona Doll and Toy Museum; 602/253-9337; it's open Sunday noon–4 P.M. and Tues.–Sat. 10 A.M.–4 P.M.; closed Mondays and in August; admission is $2.50 adults, $1 children. Beside it, the Stevens-Haustgen House (1901) provides a home for Chez Bubba, a Cajun restaurant. Next, the Bouvier-Teeter House (1899) is now the Teeter House Tea Room, 602/252-4682, which offers tea and lunch; closed Mondays. The Silva House next door dates from 1900 and was unoccupied at press time. Baird Machine Shop (1929) now houses the popular Pizzeria Bianco (pizza and salads), 602/258-8300. It's open Tues.–Sun. for dinner. The 1909 Thomas House next door is home to Bar Bianco, which belongs to the pizzeria and serves wine, beer, and appetizers.

Phoenix Museum of History

Permanent and changing exhibits illustrate important milestones in the development of early Phoenix. Wandering through the various sections, you'll learn about life at Camp McDowell, law and disorder in the pioneer days, historic floods and droughts, and construction of the old state capitol. Artifacts enliven replicas of Hancock's general store, an old ostrich farm, and a shop of Native American curios. You'll see a "lunger tent" of the type once used by tuberculosis patients, a steam locomotive from early mining operations, and an 1883 steam engine that powered one of the world's first motorcycles—a high wheeler! Interactive displays scattered through the museum will entertain the kids. A small library is available if you'd like to delve deeper into the city's early history. The museum store offers books, crafts, and souvenirs for all ages.

The museum is in Heritage and Science Park at 105 N. Fifth St.; 602/253-2734. It's open Sunday noon–5 P.M. and Mon.–Sat. 10 A.M.–5 P.M. Admission is $5 adults, $3.50 seniors (65 and older), $3 students—AAA—military, $2.50 ages 7–12; www.pmoh.org.

Arizona Science Center

"Have fun with science," suggests the Center's brochure. Here you can try some 350 different hands-on exhibits that make scientific exploration exciting! Both children and adults will find the projects challenging and fun. (Mornings, though, can be very busy with school kids.) A Play Space will entertain the age four and under set. New and improved exhibits continually appear in such fields as "All About You" (the workings of mind and body), "Networks" (finding out how things interlink), "Fab Lab" (exploring the nature of forces and movement), and "The World Around You" (studying earth sciences and aerospace). The experiments you try may be as simple as a test of perception or as complex as working the controls of an actual helicopter. Staff present special demonstrations during the day. Radio hams at station W7ASC will let you have the microphone to "work" other hams. Art exhibits and visiting exhibitions reveal beautiful and fascinating aspects of science. A planetarium will take you from the skies of Arizona to the mysteries of the universe. A giant screen iWerks theater (similar to Imax) screens impressive movies, and an interactive fountain, Water Works, may put on a show for you, too. Awesome Atom's Science Store (an intriguing gift shop) and a small food court round out the facilities.

The Center is open daily (except Thanksgiving and Christmas) 10 A.M.–5 P.M.; admission is $8 adults, $6 children 3–12 and seniors over 62. For more information call the Center at 602/716-2000, or look them up on the Web at www.az science.org. The ham radio station has a website too, www.w7asc.org

Bank One Ballpark

Baseball fans will enjoy the 75-minute tour of this amazing stadium that combines features of an old-fashioned ballpark with the latest technologies. Your guide will tell of exploits by Mark McGuire and other hitters, along with technical details such as how the retractable roof operates. You'll see the poolside "seating" beside right field, hall of fame exhibits, and party rooms, and you'll visit the Arizona Diamondbacks dugout. Ticket windows are on the west side of the stadium where the tours start: $6 adult, $4 senior 60+ and children 7–12, $2 age 4–6. It's recommended that you obtain tickets 48 hours prior, 602/462-6543 (adv. purchase), 602/462-6799 (information).

SOUTH-CENTRAL

CENTRAL AVENUE CORRIDOR

Japanese Friendship Garden and Margaret T. Hance Park

The East comes to Phoenix at this garden on the south side of Margaret T. Hance Park in north downtown. Phoenix's Japanese sister city, Himeji, helped in the design. Visitors leave their troubles at the gate to experience the simplicity and beauty of nature. Free guided tours of the garden and the Musoan ("Dream for the Future") Tea House are held Sunday 1–5 P.M., Oct.–May. For a fee you can experience an authentic Japanese tea ceremony. The ceremonies are currently held every other month, Oct.–May or June; reservations are required, 602/262-6412.

Margaret T. Hance Park runs in a long, grassy strip (actually atop the Papago Freeway tunnel) south of the central library and Culver Street. The park holds scattered monuments to Phoenix's eight sister cities, including a huge bronze panda sculpture from Chengdu, China (at the east end). Parking is plentiful off Culver Street, west of Central Avenue.

Phoenix Trolley Museum

From 1887 to 1948, streetcars rattled down the city streets to almost anywhere you'd want to go. Car No. 116 now rolls again on a short section of track at 1218 N. Central Ave. (turn west on Culver St. just north of the Margaret T. Hance Park bridge). Here you can learn about the history and workings of the old street railway. It operates on Saturdays about 11 A.M.–2 P.M. from December to early May; 602/254-0307 (recording) or 602/277-6627, www.phoenixtrolley.com. Tours cost $4.50 adult, $4 senior, and $2.50 children.

Phoenix Art Museum

This museum's extensive collection of more than 16,000 works of art will take you to many different times and places. Works in the American galleries span the years from Colonial to modern and contemporary periods and include Western landscapes and bronzes. Latin American art reveals the traditions and mixing of Spanish Colonial and indigenous forces up to the present. The exceptional Asian collection reflects the heritage of China, Japan, Tibet, and Southeast Asia over the centuries. European galleries illustrate important themes and styles as far back as the Renaissance. Fashion design exhibits emphasize American trends of the 20th century, but also include pieces by European designers. You'll marvel at the details of the famous Thorne Miniature Rooms, which re-create in intricate detail historic interiors of Europe and America at a scale of 1:12. Visiting exhibits provide a regularly changing parade of new perspectives.

Scheduled tours offer an in-depth look at selected works. An audio guide is available too. Classes and special programs for children and adults take place regularly. You can check for presentations at the video theater or drop in at the large art-research library. Kids will find art projects and some touchable pieces in the ArtWorks Gallery. The Museum Store sells crafts, art, jewelry, apparel, cards, posters, and books. A café serves creative light meals during museum hours. (You don't have to pay museum admission if you're just visiting the store or café.)

The museum, 1625 N. Central Ave., 602/257-1880, 602/257-1222 (recorded information), forms a large courtyard with the Phoenix Theatre's Main Stage and Little Theatre at the northeast corner of Central Avenue and McDowell Road. Free parking is available around the museum and in designated spaces across Coronado Road to the north. Hours are Tues.–Sun. 10 A.M.–5 P.M. (until 9 P.M. Thurs.); closed Mondays and major holidays. Admission is $7 adults, $5 full-time students over 18, $5 seniors 65 and up, $2 children 6–17; currently free on Thursday. Visit on the Web at www.phxart.org.

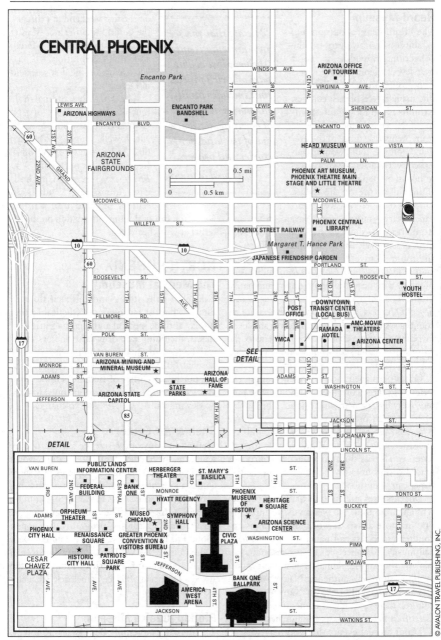

CENTRAL PHOENIX

Encanto Park

WINDSOR AVE.

ARIZONA OFFICE OF TOURISM

VIRGINIA AVE.

LEWIS AVE.

ARIZONA HIGHWAYS

ENCANTO PARK BANDSHELL

SHERIDAN ST.

ENCANTO BLVD.

ENCANTO BLVD.

ARIZONA STATE FAIRGROUNDS

HEARD MUSEUM

MONTE VISTA RD.

PALM LN.

PHOENIX ART MUSEUM, PHOENIX THEATRE MAIN STAGE AND LITTLE THEATRE

0   0.5 mi

0   0.5 km

MCDOWELL RD.

MCDOWELL RD.

WILLETA ST.

PHOENIX STREET RAILWAY

PHOENIX CENTRAL LIBRARY

Margaret T. Hance Park

JAPANESE FRIENDSHIP GARDEN

PORTLAND ST.

ROOSEVELT ST.

ROOSEVELT ST.

YOUTH HOSTEL

FILLMORE RD.

POST OFFICE

DOWNTOWN TRANSIT CENTER (LOCAL BUS)

AMC MOVIE THEATERS

POLK ST.

YMCA

RAMADA HOTEL

ARIZONA CENTER

VAN BUREN ST.

ARIZONA MINING AND MINERAL MUSEUM

SEE DETAIL

MONROE ST.

ARIZONA HALL OF FAME

ADAMS ST.

ADAMS ST.

WASHINGTON ST.

JEFFERSON ST.

ARIZONA STATE CAPITOL

STATE PARKS

JACKSON ST.

BUCHANAN ST.

DETAIL

LINCOLN ST.

TONTO ST.

BUCKEYE RD.

PIMA ST.

MOJAVE ST.

WATKINS ST.

DETAIL

VAN BUREN

PUBLIC LANDS INFORMATION CENTER

HERBERGER THEATER

ST. MARY'S BASILICA

FEDERAL BUILDING

BANK ONE

MONROE

PHOENIX MUSEUM OF HISTORY

HERITAGE SQUARE

ORPHEUM THEATER

HYATT REGENCY

ADAMS

MUSEO CHICANO

SYMPHONY HALL

ARIZONA SCIENCE CENTER

PHOENIX CITY HALL

RENAISSANCE SQUARE

GREATER PHOENIX CONVENTION & VISITORS BUREAU

CIVIC PLAZA

WASHINGTON ST.

CESAR CHAVEZ PLAZA

HISTORIC CITY HALL

PATRIOTS SQUARE PARK

JEFFERSON

BANK ONE BALLPARK

AMERICA WEST ARENA

JACKSON

SOUTH-CENTRAL

© AVALON TRAVEL PUBLISHING, INC.

Heard Museum

The Heard features outstanding exhibits on Southwest tribes. The collection provides a good overview of regional Native American groups and reveals insights into many aspects of their cultures. Exhibits illustrate the intertwining of the region's land and people from prehistoric times to the present. Clothing, tools, weapons, an Apache wickiup, and even a Navajo hogan all demonstrate the resourceful nature of the tribes. Displays of superb Native American jewelry—mostly from Navajo, Hopi, and Zuni artisans—show artistic skill and development of styles. A kachina doll collection fills an entire room. Native Americans talk about their culture in *Our Voices, Our Land,* an audiovisual program with beautiful photography and native music. The poignant *Remembering Our Indian School Days: The Boarding School Experience* recounts a system feared, hated, endured, and loved by Native American children. You'll experience the worlds of Arizona's all 21 federally recognized tribes in *We Are! Arizona's First Peoples.*

Other permanent and changing exhibit galleries hold large collections of Southwest pottery, weavings, basketry, and fine art. The Gallery of Indian Art presents contemporary Native American pieces. Families get to try hands-on and interactive projects. While visiting the galleries, you'll pass through attractive courtyards graced with fountains, native flora, and Native American sculpture.

Docents offer guided tours daily, and you can rent an audio tour. On weekends, you may see one or more artists at work and perhaps encounter a special performance of Native American music and dance. For deeper research, you can visit the extensive library. The museum's outstanding shop sells authentic Native American arts and crafts and books on Native American cultures; there's a children's corner too. Ironwood Café offers light breakfasts and lunches.

Major annual events that you may wish to catch are the World Championship Hoop Dance

> *"The art that you see in a museum is only the very last visible part of a rich process that includes family, memories, a lifetime of learning, patience, love of the land, songs, stories and prayers."*
>
> **Heard Museum**

on the first weekend in February, the Guild Indian Fair & Market on the first weekend in March, and the Celebration of Basketweaving on the first weekend in December.

The Spanish Colonial-style museum building is at 2301 N. Central Ave. (east side) between McDowell and Thomas; 602/252-8840, 602/252-8848 (recording). It's open daily 9:30 A.M.–5 P.M. except major holidays. Admission is $7 adults, $6 seniors (65 and up), $3 ages 4–12. You can find more information on the Internet at www.heard.org.

NORTH PHOENIX

The Medical Museum

Exhibits in the lobby and on each floor of Phoenix Baptist Hospital and Medical Center display antique medical and pharmaceutical artifacts, including rare drug jars, doctors' medical bags, and quack medicine items. The hospital, 6025 N. 20th Ave., 602/249-0212, is at the northwest corner of Bethany Home Road and 19th Avenue. The displays are open to public viewing daily 9 A.M.–9 P.M. No charge.

Shemer Art Center

Housed in a historic residence surrounded by sculpture, the Shemer Art Center features works of Arizona artists and craftspeople. A new show comes about once a month. Galleries close between shows, so it's best to call before coming out; 602/262-4727. The center also hosts art classes and children's programs. It's open Mon.–Fri. 10 A.M.–5 P.M. (Tuesday until 9 P.M.), and Saturday 9 A.M.–1 P.M. Admission is free. The center is near Camelback Mountain in the Arcadia District at 5005 E. Camelback Rd. (enter from Arcadia Dr.).

Plotkin Judaica Museum

The museum at Temple Beth Israel, 10460 N. 56th St. (at Shea Blvd.), 480/951-0323, illus-

© BILL WEIR

early 1890's Victorian house at the Pioneer Arizona Living History Museum

trates Jewish holidays and displays many ancient artifacts from the Holy Land. Open Sunday and Tues.–Thurs. 10 A.M.–3 P.M., and Friday after evening services; closed Sundays in summer. Admission is by donation.

Deer Valley Rock Art Center

Prehistoric tribes chipped more than 1,500 petroglyphs into the rock at this site in the Hedgpeth Hills. Scholars believe the images were created over several periods between about 5000 B.C. and A.D. 1400. Some are so old that the figures are almost covered with desert varnish. Interpretive displays in the visitor center help you gain an appreciation for the rock art from the perspectives of researchers, Native Americans, physical scientists, and archaeologists. An easy quarter-mile trail leads to viewpoints where you can see many of the petroglyphs in their natural settings. (The three boulders at trail marker #2, however, come from another location.) Rent binoculars from the visitor center to get a better look at the rock art. Signs along the wheelchair-accessible path identify local desert plants.

Kids can go on a scavenger hunt, make their own rock art, and practice drawing. Tours can be arranged with advance notice. A gift shop sells clothing, stone reproductions, jewelry with rock-art motifs, and related books. The center, 623/582-8007, is open Sunday noon–5 P.M. and Tues.–Sat. 9 A.M.–5 P.M. from October to April, then Sunday noon–5 P.M., TUES.–FRI. 8 a.m.–2 P.M., AND SATURDAY 9 a.m.–5 P.M. in summer (May–Sept.). The trail and gift shop close half an hour earlier. Guided tours begin on Saturdays Oct.–April at 10 A.M. Visit on the Web at www.asu.edu/clas/anthropology/dvrac. Admission is $4 adults, $2 seniors and students (with I.D.), $1 children 6–12. Take I-17 Deer Valley Road Exit 217B and head west 2.5 miles, keeping right at the signed fork.

Pioneer Arizona Living History Museum

The frontier comes back to life here. You'll see how residents of the territory lived from the mid-1800s to statehood in 1912. Stroll the grounds to view historic exhibits and costumed craftspeople at work. The nearly complete little town has a school, church, sheriff's office, bank, blacksmith shop, carpenter shop, opera house, ranch, cabins, and houses—including the John

Sears house, one of the first frame houses in Phoenix. Many of the 26 or so authentic buildings have been brought here from other sites; the others have been reconstructed from old photos or plans.

This museum emphasizes historical accuracy, setting it apart from "Wild West towns" based more on Hollywood fiction than on fact. Mountain men, cavalry, gunfighters, and special exhibits enliven the community on the weekend nearest its birthday (February 14). Melodrama and other productions occasionally appear in the opera house; call for times.

Pioneer Restaurant offers indoor and patio dining for breakfast on weekends, lunches daily, and possibly dinners. In the main dining room, a 29-foot mural *Over the Top* depicts a cattle drive. The magnificent bar in the next room has a colorful history.

Pioneer Arizona, 623/465-1052, is set among rocky desert foothills about 30 miles north of downtown Phoenix. Take I-17 north to Pioneer Road Exit 225 and follow signs. It's open Wed.–Sun. 9 A.M.–5 P.M. (to 3 P.M. June–Sept.). Admission is $7 adults, $6 seniors (60 and over), $5 students, and $4 children 3–5; www.pioneer-arizona.com.

WEST PHOENIX
Wildlife World Zoo

Begun in 1974 as a breeding farm for rare and endangered species, this zoo opened to the public 10 years later and today houses a large collection of exotic wildlife. You'll meet the patas monkey, fastest of all primates, which can run doglike across the ground at 35 miles per hour. Larger animals include the scimitar-horned oryx, dama gazelle, addax (an antelope of the Sahara Desert), rhino, tapir, zebra, giraffe, camel, kangaroo, and white tiger. The zoo's impressive bird collection includes pheasants, toucans, cockatoos, macaws, curassows, ostriches (all five of the world's species), and some birds exhibited nowhere else in the country. A large, walk-in aviary contains Eyton's tree ducks of Australia, black-necked stilts of North America, and other unusual birds. Penguins from South Africa keep

their "cool." Additional creatures live in the small mammal, reptile, and aquarium exhibits. Wildlife Encounters Shows and feedings take place several times daily. A Safari Train takes visitors on a narrated excursion past animals of Africa. Or you can hop on the Australian boat ride and listen to your guide point out wildlife from "Down Under." Children enjoy meeting domestic animals in a petting area and taking a spin on the carousel.

The zoo, 16501 W. Northern Ave., 623/935-9453, is open every day of the year 9 A.M.–5 P.M. From Phoenix, head west 18 miles on I-10 to Cotton Lane (Exit 124), then north six miles to Northern Avenue. From the northern Valley, it's fastest to take the 101 Loop to Northern Avenue, then follow Northern west 8 miles. Admission is $11 adults, $6 children 3–12; www.wildlifeworld.com.

West Valley Art Museum

In this gallery located northwest of Phoenix, you'll experience a lot of variety in both the local and visiting exhibitions. Shows change every month or two. On Tuesdays, except in summer, you can attend Artful Afternoon, an art or music presentation at 4 P.M. The Museum Gift Store sells some unique items. Classic Café serves Italian and American cuisine for lunch. The museum is on the north side of Bell Road between Sun City and Sun City West (turn in on Avenue of the Arts/114th Ave.). Gallery hours are Tues.–Sun. 10 A.M.–4 P.M.; closed Mondays and holidays; 623/972-0635. Admission is $5 adult, $4 senior 55 and over, $1 students. You can check www.wvam.org for exhibits, programs, and art classes.

SOUTH PHOENIX
Mystery Castle

Boyce Luther Gulley always dreamed of building his own castle. One fine day in 1930 he disappeared, leaving his wife and daughter behind. His whereabouts remained unknown until his death in 1945, when both Gulley and his castle were identified. Gulley's daughter, Mary Lou, now presides over the castle. She and assistants lead 30-minute tours through the main house (decorated with Native American baskets and rugs), the caretaker's room (with its "Stairway to the Rainbow"), the Cactus Room (built around a saguaro skeleton), the wedding chapel (with a Grand Canyon North Rim fireplace), and the Dug Out bar. Everything from Stutz-Bearcat wheels to discarded bricks went into this imaginative and whimsical mixture of American West and scrapyard—Gulley never threw away anything if it could be recycled.

The castle, 602/268-1581, is seven miles south of downtown Phoenix near the entrance to South Mountain Park. Drive south on Central Avenue, turn left (east) on Mineral Road, and continue eight blocks. Alternatively, you can drive south on Seventh Street to its end at Mineral Road, then turn left and proceed one block. It's open from October to June: Thurs.–Sun. 11 A.M.–4 P.M. (call ahead and check hours). Admission is $5 adults, $4 seniors 65 and over, $2 children 6–15.

EAST PHOENIX
Pueblo Grande Museum and Archaeology Park

Excellent exhibits here depict how life may have been for the Hohokam. Archaeologists have learned much about this ancient society by studying the plant and animal remains, artifacts, and burial sites uncovered around this large site. They know, for example, that the average Hohokam man stood five feet four inches tall, weighed 130–140 pounds, and had a 40-year life span. Many of the artifacts, along with a platform mound bearing what appear to be solstice markings, suggest that the Hohokam had a rich ceremonial culture.

A short video introduces the site and its former inhabitants, and a giant map shows the tribe's intricate canal system—one of the greatest engineering feats of prehistoric America. Tools, decorated ceramics, jewelry, and other finds show how skillfully the Hohokam lived in the desert and what crops they grew. The gallery's shows change about twice a year and spotlight archaeology, Southwest cultures, or contemporary American Native American arts.

Some children's exhibits invite hands-on exploration of archaeology.

After looking at the indoor exhibits, you'll better appreciate the ruins outside. Signs along a two-thirds-mile trail describe features of Pueblo Grande's construction and excavations. The Hohokam began construction of the platform mound at Pueblo Grande about A.D. 1150 on a terrace overlooking the Salt River. From the top of the ruins you can see an oval-shaped depression thought to be a ball court; a trail leads over to it for a closer look. On the way to the ball court, you'll pass reconstructed pithouse and adobe compounds; interiors show how the ruins might have looked when inhabited. You can borrow a *Desert Plants of Pueblo Grande* to identify species along the trails.

After your walk, you can stop in at the museum store for Native American jewelry and other crafts, children's items, and books, including the museum's excellent *Desert Farmers at the River's Edge: The Hohokam and Pueblo Grande.*

The museum sponsors events, tours, and hikes for both children and adults; staff also have information on other Southwest activities and places to visit. A research library can be used by appointment. On the second full weekend in December, Native Americans present entertainment, arts and crafts, and food at the Annual Indian Market, held at the Activity Center in South Mountain Park.

The museum and ruins lie five miles east of downtown at 4619 E. Washington St., 602/495-0900 (recording) or 602/495-0901; www.pueblogrande.com. Hours are Sunday 1–4:45 P.M. and Mon.–Sat. 9 A.M.–4:45 P.M. Admission is $2 adults, $1.50 seniors 55 and up, $1 children 6–17; free on Sunday.

Arizona Military Museum

Exhibits trace Arizona's military history—and where its soldiers have fought—from Spanish days to the present. Old maps, photos, weapons, uniforms, and other memorabilia represent each period. During World War II, the adobe museum building served as part of a prison camp detaining German submariners. A model depicts the daring "Great Escape" on Dec. 23, 1944, by 25

German officers and sailors. (They were all recaptured.) One hall features a well-armed UH-1M helicopter. An outdoor exhibit displays vehicles and artillery that range in date from World War I to Desert Storm. A library holds many books and some videos on military history.

The museum, 602/267-2676, is part of the Arizona National Guard complex at the northeast corner of E. McDowell Rd. and 52nd St., about seven miles east of downtown. Turn in off 52nd St. and look for the large building "Arizona Military Academy." It's open Tuesday and Thursday 9 A.M.–2 P.M. and Sat.–Sun. 1–4 P.M.; groups can call to schedule other times. Admission is free.

Desert Botanical Garden

If you're curious about all those strange cacti and other plants so abundant in the deserts of Arizona, this is the place to learn about them. A stroll through the extensive gardens will show how much life and beauty the desert holds.

The one-third-mile-loop Desert Discovery Trail winds past thousands of plants, including more than half the cactus species in the world. You can determine what it takes for a plant to be classified a cactus in the Cactus House and find out about succulents in the Succulent House. Short trails branch off to interpret other aspects of desert life: the Plants and People of the Sonoran Desert Trail shows how early inhabitants met their needs from the desert's resources; the Sonoran Desert Nature Trail focuses on the plants and animals here and how they interact; the Center for Desert Living Trail offers demonstration gardens, landscaping, and the Desert House to illustrate how we can live in harmony with the desert. Desert House, an actual residence, was specially designed to conserve water and energy; you can learn more from a video and exhibits nearby. A wildflower pavilion and trail lie across from the gift shop near the parking area; wildflowers along the one-third-mile-long trail represent the four deserts of the U.S.A.

All the trails have signs to identify the plants and have been graded for wheelchair access. If you arrive in spring, you'll see many plants in bloom. Lighting on the main trail and late closing hours allow for the unusual experience of strolling through the desert at night, though it's necessary to come during the day to read the plant labels or take the side trails. Inexpensive booklets offer more information on the trails and Desert House.

A Garden Activities Hotline, 480/481-8134, fills you in on the garden's many docent tours, special events, classes, and workshops; during March and April the hotline reports where you can view Arizona wildflowers. Major events include Las Noches de las Luminarias (over 7,000 luminarias with music and food) in early December, concerts (varied programs) on Sundays in spring and fall, jazz concerts on Friday evenings in summer, and landscape plant sales in mid-March and mid-October. Patio Café serves breakfast and lunch. The gift shop offers natural history books, souvenirs, and cactus specimens. A plant shop sells many types of cactus and succulents. The research library is open weekdays.

The Desert Botanical Garden, 480/941-1225, is east off Galvin Parkway in Papago Park, one-half mile north of the Phoenix Zoo. It's open daily, 8 A.M.–8 P.M. Oct.–April and 7 A.M.–8 P.M. May–Sept.; the Desert House exhibits, the plant shop, and the gift shop close at 5 P.M. Admission runs $7.50 adults, $6.50 seniors 60 and over, $4 ages 13–18 and college students, and $1.50 children 5–12; www.dbg.org.

Phoenix Zoo

More than 1,300 animals from Arizona and all over the world inhabit 125 acres of rolling hills and lakes at the Phoenix Zoo. You'll see bighorn sheep from Arizona, oryx from the Arabian desert, orangutans from Southeast Asia, lions from Africa, and spectacled bears from South America, among others.

The zoo uses moats and steep inclines instead of cages, where possible, to provide the animals with an open and natural setting. It has re-created different types of native habitat—tropical rainforest, desert mountains, savanna, wetlands, temperate woodlands—so each animal will feel at home. "Behavioral enrichment programs" make life more interesting for the animals: wildlife may have to forage for hidden food or chase and catch their dinner. The Arizona Trail section reveals many rarely seen mammals, birds, and reptiles, including some surprisingly beautiful rattlesnakes. On the Children's Trail, kids can feel sculptures of wildlife and pet tame animals. The narrated Safari Shuttle ($2 all day) will save you some walking. Special free programs include animal encounters, storytellers, and zookeeper talks. The zoo's gift shop offers books, posters, clothing, and toys. Several snack bars sell fast food. More than two million lights decorate the grounds for ZooLights on evenings from early December to early January; call for hours.

Phoenix Zoo, 602/273-1341, is east off Galvin Parkway in Papago Park; www.phoenixzoo.org. It's open daily 9 A.M.–5 P.M. from September to May, and 7 A.M.–8 P.M. June–August. In the hot months it's best to come early to see the animals when they are most active. Admission is $10 adults, $9 seniors 60 and over, $5 children 3–12 (with adult).

Hall of Flame

In the old days the position of volunteer firefighter carried great prestige. Men eagerly joined the local fire brigade, which also served as a social club. Firefighters competed in drills and marched in parades alongside their glistening machines. Today the Phoenix Hall of Flame museum houses what may be the world's largest display of firefighting gear. The equipment in this amazing collection comes from all over the world; many items are works of art in themselves.

The first gallery contains hand- and horse-drawn pumpers, hose carriers, and hook-and-ladder wagons from the 18th and 19th centuries. A second gallery displays antique motorized fire trucks. The third and fourth galleries feature historic fire-alarm systems (including the world's first computerized dispatch system), a fire-safety exhibit, and additional fire trucks. Old prints show firefighters in action. Those killed in action are honored in the National Firefighting Hall of Heroes.

Another gallery explores the world of the wildland firefighter—smokejumpers, hotshots, helitacks, air tankers, engine crews and ground crews; you'll experience a replica of a 1930s lookout cabin, interactive exhibits, and videos of firefighters in action.

The theater screens videos about steam fire engines, great fires, and the people who fight them. A gift shop sells souvenirs.

The Hall of Flame is opposite Papago Park at 6101 E. Van Buren St., 602/275-3473, www.hallofflame.org. It's open Sunday noon–4 P.M. and Mon.–Sat. 9 A.M.–5 P.M. Admission is $5 adults, $4 seniors 62 and up, and $3 students 6–17.

Salt River Project History Center

Exhibits by the Salt River Project illustrate Hohokam and modern canal systems, Hohokam life, and the construction of Theodore Roosevelt Dam. The center is at 1521 N. Project Dr., off E. Van Buren St. (turn in at the sign for the Hall of Flame), 602/236-2208. It's open Mon.–Fri. 9 A.M.–4 P.M. Admission is free.

Arizona Historical Society Museum

This large museum portrays central Arizona's modern history—the dynamic transformations of the 20th century—with some 19th-century background. As you walk into the courtyard, the sound of rushing water greets your ears. The dolomite blocks, generator, and freight wagon here come from the construction days of Roosevelt Dam; exhibits nearby and inside illustrate how the dam made possible the Valley's agricultural and industrial development. A wide-screen video, "Traces on the Land," introduces the people and geography that influenced this region. Territorial Arizona comes to life in the "Foundations of Central Arizona History" gallery, which offers reconstructed scenes and interactive exhibits. Photo exhibits and videos of "Routes: A Moving Experience" tell the story of what travel was once like for Arizonans. You can detour down the Historymakers Hall to learn about people who have helped make the state what it is today. Continue upstairs to see "Views from the Home Front" about the exciting and difficult World War II years, told from perspectives of men and women in the military, civilians supporting the war effort, Japanese-American relocatees, and German and Italian prisoners of war.

"Desert Cities" illustrates the development of the Valley of the Sun and where it could go in the future. You'll find other intriguing permanent and changing exhibits in the spacious halls too. Kids will like the museum's many projects and interactive exhibits. There's also a research library (check for hours), gift shop, guided tours (by appointment), and special programs.

The museum, 480/929-0292, is open Sunday noon–4 P.M. and Tues.–Sat. 10 A.M.–4 P.M.; free admission; www.tempe.gov/ahs. It's at 1300 N. College Ave. and Weber Dr., near the southeast corner of Papago Park. From Phoenix, you can take Loop 202 (Red Mountain Freeway), exit north on Scottsdale Road, then turn left on Curry Road or Weber Dr. to College Avenue. Alternatively, you can head east on Van Buren St., turn left on Curry Road, then left on College Avenue; if coming on Washington St., continue east (it becomes Curry Road), then turn left on College Avenue. From Tempe, head north on Mill Avenue, turn right on Curry Road, and left on College Avenue, or head north on Rural Road (becomes Scottsdale Road) and turn left on Curry Road or Weber Drive. From Scottsdale, head south on 68th St. (which becomes College Ave.) or you can go south on Scottsdale Road and turn right on Weber Drive.

PHOENIX ACCOMMODATIONS

Nowhere else in Arizona will you find such a wide selection of accommodations at such a wide range of prices—from basic motels to posh luxury resorts. Expect higher prices in the cooler months, especially in early spring when the numbers of snowbirds and other vacationers peak. On the other hand, resorts can be bargains in summer—prices may plummet more than 50 percent when the mercury soars. Seasonal savings decrease with lower-priced accommodations, but competition helps keep prices reasonable. Rates fluctuate not only through the year, but sometimes during the day if rooms are slow or quick to fill! You may get better rates by calling ahead for a reservation or by arriving in the morning. Always ask for discounts; seniors and members of AARP or AAA often get a lower price, and some places give a "super saver"

rate to everyone else. Business hotels often have a lower weekend rate. Except at small bed and breakfast places, you'll have to pay a tax of about 12 percent on room rates.

Most all national chains are represented here—many in several locations. Check motel and resort listings in the free *Official Visitors Guide* published by the Greater Phoenix Convention and Visitors Bureau. Prices below reflect approximate winter rates; categories are based on the cost for double occupancy.

Reservation Services

The sheer number of hotels and resorts in the Valley may seem overwhelming. **Phoenix Scottsdale Hotel Reservations,** 800/728-3227, www.phoenixhotelres.com, is a free service that can help you find what you're looking for and maybe save you some money, too. They arrange discounted rooms at many places; prices start around $50–100 depending on the season. **Hotel Reservations Network,** 800/715-7666 or www.hoteldiscount.com, offers similar services.

For bed and breakfast accommodations, try *Mi Casa Su Casa,* P.O. Box 950, Tempe, AZ 85280; 480/990-0682, 800/456-0682; www.azres.com; and **Arizona Trails Reservation Service,** P.O. Box 18998, Fountain Hills, AZ 85269; 480/837-4284, 888/799-4284; www.arizonatrails.com.

Hostel

Metcalf House Hostel, 1026 N. Ninth St. (between Portland and Roosevelt Sts.), 602/254-9803, offers shared rooms (separate men's and women's) that make a good choice for lowest-budget travelers.

Rarely full, the hostel is open year-round on a first-come, first-served basis with check-in at 5–10 P.M. Rates are $12 for members, $15 for nonmembers. A three-night-stay limit may apply if the hostel is crowded. Facilities include a kitchen, washer and dryer, and info-packed bulletin boards. As the only Hostelling International-affiliated place in Arizona, the hostel sells memberships and gives out the annual HI directory.

The hostel is in a run-down residential area, one mile northeast of downtown. Parking is on the street. You can walk or take a city bus to many Phoenix sights from here.

Under $50

For the lowest-priced motels, try Van Buren Street, especially downtown and the section between downtown and 40th Street. Once the major highway through Phoenix, this route was bypassed when the freeways were constructed. Many of the older places have been well maintained, while others have gone to seed. The newer motels include some well-known chains. East Van Buren looks very tattered between about 24th and 32nd Streets, so you'll feel more comfortable using a car or taxi at night. Otherwise, Van Buren makes an excellent base for many Valley attractions and it's convenient to Sky Harbor Airport.

A central place for both men and women is the **Downtown YMCA,** 350 N. First Ave., 602/253-6181. Rooms, all singles and usually all full, cost $28 s per night or $110 s per week. No reservations are taken; bathrooms are down the hall. For a small extra fee, you can use the pool, weight room, racquetball and basketball courts, running track, sauna, and hot tub.

Downtown Motels: Close to the heart of downtown are **Budget Lodge Motel,** 402 W. Van Buren St., 602/254-7247, $35 d; and **Budget Inn,** 424 W. Van Buren St., 602/257-8331, $45 d. Also downtown you'll find **Las Palmas Inn,** 765 Grand Ave., 602/256-9161, which has a pool and rates of $25 s, $30 d; and **Travel Inn 9 Motel,** 201 N. Seventh Ave., 602/254-6521, $32 d. **Desert Sun Motel,** 1325 Grand Ave., 602/258-8971, 800/227-0301, offers a pool and restaurant; $40 d. Down south two miles, **E-Z 8 Motel,** 1820 S. Seventh St., 602/254-9787, 800/655-3465, has a pool, hot tub, and restaurant; $40 s, $45 d.

East of Downtown/Airport: Heading out along E. Van Buren's "motel row," you could try **Economy Inn,** 1925 E. Van Buren St., 602/254-0181, $35 d; and **Sky Harbor Inn, 2323 E. Van Buren St., 602/685-1803, with a pool, $45 d.**

North of downtown: Near Metrocenter, between the Dunlap and Peoria Exits of I-17, is **Premier Inns of Metrocenter,** 10402 N. Black Canyon Fwy., 602/943-2371, 800/786-6835, where amenities include a pool, hot tub, and tennis; $45–66 d. At the Bell Road Exit, four miles farther north, you'll find **Motel 6 Phoenix North,** 2330 W. Bell Rd., 602/993-2353, 800/4MOTEL6, with a pool; $40 s, $46 d.

$50–100

Downtown: Los Olivos Hotel and Suites, 202 E. McDowell Rd., 602/258-6911, 800/776-5560, is close to museums and a library; $79 d room, $99 d suite.

East of Downtown/Airport: The less expensive places of this category include **Pyramid Inn,** 3307 E. Van Buren St., 602/275-3691, with a pool, $45 s, $55 d; **Parkview Inn,** 3547 E. Van Buren St., 602/273-7303, $45 s, $50 d; and **Phoenix Sunrise Motel,** 3644 E Van Buren St., 602/275-7661, $43 s, $50 d.

Some popular chains are **Rodeway Inn/Airport-24th Street,** 124 S. 24th St., 602/220-0044, $60 d; **Quality Suites,** 3101 N. 32nd St., 602/956-4900, 800/950-1688, or 800/228-5151, all with kitchenettes, $60–80 d; **Days Inn Airport** 3333 E. Van Buren St., 602/244-8244, 800/329-7466, with a pool and restaurant, $69 s, $79 d; **Super 8 Phoenix Airport,** 3401 E. Van Buren St., one mile north of airport, 602/244-1627, 800/800-8000, $65 d; **Ramada Limited Airport North,** 4120 E. Van Buren St., 602/275-5746, 800/272-6232, $60–70 d; and **Sleep Inn Phoenix Airport,** 2621 S. 47th Pl., near University Dr. and Hohokam Expressway, 480/967-7100, 800/631-3054, with a pool and hot tub, $89–99 d.

North of Downtown: The many motels off the Black Canyon Freeway (I-17) exits will be a bit of a commute for most of the sights, but they can be handy for travels to the north or west. Choices just west of the Northern Avenue Exit include **Hampton Inn I-17,** 8101 N. Black Canyon Fwy., 602/864-6233, 800/HAMPTON, with a pool and hot tub, $99 d; **Super 8 Motel,** 8130 N. Black Canyon Hwy., 602/995-8451, 800/800-8000, including a pool and hot tub, $60 s, $65 d; and **Motel 6 Phoenix Northern,** 8152 N. Black Canyon Hwy., 602/995-7592, 800/4MOTEL6, which also has a pool, $46 s,

$52 d. Farther north at Bell Road is the **Best Western Bell Hotel,** 17211 N. Black Canyon Fwy., 602/993-8300, 800/528-1234, with a pool and hot tub; $50–69 d.

$100–150

Downtown: The 1928 **San Carlos Hotel,** 202 N. Central Ave., 602/253-4121, offers rooms where Hollywood stars once stayed. The seven-story hotel emphasizes fine service and old-fashioned charm with modern facilities. In the heart of the city, it also offers an Irish pub, rooftop pool, and sundeck. Rates for rooms and suites run $129–225 s, $139–235 d. **Ramada Inn Downtown Phoenix,** 401 N. First St., 602/258-3411, 800/272-6232, has a pool and restaurant; $149 d.

East of Downtown/Airport: Holiday Inn Airport East is at 4300 E. Washington St., 602/273-7778, 800/HOLIDAY; $147 d.

North of Downtown: Best Western Executive Park Hotel, 1100 N. Central Ave., 602/252-2100, 800/528-1234, offers a fitness center, pool, and restaurant; $119 d. **Quality Hotel and Resort,** 3600 N. Second Ave., 602/248-0222, 800/256-1237, has three pools and a restaurant; $99–119 s, $109–129 d. The full-service **Lexington Hotel & City Square Sports Club,** 4000 N. Central Ave., 602/279-9811, 800/537-8483, provides a 31,000-square-foot athletic club, restaurant, and sports bar, $109 d.

$150 and up

Downtown: The **Crowne Plaza,** 100 N. First St. (at Adams), 602/333-0000, 800/359-7253, has a pool, fitness center, and a restaurant; $215 d. The 24-story **Hyatt Regency,** 122 N. Second St. (at Adams), across from Phoenix Civic Plaza, 602/252-1234, 800/233-1234, features 712 modern rooms and suites in Southwest colors, a spectacular atrium lobby, the revolving Compass Restaurant, a rooftop pool, exercise room, hot tub, and a central location; $295 s, $320 d.

North of Downtown: Four Points Sheraton, 10220 N. Metro Parkway E. (off I-17 between the Dunlap and Peoria Exits), 602/997-5900, 800/325-3535, has a pool and tennis; $139–159 d.

Biltmore Area of Northeast Phoenix: Walking into the vast atrium of **Embassy Suites,** 2630 E. Camelback Rd., 602/955-3992, 800/362-2779, you might think you're in a tropical paradise. All suites have two rooms, wet bar, and dining area; $209–229 d.

Resorts

Phoenix's grand old resort, the **Arizona Biltmore,** 24th St. at Missouri, 602/955-6600, 800/950-0086, offers a wonderful combination of atmosphere, location, and luxury. Frank Lloyd Wright handled many of the architectural details; the master's influence shows in the hotel's stained glass, geometric designs, and interplay of light and shadow. Amenities include Wright's Restaurant, a grill, two 18-hole golf courses, a putting course, five pools (one with a 90-foot water slide), two whirlpools, eight lighted tennis courts, a health spa/athletic club, and the Kids Kabana offering children's activities. The hotel is also convenient to good hiking and mountain-bike riding in the nearby Squaw Peak area. Rates run $350–550 room, $675–1800 suite from Jan. 1 to May 5; $310–465 room, $550–1465 suite May 6–22; $175–260 room, $340–960 suite from May 23 to Sept. 9; $310–465 room, $550–1465 suite from Sept. 10 to Dec. 31; www.arizona biltmore.com.

In north Phoenix, **Pointe Hilton Resort at Squaw Peak,** 7677 N. 16th St., 602/997-2626, 800/876-4683, features suites and larger, more secluded one- and two-bedroom casitas on 180 acres near Squaw Peak Park. Lush landscaping surrounds the Spanish-style buildings. The swimming pools, waterfalls, water slide, and tubing river will make a splash with the aquatic set. Kids will enjoy the water playground, game room, and other activities offered especially for them. The resort also offers four lighted tennis courts, racquetball, Tocasierra Spa, and a fitness room. Guests enjoy golf and horseback-riding privileges at Hilton's Tapatio Cliffs (see below), four miles away. Excellent dining choices include Aunt Chilada's (Mexican), Hole-in-the-Wall (Western theme), and Lantana Grille

(American/Southwestern fine dining). The Standard Rate Plan costs $199–329 mid-January to mid-May, $89–159 mid-May to mid-September, and $149–269 mid-September to mid-January; more expensive options are available; www.pointehilton.com.

The **Pointe Hilton Resort at Tapatio Cliffs,** 11111 N. Seventh St., 602/866-7500, 800/876-4683, offers two-room suites, three restaurants, a business center, an 18-hole golf course, 15 lighted tennis courts, horseback riding, hiking and mountain biking on nearby North Mountain, seven swimming pools, a 130-foot water slide, and a health spa. The Standard Rate Plan costs $229–389 mid-January to mid-May, $89–159 mid-May to mid-September, and $199–279 mid-September to mid-January; more expensive options are available; www.pointehilton.com.

The **Wigwam Resort,** 300 Wigwam Blvd., 623/935-3811, 800/327-0396, is 17 miles west of central Phoenix in Litchfield Park; head north 2.5 miles from the I-10 Litchfield Rd. Exit. The resort dates from 1929 and has a reputation for superb golf. It offers three restaurants, three 18-hole golf courses, nine tennis courts (six lighted), two swimming pools, and a fitness center. Approximate seasons and rates are $369–429 room, $429–539 casita suite from Jan to May; $185–225 room, $225–305 casita suite from June to September; and $285–335 room, $335–435 casita suite from October to December; www.wigwamresort.com.

PHOENIX CAMPGROUNDS AND RV PARKS

Many Valley RV parks cater to retired people, who come in the cooler months to spend as long as seven months under the Arizona sun. Guests enjoy an active social life then, including many craft and sport programs. Families won't fit in well at such places, but the parks listed here do accept children except as noted. RVers will find the largest selection of places to stay in Mesa and Apache Junction; the tourist offices there have lists of RV parks.

West of Downtown

Green Acres RV Park, 2605 W. Van Buren St., 602/272-7863, is close to downtown, just west of I-17; $10 RV with hookups. The adults-only **Michigan Trailer Park** is at 3140 W. Osborn (at Grand Ave.), 602/269-0122; $25 RV with hookups.

North of Downtown

Covered Wagon RV Park, 6540 N. Black Canyon Hwy., 602/242-2500, offers sites for tents ($18) and RVs ($21–36); take the I-17 Glendale Exit and go south a half mile on the west frontage road. Seventeen miles north of downtown, **North Phoenix RV,** 2550 W. Louise Dr., 623/581-3969, charges $24 RV with hookups; take the Deer Valley Road Exit off I-17, go west one block to 26th Avenue, then turn right. **Pioneer Travel Trailer Park,** 623/465-8000, 800/658-5895, sits in the desert near Pioneer Arizona Living History Museum (not affiliated), about 30 miles north of downtown Phoenix. Take I-17 Pioneer Road Exit 225; $27 RV with hookups.

Lake Pleasant County Park (about 30 miles northwest of Phoenix), **Cave Creek Recreation Area,** (about 30 miles north of Phoenix and 1.5 miles north of Carefree), and **McDowell Mountain Regional Park** (15 miles northeast of Scottsdale) all feature developed campgrounds with showers and hookups; see Valley of the Sun Recreation for details and directions.

West of Phoenix

Destiny RV Resorts is at 416 N. Citrus Rd. in Goodyear, about 25 miles west of downtown Phoenix, 623/853-0537, 888/667-2454; take I-10 Exit 124, go south on Cotton Lane to Van Buren St., then turn west to Citrus Avenue; $23 tents, $30–36 RV with hookups.

White Tank Mountain Regional Park, about 25 miles northwest of downtown Phoenix, offers camping with showers in a scenic desert setting. **Estrella Mountain Regional Park,** about 25 miles southwest of downtown Phoenix, has plenty of room for basic camping (water but no showers) plus a few RV sites with hookups. See **Valley of the Sun Recreation** for details on, and directions to, these last two places.

PHOENIX FOOD

Phoenix and the Valley hold an amazing number of restaurants. You'll also find many restaurant listings in the free weeklies *New Times, the Rep,* and *Get Out.* Other sources include the *Official Visitors Guide,* distributed free by the Visitors Bureau, and the monthly *Phoenix Magazine.* The website www.azfamily.com offers online menus, reviews, and recipes. Valley diners will find helpful descriptions in the handy book *100 Best Restaurants in Arizona.*

The area's more expensive places suggest making reservations and may have a dress code. The following list contains highlights and typical examples of the dining scene. You're rarely far from an American, Mexican, or Asian eatery, and nearly all of the resorts offer at least one elegant restaurant. A bit more than half of Phoenix's restaurants feature smoke-free dining. Except as noted, all of the following have a smoke-free room or confine smoking to the bar. Prices refer to the cost of dinner entrees; lunch specials typically cost less.

American and Southwestern

You'll glide high above the city at **The Compass,** 122 N. Second St., 602/440-3166, the Hyatt Regency's 24th-floor revolving restaurant. Open Mon.–Sat. for lunch and dinner, Sunday for brunch and dinner; $18–25, reservations suggested.

At Pointe Hilton Resort at Tapatio Cliffs, **Different Pointe of View,** 11111 N. Seventh St. and Thunderbird, 602/863-0912, presents sophisticated American and continental dining with a dazzling view of Phoenix. Open nightly for dinner (Tues.–Sat. in summer); $26–40.

Green Leaf Café, 4426 N. 19th Ave., 602/265-5992, specializes in vegetarian food and also offers chicken and fish options. Open Mon.–Sat. for lunch and Tues.–Sat. for dinner; $10–17.

Katz, 5144 N. Central Ave., 602/277-8814, fixes deli food for breakfast and lunch daily; about $7.

Miracle Mile, 9 Park Central Mall, 602/277-4783, is a kosher-style cafeteria serving good portions of excellent food. Open Mon.–Sat. for breakfast and lunch; about $6.

Mrs. White's Golden Rule Café, downtown at 808 E. Jefferson St., 602/262-9256, has real Southern cookin' and plenty of it. The menu written on the wall lists such favorites as fried chicken, pork chops, catfish, and a vegetable plate with a sampling of every kind of veggie in the kitchen. After filling up on soul food, you simply tell the cashier, perhaps Mrs. White herself, what you had—that's the golden rule. Open Mon.–Fri. for lunch; $9.

Morton's of Chicago, in The Esplanade at 2501 E. Camelback Rd., 602/955-9577, is a link in the famous steakhouse chain. Open daily for dinner; $20–34, reservations suggested.

Wright's, in the Arizona Biltmore Resort, Missouri Ave. and 24th St., 602/954-2507, presents Contemporary American cuisine with excellent service and a Frank Lloyd Wright-style decor. Patio and wine cellar dining are available too. Open daily for dinner; $27–31, reservations suggested.

Vincent Guerithault on Camelback, 3930 E. Camelback Rd., 602/224-0225, prepares imaginative Southwestern cuisine with first-rate service. Open weekdays for lunch and nightly for dinner (closed Sun.–Mon. in summer); $18–32, reservations recommended. Dress code is "business casual."

Seafood

At **The Fish Market,** 1720 E. Camelback Rd., 602/277-3474, the main restaurant downstairs features mesquite-grilled fish and New England-style seafood. It's open daily for lunch and dinner; $12–21. The upstairs "Top of the Market" room features gourmet dining; open daily for dinner only; $14–26. You can also drop by the oyster bar, sushi bar, and fresh-fish sales counter.

Steamers, in Biltmore Fashion Park at 24th St. and Camelback Rd., 602/956-3631, prepares seafood daily for lunch and dinner; $19–68 (about $24 average), reservations recommended.

Western

Harris', 3101 E. Camelback Rd., 602/508-8888, offers choice beef cuts cooked to your specifications, along with other meat and fish offerings in an elegant Southwest setting. Open Mon.–Fri. for lunch and Mon.–Sat. for dinner; $13–32, reservations recommended.

Mexican and Latin American

Aunt Chilada's has a century-old, general-store ambience. Choose from two locations: across from Pointe Hilton Resort at Squaw Peak, 7330 N. Dreamy Draw Dr., 602/944-1286; or in Pointe Hilton Resort at South Mountain, 2021 W. Baseline Rd., 602/431-6470. Both are open daily for lunch and dinner; $10–18, reservations recommended on weekends.

Blue Burrito Grille, 3118 E. Camelback Rd., 602/955-9596, features many healthful, low-fat items. Open daily for lunch and dinner; about $6.

Eliana's, 1627 N. 24th St., 602/225-2925, offers home-cooked Salvadoran food. Open daily except Monday for lunch and dinner; $8–10.

Havana Cafe, 4225 E. Camelback Rd., 602/952-1991, will give you a taste of Cuban, Spanish, and some South American foods. Open Mon.–Sat. for lunch and nightly for dinner; most $9–13.

La Parrilla Suiza prepares authentic Mexico City food, including vegetarian specials. Open daily for lunch and dinner, $6–10, at two locations: 3508 W. Peoria Ave., 602/978-8334; and 13001 N. Tatum Blvd., 602/996-6479.

Pancho's Mexican Buffet, 1003 E. Indian School Rd., 602/285-0899, offers excellent value. Open daily for lunch and dinner; about $6.

San Carlos Bay, 1901 E. McDowell Rd., 602/340-0892, specializes in Mexican seafood. Open daily for lunch and dinner; $11–16.

International

RoxSand, in Biltmore Fashion Park at 2594 E. Camelback Rd., 602/381-0444, presents food from many lands. Open daily for lunch and dinner; $20–28, reservations recommended.

French

Bistro 24, in the Ritz-Carlton, 2401 E. Camelback Rd., 602/468-0700, has a casual atmosphere in an elegant setting. Open daily for breakfast, lunch, and dinner; $18–27.

Sophisticated yet fun, **Coup des Tartes,** in a small house at 4626 N. 16th St., 602/212-1082, serves eclectic French and other cuisines. Open Tues.–Sat. for dinner; $17–25 (bring your own wine, $8 corkage fee), reservations recommended.

Italian

Avanti's, 2728 E. Thomas Rd., 602/956-0900, offers a varied menu including Italian cuisine. Open Mon.–Fri. for lunch and nightly for dinner; $17–32.

California Pizza Kitchen, in the Biltmore Fashion Park at 24th St. and Camelback Rd., 602/553-8382, prepares gourmet pizza along with pasta, soups, and salads. Open daily for lunch and dinner; $8–12.

Our Gang Pizza & Café, 9832 N. Seventh St., 602/870-4122, serves great Italian food in a New York atmosphere. Open Tues.–Sun. for dinner; $7–17.

Downtown in Heritage Square, **Pizzeria Bianco,** 623 E. Adams St., 602/258-8300, has creative pizzas, salads, and antipasti in a historic brick building. Open Tues.–Sun. for dinner; $8–12. Bar Bianco next door serves wine, beer, and appetizers.

Pronto Ristorante, 3950 E. Campbell Ave., 602/956-4049, serves regional Italian cuisine in a wood-paneled dining area decorated with antique clocks and musical instruments. Open Mon.–Fri. for lunch and nightly for dinner; $12–19, reservations recommended.

Tomaso's, 3225 E. Camelback Rd., 602/956-0836, prepares northern and central Italian and some Sicilian offerings. Open Mon.–Fri. for lunch and nightly for dinner; $12–30, reservations recommended.

Greek

Greekfest, 1940 E. Camelback Rd., 602/265-2990, serves tasty food in elegant surroundings. Open daily except Sunday for lunch and dinner; $10–25, reservations recommended.

Middle Eastern

The owner of **Mediterranean House,** 1588 E.

Bethany Home Rd., 602/248-8460, has an Israeli and Yemeni background. The restaurant is open Mon.–Fri. for lunch and Mon.–Sat. for dinner; $8–15.

Indian

Downtown, try the **Bombay Grill,** 27 W. Van Buren St., 602/256-0080, for a large selection of flavorful vegetarian and meat dishes of north India. Open Mon.–Sat. for lunch (buffet available) and dinner; $7–15.

In east Phoenix, the popular **Indian Delhi Palace,** 5050 E. McDowell Rd., 602/244-8181, offers north Indian food. Open daily for lunch with a great-value buffet and dinner; $6–18. Next door, **House of Asian Spices** sells imported groceries if you'd like to try your hand at cooking South Asian cuisine.

Nearby **Kohinoor Sweets & Snacks,** 5030 E. McDowell Rd., 602/244-0809, has a basic café where you can get south Indian masala dosas and other tasty fare, as well as heavenly sweets and spicy munchies. Open daily for lunch and Tues.–Sun. for dinner; about $4.

In north Phoenix, **Delhi Palace,** 16842 N. Seventh St. at Bell Rd., 602/942-4224, prepares excellent vegetarian and nonvegetarian food in tandoori and other north Indian styles. Open daily for lunch and dinner; $7–14. The lunch buffet is a great value.

Also in north Phoenix, **Taste of India,** 1609 E. Bell Rd., 602/788-3190, is another north Indian restaurant serving both vegetarian and meat-based entrees. Open daily for lunch (including a buffet) and dinner; $7–14.

Chinese

The **Chinese Cultural Center,** a modern "Chinatown" with distinctive architecture, offers four restaurants, a large oriental supermarket, and a few specialty shops. Look for the tile roofs at 668 N. 44th St. (west side between Van Buren and McDowell Streets). Your dining choices are: **Ichi Ban Sushi Buffet,** 602/914-9221, which offers an amazing variety and quality of Japanese and Chinese food—all served buffet style—including sushi, seafood and meat dishes, soups, and salads. It's an oriental splurge but reason-

ably priced for all you get; closed Mon.; $14 lunch, $21 dinner, less for kids. **Szechwan Palace,** 602/685-0888, fixes flavorful dishes including kung pao and Szechwan styles from their long menu of seafood, meat, and vegetable dishes. Open daily for lunch (specials Mon.–Fri.) and dinner; $6–14 (some seafood is higher). **Lao Ching Hing,** 602/286-6168, specializes in Shanghai cuisine with other popular and authentic styles too; the Peking duck ($27) must be ordered 24 hours in advance. Open daily for lunch (specials Mon.–Fri.) and dinner; $7–13 most dishes. **Sampan Seafood Restaurant,** 602/286-9888, has a nautical décor for its mostly Cantonese and some Mandarin cuisine. Tanks hold live fish, lobster, and crab for many of the menu options so you know that you're getting it fresh. You can also order meat and vegetable items including Peking duck and kung pao chicken or choose from the hot pot menu. Open daily for lunch (a buffet is available Mon.–Fri.) and dinner; $7–30. For a quick snack, you could drop in **99 Ranch Market's** deli section.

China Doll, 3336 N. Seventh Ave. (at Osborn Rd.), 602/264-0538, offers a large selection of Cantonese specialties, including lunchtime dim sum. The shrimp in garlic sauce is a favorite. Open daily for lunch and dinner; $7–10 (seafood is higher).

Golden Phoenix, 6048 N. 16th St., 602/263-8049, serves good Mandarin, Cantonese, and Szechwan styles. Open Sun.–Fri. for lunch and daily for dinner; $6–8.

Gourmet House of Hong Kong, 1438 E. McDowell Rd., 602/253-4859, has tasty food near downtown. Open Mon.–Fri. for lunch and daily for dinner; $7–12.

At **Great Wall Cuisine,** 5057 N. 35th Ave., 602/973-1112, lunch-time dim sum will come to you—just wave over a cart operator when something good catches your eye. Dinners are from the regular menu. Open daily for lunch and dinner; $6–20.

Vegetarian House has a new location at 3239 E. Indian School Rd., 602/264-3480, for its long, varied, and strictly vegetarian Chinese menu. According to the menu: "To eat vegetarian food often will be beneficial to your health, and remove miscellaneous matters from your body and help to enhance happiness and wisdom." The Suma Ching Hai Intl. Assoc. runs the restaurant and sells books and videos on their teachings; you can buy meatless ingredients, too. Open Tues.–Sat. for lunch and dinner; $6–9.

Thai

Thai Rama, 1221 W. Camelback Rd., 602/285-1123, offers inexpensive northern Thai food on a varied menu. Open Mon.–Fri. for lunch and daily for dinner; $7–10.

Vietnamese

Pho Bang, 1702 W. Camelback Rd., 602/433-9440, has great food, including some do-it-yourself grills. The simple restaurant is open daily for lunch and dinner; $4–17.

Tu Do, 7828 N. 19th Ave., just south of Northern Ave., 602/864-6759, is a good choice in the north Valley. Open daily for lunch and dinner; $4–16.

Japanese

The chefs at **Ayako of Tokyo,** Biltmore Fashion Park, 2564 E. Camelback Rd., 602/955-7007, offer teppanyaki tabletop cooking, tempura, and a sushi bar. Open Mon.–Fri. for lunch and nightly for dinner; $12–36.

Tokyo Express offers inexpensive and good fast food. Open daily for lunch and dinner at several locations, including 3517 E. Thomas Rd., 602/955-1051; 5130 N. 19th Ave., 602/433-1311; 914 E. Camelback Rd., 602/277-4666; 4105 N. 51st Ave., 602/245-1166; and 267 E. Bell Rd., 602/564-9585.

Tempe

Enterprising merchant Charles Trumbull Hayden arrived here in 1871 to set up a trading post. He liked this spot on the south bank of the Salt River because it was the safest place to cross with his freight wagons. Hayden also found it a good location for his flour mill and ferry service.

Darrel Duppa came over from Phoenix to visit Hayden's ferry one day, and he remarked that the Salt River Valley reminded him of the Vale of Tempe between Mt. Olympus and Mt. Ossa in Thessaly, Greece. Hayden liked the name and, eventually, it stuck.

Farmers settled in Tempe (tem-PEE), raising livestock, establishing a dairy, and growing a variety of crops. In 1885 the Territorial Legislature established nearby Arizona State Teachers College, now Arizona State University (ASU); it has since grown into one of the largest schools in the country. Sandwiched between Phoenix to the west and Mesa to the east, Tempe (pop. 163,000) lies just south of Scottsdale.

Downtown Tempe offers more than 140 cafés, restaurants, nightspots, bookstores, and specialty shops along and just off Mill Avenue. Brick-paved sidewalks shaded by trees invite a stroll. The Tempe Convention & Visitors Bureau, 51 W. Third St., can fill you in on local events and services.

Many of Tempe's original buildings have survived. Charles Hayden's home at First St. and Mill Ave. dates from the early 1870s and is now La Casa Vieja Restaurant. His flour mill (rebuilt in 1918 after a fire) and the 1951 grain elevator stand across Mill Avenue. Other notable historic structures downtown include the 1888 Hackett House/Tempe Bakery (now a gift shop) at 95 W. Fourth St.; the 1899 Hotel Casa Loma (now Mill Landing Restaurant) at 398 S. Mill Ave.; the Laird and Dines Building at 501 S. Mill Ave.; and the Tempe Hardware Building at 520 S. Mill Avenue. Architecture that would have surprised the pioneers lies to the east; the glass-and-steel city hall, at 31 E. Fifth St., is an upside-down pyramid, and an Arab-styled mosque stands at Sixth and Forest Streets.

Parking and Getting Around

The parking garage at Hayden Square is a good bet downtown; the nearby Visitors Bureau and other area businesses will validate your parking. Enter the garage by turning west one block on Third or Fifth Sts. from Mill Avenue. You can also park at the metered spaces in front of the visitors bureau, whose staff will reimburse you, but meters have a one-hour limit.

Parking is tight on the ASU campus, but you can use metered parking spaces (one hour maximum) or several pay lots, or search for a spot on a side street off campus. Pick up a map for campus parking areas; visitors' parking is well signed. Most of the central campus is closed to motor traffic. Valley Metro, 602/253-5000, connects the university with Tempe and the rest of the Valley. The free FLASH bus service makes a loop around campus and downtown Mon.–Fri., and FLASH LITE continues out to Papago Park on Saturday and Sunday. Cyclists will find marked bike lanes; local bike shops and the visitors bureau have maps. Both motorists and pedestrians have to be on the lookout for bicycle riders, especially at night when they may zip without lights down streets and sidewalks.

TEMPE SIGHTS

Tempe Historical Museum

This attractive museum portrays many aspects of Tempe. The large main gallery presents history as an ongoing process, from its reconstruction of a Hohokam archaeological dig to the present time. Exhibits include many historical photos, an interactive model of the Salt River and canals, a fire station, and video programs. Other facilities include a research reading room and gift shop.

The museum is at 809 Southern Ave. (at Rural Rd.), 480/350-5100, 480/350-5125 (recording); www.tempe.gov/museum. It's open Sunday 1–5 P.M. and Mon.–Thurs. and Saturday 10 A.M.–5 P.M.; closed Fridays and major holidays. Free admission; donations are welcome.

Niels Petersen House

Built in 1892, this Queen Anne/Victorian-style home used a clever ventilation system to keep the interior livable in summer. You can tour the inside, restored to its 1930s' Bungalow appearance, and learn how Neils Petersen contributed to Tempe's early growth. Outside, a small park offers picnic tables and a playground.

The house is at 1414 W. Southern Ave. (at Priest Dr.), 480/350-5151, 480/350-5100 (group tours). It's open Tues.–Thurs. and Saturday 10 A.M.–2 P.M. (last tour at 1:30 P.M.). Admission is free; donations are welcome.

Tempe Town Lake

A two-mile section of the barren gravel riverbed of the Salt River just north of Tempe has been transformed into a lake with parks on each shore. Inflatable dams hold the water in, which arrives via a canal. Visitors can bring their own non-motorized boats, rent one, or take a tour, but there's no swimming. Free outdoor concerts take place Sunday evenings in spring. Tempe Beach Park on the south shore offers picnic tables and playgrounds. Rio Lago Cruise here runs tours and rents a variety of small boats; 480/517-4050.

Hayden (Tempe) Butte

A short stiff climb will take you from downtown to the rocky summit for a panorama of Tempe and beyond. Interpretive signs describe some plants and history. The trail begins on the butte's south side near the junction of Fifth St. and College Ave., beside Sun Devil Stadium.

Guadalupe

A bit of old Mexico lies just beyond southwest Tempe. Yaqui and Mexican-Americans offer restaurants, fruit stands, bakeries, and craft shops in this small, slightly run-down community. Most of the shopping is along Avenida del Yaqui (Priest Dr.) between Guadalupe and Baseline Roads. The large white Yaqui Temple and Our Lady of Guadalupe Church can be seen one block west. For more information about the town, contact the Town Hall, 9050 S. Avenida del Yaqui, Guadalupe, AZ 85283; 480/730-3080.

ARIZONA STATE UNIVERSITY

When the Arizona Legislature founded ASU in 1885, classes met in a four-room, red-brick structure set on 20 acres of cow pasture. Today, broad lawns, stately palms, and flowering subtropical trees grace the 700-acre campus of Arizona's largest university. Growth has been spectacular in the last 30 years; the school now has more than 44,000 students and an instructional and research faculty of about 1,800. Approximately 5,000 students attend the 300-acre ASU West campus in Phoenix, while another 1,000 students take classes at the ASU East campus in Mesa. Undergraduates can choose from 88 majors, while graduate students can earn a master's degree in 97 subjects or a doctorate in 52.

Attractions on campus include the striking Gammage Auditorium, art galleries, and a variety of small museums. The well-landscaped grounds offer pleasant walking; you can learn about points of interest and flora with the *Self-Guided Walking Tour to the Main Campus* and *Arizona State University Arboretum Guide* pamphlets, both free at ASU's visitor center. Activity slows down a bit in summer—it's *hot*—but most of the galleries and museums stay open, except as noted below.

Tours of campus start at the Student Services Building and last 50–60 minutes; they leave Mon.–Fri. at 10:30 A.M. and 2 P.M.; 480/965-2604. The domed **visitor center,** 826 E. Apache Blvd. (at Rural Rd.), 480/965-0100, is open Mon.–Fri. 8:15 A.M.–4:45 P.M. and has free parking; you can pick up Arizona tourist literature too. ASU's website, www.asu.edu, lists exhibits, libraries, events, and has some enormous databases. Museum collections with maps and links are listed at www.asu.edu/museums.

Gammage Auditorium

You'll see this circular structure, commemorating a former ASU president, on the southwest corner of campus. Dedicated in 1964, the 3,000-seat auditorium was the last major building designed by Frank Lloyd Wright. Free half-hour tours are offered, Oct. 1 to mid-May, Mon.–Fri. 1–3:30 P.M.; call 480/965-4050 the day before to get on a tour. You can reach the box office at 480/965-3434. The many cultural offerings here include Broadway plays. The auditorium is easy to spot, set into a curve where Apache Boulevard meets Mill Avenue.

ASU Art Museum

The **Nelson Fine Arts Center** has galleries dedicated to American, Latin American, and con-

temporary art, prints, and crafts. The American Gallery traces themes from early portraiture to landscapes and abstract art. The other galleries usually have shows of contemporary art. You can also explore several outdoor terraces and see additional sculpture. A gift shop sells a variety of crafts. The museum is highly recommended for its quality, size, diversity, and unusual architecture.

Architect Antoine Predock designed the center to provide a "village-like aggregation of buildings" housing the arts. Aspects of the existing campus and the Southwest can be seen in the choice of materials, forms, and colors. Light coming in from skylights reflects off surfaces a total of 10 times before illuminating the artwork—a process meant to deflect the harmful qualities of daylight.

Nelson Fine Arts Center, 480/965-2787, is on the southeast corner of Mill Ave. and 10th St., on the west side of campus. Museum hours are Sunday 1–5 P.M., Tuesday 10 A.M.–9 P.M. (5 P.M. in summer), and Wed.–Sat. 10 A.M.–5 P.M.; closed Monday and major holidays. Admission is free. In addition to the museum, the Center is home to the Galvin Playhouse and University Dance Laboratory. You can park in front at the meters or in the nearby visitor parking lot. Visit on the Web at http://asuartmuseum.asu.edu.

Harry Wood Gallery

Here you can peruse exhibitions of paintings, photography, or sculpture by Master of Fine Arts students. The gallery, 480/965-3468, is in the School of Arts building and open Mon.–Thurs. 9 A.M.–5 P.M. and Fri. 9 A.M. to 3 P.M.; free admission.

Gallery of Design

Architecture aficionados can study the latest techniques here, illustrated by drawings and scale models, 480/965-6384. It's in the College of Architecture and Environmental Design, which also holds the Howe Library of Architecture. Hours are Mon.–Fri. 8 A.M.–5 P.M.; free admission.

Northlight Gallery

This gallery features photographic exhibits, both historic and contemporary. It's in Matthews Hall (behind Matthews Center), 480/965-6517. Open Sun. 12:30–4:30 P.M. and Mon.–Thurs. 10:30 A.M.–4 P.M.; free admission. The gallery closes in summer.

Museum of Anthropology

Displays illustrate prehistoric Hohokam and modern Native American cultures, archaeological techniques, and concepts of anthropology. The museum is in the Anthropology Building, next to Matthews Center, 480/965-6213. Hours are Mon., Wed., and Fri. noon–4 P.M., and Tues. and Thurs. 10 A.M.–2 P.M. (in summer, hours are Mon.–Fri. 10 A.M.–2 P.M.); free admission.

Hayden Library

The university's main library, 480/965-6164, houses the Arizona, Chicano, and East Asian special collections, along with the Labriola National American Indian Data Center and government documents. Staff can also tell you of specialized libraries at other campus locations. Computers provide access to library holdings and the Internet. Hours are Sunday 10 A.M.–midnight, Mon.–Thurs. 7 A.M.–midnight, Friday 7 A.M.–7 P.M., and Saturday 9 A.M.–5 P.M.; hours are shorter during summer and academic breaks and for the special collections; www.asu.edu/lib.

Memorial Union

This is university social center. The main floor information desk, 480/965-5728, can tell you about the latest concerts, theater performances, art shows, and sporting events. It's open daily from early morning to late at night (shorter hours in summer and breaks).

Memorial Union Art Gallery, at the north end of the building, often hosts visiting shows; it's open Mon.–Fri. 8 A.M.–5 P.M. More than a dozen eateries offer fast food along the way, or you can stop in at Union Square for regular cafeteria meals. Relax downstairs in a lounge or patio, go bowling, play a game of billiards, or see a movie.

ASU Bookstore

Offerings include general-interest books, textbooks, supplies, maps, and Sun Devils souvenirs, 480/965-4170 or http://bookstore.asu.edu.

Life Sciences Center

Meet the university's live rattlesnakes, Gila monster, and other reptiles in hallway exhibits at the Life Sciences Center, 480/965-3369. Open Mon.–Fri. 8 A.M.–5 P.M.; free admission.

Center for Meteorite Studies

See visitors from outer space in Room C-139 and the adjacent hallways of the Physical Sciences Building. This collection of more than 1,400 items is reportedly one of the world's largest of its kind. It's open Mon.–Fri. 8:30 A.M.–4 P.M.; free admission. For more information call 480/965-3576.

Geology Museum

Here you can check the six-story Foucault pendulum to see if the earth is still spinning, or watch the seismograph to learn if it's shaking. Exhibits illustrate geologic processes and identify rocks, minerals, and fossils. The museum is in F Wing of the Physical Sciences Building, 480/965-7065. It's open Mon.–Fri. 9 A.M.–noon; free admission.

ASU Planetarium

You can attend one-hour star shows at ASU's Planetarium in the Physical Sciences Building for just $2 per person. Call for show times during vacations or to arrange a group show; 480/965-6891.

Daniel E. Noble Science Library

Here you'll find books used by the nearby science and engineering departments. Computers allow you to look up collections or browse the Internet. Hikers can plan trips using the map collection and make needed photocopies. Inventors can see if they're first with a bright new idea in the U.S. Patents & Trademark Depository Library.

Hours for the main collection, during regular academic terms, are Mon.–Thurs. 7 A.M.–midnight, Friday 7 A.M.–7 P.M., Saturday 9 A.M.–5 P.M., and Sunday 10 A.M.–midnight. The map collection is open Mon.–Thurs. 8 A.M.–8 P.M. and Friday 8 A.M.–5 P.M. (closed weekends). For more information call 480/965-7607, 480/965-3582 (map collection), or 480/965-3415 (recorded hours); www.asu.edu/lib/noble.

Sports

ASU has fielded some top teams. Trophies, clippings, and photos are on display at the **Sports Hall of Fame,** housed in the circular corridor of the Wells Fargo Arena; open Mon.–Fri. 8 A.M.–5 P.M. The giant 74,000-seat Sun Devil Stadium hosts football games, while the 14,000-seat Wells Fargo Arena serves ASU's basketball squads. Baseball plays in the 8,000-seat Packard Stadium. Buy tickets to games in front of the stadium at the Sun Devils Athletic Ticket Office; 480/965-2381; www.thesundevils.com. Tours of the Wells Fargo Arena and Sun Devil Stadium are available; 480/965-3933.

TEMPE ACCOMMODATIONS

$50–100

University Motel, 902 S. Mill Ave., 480/966-7221, features a pool and a great location for downtown and ASU; $55–75 s, $65–80 d. East of ASU, **Hideaway Lodge Motel,** 1461 E. Apache Blvd., 480/829-8829, offers a pool and some kitchenettes; $50 d room, $55 d kitchenette. About two miles east of ASU is **Econo Lodge of Tempe,** 2101 E. Apache Blvd., 480/966-5832, 800/207-1317, with a pool, $59–69 s, $79–89 d. About a mile southwest of downtown and ASU is **Motel 6,** 513 W. Broadway Rd., 480/967-8696, 800/4MOTEL6, with a pool, $50 s, $56 d. Just east of ASU, **Tempe Travelodge,** 1005 E. Apache Blvd., 480/968-7871, 800/578-7878, has two pools; $50 d. Also nearby with pool and hot tub are **Super 8,** 1020 E. Apache Blvd., 480/967-8891, 800/800-8000, $48 s, $58 d; and **Days Inn,** 1221 E. Apache Blvd., 480/968-7793, 800/329-7466, $79 d.

$100–150

Holiday Inn, 915 E. Apache Blvd., 480/968-3451, 800/HOLIDAY, is just southeast of ASU and has a pool, hot tub, and Ducks Restaurant; $119–124 d.

Fiesta Inn, 2100 S. Priest Dr., 480/967-1441, 800/528-6481, has a pool, hot tub, and tennis courts in western Tempe; $135 d.

Country Suites by Carlson, 1660 W. Elliot Rd., 480/345-8585, 800/456-4000, is in the southwestern part of town convenient to I-10. Guests have a pool, hot tub, and nearby fitness center; $109 d for a studio and $119–139 d for a suite.

$150 and up

Tempe Mission Palms, 60 E. Fifth St., 480/894-1400, 800/547-8705, has an ideal location close to both ASU and downtown. Amenities include a pool, exercise room, and tennis courts. The Mission Grill serves Southwestern food. Deluxe rooms ($219–269 d) overlook a courtyard with pool and gardens, standard rooms ($169–199 d) face outside.

Towering seven floors just south across from ASU, **Twin Palms Hotel,** 225 E. Apache Blvd., 480/967-9431, 800/367-0835, offers guests a pool and use of ASU recreation facilities; $139–159 s, $149–169 d.

Courtyard by Marriott, 601 Ash Ave., 480/966-2800, 800/321-2211, features spacious rooms, a pool, and a Jacuzzi near downtown and ASU, $179 d.

Sheraton Airport Hotel, 1600 S. 52nd. St. in western Tempe, 480/967-6600, 800/325-3535, has a pool and a hot tub; $196 d.

The Wyndham Buttes Resort, 2000 Westcourt Way, 602/225-9000, 800/WYNDHAM, has a scenic setting among the Tempe Buttes with restaurants, a health club, pool, and tennis. It's near the southeast corner of Broadway and 48th St., convenient to Tempe and the airport; $189 d room, $475 d suite.

TEMPE RV PARKS

The adult **Green Acres RV Park III,** 1890 E. Apache Blvd., 480/829-0106, lies one mile east of the ASU campus; $20 RV with hookups. Two others are nearby: **Apache Palms RV Park,** 1836 E. Apache Blvd., 480/966-7399, $22 and $29 RV with hookups; and the adults-only **Tempe Travel Trailer Villa,** 1831 E. Apache Blvd., 480/968-1411, about $20 RV with hookups.

TEMPE FOOD

American

Gentle Strength Cooperative, 234 W. University Dr., near ASU, 480/968-4831, fixes tasty and healthy vegetarian food in their Desert Greens Café. Open Sunday for brunch, daily for lunch, and Mon.–Sat. for a light dinner; $1–5.

At **House of Tricks,** 114 E. Seventh St., 480/968-1114, chef-owners Robert and Robin Trick offer Contemporary American Eclectic cuisine. Open Mon.–Sat. for lunch and dinner; $16–22.

Pita Jungle, 1250 E. Apache Blvd., 480/804-0234, makes some of the best vegetarian food around. Open daily for breakfast, lunch, and dinner; $4–10.

Seafood

At **Rusty Pelican,** 1606 W. Baseline Rd., 480/345-0972, the decor and food will convince you that you're beside the ocean. Open daily for lunch and dinner; $15–36.

Western

Monti's La Casa Vieja specializes in steaks for an appreciative crowd. Other meats, pasta, and seafood fill out the menu. The restaurant occupies the large, rambling 1871 Charles Hayden house; it's at Mill Ave. and First St. in the north end of downtown; 480/967-7594. Open daily for lunch and dinner; $9–25.

Middle Eastern

Close to ASU and downtown, **Phoenicia Café,** 616 S. Forest Ave., 480/967-8009, offers tasty Middle Eastern food, including vegetarian or meat pita boats. Open daily for lunch and dinner (from noon–7 P.M. Sunday); $3–7.

Tasty Kabob, 1250 E. Apache Blvd., 480/966-0260, brings flavors of the Persian Empire to the Valley. Open daily except Monday for lunch and dinner; $7–14.

Haji-Baba, 1513 E. Apache Blvd., 480/894-1905, prepares excellent and inexpensive Middle Eastern meals and also sells groceries, magazines, and music from that region. Open daily for lunch and dinner (closes Sunday at 6 P.M.); $5–10.

Indian

Delhi Palace, 933 E. University Ave., 480/921-2200, prepares excellent vegetarian and nonvegetarian food in tandoori and other northern Indian styles. Open daily for lunch and dinner; $7–14. The lunch buffet is a great value.

Chinese

P.F. Chang's China Bistro, 740 S. Mill Ave. (at University Dr.), 480/731-4600, combines a menu reflecting many regions of China with American hospitality—you can have coffee, wine, or dessert with your meal. Open daily for lunch and dinner; $6–14.

Vietnamese

Saigon Healthy Deli, 820 S. Mill Ave. (at University), 480/967-4199, is a simple café offering a good selection of both meat and vegetarian dishes at bargain prices. Open Mon.–Sat. for lunch and dinner; $4–6.

Japanese

Saki's Pacific Rim Café & Sushi Bar, in Centerpoint at 740 S. Mill Ave., 480/968-7300, offers contemporary presentation and decor for its Japanese and other Asian dishes. Open nightly for dinner; $8–18.

Korean

Korean Garden, near ASU at 1324 S. Rural Rd., 480/967-1133, offers authentic food in a pleasant environment. Open Mon.–Fri. for lunch and Mon.–Sat. for dinner; $11–16.

Scottsdale

Chaplain Winfield Scott, Scottsdale's first resident, fell in love with the Valley when he homesteaded here in the 1880s. During his frequent travels, he promoted the land as "unequaled in greater fertility or richer promise." A small close-knit community soon formed at Brown Avenue and Main Street.

Today the little village has grown up—215,000 people now live here. Scottsdale, once billed as "The West's Most Western Town," boasts innumerable porch-fronted shops selling Western and Native American art, international art, crafts, and Western clothing. Both residents and visitors enjoy the top-notch specialty shops, art galleries, cultural events, restaurants, resort hotels, and beautiful landscaping. Scottsdale, just east of Phoenix and just north of Tempe, serves as an ideal base for a stay in the Valley.

The Civic Center Mall area downtown makes a good starting or resting place with its fountains, sculpture, and flowers. The Scottsdale Historical Museum, tourist office, Scottsdale Center for the Arts, Museum of Contemporary Art, and a large library surround the central plaza. Scottsdale welcomes you with lots of free parking surrounding the Civic Center. Shoppers need only cross Brown Avenue to the west to visit Old Town Scottsdale's many shops and restaurants; they're centered on Brown Avenue, First Street, and Main Street. Many of the galleries stay open late and offer artist demonstrations for the Scottsdale Artwalk on Thursdays 7–9 P.M.; 480/990-3939; www.scottsdalegalleries.com.

The Scottsdale Downtown Roundup, 480/312-7696, offers a free shuttle service to central shopping areas Mon.–Sat. from mid-November to the end of May.

SIGHTS IN DOWNTOWN SCOTTSDALE

Scottsdale Historical Museum (The Little Red Schoolhouse)

Scottsdale was so small when this schoolhouse was built in 1909 that all the town's children could fit into its two classrooms. From the 1920s into the '50s, Mexican agricultural workers used the building as a schoolhouse and community center. Today, photos and artifacts in the Little Red Schoolhouse remind us of the town's past. Located near the center of the original Scottsdale, the schoolhouse makes a good place to begin a tour of the modern city. It's at 7333 E. Scottsdale Mall in the Civic Center complex, just east of the intersection of Brown Ave. and Main St.; 480/945-4499; www.scottsdalemuseum.com. Hours are Sunday noon–4 P.M. and Wed.–Sat. 10 A.M.–5 P.M.; closed July–August. You can pick up a self-guided walking-tour map of Old Town Scottsdale at the schoolhouse or the chamber of commerce.

Scottsdale Center for the Arts and Museum of Contemporary Art

Scottsdale residents have always had a keen interest in the arts. Two large buildings of this facility contain galleries of contemporary art, an 800-seat performing arts theater, a cinema, and an outdoor amphitheater. Call 480/994-2787 to find out what's coming up, or check the website at www.scottsdalearts.org. Each building has a museum store, often selling items related to current exhibits.

The center is at 7380 E. Second St. in the Civic Center complex (two blocks east of Scottsdale Rd. and two blocks south of Indian School Rd.) between the Scottsdale Historical Museum and the library. The museum is open Sunday noon–5 P.M., Tues.–Wed. 10 A.M.–5 P.M., Thurs. 10 A.M.–8 P.M., and Fri.–Sat. 10 A.M.–5 P.M.; call for extended hours in winter. Admission is $7 adult, $5 students, and free for ages 15 and under; everyone gets in free on Thursdays.

McCormick Railroad Park

Rail buffs of all ages will want to hop on a five-twelfths-scale train for a ride around this unusual park's grassy acres. You can also see a standard gauge, Mogul-type Baldwin steam engine and historic railway cars on display. The reconstructed

Stillman Station sells tickets and souvenirs. Two old railway stations house shops with souvenirs, model-train supplies, railroad books, and mementos. A Southern Pacific caboose offers snacks. On Sunday afternoons you can visit several model railroad clubs, each running a different scale train, and see live steamers. Other attractions here include playgrounds, the small Xeriscape Arboretum, and reservable picnic ramadas.

The park is at 7301 E. Indian Bend Rd., just east of Scottsdale Rd., 480/994-2312. The train rides and a 1950 carousel operate daily. Rides start at 10 A.M. The park closes between 5:30 and 7:30 P.M., depending on the month; call for summer hours.

SIGHTS NORTH OF DOWNTOWN SCOTTSDALE
Cosanti

Italian-born Paolo Soleri first came to Scottsdale in 1947 to study architecture with Frank Lloyd Wright. In 1956 Soleri started the Cosanti Foundation to design energy- and space-efficient cities. He uses the word *arcology*, a combination of "architecture" and "ecology," to describe his work.

At Cosanti, you can see some of Soleri's unique structures and learn about his ideas for making the world a better place. The gallery/gift shop sells books, a video, drawings, sculpture, and Soleri's famous windbells to help finance the foundation.

Cosanti is in Paradise Valley at 6433 E. Doubletree Ranch Rd. (look for the sign "Soleri" on the south side of the street), 480/948-6145. From central Scottsdale, go north five miles on Scottsdale Road, then turn left on Doubletree Ranch Road and continue one mile. Open Sun. 11 A.M.–5 P.M. and Mon.–Sat. 9 A.M.–5 P.M.; donations welcome.

You can also visit Soleri's town-in-the-making, Arcosanti, 65 miles north of Phoenix (described at the end of the North-Central Arizona chapter).

Rawhide Wild West Town

This replica of an 1880s' Old West town features about 25 buildings that look like a movie set. Desperadoes and other characters regularly enliven the scene, and horse-drawn carriages add a touch of retro-realism. Among the highlights are Bob Boz Bell's Wild West Museum with entertaining and informative exhibits; the Six Gun Theater's stunt action shows; and performances in the Native American village. A haunted hotel and Lost Dutchman's Mine provide additional thrills. Along with the requisite saloon and blacksmith, you'll find shops selling Western-theme goods and displaying antiques and interesting items like Tom Mix's hat and boots. Kids may have a hard time passing up the petting zoo, shooting gallery, ice cream parlor, and candy store. And when they get done there, you can buy them a ride on a stagecoach, train, horseback, or pony.

Rawhide Steakhouse serves up dinners of steak, chicken, ribs, shrimp, trout, and—for the adventurous—rattlesnake and Rocky Mountain oysters. There's even a veggie plate. Entrees range $6–26 and come with cowboy beans, corn cobette, and salad. Lunch is served Fri.–Sun. from October to May. Country Western musicians entertain in the evenings.

The Sundown Cookout and Western Luau begins with a hay-wagon ride to the cookout site for food and song; $28 adults, $16 children under 12, call for the seasonal schedule and to make reservations.

Rawhide, 480/502-1880, 800/527-1880, is at 23023 N. Scottsdale Rd., about 13 miles north of central Scottsdale. (Follow Scottsdale Road four miles north from downtown and look for it north of Bell Road and one block before Pinnacle Peak Road.) The town is open evenings 5–10 P.M. all year, extended on Fri.–Sun. to 11 A.M.–10 P.M. from October to May. There's an admission fee that depends on what package of attractions and shows that you purchase. See the latest info online at www.rawhide.com.

sculpture in front of Rawhide Wild West Town

SOUTH-CENTRAL

Heard Museum North

The Heard Museum offers a gallery and gift shop in El Pedregal Festival Marketplace, 34505 N. Scottsdale Rd. (at Carefree Hwy.), 480/488-9817. It's open Sun. noon–5 P.M. and Mon.–Sat. 10 A.M.–5:30 P.M. (5 P.M. in summer); admission is $2 adults, $1 children 5–12.

Cave Creek and Carefree

The adjacent towns of Cave Creek and Carefree lie in the foothills about 25 miles northwest of downtown Scottsdale and 30 miles north of downtown Phoenix. They fit well into a scenic drive between northern Scottsdale and northern Phoenix.

Carefree has one of the world's largest sundials, many art shops, and several restaurants. This is your chance to be on "Easy Street" and to find out what happens where Ho and Hum Roads meet!

In Cave Creek, the **Cave Creek Museum** offers a look at the town's past. The museum's Ar-chaeology Wing holds a fine collection of pottery, baskets, and other crafts from prehistoric and modern times. The Pioneer Wing displays aspects of early mining, ranching, and home life. Walk out back to see an early 1920s' tubercular cabin and a small church. There's a well-preserved mining arrastre (ca. 1900) in front. A gift shop offers books and crafts of Native Americans and the Southwest. The museum is on Basin Road, a quarter-mile south of Cave Creek Road, 480/488-2764. It's open Oct.–May, Wed.–Sun. 1–4:30 P.M.; admission is free.

About one mile east of Cave Creek Museum, **Gateway Desert Awareness Park** offers a short nature trail with interpretive signs (the museum may have a trail booklet). From Cave Creek Road, turn north one block on Vermeersch Road (beside the Jackalope Café), then park on the right before the road crosses a wash. Continue on foot along the road across the wash, then look for the trail on the left. The trail ends across from the **Desert Heritage Center,** which has some exhibits, the short Saguaro Trail, and an amphitheater.

The **Carefree/Cave Creek Chamber of Commerce** is in Carefree's Marywood Plaza, at the southeast corner of Tom Darlington and Cave Creek Rds. (P.O. Box 734, Carefree, AZ 85377), 480/488-3381. It's open Mon.–Fri. 9 A.M.–4 P.M.; www.arizonaguide.com/cfcc.

To reach Cave Creek and Carefree from Scottsdale, follow Scottsdale Road (turns into Tom Darlington) north to its end. From Phoenix, drive north on Cave Creek Road, or take I-17 north to Carefree Highway/AZ 74 (Exit 223), and head east 10.2 miles.

Bartlett Reservoir

Bartlett, and Horseshoe Reservoir upstream on the Verde River, offer fine scenery and outdoor recreation. People come to fish in both lakes for largemouth bass, catfish, crappie, bluegill, and carp. Horseshoe also supports endangered razorback sucker and Colorado pikeminnow, which must be returned to the water. At each reservoir, you'll need to pay daily use fees at vending machines of $4/vehicle and $2/boat, but there's no additional charge for camping. For more information, contact the **Cave Creek Ranger Station,** 40202 N. Cave Creek Rd. (Scottsdale, AZ 85262), 480/595-3300, open Mon.–Fri. 8 A.M.–5 P.M.; www.fs.fed.us/r3/tonto. You'll pass the ranger station on the left just after turning off Cave Creek Road toward the reservoirs.

The main road to Bartlett ends at Jojoba Boating Site, which has a paved boat ramp. A sign says that RV camping is permitted here from Oct. 31 to May 1. The nearby sheriff's office is staffed on summer weekends and has an emergency phone. **Jojoba Trail** begins on the north side of the parking area here and winds north about one mile through granite boulders and desert plants. The Mazatzal Mountains soar into the sky across the lake. Bartlett Lake Marina, just south of Jojoba Boating Site, provides two convenience stores, pontoon boat rentals, wet and dry storage, auto and boat fuel, and bait and tackle year-round; 602/316-3378; www.bartlettlake.com. Continue south 2.1 miles

past the marina turnoff on an unpaved road through boulder-strewn hills for Riverside Campground (vault toilets but no drinking water) below the dam.

North Lake Road (Forest Road 459) leads to recreation areas on the lake; the turnoff from the main road is half a mile before Jojoba Boating Site. In 0.6 mile you'll reach the entrance for Rattlesnake Cove Recreation Site, a day-use area with water, shaded tables, grills, restrooms, and fishing pier. Pavement ends in another 2.5 miles at Yellow Cliffs Boating Site, which has a paved boat ramp, water, and restrooms. Primitive camping is just beyond at S. B. Cove. The road ends 0.7 farther at Bartlett Flat, popular with boaters and campers; outhouses are the only facilities.

From the town of Cave Creek, go east seven miles on Cave Creek Road, turn right and drive six miles on Forest Road 205, then continue eight miles on Forest Road 19 to the lake. These roads are paved and make a great scenic drive, especially on weekdays when traffic is light.

Horseshoe Lake

Upstream from Bartlett, this reservoir offers a quieter experience. The road is unpaved and facilities are very basic. Personal watercraft and water-skiing are not permitted, and there's a 15-mph speed limit. Follow directions to Bartlett except turn left at the intersection of Forest Roads 19 and 205 and take unpaved Forest Road 205 for 10 miles all the way to the dam. You can stay on the Verde River at Mesquite Recreation Site, which has tables, grills, and outhouses in a mesquite grove; the turnoff is 8.2 miles in on your right. Horseshoe Campground offers similar facilities near the river 1.5 miles farther. Catfish Point nearby has river access just below the dam; you can hand launch boats here. Canoeists enjoy the eight miles of river between Horseshoe and Bartlett. (For information on flow and lake levels, call the Salt River Project at 602/236-5929.) A few shaded picnic tables overlook the lake near road's end. The boat ramp here is paved, but narrow and only usable at higher lake levels. Visitors pay the same daily fees as at Bartlett: $4/vehicle and $2/boat.

Sears-Kay Ruin

About 900 years ago, the Hohokam built this hilltop village, one of a series between the Valley and the mountains to the north. A one-mile loop trail climbs to the 40-room pueblo and its main plaza, laboriously constructed with a retaining wall. On top, you'll enjoy a great view of Weaver's Needle in the Superstitions, Four Peaks, the fountain in Fountain Hills, and more hills to the north. The trailhead has a few covered picnic tables for day use only; no water or fee. Follow Cave Creek Road east from Carefree, turn left (north) 2.6 miles on Forest Road 24 at the Bartlett Lake junction (the last one-third mile of Forest Road 24 is gravel), then right at the sign.

Mistress Mine

In another 1.3 miles north of the Sears-Kay Ruin, you can stop on the left to visit a rock shop, see a little museum near the old mine shaft, or do some gold panning. It's open daily 10 A.M.–6 P.M.; 480/488-0842.

Seven Springs Campground

Large sycamore and ash trees provide shade for this and adjacent **CCC Campground** among hills of the Tonto National Forest, north of the Valley. Sites have picnic tables and pit toilets but no drinking water; $4/vehicle. From the town of Cave Creek go seven miles east on Cave Creek Road to a junction, then keep left on Forest Road 24. It becomes dirt after 2.3 miles, then it's another 11 miles of scenic, winding road to the two campgrounds. **Cave Creek Campground,** a mile farther, is a group fee area requiring reservations; 480/595-3300. The Cave Creek Trail System offers about 30 miles of trails for hikers, horseback riders, and mountain bikers.

Bloody Basin Road

Drivers with high-clearance vehicles can leave the crowds behind on this 60-mile scenic back road through the Tonto National Forest. The road connects Carefree/Cave Creek with I-17 Exit 259 (Bloody Basin/Crown King). You'll enjoy views of the Mazatzals, rugged high-desert hill country, and wooded canyons. In Bloody Basin, 26 miles from I-17, a very bumpy side road goes southeast 12 miles to the Verde River and Sheep Bridge, where hikers can head into the Mazatzal Wilderness. Primitive camping is possible almost anywhere in Tonto National Forest, or you can stop at Seven Springs or CCC Campgrounds near the southern end of Bloody Basin Road. Follow directions to Seven Springs Campground above, then continue north on Forest Road 24.

SIGHTS EAST OF DOWNTOWN SCOTTSDALE

Taliesin West

Considered one of renowned architect Frank Lloyd Wright's greatest masterpieces, Taliesin West began in 1937 as a winter home for Wright's school of architecture. The apprentices lived in tents and simple shelters on the property and today, more than 60 years later, they still do. Wright didn't just design buildings according to plan; he let them "grow" from the inside out. He used a similar method for training his student architects, encouraging them to grow and develop far beyond facts and formulas. Nature inspired many of Wright's ideas, which still look contemporary many decades later.

Though Wright died in 1959, the Frank Lloyd Wright School of Architecture and Taliesin Architects carry on his high standards here. Most students stay 3–5 years, living and working closely with one another and the faculty. Tour guides, docents, or (occasionally) apprentices lead a variety of walking tours through the complex.

The one-hour "Panorama" tour ($16 adults, $14 seniors and students, $3 children 4–12) takes in some of the grounds and buildings. You'll also see highlights of Wright's work in models and photos.

On the 90-minute "Insights" tour ($22 adults, $18 seniors, students, and 15 children 4–12), you also visit Wright's magnificent living room. "Desert Walks" ($20), introduce visitors to the Sonoran Desert that so inspired Wright; they last 90 minutes and run only Nov. 1 to April 15; reservations are requested and there's a discount if taken with the Panorama tour.

On the two-hour "Apprentice Shelter" tour, an apprentice will take you to the individually designed structures in the desert; tours go only on Saturdays from Dec. 1 to April 14 and cost $30; reservations are requested.

In-depth (about three hours) "Behind the Scenes" tours ($35, reservations requested) provide the most personal and best experience if you have the time and funds. Associates—some who actually worked with Wright—give presentations on life and architecture at Taliesin West as you make an extensive tour of the buildings.

Tours are less expensive and offered less frequently in summer. At any time of year, it's a good idea to call ahead and check the current schedule; 480/860-8810 (recorded information) or 480/860-2700, ext. 494 or 495. The website www.franklloydwright.org provides tour information and illustrates some of the work done here. There's a remarkable selection of related books, videos, prints, and gift items in the visitor center.

Taliesin West is set in the western foothills of the McDowell Mountains, northeast of Scottsdale. From central Scottsdale, go north seven miles on Pima Freeway 101 or Scottsdale Road, turn right about five miles on Cactus Road, cross Frank Lloyd Wright Blvd. and continue one mile farther on Taliesin Drive. From the west, you can take Bell Road/Frank Lloyd Wright Boulevard and turn left at the Cactus Road junction. From the east, take Shea Boulevard, turn north on 114th Street/Frank Lloyd Wright Boulevard, then turn right at the Cactus Road junction.

Fountain Hills

One of the world's highest artificial fountains shoots 560 feet into the air in this community 18 miles northeast of Scottsdale. A 15-minute display takes place daily on the hour, 9 A.M.–9 P.M. and is lit up at night. The surrounding park is a fine place for a picnic or stroll. From Scottsdale, go north six miles on Pima Freeway 101 or Scottsdale Road, east 12 miles on Shea Blvd., and north 2.5 miles on Saguaro Boulevard. Fountain Hills Chamber of Commerce is at 16837 E. Palisades Blvd. (P.O. Box 17598, Fountain Hills, AZ 85269), 480/837-1654, open

Mon.–Fri. 8 A.M.–5 P.M.; www.fhchamberof commerce.org.

Out of Africa Wildlife Park

This unusual zoo features big cats from all over the world in both near-natural habitats and shows. In the very popular Tiger Splash show, handlers jump in a pool and encourage the tigers to follow. Cubs may put in an appearance in other demonstrations. Colorful birds include cockatiels and a keel-billed toucan. Powerful gray and arctic wolves roam their territories. Pythons, a king cobra, and other scaly friends dwell in the reptile exhibits. Creatures such as coati, gray fox, javelina, and black-tailed prairie dogs represent Arizona wildlife. Facilities include a primitive playground, patio café, and gift shops.

Out of Africa lies east of Fountain Hills, opposite the turnoff for the Fort McDowell Indian Reservation. Take the Beeline Highway north two miles from the intersection with Shea Blvd. and turn south on Fort McDowell Road. In Oct.–May, hours are Tues.–Sun. and major holidays (except Thanksgiving and Christmas) 9:30 A.M.–5 P.M.; summer hours run Sun. 9:30 A.M.–5 P.M., Wed.–Fri. 4– 9:30 P.M., and Sat. 9:30 A.M.–9:30 P.M. A variety of shows run through the day, so you'll get the most out of a visit with an early start. Admission costs $15.25 adults, $14.15 seniors 65 and up, $5.41 children 3–12. For more information call 480/837-7779 (recording), 480/837-6683 (office), or visit www.out ofafricapark.com.

Hoo-hoogam Ki Museum

Pima and Maricopa on the Salt River Indian Reservation exhibit baskets, pottery, historic photos, and other artifacts at this museum just east of Scottsdale. The museum building incorporates adobe, desert plants, and stone in a traditional "sandwich"-style construction. A gift shop sells crafts from many tribes, and a kitchen in back serves breakfast and lunch weekdays on a patio.

The museum is at 10005 E. Osborn Rd., 480/850-8190. To get there, take Thomas or McDowell Roads east from Phoenix or Scottsdale to Longmore Road, then turn north. Hours are

Mon.–Fri. 10 A.M.–4:30 P.M. (also Saturday 10 A.M.–2 P.M. Oct.–May); closed on tribal and major American holidays; donations welcome.

SCOTTSDALE ACCOMMODATIONS

$50–100

Motel 6, 6848 E. Camelback Rd., 480/946-2280, 800/4MOTEL6, has a pool; $60 s, $68 d.

$100–150

Econolodge Scottsdale, 6935 E. 5th Ave., 480/994-9461, 800/553-2666, offers a pool and a location close to shopping; $109–117 d. **Scottsdale Pima Inn & Suites,** 7330 N. Pima Rd., 480/948-3800, 800/344-0262, has a pool, two hot tubs, sauna, and exercise center; $119 d room, $169 d suite. **Rodeway Inn,** 7110 E. Indian School Rd., 480/946-3456, 800/228-2000, offers a pool and hot tub; $109 d. **Days Inn Scottsdale Fashion Square Resort,** 4710 N. Scottsdale Rd., 480/947-5411, 800/325-2525, offers a pool, hot tub, and tennis; $124 d.

$150–200

Old Town Hotel & Conference Center, 7353 E. Indian School Rd., 480/994-9203, 800/695-6995, puts you in the heart of downtown Scottsdale next to shopping and the Civic Center Mall. Amenities include a pool, hot tub, tennis court, and health-club privileges; $145 s, $155 d. **Hospitality Suite Resort-Scottsdale,** 409 N. Scottsdale Rd., 480/949-5115, 800/445-5115, has three pools, a hot tub, tennis, and other activities; $79–109 d studio, $109–139 d suite. The Frank Lloyd Wright-style **Ramada Hotel Valley Ho Resort,** downtown at 6850 Main St., 480/945-6321, 800/272-6232, is near shopping and has three pools, three hot tubs, tennis, and a fitness center; $175 d room, $200 suite.

Resorts

The Phoenician, 6000 E. Camelback Rd., 480/941-8200, 800/888-8234, sits on 250 landscaped acres at the base of Camelback Mountain. The Valley's most lavish resort, it's rated by *Condé Nast Traveler* magazine as one of the top 10 resorts

in the world. Fountains, pools, and waterfalls grace the grounds, which also hold a 27-hole golf course, nine pools, a 165-foot water slide, and a tennis garden with 11 lighted courts. Other amenities include nine dining areas, afternoon tea, a mineral water/juice bar in the spa, poolside snacks, and an ice cream parlor. The Center for Well Being offers a fitness center, spa treatments, and a beauty salon. Kids will love the water and the Funicians Club activities. Rooms range $595–695 from Dec. 22 to May 5, $495–550 from May 6 to June 2, $245–295 from June 3 to Sept. 15, and $495–550 from Sept. 16 to Dec. 21. Incredibly luxurious suites are also available; www.thephoenician.com.

Marriott's Camelback Inn Resort, Golf Club & Spa, 5402 E. Lincoln Dr., 480/948-1700, 800/242-2635, opened in 1936 as Marriott's first resort. It features pueblo-styled casitas and suites, some with private sundecks or pools. Dining options include the Chaparral restaurant for continental fine dining, the Navajo Room for Southwest cuisine, and four other restaurants and cafés. Guests enjoy two 18-hole golf courses, six lighted tennis courts, three pools and whirlpools, and a health spa/fitness center. Rates run about $460 for casitas and $710–1135 suites from Jan. 1 to May 31, $149–240 casitas and $315–550 suites from June 1 to Sept. 11, and $309 casitas and $525–850 suites from Sept. 12 to Dec. 31; www.camelbackinn.com.

Marriott's Mountain Shadows Resort and Golf Club, 5641 E. Lincoln Dr., 480/948-7111, 800/782-2123, offers four restaurants (including an oyster bar and seafood restaurant), a lounge, an 18-hole executive golf course, three pools, two whirlpools, eight lighted tennis courts, volleyball, and a fitness center. The informal atmosphere here appeals to families and younger guests. Rooms with breakfast run $189–269 from Jan. to mid-June, $99 mid-June to mid-Sept., and $199 mid-Sept. to mid-Jan.; one-bedroom suites cost nearly double, while two-bedroom suites go for nearly triple the room rate; www.mountainshadows.net.

Orange Tree Golf Resort, 10601 N. 56th St., 480/948-6100, 800/228-0386, offers one-bedroom suites on 128 acres. Amenities include two restaurants, a café, 18 holes of golf, two pools, a hot tub, fitness center, and nearby tennis and racquetball courts. Rates run about $225 from Dec. 26 to April 15, $185 from April 16 to May 31, $125 from June 1 to Aug. 31, and $185 from Sept. 1 to Dec. 25; www.orange treegolfresort.com.

Millennium Resort Scottsdale McCormick Ranch, 7401 N. Scottsdale Rd., 480/948-5050, 800/243-1332, offers hotel rooms and two-and three-bedroom villas in a lakeside setting only three miles from Scottsdale city center. All accommodations have a patio or balcony. Amenities include a restaurant, two 18-hole golf courses, a pool and whirlpool, three lighted tennis courts, plus sailboats, paddleboats, and canoes on Camelback Lake. Hotel rooms cost $200–289 from Jan. 1 to April 30, $145–229 in May, $62–109 from June 1 to Sept. 16, and $145–229 from Sept. 17 to Dec. 31; villa rates are higher; www.millennium-hotels.com.

Scottsdale Conference Resort, 7700 E. McCormick Pkwy. in north Scottsdale, 480/991-9000, 800/528-0293, has guest rooms and suites in the three-story main building and in private casitas along the golf course. Amenities include the Palm Court restaurant for fine dining, a cocktail lounge, two 36-hole golf courses, two swimming pools, five lighted tennis courts, and a sports and fitness center. Room rates run about $360 from Jan. 5 to April 1, $250 from April 2 to May 22, $175 from May 23 to Sept. 7, $250 from Sept. 8 to Nov. 20, and $175 from Nov. 21 to Jan. 4; www.scottsconf.com.

Fairmont Scottsdale Princess, 7575 E. Princess Dr. in northern Scottsdale, 480/585-4848, 800/344-4758, features guest rooms and suites on 450 acres. The Marquesa restaurant (closed June–Aug.) prepares exceptional Spanish/Mediterranean cuisine, and the less expensive La Hacienda (closed Aug.) serves Mexican food accompanied by music from a mariachi band. Guests enjoy two other restaurants, six bars and lounges, a business center, two 18-hole golf courses, four pools, two waterslides, nine lighted tennis courts, racquetball, squash, basketball, a fitness trail, and a spa and fitness center. Players and spectators come for the Phoenix Open and a professional tennis tournament. Kids try their luck in the fishing pond. Peak season (Jan. 1–April 23) rates are $359–519 rooms, $469–569 casitas, $569–3,200 suites. Mid season (April 24–May 31 and Sept. 6–Dec. 31) runs $229–359 rooms, $339–409 casitas, $439–3,200 suites. And in summer (June 1–Sept. 5) rates drop to $159–269 rooms, $269–319 casitas, $369–3200 suites; www.fairmont.com.

The Boulders, 16 miles north of downtown Scottsdale, 480/488-9009, 800/553-1717, features a picturesque setting among natural rock formations. Dining options include the formal Latilla Room for American cuisine, the Palo Verde for Southwestern food, and Boulders Country Club for meat and seafood. Known as a premier golf and spa resort, The Boulders features two 18-hole golf courses, a driving range, four pools, eight tennis courts, jogging and hiking trails, and the Golden Door Spa with a fitness center. Individual casitas and pueblo villas fit in with the natural terrain and offer fully stocked mini-bars, patios or balconies, and wood-burning fireplaces. The resort is in Carefree, one-third mile north of el Pedregal and the Scottsdale Road-Carefree Highway junction; the business office is at el Pedregal, 34505 N. Scottsdale Rd., #K-1. In the high season (Jan. 14–April 28), casitas run $475–595 and pueblo villas go for $655–805/one bedroom, $875–1045/two bedroom, $1095–1235/three bedroom; prices decrease by about half in midsummer; www.wyndham.com.

SCOTTSDALE FOOD
American

In Old Town Scottsdale, **Arcadia Farms,** 7014 E. First Ave., 480/941-5665, creates fancy sandwiches, salads, and desserts daily for lunch. Open daily with indoor and patio seating; $9–12, reservations recommended.

Original Pancake House, 6840 E. Camelback Rd., 480/946-4902, serves some of the best breakfasts in the Valley. Open daily until 2 P.M.; $3–8.

In Old Town Scottsdale, **Sugar Bowl,** 4005 N. Scottsdale Rd. (at First Ave.), 480/946-0051, offers a myriad of tempting treats for sweet tooths in an old-fashioned ice-cream parlor. It also serves home-style meals daily for lunch and dinner; $4–8.

Seafood
Landry's Pacific Fish Company, 4321 N. Scottsdale Rd., 480/941-0602, is a good place for fresh seafood in a nautical setting. Many items are broiled over mesquite charcoal. Open daily for lunch and dinner; $19–56.

Western
Don & Charlie's, 7501 E. Camelback Rd., 480/990-0900, features top-notch steak and barbecue. Open nightly for dinner only; $13–36.

Pinnacle Peak Patio, 10426 E. Jomax (at Alma School Rd.), 480/585-1599, serves mesquite-broiled steaks and chicken in a strictly cowboy atmosphere—if you wear a tie inside, it'll be snipped off and added to the large collection hanging from the rafters. Musicians play country tunes nightly. Open Sunday for lunch and daily for dinner; $15–29. It's in the foothills of the McDowell Mountains about 20 miles northeast of Scottsdale; take Pima Road north, turn east on Happy Valley Road, then north on Alma School Road.

Rawhide Steakhouse and Saloon, 23023 N. Scottsdale Rd., 480/502-1880, offers live country-western music every night and cooks up steak, chicken, ribs, and other Western fare. It's open for lunch Fri.–Sun. from October to May and daily for dinner year-round; $6–26. Some evenings you can take a hay-wagon ride to the Sundown Cookout and Western Luau; $28 adults, $16 children under 12, call for reservations. The restaurant is 13 miles north of central Scottsdale in Rawhide Wild West Town.

Mexican
Just south of Old Town Scottsdale, **Carlsbad Tavern,** 3313 N. Hayden Rd., 480/970-8164, offers a New Mexican menu in a casual restaurant/bar setting. Open daily for lunch and dinner; $6–22.

In north Scottsdale, **Havana Patio Cafe,** 6245 E. Bell Rd., 480/991-1496, will give you a taste of Cuban, Spanish, and other Latin American foods. Open Mon.–Sat. for lunch and nightly for dinner; most entrees $9–28.

Los Olivos has offered fine food in Scottsdale since 1949. It's open daily for lunch and dinner; $7–14. Two locations: in Old Town at 7328 E. Second St., 480/946-2256; and at 15544 N. Pima Rd., 480/596-9787.

International
Marco Polo Supper Club, 8608 E. Shea Blvd., 480/483-1900, combines the flavors of Italy and Asia with great success. Open nightly for dinner; $15–30, reservations recommended.

French
Voltaire, 8340 E. McDonald Dr., 480/948-1005, is known for its superb food and friendly atmosphere. Open Mon.–Sat. for dinner only; $16–24, reservations recommended. Closed June 1–Sept. 30.

Italian
Avanti's, 3102 N. Scottsdale Rd., 480/949-8333, prepares a varied menu of Italian cuisine plus some Spanish and French items. Open nightly for dinner; $16–26.

California Pizza Kitchen, 10100 N. Scottsdale Rd., 480/596-8300, offers gourmet pizza along with pasta, soups, and salads. Open daily for lunch and dinner; $8–12.

In northern Scottsdale, **La Locanda,** 10201 N. Scottsdale Rd. (south of Shea Blvd.), 480/998-2822, serves highly rated food. Open nightly for dinner only; $14–26, reservations recommended.

Mancuso's, at the Borgata Shopping Center, 6166 N. Scottsdale Rd., 480/948-9988, cooks outstanding northern Italian and continental cuisine prepared from family recipes. Open Mon.–Sat. for lunch and nightly for dinner; $17–45, reservations recommended.

Pizzafarro's, 7120 E. Mercer Lane, 480/991-0331, rates as one of the Valley's best for pizza. Open Tues.–Fri. for lunch and Tues.–Sun. for dinner; $5–18. Also in Carefree at 36889 N. Tom Darlington Dr., 480/488-0703.

Spanish
Marquesa, in the Fairmont Scottsdale Princess, 7575 E. Princess Dr., 480/585-4848, serves fine cuisine from Catalan and the Basque

region in a Spanish-colonial decor. Open for dinner nightly and for Sunday brunch from Sept. to May; $29–43, reservations and natty attire recommended.

Indian

Jewel of the Crown, 7373 Scottsdale Mall (near Scottsdale Center for the Arts), 480/949-8000, prepares both vegetarian and meat dishes in tandoori and other north Indian styles. Open daily for lunch (there's a buffet Sat.–Sun.) and dinner; $8–16.

Chinese

China Gate, 7820 E. McDowell Rd., 480/946-0720, is a Valley favorite with the best in Mandarin, Szechuan, and Hunan cuisines. Open Mon.–Fri. for lunch and daily for dinner; $7–15.

   Sesame Inn, 13610 N. Scottsdale Rd., 480/483-9696, prepares varied cuisines. Open daily for lunch and dinner; $5–13. Another branch is farther north near Carefree at 34482 N. Scottsdale Rd., 480/595-8888.

Thai

In Old Town Scottsdale, **Mallee's on Main,** 7131 E. Main St., 480/947-6042, offers many tempting dishes of gourmet Thai food. Open Mon.–Sat. for lunch and daily for dinner; $9–20.

   Royal Barge, 8140 N. Hayden Rd., 480/443-1953, features a great selection of tasty Thai food. Open Tues.–Fri. for lunch and Tues.–Sun. for dinner; $8–15.

Japanese

RA, 3815 N. Scottsdale Rd. and First St. in Old Town Scottsdale, 480/990-9256, offers a long list of sushi items at its bar and a selection of noodle, meat, and fish entrees. Open Mon.–Fri. for lunch and nightly for dinner; $10–21.

   Sushi on Shea, 7000 E. Shea Blvd. in northern Scottsdale, 480/483-7799, offers sushi, noodles, and teriyaki dishes with a contemporary decor. Open nightly for dinner; $13–25.

Korean

Korean Restaurant, in Papago Plaza at the southwest corner of Scottsdale and McDowell Rds., 480/994-5995, serves flavorful bulkogi (barbecued beef) and other specialties; try the tangy kimchee (marinated vegetables). Open Mon.–Sat. for lunch and daily for dinner; $8–15.

Mesa

In March 1877, when a group of 84 Mormon settlers arrived here, they found a land of desert with only thin strips of vegetation lining the Salt River. The eager families immediately began rebuilding the old Hohokam irrigation canals, hoping to make the desert green and start a prosperous new life under the warm Arizona sun. Because the land reminded them of a tabletop, they named the settlement Mesa. From the tiny adobe fort used by pioneers in the first years, Mesa has grown into Arizona's third-largest city, with a population approaching half a million. More people arrive in winter to enjoy the sunny climate, the lakes, and the Superstition Mountains. Mesa, next door to Tempe and 15 miles east of Phoenix, is easily reached by the Superstition Freeway.

SIGHTS

Mesa Southwest Museum

Step into the past to experience the region and its peoples from the beginning of time to the modern era. The exhibits, greatly expanded in 2000, can be followed chronologically or in any order you like. Turn right in the lobby to enter the Tunnel of Time and see meteorites and astronomy exhibits about the universe. Next, the Hall of Minerals has some beautiful specimens along with illustrations of how rocks formed. You'll come out at Dinosaur Mountain, a towering rock face inhabited by lifelike animated beasts. Periodic thunderstorms unleash flash floods that roar down the mountain. Pictures, fossils, and realistic models trace the development of early life. Families can detour into the Discovery Resource Center to check out the hands-on exhibits and projects. Skeletons in Dinosaur Hall represent over 20 species, including a giant plant-eating Camarasaurus. Continuing to the upper gallery, you'll have another perspective of Dinosaur Mountain, see a gallery of impressive Arizona Highways photos, and go through Sonoran Desert exhibits. On entering the Paleo-Indian room, you'll pass archaeology displays and a skeleton of a mammoth. Beyond is a recreated Hohokam village with rooms furnished as if still inhabited. A gallery of Mesoamerican art contains figurines and other ceramics.

Spanish influence is seen in a replica of the Guevavi Mission (1701–1774), the first in Arizona. A short side trip leads to a grim territorial jail. A door leads to the courtyard outside where you can see a mine replica and try some gold panning. Back inside you can enter the tunnel of the Lost Dutchman Mine and discover some of its facts and mysteries. The modern era begins with exhibits of Apache and Pima and storefronts of early Mesa. The historic displays end with an entertaining "Arizona and the Movies" room. Several changing galleries and a theater room host a variety of shows about the Southwest and beyond.

A gift shop sells books and souvenirs. Staff can tell you about Mesa Grande Ruins, a nearby Hohokam village excavation that can be visited by appointment. The museum is downtown at 53 N. Macdonald St., on the corner of W. 1st St.; from the Superstition Freeway/US 60, turn north on Country Club Drive, then right on 1st Street. It's open Sun. 1–5 P.M. and Tues.–Sat. 10 A.M.–5 P.M.; admission is $6 ages 13–54, $5 seniors and students, and $3 ages 3–12; 480/644-2230 (recording).

Sirrine House

Joel Sirrine built this Queen Anne Victorian-style house in 1896 with a wraparound porch. The house contains period antiques from the early 20th century, including a 1906 washing machine. You can tour the house, one of the finest surviving from Mesa's early years, from October to late March, Sat. 10 A.M.–5 P.M. and Sun. 1–5 P.M. The tours are free. The house is downtown at 160 N. Center St., 480/644-2760.

Mesa Arts Center

Juried contemporary art exhibits from Arizona and across the country arrive here every 4–6 weeks. The Center, downtown in Galeria Mesa, 155 N. Center St., 480/644-2056, also offers concerts, classes, movies, and the Mesa Youtheatre. Gallery hours are Tues.–Fri. noon–8 P.M., Sat. noon–5 P.M.; closed the first three weeks in August. The Center will be moving to a new facility on the southeast corner of Main and Center Sts. in 2003 or 2004.

Arizona Museum for Youth

Here children can participate in art programs and view art exhibits presented just for them. Drop-in workshops take place as well. The museum is in downtown Mesa at 51 E. Main St., but it may move back to the old location, three blocks away, at 35 N. Robson St.; 480/644-2467. It's open Sun. 1–5 P.M., Tues.–Fri. 1–5 P.M. (9 A.M.–5 P.M. in summer), and Sat. 10 A.M.–5 P.M. Admission is $2.50 ages two and up; call for the exhibit schedule, which changes three times a year, and to verify the address.

Arizona Temple

Rising from beautifully landscaped gardens, the Arizona Temple of the Mormon Church rates as Mesa's most notable landmark. Workers completed the structure, based on classical Greek architecture, in 1927. Friezes at the top four corners of the exterior represent the gathering of church members from different regions of the world; brochures at the visitor center explain each of the eight scenes and the temple's history.

Marriages and other sacred ceremonies take place inside the temple, so it's not open for tours. But you're welcome to wander among the exotic plants in the gardens and view exhibits in the visitor center just north of the temple. A variety of free tours in the visitor center present the basic doctrines of the Mormon church (the Church of Jesus Christ of Latter-day Saints) through a series of videos and animated dioramas. The presentations explain the importance of

© BILL WEIR

Sentimental Journey B-17G of the Confederate Air Force, Arizona Wing, taxis in.

temples, families, the Book of Mormon, prophecy, and other aspects of Mormon beliefs. The half-hour tours run daily 9 A.M.–9 P.M. (10 A.M.–10 P.M. in December).

Special events at the Temple include the Easter Pageant during the week preceding Easter and the display of Christmas lights (600,000 of them!) that brighten the grounds from late November through December. Also during the Christmas holidays, 30-minute musical programs take place nightly at 7 P.M. If you'd like to know more about the Mormon religion, ask to see the other movies and videotapes at the visitor center, or visit www.lds.org. The Arizona Temple is at 525 E. Main St., just east of downtown; 480/964-7164.

Across the street from the temple grounds, the **Mesa Family History Center,** 41 S. Hobson, 480/964-1200, attracts many people who enjoy tracing their roots; open Mon. and Sat. 9 A.M.–5 P.M. and Tues.–Fri. 9 A.M.–9 P.M. Free admission. An introductory video will help you get started.

Mesa Historical Museum

The people of Mesa put together this remarkable collection of pioneer memorabilia and antique farm equipment. Each of the many rooms has a different theme. A video recounts Mesa's history. On guided or self-guided tours, you'll see ornate saddles, harnesses, furniture, kitchens, a gristmill, and pioneer photos. Auditorium murals depict Southwest history. The one-eighth-scale Fort Utah illustrates the history of the area's first pioneer building. An exhibit on Roosevelt Dam illustrates how the project changed the lives of those in Mesa. Antique farm machinery rests along the side and back. You can visit the museum, housed in a 1913 school building, on Tues.–Sat. 10 A.M.–4 P.M. from September to May; summer hours are Tues.–Sat. 9 A.M.–1 P.M. The museum is in north Mesa at 2345 N. Horne, 480/835-7358; www.mesaaz .org. Admission and tours are free.

On the way, you may want to stop at **Park of the Canals,** 1710 N. Horne, to see three ancient Hohokam canals. Pioneers cleared out and reused the system in 1878. The park also has picnic tables, a playground, and a small desert botanical garden; free admission.

Confederate Air Force-Arizona Wing

The World War II B-17G bomber "Sentimental Journey" stands out as the centerpiece of a remarkable collection of vintage aircraft here. The B-17G and other aircraft may be open for tours or you may be lucky enough to see one roar down the runway and take off into the skies. Even more exciting is a ride in one! Call to check on the flying schedule. Other World War II planes in the collection include a B-25 Mitchell bomber that flew missions out of Corsica, a German Heinkel HE-111 bomber, a C-45 transport, and a SNJ trainer. The hangar also houses photo exhibits, engines, and displays of radio, navigation, and gunnery equipment. The museum is at Falcon Field on the northeast corner of Greenfield and McKellips Rds. (enter from Greenfield), 480/924-1940; www.arizonawing-caf.org. It's open daily 10 A.M.–4 P.M.; admission is $5 adults, $2 ages 6–14.

Champlin Fighter Aircraft Museum

Aircraft from World War I, World War II, and the jet age draw visitors to this unique collection. Here you'll also learn about the men who flew them. Autographed photos accompany stories of fighter pilots who flew in conflicts from World War I to Vietnam. Realistic paintings show aircraft in action.

The planes themselves stand poised in three giant hangars. You'll see replicas—a 1911 Mercedes-powered Rumpler Taube—the world's first combat aircraft—and a Fokker Dr-1 triplane like the one flown by Manfred von Richthofen, the "Red Baron." Other beautifully preserved planes in the collection include a British Sopwith Camel, an extremely rare German Messerschmitt 109E, a Supermarine Spitfire Mk IX, and an American P-51D Mustang. Famous aircraft engines on display include the 1941 rocket engine used in the Messerschmitt 163 Komet and one of the eight engines used on Howard Hughes's *Spruce Goose*. In the jet aircraft hangar, a U.S. Navy F4 Phantom dwarfs a F86 Sabre and a trio of Russian MiGs.

Falcon Field began life as a secret training base for Royal Air Force crews in 1941, when Arizona skies offered friendlier flying and better weather than in England; the hangars that now house World War I and World War II aircraft date from this time. You can peek into the restoration area

where mechanics keep these antique craft in flying condition. In a video presentation, you'll hear aces tell how they flew and fought, and you'll see actual combat footage filmed during World War II and in Korea and Vietnam. Docents offer tours of the planes. A gift shop sells aircraft models, posters, and books.

Falcon Field is off McKellips Road in northeast Mesa, about seven miles from downtown. The museum, 480/830-4540, is open daily 10 A.M.–5 P.M. Sept. 16–April 14, and daily 8:30 A.M.–3:30 P.M. April 15–Sept. 15. Admission is $6.50 adults, $3 children 5–12. NOTE: The collection has been purchased by the Museum of Flight in Seattle and will move there in mid- to late 2003.

Buckhorn Wildlife Museum

Over 400 stuffed and mounted animals, most native to Arizona, can be seen here. Birds hang from the rafters, javelinas glare from the walls, a coyote snarls from behind a couch. The collection is open Tues.–Sat. 9 A.M.–5 P.M. (call for summer hours). Admission is $4 adults, $2 children under 12. Buckhorn Mineral Wells here no longer offer baths, but you can stay in the 1940s cottages ($45 d). The museum and cabins are at 5900 E. Main St., seven miles east of downtown Mesa at the northwest corner of Main St. and Recker Rd.; 480/832-1111.

Chandler Museum

Historical exhibits at this museum in the town of Chandler, just south of Mesa, display Native American artifacts and memorabilia of pioneer life and early agriculture. You'll learn about Dr. Alexander J. Chandler (1859–1950), who pioneered irrigation here, opened the nearby San Marcos Hotel, and founded the town named for him. There's also a photo of the Gila River Relocation Center south of Chandler, where West Coast Japanese-Americans did time in 1942–1944.

The museum, 178 E. Commonwealth Ave., 480/782-2717, is just east of A.J. Chandler Park in downtown Chandler. Hours are Mon.–Sat. 11 A.M.–4 P.M. To get there from Mesa, head south on Country Club Drive (AZ 87), which becomes Arizona Avenue and is the main street through Chandler. Go east one block on Buffalo

St. (also signed "City Complex"), south one block on Arizona Place, then east one block on Commonwealth Avenue.

Arizona Railway Museum

Railroad enthusiasts have preserved a 1906 steam locomotive and a wide variety of other historic rolling stock in Chandler. You may be able to enter some of the Pullman cars and a caboose. The museum building, which resembles an early Southwest railroad depot, holds a 1950s' Traffic Control Center (push the button to see it work) and railroad memorabilia. It's at 399 N. Delaware St., 480/821-1108. Open Sat.–Sun. noon–4 P.M. (closed in summer); free admission.

Gilbert Historical Center

In the small agricultural town of Gilbert (south of Mesa and east of Chandler), exhibits in eight rooms of the 1913 Gilbert Grammar School tell the town's story from prehistory to the present. A lineup of antique farm machinery sits outside. The center is at 10 S. Gilbert Rd. (enter from Elliot Rd.), 480/926-1577. Hours run about Tues. and Sat. 9 A.M.–4 P.M. from Oct. to May, but it's best to call and check; free admission.

ACCOMMODATIONS

$50–100

Downtown Area: Mesa Travelodge, 22 S. Country Club Dr., 480/964-5694, 800/578-7878, offers a pool; $60 d. **Budget Suites Motel,** 537 S. Country Club Dr., 480/969-5248, has all studios and a pool; $49 s, $59 d. **Motel 6,** 630 W. Main St., 480/969-8111, 800/4MOTEL6, has a pool; $44–49 s, $50–56 d. **Quality Inn Royal-Mesa,** 951 W. Main St., 480/833-1231, 800/333-5501, offers a pool, hot tub, and exercise room; $69–99 d.

West of Downtown: Tri-City Inn, 1504 W. Main St., 480/969-7241, is near the Tri-City Mall; $40 d. **Mesa Oasis Inn,** 2150 W. Main St., 480/962-5051, features all kitchenettes and a pool; $55–60 d.

East of Downtown: Days Inn East Mesa, 5531 E. Main St., 480/981-8111, 800/329-7466, includes a pool and hot tub; $55 s, $60 d.

Holiday Inn Express, 5750 E. Main St., 480/985-3600, 800/888-3561, has a pool and hot tub; $79–109 d. **Super 8,** 6733 E. Main St., 480/981-6181, 800/800-8000, also has a pool and hot tub; $60 s, $65 d.

South of Downtown: Holiday Inn Hotel & Suites, 1600 S. Country Club Rd., 480/964-7000, 800/HOLIDAY, features a pool, hot tub, and fitness room; $89 d room, $129 d suite.

$100 and up

Sheraton Mesa, downtown at 200 N. Centennial Way (off University between Center and Mesa), 480/898-8300, 800/456-6372, has a pool, hot tub, exercise room, and two restaurants; $139 d. **Hampton Inn Mesa,** 1563 S. Gilbert Rd., 480/926-3600, 800/HAMPTON, offers a pool and hot tub; $109 s, $119 d. **Country Inn & Suites by Carlson,** 6650 E. Superstition Springs Blvd., 480/641-8000, 800/456-4000, offers a pool, hot tub, and exercise room; $139 d room, $159 d suite. **Hilton Phoenix East/Mesa,** 1011 W. Holmes Ave. in the southwestern part of town (near the Alma School Rd. Exit from Superstition Fwy.), 480/833-5555, 800/544-5866, has a pool, hot tub, and fitness center; $220 s and $235 d standard room, or $250 s and $265 d suite.

Resorts

Saguaro Lake Ranch Resort, 13020 Bush Hwy., 480/984-2194, has a beautiful setting overlooking the Salt River below Saguaro Lake. Perhaps the Valley's most rustic resort, the facility has a main lodge and dining rooms with fireplace, a swimming pool, and hiking and riding trails. Horseback riding, kayaking, tubing the Salt River, mountain biking, and jeep tours can be arranged too. Bed and breakfast rates are $90 s, $125 d Dec. 15-May 31, and $75 s, $95 d the rest of the year. The American Plan, available during the cooler months only, includes room and three meals: $135 s, $225 d Dec. 15-May 31, and $125 s, $200 d Sept. 15–Dec. 14.

When the **Sheraton San Marcos Resort** opened in Chandler in 1912, it was the only resort in the state to offer the full set of amenities—golf, horseback riding, tennis, and polo! The San Marcos has competition now—and the horses and polo players have departed—but it retains old Arizona charm while providing modern facilities. Spread over 123 acres, the resort has a Southwestern restaurant, a café, 18-hole golf course, two pools, a hot tub, tennis courts, and an exercise room. It's in central Chandler (just south of Mesa) at 1 San Marcos Place, 480/812-0900, 800/528-8071; www.sanmarcos resort.com. In season, the deluxe rooms are $119–139 d and the suites go for $219–240.

CAMPGROUNDS AND RV PARKS

Mesa

Green Acres I, 2052 W. Main St., 480/964-5058, is close to Mesa; $21 RV with hookups, $23 in the adult section. Four miles east of downtown, **Goodlife RV Resort,** 3403 E. Main St., 480/832-4990, 800/999/4990, has more than 1,100 spaces. It's designed for people 55 and over and has a pool, hot tubs, and many seasonal activities; $32 RV with hookups. Farther out, **Mesa Regal RV Resort,** 4700 E. Main St., 480/830-2821, also provides a pool, hot tub, exercise room, and wintertime programs for guests 55 and over; $33 RV with hookups. **Usery Mountain Recreation Area,** 12 miles northeast of downtown Mesa, has camping with hookups and showers; see "Valley of the Sun Recreation" for details and directions.

Apache Junction

Lost Dutchman State Park, 480/982-4485, has a spectacular setting in the foothills of the Superstition Mountains, six miles northeast from US 60/89 on AZ 88; $10 tent or RV (showers but no hookups). Both tents and RVs are also welcome at **Mesa-Apache Jct. KOA,** 1540 S. Tomahawk Rd. (one mile north from Superstition Fwy. Exit 197), 480/982-4015, 800/562-3404 (reservations); $18 tent, $22–24 RV with hookups. **Lost Dutchman RV Resort,** in town at 400 N. Plaza Dr., 480/982-4173, caters to folks 55 and older with a pool, hot tubs, and planned seasonal activities; $36 RV with hookups. **Rock Shadows Travel Trailer Resort,** 600 S. Idaho Rd.,

480/982-0450, provides a pool, hot tubs, and seasonal programs for seniors 55 and over; $28 RV with hookups.

FOOD
American

The Landmark Restaurant, 809 W. Main, 480/962-4652, draws customers for favorites such as prime rib, New York steak, pot roast, and pork chops. Its Salad Room, one of the Valley's best salad bars, has over 100 items. Open daily for lunch and dinner (on Sunday the dinner menu is served all day); $13–25.

Ripe Tomato Cafe, 745 W. Baseline, 480/892-4340, is famous for its tasty omelets, pancakes, burgers, chimichangas, and other fare served in generous quantities. Open daily for breakfast and lunch; prices average about $6.

Western

In south Mesa, **Rockin' R Ranch,** 6136 E. Baseline, 480/832-1539, dishes up barbecued beef or chicken with 'taters, beans, biscuits, and coffee. After dinner the wranglers entertain with Western music and humor. Open all year, call for reservations and times; $23 adults, $21 seniors 65 and older, and $12 kids 3–12; www.rockinr.net.

Barleen's Arizona Opry, 2275 Old West Hwy. in Apache Junction, 480/982-7991, presents dinner and a lively show during their Nov.–April season; $19.75 adult, $13.25 children 12 and under.

Mining Camp, 480/982-3181, offers great Western grub, much of it all-you-can-eat, served family-style in a replica of an old mining camp's cook shanty. It's a great place for the kids. Open daily for dinner and Sunday for lunch during the Oct.–June season; $17–19 adults (10 percent off for seniors), $8.45 children 6–12, reservations recommended. The restaurant is four miles northeast of Apache Junction on AZ 88, then one mile right at the sign.

Mexican

Garcia's, 1940 E. University Dr.; 480/844-0023, is a long-running favorite. Open daily for lunch and dinner; $6–13, reservations recommended.

Pancho's Mexican Buffet, 1050 S. Country Club Dr. and Southern Ave., 480/833-1144, offers excellent value in a buffet with initial serving cafeteria style and seconds brought to you when you raise the miniature flag at your table. Open daily for lunch and dinner; about $6.

Italian

Anzio Landing Italian Restaurant, 2613 N. Thunderbird Circle, 480/832-1188, has a great reputation for northern and southern Italian food. It's on the north side of Falcon Field near the corner of Higley and McDowell Roads. Open Mon.–Sat. for lunch and dinner; $12–20.

German

Zur Kate, 4815 E. Main St., 480/830-4244, serves hearty schnitzels and wursts along with beers from the Old Country. Live music entertains on weekends. Open Mon.–Sat. for lunch and dinner, call for summer schedule; $6–11.

Chinese

China Gate, 2050 W. Guadalupe Rd., 480/897-0607, is a Valley favorite for fine Mandarin, Szechuan, and Hunan cuisines. Open daily for lunch and dinner; $7–15.

Japanese

Tokyo Express, 1120 S. Dobson Rd., 480/898-3090, has inexpensive and good fast food. Open daily for lunch and dinner; under $5.

Valley of the Sun Entertainment

© BILL WEIR

Novelist Tony Hillerman had an appreciative audience for his talk and book signing at the Arizona Book Festival in Phoenix.

EVENTS

Concerts, festivals, shows, and other special events happen nearly every day in the Valley. The Arizona Office of Tourism publishes a comprehensive event listing that's available at local tourist offices and online at www.arizonaguide.com. In Phoenix, you can stop by the Greater Phoenix Convention & Visitors Bureau at 50 N. 2nd St. or call the Visitor Information Line at 602/252-5588; www.phoenixcvb.com.

Here are some of the best-known annual happenings.

January

Celebrations continue around the **Tostitos Fiesta Bowl,** which kicks off the year on or near January 1; www.tostitosfiestabowl.com. **Glendale Glitters Holiday Extravaganza** continues until mid-month. Competitors put their best stock forward during the **Arizona Stock Livestock Show and Rodeo** in late December and early January. Top PGA golfers compete in the **Phoenix Open.** The **Scottsdale Celebration of Fine Art** brings together more than 100 artists, many of whom can be seen at work, at Scottsdale Road and Mayo

© BILL WEIR

Luke Day at Luke Air Force Base

Boulevard (one mile north of Bell Rd.) from mid-January to late March; www.celebrateart.com. In late January or early February, the **Parada del Sol** in Scottsdale features the world's longest horse-drawn parade and a big rodeo.

February

Scottsdale Celebration of Fine Art continues. The Heard Museum sponsors fast-paced competition in the **World Championship Hoop Dance Contest** by Native Americans on the first weekend; www.heard.org. The horsey set enjoys Scottsdale's **Arabian Horse Show** at WestWorld; this venue has many other horse shows and sales through the year. Native Americans host the **O'odham Tash Indian Pow Wow** near the city of Casa Grande, 45 miles south of Phoenix, with a parade, rodeo, dances, and crowning of the O'odham queen. Fountain Hills hosts the **Great Fair,** featuring a hot-air balloon race, 5K and 10K runs, and the Southwest Arts and Crafts Show. **Lost Dutchman Days and Rodeo** presents a parade, rodeo, and bluegrass festival in Apache Junction. Step back to the 16th century for the **Arizona Renaissance Festival,** when a vast site southeast of

Apache Junction becomes a medieval playground of tournament jousting, theater, crafts, food, and costumed performers; it begins early in the month and runs to late March on each Sat.–Sun. and Presidents' Day; www.royalfaires.com. **VNSA Used Book Sale,** sponsored by the Volunteer Nonprofit Service Association, presents a huge selection on the second weekend at the Arizona State Fairgrounds; proceeds go to charities; www.vnsabooksale.org. Glendale hosts the **Chocolate Affaire** with chocolate, gourmet cuisine, chocolate-factory tours, and entertainment.

March

The **Arizona Renaissance Festival** and the **Scottsdale Celebration of Fine Art** continue. The **Heard Museum Guild Indian Fair and Market** brings nearly 500 Native American artists to show and demonstrate their work, along with entertainment, food, and children's activities, on the first weekend; www.heard.org. Baseball's **Cactus League** plays spring training games at many stadiums in the Valley. **Scottsdale Arts Festival** celebrates with juried craft booths, music, food, and children's activities.

THE ARIZONA RENAISSANCE FESTIVAL

For eight consecutive weekends each year in February and March, a merry town comes to life on the east side of the Valley of the Sun. Modern cares fade away as one walks through the gate into a 16th-century world of magicians, story tellers, comics, jugglers, and music makers. Entertainers on a dozen stages provide amusement for their audiences throughout the day, plus you'll meet many costumed actors engaged in song, dance, or other festivities elsewhere on the 30-acre park. The emphasis is on fun—and joining in on the non-stop activities. Artisans demonstrate their glass blowing, weaving, pottery, armor making, and other skills as you watch.

Kids have many games of skill and chance. Jousting knights, dressed in armor and mounted on powerful horses, battle each other three times a day in the King's Arena, with the last match a "joust to the death."

Actors in some of the stage shows have been know to toss out some risqué humor, but the program schedule lets you know which ones these are! Even in a full eight-hour day, you cannot see everything. An early start helps, and you can ask staff which shows are so popular as not to be missed. Kitchens turn out such offerings as turkey drumsticks, steak on a stake, stews, and pizza. Pastries and chocolates may tempt you too.

Old Town Tempe's **Spring Festival of the Arts** features work by some of the Southwest's best artists and craftspeople, along with food treats and live performances on Mill Avenue. Chandler hosts the annual **Ostrich Festival** with ostrich races and arts and crafts booths. Williams Gateway Airport in Mesa hosts an **Air & Motor Spectacular** with aircraft acrobatics in the sky and powerful truck and car events on the ground; coxairshow.com. The Arizona Temple in Mesa puts on an **Easter Pageant** during the week preceding Easter.

April

Maricopa County Fair features entertainment, rides, and agricultural exhibits at the Arizona State Fairgrounds; www.maricopacountyfair.org. **Arizona Book Festival** is the place to meet authors—both local and nationally known—and listen to their experiences at Margaret T. Hance Deck Park in Phoenix; www.azbookfestival.org. **Sunday on Central** is a huge street fair with entertainment, community booths, and food on Central Avenue. **Luke Day** features a big air show with the U.S. Air Force's Thunderbirds aerial demonstration team, the U.S. Army's Golden Knights parachute team, civilian plane acrobatics, and ground displays; the event doesn't happen every year but it's worth seeing when it does. Golfers 50 and over play in **The Tradition,** a Senior PGA tournament. The **Par-**

adise Valley Jazz Party draws top performers; www.paradisevalleyjazz.com. The **Glendale Jazz and Blues Festival** plays in Murphy Park in downtown Glendale.

The **Yaqui Indian Easter Celebration** begins on Ash Wednesday and continues every Friday until Holy Week, then Wednesday to Easter Sunday. Dancers wear special masks and costumes in a reenactment of the crucifixion. The ceremonies, believed to be nearly 300 years old, symbolize the battle between good and evil. The Yaqui community sponsors the celebration at the Church Plaza between Iglesia and San Angelo roads in Guadalupe, southeast of Phoenix; 480/730-3080 (town hall).

May

Mexican music, dancing, and food mark **Cinco de Mayo,** the anniversary of Mexico's 1862 expulsion of the French; it's celebrated on the weekend nearest the fifth.

June to September

It's hot! Valley residents head for the nearest swimming pool or drive to the high country. Those who stay enjoy programs of musicals, plays, and concerts held at various locations. **July 4th Fireworks** explode in the night skies at Wesley Bolin Plaza in front of the state capitol and in Glendale.

The festival runs rain or shine: 10 A.M.–6 P.M. on Saturday and Sunday, plus Presidents' Day, from early February to late March. Entry fees are $16 adults, $14 seniors 55 and over, $6 kids 5–12. Also budget some money for meals (no outside food is allowed) and tips for the performers. Call 520/463-2700 or check www.royalfaires.com for days and times. From Phoenix, take the Superstition Freeway (US 60) east past Apache Junction and the Gold Canyon Resort to the festival village, which will be on your right. If you're driving from Tucson, follow either the Pinal Pioneer Parkway (AZ 79) or take highways I-10, AZ 87, AZ 287, and AZ 79 to Florence Junction, then continue northwest seven miles.

© BILL WEIR

SOUTH-CENTRAL

October

The **Arizona State Fair** in Phoenix features exhibits of the state's best in agriculture, livestock, and home crafts, along with concerts, rides, and games; www.azstatefair.com. The Phoenix Art Museum puts on a **Cowboy Artists of America Sale & Exhibition;** www.phxart.org. **Rodeo Showdown** features some of the best riders in a world finals at America West Arena in Phoenix.

November

Bright colors fill the sky during the **Thunderbird Balloon Classic** at WestWorld in Scottsdale; www.t-birdballoonclassic.com. Murphy Park in downtown Glendale glows under a canopy of half a million lights in the **Glendale Glitters Holiday Light Display** from the day after Thanksgiving until mid-January.

December

Holiday celebrations include **Festival of Lights** (a festival and electric light parade in downtown Phoenix), **Glendale Glitters Holiday Light Display,** Heritage Square's **Victorian Holiday,** the Desert Botanical Garden's **Noche de las Luminarias,** the Phoenix Zoo's **ZooLights,** and the Arizona Temple's **Christmas Lights** display (600,000 of them from late November through December). On the first weekend, **Celebration of Basketweaving** attracts skilled Native American artisans to the Heard Museum; www.heard.org. Tempe's Old Town hosts the **Fall Festival of the Arts** to exhibit the work of local and visiting artists, along with food, music, dance, and children's entertainment. On the second full weekend, Native Americans present entertainment, arts and crafts, and food in the **Annual Indian Market,** sponsored by the Pueblo Grande Museum and held at the Activity Center in South Mountain Park; www.pueblogrande.com. **Tostitos Fiesta Bowl** activities in late December include an impressive parade, the National Band Championship, and sports events, all leading up to the big game on or near New Year's Day; www.tostitosfiestabowl.com.

MOVIES, THEATER, AND CONCERTS

To find out what's happening in the Valley, call the Visitor Information Line at 602/252-5588 (recording). Newspapers, especially the weekly *New Times, the Rep,* and *Get Out* (all free at newsstands), review the entertainment scene. Good websites for listings include www.phoenixnew times.com and www.azcentral.com.

Movie Theaters

Gigaplexes with large numbers of screens and comfy seats have hit the Valley. AMC has a— count 'em—30-screen theater in the Deer Valley area at the southwest corner of I-17 and Loop 101, as well as 24-screen theaters downtown at Arizona Center and at Awatukee (I-10 and Ray Rd.), and 14 screens in Phoenix (Esplanade at 24th St. and Camelback Rd.) and in Glendale (75th Ave. and Bell Rd); all 602/956-4262. The papers mentioned above list the films playing at these and other Valley theaters, including a couple of drive-ins.

Imax and iWerks

These systems use a projection screen six stories tall and a projection film with 10 times the area of 35 mm film to project a sharp, realistic image. Some movies feature 3D for an even bigger impact. **Arizona Mills Imax** is near the junction of I-10 (take Baseline Rd. Exit east) and Superstition Freeway (take Priest Dr. Exit south); 480/897-1453. The **Arizona Science Center,** 602/716-2000, in downtown Phoenix has a similar iWerks big-screen theater. Most films in these formats run about 45 minutes.

Phoenix

Arizona Theatre Company performs classic and contemporary plays and some musicals from September to May at Herberger Theater Center, 222 E. Monroe St., 602/256-6995 (Arizona Theatre Company box office) or 602/252-8497 (Herberger Theater box office); www.aztheatre co.org. **Phoenix Theatre,** 602/254-2151, opened in 1920 and is the longest continuously running theater in the country. Besides performances for adults, the theater offers children's programs by the Cookie Company. The theater building forms a courtyard with the Phoenix Art Museum on the northeast corner of Central Avenue and Mc-Dowell Rd.; www.phoenixtheatre.net.

The **Phoenix Symphony,** 602/495-1999, offers a variety of concerts during its Sept.–May season, when the music resounds at Symphony Hall in downtown Phoenix and at Scottsdale Center for the Arts; www.phoenixsymphony.org. **Ballet Arizona,** 602/381-0184, productions run from October to May, mostly at Herberger Theater Center and some at Symphony Hall; www.balletaz.org. Symphony Hall is in the downtown Phoenix Civic Plaza at 225 E. Adams Street. **Arizona Opera,** 602/266-7464, presents productions October to April at Symphony Hall; www.azopera.com.

The **Cricket Pavilion** hosts major music events in an open-air, 20,000-seat amphitheater in far western Phoenix, one-half mile north of I-10 between 79th and 83rd Aves.; contact the Info Line 602/254-7599, Ticketmaster 480/784-4444, 520/321-1000, or check the Web at www.azconcerts.com.

Celebrity Theatre, 440 North 32nd St., 602/267-9373, brings in top names of a wide spectrum of popular music.

The city of Phoenix, 602/261-8991, presents free **Coffeehouse Concerts** on Wednesday evenings year-round at the south clubhouse patio in Encanto Park.

Scottsdale

The **Scottsdale Center for the Arts,** 480/994-2787, sponsors diverse musical and theatrical offerings and contemporary art exhibits at 7380 Scottsdale Mall, one block south of Indian School Road and two blocks east of Scottsdale Road; www.scottsdalearts.org. **Kerr Cultural Center,** 480/965-5377, offers musical ensembles and theatrical productions all year in a charming adobe recital hall; art exhibits, which change each month, are open Mon.–Fri. 8:30 A.M.–5 P.M.; the center is near Rose Lane off 6110 N. Scottsdale Road and south of the Borgata.

Tempe

On the ASU campus, **Gammage Center for the Performing Arts,** 480/965-3434, presents a varied program of theater, concerts, and dance in a distinctive rotunda structure. **Red River Music Hall** features performances by world-famous singing artists of country, western, gospel, jazz, bluegrass, rock and roll, and nostalgia, plus a

Christmas show; all seats are reserved. It's at 730 N. Mill Ave., on the southwest corner of Mill and Washington/Curry, one block north of the Mill Avenue bridge; 480/829-6779, 800/466-6779; www.redrivermusichall.com.

Sun City

ASU Sundome Center for the Performing Arts, 623/975-1900, frequently hosts big-name performers in a 7,000 seat facility, said to be the world's largest single-level theater, during the September to May season. The center is at 19403 R.H. Johnson Blvd. (north of Bell Rd.) in Sun City West.

NIGHTLIFE

The Valley moves to many different beats. Check out the weekly *New Times, the Rep,* and *Get Out* (all free at newsstands) for what's playing. On the Web, visit www.phoenixnewtimes.com and www.azcentral.com.

Country-Western

The music sets many toes to tapping at **Mr. Lucky's,** 3660 Grand Ave. (two blocks north of Indian School Rd.) in Phoenix; 602/246-0686. Inside you'll find vast dance floors and all-you-can-eat barbecue; outside, an arena hosts live bull riding on the weekends. Steakhouses with live entertainment include **Rawhide** at 23023 N. Scottsdale Rd. in Scottsdale, 480/502-1880; **Rockin' R Ranch** at 6136 E. Baseline in Mesa, 480/832-1539; and **Rustler's Rooste,** 7777 S. Pointe Parkway in Phoenix, 602/431-6474.

Nightclubs

Catch local and national acts at **The Bash on Ash,** 5th St. and Ash Ave. in Tempe; 480/966-8200.

Comedy

The Improv, 930 E. University Dr. in Tempe, 480/921-9877, showcases top talent.

Jazz

Swing to the music at **J. Chew & Co.,** 7320 E. Scottsdale Mall in Old Town Scottsdale; 480/946-2733.

Blues

Hear cool sounds in **The Rhythm Room,** 1019 E. Indian School Rd. in Phoenix, 602/265-4842; **Char's Has the Blues,** 4631 N. 7th Ave. in Phoenix, 602/230-0205; and **Warsaw Wally's,** 2547 E. Indian School Rd. in Phoenix, 602/955-0881.

Latin and Flamenco

Move to music at **Pepin,** E. 7363 Scottsdale Mall in Scottsdale; 480/990-9026.

Rock

Nita's Hideaway, 1816 East Rio Salado Parkway in Tempe, 480/966-7715, features top cutting-edge bands. **Modified,** 407 East Roosevelt in Phoenix, 602/252-7664, is unusual in having no alcohol or game machines, so the appreciative audience can better devote themselves to the music. For rock 'n' roll, try **Mr. Bolo's** at 330 S. Gilbert Rd. in Mesa; 480/649-1650.

Sports Bars

Majerle's Sports Grill, 24 N. 2nd St. (across from the America West Arena) in Phoenix, 602/253-9004, attracts the downtown crowd, including the Phoenix Suns.

Pubs

George & Dragon Restaurant, 4240 N. Central Ave. (at Indian School Rd.) in Phoenix, 602/241-0018, creates authentic English pub food such as steak and kidney pie, fish and chips, and Cornish pasties, and keeps more than a dozen brews on tap; open daily for lunch and dinner.

Seamus McCaffrey's Irish Pub & Restaurant, 18 W. Monroe St. in downtown Phoenix, 602/253-6081, serves Guinness and traditional foods. Irish musicians often perform on Friday and Saturday.

Casinos

Fort McDowell Casino is in the northeast

SOUTH-CENTRAL

THE CACTUS LEAGUE: SPRING TRAINING UNDER THE SUN

Ten major-league baseball teams—known as the "Cactus League"—currently warm up for the season in spring training camps under Arizona's blue skies. For fans, who enjoy watching players practice and play exhibition games in Valley of the Sun or Tucson stadiums, the time is one of welcoming back their teams after a long winter. Low ticket prices and many new or renovated stadiums add to the pleasure of watching the teams begin their play. Admission prices run $3–18 depending on team and seating. The action takes place in March, with the possibility of some games at the end of February or beginning of April.

You can get the schedules and venue information for all of the teams from the Mesa Convention & Visitor's Bureau, 120 N. Center, Mesa, AZ 85201; 480/827-4700 or 800/283-6372; www.mesacvb.com. The office is open Mon.–Fri. 8 A.M.–5 P.M. Staff will mail or fax you the information, or you can get it from the website.

Sports sections of the *Arizona Republic*, the *Tribune*, the *Arizona Daily Star*, and other newspapers will have the latest spring-training write-ups and schedules. The website www.cactus-league.com also has detailed listings of teams, stadiums, game dates, and sources of tickets.

Teams and Venues

The **Anaheim Angels** play ball at Tempe Diablo Stadium, 2200 W. Alameda Dr. in Tempe; it's off 48th St., one mile south of I-10 Exit 153.

The **Arizona Diamondbacks** play at the Tucson Electric Park, 2500 E. Ajo Way in Tucson; take I-10 Kino Pkwy. Exit 263 and turn east on Ajo Way.

The **Chicago Cubs** are at Hohokam Stadium, 1235 N. Center St. in Mesa, 1.5 miles north of downtown.

The **Chicago White Sox** train at Tucson Electric Park, 2500 E. Ajo Way in Tucson; take I-10 Kino Pkwy. Exit 263 and turn east on Ajo Way.

The **Colorado Rockies** swing at Hi Corbett Field in Randolph Park, east of downtown Tucson at 3400 E. Camino Campestre; take the I-10 Broadway/Congress Exit 258 and go east four miles.

The **Milwaukee Brewers** play at the Maryvale Baseball Park, 3600 N. 51st Ave. in west Phoenix; take I-10 51st Ave. Exit 139 and go north 1.5 miles (the park is on the left just before Indian School Rd.), or, from I-17, take Indian School Exit 202 and head west 4.5 miles on Indian School Road.

The **Oakland Athletics** practice at Phoenix Municipal Stadium on the south side of Papago Park, 5999 E. Van Buren St. in east Phoenix; from the 202 Red Mountain Freeway, take the Van Buren St. exit (if eastbound) and go one mile east on Van Buren St. or take the Priest Drive exit (if westbound) and go one mile north on Priest Drive.

The **San Diego Padres** play at the Peoria Stadium, 16101 N. 83rd Ave., northwest of Phoenix in Peoria; take the I-17 Bell Road Exit 212, go west 8 miles on Bell, then left on 83rd Avenue.

The **San Francisco Giants** train at the Scottsdale Stadium, 7408 E. Osborn Rd. in downtown Scottsdale; the stadium is on the northeast corner of Osborn and Civic Center Plaza, half a mile east of Scottsdale Road.

The **Seattle Mariners** sail at the Peoria Stadium, 16101 N. 83rd Ave., northwest of Phoenix in Peoria; take the I-17 Bell Road Exit 212, go west 8 miles on Bell, then left on 83rd Avenue.

corner of the Valley at AZ 87 and Fort McDowell Rd.; 800/THE-FORT. **Harrah's Phoenix Ak-Chin Casino** is 25 miles south of Phoenix near the town of Maricopa; take I-10 Queen Creek Rd. Exit 164 and head southeast 17 miles; 480/802-5000, 800/HARRAHS.

SPORTING EVENTS

Pro Sports

The **Arizona Diamondbacks** play major league baseball in their spacious home at Bank One Ballpark; 602/514-8400, 888/777-4664 (ticket office), 602/462-6500 (general information); www.azdiamondbacks.com. The NBA **Phoenix Suns**, 602/379-SUNS, professional basketball team plays home games in the America West Arena, 201 E. Jefferson St.; www.nba.com/suns. Women basketball players of the **Phoenix Mercury** WNBA team, 602/252-9622, play at America West Arena; www.wnba.com/mercury. The NFL's **Arizona Cardinals**, a professional football team, play home games at Arizona State University's Sun Devil Stadium in Tempe; 480/379-0102, 800/999-1402 (ticket office); www.azcardinals.com.

The **Phoenix Coyotes**, 480/563-7825, 888/255-7825, play NHL ice hockey Oct.–April at the America West Arena; www.nhlcoyotes.com. The **Phoenix Open**, 480/870-4431, attracts big-name professional golfers each January to the Tournament Players Club in Scottsdale; www.phoenixopen.com.

College Sports

The Arizona State University **Sun Devils**, 480/965-2381, battle opponents in an active program of football, baseball, basketball, swimming, gymnastics, archery, and other sports; www.thesundevils.com.

Motor Sports

Engines roar as cars strain for the finish line February to November at **Manzanita Speedway**, 35th Ave. and West Broadway; 602/276-7575. **Phoenix International Raceway**, 707 S. 115th Ave., 602/252-3833, schedules several major events each year. **Firebird International Raceway**, 602/268-0200, offers both land and water racing with several courses including a professional NHRA dragstrip and a 120-acre water-sports lake 12 miles southeast of Phoenix off I-10 at Exit 162A.

At the Races

Dogs run the track at **Phoenix Greyhound Park**, 3801 E. Washington (at 40th St.), 602/273-7181, nightly at 7:30 P.M. year-round; stay cool in the air-conditioned grandstands and clubhouse. In Apache Junction, **Apache Greyhound Park**, 2551 W. Apache Trail, 480/982-2371, offers race events at 1 P.M. Wed. and Fri.–Sun., from late November to early April; off-track betting is offered daily year-round.

Thoroughbreds and quarter horses race at **Turf Paradise**, 1501 W. Bell Rd. and 19th Ave., 602/942-1101, from late September to early May, usually Fri.–Tues. with simulcast racing on the other days.

Valley of the Sun Recreation

Valleyites take their sports seriously and enjoy the many recreational facilities in the area. You can play golf, tennis, or racquetball, go horseback riding, jump in the pool, tube the Salt River, and even go surfing. The **Phoenix Parks and Recreation Department,** 602/262-6861, sponsors some excellent parks and a variety of educational and recreation programs for children, adults, and seniors. The website "Phoenix at Your Fingertips" (www.ci.phoenix.az.us) lists many facilities. Large county parks ring the Valley, providing additional opportunities to enjoy nature; for information call the **Maricopa County Parks and Recreation Department,** 602/506-2930; www.maricopa.gov. The book *Day Hikes and Trail Rides In and Around Phoenix* by Roger and Ethel Freeman offers detailed trail descriptions for hikers and horseback riders.

SPORTS
Golf and Tennis
Both golf and tennis are extremely popular in the Valley. Enthusiasts often spend entire vacations at resorts offering top-notch facilities and professional instructors. Four Phoenix city parks feature golf courses and many offer tennis courts, as well as two tennis centers. Newsstands may have the free *Sun Tennis* and *Sun Golf* magazines. The Visitors Bureau provides many free publications and brochures of public and private golf courses.

Swimming
Phoenix alone offers 28 public pools; see the Phoenix Yellow Pages under "Swimming Pools." If you're looking for waves and water slides, try the places listed below.

Kiwanis Recreation Center, 480/350-5201, features an indoor wave pool (closed Dec.), gym, and tennis courts at 6111 S. All-America Way in the southeast corner of the large Kiwanis Park, reached by Mill Ave. between Baseline and Guadalupe Roads in Tempe.

Big Surf, 480/947-7873, has artificial waves 3–5 feet high that come crashing onto the beach.

You can rent rafts and, for added thrills, try the water slides. Small children can play in a shallow pool. The season runs daily between Memorial Day and Labor Day weekends. Big Surf is in northern Tempe at 1500 N. McClintock Dr., south of McKellips Road.

Golfland-Sunsplash, 480/834-8318, offers a wavepool and 10 water slides for fun and excitement plus rental rafts, three 18-hole miniature golf courses, video games, bumper boats, Indy race cars, and other amusements in Mesa at 155 W. Hampton Ave. (north one block on Country Club Drive from Superstition Freeway, then right on Hampton).

Waterworld Safari, 623/581-1947, contains a wave pool, water slide, and the "Lazy River" to cool you off; shallow pools cater to small children. The park is open from Memorial Day weekend to Labor Day weekend. From downtown Phoenix take I-17 north 17 miles to Pinnacle Peak Road, then go west two miles on Pinnacle Peak Road.

Tubing Down the Lower Salt River
Cool off in the summer on a leisurely float down the Salt River east of Mesa. Salt River Recreation, 480/984-3305, rents inner tubes and provides a shuttle bus service back to the put-in point for $10 per person ($6 shuttle pass only); www.saltrivertubing.com. The season runs May–Sept., weather and water permitting. The shuttle bus serves four points along the river, with a choice of floats lasting from 90 minutes to a half day.

An extra tube will carry your cooler of cold drinks, but don't bring glass containers. Weekends often see large crowds, and the Salt becomes one big party. Wear tennis shoes to protect your feet when walking in the river. Life jackets are a good idea—a necessity with children. Don't tie your tubes together; rather, lock your feet into each other's tubes.

Canoeists can enjoy the trip spring through autumn (there's no flow in winter). You can beat the summer tubing crowds by starting at sunup.

Below Granite Reef Dam, the Salt is a river no more—the water is channeled into canals, leaving only a dry riverbed downstream. See "Tonto National Forest Recreation Areas" below for other things to see and do along the lower Salt River. From the east edge of Mesa, take Bush Highway north to the Salt River.

Horseback Riding

The Phoenix area offers miles of scenic trails suitable for horses. Many of the stables can arrange lessons, breakfast rides, steak cookouts, hayrides, overnight trips, and boarding. Riding season runs about October to May. Reservations are advised. For trips into South Mountain Park, contact **South Mountain Stables**, 10005 S. Central Ave., 602/276-8131; **Ponderosa Stables**, 10215 S. Central Ave., 602/268-1261; or **All Western Stables**, 10220 S. Central Ave., 602/276-5862. All three lie just outside the park entrance.

Near Papago Park, you can go with **Papago Riding Stable**, 400 N. Scottsdale Rd. (turn in at Club Rio) in Tempe; 480/966-9793.

In Cave Creek, ride with **MacDonald's Ranch**, 26540 N. Scottsdale Rd., 480/585-0239; www.macdonaldsranch.com.

For guided hourly, all-day, and overnight pack trips into the wild Superstition Mountains and other desert areas, see **O.K. Corral Stables**, two miles northeast of Apache Junction on AZ 88, then left at Tomahawk Road, 480/982-4040; their season runs Oct.–May, then the horses move to stables near Pine (north of Payson) for the summer; www.okcorrals.com.

Ben Avery Shooting Facility

Shooters and archers can practice at this fine facility run by Arizona Game and Fish. Users also enjoy picnicking and camping. The range operates Wed.–Sun. 7 A.M.–dark; the trap and skeet range is available some nights (check for hours). It's 26 miles north of downtown Phoenix, west off I-17 Carefree Hwy. Exit 223; 623/582-8313 for the rifle and pistol range, 602/287-1019 for the Black Canyon Trap and Skeet Club.

CITY PARKS

City parks offer everything from a tranquil Japanese garden to challenging mountain hiking, as well as many recreation facilities. Tourist offices may have brochures, and you can contact the main Parks, Recreation, and Library Dept. office, open Mon.–Fri. 8 A.M.–5 P.M. in the Phoenix City Hall, 200 W. Washington St., 16th Fl., Phoenix, AZ 85003; 602/262-6861. The website "Phoenix at Your Fingertips" www.ci.phoenix .az.us has lots of information, including a clickable map that lists parks near you. City parks have free admission; they're for day use only.

Encanto Park

This 222-acre oasis of lakes and trees features picnic areas and many recreation facilities. The southern section has tennis, racquetball, volleyball, basketball, a swimming pool, playgrounds, and picnic areas. Free **Coffeehouse Concerts** entertain on Wednesday evenings year-round at the south clubhouse patio. You can check out sports equipment from the Recreation Building south of the swimming pool; parking is off 15th Avenue south of Encanto Boulevard.

Enchanted Island, a family amusement park, 602/254-1200, has a carousel, train, and other rides on weekends and some weekdays. Rides have a charge. Parking is north of Encanto Boulevard between 7th and 15th Avenues.

The northern section of Encanto has a clubhouse for special events (check the bulletin board or call 602/261-8991), picnic areas, playgrounds, a small lake with boat rentals (602/254-1520), an urban fishing program, and a golf driving range; parking is off 15th Avenue north of Encanto Boulevard. Two golf courses lie farther north: an 18-hole course at 2775 N. 15th Ave., 602/253-3963; and a nine-hole course—excellent for beginners—at 2300 N. 17th Ave., 602/262-6870. The park office is in the Norton House, 2700 N. 15th Ave., between Encanto Boulevard and Thomas Rd., 602/261-8991. Encanto Park lies just two miles north of downtown Phoenix at N. 15th Avenue and Encanto Boulevard.

Papago Park

Previously a national monument because of its desert flora and Native American history, this large area on the east edge of Phoenix offers numerous attractions in and near the park, such as the Phoenix Zoo, Desert Botanical Gardens, Arizona Historical Society Museum, Hall of Flame, an 18-hole golf course, Phoenix Municipal Stadium, and a baseball field. Enter Papago Park from Galvin Parkway, which runs between McDowell Road and Van Buren Street/Mill Avenue; 602/261-8318.

The park also features a recreation area with picnicking, easy hiking, a bike trail, and a small lake where children 15 and under may fish without a license. Hole in the Rock provides a scenic window onto Phoenix; you can hike up into it on a short trail. Continue to road's end for the short walk to the white-tiled pyramid tomb of George W.P. Hunt, seven times governor of Arizona. The recreation area is east off Galvin Parkway; turn in at the zoo entrance, then turn left.

Squaw Peak Park

Squaw Peak crowns a group of desert hills in Phoenix Mountains Preserve, nine miles northeast of downtown Phoenix. The park offers some great hiking trails and picnicking areas with water and shaded tables. Saguaro cactus, palo verde, creosote bush, and barrel and cholla cactus thrive on the rocky hillsides. Turn onto Squaw Peak Drive from Lincoln Boulevard between 22nd and 23rd Streets; 602/262-6696.

Summit Trail #300 climbs to the top of 2,608-foot Squaw Peak in 1.2 miles with a 1,200-foot elevation gain. You'll enjoy a superb panorama and lots of company—it's probably Phoenix's most popular trail. The path has steep sections, but it has been well graded and is easy to follow. On Sunday the peak hosts a remarkable crowd of teenagers, families, joggers wearing headsets—all puffing along. No dogs or bicycles allowed, though. In the warmer months, be sure to carry water and get an early start. An alternative Summit Trail for the lower section and a connection with Squaw Peak Circumference Trail #302 provide options for some loop hikes.

Squaw Peak Circumference Trail #302 makes a scenic 3.7-mile loop—it's one of Phoenix's best hikes. In some of the beautiful valleys you may forget that you're in the middle of an urban area. The trail climbs two saddles, so you'll get a good workout and gain 720 feet at the highest saddle, where you'll be on the Summit Trail; from here the summit lies 488 higher. Begin the Circumference Trail on either of the summit trails and turn left at the saddle or continue to the end of the park road and start down either end of the Squaw Peak Nature Trail (take the trail that descends into the wash for the most direct route). Note that dogs cannot go on the Summit Trail section.

Squaw Peak Nature Trail #304 makes a 1.5-mile loop from the end of the road. Signs identify some plants, but the beautiful desert scenery will be the main attraction; you'll gain just 180 feet.

Camelback Mountain Trail and Echo Canyon Recreation Area

The steep, rough trail to the 2,704-foot summit of Camelback Mountain will challenge kids and a lot of adults, yet most seem to make it to enjoy the spectacular views. The adventure starts on the northwest side of the mountain in Echo Canyon Recreation Area. In 0.3 mile you'll reach a minor ridge; continue up along the base of 200-foot cliffs to the Camel's Neck, from which more steep climbing takes you to the summit, 1.16 miles one way total and a 1,300-foot elevation gain. On a clear day you can take in countless aspects of the vast Valley; you won't need a map to identify the edge of the Salt River Indian Reservation to the east—it's the line where the city ends and irrigated fields begin. For a much easier walk, there's a short trail to Robby's Rock, a popular area with rock climbers. Beautiful rock formations provide a bonus for either hike. Carry at least a quart of water on the summit trail; it's a good idea to get a very early start in summer and avoid the trail after rain, when it becomes slippery.

From Phoenix, head north on 44th Street, which curves east and becomes McDonald Drive, then turn right (south) on E. Echo Canyon Parkway just 200 feet past the Tatum Boulevard junction. The Recreation Area has water but no

© BILL WEIR

the view east from the summit of Camelback Mountain

restrooms or other facilities. On weekends and holidays, you'll either be lucky or wait a long time to get a parking space.

Cholla Trail climbs from a trailhead at about 6200 E. Cholla Lane approximately 1.5 miles one-way; the first section is easy, then the going becomes very steep. Some parking is available along the west side of Invergordon (64th St.). Parks and Recreation, 602/262-4837, can provide information on Camelback Mountain and its facilities.

North Mountain Recreation Area

This desert park features many family and group ramadas along a loop road, plus a playground and basketball and volleyball courts. The easy **Penny Howe Barrier-Free Trail #40** has interpretive signs about plants along its one-third-mile loop; the trail starts from the northwest corner of the Havasupai parking lot. For a workout, many locals head up **North Mountain Trail #44** from Maricopa Picnic Area at the north end of the road loop; it climbs to a road that leads to the summit (2,104 feet). You can make a loop by taking Trail #44A to the left of the towers and

southeast along ridges to the Quechan Picnic Area on the southwest part of the loop road. The hike is about 1.6 miles long (one-way or the loop) with an elevation gain of 514 feet. North Mountain's entrance is at 10600 N. 7th St.; call 602/262-6696 (Northeast District) for information and ramada reservations.

Christiansen Trail #100 offers more areas to explore for hikers, cyclists, and horseback riders. You can start from a trailhead opposite the Pointe Hilton at Tapatio Cliffs, one mile north of the North Mountain entrance on 7th Street; the trail leads west to Shaw Butte and southeast to Squaw Peak in the Phoenix Mountain Preserve. Altogether, the easy-to-moderate trail is 10.7 miles one-way, with elevations ranging from 1,290 to 2,080 feet; many other trails loop off it. The west trailhead is on the north side of Mountain View Park at 7th Avenue and Cheryl Drive. East trailheads are at Dreamy Draw Recreation Area, 40th Street (south from Shea), and Tatum Boulevard (opposite Tomahawk Dr.).

South Mountain Park

The world's largest city park, South Mountain

encompasses 16,500 acres of desert mountain country. A paved road winds to the top for great views of the Valley. On the way you'll pass several picnic areas and trailheads. More than 50 miles of hiking and horseback trails lead through the backcountry. A park map shows roads, facilities, lookouts, and hiking trails; pick one up outside the ranger station or at the visitor center. Stables rent horses just outside the park's entrance, and there's an equestrian area inside the park. An activity center on the left just inside the entrance hosts special events. A visitor center, just past the ranger station, offers maps, literature, and some exhibits; you can also reserve picnic areas here, 602/495-0222 (daily 9 A.M.–4 P.M.). A short nature trail begins nearby; signs introduce the desert's flora and fauna. South Mountain Park lies seven miles south of downtown Phoenix on Central Avenue.

After the ranger station, roads branch off on both sides to covered picnicking areas, some of which can be reserved. San Juan Road forks right two miles inside the park, leading four miles through a valley to a trailhead and a low overlook of Phoenix. Take the Summit Road left at the fork to reach the heights. The road climbs to Telegraph Pass, then on past several lookouts on the left, of which Dobbin's has the best views of the Valley. Continue to the end of TV Towers Road for panoramas to the south from Gila Valley Overlook.

Hikers will enjoy some of the 18 trails, many of which form loops. Besides the views, you're likely to see prehistoric petroglyphs. **National Trail** extends the length of the park, climbing from low elevations at each end to high ridges in 14.3 miles one-way. **Hidden Valley,** a popular half-day trip through a landscape of giant granite boulders and stately saguaros, is 3.5 miles roundtrip via National Trail. To reach the trailhead, go two miles past the park entrance gate, turn left onto Summit Road and—following it four miles and keeping right past the turnoffs for two lookout points—then stay left at the next fork to Buena Vista Lookout. The first quarter mile of trail follows a ridge east with good views before gently dropping into a valley. After a mile or so, some large slick rocks must be ne-

gotiated before entering wide, bowl-shaped Hidden Valley. Near the lower end of the little valley, you'll pass through a natural tunnel about 50 feet long. This makes a good turnaround point, or you can explore more of the valley and surrounding hills. In summer carry extra water and avoid the heat of the day.

MARICOPA COUNTY PARKS

Large county parks, most with campgrounds and hiking trails, ring the Valley. The main county office will send you maps and brochures, though staff may not have first-hand knowledge of all areas; it's open Mon.–Fri. 8 A.M.–5 P.M. at 411 N. Central Ave. (Phoenix, AZ 85004), 602/506-2930; www.maricopa.gov. You can usually reach individual park offices seven days a week, though staff will all be out on patrol at times. Camp hosts can also help with park information. The entry fee of $3/vehicle for day-use fee ($5 at Lake Pleasant) is credited toward camping fees of $8, or $15 if the site has electricity. A 14-day stay limit applies. There's also a $50 day-use pass good for one year at all of the areas except Lake Pleasant. Weekends in the cool season, especially in early spring, see the most visitors; you'll find more solitude on weekday visit. Few people visit in summer, and sections of parks may close.

Estrella Mountain Regional Park

Spanish explorers named the range Estrella ("Star") after the pattern of deeply carved canyons radiating from the summits. This 19,840-acre recreation area southwest of Phoenix offers picnicking, camping, 34 miles of trails, a rodeo arena, and a golf course. The huge, grassy picnic area has a playground and many covered picnic tables. It's also popular with groups, who can rent picnic ramadas, the two ballfields, an amphitheater, the rodeo arena, and arrange camping. You may catch a rodeo or horse show at the rodeo arena. Ranger-led hikes go out on Sunday at 2 P.M. in the cooler months. Families and individuals can use the small number of RV sites with hookups ($15/night) and do basic camping ($8; water but no showers or established sites). Day-users pay $3/vehicle. The park office is at 14805

W. Vineyard Ave. in Goodyear; 623/932-3811. From Phoenix, take I-10 about 20 miles west to Estrella Parkway Exit 126, go south about five miles on Estrella Parkway, then turn left on Vineyard Avenue just after the Gila River bridge; the golf course entrance is on the right after half a mile and the park entrance is just beyond.

The rocky foothills of the range provide a scenic backdrop for the trails, all of which loop back or form loops with other trails. The Estrella summits themselves have no roads or trails—they're as rough and forbidding as when the Spanish explorers passed by! Climbing them can be hazardous. Although all trails are shared-use, hikers tend to favor the Gila Trail (2-mile loop; 200-foot elevation gain) and the Rainbow Loop (up to 14.6 miles; 460-foot elevation gain). Mountain-bike riders like the central loop of about six miles formed by the Rock Knob Buggy, Pack Saddle, and Rainbow Valley. Equestrian riders particularly enjoy the Gadsden Trail (7.4 miles; 320-foot elevation gain) and Pack Saddle Historical Trail (2.4 miles; 270-foot elevation gain), both in the eastern section of the park. You can camp in the back-country with a permit.

Estrella Mountain Golf Course, in the northwest corner of the park, 623/932-3714, has 18 holes, a pro shop, and snack bar.

White Tank Mountain Regional Park

Extensive trails at this park wind back into the White Tank Mountains on the west side of the Valley. Infrequent flash floods have roared down the canyons, scouring out depressions (tanks) in the white granite, giving the park its name. Elevations range from 1,402 feet at the park entrance to 4,083 feet on the highest peak. Archaeologists have identified seven Hohokam village sites and numerous petroglyphs. The county's largest park at 26,337 acres, it offers visitors year-round use of picnic areas (some with covered tables), group ramadas, family and group campgrounds, and four major interconnecting trails. Campers can watch the vast spread of lights coming on across the Valley at sunset, then the golden illumination of the mountains at sunrise. The family campground ($8/night) and one

of the group campgrounds have showers; a few sites have hookups for $15. Saturday evening campfire programs at 7 P.M. run during the cooler months. Day use costs $3/vehicle.

Hiking trails range from two short barrier-free trails to a 6.5-mile rugged loop high into the hills. The popular Waterfall Trail leads to pools and a waterfall deep in a box canyon; it's a cool spot even in summer, though there's not always a flow. Petroglyphs cover some of the big boulders along the way. The first 0.4 mile to Petroglyph Plaza has barrier-free access. You can also start from Black Rock Trail; it's a 1.3-mile loop with a short connector trail to Waterfall Trail. Black Rock has a half-mile, barrier-free interpretive trail loop. For a longer hike, consider Ford Canyon (8.8 miles roundtrip) and Mesquite Canyon to Willow Springs (five miles roundtrip). A new trail connects the upper ends of these two trails. For views and a challenging hike, Goat Camp Trail loops high into the range (6.5 miles, but trailheads are an additional 2.5 miles apart by road). Mountain-bikers zip down the Sonoran Loop Competitive Track with several loop possibilities of 2.9-5 miles; hikers can use the trail too, but they need to be aware of the bikers. Equestrians have a staging area but only short sections to ride, as most trails get too rough higher up. Backcountry campers must register first.

To reach the park from Phoenix, head west on I-10 to Cotton Lane Exit 124, go north seven miles to Olive Avenue, then west five miles. From the north Valley, take the 101 Loop to Olive Avenue, then turn west. For more information, contact the park administration at P.O. Box 91, Waddell, AZ 85335; 623/935-2505.

Lake Pleasant Regional Park

This large reservoir just northwest of the Valley sits among saguaro-studded hills with a backdrop of the rugged Bradshaw Mountains. Fishing and camping draw visitors during the cooler months, and boaters stream in to cool off in summer. The lake's open waters provide excellent conditions for sailing; races are sponsored by the Arizona Yacht Club and Lake Pleasant Sailing Club. Anglers seek out largemouth bass, white bass, catfish, bluegill, sunfish, and crappie. Jet-ski races, sailing regattas, and fishing tournaments take place annually.

Completion of the present Waddell Dam in 1993 raised the lake level to about 1,700 feet in elevation; the lake's surface area is about 10,000 acres when full. From the high levels in March and April, the lake drops 100 feet or so by September or October of each year as the water goes out to irrigate west Valley fields. Eagles nest in the Agua Fria River area in the northeast from mid-December to mid-June, when no visitors may enter. Few people come to the lake for hiking, but you can follow Pipeline Canyon Trail between the north and south recreation areas on the west shore. Staff may have a handout on the more than 50-mile-long Black Canyon Trail east of the lake, or you can contact the BLM Phoenix Field Office at 2015 W. Deer Valley Rd., Phoenix, AZ 85027; 602/580-5500.

The county's regional park offers year-round camping, picnicking, boating, and fishing on the west shore. (Pleasant Harbor runs a deluxe marina and RV resort on the southeastern shore with a separate entrance and fees; see below for details.) Take the main entrance for the Waddell Dam Overlook, which has a visitor center, gift shop, and a great panorama of the lake; exhibits cover the Central Arizona Project, dam, and wildlife. A 10-lane boat ramp, marina, picnic areas, and two campgrounds are nearby. The marina offers fishing, pontoon boat and jet-ski rentals, and parasailing. You'll find food stands here and elsewhere around the park. Desert Tortoise Campground has showers and sites for both tenters ($8) and RVers ($15 with water and electricity) on a first-come, first-served basis. Roadrunner Campground serves as an overflow area with showers and water/electric hookups; all $15. Primitive camping is possible for boaters along the lakeshore. From the north entrance, you can use Cottonwood Day Use picnic area, shoreline campsites, and a four-lane boat ramp.

Day use costs $5/vehicle, $2/watercraft, and $1/cyclist; annual passes cost $60 for Mon.–Thurs. use or $120 for all days. Passes and further information are available from the park office, 41835 N. Castle Hot Springs Rd., Morristown, AZ 85342; 928/501-1702 (main office) or 928/501-

hikers on Waterfall Trail, White Tank Mountain National Park

© BILL WEIR

1710 (gate). Lake Pleasant is about 30 miles northwest of Phoenix; take I-17 north to AZ 74 (Exit 223), go west 11.5 miles on AZ 74, north 2.2 miles on Castle Hot Springs Road, then turn right into the park. The north entrance is three miles farther north on Castle Hot Springs Road. To reach Lake Pleasant from Sun City, head north 15 miles on 99th Avenue to AZ 74 and follow signs.

Pleasant Harbor

A marina and RV resort on the east shore provide more luxury at a higher cost than the county facility across the lake. The RV campground has showers, a convenience store, game room, horseshoe pits, volleyball, a pool, and hot tub; $25–31 with hookups, depending on size. For information call 602/269-0077 or, outside the Phoenix area, 800/475-3272. The full-service marina offers a ship's store and rentals of fishing, ski, patio, and jet-ski boats; 623/566-3100, 928/510-3100. The

Desert Princess, an 1880s Mississippi River boat replica, offers lunch or dinner cruises many days year-round and scenic tours in summer; 623/815-2628. Follow directions to Lake Pleasant Regional Park, but turn north at the sign before crossing the Agua Fria riverbed and continue 2.2 miles. A $6 entry fee is collected for each vehicle and watercraft (additional watercraft cost $2 each).

Cave Creek Recreation Area

The rocky hills west of Cave Creek hold campgrounds, picnic areas, a rodeo arena, and hiking trails. Elevations range from 1,880 feet in the camping area to 3,060 feet atop the park's highest peak. The family campground has showers and water/electric hookups at all sites for $15; there's a dump station near the entrance. Groups can reserve a separate campground and picnic ramadas. Equestrians like the trails, which are also open to hikers and mountain bikers. Be aware that the several mine shafts in the park are dangerous to enter. For an easy walk, try Clay Mine Trail (0.9 mile one-way) from the campground area or the Slate (1.6 miles one-way) and Flume (1.5 miles one-way) Trails from the day-use area. Go John (4.8-mile loop) and Overton (2.1-mile loop) Trails each circle a hill from the day-use area. The horse staging area and Cave Creek Riding Stables (602/465-9559) are also here.

Day use costs $3/vehicle. The park is open year-round at 37904 N. Cave Creek Pkwy., Cave Creek, AZ 85331; 480/465-0431. From the Carefree Highway between I-17 and Cave Creek Road, turn north on 32nd St. and continue 1.6 miles.

McDowell Mountain Regional Park

You'll enjoy beautiful vistas from near the eastern McDowells, 15 miles northeast of Scottsdale. A wide variety of desert plants grows at the 1,600- to 3,000-foot elevations, though two-thirds of the 21,000-acre park burned in the lightning-caused Rio Fire of July 1995. You can compare areas and see how the desert has recovered. From 1870 to 1890, the Stoneman Military Road ran through the park, connecting nearby Fort McDowell with Fort Whipple near Prescott. Day-use

areas stay open all year, though the campground may close between Memorial and Labor Day weekends. The family campground has showers and water/electric hookups for $15; an overflow area may be available if the campground is full. There's also a dump station. Groups can reserve their own campground and picnic ramadas. Day use costs $3/vehicle; contact the park at P.O. Box 18415, Fountain Hills, AZ 85269; 480/471-0173. Take Shea Boulevard from Scottsdale or AZ 87 from Mesa to Fountain Hills, then turn north on Saguaro Boulevard (passes near the fountain), Fountain Hills Boulevard, or Palisades Boulevard, all of which join Fountain Hills Boulevard and become McDowell Mountain Road. Entrance is on the east side of the park, four miles beyond Fountain Hills.

Thirty-five miles of trails for hikers and horseback riders wind through the foothills and lower slopes, though not up the McDowells themselves. The popular and gentle North Trail (no horses) loops 3.1 miles through an unburned area with interpretive signs. The 1.2-mile Lousley Hill Trail loop (hikers only) offers good panoramas of the McDowells, Mazatzals, Four Peaks, and Superstitions. Wagner Trail from the family campground offers several easy loops of 1.6-4 miles. The 15.3-mile loop Pemberton Trail is too long for most hikers, but will give mountain bikers and horses a good workout. Scenic Trail makes a 2.8-mile loop via a wash (too sandy for most bikers) and a ridge. In the southern section of the park, the McDowell Competitive Track offers three interconnected loops for mountain bikers, runners, and trotting horses; the Sport Loop is three miles long; the Long Loop is 8.2 miles; and the difficult Technical Loop is 2.9 miles long. Slower users yield to faster on these loops.

Usery Mountain Recreation Area

Visitors enjoy this scenic setting with camping, picnicking, trails, abundant wildlife, and fantastic sunsets over the Valley. The park, about 12 miles northeast of downtown Mesa, includes more than 3,600 acres of Sonoran Desert with elevations from 1,700 to 2,750 feet. It takes its name from Usery Mountain in the northwest corner; King Usery, a desperado and horse thief, lived in the area in the late 1800s. Mexican and Basque shepherds still herd flocks of sheep across Usery Pass in the spring and autumn. Picnic areas offer shaded tables. The family campground has showers and water/electric hookups. It's open Oct.–April and sometimes in summer; $15. If it's full, you can stay in overflow sites (no hookups); $8. A dump station is near the campground entrance. Groups can reserve their own campground and picnic areas. Day use costs $3/vehicle. Contact the park at 3939 N. Usery Pass Rd., #190, Mesa, AZ 85207; 480/984-0032. From US 60 in Apache Junction, turn north on Ellsworth Road, which becomes Usery Pass Road; the park entrance is on the right. The road continues over the pass with good views and descends to the lower Salt River Recreation Area.

The park has trails to suit almost anyone. The popular Wind Cave Trail climbs 800 feet in 1.6 miles to shallow caves in the cliffs of Pass Mountain. The trail, for hikers only, offers panoramas all along the way. Volcanic ash formed these light-colored cliffs of tuff, which are capped by a layer of basalt. Hikers, skilled mountain bikers, and equestrians can do Pass Mountain Trail, a rugged 7.1-mile loop around Pass Mountain; going clockwise works best as you'll be going down instead of up one steep 500-foot grade. Blevins Trail, in the southern area of the park, makes an easy 2.9-mile loop good for beginner mountain bikers; several other loops branch off for longer trips. For an easy stroll, try the Merkl Memorial Trail—a 0.9-mile loop around a rocky hill in the picnic area. Signs along the trail identify plants. A spur trail follows a ridge 0.4 mile between the north and south ends of the Merkl loop; it has a 90-foot climb. A half-mile loop in the family campground provides another easy ramble. Kids can frolic in the playgrounds, too. Equestrians have a horse-staging area. Archers can practice at a range near the entrance station. The Usery Mountain Shooting Range of the Rio Salado Sportsman's Club is one-third mile north of the park entrance; 480/984-9610.

TONTO NATIONAL FOREST RECREATION AREAS

The Salt River and its Saguaro Lake bring greenery and water sports to the eastern part of the Valley of the Sun. Additional areas to explore in the Tonto National Forest lie north of the Valley—see "Scottsdale Sights" above. You can also visit the Salt River Canyon east of the Valley on the exciting Apache Trail scenic drive—see "East of Phoenix: The Apache Trail Loop" below.

Lower Salt River Recreation Area

The Salt's final run below Saguaro Lake offers a glimpse of what the riparian life of the Valley looked like before the coming of modern irrigation canals. Visitors come to enjoy tubing in the Salt during the warm months, camping in winter (only), and fishing and picnicking year-round. Day use is free, but campers pay $6. Recreation areas have vault toilets but no drinking water. The Bush Highway connects the area with Mesa to the south and AZ 87 to the north. If coming from Mesa, you'll first reach the turnoff for Phon D. Sutton Recreation Area; it's 1.2 miles in and has lots of parking for RVs. The Lower Salt River Nature Trail, an easy 2.3-mile loop, begins at the downstream end of Phon D. Sutton, follows the shore downstream, turns inland through cottonwood and mesquite woodlands, then returns via some desert uplands; signs tell of life here and the changes that settlement has brought.

Coon Bluff Recreation Area is one mile east on Bush Highway past the Sutton turnoff, then one mile in. Picnic tables under the trees overlook the river. This is an especially good spot for tent camping.

Goldfield Recreation Area is 1.3 miles past the Coon Bluff turnoff, then 1.3 miles in. Tube rental and the shuttle-bus center are near the turnoff. Usery Pass Road ends at this junction; turn south for Usery Mountain Recreation Area and good views back to the Salt River Valley.

The Bush Highway crosses the Salt on Blue Point Bridge, 2.5 miles east of the Goldfield turnoff; there's a recreation area on the north shore. Another two miles east takes you to Water Users Recreation Area and some impressive canyon scenery. A short trail leads to the river. Continue up a hill on the Bush Highway to the turnoff for Saguaro Lake.

Saguaro Lake

The scenery, fishing, and boating on Saguaro Lake attract people year-round. The 10-mile-long, 1,100-acre lake within Tonto National Forest is the last in the chain of lakes on the Salt River and the closest to Phoenix. Anglers catch largemouth and yellow bass, channel catfish, bluegill, and walleye. **Lakeshore Restaurant,** 480/984-5311, serves breakfast and lunch daily and dinner Wed.–Sun., either indoors or out on the patio (great views). **Saguaro Lake Marina** offers boating supplies and rentals of fishing, patio, and ski boats; 480/986-5546 (marina), 480/986-0969 (rentals).

The adjacent **Saguaro del Norte** area provides day-use boat ramps, picnic areas with covered tables, and Saguaro Lake Vista Trail, but no water; $4/vehicle and $2/boat. **Butcher Jones Recreation Area** offers a picnic area and hiking along the northern lakeshore, but no boat ramp; $4/vehicle day use. Butcher

Jones Trail follows the shore—the first quarter mile is paved for wheelchair fishing access—and crosses a peninsula (115-foot climb) to Burro Cove in 2.5 miles one-way. The road to Butcher Jones turns off the Bush Highway one mile north of the marina. Picnic and boating areas almost always fill up on Sunday and sometimes on Saturday from mid-spring to mid-summer; try to arrive by early morning. Only boaters can reach **Bagley Flat Campground,** about four miles from the marina; it has tables and pit toilets, but no water or fee. Dispersed camping is also permitted, but again, you'll need a boat.

To reach Saguaro Lake, take the Bush Highway or AZ 87 from eastern Mesa. The **Mesa Ranger District** office of the Tonto National Forest stocks recreation information for the Saguaro Lake, lower Salt River, Superstitions, and Four Peaks areas. It's at 26 N. Macdonald St. in Mesa (AZ 85201), 480/610-3300; open Mon.–Fri. 7:45 A.M.–4:30 P.M. You can also contact the main Tonto office at 2324 E. McDowell Rd. (Phoenix, AZ 85006), 602/225-5200; open Mon.–Fri. 8 A.M.–4:30 P.M.

Valley of the Sun Shopping and Information

SHOPPING

The Valley features thousands of shops eager to sell you something. Glittering department stores and boutiques display the latest in fashion. Or you can visit rustic, porch-fronted shops and be outfitted in Western duds from boots to bolo ties. Western and Native American art make distinctive gifts. Anglo and Hispanic artists recall the frontier days in painting and sculpture, while Native American artists reveal their heritage in arts and crafts. Mexican import shops represent skilled craftspeople from south of the border.

Old Town Scottsdale

Arts, crafts, clothing, and restaurants—many with an Old West theme—abound in the area centered around Brown Avenue, Main St., and 1st St., just west of Scottsdale's Civic Center.

You'll also find an outlet for Arizona Highways, whose publications feature beautiful photography and excellent creative writing, at 7235 E. 1st Avenue. Many galleries open Thursday evenings for the **Scottsdale Artwalk,** which presents exhibitions, demonstrations, and entertainment; it takes place 7–9 P.M. year-round; www.scottsdalegalleries.com.

Fifth Avenue

Scottsdale's biggest shopping area is centered along this curving street between Scottsdale Road and Indian School Road. Local merchants promote the huge selection of shops here as "Arizona's ultimate shopping experience."

The Borgata

This elegant shopping center is modeled after the Tuscan village of San Gimignano, complete

artist at work during the Scottsdale Celebration of Fine Art

© BILL WEIR

with cobblestone paths, courtyards, and medieval towers and archways. Your credit cards will take a beating in most of these stores, but window shopping is fun. The Borgata, 6166 N. Scottsdale Rd., 480/998-1822, is two miles north of Old Town Scottsdale.

Glendale—"Arizona's Antique-Shopping Capital"

Glendale, the fourth largest city in Arizona, lies northwest of downtown Phoenix; take I-17 Glendale Exit 205 west five miles or head northwest on Grand Avenue/US 60.

Downtown Glendale's **Old Towne Shopping District,** on Glendale Avenue east of 59th Avenue, offers a host of antique stores and other specialty shops. Murphy Park, at Glendale and 58th Avenues, hosts a Saturday crafts market 9:30 A.M.–4:30 P.M. from October to May.

The **Historic Catlin Court Shops,** downtown between Myrtle and Palmaire Avenues, from 57th to 59th Avenues, hold more treasures for shoppers. The Glendale Town Trolley makes a loop through both the Old Towne and

Catlin Court shopping districts and rolls on to Cerreta's Candy Company, most days Oct–April; free.

Visitors with a sweet tooth won't want to miss **Cerreta's Candy Company,** 5345 W. Glendale Ave., 623/930-1000, which offers tours of their factory.

The **Glendale Visitor Center,** 5800 W. Glenn Dr., Suite 140 (Glendale, AZ 85301), 623/930-4500, 877/800-2601, has lots of information on sights, shopping, events, and other aspects of their city. Hours run Mon.–Sat. 10 A.M.–5 P.M.; tour.glendaleaz.org. **Glendale Special Events Hotline** has a recording of upcoming happenings; 623/930-2299.

Other Shopping Malls

Metrocenter (exit west at Dunlap or Peoria Aves. from I-17 in north Phoenix), 602/997-2641, is *big*—five major department stores, more than 200 specialty shops and eateries, a 14-screen movie theater, and banks; adjacent to Metrocenter, you'll find hotels, many restaurants, and two movie theaters. **Biltmore Fashion Park,** Camelback

Rd. and 24th St. in Phoenix, 602/955-8400, features about a dozen restaurants and 60 luxury stores, including Saks Fifth Avenue, Polo/Ralph Lauren, Gucci, and Macy's.

Scottsdale Fashion Square, 7014 E. Camelback Rd. (at Scottsdale Rd.), 480/941-2140, has four major department stores, about 150 specialty stores, a food court, five full-service restaurants, and two cinemas. **el Pedregal Festival Marketplace at the Boulders,** 34505 N. Scottsdale Rd., 480/488-1072, offers boutique shopping in a Moroccan festival-style marketplace offering 35 restaurants, galleries, and shops, including an exhibit gallery and a shop of the Heard Museum. Two miles north of el Pedregal in Carefree, shops in **Spanish Village,** Tom Darlington Dr. and Cave Creek Rd., 480/488-0350, offer Western and Native American art and crafts in a relaxed atmosphere. **Superstition Springs Center,** 6555 E. Southern Ave. in Mesa, 480/396-2570, has five department stores, over 120 specialty stores, an eight-screen cinema, and a 36-horse carousel.

Outlet Malls

Arizona Mills, 480/491-7300, brings "Shoppertainment" to the Valley with many factory and specialty shops, a 24-screen theater, Imax theater, games arcade, and a food court. Two information desks offer Arizona tourist literature as well as a map of Arizona Mills. Check out the exotic decor in the Rainforest Cafe's family restaurant and juice bar!

To the north, **Outlets at New River,** 4250 W. Anthem Way, 623/465-9500, sells many big-name brands at bargain prices in more than 80 stores (and there's a food court too). To get there go 15 miles north of Bell Road on I-17 to Anthem Way Exit 229.

Outdoor Supplies

REI offers two co-op stores in the Valley. Both stock an excellent selection of gear for hiking, backpacking, bicycling, river-running, downhill skiing, cross-country skiing, and other sports; rentals available too. Experts give regular talks on outdoor adventures and skills. Optional lifetime memberships, available for a small fee, pay dividends of about 10 percent of all purchases at the end of each year. The Tempe store is at 1405 W. Southern Ave. across from the Neils Peterson house; 480/967-5494. In Paradise Valley, REI is at 12634 N. Paradise Village Pkwy. W., one long block north of Cactus Road, across the street from Paradise Valley Mall; 602/996-5400. REI has a Web page of upcoming events for each store at www.rei.com. **Arizona Hiking Shack** also has a fine array of outdoor gear and rentals at 11649 N. Cave Creek Rd. (a quarter mile south of Cactus Rd.) in north Phoenix; 602/944-7723.

Native American Music

Drumbeat Indian Arts, 4143 N. 16th St. in Phoenix, 602/266-4823, stocks hundreds of different Native American music titles from many American tribes.

Books and Maps

The Book Store, 4230 N. 7th Ave., 602/279-3910, has not only many used books, but out-of-town newspapers and one of the best selections of magazines in the state. **Bent Cover Bookstore,** 12428 N. 28th Dr. (one block west of I-17, just north of the Cactus Rd. Exit), 602/942-3778, offers used hardback and paperback books. **Book Gallery** stocks a large selection of used books in Phoenix at 169 W. Camelback Rd. (602/263-8353) and at 3740 E. Indian School Rd. (602/253-6922).

Changing Hands, 480/730-0205, carries a large selection of new and used books at the southwest corner of 6328 S. McClintock Dr. (#101) and Guadalupe. **Old Town Books,** 518 S. Mill Ave., 480/968-9881, features a small but select inventory of used books. **Half Price Books,** 1245 W. Elliot Rd. in Tempe, 480/961-9477, has many clearance and used-book bargains. **Bookman's,** 1056 S. Country Club Dr. in Mesa, 480/835-0505, boasts 22,000 square feet of used books, magazines, CDs, LPs, tapes, videos, and software. **Mesa Bookshop,** 50 W. Main St. in downtown Mesa, 480/835-0757, has a great selection of art, music, philosophy, Latin America, and fiction. Shopping malls house the popular book chains.

For maps of Arizona and the world along with some regional books, see **A Wide World of Maps** in Phoenix at 2626 W. Indian School Rd., 602/279-2323, 800/279-7654 and in Mesa at 1444 W. Southern Ave., 480/844-1134. Topo maps are also sold by **REI**, in Tempe at 1405 W. Southern Ave., 480/967-5494, and in Paradise Valley at 12634 N. Paradise Village Parkway West, 602/996-5400, and by **Arizona Hiking Shack**, 11649 N. Cave Creek Rd. in north Phoenix, 480/944-7723.

INFORMATION

Tourist Offices

Greater Phoenix Convention & Visitors Bureau has a free *Official Visitors Guide* and many brochures downtown at 50 N. 2nd St. (Phoenix, AZ 85004). It's open Mon.–Fri. 8 A.M.–5 P.M.; 602/254-6500, 877/225-5749, www.phoenixcvb.com. You can park at 15-minute meters in front. For Valley event news and other services, call the Visitor Information Line at 602/252-5588. The Visitors Bureau maintains a branch office in Biltmore Fashion Park at 24th St. and Camelback Rd.; open daily during shopping center hours.

Scottsdale Convention & Visitors Bureau is at 7343 Scottsdale Mall (Scottsdale, AZ 85251), open Sun. 11 A.M.–4 P.M. (Oct.–April), Mon.–Fri. 8:30 A.M.–6 P.M., and Sat. 10 A.M.–4 P.M.; 480/945-8481or 800/877-1117; www.scotts dalecvb.com.

Tempe Convention and Visitors Bureau at Hayden Square in Old Town Tempe, off Mill Ave. (51 W. 3rd St., Suite 105, Tempe, AZ 85281) is open Mon.–Fri. 8:30 A.M.–5 P.M.; 480/894-8158, 800/283-6734; www.tem pecvb.com.

Mesa Convention & Visitors Bureau at 120 N. Center (Mesa, AZ 85201) is open Mon.–Fri. 8 A.M.–5 P.M.; 480/827-4700, 800/283-MESA; www.mesacvb.com.

Carefree/Cave Creek Chamber of Commerce at Marywood Plaza (P.O. Box 734, Carefree, AZ 85377) is open Mon.–Fri. 9 A.M.–4 P.M.; 480/488-3381; www.arizona guide.com/cfcc.

Apache Junction Chamber of Commerce at 567 W. Apache Trail (Apache Junction, AZ 85220) is open Mon.–Fri. 8 A.M.–5 P.M. and Sat. (except in summer) 9 A.M.–2 P.M.; 480/982-3141, 800/252-3141; www.apachejunction coc.com.

Fountain Hills Chamber of Commerce at 16837 E. Palisades Blvd. (P.O. Box 17598, Fountain Hills, AZ 85269) is open Mon.–Fri. 8 A.M.–5 P.M.; 480/837-1654, www.fhchamberof commerce.org.

Glendale Visitor Center, 5800 W. Glenn Dr., Suite 140. (Glendale, AZ 85301), 623/930-4500, 877/800-2601, is open Mon.–Sat. 10 A.M.–5 P.M.; tour.glendaleaz.org.

The **Arizona Office of Tourism** offers information on every region of the state—ask for their free travel kit. You can find most of their literature at other tourist offices, but this one has the best selection. It's at 1110 W. Washington Street, Suite 155, Phoenix, Arizona 85007; open Mon.–Fri. 8 A.M.–5 P.M.; 602/364-3700, 888/520-3434, fax 602/240-5475. The excellent website www.arizonaguide.com has travel tips, event listings, and links to many chamber of commerce sites.

Arizona Public Lands Information Center

The center's helpful staff should be able to meet all your needs for recreation information on federal and state lands in Arizona. You can ask questions and purchase books on scenic drives, camping, hiking, mountain biking, off-highway trails, river running, regional history, Native Americans, natural history, travel, and other topics. Maps on hand include those of Arizona's national forests and BLM lands, plus topographic, city, and state. The center can also print out custom topographic and land-use maps. Staff sell fishing and hunting licenses, national and state park passes, and national forest recreation permits. The center is open Mon.–Fri. 8:30 A.M.–4:30 P.M. at 222 N. Central Ave., Suite 101 (Phoenix, AZ 85004); 602/417-9300; www.publiclands.org. The office is in downtown Phoenix inside the Security Center Bldg., across Central Avenue from the tall Bank One building. You can park around the corner on the south side of Van Buren across from the city bus terminal and get a one-hour validation.

Tonto National Forest

You can camp, hike, and boat in the Tonto's 2.9 million acres of forests and cacti that stretch north and east of the Valley. The forest includes the Superstition and Mazatzal Ranges and the lakes along the Verde and Salt Rivers. The Supervisor's Office is at 2324 E. McDowell Rd. (Phoenix, AZ 85006), 602/225-5200; it's open Mon.–Fri. 8 A.M.–4:30 P.M.; www.fs.fed.us/r3/tonto. The website www.gorp.com also has lots of national forest recreation information.

The **Cave Creek Ranger District** office of the Tonto National Forest knows about Bartlett and Horseshoe Lakes, the Cave Creek Trail System, and other areas north of the Valley. The office, at 40202 N. Cave Creek Rd., Scottsdale, AZ 85262, is open Mon.–Fri. 8 A.M.–5 P.M.; 480/595-3300. It's in the extreme north part of town; head northeast on Cave Creek Road, turn right on Bartlett Lake Road, then it's on your left.

The **Mesa Ranger District** office of Tonto National Forest stocks recreation information for the Saguaro Lake, lower Salt River, Superstitions, Four Peaks, and other areas east of the Valley. The office, at 26 N. Macdonald St., Suite 120, Mesa, AZ 85201, is open Mon.–Fri. 7:45 A.M.–4:30 P.M.; 480/610-3300.

Bureau of Land Management

The Phoenix Field Office, 21605 N. 7th Ave. (Phoenix, AZ 85027), 623/580-5500, provides information on BLM areas in most of central and northern Arizona; It's open Mon.–Fri. 7:30 A.M.–4:15 P.M. and is south of Deer Valley Rd.

Arizona State Parks

The staff here provide outdoor recreation information and publications for the entire state, as well as their own areas. The main office has an information desk and gift shop at 1300 W. Washington, Phoenix, AZ 85007; open Mon.–Fri. 8 a.m-5 P.M.; 602/542-4174 or, if in Arizona outside the Phoenix area, 800/285-3703; fax 602/542-4188; www.pr.state.az.us.

Arizona Game and Fish

The office has information and sells licenses for fishing, hunting, and boat registration; you can also learn about off-highway vehicle travel. The main office is at 2221 W. Greenway Rd. (Phoenix, AZ 85023); it's open Mon.–Fri. 8 A.M.–5 P.M.; 602/942-3000. The office for central Arizona is at 7200 E. University Dr. (Mesa, AZ 85027); 480/981-9400; www.azgfd.com.

Libraries

The **Phoenix Central Library** looks like a giant glass and metal cube. Once inside the five-story atrium, you'll have much to explore in the spacious facility; a map lists what's on each floor and describes some of the unusual design features of the building. The Friends Place near the entrance sells gift items and surplus books. First floor has fiction, foreign languages, and children's books. Second floor houses periodicals, Internet computers, and a copy center. The Arizona Room (closed Mon. and Fri.) on the fourth floor has great reading on the state's history, travel, and natural life; this is the place to pore over maps and books about lost-mine legends before setting off on your own treasure hunt! You'll need an appointment to see the Rare Book Collection, located across from the Arizona Room. Nonfiction hangs out on the fifth floor, claimed to be the largest reading room in North America. The library is two blocks south of McDowell Road at 1221 N. Central Ave. and Willetta St.; it's open Sun. noon–9 P.M., Mon.–Thurs. 9 A.M.–9 P.M., and Fri.–Sat. 9 A.M.–6 P.M.; 602/262-4636. On the Internet, you can access the 1.8 million holdings of the Phoenix public libraries at www.phoenixlibrary.org. See the blue pages in the phone book under Phoenix libraries for information on the 12 branches scattered around town.

The **State Capitol** has a research library on Arizona history, maps, state documents, federal documents, and genealogy at 1700 W.

Washington, Room 300; it's open Mon.–Fri. 8 A.M.–5 P.M.; 602/542-3701; www.lib.az.us.

The **Scottsdale Public Library** at 3839 Civic Center Blvd. is open Sun. 1–5 P.M., Mon.–Thurs. 9 A.M.–9 P.M., and Fri.–Sat. 10 A.M.–6 P.M.; 480/994-2474; library.ci.scottsdale.az.us. Scottsdale has branch libraries at 10101 N. 90th St. (south of Shea), 480/391-6061; at 10187 E. McDowell Mt. Ranch Rd., 480/391-6200; and at 12575 E. Via Linda, Suite 102 (north of Shea); 480/391-6100.

The **Tempe Public Library** sits next to the Tempe Historical Museum on the southwest corner of 3500 S. Rural Rd. and Southern Ave.; it's open Sun. noon–5:30 P.M., Mon.–Thurs. 9 A.M.–9 P.M., and Fri.–Sat. 9 A.M.–5:30 P.M.; 480/350-5555 (information recording) or 480/350-5511 (reference); www.tempe.gov/library. You can also use libraries on the ASU campus.

The **Mesa Public Library** is downtown at 64 E. 1st St.; it's open Sun. 1:30-5:30 P.M., Mon.–Thurs. 9:30 A.M.–9 P.M., and Fri.–Sat. 9:30 A.M.–5:30 P.M.; 480/644-3100 (recording) or 480/644-2207 (reference); www.ci.mesa.az.us/library.

The **Apache Junction Public Library** is north of the city hall complex at 1177 N. Idaho Rd.; hours run Mon., Wed., and Fri. 9 A.M.–5 P.M., Tues. and Thurs. 9 A.M.–8 P.M., and Sat. 9 A.M.–5 P.M.; 480/474-8555; www.ajcity.net.

Newspapers and Magazines

The *Arizona Republic* comes out every morning and features a big Sunday edition; the paper also does a free weekly entertainment guide, *the Rep* and maintains an excellent website, www.azfamily.com. The *Tribune* serves the East Valley and publishes a free Valley-wide weekly paper, *Get Out.* The weekly *New Times,* also free, presents hard-hitting journalism, local news, and extensive entertainment coverage. Newsstands can be a treasure-trove of free information on golf, tennis, bicycling, running, New Age, and many other topics.

Phoenix Magazine comes out monthly with news and useful information about the Valley. Scottsdale has its own magazines—*Scottsdale Scene* and *Scottsdale Magazine.* The monthly

Carefree Enterprise has an interesting mix of general reading and local news.

SERVICES

The Phoenix downtown **post office** is at 522 N. Central Avenue. Other post offices include Scottsdale's at 7242 E. Osborn Rd.; Tempe's at 1962 E. Apache Blvd., with a downtown branch at 500 S. Mill; and Mesa's at 135 N. Center. For postal information or to get the address of the post office nearest you, call 800/275-8777. General Delivery mail can be sent to you at the Rio Salado Station on 1441 E. Buckeye Rd.; address it with your name, General Delivery, Phoenix, AZ 85034.

American Express handles currency exchange in the Biltmore Fashion Park at 2508 E. Camelback Rd., 602/468-1199, and at the Scottsdale Fashion Square, 6900 E. Camelback Rd., 480/949-7000.

Need a doctor? **Maricopa County Medical Society** will refer you to one. It's open weekdays 8 A.M.–5 P.M., 602/252-2844.

TRANSPORTATION

Tours

The Valley of the Sun features many tour operators. Drop by one of the Visitors Bureau offices for the latest brochures and *Official Visitors Guide* listings. The Sunday *Arizona Republic* travel section advertises travel deals.

The **Gray Line** runs tours of the Phoenix area including the Heard Museum (4 hours, $41), Sedona/Oak Creek Canyon (nine hours, $58), Nogales (10 hours, $85), and the Grand Canyon (14 hours, $99); two-day trips visit the Grand Canyon ($198 d); longer trips roll to other areas of the Southwest. You'll find the Gray Line office at 1243 S. 7th St., Phoenix, AZ 85034; 602/495-9100, 800/732-0327; www.graylinearizona.com.

Local Bus

Valley Metro will ride you around the Valley, visiting parks, shopping areas, most of the sights, and the airport—all for just $1.25 ($1.75 express); transfers are free when requested upon boarding. All-day passes cost $3.60; you can purchase them at the downtown terminal at Van Buren St. and Central Ave.; 602/253-5000. The *Bus Book* available free at the terminal and many tourist offices has a map and timetables; it's on the Internet at www.valleymetro.maricopa.gov. Most buses head for home between 6 P.M. and 10 P.M.; only a handful operate on Sunday and major holidays. In the downtown area you can ride the **Downtown Area Shuttle** (DASH) for free; 602/257-0338.

Long-Distance Bus

The **Greyhound** bus terminal is near the airport at 2115 E. Buckeye Rd.; 602/389-4200 (local) or 800/231-2222 (national fare and schedule info); www.greyhound.com. You'll find other Greyhound stations in northwest Phoenix at 2647 W. Glendale Ave., 602/246-4341; and in Mesa at 1423 S. Country Club Dr., 480/834-3360.

Buses of **White Mountain Passenger Lines** heads from Phoenix (319 S. 24th St.; 602/275-4245) to the cool pines of the Mogollon Rim with stops at Mesa (Greyhound depot at 1423 S. Country Club Dr.; 480/834-3360), Payson, Heber, Snowflake, and Show Low; services are once daily in each direction Mon.–Sat.; the main office, 928/537-4539, is in Show Low.

Auto Rentals

The Valley moves on wheels; if you need some, check the Yellow Pages or the Visitors Bureau's *Official Visitors Guide.* Rental companies offer many different plans; most maintain offices at the airport or make free pickups. You can rent RVs too.

Driveaways

These are autos requiring delivery to another city. If a car's going to a place you're headed, a driveaway's like a free car rental, but you'll still have to pay for gas. You must be at least 21 years old and pay a deposit of $75–150. There are also time and mileage limits. Ask for an economy car for the lowest costs. See the Yellow Pages under "Automobile Transporters and Driveaways."

Train

Amtrak's routes no longer go through Phoenix, but connecting buses will take you to the **Sunset Limited/Texas Eagle,** which runs three eastbound and three westbound departures each week across southern Arizona, or to the **Southwest Chief,** which runs both east and west daily across the northern part of the state. Both the Texas Eagle and Southwest Chief trains go between Los Angeles and Chicago. The Sunset Limited splits off in Texas for Orlando. The terminal is downtown at 401 W. Harrison St. and 4th Avenue. For reservations and information, call 800/872-7245 (USA-RAIL) or visit www.amtrak.com.

Air

Commercial flights land at Sky Harbor Airport, just three miles east of downtown Phoenix. The west entrance off 24th St. and I-10/Papago Freeway is closer to downtown. The east entrance off 44th St. and Hohokam Expressway/143 serves Scottsdale, Tempe, and other east Valley areas. Sky Harbor has three separate terminals connected by a free 24-hour shuttle bus. The busy airport is well organized but you'll have to do some walking. It's on the Web at www.phxskyharbor.com. International flights serve Mexico, Canada, and Europe.

The **City of Phoenix** staffs information desks in Terminals 2, 3, and 4. Free telephones near the baggage claims connect to many Valley hotels and motels.

Taxis waiting outside charge widely varying fares—shop around. **SuperShuttle** provides door-to-door service from homes and hotels to or from the airport; on arrival at Sky Harbor, step outside any of the terminals to locate a representative; for a ride to the airport, call 24–48 hours in advance at 602/244-9000, 800/331-3565; fares start at $6–12 for downtown and increase with distance. **Valley Metro** buses are the cheapest way into town; they leave the airport about every 30 minutes (every hour on Sun.) from early morning to late evening; 602/253-5000.

East of Phoenix: The Apache Trail Loop

Driving east through Phoenix, Tempe, Mesa, and Apache Junction, you might think the city will never end. But as soon as you turn onto AZ 88 in Apache Junction, the shopping centers, gas stations, and hamburger stands fade away, and you're left with just the desert, lakes, and mountains. Here begins a 200-mile loop through some of the most rugged country in the West. Allow six hours to drive this circuit around the rugged Superstition Mountains, taking AZ 88, "The Apache Trail," and AZ 188 to Globe, then returning to Apache Junction via US 60/70. Besides the wild scenery, you can enjoy hiking and horseback riding in the Superstition Wilderness, boating on a chain of lakes within the Salt River Canyon, stepping inside prehistoric cliff dwellings in Tonto National Monument, seeing copper-mining operations near Globe, Miami, and Superior, and visiting the Boyce Thompson Arboretum—an amazing collection of plants from all over the world.

Information

The Tonto National Forest provides recreation information for the Apache Trail and many of the places of interest along it, such as the Superstition Wilderness and Roosevelt Lake. Offices sell maps and hand out flyers on campgrounds, trails, and boating. The **Supervisor's Office**, 2324 E. McDowell Rd. (Phoenix, AZ 85006), 602/225-5200, is open Mon.–Fri. 8 A.M.–4:30 P.M. The **Mesa Ranger District** office, 26 N. Macdonald St. (Suite 120, Mesa, AZ 85201), 480/610-3300, covers the Superstition and Four Peaks Wilderness Areas and the Apache Trail's western and central parts; hours are Mon.–Fri. 7:45 A.M.–4:30 P.M. **Roosevelt Lake Visitor Center,** in Roosevelt south of the dam on AZ 188 (HC 02, Box 4800, Roosevelt, AZ 85545), 928/467-3200, looks after Burnt Corral Recreation Site and the eastern end of the drive, as well as the Roosevelt Lake area. It's open daily 7:45 A.M.–4:30 P.M. Online, you'll find Tonto National Forest info at www.fs.fed.us/r3/tonto.

SUPERSTITION WILDERNESS

Some of the Southwest's best desert hikes wind through the canyons and mountains of this 160,200-acre wilderness. It lies south of the Salt River Canyon and Apache Trail, about 40 miles east of Phoenix. Elevations range from about 2,000 feet along the west boundary to over 6,000 feet in the eastern uplands. Desert vegetation dominates, but a few pockets of ponderosa pine hang onto the highest slopes. Wildflowers may put on colorful extravaganzas in early spring and following summer rains.

Gold Fever

Legends tell of Don Miguel Peralta discovering fantastic amounts of gold somewhere in the Superstitions in 1845. He and his miners, however, met their deaths at the hands of Apache and took the location of Peralta's Sombrero Mine to their graves. At least one member of Peralta's party survived the massacre, the stories go, and some 30 years later revealed the location of the mine to a German immigrant, Jacob Waltz. Locally known as The Dutchman, Waltz worked the mine without ever revealing its location. Those who tried to follow him into the Superstitions were either lost in the maze of canyons or found murdered. The power of the Lost Dutchman legends have intensified since the prospector's death in 1891.

The stories about Jacob Waltz and his Lost Dutchman Mine may be just tall tales. Despite the efforts of thousands of gold-crazed prospectors, no major finds have ever been confirmed. Geologists studying the mountains say that they are remnants of volcanic calderas, an unlikely source of rich veins of precious metal. Perhaps the crafty Dutchman worked as a fence for gold thieves employed in the Vulture Mine near Wickenburg. Miners stealing nuggets wouldn't be able to sell their loot in Wickenburg, so Waltz may have run a gold-laundering operation by caching the Vulture gold in the Superstitions. If so, he still has a lot of people fooled, even after 100 years!

Climate

Spring and autumn bring the most pleasant weather for a visit to the Superstitions. Winter is often fine at lower elevations, though snow and cold hit the higher areas. Summer, which lasts from May to October, can get unbearably hot. Temperatures can exceed 115°F in the shade—and there's precious little shade. You can venture into the Superstitions in the summer on a crack-of-dawn journey, then be out by late morning when the heat hits. Carry plenty of water, especially in summer when springs and creeks dry up.

Hiking

Twelve trailheads and 180 miles of trail offer all kinds of possibilities. Because they're so close to Phoenix, the Superstitions get unusually heavy traffic for a wilderness area. The west half, especially near the Peralta and First Water trailheads, receives the most visitors. You're more likely to see javelina, desert mule deer, mountain lion, black bear, and other wildlife in the eastern part of the range. You don't need a permit to hike or camp in the Superstitions; just leave the area as you found it and limit groups to 15 people, stays to 14 days. Horses are allowed; bring feed, as grazing is prohibited. Laws protect the wilderness from prospecting involving surface disturbance; no one can file new claims. For additional information, check with the Forest Services offices listed above and take a look at guidebooks such as *Hikers Guide to the Superstition Wilderness* by Jack Carlson and Elizabeth Stewart.

FOUR PEAKS WILDERNESS

This wilderness area covers 60,743 acres in the southern Mazatzal Mountains. The Salt River Canyon, now filled with Canyon and Apache Lakes, separates it from the Superstition Mountains. Four Peaks, visible over a large section of central Arizona, have long been a major landmark. From their deeply incised lower slopes along Canyon Lake at an elevation of 1,600 feet, the mountains top off at Browns Peak, northernmost of the four at 7,657 feet.

Vegetation ranges from saguaro cactus at the base to ponderosa pine, Douglas fir, and aspen near the top. Javelina, deer, black bear, mountain lion, and smaller animals inhabit the slopes. Arizona's highest concentration of black bear live here; wise campers hang food out of reach at night. Trailheads can be reached from AZ 87 on the west (northeast of Mesa) and from AZ 188 on the east (northwest of Roosevelt Dam). A huge fire in 1996, caused by two careless campers near Lone Pine Saddle, burned 61,000 acres and badly damaged several trails. Forest Service staff can advise on current conditions.

APACHE JUNCTION TO THEODORE ROOSEVELT DAM

Once a raiding route for Apache, the Apache Trail (AZ 88) still has a primitive and imposing character. It twists and climbs as it tries to find a way through the rugged land. Jagged ridges, towering cliffs, and the desert itself inspire awe among travelers. Much of the Apache Trail, now designated a National Scenic Byway, is graded dirt. Due to narrow bridges and blind curves, the road isn't recommended for large trailers or large RVs. From the Phoenix area, take the Superstition Freeway or other roads east to Apache Junction and follow signs for AZ 88. Mileages given are from the beginning of AZ 88 in Apache Junction.

Horsin' Around

Two miles from Apache Junction on AZ 88, you'll come to Tomahawk Road, the turnoff to **O.K. Corral Stables** (it's 1.7 miles to the left down Tomahawk), 480/982-4040; www.okcorrals.com. The stables offer a variety of guided horseback rides in the Superstition and Goldfield Mountains. There's an RV park here too.

Goldfield Ghost Town and Mine Tours

The original mining camp of Goldfield boomed in the mid-1890s with the discovery of gold. Its population peaked at 5,000 before drifting away after mining yields dwindled in 1915. Nothing remains of the tent and adobe buildings, and the actual mine is too dangerous to enter, but you can see a lot of history and artifacts in today's reconstruction on the site (Mile 4.5 along the Trail).

The weathered buildings and mine exhibit of Goldfield, 480/983-0333, feature one of the best displays of mining equipment in the Southwest along with many activities and exhibits. Admission is free—you just pay for what interests you. Goldfield Ghost Town and Mine Tours is open daily all year about 10 A.M.–5 P.M.; things slow down in summer when some businesses may go to shorter hours or close weekdays.

Look for the 20-stamp mill behind the Goldfield Livery building. Other outdoor exhibits include a five-stamp mill, engines, and old trucks. The underground mine is modeled after the nearby Mammoth Mine, one of the world's richest until closed by flooding. A guide takes you on a 25-minute tour and explains how miners tunneled and worked in the stope. An authentic headframe, hoists, ore cars, and miners' tools add to the atmosphere. Open daily 10 A.M.–5 P.M.; admission is $5 adults, $3 children 6–12. A nearby shop offers gold panning and gold nugget jewelry.

Superstition Mountains Museum, 480/983-4888, features exhibits about wildlife, prehistoric tribes, prospectors, miners, cowboys, and how the Superstitions formed. A video tells the legends of the Lost Dutchman Mine. The gift shop offers a great selection of regional books. Open daily 9 A.M.–4 P.M. from Sept.–May, then Mon.–Fri. 9 A.M.–3 P.M. in summer. Admission is $3 adults, $2.50 seniors 55 and up, $1 students grades 1–12; www.superstitionmountainmuseum.org. In the future, the museum plans to move to a new building three-quarters of a mile back towards Apache Junction on the Apache Trail.

Superstition Scenic Railroad rolls down its narrow-gauge tracks with a narrated tour of the history and geology of the Goldfield area; it runs daily (Thurs.–Sun. from June to Oct.) 10 A.M.–5 P.M. Up on the hill at the **Bordello Museum,** you can find out how lonely miners of bygone years entertained themselves; open daily 10 A.M.–5 P.M. Other attractions at Goldfield include horseback and carriage rides (both closed in summer), a live reptile exhibit, and a photo studio. Gunslingers shoot up the town from January to April. You can shop for Western duds, crafts, jewelry, rocks, and sweets. **Apache Trail Tours,** 480/982-7661, offers day and overnight hiking trips in the Superstition Wilderness, driving tours on the Apache Trail, and backcountry drives.

If you'd like to stay the night in the ghost town, **Goldfield Boarding House,** 480/986-7680, offers old-style rooms. If you get a hankerin' for some grub, **Mammoth Steakhouse and Saloon,** 480/983-6402, serves lunch and dinner daily but lacks a non-smoking area; bands entertain some nights. A bakery down the street prepares breakfasts and lunches.

A better place nearby for dinner is the **Mining Camp Restaurant,** 480/982-3181, which offers Western fare in a replica of an old mining camp's cook shanty. It's open Oct.–June daily for dinner and Sunday for lunch; $17–19 adults (10 percent off for seniors), $8.45 children 6–12, reservations recommended; from Goldfield, head 0.2 mile back toward Apache Junction, then turn left one mile at the sign.

Lost Dutchman State Park

At Mile 5.4, the park offers picnicking, day hiking, and camping at the base of the Superstition Mountains. Staff present interpretive programs Oct.–April, including evening talks (usually Fridays) and guided hikes (usually Saturdays). The Native Plant Trail loop near the park entrance identifies desert plants on a paved and wheelchair-accessible path. Longer trails loop onto the slopes of the adjacent Superstition Mountains in the Tonto National Forest; ask for a map at the ranger station. Treasure Loop Trail has views and a variety of desert plants along its 2.4-mile length. Connecting trails allow for a variety of other loops too, and extend north to First Water Road and south and east to Hieroglyphic Canyon and Peralta Trailhead. Siphon Draw Trail climbs for the high country, 3.2 miles roundtrip to a basin at an elevation of 3,100 ft.; adventurous hikers can continue up a rough route to the Flatiron (4,862 feet), a five-hour, five-mile total roundtrip.

Individual campsites are first-come, first-served; only groups can reserve areas. The popular campground often fills Jan. to mid-April, so plan to arrive early then. Overflow camping may be available, especially on weekdays. Entry costs $5/vehicle for day use or $10/vehicle for camping with water, showers, and a dump station, but no hookups; 480/982-4485.

Just down the highway from the park you'll enter **Tonto National Forest.** and come to the turnoff to **First Water Trailhead,** (three miles in on the right), a popular starting point for hikes in the Superstition Wilderness; $4/day parking fee.

Different Points of View

At Mile 7.8, **Needle Vista Viewpoint** provides a good look at Weaver's Needle in the Superstitions. The Lost Dutchman Mine is said to lie in the shadow of this striking 4,535-foot pinnacle, which still beckons to gold seekers. The pinnacle's name honors frontier scout Pauline Weaver. Local Apache had a different appellation for it, likening it to a certain part of a stallion's anatomy.

Farther down the highway you'll come to **Canyon Lake Vista Point** (at Mile 12.5). The series of lakes along the Salt River provides fishing and boating for visitors and precious water for Phoenix. Past the viewpoint, the road sweeps down from the heights to the lakeshore.

Canyon Lake

Mormon Flat Dam, completed in 1925, created Canyon Lake. Anglers here have hooked largemouth and yellow bass, trout, catfish, bluegill, carp, walleye, and crappie. During the busy midspring to mid-summer season, Sunday crowds sometimes fill all available parking places in the Canyon Lake area; try to arrive early.

Acacia Picnic Site (at Mile 14.5) offers swimming at a gravel beach and fishing; $4/vehicle. Nearby **Palo Verde Boating Site** (Mile 14.7) has a boat ramp and restrooms but no picnic tables; $4/vehicle and $2/watercraft. **Boulder Recreation Site** (Mile 14.9) provides a swimming beach, picnic tables, and wheelchair-accessible fishing; $4/vehicle.

At Mile 15.2, you'll come to **Canyon Lake Marina,** 602/986-5546. The marina offers boat rental and storage, fishing supplies, a campground, and a restaurant. Laguna Beach Campground here is open all year for picnicking ($10), tent camping ($12), and RV camping ($15 with no hookups, $25 with hookups); showers in-

cluded. Another camping area, **the Point,** is accessible only to boaters; it's on the left, three miles upstream from the marina. The marina restaurant serves breakfast Sat.–Sun., lunch daily, and dinner Fri.–Sun.; the dinner menu lists steak, chicken, and seafood. Also here, the **Dolly Steamboat** takes visitors on scenic 90-minute narrated nature cruises ($14.80 adults, $8 ages 6–12), 90-minute lunch cruises, and 2.5–3.5-hour dinner cruises; call 480/827-9144 for times and to make the required dinner reservations. The vessel's double decks have both indoor and outdoor seating; www.dollysteamboat.com.

Boulder Canyon Trail #103 begins across the highway from the marina and climbs up a ridge to spectacular views of the Superstitions and Canyon Lake area. The trail continues on through La Barge and Boulder Canyons, linking with several other trails in the Superstition Wilderness.

Continuing down the highway, you'll soon come to **Laguna Boating Site** (Mile 15.5); $4/vehicle and $2/watercraft.

Tortilla Flat and Vicinity

Tortilla Flat (pop. six) is just a tiny community, but it's the only one along this section of road (Mile 17.3). The faded Western-style buildings—including a café, post office, country store, and curio shop—look as though they're out of a movie set. Old mining and farming relics lie around. You may see a dummy outlaw swinging in the breeze. A hungry pioneer, who perceived the surrounding rock outcrops as stacks of tortillas, reportedly gave the place its name.

The country store has an ice cream parlor—try a scoop of prickly pear. The café, 480/984-1776, wallpapered with dollar bills, serves American and Mexican meals. During winter, barbecued food is served on the patio.

Tortilla Campground (elev. 1,752 feet) across the highway is popular with RVers; the season runs Oct.–April; $12 per night. Reservations can be made with the Mesa Ranger District office; 480/610-3300.

Continuing down the highway, you'll reach the end of the pavement at Mile 23.0 and the beginning of 21 miles of graded dirt road to

Roosevelt Dam. A mile farther, **Tortilla Trailhead** for the Superstition Wilderness is on the right.

Fish Creek Hill to Apache Lake

At Mile 24.9, **Fish Creek Hill Scenic Vista** on the left is well worth a stop. The paved path leads to overlooks of rugged canyons. Four Peaks stand to the north. There's a restroom.

The descent down Fish Creek Hill provides a thrill, especially for the driver, who must negotiate sharp bends as the road traverses a cliff face and drops 1,500 feet in three miles. Fish Creek, near the bottom, is said to have native Gila chub and Gila topminnow. Hikers can head up Fish Creek Canyon.

At Mile 30.6, hikers might wish to turn right onto Forest Road 212 and continue three bumpy miles to Reavis Trailhead. **Reavis Ranch Trail #109** crosses the eastern part of the Superstition Wilderness through ponderosa pine forests to Reavis Ranch; other trails branch off for a variety of hikes. Elisha Reavis lived a hermit's life on his ranch from 1872 until his death in 1896.

At Mile 32.4, **Apache Lake Vista** provides views of the lake in the canyon below. Held back by Horse Mesa Dam, Apache Lake reaches nearly to Roosevelt Lake—a distance of 17 miles. Turn down the road 1.3 miles here for **Apache Lake Marina and Resort,** 928/467-2511. The motel offers rooms ($60–70 d) and suites with kitchens ($75–85 d). RV sites go for $20, including hookups and showers. The restaurant features steak, chicken, and seafood among other American and some Mexican items; it's open daily for breakfast, lunch, and dinner. Other amenities include a swimming beach, store with fishing and camping supplies, boat ramp, fishing- and pontoon-boat rentals, car and boat fuel, and boat storage. Anglers can catch smallmouth and largemouth bass, trout, yellow bass, catfish, sunfish, and walleye. Officers staff the **Maricopa County Sheriff Aid Station,** 928/467-2619, at the lake on weekends and holidays.

At Mile 34.5, unpaved Forest Road 250 leads one mile down to **Davis Wash** on the lake; this undeveloped area has outhouses and costs $4/vehicle day use or camping, $2/watercraft. The riparian vegetation here lies on a floodplain

surrounded by desert hillsides. The turnoff may not be signed; look for it between Mileposts 231 and 232.

At Mile 39.5 you'll pass the sign for **Burnt Corral Recreation Site,** which lies one-third mile to the left on a paved road. Mesquite trees shade the picnicking and camping sites on the shore of Apache Lake at an elevation of 2,060 feet. Visitors enjoy the delightful setting and well-spaced sites in addition to a beach, drinking water, and paved boat ramp. Camping costs $9 for a single space; doubles, triples, and quintuples are also available. Day use costs $4/vehicle and $2/watercraft. Sites tend to fill on most weekends except in winter. Dispersed camping is possible along the shore at the adjacent **Lower Burnt Corral,** but this area is a floodplain; turn left after the fee station and go across the cattle guard. At Mile 40.2, **Upper Burnt Corral** offers a primitive lakeshore area on a small cove; drive 0.7 mile on the Apache Trail beyond the Burnt Corral junction, then turn left half a mile on unpaved Forest Road 57, which may not be signed. **Three Mile Wash** is another primitive area a bit farther up the lake at Mile 42.3; the unsigned turnoff is at a bend of the Apache Trail near Milepost 239. A bumpy dirt road leads 0.2 mile down to the lake in a floodplain area. These undeveloped sites have a $4/vehicle and $2/watercraft fee for day or overnight use; outhouses are the only facilities, but you can get water at Burnt Corral. The Roosevelt Lake Visitor Center, 928/467-3200, has information on this area.

From Three Mile Wash, the Trail begins a climb through Apache Lake Gorge to Roosevelt Dam. Viewpoints with interpretive signs before and after the dam are worth a stop to admire the structure and its surroundings.

Theodore Roosevelt Dam

An engineering feat in its day, the 284-foot-high structure is still the world's highest masonry dam. The arduous task of cutting and placing the stone blocks lasted from 1903 to 1911, when President Teddy Roosevelt motored over the Apache Trail for the dedication ceremony. By the late 20th century, engineers worried that the original dam couldn't survive a moderate earthquake or a massive flood, so a new concrete dam was built over the old structure. It now towers 77 feet higher than before and raises the operating high water level by 15 feet. A graceful arched suspension bridge spans the lake just above the dam.

THEODORE ROOSEVELT LAKE

Fed by Tonto Creek from the north and the Salt River from the east, the reservoir stretches 23 miles long and as much as two miles wide. With approximately 19,199 surface acres when full, it's the largest of the four Salt River lakes. Summers at Roosevelt's 2,151-foot elevation are as hot as those in the Valley, but water-skiing and boating attract many visitors. Anglers enjoy the rest of the year, when it's cooler. Known as a good bass and crappie lake, Roosevelt also contains catfish and sunfish.

Great Basin Canada geese take up residence during the winter at Bermuda Flat on the north arm. Part of this area is closed to the public November 15–February 15, but you can view the geese from the highway. Bald eagles use the middle third of the north shore for nesting and foraging; no camping is allowed here.

Fluctuating lake levels determine which boat ramps and recreation sites will be open, so it's a good idea to check with the Roosevelt Lake Visitor Center before coming out. The Forest Service offers developed campgrounds, primitive camping areas, and boat ramps along the west shore. Camp hosts can be found at the developed and some primitive camping areas except in summer. Daily fees run $11 for the developed campgrounds, $4 for day or overnight use of primitive areas, and $2 per watercraft. You'll find fish-cleaning stations at Grapevine, Schoolhouse, Cholla, and Windy Hill. Dump stations are on AZ 188 opposite the Cholla Recreation Site and between the Windy Hill and Grapevine Recreation Site turnoffs.

If you'd like more solitude and don't mind driving on unpaved roads, you can head over to the east side of the lake via the A-Cross Road; this route runs between AZ 188 at the north end of the lake (a ford over Tonto Creek may be too high at times) and the Young Road (AZ 288).

Hikers can visit pools of Salome (SAL-oh-may) Creek in the south end of Salome Wilderness from A-Cross Trailhead on A-Cross Road.

Information

Interpretive staff at the **Roosevelt Lake Visitor Center** in Roosevelt, 1.3 miles southeast of the dam on AZ 188, can tell you about area facilities, fishing, hiking, camping, and boating. They sell annual passes for the Roosevelt Lake recreation sites. The exhibit room has displays of wildlife and illustrates the history of the Tonto Basin's peoples from prehistoric Salado residents to the dam's construction workers. A bookstore has a good selection of regional titles and maps. A few picnic tables are outside. The visitor center is open daily 7:45 A.M.–4:30 P.M. Write to HC 02, Box 4800, Roosevelt, AZ 85545, or call 928/467-3200; www.fs.fed.us/r3/tonto.

Recreation Areas

Cholla Recreation Site (5.8 miles northwest of Roosevelt) and **Windy Hill Recreation Site** (2.5 miles southeast of Roosevelt, then north two miles on a paved road) offer campgrounds with water, solar showers, boat ramps, and playgrounds, but no hookups; sites cost $11. Blevins Picnic Site in Windy Hill Recreation Site costs $4/vehicle. **Grapevine Group Site** (5.5 miles southeast of Roosevelt, then north 2.5 miles) has paved roads, a boat ramp, and showers; reservations are required, 928/467-3200. Grapevine Wash (open gate on left just before the Grapevine Group Site) is a primitive camping area and costs $4/vehicle. **Schoolhouse Recreation Site** (6.7 miles southeast of Roosevelt, then north three miles) lacks showers.

Vineyard Picnic Area is 3.5 miles northwest of Roosevelt and costs $4/vehicle. Primitive camping areas include Bachelor Cove (5.1 miles northwest of Roosevelt), Cholla Bay (5.6 miles northwest of Roosevelt), and Bermuda Flat (about eight miles northwest of Roosevelt; closed Nov. 15–Feb. 15 for the Canada geese); these have a $4/vehicle and $2/watercraft daily fee.

Diversion Dam Recreation Area is on the Salt River just above its entrance to Roosevelt Lake. Several river access points provide a place for river runners to take out above a diversion dam and put in below the dam. People also come for picnicking, birding, fishing, and playing in the water. The recreation area has toilets but no drinking water or charge. From the AZ 188-AZ 288 junction 14 miles southeast of the dam and 15 miles northwest of Globe, turn north four miles on AZ 288, then turn left about one mile on Forest Road 465; another access point (unsigned) is across the Salt River Bridge 1.2 miles farther on AZ 288; the Roosevelt Lake Visitor Center has a map.

Services

Roosevelt Marina, 1.3 miles southeast of the dam in Roosevelt, 928/467-2245, has a primitive campground ($6 plus $2/watercraft), boat rentals (fishing and pontoon), wet and dry boat storage, a paved boat ramp, a snack bar, gasoline for boats, and a store. **Lakeview Mobile Home Park,** across the highway, 928/467-2203, has RV spaces with hookups ($21).

Spring Creek RV Park & Motel, 8.4 miles southeast of Roosevelt and 0.6 mile north of the resort turnoff, 928/467-2888, offers rooms at $45 d ($65 d with kitchen), RV sites at $20 with hookups, and a nine-hole golf course; www.rooseveltlake.com. The nearby **Quail's Nest Bar & Grill,** 928/467-2106, serves grilled food, pasta, sandwiches, soups, and salads daily except Tuesday for lunch and dinner. **Spring Creek Store** sells groceries, gasoline, and camping and fishing supplies. **Roosevelt Post Office** lies across the highway.

Roosevelt Lake Resort is nine miles southeast of Roosevelt (17 miles northwest of Globe), then east 0.6 mile, 928/467-2276. Rooms cost $30 s, $35 d; cabins have kitchens (bring your own cookware) and run $35 s, $40 d. Expect to pay more on summer weekends. The restaurant serves breakfast, lunch and dinner, though it doesn't open until 10 A.M. Mon.–Friday.

Rock House Grocery, 5.5 miles north on AZ 288 (Young Hwy.), offers provisions, gasoline, and a trailer park (usually full); 928/467-2484.

In Punkin Center, a village 20 miles northwest of Roosevelt off AZ 188, you can stay at **Punkin**

Center Lodge, 928/479-2229. Rates for up to four people run $38 ($50 kitchenette). Next door, the **Steakhouse,** 928/479-2627, is open daily for lunch and dinner; there's live entertainment on Friday and Saturday. RV parks are nearby.

TONTO NATIONAL MONUMENT

Two well-preserved cliff dwellings constructed by the prehistoric Salado overlook the blue waters of Roosevelt Lake. The Salado lived in this part of the Salt River Valley about A.D. 1150–1450. Skillful farmers, they dug irrigation canals to water their corn, squash, beans, grain amaranth, and cotton. They also roamed the desert hills for cactus fruits, mesquite beans, deer, pronghorn, and many other wild foods. Crafts included beautiful polychrome pottery and intricately woven cotton cloth.

At first they built small, scattered pueblos along the river, but about A.D. 1250 some Salado began living on more defensible ridgetops. From A.D. 1300 until their departure soon after A.D. 1400, part of the population moved into caves like those in the monument.

Visitor Center and Cliff Dwellings

Exhibits illustrate how the Salado lived and what we know of their history. Stone tools, pottery, cotton cloth, and other artifacts reveal their artistic talents. You can watch a video introduction and shop for books and maps. A nature trail near the visitor center identifies desert plants. The self-guided trail on the hillside above and behind the visitor center leads up to the Lower Cliff Dwelling. Originally the cave contained 19 rooms, with another 12 in the annex outside, but those exposed to the weather have worn away. Allow one hour for the trip; you'll climb 350 feet on a paved path.

The Upper Cliff Dwelling, reached by a different trail, is about twice the size of the Lower, but it's farther away and requires advance planning. You can visit the Upper Cliff Dwelling only on ranger-guided tours, which are conducted Nov.–April; call or write to check on days and times. The free tours last about three hours and involve a three-mile roundtrip hike with an elevation gain of 600 feet.

The monument, 928/467-2241, is open daily 8 A.M.–5 P.M., but the trail closes one hour earlier. The visitor center is south one mile off AZ 188, 1.8 miles southeast of Roosevelt and 24 miles northwest of Globe; entrance fee is $3/person age 16 and up. For more information, write Tonto National Monument, HC 02, Box 4602, Roosevelt, AZ 85545; www.nps.gov/tont. A picnic area with water is on the left, halfway in from the highway to the visitor center. If you're driving the Apache Trail Loop, this is the halfway point in time; Apache Junction is 2–3 hours away.

SALT RIVER CANYON WILDERNESS

Fifty-one miles of lively whitewater dance through the Salt River from the US 60 bridge north of Globe down to the AZ 288 bridge near Roosevelt Lake. Boaters can raft or kayak on one- or two-day trips on the upper section, or run the entire stretch in 3–5 days. Midweek travel gives the best chance for solitude, especially in the upper section. Only experienced river-runners should attempt this wild water, as several rapids through the twisting canyons have a rating of Class IV. The bigger rapids have earned names such as "Baptism," "Maytag Chute," "Reforma," "Overboard," "Cliff Hanger," and "Wakeup." Rafting companies (see below) supply skilled crew and all the equipment so that anyone in good health can go through. Trips use paddle rafts (everyone participates in paddling), oar boats (only the guide rows), and combinations of the two. The companies request several weeks' advance notice on all the trips.

The Forest Service requires visitor groups to be no more than 15, to use suitable nonmotorized craft, and to practice "no trace" camping. Large rafts over 15 feet can be too unwieldy; open canoes will swamp. Because the Salt has become very popular, all river users must use a fire pan, carry out all non-burnable trash, and pack out all human solid waste.

Flow levels depend on the winter snowpack, so spring affords the best chance of sufficient

SOUTH-CENTRAL

© BILL WEIR

Horseshoe Bend

water. The liveliest rapids (Class III–IV) most commonly occur mid-March to early April, and the weather is usually reliable after late March. Bridge-to-bridge trips depend on water level—fast flows in early season (March and April) make it a three-day float; lower flows later in the season (May or June) make for four- or five-day trips. The Salt River Project has a recording of flow rates, 602/236-5929, or you can check the USGS website at water.usgs.gov/real-time.html. Generally for the Salt River, 750 cubic feet per second is considered low water and 4,000 cfs or above is high water.

Permits

Rafting companies take care of the needed permits for their trips. Private parties must plan well ahead. You'll need a tribal permit along the upper stretch because part of the south shore belongs to the San Carlos Apache tribe and the north shore to the White Mountain Apache, who issue the permits; permits won't be required if you start from Horseshoe Bend and maybe from Gleason Flat (check). The store near the US 60 bridge and other outlets on the reservation sell tribal permits, which are easily obtained. For information on the tribal permits, contact the Hon-Dah Ski and Sport Shop, 928/369-7669, or the White Mountain Game & Fish Dept., P.O. Box 220, White River, AZ 85941; 928/338-4385. The Forest Service requires a permit March 1–May 15 for the wilderness section between Gleason Flat and Roosevelt Lake. Since demand far exceeds available dates, permits are issued by a lottery system; contact the Globe Ranger District office, 7680 S. Six Shooter Canyon Rd., Globe, AZ 85501; 928/402-6200. Both the Globe Ranger District and Phoenix Supervisors (602/225-5200) offices have a detailed booklet on the Upper Salt River.

Rafting Tours

Blue Sky Whitewater offers Salt River trips from the Salt River Bridge to Salt Draw in one day (12 miles, $100), to Gleason Flat in two days (22 miles, $255), and all the way through to the AZ 288 bridge in 3–5 days ($125/day). Spring trips (March–April) use wetsuits (in-

cluded); camping gear can be rented for the multi-day trips. Gila River trips are offered too. Contact the office at 143 N. High St., Globe, AZ 85501; 928/425-5252, 800/425-5253; www.gobluesky.com.

Far Flung Adventures offers Salt River trips March through May, with choices of one-day trips from the Salt River Bridge to Salt Banks ($95–99), two days to Gleason Flat ($300), or all the way to the AZ 288 bridge in three ($425–450) or five ($700) days. The company, based in New Mexico, also runs trips there and in Colorado, Texas, and Mexico. Local office is at P.O. Box 2804, Globe, AZ 85502; 928/425-7272, 800/231-7238; www.farflung.com.

Desert Whitewater runs Salt River trips during the March to May season. Day trips from the Hwy. 60 Bridge to Mescal Falls cost $99; two-day runs continue down to Gleason Flat ($290). Three-day trips usually start at Gleason Flat and go to the Hwy. 288 Bridge ($420), while five-day ($650) trips cover the whole distance. Camping gear can be rented. For more information, contact the company at P.O. Box 3493, Flagstaff, AZ 86003; 928/774-1743, 800/272-3353; www.desertwhitewater.com.

Mild to Wild offers rafting trips of one and two days in the Salt River Canyon from late February to May; costs run $98 for a one-day float from Salt River Bridge to below Salt Banks (12 miles), and $275 for two days from the bridge to Gleason Flat (22 miles). Wetsuits and camping gear may be rented. Mild to Wild also offers trips on the Verde River in Arizona and on rivers in Colorado. There's a local office in Globe in season, but you can contact the main office at 1111 Camino del Rio, Durango, CO 81301; 800/567-6745; www.mild2wildrafting.com.

GLOBE

Tucked into a narrow valley between the Apache Mountains to the northeast and the Pinal Mountains to the south and west, Globe is a handy stopping place for travelers. The town's 3,500-foot elevation provides a pleasant climate most of the year. Though its years of glory as a big copper-mining center have long passed, Globe still has a

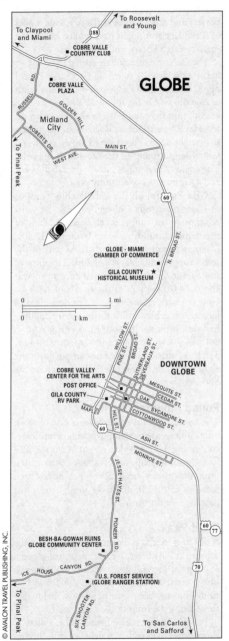

GLOBE

To Roosevelt and Young

To Claypool and Miami

COBRE VALLE COUNTRY CLUB

COBRE VALLE PLAZA

Midland City

GOLDEN HILL

RUSSELL RD.

ROBERTS DR.

MAIN ST.

WEST AVE.

To Pinal Peak

60

GLOBE - MIAMI CHAMBER OF COMMERCE

N. BROAD ST.

GILA COUNTY ★
HISTORICAL MUSEUM

0   1 mi
0   1 km

WILLOW ST.
PINE ST.
BROAD ST.
SUTHERLAND ST.
DEVEREAUX ST.

DOWNTOWN GLOBE

COBRE VALLEY CENTER FOR THE ARTS
POST OFFICE
GILA COUNTY RV PARK

MESQUITE ST.
OAK CEDAR ST.
SYCAMORE ST.
COTTONWOOD ST.
MAPLE
HILL ST.

60

ASH ST.

MONROE ST.

JESSE HAYES ST.

PIONEER RD.

BESH-BA-GOWAH RUINS
GLOBE COMMUNITY CENTER

ICE HOUSE CANYON RD.

60 77

70

U.S. FOREST SERVICE
(GLOBE RANGER STATION)

SIX SHOOTER CANYON RD.

To Pinal Peak

To San Carlos and Safford

lot of character. On a drive down Broad Street you can visit its museum, view ruins of the Old Dominion Copper Mine, and see many buildings dating from the early 1900s.

The chamber of commerce, also on Broad Street, offers a *Walking Tour of Historic Downtown Globe* leaflet that details the history of these old structures. You can also pick up a *Globe-Miami Drive Yourself Highway Mine Tour* leaflet describing six mines, historic and modern, visible from US 60 in the Globe and Miami areas; none of the mine sites is open to the public. Antique, craft, and gift shops abound in Globe; the chamber has a list.

History

In 1875, prospectors struck silver in the hills of the western part of the San Carlos Apache Indian Reservation. The most remarkable find, a globe-shaped silver nugget, reportedly had the rough outlines of the continents scarred on its surface. Miners converged on the area, which was officially sliced off the reservation, then set up camp on the east bank of Pinal Creek. Their presence didn't go over well with the Apache, who regularly menaced the camp until Geronimo's surrender in 1886.

The silver began to give out after only four years, but by then rich copper deposits had been discovered beneath the silver lodes. The Old Dominion Copper Company moved in, and during the early 1900s its copper mine ranked as one of the greatest in the world. Globe prospered too—its 50 restaurants and saloons never closed, and about 150 sporting women worked out of little shacks along N. Broad Street. George W.P. Hunt arrived in 1881 as a young man and worked his way up to become a leading merchant and banker before going on to serve as Arizona's first governor. Labor troubles and declining yields began to eat into mining profits, and the Depression shut down the Old Dominion completely in 1931. Copper mining shifted to nearby Miami, leaving Globe as a quiet county seat.

Gila County Historical Museum

This small but varied collection includes Native American, pioneer, and mining artifacts. The

SOUTH-CENTRAL

Indian Room displays prehistoric pottery from the area and some fine modern baskets. Period exhibits—Governor Hunt's bedroom, ranch room, printing shop, and mine superintendent's office—recall life in early Globe. Ore cars and large machinery sit outside. The museum building, which dates from 1914, served as the company's mine rescue station for many years. You can visit Mon.–Fri. 10 A.M.–4 P.M. and Sat. 11 A.M.–3 P.M.; donations welcome; 928/425-7385. It's at 1330 N. Broad St., next door to the chamber of commerce and opposite the Old Dominion Copper Co. Mine.

Cobre Valley Center for the Arts

Local artists have banded together to open an art gallery and gift shop in the old Gila County Courthouse, built in 1906–07. Doing much of the restoration themselves, local volunteers also added a theater used by the Copper Cities Community Players. You can see the art exhibits (some rotate monthly) Sunday noon–5P.M. and Mon.–Sat. 10 A.M.–5 P.M.; free. Go downstairs to see works of the Handweavers Studio and a stained-glass studio. It's downtown at the corner of Broad and Oak Sts.; 928/425-0884. Handicap access is on Oak Street.

Besh Ba Gowah

Archaeologists count 200 rooms at this pueblo, built and inhabited between A.D. 1225 and 1450, at a time when Salado villages lined both sides of Pinal Creek. An earlier village of pithouses associated with the Hohokam stood on this site about A.D. 600–1150. Exposed to both the elements and humans, Besh Ba Gowah has been weathered more than the Tonto National Monument cliff dwellings, but its extensive foundations and few remaining walls testify to its original size. The name Besh Ba Gowah comes from an Apache word meaning "metal camp."

A self-guided trail winds through the ruins, some restored, some only stabilized, some still unexcavated. The restored rooms contain baskets, pots, ladders, and other implements, arranged as if the Salado were still living here. An ethno-botanical garden displays native and cultivated plants used by prehistoric tribes. The

museum offers an introductory video, displays of pottery and other Salado artifacts, a scale model of the village as it might have looked in 1325, a small research library, and a gift shop.

The museum and ruins are open daily 9 A.M.–5 P.M.; 928/425-0320. Admission is $3 ages 12 and up, $2 seniors. Besh Ba Gowah is 1.5 miles south of downtown Globe; follow S. Broad Street to its end, turn right across the bridge, curve left on Jess Hayes Street/Pioneer Road one mile, make a sharp right up to Globe Community Center, and follow signs around to the far side of the ruin. The adjacent park offers picnic tables, ball fields, and a summertime swimming pool.

Gila Pueblo, on the Gila Pueblo Campus of Eastern Arizona College, can also be visited, though the ruin is much smaller. Many of the campus buildings date from the 1930s, when archaeologists reconstructed part of the ruin to appear much as it had during the time of the Salado. The village perished due to war about 1440, perhaps at the hands of Besh Ba Gowah warriors during a time of drought and famine. An exhibit inside the two-story building has some artifacts. It's open Mon.–Fri. 8 A.M.–5 P.M. (to 7 P.M. during main terms); 928/425-3151. Admission is free. The campus is on the right, one mile beyond Besh Ba Gowah on Six Shooter Canyon Road.

Round Mountain Park

The conical hill on the northeast side of town offers hiking, views, and picnicking. Four interconnecting trails provide a way to the top (a 426-foot climb) in loops of 1.7, 2.4, or three miles. From downtown, head east on Ash Street, then turn left (north) 0.6 mile on South Street, just past the Comfort Inn.

Pinal Peak

A dirt road winds up the timber-clad slopes to the summit at 7,812 feet. Weather permitting, you'll enjoy great views, hiking, picnicking, and two of the coolest campgrounds in the Tonto National Forest. See "Campgrounds" below for those along the summit road and nearby.

For the 18-mile drive from Globe, follow S. Broad Street to its end, turn right across the bridge, curve left on Jess Hayes Street/Pioneer Road to the junction of Ice House Canyon and Six Shooter Canyon Rds., turn right 2.5 miles on Ice House Canyon Road, turn right three miles on Kellner Canyon Road/Forest Road 55 (pavement ends), and then left 12.5 miles on Forest Road 651 to the summit. An alternative way in follows Russell Road from US 60 (opposite the AZ 188 turnoff). Keep right on Russell Road at a fork 0.3 mile in and continue south on what becomes Forest Road 55. Pavement ends 2.3 miles from US 60 and the road climbs up to the junction of Forest Road 651 in another 3.4 miles.

In summer, you can drive all the way to the top of Signal Peak, the highest point; at other times you walk the last bit. Ice House Canyon, Six Shooter, Telephone, Kellner Canyon, Squaw Spring, Bobtail Ridge, and Mill Creek Trails climb steeply from the valleys below. The Globe Ranger District office has trail descriptions and maps.

Accommodations

You'll find Globe's motels along US 60 (N. Broad, Willow, and E. Ash Streets). The older places offer the lowest rates.

Under $50: Listed from west to east are **Copper Hills Inn & Suites,** US 60 between Miami and Globe, 928/425-9232, $39 s, $44 d and up; **Belle-Aire Motel,** 1600 N. Broad St., 928/425-4406, with a pool, $22 s, $30 d; **Economy Inn,** 1105 N. Broad St., 928/425-5736, with a pool, $25 s, $32 d; **Willow Motel,** 792 N. Willow St., 928/425-9491, $20 s, $28 d; **Copper Manor Motel,** 637 E. Ash St., 928/425-7124, with a pool, $45–48 d; and **El Rancho Motel,** 1300 E. Ash St., 928/425-5757, $25 s, $32 d.

$50–100: Newer motels usually fall into this category. From west to east, these are **Holiday Inn Express,** 2119 Hwy. 60 on the west side of Globe, 928/425-7008, 800/HOLIDAY, $65 d; **Comfort Inn,** E. Ash and South St., 928/425-7575, 800/228-5150, with a pool and hot tub, $59 s, $69 d; **Days Inn,** 1630 E. Ash St., 928/425-5500, 800/329-7466, has a pool and hot tub, $55 d; **Ramada Limited,** 1699 E. Ash St., 928/425-5741, 800/256-8399, has a pool and hot tub, $58 d; and **Best Western**

Apache Gold Hotel & Casino, seven miles east on US 70, 928/402-5600, 800/272-2438, with restaurants, golf, pool, hot tub sauna, and exercise room, $59 d ($69 d Fri.–Sat.) or $99 d Jacuzzi room.

Bed and breakfast inns in town include **Noftsger Hill Inn,** housed downtown in a 1907 schoolhouse at 425 North St., 928/425-2260, $55–75 d; **Cedar Hill B&B,** downtown at 175 E. Cedar St., 928/425-7530, $50 d; and **The Hideaway,** Ice House Canyon Rd., 928/402-0454, $50 d (also apartments for $50 d but no breakfast).

Campgrounds

Gila County RV Park has dry sites for tents or RVs ($5) and hookup sites ($16). It's near downtown at 300 S. Pine St.; 928/425-4653. Take the Maple Street Exit from the Hwy. 60 bypass. RVs can park at **Apache Trail Mobile Park,** four miles north on AZ 188, then right on old State 88, $16 with hookups, 928/425-7979; and nearby **Holiday Hills Mobile Home Park,** $17 with hookups, 928/425-8585.

Tent campers and small RVs can head south to one of the Tonto National Forest campgrounds in the Pinal Mountains. **Sulphide del Rey** (elev. 4,500 feet) is 10 miles southwest of Globe via Jess Hayes Road, Ice House Canyon Road, Kellner Canyon Road/Forest Road 55, and Forest Road 651; open all year, no water or fee. **Lower Pinal** and **Upper Pinal** (elev. 7,500 feet), accessible April–Dec., are about 4.5 miles past Sulphide del Rey; Upper Pinal has water from about May to October; no fees. There are also Forest Service sites at **Pioneer Pass** (elev. 6,000 feet), accessible May–Nov., nine miles south via Jess Hayes Road and Ice House Canyon Road/Forest Road 112. No water or fee. The upper site has horse corrals. **Jones Water Campground** (elev. 4,500 feet) offers sites in oaks and cottonwoods 15 miles northeast of town on US 60; no water or fee. **Timber Camp** has sites in the cool pines at an elevation of 6,000 feet, 27 miles northeast of town on US 60; no water or fee.

Oak Flat (elev. 4,200 feet) offers year-round camping west on US 60 near Superior; no water or fee. The Globe Ranger District office has the

Tonto Forest map and recreation information; 928/402-6200.

Food

Family cafés that serve breakfast, lunch, and dinner daily include **Judy's Cook House,** in Cobre Valley Plaza on the west side of town, 928/425-5366; and **Country Kitchen,** 1505 E. Ash St. on the east side, 928/425-2137. **Java Junction** (closed Sunday) offers a selection of coffees, sandwiches, and desserts downtown at Cedar and Broad Sts., 928/402-8926. For pizza, it's **R&R Pizza Express,** 1100 N. Broad St. downtown, 928/425-8575 (closed Sunday); and **Pizza Hut,** 1497 E. Ash St., 928/425-4401. For Mexican and American cuisine, try **El Ranchito** (closed Mon.), 686 N. Broad St., 928/402-1348; **Guayos on the Trail,** (closed Tues.) 1.2 miles north on AZ 188, 928/425-9969; **La Luz del Dia Restaurant and Bakery** (breakfast & lunch; closed Sun.), 304 N. Broad St., 928/425-8400; **Gen's Café** (breakfast & lunch; closed Sun.), 247 S. Broad St., 928/425-4707; and **La Casita East,** 1960 E. Ash St., 928/402-9279. **China Taste,** 338 E. Ash St., 928/402-8448, offers oriental flavors in a variety of styles.

Popular restaurants without a non-smoking section include **Mesquite Restaurant,** serving steak, ribs, and Italian food (closed Sun.–Mon.), 598 N. Broad St. downtown, 928/425-6707; **Crestline Steak House** (dinner only), 1901 E. Ash St., 928/425-6269; and Mexican at **El Rey Cafe,** 999 N. Broad St. downtown, 928/425-2054.

Entertainment and Events

Globe Theatre screens current movies at 141 N. Broad St.; 928/425-5581.

Gila County Gem and Mineral Show sparkles in late January. **Historic Home and Building Tour,** accompanied by the **Antique and Quilt Show,** is in February; **Mining Country Boomtown Spree,** an arts and crafts fair in Miami, runs in April. **Copper Dust Stampede Rodeo, Dance, and Parade** shake up April or May. **Cinco de Mayo** brings entertainment and food to the weekend nearest May 5th. The **Golden Oldies Car Show** glit-

ters in May. **Fourth of July Fireworks** enliven midsummer. The **Gila County Fair** entertains in September. **Horse races** run on the first and second weekends in October. **Apache Jii** (Days) on the fourth Saturday in October honor the nearby Native American community with dances, crafts, and food by Apache and other Native American groups. **Veterans Pageant, Fair, and Rodeo** take place 19 miles east in San Carlos on Veterans Day weekend in November. **Christmas Light Parade** in mid-December and **Festival of Lights** at Besh Ba Gowah on the Sunday before Christmas add to holiday cheer.

Recreation

Globe Community Center has a swimming pool, picnic areas, and ball fields 1.5 miles south of downtown Globe; follow S. Broad Street to its end, turn right across the bridge, curve left on Jess Hayes Street/Pioneer Road one mile, then make a sharp right at the sign.

Cobre Valle Country Club, 928/473-2542, is open to the public with a nine-hole golf course and tennis and racquetball courts; it's just north on AZ 188 between Globe and Miami.

Information and Services

The very helpful **Globe-Miami Chamber of Commerce** is at 1360 N. Broad St. (P.O. Box 2539, Globe, AZ 85502); 928/425-4495, 800/804-5623. Stop by and pick up descriptions of historic walking tours of Globe and Miami and a highway driving tour past six local mines. It's open Mon.–Fri. 8 A.M.–5 P.M. and, from October to April, also Sat.–Sun. 10 A.M.–4 P.M.; www.globemiamichamber.com.

The **Globe Ranger District** office, 7680 S. Six Shooter Canyon Rd. (Globe, AZ 85501), 928/402-6200, provides details on camping, backcountry drives, an off-highway vehicle area, and hiking trails (which tend to be steep). It's two miles southeast of downtown; follow S. Broad Street to its end, turn right across the bridge, curve left on Jess Hayes Street, which becomes Pioneer Road, then Six Shooter Canyon Road. Hours are Mon.–Fri. 7:45 A.M.–4:30 P.M.; www.fs.fed.us/r3/tonto.

© BILL WEIR

"Wing Nut" at the oars, Gila River float trip above Winkelman

SOUTH-CENTRAL

The **Globe Public Library** is downtown at 339 S. Broad St.; 928/425-6111. The main **post office** is downtown at 101 S. Hill and Sycamore Streets; 928/425-2381. **Cobre Valley Community Hospital** is south of the US 60-AZ 188 junction on the west side of town; 928/425-3261.

Tours and Transportation

The Salt River north of town has beautiful canyon scenery and exciting whitewater. Rafters and kayakers can do trips of one to five days; see "Salt River Canyon Wilderness" above. Many of the commercial river companies on the Salt operate out of Globe.

Greyhound offers several westbound and eastbound buses daily from the station at 1666 E. Ash St.; 928/425-2301.

WINKELMAN AND THE COPPER BASIN

Copper mining and smelting continue on a large scale in several areas near the town of Winkelman, between Globe and Tucson on AZ 77. Mountain and desert scenery provide the biggest

attractions for visitors; AZ 77 between Winkelman and Globe follows a beautiful section of the Gila River (just north of Winkelman) and winds through the Mescal Mountains. AZ 177 between Winkelman and Superior also crosses rugged mountains, where you can stop at an overlook of ASARCO's Ray Mine, a vast open-pit copper mine. **White Canyon Wilderness** is west of AZ 177 via some rough roads; contact the Bureau of Land Management's Phoenix Field Office, 602/580-5500, for information on this area. **Aravaipa Canyon Wilderness** has a western trailhead off AZ 77 south of Winkelman. Note that even day-hikers must obtain a permit to visit here.

Winkelman and Vicinity

Smelter smokestacks tower over this community and its twin, Hayden. A park beside the Gila River offers picnicking and camping amid giant cottonwood trees; turn in at the AZ 77-AZ 177 junction.

Gila River

Boating offers the best way to enjoy the scenery and wildlife along a 10-mile section of the Gila

River upstream from Winkelman. This float has only gentle rapids, so it's good for beginners and families, too. Canoes, kayaks, and small rafts can run the river in 2–3 hours, depending on put-in location, river flow, and winds. Fallen trees and other hazards make tubing dangerous, however. Unlike most rivers of the region, the Gila flows all summer thanks to irrigation releases from Coolidge Dam. The boating season lasts from about March to August. Try to get a morning start, as afternoon headwinds can slow progress.

Put-in points can be tricky to find as they're unsigned and may require high-clearance, 4WD vehicles to reach. No permit is needed for a six-mile trip starting near the tiny community of Christmas on BLM land. If you have a state recreation permit, you can put in near Dripping Springs for a 10-mile run, as do the commercial trips. Recreation permits for this state trust land can be purchased in Tucson (520/628-5480) and Phoenix (602/542-4631). Needles Eye Wilderness farther upstream has no river access because of sacred sites on the San Carlos Indian Reservation and bald eagle nests.

Take-out is normally at the park in Winkelman. You can sign up for rafting tours with **Blue Sky Whitewater,** in Globe, 928/425-5252, 800/425-5253; www.gobluesky.com; and with **Chandelle Adventure Tours,** in Tucson, 520/577-1824, 800/242-6335; chandelletours.com.

GLOBE TO APACHE JUNCTION
Miami and Claypool
A strange landscape greets you on the approach to these two towns west of Globe. Many-tiered terraces of barren, buff-colored mine tailings and dark slag dumps dominate the view. Miami and Claypool stretch along Bloody Tanks Wash, named for a massacre of Apache in 1864 by a band of whites and allied Maricopa. Developers arrived in 1907 to lay out a town site named after Miami, Ohio. Giant copper-ore reduction plants built by the Miami Copper and Inspiration Companies resulted in the nickname "Concentrator City." Miami has had its ups and downs since, following the rise and fall in copper prices,

Saguaro cactus in bloom near the Gila River

© BILL WEIR

but production continues. The town has some historic buildings and a few restaurants.

Miami to Superior
Highway 60 climbs over jagged mountains between these two towns. Six miles west of Miami you'll see the vast workings of the open-pit Pinto Valley copper mine. The road continues climbing to the small community of "Top of the World," then descends into Devils Canyon. **Oak Flat Campground** (elev. 4,200 feet) lies in more open country nearby; turn south a half mile on Magma Mine Road at the sign near Milepost 231; open all year; no water or fee. West of Oak Flat, the highway drops through scenic, steep-walled Queen Creek Canyon to Superior.

Superior
Opening of the rich Silver King Mine in 1875, followed by development of the Silver Queen, brought streams of fortune hunters into this min-

eral-laden region. As at Globe, miners found rich deposits of copper when the surface silver began to play out. Superior lies just west of scenic Queen Creek Canyon in a valley surrounded by rugged mountains.

North of town you'll see the high smokestack of an idle smelter and extensive tailings from the Magma Copper Mine, where shafts plunge nearly 5,000 feet underground. The mine was closed at press time, though exploration continues. Perlite is also mined and processed in the area.

All travelers' facilities lie along US 60, which bypasses downtown. **El Portal Motel** has basic rooms at $35–45 d; 520/689-2886. **Superior RV Park** offers a quiet spot for adults just west of town with tent sites ($8), RV sites ($15 with hookups), coin showers, laundry, and a dump station; 520/689-5331. **Buckboard City** next door has a restaurant (breakfast and lunch daily), rock and gift shops, and the **"world's smallest museum,"** which packs local, natural, and cultural history into a tiny building; donation; 520/689-5800; www.worldssmallestmuseum.com. **Ed's La Casita Café West** serves Mexican and American food for lunch and dinner; closed Monday. **Eduardo's Pizza** is across the street. **Los Hermanos Restaurant** is a Mexican-American café open daily for breakfast, lunch, and dinner, but it lacks a smoke-free dining area. Nearby on US 60 you'll find a park with a red caboose and picnic tables.

Main Street in downtown Superior practically looks like a ghost town—paint peels from the closed shops. **Bob Jones Museum,** named after Arizona's sixth governor and housed in his former home, has a small historical collection at Main and Neary; it's open some days.

Boyce Thompson Arboretum State Park

You can see more than 3,200 different desert plants here in Arizona's oldest (1920s) and largest (323 acres) botanical garden. Exotic species from around the world thrive alongside native Sonoran Desert plants. Short trails lead through Sonoran and Chihuahuan desert areas, a cactus garden, riparian areas, an Australian forest, and herb and rose gardens. Buy or borrow the booklet for the Main Trail, a scenic 1.5-mile loop in Queen Creek

Canyon; handouts offer additional information on many of the other trails and gardens. Most of these trails branch off from the first part of the Main Trail, so you don't have to walk far to see the highlights. Much of the trail system is wheelchair-accessible. The Curandero/Sonoran Desert Trail describes traditional herbal medicines of the Sonoran Desert. (Curanderos are traditional healers in Mexican culture.) Greenhouses contain cacti and succulents that might not otherwise survive winter cold at this 2,400-foot elevation. The Smith Interpretive Center, between the display greenhouses, has exhibits on plants and local history. A Demonstration Garden offers tips and examples of water-efficient landscaping design.

More than 200 bird and 72 terrestrial species have been seen in the area. Ayer Lake and Queen Creek on the Main Trail are good places to watch for wildlife; you may see endangered Gila topminnow and desert pupfish in the lake. Nearby Picket Post Mountain (4,400 ft.) soars above the gardens. A heliograph station, equipped with mirrors to flash the rays of the sun, operated atop the peak during the Apache wars. No developed trails go to the summit and there's no access from the arboretum.

The visitor center offers some exhibits and a gift shop with snacks, books, prints, posters, and seed packets. You can also purchase cactus, other succulents, trees, shrubs, ground cover, and herbs. The cooling-tower exhibit at the visitor center creates a cool microclimate; its 30-foot tower functions as a giant evaporative cooler.

Scheduled events include an **Arid Land Plant Show** on the first weekend in April and a **Fall Landscaping Festival.** A picnic area near the parking lot is available to visitors. Today the University of Arizona, the State Parks Board, and the nonprofit Arboretum Corporation manage the arboretum. It's open daily except Christmas 8 A.M.–5 P.M.; $5 adults, $2 children 5–12; 520/689-2811 (recording); http://arboretum.ag.arizona.edu. The arboretum is three miles west of Superior, 60 miles southeast of Phoenix, and 101 miles north of Tucson.

Arizona Trail

Picket Post Trailhead, about five miles west of

Superior off US 60, provides access to a 15-mile segment of the Arizona Trail. From the trailhead (elev. 2,400 feet), the trail winds north to Montana Mountain Saddle (elev. 5,500 feet), then drops to Rogers Trough Trailhead (elev. 4,883 feet) on the south boundary of the Superstition Wilderness. From here the Arizona Trail continues north and east through the wilderness to Roosevelt Dam. You can also head south on the Arizona Trail from Picket Post Trailhead. The Globe Ranger District office, 928/402-6200, has a map with trailhead directions that you'll need, as there may not be any signs on US 60.

Florence Junction

Not a town at all—just a junction. The *town* of Florence, home to McFarland State Historic Park and the Pinal County Historical Museum, lies 16 miles south on AZ 79.

Peralta Trailhead

One of the most popular trailheads for the Superstition Wilderness lies off US 60 about nine miles northwest of Florence Junction or eight miles southeast of Apache Junction. Follow graded-dirt Forest Road 77 in for seven miles; a $4/day parking fee is charged. You'll also see the Dons Camp on the left just before the trailhead. The Dons Club, an organization devoted to promoting the legends and beauty of the Southwest, hosts a big one-day event here, usually in March, when thousands of people descend on the Superstitions for hikes, demonstrations, and entertainment; 602/258-6016; www.donsofarizona.org.

There's good hiking here, with three trails branching off into the wilderness. One of them, **Peralta Trail #102,** goes up Peralta Canyon to Fremont Saddle, where you get a great view of Weaver's Needle. It's four miles roundtrip and a 1,400-foot climb to the pass; carry water and avoid the heat of a summer day. Peralta Trail continues down the other side past the base of Weaver's Needle, connecting with other trails in the Superstitions.

South of Phoenix

On the drive between Phoenix and Tucson you'll cross desert plains with views of the Superstitions, Picacho Peak, Santa Catalina Mountains, and other rugged ranges. Desert plants along the roadside sometimes bloom in blazes of bright color in spring. Several spots are worth a visit, whether you take the old Pinal Pioneer Parkway (AZ 79) or the speedier I-10.

FLORENCE

Florence, one of the oldest white settlements in Arizona, dates back to the arrival of Levi Ruggles in 1866. Ruggles found a safe ford on the nearby Gila River and believed the valley suitable for farming. He laid out a town site that soon became a trade center and stage stop for surrounding army camps.

Some people advocated Florence as the Arizona territorial capital, but the town had to settle for designation as the Pinal County seat. The first county courthouse went up in 1878, and is now open as McFarland State Historic Park. The second county courthouse, completed in 1891 with an ornate cupola, stands as Florence's chief landmark. Funds ran out before the clock could be installed in the cupola, so workers attached the hands at a permanent 11:44!

Not everybody comes to Florence by choice—the Arizona State Prison sits at the edge of town. Convicts completed the prison in 1909, replacing the territorial prison at Yuma. Inmates now number over 8,000—more than double the town's 3,800 inhabitants.

Florence has two museums and a large number of historic buildings—over 150 listed with the national register. Old porch-fronted shops line Main Street. You can pick up a guide at the visitor centers or at the museums.

Pinal County Historical Museum

This diverse collection portrays the area's long

"MAJOR" PAULINE CUSHMAN

Pauline Cushman agreed to serve as a Union spy during the Civil War. Sent to Tennessee on assignment, she was captured by the confederacy and sentenced to hang as a spy. After a hasty retreat by Confederate troops left her free, she rode north dressed in a military outfit with an insignia of a cavalry major. It's uncertain whether she assumed this rank or was somehow awarded it, as no women were in the military at the time. Widowed a second time in San Francisco, she worked in redwood logging camps before meeting Jerry Fryer and moving to Arizona in 1879. They married, ran a hotel and livery, and Jerry became the Pinal County sheriff. Home life fell apart in 1890 and Pauline returned to San Francisco, where she died of a pain medicine overdose three years later.

history. Native American pottery, baskets, and stone tools come from prehistoric and modern tribes of the area. An 1880 horse-drawn opera coach offers a taste of early pioneer elegance. Tools, mining gear, household items, and clothing exhibits portray the life of the early settlers. News clippings describe the tragic death of silent-screen hero Tom Mix, killed in a car accident nearby. Bullet aficionados will find hundreds of different types on display. Outdoor exhibits include farming and mining machinery, a blacksmith shop, and a homesteader shack.

The prison exhibits are sobering: hangman's nooses framing photos of their victims, a hanging board, gas-chamber chair, massive prison registers from Yuma and Florence, and the story of murderess Eva Dugan, hung and simultaneously decapitated in 1930. A research library has additional information on local history. The museum, 715 S. Main St., 520/868-4382, is open Sunday noon–4 P.M. and Tues.–Sat. 11 A.M.–4 P.M. except closed July 15–Aug. 31; donations are welcomed. **Main Street Park** has picnic tables across from the museum.

McFarland State Historic Park

This adobe building served as Pinal County's first courthouse, sheriff's office, and jail from 1878 to 1891, then functioned for 50 years as the county hospital. In 1883 an angry mob took two murder suspects from the jail and hung them in a corridor. Exhibits illustrate the lives and personalities of Florence's pioneers—describing the town's good guys and bad guys—and detail construction of the town's hospital and courthouse. Photos show the Florence POW camp through which 13,000 Italian and German prisoners passed in 1942–45. You'll also learn about Ernest McFarland (1894–1984), who began his political career in 1925 as Pinal county attorney, then rose to serve as U.S. senator, Arizona governor, and chief justice of the State Supreme Court. The park is near the north end of Main Street at Ruggles Street; 520/868-5216. It's open Thurs.–Mon. 8 A.M.–5 P.M.; admission is $2 adults, $1 ages 7–13. A city park just to the north offers shaded tables, playground, ball fields, and a pond.

Poston's Butte

Charles Poston explored and mined in what is now Arizona from 1853 to 1861, but his greatest achievement was successfully lobbying in Washington, D.C., for a territorial government in 1863. Poston went on to become the first superintendent of Indian affairs in Arizona and one of the first Arizona delegates to Congress.

His congressional term finished, Poston traveled to India and became a fire worshipper. Upon returning to Arizona in 1878, he built a continuous fire—a sort of temple of the sun—atop a hill, naming it Parsee Hill. The flames died out several months later, ending a project that disbelievers mocked as "Poston's Folly." Today, Poston lies buried in a pyramid-shaped tomb on the summit of the hill, renamed Poston's Butte, northwest from Florence across the Gila River.

A trail—steep and with some loose rock—leads to the top. If you'd like some exercise and views, drive north a bit over a mile from downtown on AZ 79, cross the Gila River Bridge and continue 0.1 mile, turn left (near Milepost 136) 1.3 miles on the Hunt Highway, then turn right onto an unpaved road leading under the railroad tracks. Depending on your vehicle, you may wish to park here and walk. After the underpass, park on the left and walk half a mile (one way) on the track up the hillside; elevation gain is about 300 feet. It's possible to reach the summit with a 4WD vehicle, but the way is very bumpy.

Box Canyon

This beautiful canyon attracts picnickers, hikers, and photographers. Desert plants, volcanic rock walls, and an intermittent stream make for delightful exploring. Loose sand and gravel can trap cars on the way, so it's best to have 4WD. From Florence, drive north on AZ 79 across the Gila River bridge and continue 0.3 mile, then turn right 14 miles on a dirt road (before the railroad tracks). On the way in you'll parallel the Gila River past fields, an orchard, and, at 9.4 miles, the Ashurst-Hayden Diversion Dam. The road curves northeast, crosses some washes (cars may have trouble here), and enters Box Canyon. Some drivers manage to get all the way through the canyon in another 13 miles and come out on AZ 79 or US 60 to the north, though this route requires difficult four-wheeling.

St. Anthony's Greek Orthodox Monastery

Copper domes of the chapel gleam in the sun in this picturesque desert setting about 10 miles southeast of Florence. Father Ephraim, a spiritual leader from Mt. Athos in Greece, chose the spot for its serenity and isolation from the distractions of the world. Since its founding in July 1995, the monastery has grown to about 30 monks who follow a rigorous schedule of work and prayer, including praying while working. Visitors interested in the monastery and its religion may drop by for a visit from 10 A.M.–4 P.M. daily. Come to the bookstore, just inside the entrance, and someone will show you around; 520/868-3188. From AZ 79 just south of Milepost 124, turn east 2.3 miles on Paisano Road.

Tom Mix Monument

October 12, 1940, was a sad day for fans of movie hero Tom Mix. Speeding north from Tucson in his big Cord, he lost control of the car and rolled over in a ditch, subsequently renamed Tom Mix Wash. A roadside monument, topped by a riderless horse, marks the spot, 17 miles south of Florence on AZ 79, between Mileposts 115 and 116. A rest area here has picnic tables.

Accommodations and Camping

On the east side of town at the junction of AZ 79 and AZ 287, **Blue Mist Motel,** 520/868-5875, has a pool, and there's a café next door; $35–40 s, $40–50 d. **Taylor's Bed & Breakfast Inn,** 321 N. Bailey St., 520/868-3497, is in one of Florence's 19th-century buildings downtown. The rooms have many antiques; $55 d shared bath, $75 d private bath.

Rancho Sonora Inn & RV Park, about five miles south of town on AZ 79 at Milepost 128, 520/868-8000, 800/205-6817, offers a Southwestern atmosphere in the adobe buildings of a 1930's guest ranch. Amenities include a pool and hot tub. Courtyard rooms cost $74 d, one-bedroom cottages are $105 d, and two-bedroom cottages run $150 d, with lower prices in summer. The pleasant campground has showers and a clubhouse; $18 tent, $22 RV with hookups, also with lower rates off season.

Desert Garden RV Park, five miles south on AZ 79 near Milepost 128, 520/868-3800, 888/868-4888, is in an attractive desert setting amidst saguaro and cholla. Guests also enjoy a club house, craft room, and planned activities (in winter). Reservations are recommended Dec. to March; $15 RV w/hookups; long-terms sites are available too; www.desertgardensrvpark.com.

Food

Murphy's Soup & Salad, 310 N. Main St., 520/868-0027, fixes homestyle lunches on weekdays. **Old Pueblo Restaurant,** 505 S. Main St., 520/868-4784, offers American and Mexican food Sun.–Fri. for breakfast, lunch, and dinner. The nearby **L&B Inn** has a similar menu but lacks a smoke-free area.

For Italian dining, try **A&M Pizza,** 445 W. Hwy. 287, 520/868-0170, which prepares pasta and chicken dishes as well as pizza and subs. It's open daily for lunch and dinner. Five and a half miles south of town on AZ 79, **Yolanda's Chuckwagon,** 520/868-9727, serves up steak, prime rib, seafood, and a salad bar. It's open for lunch buffet Tues.–Fri. and Sun., and for dinner Tues.–Sunday.

Events

The **Tour of Historic Florence** visits private and public buildings in February; you can walk or take a shuttle. **Pinal County Fair** brings fun and exhibits to the town of Casa Grande from the last Wednesday in March through the following Sunday. The Assumption Church sponsors a **Cinco de Mayo** parade on the weekend preceding May 5. Fireworks go off for the **July 4th Festivities.** The **Junior Parada** on Thanksgiving weekend celebrates with a rodeo, parade, entertainment, and food.

Information and Services

Florence Visitors Center, operated by the Greater Florence Chamber of Commerce, offers lots of information on local history and sights as well as places farther afield in Arizona; some books are sold. The center is in an 1890 brick commercial building one block east of N. Main on Eighth St. (P.O. Box 929, Florence, AZ 85232), 520/868-9433, 800/437-9433; florenceaz.org. Hours are Mon.–Fri. 10 A.M.–4 P.M. year-round.

One block south and east from the courthouse, the **Pinal County Visitor Center,** 330 E. Butte Ave. (P.O. Box 967, Florence, AZ 85232), 520/868-4331, 888/469-0175, will also help you with local and state travel. It's open Mon.–Fri. 10 A.M.–5 P.M. and possibly weekends.

The **Prison Outlet,** 520/868-3014, on AZ 79 diagonally across from the Blue Mist Motel, sells arts and crafts produced by the inmates; open Fri.–Mon. year-round and daily in December.

CASA GRANDE RUINS NATIONAL MONUMENT

Arizona's biggest and most perplexing prehistoric building contains 11 rooms and rises four stories above an earthen platform. An estimated 3,000 tons of mud went into the rectangular structure, whose walls range in thickness from 4.5 feet at the base to 1.8 feet near the top.

Archaeologists don't know the purpose of Casa Grande, but some speculate that it was used for ceremonies or astronomical observations; certain holes in the walls appear to line up with the sun at the summer solstice and possibly with the moon during selected lunar events. Smaller structures and a wall surround the main building. Hohokam, who had farmed the Gila Valley since about 200–300 B.C., built Casa Grande around A.D. 1350. This is the only structure of its type still standing.

By about 1450, after just a few generations of use, the Hohokam abandoned Casa Grande along with all their other villages. The Jesuit priest Eusebio Kino recorded the site in 1694, giving it the Spanish name for "great house."

At the monument's visitor center, exhibits introduce you to the Hohokam and their irrigation canals, farming tools, jewelry, and ball courts. You'll learn some of the various theories that account for their disappearance. Models show how the Great House may have looked. Rangers lead tours of Casa Grande, or you can set off on the self-guided trail. Signs identify cactus and other desert plants. The visitor center sells books on Arizona's tribes, settlers, and natural history.

The monument, 1100 Ruins Dr. (Coolidge, AZ 85228), 520/723-3172, is one mile north of downtown Coolidge off AZ 87. (These ruins shouldn't be confused with the modern town of Casa Grande, which is about 20 miles away.) It's open daily 8 A.M.–5 P.M.; admission is $2 per person, maximum $4 per vehicle; www.nps.gov/cagr.

Coolidge

Two small museums encourage a detour east off the highway onto the quiet streets of this small town. **Golden Era Museum,** 520/723-5044, displays a collection of antique toys and trains open Sat.–Sun. at 297 W. Central Avenue. The **Coolidge Museum,** 520/723-3588, has historic exhibits open by appointment at 161 W. Harding Avenue. Travelers will find two motels on the north side of town and two adult RV parks on the south side along the main highway, AZ 87/Arizona Boulevard. The **Coolidge Chamber of Commerce,** 520/723-3009, offers local info Mon.–Fri. 8 A.M.–5 P.M. beside a city park at 320 W. Central Ave. (Coolidge, AZ 85228); www.coolidgeaz.org.

Blackwater Trading Post and Museum

Drop in to see fine Hohokam pottery, baskets by Tohono O'odham and Pima, and artifacts of other Southwestern tribes. You can shop for Native American jewelry and crafts. It's on the north side of AZ 87; head west 4.3 miles from the AZ 287-87 junction or, from I-10, you can go east 9 miles on AZ 387 and AZ 87; 520/723-5516. Open daily; donations welcome.

GILA INDIAN CENTER

This cultural center on the Gila River Reservation makes a fine break from freeway driving. About 12,000 Pima and Maricopa live on the 387,000-acre reservation, which was founded in 1859. A museum displays artifacts of the tribes and interprets local history. Photo exhibits include Snaketown, a 200-acre Hohokam site, and the 1942–45 Gila River Internment Center that held Japanese-Americans. Crafts in the gift shop include pottery of Maricopa and New Mexican tribes, Tohono O'od-

ham baskets, Hopi kachina dolls, and Navajo rugs. Jewelry, paintings, and prints come from many tribes. An inexpensive restaurant offers fry bread and some Mexican and American items daily for breakfast and lunch.

Outside, Heritage Park contains traditional structures of the Hohokam, Pima, Maricopa, Tohono O'odham, and Apache tribes; a booklet available at the gift shop describes each group. Gila Indian Center is open daily except some holidays 8 A.M.–5 P.M.; donations welcome; 480/963-3981. Native American craft demonstrations and performances take place during the Thanksgiving Celebration (weekend following Thanksgiving) and the Anniversary Celebration (third weekend in March). From I-10 Exit 175, go west half a mile on Casa Blanca Road; the exit is 26 miles southeast of Phoenix and 85 miles northwest of Tucson.

CASA GRANDE

Once a small, sleepy agricultural town, Casa Grande has been discovered by winter visitors. Originally, no town was planned here. It was just a spot where the railway stopped laying tracks during the summer of 1879. Shipping agents then dropped off agricultural and mining supplies beside the track. When the tracks continued on to Yuma, people stayed and the town grew to a population of 500 by 1882, but the national mining slump in the 1890s caused Casa Grande to dwindle to just a mercantile store, a saloon, and two small businesses. Agriculture became the mainstay, with livestock, vegetables, alfalfa, wheat, barley, citrus, and cotton contributing to the local economy. Now, the town depends just as much on the winter visitors who patronize the resort, motels, and RV parks. Casa Grande's population has passed 26,000 and continues to grow.

Casa Grande Valley Historical Museum

The museum takes you back to the days of the early tribes and pioneers. You'll learn about area mining and view period living rooms, bedrooms, and kitchens. The collection and a gift shop are open Mon.–Sat. 1–5 P.M. from September 15 to

May 15; $2 admission. The museum is downtown at 110 W. Florence Blvd. (behind a 1927 stone former church); 520/836-2223.

Casa Grande Art Museum

This small gallery offers a chance to enjoy paintings, sculpture, photographic displays, and ceramics as well as an outdoor sculpture garden. Most work is for sale. Exhibits change about once a month. It's at 319 W. 3rd. St., one block south and east from the historical museum; 520/836-3377; call for days and hours; closed in summer.

Accommodations

The **Francisco Grande Resort and Golf Club** offers accommodations with an 18-hole golf course, pool, hot tub, tennis, and restaurant. It's five miles west of downtown at 26000 Gila Bend Hwy.; 520/836-6444, 800/237-4238; www.franciscogrande.com. Motels, restaurants, and many RV parks lie scattered around town or near I-10.

Information and Services

The **Greater Casa Grande Chamber of Commerce** is at 575 N. Marshall St. (Casa Grande, AZ 85222); turn south from Florence Blvd. at the Dairy Queen; 520/836-2125, 800/916-1515. It's open Mon.–Fri. 9 A.M.–5 P.M.; www.casagrandechamber.org.

Shoppers enjoy **Tanger Factory Outlet Center,** which holds about 38 shops at I-10 Exit 198, 520/836-9663, 800/405-5016; and **Factory Stores of America,** with more than a dozen shops at I-10 Exit 194.

Casa Grande Regional Medical Center is at 1800 E. Florence Blvd., 520/426-6300.

PICACHO PEAK STATE PARK

Picacho Peak has long served as a landmark for tribal groups, Spanish explorers, American frontiersmen, and modern-day motorists. Park visitors enjoy hiking, camping, and picnicking in this scenic area. Saguaro and other plants of the Sonoran Desert thrive on the rocky hillsides. Mexican gold poppies can blanket the hillsides in spring

after a wet winter. Monuments near the flagpole commemorate the Battle of Picacho Pass (where I-10 now runs) and the building of a road by the Mormon Battalion.

The Battle of Picacho Pass, on April 15, 1862, was the most significant conflict of the Civil War this far west. Confederate forces killed Lieutenant James Barrett, leader of the Union detachment, and two privates. Aware that Union reinforcements would soon arrive, the Confederates retreated back down the Butterfield Road to Tucson.

Civil War in the Southwest

This reenactment takes place on the second weekend in March. Infantry and cavalry fight three historic engagements to commemorate two battles that took place in New Mexico plus the Battle of Picacho Pass. Smoke spreads over the desert as the crack of rifles and roar of cannons echo off the hillsides. In calmer moments between the conflicts, you can visit the encampments of each side and see how the soldiers and civilians lived.

Practicalities

The park, 520/466-3183, offers trails, picnic areas, campgrounds with showers, and a dump station. Fees are $5 per vehicle for day use, $10 for camping in non-hookup sites, or $17 with water and electric hookups. No reservations are taken, but it's rare for all sites to fill. Groups can reserve picnic and camping areas. To get there, take I-10 Exit 219 (70 miles southeast of Phoenix and 41 miles northwest of Tucson) and follow signs a half mile.

Hiking Trails

Hunter Trail climbs 1,500 feet to the summit of 3,374-foot Picacho Peak, a tilted remnant of ancient lava flows. This rugged four-mile roundtrip requires 4–5 hours. (For a shorter but still strenuous hike, also with expansive views, take the Hunter Trail just as far as the saddle, a two-mile roundtrip of 1.5 hours.) Be careful on the backside where the trail crosses some loose rock; posts and cables provide handholds in the rougher spots. **Sunset Vista Trail** traverses the back of the peak in a 6.2-mile roundtrip to the summit;

it has fewer hikers and a more secluded setting as I-10 is out of view most of the way. Good shoes, plenty of water, and sun protection will help make an enjoyable and successful climb on either of these trails. If you hike up one trail and down the other, you'll have to arrange a shuttle or walk the 2.2 miles between the two trailheads to get back to your car.

Calloway Trail is an easier climb to a low pass between Bugler's and Picacho peaks, 1.5 miles roundtrip, requiring an hour. A half-mile-loop **nature trail** introduces desert plants; you can begin from Memorial Plaza near the contact station or from the hookup campground. Rangers offer trail maps.

GILA BEND

The town of Gila Bend (pop. 2,000) sits near the Gila River 68 miles southwest of Phoenix.

Father Kino, who came through here in 1699, found a prosperous Maricopa village with irrigated fields yielding two harvests annually. The Butterfield stagecoach first rolled through in the early 1850s, and a town later grew up around its station.

Today Gila Bend serves as an agricultural center and a travelers' stop. Surrounding farms raise cotton, wheat, barley, and other crops. San Lucy, a Tohono O'odham village, lies just north of town. On Business Loop I-8, the main street through town, you'll find seven motels, one RV park, and a variety of restaurants.

The **Gila Bend Museum and Tourist Center,** on Business Loop I-8 at 644 W. Pima St. (P.O. Drawer A, Gila Bend, AZ 85337), 928/683-2002, offers historical exhibits and travel information. It's usually open daily 8 A.M.–4 P.M. The **public library** is a couple of blocks off the highway at 202 N. Euclid.

Northwest of Phoenix

WICKENBURG

You still get a sense of the Old West in easygoing Wickenburg, where Western-style buildings line the downtown streets. Even a bit of gold fever lingers, still drawing prospectors to mine-scarred hills. Cowboys continue to work the range, though joined now by riders from local guest ranches. The picturesque rocky hills around Wickenburg offer ideal horseback riding. Not surprisingly, the town has a good selection of shops specializing in Western apparel, Western art, Native American arts and crafts, and antiques.

Wickenburg's cool and sunny weather lasts from November to May. Summers at the town's 2,100-foot elevation can get very hot; average highs in July run 103°F. It's 58 miles northwest of Phoenix; you can get here from Phoenix via US 60 (Grand Ave.) or the longer but less congested route past Lake Pleasant via I-17 and AZ 74.

History

Henry Wickenburg had roamed the hills of Arizona for a year in search of gold before striking it rich at the Vulture Mine in 1863. According to one legend, he noticed the shiny nuggets when reaching down to pick up a vulture he'd shot; others claim he glimpsed the gold while picking up a rock to throw at his burro. Either way, Wickenburg set off a frenzied gold rush.

The Vulture Mine lacked water needed for processing, so miners hauled the ore 14 miles northeast to the Hassayampa River. In just a few years, the town that grew up around the mills became Arizona's third-largest city. It missed becoming the territorial capital in 1866 by only two votes.

Prospectors discovered other gold deposits in the Wickenburg area until more than 80 mines operated at the height of the gold rush. Mining for gold and other minerals continues today, though on a smaller scale.

Desert Caballeros Western Museum

This fine museum takes you back to Wickenburg's Wild West days. Dioramas illustrate the history of the Vulture Mine and the early mining community. Period rooms and a street scene indicate how Wickenburg actually looked.

A Native American Room displays a varied collection of prehistoric and modern crafts, including kachina dolls, pottery, baskets, and stone tools. Precious stones and minerals glitter in the Mineral Room. A large art gallery features outstanding Western paintings and sculpture by Remington, Russell, and other inspired artists. Temporary exhibits appear, too. Walk over to a small park behind the museum to see *Thanks for the Rain*, a bronze sculpture by Joe Beeler.

The museum, art gallery, and a gift shop are at 21 N. Frontier St., one block west of the downtown highway junction, 928/684-2272/7075. Open Sunday noon–4 P.M. and Mon.–Sat. 10 A.M.–5 P.M.; admission is $5 adults, $4 seniors 60 and over, $1 children 6–16; www.westernmuseum.org.

Old Jail Tree

The town lacked a jail in the early days, so prisoners were shackled to this old mesquite tree. The tree stands behind the Circle-K store at the highway junction downtown.

Hassayampa River

Normally you'll see just a dry streambed through town. The river's Apache name means "river that runs upside down," because its waters flow beneath the sandy surface. A wishing well and sign at the west end of the highway bridge relate the legend that anyone drinking from the stream will never tell the truth again. See for yourself!

Hassayampa River Preserve

The river pops out of the ground along a five-mile section of riverbed below town, watering lush vegetation. The Goodding willow-Fremont cottonwood forest along the banks is one of the rarest forest types in North America.

Spring-fed Palm Lake attracts many waterfowl not normally seen in the desert. Visitors have counted more than 230 species of birds, including zone-tailed and black hawks that fly up from Mexico to nest. The preserve, managed by the Arizona chapter of the Nature Conservancy, provides a sanctuary for these hawks and other wildlife. Visitors can enjoy quiet walks through

the natural settings, reflecting on the fact that of Arizona's streamside habitats existing a century ago, only about 10 percent exist today.

Check in at the visitor center/gift shop to pick up trail information, regional and natural history books, or literature on environmental concerns. The four-room adobe core of the visitor center, built in 1860, has served as ranch, stagecoach way station, and one of Arizona's first guest ranches. Three trails, each a half-mile loop, begin near the visitor center and wander through the woodlands, along the riverbank, or around Palm Lake.

You can visit Wed.–Sun. (Fri.–Sun. from May 15 to Sept. 14) 8 A.M.–5 P.M.; a $5 suggested donation by nonmembers is appreciated. The preserve offers guided nature walks on the last Saturday of each month; call for time and reservations. Hassayampa River Preserve lies three miles southeast of Wickenburg on US 60 near Milepost 114, 928/684-2772; www.tncarizona.org.

Guest Ranches

Rancho de los Caballeros, 1551 S. Vulture Mine Rd., Wickenburg, AZ 85390, 928/684-5484, 800/684-5030, is the largest and most elegant of the group. Guests enjoy horseback riding, an 18-hole golf course, pool, tennis, hot-air balloon rides, children's activities, and fine dining. The season runs early Oct. to mid May. Rates are $239–399 s, $379–509 d in high season (Feb.–April); $217–309 s, $329–419 d in low season (Oct.–Jan. and May). www.sunc.com. From Wickenburg, go 3.5 miles west on US 60, then turn left (south) two miles on Vulture Mine Road.

Flying E Ranch, 2801 W. Wickenburg Way, Wickenburg, AZ 85390, 928/684-2690, 888/684-2650, still works cattle at a nearby spread. It has an informal atmosphere where guests can ride, play tennis, enjoy family-style meals, work out in the fitness room, or relax around the pool and hot tub. It's open Nov. 1–April 30. Rates are $145–175 s, $230–295 d; flyingeranch.com. To get to the ranch go four miles west on US 60, then one mile south.

Kay El Bar Ranch, P.O. Box 2480, Wickenburg, AZ 85358, 928/684-7593, 800/684-7583, has been around so long it's on the

National Register of Historic Places. It began as a cattle ranch in the early 1900s, then became a guest ranch in 1926. The adobe lodge and casitas help create a Western experience for guests, who ride, receive riding instruction, hike a scenic trail, enjoy the pool and hot tub, and have family-style meals and cookouts. Rates include all meals, riding, and ranch facilities: $170 s, $300 d in lodge rooms, $300 d in Casa Monterey, $330 d in Casa Grande, or $660/four in Homestead House; www.kayelbar.com. The ranch is open October 12 to May 1. Go 2.5 miles northwest on US 93 and turn right on Rincon Road at the sign.

Williams Family Ranch, P.O. Box 3855, Wickenburg, AZ 85358, 928/308-0589, offers the experience of a working cattle ranch in a remote area along the Hassayampa River, 16 miles northeast of Wickenburg. Guests can come out just for the day to ride ($85 with lunch; two-person minimum) or stay in a bunkhouse and dine family-style in the main ranch house. Rates with accommodations, meals, riding, and transportation from Wickenburg are $110 s, $210 d ($700/week s, $1,350/week d); www.williamsfamilyranch.com. A stay of at least three days is recommended if you'd like to try your hand with the cattle. The season runs September to May.

Other Accommodations in the Countryside

Across the Hassayampa River from Kay El Bar Ranch, **Rincon Bed & Breakfast,** 928/684-2328, 888/684-2338, offers casita accommodations from mid-November to April; $90 d. Go 2.5 miles northwest on US 93, then right 1.5 miles on Rincon Road. If the river is flooding or if you'd like a very scenic drive through desert hills on mostly unpaved roads, head northeast 3.2 miles on Constellation Road from E. Wickenburg Way, turn left 5.4 miles on Blue Tank Road (High Water Rd.) to its end, then left 0.3 mile on Rincon Road.

Rancho Casitas, 56550 Rancho Casitas Rd., 928/684-2628, provides comfortable accommodations with kitchens and patios in a hilltop setting five miles north of town; you can bring

your own horse. Open Oct.–May with a one-week minimum stay, which starts at $550 d.

Accommodations in Town

You'll find most of the motels in town along US 60, named Wickenburg Way. The winter/spring rates listed here come down in summer. Coming from Phoenix, you'll pass **AmericInn,** 850 E. Wickenburg Way, 928/684-5461, 800/634-3444, $64 s, $70 d; and **Best Western Rancho Grande,** 293 E. Wickenburg Way, 928/684-5445, 800/854-7235, $71 s, $74 d.

Continuing west from downtown you'll see the **Capri Motel,** 521-A W. Wickenburg Way, 928/684-7232, $56–81 d; and **Log Wagon Inn,** 573 W. Wickenburg Way, 928/684-2531, $36.50 s, $41.50 d.

North on Tegner St. (US 93) are a **Super 8 Motel,** 975 N. Tegner St., 928/684-0808, 800/800-8000, $55 s, $60–65 d; and **Los Viajeros Inn,** 1000 N. Tegner St., 928/684-7099, 800/915-9795, $85 s, $95 d.

Camping

RVs can stay at **Horspitality RV Park and Boarding Stable,** two miles southeast on US 60, 928/684-2519, $20 RV with hookups including showers; **Aztec Mobile Home and RV Park,** 401 E. Wickenburg Way, 928/684-2481, $14 with hookups and showers; **Desert Cypress Trailer Ranch,** behind McDonald's at 610 Jack Burden Rd., 928/684-2153, adults only, $20 with hookups, showers, and tax; or **Constellation Park,** one mile northeast on Constellation Road, where sites for self-contained rigs (no tents) are only $2 but have no water or facilities.

Another possibility for both tents and RVs is camping out in the desert. Avoid washes, and be sure you're on public land.

Food

For good American fare, try **Homestead Restaurant,** 222 E. Wickenburg Way, 928/684-0648; **Country Kitchen,** 495 E. Wickenburg Way, 928/684-3882; and **Willows Restaurant,** 850 E. Wickenburg Way in AmericInn, 928/684-5461. More American food is available at the **Cow-**

boy Cafe, 445 N. Tegner St., 928/684-2807; **Charley's Steak House,** 1187 W. Wickenburg Way, 928/684-2413; and **Chicken Noodle Café** (breakfast and lunch), 2021 W. Wickenburg Way in West Plaza Shopping Center, 928/684-2294. Try brunch and lunch at **The March Hare,** in a historic house at 170 W. Wickenburg Way, two blocks west of Tegner St., 928/684-0223.

You can dine Mexican downtown at **Anita's Cocina,** 57 N. Valentine (around the corner from the Homestead Restaurant), 928/684-5777. Pick up pizza at **Sangini's,** 107 E. Wickenburg Way, 928/684-7828. **House Berlin** prepares German food and other continental cuisine for lunch and dinner at 169 E. Wickenburg Way, 928/684-5044; closed Monday. The **Sizzling Wok** serves Chinese cuisine at 621 W. Wickenburg Way, 928/684-3977.

Rancho de los Caballeros, 928/684-5484, offers buffets and ala carte items to the public by reservation.

You'll find several fast-food places on E. Wickenburg Way. **West Plaza Shopping Center** on the west edge of town and **Bashas' Frontier Center** on N. Tegner St. have supermarkets and other stores.

Entertainment and Events

Saguaro Theater screens current films at 176 E. Wickenburg Way; 928/684-7189. **Gold Rush Days** celebrates Wickenburg's Western heritage with a shootout, parade, rodeo, concerts, "mellerdramas," a gold-panning contest, and other activities on the second full weekend in February. **July 4th** brings fireworks and a watermelon feed. **Fiesta Septiembre,** on the first Saturday of September, celebrates Hispanic culture with dances and music in the park behind Desert Caballeros Western Museum. The **Wickenburg Bluegrass Festival** brings foot-tapping music and dancing to town on the second full weekend in November. A **Cowboy Poets Gathering** on the first full weekend in December presents the rich heritage of those who work the range. The **Christmas Light Parade** brightens the evening on the second Friday in December.

Recreation

Coffinger Park offers picnicking, a swimming pool, tennis courts, and a ball field off N. Tegner St., just across the Sols Wash bridge. **Sunset Park,** four miles west of town on US 60, has picnicking, tennis courts, a basketball court, and ball fields. Play golf year-round at the nine-hole **Wickenburg Country Club** course (go two miles west on US 60, then north on Country Club Rd., 928/684-2011) or the 18-hole course at **Rancho de los Caballeros** (3.5 miles west on US 60, then south two miles on Vulture Mine Road, 928/684-5484).

Information and Services

The helpful **Wickenburg Chamber of Commerce** is in the 1895 railroad depot at 216 N. Frontier St. (Wickenburg, AZ 85390), one block west of N. Tegner St.; 928/684-5479; www.wickenburgchamber.com. It's open Sunday 10 A.M.–2 P.M., MON.–FRI. 9 a.m.–5 P.M., and Saturday 10 A.M.–3 P.M. (until 2 P.M. June–Sept.), The **public library** is at 164 E. Apache St., one block north of Wickenburg Way and just west of the river; 928/684-2665. It's open Mon.–Fri. 8 A.M.–7 P.M. and Saturday 8 A.M.–noon.

D&J Maps, Etc. has the maps, regional books, and gold panning supplies to get you started on a tour of the backcountry for fun or gold—or both! It's downtown at 18 N. Tegner St., 928/684-0096.

The **post office** is in the West Plaza Shopping Center on W. Wickenburg Way; 928/684-2138. **Wickenburg Regional Medical Center** is at 520 Rose Lane, 0.8 mile north off Tegner Street from Wickenburg Way; 928/684-5421.

Tours and Transportation

Check with the Wickenburg Chamber of Commerce for backcountry driving tours and trail rides.

Greyhound and **K-T Services** buses stop at the Subway restaurant on E. Wickenburg Way; 800/231-2222. Greyhound runs at least twice daily east to Phoenix, northwest to Las Vegas, and west to California. K-T Services travels daily to Phoenix and Las Vegas via Parker, Lake Havasu City, and Laughlin.

VICINITY OF WICKENBURG

Vulture Mine

Ruins of the Vulture Mine and the adjacent ghost town of Vulture City are remarkably well preserved. They present a rare opportunity to visit a historic mine that has been neither reconstructed nor destroyed. The site was mined from the time of Henry Wickenburg's discovery in 1863 until wartime priorities in 1942 shut the mine down. Gold and silver still lie in underground veins and may be mined again.

You can walk the self-guided, quarter-mile loop past the assay office, glory hole, headframe and main shaft (more than 2,000 feet deep), blacksmith shop, ball mill, power plant, apartment houses, mess hall, and other structures. Be sure to stay on the marked trail—some areas and buildings are dangerous to enter—and wear good shoes. It's open daily 8 A.M.–4 P.M. Sept.–May, then weekends only in June and July; closed August. Admission is $7 adults, $5 seniors 62+ and children 6–12. Group tours can be scheduled; call 602/859-2743. From Wickenburg, head west 2.5 miles on Wickenburg Way, then turn south 12 miles on paved Vulture Mine Road; the mine is on your right.

Robson's Mining World

The Nella-Meda Mine is a reconstructed ghost town with about 30 buildings, including an antique print shop, blacksmith shop, saloon, general store, and miners' cabins. Miners dug gold ore here from the early 1900s until WW II, and there's evidence that the Spanish worked the site much earlier. A self-guided walking-tour map explains the use and history of many of the buildings and the pieces of machinery in what's claimed to be the world's largest collection of antique mining equipment. You can step inside the buildings, which are opened on request. Hikers enjoy a scenic walk up a nearby canyon to Black Tanks, natural pools where prehistoric tribes left behind petroglyphs and holes in the streambed; it's about three miles roundtrip and a bit rugged in the upper part. There's a small admission fee. Mining World, 928/685-2609, is open Oct.–April weekdays 10 A.M.–4 P.M. and weekends 8 A.M.–6 P.M.

A bed and breakfast here has rooms and suites. The restaurant serves breakfast and lunch; you can arrange dinners (steak, chicken, or fish) and cowboy cookouts by reservation. The mine is 31 miles northwest of Wickenburg on AZ 71, near Milepost 90; head west 25 miles on US 60, turn north four miles on AZ 71, then turn west 1.7 miles at the sign. The mailing address is P.O. Box 3465, Wickenburg, AZ 85358.

Stanton

Originally called Antelope Station, this settlement began in 1863 when prospectors found placer gold in Antelope Creek. Five years later, the population reached 3,500. The gold began to play out by the early 1900s, and Stanton started fading away. The stage stop, hotel, and opera house survive from the old days.

Members of the Lost Dutchman Mining Association now own the site, where they continue the tradition of gold mining in Antelope Creek as a hobby. Ask permission to look around Stanton; there's no charge, though you can make a donation.

From Wickenburg follow AZ 89 north 18 miles, two miles past Congress, then turn right 6.5 miles on a graded dirt road signed for Stanton. You'll see old shacks, mine tailings, rusting machinery, and some new operations along the road, as well as a large dairy. After entering Stanton, turn left through the Lost Dutchman's Mining Association gate. The main road continues another mile to the site of Octave (signed No Trespassing), then becomes too rough for cars. On Rich Hill, between Stanton and Octave, prospectors reportedly picked up gold nuggets the size of potatoes, just lying on the ground.

Drivers with high-clearance vehicles can turn left just past Stanton and climb five miles up the valley past more mining operations to AZ 89 at the top of Yarnell Hill. The road comes out just north of St. Mary's Catholic Church. It's fun to search out some of the old gold mines and ghost towns surrounding Wickenburg. Caution is needed on these dirt roads; get local advice on conditions and avoid traveling after heavy rains.

Yarnell Hill Lookout

Southbound travelers can stop at a pullout for a sweeping view of the desert and distant mountains below. The lookout lies 25 miles north of Wickenburg and a half mile south of Yarnell on AZ 89. Northbound travelers don't have access to this stop.

Shrine of St. Joseph

A short trail with steps climbs past statues and plaques depicting the Stations of the Cross. Giant granite boulders weathered out of the hillside add to the beauty of the spot; donations welcome. Turn west one-half mile at the sign in central Yarnell.

Yarnell and Peeples Valley

Yarnell offers the **Oak Park Motel & RV Park,** 928/427-6383; $40 s, $45 d, $18 RV w/hookups, showers, and laundry; tenters can pitch on the gravel spaces for $10. Several cafés are around town too. **Yarnell Daze** in May celebrates with a parade, car show, games, and barbecue. The **Yarnell-Peeples Valley Chamber of Commerce** can tell you about the area; it's sponsored by Hill Top Realty, 928/427-3301.

Joshua Forest

Joshua trees *(Yucca brevifolia)* line US 93 for 18 miles between Mileposts 180 and 162. You'll see the first ones about 22 miles northwest of Wickenburg. Large clusters of pale-green flowers appear from early February to early April.

Burro Creek Recreation Site

A perennial stream flows through this scenic canyon area (elev. 1,960 feet), feeding deep blue pools and lush greenery in the desert. Open all year, it's a great place to take a break from the long drive on US 93. Visitors enjoy camping, picnicking, birding, swimming, hiking, four-wheeling, and rockhounding for agates and Apache tears. A cactus garden and interpretive signs introduce life of the desert. Hikers can head up the creekbed if the water isn't too high—the creek extends some 40 miles upstream and goes through the heart of Burro Creek Wilderness; downstream is private land. Day use is free. The campground has drinking water, flush toilets, and a dump station, but no showers; $10 per night. For information and group campsite ($30) reservations, contact the Kingman Field Office of the BLM at 2475 Beverly Ave., Kingman, AZ 86401, 928/692-4400, kingman.az.blm.gov. Head northwest 63 miles from Wickenburg or southeast 65 miles from Kingman on I-40 and US 93, then turn west 1.3 miles at the sign. An overlook on the west side of the highway near the bridge provides a fine panorama of the area.

Eastern Arizona

Eastern Arizona will surprise you. Instead of the arid desert country you might expect, you'll find 2,000 square miles of forested peaks, placid lakes, and sparkling streams in the White Mountains. Residents and visitors enjoy the cool summer climate, abundant trout-filled waters, and winter sports. Mount Baldy, Arizona's second-highest mountain, crowns the range at 11,403 feet; it's sacred to the Apache tribe. Sunrise Ski Resort, several miles north, features some of the most challenging downhill runs in the Southwest. Cross-country skiers and summer hikers can find solitude almost anywhere in these mountains.

For a wildly scenic drive in the high-country, try the Coronado Trail between Springerville and Clifton. Slow and winding, the route offers almost unlimited picnicking, hiking, and camping possibilities. Over to the west, another highway presents a different surprise—you're driving along southwest of Show Low when suddenly the road begins to descend into a magnificent chasm. It's the Salt River Canyon, a smaller but equally colorful version of the Grand Canyon.

Traveling north from the White Mountains, you'll notice the scenery changing from mountain firs and pines to junipers and vast rangelands, then to the multihued, barren hills of the Painted Desert. Petrified Forest National Park protects its famous fossilized wood amid striking desert country.

A beard growing contest at the rodeo in Winslow, 1948.

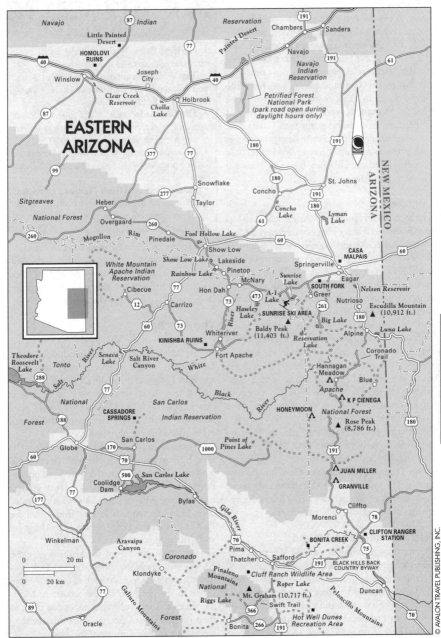

Southward from the White Mountains, the range in elevation is even greater—you'll be in cotton country along the Gila River, while "islands" of high mountains, such as Mt. Graham (10,717 feet) near Safford, soar into the sky from the desert plains. A paved road runs nearly to the top of Mt. Graham, taking you from the Lower Sonoran Zone to the Hudsonian. The Galiuro Mountains to the west form a rugged wilderness with several peaks over 7,000 feet. Perennial streams add beauty to desert canyons in such places as Aravaipa Canyon Wilderness west of Safford and the Gila Box Riparian National Conservation Area east of town.

Climate

The high country provides welcome relief in summer from the searing heat of the deserts. Most eastern Arizona resort areas lie at elevations of 6,000–8,500 feet, where average summer temperatures run in the 60s and 70s (°F), and highs rarely exceed the mid-80s. Early summer is the driest time of year. Afternoon thunderstorms drench the forests almost daily from mid-July to early September, bringing about one-third of the area's 15 or so inches of annual precipitation. Winter sees heavy snowfalls and lows in the teens—camping above 6,000 feet becomes difficult. Skiers enjoy the often bright and sunny winter days, when highs can reach the mid-40s. You may even see some anglers come out and chop holes in the lake ice to get at elusive trout.

Petrified Forest National Park and the surrounding high-desert country can be hot in summer and cold in winter, but they are usually free of snow. The low desert south of the White Mountains enjoys mild winters and rarely receives snow. As in the rest of eastern Arizona, the deserts see frequent thunderstorms in late summer.

Getting There and Around

Private transportation is virtually a necessity in eastern Arizona. Only a few bus and train connections serve the area. White Mountain Passenger Lines maintains the most extensive bus routes, connecting Show Low and Heber in eastern Arizona with Payson and the Phoenix area. Greyhound buses stop in Winslow and Holbrook on

---

EASTERN ARIZONA HIGHLIGHTS

- **Petrified Forest National Park:** Fallen trees have been transformed into colorful stone.
- **The White Mountains:** Conifer-clad peaks and valleys offer hiking, back-road drives, mountain biking, fishing, and skiing.
- **The Coronado Trail:** One of America's most spectacular scenic drives, this highway twists through rugged mountains.
- **Aravaipa Canyon Wilderness:** A perennial creek brings life to the desert in a pretty canyon near Safford.
- **Mount Graham Drive:** This mountain road ascends more than 6,000 feet from the high desert to alpine country atop a "sky island."

---

runs across northern Arizona and at Globe and Safford on a southern route. Winslow is the only town served by Amtrak trains. Show Low has a commuter airline, providing the only scheduled commercial air service in the area.

The Apache

Close relatives of the Navajo, the Apache have a similar language and customs. Groups of Apache are thought to have migrated from Canada, arriving in Texas and New Mexico in the 16th century. A few moved west, forming the tribes that now live on the White Mountain and San Carlos Reservations in eastern Arizona and three small reservations in central Arizona.

The early Apache lived a nomadic life—the men hunted game while the women gathered wild plant foods. They had few material possessions, and they probably lived in small conical huts covered with animal skins. Cultivation of corn, beans, and squash, learned from either the Pueblo or Navajo, later supplemented hunting and gathering.

Horses obtained from the Spanish gave the Apache great mobility, and by the mid-18th century their raiding routes stretched from the Hopi mesas in the north to central Sonora in Mexico. Their predatory habits did not endear them to their neighbors—in fact, the name Apache may have come from a Zuni word for "enemy."

APACHE RESERVATION LIFE

Attempts over the years by the Spanish, the Mexicans, and finally the Americans to exterminate the Apache caused the tribes to retaliate with a murderous vengeance. By 1870, the U.S. government finally realized that a military solution just wouldn't work. The government then initiated a "Peace Policy," which placed all Native Americans on reservations and taught them to farm and raise livestock. The San Carlos Reservation, created in 1871 just south of the White Mountains, became home for various tribes—Mohave, Yavapai, Yuma, and several different groups of Apache.

Officials thought the tribes would be easier to control if centralized on one reservation, but their plan may actually have extended the Apache wars. Quarrels developed between the different groups, attempts at farming fared poorly, and government agents frequently cheated the tribespeople. Geronimo and other war chiefs fled the reservation at times to lead raids against settlements in southern Arizona and northern Mexico. By the time Geronimo surrendered in 1886, the federal government recognized that the San Carlos Reservation had failed, and it removed all tribes except the San Carlos Apache. Meanwhile, many of the White Mountain and Cibecue Apache had succeeded in holding onto part of their own territory to the north, which became a reservation in 1897.

In 1918, a ranching program issued five head of cattle to each of 80 Apache families. Although the program nearly failed, the herds on the Fort Apache Reservation grew to 20,000 by 1931. Still, it wasn't until 1936 that white people finally removed the last of their own cattle from the reservations. Recognizing the recreational value of their lands, in the 1950s the White Mountain Apache began to build access roads, reservoirs, campgrounds, marinas, motels, restaurants, and a ski resort. They also own and operate a large lumber industry. During this development, the tribe has preserved their land's great natural beauty. San Carlos Apache have provided visitors' facilities on their lands as well, though on a smaller scale.

The High Desert

WINSLOW AND VICINITY

Founded in 1882 as a railroad terminal, the town commemorates General Edward Francis Winslow, president of the St. Louis and San Francisco Railroad, associated with the Atlantic and Pacific line that ran through here. Navajos called the place Beeshsinil ("Iron lying down"). Ranchers turned the community into a major stock-raising center and shipping point. By the early 20th century, Winslow had become the most important community in northern Arizona. Route 66, formed in 1926 when new and existing roads connected Chicago with the West Coast, brought America's motorists to the busy downtown. Charles Lindbergh came to design Winslow Airfield as a midway stop for flights between Chicago and Los Angeles, then made the inaugural flight in 1930. The Santa Fe Railroad and Fred Harvey Company opened a fabulous resort hotel, La Posada, also in 1930.

But alas, by the 1970s commercial flights had long bypassed the airfield, train passenger traffic had dried up, and I-40 bypassed downtown. Winslow lay tattered and nearly forgotten. Now visitors have started to discover the history and atmosphere of the old town. La Posada, nearly lost, has been dusted off, restored, and reopened as the grand Southwest hotel it once was. The airfield and a piece of Route 66 also survive, as do prehistoric ruins nearby in Homolovi Ruins State Park. The Old Trails Museum downtown portrays Winslow's colorful history with many old photos and artifacts.

Trade and the railroad remain important to the community, though tourism, trucking, and a state prison boost the economy, too. Winslow (pop. 11,215) lies in the Little Colorado River Valley at an elevation of 4,850 feet. Travelers

© OLD TRAILS MUSEUM, WINSLOW

Interior of Winslow's famed Harvey House, La Posada, in 1930. It included the busy newstand in the background.

find it a convenient stopover; Meteor Crater is 25 miles west, the Hopi and Navajo reservations lie to the north, Petrified Forest National Park is 50 miles east, and the Mogollon Rim forest and lake country is 40 miles south.

La Posada

Almost immediately after its 1930 opening, La Posada became *the* place to stay for movie stars and other rich and famous people who came for a relaxing getaway in splendid surroundings. Architect Mary Colter let loose her imagination, creating not so much a hotel as a grand hacienda that would have made an 18th-century Spanish don proud. She designed and oversaw construction of the magnificent arches, acres of exotic gardens, a ballroom, antiques "from their travels," and rustic furniture "made by the ranch hands." Colter considered it her masterpiece. People staying here felt as though they were personal guests of the fictional don.

La Posada turned out to be the last great railroad hotel built in the United States. The Depression hurt business in the 1930s, then the post-war decline of the railroads forced the hotel to close in 1957. The Santa Fe Railroad converted some of it to offices. The building might have been torn down had not some people discovered this "lost treasure" and set to work restoring it. Now, after 40 years of lying dormant, La Posada once again welcomes guests to the spacious halls, dining area, lounge, and rooms. Patios and libraries invite guests to sit down and relax. A

gift shop sells Southwestern items including Native American work, Mimbreño ware (with prehistoric designs), and books. Unless a special event is going on (it's a great place for weddings), you're welcome to drop by and take a self-guided walking tour of the grand public areas. The hotel is online at www.laposada.org.

Old Trails Museum

This fun little museum reveals life in the Winslow area from Stone Age to modern times. Popular exhibits include Homolovi pottery, railroad memorabilia, La Posada and Harvey Girls displays, Route 66 history, and territorial doctors. The moonshine still, used by Italian immigrant Frank Ianni from the 1920s to the 1980s, is here. And you may see clothing worn by stage actress Norma Deane (1897–1926), a local girl who made it big in the theater, was engaged to famed star Victor Jory, then died on a visit home while trying to cross a flooded wash.

The collection is downtown in a 1921 commercial building at 212 Kinsley; 928/289-5861. Open Tues.–Sat. 1–5 P.M. (closed Wed. from Nov. to Feb.); donations welcome. Regional books are sold.

The Corner

"Take it Easy," a hit single recorded by The Eagles in the early 1970s, inspired the little park near the museum with the lines "Standin' on a corner in Winslow, Arizona, such a fine sight to see. It's a girl, my Lord, in a flatbed Ford, slowin' down to take a look at me." Look for the statue and mural at the northwest corner of Route 66 (Second St.) and Kinsley Avenue.

Brigham City

In 1876 Mormon pioneers arrived to establish this new settlement on the Little Colorado. They had been called by their church to provide a new place for members to live and work. The colonists' early optimism for the farming potential of bottomland along the Little Colorado soon faded as floods washed away dams and irrigation systems. Fear of Native American attacks caused residents to protect their community with walls 200 feet long and seven feet high. Al-

These are some of the 400 children who dressed up in hand-made crepe-paper costumes in 1931 for the musical production, "The Awakening of Spring." Different groups represented fairies, flowers, butterflies, winter wind, rain, and snow.

though never attacked, settlers abandoned Brigham City in 1881 because of the irrigation difficulties. It's slowly being reconstructed on the site just northeast of Winslow; ask at the nearby chamber office. Old Trails Museum has a model of the settlement.

Homolovi Ruins State Park

Ancestral Puebloans lived in pithouses and later at six pueblo villages near present-day Winslow from about A.D. 600 to 1390. The inhabitants, it's believed, then moved north to the Hopi mesas. Oral traditions passed down through generations of Hopi relate how ancestors emerged from a world beneath the present one and migrated in stages to their present home. Clan elders guided the migrations through revelations from dreams and meditations. The Hopi consider these ruins sacred and still leave *pahos* (prayer feathers) here for the spirits. Site visitors mustn't take or disturb anything; federal and state laws prohibit removal of artifacts. Even the tiniest potsherd must be left in place to preserve the sacred character of the sites.

The name Homolovi ("Place of the Little Hills") applies to all sites in the Winslow area. Serious archaeological studies began only in 1984; you're welcome to watch the archaeologists when they're working here. The **visitor center** makes a good place to start with its exhibits, videos (shown on request), and information desk; you can purchase Hopi crafts and books on Native Americans. Staff offer workshops on crafts, gardening, archaeology, wildlife, and storytelling. Archaeology Day, the last Saturday in July, features tours and arts and crafts demonstrations. A pithouse village site lies behind the visitor center, but the shallow depressions can hardly be seen.

A sign at the visitor center parking area points the way toward **Sunset Cemetery,** a half-mile-roundtrip walk. Lot Smith founded Sunset in 1876 beside the Little Colorado River, though floods and droughts forced abandonment of the Mormon settlement 11 years later.

Take I-40 Exit 257 for AZ 87 (just east of Winslow), go north 1.3 miles to the park entrance, then turn left 2.1 miles to the visitor center; on the way in you'll pass the turnoff for the campground and Homolovi I on the left, then the Homolovi II turnoff on the right just before the visitor center. The park is open daily 7 A.M.–7:30 P.M. (8 A.M.–5 P.M. for the visitor center) except Christmas; 928/289-4106. Admission is $4 per vehicle (up to four people).

The **campground** has showers, tent pads, dump station, and water and electric hookups for $10 ($15 if you use hookups) including park admission; there's a discount for weekly stays. Water hookups are available only from mid-April to mid-October. The campground usually has room; no reservations are taken.

Homolovi II is the largest site and forms the main section of the state park. Though badly weathered, the ruins show what a prehistoric site looks like before extensive excavation or reconstruction. A quarter-mile loop trail, suitable for wheelchairs, leads along the top of a mesa past the ruins. Signs interpret and describe the village. Ancestral pueblo people occupied it from 1250 to 1390 with a population as high as 3,000. The village comprised more than 1,200 rooms arranged around three plazas and probably stood two or three stories high. A group of five rooms in the West Plaza and a kiva in the Central Plaza have been excavated and stabilized to show the original floor plans. The village served as a major trade center and staging area for northward migrations. Waters of the Little Colorado River below attracted game and nourished crops and wild plant foods. The trailhead for Homolovi II is 3.1 miles north of the visitor center on a paved road; a few picnic tables lie along the way in. You can also stop at the Tsu 'vö Loop Trail, a half-mile interpretive loop to a saddle between twin buttes; a trail leaflet helps you locate early petroglyphs and other features beside the trail. At the beginning of the loop another trail heads north to a prairie dog town where you may also see burrowing owls in a half-mile roundtrip. Near the end of the loop, you can turn off to Dine Point atop a hill for views of the park and beyond in 1.5 miles roundtrip.

Homolovi I, a pueblo of over 1,000 rooms near the Colorado River, takes some imagination because you can see only outlines of the

sifting through the diggings at Homolovi I, Homolovi Ruins State Park

walls. Follow the paved road 1.5 miles, then walk along a short dirt trail to reach it.

Homolovi III and IV lie west across the Little Colorado River from Homolovi II. Homolovi IV may be visited and has some fine petroglyphs; stop first at the visitor center to obtain directions. There's nothing to see at Homolovi III; the ruins have been buried to protect them from erosion. **Chevelon Ruins** are the farthest out, about 15 miles southeast of Winslow, and open only for occasional tours.

Little Painted Desert County Park

Enjoy the views and beautiful sunsets from this park, 13 miles northeast of Winslow on AZ 87 (I-40 Exit 257). Facilities include a scenic rim viewpoint overlooking colorful desert hills, a hiking trail, and picnic tables.

McHood Park

Situated on both banks of Clear Creek Reservoir, McHood features swimming, boating, fishing, and picnicking. Anglers catch trout, bass, and catfish. Boaters may use the launch ramp and head 2.5 miles upstream into a scenic canyon with 200-foot cliffs; look for petroglyphs. The area has good birdwatching, too.

Park gates are open 8 A.M. to between 6 and 8 P.M. April 1 to October 31 and 8 A.M.–5 P.M. the rest of the year. At press time there were no fees or campground, though future improvements may reinstate both; 928/289-3411 (city offices).

From Winslow, head south 1.2 miles on AZ 87, then left 4.3 miles on AZ 99 to the park. Turn left before the reservoir bridge to reach the boat ramp and swimming area, or continue across the bridge and turn left to the picnic area.

Accommodations

Winslow has a good selection of motels, which can be very good values. You'll find them along old Route 66 (Business I-40) between I-40 Exits 252 and 255 and on North Park Drive near I-40 Exit 253. The I-40 business route splits downtown into Route 66, formerly Second Street, (eastbound) and Third Street (westbound). Bargain-priced motels abound on Route 66 and Third Streets. Many places run well under $35 even in the peak summer months, though a few establishments look like they're on their last legs.

Under $50: Some of the better ones in this price category include, from west to east, **Travelodge** with an outdoor pool at 1914 W. Third St., 928/289-4611, 800/578-7878, $39 s, $44 d; **Motel 10,** 725 W. Third St., 928/289-3211, 800/675-7478, $35 s, $37 d incl. tax; and **Winslow Inn,** 701 W. Third St., 928/289-9389, $27 s, $29 d.

$50–100: Days Inn, 2035 W. Hwy. 66, 928/289-1010, 800/329-7466, sports an indoor pool and hot tub; $55–60 d. **Super 8 Motel,** 1916 W. Third St., 928/289-4606, 800/800-8000, costs $47 s, $51–57 d. **Econo Lodge,** 1706 N. Park Dr. (just south of I-40 Exit 253), 928/289-4687, 800/553-2666, has an outdoor pool; $50 s, $60 d. **Best Western Adobe Inn,** 1701 N. Park Dr. (just south of I-40 Exit 253), 928/289-4638, 800/528-1234, features an indoor pool, hot tub, and restaurant; $72 d. **Holiday Inn Express,** Transcon Lane (just north off I-40 Exit 255), 928/289-2960, 800/HOLIDAY, includes an indoor pool and hot tub; $79 s, $89 d.

La Posada, downtown at 303 E. Second St., 928/289-4366, once again welcomes guests to its distinctive rooms and spacious halls decorated with art and hand-crafted furniture. All rooms have private baths, which was a rarity back in 1930. Rates run $79–99 d depending on size; www.laposada.org. The Turquoise Room restaurant has some of the best food in northern Arizona. Amtrak passengers have only a short stroll to the hotel doors.

Campgrounds

Freddie's RV Park has RV sites ($14.50 with hookups) just north of I-40 Exit 255 on the east side of town; 928/289-3201. Homolovi Ruins State Park offers sites with hookups; see description above.

Food

La Posada's **Turquoise Room** restaurant, named for the private dining car on the Santa Fe Super Chief, serves retro Fred Harvey and contemporary Southwestern cuisine daily except Tues. for breakfast, lunch, and dinner; 928/289-2888. In the late 1800s and early 1900s, Fred Harvey restaurants served the region's best cuisine. Specialties popular back then included baked egg dishes, which you'll find on the breakfast menu. Dinners, about $12–20, feature a changing selection of steak, prime rib, lamb, chicken, seafood, and pasta. The signature soup is corn on one side and bean on the other, with a signature on top! The Martini Lounge lies just off the dining room.

Entre Restaurant, 1919 W. Second St., 928/289-2141, offers Chinese and American fare daily for lunch and dinner; there's also a lunch buffet Mon.–Friday. **Sue's Place Family Restaurant,** 723 W. Third St., 928/289-1234, has American favorites and some Mexican items for breakfast, lunch, and dinner; closed Sat. dinner and all day Sunday. **Port Java,** at the Winslow-Lindbergh Regional Airport terminal, 928/289-0850, prides itself on hamburgers, desserts, and coffees; open daily. **Casa Blanca**

Café, 1201 E. Second St., 928/289-4191, serves up Mexican and American food daily for lunch and dinner.

Restaurants just north of I-40 Exit 253 off North Park Dr. near Wal-Mart include a 24-hour **Denny's,** a 24-hour **Señor D's** (Mexican-American at Pilot truck stop), **Captain Tony's Pizza & Pasta Emporium, Pizza Hut,** and **Arby's.**

On the east edge of town, just off I-40 Exit 255, you can dine Chinese at **China Inn,** north of I-40, 928/289-2086, open daily for lunch and dinner; or try American fare at the **Country Market,** a restaurant in the Flying J truck stop south of I-40 Exit 255, 928/289-5330, for daily buffets of breakfast, lunch, and dinner, plus a 24-hour menu service.

Bashas' and **Safeway** supermarkets are on N. Park Dr., one block south of I-40 Exit 253.

Events

Fireworks and local entertainers help celebrate **July Fourth.** Cowboys and cowgirls show their stuff in the **West Best Rodeo** on the second Saturday in September. The **Christmas Parade** starts off the holiday season on the third Saturday in November.

Recreation

Winslow City Park, at the corner of Colorado Ave. and Cherry St., has indoor and outdoor pools, tennis and racquetball courts, ball fields, weight rooms, and sports programs; 928/289-5714 (parks and recreation), 928/289-4543 (indoor pool), or 928/289-4592 (outdoor pool). Play golf at the nine-hole **Santa Fe Golf Course,** one block east on North Road from North Park Dr.; 928/289-6737.

Information and Services

The **Winslow Chamber of Commerce,** just north of I-40 Exit 253 (look for the giant Native American statue), 928/289-2434, provides maps and information on area sights and facilities. An exhibit room introduces the land and people of northeastern Arizona. The office is open Mon.–Fri. 8 A.M.–5 P.M. For more information, write the chamber at 300 W. North Rd., Winslow, AZ 86047; winslowarizona.org.

For Native American art and crafts, drop in at the historic **Hubbell Trading Post,** 523 W. Second St., 928/289-3986, to see work by the Arizona Indian Arts Cooperative; closed Sunday.

The **public library,** 420 W. Gillmore St., 928/289-4982, has a good collection of books on Arizona and the Southwest; open Tues.–Sat. 10 A.M.–5 P.M. (Wed. and Thurs. until 7 P.M.). The **post office** is at 223 Williamson Ave. between Route 66 and Third St.; 928/289-2131. **Winslow Memorial Hospital** is on the north edge of town at 1501 Williamson Ave. (take I-40 Exit 253); 928/289-4691.

Transportation

Amtrak offers rail service but there's no agent in town; call 800/872-7245 for schedule and ticket information. The station, next to La Posada, is open during the day. **Greyhound** buses stop downtown at the Circle K, 323 N. Williamson Ave., 928/289-2358, 800/231-2222.

Joseph City

Mormons established the farming community of Allen's Camp in 1876 under great difficulty. Attempts to dam the Little Colorado for irrigation failed repeatedly, leaving crops to wither away. Although four other Mormon settlements along the Little Colorado were abandoned, this town, renamed Joseph City, persevered. It is the oldest Anglo community in Navajo County.

On the east side of town, **Norma's RV Park,** 928/288-3273, has spaces for self-contained units; $15 with hookups. **Subway** and **A&W** restaurants are on the east end of town (I-40 Exit 277).

HOLBROOK

When the railroad reached this site in 1881, Eastern investors recognized the surrounding rangelands as prime cattle country and wasted no time in seeking grazing rights. Within two years, the Aztec Land and Cattle Company based near Joseph City ran 60,000 head of cattle. The Aztec, better known as the Hashknife outfit after the shape of its brand, became the third-largest cattle empire in the United States.

In 1948, Winslow's famous Santa Fe Indian Band played a concert to welcome the railroads gleaming new "Train of Tomorrow."

Its cowboys worked the longhorns across one million acres. On holidays, the cowpokes, looking for a good time, rode into Holbrook with guns blazing. Rustling and poor management troubled the Hashknife operation until it shut down about 1900, but Holbrook (pop. about 5,700) remains a ranching center. Travelers often use Holbrook as a base for visiting the nearby Petrified Forest National Park and the Navajo and Hopi lands.

Navajo County Museum

You can relive some of the area's Wild West history in the 1898 former county courthouse downtown. Period rooms and artifacts trace the changes from the prehistoric era to lawless frontier days to modern times. Head upstairs to see the courtroom, with its decorative metal ceiling, and some restored offices. Don't miss the dungeon-like jail downstairs.

Exhibits are open daily 8 A.M.–5 P.M.; donations welcome. The Holbrook Chamber of Commerce office is here too, open identical hours and with the same telephone numbers, at the corner of 100 E. Arizona St. and Navajo Blvd.; 928/524-6558, 800/524-2459.

International Petrified Forest

Several attractions at this private museum invite a stop. The Museum of the Americas has a large collection of prehistoric Meso-American and Southwestern effigies and pottery, plus jewelry, tools, and other finds. A two-room reconstructed pueblo stands in the middle of the museum. A fossil display has some huge dinosaur bones, eggs, and dung; the unusual green petrified wood gets its color from chromium. Outside, a small herd of buffalo and a few life-size dinosaurs will interest the kids. A four-mile loop drive leads past colorful hills covered with large petrified logs. The gift shop offers petrified wood and other souvenirs. Hours run daily 8 A.M.–5 P.M. in winter, 8 A.M. to 6 P.M. in spring and autumn, and 7 A.M.–7 P.M. in summer; 928/524-9178, 888/830-6682, www.petrifiedforest.com. Admission is $5 per vehicle. Head east about three miles on I-40 from Holbrook to Exit 292; the museum is just south of I-40.

Accommodations

Holbrook offers some 25 motels and 25 restaurants along W. Hopi Dr. and Navajo Boulevard. The two streets meet downtown, where their

EASTERN ARIZONA

numbering begins; W. Hopi Dr. heads west to I-40 Exit 285; Navajo Blvd. goes north to I-40 Exit 286, then curves east back to I-40 at Exit 289. Addresses on Navajo Blvd. over 1200 are between Exits 286 and 289. Many of the motels post bargain rates year-round.

Under $50: Of the large selection in this category, the **Wigwam Motel**, 811 W. Hopi Dr., 928/524-3048, stands out as a Route 66 icon and favorite of both kids and adults. Although dating from the late 1940s, the wigwams are both comfy and cozy and have original hickory furniture; $36 one bed, $42 two beds including tax. A small museum of Native American artifacts and petrified wood is off the lobby.

Others in the Under $50 category include: **Budget Host Holbrook Inn**, 235 W. Hopi Dr., 928/524-3809, 800/283-4678, $22–26 d; **Sun & Sand Motel,** with a pool at 902 W. Hopi Dr., 928/524-2186, $25 d; **Budget Inn Motel,** 602 Navajo Blvd., 928/524-6263, $20 d; **Western Holiday Motel,** 720 Navajo Blvd., 928/524-6216, $20 s, $26 d; **El Rancho Motel,** 867 Navajo Blvd., 928/524-3332, $39 d; **Best Inn,** 2211 Navajo Blvd., 928/524-2654, $41 d; **Sahara Inn,** 2402 Navajo Blvd., 928/524-6298, $20 d; **Relax Inn,** 2418 Navajo Blvd., 928/524-6815, $23 s, $26 d; **Econo Lodge,** with a pool at 2590 Navajo Blvd., 928/524-1448, 800/55-ECONO, $40 s, $45 d; and **Ramada Limited,** featuring an indoor pool and hot tub at 2608 Navajo Blvd., 928/524-2566, 800/272-6232, $35 s, $45.50 d.

$50–100: Choices in this category include **Best Western Adobe Inn** with a pool at 615 W. Hopi Dr., 928/524-3948, 800/528-1234, $46 s, $50 d; **Holiday Inn Express,** 1308 Navajo Blvd., 928/524-1466, 800/465-4329, featuring an indoor pool and hot tub, $77 s, $82 d; **Super 8,** with a pool and hot tub at 1989 Navajo Blvd., 928/524-2871, 800/800-8000, $48 s, $55 d; **Best Western Arizonian,** 2508 Navajo Blvd., 928/524-2611, 800/528-1234, with a pool, $59 s, $65 d; **Days Inn** sporting an indoor pool and hot tub at 2601 Navajo Blvd., 928/524-6949, 800/329-7466, $52 s, $62 d; and **Comfort Inn,** with a pool at 2602 Navajo Blvd., 928/524-6131, 800/228-5150, $69 s, $74 d.

Heward House Bed & Breakfast, 108 Crestview, 928/524-3411, has a great panorama atop a butte north of downtown; $75d.

Campgrounds

OK RV Park, just north of I-40 Exit 286 at the corner of Roadrunner and Buzzard, 928/524-3226, is open all year with showers and a laundry; $13.50 tent or RV without hookups, or $21 with hookups, including tax. You'll find the **KOA** campground at 102 Hermosa, just off Navajo Blvd., for $19 tent or RV no hookups, $28 RV with hookups, and $32 kamping kabins plus tax; 928/524-6689. Guests can take in pancake breakfasts and cowboy cookouts and have access to the pool in summer as well as the year-round store, game room, playground, showers, and laundry. Take I-40 Exit 286 or 289.

Cholla Lake County Park, 10 miles west of Holbrook near a power plant, offers picnicking, camping, fishing, water-skiing, windsurfing, and swimming. Anglers pull largemouth bass, catfish, and sunfish from the 360-acre lake. A swim area and fishing dock are wheelchair accessible. Day-use fee is $3 ($2 for county residents). The campground, open year-round, includes showers and costs $10 per night or $14 with water and electric hookups; 928/288-3717 (park) or 928/524-4250 (county office). Take I-40 Exit 277 and follow signs for about a mile.

Food

Some of the downtown cafés tend to be smoky. Two places that serve American and Mexican food and provide a nonsmoking area are **Mr. Maestas,** 502 Navajo Blvd., 928/524-6000, and **El Rancho Restaurant,** 867 Navajo Blvd., 928/524-3332; both open daily for breakfast, lunch, and dinner, though El Rancho closes on Monday. Old West décor and steer horns welcome you at **Butterfield Stage Co. Steakhouse,** 609 W. Hopi Dr., 928/524-3447; open daily for dinners of steak, prime rib, barbecue, and seafood.

Other good bets lie along Navajo Blvd. between I-40 Exits 286 and 289: **Roadrunner Café,** 1501 Navajo Blvd., 928/524-2787, and

Jerry's Restaurant, 2600 Navajo Blvd., 928/524-2364, serve American favorites daily for breakfast, lunch, and dinner. For Chinese and American, try **Mandarin Beauty Restaurant,** 2218 Navajo Blvd., 928/524-3663; it's open for lunch (buffet available Mon.–Fri.) and dinner; may close Sunday. **Mesa Italiana Restaurant,** 2318 Navajo Blvd., 928/524-6696, prepares fine Italian cuisine with veal, chicken, shrimp, pasta, and pizza; there's a wine list too; open daily except Mon. for lunch and dinner. **Mesa Grill & Sports Bar,** 928/524-6697, is open evenings next door. Many popular fast-food places lie along this section of Navajo Blvd., too. **Safeway** supermarket is at 702 W. Hopi Drive.

Events

Pow-wow-style **Native American Dances** take place nightly Mon.–Fri. during part of summer on the lawn next to the old courthouse; check with the chamber for the schedule and times. The **Hashknife Pony Express** hits the trail every year in late January, when riders carry the mail from Holbrook to Scottsdale. You can send a letter along, too, by affixing the usual postage and marking the lower left corner "Via Pony Express." Enclose in a second envelope and send to Postmaster, Holbrook, AZ 86025. **Old West Days,** on the second weekend in June, features Bucket of Blood foot and bicycle races along with Old West reenactors, arts and crafts exhibits, music, and dancing. Fireworks and "the state's best barbecue" mark **July Fourth.** The **Quilt Festival** stitches up in late July or early August. **Navajo County Fair** runs on in September. Townspeople decorate a room full of trees for the **Festival of Trees,** on Thurs.–Sat. of the first weekend of December. A nighttime **Christmas Parade of Lights** brightens downtown on the first Saturday in December.

Shopping

Although it's strictly forbidden to remove anything from Petrified Forest National Park, you can shop in Holbrook for samples of the strange wood-turned-to-stone that have come from private lands. Small pieces cost just pennies; larger, polished specimens run from a few dollars into the thousands. Turquoise, geodes, and other treasures are available as well. **Jim Gray's Petrified Wood Co.** has an enormous selection just south of town at the junction for US 180, on the way to the south entrance of Petrified Forest National Park; look for huge petrified logs surrounding the store. Also try the **Rainbow Rock Shop** at 101 Navajo Blvd., other shops on Navajo Blvd., or those just outside the south entrance of the national park. **Julien's Roadrunner** at 109 W. Hopi Dr. is full of Route 66 memorabilia. For Native American crafts, look into **Nakai Indian Jewelry** at 357 Navajo Blvd., **Linda's Indian Arts & Crafts** at 405 Navajo Blvd., **Pow Wow Trading Post** at 752 Navajo Blvd., and **McGee's Beyond Native Tradition** at 2114 Navajo Boulevard.

Recreation

Hunt Park features a picnic area, playground, outdoor swimming pool, and tennis courts; turn east on Florida Street from Navajo Blvd.; 928/524-3331 (pool). The nine-hole **Hidden Cove Golf Course** lies about three miles west of town; take I-40 Exit 283 and turn north on Golf Course Rd.; 928/524-3097.

Information and Services

The helpful **Holbrook Chamber of Commerce** offers both local and statewide literature in the old county courthouse along with Navajo County Museum historical exhibits. Both are open Mon.–Fri. 8 A.M.–5 P.M., downtown at the corner of Navajo Blvd. and Arizona St. (100 E. Arizona St., Holbrook, AZ 86025); 928/524-6558, 800/524-2459; azjournal.com. The **public library** is at 451 N. First Ave.; it's open Mon. 10 A.M.–5 P.M., Tues.–Thurs. 10 A.M.–7 P.M., Fri. 1–5 P.M., and Sat. 10 A.M.–2 P.M.; 928/524-3732. The **post office** is at 100 W. Erie St.; 928/524-3311.

Transportation

Greyhound buses stop at Circle-K near the corner of 101 Mission Lane and Navajo Blvd.; 928/524-3832, 800/231-2222.

Petrified Forest National Park

Like the Grand Canyon, Petrified Forest National Park presents an open book to the earth's past. The park lies in the Painted Desert, whose colorful hills provide a world-famous resource of petrified wood and related fossils. Layers of the Chinle—a widespread geologic formation delicately tinted with reds, grays, oranges, and whites—have eroded to reveal remains of life frozen in stone from 225 million years ago. Rivers in that period carried fallen trees, some of which towered almost 200 feet high, onto the floodplains. Waterborne minerals transformed the logs to stone, replacing wood cells and filling the spaces between with brightly colored quartz and jasper crystals. This now-arid land would be unrecognizable today to its ancient inhabitants: primitive fish, massive amphibians, and fearsome reptiles.

Some of the strange animals that once crawled and swam here became fossils, now on display in park exhibits, though the trees have traditionally attracted the most attention. In the late 1800s, collectors carted away vast quantities of petrified wood logs for souvenirs or dynamited the stone trees to retrieve their crystals. This loss led to a battle for preservation, won in 1906 when President Theodore Roosevelt signed a bill establishing the Petrified Forest National Monument. A 1958 act of Congress, followed by acquisition of new lands, changed the status of the land to a national park in 1962.

Research continues today to unravel the mysteries of how early life developed here those millions of years ago. Archaeologists attempt to trace the early human history of the park, which extends back about 10,000 years ago to nomadic groups, some of whom later settled in pueblo farming communities before moving on about 1400.

Flora and Fauna

A surprising amount of life exists today in the park, despite the meager nine-inch annual rainfall and lack of permanent water. Evening primrose, Indian paintbrush, mariposa lily, sunflowers, and other plants bloom when they receive sufficient moisture. Snakeweed and rabbitbrush are common and especially conspicuous in autumn when their bright yellow blooms can be seen covering the hills throughout the park. Other plants you're likely to see include buckwheat—a shrub that turns orange-brown in autumn—and saltbush, named for the tiny salt crystals formed on its leaves to conserve moisture.

Lizards often sun themselves atop petrified logs, but snakes will probably sense you before you see them; the western rattlesnake is the only poisonous species found here, and it's seldom encountered. The collared lizard may attain a length of 14 inches and sometimes has bright yellow and green coloration along with its signature black-and-white neck band. Also commonly seen, the plateau striped whiptail lizard's sleek body has black-and-white stripes and a bluish tail. Most bird species found in the park visit only during spring and autumn while migrating between north and south. Hardy residents that you're likely to sight anytime include ravens, rock wrens, and horned larks. Prairie dogs, black-tailed jackrabbits, and desert cottontails are often sighted, but pronghorn, coyotes, and bobcats also live here. The visitor center and museum offer checklists for birds and other animals.

The Three Sections

The southern section—the original national monument—features some of the finest petrified wood in the world. The central section contains the greatest number of prehistoric Native American sites. During their stay from about A.D. 300 to 1400, the ancestral pueblo people progressed from seminomadic hunters and gatherers to farmers who lived in permanent pueblos and likely had a complex ceremonial life. Scientists examining the numerous petroglyphs have discovered some that function as solar calendars.

The northern section of the park has many viewpoints of the Painted Desert, famed for its landscape of ever-changing colors—the effect of the sun playing on hills stained by iron, manganese, and other minerals. Colors become most vivid early and late in the day, fading toward noon. Added in 1932, this northern section is the largest part of the park.

Visiting the Park

Sightseeing in the park can be enjoyable at any time of year; just protect yourself from the sun in the warmer months. You can begin the paved 28.6-mile scenic drive through the park at either end. If eastbound, you'll save miles by using the south entrance off US 180 from Holbrook, then continuing east on I-40 from the north entrance after visiting the park. If westbound, the north entrance offers shorter access. The drive takes 45 minutes non-stop; the average visit runs about two hours, but you could easily spend all day by visiting each stop and doing some short hikes.

The park is open daily 8 A.M.–5 P.M. except Christmas, with extended hours likely in the summer and shoulder seasons. Winter snow or ice storms occasionally close the road. Start early, as you can easily spend a full day enjoying all the walks, views, and exhibits. Pets can come along if they're leashed and don't go into buildings or off paved surfaces. Admission, good for seven days, is $10 per vehicle ($5 per visitor by motorcycle, bicycle, or foot); free with a Golden Eagle, Golden Age, or Golden Access pass. For more information, contact Park Headquarters at P.O. Box 2217, Petrified Forest, AZ 86028; 928/524-6228; www.nps.gov/pefo.

The visitor center near the north entrance and the museum near the south entrance offer exhibits illustrating park geology, fossils, ecology, and human history. They also sell books, videos, postcards, posters, and maps. A list of the day's ranger talks and walks will be posted. You can also talk with a ranger, pick up a bird list and leaflets on special topics, and obtain backcountry permits. Don't remove any petrified wood or other objects from the park—officials have a "zero-tolerance policy" toward thieves. Rangers estimate that tons of petrified forest would be lost every year if visitors were to pocket even tiny illicit souvenirs.

Holbrook's International Petrified Forest invites a stop, especially if you're traveling with kids. The fossil display at the Museum of the Americas has some huge dinosaur bones, eggs, and, always fun for the youngsters, dung.

Services

The park has no campgrounds or lodging. Two gift shops just outside the south entrance offer primitive camping. Holbrook to the west of the park has the most extensive accommodations in the area. Picnic fixings come in handy, as the park offers picnic areas near the south and north ends. There's a restaurant near the north entrance and a snack bar across from Rainbow Forest Museum inside the south entrance. Only the developed areas have water; you'll probably want to carry something to drink. Shops sell souvenirs outside the park near the south entrance, inside the park at the Rainbow Forest complex, and next to the visitor center at the north entrance station. Shops are the place to obtain petrified wood souvenirs, as the wood comes from private land outside the park boundaries.

Backcountry Travel

The wilderness remains relatively undiscovered—only one of a thousand park visitors strays more than a short distance from pavement. You're free to roam across the landscape and make your own discoveries. Few trails exist, but natural landmarks help guide your way. Carry water (no springs) and wear a hat for protection from the sun. Topo maps will be handy as the wilderness lacks signs. Rangers can give advice, suggest places to see, provide directions, and offer a hiking leaflet. They also issue the free permits required for overnight trips.

Campsites must be within the wilderness and at least one mile from the road. Even if you're planning only a long day hike, it's a good idea to discuss your plans with a ranger. Riding horses and pack animals are permitted, with a limit of six animals per party; carry feed and water. All back-country users should note rules against camp-fires, pets, and firearms.

Painted Desert Wilderness in the north contains 43,020 acres of colorful mesas, buttes, and badlands. You can visit Native American sites and petroglyphs. Onyx Bridge, a 50-foot-long petrified tree in the Black Forest, about four miles roundtrip, is a good destination. Pilot Rock (elev. 6,295 feet), about seven miles northwest of the trailhead, stands as the highest point in the park. Kachina Point Trailhead provides access behind Painted Desert Inn.

SCENIC DRIVE

This description runs from south to north, but you can drive the road in either direction. Numbers in parentheses indicate distances from the north end of the drive. Mileages apply to the drive only and don't include side trips:

Mile 0 (28.6): Beginning of the scenic drive from US 180.

Mile 0.1 (28.5): **Petrified Forest Museum Gift Shop** (928/524-3470) and **Crystal Forest Museum and Gift Shop** (928/524-3500) stand on opposite sides of the road just outside the park's south entrance. Although neither edifice is connected with the park, both exhibit dazzling collections of polished petrified wood, including giant log cross-sections and carvings. You can buy most pieces, along with unpolished petrified wood and other minerals, rocks, fossils, and Native American crafts. Both shops allow free primitive camping for tents and RVs; electric hookups are an optional $10 (free with $50 purchase).

Mile 0.2 (28.4): **South Entrance Station.** A ranger collects fees and gives out park brochures. If you've brought in unpolished wood or other objects, ask the ranger to mark or bag them to avoid any misunderstandings about the source. It's against the law to take *anything* from the park.

Mile 2.4 (26.2): **Rainbow Forest Museum.** You're likely to be greeted by the cast of a huge

skeleton on entering the museum. It might be a ferocious phytosaur, a large crocodile-like reptile that lurked in the forests and swamps here during the Triassic Period 225 million years ago, or a placerias, a two- to three-ton reptile that roamed in herds during the same time. The skeletons and other exhibits provide a look at the strange environment of cycads, ferns, fish, amphibians, reptiles, and other early life that existed then. Rangers provide information and backcountry permits. You can purchase books, videos, posters, postcards, and maps. A "Conscience Wood" exhibit contains stolen petrified wood, returned with apologetic and remorseful letters.

The **Giant Logs Trail** begins behind the visitor center, winding in a half-mile loop past monster-sized logs—a rainbow of reds, yellows, grays, whites, blacks, pinks, and oranges. The base of one fallen tree stands higher than a man. **Fred Harvey's Rainbow Gift Shop and Fountain** offers Native American crafts, souvenirs, and a snack bar across the road from the museum.

Mile 2.5 (26.1): **Picnic area.**

Mile 2.6 (26.0): **Long Logs Loop Trail** and **Agate House Trail** turnoff, then a half mile to parking. Each trail is an easy half-mile walk, a good opportunity to look closely at the ancient trees. The jumble of logs here may have been a logjam, buried in mud, sand, and volcanic ash. Many logs measure more than 100 feet long. Prehistoric tribes built the unusual Agate House entirely with chunks of colorful petrified wood. One of its seven rooms has been reconstructed to show their original size.

Mile 8.1 (20.5): **Crystal Forest Loop Trail.** Some of the prettiest and most concentrated petrified wood in the park lies along this paved half-mile trail.

Mile 9.9 (18.7): **Jasper Forest** turnoff, then a half mile to parking. The overlook provides great views to the west and north. Below lie pieces of petrified wood eroded from the hillsides.

Mile 10.1 (18.5): **Agate Bridge.** Erosion carved out a gully beneath a large log, leaving a bridge. In years past, a Hashknife cowboy rode his horse across the log on a $10 bet. Rangers won't let you do this today—it's unsafe. Because of cracking, the log was braced with a concrete beam in 1917.

Mile 12.9 (15.7): **Blue Mesa** turnoff, then three miles to parking. Blue Mesa offers several panoramic overlooks and a one-mile-loop interpretive trail. The trail provides a good introduction to the Chinle Formation and its badlands topography.

Mile 14.5 (14.1): **The Tepees.** Symmetrical, cone-shaped hills are visible from the pullout.

Mile 16.5 (12.1): **Newspaper Rock** turnoff, then 0.3 mile to parking. An impressive collection of ancient petroglyphs covers a huge sandstone boulder. The drawings have not been interpreted, but they seem to represent animals and spiritual figures. Bring binoculars to better examine the artwork or use the free telescopes.

Mile 17.4 (11.2): **Puerco Pueblo.** Before A.D. 1100, local Native Americans lived in small scattered settlements. The building of larger pueblos, such as Puerco, indicates a change to an agricultural lifestyle requiring greater pooling of efforts. The broad, meandering Puerco River provided reliable water all year, and its flood plain had rich soil for farming. The river also attracted birds, pronghorn, and other game. Native Americans built a one-story pueblo with about 100 rooms. You can see the foundations of these rooms and one of the kivas built around a rectangular plaza. Archaeologists believe that this site was occupied between A.D. 1100 and 1200 and again from about 1300 to 1400. The last occupants appear to have packed up and left peaceably, perhaps over a period of years.

Help protect the site by remaining on the trail. Many fine petroglyphs cover the boulders below the village. Though more scattered, they're comparable with the petroglyphs at Newspaper Rock. One of the Puerco petroglyphs marks the summer solstice. About 14 other sites with solar markings have been discovered in the park.

Mile 17.7 (10.9): **Puerco River bridge.** The scene was probably far different when Native Americans occupied the pueblo. Records indicate that cottonwood trees grew along the floodplain as late as the 19th century. Ranchers took advantage of the abundant grasslands in the late 1880s, but drought in 1891–94 dried up the grass, and gross overstocking destroyed the range. Runoff carried high concentrations of salts into the river, killing less salt-resistant plants. Floods have taken their toll, scouring and widening the river and leaving loads of silt in their wake. Now the river is dry much of the year.

Mile 18.1 (10.5): **Bridge over the railroad tracks.** The Petrified Forest first gained national attention with the completion of the Atlantic and Pacific Railroad (later the Santa Fe) across northern Arizona. Train travelers disembarked at the nearby Adamana Station, now abandoned, to visit the "trees turned to stone."

Mile 23.6 (5.0): **Lacey Point Overlook** of the Painted Desert.

Mile 24.1 (4.5): **Whipple Point Overlook** of the Painted Desert. One of the first white people to visit the Petrified Forest, Lieutenant A.W. Whipple arrived in 1853.

Mile 24.3 (4.3): **Nizhoni Point Overlook** of the Painted Desert. In sunlight, the hillside below appears to be covered with shards of glass. These are natural pieces of selenite gypsum, a very soft mineral you can scratch with your fingernail.

Mile 25.4 (3.2): **Pintado Point Overlook** of the Painted Desert. You're now on a volcanic lava flow, which covers the entire rim and protects the underlying softer Chinle Formation from erosion.

Mile 26.0 (2.6): **Chinde Point Overlook and Picnic Area** turnoff, then 0.3 mile in. Restrooms are available in the summer months.

Mile 26.2 (2.4): **Painted Desert Inn** and **Kachina Point Overlook.** Herbert Lore built the original inn with Native American labor and local materials in 1924. Travelers bumping their way across Arizona on Route 66 stopped for meals and shopped for Native American crafts. After the National Park Service bought the inn and surrounding land in 1936, Civilian Conservation Corps workers rebuilt and enlarged the structure in a pueblo style. It served as a park concession and information station, but the six sleeping rooms were not used after WW II. Hopi artist Fred Kabotie painted the murals in the 1940s. Also look for the carved beams, handmade furniture, metal lamps, and decorated skylights created by the Civilian Conservation Corps. The inn closed when the Painted Desert Visitor Center opened in 1962 and the old building faced demolition, but people recognized its unique Southwestern architecture—a mixture of Spanish and Native American pueblo styles—and saved it.

Now a national historic landmark restored to its 1940s appearance, Painted Desert Inn contains rotating historical and cultural exhibits. A bookstore specializes in Native American books, posters, and crafts. Open daily 9 A.M.–4 P.M. with extended hours possible in summer. You can follow the easy **Rim Trail** between here and Tawa Point Overlook. The trailhead for **Painted Desert Wilderness** (Onyx Bridge, Black Forest, etc.) begins near Kachina Point, behind the inn.

Mile 26.7 (1.9): **Tawa Point Overlook** offers a Painted Desert panorama and a trailhead for the Rim Trail to Kachina Point.

Mile 27.5 (1.1): **Tiponi Point Overlook** of the Painted Desert.

Mile 28.1 (0.5): **Painted Desert Visitor Center** and **North Entrance Station.** A 20-minute movie, shown on the hour and half-hour, illustrates the park's features and describes the formation of petrified wood. A few exhibits have plant and animal fossils, and you can view a "Conscience Wood" display. A ranger will answer your questions and issue backcountry permits. **Fred Harvey Painted Desert Oasis** has a cafeteria, curio shop, and gas station.

Mile 28.6 (0.0): **Junction with I-40.**

South of Holbrook

SNOWFLAKE AND TAYLOR

Heading south from Holbrook, you'll notice the gradual transition from sparsely vegetated desert plains to grasslands and juniper woodlands near the twin towns of Snowflake and Taylor, then the pinyon and ponderosa pines at Show Low, Lakeside, and Pinetop. Mormon settlers established Snowflake in 1878 and built a solid community that thrives to this day. The town's name refers not to the weather, but to a traveling Mormon official, Erastus Snow, and the leader of the settlement, William Flake. The wide streets and numbering system around the central church follow the Mormons' City of Zion plan. Citizens take great interest in their pioneer heritage. A *Historic District Brochure* lists and maps more than 50 structures built in the late 1800s and early 1900s. You can see these on a self-guided or guided tour, with the guided tour having the advantage of taking you inside some buildings not otherwise open. It's easy to get around town once you've become accustomed to the street naming system, which counts out in the four directions from the junction of Main Street (AZ 77) and Center.

Mormons also founded Taylor, just to the south, in 1881, and named it after a church president.

Stinson Pioneer Museum

The two adobe buildings, later joined, that form the museum date from about 1873 and are the oldest in Snowflake. William Flake purchased them from cattleman James Stinson to establish the Mormon community. The first settlers held church meetings, school, and court here. Exhibits show many aspects of pioneer life. Silver Creek Forge in back has a working blacksmith shop that may be in operation when you visit. The museum, 928/536-4881, is open Tues.–Fri. 10 A.M.–4 P.M. and Sat. 10 A.M.–3 P.M. year-round;

donations welcome. It's on your left, one block east of Main Street on First Street North.

The guided **Historic Home Tour** begins here and visits the interiors of the 1895 James M. Flake Home, 1860s William J. Flake cabin, John Freeman Home, and the Jesse N. Smith Home; other structures are also described on the tour, but you don't go inside. A self-guided tour leaflet is available too, if you'd like to explore on your own.

Accommodations and Food

You can stay in an 1890 pioneer house at the **Osmer D. B&B,** 161 N. Main St., 928/536-3322; each room has a different antique décor and a bath; $65–120 d. **Cedar Motel,** 39 S. Main St., 928/536-4606, is also in downtown Snowflake; 40–60 d. **Silver Creek Inn,** 825 N. Main St. in Taylor, 928/536-2600, 888/246-5440, is just south of Snowflake; $70 d.

Local cafés include **Katie's Country Kitchen** at 205 N. Main in Snowflake, 928/536-5450; and **Trapper's Café** at 9 S. Main in Taylor, 928/536-7758. **Pizza Hut** and several fast food places lie along the highway between the two downtowns.

Events

Snowflake Pioneer Days Celebration honors the founding anniversaries of both Salt Lake City and Snowflake on the Thurs.–Sat. closest to July 24; highlights include a rodeo, parade, arts and crafts, a barbecue, fireworks, and a dance.

Recreation

Snowflake has a large city park on N. Main and a swimming pool. **Snowflake Golf Course** offers 18 holes year-round at 90 N. Country Club Dr., three miles west of downtown on AZ 277; 928/536-7233.

Information

The **Snowflake-Taylor Chamber of Commerce** in the 1893 John Freeman House has maps of the historic district and information about the places open to the public. It's open Mon.–Fri. 9 A.M.–3 P.M. and Sat. 9 A.M.–3 P.M. year-round on the corner of Main St. and First St. N, beside a supermarket and across from the church; you can write P.O. Box 776, Snowflake, AZ 85937, or call 928/536-4331.

Transportation

White Mountain Passenger Lines goes Mon.–Sat. from the stop at NAPA Auto Parts on 821 S. Main St., 928/536-4251, to Show Low (the main office, 1041 E. Hall St., 928/537-4539), Heber, Payson, Mesa, and Phoenix.

SHOW LOW

With so many recreation opportunities in the nearby Mogollon Rim country and White Mountains, Show Low has become an important year-round resort. Attractions include excellent trout fishing, hiking, camping, horseback riding, golf, scenic drives, big-game hunting, and skiing. The town of 9,200 (more than double in summer) sits on the pine-forested Mogollon Rim at an elevation of about 6,400 feet.

Show Low got its name from a poker game played in 1876. Corydon Cooley, a noted Indian scout, and his partner, Marion Clark, established a 100,000-acre ranch here in 1870, but found the place wasn't big enough for both of them. Agreeing to settle their differences with a game of cards, they sat down at Cooley's kitchen table for a game of "seven up." The two played through the night until finally Clark said, "Show low and you win." Cooley pulled out an unbeatable deuce of clubs and took the ranch.

Several years later, Mormons bought the property, and their church now occupies the gaming site. Show Low's main street took its name, Deuce of Clubs, from the winning card.

Show Low Historical Society Museum

You can learn about the town's past from Native American artifacts, old photos, post office, kitchen, and changing exhibits at 541 E. Deuce of Clubs. The museum, 928/532-7115, is open Tues.–Fri. 1–5 P.M. and Sat. 10 A.M.–2 P.M. from mid-April to mid-October; donations welcome. Visits by appointment (phone numbers are on the door) also can be arranged. A gift shop sells handicrafts.

Fool Hollow Recreation Area

The 140 acre, U-shaped lake contains trout, smallmouth and largemouth bass, catfish, northern pike, bluegill, and a few walleye. Ponderosa

EASTERN ARIZONA

pines and junipers surround the cool waters at an elevation of 6,300 feet. East and west shores have boat ramps and there's a fish-cleaning station. Boaters can use motors up to eight horsepower. The campground, which fills on many summer weekends, has sites with and without hookups, showers, and a dump station. Group day-use areas can be reserved. Interpretive programs take place on Saturdays in summer. Kids have playgrounds in both the day-use and camping areas. It's a multiagency park, open year-round with Arizona State Parks operating the facilities. Camping fees run $10 tent or RV with no hookups, $17 at sites with hookups. Day use costs $5 per vehicle, $1 pedestrian or bicyclist; 928/537-3680. It's just three miles northwest of Show Low; take Hwy. 260 west almost two miles, turn right on Old Linden Road and follow the signs one mile.

Show Low Lake

Known for its walleye, the lake also contains channel catfish, trout, largemouth bass, and bluegill. Fishermen have a boat ramp and can use motors to eight horsepower. The Navajo County campground on the lake's west side is open year-round with water, showers, and a playground; $8–10 no hookups, $16 w/electicity. Picnicking in the campground costs $2. Groups can reserve ramadas; 928/537-4126. The store offers supplies and rents fishing and paddle boats; it's open year-round, weather permitting. The lake lies about five miles south of Show Low; go south four miles on AZ 260, then turn east 1.3 miles at the hospital onto Show Low Lake Road.

Pintail Lake

A natural volcanic depression filled with treated wastewater attracts waterfowl and other wildlife north of Show Low. Artificial islands serve as nesting sites. Go north 3.5 miles on AZ 77 from the east edge of town, then turn right 0.4 mile on Pintail Lake Road (between Mileposts 345 and 346). A paved 0.3-mile trail (wheelchair accessible) leads to a viewing blind. A side trail leads to another viewing platform.

Accommodations

Show Low's motels, listed west to east in each cat-

egory, lie along Deuce of Clubs. The summer rates shown usually come down a bit in winter.

Under $50: Kiva Motel, 261 E. Deuce of Clubs, 928/537-4542, offers a pool, hot tub, and sauna, $38 s, $45 d; **Thunderbird Motel,** 1131 E. Deuce of Clubs, 928/537-4391, has some kitchenettes, $33 d and up; and **Snowy River Motel,** 1640 E. Deuce of Clubs, 928/537-2926, $39–49 d.

$50–100: Sleep Inn, 1751 W. Deuce of Clubs, 928/532-7323, 800/SLEEP-INN, offers an indoor pool and hot tub, $50–80 s, $54–80 d; **Paint Pony Lodge (Best Western),** 581 W. Deuce of Clubs, 928/537-5773, 800/528-1234, $70 d; **Show Low Days Inn,** 480 W. Deuce of Clubs, 928/537-4356, 800/329-7466, has a year-round pool and hot tub, $57 s, $65 d, add $10 Fri.–Sat.; **Holiday Inn Express,** 151 W. Deuce of Clubs, 928/537-5115, 800/HOLIDAY, offers an indoor pool and Jacuzzi, $89.50 d; **KC Motel,** 60 W. Deuce of Clubs, 928/537-4433, 800/531-7152, has a hot tub and fridges, $52–62 d; and **Motel 6,** 1941 E. Deuce of Clubs, 928/537-7694, 800/466-8356, $45 s, $50 d.

Campgrounds

All of the area campgrounds are open year-round and offer showers, except as noted. Both tenters and RVers can camp at Fool's Hollow Lake and Show Low Lake, described above, which are also the best choices for families. RVs may also choose from **Country Lane RV Park** (adult), open May–Sept., 0.75 mile north of Deuce of Clubs at 1051 N. Central Ave., 928/537-5161, $12 RV with hookups; **K-Bar RV Resort** (adult), 300 N. 16th Ave., 928/537-2886, $23.50 RV with hookups; **Venture In RV Resort** (adult), open May–Oct., 1.3 miles west on AZ 260 at 270 N. Clark Rd., 928/537-4443, $25 RV with hookups; **Ranchero RV Mobile Home Park** (adult), 2.9 miles south on AZ 260 at 3860 S. White Mountain Rd., 928/537-4479, $25 RV with hookups; **Pine Shadows Mobile Home Park** (adult), open May–Oct., 3.7 miles south on AZ 260 at 4951 S. White Mountain Rd., 928/537-2895, $19 RV with hookups; **Waltner's RV Resort** (adult), open May–Oct. 15, four miles south on AZ 260, left half a mile on Show Low Lake Road, then left to 4800 S. 28th St., 928/537-4611, $28 RV with hookups and tax; and **Rim Crest RV Resort** (adult), open April 15 to Oct. 15, 4.4 miles south on AZ 260, 928/537-4660, $20 RV with hookups.

Food
Look for restaurants along Deuce of Clubs and south on AZ 260. You can find American food at **JB's Restaurant,** 480 W. Deuce of Clubs, 928/532-1266; Country Kitchen, 201 E. Deuce of Clubs, 928/537-4774; and **Branding Iron Steak House,** 1251 E. Deuce of Clubs, 928/537-5151. For Mexican dining try **Licano's Mexican Food & Steakhouse,** 581 W. Deuce of Clubs, 928/537-3365; **La Casita,** four miles south on AZ 260 at 5000 S. White Mountain Rd., 928/537-5179, closed Monday; and **White Mountain Restaurant,** 2101 E. Deuce of Clubs, 928/537-9880.

Chinese food is served at **Asia Garden Restaurant,** 59 W. Deuce of Clubs, 928/537-9333, closed Monday; **China Cafe,** 1201 E. Deuce of Clubs, 928/537-5407; and **China Moon Buffet,** four miles south on AZ 260 at 4817 S. White Mountain Rd., 928/537-8828, may close Sunday.

Pick up pizza at **Pat's Place,** 981 E. Deuce of Clubs, 928/537-2337, which also serves breakfast; **Pizza Factory,** 100 N. White Mountain Rd., 928/537-7771, closed Sun.; or **Pizza Hut,** 4481 S. White Mountain Rd. in Pineway Center, 928/537-5306. Show Low offers plenty of the usual fast-food places, too.

Entertainment and Events
Enjoy movies at **Winchester Theater,** one mile south on AZ 260 at 1850 S. White Mountain Rd.; 928/367-7469. **Thunder Raceway** offers a variety of automotive racing at 4701 E. Deuce of Clubs from March to October; 928/537-1111.

Show Low celebrates **July Fourth** with a parade and fireworks. Loosen up at the **Square Dance Festival** on the second weekend in July. In December, the town hosts an **Electric Parade,** dressing up in bright lights to celebrate the holidays. Softball tournaments and other events take place throughout the year; consult the Show Low Chamber of Commerce.

Recreation
The **city park** offers a year-round program of activities, an indoor swimming pool, picnic areas with ramadas, a playground, and tennis, basketball, softball, racquetball, and volleyball courts; 928/532-4130 (Family Aquatic Center), 928/532-4140 (Show Low Parks and Recreation). Turn in at 951 W. Deuce of Clubs or off E. Hwy. 260.

Play golf at the 18-hole **Show Low Golf Club,** 860 N. 36th Dr. (near the intersection of AZ 260 and Old Linden Road on the west side of town), 928/537-4564, or at **Silver Creek Golf Club's** 18 holes at White Mountain Lakes, five miles east on US 60, then 7.5 miles north on Bourdon Ranch Road, 928/537-2744.

Information and Services
Folks at the **Show Low Regional Chamber of Commerce** can help you find accommodations and other services; it's open Mon.–Fri. 9 A.M.–5 P.M. and Sat.–Sun. 9 A.M.–3 P.M. at 951 W. Deuce of Clubs (P.O. Box 1083, Show Low, AZ 85902); 928/537-2326, 888/746-9569 (888/SHOW-LOW); www.showlowchamberofcommerce.com. The **public library** is at 20 N. Sixth St. and E. McNeil; 928/537-2447.

The **post office** is at 191 W. Deuce of Clubs; 928/537-4588. **Navapache Regional Medical Center,** 2200 E. Show Low Lake Rd., 928/537-4375, lies next to Wal-Mart, four miles south of Show Low on AZ 260 on the way to Pinetop–Lakeside.

Transportation
Airline service may be available—check with the chamber. **White Mountain Passenger Lines** offers bus service Mon.–Sat. from Show Low to Snowflake, Heber, Payson, Mesa, and Phoenix; the main office is at 1041 E. Hall St. (P.O. Box 460, Show Low, AZ 85902); 928/537-4539. **Four Seasons Bus Connection** serves local routes in the Show Low and Pinetop-Lakeside areas and goes to Hon-Dah; 928/537-0627.

PINETOP–LAKESIDE
The name well describes the lakes and pine forests surrounding the previously twin towns near the edge of the Mogollon Rim, some eight miles

southeast of Show Low. In 1880, Mormon pioneers named their new community Fairview, but renamed it Lakeside upon the completion of Rainbow Lake. Several smaller lakes have been added since, until the area now seems to consist as much of water as of land. Soldiers undertaking the long climb up the Mogollon Rim from Fort Apache in the 1870s often stopped to rest at a place they christened Pinetop; Mormon ranchers founded a settlement there in 1878.

Lakeside (elev. 6,745 feet) on the north and Pinetop (elev. 7,279 feet) just to the south have incorporated as Pinetop-Lakeside, a major recreational center dotted with innumerable summer cabins and resorts. The year-round population of 8,000 jumps to 25,000 in summer.

Mogollon Rim Overlook and Nature Trail

An easy one-mile walk, wheelchair-accessible, offers great views of forested valleys and ridges. Signs describe the area's forests, medicinal plants, and history. The trailhead lies just west of AZ 260, three miles north of the Lakeside Ranger Station. Or, from Show Low, head south 5.5 miles on AZ 260 from Deuce of Clubs.

Big Springs Environmental Study Area

A pleasant half-mile nature trail winds through a variety of wildlife habitats. The trail offers interpretive signs and is quite an easy hike, though muddy after rain or snow. Turn south half a mile on Woodland Road from AZ 260, then look for the parking area on the left.

Rainbow Lake

This 80-acre reservoir in Lakeside just west of AZ 260 is stocked with rainbow trout, brown trout, and some smallmouth bass and catfish. You can fish from the shore near the dam or rent a boat; the lake has an eight-hp motor limit. Nearby Lakeside Campground ($9) is open May to Oct.; you can reserve sites at 877/444-6777; reserveusa.com.

Scott Reservoir

A slightly smaller fishing lake of 70 acres, Scott lies about three miles northeast of Lakeside.

Take Porter Mountain Road (turnoff is one block south of Lakeside Ranger Station) east and north 1.4 miles, turn east 0.6 mile, then right to the reservoir. It offers a boat ramp and a small campground with no drinking water or fee. Only electric motors are permitted.

Woodland Lake

This 18-acre, lake has rainbow and brown trout and some largemouth bass, catfish, and green sunfish; electric boat motors are okay. Woodland Lake Park offers a fishing pier, picnicking, trails, tennis courts, volleyball, softball, and playgrounds, but no camping. Groups can reserve ramadas with Pinetop-Lakeside Parks and Recreation; 928/368-6700. Trails circle the lake (one mile) and go to other destinations. From White Mountain Boulevard, turn in about a half mile on Woodland Lake Road at the Chevron Station.

White Mountain Trail System

Eleven loops, many interconnected, wind through the forests in the Pinetop-Lakeside area. They total about 180 miles and are open to hikers, mountain bikers, and equestrians. In winter, cross-country skiers can glide down the paths. Drop by the Lakeside Ranger Station for maps and trail descriptions. The Pinetop-Lakeside Chamber of Commerce also may have this material.

Accommodations

In this, the largest resort area in the White Mountains, you have a choice of many motels, cottages, cabins, and bed and breakfasts, all nestled in cool pine forests. Rates tend to run higher on summer weekends, when reservations are a good idea. The Pinetop-Lakeside Chamber of Commerce maintains a longer list of places to stay and can help you find what you're looking for.

Under $50 (Lakeside): Bear's Paw Motel, 4229 Valley Lane, 928/368-5231, runs $37 d ($47 d Fri.–Sat.), plus $8 for a kitchen. **Forest House Motel,** 2990 W. White Mountain Blvd., 928/368-6628, 888/440-2220, has a variety of rooms, some with kitchenettes, at $35–75 d (add $10 Fri.–Sat.).

Under $50 (Pinetop): Pinetop Lodge, 593 E. White Mountain Blvd., 928/367-3510, offers a variety of rooms, some kitchenettes and fireplaces;

$35–55 d. **Bonanza Motel,** 858 E. White Mountain Blvd., 928/367-4440, 888/577-4440, has some kitchenettes; $42 s, $45 d. **Blue Ridge Motel and Cabins,** 2012 E. White Mountain Blvd., 928/367-0758, offers log-cabin-style motel units and cabins; $39 d ($45 d Fri.–Sat.) rooms, $42 d ($49 d Fri.–Sat.) small cabins with kitchenettes, and $72 d large cabins with fireplaces and kitchenettes. **Nine Pines Motel,** 2089 E. White Mountain Blvd, 928/367-2999, 888/597-4637, contains rustic pine-log furniture; $37–60 d ($42–69 d Fri.–Sat.).

$50–100 (Lakeside): The Place Resort, 3179 W. White Mountain Blvd., 928/368-6777, has cottages with kitchenettes and fireplaces; $72 d studio, $86 d one bedroom, and $109 (4 people) two bedroom. **Lake of the Woods Resort,** 2244 W. White Mountain Blvd, 928/368-5353, is a great place for families with cabins, all with kitchenettes and fireplaces, plus a private lake, boats, two hot tubs and a sauna; $81–113 d. **Lazy Oaks Resort,** 1075 Larson Rd., 928/368-6203, has a lakeside setting for its cabins, all with kitchenettes and fireplaces; $64–80 d one-bedroom, $94–118 two bedrooms; there's a five-night minimum in summer. **Walker's Rainbow Lake Log Cabin Resort,** 1638 W. White Mountain Blvd., 928/368-6364, 800/932-2246, offers cabins, all with kitchenettes, and a hot tub; $85 d.

$50–100 (Pinetop): Best Western Inn of Pinetop, 404 E. White Mountain Blvd., 928/367-6667, 800/528-1234, has a hot tub; $59–89 d ($89–109 d Fri.–Sat.). **Buck Springs Resort,** 6036 Buck Springs Rd., 928/369-3554, features cottages with kitchens and fireplaces; $85 d one bedroom, $155 three bedrooms. **Cozy Pine Cabins,** 1211 S. Ravens Way Dr., 928/367-4558, has kitchens and some fireplaces; $60–110. **Comfort Inn,** 1637 E. White Mountain Blvd., 928/368-6600, 800/843-4792, has some fireplaces and a hot tub; $65 d ($75 d Fri.–Sat.). **Meadows Inn,** off Woodlands Rd., 928/367-8200, offers bed and breakfast; $85–125 d. **Moonridge Lodge and Cabins,** 596 W. White Mountain Blvd., 928/367-1906, features cabins with kitchenettes and fireplaces, plus a few rooms and cottages; $63–75 d cabins, $25–35 d rooms, $40 d cottages. **Mountain Hacienda Lodge,** 1023 E. White Mountain Blvd., 928/367-4146, 888/567-4148, has rooms from

$49 d ($65 d Fri.–Sat.). **Mountain Haven Inn,** 1120 E. White Mountain Blvd., 928/367-2101, 888/854-9815, has all nonsmoking rooms including some kitchenettes for $44–109 d and houses for $125–150. **Woodland Inn & Suites,** 458 E. White Mountain Blvd., 928/367-3636, 866/PINETOP, includes a hot tub; $89 d ($99 d Fri.–Sat.). **Northwoods Resort,** 165 E. White Mountain Blvd., 928/367-2966, 800/813-2966, offers cabins, all with kitchens and fireplaces, and a Jacuzzi; $99 d studio, $119 d one bedroom, $149 two bedroom. **Super 8 Motel,** 1202 E. White Mountain Blvd., 928/367-3161, 800/800-8000, features an indoor pool and hot tub plus several kitchenettes; $55–100 d ($65–125 d Fri.–Sat.). **Holiday Inn Express,** 431 E. White Mountain Blvd., 928/367-6077, 800/HOLIDAY, offers rooms with microwave and refrigerator plus a hot tub, sauna, and exercise room; $90 d ($109 d Fri.–Sat.). **Whispering Pines Resort,** 237 E. White Mountain Blvd., 928/367-4386, 800/840-3867, features cabins with kitchenettes and fireplaces; $77–125 d.

Campgrounds

Tenters and RVers can stay in the ponderosa pine forests at **Lakeside Campground,** across from the Lakeside Ranger Station in town, 928/368-5111 (Lakeside Ranger Station). There's water and a $9 fee from May to October. It usually has room. **Scott Reservoir** has a small campground three miles northeast of Lakeside on Forest Road 45 via Porter Mountain Road; the turnoff from AZ 260 is one block south of the Lakeside Ranger Station. No drinking water or charge but it often fills in summer. **Show Low Lake,** 928/537-4126, is open year-round with water, showers, a playground, and a store; $8–10 no hookups, $16 w/electricity. Groups can reserve ramadas. Go four miles north of Lakeside, then turn right 1.3 miles at the hospital onto Show Low Lake Road. Another possibility is to head for the woods—you can camp free almost anywhere in the Sitgreaves National Forest. People at the Lakeside Ranger Station can suggest areas.

Lakeside RV parks include: **Rainbow Forest RV Park,** 3720 Rainbow Lake Dr.,

928/368-5286, $19; **Ponderosa RV Resort** (adult), 1666 Ponderosa Lane, $18, open April 15–Oct. 15, 928/368-6989; and **Running Bear Mobile Resort,** 2458 Running Bear Rd., 928/368-6660, $10.

Food

Restaurants are surprisingly good for such small communities. In Lakeside, you can dine American at **Christmas Tree,** 455 N. Woodland Rd., 928/367-3107, open Wed.–Sun. for dinner; and **Chuckwagon Steak House,** on Porter Mountain Rd. (1.5 miles in from Hwy. 260), 928/368-5800, open daily for dinner (closed Mon.–Tues. in winter). For Mexican and American, head over to **Matta's Too,** 1676 W. White Mountain Blvd., 928/368-6969, open daily for lunch and dinner.

In Pinetop, American choices include **Charlie Clark's Steakhouse,** 1701 E. White Mountain Blvd., 928/367-4900, daily for dinner; and **Chalet Restaurant,** 348 W. White Mountain Blvd., 928/367-1514, open Tues.–Sat. for dinner. Dine Mexican at **El Rancho,** 1523 E. White Mountain Blvd., 928/367-4557, open daily for lunch and dinner. The **Lotus Garden,** 984 E. White Mountain Blvd., 928/367-2568, serves Chinese cuisine daily for lunch and dinner.

Entertainment and Events

Enjoy movies at **Lakeside Cinema,** 20 E. White Mountain Blvd.; 928/367-7469. The **White Mountain Native American Art Festival and Indian Market** in July attracts Native Americans from all over the Southwest for dances, music, art, crafts, demonstrations, and food. August brings the **White Mountain Bluegrass Music Festival.** The **Fall Festival** on the last full weekend of September features a colorful parade, arts and crafts show, and other presentations to mark the end of summer. The small **Octoberfest** takes place on the second weekend of October with German-inspired music, food, and beer.

Recreation

You can go horseback riding from May to September with **Porter Mountain Stables,** 4048 Porter Mountain Rd., 928/368-5306; and **Pinetop Lakes Equestrian Center,** Bucksprings Road near the Pinetop Country Club, 928/369-1000. Play golf on the 18-hole executive course at **Pinetop Lakes Golf & Country Club,** one-quarter mile east on Bucksprings Road from White Mountain Blvd., 928/369-4531; the season runs April to October.

Information

Visit or write the **Pinetop-Lakeside Chamber of Commerce,** 102-C W. White Mountain Blvd. (P.O. Box 4220, Pinetop, AZ 85935), 928/367-4290, 800/573-4031, to obtain the latest information, including that of the national forest lands and the town of Greer. The office is centrally located next to Safeway on the main highway. It's open in summer Mon.–Fri. 9 A.M.–5 P.M., Sat.–Sun. 9 A.M.–1 P.M., then the rest of the year Mon.–Fri. 9 A.M.–4 P.M.; www.pinetoplakesidechamber.com

Staff at the **Lakeside Ranger Station,** 2022 W. White Mountain Blvd. (Lakeside, AZ 85929), 928/368-5111, will share information on camping, hiking, driving, and fishing in Apache-Sitgreaves National Forest. The office is across the highway from Lakeside Campground and open Mon.–Fri. 8 A.M.–4:30 P.M.; www.fs.fed.us/r3/asnf.

Arizona Game and Fish, 2878 E. White Mountain Blvd., 928/367-4281, provides wildlife information and sells fishing and hunting licenses; open Mon.–Fri. 8 A.M.–5 P.M.; www.azgfd.com.

Larson Memorial Library, 1595 W. Johnson Lane, 928/368-6688, is near the corner of White Mountain Blvd. and Woodland Rd.; closed Sunday.

Services

The **Pinetop Post Office** is at 712 E. White Mountain Blvd.; 928/367-4756; **Lakeside Post Office** is at 1815 W. Jackson Lane, one block off White Mountain Blvd.; 928/368-6686. Several shops along the highway sell and rent **skiing and snowboarding equipment** in season. **Paradise Creek Anglers/The Skier's Edge** provides a large selection of equipment for camping, hiking, skiing, snowboarding, and fly-fishing at 560 W. White Mountain Blvd.; 928/367-6200, 800/231-3831.

Transportation

In nearby Show Low, an airline usually offers flights to Phoenix, and **White Mountain Passenger Lines** has bus connections with Heber, Payson, Mesa, and Phoenix. **Four Seasons Bus Connection** serves Show Low, Pinetop-Lakeside, and Hon-Dah; closed Sunday; 928/537-0627.

White Mountain Apache Reservation

When the Warm Springs Apache were moved in 1877 to San Carlos, across the river from the White Mountain Reservation, Chief Victorio and a small band escaped. He led a brutal campaign against Americans and Mexicans in 1879–1880, killing nearly 1,000 people before being shot by a Mexican bounty hunter.

Some of Arizona's best outdoor recreation can be found on the White Mountain Apache Reservation, which spans more than 1.6 million acres. You have choices among many campsites, fishing streams, lakes, ski runs, and hiking trails. Far-sighted planning and development by the White Mountain Apache resulted in the high-quality recreation available today. Though tribal permits are required for almost any activity, costs are reasonable. You don't need state licenses for fishing, boating, or hunting—just the tribal permits. Some areas, such as the summit of sacred Baldy Peak, are closed or require a special use permit. All Native American ruins, except for Kinishba, are closed.

Information

Staff at **Hon-Dah Ski and Outdoor Sport,** three miles south of Pinetop, 928/369-7669, 877/226-4868, is the best source of information for recreation on the reservation; you can also obtain permits here; www.wmatoutdoors.com. It's open daily year-round on the east side of the Hon-Dah Casino complex. You can also obtain information directly from the **Game and Fish Department,** next to the White Mountain Apache Motel in Whiteriver; 928/338-4385/4386. The free annual newsletter *White Mountain Apache Tribe Outdoor Recreation Regulations* can be picked up at the two places above and at many area businesses and tourist offices, or write P.O. Box 220, Whiteriver, AZ 85941. Other year-round places for permits on the reservation are Sunrise Service Station and Salt River Canyon Trading Post. In summer, you can also secure permits at Horseshoe Lake, Reservation Lake, and Hawley Lake. Off-reservation sources include Pinetop Sporting Goods in Pinetop, Popular Outdoor Outfitters and K-Mart in Show Low, Circle B Market in Greer, Western Drug in Springerville, and Tempe Marine in Chandler.

Watch for logging trucks on the reservation's many back roads. Some roads may be too rough for cars, especially after rain or snow. Staff at the Hon-Dah Ski and Outdoor Sport store or at Game and Fish can advise on current conditions. Most road junctions have signs, but it's a good idea to consult a map in finding your way around the back roads.

EASTERN ARIZONA

The Apache and the federal government disagree on the name of the reservation; government officials tend to use the term Fort Apache, while the Apache understandably prefer White Mountain Apache.

Events

The Apache enjoy participating in and attending rodeos, which take place on many weekends through the warmer months. The **Tribal Fair and Rodeo** on Labor Day weekend is the major annual event. Rodeos, powwows, and other area events are listed in the local paper, the *Fort Apache Scout.*

Sightseeing, Camping, and Skiing

You'll need a $6 vehicle permit for a picnic or sightseeing stop on the reservation unless you've already obtained a tribal permit for camping, fishing, or other recreational activity; hikers, cyclists, or bus passengers pay $3 each. Camping facilities are basic, usually just picnic tables, fireplaces, and toilets, though some campsites offer drinking water. Backpacking is permitted in certain areas with the proper permit. Camping fees of $8/vehicle per night or $150/vehicle for 30 days must be paid in advance; hikers, cyclists, and bus passengers pay $3 each.

Sunrise Ski Area, with its many downhill runs, attracts ski enthusiasts in winter. Sunrise also offers snowboarding, cross-country skiing, tubing, and snowmobiling. The tribe prohibits ATVs, horseback riding (except with authorized concessions), and swimming (except at hotels) everywhere on the reservation.

Boating and River Running

If you use a boat, you'll need a boat permit— $5 per day or $20 yearly for lake use. Sunrise is the only lake where gas motors (10 hp limit) are allowed; everywhere else you're limited to electrics.

Kayakers and rafters can enjoy a section of the Salt River Canyon, usually best run during the winter snowmelt from March to May. River runners doing the Salt River must obtain the proper permit, available at Salt River

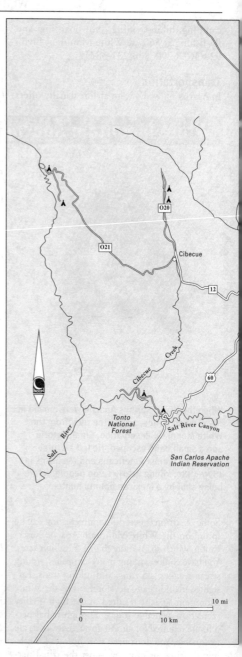

WHITE MOUNTAIN APACHE RESERVATION

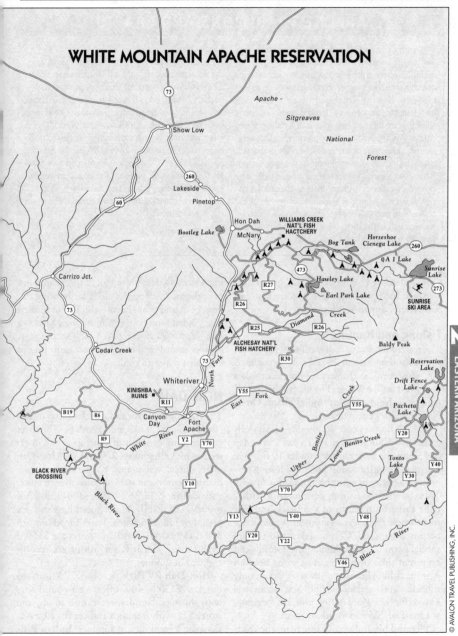

Apache -

Sitgreaves

National

Forest

73

Show Low

260

Lakeside

Pinetop

60

Hon Dah

Bootleg Lake

McNary

WILLIAMS CREEK
NAT'L FISH
HACTCHERY

Bog Tank

Horseshoe
Cienega Lake

260

A 1 Lake

473

R27

Hawley Lake

Earl Park Lake

Sunrise
Lake

SUNRISE
SKI AREA

273

Carrizo Jct.

R26

73

R25

Diamond   Creek

R26

ALCHESAY NAT'L
FISH HATCHERY

R30

Baldy Peak

Cedar Creek

73

North Fork

Reservation
Lake

Whiteriver

Y55   Fork

Creek

Drift Fence
Lake

KINISHBA
RUINS

R11

East   Fork

Y55

Pacheta
Lake

B19

R6

Canyon
Day

Fort
Apache

Y2

Y70

Upper Bonito

Lower Bonito Creek

Y20

R9

Y10

White   River

Tonto
Lake

Y40

BLACK RIVER
CROSSING

Y30

Black River

Y13

Y40

Y48

Y20

Y22

Black   River

Y46

© AVALON TRAVEL PUBLISHING, INC.

EASTERN ARIZONA

APACHE TRADITIONS AND CRAFTS

Driving through the Apache homeland, you might think their culture is gone—you see members of the tribe living in modern houses, frequenting the shopping centers, and working at regular jobs. But the Apache continue to use their own language and preserve the old traditions. Boys still study under medicine men to learn the prayers, rituals, and medicinal plants used in healing ceremonies. Elaborate coming-of-age ceremonies still mark the passage of young women into adulthood. Known as Sunrise Dances, these rites usually take place on weekends during summer; check local papers for dates or ask at the tribal offices in Whiteriver and San Carlos. Buckskin dresses, worn by women before the introduction of calico, are occasionally seen at Sunrise Dances.

Crafts

Frequently on the move in pre-reservation days, the Apache created only a few utilitarian crafts. They still make some of their products today—baskets, cradleboards, and beadwork. Attractive designs in beadwork decorate necklaces, bolo ties, and other adornments. Woodcarvers have recently begun fashioning realistic dolls depicting the dance movements of the Apache Spirit Dancers. Craftspeople on the San Carlos Reservation set peridot (a transparent yellow-green gemstone) in bolo ties, necklaces, earrings, and other jewelry. Look for all these at shops on the reservations.

Canyon Trading Post on US 60, and have a suitable boat (no open canoes) and equipment. See **Salt River Canyon Wilderness.**

Fishing and Hunting

The reservation includes 400 miles of mountain streams and more than 25 lakes. Anglers can go out year-round; ice fishing is popular on lakes not closed for the winter. The waters are stocked with trout from Alchesay and Williams Creek National Fish Hatcheries.

Fishing licenses cost $6 per day or $65 calendar year. Children ages 10–14 pay $3 per day or $32 for the year; children under 10 fish free but must be with an adult holding a fishing permit. An agreement with the San Carlos Apache Tribe honors the fishing permits from either tribe along both banks of the Black and Salt rivers where the reservations meet; a special use permit is required. Certain lakes also require special permits; check regulations. Groups can even rent their own lakes. You won't need an Arizona fishing license on the reservation; only tribal fees and regulations apply. You can arrange a guide for fishing or hunting trips; ask for names at Hon-Dah Ski and Outdoor Sport.

Plentiful big and small game roam the reservation. The tribe has established regular hunt-

ing seasons for elk, mountain lion, javelina, and pronghorn. You'll need a guide for hunting elk, lion, bear, and pronghorn—also lots of money. The guided hunts can run more than $1,000 a day, but participants report a high success rate. Smaller animals and birds are more easily bagged and don't require a guide.

HON-DAH

The Apache name for this traveler's stop means "Be My Guest." It's 19 miles north of Whiteriver and three miles south of Pinetop at the intersection of AZ highways 260 and 73. Hon-Dah offers a hotel, restaurants, RV park, store/information center, gas station/convenience store, and casino; 928/369-0299, 800/929-8744 (800/WAY-UP-HI). Hotel guests have use of a pool, hot tub, and sauna. Rates for rooms run $79 d ($99 d Fri.–Sat.) and suites are $150 d ($180 d Fri.–Sat.). Reservations are recommended in summer.

Hon-Dah RV Park, across AZ 73 from the hotel, 928/369-7400, offers year-round sites with showers, laundry, recreation room, and store; $21 with hookups (no tents). Reservations are a good idea in summer. **Indian Pine Restaurant** off the casino serves dinners of

© BILL WEIR

The Apache regard the Salt Banks beside the Salt River as sacred, so no visits are permitted, but you can see them on a raft trip.

steak, ribs, chicken, seafood, and pasta; you can also enjoy buffets daily for breakfast, lunch, and dinner; 928/369-7552. The adjacent **Timbers Lounge** hosts a big Sunday brunch and presents live entertainment in the evenings Tues.–Sunday.

Hon-Dah Ski and Outdoor Sport provides information for recreation on the reservation and sells permits, sporting goods, and clothing. In winter, it offers a full-service ski and snowboard shop. Open daily year-round on the east side of the Hon-Dah Casino complex; 928/369-7669, 877/226-4868; www.wmatoutdoors.com.

EAST OF HON-DAH

McNary

Though there's not much to see, this old lumber town has an unusual history. Back in 1916, an energetic Flagstaff businessman named Tom Pollock chose the spot for a new lumber enterprise. Leasing the land from the Apache, he ran a railroad line in and named the place "Cooley,"

after Corydon E. Cooley of the famous Show Low card game.

Meanwhile, 1,000 miles east in McNary, Louisiana, the W.M. Cady Lumber Co. was quickly running out of timbered land. So in 1924 Cady bought out Pollock's Apache Lumber Co. and moved practically the whole town westward to Cooley. Renamed McNary, the town became known for its harmonious mixture of blacks, whites, Latins, and Native Americans. When fire destroyed the sawmill in 1979, owners rebuilt 40 miles east near Eagar.

Shush Be Zahze Lake

If you can't pronounce the Apache words, just call the place "Little Bear." The 15-acre lake, at an elevation of 7,900 feet, has a small campground, and you can fish for rainbow, brown, and brook trout. Go 11 miles east of Hon-Dah on AZ 260 and turn north 0.8 mile; keep left at the fork.

Shush Be Tou Lake

The name is Apache for "Big Bear." The 18-acre

lake has a campground and offers fishing similar to conditions on nearby Shush Be Zahze Lake. The directions are the same, except this time take the right fork.

Hawley Lake

Trout swim in the waters of this 260-acre lake; in winter you can fish through the ice. Constructed in 1957, this was the first lake on the reservation designed for recreation. Facilities include a boat dock with rentals, service station/grocery store, campground ($8) and trailer park ($20); 928/335-7511. You can stay in cabins ($109–159) and lodge rooms ($85–110) too; make reservations at 928/369-1753. Permits for fishing, camping, and other activities are available at the store. Facilities are open from about May to October.

From AZ 260, 11.3 miles east of Hon-Dah, turn south 11 miles on AZ 473; the first nine miles are paved. Despite the 8,500-foot elevation, the road is kept open year-round.

Earl Park Lake (47 acres), a half mile southeast of Hawley Lake, also offers catch-and-release fishing (artificial lures and flies only).

Horseshoe Lake

You can fish on this 121-acre lake (elev. 8,100 feet) for rainbow, brown, and brook trout. Information, camping and fishing supplies, boat rentals, and permits are available at the boat dock and store, open from about mid-May to mid-Sept.; 928/521-2613. The road is cleared in winter for ice anglers. Go 13.5 miles east of Hon-Dah on AZ 260, turn south at the sign, and follow the road one mile across the dam to the south side of the lake.

Bog Tank

This 12-acre lake (elev. 8,100 feet) is stocked with rainbow, brown, and brook trout. Day use only. Bog Tank lies 14 miles east of Hon-Dah on AZ 260, then 0.3 mile north. Nearby Horseshoe Lake has groceries and fishing supplies.

A-1 Lake

Stocked with rainbow and brook trout, this 24-acre lake is open all year. It's 18 miles east of Hon-Dah on AZ 260, on the south side of the highway.

Sunrise Lake

Anglers prize this 891-acre lake (elev. 9,200 feet) for its large brook trout. This is the only lake on the reservation where you can use gas motors, though limited to 10 horsepower. **Sunrise Marina** offers boat and fishing-pole rentals, a paved boat ramp, and a few fishing supplies in summer. It's behind Sunrise Park Hotel; call 928/735-7669 and ask for the marina.

Sunrise Park Lodge, 928/735-7669, 800/554-6835 (800/55-HOTEL), offers a restaurant (open daily for breakfast, lunch, and dinner), indoor pool, indoor and outdoor hot tubs, a sauna, and a volleyball area. The lodge closes for about six weeks at the end of the ski season in April, reopens for summer visitors from Memorial Day to mid-September, then closes again until the ski season starts. Summer rates run $59 d. From AZ 260, 20 miles east of Hon-Dah or 18 miles west of Springerville, turn south 3.5 miles on AZ 273 to the hotel.

Scenic Lift Rides at the ski area take you to the heights on Sat.–Sun. 10 A.M.–4 P.M. from about May 20 to Oct. 15; $8 adult, $4 age 12 and under. Mountain bikes and boards can be rented at the Sports Shop located at the ski lift.

Sunrise General Store, on the highway a half mile south of the lodge, 928/735-7335, sells groceries, permits, and gas. In winter, the store rental cross-country skis and snowshoes.

Lee Valley Stables, 928/735-7454, offers guided rides, hay rides, cookouts, and winter sleigh rides near Sunrise General Store.

An **RV campground** ($9) across the road from the store has electric hookups. **Sunrise Campground** ($8) is nearby, on the left just after turning onto the Sunrise Ski Area road.

Sunrise Park Resort Ski Area

This cluster of three peaks—Sunrise, Apache, and Cyclone Circle—boasts more than 65 ski runs winding through pine and aspen forests of the White Mountains. The resort is largely geared to family skiing, with about 40 percent beginner, 40 percent intermediate, and 20 percent advanced terrain. A combination of one high-speed quad, two regular quads, four triples, one double, and two surface lifts keeps lines short. Snow-making machines add to the natural snowpack for a season lasting from late November to mid-April. Sunrise also offers a snowboard park, Nordic trails system, tubing park, horse-drawn sleigh rides, and snowmobiling (tracks and tours).

Lift rates are $34 full day ($19 juniors 12 and under), $27 half day ($14 juniors 12 and under), $13 seniors 65–69, and free seniors 70 and up. A season pass costs $295 ($195 juniors 12 and under) if purchased before November 1, then $475 ($295 juniors 12 and under). The resort offers a variety of group and private lessons. Shops rent equipment and offer sales and repairs. Child-care services feature indoor and outdoor activities for children ages 3–6 and babysitting for infants up to age two.

Sunrise Ski Area offers package deals and family plans that include room and lift tickets. Room-only rates start at $59 d, jumping to $95 d during the holiday season (mid-December to early January) and on Friday, Saturday, and holidays at other times. For the latest accommodation and skiing information, contact Sunrise Ski Area, P.O. Box 217, McNary, AZ 85930; 928/735-7669; www.sunriseskipark.com. For recorded ski conditions or lodge reservations, phone 800/554-6835.

Shuttle buses connect Sunrise Park Hotel with the ski lifts and Sunrise Day Lodge about every 15 minutes. Accommodations are tight during the ski season, and many skiers stay at Greer (15 miles to the east), Springerville (22 miles east), or Pinetop-Lakeside (30 miles west).

Pacheta Lake

The best campsites lie on the east side of this 68-acre lake (elev. 8,170 feet). Drinking water is available. Anglers seek out trophy rainbow and brown trout; catch-and-release with artificial lies and lures only. People say the name Pacheta came from two card-playing cowboys who were caught cheating around 1900; they were dubbed the "pair-of-cheaters," which became Pacheta.

There are three ways to get here: follow the signs 40 miles east from Fort Apache on Indian Routes Y-70 and Y-20; take Y-55 east from Fort Apache; or drive the better roads—AZ 273, Forest Road 116, and Y20—south from AZ 260 past Sunrise and Reservation Lakes. Pacheta Lake lies several miles east of the junction of Y-20 and Y-55.

Drift Fence Lake

Cowboys gave this lake its name: During cattle roundups, stock drifted along the fence on the west side of the lake to reach lower pastures. The 16-acre lake lies close to the road between Pacheta and Reservation Lakes; elevation 8,900 feet. You'll find small campsites at each end of the lake; large vehicles have more room at the north end.

Reservation Lake

This 280-acre lake, the second largest on the reservation, offers good fishing for rainbow, brown, and brook trout. Cool forests of aspen, fir, and spruce grow at the 9,000-foot elevation. A marina offers rental boats, supplies, and permits from late May to early September; 928/521-7458. Several campgrounds surround the lake.

The easiest way in is from the north: from Hon-Dah, take AZ 260 east 20 miles to AZ 273, head southeast on AZ 273 for 14 miles, turn south 10 miles on Forest Road 116, then turn right a half mile and cross a cattleguard to the lake. From Fort Apache, drive 46 miles east on Indian Routes Y-70 and Y-20 or take Y-55 and Y-20.

SOUTH OF HON-DAH

Alchesay and Williams Creek National Fish Hatcheries

These hatcheries keep the streams and lakes of the reservation stocked with trout. Williams Creek receives eggs from four or five species of trout, then raises the hatchlings to sportfishing size; large brood trout inhabit the raceways. Alchesay specializes in raising small native, rainbow, brown, and cutthroat trout of 6–8 inches. Visitors are welcome to view exhibits and stroll along a self-guided tour on weekdays 7 A.M.–3:30 P.M. at both hatcheries; closed holidays. Alchesay also has a picnic area.

EASTERN ARIZONA

The turnoff for Alchesay Hatchery is four miles north of Whiteriver between Mileposts 342 and 343 of AZ 73; a signed paved road heads northeast along the White River 4.6 miles to the site. Roads to Williams Creek Hatchery turn off 13 miles north of Whiteriver, between Mileposts 351 and 352, and 15 miles north of Whiteriver (four miles south of Hon-Dah) between Mileposts 353 and 354; follow signs nine miles in on gravel roads.

Diamond Creek
Rainbow and a few brown, brook, and native trout lurk in this creek. No camping. Take the turnoff for Alchesay Fish National Hatchery, four miles north of Whiteriver, then turn right onto Indian Route R-25.

North Fork of the White River
The river is stocked with rainbow and brown trout, and you might catch a few brook and cutthroat. Take the parallel Upper Log Road to reach fishing spots along this stream. Take the Williams Creek Hatchery turnoff (Log Road) between Mileposts 351 and 352, 13 miles north of Whiteriver, or the turnoff between Mileposts 353 and 354, 15 miles north of Whiteriver and four miles south of Hon-Dah.

Bootleg Lake
At one time you could buy illegal booze here; today your best bet is largemouth bass, rainbow trout, channel catfish, and sunfish. The lake is managed for trophy bass; and you'll need a special permit here. Day use only. Elevation of the 10-acre lake is 6,800 feet. Turn west off AZ 73 at Milepost 355, three miles south of Hon-Dah, and go in 2.2 miles.

WHITERIVER
The administrative center of the White Mountain Apache lies south of Hon-Dah in a valley at 5,000 feet, surrounded by high forested hills. It's easy to confuse the name of the town with that of the river flowing beside it, but the town is spelled as one word. Whiteriver has a trading post, motel, restaurants, shopping center, Indian Health Service Hospital, and tribal offices. The tribe owns and operates the giant Fort Apache Timber Company mill on the south edge of town.

Practicalities
White Mountain Apache Motel, just south of the shopping center, 928/338-4927, features modern rooms ($55 d), restaurant, and a gift shop. The motel's restaurant served breakfast, lunch, and dinner daily. You can obtain information and permits next door at the tribal **Game and Fish Department** (P.O. Box 220, Whiteriver, AZ 85941), 928/338-4385/4386; open Mon.–Fri. 8 A.M.–5 P.M. **White Mountain Apache Shopping Center,** just south of the town center, includes a supermarket, stores, and post office.

Fort Apache and the Apache Cultural Center
In 1869, Major John Green selected this site near the confluence of the north and east forks of the White River as a supply base for troops in the field. Although the White Mountain Apache proved friendly, army officers thought it wise to keep an eye on them, meanwhile preventing white settlers from encroaching on Native American land.

Originally established as Fort Ord in 1870, the post's name changed to Camp Mogollon, then to Camp Thomas, and finally to Camp Apache—all within one year! Troops and Apache scouts rode out to subdue rebellious Apache in the Tonto Basin (1872–73), and then to fight Victorio (1879) and Geronimo (1881–86).

Alchesay, the most prominent Apache scout, became known for his honesty and dedication to both the army and his people. He helped put down rebellions of hostile tribes and assisted General Crook in making peace with Geronimo in 1886. Fort Apache saw its last major action during the Mexican Campaign (1916–17). In 1922, the U.S. Indian Service converted the fort to a boarding school, naming it in honor of President Theodore Roosevelt. Most of the first students were Navajo, though local Apache enrolled later. About 100 students now attend the school.

Venerable buildings still standing include the commanding officer's quarters (built of logs in 1871) used by General Crook, the adjutant's office (adobe, 1875), and officers' row (stone, 1890s). The commanding officer's quarters are open Mon.–Fri. 8 A.M.–5 P.M. with visitor information and exhibits about the history of the fort's scouts and soldiers.

Drop into the nearby **Apache Cultural Center and Museum**, 928/338-4625, recognizable by its conical roof, to learn about Apache history and culture; exhibits display fine examples of Apache crafts. Open Mon.–Fri. (and Sat. in summer) 8 A.M.–5 P.M.; admission is $3 adults, $2 seniors 65 and older and students 7–17; www.wmat.nsn.us. Go southwest about five miles on the highway from the motel in Whiteriver, turn 0.7 mile left across the river, then left at the sign.

Kinishba Ruins

Kinishba is Apache for "Brown House." Prehistoric tribes built two large pueblos and smaller buildings here between A.D. 1232 and 1320. The mixed population came from areas of the Little Colorado, central Gila, and Salt Rivers. Residents abandoned the village about 1350, possibly because of insufficient water.

A University of Arizona team excavated the ruins from 1931 to 1939 and found 14 types of pottery and a great wealth of shell jewelry scattered across more than 700 rooms. Only one of the large structures has survived. Because it has not been stabilized, you may not enter, but you can view the ruins by walking around outside. It's best to check in with the Apache Cultural Museum before coming out here. From Whiteriver, go southwest six miles on the highway, then turn right on a dirt road; the ruins are two miles in (keep left at the fork 1.7 miles in).

EAST OF WHITERIVER
East Fork of the White River

The stream offers rainbow and brown trout. The upper reaches are closed to fishing. From the turnoff east of Fort Apache, head east on Indian Route Y-55. Day use only.

Upper and Lower Bonito Creek

Bonito is Spanish for pretty. This stream offers rainbow and brown trout; you'll need a special use permit for some sections. From the junction for Indian Route Y-70, two miles east of Fort Apache, turn in at the sign reading Tonto Lake-Pacheta Lake-Maverick-Drift Fence Lake-Hurricane Lake-Reservation Lake. The road soon turns to gravel, offering fine views of the White River Valley as you climb Seven-Mile Hill. After 11.7 miles, turn left and drive three miles on Y-70 for Upper Bonito (day use only) or continue straight three miles on Y-40 for Lower Bonito.

WEST OF WHITERIVER
Cibecue

This small town in the western part of the reservation serves as the center for the Cibecue Apache, a group distinct from the White Mountain and San Carlos Apache. For administration purposes, though, the Cibecue area is considered part of the White Mountain Reservation. Visitors can enjoy camping and good fishing for rainbow and brown trout in the upper 15 miles of nearby Cibecue Creek. The first fishing and camping spots lie five miles north of town on a dirt road paralleling the creek. Elevations average about 6,000 feet. You need a special use permit to drive past the town. Apache Traders in Cibecue offers gas and supplies. To reach Cibecue, turn northwest on Indian Route 12 from US 60, eight miles south of Carrizo.

In the winter of 1880, a Cibecue medicine man named Noch-ay-del-klinne began preaching a new religion that predicted the expulsion of all white people. He soon gathered an enthusiastic following, worrying officers at Fort Apache. In August 1881, officers dispatched troops and 23 Apache scouts to arrest the medicine man. Fighting broke out upon their arrival at Cibecue, and Noch-ay-del-klinne was killed. The scouts then mutinied, joining the attack on the troops. Angry Apache pursued the survivors the entire 40 miles back to the fort. Captain Hentig and six other soldiers died in what's believed to be the only revolt by Apache scouts in their 75 years with the army.

Salt River Canyon

Father Eusebio Francisco Kino visited this colorful canyon in 1698, naming it Salado for the salt springs in the area. There are great views of the canyon from US 60 as the highway swoops down to a bridge 48 miles southwest of Show Low. You can explore further by driving on the dirt road that parallels the river. This route is highly scenic, with towering cliffs above and the river below. Take the turnoff just north of the highway bridge until you come to a fork. At the fork, you can turn left and drive under the bridge a half mile upriver to **Apache Falls,** or bear right four miles on the road downstream to Cibecue Creek. The road is rough in spots but passable for cautious motorists.

The desert country here at 3,000 feet contrasts sharply with the White Mountains, a short drive north. Saguaro cacti grow on the slopes to

the right past the ford on Cibecue Creek. Don't cross if the water is fast-flowing and muddy.

The Salt Banks, three miles past Cibecue Creek, are a long series of salt springs that have deposited massive travertine formations. Minerals and algae color the springs orange, red, and dark green. This site has long been sacred to the Apache, who draw salt here and perform religious ceremonies. It's closed to the public. Past the Salt Banks, the road begins a steep climb, becoming too rough for cars. The White Mountain Apache have established several primitive campsites (no drinking water) along the Salt River between the highway bridge and Cibecue Creek. Salt River Canyon Trading Post, near the highway bridge, stocks supplies and permits. Anglers on the Salt River catch mostly channel catfish and some smallmouth bass and bluegill.

The Low Desert

SAN CARLOS APACHE RESERVATION

The San Carlos Reservation offers scenery for every season: cool pine forests in the northeast, grasslands and wooded ridges in the center, and cactus-studded desert in the southwest. In winter you'll probably want to stick to the low country around San Carlos Lake, then head for the hills in summer. The Black and Salt Rivers form a natural boundary with the White Mountain Apache Indian Reservation to the north. Much of the land is fine cattle-grazing country and supports large tribal herds.

You can reach San Carlos Lake and Seneca Lake by paved highways, but roads to other recreation areas may be too rough for cars, especially after rains or snowmelt.

Permits and Information

You need a recreation permit ($7/day or $10/day family) to camp, picnic, hike, or venture onto back roads unless you have a fishing, hunting, or special-use permit. Family permits include parents and kids 18 and under. Visitors to the Black

harvesting desert cotton

and Salt Rivers or Bear Wallow Creek must have a special permit. One-day permits are good for 24 hours from midnight to midnight. No permit is needed for driving through on US 60, US 70, Road 800 to San Carlos, or Road 500 to Coolidge Dam.

Fishing licenses cost $7 per day or $75 per calendar year; free if under 12 and with a permit-holding adult. Obtain the Black and Salt River permit instead if you'll be fishing in those rivers or Bear Wallow Creek; it costs $10 per day for ages

12 and up. Boat permits are $3 per day or $30 per calendar year; a combined fishing and boat permit runs $100 for a calendar year. Water-skiing/personal watercraft permits are $7 per day or $75 yearly; free if under age 12 with a permit-holding adult.

For permits and the latest regulations, facilities, fees, and road conditions, contact the **San Carlos Recreation and Wildlife Department** office near the corner of Moon Base Road and US 70 between Mileposts 272 and 273, 1.5 miles east of the AZ 170 junction for San Carlos; 928/475-2343, 888/475-2344; it's open Mon.–Fri. 8 A.M.–4:30 P.M. and Sat. 7 A.M.–3 P.M.; P.O. Box 97, San Carlos, AZ 85550.

Other sources for permits include **Apache Gold Casino's** convenience store, 928/475-7800, ext. 3658; **Express Stop** in Globe, 928/425-3911; **Circle K Store #423** in Globe, 928/425-5952; **Minit Market #4** in Pima, 928/485-3040; **Pinky's Bait & Tackle** in Safford, 928/428-0056; **Bob Keen's Store** in Fort Thomas, 928/485-2261; and **Tempe Marine** in Mesa, 480/782-6813.

Recreation

Campsites are usually open all year. Recreation permits must be bought beforehand. In summer, observe fire restrictions.

Fishing is the big attraction for most visitors— San Carlos Lake is known as Arizona's hottest bass spot. Farther north you can catch trout, catfish, or bass in Point of Pines Lake, Seneca Lake, Dry Lake, and the Black River.

Gasoline motors can be used at San Carlos and Talkalai Lakes; at other lakes you're restricted to a single electric motor. The tribe doesn't allow ATVs or river running; the White Mountain Apache, however, do allow river running on the Salt River from their shore.

Hunters can pursue big and small game with the appropriate licenses. Certain areas of the reservation may be open only to tribal members. Some hunts require licensed guides.

San Carlos

This small community is very much a government town. Rows of office buildings and apartments line the main street. Here you'll find most tribal offices, post office, grocery store, San Carlos Café, and a service station. It's four miles north of US 70 on AZ 170 or you can take Road 800 from just east of Apache Gold Casino.

Shops sell Apache crafts, such as baskets, beadwork, cradle boards, and peridot jewelry. Peridot is a deep yellow-green, transparent mineral; the cut stones, sold mounted or loose, resemble emeralds. Check for crafts at the **Cultural Center** on US 70, just east of the AZ 170 junction, and at **Apache Gold Casino** on US 70, seven miles east of Globe.

Apache Cultural Center

The San Carlos Apache tell their history from their creation to the present, using stories, photos, and dioramas. A gift shop sells books, paintings, and Apache crafts such as jewelry, beadwork, baskets, cradleboards, and wood carvings of crown dancers. The center is just east on US 70 from the AZ 170 junction, near Milepost 272; open about Mon.–Fri. 9 A.M.–5 P.M.; $3 adult, $1.50 seniors, $1 students, free under 12; 928/475-2894.

San Carlos Lake

The 19,500-acre lake, when full, measures 23 miles long by two miles wide, making it the largest lake lying completely within Arizona. Though famed mostly for its prolific bass population, the waters have produced state-record specimens of flathead catfish, crappie, and bluegill. People come year-round despite the hot summers at the 2,425-foot elevation. Pullouts atop the 880-foot-high Coolidge Dam, dedicated by President Coolidge himself in 1930, allow you to view the dam and the canyon below.

San Carlos Lake Store, 9.5 miles south of US 70/Peridot and two miles north of the dam, 928/475-2756, provides information, fishing supplies, groceries, snacks, and gasoline; it's open daily. A small RV park lies across the parking lot, $15 with hookups. A paved road just north of the store leads one mile down to **Soda Canyon Point Campground** (views, tables, and water) and the marina, which has a paved boat ramp, rentals (pedal boats, pontoon boats, and bass boats), boat slips, some fishing tackle, ice, and gas. Other campgrounds lie on both the north and south sides of the lake.

Other Recreation Areas

Talkalai Lake: Chief Talkalai served as an Indian scout with the army and helped capture Geronimo. Talkalai Lake has given up some sizable largemouth bass, flathead and channel catfish, crappie, and bluegill. Gas motors up to 15 hp are permitted. The lake and campground (no drinking water) lie about three miles north of the town of San Carlos; the last half is unpaved.

    Cassadore Springs: This small picnic area and campground offers spring water about 12 miles north of the town of San Carlos.

    Point of Pines: The 35-acre trout lake and campground (no drinking water) are in the eastern part of the reservation. From US 70, five miles east of the San Carlos turnoff, head northeast 55 miles on Indian Route 1000 to the campground; all but the last few miles or so are paved.

    Seneca Park: Anglers catch trout, catfish, and largemouth bass in 27-acre Seneca Lake. The lake and campground (no drinking water) are in the northwest corner of the reservation just off US 60/AZ 77, 33 miles north of Globe and five miles south of the Salt River Canyon bridge.

Best Western Apache Gold Hotel & Casino

The hotel, 928/402-5600, 800/272-2438 (800/APACHE8), offers includes an 18-hole golf course, a pool, hot tub, sauna, and workout room seven miles east of Globe on US 70; www.apachegold.com. Rooms start at $59 d Sun.–Thurs. and $69 d Fri.–Sat.; Jacuzzi rooms go for $99 d. The nearby RV park has sites in a sea of asphalt for $17 with hookups. Restaurants fail to provide nonsmoking sections; the **Apache Grill** serves breakfast, lunch, and dinner daily; the **Wickiup Buffet** does lunch and dinner daily and breakfast on Sat.–Sun.; both lie off the casino.

Events

Look for Apache dances, crafts, foods, and cowboys showing off their riding skills at the **Bylas Rodeo** in April and at the **Veteran's Memorial Fair and Rodeo** on Veteran's Day weekend in November. **Traditional dances** are held during the summer; call the tribal office (928/475-2361) or Cultural Center (928/475-2894) for dates and places. The **Sunrise Ceremony,** marking the coming-of-age of young women, occurs most frequently, usually on summer weekends.

SAFFORD

Surrounded by the rugged Pinaleno, Gila, and Peloncillo mountain ranges, Safford (elev. 2,900 feet) lies in the broad Gila River Valley. Hohokam, Mogollon, and Anasazi sites in the valley date from about 300 B.C. to A.D. 1200. The Apache arrived about 1700 and managed to discourage European settlers until 1874. In that year four Civil War veterans founded a town named after Anson P. Safford, territorial Arizona's third governor. Five years later Mormon settlers arrived to farm the valley, founding Smithville, later renamed Pima. Mormons also settled in Thatcher, Central, Eden, Graham, and Bryce.

    The Jewish merchant Isadore Elkan Solomon arrived in a town later named for him. He opened a store and other businesses, then helped start Gila Valley Bank, which later evolved into the Valley National Bank.

    Though small, Safford (pop. 9,500) serves as the Graham County seat and as the main retail and service center for a large area of southeastern Arizona. Though cotton, especially in Pima, is king, the irrigated bottomland also supports wheat, barley, alfalfa, and other crops.

    Visitor highlights include the scenic Mt. Graham Drive into the 10,000-foot-plus Pinaleno Mountains (hiking, fishing, and camping), Aravaipa and Bonita Canyons (wildlife and scenery along a perennial stream), the Galiuro Wilderness (for adventurous hikers), Discovery Park (science exhibits), and the Graham County and Pima historical museums.

Discovery Park

Safford's science center continues to develop on 200 acres at the south end of town. The **Gov Aker Building** features astronomy exhibits that detail everything from early concepts of the universe by different cultures to cutting-edge research. One gallery illustrates the history of astronomy. Videos and interactive exhibits explain the workings of telescopes and the nature of the waves received from space. The Shuttlecraft Polaris motion simulator "departs" for scheduled tours of the solar system. You can view surroundings by day through the world's largest Camera Obscura, and by night with a 20-inch astronomical telescope. A gift shop sells posters and science toys. New mining and agriculture museums may be completed by the time of your visit.

Outdoors, you can hop on a train for a narrated ride through the extensive park grounds until dusk. A wildlife area, reached by trail or the train, has wetlands with bird blinds. Tours of the Mt. Graham International Observatory are available from about mid-May to mid-November and require advance reservations. From US 70 on the west side of town, take 20th Avenue 2.4 miles south to the entrance; or, from US 191 south of Safford, turn west on Discovery Park Boulevard to 20th Avenue, then turn left. Open Tues.–Sat. 1–10 P.M.; $4 age 12 and up, $3 youth 6–11; the railroad tour costs $1 and the motion simulator is $6; 928/428-6260; www.discoverypark.com.

Graham County Historical Museum

Native American artifacts in the Prehistory Room include pottery and stone tools from early residents. As you continue through the rooms, you'll see displays of pioneer home life and ranching, school and community, and galleries dedicated to vintage clothing and a doll collection. The museum, 928/348-0470, is open Mon. 2–8 P.M., THEN TUES. AND SAT. 10 A.M.–5 P.M.; free admission. It's in the 1917 Thatcher Public School building at 3430 Hwy. 70 (park on 4th St.) in downtown Thatcher, just west of Safford.

Cotton Gin Tours

All that cotton in Graham County fields comes to two cotton gins in the Safford area. Both offer tours during the ginning season, from early October through December and sometimes into January. Call in advance to **Safford Valley Cotton Growers Co-op,** off US 191 in Safford,

928/428-0714, or **Glenbar Gin** just west of Pima, 928/485-9255.

Accommodations

Safford's motels line US 70, also signed on the west side of town as Thatcher Boulevard and on the east side as Fifth Street. Each motel includes air-conditioning and most also have swimming pools—you may want both in summer, when highs push 100°F.

Under $50: Check out **Tour Rest Motel,** 110 Fifth St., 928/428-3881; $24 s, $28 d (slightly more in winter). Also try **Motel Western,** 1215 Thatcher Blvd., 928/428-7850, with a pool, $33 s, $35 d; or **Econo Lodge,** 225 E. Hwy. 70, 928/348-0011, 800/553-2666, with a pool, $40 s, $45 d.

$50–100: Best Western Desert Inn, 1391 Thatcher Blvd., 928/428-0521, 800/528-1234, offers a pool and restaurant, $59 s, $65 d, $92 suite; **Comfort Inn,** 1578 Thatcher Blvd., 928/428-5851, 800/221-2222, also has a pool and restaurant, $56 s, $66 d; and **Day's Inn,** 520 E. Hwy. 70, 928/428-5000, 800/329-7466, includes a pool and hot tub, $65 s, $80 d.

$100–150: Ramada Inn Spa Resort, 420 E. Hwy. 70, 928/428-3200, 800/272-6232, features an indoor pool, indoor hydro-therapy pool, outdoor hot tub, saunas, putting green, and a pizza restaurant; $85 s, $95 d (add $15 for rooms with hot tubs), $115–165 d suite.

Hostel and Campgrounds

Essence of Tranquility, 928/428-9312, 877/895-6810, features hot spring mineral baths, teepee rentals ($20–60, depending on size), and tent camping ($10/person) including use of baths, rec. room, kitchen, and showers; health treatments can be arranged too. From Safford, head south about five miles on US 191, turn right (west) on Lebanon Road, then left (south) where the road curves to 6074 S. Lebanon Loop Road.

RVers can stay at: **Desert Hill Mobile Home Park,** 326 Eighth Ave., just north of US 70, 928/428-1930, $10 with hookups; **Sunrise Village Mobile Home Park,** 900 E. Hollywood Rd., with pool and hot tub, 928/428-1895, $15 with hookups; **Tower Mobile Park,** 1.5 miles east at 2056 E. US 70, 928/428-6997, $14 with hookups; **Safford Ranch Mobile Home Park** (adults 55 and over), three miles east at 3201 E. Hwy. 70, 928/428-3828, $15 with hookups; **Lexington Pines RV Resort** (adults 55 and up), 1535 W. Thatcher Blvd., 928/428-7570, $17 with hookups; and **Red Lamp Mobile Home Park,** three miles west at 3341 W. Main St. in Thatcher, 928/428-3382, $15/hookups.

Food

The **Branding Iron** serves up Western-style dinners with a view of the city about 2.5 miles north of downtown; go north on Eighth Avenue, then left on River Road; closed Monday; 928/428-6252. **Brick's Steakhouse,** 4367 S. Hwy. 191, 928/348-8111, brings in the crowds with good food. Country Manor Restaurant, 415 E. Hwy 70 (across from the Ramada), 928/428-7148, is an attractive place for both American and Mexican food, open daily for breakfast, lunch, and dinner. **Golden Corral Family Steak House** is a popular place in Gila Valley Plaza at 2019 W. Thatcher Blvd., open daily for lunch and dinner and Sat.–Sun. for breakfast with menu and buffet offerings; 928/428-4744. **JB's Restaurant** dishes up American favorites daily for breakfast (buffet available), lunch, and dinner at 1391 W. Thatcher Blvd.; 928/348-9083. **Jerry's Restaurant** does American fare 24 hours a day at 1612 W. Thatcher Blvd.; 928/428-5613.

For Chinese cuisine, try the **Jumbo Chinese Restaurant** (Cantonese and Szechuan with a lunch buffet) at 817 W. Thatcher Blvd., 928/428-2888; or **Super Wok** (has a lunch buffet) at 1275 W. Thatcher Blvd., 928/348-9452. Dine Mexican at **Casa Mañana** (closed Sun.), corner of US 70 and First Ave., 928/428-3170; **El Charro** (closed Sun.), 601 Main St., 928/428-4134; **Chalo's La Casa Reynoso,** 611 Sixth Ave., 928/348-9889; **La Casita,** west in Thatcher at 3338 Main St., 928/428-1882; or **La Paloma** (closed Sun.), five miles east in Solomon, 928/428-2094.

You can pick up pizza and pasta at **R&R Pizza Express,** 628 Main St., closed Sun., 928/428-7775; **Pizza Hut,** 1305 W. Thatcher Blvd., 928/428-4320; **Pizzarama,** 2049 W. Thatcher

Blvd. (behind Golden Corral in Gila Valley Plaza), 928/428-4748; and **Picadilly Circus,** inside the Ramada Inn at 420 E. Hwy. 70, 928/428-3200.

You'll find supermarkets and several fast-food restaurants in the Mt. Graham and Gila Valley Plaza shopping centers on US 70 west of downtown.

Events

The **Old-Time Fiddlers Contest** livens up February. **Horse racing** takes off at the county fairgrounds on the last weekend of March and the first weekend of April. **Bylas Rodeo and Pow Wow** in April occurs 43 miles northwest on the San Carlos Apache Indian Reservation. **Cinco de Mayo** and **Cotton N' Copper Stampede** celebrate on the weekend nearest May 5th with a parade, PRCA rodeo, and entertainment. **Pioneer Day** rolls out with a parade, barbecue, and entertainment on the weekend nearest July 24th; the event rotates between Safford, Thatcher, and Pima.

Cowpunchers describe their feelings in **Cowboy Poet Roundup** in September. The **Graham County Fair** features entertainment, local agricultural accomplishments, and crafts on the second weekend of October. You can shop at the **Cowboy Christmas Arts and Crafts Festival** on the weekend after Thanksgiving. Contact the chamber of commerce for additional info; 928/428-2511.

Recreation

You'll find an outdoor public **swimming pool,** open from Memorial Day to Labor Day, in Firth Park behind the chamber of commerce at 1111 Thatcher Blvd.; 928/348-3222. **Tennis** players can use the lighted courts at Graham County Park, two miles south on US 191, or at the junior high school, 520 11th Street. **Graham County Park** also offers racquetball, basketball, ball fields, a jogging track, and picnicking; all but the track are lit for night use. Play golf year-round at the 18-hole **Mount Graham Golf Course,** four miles southwest of town, 928/428-1260; turn south on 20th Avenue and follow signs. **Swings & Things Sports Park,** 520 E. Hwy. 70,

928/348-8333, features two 18-hole miniature golf courses and a driving range.

Feeling run-down with too many aches and pains? Then take the waters at **Essence of Tranquility,** five miles south of Safford at 6074 S. Lebanon Loop Rd. (turn west off US 191 on Lebanon or Cactus Roads); 928/428-9312. Massage and other treatments can be arranged, and visitors may stay in a teepee or their own tent. Hot baths are also available at **Kachina Mineral Springs,** a hot springs spa six miles south of Safford on US 191, then west at the sign; 928/428-7212.

Information

The **Graham County Chamber of Commerce** is very helpful and well stocked with literature and maps. It's on US 70 just west of downtown at 1111 Thatcher Blvd. (Safford, AZ 85546); 928/428-2511, 888/837-1841. An exhibit room has a detailed diorama of 11,000 years ago when man first arrived in the Southwest, a diorama of a pueblo village about A.D. 1400, photos and telescope models of Mt. Graham International Observatory, and displays on local cotton, mining and minerals, recreation, and prehistoric Native American finds. Hours run Mon.–Fri. 8 A.M.–5 P.M. and Sat.–Sun. 9 A.M.–3 P.M.; www.graham-chamber.com or www.visitgrahamcounty.com. A rest area with picnic tables lies just outside and there's a public swimming pool out back.

Safford Ranger Station of the Coronado National Forest has travel and recreation information on Mt. Graham Scenic Drive in the Pinaleno Mountains, the Galiuro Wilderness, and the lesser-known wildernesses of Santa Teresa and Winchester; it's open Mon.–Fri. 8 A.M.–5 P.M. on the third floor of the post office, downtown at the corner of US 70 and Fifth Ave.; or write P.O. Box 709, Safford, AZ 85548; 928/428-4150.

The **Bureau of Land Management** (BLM) office provides information on many backcountry areas around Safford, including Aravaipa Canyon (for which you'll need a permit). Rockhounds can pick up brochures about the Black Hills (between Safford and Clifton) and Round Mountain (south of Duncan) areas, a source of fire agates. The BLM office is at 711 14th Ave., Safford, AZ 85546, across the road from the high school. It's open weekdays 7:45 A.M.–4:15 P.M.; 928/348-4400.

The **public library** has an Arizona collection at 808 Seventh Ave.; 928/428-1531. The **Alumni Library** includes a media center at Eastern Arizona College on the northwest corner of Church St. and College Ave. in Thatcher; it's closed early July to mid-August; 928/428-8304.

Services

The **post office** occupies the corner of US 70 and Fifth Ave.; 928/428-0220. **Mount Graham Community Hospital** lies southwest of downtown at 1600 S. 20th Ave.; 928/348-4000. **Gila Outdoor,** 408 Main St., 928/348-0710, offers topo maps, book, supplies, and clothing.

Tours and Transportation

Check with the chamber office for outdoor adventure tour operators. **Greyhound** buses stop several times a day in each direction on a route between El Paso, Texas, and Phoenix. The station is at the corner of 404 Fifth St. and Hwy. 70; 928/428-2150.

VICINITY OF SAFFORD

Eastern Arizona Museum and Historical Society (Pima)

You can learn about the Native Americans and pioneers of the area from this large collection. Open Wed.–Fri. 2–4 P.M. and Saturday 1–5 P.M.; visits can be arranged at other times, too; admission is free; 928/485-9400, 928/485-3032. Exhibits reside in an early Pima bank and town hall building on US 70, nine miles west of Safford.

Cluff Ranch Wildlife Area

The Arizona Game and Fish Department maintains the 788-acre Cluff Ranch as a wildlife and recreation area. Streams from Mt. Graham fill two or three ponds and support lush riparian vegetation. Anglers catch trout in winter and largemouth bass, channel catfish, crappie, and bluegill year-round. Boats—oar, sail, or electric—can be used. Visitors may do primitive

THE MOUNT GRAHAM RED SQUIRREL

This subspecies *(Tamiasciurus hudsonicus grahamensis)* lives only in the Pinaleno Mountains (Mt. Graham) of southeastern Arizona. It became isolated here at the end of the Pleistocene glacial periods when the surrounding plains no longer supported conifer forests. In the 1950s, scientists thought the subspecies had become extinct, but small numbers were rediscovered in the 1970s. The population has continued to recover despite construction of the Mt. Graham International Observatory, which some experts thought would threaten the squirrels' survival. Work on the observatory

seems to have no effect on the squirrels. Rather, their numbers correspond to the availability of conifer seeds, their primary food. The squirrels prefer the mixed conifers on Mt. Graham between 8,500 and 10,000 feet, but they also live in the spruce-fir forest at the higher elevations on the mountain. They're only 12–14 inches in total length, with dark gray fur tinged with red and with white under parts; a narrow black stripe runs down each side where the gray and white meet. You may hear their noisy calls in the forest.

The Mt. Graham International Observatory Controversy

One might think that construction of an observatory on a small corner of a long summit ridge wouldn't be a problem for anyone. For the University of Arizona, however, plans for building this

BOB RACE

Tamiasciurus hudsonicus grahamensis

camping at the ponds; Pond Three has a vault toilet. Birding is good and you're almost sure to see some free-roaming deer or javelina. Strips of grain crops are planted for wildlife.

Cluff Ranch, 928/485-9430, is open all year;. From US 70 in Pima, nine miles west of Safford, turn south 1.5 miles on Main Street; the road curves west and becomes Cottonwood Road; continue another 0.4 mile, then turn south 4.5 miles.

Roper Lake State Park

The shores of this pretty lake offer camping, picnicking, swimming, and fishing. The island, connected by a walking path, offers grass, shade trees, and a beach; it's for day use only. Anglers can launch boats (electric motors okay) and try for trout (in winter), catfish, bass, bluegill, and crappie. Hedonists can relax in the hot tub, fed by a natural spring. Mariah Mesa Nature Trail begins near the hot tub and makes a half-mile loop up the mesa with good views; a trail leaflet and numbered posts identify desert plants. The park has separate campground loops with and

without water/electric hookups, and an area for groups; there's usually room, though hookup sites can fill in winter. Campers can use showers and a dump station. Admission runs $5 day use or $10 camping ($17 with water and electric hookups). The park is open all year; 928/428-6760. Roper Lake lies six miles south of Safford off US 191.

Dankworth Ponds Unit day-use area also offers good picnicking, fishing, and hiking. Warm water from an artesian spring feeds a large pond. A 1.75-mile-roundtrip trail winds along the pond, crosses riparian areas and a mesquite bosque, climbs a little mesa to replicas of Native American dwellings, then continues to a dry wash. Admission fees cover both units of the Roper Lake State Park; Dankworth lies 2.7 miles farther south on US 191 (0.7 mile south of the Swift Trail junction).

Mount Graham Drive and the Pinaleno Mountains

Mount Graham (10,720 feet) in the Pinaleno Mountains soars nearly 8,000 feet above Safford—the greatest vertical rise of any mountain in Arizona. Visitors enjoy the views, cool

EASTERN ARIZONA

new facility turned into a public-relations nightmare. Mt. Graham had been selected as the best of 280 potential mountain sites for the observatory due to its clear skies, low light pollution, dry air, and ease of access. The Arizona Wilderness Act of 1984 had designated 3,500 acres atop the Pinalenos as a potential astrophysical research study area. Four years later, the Arizona-Idaho Conservation Act of 1988 authorized the University of Arizona and its partners to build three telescopes and an access road; if subsequent studies showed no harm to the endangered Mt. Graham red squirrel, four more telescopes could be built on a maximum of 24 total acres of land.

Environmentalists decried the cutting of trees that might drive the Mt. Graham red squirrel and other wildlife into extinction. Apache protested that sacred land would be desecrated by buildings and made inaccessible to tribal members who wished to collect herbs and water for ceremonies. Legal actions to halt construction began with a nine-claim lawsuit by the Sierra Club Legal Defense Fund in 1989. Community support from local towns and the Board of Supervisors of Graham and Cochise Counties weighed in on the side of the observatory. Eventually the University of Arizona and it partners survived the claims and appeals by opposing groups. Construction has gone ahead and the first instruments have become operational. The University of Arizona continues to work with the Forest Service and U.S. Fish and Wildlife Service to minimize harmful effects on the land and wildlife; officials have also met with Apache groups to provide access to land near the observatory. A team of biologists funded by the university monitors the Mt. Graham red squirrels.

breezes, hiking, picnicking, camping, and fishing. A gate just past Shannon Campground closes during the snow season of Nov. 15 to around April 15 or later.

A good road, called the Swift Trail (AZ 366), ascends the eastern slopes through a remarkable range of vegetation and animal life. Starting among cactus, creosote bush, and mesquite of the upper Sonoran Desert, you'll soon arrive at pygmy forests of juniper, oak, and pinyon pine. Higher on the twisting road, you'll enter dense forests of ponderosa pine, Douglas fir, aspen, and white fir. Thick stands of Engelmann spruce dominate the highest ridges. The Mt. Graham red squirrel, Mt. Graham pocket gopher, white-bellied vole, and Rusby's mountain fleabane (a wild daisy) are found only in the Pinaleno Mountains.

Fire-lookout towers on two peaks offer superb views. **Heliograph Peak** (elev. 10,028 feet) offers one of the best panoramas in the region; on a clear day you can see most of southeastern Arizona. The 2.2-mile road to the lookout is gated, but you can walk up it or take Arcadia Trail #328 one mile from Shannon Campground, then turn up Heliograph Trail #328A one mile. The army built a heliograph station here in 1886 using mirrors and sunlight to relay messages to troops.

Columbine Visitor Information Station, at mile 29 on the Swift Trail, is in an old CCC building that once housed forest workers and firefighters; it may be open in summer.

Webb Peak (elev. 10,086 feet) offers a better view of the Gila River Valley and surrounding mountains; you can reach the summit by ascending one mile on Web Peak Trail #345 from Columbine public corrals, by walking a 1.7-mile gated road, or by making a loop on both.

You can stop for a picnic along the way at **Noon Creek** (seven miles up; elev. 5,200 ft.), **Round the Mountain** (7.5 miles; elev. 5,300 ft.; also has corrals and popular trailhead), **Wet Canyon** (10 miles; elev. 6,100 ft.), and **Clark Peak Trailhead** (36 miles; elev. 9,000 ft.). There's no water or charge at these places, but you would have to pay if picnicking at a campground. If you're driving AZ 266 south of Mt. Graham, **Stockton Pass Picnic Area** offers views and water at an elevation of 5,600 feet; free. To get there, head south 17 miles from Safford on US 191, then turn right (southwest) 12 miles on AZ 266; it's also the lower trailhead for the Shake Trail #309, which descends from the Pinelenos.

Six developed campgrounds have drinking water and a $10 fee from mid-May to late

October. Campground elevations range from 6,700 feet at Arcadia to 9,300 feet at Soldier Creek. Anglers can camp and try for trout in Riggs Lake, near the end of the Swift Trail.

Equestrians can use corrals, trails, camping, and parking at Round the Mountain, Cunningham, Columbine, and Clark Peak Trailhead. Round the Mountain may have stock water; Columbine offers both drinking and stock water.

To drive the 35-mile-long **Swift Trail Parkway,** go seven miles south from Safford on US 191, or 26 miles north from I-10, and turn west at the sign. The first 21 miles is paved, followed by 14 miles of gravel to Clark Peak trailhead. This last section of road is gated Nov. 15–April 15 because of snow and the need to protect the red squirrel habitat. The drive from Safford and back takes about 4.5 hours. Stock up on gas and supplies before leaving town.

The Safford Ranger Station has an auto tour to the features of the Swift Trail, maps of the Coronado National Forest (Pinaleno Range), and information sheets on picnic areas, campgrounds, and trails. Hikers can choose among many trails but should be prepared for steep sections.

Mt. Graham International Observatory has a series of large telescopes atop Emerald Peak. Initial construction includes the Columbus Project, a 12-meter-equivalent binocular telescope, a 10-meter Submillimeter Telescope, and a 1.8-meter Lennon Telescope. See the Discovery Park description above for tours and website links. Protecting red squirrel habitat is a major concern—and controversy—in the development of the telescope site. High Peak, the summit of Mt. Graham, closed to protect the red squirrel.

Galiuro Mountains

Rugged and brush-covered, the Galiuro Mountains rise above the desert in two parallel ranges. Prominent peaks along the east ridge are Bassett (7,671 feet), Kennedy (7,540 feet), and Sunset (7,094 feet); along the west ridge stand Rhodes (7,116 feet), Maverick (6,990 feet), and Kielburg (6,880 feet). The terrain is so rough and steep that hikers stick mostly to the network of 10

trails, which total 95 miles. On the east side near the end of Forest Road 253, Deer Creek Trailhead is popular and sometimes accessible by car. Jackson Cabin Road (Forest Road 691) provides access from Willcox to the southeast via Cascabel Road and Muleshoe Ranch. The remote location and unpaved roads to this little-known range mean that you're likely to have solitude, though the area has been getting more popular. The Galiuros lie about 45 miles southwest of Safford, on the other side of the Pinalenos.

The **Galiuro Wilderness** of the Coronado National Forest protects 76,317 acres of the range. Another 6,600 acres just to the south lies within the Bureau of Land Management's **Redfield Canyon Wilderness.** Redfield Canyon offers scenic hiking through a narrow red-walled chasm.

These two wilderness areas, along with lands to the south, make up the 49,000-acre **Muleshoe Ranch Cooperative Management Area,** a collaborative effort of the Bureau of Land Management, Coronado National Forest, and The Nature Conservancy. The many perennial streams support wildlife and plant species in this remote region. You're welcome to stop in to see the visitor center exhibits operated by The Nature Conservancy. Walks nearby include a 0.75-mile interpretive trail loop, a three-mile loop through a riparian habitat, and a six-mile vista trail loop. Popular with birders and hikers, Muleshoe is open year-round Thurs.–Mon. 8 A.M.–5 P.M.; a $5 donation is suggested for nonmembers; 520/586-7072. You can stay at casitas, $70 d, $90 d, and $100 d; closed June–August. An information kiosk marks the beginning of the Jackson Cabin Road, a primitive road leading north toward the two wilderness areas.

Vegetation depends on the elevation and slope orientation. The south and west slopes have dense growths of manzanita, live oak, and other brush, with juniper, pinyon, and oak trees higher up. The higher canyons and north-facing slopes support Arizona cypress, ponderosa pine, Chihuahua pine, Mexican white pine, Douglas fir, and some white fir. Sycamore, alder, aspen, and other deciduous trees grow along streambanks. Mule deer, white-tailed deer, black bear, javelina, and mountain lion roam the rugged hillsides and canyons.

The old Power's cabin (built 1910), mine shafts, and ore-milling machinery lie along Rattlesnake Canyon. Power's Garden cabin, also in Rattlesnake Canyon, may be open to hikers— check with the Forest Service.

Streams usually dry up during late spring and early summer. The more reliable springs include Power's Garden, Mud, Corral, Holdout, Cedar, Jackson, Juniper, and South Field. See the Forest Service office in Safford for latest water, trail, and road conditions.

Aravaipa Canyon Wilderness

A jewel in the desert, Aravaipa Canyon is renowned for its scenery and variety of wildlife. The waters of Aravaipa Creek flow all year, a rare occurrence in the desert, providing an oasis for birds and other animals. Giant cottonwood, ash, sycamore, and willow trees shade the canyon floor. Rocky hillsides, dotted with saguaro cactus and other desert plants, lie only a few steps from the lush vegetation along the creek. Birders have sighted about 200 species in the canyon, including bald eagle and peregrine falcon. Mule and white-tailed deer, javelina, and coatimundi frequent the area; you might even see a mountain lion or bighorn sheep. Remember to keep an eye out for any of several species of rattlesnakes.

Although there's no established trail, hiking is easy to moderate along the gravel creekbed. Tributary canyons invite side trips—Hell Hole Canyon is especially enchanting. You'll be wading frequently across the creek, so wear tennis shoes or other shoes that can get wet. Grassy terraces make inviting campsites.

To visit the 11-mile canyon—even for day-hikes—you must get a permit from the BLM office in Safford. You can make reservations up to 13 weeks in advance by phone or mail, which is especially important for the very popular spring and autumn weekends, when it's best to call first thing in the morning; be sure to cancel if you or any of your party won't be coming. Only 50 people per day are permitted in the canyon. The BLM has a two-night (three-day) stay limit. Horseback riders are welcome but, on overnight trips, must camp with their horses on the uplands above the riparian canyon. Each group is limited to five animals. Hikers have a ten-person size limit. Pets are prohibited. Visitors must sign in at one of the trailheads and pay a fee of $5 per person per day.

Trailheads, though only 11 trail miles apart, are separated by 160 driving miles. The East Trailhead requires a high-clearance vehicle (no cars) for the half dozen or so stream crossings; it's reached by Klondyke Road (turn off US 70 about 15 miles northwest of Safford between Mileposts 313 and 314) or Fort Grant Road (turn off US 191 19 miles south of Safford or 17 miles north of I-10's Willcox Exit 336). A ranger is stationed in Klondyke, a settlement 10 miles before the trailhead. Two veteran Yukon prospectors established Klondyke in the early 1900s. **Klondyke Country Store**, 928/828-3335, 877/728-3335, is open all year with supplies and a housekeeping unit, available from one ($75) to five bedrooms ($250); amenities include a hot tub and corrals; www.klondykestore.com. The store may be able to arrange horseback riding and wildlife tours in this remote location. **Fourmile Campground** nearby has drinking water year-round and a $5 fee; turn left in Klondyke at the sign. With 4WD, you can also camp along Turkey Creek Canyon (no facilities or fee), a pretty tributary of Aravaipa Creek near the East Trailhead.

The West Trailhead is much closer to Phoenix (120 miles) and Tucson (70 miles). A ranger station is located at Brandenburg, three miles before the trailhead. There's no camping at the trailhead. From the junction on AZ 77 near Milepost 124, about 11 miles south of Winkelman, turn east 12 miles on Aravaipa Road to the trailhead.

Bonita Creek

This perennial stream flows through a pretty canyon in the Gila Mountains, about 25 miles northeast of Safford. Primitive roads provide access to the creek; one road follows the riparian canyon for about two miles. Summer flash floods can take out the road, which has many stream crossings, so it's a good idea to first check conditions and routes with the BLM office.

You may spot prehistoric cliff dwellings— most served as granaries—in the canyon, but they are too fragile and footing on the steep hill-sides too precarious to approach closely. Birding and hiking are best on weekdays. You can camp almost anywhere except at the mouth—just keep well above the washes to avoid being surprised by a flash flood.

From Safford, travel east about five miles on US 70 to the town of Solomon, then turn left (north) seven miles on Sanchez Road. At the sign for Gila Box Riparian National Conservation, turn left 2.5 miles on a graded dirt road to the west entry sign and continue, following signs for Bonita Creek. Other roads lead north to the trailhead for Lee Trail, a midway access point in Bonita Creek, and to Red Knolls Road, which crosses upper Bonita Creek.

A restored pioneer cabin from the 1920s marks the joining of Bonita Creek and the Gila River. There's also a wildlife-viewing platform. **Riverview Campground** nearby is open year-round with water, shade ramadas, and a $5 fee. **Flying W Group Day Use Area** is in the area too.

The lower 15 miles of Bonita Creek and a 23-mile section of the Gila River, including the Gila Box, receive protection as the **Gila Box Riparian National Conservation Area.** Stop by the BLM in town for a brochure that includes a detailed map of the roads and facilities in the Gila Box.

Safford–Morenci Trail

Pioneer ranchers and farmers built this trail in about 1874 to haul their products to the booming mines of the Morenci area. The trail fell into disuse with the advent of the automobile during the early 1900s. Today it receives little use and is often difficult to follow—you'll need topo maps and a compass.

Hikers and horseback riders enjoy the variety of desert and riparian environments along the way. The trail is 14 miles one-way with an elevation range of 3,700 to 6,200 feet. Bonita Creek, crossed about midway, makes a good camping spot; creek water must be treated. Roads to both the west and east trailheads may require 4WD vehicles in wet weather. Contact the BLM office in Safford for more information.

Hot Well Dunes Recreation Area

Sand dunes and a hot-water artesian well attract visitors to this remote spot southeast of Safford. Off-highway vehicle enthusiasts come to ride the dunes of the 2,000-acre recreation area, which offers campsites and hot tubs; $3/vehicle or $30 annual permit. Drillers seeking oil in the 1920s hit hot water, which flows at more than 250 gallons per minute at 106° F. From Safford, you can head east seven miles on US 70, then turn south (between Mileposts 347 and 348) 25 miles on Haekel Road. Or drive 17 miles south from Safford on US 191, turn east (near Milepost 105) 12 miles on Tanque Road, then right eight miles on Haekel Road. From Bowie on I-10 (Exits 362 or 366), turn north two miles on Central Avenue, turn right eight miles on Fan Road; then turn left nine miles on Haekel Road. The BLM office in Safford has information on the area.

Black Hills Back Country Byway

You can take this 21-mile scenic drive in dry weather. A high-clearance vehicle is best, though cautiously driven cars may be able to make it, too. Start from US 191, either east of Safford or south of Clifton. At each end of the drive you'll find a National Back Country Byway kiosk with historical and road information. Based on mileage from the Safford (southwestern) end of the drive, a BLM brochure describes history, geology, and natural resources at various points along the drive. Audiocassettes that interpret the colorful history of the byway are available from the chambers of commerce in Clifton and Safford and from the BLM in Safford. Visitors with long trailers or RVs should leave them at the information kiosks.

The Black Hills make up the northern end of the Peloncillo Mountains, a volcanic range with alluvial sand and gravel on its flanks. Both ends of the byway begin on the sand and gravel, then climb into volcanic rock in the higher, central part of the drive. Lava flows consist of dark gray and gray brown andesite, rhyolite, and dacite interlayered with multicolored ash both from wind-blown falls and ash flows. Ash deposits range in color from red or yellow to gray.

The low sections of the drive pass through a desert scrub plant community with much creosote. Animals include diamondback rattlesnakes, whip-tailed lizards, kangaroo rats, and various species of raptors. Higher elevations include desert grasslands populated by Gambel's quail. Juniper, pinyon pine, and oaks grow along the highest section of the drive. Here you may see mule deer, javelinas, black-tailed rattlesnakes, and migratory birds.

The Canyon Overlook Picnic Area lies midway through the drive at a high point overlooking the Gila River Canyon. At 17.1 miles from the southwest end, you'll find a picnic area on the north side of the Old Safford Bridge, built in 1918. The riverbank below the south side of the bridge serves as the boat put-in for kayaks, rafts, and canoes floating the Gila Box Riparian National Conservation Area. **Owl Canyon Campground,** located on a cliff overlooking the river northeast of the bridge, offers sites with shade ramadas; there's a fee of $5, but no drinking water is supplied. Dispersed camping is allowed along the Byway except in riparian areas near the bridge.

Floating the Gila River

Boaters enjoy the solitude, sheer cliffs, and abundant bird life on this 23-mile trip through the Gila Box Riparian National Conservation Area northeast of Safford. You may see bighorn sheep, beaver, and other wildlife, too. The Gila River runs year-round, but flow volume and season determine river-running conditions. January through April has the highest flows but very cold water temperatures. Levels usually drop in May and June, then pick up again after the July–Sept. rains. Autumn can be fine with cooler temperatures and the cottonwoods turned to gold.

At low flows of 150–500 cfs, conditions are excellent for beginners, who can take inflatable kayaks; boats may have to be pulled through short shallow sections. Flows of 500–1,500 cfs allow rafts up to 14 feet as well as canoes and hard and inflatable kayaks. At 1,500-3,500 cfs, 12-foot and larger rafts do well; kayakers (hard and inflatable) find more challenging conditions. Flows of 3,500-6,000 cfs require experienced rafters and very experienced kayakers for the Class II and III rapids and debris in the water. Only very experienced rafters with rafts 14 feet or larger should go at 6,000-10,000 cfs, when swift currents create many Class III rapids. Above 10,000 cfs, the river becomes hazardous and running it is not recommended.

Put in is on the south side of the Old Safford Bridge on the Black Hills Back Country Byway. Take out is at Dry Canyon, reached via Sanchez Road from Safford. The required river permits can be obtained at self-service pay stations at the launch site. The BLM office in Safford can advise on flows, access, and availability of commercial trips. You can also obtain flows on the Web at http://water.usgs.gov/realtime.html.

The Coronado Trail

Seeking treasures of the legendary Seven Cities of Cíbola, in 1540 Francisco Vásquez de Coronado and his men struggled through the rugged mountains of eastern Arizona. Though the Spaniard's quest failed, the name of this scenic highway recalls his effort. You'll discover the area's real wealth on a drive over Coronado's old route—rugged mountains covered with majestic forests rolling in blue waves towards the horizon. The blazing gold of aspen in autumn is matched only by the dazzling display of wildflowers in summer. The 123 miles of paved highway between Clifton and Springerville twist over country little changed from Coronado's time. When exploring this region, hikers, anglers, and cross-country skiers will find themselves far from the crowds. Visitors might even spot some of the Mexican wolves released between Clifton and Alpine. They're about German shepherd size—larger and heavier than coyotes. A few backcountry areas frequented by the wolves may be closed.

A look at the Apache-Sitgreaves National Forest map shows many scenic backcountry loops. Allow enough time for the journey through this high country—even a nonstop highway drive requires three and a half hours. With some 460 curves between Morenci and Alpine, this route certainly isn't suitable for those in a hurry. And you'll probably want to stop often to enjoy the views, walk around, and maybe have a picnic. Drivers should stock up on groceries and gas before attempting the 89 miles from Morenci to Alpine; there are no towns along this stretch, though Hannagan Meadow Lodge offers a small store/gas station.

Winter snows can close the highway from just north of Morenci to Alpine between mid-December and mid-March, though the section from Springerville to Alpine remains open. Miles of fine cross-country ski trails attract winter visitors to the forests near Alpine and Hannagan Meadow.

CLIFTON AND MORENCI

Coronado's expedition marched through this area in 1540, unaware of the gold deposits and abundant copper ore lying deep within these hills. Mexican miners discovered gold in 1867 and began small-scale placer operations. As the gold played out, Eastern prospectors took an interest in the copper deposits. They registered claims and by 1872 had staked out the town of Clifton. The nearby mining towns of Joy's Camp (later renamed Morenci) and Metcalf also date to this time. Miners faced great difficulties at first, as the nearest railhead was far away in Colorado and frequent Apache raids interrupted work.

In 1878, Arizona's first railroad connected the smelter in Clifton with the Longfellow Mine at Metcalf, nine miles north. Mules pulled the empty ore cars uphill to the mine; on the way down, the mules got a free ride. Three tiny locomotives, one on display in Clifton, later replaced the mules. Miners worked underground during the first six decades; in 1937, after a five-year Depression-era hiatus, all mining shifted to the surface, where it continues today.

Both Metcalf and old Morenci are gone now—Metcalf abandoned and destroyed, and old Morenci quarried away. The new Morenci has a modern appearance but lacks the character of an old mining town. Clifton, the Greenlee County seat, still has its old buildings and the Copper Head locomotive, built in the 1880s. Booze joints and brothels, where desperados engaged in frequent shootouts, once lined Chase Creek Street. Today the street is quiet and the old jail empty, but Clifton remains one of Arizona's more historically distinctive towns. Clifton also claims fame as the birthplace of the Apache warrior Geronimo.

Sights

Clifton's old jail, close to the old train depot/Chamber of Commerce, was built in 1881 by blasting and hacking a hole into the hillside. The jail's first occupant turned out to be the man who built it, Margarito Verala. After doing a fine job on the construction, Verala received his pay, got drunk on mescal, and proceeded to shoot up the town. You're welcome to step inside the gloomy interior. If the gate's locked, check at the city hall or police station for the key. The Copper Head locomotive of the old Coronado Railroad rests next to the jail. Tours by the Phelps Dodge Company provide a close-up look at the copper mine operations in Morenci.

Strolling along Chase Creek Street, you can imagine how it once looked—when the boisterous miners of old came looking for a good time. The street parallels US 191 on the opposite side of the creek. Drop into the **Greenlee Historical Museum** at 317 Chase Creek St. to see exhibits and artifacts of the old days; a large model (circa 1915) shows the ore deposits and mines of the area; some fascinating local history books can be purchased. The museum is open Tuesday, Thursday, and Saturday 2–4:30 P.M. or by appointment; donations welcome; 928/865-3115.

Accommodations and Food

Two women purchased an old saloon with their credit card for $10,000, then restored the former brothel rooms into a comfortable boardinghouse. Rooms cost $35 s and $45 d, dormitory beds run $15; rates drop with stays of four days or more. Baths and a small kitchen are shared. It's at 265 Chase Creek St.; 928/865-3891.

Rode Inn Motel, 186 S. Coronado Blvd., 928/865-4536, is in south Clifton; $45 s, $50 d. **Morenci Motel,** 928/865-4111, lies six miles up the highway from Clifton; $69 d.

Clifton gives you a choice of the little Mexican café **Casa Muñoz,** where the upper end of Chase Creek Street meets US 191, and the smoky Mexican-American **PJ's Restaurant** in the south part of town at 307 S. Coronado Blvd. (US 191), or several fast-food places along the highway. Another option is a picnic—you'll find tables just off US 191 in Clifton south of the San Francisco River bridge and north of the Rode Inn.

Morenci has the **Copperoom Restaurant** with American and Mexican dining in the Morenci Motel. **R&R Pizza Express** and a **Dairy Queen** lie across the street in the shopping plaza. The **Kopper Kettle Kafe** in the plaza is smoky.

Stock up on groceries at **Bashas'** in the shopping plaza, especially if headed north, as no supplies or gas are available for the next 67 miles to Hannagan Meadow.

Events

Horse races run during March at the fairgrounds in Duncan. The **Greenlee County Fair and Rodeo** entertains during late Sept./early Oct. in Duncan.

Recreation

Cool off in outdoor **swimming pool** near the plaza in Morenci; 928/865-2003. Play golf at the nine-hole **Greenlee Country Club** course in York Valley, 12 miles southeast of Clifton via US 191 and AZ 75; 928/687-1099.

Information and Services

The **Greenlee County Chamber of Commerce** provides information on the history, sights, and facilities of the area. You can see old photos of Morenci, taken before it disappeared, and of Clifton in its busier days. Rockhounds can obtain directions to several agate digs. The office, in Clifton's 1913 train depot, is open Mon.–Fri. 9 A.M.–5 P.M.; P.O. Box 1237, Clifton, AZ 85533; 928/865-3313.

For hiking and camping information on the south half of the Coronado Trail, see the **Clifton Ranger District** office of the U.S. Forest Service at Three Way, nine miles south of Clifton. It's open Mon.–Fri. 8 A.M.–4:30 P.M.; Box HC1-733, Duncan, AZ 85534; 928/687-1301/1314. Clifton's **public library** is across from the county courthouse at 102 School St., 928/865-2461.

Morenci's **public library** is in the Phelps Dodge Mercantile and shopping plaza, 928/865-2775. **Post offices** are at N. Coronado Blvd. in Clifton and in the shopping plaza in Morenci. **Morenci Healthcare Center,** 928/865-4511, provides clinic and 24-hour medical services at Coronado Blvd. and Burro Alley.

SIDETRIPS FROM CLIFTON

Mule Creek Road

Highway AZ 78 winds into the pinyon-juniper forests of the Big Lue Mountains east of town and continues into New Mexico. Ponderosa pine and oak grow at the higher elevations near the campgrounds. Begin at the "Three Way" junction nine miles south of town. You can stay at **Black Jack Campground** (elev. 6,300 feet) about 11 miles in and at **Coal Creek Campground** (elev. 5,900 feet) five miles farther. These small campgrounds can usually be reached year-round; no water or fee.

San Francisco River Scenic Drive

Forest Road 212 winds from Clifton east up along the San Francisco River past ranches, old mines, and canyon scenery to Evans Point. Cars can travel at least a few miles and high-clearance 4WD vehicles farther. Head up Frisco Avenue on the west side of the river, cross the river on a concrete bridge, and continue upstream. Staff at the Clifton Ranger District office and Greenlee County Chamber of Commerce can advise you on this and other backcountry drives and hikes.

BELOW THE MOGOLLON RIM

Morenci Mine Overlook

From this high vantage point, 10 miles north of Clifton, you can gaze into one of the biggest man-made holes in the world. Giant 210-ton trucks look like toys laboring to haul copper ore out of the ever-deepening pit. On the drive up from Clifton (elev. 3,502 feet) and modern Morenci (elev. 4,080 feet), you'll pass a giant smelter (now closed), concentrators (also now closed), and a solvent extraction/electrowinning plant. At press time, no mine tours were offered.

The old town of Morenci has vanished.

When it got in the way of the mine, Phelps Dodge built a new community and quarried away the old one. The company could make the move, completed in 1969, because it owned the town as well as the mine. You can see photos and artifacts of old Morenci in the Greenlee Historical Museum on Chase Creek Street in Clifton.

Granville Campground/ Cherry Lodge Picnic Area

Both of these places lie in a wooded canyon at an elevation of 6,800 feet and make pleasant stops. The camp and picnic sites are open all year; there's drinking water from early April to late October; free. The campground and picnic area lie on opposite sides of the road, about 20 miles north of Clifton between Mileposts 178 and 179.

Honeymoon Campground

As its name suggests, this is a secluded spot at the end of the 22-mile dirt Upper Eagle Creek Road. Elevation is 5,400 feet. No drinking water or fee; you'll need to carry out trash. You can fish for trout in Eagle Creek, stocked from May to September. Turn west onto Forest Road 217 near Milepost 188 of the Coronado Trail. Many of the ranches along the way date back to the late 1800s.

Juan Miller Campgrounds

The season runs year-round when not blocked by snow at the upper (elev. 5,800 feet) and lower (5,700 feet) campgrounds; no drinking water or fee. Head east one mile from the Coronado Trail on Forest Road 475. The turnoff is near Milepost 189, 33 miles north of Clifton and 35 miles south of Blue Vista. Forest Road 475 continues east to Blue River, another 15 miles, passing many small canyons and ridges good for day hiking.

Rose Peak

At an elevation of 8,786 feet, Rose Peak offers great views north to the Mogollon Rim, east and southeast to the Blue River area and far into New Mexico, south to the Pinalenos, and west across the Apache reservations. It's also a good place for birdwatching. The turnoff lies near Milepost 207, about 51 miles north of Clifton and 17 miles south of Blue Vista. You can reach the forest lookout tower on a one-mile trail or by driving up a steep, narrow, 1.4-mile road (high-clearance needed); the road and trail could be hiked as a 2.4-mile loop.

Strayhorse Campground

This free campground at an elevation of 7,600 feet offers spring water. It's 64 miles north of Clifton and four miles and 1,600 feet below Blue Vista; turnoff is near Milepost 221. **Raspberry Creek Trail #35** leads east to Blue River in the Blue Range Primitive Area. **Highline Trail #47** goes west 14.5 miles, linking with several other trails. Trails in this area, west of Strayhorse Campground, tend to be harder to follow.

ATOP THE MOGOLLON RIM

Blue Vista Overlook

In clear weather you can see countless ridges rolling away to the horizon from this 9,184-foot vantage point. Signs identify many of the mountain ranges, including Mt. Graham (elev. 10,717 feet), the highest peak of the Pinaleno Range, 70 miles to the south. A short trail through the mixed conifer forest goes farther out on the ridge, though trees obscure the views.

The overlook sits at the very edge of the Mogollon Rim, 68 miles north of Clifton and seven miles south of Hannagan Meadow. Turn 0.3 mile southwest at the sign to paved parking, picnic tables, an outhouse, and wheelchair-accessible views. A gate blocks the road to the parking area in winter, but you can park outside and walk in.

Bear Wallow Wilderness

This area west of the Coronado Trail contains 11,000 acres, including what's thought to be the largest stand of virgin ponderosa pine in the Southwest. **Bear Wallow Trail #63** follows Bear Wallow Creek downstream through the wilderness west to the San Carlos Indian Reservation boundary, 7.6 miles one-way; elevations range from 8,700 feet at the trailhead to 6,700 feet at the reservation boundary. You can hike on the reservation with a tribal Black and Salt River permit, which costs $10/day ages 12 and up; see **San Carlos Apache Reservation.**

Two shorter trails drop down to the trail and creek from the north. **Reno Trail #62** (1.9 miles one-way) meets Bear Wallow Trail at Mile 2.6; **Gobbler Point Trail #59** (2.7 miles one-way) meets Bear Wallow Trail at Mile 7.1.

Reach upper trailheads from Forest Road 25, which turns off US 191 opposite the road for K.P. Cienega Campground. Foresters at the Alpine Ranger District office have trail descriptions and can advise on current conditions.

K.P. Cienega Campground

Sites in this idyllic spot overlook a large meadow (*cienega* is Spanish for meadow) and a sparkling stream; water is often available in summer; no charge. From the Coronado Trail two miles north of Blue Vista Overlook and five miles south of Hannagan Meadow, turn east 1.5 miles on a dirt road to the campground. On the way, you'll pass the trailhead for **K.P. Trail #70,** heads into the Blue Range Primitive Area.

HANNAGAN MEADOW AND VICINITY

Splendid forests of aspen, spruce, and fir surround the tiny village of Hannagan Meadow (elev. 9,100 feet), 22 miles south of Alpine. A network of trails offers some great hiking; several trails also lead into the adjacent Blue Range Primitive Area. Here, in areas relatively unknown, you'll find some of the best cross-country skiing and snowmobiling in all of Arizona. The road from Alpine is normally open in winter, though storms occasionally shut it down for a few days.

EASTERN ARIZONA

Hannagan Meadow Campground and Trails

This national forest campground 0.3 mile south of the lodge on the highway stays open from mid-May to mid-September; no drinking water (water is available from a hose in front of the store) or fee. The **Acker Lake Trail** starts at the campground between campsites #6 and #7; it offers access to both Acker Lake, 3.5 miles, and the more remote areas of the Blue Range Primitive Area. **Fish Creek Trail** follows the creek all the way from Acker Lake to the Black River, about 12 miles one-way. The upper trailhead is reached from Hannagan Meadow; a half-mile access trail connects the lower trailhead to Fish Creek, about five miles above the confluence with the Black River. Other trails start across the road from the campground.

Hannagan Meadow Lodge

The cozy rooms and rustic cabins at this remote lodge offer comfortable year-round accommodations; all have private bath. Rooms and suites in the lodge run $60–100 d, and log cabins go at $80–125 for up to four people. The lodge dining room serves breakfast, lunch, and dinner daily; the dinner menu includes steak, prime rib, chicken, trout, seafood, and pasta. A small gas station/store sits next door. A stable offers horseback riding in the warmer months. You can reach Hannagan Meadow Lodge at HC 61, P.O. Box 335, Alpine, AZ 85920; 928/339-4370; www.hannaganmeadow.com.

Winter Sports

Cross-country skiers in the Hannagan Meadow area can glide along four marked trails totaling about 27 km during the late November to late March season. The Alpine Ranger District office and Hannagan Meadow Lodge have maps. A snowmobile trail starts from the north end of the lodge area.

BLUE RANGE PRIMITIVE AREA

This rugged wilderness country lies south of Alpine along the Arizona-New Mexico border. The south-flowing Blue River, fed by several perennial streams, neatly divides the primitive area. The Mogollon Rim, with high cliffs forming the south boundary of the Colorado Plateau, crosses the area from west to east. Geologic uplifting and downcutting have created spectacular rock formations and rough, steep canyons. Elevations range from 9,100 feet near Hannagan Meadow to 4,500 feet in the lower Blue River.

Hiking down from the rim, you'll find spruce, fir, and ponderosa pine forests giving way to pinyon pine and juniper. Wildlife includes Rocky Mountain elk, Coues white-tailed deer, mule deer, black bear, mountain lion, javelina, and bobcat. You may also see such rare and endangered birds as the southern bald eagle, spotted owl, American peregrine falcon, aplomado falcon, Arizona woodpecker, black-eared bushtit, and olive warbler. The upper Blue River and some of its tributaries harbor small numbers of trout.

Hiking

Hikers usually enjoy the best weather from April to early July and from September to late October. Violent thunderstorms lash the mountains in July and August. Snow covers much of the land from November to March. Many day-hikes and backpacking trips are possible on Forest Service trails. You can hike from trailheads along the Coronado Trail (US 191), Forest Road 281 (Blue Rd.), and Forest Road 567 (Red Hill Rd.). Other trailheads lie to the east in New Mexico and to the south off Forest Road 475. The Forest Service office in Alpine has maps and trail descriptions.

ALPINE

Mormon settlers founded this town in 1879, naming it Frisco for the nearby San Francisco River. Later, believing their mountains resembled the Alps, settlers renamed the community Alpine. The setting is pretty—a high mountain valley (elev. 8,046 feet) surrounded by extensive woodlands—but the Alps it's not.

Alpine (pop. 600) is an excellent base for hiking, mountain biking, fishing, hunting, horseback riding, golfing, scenic drives, and—in winter—cross-country skiing, sledding, and snowmobiling.

Accommodations

Places tend to fill up on summer weekends, when you'll need reservations.

Under $50: Alpine Cabins, just east on US 180 from the highway junction, 928/339-4440, has a variety of kitchenettes at $45–50 up to four persons. **Mountain Hi Lodge,** a half mile east on Main St., 928/339-4311, provides rooms at $34–41 d ($39–46 d Fri.–Sat.) and kitchenettes at $44–51 d ($49–56 d Fri.–Sat.). **Coronado Trail Cabins & RV,** a half mile south of town on US 191, 928/339-4772 has cabins with kitchenettes are open year-round at $45 d; RV spaces are open April–Oct. and cost $17 with hookups.

$50–100: Sportsman's Lodge, US 191 just north of the highway junction, 928/339-4576, 888/202-1033, offers motel rooms for $50 d and kitchenettes for $75 d. **Alpine Country Club Inn,** 928/339-1840, has condos overlooking the golf course ($80 d) and a cabin in town ($70; add $10 to rates on Fri.–Sat.). **Tal-Wi-Wi Lodge,** three miles north of Alpine, 928/339-4319, features year-round motel rooms at $65 d, $75 d with fireplace, $85 d with hot tub, and $95 d with fireplace and hot tub; the restaurant is open May–late Nov. with breakfast Sat.–Sun. and dinner Wed.–Saturday. **Black River RV Park,** 928/333-4984, offers cabin rentals ($65 d) and RV sites ($10) along with horseback riding; from Alpine, head south 14 miles on US 191, west seven miles on Forest Road 26, then right at the sign. Members of the same family operate **Sprucedale Ranch,** 928/333-4984, which offers accommodations at a working cattle and horse ranch at an elevation of 8,000 feet. Minimum stays are six days at $385 adult with a reduced rate for children. From Alpine, drive 14 miles south on US 191, turn right nine miles on Forest Road 26, then right one mile on Forest Road 24 to the ranch turnoff; P.O. Box 880, Eagar, AZ 85925; www.sprucedaleranch.com.

Campgrounds

Alpine Divide Campground is set in a forest of ponderosa pine and Gambel oak four miles north of Alpine. It offers sites with drinking water from mid-May to mid-September, $7.

The rest of the year, camping is on a pack-in/pack-out basis and free.

Luna Lake Campground, four miles east of Alpine on US 180 near the New Mexico border, lies in a ponderosa pine forest; it's open with drinking water from mid-May to mid-September, $8; reservations can be made at 877/444-6777; reserveusa.com. Luna Lake (75 acres) has a boat launch, boat rentals, and a small store and is open all year. Anglers go after trout in all four seasons—even through the ice in winter.

Coronado Trail Cabins & RV, a half mile south of town on US 191, 928/339-4772, offers RV spaces from April–Oct. for $17 with hookups. **Outpost RV & Trailer Park,** on US 180 near Luna Lake, 928/339-4854, has RV sites from April 15 to Oct. 15 for $12.50 with hookups. **Alpine Village Trailer Park,** in town on US 180, 928/339-1841, offers sites year-round at $5 for tents, $15 for RVs with hookups; showers cost an extra $3 per person. **Meadow View RV Park,** in town one block north of the junction of US 191 and US 180, 928/339-1850, has RV sites year-round at $14 but no showers. **Black River RV Park** has spaces southwest of town on Forest Road 26.

Food

Bear Wallow Café, just east on US 180 from the highway junction, 928/339-4310, serves American food in town. **Tal-Wi-Wi Lodge** offers a restaurant three miles north of Alpine; it's open May–late Nov. with breakfast Sat.–Sun. and dinner Wed.–Sat.; 928/339-4319. The **Alpine Country Club's** restaurant is open during the warmer months; head east three miles on US 180, then turn south two miles and follow signs about two miles; 928/339-4944. **Alpine Country Store** sells groceries on US 180 in town.

Events

Bush Valley Craft Fair takes place on Memorial Day weekend in May. **Luna Lake Trout Derby** fishes in June. Worms strain for the finish line in **Worm Races and Parade** on the second full weekend in July. Vehicles glitter in the **Classic Car Show** in August. The **CASA Chili Cookoff** spices up August. Shop early in the **Bush Valley Christmas Bazaar** on Labor Day weekend.

Recreation

You can **ride horses** with outfitters at **Sprucedale Ranch and Hannagan Meadow Lodge. Cross-country skiers** roam the groomed trails northwest of town in Williams Valley or south of town at Hannagan Meadow. You can rent cross-country ski gear at the **Tackle Shop,** which also has outdoor supplies; 928/339-4338.

See how far you can hit a golf ball through the thin mountain air at **Alpine Country Club,** which offers an 18-hole course and a restaurant; closed in winter. Head east three miles on US 180, then turn south two miles and follow signs; 928/339-4944.

Information and Services

The **Alpine Chamber of Commerce** maintains a list of accommodations and services; write P.O. Box 410, Alpine, AZ 85920; 928/339-4330 (answering machine); www .alpine-az.com. People at the **Alpine Ranger District** office of the Apache-Sitgreaves National Forest are very helpful with information on scenic drives, fishing, hiking, mountain biking, camping, and cross-country ski trails. The district covers the north half of the Coronado Trail, including Escudilla Mountain and most of the Blue Range Primitive Area. You can also obtain local tourist information and purchase books and maps. The office is open Mon.–Fri. 8 A.M.–4:30 P.M.; 928/339-4384. (People with hearing impairments can call the TDD 928/339-4566.) It's on US 191 in town opposite the turnoff for US 180; P.O. Box 469, Alpine, AZ 85920.

Alpine's **public library** is on US 180; 928/339-4925. The **post office** is on US 191 just north of the junction.

VICINITY OF ALPINE

The **East and West Forks of the Black River** west of town have fishing, hiking, and campgrounds; continue west for Big Lake, Crescent Lake, and other recreation areas.

Blue River-Red Hill Scenic Loop

On this backcountry drive you'll roll by the Blue River, remote ranches, and rugged hill country. The Forest Service maintains two small campgrounds along the way—Upper Blue, with spring water, and Blue Crossing. Both lie near the Blue River at an elevation of 6,200 feet; no charge.

From Alpine, head east three miles on US 180 and turn south on Forest Road 281 (Blue Road). After 10 miles you'll reach the Blue River; follow it downstream nine miles to the junction with Forest Road 567 (Red Hill Road). A river ford here can be impassable in high water. Red Hill Road twists and climbs out of the valley, often following ridges with good views, to US 191, 14 miles south of Alpine. If driving in the other direction, you'll find the Red Hill Road turnoff between Mileposts 239 and 240 on US 191. The forest roads are gravel and should be okay in dry weather for cautious drivers. See the Alpine Ranger District office for more information on this and other scenic drives in the area.

Hikers may want to try **Red Hill Trail #56;** this 7.6-mile trail follows a jeep track to the Blue Range Primitive Area, descends along ridges via Red Hill (elev. 7,714 feet), drops into Bush Creek, and follows it to Tutt Creek. **Tutt Creek Trail #105** connects the lower end of Red Hill Trail with Red Hill Road, 0.8 mile to the east. The upper trailhead (elev. 8,000 feet) is on Forest Road 567 one mile east of US 191; the lower trailhead (5,800 feet) is on Forest Road 567 a half mile before the Blue River.

Mountain Bicycling

The Apache-Sitgreaves National Forest offers many good areas for mountain biking. Marked trails on the Alpine District include upper (8 miles) and lower (2.5 miles) loops near Luna Lake, Georges Lake near Alpine (4.5 miles, 7.5 miles without shuttle), Terry Flat Loop (six miles) at Escudilla Mountain, Hannagan Meadow Loop (5.5 miles) south of Alpine, and Williams Valley (five miles) northwest of Alpine. You can rent bikes in Springerville and Alpine.

Escudilla Mountain and Wilderness

In 1540, Coronado spotted the 10,912-foot

summit of this ancient volcano; perhaps a homesick member of his expedition named the mountain after an *escudilla,* a soup bowl used in his native Spain.

In 1951 a disastrous fire burned the forests on the entire north face of Escudilla. Aspen trees then took over where mighty conifers once stood, the normal sequence after a mountain fire. Raspberries, snowberries, currants, elderberries, strawberries, and gooseberries now flourish here too.

The forests of spruce, fir, and pine on top escaped the fire; lower down you'll find surviving woodlands of aspen, Rocky Mountain maple, ponderosa pine, and Gambel oak. Elk, deer, black bear, and smaller animals roam the hillsides. Escudilla was once grizzly country, but the last animal was killed by the 1930s.

Now a wilderness area of 5,200 acres, Escudilla offers excellent hiking. Outstanding views from the fire lookout—the highest in Arizona— reward those who make the climb. The actual summit (10,912 feet)—Arizona's third highest— lies a half mile to the north and 36 feet higher, but trees there completely block the views.

Escudilla National Recreation Trail, a well-graded, 3.3-mile trail from Terry Flat (elev. 9,600 feet), ascends to Escudilla Lookout through aspen, meadows, and conifers. The old Government Trail originally began at Hulsey Lake and, though shown on some maps, it's no longer maintained and isn't recommended.

From US 191 between Mileposts 420 and 421, about six miles north of Alpine and 21 miles south of Springerville, turn east 4.6 miles on Forest Road 56 to Terry Flat Loop, then take the left fork 0.4 mile to the trailhead. **Terry Flat Loop** is a worthwhile destination in itself; the six-mile dirt road encircles Terry Flat Meadow with many fine views of Escudilla Mountain; cautious drivers can usually make the trip with cars in dry weather.

Nelson Reservoir

Rainbow, brown, and brook trout live in this 60-acre lake surrounded by a woodland of pinyon pine and juniper. It's just west of US 191, 11 miles north of Alpine and 10 miles south of Springerville. Restrooms, a paved boat ramp, and handicapped fishing station are provided at the north end; no fires or camping. Winter visitors can fish through the ice. Escudilla Mountain, the large rounded peak to the south.

Springerville and Eagar

Since Henry Springer's trading post opened in 1879, Springerville has grown into an important trade, ranching, and lumbering center. Today the town is a handy stop for travelers. Springerville and the adjacent town of Eagar lie in Round Valley beside the Little Colorado River at an elevation of 6,965 feet. Rolling grass-covered hills surround the valley.

The *Madonna of the Trail,* an 18-foot statue in Springerville, commemorates the hardy pioneer women of yesteryear. You can't miss the giant dome of the Round Valley Ensphere in Eagar; this multipurpose building has a total floor area of 189,000 square feet, unusually large for such a small community. It is said to be the only domed high school football field in the country.

Casa Malpais

This prehistoric ruin offers some unusual features. The Mogollon people built the village, believed to be a major trade and ceremonial center, between A.D. 1260 and 1440. It sits on a series of terraces at the edge of a large lava flow, just north of present-day Springerville. Huge cracks—more than 100—under the site served as ceremonial and burial chambers, referred to as "catacombs" by some archaeologists.

The masonry pueblo at Casa Malpais ("House of the Badlands") rose two and three stories with more than 120 rooms. The impressive Great Kiva, square in the Mogollon style, measures 55 by 62 feet; archaeologists believe it once had a roof. Other features at the site include rock art, masonry stairways, and an oval wall enclosing what is thought to have been an astronomical observatory.

You can view excavated artifacts at a museum and visit Casa Malpais on tours sponsored by the city of Springerville. The tours, the only way to enter the ruins, last about 1.5 hours and involve 1.5 miles of walking and a 250-foot climb; bring water and a hat in summer. Ongoing excavations are often visible in spring, summer, and autumn. Because of their sacred nature, the underground chambers are closed to the public.

Meet at the museum, 928/333-5375, before going to the site, 318 E. Main St. in Springerville; it's open Mon.–Fri. 8 A.M.–6 P.M. and Sat.–Sun. 8 A.M.–4 P.M. year-round, tours usually leave at 9 A.M., 11 A.M., and 2 P.M. in good weather; additional tours may be added in summer. Tours or general admission run $5 adults, $4 seniors 55 and up and students 12–18, $3 children 11 and under; www.casamalpais.com. Dinosaur tours to a local excavation site may be available too.

Renee Cushman Art Collection

Renee Cushman willed her valuable collection of European art and furniture to the LDS Church in Springerville. Three display rooms house her goods, which range from Renaissance to early 20th century. Call for an appointment to see the collection; 928/333-4514. It's at the Springerville LDS Church at 150 N. Aldrice Burk, 1.5 blocks off Main Street.

Accommodations

Under $50: White Mountain Motel, 333 E. Main St., 928/333-5482, offers simple lodging at $30 s, $34 d; weekly rates for kitchenettes run $145 d. **El Jo Motor Inn,** 435 E. Main St., 928/333-4314, costs $36 s, $39.50 d, and up. **Reed's Motor Lodge,** 514 E. Main St., 928/333-4323, 800/814-6451, offers a variety of rooms at $28–39 s, $34–50 d, and $55–80 suites; the hosts enjoy art and have a gallery and some rooms decorated by regional artists; guided hike and horse tours can be arranged. **Super 8 Motel,** 123 W. Main St., 928/333-2655, 800/800-8000, costs $36 s, $42 d.

$50–100: Rode Inn, 242 E. Main St., 928/333-4365, offers deluxe lodgings at $45 s, $60 d ($60 s, $70 d Fri.–Sat.); suites run $145 d. In Eagar you can stay at the **Best Western Sunrise Inn,** 128 N. Main St., 928/333-2540, 800/528-1234, with a hot tub and exercise room, for $55 d ($69 d Fri.–Sat.). Also in Eagar, **Paisley Corner Bed and Breakfast,** 287 N. Main St., 928/333-4665, has rooms in a 1910 house at $65–95 (all with private bath).

Campgrounds

Casa Malpais Campground, one mile northwest on US 60, 928/333-4632, runs $10 tent or $16 RV with hookups and has showers. Nearby Becker Lake offers trout fishing. **Bear Paw RV Park,** 425 E. Central Ave. in Eagar, 928/333-4650, is open all year for self-contained rigs; $11 RV with hookups.

Food

For American and Mexican food in Springerville, try **Booga Red's,** 521 E. Main St., 928/333-2640; open daily for breakfast, lunch, and dinner. **Safire Restaurant** 411 E. Main St., 928/333-4512, fixes American and a few Mexican items nearby daily for breakfast, lunch, and dinner. Locals also dine at **Mike's Place,** corner of E. Hwy. 60 at D St., 928/333-4022, for steak and other American cuisine. **Lil' Ranglers Café,** 173 W. Main St., 928/333-4826, also serves steaks along with other American and Mexican food daily for breakfast, lunch, and dinner. **R&R Pizza Express,** 181 W. Main St., 928/333-3033, dishes up pizza and pasta Mon.–Sat. for lunch (buffet available) and dinner.

Events

The community celebrates **July 4th** with a parade, rodeo, barbecue, dance, and fireworks. **Eagar Daze,** the first weekend in August, features talent show, games, barbecue, and dance. A **Christmas Lights Parade and Crafts Fair** is held on the first or second Saturday in December.

Recreation

Springerville Park offers shaded picnic tables and a playground near the White Mountain Historical Society Park; turn south three blocks on Zuni from Main. Old buildings of the historical park may be open, ask at the chamber office.

The **Sweat Shop,** 74 N. Main St. in Eagar, 928/333-2950, rents mountain bicycles and cross-country skis.

Eagar has the indoor **Round Valley Swimming Pool** at 116 N. Eagar St.; 928/333-2238.

Shopping

Round Valley Plaza, just south of downtown Springerville on S. Mountain Ave., has a supermarket and other stores. **Stuart Books,** 319 E. Main St. in Springerville, 928/333-2587, offers new and used books. Pick up fishing, hunting, and camping supplies in Springerville at **Western Drug and General Store,** 105 E. Main St., 928/333-4321; or at **Sport Shack,** 329 E. Main St., 928/333-2222.

Information and Services

Staff at the **Round Valley Chamber of Commerce,** 318 E. Main St. in downtown Springerville, 928/333-2123, can tell you about the area and services; it's open Mon.–Sat. 9 A.M.–5 P.M.; P.O. Box 31, Springerville, AZ 85938; www.az-tourist.com.

For maps and the latest information on recreation and road conditions in the Apache-Sitgreaves National Forest, visit either of the two **U.S. Forest Service** offices on S. Mountain Avenue. The **Springerville Ranger District Office,** 165 S. Mountain Ave. (just north of Round Valley Plaza), 928/333-4372, has specific information and forest maps on Big Lake, Mt. Baldy, Greer, South Fork, and other areas of the district; it's open Mon.–Fri. 7:30 A.M.–4:30 P.M.; P.O. Box 760, Springerville, AZ 85938. The **Supervisor's Office,** just south of Round Valley Plaza, 928/333-4301, has general information on Apache-Sitgreaves National Forest; it's open Mon.–Fri. 7:30 A.M.–4:30 P.M.; P.O. Box 640, Springerville, AZ 85938.

The **public library** is in Eagar Plaza behind Dairy Queen; 928/333-4694. **White Mountain Regional Medical Center** is in downtown Springerville at 118 S. Mountain Ave.; 928/333-4368.

West of Springerville

SOUTH FORK

An entertaining museum, a campground, and cabins lie in the meadows and forests along the South Fork of the Little Colorado River. Turn south on Apache Co. 4124 from AZ 260 between Mileposts 390 and 391, about five miles west of Springerville/Eagar.

Little House Museum

Exhibits in a series of buildings at X Diamond Ranch, including a cabin and a granary dating from the 1890s, illustrate the history of the region. Your guide uses photos and heirlooms to tell stories of the pioneers. Working nickelodeons and other music machines from the past provide musical interludes. The 90-minute tours go May 25-Labor Day: Thurs.–Sat. at 11 A.M. and 1:30 P.M. and Sun.–Mon. at 1:30 P.M. only, closed Tuesday and Wednesday; open in winter by reservation; 928/333-2286. Admission is $4 adults, $1.50 children.

The X Diamond Ranch also offers log cabins ($80–125 up to four), rock-art tours (hiking or horseback), archaeology programs, a salon with skin-treatment programs, and private fishing access (with both catch-and-release and catch-and-keep areas; fishing equipment can be rented, too). Five-member teams on horseback play cowboy golf in the X Diamond Ranch Cowboy Charity Golf Tournament on the weekend before the summer solstice; a western art show accompanies the tournament. Turn in 2.4 miles on Apache Co. 4124, then right 0.7 mile at the sign.

South Fork Guest Ranch

Guests stay in cabins and can use a private pond in South Fork Canyon, 2.4 miles south of AZ 260 on Apache Co. 4124, 928/333-4455; open all year, $35–120 d.

South Fork Campground

Campsites in the ponderosa pines cover both sides of the stream at an elevation of 7,520 feet. They're open with water from mid-May to the end of October; $6. Turn south 2.8 miles on Apache Co. 4124 to road's end. From the campground you can follow South Fork Trail #97.

GREER

This little town sits in a pretty valley high in the White Mountains at 8,500 feet. Settlers first arrived in 1879, then later named their community for Americus Vespucius Greer, a prominent Mormon pioneer.

Today Greer comes to life in the summer, when visitors enjoy fishing, forest walks, and the cool mountain air. Winter is also a busy season—snow worshippers flock to the slopes of nearby Sunrise Ski Area or put on their skinny skis to glide along the miles of marked cross-country ski trails just outside town. The quietest times are mid-April to early May, when the first signs of spring appear; and autumn, when days are crisp and aspens turn gold. Greer lies 15 miles east of Sunrise Ski Area, 16 miles west of Springerville and 225 miles northeast of Phoenix. From the junction on AZ 260, turn south five miles on AZ 373.

You can fish for trout in the waters of the Little Colorado River in and near town and in the **Greer Lakes,** three small reservoirs offering boating (electric motors okay) and picnicking north of town; turn east off AZ 373 opposite Hoyer Campground.

Butler Canyon Trail (cross-country ski trail in winter) is a one-mile, self-guided nature trail just north of town; turn east 0.1 mile off AZ 373 at the sign for Montlure Camp and Nature Trail, 0.7 mile south of Circle B Market.

Cross-country skiers can enjoy a variety of loop trails in the woods northwest of town. **Pole Knoll** offers additional cross-country skiing farther west; you can reach it by skiing from Greer or by parking on the south side of AZ 260 near Milepost 383. You can obtain ski-trail maps from local businesses or from the **Springerville Ranger District** office in Springerville; 928/333-4372.

Butterfly Lodge Museum

This 1913 cabin recalls the extraordinarily colorful lives of two residents. James Willard Schultz (1859–1947) came west in his youth, married a Blackfoot maiden, then later became a noted explorer, storyteller, archaeologist, Native American-rights advocate, and popular author. He wrote 37 adventure stories, beginning with *My Life as an Indian.* Schultz set three books in Arizona, where he got to know the Hopi, Navajo, and Apache tribes. Although an outsider to the close-knit Mormon village of Greer, he enjoyed life at his cabin and hunting trips in the wilderness. His son, Lone Wolf (Hart Merriam Schultz; 1882–1970), also roamed the West before receiving encouragement from artist Thomas Moran in 1906 to take formal art training. Lone Wolf enjoyed great success by the 1920s with his Western paintings and sculpture; he often stayed here at the cabin.

Exhibits in the restored cabin tell about their lives and families. You'll also see writings of the father and artwork of the son. A gift shop sells articles, cards, and books, including *On the Road to Nowhere, A History of Greer, Arizona 1879–1979,* by the museum's curator, Karen M. Applewhite.

The museum is half a mile south of the Circle B Market, then east at the sign; 928/735-7514. It's open Fri.–Sun. 10 A.M.–5 P.M. from Memorial Day to Labor Day weekend; admission is $2 adults, $1 ages 12–17.

Accommodations

Greer resorts offer lodge rooms and rustic cabins; most cabins have kitchens and cozy fireplaces.

Under $50: Circle B Motel, next to the market of the same name on the way into town, costs $49 d; 928/735-7540. Established in 1910, **Molly Butler Lodge,** in town, 928/735-7226, is the oldest guest lodge in Arizona. It's open year-round with rooms at $35 d and $45 d and a restaurant.

$50–100: Greer Mountain Resort, 2.7 miles north of town; 928/735-7560, offers apartments ($60 d), cabins ($85 d and $100 d), and a restaurant. **The Aspens,** 928/735-7232, has cabins for $60–80 d. **Snowy Mountain Inn,** three miles north of town, has a restaurant, fishing pond, jacuzzi, and horse boarding. Rooms run $85–100 d, cabins start at $110; 928/735-7576. **White Mountain Bed & Breakfast/Cabins** offers rooms with private baths in an 1892 farmhouse ($69–89 d with breakfast), cabins ($85–195 d), and fishing in the Little Colorado River and beaver pond in back; 928/735-7568, 888/493-7568; www.wmonline.com/wmlodge. **Cattle Kate's Lodge B&B** also has a fishing pond. Rates run $85 d and $95 d for rooms and $135 d for a suite; 928/735-7744. The Little Colorado River runs through the property at **Four Seasons,** 928/735-7333, where cabins are open all year for $95–100.

$100–150: Greer Lodge, 928/735-7216, 888/475-6343, features luxurious rooms and cabins, a restaurant, and a private trout pond. It's open all year at $120 d in the lodge and $75–120 d for cabins. **The Peaks Resort Hotel,** 928/735-7777, 800/556-9997, has a restaurant and offers deluxe rooms at $109 d, suites for $149 d, and cabins at $109 d; it's all nonsmoking. The award-winning **Red Setter Inn Bed and Breakfast,** 928/735-7441, 888/994-7337, features rooms in a log lodge ($130–195 d) and a four-bedroom housekeeping cabin ($550 per night); www.redsetterinn.com.

Campgrounds

You'll pass the two national forest campgrounds of **Benny Creek** ($6) and **Rolfe C. Hoyer** ($12) on the way in to Greer. Both nestle in ponderosa pines at an elevation of about 8,250 feet with water during the season of about mid-May to the end of September. Hoyer Campground is larger with a nature trail, showers, and dump station. Sites at both campgrounds can be reserved at 877/444-6777; reserveusa.com. **Mountain Aire RV Park,** across from Big Ten Resort, 928/735-7524, has RV sites at $25 from May 1-early October.

Food

Peaks Restaurant, 928/735-7777, cooks country-style food daily for breakfast, lunch, and dinner in summer, then Wed.–Thurs. for lunch and dinner the rest of the year.

Molly Butler Lodge, 928/735-7226, offers breakfast and lunch some days and dinner daily.

Amberon's at Greer Lodge, 928/735-7217, prepares breakfast and lunch daily May–Oct. (weekends only in winter) and dinner nightly year-round.

Greer Mountain Resort, 2.7 miles north of town, 928/735-7560, has breakfast and lunch daily.

Services

Circle B Market, 928/735-7540, offers groceries, fishing gear, camping supplies, boat rentals, and cross-country ski rentals. Greer also has a post office and a library. For tourist information, you can visit the Round Valley Chamber of Commerce office in Springerville or check www.az-tourist.com

MOUNT BALDY WILDERNESS

The pristine forests and alpine meadows of 11,590-foot Mt. Baldy present a fine opportunity to visit a subalpine vegetation zone. You'll see magnificent forests untouched by commercial logging. Engelmann and blue spruce dominate, but quaking aspen, white fir, corkbark fir, Douglas fir, southwestern white pine, and ponderosa pine also cover the slopes. You might catch a glimpse of elk, mule or white-tailed deer, black bear, beaver, wild turkey, blue grouse, or other wildlife. Mount Baldy is an extinct volcano eight or nine million years old, worn down by three periods of glaciation.

West Fork #94 and **East Fork #95** trails follow the respective branches of the Little Colorado River on the northeast slopes of Mt. Baldy. Each trail is 6.5 miles long; they meet on the grassy summit ridge. The summit is another mile away, but the last half mile of trail crosses White Mountain Apache land, which is closed to outsiders. The Apache vigorously enforce this closure—errant hikers have been arrested, their gear confiscated—so don't try to sneak in! Apache still make pilgrimages to this sacred peak.

Hiking season stretches from June to October, but plan to be off the ridges in early afternoon in July and August to avoid thunderstorms. The trailheads, about four miles apart by road, are easily reached from Sunrise, Big Lake, or Greer. In fact, both trails also go north to Greer, about five miles away.

The West Fork Trailhead (elev. 9,240 feet) lies just outside the wilderness boundary at the end of Forest Road 113J, a half mile in from AZ 273. The East Fork Trailhead (elev. 9,400 feet) begins near the Phelps Cabin site, 0.2 mile in from AZ 273. An all-day or overnight loop hike uses a 3.3-mile connecting trail that joins the lower ends of West Fork and East Fork trails. This trail, which may not appear on maps, goes from the West Fork Trail (0.3 mile up from the trailhead) to the Phelps Cabin site area.

Horseback riders are welcome on the trails, too. They'll appreciate the corrals at **Gabaldon Campground,** which offers basic camping—no water, tables, or fee—in spruce trees off AZ 273, just east of Phelps Trailhead. Trail #95 connects the campground and trailhead. The season runs about June to September at this 9,400-foot elevation.

Anglers catch brook, rainbow, and a few native cutthroat trout in the creeks. The Forest Service asks visitors to limit hiking and riding groups to 12 people and camping groups to six. Forest Service offices sell a topo map of Mt. Baldy Wilderness.

BIG LAKE

Rolling mountain meadows and forested hills of spruce and fir surround this pretty lake. Top-rated for trout by many anglers, Big Lake (575 acres) boasts a marina, campgrounds, hiking trails, and a riding stable. The marina offers rental boats, motors, fishing supplies, gas, and groceries from late April/early May to mid-November. A fish-cleaning station lies across the parking lot, and a public boat ramp is a short drive away.

Nearby **Crescent Lake** (197 acres) features trout fishing and a smaller marina—boat rentals and snacks—but no campgrounds. The Forest Service operates a visitor center on the main road between the two lakes; check out the naturalist programs, displays, books, and maps.

At Big Lake you have a choice of four campgrounds: **Rainbow** ($10–20), **Grayling** ($10), **Brookchar** ($8), and **Cutthroat** ($8). All have drinking water. Both RVers and tenters can stay at Rainbow and Grayling, but only tents are allowed at Brookchar and Cutthroat. Showers and a dump station are available. Camping season with water lasts mid-May to mid-September; Grayling, Brookchar, and Cutthroat stay open mid-April to Thanksgiving if weather permits. Expect cool nights at the 9,100-foot elevation even in midsummer. Reserve campsites at 877/444-6777; reserveusa.com.

Big Lake lies about 20 miles south of AZ 260 via paved AZ 261 and AZ 273; the turnoff is at Milepost 393, seven miles east of the Greer junction and three miles west of Springerville. The Apache-Sitgreaves Forest map shows other ways in.

Vicinity of Big Lake

Mountain bikers can enjoy the marked **Indian Springs Trail #627,** a 7.5-mile loop south of Big Lake; the three-mile (one-way) **West Fork Destination Trail** branches off the loop to the

West Fork of the Black River. There are many other fine rides on the forest roads as well.

Lee Valley Lake (35 acres) contains brook trout—best early and late in the season—and great scenery at an elevation of 9,400 feet near Mt. Baldy Wilderness; it's off AZ 273 between Big Lake and Sunrise. **Winn Campground** sits at the end of Forest Road 554, two miles in from AZ 273. Greer, Lee Valley Lake, Sunrise Lake, Big Lake, and Crescent Lake all lie within a 10-mile radius. Camping season at the 9,320-foot elevation runs from mid-May to the end of September; sites have drinking water and an $10 fee; they and **Winn Group** area can be reserved by contacting 877/444-6777; reserveusa.com.

East Fork of the Black River offers fishing for rainbow trout. Stay at **Diamond Rock, Aspen,** or **Buffalo Crossing campgrounds;** free, with drinking water at Diamond Rock only. The season runs from early May to the end of October. The area is nine miles southeast of Big Lake and 10–14 miles southwest of Alpine.

West Fork of the Black River has fishing for rainbow and brown trout. **West Fork Campground** beside the stream is free but lacks drinking water. An eight-mile hike leads downstream from Forest Road 116 to West Fork Campground. The Apache-Sitgreaves National Forest map shows back roads in the area.

North of Springerville

Lyman Lake State Park

Rain and snowmelt from the White Mountains flow down the Little Colorado River and fill this 1,500-acre lake. Juniper trees and other high-desert vegetation grow in the wide valley at an elevation of 6,000 feet. Though it's cold here in winter, anglers come year-round to try for channel catfish, largemouth bass, and walleye. Lyman Lake is large enough for sailing and waterskiing; there are no motor restrictions. Water skiers test their skills in a ski slalom course near the dam. Anglers enjoy a section of the west end designated as a no-wake area.

Two small peninsulas, with a protected swim area in between, jut out into the lake from the campground and day-use areas. The north peninsula has a store, day-use area, two paved boat ramps, a boat dock, fishing pier, group camp area, and 1.2 miles of hiking trails with views and lake access; hikers can start from either the day-use or group areas. The store offers groceries, snacks, fishing supplies, and boat rentals from about April to October; it may close on Mondays. Some fine petroglyph panels and views on the south peninsula attract visitors to the pair of trail loops here, totaling 1.5 miles. Another trail goes out to the buffalo pen, a half-mile one-way, or up the mesa behind the ranger residences for a panorama of the lake.

An excellent year-round campground includes restrooms, showers, hookups, and a dump station. Boaters can also use undeveloped campsites on the shore. Campers should prepare for strong winds on the open terrain. Charges per vehicle run $4 day use, $10 camping, or $15 with electric and water hookups.

From the first weekend in May to the last one in September, rangers lead 90-minute tours across the lake to the Ultimate Petroglyph Trail on Sat.–Sun. at 10 A.M. and one-hour tours to the Rattlesnake Point Pueblo on Sat.–Sun. at 2 P.M.; reservations recommended. You can also visit these sites on your own, but you'll need a boat to reach the start of the Ultimate Petroglyph Trail. Fireworks on July Fourth light up the skies in a "Fire Over the Water" display.

The park lies 17 miles north of Springerville and 10 miles south of St. Johns on US 180/191 between Mileposts 380 and 381, then east 1.3 miles; 928/337-4441. Look for buffalo near the entrance. The contact station has photos and artifacts of prehistoric Native American sites from the area, including Rattlesnake Point Pueblo.

St. Johns

Spanish explorers named this spot on the Little Colorado River El Vadito (Little River Crossing). In 1871, Solomon Barth founded a settlement

along Ultimate Petroglyph Trail, Lyman Lake State Park

© BILL WEIR

EASTERN ARIZONA

along the river with his brothers and some Mexican families, then moved six miles upstream to the present site the following year. Residents named the community San Juan after its first female resident, Señora Maria San Juan de Padilla de Baca. Postal authorities supposedly refused to accept a foreign name, so it was changed to Saint John, with an "s" added for phonetic effect. Mormon settlers arrived in 1879 from Utah. Today, St. Johns (pop. 3,300) serves as the Apache County seat, 27 miles north of Springerville and 44 miles southeast of Petrified Forest National Park.

You can learn more about the area's history and see pioneer and Native American artifacts in the **Apache County Museum,** 180 W. Cleveland (US 180/AZ 61), 928/337-4737; it's open Mon.–Fri. 9 A.M.–5 P.M. (closed holidays); donations are welcomed. Archaeological highlights unearthed in the area include tusks and a jaw from a mammoth and a leg bone from a giant camel. Out back, you'll find a petroglyph panel, jail, log cabin (circa 1881), adobe building reconstruction, and farm equipment. The **St. Johns Chamber of Commerce,** 928/337-2000, is also

in the museum and open Mon.–Fri. 8 A.M.–5 P.M.; P.O. Box 178, St. Johns, AZ 85936.

St. Johns has a **Budget Inn** at 75 E. Commercial St., 928/337-2990, $40 s, $43 d; and a **Days Inn** at 125 E. Commercial St., 928/337-4422 or 800/DAYSINN, $46-50 d. Cafés in town include the **Inn & Out Grill** near the museum at 106 W. Cleveland, 928/337-2505; and the Mexican **El Camino** (closed Sun.) on the road from Springerville at 277 White Mountain Dr., 928/337-4700.

The **San Juan Fiesta** in mid-June, celebrates with a parade, barbecue, dances, and games. A **July Fourth** festival features a barbecue, games, and fireworks. **Pioneer Day,** on the weekend nearest July 24, has a parade, rodeo, pageant, barbecue, and dances. The **Apache County Fair** in September presents exhibits and horse races. In mid-December, a large community choir forms a living Christmas tree. Also in December, the museum offers a tour of historic houses not normally open to the public.

The pleasant **city park** includes covered picnic tables, playground, outdoor pool, and courts for tennis, volleyball, racquetball, and handball at Second West and Second South; from near the museum, turn south two blocks on Second West. The **public library** is at 245 West and First South; 928/337-4405.

Kolhuwalawa

Arizona's 23rd Indian reservation was created in 1985, returning to the Zuni (ZOO-nee) their heaven. The Zuni believe these 1,400 acres, 14 miles north of St. Johns, to include the place where human spirits return after death. Anthropologists think that Zuni religious leaders have held sacred dances and ceremonies here since at least A.D. 900, when ancestors of the tribe began migrating from pueblos in Arizona to New Mexico.

The Zuni people, like the Hopi, still live in pueblos and maintain many of their old traditions. You can visit Zuni Pueblo, one of the fabled Seven Cities of Cíbola sought by Coronado in 1540. Zuni is in New Mexico, 58 miles northeast of St. Johns.

Concho Lake

Concho is stocked with trout. The adjacent **Concho Valley Country Club** features an 18-hole golf course, 928/337-2622 (golf shop), or 800/658-8071 (golf reservations). **Concho Valley Motel**, 928/337-4644, has rooms for $30–60 s, $40–80 d; the restaurant is open weekends for breakfast and daily for lunch during the golfing season of May to October.

Southern Arizona

Forested mountains tower above the vast desert and grasslands of Southern Arizona. The Sonoran Desert with its giant saguaro and other hardy plants cover lands from Tucson west to the Colorado River Valley. Desert grasslands fill most valleys to the east. Climate varies dramatically with elevation. Expect mild winters and very hot summers on the desert, slightly cooler and wetter weather on the grasslands. Four ranges—the Santa Catalinas, Santa Ritas, Huachucas, and Chiricahuas—have peaks over 9,000 feet and offer delightful summer weather and deep snow during the winter. Mount Lemmon, in the Santa Catalinas near Tucson, has downhill ski runs. Astonishing varieties of birds, animals, and plants find niches in southern Arizona's varied topography. Some species, such as the whiskered senita cactus and the colorful trogon bird,

have migrated north from Mexico and are rarely seen elsewhere in the United States. The combination of clear, dry air and the many mountain ranges provides excellent observing conditions for astronomers. It's said that more of them live within a 50-mile radius of Tucson than in all the rest of the world!

Tumacacori National Historic Park

© BILL WEIR

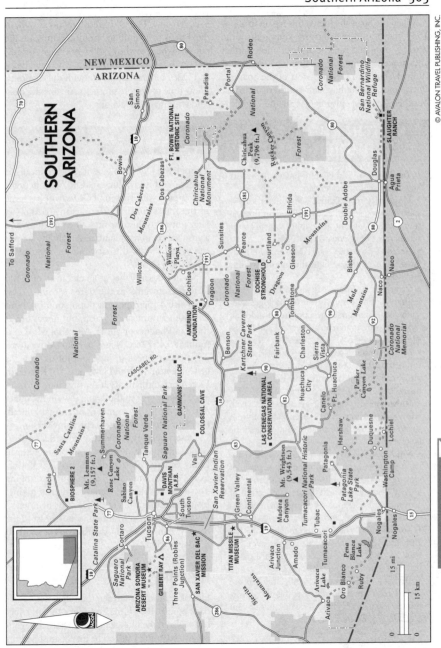

© AVALON TRAVEL PUBLISHING, INC.

SOUTHERN ARIZONA

When the Spanish entered this region in about 1539, they found several tribes, among them the warlike, nomadic Apache and the more settled and peaceful Tohono O'odham (Papago) and Akimel O'odham (Pima). Most of the Spanish, Pima, and Apache have left southern Arizona, but their legacy of culture, place names, and leg- ends remains. The Old West lives on as well, in the dozens of abandoned mining camps, on the ranches where cowboys still work huge spreads, and on the streets of Tombstone where the Earps and Doc Holliday shot it out with the Clantons. Allow time to explore southern Arizona. It's a big land with many attractions.

SOUTHERN ARIZONA HIGHLIGHTS

- **Tucson:** The "Old Pueblo" has a long history and a lively cultural calendar.
- **University of Arizona:** Museums, theaters, sports venues, and an energetic student popula- tion create a vibrant atmosphere at this large school just east of downtown Tucson.
- **Arizona-Sonora Desert Museum:** Highly rated zoo exhibits spotlight the region's wildlife and flora.
- **Pima Air & Space Museum:** Civilian and military aircraft display great technological ad- vances at the nation's largest privately funded air museum; you can tour an authentic Titan II mis- sile site, too.
- **Mt. Lemmon:** A scenic drive winds to near the top of this 9,157-foot peak past views, picnic areas, campgrounds, trails, and the southern- most ski area in the United States.
- **Biosphere 2:** The giant greenhouses, which you're welcome to visit, have been sealed off from the rest of the world to create a unique scientific laboratory.
- **San Xavier del Bac:** This well-preserved Span- ish mission continues to be an active place of worship for the Tohono O'odham Indians.
- **Kitt Peak:** The world's largest collection of astronomical telescopes is complemented by a visitor center, tours, and panoramic views.
- **Tombstone:** "The town too tough to die" has authentic 1880s' Old West atmosphere; you can stroll into the OK Corral, saloons, an 1881 dance hall, and other reminders of the past.
- **Bisbee:** Elegant early 1900's architecture tucked into narrow canyons gives this old copper- mining town lots of character; you can ride into an underground mine, too.

Tucson

Though the Old Pueblo, as it's known locally, is modern and lively, Tucson's Old West heritage will surprise you. Tucson (TOO-sawn) has some of the finest cultural offerings in Arizona—a large university, historic sites, fine museums, and a great variety of restaurants and nightlife. Yet you can actually walk this city and see most of its downtown sights.

Set in a desert valley at an elevation of 2,400 feet, Tucson ranks as the state's second-largest city, with a metropolitan population of about 840,000. Summers are warm, but not as hot as those in Phoenix or Yuma. And cool Mt. Lem- mon, at 9,157 feet, is just an hour's drive away. Temperatures peak in June and July with highs generally near 98°F and lows near 70° F. Even in December and January it's spring-like, with av- erage highs in the mid-60s and lows in the upper 30s. Of the 11 or so inches of annual rainfall, over half falls in the July–Sept. rainy season.

Desert vegetation, with paloverde, cotton- wood, and mesquite trees, is surprisingly lush. Many varieties of cacti display brilliant flowers from April to late May. The mountains ringing Tucson offer splendid scenery and great hiking. In just minutes, hikers can get out of town— west to the Tucson Mountains, northeast to the Santa Catalinas, east to the Rincons or south to the Santa Ritas.

HISTORY

Hohokam Indians farmed the valley floor as far back as A.D. 100. Pima and other Indian tribes had replaced the Hohokam long before the Span- ish arrived in the 1500s. The first Spanish visitors found a Pima Indian village, Stjuk-shon (*stjuk* means "dark mountain"; *shon,* "foot of"), at the base of Sentinel Peak, the hill with the large "A" now painted on it. The Spanish adopted the name as "Tucson" when laying out the Presidio of San Agustín del Tucson in 1775.

Attacks by roving Apache made fortifications necessary, so adobe walls 12 feet high and 750 feet long enclosed the new settlement. Mexico inherited Tucson from Spain after the 1821 revolution, but little changed except the flag.

Americans Arrive

Tucson joined the United States with the Gadsden Purchase in June 1854, but 21 months of boundary-marking and bureaucratic delays passed before the arrival of American officialdom in the form of the army's First Dragoons. Although Apache continued to menace settlers and travelers, Americans began to arrive in force, and the Butterfield Overland Stagecoach soon opened service to Tucson.

To cope with the desert climate, Anglos adopted much of the food, building techniques, and other customs of the Mexicans. You'll see the results of these practices, as well as of Anglo-Mexican intermarriage, in Tucson's cultural mix.

Wars and the Wild West

Confederate cavalry under the command of Captain Sherrod Hunter captured Tucson in February 1862. Union troops led by Colonel James Carleton marched in from California two months later, clashing with the Confederates at Picacho Pass, on the Butterfield Road about 42 miles northwest of Tucson. After this battle, the most westerly significant skirmish of the Civil War, the outnumbered Confederates retreated.

The 1860s were Tucson's Wild West years. Men rarely ventured unarmed onto the dusty streets, and shootouts were frequent. Still, the town prospered, serving as the territorial capital from 1867 to 1877. By 1880, when the first train rolled in, the population had grown to over 7,000.

The Arizona Territorial University opened its doors in 1891 on land donated by a saloonkeeper and a pair of gamblers. Davis-Monthan Field

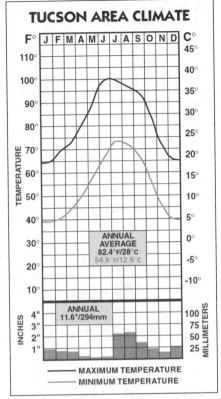

TUCSON AREA CLIMATE

ANNUAL AVERAGE
82.4°F/28°C
54.6°F/12.6°C

ANNUAL
11.6"/294mm

——— MAXIMUM TEMPERATURE
——— MINIMUM TEMPERATURE

brought Tucson into the aviation age and became an important training base during World War II. Many of the airmen and others passing through the city during those hectic years returned to settle here. With new postwar industries and the growth of tourism, the Old Pueblo has boomed ever since.

HISTORICAL WALKING TOUR
Northern Section

The historical walking tour provides a look at the Spanish, Mexican, and Anglo legacies of Tucson. Tucson Museum of Art and Historic Block is the main attraction and a convenient place to start. It doesn't open until 10 A.M. (noon on Sundays), so you may wish to visit at the end of your walk. You can park in the museum's lot west across Main Avenue (enter from Paseo Redondo), the underground lot south across Alameda St., the multilevel lot just to the east, or the large outdoor lot two blocks north along Court Avenue.

Tucson Museum of Art and Historic Block displays art of the Americas, including Precolumbian artifacts, Spanish colonial paintings and furnishings, Latin American folk art, and works by Western, modern, and contemporary artists. Special exhibitions appear 12–15 times a year. Spacious galleries of the main museum building host modern and contemporary art. Nearby on the same block, galleries in historic houses offer art and history exhibits of the West and Latin America. Docents lead tours of the collections daily; call for times. You can also join walks from October to April of the Museum Highlights, the Corbett House, or the historic block. The Plaza of the Pioneers and adjoining courtyards provide a space for fiestas, concerts, markets, or just relaxing. A large gift shop off the lobby in the main museum building sells a variety of crafts. The art library to the east of the main museum building is open Mon.–Fri. 10 A.M.–3 P.M. The Tucson Museum of Art School offers a variety of noncredit classes for children and adults on creating and appreciating art. The museum is open Mon.–Sat. 10 A.M.–4 P.M. and Sunday noon–4 P.M., except closed Monday in summer. Admission costs $5 adults, $4 seniors 60 and over, $3 students over 12, free for children 12 and under, and free entry for all on Sunday. The price includes tours and entry to the historic Fish, Stevens/Duffield, and Corbett Houses and La Casa Cordova, all of which stay open the same hours as the museum. Tucson Museum of Art is downtown at 140 N. Main Ave. and Alameda St.; 520/624-2333, www.tucsonarts.com.

In the main museum galleries, exit west across Moore Courtyard to visit the **Edward Nye Fish House,** built by a rich businessman in 1868 with 15-foot ceilings and solid adobe walls more than 2.5 feet thick. It now houses the Goodman Pavilion of Western Art; step inside to see the gallery's high-quality artwork, mostly from the Southwest. From the central Plaza of the Pioneers,

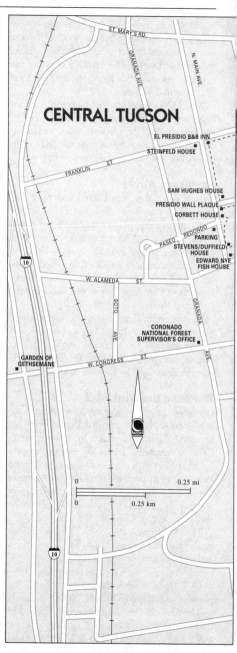

CENTRAL TUCSON

© AVALON TRAVEL PUBLISHING, INC.

W. 6TH ST.

N. MEYER AVE.
N. COURT AVE.
N. CHURCH AVE.
N. 9TH AVE.
ASH ALLEY
N. STONE AVE.
N. 7TH AVE.
TOOLE AVE.
E. 6TH ST.
BUS. 10
ARIZONA AVE.
N. 5TH AVE.
HERBERT AVE.
N. 4TH AVE.
HOFF AVE.

PIPIAN'S
ATHENS ON 4TH AVE
CARUSO'S
ANTIGONE BOOKS
FOOD CONSPIRACY CO-OP

EL CHARRO
PARKING

STORK'S NEST
COUNCIL ST.
E. 7TH ST.

ROMERO HOUSE
OLD TOWN ARTISANS, LA COCINA
LA CASA CORDOVA
YMCA (LOHSE)
E. ALAMEDA ST.
E. 8TH ST.
STEVENS AVE.
PARKING

TUCSON MUSEUM OF ART & HISTORIC BLOCK
PIMA COUNTY COURTHOUSE
PUBLIC LIBRARY
E. 9TH ST.

PARKING
E. PENNINGTON ST.
AMTRAK

ALLANDE FOOTBRIDGE
EL PRESIDIO PARK
TRANSIT CENTER
E. 10TH ST.
CONGRESS HOTEL

GARCÉS FOOTBRIDGE
E. CONGRESS ST.
BANK ONE
GREYHOUND BUS

VEINTE DE AGOSTO PARK
BROADWAY BLVD.

LA PLACITA VILLAGE
TUCSON VISITORS CENER
EL CENTRO CULTURAL DE LAS AMERICAS
POST OFFICE BRANCH

JACKSON ST.
BUS. 10

MUSIC HALL
TUCSON HISTORIC WALKING TOUR
OCHOA ST.
E. 12TH ST.

LEO RICH THEATRE
ST. AUGUSTINE CATHEDRAL
AVE.

SOZA-CARRILLO-FREMONT HOUSE MUSEUM
TUCSON CHILDREN'S MUSEUM
CORRAL ST.
E. 13TH ST.

ARENA
McCORMICK
TEMPLE OF MUSIC AND ART

TUCSON CONVENTION CENTER
TUCSON POLICE DEPARTMENT
E. 14TH ST.

CUSHING
MONTIJO HOUSE
CUSHING STREET BAR & RESTAURANT

EL TIRADITO
AMERICA WEST GALLERY
E. 15TH ST.

TEATRO CARMEN
MEXICAN TORTILLA FACTORY
SIMPSON

S. CHURCH AVE.
S. STONE AVE.
S. SCOTT AVE.
S. 6TH AVE.
S. 5TH AVE.
S. 4TH AVE.

SOUTHERN ARIZONA

walk west to enter the **Stevens/Duffield House,** part of which dates from 1856. Hiram Sanford Stevens was a good friend of Edward Fish, and much of Tucson's social life centered on their houses. The Stevens/Duffield House contains the Palice Pavilion/Art of the Americas Galleries, which displays Precolumbian, Spanish Colonial, and folk art. Café à la C'Art serves creative sandwiches and salads here for lunch Mon.–Friday.

You can walk around to the street side of the Stevens/Duffield House and continue north to the **Corbett House** next door. This restored Mission Revival bungalow represents a middle-class house of the early 1900s. J. Knox Corbett came to Arizona to recover from tuberculosis in 1880 and built this house in 1906–1907. He was a successful businessman and served 23 years as the Tucson Postmaster. Come inside to see the beautiful Arts and Crafts furnishings on a self-guided tour.

Head east across the Plaza of the Pioneers to see **La Casa Cordova,** built of adobe and one of the oldest houses in the area, dating from about 1848. Interior rooms have been restored to reflect life in the 1800s; historic exhibits relate the story of the Tucson presidio. From November to March you can enjoy *El Nacimiento*—more than 400 hand-painted terra cotta figurines that form a tableau illustrating biblical scenes and traditional Mexican life. The **Romero House** north of La Casa Cordova was built in the 1860s and modified many times. It's now used by the Tucson Museum of Art School.

You may wish to detour east across Meyer Avenue to visit the arts and crafts shops of **Old Town Artisans,** worth a look even if you're not buying. The shops display colorful sculptures, paintings, prints, and crafts in Western, Indian, and Mexican styles. Old Town Artisans is open Mon.–Sat. 9:30 A.M. (10:30 A.M. in summer)–5:30 P.M. and Sunday noon–5 P.M.; 520/623-6024, 800/782-8072, www.oldtownartisans.com. **Saguaro Artisans** offers more handicrafts north across Washington Street. Both places date from the 1800s and have adobe walls and saguaro-rib ceilings. **La Cocina Restaurant,**

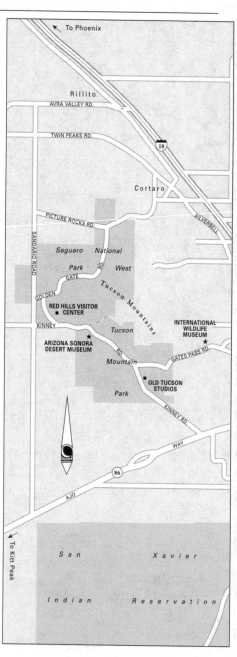

To Biosphere 2 and Florence

Catalina
State
Park

TUCSON VALLEY

Mt. Lemmon
(9,157 ft.)

Summerhaven

Rose Canyon
Lake

Santa Catalina Mountains

MOORE   RD.
TANGERINE   RD.
NARANJA   RD.
MESA VERDE
LA CHOLLA BLVD.
LA CANADA

77

TOHONO
CHUL PARK

INA   RD.
ORANGE GROVE RD.
ORACLE
1ST AVE.
SKYLINE   DR.
SUNRISE DR.

DEGRAZIA GALLERY
IN THE SUN

Sabino Canyon
Bear Canyon

SABINO CANYON
VISITOR CENTER

CATALINA HWY.

SKY ISLAND
SCENIC BYWAY

RIVER   RD.
ROGER RD.
SWAN
CRAYCROFT

H.H. FRANKLIN
FOUNDATION MUSEUM

FORT LOWELL RD.

FORT LOWELL
MUSEUM

77

GRANT

CAMPBELL
COUNTRY CLUB
ALVERNON WAY
RD.
RD.
WILMOT
KOLB

TANQUE VERDE RD.

TANQUE VERDE
GUEST RANCH

BUREAU OF
LAND MANAGEMENT

TUCSON BOTANICAL
GARDENS

UNIVERSITY OF
ARIZONA

SPEEDWAY   BLVD.

BROADWAY   BLVD.

HARRISON

FREEMAN

Saguaro   National

'A' Mountain

DOWNTOWN

KING HWY.
PARK AVE.
AVE.

TUCSON

REID PARK
ZOO

22ND

OLD   ST.
SPANISH

TRAIL

Park

MISSION RD.

BUS.
10

BUS.
19

PALO   VERDE   RD.

Davis

Monthan

GOLF LINKS

ESCALANTE

IRVINGTON   RD.

MAIN GATE

SAGUARO NATIONAL
PARK VISITOR CENTER

East

Rincon
Mountains

VALENCIA RD.

CASINO
OF THE
SUN

DESERT
DIAMOND
CASINO

MISSION SAN XAVIER
DEL BAC

NOGALES AVE.

ALVERNON
LOS   WAY

TERMINAL

TUCSON
INTERNATIONAL
AIRPORT

HUGHES ACCESS RD.

PIMA AIR &
SPACE
MUSEUM

REALES RD.

WILMOT RD.
KOLB   RD.

A.F.B.

HOUGHTON   RD.

VALENCIA   RD.

OLD   SPANISH   TRAIL

19

10

To Nogales

0   5 mi
0   5 km

To Tombstone and
Bisbee

To Colossal Cave
and I-10

© AVALON TRAVEL PUBLISHING, INC.

SOUTHERN ARIZONA

St. Augustine Cathedral

Built between 1889 and 1896, the **Julius Kruttschnitt House** blends the Mexican style of adobe construction and a *zaguan* (a central hall connecting the entrance on the street side with a patio in back) with an Anglo-American verandah and landscaped yards. It's now the El Presidio Bed & Breakfast Inn; see Accommodations below.

If you walk two blocks east to Court Avenue, you'll find the house built by French stonemason Jules le Flein, now **El Charro Café.** Le Flein came to Tucson in the late 1800s to remodel the St. Augustine Cathedral. In 1900 he built this house for his family, using volcanic stone from Sentinel Peak. His daughter, Monica, founded the Mexican restaurant in 1922.

One block south is the **Stork's Nest,** so called because it served as Tucson's first maternity ward. It was first recorded after the fire of 1883 as an adobe dwelling with attached ramada. The building houses the **Southwest Parks and Monuments Association** office.

Turning left on Alameda and south on Church, you come to **Pima County Courthouse,** a colorful building constructed in 1928 in a mix of Southwest, Spanish, and Moorish architectural styles. A small exhibit in the Assessor/Treasurer office (turn left from the courtyard) contains adobe bricks from the original presidio wall.

in Old Town Artisans, serves mesquite-grilled meats, fish, and vegetables, along with soups, salads, and sandwiches—on the patio or indoors. It's open daily for lunch; 520/622-0351.

Follow Washington St. west to the corner with Main Avenue, where a sign marks the site of the original presidio wall's northwest corner. Across Washington is the **Sam Hughes House,** now a series of garden apartments. Hughes came to Tucson for his health in 1858 and became an important businessman and developer in early Tucson. He moved into this house with his bride in 1864, expanding it considerably over the years to accommodate their 15 children. Hughes and his wife lived to celebrate their 50th wedding anniversary here.

The **Steinfeld House** is a California Mission Revival brick-and-stucco house dating from 1900, and is known as the site of one of Tucson's first bathtubs with piped-in water. The mansion has been restored for use as offices.

Southern Section

Strolling two blocks south on Church Avenue, you'll reach the small **Veinte de Agosto Park,** dominated by an equestrian statue of Gen. Francisco "Pancho" Villa, the Mexican revolutionary. Originally part of the Plaza de la Mesilla, the park's name now commemorates the founding date of the Tucson presidio on August 20, 1775. Architecture enthusiasts may enjoy a side trip one block east on Congress to see Tucson's first skyscraper, an attractive 10-story tower of brick and stone with a handsome lobby. The structure now houses Bank One.

For a break or to obtain tourist information, you can turn into of **La Placita Village** across Broadway Boulevard. Signs point the way between the brightly colored buildings to the Tucson Visitors Center, where you'll also find cafés

© BILL WEIR

SOUTHERN ARIZONA

and the Pima County Sports Hall of Fame facing a little park.

Head east on Broadway Boulevard for the **Charles O. Brown House,** now occupied by El Centro Cultural de Las Americas. Brown owned the Congress Hall Saloon, a popular watering hole and gambling spot for politicians of the day. The oldest part of the house, on Jackson St., dates from about 1858. Between 1868 and 1888 Brown built on Broadway (then Camp St.) and connected the two sections with an attractive patio and garden.

Continuing around the corner and two blocks south on Stone Avenue, you come to **St. Augustine Cathedral,** constructed in 1896. Its impressive sandstone facade, fashioned after the Cathedral of Querétaro in Mexico, was added in the late 1920s, as were the stained-glass windows. A bronze statue of St. Augustine stands watch above the doorway. Southwestern symbols mix with traditional elements on the facade.

The **Tucson Police Department,** in a large concrete building two blocks south on Stone Avenue, has police-related exhibits in its lobby; highlights include a collection of antique law-enforcement equipment and a submachine gun once owned by "public enemy number one," John Dillinger.

Turn right on Cushing Street to **Montijo House,** which preserves the name of the well-known Mexican ranching family that once owned it. The house was completed during the Civil War, then remodeled in the 1890s in an ornate Victorian style.

The **Cushing Street Bar & Grill** features an attractive 1880s' decor with beautiful wood furnishings. Joseph Ferrin lived here and operated a general store about 100 years ago. Next door around the corner is **America West Gallery,** home in the 1860s to rancher Francisco Carrillo. The well-preserved house contains exotic antiques and primitive art gathered from many countries. The patio features a collection of Mexican millstones. The gallery is usually open Mon.–Fri. 10 A.M.–4 P.M.; 520/623-4091. **Teatro Carmen** across the street hosted many Spanish-language productions after its opening in 1915. Around the corner on Main Avenue is a traditional **Mexican flour tortilla factory;** pick up fresh tortillas or just watch them being made, but you'll have to be early as workers finish by late morning; closed Sunday.

El Tiradito, or Wishing Shrine, commemorates a tragic love triangle. The story has many versions, but one account tells of a love affair between young Juan Olivera and his mother-in-law. Juan was caught and killed by his father-in-law on this spot in 1880. Because of his sins, the dead Juan could not be laid in consecrated ground, and so he was buried where he fell. The pious lit candles and prayed for his soul at the site. Later, parents came to pray for their errant daughters. The custom then developed that anyone could light a candle on the grave and make any kind of wish. If the candle burns to its base, the wish will be granted. The shrine is said to be the only one in North America dedicated to a sinner.

Follow the sidewalk around the Exhibit Hall and Arena of the Tucson Convention Center to the **Sosa-Carrillo-Fremont House Museum.** The adobe building, constructed in about 1880 by the Carrillo family on land purchased from the Sosas, was saved in 1969 when surrounding houses were torn down. The old structure takes its name from the fifth territorial governor, John C. Fremont, who rented it in 1881. Inside the restored rooms, you can imagine the life of a wealthy Tucson family in the 1880s. A self-guided tour explains the architectural features of the house. Five different types of ceiling were used: saguaro rib, ocotillo, cane, painted cloth (looks like plaster), and redwood. Short videos on Arizona history are shown on request. A gift shop sells history books. Staff lead two-hour guided tours of El Presidio Historic District on Saturday mornings, Nov.–March; $5; call for reservations and times. The museum is at 151 S. Granada Ave. between the Music Hall and Arena in the Tucson Convention Center; 520/622-0956. Open Wed.–Sat. 10 A.M.–4 P.M.; free admission. You can park in front; free for museum visitors.

As you leave the Fremont House, turn right and walk up the steps alongside the **Music Hall** into an oasis of gardens, trees, and fountains. The small building ahead to the east is the **Leo Rich Theatre.** Turn left and walk through **La**

Placita Village Continue on to the Garcés Footbridge across Congress St., then the Allande Footbridge across Pennington St. to El Presidio Park. These modern bridges honor early Spaniards. Francisco Garcés, an explorer and Franciscan priest, was the first missionary to visit the Pima Indian village at the base of Sentinel Peak. Pedro Allande, first resident commander of the Tucson presidio, once led a spirited defense against 600 warring Apache. Despite a severe leg wound, he continued to direct his 20 presidial soldiers, eventually saving the settlement.

El Presidio Park was known as Plaza de las Armas in the original presidio. Soldiers drilled and held holiday fiestas on this spot 200 years ago. The soldiers have gone, but residents still enjoy fiestas. The park offers a quiet spot to rest and enjoy the sculptures and fountains. The Tucson Museum of Art and Historic Block is just a short walk away and marks the end of your journey.

SIGHTS BETWEEN DOWNTOWN AND THE UNIVERSITY OF ARIZONA

Tucson Children's Museum

Full of things to do, this museum has been designed especially for kids ages 2–11 (who must be with an adult). Children have fun exploring the world, conducting scientific experiments, learning about different careers, discovering new cultures, and getting behind the wheel of a real fire truck. Wee World offers a play area for the 5 and under set. A gift shop sells souvenirs. Special activities take place on weekends and you can rent a room for a birthday party.

The museum is in the historic 1901 Carnegie Library building at 200 S. Sixth Ave., between 12th and 13th Sts.; 520/792-9985, www .azstarnet.com/~tuchimu. Open Tues.–Sat 10 A.M.–5 P.M., and Sunday noon–5 P.M.; closed Monday (except some holidays). Admission costs $3.50 children 2–16, $5.50 adults, and $4.50 seniors.

Fourth Avenue

The Bohemian heart of Tucson lies along this street located between downtown and the university. Ethnic cafés, restaurants, galleries, and thrift shops line both sides from University Boulevard south to 9th Street. Old Pueblo Trolley runs antique electric streetcars along 4th Avenue and University Boulevard on Fri. evenings, Sat. afternoons and evenings, and Sun. afternoons; 520/792-1802, www.oldpueblotrolley.org. You can learn more about 4th Avenue, its March and Dec. street fairs, and other activities by calling 520/624-5004, www.avefun.com.

The Postal History Foundation

An ornate 100-year-old postal counter from Naco, Arizona, and rotating exhibits greet you upon entering the little museum here. A philatelic center sells a large variety of current stamps—and you probably won't have to wait in line! Stamp enthusiasts can delve into the large research library. The foundation actively promotes postal research and education. It's just west of the university at 920 N. 1st Ave.; 520/623-6652, www.azstar net.com/~phf/phf.htm. Open Mon.–Fri. 8 A.M.–3 P.M. Admission is free (donations welcome); free parking is available in back.

Arizona Historical Society Museum

Wonderful exhibits take you through Arizona's times of Spanish, Mexican, Mountain Men, Territorial, and Early Statehood. Period rooms, artifacts, and photos bring history to life. Temporary exhibits and special programs interpret aspects of the past. Visitors of all ages enjoy the early 1900s copper mine exhibit, where you can walk through a realistic mine complete with sound effects, emerging at a giant stamp mill and other processing machinery. Brightly colored minerals on display reveal the state's underground wealth and beauty. A gift shop provides a good selection of books and crafts. The Arizona Historical Society's research library is open to the public.

The museum is at 949 E. 2nd St. and Park Ave., just west of the University of Arizona; 520/628-5774, http://w3.Arizona.edu/~azhist. Hours are Mon.–Sat. 10 A.M.–4 P.M. and Sunday noon–4 P.M. (the library closes at 1 P.M. on Saturday and is closed all day Sunday). Admission is free but donations are welcome. You can park for free at the Arizona Historical Society spaces in the parking garage one block west on 2nd St.; pick up a parking pass at the museum information desk.

UNIVERSITY OF ARIZONA

In 1885, the 13th Territorial Legislature awarded Tucson $25,000 to establish Arizona's first university. Most townspeople didn't think much of the idea; they wanted the territorial capital, awarded to Prescott, or at least the territorial insane asylum, awarded to Phoenix. It was left to a handful of determined citizens to get the school built. The walls went up after a saloonkeeper and two gamblers donated the land, but money ran out before the roof was finished. A federal loan completed the structure, and the university opened in 1891. The one building, today known as Old Main, contained the classrooms, library, offices, and dorms.

Six faculty taught 32 students the first year, nearly all in the Preparatory School. Like many other states at the time, Arizona suffered from a lack of secondary schools. The university has since expanded to 34,000 students with a faculty and staff of about 12,000. Fourteen colleges and eight schools offer 131 undergraduate, 138 masters, and 95 doctoral degree programs.

Visitors can enjoy theater and concert performances, the Flandrau Planetarium, sporting events, and several museums. The university's website (www.arizona.edu) offers a great deal of information on these and other aspects of the school. FM radio stations offer public-radio programs with classical music (KUAT 90.5) and jazz (KUAZ 89.1).

The campus lies about a mile east of downtown; 520/621-2211 (switchboard). Parking is tight; look for metered street spaces or signs directing you to visitor lots. Free shuttle buses make loops around campus on weekdays, and Sun Tran offers good bus connections to other parts of Tucson.

Visitor Center and Tours

The campus visitor center, 520/621-5130, is on the east side of campus close to Flandrau Plane-

tarium, the Main Library, and stadiums; turn in one block on University from Campbell. It may move in 2002, however, so calling ahead or checking the website www.arizona.edu would be a good idea. Open Mon.–Fri. 8 A.M.–5 P.M. (to 4 P.M. in summer), the center offers free literature, listings of U of A events, video programs, a few exhibits, an Internet terminal, and maps. You can purchase a one-day parking permit at the center or use metered spaces nearby.

The **Visitor Information Program** offers 90-minute walking tours that leaves from the visitor center on Thursday and Saturday at 9:30 A.M., Sept.–May; 520/621-5130; reservations required. Prospective students and parents will be interested in the 60- to 90-minute **campus walking tours** that leave from the Nugent Building; call 520/621-3641 for information.

Arizona State Museum

This is a great place to learn about archaeology and Arizona's Native American peoples. Founded in 1893, the museum houses an extensive collection of artifacts from prehistoric, historic, and contemporary tribes. The exceptional *Paths of Life: American Indians of the Southwest* exhibit explores the cultural traditions and current lifestyles of 10 Indian peoples of Arizona and northern Mexico. Changing exhibits appear too. A gift shop sells books and a good selection of Indian crafts. To learn more, you can head upstairs to the museum's library of books on archaeology and anthropology. In February, the museum hosts the Southwest Indian Art Fair with demonstrations, dancing, storytelling, and traditional foods. It's on campus at the corner of E. University Blvd. and N. Park Ave.; 520/621-6302, www.statemuseum.arizona.edu. Hours are Mon.–Sat. 10 A.M.–5 P.M. and Sunday noon–5 P.M., closed major holidays; admission is free.

Museum of Art

The diverse collection here spans the years from the Renaissance to the present. Changing exhibitions come from the university and other institutions. A small gift shop sells books, magazines, posters, and cards.

The museum is open during the school year, Mon.–Fri. 9 A.M.–5 P.M. and Sunday noon–4 P.M.; hours in summer (mid-May to mid-August) are Mon.–Fri. 10 A.M.–3:30 P.M. and Sunday noon–4 P.M., 520/621-7567, artmuseum.arizona.edu. Admission is free. You can park in the Park Avenue Garage, north of Speedway Boulevard, and use the pedestrian underpass.

Center for Creative Photography

Drop in to view exhibitions of photographs by Richard Avedon, Ansel Adams, Paul Strand, and other famous artists. The center holds some 60,000 prints by more than 2,000 photographers plus an archive of manuscripts, photography materials, and artifacts. With prior notice, you can arrange to see original works of your choice in the PrintViewing Room. Binders at the center and the center's Internet site list collections and artists. An extensive photography library lies across the lobby from the exhibition gallery. There's also a small gift shop. Staff can direct you to other photographic exhibits in town. The center is just southeast of the Museum of Art on Olive; 520/621-7968. It's open Mon.–Fri. 9 A.M.–5 P.M. and Sat.–Sun. noon–5 P.M.; donations welcome. The website www.creativephotography.org has an exhibition schedule and resources.

Student Union

This building in the center of campus is a good place to meet students and learn what's going on. You'll find cafeterias, a variety of cafés, student services, and recreation areas here. Travelers can check the ride board; photographers can pick up film at the photo shop. The first floor offers several eating establishments, an information desk (520/621-7755), and an art gallery.

In the basement, the Cellar often jumps to live music during lunch hour. Sam's Place, nearby, is packed with students playing pocket billiards, table tennis, and other games; a computer lab is on the far side. The basement also has a post office and copy center.

Cafeterias are on the first and second floors. On the second floor is the USS *Arizona* Collection, consisting of photographs, a model, and artifacts from the battleship *Arizona,* destroyed at Pearl Harbor on December 7, 1941. The Cactus Lounge lies between the second and third floors. Union Club, on the third floor, offers lunch and sweeping views of the campus and mountains. Gallagher Theatre, at the east end of the building, shows popular movies nightly. On the west end is the ASUA Bookstore, well stocked with textbooks, general reading matter, school supplies, and University of Arizona clothing; a computer store is upstairs (take the outdoor stairs).

Flandrau Science Center and Planetarium

Flandrau offers engaging science exhibits for visitors of all ages. Kids have their own projects to do. You can explore visiting shows and the permanent astronomy displays, or head downstairs to the Mineral Museum's beautiful specimens. A gift shop sells books, posters, and astronomy souvenirs.

Inside the planetarium theater, amateur stargazers can experience dynamic and entertaining programs on astronomy, Native American sky lore, and wonders of the universe. Call for show times and topics, or check the website www.flandrau.org. Theater shows cost $5 adult, $4.50 students and seniors, $4 children 3–13.

Flandrau is at North Cherry Ave. and University Blvd.; 520/621-STAR. Parking is available across E. University Boulevard; turn in from N. Campbell Avenue. Hours are Mon.–Sat. 9 A.M.–5 P.M., Sun. 1–5 P.M., and evenings Wed.–Sat. 7–9 P.M. The center's 16-inch telescope is available for free public viewing of the stars, planets, and galaxies Sept.–March, Wed.–Sat. 7–10 P.M., and April–Aug., Wed.–Sat. 8–10 P.M.

Admission to the center is included with purchase of a theater ticket; otherwise $3 adults, $2 children 3–13.

Students for the Exploration and Development of Space has a local chapter and a good website, www.seds.org.

Library

With about eight million items and access to more than 1,600 databases, the school library offers serious research possibilities. The Main Library's second floor (main entrance) has an information desk, periodicals, a reference section, computer terminals, and a copy center. The map collection is downstairs; government documents are up on the third floor. Special Collections & Southwest Folklore Center has a separate entrance in front of the Main Library. Other specialized libraries on campus include: Science-Engineering, Architecture, Center for Creative Photography, Music, and Oriental Studies.

Hours vary with seasons; call 520/621-6441 for more information. Library catalogs and hours are also available on the Internet at www.library.arizona.edu.

Wildcat Heritage Gallery

See photos of Wildcat teams and players dating from 1897 to the present at this gallery on the first and second floors of the west side of McKale Memorial Center. It's open Mon.–Fri. 8 A.M.–5 P.M. The Center's ticket office and sports shop are on the south side, where you'll also find parking on the street. In cyberspace, you can check out the Wildcats at www.arizcats.com.

The History of Pharmacy Museum

Exhibits in the College of Pharmacy Building, four blocks north of the main campus at Warren Ave. and Mabel St., 520/626-1427, trace the history of Arizona pharmaceuticals with drugstore paraphernalia, old-time cure-alls, and antique medicine bottles. Look for displays near the elevators on the first through fourth floors and off the hallway between the third-floor elevator and the Dean's Office. The building is open Mon.–Fri. 8 A.M.–5 P.M.; admission is free. You can pick up a walking-tour guide to the exhibits when you get there, or take the virtual tour at www.pharmacy.arizona.edu/museum. A visitor parking lot is at Campbell and Mabel.

WEST OF DOWNTOWN
Garden of Gethsemane

While lying wounded on a World War I battlefield, Felix Lucero made a vow to dedicate his life, if he lived, to the creation of religious statues. He lived, and kept his vow; today, his life-size sculptures of the Last Supper and other subjects can be seen at the northeast corner of W. Congress St. and Bonita Ave., just west of I-10. Open daily; free admission.

"A" Mountain

You can't miss this small peak just west of downtown. In earlier days soldiers used it as a lookout point for hostile Indians, which explains its original name, Sentinel Peak. The giant "A" dates from October 23, 1915, when the local university football team beat Pomona College by a score of 7–3; jubilant sports fans immediately headed out to paint the "A." The painting became a tradition, and every year freshmen whitewash the giant letter—and themselves—for all to see.

To enjoy the panorama from the top of the peak, drive west 0.6 mile on Congress St. to just before it ends, then turn left on Cuesta, which becomes Sentinel Peak Road. The road loops around the summit; there's a large parking area on the west side, from which the summit is a short walk up.

International Wildlife Museum

This natural history museum displays over 400 kinds of mounted mammals, birds, and insects from all over the world. Many appear in naturalistic habitat dioramas and illustrate animal behavior. Arizona creatures reveal themselves in both nocturnal and daytime settings. Elsewhere, wild sheep and goats inhabit a 30-foot mountain in an impressive exhibit. You'll see rare species such as birds of paradise from Papua New Guinea and extinct ones such as the passenger pigeon from the U.S.A. Imposing recreations of an Irish elk and a woolly mammoth show prehistoric life. The insect collection reveals dazzling butterflies.

Kids can explore touch tables, try the interactive computers, and do other projects. A theater screens full-length wildlife movies on the hour. An extensive gift shop sells crafts from the far corners of the world. The restaurant serves light meals.

The museum is at 4800 W. Gates Pass Rd., 520/617-1439 (recording), www.thewildlifemuseum.org. To get there, head west five miles on Speedway Boulevard from I-10 in Tucson. This section of road is fine for large vehicles and trailers. Museum hours are Mon.–Fri. 9 A.M.–5 P.M., Sat.–Sun. 9 A.M.–6 P.M. Admission costs $7 adults; $5.50 students 13–17, military, and seniors 62 and over; $2.50 children 6–12.

Tucson Mountain Park

The park in these rugged mountains just eight miles west of town contains over 17,000 acres, a network of interconnecting hiking trails, a couple of picnic areas, Gilbert Ray Campground, Old Tucson Studios, and the Arizona-Sonora Desert Museum. Saguaro National Park provides additional scenic backcountry just to the north. The campground and area attractions may have a map of the park. Unless you're driving a big rig, the best route in is Gates Pass Road, reached from Tucson via Speedway Boulevard; the pass has a great view and makes a fine place to watch the sunset. RVs over 25 feet or vehicles with trailers should take Ajo Way and Kinney Road.

Old Tucson Studios

The West has been won many times over at this famous movie location, which re-creates Tucson of the 1860s with weathered adobe or frontier buildings, board sidewalks, and dusty streets. The set began back in 1939 as the setting for the Columbia Pictures film *Arizona*. More than 350 movies and video projects have been filmed here since, including *Dirty Dingus Magee, Rio Lobo, Death of a Gunfighter,* and *Young Guns II.* Filmmakers have shot such well-known TV shows as *Gunsmoke* and *Little House on the Prairie* here as well.

Today, adults and kids can enjoy a wide variety of shows and rides. A miniature train chugs around Old Tucson on a narrated excursion, providing a good introduction. Arizona Theatre, near the entrance, plays movie clips of past cowboy action filmed here. Stunt people wearing period clothing stage blazing gunfights at several locations. Step into the Grand Palace Saloon for uproarious entertainment. Hear Southwestern lore in the Storytellers Theater. The Iron Door Mine, stagecoach, carousel, old-time car, and trail rides provide additional excitement. Children meet tame animals in the petting zoo. You'll find food at several eateries, a sweet shop, and an ice cream parlor. You can also bring a picnic (no alcohol). Pets on leash are welcome.

Old Tucson is 12 miles west of Tucson in Tucson Mountain Park; 520/883-0100, www.oldtucson.com. Drive west on Speedway Boulevard/Gates Pass Road (not suited for large rigs) or take Ajo Way and Kinney Road. It's open daily 10 A.M.–6 P.M. except Thanksgiving and Christmas; may close Mon. in summer. Rates with tax are $16 adults and $10 children ages 4–11; seniors and Pima County residents get a 10 percent discount. Admission includes all activities and shows except for gold panning, mine tour, arcade games, and trail rides. Special events take place occasionally. On weekend evenings in October, Old Tucson becomes a haunted town after regular park hours.

Arizona-Sonora Desert Museum

This world-famous living museum contains animals and plants native to the Sonoran Desert of Arizona, the Mexican state of Sonora, and the Gulf of California region. Mountain lions, bighorn sheep, javelinas, and over 385 other types of animals as well as 1,400 species of plants dwell in nearly natural surroundings. The setting is superb, with great views over the Avra Valley. Baboquivari Peak (7,730 feet), sacred to the O'odham Indians, and the nearer Kitt Peak (6,875 feet), site of important astronomical observatories, stand to the southwest.

Watch frolicking otters and busy beavers through underwater panels. Try to spot the birds in the walk-in aviaries—not as easy as you'd expect, as many desert birds blend in well with their surroundings. Meet rattlesnakes, Gila monsters, scorpions, and other desert dwellers face to face. The Life Underground exhibit lets you step below the surface to observe wildlife in their burrows. A realistic limestone cave and earth science exhibits take you even deeper underground and far back in time. You'll find desert flora well represented and labeled in the gardens. The Pollination Garden has areas to attract bees, butterflies, moths, and bats.

Bring a sun hat and good walking shoes; it requires a half day to see all the exhibits. Animals are more active in the morning, which is a good time to visit. Special programs, scheduled daily, introduce you to some of the creatures living here. The popular Birds in Flight program (Nov.–April) brings out raptors such as owls and hawks to demonstrate their flying and hunting skills. You'll have many opportunities to meet docents and see their presentations. Gift shops, a restaurant, and a snack bar are on the museum grounds. A picnic area lies just to the east in Tucson Mountain Park, and you'll find several more in nearby Saguaro National Monument West.

Arizona-Sonora Desert Museum is in Tucson Mountain Park, 14 miles west of Tucson; 520/883-2702 (recording). Take Speedway Boulevard west across Gates Pass. Large RVs and trailer-rigs must take Ajo Way and Kinney Road. Hours are Oct.–April, daily 8:30 A.M.–5 P.M.; and March–Sept., daily 7:30 A.M.–6 P.M. On "Summer Saturdays," the museum stays open until 10 P.M. so visitors can enjoy the evenings. Admission costs $9.95 adults, $1.75 ages 6–12. No pets permitted. The excellent website (www.desertmuseum.org) has exhibit, event, wildlife, and plant information.

Saguaro National Park West

The Tucson Mountains District of Saguaro National Park contains vigorous stands of saguaro cactus, as well as an abundance of other desert life. Stop at the **Red Hills Visitor Center** to view exhibits and a video about the Sonoran Desert; 520/733-5158, www.nps.gov/sagu. The center's gift shop/information desk sells books, maps, videos, and posters and offers hiking tips and suggestions. Special programs and nature walks are occasionally offered, most frequently Dec.–April. Visitor center hours are daily 8:30 A.M. until 5 P.M. To get here from Tucson, continue two miles past the Arizona-Sonora Desert Museum. If coming from Phoenix, take the I-10 Avra Valley Road Exit 242 and follow signs 13 miles.

The six-mile **Bajada Loop Drive** takes in some of the scenic countryside with two picnic areas and several trailheads along the way; the visitor center sells an interpretive guide to the drive. Part of the graded dirt road has a one-way section. The drive and other unpaved roads in the park close from sunset to 6 A.M.

Hikers will find many interesting trails in the park. The short, paved, and wheelchair-accessible **Cactus Garden Trail** beside the visitor center introduces the unique saguaro and other plants of the Sonoran Desert. **Javelina Wash Trail** makes a short loop behind the visitor center. **Desert Discovery Nature Trail** is an easy paved half-mile loop that's wheelchair-accessible; the trailhead is 0.9 mile northwest of the visitor center. **Valley View Overlook Trail** begins 0.2 mile past the start of the one-way section of the Bajada Loop Drive and climbs to a fine panorama; signs tell of plant and animal life; it's 0.8 mile roundtrip. Farther along the loop drive, you can take a short detour to Signal Hill picnic area, then climb the easy 0.25-mile roundtrip **Signal Hill Petroglyphs Trail.** Interpretive exhibits tell of the peoples who have come through this land.

Other trails, many interconnecting, wind through the scenic Sonoran Desert past petroglyphs, old mines, and springtime wildflowers. A map available at the visitor center shows trails, trailheads, and distances. You can reach the summit of Wasson Peak (elev. 4,687 feet), the highest in the Tucson Mountains, from several trailheads. King Canyon Trail provides the shortest way to the top in 7 miles roundtrip with an elevation gain of about 1,900 feet. It begins across Kinney Road from the Arizona-Sonora Desert Museum and goes northeast in a gradual 0.9-mile climb to Mam-a-Gah picnic area; the path steepens to a moderate grade for the next 1.4 miles to a ridge with views of the Catalinas, then switchbacks 0.9 mile to the Hugh Norris Trail, on which you turn right 0.3 mile to the summit. Coming down, you can make a loop by continuing on the Hugh Norris Trail 1.9 miles past the King Canyon Trail junction, down a set of switchbacks, and along a ridge, left one mile down the Sendero Esperanza Trail to the workings of the abandoned Gould Mine, then right 1.1 miles on the Gould Mine Trail back to the King Canyon Trailhead.

BIOSPHERE 2: THE NEXT GENERATION

Thirty miles north of Tucson, a huge glass dome looms over the Arizona desert. The impressive structure, called Biosphere 2, got its start as the brainchild of John Allen, a controversial figure labeled a visionary by some and a new-age cult leader by others. In the early 1970s, Allen and a group of like-minded souls predicted that humanity—faced with the impending destruction of the earth's environment—would be forced to colonize Mars. In order to study how this colonization might be accomplished, Allen envisioned creating a prototype colony here on earth.

His plan was to build a giant greenhouse of sorts that could be completely sealed off from the outside atmosphere. He would then recruit a volunteer crew of "colonists" to live for two years wholly within the three-acre, glass-enclosed world. This little world would resemble our larger world—Biosphere 1—with tropical rainforest, savanna, desert, farmland, marsh, ocean, and human-habitat ecosystems. Everything necessary to support life—all water, food, and air—would be recycled or produced within the walls on a completely self-sustaining basis.

In 1974, Allen recruited Texas oil billionaire Edward Bass to back the multimillion-dollar Biosphere 2 project. Construction began in 1986, and

on September 26, 1991, the first crew of four men and four women stepped through the airlock and were sealed into their new, space-age mini-world.

Well, as so often happens out here in the uncertain, uncontained world of Biosphere 1, things inside Biosphere 2 didn't proceed as planned. One crew member left the grounds briefly for minor medical treatment and returned with spare computer parts, putting a dent in the self-sustainability premise. And when mites and unusually cloudy weather inhibited their crops, the Biospherians depleted their stored food supplies. Members lost an average of 15 percent of their body weight. Declining oxygen levels added to their fatigue and forced project directors to pump in fresh gas. To top it off, the crewmembers had to spend time battling ants and cockroaches, which took time away from research and hardly boosted morale. A Biospherian later admitted that the work just to survive left little time for scientific studies. Meanwhile, the project was coming under attack from critics, who accused Biosphere 2 of being less a scientific project than the expensive material manifestation of a new-age cult.

The original Biospherians emerged from their two-year journey and were replaced shortly there-

NORTH OF DOWNTOWN

H.H. Franklin Foundation Museum

This unusual museum specializes in the Franklin, a luxury car produced from 1902 until the financial woes of the Depression ended work in 1934. Gleaming antique cars reveal the elegance and amazing engineering of a time gone by. Franklin innovations included air-cooled engines, the first auto assembly line for luxury cars, extensive use of die-cast aluminum parts to save weight and improve fuel efficiency, and one of the first starter/generators. The 20 or so Franklins on display illustrate the evolution of the auto during these years. The cars still run well and appear in regional auto shows.

The museum is at 3420 N. Vine Ave., between E. Fort Lowell and E. Prince Rds. (about

two miles north of the University of Arizona). It's open October 15 to late May; call 520/326-8038 for hours. Donations are welcome. The website www.franklincar.org/foundation.htm has photos and info on the cars.

Tohono Chul Park

The name means Desert Corner in the Tohono O'odham language. Here you can enjoy natural desert beauty in northwest Tucson. Nature trails wind through the 49-acre grounds, past about 500 plants from the Southwest and northern Mexico. Signs illustrate some of the many bird species that you may see. Javelina, desert tortoise, collared lizard, chuckwalla, ground squirrel, desert cottontail, and blacktailed jackrabbit also inhabit the park. The Ethnobotanical Garden displays plants that

© BILL WEIR

after by another group of voyagers, but the project was beginning to unravel. In 1993, all 11 members of the scientific advisory committee resigned, citing lack of progress. And by April 1994, the experiment completely succumbed to chaos. Bass was busy firing members of the board, and two of the original Biospherians, who had been thrown off the site, were later arrested and accused of participating in a raid designed to sabotage the site.

Looking past the administrative wrangling, Columbia University scientists—who had been invited to help solve the mystery of the low oxygen levels—took an interest in the research potential of the project. On January 1, 1996, Columbia University's Lamont-Doherty Earth Observatory stepped in to manage Biosphere 2 and has been doing so ever since.

More than 200 scientists and researchers have worked on the $200 million project with the hope that it will provide valuable information on how to preserve the earth's ecosystem. Current research is studying the interaction of plants, carbon dioxide, water, and pests; the relationship between coral reefs and the atmosphere; and the effect of global warming on ecosystems. No crews have been sealed inside since the first missions in 1991–1994, but the option hasn't been ruled out for the future.

native people have used for food, fiber, medicine, or dyes. The Demonstration Garden provides ideas for landscaping. The Geology Wall, in the Demonstration Garden, has rocks from more than two dozen geologic formations in the Santa Catalina Mountains; panels tell how the rocks formed. Garden for Children encourages kids to explore the natural world; gift shops sell a booklet with additional projects and games. Art and Indian craft shows in the Exhibit House change every 6–8 weeks. The Park Greenhouse has plants for sale. Two museum shops sell handcrafts, jewelry, and some books. Staff offer park, birding, and wildflower tours, lectures, and concerts; call for times. The Tea Room's indoor and outdoor areas offer a pleasant place for breakfast, lunch, and afternoon tea daily 8 A.M.–5 P.M.; 520/797-1222.

You can picnic at one of the shaded tables scattered through the park.

The park is at 7366 N. Paseo del Norte; 520/575-8468 (recording), 520/742-6455 (office), www.tohonochulpark.org. From the junction of Ina and Oracle Rds. in north Tucson, head west on Ina and turn north at the first stoplight. Park grounds are open daily 7 A.M.-sunset; the Exhibit House hours run Mon.–Sat. 9:30 A.M.–5 P.M. and Sunday 11 A.M.–5 P.M.; a $2 donation is appreciated since the park is a nonprofit foundation.

Catalina State Park

This 5,500-acre park in the western foothills of the Catalinas offers picnicking, camping, birding, hiking, and horseback riding. All the trails offer mountain views and a chance to see desert birds, other animals, and wildflowers. Staff lead guided hikes, bird walks, and wildflower walks Oct.–April. Hikers can walk easy loops within the park, explore nearby canyons, or climb all the way to the top of Mt. Lemmon. The ranger station offers free trail maps of the park area, a birdlist, and sells detailed topo maps to all the Catalinas.

The one-third-mile **Romero Ruins Interpretive Trail** climbs a low ridge and makes a loop through a Hohokam village site and the ruins of Francisco Romero's mid-19th-century ranch. The one-mile **Nature Trail** loop has interpretive signs about desert life. **Birding Trail** offers good opportunities for sightings on its one-mile loop. These first three loops are open to foot travel only, but the 2.3-mile **Canyon Loop Trail** is open to hikers, cyclists, and equestrians.

Romero Canyon Trail and **Sutherland Trail** head east deep into the Catalinas. The trails narrow and steepen where they leave the state park and enter Pusch Ridge Wilderness and a Bighorn Sheep Management Area. At this point, cyclists and dogs—both prohibited in the Wilderness—have to turn back. The trails also become too rough for most equestrians. Natural pools along the lower part of the popular Romero Canyon Trail make good day-hike destinations; in spring, the creeks in Montrose and Romero Canyons will be running and have small waterfalls. Montrose Pools lie a short, steep descent off Romero Canyon Trail just 1.1 miles up. Romero Pools, 2.8 miles one-way with a 900-foot elevation gain, can be deep enough for swimming. The Romero Canyon and Sutherland Trails meet the Mt. Lemmon Trail that leads to the summit (14 strenuous miles one-way) and other destinations. Sabino Canyon is about 17 strenuous miles away via Romero Canyon Trail and the 6,000-foot Romero Pass.

Equestrians especially like the **Fifty-Year Trail,** though hikers and mountain bikers enjoy it, too; the six-mile (one-way) trail heads northeast from the Equestrian Center across rolling foothills to connect with Sutherland and other National Forest trails. Experienced mountain bikers can do a challenging loop of about nine miles on Fifty-Year, a trail link, and Sutherland Trail.

Catalina State Park is 14 miles north of downtown Tucson off Oracle Road (AZ 77); 520/628-5798. Admission costs $5/vehicle for day use, $10/vehicle camping no hookups, or $15/vehicle at sites with electric and water hookups. Facilities include showers and a dump station. The campground fills nearly every day Jan.–April. Sites are allocated on a first-come, first-served basis, so arrive early in the day for the best chance of snagging one. Groups can reserve their own areas. Your horse is welcome to stay at the Equestrian Center, in which case you would camp here. Special events include a March open house at Romero Ruins site, Easter sunrise service, and a Solar Expo and Potluck in May.

Biosphere 2 Center

You're welcome to take a peek into this unusual scientific compound, 30 miles north of Tucson, and to witness its strides toward understanding Biosphere 1—our planet Earth.

Begin in the visitor center, where you'll hear an introductory talk and view a short film about research at Biosphere 2. You'll learn that it's the world's largest greenhouse, up to 91 feet high and enclosing 3.15 acres. A detailed model shows the interior chambers and equipment rooms that keep this little world running.

The well-marked tour route can also be followed on your own—you can freely join and leave the groups. You'll walk past the original quarantine rooms to the test module, Biosphere 2's prototype and first sealed system. Next, you walk through the Demonstration Laboratories, a series of greenhouses. This smaller-scale version of Biosphere 2 has tropical, temperate, desert, and garden areas; some animals can be seen here, too.

Finally, you get to investigate the amazing structure of Biosphere 2 itself, which is sealed in with triple-pane glass, a pair of air-chamber "lungs," and a stainless steel underpan. You'll see some of the living and working quarters of the Biospherians—the well-equipped kitchen, dining room, an apartment, and computer center.

Technicians still man the computers, keeping the life-support system operating for the more than 3,000 species of plants and animals inhabiting the intensive agriculture bay and the five "biomes" (self-sustaining communities of living organisms). Those represented here are tropical rainforest (the largest and highest section), desert, savanna, marsh, and ocean. The old animal bay and some former recreation and work areas now contain photo exhibits and interactive computers; here you can discover the facts and mysteries of the Earth's climate and how we're finding ways to counteract global warming and air pollution. You'll also learn about current experiments.

Visitors may walk through one glassed-in chamber—the orchard—of Biosphere 2, peer in at the different biomes from the outside, and enter an underwater viewing gallery to see the tropical fish and corals inhabiting the one-million-gallon "ocean." After the tour, you can drop in the Biosphere Theater, across from the Demonstration Laboratories, to see a program about the Center's work.

Allow at least two hours for the walking tour, which is a mile-and-a-half long and wheelchair accessible. Much of the route is outdoors, so bring a hat and sunscreen; also be prepared for winter cold at the 4,000-foot elevation.

If you'd like to see the inner workings of Biosphere 2, sign up for an **Under the Glass** tour. Your guide takes you through an airlock into the basement filled with pipes and machinery that create the climates of the biomes. You then follow a narrow passageway into one of the giant "lungs." This tour lasts about 45 minutes and involves walking on wet pavement; it's not suitable for small children or wheelchairs. There's an extra $10/person charge.

Other visitor facilities include gift shops at several locations; the Lion's Den Café with snacks near the Demonstration Laboratories; the Cañada del Oro Restaurant, serving American food daily for continental breakfast, lunch, and dinner; and the **Biosphere Hotel and Conference Center,** offering comfortable accommodations with great views for $129 d Dec.–April, $79 d May–Aug., and $99 Sept.–November. The hotel also offers package deals including room, breakfast, dinner, and Biosphere 2 Center admission.

Biosphere 2 Center, 520/896-6200 (local), 520/825-1289 (Tucson), or 800/828-2462, is

about a 45-minute drive from Tucson or a two-hour drive from Phoenix. From Tucson, head north 25 miles on Oracle Road/AZ 79 to Oracle Junction, turn northeast 5.5 miles on AZ 77 to the sign, then go south 2.7 miles to visitor parking. The best route from the Phoenix area is via Florence and AZ 79 to Oracle Junction. Alternatively, you can take I-10 to the Ina Road Exit, go east on Ina Road to Oracle Road/AZ 79, then north to Oracle Junction.

Hours are daily 9 A.M.–5 P.M.; call or check the Web for tour times. Admission is $12.95 adults, $11.50 college students and seniors 62 and over, $8.95 youth 13–17, and $6 ages 6–12. The project's website (www.bio2.edu) features a cybertour and contains information on the Center's education, research, and visitor facilities.

Oracle

This small town lies at an elevation of 4,514 feet in the northern foothills of the Catalinas, 37 miles from Tucson. American Drive, the main road through Oracle, makes a loop off AZ 77.

Acadia Ranch Museum has some historic exhibits and a reading room in an 1880 adobe ranch house that later expanded to become a boardinghouse, then a sanitarium. It's on Mt. Lemmon Road near American Ave. in the town center; 520/896-9609. Open Saturday 1–5 P.M. (except major holidays) and by appointment.

Residents celebrate **Oracle Oaks Festival** in April with a parade, car show, dance, and carnival. Oracle also has a couple of places to stay, restaurants, and a library. To get to Peppersauce Campground in the Coronado National Forest, turn off on Mt. Lemmon Road.

Oracle State Park, Center for Environmental Education

Birders and other nature lovers enjoy a visit to this park, 520/896-2425, which occupies nearly 4,000 acres of rolling hills wooded in oaks. Facilities are day-use only and include picnic tables, interpretive walks, and more than 10 miles of trails. Longer trails, including a section of the Arizona Trail, head off into the Coronado National Forest. You can also reach the Arizona Trail from trailheads off American

Avenue just south from AZ 77 and off the Mt. Lemmon Road.

Call for the tour schedule of the Kannally Ranch House, a late 1920s Italian Revival adobe. From Tucson or Phoenix, drive to Oracle Junction, then follow AZ 77 northeast for nine miles, turn right two miles on the road to Oracle's business district, turn right one mile on Mt. Lemmon Hwy., then left into the park entrance. Open daily, $4/vehicle, $1/person for nonmotorized travel.

NORTHEAST OF DOWNTOWN

Tucson Botanical Gardens

You'll enjoy a visit here for the wide variety of beautiful flora, both native and exotic. Places to explore include an herb garden, a tropical greenhouse, a cactus and succulent garden, a low-moisture (xeriscape) demonstration garden, a Native American crops garden, butterfly garden, typical Mexican-American barrio garden, and an iris garden. A Sensory Garden invites you to smell, touch, listen, look, or just be curious. There's a picnic area too. You can attend classes, workshops, tours (except in summer), and a variety of special events. For schedule information, call 520/326-9255 (recording) or 520/326-9686, or check the website at www.tucsonbotanical.org.

The gardens are about six miles northeast of downtown at 2150 N. Alvernon Way, just south of Grant Road. The garden and gift shop are open daily 8:30 A.M.–4:30 P.M. Admission is $4 adults, $3 seniors 62 and older, $1 children 6–11. The research library is open Monday, Wednesday, and Friday 2–4:30 P.M. A nursery sells plants Fri.–Sun. 10 A.M.–4 P.M.

Fort Lowell Museum

U.S. Army troops chasing troublesome Apache in the 1860s needed a base. So they built Camp Lowell on the outskirts of Tucson in 1866 and named it in honor of an officer killed in the Civil War. The camp moved to its present site in 1873 and became a fort in 1879. Patrolling, guarding, and offensive operations kept it a busy place during the Geronimo campaigns, which ended with the famous Apache leader's surrender in

September 1886. With the Indian wars finally over, the army abandoned the fort in 1891.

The commanding officer's quarters and nearby kitchen building have been reconstructed as a museum. Inside the quarters you'll find a period room, a model, equipment used by the army, and many photos with the stories of officers, enlisted men, wives, children, and Apache scouts. The kitchen has some excavated artifacts and exhibits about life of the enlisted men. The adobe house visible across the street is an original officer's quarters. Martha Summerhayes stayed here in 1886 with her husband, a regimental quartermaster, and later wrote of her experiences in *Vanished Arizona* (see Suggested Reading). Currently the house is a private residence and closed to the public. Signs with maps lead around the park to an equestrian statue and ruins of the adobe hospital and other buildings. In early February, **La Reunión de El Fuerte** presents cavalry drills, music, and self-guided tours to historic sites in Fort Lowell Park and the surrounding community, including places not normally open to the public. The museum, 2900 N. Craycroft Rd., 520/885-3832, is in Fort Lowell Park just south of the Fort Lowell Road junction (about eight miles northeast of downtown). It's open Wed.–Sat. 10 A.M.–4 P.M. with free admission, but donations are welcome. The city park also has picnicking, reservable ramadas (520/791-4873), a playground, pool, and ball fields.

De Grazia Gallery in the Sun

A work of art in itself, the adobe gallery blends into the desert. You enter through a gate patterned after the one at Yuma Territorial Prison, then pass through a short mine tunnel.

Ettore "Ted" De Grazia, born in the Arizona mining district of Morenci, became fascinated at an early age by the desert colors and cultures of the Southwest. In a short video, he narrates the story of his life and work. He earned fame for his paintings, but created ceramics, sculpture, and jewelry and wrote books as well. Since his death in 1982, the gallery has continued as a museum. The many exhibit rooms illustrate his varied interests, themes, and techniques. A gift shop sells his prints, sculpture, and books.

De Grazia built Mission in the Sun, the adobe chapel outside to the west, as his first project on this site in the early 1950s. He dedicated it to Our Lady of Guadalupe, patron saint of Mexico. You can step inside to see the murals and seating illuminated by the open sky. Local artists display work nearby in the Little Gallery, open Nov.–April.

Gallery in the Sun is at 6300 N. Swan Rd., 520/299-9191, 800/545-2185. From downtown, head east four miles on Broadway to Swan Rd,, then turn north six miles; the gallery is just before Skyline Drive. It's open daily 10 A.M.–4 P.M.; free admission.

SANTA CATALINA MOUNTAINS

The Santa Catalinas, crowned by 9,157-foot Mt. Lemmon, rise in ragged ridges from the north edge of Tucson to cool forests atop the higher slopes. A paved road, the Catalina Highway/Sky Island Scenic Byway, winds high into the mountains past many vistas and recreation areas. A tram ride or easy walk takes you into Sabino Canyon, an oasis of greenery beneath rock walls covered with saguaro cactus. Catalina State Park offers trails and vistas beneath the imposing western face of the Catalinas.

Hikers can choose among trails totaling over 150 miles in length and ranging from easy strolls to extremely difficult climbs. Much of the hiking lies within the **Pusch Ridge Wilderness,** which protects most of the western part of the range. Hikers in the wilderness must heed special regulations to protect the desert bighorn sheep by not going more than 400 feet off trail from January 1 to April 30, not bringing in dogs (seeing-eye or handi-dogs are ok), and not exceeding group sizes of 15 for day use or 6 camping. The *Santa Catalina Mountains* topo map shows the main trails, distances, and trailheads; it's sold at Forest Service offices and hiking stores. Volunteers and foresters of the Santa Catalina Ranger District office provide information on the Santa Catalinas. Contact them at the Sabino Canyon Visitor Center, 5700 N. Sabino Canyon Rd. (Tucson, AZ 85750), 520/749-8700. The office is open Mon.–Fri. 8 A.M.–4:30 P.M., Sat.–Sun.

8:30 A.M.–4:30 P.M. The excellent website www.fs.fed.us/r3/coronado/scrd has details on recreation in the district.

History

In 1697, the tireless Jesuit priest Eusebio Francisco Kino visited a Tohono O'odham village in what's now Tucson. He named it, and the high ranges to the north and east, Santa Catarina. Spanish prospectors found gold in Cañada del Oro; they also reportedly mined gold in the Mine with the Iron Door and silver in La Esmeralda, both lost mines lying somewhere in the range.

Raiding Apache discouraged mining until the late 1870s, when Anglo goldseekers began placer operations in Cañada del Oro, tunneling into the hillsides. Most of the mines lie in the northeastern part of the mountains.

Mount Lemmon honors botanist Sara Lemmon, who, with her husband John, discovered many species of plants on an 1881 expedition to the summit. As trails into the mountains improved, the citizens of Tucson headed to the hills more often for the cool air and scenery. The highway to the top, built largely by federal prisoners, was completed in 1951.

Catalina Highway/ Sky Island Scenic Byway

In just an hour, this scenic drive will take you from fine stands of saguaro in the deserts of the Lower Sonoran Zone up to the forests of the Canadian Zone, where meadows bloom with wildflowers in spring and summer. Superb panoramas and fanciful rock pinnacles line much of the drive. Up on top, you'll enjoy camping, picnicking, and hiking in the warmer months, skiing in winter. The 40-mile drive from downtown Tucson leaves the saguaro, paloverde, and cholla behind, passes through woodlands of oak, juniper, and pinyon, and then enters pine forests at about 7,000 feet. Fir and aspen cling to the cool, north-facing slopes above 8,000 feet. The many vista points and picnic areas along the way offer places to stop but you'll need to bring water. Some of the shorter hikes are mentioned here; the *Santa Catalina Mountains* topo map shows the extensive interconnecting trail system. Some trails are suitable for mountain bikers and equestrians; see the website or visitor centers for ideas. *Be sure to fill up with gas before leaving Tucson,* as none is available on the Catalina Highway. It's also a good idea to check for road closures due to construction or storms. The drive begins from the northeast corner of Tucson; head east on Tanque Verde Road, then turn left on the Catalina Highway. After 4.3 miles, you'll enter the Coronado National Forest and the start of the highway's mileposts. If driving, keep an eye out for cyclists who enjoy the challenging ride.

Unless you're going straight through to Summerhaven or Ski Valley, you'll need to purchase a recreation pass from the Forest Service for use of any roadside parking area, picnic or camping area, toilets, trailheads, or vista points at $5/day, $10/week, or $20/year per vehicle (half price for Golden Age and Golden Access holders). The passes also include visits to Sabino Canyon and can be purchased from a booth at Mile 5.1 on the highway, as well as from Sabino Canyon Visitor Center, Palisades Visitor Center, and some other concessionaires. Cyclists don't need a pass.

Babad Do'ag, the first signed vista point, is on the right at Mile 2.6. The Tohono O'odham name means "Frog Mountain," which the Santa Catalinas resemble when viewed from the south. All of Tucson Valley lies at your feet from this 3,450-foot perch.

The highway turns north between the rugged cliffs of Molino Canyon to **Molino Canyon Vista** on your right at Mile 4.3. Two short trails, one paved for wheelchair access, lead to viewpoints of the canyon; the seasonal creek below cascades into pools. Look for the transformation of plants as the Sonoran Desert begins to give way to oaks and grasslands.

Molino Basin, on the left at Mile 5.7, is the first campground on the drive and 18 miles from downtown Tucson. Summers get hot at the 4,370-foot elevation, so it's open only from mid-October to the end of April. You'll need to bring drinking water; cost is $5 for camping, free for day use. Hikers can head along the Arizona Trail.

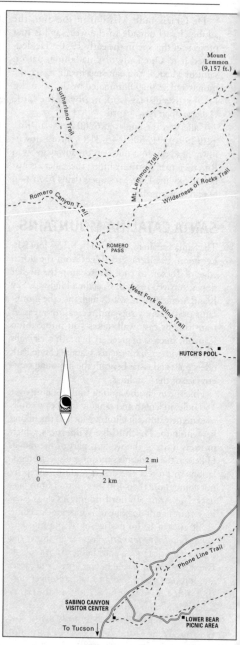

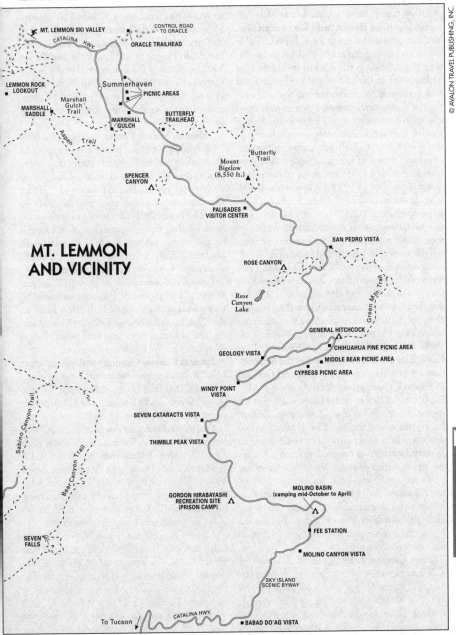

MT. LEMMON
AND VICINITY

MT. LEMMON SKI VALLEY

CATALINA HWY.

CONTROL ROAD
TO ORACLE

ORACLE TRAILHEAD

LEMMON ROCK
LOOKOUT

Summerhaven

PICNIC AREAS

Marshall
Gulch
Trail

MARSHALL
SADDLE

MARSHALL
GULCH

BUTTERFLY
TRAILHEAD

Aspen   Trail

Butterfly
Trail

SPENCER
CANYON

Mount
Bigelow
(8,550 ft.)

PALISADES
VISITOR CENTER

SAN PEDRO VISTA

ROSE CANYON

Rose
Canyon
Lake

Green Mtn. Trail

GENERAL HITCHCOCK

GEOLOGY VISTA

CHIHUAHUA PINE PICNIC AREA

MIDDLE BEAR PICNIC AREA

CYPRESS PICNIC AREA

WINDY POINT
VISTA

Sabino Canyon Trail

SEVEN CATARACTS VISTA

THIMBLE PEAK VISTA

Bear Canyon Trail

MOLINO BASIN
(camping mid-October to April)

GORDON HIRABAYASHI
RECREATION SITE
(PRISON CAMP)

SEVEN
FALLS

FEE STATION

MOLINO CANYON VISTA

SKY ISLAND
SCENIC BYWAY

To Tucson

CATALINA HWY.

BABAD DO'AG VISTA

© AVALON TRAVEL PUBLISHING, INC.

SOUTHERN ARIZONA

Prison Camp Road, on the left at Mile 7.4, leads to **Gordon Hirabayashi Recreation Site.** You can picnic and camp here, but there's no water; a camping fee may be added in the future. A trailhead on the left just inside the gate and another at the end of the road (one-third mile in) gives access to the Arizona Trail and a variety of hiking destinations. Horse corrals are at the end of the road too. The recreation site's name honors a Japanese-American held here during World War II after being convicted for disobeying curfew and relocation orders. You'll see foundations and other remnants of the prison camp established in 1933. Prisoners labored 18 years to construct the Catalina Highway until its completion in 1951. The camp housed juvenile offenders until it closed and the buildings were razed in the mid 1970s. Interpretive signs tell the story of the camp and its people.

In another mile, you'll pass **Thimble Peak Vista** on the left with fine views west across Bear Canyon—the largest drainage of the Santa Catalinas. **Seven Cataracts Vista,** 0.6 mile farther on the left, takes in a series of cascades across Bear Canyon. Cypress and Middle Bear Picnic Areas on the right, then Chihuahua Pine Picnic Area on the left lie tucked in the forest beginning at Mile 11.5. The year-round **General Hitchcock Campground,** on the right at Mile 12, lies at 5,920 feet under pines, oaks, and junipers. It's 21 miles from downtown Tucson, has no water, and there's a $5 camping fee (free day use). In another two miles you'll come to **Windy Point Vista** on the left (parking is on the right), which provides sweeping panoramas of the Rincons, Santa Ritas, southern foothills of the Catalinas, and the Tucson Valley. The granite pinnacles here attract rock climbers and camera buffs. **Geology Vista,** a bit farther on the right, offers more pinnacles and good views to the east and southeast.

Rose Canyon Lake lies at an elevation of 7,200 feet amid ponderosa pines; turn left near Mile 17. Its seven acres offer trout fishing and a one-mile lakeside trail loop, but no swimming or boating. The nearby campground, 33 miles from downtown Tucson, is open Easter weekend to the end of October and has drinking water, in-terpretive programs, and a $15 fee. Day use runs $5 for parking at the lake or picnicking.

You can see the Galiuros and many other mountain ranges to the east from **San Pedro Vista,** on the right 0.4 mile beyond Rose Canyon turnoff. **Green Mountain Trail** connects San Pedro Vista with General Hitchcock Campground to the south. Allow three hours for the four-mile (one-way) hike.

Palisades Visitor Center, on the left at Mile 19.9, is open as staffing permits. Inside, you can see exhibits on the many life zones that you're passing through; books and maps are sold. Across the highway, you can hike to the top of 8,550-foot **Mt. Bigelow,** a 1.5-mile roundtrip climb of 600 feet. The **Butterfly Trail** also begins at this trailhead, winding through ponderosa pine, Douglas fir, and juniper-oak woodlands to Butterfly Trailhead (Mile 22.8), 5.7 miles one way to the northwest; allow 4–5 hours between trailheads.

Groups can reserve nearby Showers Point and Whitetail Campgrounds. Primitive camping (no facilities) is possible along Mt. Bigelow Road on the right, 1.1 miles beyond Palisades Visitor Center, and at Lizard Rock and Incinerator Ridge; these areas receive heavy use, however.

Spencer Canyon Campground, on the left at Mile 21.7, offers cool mountain air at an elevation of 8,000 feet; it's 38 miles from Tucson, open May to mid-October, and has drinking water; $12 for camping, $5 for day use.

One mile farther at an elevation of about 8,000 feet, you'll pass Sykes Knob and Inspiration Rock Picnic Areas on the left, then Box Elder, Alder, and Loma Linda Picnic Areas on the right. **Aspen Vista Point,** on the right at Mile 23 between Sykes Knob and Inspiration Rock Picnic Areas, overlooks the San Pedro Valley and many hills beyond; a copper mine is visible in the valley.

Control Road (Forest Road 38), on the right half a mile past Loma Linda and one-third mile before the Ski Valley turnoff, offers an adventure for drivers with high-clearance vehicles. The unpaved road bounces steeply down the northeast side of the Catalinas, past Oracle Ridge Mine to Peppersauce Campground (described below). The 21 miles to the campground takes about two hours, then the road continues another eight miles to Oracle. The first nine miles is especially steep and rough—4WD might be handy. Cars may be able to make it one-third mile down the Control Road to a parking area at a trailhead for the Arizona Trail/Oracle Ridge Trail #1, which winds north down to Oracle in 12.5 miles one way. Winter snow usually closes the road.

Nearing Mile 25, you'll come to a highway junction; turn right 1.5 miles to Ski Valley or continue straight a quarter mile for the village of Summerhaven.

Summerhaven offers year-round lodgings, restaurants, stores, gift shops, and a post office convenient for skiers and summer visitors. You'll first come to **Mt. Lemmon Café** on the left; it's open daily for breakfast in summer and lunch year-round; the café has a large patio and is known for its pies—this may be your only chance to have a sour cream apple pie; 520/576-1234. The post office is next door. **Alpine Lodge,** a small hotel a bit farther down on the right, has rooms at $69 d Sun.–Thurs., $89 d Fri.–Sat. and holidays; 520/576-1544. The lodge's restaurant offers breakfast on summer weekends, light lunches and dinners daily, and full-course dinners Fri.–Saturday. **Mt. Lemmon Suites,** on the left, runs $99–129 d weekdays and $129–159 d weekends and holidays; 520/576-1664. There's a little grocery store here—The Village Market. Next door, the **Summerhaven Coffee House,** 520/576-1586, fixes sandwiches, quiches, soups, salads, baked goodies, and coffees daily for breakfast and lunch. Next on the left, you'll find the Mt. Lemmon General Store, which has groceries, some camping supplies, a rental cabin ($145), gift shop, and a fudge shop; 520/576-1468. Next, on the right, **Cabins & Cookies** offers five rooms in a mountain inn at $120 d; people also come for the large cookies sold here; 520/576-1542. **Aspen Trail Bed & Breakfast** provides a romantic getaway in a secluded setting off Carter Canyon Road; guests have a full breakfast, dinner is available, and each room has a spa; rates run $170–195 d with weekday and multi-day discounts; cabin rentals are available too; 520/576-1558; you can see rooms on the Web at www.mt-lemmon.com.

A half mile beyond Summerhaven, you'll reach **Marshall Gulch Picnic Area** on the left. (A gate blocks the road in winter, when you'll have to park outside and walk the last bit.) The 3.8-mile **Aspen Loop Trail** begins across the road and offers a good introduction to the high country; it's open about May to October. A sign "Aspen Trail #93, Marshall Saddle 2.5," marks the start. The trail climbs through aspen, fir, and ponderosa pine and offers some good views. At Marshall Saddle, turn right down Marshall Gulch and walk 1.3 miles back to the picnic area.

Mount Lemmon Ski Valley, the southernmost ski area in the United States, sweeps winter skiers and summer visitors from 8,200 to 9,157 feet on a double chairlift. The ski season lasts from about mid-December to mid-April. Skiers have a choice of 20 runs, including "bunny slopes" for beginners. Rental packages (skis, boots, and poles) cost $17; snowboards cost $27. Lessons, all 90 minutes, are $50 for private, $40 for semi-private, or $18 for group. Lift tickets cost $32 per day ($27 half day) for adults, $14 ($11 half day) for children 12 and under. After the ski season, you can take the Skyride up to enjoy the views and cool forests; $7.50 adult, $3.50 children 4–12. The ski area has a snack bar, fudge shop, and a gift shop near the lifts. The large decks provide the venue for an Octoberfest on the last two weekends of September and the first two weekends of October with a German band, dancing, beer, and food. **Iron Door Restaurant,** across the highway, is renowned for its chili and cornbread; open Sat.–Sun. for breakfast and daily for lunch with indoor and outdoor seating. For more information, call 520/576-1400 (recording of current ski conditions), 520/576-1321 (business office), or 520/547-7510 (Pima County Sheriff's road condition hotline).

A hiking trail, open about May to October, goes from the bottom of the ski lift through fir and aspen forests to the summit in 1.5 miles one way. It's unsigned, so ask someone to point out the start. You could also take the Skyride up and walk down.

An unimproved continues past Mt. Lemmon Ski Valley to an infrared observatory near the top of Mt. Lemmon. Except in winter, you may be able to drive 1.7 miles up the road to a trailhead for Mt. Lemmon Trail and other high-country walks. The observatory area is gated and fenced.

Peppersauce Campground lies in a shallow canyon of the northeastern foothills at an elevation of 4,700 feet. Large sycamore and walnut trees shade the sites, which have water and cost $8 for camping, $2.50 for day use year-round. If all spaces are taken, seek dispersed camping along Forest Road 29 starting opposite the campground entrance. Groups can stay at a group campground that's reservable through the district office, 520/749-8700; if not reserved, then it's available first-come, first served. From Oracle, head southeast 8.4 miles on the Mount Lemmon Road/Forest Road 38; halfway to the campground you will see gateways to the **Arizona Trail.** Drivers with high-clearance vehicles can follow the rough, 21-mile Control Road (Forest Road 38) through a mining area from the Catalina Hwy.; the turnoff is just before the junction for Ski Valley.

Peppersauce Cave is an undeveloped limestone cavern 2.2 miles past the campground turnoff on the road from Oracle. Despite the road warning sign, you can usually negotiate this stretch in a car and reach the one-lane bridge, where you'll find parking. Walk about 300 feet up the wash, then bear right along the second well-trod path to the cave entrance. Take at least two flashlights per person and expect to do some crawling in muddy passageways. Many of the cave decorations have been lost. A 1948 *National Geographic* photograph shows cave explorers hauling out smashed-off remains of once-beautiful cave formations.

Sabino Canyon

Sabino Creek, deep in the southern foothills of the Santa Catalina Mountains, begins its journey on the slopes of Mt. Lemmon, bouncing down through the canyon and supporting the lush greenery and trees in which deer, javelina, coyotes, birds, and other animals find food and shelter.

In the **Sabino Canyon Visitor Center,** at the entrance to the canyon, you'll see exhibits on the canyon and Santa Catalina Mountains. You can buy books and maps of the area at the center, and join naturalists on scheduled walks. The self-guided **Bajada Nature Trail** identifies desert plants on a loop behind the center; it's graded for wheelchairs. The visitor center, 520/749-8700 (Santa Catalina Ranger District office), is open weekdays 8 A.M.–4:30 P.M. and weekends 8:30 A.M.–4:30 P.M.; www.fs.fed.us/r3/coronado/scrd. Sabino Canyon lies 13 miles northeast of downtown Tucson. The parking fee charged here also covers the Catalina Highway; $5/day, $10/week, or $20/year per vehicle (half price for Golden Age and Golden Access holders). Take Tanque Verde Road to Sabino Canyon Road, then turn north and drive 4.5 miles to the canyon entrance. Skyline and Sunrise Rds., west of the visitor center, offer a scenic alternative. An early arrival will beat the crowds both at parking and on the trail.

A road winds up through Sabino Canyon for 3.8 miles, crossing the creek many times. You can explore the canyon by hiking, horseback riding, or taking a shuttle tram. Private motor vehicles are prohibited beyond the visitor center. Because Sabino Canyon receives a large number of visitors, bicycles are prohibited all day on Wednesday and Saturday and from 9 A.M. to 5 P.M. the rest of the week. No pets, glass containers, or alcohol are permitted in the canyon.

The **shuttle** leaves the visitor center daily every half hour 9 A.M.–4:30 P.M.; fares are $6 adults, $2.50 ages 3–12. Call 520/749-2861 (recording) or visit www.sabinocanyon.com to check schedules. The narrated ride lasts 45–50 minutes roundtrip; you can get on and off as often as you choose at any of the nine stops.

Hiking, birding, picnicking, and swimming attract the most visitors. The Forest Service provides picnic areas and restrooms, though you'll find drinking water only at the visitor center and the first two stops. Visitors can bring a picnic and spend all day relaxing by the water. Groups can reserve Cactus Ramada picnic area near the visitor center. Camping is not allowed in the canyon; to camp, backpackers must hike at least a quarter mile in from trailheads.

Hikers have a choice of many destinations at the last stop: back to the visitor center via the **Phone Line Trail,** high on the east slopes of

Sabino Canyon (5.5 miles one-way); to lower Bear Canyon via Seven Falls (12 miles one-way); up the West Fork of Sabino Canyon to Hutch's Pool (8.2 miles roundtrip); or to Mt. Lemmon's summit (13 hard miles one-way).

Enjoy the special magic of Sabino Canyon on a **moonlight ride,** offered when the moon is full, April–June and Sept.–December. The Moonlight Shuttle fare is $6 adults, $2.50 children 3–12. Reservations and prepayment are required; 520/749-2327.

Bear Canyon

This beautiful desert canyon east of Sabino features Tucson's most popular hiking destination—Seven Falls, a series of waterfalls, each with a pool at its base. Some of the pools are large enough for swimming, a great way to cool off in the warmer months.

Seven Falls, cascading from pool to pool, is one of the prettiest spots in the Catalinas.

To reach the falls, you can either hike from the visitor center or take the Bear Canyon shuttle for the first 1.5 miles. Bear Canyon Trail begins just south of the Sabino Canyon Visitor Center, crosses some rolling foothills to Bear Canyon (1.5 miles one-way), then turns up the canyon to Seven Falls (3.8 miles total, one-way). The trail continues 4.3 miles to connect with other trails in the Catalinas. On the hike to Seven Falls you'll cross the creek seven times, make a gentle climb onto the east hillside, then descend to the falls. The water-polished rock surrounding the pools requires care in walking as it's very slippery. Allow about 4.5 hours for the roundtrip or 3.5 hours from the Bear Canyon shuttle terminus; elevation change is 650 feet. Picnic tables nestle beside Sabino Creek and at Bear Canyon Overlook along the way.

Those who wish to skip the first 1.5 miles of hiking can pick up the shuttle bus at the visitor center for the short ride east to Bear Canyon; the canyon scenery doesn't begin until you leave the road, so there's no point in taking this shuttle unless you plan on hiking. The shuttle (no narration) leaves the visitor center every hour on the hour, daily 9 A.M.–4 P.M.; fare is $3 adults, $1 ages 3–12. Bicyclists may not ride into Bear Canyon because it lies in Pusch Ridge Wilderness, but they may take the road to the mouth of the canyon.

EAST OF DOWNTOWN

Reid Park Zoo

This small but satisfying collection displays flamingos, lions, tigers, hippos, polar bears, and other exotic life. A walk-in aviary features birds from the far corners of the world. The South America loop has 12 exhibits, including its own walk-in aviary. Landscaping and plants add beauty and provide a natural setting for the different habitats. Zoo staff breed anteaters and other rare animals and participate in a species survival program. The zoo has a snack bar, gift shop, and, on the west side in Reid Park, a picnic area. It's open daily 9 A.M.–4 P.M.; $4 adults, $3 seniors 62 and over, 75 cents children 5–14; 520/791-4022 (recording) or 520/791-5064. Reid Park lies 3.5

miles east of downtown. Enter from 22nd St. just east of Country Club Road.

Pima Air & Space Museum

The more than 250 historic aircraft here illustrate the dramatic advances in aviation technology. This museum, the nation's largest private collection, displays many famous planes from World War II through the present on 75 acres. The first building that you'll enter introduces aviation with a full-scale replica of the Wright brothers' 1903 Wright Flyer and an amazing variety of flying machines. You'll see the contrast in flight trainers from the World War II Link to the Boeing 707. A motion simulator "takes off" for exciting rides (extra charge). Outside, you can see some VIP aircraft and take a tour the VC-118A/DC-6A presidential plane used by Kennedy and Johnson. A few civilian airliners are on display, but it's the military planes that will most impress you with their history, size, and diversity. The 390th Memorial Museum in a separate building on the grounds features a World War II B-17 bomber surrounded by many photos of crews and planes; a diorama and a video show aerial dramas. Exhibits around a gleaming B-24 and a B-29 in another hangar also have many stories to tell. Fighters show developments from World War II to early jets, through the F-100 series, to some current models; there's also a lineup of Migs. Huge transports, three B-52 bombers, many helicopters, and a speedy SR-71 Blackbird stand at rest. The Space Exploratorium & Challenger Learning Center traces the journey into outer space with full-size mockups of Robert Goddard's 1926 liquid-fuel rocket, an X-15, and Mercury and Apollo capsules along with models, rocket engines, and a video of NASA's history; school kids participate in space missions, which staff explain on free tours. The Arizona Aviation Hall of Fame next door recounts the contributions of state aviators.

Free walking tours take you around to many of the indoor exhibits. The Cactus Hopper Tram offers a narrated 45-minute tour of the aircraft outside with stops at the hangars, where you can get on and off; it's a great introduction to the museum and makes it easier for people who can't walk long distances; $3 extra. A gift shop sells aircraft models, books, and posters. There's an inexpensive snack bar. Researchers can make an appointment to use the library. The museum, 520/574-0462, lies about 12 miles southeast of downtown. Take I-10 southeast to Valencia Road Exit 267, then drive east two miles. Hours are 9 A.M.–5 P.M. daily; admission is $7.50 adults, $6.50 seniors 62 and older and active military, $4 ages 7–12. Combination tickets for the museum, Titan Missile Museum, and AMARC tours (see below) save money. For more information about the museum, check out their website at www.pimaair.org.

Davis-Monthan Air Force Base and AMARC Tours

Charles Lindbergh dedicated Davis-Monthan in 1927 as the country's first municipal airport. During World War II it became a training ground for crews of B-17 bombers and other aircraft. The base now trains pilots in combat and electronic reconnaissance aircraft.

A tenant at the base, AMARC (Aerospace Maintenance And Regeneration Center), stores a staggering number—more than 5,000—of surplus planes. The great variety of fighters, transports, and bombers extends across 2,600 acres. You can see them on scheduled bus tours that depart Mon.–Fri. from Pima Air & Space Museum; reservations are recommended in the cooler months.

Saguaro National Park East

In the foothills of the Rincon Mountains, this older and larger unit of the park features many huge saguaros. These cacti require about 25 years to grow just two feet and need protective shade. Arms don't appear until the saguaro is about 75 years old. Old-timers may live more than 200 years and reach 50 feet in height. Creamy white blossoms, the state flower, appear in early May. The fruit, which matures in midsummer, resembles a flower with shiny, black seeds surrounded by a bright red shell.

Until this land received protection, young saguaro had a hard time. Grazing cattle trampled them and woodcutters took many of the "nurse plants" that shaded and sheltered the young ones. Today the area contains mostly very old and very young specimens.

The **visitor center,** just inside the park entrance, contains exhibits of desert geology, ecology, flora, and fauna. A 15-minute slide program shown every half-hour illustrates the biotic communities of the park and the influence of the encroaching city. Naturalists offer special programs and walks, especially during the cooler months. Staff have books, maps, and hiking information. Outside, the **Cactus Garden** displays a variety of labeled desert plants.

Saguaro National Park East is just off Old Spanish Trail, about 16 miles east of downtown. Bicyclists can reach the park on a bike path that parallels Old Spanish Trail. The visitor center is open daily 8:30 A.M.–5 P.M. year-round; 520/733-5153, www.nps.gov/sagu.

Cactus Forest Drive, an eight-mile paved road, begins near the visitor center and winds through the foothills of the Rincon Mountains with many fine views. It's open from 7 A.M. to sunset and costs $6 vehicle admission, $3 for bicyclists or foot travelers. After you've driven about 2.2 miles along this one-way route, you'll come to the turnoff for **Mica View Picnic Area** on the left; it has picnic tables and an outhouse but no water. Another 0.3 mile past the turnoff, look for the **Desert Ecology Trail.** On this paved quarter-mile trail (wheelchair-accessible), you'll learn how plants and animals cope with the environment.

Freeman Homestead Nature Trail begins on the right, 200 yards down the spur road to Javelina Picnic Area. The trail makes a one-mile loop through huge saguaro and along a wash filled with mesquite; interpretive signs describe homesteading in the desert. **Javelina Picnic Area** has some shaded picnic tables and outhouses but no water.

Cactus Forest Trail System offers about 128 miles of interconnecting trails with many loop possibilities in the desert hills; ask for a trail brochure at the visitor center. Mountain bikers particularly enjoy the system's namesake, the 2.5-mile-one-way Cactus Forest Trail through the heart of the cactus forest between the north and south sides of the drive; it's wide and heavily used, shared by hikers, cyclists, and equestrians. Hiking trails north of Cactus Forest Drive follow gentle terrain and can be reached from several trailheads on the north side of the drive. For more rugged and scenic country, try the trails to the east of Garwood Trail. You can see an unusual mix of saguaro amidst juniper and grasslands in some areas here. Douglas Spring Trailhead at the east end of Speedway Boulevard is the closest access point for this area. Bridal Wreath Falls is a good destination during runoff; follow Douglas Spring Trail 2.5 miles in, then turn right 0.3 mile at the sign to the falls.

Tanque Verde Ridge Trail begins near the Javelina Picnic Area and climbs into the rugged **Saguaro Wilderness** of the Rincon Mountains. The trail continues with lots of ups and downs to Mica Mountain, at 8,666 feet the highest peak in the wilderness and 17.5 miles away by trail. Several other trailheads provide access to Mica Mountain, though hiking distances are also too far for day trips. Spring and autumn are the best seasons for a visit as the wilderness is especially dry and unforgiving in the heat of summer; winter can bring snow. A free permit from the visitor center is needed for backcountry camping, which is permitted only at designated sites. Carry water (one gallon per day) and topo maps.

Colossal Cave Mountain Park

Tour guides lead you deep underground to the large formations in this dry, limestone cave. You'll learn about the cave's history and geology, but not where outlaws hid their $60,000 in gold! The tour covers a half-mile and requires a great deal of stair climbing—a total of 363 steps—at a leisurely pace. The cave stays a comfortable 70° F year-round. Tours leave frequently and last 45–55 minutes; you can usually get in within a half hour. Ladder Tours operate some days by reservation; you'll don a hard hat and follow the guide to areas off the normal tour route. A snack bar and gift shop await outside the entrance. Civilian Conservation Corps workers laid the cave's flagstone pathways and constructed the buildings outside in the mid-1930s.

While in the park, you can visit **La Posta Quemada,** a working ranch that dates back to the

SOUTHERN ARIZONA

1870s. It offers a museum, hiking, horseback riding (520/647-3450), a research library, and a café. Museum exhibits illustrate the cave's formation, life, and prehistoric artifacts found inside. Historical displays tell of the ranch's history. The park also offers picnic areas and a playground. You can camp (limited to one night) in the picnic areas at no extra charge, but you'll need to arrive in the park before closing time.

Cave entry runs $7.50 adults, $4 children ages 6–10. You'll also need to pay the park entry fee of $3 per car, $2 motorcycle, or $1 bicycle; 520/647-7275 (cave) or 520/647-7121 (ranch), www.colossalcave.com. Colossal Cave Mountain Park lies 22 miles southeast of downtown Tucson. Take I-10 east to Vail-Wentworth Exit 279, then go seven miles north; or take the Old Spanish Trail to Saguaro National Monument East, then go 12 miles south. The park is open mid-September to mid-March, daily 9 A.M.–5 P.M. (until 6 P.M. Sunday and holidays), then mid-March to mid-September, daily 8 A.M.–6 P.M. (until 7 P.M. Sunday and holidays).

Redington Pass

The bumpy, unpaved Redington Road offers a scenic "back door" to the eastern Tucson Valley. You'll enjoy panoramas of Tucson as the road winds up to the high-desert Redington Pass, which separates the Santa Catalinas and the Rincons; side roads lead to trailheads for the Arizona Trail and other paths into the mountain ranges.

From Tucson, head east on Tanque Verde Road; pavement runs out 2.7 miles past the Wentworth Road junction, then it's 9 miles to the pass via the Redington Road. On the east side, the road gradually descends 17.5 miles from the pass into the San Pedro Valley, where you can turn north to San Manuel (17 miles) or south to Gammon's Gulch (30 miles) and Benson (42 miles) on partly paved roads.

ACCOMMODATIONS

Tucson has more than 100 hotels, motels, bed and breakfasts, and resorts—near the freeway, downtown, at the airport, near the university,

and scattered around the valley. Look for lodging listings in the *Tucson Official Visitors Guide* distributed free by the Tucson Convention and Visitors Bureau.

Prices rise during the cooler months, especially during February and March when the weather and popular events, such as the Gem and Mineral Show and Fiesta de los Vaqueros, draw huge numbers of visitors. Reservations will come in handy then. Also, take the motel prices with a grain of salt—prices rarely stay still long except in the summer doldrums. The rates listed below reflect those in the spring high season; rates go higher at many places during the Gem and Mineral Show and lower in the hot months. Add about 9.5 percent tax to rates at all accommodations except perhaps the smallest bed and breakfasts.

Bed and Breakfast Inns

These are private houses open to travelers in the European tradition. The degree of luxury varies, but the hosts offer a personal touch lacking in most motels. Advance reservations are usually necessary. Some B&Bs close for a month in summer. Check the Visitor Center for brochures describing local establishments or the *Tucson Official Visitors Guide.*

Free reservation services can help match you to a suitable place. **Mi Casa Su Casa** (Spanish for "My house [is] your house"), P.O. Box 950, Tempe, AZ 85280, 520/990-0682, 800/456-0682, has a variety of statewide listings in the Tucson area with rates usually in the $75–125 d range; singles may cost about $10 less. **Arizona Trails Bed & Breakfast Reservation Service** (P.O. Box 18998, Fountain Hills, AZ 85269) offers Tucson places among their statewide listings; 602/837-4284, 888/799-4284; www .arizonatrails.com.

Several bed and breakfasts lie close to downtown and the university. **The Adobe Rose Inn,** 940 N. Olsen Ave., 520/318-4644, 800/328-4122, offers a 1933 adobe with Southwestern furnishings and a pool; $90–125 d in winter, less in summer; www.aroseinn.como. **Casa Alegre Bed and Breakfast Inn,** 316 E. Speedway Boulevard, 520/628-1800, 800/628-5654, occupies a 1915 craftsman-style bungalow with a pool and hot tub; $80–135 d; www.casaalegreinn.com. **Catalina Park Inn,** 309 E. 1st St., 520/792-4541, 800/792-4885, is in a 1927 house with beautiful interiors; $114–144 d, less in shoulder seasons; closed June–Aug.; www.catalinaparkinn.com. **El Presidio Bed and Breakfast Inn,** 297 N. Main Ave., 520/623-6151, 800/349-6151, offers rooms in a historic adobe house; $95–125 d. **La Posada del Valle,** 1640 N. Campbell Ave., 520/795-3840, 888/404-7113, has rooms in a 1920s' inn; $109–149 d in Feb.–March, less the rest of the year; www.bbhost.com/laposadadelvalle. Two blocks from the Tucson Convention Center, the vintage-1900 **Meyer Street House,** 562 S. Meyer St., 520/629-0361, offers full-size adobe apartments with individual patios; $95 d. **Peppertrees Bed and Breakfast Inn,** 724 E. University Blvd., 520/622-7167, 800/348-5763, offers rooms in a 1905 house and three newer houses nearby; $108–175 d, less in summer.

About 5.5 miles northeast of downtown in a central location, **Hacienda Bed & Breakfast,** 5704 E. Grant Rd., 520/290-2224, 888/236-4421, features a pool, spa, and exercise room; $85–125 d; www.tucsonhacienda.com. **Casa Tierra Adobe B&B Inn,** 11155 W. Calle Pima, 520/578-3058, 866/254-0006, offers an adobe house with courtyards and fountains in the desert 16 miles west of town; $135–300 d, closed June 15–Aug. 15.

Hostels

The Roadrunner Hostel, 346 E. 12th St., 520/628-4709, www.roadrunnerhostel.com, has a 1900 adobe house in the downtown neighborhood of Amory Park. Amenities include big-screen TV, free Internet computers, air conditioning, a kitchen, laundry, and no curfew. Beds run $16/night and $95/week; a private room is $35 d/night and $210 d/week. The hostel is just a short walk from the bus and train stations or you can call for a free pickup; transport cost from the airport is $10.

The **Hotel Congress** has a hostel as well as regular rooms downtown; see the listing below.

Motels and Hotels: Downtown

Under $50: Motel 6, 960 S. Freeway, 1-10 Congress St. Exit 258, 520/628-1339 or 800/466-8356, has a pool; $38–40 s, $44–46 d.

$50–100: In the heart of downtown, **Hotel Congress,** 311 E. Congress St., 520/622-8848 or 800/722-8848, opened in 1919 to serve passengers of the Southern Pacific Railroad. It's a short walk from the Amtrak, Greyhound, and local bus stations. All of the rooms have 1930s decor and furnishings—you'll get a radio and an old-fashioned telephone—along with a bath or shower; rates run $62 s, $75 d Jan.–April, then decrease to a low of $30 s, $35 d June–Aug. (only evaporative cooling). The hotel also has a **youth hostel** ($16/bunk, passport required, no reservations accepted), café, nightclub (expect some noise in the rooms), and an Internet bar; hotcong.com.

Four Points Hotel by Sheraton, 350 S. Freeway, I-10 Congress St. Exit 258, 520/622-6611 or 800/551-1466, offers a pool, hot tub, and fitness center; $79–109 d. **Innsuites Hotel & Resort,** 475 N. Granada Ave., 520/622-3000 or 800/842-4242, includes a breakfast buffet; $90–160 d. **Howard Johnson Inn,** 1010 S. Freeway, I-10 22nd St./Staff Pass Blvd. Exit 259, 520/622-5871 or 800/446-4656, has a pool; $79 d. **Holiday Inn Express,** 750 W. Starr Pass Blvd., I-10 22nd St./Starr Pass Blvd. Exit 259, 520/624-4455 or 800/HOLIDAY, offers a pool and hot tub; $89 d. **Comfort Inn,** 715 W. Star Pass Blvd., I-10 22nd St./Starr Pass Blvd. Exit 259, 520/791-9282 or 800/228-5150, has a pool and hot tub; $59 s, $65 d.

$100–150: Clarion Inn & Suites, 88 E. Broadway Blvd., 520/622-4000 or 800/CLARION, provides a pool, sauna, and whirlpool; $109 d. **Radisson Hotel City Center,** 181 W. Broadway Blvd., 520/624-8711 or 800/448-8276, has a pool and fitness room; $129 d.

Motels and Hotels: North of Downtown

Good hunting grounds for the older, less expensive motels north of downtown lie along the zigzag Business Route north along Stone Avenue from Speedway Boulevard, west on Drachman Street, north along Oracle Road, then finally west on Miracle Mile to 1-10 Exit 255.

Under $50: On Drachman Street check out **Copper Cactus Inn,** 225 W. Drachman St., 520/622-7411, with a pool and kitchenettes, from $30 d; and **Frontier Motel,** 227 W. Drachman St., 520/798-3005, also with a pool and kitchenettes, $40 d.

On Oracle Road, you can try **La Siesta Motel,** 1602 N. Oracle Rd., 520/624-1192, $30 s, $35 d; **Hacienda Motel,** 1742 N. Oracle Rd., 520/623-2513, $35 s, $38 d; **Highland Tower Motel,** 1919 N. Oracle Rd., 520/791-3057, with a pool and kitchenettes, $30 s, $35 d; and **Tiki Motel,** 2649 N. Oracle Rd., 520/624-0956, with a pool and kitchenettes, $45 d and up.

Miracle Milers include **Arizonan Motel,** 437 W. Miracle Mile, 520/623-8702, $25 d; **Sunland Motel,** 465 W. Miracle Mile, 520/792-9118, with a pool, $25 s, $30 d; **Wayward Winds Lodge,** 707 W. Miracle Mile, 520/791-7526, also with a pool, $45 d; **Mountain View Motel,** 741 W. Miracle Mile, 520/628-7585, $50–75 d; and **Amazon Motel,** 1135 W. Miracle Mile, 520/622-7725, with a pool and kitchenettes, $39 s, $45 d.

$50–100: On Stone Avenue you'll find **University Inn,** 950 N. Stone Ave., 520/791-7503 or 800/233-8466, with a pool, $39 s, $50 d and up; **Super 8,** 1248 N. Stone Ave., 520/622-6446 or 800/800-8000, with a pool, $49 s, $52 d; and **Flamingo Hotel,** 1300 N. Stone Ave., 520/770-1910 or 800/300-3533, offering a pool, hot tub, and continental breakfast, $59–99 d. **Best Western Executive Inn,** 333 Drachman St., 520/791-7551 or 800/800/255-3371, has a pool; $80 s, $90 d. **Ghost Ranch Lodge,** 801 W. Miracle Mile, 520/791-7565 or 800/456-7565, spreads out on 8 acres of gardens and has a restaurant, pool, and hot tub; $78 s, $86 d and up; www.ghostranchlodge.com.

$100–150: Best Western Royal Inn, 1015 N. Stone Ave., 520/622-8871 or 800/528-1234, has a pool and hot tub, $109 d room, $129 d suite. **Ramada Inn University,** 1601 N. Oracle Rd., 520/623-6666 or 866/882-7661, has a pool and full breakfast; $129 d.

Motels and Hotels: East of Downtown

$50–100: La Quinta, 6404 E. Broadway Blvd., 520/747-1414 or 800/531-5900, features a pool, hot tub, and health-club pass; $62 d.

$100 and up: Doubletree Guest Suites, 6555 E. Speedway Blvd., 520/721-7100 or 800/222-8733, offers a pool, hot tub, and fitness center; $125–160 d. **Viscount Suite Hotel,** 4855 E. Broadway Blvd., 520/745-6500 or 800/527-9666, has a pool and hot tub; $109 d. **Embassy Suites on Broadway,** 5335 E. Broadway Blvd., 520/745-2700 or 800/362-2779, includes a pool, hot tub, and full breakfast; $99–159 d. **Smugglers Inn Motor Hotel,** 6350 E. Speedway Blvd., 520/296-3292 or 800/525-8852, has a restaurant, pool, and hot tub; $119 d. **Residence Inn by Marriott,** 6477 E. Speedway Blvd., 520/721-0991 or 800/331-3131, provides a pool, hot tub, and breakfast buffet; from $129 d.

$150 and up: Across from the University of Arizona, **Sheraton Four Points,** 1900 E. Speedway Blvd., 520/327-7341 or 800/843-8052, offers a pool and whirlpool; $109 d and up. **Lodge on the Desert,** 306 N. Alvernon Way, 520/325-3366 or 800/456-5634, features a hacienda atmosphere, some fireplaces, and a pool; $189 d and up. **Doubletree Hotel at Reid Park,** 445 S. Alvernon Way, 520/881-4200 or 800/222-8733, has a pool, and exercise room; $149–169 d. **Sheraton Tucson Hotel & Suites,** 5151 E. Grant Rd., 520/323-6262 or 800/325-3535, includes a restaurant, pool and fitness center; $109 d and up.

Motels and Hotels: South of Downtown and Airport

The south side of town isn't much to look at, but you'll be close to I-10 and the airport. Bargain hunters can find good deals just north of Exit 261, and along the old Benson Highway, which parallels I-10 between Exits 261 and 267. Many of the old motels along here offer low weekly rates as well and will more likely have vacancies than will places closer to downtown.

Under $50: In South Tucson, a separate city with a strong Mexican flavor, try the **Arizona Motel**, 1749 S. 6th Ave., 520/622-7768, with a pool and kitchenettes; $25 s, $29 d. Farther south and just north of I-10 Exit 261 are the **Econo Lodge**, 3020 S. 6th Ave., 520/623-5881 or 800/553-2666, with a pool and hot tub, $40 s, $45 d; **Star Motel**, 3031 5. 6th Ave., 520/792-0712, $30 s, $35 d; and **Budget Inn**, 3033 S. 6th Ave., 520/884-1470, $37 s, $43 d.

Just south of I-10 Exit 262, you'll find **Economy Inn**, 220 E. Benson Hwy., 520/622-9737; $30 s, $35 d; and **Lazy 8 Motel**, 314 E. Benson Hwy., 520/6223336, with a pool, $36 s, $45 d. Motels east along the Benson Highway between I-10 Exits 262 and 267 include **Western Motel**, 3218 E. Benson Hwy., 520/746-9892, $30–45 d; and **Redwood Lodge**, 3315 F. Benson Hwy., 520/294-3802, with a pool and weekly kitchenettes, $35 d.

$50–100: Moving up to the newer motels, choices include **Howard Johnson Lodge-Airport**, 1025 E. Benson Hwy., 520/623-7792 or 800/446-4656, with a pool, hot tub, and sauna, $69 s, $75 d; **Holiday Inn Tucson Airport**, 4550 5. Palo Verde Blvd., 520/746-1161 or 800/HOLIDAY, $76 d; **Ramada Inn & Suites**, 5251 S. Julian Dr. (Palo Verde at I-10), 520/294-5250 or 800/272-6232, with a pool, hot tubs, and exercise room, $89 d and up.

$100 and up: Clarion Hotel Airport, 6801 5. Tucson Blvd., 520/746-3932 or 800/526-0556, offers a pool and hot tub; $99–139 d. **The Inn at the Airport**, 7060 S. Tucson Blvd., 520/746-0271 or 800/772-3847, has a pool and hot tub; $69–79 d. **Embassy Suites Hotel and Conference Center**, 7051 S. Tucson Blvd., 520/573-0700 or 800/EMBASSY, includes a pool, hot tub, and exercise room; $169 d.

Guest Ranches

The Tucson area features one of the world's largest concentrations of guest ranches, where you can enjoy Western hospitality and activities as well as high-quality accommodations and food. Popular activities include horseback riding, swimming, tennis, hiking, birding, socializing, and just relaxing. Meals, served family-style at some places, are included with your stay. Figure on adding an extra 16 percent gratuity and around 7.5 percent tax to the rates listed below. Most guest ranches close during the hot summers, though a few remain open for hardy visitors.

Tanque Verde Guest Ranch, 14301 E. Speedway (Tucson, AZ 85748), 520/296-6275 or 800/234-3833, lies in the foothills of the Rincon Mountains 10 miles east of Tucson. The luxurious ranch dates from the 1880s and offers a host of amenities and activities, including horseback riding, indoor and outdoor pools, a Jacuzzi and saunas, an exercise room, five tennis courts, and nature walks. Guests feast on the dining room's buffets and on cookouts. Prices include meals, riding, and ranch activities. Daily rates during the peak season (Dec. l6–April 30) are $280–360 s, $330–435 d; summer rates (May–Sept.) drop to $220–290 s, $260–345 d; autumn (Oct. to Dec. 15) runs $230–300 s, $270–355 d; www.tanqueverderanch.com.

Lazy K Bar Guest Ranch, 8401 N. Scenic Dr. (Tucson, AZ 85743), 520/744-3050 or 800/321-7018, is an informal family ranch 16 miles northwest of downtown. The ranch lies at the foot of the Tucson Mountains, next to Saguaro National Park West. Guests can enjoy horseback riding, a swimming pool, whirlpool, volleyball, basketball, hiking, and family-style meals. Inclusive rates run $181 s, $290 d during the Dec.–April peak season; less other months. A three-day minimum stay is requested. The ranch is closed June 20–Sept. 15; www.lazykbar.com.

White Stallion Ranch, 9251 W. Twin Peaks Rd., Tucson, AZ 85743, 520/297-0252 or 888/977-2624, sprawls over 3,000 acres some 17 miles northwest of Tucson. The ranch offers horseback riding, a pool, hot tub, two tennis courts, nature trails, and varied ranch activities. Breakfast, buffet lunch, and family-style dinner are included in the rates of $165 s, $252–354 d in spring, then slightly less in autumn and a bit more over the Christmas holiday; there's a four-night minimum in winter. The ranch closes June–August; www.wsranch.com.

Rancho de la Osa Guest Ranch, P.O. Box 1,

Sasabe, AZ 85633, 520/8234257 or 800/872-6240, dates back 250 years to a Spanish land grant; it's 66 miles southwest of Tucson near the Mexican border. Guests will enjoy horseback riding, a pool, hot tub, birding, hiking, biking, and lots of peace and quiet. The adobe buildings feature artwork and colorful Mexican-inspired decor. The dining room serves gourmet Southwestern cuisine. Inclusive rates are $200 s, $320 d from September to May, then $160 s, $275 d in June and July; there's a three-night minimum stay. Weekly rates and deluxe rooms are available. The ranch closes in August. For more information, check out www.ranchodelaosa.com.

Resorts

Northeast of the University of Arizona, **Arizona Inn,** 2200 E. Elm St., Tucson, AZ 85719, 520/325-1541 or 800/933-1093, opened in 1930 and continues to combine old Arizona elegance with modern luxury. The 14 acres of peaceful grounds offer gardens, a pool, two clay tennis courts, and croquet. The restaurant serves continental fare. Highseason rates (Jan.–April) run $195–295 d for a room and $299–349 d for a suite; by summer, rates have dropped to $134– 174 d for a room and $184–224 d for a suite; www.arizonainn.com.

Canyon Ranch Spa, 8600 E. Rockcliff Rd. (Tucson, AZ 85750), 520/7499000 or 800/742-9000, is a health-and-fitness vacation resort with an active program of exercise classes, tennis, racquetball, swimming, hiking, biking, yoga, and meditation. Chefs prepare healthy gourmet meals from natural ingredients; no alcohol is served. The 70-acre grounds lie northeast of town near Sabino Canyon. There's a four-night minimum stay during the high season, though the spa recommends a seven-day visit. A four-night package in winter goes for $3,272– 12,102 s ($2,651 –7,680/person, double occupancy) with meals and many services; www.canyonranch.com.

Omni Tucson National Golf & Spa Resort, 2727 W. Club Dr. (Tucson, AZ 85742), 520/297-2271 or 800/278-5880, spreads over 650 acres at the base of the Catalinas on the northwest side of the city. The resort is the Tuc-

son home of the PGA and features a 27-hole golf course, lakes, full-service spa services, an exercise room, four tennis courts, two pools, volleyball, basketball, and fine dining. In high season (Jan.–mid-May), rates are $275–389 d; spring and autumn rates are lower, and they drop in summer to $115– 195 d; www.tucsonnational.com.

On the north edge of town next to the Catalinas, the **Westin La Paloma,** 3800 E. Sunrise Dr. (Tucson, AZ 85718), 520/742-6000 or 800/228-3000, features a 27-hole golf course, health center, many tennis courts, racquetball courts, two giant pools, a water slide, and a selection of restaurants. The high-season (Jan.–late May) rate is $480 d; summer (late May–early Sept.) runs $250 d; autumn (early Sept. –Dec.) goes for $440 d; www.westin.com.

On the northwest side of town below the Catalinas is **Sheraton Tucson El Conquistador Resort and Country Club,** 10000 N. Oracle Rd. (Tucson, AZ 85737), 520/544-5000 or 800/325-7832. The resort offers 45 holes of golf, 32 lighted tennis courts, racquetball courts, an athletic club, 4 pools, hot tubs, horseback riding, and Western, Mexican, and continental dining. Rack rates are $380-850 d year-round, but you can often find specials; www.sheraton.com.

Nestled in the foothills of the Catalinas north of the city is **Loews Ventana Canyon Resort,** 7000 North Resort Dr. (Tucson, AZ 85750), 520/299-2020 or 800/234-5117. The 93-acre grounds enclose a natural waterfall, two 18-hole golf courses, eight lighted tennis courts, two swimming pools, a hot tub, health club, and several restaurants. Rates range $295–325 d in the Jan. 8–May 20 high season; $175– 185 d in the May 21 –Sept. 8 summer season; and $295–325 d in the Sept. 9–Jan. 7 autumn season; www.loewshotels.com.

Westward Look Resort, 245 E. ma Rd. (Tucson, AZ 85704), 520/297-1151 or 800/722-2500, began in 1929 as a dude ranch and now rates as one of the area's best value resorts. It's on 80 acres near the north edge of town, beneath the Catalinas. Guests enjoy eight (5 lighted) tennis courts, three pools, three hot tubs, a jogging trail, fitness center, aerobics, massage therapy, volleyball, and basketball. Diners sample continental cuisine in the Gold Room. High season (mid-January to March) rates run $269–329 d; summer rates drop to $179–139 d; suites are available too; www.westwardlook.com.

Campgrounds and RV Parks

All of the following welcome families except as noted. Both tenters and RVers will find especially scenic settings at Catalina State Park, in the Coronado National Forest, and at Gilbert Ray Campground. Seniors have many RV parks catering just to them with recreation facilities and activities. The *Tucson Official Visitors Guide* and the Yellow Pages list other RV parks and campgrounds.

Catalina State Park, 12 miles north of Tucson on Oracle Road (US 89), offers campsites in the foothills of the Santa Catalinas, 520/628-5798. Rates are $10, $17 with electricity; showers are available. You and your horse can camp in the equestrian center.   Several Coronado National Forest campgrounds line the Catalina Highway; the closest to Tucson is 18 miles away at **Molino Basin,** 520/749-8700; see the Santa Catalina Mountains section above.

Gilbert Ray Campground has a desert setting in Tucson Mountain Park, eight miles west of town; cars can take Speedway Boulevard (I-10 Exit 257) west over Gates Pass, but large rigs should follow Ajo Way and Kinney Road. Rates are $7 for tent camping, $12 for RV sites with electric hookups, 520/883-4200. The campground has a dump station but no showers. In spring, you'll often find vacancies here when other places fill.

Justin's RV Park (adult) is in the same area at 3551 S. San Joaquin Rd., 520/883-8340. Children are welcome May–Sept. when the adjacent Justin's Water World is open. Sites with hookups cost $12.50.

Prince of Tucson RV Park is four miles northwest of downtown on the west side of I-10 at 3501 N. Freeway; take Prince Road Exit 254, 520/887-3501 or 800/955-3501. The park has a swimming pool, hot tub, and recreation room; $25 RV with hookups, $20 tent (but only

April–Aug.). The nearby **Tratel Tucson RV Park** at 2070 W. Fort Lowell Rd. caters mainly to seniors, 520/888-5401. The park has a pool and recreation room. RV sites with hookups cost $18. To get there, take I-10 Exit 254 (Prince Rd.), then go a half mile south on the west frontage road.

Whispering Palms RV Trailer Park is at 3445 N. Romero Rd., 520/888-2500 or 800/266-8577. Reach it via I-10 Prince Road Exit 254, head east, then south on Romero. Tent sites cost $17.85, RV sites with hookups go for $21.16.

Crazy Horse RV Campground, 6660 S. Craycroft Rd., 520/574-0157 or 800/279-6279, is southeast of downtown; take I-10 Exit 268, then drive a quarter mile north on Craycroft. Amenities include a heated pool and recreation room. Rates are $18.50 tent, $20.20 RV with hookups.

Cactus Country RV Resort, 10 195 S. Houghton Rd., 520/574-3000 or 800/777-8799, welcomes seniors and families with a pool, hot tub, and organized winter activities. It's 16 miles southeast of downtown off I-10; take Exit 275, then go 0.2 mile north. Rates are $16.50 tent, $27 RV with hookups.

Seniors can enjoy a wide range of recreation and entertainment programs at large RV resorts. These include **Rincon Country West RV Resort,** four miles south of Tucson at 4555 S. Mission Rd. (take I-19 Ajo Way Exit 99), $28 RV with hookups, 520/294-5608 or 800/782-7275; **Western Way RV Resort,** 3100 S. Kinney Rd., west from 1-19 Ajo Way Exit 99, $32.64 RV with hookups, 520/578-1715 or 800/292-8616; and **Voyager RV Resort,** 8701 S. Koib Rd. (near I-10 Kolb Rd. Exit 270), $36.60 RV with hookups, 520/574-5000 or 800/424-9191.

FOOD

Diners give high marks to Tucson's Mexican food. Visitors can also choose from American, Chinese, Middle Eastern, Indian, Greek, Italian, German, and French. The more expensive places may have a dress code; ask when making reservations.

Of course Tucson offers plenty of cowboy food—the old standbys of steak, potatoes, beans, and biscuits. The following is only a small selection of Tucson eateries; see the *Tucson Weekly* and the *Tucson Official Visitors Guide* for more listings. The price ranges given below are for dinner entrées.

American and Southwestern

Oasis Vegetarian Eatery & Food Co., 1523 N. Park Ave., 520/884-1616, features homemade veggie burgers and a long list of sandwiches and salads. Open Mon.–Sat. for lunch and dinner; $4–7. A downtown branch at 216 E. Congress St., 520/670-1616, is open Mon.–Fri. for lunch.

La Cocina Restaurant, in the Old Town Artisans block at 201 N. Court, 520/622-0351, serves mesquite-grilled meats, fish, and vegetables, along with soups, salads, and sandwiches on the patio and indoors. Open daily for lunch; $7–13.

Cushing Street Bar & Restaurant, 198 W. Cushing St. (at Meyer, just south of the Tucson Convention Center), 520/622-7984, offers steak, seafood, quesadillas, and salads in an attractive 1880s' setting. Open Mon.–Sat. for lunch and dinner; $9–16. The former general store is in the historic Barrio Viejo.

Epic Café, 745 N. 4th Ave. (near downtown and the U of A), 520/624-6844, offers a great choice of sandwiches and salads along with their famous scones and cranberry couscous. Open daily for breakfast, lunch, and dinner; about $5.50.

Garland, 119 E. Speedway Blvd. (0.75 mile northeast of downtown, between 6th and Stone Ayes.), 520/792-4221, makes a good place for American, Italian, Greek, French, Mexican, and vegetarian food. Open daily for breakfast, lunch, and dinner; $6–15.

The elegant dining room at **Arizona Inn,** 2200 E. Elm St. between Campbell and Tucson Blvd. (two miles northeast of downtown), 520/325-1541, serves continental cuisine. Open daily for breakfast, lunch, and dinner and a Sunday brunch; $21–32.

In the Westin La Paloma, **Janos,** 3770 E. Sunrise Dr., 520/615-6100, prepares exceptionally good and creative New Southwestern cuisine

with influences from France, the Mediterranean, and Asia. Open Mon.–Sat. for dinner; $26–45.

Eight miles east of downtown, **Jonathan's Tucson Cork,** 6320 E. Tanque Verde Rd., 520/296-1631, rates as one of the best steakhouses in Tucson. It also serves ostrich, buffalo, chicken, seafood, and prime rib daily for dinner; $14–35.

Kingfisher, 2564 E. Grant Rd. (northeast of downtown), 520/323-7739, has an extensive seafood menu plus some meat and vegetarian items. It's open Mon.–Fri. for lunch and daily for dinner; $12–28.

Little Anthony's Diner, behind the Gaslight Theatre on the southwest corner of 7010 E. Broadway Blvd. and Kolb Rd. (eight miles east of downtown), gives you many choices of burgers, sandwiches, chicken dishes, and deserts in a 1950s setting. The menu advertises blue plate specials "just like mom's." Grandma Tony's Pizza is available here too, for dine in or take out. Open daily for lunch and dinner, and on weekends for breakfast, $4–13.

Pinnacle Peak Steakhouse, 6541 E. Tanque Verde Rd., 520/296-0911, is a family-style steakhouse with a cowboy atmosphere. Don't wear a tie here, or it may join the thousands of severed ties that decorate the ceilings. Open nightly for dinner; $8–14 adults, $2.25–6 children. No reservations taken, but you can avoid peak-season lines by arriving early or late. A museum, children's train, and nightly gunfights provide entertainment. The restaurant, along with two others, shops, and oldtime photo galleries are in Trail Dust Town, a recreated Old West town eight miles east of downtown.

The Ranchers Club, in the Sheraton Hotel at 5151 E. Grant Rd., 520/321-7621, serves some of the best steaks in town along with seafood in an Old West atmosphere. Open Mon.–Fri. for lunch and Mon.–Sat. for dinner; $23–25.

CCC Chuckwagon Suppers, 8900 W. Bopp Rd., 520/883-2333 or 800/446-1798, dishes up generous quantities of real cowboy beef, beans, and other trappings, accompanied by Western music; $17–22 adults, $9–14 children. Open Tues.–Sat. for dinner from late December to mid-April. Reservations recommended. It's near the Tucson Mountains about 12 miles west from downtown via Ajo and Kinney Roads.

Mexican Cafe

Poca Cosa prepares traditional Mexican cuisine in the dining room of the Clarion Hotel. Open Mon.–Sat. for lunch and dinner; $13–18. Downtown at 88 E. Broadway; 520/622-6400.

Garcia's serves fajitas and other tasty food. Open daily for lunch and dinner; $6–1 5. Downtown in the historic 1890 El Paso-Southwestern Depot at 419 W. Congress; 520/628-1956.

El Charro has been a popular dining spot since 1922. Open daily for lunch and dinner with patio and indoor areas; $4.50–14. In the historic Le Flein House downtown at 311 N. Court Ave.; 520/622-1922. Also in El Mercado at 6310 E. Broadway Blvd.; 520/745-1922. An airport branch serves travelers and an underwater affiliate on the USS *Tucson* submarine serves crew.

El Parador's dining room features a garden atmosphere. Open Mon.–Sat. for lunch and daily for dinner; $9–16. It's two miles east of downtown at 2744 E. Broadway Blvd.; 520/881-2808.

El Saguarito prepares healthy Mexican food cooked with canola oil. Open Mon.–Fri. for breakfast, lunch, and dinner; $3.50–9. Located just east of downtown at 1012 E. 6th St. (near Park Ave.); 520/297-1264.

El Torero draws diners with generous servings for lunch and dinner; $6–11. Closed Tuesday. It's in South Tucson at 231 E. 26th St., near S. 4th Ave.; 520/622-9534. You'll find other Mexican restaurants in the same neighborhood; South Tucson is a one-mile-square city-within-a-city just south of downtown Tucson.

La Fuente Restaurant has a garden setting for fine dining with choices of meat, seafood, and vegetarian food. Musicians serenade diners in the evenings. Lunches feature a tostada-taco bar Mon.–Thurs. and a buffet on Friday; a champagne brunch with music is offered on Sundays. Open daily for lunch and dinner, except closed Mon. in summer; $10–23. North of downtown at 1749 N. Oracle Rd.; 520/6238659.

making tortillas at the Tucson Museum of Art

International

Govinda's Natural Food Buffet offers a flavorful vegetarian menu with indoor and patio dining at 711 E. Blacklidge Dr., east off 1st Avenue between Glenn and Fort Lowell, 520/792-0630. Open Wed.–Sat. for lunch and Tues. –Sat. for dinner. Tuesday is East Indian night and Thursday is vegan; $8 lunch buffet, $9 dinner buffet, with lower children's prices and salad-bar options. You can join the Hare Krishna community for a Sunday Feast and Festival with chanting, meditation, discussion, and a meal on Sunday 5:30–8 P.M.

Continental

The **Gold Room's** excellent food and service accompany a sweeping view of the city. Open daily for breakfast, lunch, and dinner; $19–35. Reservations recommended for dinner. It's at the Westward Look Resort, nine miles north of downtown, 245 E. ma Rd.; 520/297-0134, ext. 413.

The **Tack Room** serves highly rated Southwest/continental food in an adobe hacienda. Open nightly except Monday for dinner (also closed Tuesday July–Oct.); $27–49; reservations recommended. It's 10 miles northeast of downtown at 7300 E. Vactor Ranch Trail off N. Sabino Canyon Rd.; 520/722-2800.

French

Le Rendez-Vous offers fine French food in a formal setting Tues. –Fri. for lunch and Tues. –Sun. for dinner; $20–29, also *prix fixe* options, reservations recommended. Go six miles northeast

SOUTHERN ARIZONA

of downtown to 3844 E. Fort Lowell Rd.; 520/323-7373.

Italian

Caruso's serves southern Italian cooking; this Tucson institution dates back to the 1930s. Open Tues.–Sun. for dinner; $7–10. Located just east of downtown at 434 N. 4th Ave.; 520/624-5765.

Daniel's Restaurant and Trattoria serves cuisine of northern Italy daily for dinner; $20–30, reservations recommended. Located about seven miles northeast of downtown in St. Philip's Plaza at 4340 N. Campbell Ave.; 520/742-3200.

Pizza

Magpies Gourmet Pizza has long been top rated for its quality and variety. Open daily for lunch and dinner; $7–25. It's near downtown at 605 N. 4th Ave.; 520/628-1661.

Mediterranean

Athens on 4th Avenue presents Greek cuisine cooked with many imported ingredients; also has patio dining. Open Mon.–Sat. for dinner; $10.50–20. It's half a mile from downtown at 500 N. 4th Ave.; 520/624-6886.

Evangelo's has a fine reputation as one of the best restaurants in town, with a wide selection of entrees and an extensive wine list. Open daily for lunch and dinner; $15–21, reservations requested. Six miles west of downtown at 4405 W. Speedway Blvd.; 520/624-8946.

Olive Tree serves generous portions of Greek and other Mediterranean food with a choice of indoor or patio tables. Open daily for dinner; $14–27. Head seven miles east of downtown to 7000 E. Tanque Verde Rd.; 520/298-1845.

Indian

Gandhi prepares seafood, meats, and vegetarian food in tandoori and other north Indian styles. Open daily for lunch (buffet available) and dinner; $6– 13. North of downtown at 150 W. Fort Lowell, near Stone Ave.; 520/292-1738.

New Delhi Palace offers north Indian cuisine, including tandoori. Open daily for lunch (buffet and ala carte) and dinner; $6–14. It's six miles east of downtown at 6751 E. Broadway Blvd.; 520/296-8585.

Chinese

Jasmine Garden serves Cantonese food daily for lunch and dinner with a buffet option; you can order dim sum Sat.–Sun. for lunch; $5–25. Four miles northeast of downtown at 1145 N. Alvemon Way (northwest corner with Speedway Blvd.); 520/325-5353.

Lotus Garden features a long menu of Cantonese and Szechuan specialties. Open daily for lunch and dinner; $6–15. Six miles northeast of downtown at 5975 E. Speedway Blvd.; 520/298-3351.

Thai

China-Thai Cuisine cooks tasty Thai, Mandarin, and Szechwan food. Open Mon. –Sat. for lunch and daily for dinner; $6–14. Seven miles northeast of downtown at 6502 E. Tanque Verde Rd.; 520/885-6860.

Japanese

Shogun has attractive decor with a choice of tables or tatami booths. There's a sushi bar too. Open Mon.–Sat. for lunch and daily for dinner; $11 –18. North of downtown in River Village Center at 5036 N. Oracle Rd.; 520/888-6646.

ENTERTAINMENT

You'll find club, movie, and performance listings in the *Tucson Weekly,* free at newsstands, and in the entertainment sections of the *Arizona Daily Star* and *Tucson Citizen.*

Nightlife

Club Congress presents local and national artists on Friday, then DJ music the rest of the week. The action (for ages 21 and up) takes place downtown in the Hotel Congress, 311 E. Congress; 520/622-8848. **Berky's Bar** features blues with some rock and roll nightly at 5769 E. Speedway; 520/296-1981. **Chicago Bar** moves to sounds of reggae, blues, and rock nightly at 5954 E. Speedway; 520/748-8169. **O'Malley's** is a popular bar downtown with a variety of live music Thurs.–Sat. at 247 N. 4th Ave.; 520/623-8600.

You can enjoy country-western music and dancing Tues.–Sat. at **The Maverick,** 4702 E. 22nd St. at Swan; 520/748-0456. Bands play mariachi or Latin favorites at **La Fuente Restaurant** nightly at 1749 N. Oracle Rd., 520/623-8659; you can dine Mexican or sit at the lounge. For jokes, it's **Laffs Comedy Caffé** on Wed.–Sat. at 2900 E. Broadway Blvd.; 520/323-8669.

Movies

Loft Cinema screens independent and foreign films at 3233 E. Speedway Blvd.; 520/795-7777; desert.net/loft/. See newspapers for listings of other area theaters.

Theater and Concerts

The **Arizona Repertory Theatre** offers many fine productions Sept.–June at the University of Arizona's Marroney and Lab Theatres; 520/621-1162 (Fine Arts box office).

The **University of Arizona Artist Series** brings prominent performers to Centennial Hall, on campus just inside the main (east) gate on University Blvd.; 520/621-3341 (box office).

Many performances take place at the **Tucson Convention Center** Music Hall, Leo Rich Theatre, and Arena; 520/791-4101, www.ci.tucson.az.us/tcc. You can attend performances

at the Tucson Convention Center (TCC) of the **Ballet Arizona** Oct.–May, 888/322-5538; the **Tucson Symphony,** Thursday and Friday evenings Sept.–May. (also Sun. Jan–April), 520/882-8585, www.tucsonsymphony.org; the **Arizona Opera,** Oct.–March, 520/293-4336, www.azopera.com; **Arizona Friends of Chamber Music,** Oct.–April, 520/577-3769; and the Theater League's **Broadway musicals;** 800/776-7469, www.theaterleague.com.

Pima Community College's Center for the Arts offers a large variety of theatrical and musical performances produced not only by the college but by many of the area's cultural organizations. The college's facilities include **Proscenium Theatre, Black Box Theatre, Recital Hall,** and a small art gallery just west of downtown at 2202 W. Anklam Rd. (head west on Sixth St., which turns into St. Mary's Rd., then into Anklam Rd.); 520/206-6988.

The professional **Arizona Theatre Company** presents a series of plays Sept.–May at the Temple of Music and Art, 330 S. Scott Ave.; 520/622-2823. The experimental **Invisible Theatre** offers performances Sept.–June; it's one mile northeast of downtown at 1400 N. 1st Ave. and Drachman St., 520/882-9721. For hilarious family entertainment, take in an old-fashioned melodrama at the **Gaslight Theatre,** Wed.–Sun. year-round, southwest corner of 7010 E. Broadway Blvd. and Kolb Road, eight miles east of downtown; 520/886-9428.

Casinos

The Tohono O'odham's **Desert Diamond Casino** is just south of town near the airport at 7350 S. Nogales Hwy. one mile south of Valencia Rd.; 520/294-7777. The Pascua Yaqui tribe offers the **Casino of the Sun** on the southwest edge of town at 7406 S. Camino de Oeste; 520/883-1700.

Sporting Events

The University of Arizona **Wildcat** teams compete in football, basketball, baseball, tennis, swimming, track and field, and other sports during the school year. For ticket information call the McKale Center at 520/621-2287, 800/452-2287; www.arizcats.com. The Tucson Electric Park at

2500 E. Ajo Way hosts the **Tucson Sidewinders** minor-league baseball team early April-early Sept.; 520/434-1021; www.tucsonsidewinders.com. **Spring training** in March brings the major-league baseball teams Arizona Diamondbacks and Chicago White Sox to the Tucson Electric Park, 520/434-1000, and the Colorado Rockies to Hi Corbett Field, 520/327-9467.

Greyhounds hit the track at **Tucson Greyhound Park** year-round in South Tucson at 2601 S. 3rd Ave. at E. 36th St.; call 520/884-7576 or check the Web at www.tucdogtrak.com for the schedule. Stock cars (mostly) roar toward the finish line at **Tucson Raceway Park** on Saturday nights from the first Saturday in April to the first Saturday in October; take the I-10 Rita Road Exit 273, turn south, make the first left, and follow signs; 520/762-9200; www.daytonausa.com.

EVENTS

Something's happening nearly every day in the cooler months, and the visitors bureau knows what it is. See the events listings in the *Tucson Official Visitors Guide.* Some of the best-known annual happenings are listed below.

January: Southern Arizona Square and Round Dance and Clogging Festival attracts more than 3,000 dancers. **Tucson Quilters Guild Show** takes place mid-month. The **PGA Tucson Open Golf Tournament** draws more than 100 professional golfers.

February: The giant **Tucson Gem, Mineral, and Fossil Showcase** features more than 25 shows over a two-week period beginning in late Jan. and climaxing with the three-day **Tucson Gem and Mineral Show** (www.tgms.org), which has museum exhibits and hundreds of dealers; contact the Visitors Bureau for event listings and maps. **La Reunión de El Fuerte** in the Old Fort Lowell Neighborhood presents cavalry drills, band music, and self-guided tours to historic sites in Fort Lowell Park and the surrounding community, including places not normally open to the public. About 500 horses display their hunter/jumper skills in the **Tucson Winter Classic Horse Show.** Cowboys and cowgirls get together for a big rodeo and a colorful nonmotorized parade in **La Fiesta de los Vaqueros** on the last full weekend; www.tucsonrodeo.com. At Arizona State Museum's **Southwest Indian Art Fair,** Native Americans offer demonstrations, dancing, storytelling, and traditional foods.

Bluegrass musicians play and compete in the **Fiddler's Contest.**

March: Spring training by the major-league baseball Arizona Diamondbacks and White Sox teams at Tucson Electric Park (520/434-1000) and the Colorado Rockies at Hi Corbett Field (520/327-9467). **St. Patrick's Day Parade and Festival** celebrates Irish heritage on or near the 17th. **Wa:k Pow Wow** attracts Southwestern Indian groups to San Xavier Mission for traditional and modern singing and dancing. Top golfers compete in the **LPGA Welch's/Circle-K Championship.** The **Fourth Avenue Street Fair** late in the month features artists, craftspeople, entertainers, and food on N. 4th Avenue between University and Eighth St.; the fest repeats in December; www.avefun.com. Yoeme (Yaqui) Indians of Pascua Village in Tucson stage the **Yaqui Easter Lenten Ceremony,** a Passion play, the Friday before Palm Sunday during the Easter season; the ceremony is a mixture of Catholic and tribal ritual concerning the forces of good overcoming those of evil.

April: "Simon Peter" Passion Play is a three-hour Easter pageant. During **Spring Fling,** university students stage a carnival featuring rides, games, and food. The **Pima County Fair** offers circus events, concerts, carnival rides and games, exhibits, and livestock shows at the Pima County Fairgrounds; www.pimafair.com. The **Tucson International Mariachi Conference** presents concerts, a parade, art exhibit, and golf tournament.

May: The Hispanic community celebrates **Cinco de Mayo** on or near the fifth with art, music, dances, and food.

June: The African American community celebrates a **Juneteenth Festival** mid-month.

July: Parades, picnics, and fireworks commemorate **Independence Day** on the fourth.

August: Fiesta de San Agustín honors the

birthday of Tucson's patron saint with music, dancing, and food.

September: The **Mexican Independence Day Celebration** is a traditional Mexican fiesta with music, folkloric dancers, arts, and food. **Oktoberfest** brings German music, food, and beer to Mt. Lemmon Ski Valley on the last two weekends of September.

October: Oktoberfest at Mt. Lemmon Ski Valley continues on the first two weekends of October. Experience Tucson's ethnic diversity in art, music, dance, and food during **Tucson Heritage Experience Festival.** The **Tohono O'odham All-Indian Rodeo and Fair** features a parade, singing, dancing, crafts, and food—all offered by the tribe on their reservation near Sells, 58 miles southwest of Tucson. German bands, dancers, and food mark **La Fiesta de los Chiles** celebrates the chili pepper with entertainment, food, and crafts at Tucson Botanical Gardens late in the month; www.tucsonbotanical.org.

November: Western Music Festival brings top Western musicians for concerts and workshops. Thousands of bicyclists challenge the clock and each other in **El Tour de Tucson** races on the Saturday before Thanksgiving.

December: Luminaria Nights brightens Tucson Botanical Gardens with 20,000 luminarias and entertainment on the first full weekend; www.tucsonbotanical.org. **Fourth Avenue Street Fair** early in the month brings artists, craftspeople, entertainers, and food outdoors to N. 4th Avenue between University and Eighth Streets; www.avefun.com. **Winterhaven Festival of the Lights** has the residents and town dressed up for the holidays for 10 days beginning the Saturday before Christmas.

RECREATION
Reid Park
This spacious green park in the middle of Tucson holds a zoo, Hi Corbett baseball field, a soccer field, rose garden, lakes, and picnic areas. The park is three miles east of downtown; enter from Country Club Rd., 22nd St., or Camino Campestre. The **Tucson City Parks and Recreation** office, in the park at 900 S. Randolph

Way, offers information on facilities and programs centered at Reid and other parks; 520/791-4873; www.ci.tucson.az.us/parksandrec.

Lohse YMCA
The extensive facilities at this downtown center include an covered outdoor pool, fitness center, racquetball/handball courts, an indoor track, sauna, and whirlpool. Various fitness classes are offered. Daily passes cost $7 or you can purchase an annual membership. It's located at 60 W. Alameda; 520/623-5200. There's a parking garage above the center.

Swimming
Tucson Parks and Recreation maintains 21 swimming pools, most open during the summer only, but you can swim year-round at Archer, Catalina High School, Fort Lowell, Himmel, and Udall. Look up addresses and phone numbers in the telephone book under Tucson City Government.

You can also swim in the covered outdoor pool at Lohse YMCA, 60 W. Alameda, 520/623-5200, and in the outdoor pool at University of Arizona's McKale Center, 520/621-2599.

Tennis
With over 300 courts in town, it's not hard to find a place to play. The Visitors Bureau's *Tucson Official Visitors Guide* lists some of the public ones. The **Randolph Recreation Complex** offers 25 lighted tennis courts, instruction, and a pro shop, as well as 10 lighted racquetball courts. It's three miles east of downtown at 50 S. Alvernon Way, just south of E. Broadway; 520/791-4896.

Golf
The City of Tucson offers five 18-hole courses and there are about two dozen private and resort clubs in town; see the *Tucson Official Visitors Guide for listings.*

Horseback Riding
The countryside surrounding Tucson has some fine riding. Stables may close in summer or ride only early and late in the day. Reservations are recommended at all of the following. **Walking Winds Stables** at 10811 N. Oracle Rd., 520/742-

4200, and **Pusch Ridge Stables** at 13700 N. Oracle Rd., 520/825-1664, offer rides, cookouts, and hay-wagon rides year-round in the Santa Catalina foothills, about 13 miles north of downtown. **Cocoraque Ranch Horse Rides** west of the Arizona-Sonora Desert Museum, 520/682-8594, has rides and other activities on a working cattle ranch. **Colossal Cave Mountain Park Stables,** on the east edge of town, 520/647-3450, is also a working cattle ranch with a variety of rides.

Southern Arizona Hiking Club

About 2,000 members belong to this active group, which organizes about 50–60 hikes monthly. Hikes range from easy to challenging. The club schedules day-hikes, backpacks, climbs, river trips, ski tours, and snowshoe trips. Members also promote conservation and build trails. Visitors are welcome on hikes. Contact the club for membership information by sending a self-addressed, stamped envelope to P.O. Box 32257, Tucson, AZ 85751. You can also call 520/751-4513 for recorded information or check the Website www.sahcinfo.org.

Skiing

At **Mount Lemmon Ski Valley** in the Santa Catalina Mountains you can enjoy downhill skiing during the mid-December to mid-April season. Two double chairlifts take skiers up the slopes. The longest run is three-quarters of a mile, dropping from 9,150 to 8,200 feet through fir and aspen forests; 520/576-1321. To check on snow and road conditions, call 520/576-1400 for a recorded message.

SHOPPING

Fourth Avenue

The section of 4th Avenue between 4th and Seventh Sts. has many ethnic restaurants and a variety of craft, thrift, and antique shops. Big street fairs take place here in late March and early December. The **Food Conspiracy Co-op** has been running since 1971; it's open daily and nonmembers are welcome at 412 N. 4th Ave., between Sixth and Seventh Sts.; 520/624-4821. **Old Pueblo Trolley** runs a historic trolley along

4th Avenue and University Boulevard. Fri.–Sun.; 520/792-1802. You can find out more about 4th Avenue activities and business at the website www.avefun.com.

Shopping Centers

Tucson has four giant malls, all enclosed, airconditioned, and open daily with department stores, specialty shops, restaurants, and movie theaters (either inside or adjacent).

El Con Mall is three miles east of downtown at 3601 E. Broadway Blvd. (between Country Club Rd. and Alvernon Way); 520/795-9958. **Park Place** is six miles east of downtown at 5870 E. Broadway Blvd. (between Craycroft and Wilmot Rds.); 520/748-1222. **Tucson Mall** is one of the largest in the state, with more than 200 stores, 4.5 miles north of downtown at 4500 N. Oracle and Wetmore Rds.; 520/293-7330. **Foothills Mall—Outlets, Entertainment & More** has many shops, 10 miles north of downtown at 7401 N. La Cholla Blvd. and W. Ina Rd.; 520/219-0650.

Art Galleries

Be sure to see **DeGrazia Gallery in the Sun** (see **Northeast of Downtown,** above). **Old Town Artisans,** in the middle of the downtown El Presidio District, offers a large selection of crafts and art produced by local, Indian, Mexican, and international artists. Open Mon.–Sat. 9:30 A.M. (10:30 A.M. in summer)–5:30 P.M. and Sunday noon–5 P.M.; 520/623-6024, 800/782-8072, www.oldtown artisans.com. It's on the corner of 186 N. Meyer Ave. and Telles St., near the Tucson Museum of Art. The Visitors Bureau has many listings for arts, crafts, and antiques in its *Tucson Official Visitors Guide.*

Bookstores

Bookman's Used Books claims to be Arizona's largest used-book store, with some music, video, and new titles, too. It's at 1930 E. Grant Rd. at Campbell, 520/325-5767; and at 3733 W. Ina Rd., 520/579-0303. The **Book Stop** offers used hardbound books and some used paperback

© BILL WEIR

Mission at DeGrazia Gallery in the Sun

books and magazines at 2504 N. Campbell Ave.; 520/326-6661.

You'll find huge selections of new books at **Borders Books & Music,** 4235 N. Oracle Rd., 520/292-1331, and in Park Place on 5870 E. Broadway Blvd., 520/584-0111.

Audubon Nature Shop, at 300 E. University Blvd., offers books on nature and birdwatching along with binoculars and other supplies; 520/629-0510; closed Sunday.

The **University of Arizona** bookstore sells Arizona and Southwest titles along with general reading material and textbooks. It's at the west end of the Student Union, 520/621-2426; www .uofabookstore.com.

Outdoor Supplies and Maps

For hiking, camping, and climbing gear, try **Summit Hut,** 5045 E. Speedway Blvd., 520/ 325-1554, www.summithut.com; or the three stores of **Popular Outfitters,** at Campbell and Glenn (520/326-2520), Broadway and Wilmot (520/290-1644), or at Oracle and Orange Grove (520/575-1044).

Summit Hut also carries hiking, national forest, state, and Mexico maps. Another good source is **Tucson's Map & Flag Center** at 3239 N. 1st Ave., 520/887-4234; closed Sunday.

Cactus

B&B Cactus Farm sells a great variety of cacti and succulents from tiny potted arrangements to huge saguaro on the east edge of town at 11550 E. Speedway Blvd., 520/721-4687; closed Sunday. Also in far east Tucson, **Tanque Verde Greenhouses** has thousands of cacti of many sizes and from many lands at 10810 E. Tanque Verde Rd., 520/749-4414; closed Sunday.

INFORMATION

Tourist Office

The very helpful folks at **Metropolitan Tucson Convention & Visitors Bureau** provide the excellent *Tucson Official Visitors Guide* and many brochures of area sights and services; you can find them downtown in the Visitor Center at 110 S. Church Ave., Suite 7199; 520/624-1817,

800/638-8350; fax 520/884-7804; www.visit-tucson.org. (Mailing address is 100 S. Church Ave., Tucson, AZ 85701.) The office is open Mon.–Fri. 8 A.M.–5 P.M. and Sat.–Sun. 9 A.M.–4 P.M.; you can pick up the visitor guide outside when the office is closed. Closest parking is in a garage across Church Avenue.

Coronado National Forest

The **Supervisor's Office** contains general information on all the districts in the Coronado, including many of the most scenic areas in southeastern Arizona. It's downtown in room 6A (sixth floor) of the Federal Building, 300 W. Congress St. (Tucson, AZ 85701); 520/670-4552, www.fs.fed.us/r3/coronado. Open Mon.–Fri. 8 A.M.–4:30 P.M.

For specific information on the campgrounds, trails, and backcountry regions of the Santa Catalinas, contact the **Santa Catalina Ranger District** office; open Mon.–Fri. 8 A.M.–4:30 P.M. and Sat.–Sun. 8:30 A.M.–4:30 P.M. It's in the Sabino Canyon Visitor Center, 5700 N. Sabino Canyon Rd. (Tucson, AZ 85750); 520/749-8700; www.fs.fed.us/r3/coronado/scrd.

Bureau of Land Management

For information about recreational opportunities on land administered by the BLM in southeastern Arizona, including the Ironwood Forest Natl. Monument, Las Cienegas Natl. Conservation Area, San Pedro, and Middle Gila River areas, contact the Tucson office Mon.–Fri. 8 A.M.–4 P.M. It's way out of town at 12661 E. Broadway (Tucson, AZ 85748); 520/722-4289; www.az.blm.gov.

Mexican Consulate

The Consulado de Mexico has information for visiting and driving in Mexico. Some tourist literature may be available, too. Open Mon.–Fri. 8 A.M.–2 P.M.; 520/882-5595, 520/882-5596. It's just south of downtown in an 1860s' building at 553 S. Stone (Tucson, AZ 85701); www.embassyosmexico.org.

Libraries

The **City of Tucson Main Library** is downtown at 101 N. Stone between Pennington and Alameda; look for a large white and gray marble building. It's open Mon.-Wed. 10 A.M.–9 P.M., Thurs. 9 A.M.–6 P.M., Friday 10 A.M.–5 P.M., Saturday 9 A.M.–5 P.M., and Sunday 1–5 P.M.; 520/791-4393 (recording) or 520/791-4010 (Infoline); www.lib.ci.tucson.az.us. You can park in the underground garage, two hours free with validation; enter from Alameda. The library has 18 branches.

University of Arizona libraries are open to the public and include some outstanding collections. Hours vary with seasons; 520/621-6441. The website www.library.arizona.edu provides access to library catalogs and hours.

Newspapers

Tucson's major dailies are the *Arizona Daily Star* in the morning and the *Tucson Citizen* in the afternoon; only the *Star* publishes a Sunday edition. The Friday "Caliente" section of the *Star* reports on nightlife, concerts, theater, and dancing. Web address is www.azstarnet.com.

The *Tucson Citizen* includes local happenings and movies in its "Living" section Mon.–Sat., with more detailed reports in the Thursday "Calendar" section; www.tucsoncitizen.com.

The *Tucson Weekly's* lively pages report on most everything that's happening in Tucson, along with feature articles and restaurant listings. It's free at newsstands or you can visit the website, www.tucsonweekly.com, which also has the annual "Best of Tucson" reviews.

SERVICES

The **main post office** is 2.5 miles southeast of downtown at 1501 S. Cherrybell Stravanue; General Delivery mail can be sent here (Tucson, AZ 85726); 800/275-8777. The downtown branch is at 141 S. Sixth Avenue. You'll find another branch at 911B E. University Blvd., between Tyndall and Park Avenues.

Banks no longer provide a foreign exchange service except unless you have an account, but ATM machines are widespread and usually accept foreign cards. **Arizona Stamp & Coin** will buy and sell Mexican pesos at 4668 E.

Speedway Blvd. and Swan, 520/795-1594; closed Sunday.

Pima County Medical Society will refer you to any sort of doctor you might need. It's open Mon.–Fri. 8:30 A.M.–4:30 P.M.; 520/795-7985.

TOURS AND TRANSPORTATION

Tours

Gray Line Tours offers day-trips of the city (Bario Historico, Old Town Artisans, and San Xavier, 3.5 hours), San Xavier/Desert Museum (four hours), Biosphere 2 (five hours), Tubac/Nogales (eight hours), and Tombstone/Bisbee (eight hours). Two- and three-day tours visit the Grand Canyon; fares depend on group size. The office is downtown 181 W. Broadway (P.O. Box 1991, Tucson, AZ 85702); 520/622-8811, 800/276-1528; www.graylinearizona.com.

Old Pueblo Tours, 520/795-7448, conducts downtown tours of about two hours beginning from the Visitor Center. **Trail Dust Adventures Jeep Tours,** 520/747-0323, takes in scenery and petroglyphs on a private jeep trail in the Tortolita Mountains northwest of Tucson.

Chandelle Tours runs river trips on a scenic section of the Gila River near Winkelman, a bit over an hour's drive north, from mid-March to mid-Sept.; you'll travel in rafts or inflatable kayaks on a gentle float with a good chance of seeing wildlife; trips include about four hours on the water plus lunch at $79. You can also sign up for day-long rafting trips on the Salt River from about early March to mid-May. Tours to Karchner Caverns are offered too; 520/577-1824, 800/242-6335; www.azcaverntours.com.

For hot-air balloon flights in the Tucson area call **Fleur de Tucson Balloon Tours,** 520/529-1025, **Balloon Rides USA,** 520/299-7744, or **Southern Arizona Balloon Excursions,** 520/624-3599, 800/524-3599.

Taxis

Taxis companies include **Allstate Cab,** 520/798-1111; **Yellow Cab,** 520/624-6611; and **Ameri-Cab,** 520/797-7979.

Local Bus

Sun Tran takes you to the parks, sights, and shopping areas of the city and to the airport for only $1; you must have exact change. Transfers are free; ask the driver before you pay your fare. Drivers also sell a $2 day pass.

Buses congregate at the Ronstadt Transit Center, downtown at Congress and Sixth Ave.; the Tohono Tadai Transit Center in the north at 4540 N. Stone; and at Laos Transit Center in the south at 205 W. Irvington Road. For Sun Tran information call 520/792-9222 or check the Web at www.suntran.com. The Visitors Bureau has free schedules.

Old Pueblo Trolley runs a historic trolley along 4th Avenue Fri.–Sun.; 520/792-1802.

Long-Distance Bus

Greyhound offers frequent service to many cities from its terminal downtown at 2 S. 4th Ave. at E. Broadway; it's open 24 hours and has lockers and a coffee shop; 800/231-2222 (fares and schedules) or 520/882-4386 (local terminal); www.greyhound.com.

Golden State/Crucero connects the Greyhound terminal with Nogales many times daily with stops at Green Valley and other communities along I-19; daily services also go from Tucson to Phoenix and from Tucson to Douglas via Sierra Vista, and Bisbee. Some buses continue past Nogales into Mexico; 520/623-1675.

Train

Amtrak schedules three eastbound and two westbound departures every week on the Sunset Limited/Texas Eagle. The train connects Los Angeles with Chicago (Texas Eagle) and Orlando (Sunset Limited), splitting or joining in Texas. Amtrak's terminal is downtown at 400 E. Toole Ave., two blocks north of the Greyhound station; for reservations and information call 800/872-7245 or check the website, www.amtrak.com. Fares depend on availability, so you'll get the lowest fares in off-peak times or by calling 8–10 weeks (or more) ahead.

Air

The **Tucson International Airport** is 8.5 miles

south of downtown. About ten airlines touch down here with nonstop service to 15 cities in the United States, as well as to Hermosillo in Mexico. The website www.tucsonairport.org has airport information and links to airlines. Information counters at both ends of the airport have brochures. Sun Tran Bus numbers 11 and 25, airport shuttles, and taxis connect the airport with downtown. **Arizona Stagecoach**

provides 24-hour shuttle service between the airport and your destination in the Tucson and Green Valley areas; for a ride to the airport, call 520/889-1000 24 hours advance. **Arizona Shuttle Service** runs hourly day and evening to Sky Harbor Airport in Phoenix from 5350 E. Speedway Blvd., the University of Arizona (6th St. and Cherry Ave.), and I-10 and Ina Rd.; 520/795-6771.

West to Organ Pipe Cactus National Monument

TOHONO O'ODHAM RESERVATION

Twenty-five miles west of Tucson on AZ 86 lies the main Tohono O'odham Reservation. The land appears inhospitable—dry sandy washes and plains, broken here and there by rocky hills or mountains. The first white people couldn't believe that humans could live in such wild and parched desert, yet the Tohono O'odham have thrived here for centuries.

Most Tohono O'odham are friendly, but the tribe has shown little interest in tourism. The vast reservation has hardly any visitor facilities and not a single motel, tourist office, or tribal museum. Two attractions, in addition to the desert scenery, make a visit worthwhile: the world-famous Kitt Peak Observatory and the Tohono O'odham All-Indian Rodeo and Fair.

KITT PEAK

Large white domes perched atop the 6,875-foot summit enclose instruments that unravel the mysteries of the universe. You're welcome to drive up and see the observatory and astronomy exhibits. The 24 telescopes come in many sizes and types, including two that use radio waves. The Association of Universities for Research in Astronomy (AURA) operates these National Optical Astronomy Observatories for the National Science Foundation.

Visitor Center

Here you can see an introductory video and ex-

hibits that illustrate the nature of light and the workings of telescopes. The visitor center gift shop sells Tohono O'odham basketry at very good prices, as well as astronomy-related books, posters, videos, and T-shirts. Kitt Peak National Observatory is open daily 9 A.M.–4 P.M. (to 3:45 P.M. for the visitor center) except New Year's Day, Thanksgiving Day, and Dec. 24–25; free admission (donations welcome). Check schedules, basic information, and winter road conditions by calling 520/318-8200 (recording) or 520/318-8726 (visitor center); www.noao.edu.

The air is cool up here—15-20° colder than Tucson—so a jacket or sweater will usually be needed. Kitt Peak lies 56 miles southwest of Tucson via AZ 86 and AZ 386. The last 12 miles are on a paved and well-graded mountain road, though winter storms can close it for short periods. Visitors need to come prepared with warm clothing, food, and a full tank of gas—there's no restaurant or store here. On the drive up, you'll pass a picnic area entrance on the left (1.5 miles before the visitor center) with a picnic ramada, tables, drinking water, and restrooms in an oak forest.

Tours and Visitor Programs

Pick up a map at the visitor center for the self-guided tour of the grounds that passes some of the most impressive telescopes. Visitors may enter viewing galleries of three telescopes and read signs about workings of others. Free one-hour tours present more background and details; they leave the visitor center daily at 10 A.M., 11:30 A.M., and 1:30 P.M. Stargazing programs take place nightly using the 16-inch telescope located directly above the entrance to the visitor center. You'll need to make a reservation (at least two weeks ahead, if possible) and pay $35 ($30 children under 18, students, and seniors). The Advanced Observing Program enables one or two amateur astronomers to use telescope equipment with professional guidance. You'll need to make reservations and pay $330 one person or $385 for two persons; rates include room and board but there are no rainchecks! Visitor center staff and the website www.noao.edu have details on these programs.

The Telescopes

Before Kitt Peak was built, students and women found it almost impossible to secure time at a major telescope; here they have an equal chance. Astronomers use the equipment free of charge, but receive no rain checks. People learn to be philosophical, waiting many months only to be clouded out.

Computers control the instruments; CCD (charge-coupled device) image sensors convert light into digital form and store it on computer tape for later analysis. It's rare for an observer to actually look through a telescope these days, and few instruments even feature an eyepiece. Most telescopes at Kitt Peak have designs to maximize their light-gathering power rather than their magnification—a distant star looks the same size through even the biggest scopes. The McMath-Pierce Solar Telescope, however, produces a 30-inch image of the sun by using mirrors in a slanted 500-foot corridor, about 300 feet of which run below ground. You can go inside to inspect the interior; a TV screen displays the sun's image. This telescope won an architectural award in 1962, a rare accolade for an observatory.

The 2.1-meter (84-inch) telescope nearby was the first large instrument on Kitt Peak for nighttime viewing; a viewing gallery and exhibits are inside. Astronomers use the scope to observe distant stars and galaxies in both the visible and infrared spectra. The Mayall four-meter (158-inch), one of the world's largest telescopes, requires a building 18 stories high. An elevator takes you to the 10th-floor observation deck, offering panoramic views of southern Arizona and northern Sonora. Spacewatch, a group at the University of Arizona's Lunar and Planetary Laboratory, explores the solar system for small objects—including Earth-orbit-crossing asteroids—with 1.8-meter and 0.9-meter telescopes. Visit www.lpl.arizona.edu/spacewatch/ for details. If you stop at the picnic area, you can get a close look at a giant radio telescope of the Very Long Baseline Array; it's one of 10 spaced between Hawaii and the Caribbean that link to form a single antenna with an amazing resolution; a sign explains how this works.

SELLS

Sells, the largest town on the Tohono O'odham Reservation, serves as tribal headquarters. The dependable water here has made the place a popular stop for travelers since prehistoric times. Originally known as Indian Oasis, the settlement took its present name in 1918 to honor Indian Commissioner Cato Sells. The town lies 58 miles southwest of Tucson via AZ 86, 20 miles past the turnoff for Kitt Peak. Offices, schools, and a shopping center line a business loop just south of the main highway.

Sells Shopping Center has a shop with Tohono O'odham baskets and other Indian crafts, a **Basha's** supermarket and bakery, and a post office. The **Papago Café** and another crafts shop lie on the main highway just west of the business loop. You'll find another trading post with Tohono O'odham crafts 22 miles west at Quijotoa.

Tohono O'odham All-Indian Rodeo and Fair

Tohono O'odham cowboys show off their riding and roping skills in the tribe's big annual event, held in late January or early February. The Tohono O'odham put on a parade, exhibit crafts, serve Indian fry bread, and perform songs and dances. Obtain the dates from the tribal office in Sells, 520/383-2221, or the Visitors Bureau in Tucson, 520/632-6024, 800/638-8350.

Before camping or exploring the backcountry, check to see if you'll need a permit from one of the 11 districts of the reservation; the **Tohono O'odham Tribe Administration,** Sells, AZ 85634, 520/383-2221, can advise you on which district to contact and give you its telephone number. The administration office is in an all-white building with a man-in-the-maze symbol, near schools on the north side of the business loop; enter from the back. Ask about road conditions if you plan to venture off the main highway; dirt roads can become impassable after rains.

ORGAN PIPE CACTUS NATIONAL MONUMENT

The Sonoran Desert puts on its finest show in this remote area of Arizona. Some desert plants, such as the senita cactus and elephant tree, grow only here and in Mexico. The name of Arizona's largest national monument honors the giant organ pipe cactus, which thrives in this area. In appearance it's similar to the saguaro, though the organ pipe's many branches all radiate from the base.

Animals adapt to the heat by hiding out during the hottest part of the day. They're most active morning, evening, and night. Wildlife you might see include lizards, birds, kangaroo rats, kit foxes, bobcats, javelina, bighorn sheep, and pronghorn. The six species of rattlesnakes are nocturnal during hot weather—a good reason to use a flashlight at night. About 40 species of birds stay year-round; more than 230 others drop in while migrating. Quitobaquito Oasis offers prime birding (see **Puerto Blanco Scenic Drive,** below).

If you're lucky enough to arrive in March or April after a wet winter, you'll see the desert ablaze with flowers in yellow, blue, red, and violet. Annual plants bloom first as they must quickly germinate and produce seeds before the onslaught of the summer heat. The smaller cacti, such as cholla and prickly pear, come next. And lastly, the big saguaro and organ pipe blossoms appear, peaking in May or June. A wildflower hotline provided by the Desert Botanical Garden

in Phoenix tells what's happening during the spring; 602/754-8134.

Summer is the quiet season at the monument, as daytime highs commonly range from 95° to 105°F. Thunderstorms arrive in late summer, bringing about half the annual 9.5 inches or so of rain. Winters run cool to warm, with occasional gentle rains.

Visitor Center

For an introduction to the highly adaptable plants and wildlife that live here, start at the visitor center, located 22 miles south of Why. A slide presentation gives an overview of the area. Exhibits describe plants and animals of the region and the effects of humans on the desert. Just outside, a short paved nature trail identifies common plants and provides more information on the desert environment.

Rangers can answer your questions and issue camping permits. Staff sell books, prints, and topo maps. Naturalists offer programs during the cooler months at the visitor center, on trails, and at the campground. **Tohono O'odham Day** takes place Saturday on the third weekend in March with craft demonstrations, food, and programs. The visitor center is open daily 8 A.M.–5 P.M.; 520/387-6849; www.nps.gov/orpi. Monument admission is $5 per vehicle.

Puerto Blanco Scenic Drive

Varied desert environments, Quitobaquito Oasis, and rare desert plants of the Senita Basin are highlights of this 53-mile loop. A pamphlet explains features at numbered stops; pick one up at the visitor center or at the start of the drive just west of the visitor center. Nearly the entire route is graded dirt designed for slow speeds—allow at least a half day. Note that a section of the drive is one-way (counterclockwise) and that you can't turn back. Picnic tables and three short hiking trails invite longer visits. Mountain bikers can ride the drive in either direction, though it's a bit long to do the whole loop.

Red Tanks Tinaja Trail, 1.2 miles round-trip, winds through pretty desert hills to some small natural pools in a wash. It starts 600 feet before Stop 3 (where you park), four miles in

THE GILA MONSTER

(Heloderma suspectum)

This venomous lizard spends more than 95 percent of its solitary life underground or beneath rocks. In spring, during summer monsoons, and in autumn it comes out to feed on eggs—especially of Gambel quail—and small prey such as birds, young rabbits, and rodents. Fat reserves in the tail see it through the winter. Gila monsters mate in early summer, then the female lays her eggs in cool, moist soil in arroyos.

Although active during the day and on some warm summer nights, the "monster" is seen by few people. You can recognize it by its beadlike scales in black, yellow, orange, or pink patterns. Adults grow to a length of 18–24 inches and weigh up to two pounds. Each individual keeps to a small range, but the species extends over much of southern and western Arizona in desert foothills. A larger and darker cousin, the Mexican beaded lizard *(Heloderma horridum)* roams farther south in Mexico.

The Gila monster, despite its name, is shy and gentle—it becomes dangerous only if picked up or cornered. When threatened, it gets nasty by clamping down with powerful jaws; venom produced in the lower jaw then seeps through grooves in the teeth. The lizard may try to hang on and on while the painful poison works its way into the wound. Methods of loosening the grip include using a stick in the mouth and pushing back, applying a flame under the jaw, immersing the lizard in water, or in desperation, yanking the lizard off by its tail. First aid and a physician will be needed to clean the wound and treat the pain, bleeding, swelling, and lowered blood pressure.

Both common sense and Arizona law protect the Gila monster.

on the drive. **Dripping Springs Mine Trail,** two miles roundtrip, climbs gentle slopes with views to a 1918 claim. It begins at Mile 11.9 on the drive; park here or at the Little Continental Divide at Mile 11.5. **Senita Basin Trail** makes a 2.5-mile loop from the end of the spur road to Senita Basin.

Quitobaquito, one mile off the loop, features a large artificial pond surrounded by tall cottonwoods. The springs lie 100 yards north up a trail. Ducks and other waterfowl—not what you'd expect in the desert—drop in during the spring and autumn. Coots stay here year-round. Father Kino and other early Spanish missionaries and explorers stopped here on their way to the Colorado River. The '49ers headed for the California goldfields came by too, favoring a southern route to avoid hostile Indians roaming farther north. Many goldseekers perished of thirst on the fearsome Camino del Diablo or Devil's Highway between Sonoita and the Colorado River. Quitobaquito provided one of few sources of water on the route. Vehicle break-ins occur occasionally here and all along the Mexican border; don't leave valuables in the car when parked here.

Senita Basin, four miles off the loop, is home to the senita cactus and elephant tree. Similar in appearance to organ pipe cactus, the senita is distinguished by its gray whiskers and sparse arm ribs. The elephant tree looks like the root system of an upside-down tree. Examples of a senita and an elephant tree are at stop 24.

Ajo Mountain Drive

Heading into the more rugged country of the eastern part of the monument, this drive skirts the base of 4,808-foot Mt. Ajo with many spectacular views. Most of the 21-mile gravel loop road is one-way; pick up a pamphlet describing the drive at the visitor center or at the start of the loop, just across the highway from the visitor center; allow at least two hours. Mountain bikers enjoy the loop, which they can ride in either direction.

Estes Canyon-Bull Pasture Trail, off Ajo Mountain Dr., is the most spectacular established trail. The Estes Canyon segment follows the canyon; the Bull Pasture part climbs a ridge. The trails meet and then continue to Bull Pasture, where ranchers once grazed cattle. The entire loop, including the spur trail to Bull Pasture, is

SOUTHERN ARIZONA

4.1 miles roundtrip with some steep sections and loose rock; carry water.

Hiking

Besides the trails along the scenic drives, you have several options near the campground, 1.5 miles from the visitor center. On the 1.2-mile **Desert View Nature Trail** loop, you'll travel up a wash, then climb onto a ridge with a good panorama. **Victoria Mine Trail,** 4.5 miles roundtrip, takes you to a historic mine that produced lead, silver, and gold. Also beginning at the campground are a one-mile trail encircling the camping area and a 1.3-mile trail to the visitor center. New interconnecting trails provide a variety of loop possibilities from the campground, Puerto Blanco Drive and Senita Basin Road. Hikers can do countless cross-country trips in the monument's open terrain. Rangers can help you plan. The visitor center sells an inexpensive *Explorer's Guide to Walks, Routes, and the Back Country.* You'll need a permit for any overnight hikes.

Accommodations, Campgrounds, and Food

The 208-site campground near the visitor center is open all year, with room for trailers to 35 feet. There's drinking water but no hookups or showers; sites cost $10 per night. It fills most days during the busy season after Christmas to early April, when campers should try to arrive by 11 A.M.

Tenters who want to leave the asphalt and flush toilets behind can camp at **Alamo Canyon Primitive Campground,** 14 miles away. This pretty spot is also a good base for day hikes. You'll need to register first at the visitor center and pay $6. No trailers or RVs permitted.

For motels, stores, gas stations, and restaurants you must leave the monument. Nearest services are at Lukeville, Arizona (five miles south); Sonoita, Mexico (two miles farther); and Why (22 miles north).

VICINITY OF ORGAN PIPE CACTUS NATIONAL MONUMENT

Lukeville

Just a wide spot on the road next to the Mexican border, Lukeville honors WW I flying ace Frank Luke. Besides the immigration and customs offices, Lukeville has a gas station, supermarket/general store, café (breakfast, lunch, and dinner daily), and the **Gringo Pass Motel and Trailer Park;** 520/387-5507. Rooms here cost $55.70 s, $65 d. The campground, which closes in summer, has showers and costs $11 for RV and tent sites.

Sonoita, Mexico

Several restaurants, motels, curio shops, and an attractive little plaza lie two miles southwest of the Mexican border in Sonoita. Beaches, fishing, and seafood lure many visitors 63 more miles to Puerto Peñasco on the Sea of Cortez. There you'll find seaside motels, restaurants, and trailer parks. A permit is required for travel beyond Sonoita. You can buy Mexican auto insurance on both sides of the border, in Why, and in Ajo.

Why

Why Why? Because motorists used to call it "the Y." Why centers on the junction of AZ Highways 85 and 86 north of Organ Pipe Cactus National Monument. The **Why Not Travel Store** downtown offers gas, snacks, groceries, Mexican insurance, and a post office. A gas station across the street also has snacks and groceries. A few RV parks and cafés round out the town's offerings.

Las Palmas RV Park, just west of the junction, has showers. Sites run $10 tent, $16.50 RV with hookups; 520/387-6304. On the east side of town, try **Coyote Howls Trailer Park** with senior activities and coin showers. No hookups, but a water fill and a dump station are available. Sites cost $5 for a tent, van, or pickup camper, $8 for larger units; 520/387-5209. Continue 1.5 miles east from Why to **Hickiwan Trails RV Park** on the north side of AZ 86, behind a gas station/convenience store. Sites have showers and cost $7.50

© BILL WEIR

cristate growth on an organ pipe cactus

for dry camping for tent or RV, $15 with hookups; 520/362-2923, 520/362-2918. Another campground is across the highway. To camp free of charge, you might ask people at Why for suggestions. RVs park on BLM land at Gunsight Wash, 1.9 miles south of Why on Hwy. 85 just after the bridge, though there's talk of cutting back on overnight use here.

AJO

This pleasant small town appears lost in a sea of desert. It's 10 miles northwest of Why and 42 miles south of Gila Bend. The town's name (pronounced "Al-I-ho") may have come from the Tohono O'odham word for paint; Indians collected copper minerals here to use in painting their bodies.

Prospectors settled as early as 1854, but Ajo didn't really get going until the dawn of the 20th century, when suitable ore-refining techniques became available. The New Cornelia Copper Company was founded in 1917 and later bought by Phelps Dodge. Squeezed between low copper prices and high costs, Phelps Dodge shut down the mine and smelter in 1985. After weathering some hard times, Ajo has been discovered by retirees and winter visitors. There are now plans for resuming mining in the giant open pit, though opening will depend on the price for copper.

Graceful palms and flowering trees surround the Spanish colonial-style plaza and many public buildings downtown. Greenery and trees grow around the miners' tiny houses.

Sights

The **New Cornelia Open Pit Mine** just south of town ranks as one of the world's largest, 1.5 miles across. A tiny visitor center here has a few exhibits and a copper mining video; it's open daily from October to April. To reach the mine lookout from downtown, turn southwest on La Mina Avenue, then turn right on Indian Village Road and follow signs. The nearby **Ajo Historical Museum** houses mining, mineral, pioneer, and Indian exhibits in a former St. Catherine's Indian Mission (1942–68). It's open daily about noon–4 P.M. Oct.–April; from the mine overlook, continue to the end of Indian Village Road and turn left; 520/387-7105.

SOUTHERN ARIZONA

Accommodations

Peak winter/early spring rates are listed here. **Under $50:** The town's motels lie north of town on 2nd Ave./Hwy. 85: **Marine Motel,** 1966 N. 2nd Ave. (Hwy. 85), 520/387-7626, $55–65 d; and **La Siesta Motel,** 2561 N. Hwy. 85, 520/387-6569, $54 d (less expensive trailers can be rented too).   **$50– 100: The Guest House Inn** offers bed and breakfast at 700 Guest House Rd., 520/387-6133; $79 s, $89 d.

Campgrounds

Local campgrounds, all with showers, include **Shadow Ridge RV Resort,** 431 N. Hwy. 85, 520/387-5055; **Ajo Heights RV Park,** 2000 N. Hwy. 85, 520/387-6796; **Belly Acres RV Park,** 2030 N. Hwy. 85, 520/387-5767; and **La Siesta Motel,** 2561 N. Hwy. 85, 520/387-6569.

Food

Don Juan's, southwest of the plaza across the road, serves Mexican-American food daily except Wednesday for breakfast, lunch, and dinner; 520/387-3100. **Pizza Hut,** 627 N. 2nd Ave., 520/387-6842, offers lunch (buffet available) and dinner daily. **Señor Sancho's,** 663 N. 2nd Ave., 520/387-6226, cooks Mexican fare for lunch and dinner daily. **Dairy Queen,** 1304 N. Hwy. 85, has snacks and treats. **Bamboo Village,** 1810 N. 2nd Ave., 520/387-7536, fixes Chinese food for lunch and dinner daily except Monday.

Golf

The **Ajo Country Club** has a nine-hole golf course and a restaurant open daily for breakfast and lunch and Friday for dinner. It's seven miles northeast of town via Well and Mead Rds.; 520/387-5011.

Information and Services

The **Ajo District Chamber of Commerce,** 400 Taladro (Ajo, AZ 85321), 520/387-7742, is on the main highway one block southeast of the plaza. It's open Mon.–Fri. 8:30 A.M.–4:30 P.M.; also Saturday 10 A.M.–3 P.M. in the cooler months if staffing permits.   **Si Como No** ("yes, why not") sells regional books and topo maps as well as gift and clothing items at 207 Taladro, just southeast of the plaza. **Ajo Stage Line,** 321 Taladro, 520/387-6467 or 800/942-1981, offers many trips in Mexico and the Western U.S., including popular day tours to Rocky Point; www.ajostageline.com. Agencies in town advertise Mexican insurance. Ajo's **post office** and **public library** are by the plaza.

CABEZA PRIETA NATIONAL WILDLIFE REFUGE

The 860,000 acres of desert wilderness west of Organ Pipe Cactus National Monument hasn't changed much since white people arrived. The region has no facilities, no paved roads, no running water.

Desert bighorn sheep, for which the refuge was founded in 1939, and the endangered Sonoran pronghorn receive protection here. Much of the refuge has wilderness designation. Twelve small mountain ranges rise above the desert floor. Wildlife and vegetation are similar to those in Organ Pipe Cactus National Monument, but the climate is harsher. Cabeza Prieta's annual rainfall averages about nine inches in the east and three inches in the west. Some areas go more than a year without rain.

Only jeep tracks and remnants of the old El Camino del Diablo (Devil's Highway) traverse the landscape. Allow at least two days to cross the refuge on the roads between Ajo and Wellton; distance is 124 miles one-way, 59 miles in the refuge. An alternate connecting route, the Christmas Pass/Tacna Road from I-8, closes for two weeks in March or April for military training. A shorter trip to the Growler Mountains, 20 miles (two hours) west of Ajo via Charley Bell Pass Road, offers a chance to see pronghorn on the plains and desert bighorn sheep in the mountains; the road ends at Charley Bell Pass, where there's hiking.

Visitors must obtain a permit for entry and sign a liability release. You'll need a four-wheel-drive vehicle as anything else will get stuck in the loose sand. Vehicles must stay on designated roads. Be aware that Cabeza Prieta's rough roads can be very hard on vehicles; also, heavy brush can scratch up vehicle paint ("Arizona pin-striping"). Carry desert travel supplies and plenty of extra water. Be sure to talk with a refuge officer before your trip to find out current conditions. Summer temperatures can be downright dangerous.

The Cabeza Prieta National Wildlife Refuge visitor center is at 1611 N. Second Ave. (Ajo, AZ 85321), on the highway just north of town; 520/387-6483. It's open Mon.–Fri. 7:30 A.M.-noon and 1–4:30 P.M. Inside you'll find wildlife exhibits, videos, and a slide presentation.

South from Tucson to Mexico

Mexico lies at the end of a short drive south from Tucson via I-19, just 63 miles or 100 km—all of I-19 is signed in metric. Except for the speed limits, that is—the Highway Patrol doesn't want motorists feigning confusion at the sight of "120 kph" signs.

You'll follow the Santa Cruz River Valley, one of the first areas in Arizona colonized by the Spanish. The Jesuit priest Eusebio Francisco Kino began mission work at Guévavi and Tumacacori in 1691, then moved to San Xavier and other sites. Livestock, new crops, and the new religion introduced by Kino and later padres greatly changed the lives of the Indians. You may wish to stop at some of the many historic and scenic sights on the way. Some fine resorts, guest ranches, and inns lie along the route; low-budget travelers may prefer to check out the campgrounds here or stay in Tucson or Nogales motels.

MISSION SAN XAVIER DEL BAC

This gleaming white church rises from the desert as a testimonial to the faith of early Spanish missionaries and the Tohono O'odham Indians. One of the finest pieces of Spanish colonial architecture in the United States, its beauty has given rise to the name White Dove of the Desert. Padre Kino first visited the site in 1692, and a chapel went up in 1700. The church's name honors Kino's patron saint. The Indian village name of Bac or *Wa:k* means "where the water comes out of the ground."

The mission often lacked a resident priest and suffered many difficulties during its early years. Pima Indian revolts in 1734 and 1751 caused serious damage. Raiding Apache harassed resi-

dents and stole livestock. The oldest surviving part of the mission dates from 1757-63, when the Jesuit Father Alonso Espinosa built a large, flat-roofed adobe church. This structure was later moved and butted up against the east bell tower of the present church, and it is now part of the south wing of the mission.

Franciscan missionaries began construction of the present church, a marvelous example of Mexican folk baroque architecture, in 1783. Shortage of materials and skilled artisans resulted in the folksy character of the building. There was no marble, so the main altar was painted to look like marble; no glazed tiles, so the dadoes were painted to look like tiles; and few fine fabrics, so curtains were painted on.

A bit of mystery surrounds the church. No one knows for sure who designed it. Legends give various reasons for why the east bell tower and other parts were left unfinished, but records state that friars ran short of construction funds.

You're welcome to step inside the church and admire the many paintings, statues, and embellishments. A statue of St. Francis Xavier above the altar, ordered from Mexico in 1759, predates the church and is the most famous of the 50 or so statues inside. Above him stands the Virgin of the Immaculate Conception; highest of all is a figure representing the Catholic God. Another figure of St. Francis Xavier reclines in the west alcove where it receives much veneration. You can take flash photos unless a service is in progress; worshippers shouldn't be photographed. The church is still a spiritual center for the Tohono O'odham. Masses are held Sunday at 8 A.M., 11 A.M., and 12:30 P.M.; Tues.–Fri. at 8:30 A.M., and Saturday at 5:30 P.M.

SOUTHERN ARIZONA

The **mission museum** introduces the people of Wa:k and the Spanish missionaries, then tells the church's history with architectural plans, photos, religious art, priests' vestments, and furnishings; a video illustrates how the artwork has been brought back to life in a major restoration project. Exhibits are open daily with hours depending on the season. A **gift shop** on the east side sells religious and Southwest souvenirs, San Xavier and regional books, and some Indian crafts. **San Xavier Plaza** across from the mission includes the **Wa:k Snack Shop** (Mexican, Indian, and American food) and shops selling crafts of Tohono O'odham, Zuni, Hopi, Navajo, and other tribes. Indians set up food stalls outside, especially on Sunday and religious holidays.

To the west stands a former mortuary chapel where two early Franciscan friars lie buried. The small hill to the east features a replica of the Grotto of Lourdes. Major religious celebrations are the Feast of St. Francis of Assisi on October 4th (2 days) and the Feast of St. Francis Xavier on December 3rd (3 days). In March, usually on the 2nd weekend, the Wa:k Pow Wow attracts Southwestern Indian groups to San Xavier Mission for traditional and modern singing and dancing.

Mission San Xavier del Bac is open daily 7 A.M.–5 P.M., donations welcome; 520/294-2624. It's 10 miles south of downtown Tucson; take I-19 south to Exit 92 and follow signs west and north 1.2 miles.

GREEN VALLEY AREA

Green Valley (pop. 26,000) is a retirement area nestled in rolling hills overlooking the Santa Cruz Valley, 25 miles south of Tucson; take I-19 Exits 63, 65, or 69. Pecan orchards grow to the northeast, and a several major sights lie nearby.

Asarco Mineral Discovery Center and Mine Tours

The terraced white hills west of I-19 conceal giant open-pit and underground copper mines. You can learn about the fascinating process of mining from exhibits at the Mineral Discovery Center and take a tour to the giant Mission

Saint Antonio, San Xavier del Bac

© BILL WEIR

Mine. Video programs and exhibits illustrate the techniques used to dig the ore and purify it. Outdoor exhibits include haul trucks, an early 20th-century mine headframe, and other historic mine equipment. You can enjoy your lunch at a landscaped picnic area. A gift shop offers excellent Southwestern crafts, many made of copper, and books. Arizona tourist literature is available too.

The Center is just off I-19 Exit 80 (head west 300 feet on Pima Mine Road, then turn left through the gate and continue 0.2 mile). It's open Tues.–Sat. 9 A.M.–5 P.M. with free admission, but tours cost extra; 520/625-7513 (recording) or 520/625-8233 (tour reservations). Check the Web at www.mineraldiscovery.com

If you'd like to see the actual working mine for yourself, sign up for a tour to the edge of the Mission Mine Complex pit and inside one of the mills. Your guide will point out and explain features of the operation. The ore here averages only 0.6 percent copper, so the mine must operate on a large scale to be profitable. The pit is a quarter mile deep and up to two miles across, and miners will continue digging at least another 700 feet down. Giant shovels load the huge trucks, some of which can carry 320 tons of earth. At 4 P.M. on weekdays, you may get to see a mine blast on the last tour. Inside the mill you'll see machinery that grinds and concentrates the ore in several stages to achieve a 28 percent copper content, ready for shipment to smelters elsewhere. Tours (wheelchair accessible) depart from the Mineral Discovery Center, 9:30 A.M. to 3:30 P.M. on the Center's open days; $6 adult, $5 seniors 62 and over, and $4 ages 5–12. Only large groups need to make reservations.

Titan Missile Museum

You may think that you're trespassing on a top-secret military installation—official Air Force vehicles, a helicopter, giant antenna, and refueling equipment look ready for action. But this once top-secret facility has thrown open its heavy doors to the public. You'll descend past security gates and a pair of blast doors to the control room, where the guide demonstrates the launch sequence. Then you walk through another set of blast doors and down a 200-foot tunnel for a close look at the awesome Titan II missile. In use from 1963-82, the site has been designated a National Historic Landmark.

One-hour tours depart daily 9 A.M.–4 P.M. from November 1 to April 30, then Wed.–Sun. 9 A.M.–4 P.M. the rest of the year; closed Christmas and Thanksgiving. Call 520/625-7736 for reservations, though walk-ins can usually get on the next tour. Admission is $7.50 adults, $6.50 seniors and military, $4 ages 7–12. An elevator allows access for wheelchairs and people unable to climb the stairs. To reach the museum, take I-19 Duval Mine Road Exit 69, then turn west 0.6 mile to the entrance.

Accommodations and Camping

Holiday Inn Express offers a breakfast buffet and an indoor pool and spa; take I-19 Exit 69, then turn south on the west frontage road; 520/625-0900. **Green Valley Best Western** has a restaurant, pool, and spa at 111 S. La Canada Dr.; take I-19 Exit 65, turn west on Esperanza, then south on La Canada; 520/625-2250, 800/344-1441. **Fairfield Green Valley Lodge** provides spacious suites and rooms near San Ignacio Golf Club at 1861 W. Demetrie Loop, south and west of I-19 Exit 63; 520/393-5700, 888/450-5444.

Green Valley RV Resort is an adult park with a large recreation center, pool, and spa; $30 RV with hookups ($20 in summer). It's just west from I-19 Duval Mine Road Exit 69; 520/625-3900, 800/222-2969.

Food

The town features several fine restaurants. They include **Los Amigos** with a long Sonoran/Mexican menu at 249 W. Esperanza Blvd. (west of I-19 Exit 65), 520/638-0344; **Arizona Family Restaurant** for American food at 80 W. Esperanza Blvd., 520/625-3680; and **Mesquite Willy's Rib House** for barbecue at 190 W. Continental Rd. (west of I-19 Exit 63), 520/648-0988.

Information

Green Valley Chamber of Commerce, 520/625-7575, 800/858-5872, provides information on the sights and services of the area. It's open Mon.–Fri. 9 A.M.–5 P.M. and Saturday 9 A.M.–noon (closed Saturday May–Aug.). Drop by the office at 270 W. Continental Rd., adjacent to the Continental Shopping Plaza just west of I-19 Exit 63; or write P.O. Box 566, Green Valley, AZ 85622. Or, visit on the Web at www.greenvalleyazchamber.com.

SANTA RITA MOUNTAINS

Mount Wrightson (elev. 9,453 feet) tops the range and makes a challenging day-hike that offers some of the best mountain scenery and views in the Tucson area. About 90 miles of hiking trails web the Santa Ritas and many are suitable for horseback riding. Most of the highest mountains lie within the **Mt. Wrightson Wilderness.** Below on the western slope, the forests and a perennial creek of Madera Canyon attract many species of birds and other wildlife. Many trails, some wheel-chair accessible, wind

COLD WAR DEFUSED—THE TITAN MISSILE MUSEUM

When the SALT treaty called for the deactivation of the 54 Titan missiles buried deep below ground in Arizona, Kansas, and Arkansas, the people at Pima Air and Space Museum asked that one site remain open for public tours. After complex international negotiations, the request was granted. And so today the Green Valley complex of the 390th Strategic Missile Wing has been declassified and opened to the public.

Here you can watch a tape of an Air Force crew going to work, prepared for a command that fortunately never came. Had they launched their nuclear missile, in less than an hour its 440,000 pounds of thrust could have taken it from its blastproof Arizona silo to a target 8,000 miles away.

You can sit behind the consoles where two officers once waited for the command that would tell them to use two sets of keys in two combination locks to retrieve launch codes that would incinerate millions of people. The hardened command center is mounted on springs to withstand anything but a direct hit. You'll pass through a pair of 6,000-pound blast doors to approach the missile itself—110 feet tall and weighing 170 tons when fully fueled and ready to fly.

© BILL WEIR

Ralph Hoemke, a former missile silo worker, demonstrates the launch sequence in the control room.

along the creek or climb to lofty vistas. Easy access 38 miles south of Tucson and good facilities make the canyon a popular and rewarding destination. It's open all year.

A paved road from I-19 Continental Exit 63 crosses the Santa Cruz Valley and enters Madera Canyon in 11.5 miles, then continues about two miles to Roundup Picnic Area at the end of the road. You'll leave the mesquite, ocotillo, and cacti of the desert behind as you drive through forests of juniper, oak, and pine. Friends of Madera Canyon may request a small donation near the canyon entrance. The Nogales Ranger District of the Coronado National Forest has maps and trail information near Nogales; 520/281-2296. You can also obtain information at Santa Rita Lodge's gift shop, at some trailheads, and from the Supervisor's Office in Tucson; 520/670-4552. *Tucson Hiking Guide,* by Betty Leavengood, contains detailed trail descriptions and maps. *Santa Rita Mountains, Arizona—A Trail and Recreation Map* covers the entire range with trail names and distances.

Madera Canyon

Birdwatchers flock here to see abundant and unusual wildlife, of which the coppery-tailed elegant trogon bird *(Trogon elegans)* is the star attraction. During summer this colorful, parrotlike bird flies in from Mexico to nest in tall trees in the canyon bottoms. More than 200 other bird species have been spotted in Madera Canyon, including 13 species of hummingbirds. Mid-March to mid-September is the best time for birdwatching. Bear, deer, mountain lion, coatimundi, and javelina also share the spring-fed canyon.

Proctor Parking Area, on the right at the entrance to the canyon (elev. 4,400 feet), offers views of the mountains and the cottonwoods and other trees along the creek. Interpretive signs line a paved path (wheelchair accessible) that winds upstream and makes a loop, 0.8 mile roundtrip. Benches along the way offer places to rest and contemplate. A crumbling adobe wall of White House Ruins lies just off the trail. A narrow trail continues upstream to trailheads at White House Picnic Area in 0.75 mile, Madera Picnic Area in 1.2 miles,

Santa Rita Lodge in 1.4 miles, the Amphitheater in 1.7 miles, and trail's end at Roundup Picnic Area in 4.4 miles one way.

White House Picnic Area on the right a bit farther up the canyon offers tables in a woodland and an easy 0.4-mile paved loop trail that's wheelchair accessible. **Madera Picnic Area,** about half way up Madera Canyon at Milepost 12, has tables in the forest on both sides of the road at an elevation of 4,820 feet. **Roundup Picnic Area** (elev. 5,400 feet) offers two areas with tables under the trees; you have a choice of taking the right fork to the upper end of the Nature Trail or turning left for Old Baldy, Super, and Vault Mine Trailheads. The **Nature Trail** has interpretive signs as it winds down the valley 2.7 miles one way to the Amphitheater trailhead. You could also continue on trails down as far as Proctor Parking Area in 4.4 miles total one way with a 1,000-foot elevation drop.

Bog Springs-Kent Spring Loop Trail

One of Madera Canyon's prettiest hikes begins from Madera Picnic Area. The moderate 5.8-mile trail has an elevation gain of 1,600 feet with fine views of the Santa Ritas, Madera Canyon, and far across the Santa Cruz Valley. Three springs along the way usually have water (treat before drinking) that attracts birds and other wildlife and supports large sycamore trees. The path climbs gently 0.7 mile from the east side of the picnic area to the start of the loop; turn left for Bog Springs, another 0.8 mile. The trail steepens to its highest point just before Kent Spring (elev. 6,620) 1.2 miles farther. The way then follows an old jeep road, steeply downhill at first, to Sylvester Spring in 0.5 mile, swings over into another seasonal drainage, curves back to the start of the loop in 1.9 miles, and back to the picnic area in 0.7 mile. You can save a bit of hiking by starting from the trailhead at Bog Springs Campground, but there's no hiker parking here—you'd have to pay the campground fee.

Mt. Wrightson Trails

On a clear day at the top, you'll see most of southeastern Arizona and well into Mexico. Don't climb if thunderstorms threaten—another good reason to get an early start in summer. Usually May–Nov. offers the best hiking, especially if you get an early start. Pines begin to appear at trailhead elevations, then become more numerous higher up. Douglas fir and aspen groves thrive in protected areas. Only hardy trees hang onto the wind-blasted ridges.

Two trails to the summit start from Madera Canyon's Roundup Picnic Area (elev. 5,400 feet) on the west side of the range. **Super Trail #134** has a relatively gentle grade that's easy on the body, but the trail is long (16.2 miles) and offers little shade. **Old Baldy Trail #372** is steeper, but it's also shorter (10.8 miles roundtrip) and offers lots of shade through much of the day. Many hikers go up one trail and descend the other to make a figure-eight loop. The trails cross at Josephine Saddle (elev. 7,250 ft.)—a major junction southwest of the peak—then meet again at Baldy Saddle (elev. 8,800 ft.), just below the peak's north face. From here it's just 0.9 mile more to the summit. Most of both trails lie in the wilderness, where mountain bikes are prohibited.

Hikers with a high-clearance 4WD vehicle can reach the trailhead for the **Gardner Canyon Trail** on the east side of the Santa Ritas. This good trail is slightly shorter with a bit less climb than the ascent from Madera Canyon. From Tucson, head east about 21 miles on I-10 to Exit 281, turn south about 21 miles on AZ 83, then turn west about 11 miles on Gardner Canyon Road (Forest Road 92). You'll pass Apache Springs Ranch and trailheads for the Arizona Trail before reaching the Gardner Canyon Trailhead at road's end. The last several miles have several creek fords and hill climbs that can be rough. At the trailhead (elev. 6,070 ft.), follow Gardner Canyon Trail #143 three miles to the Super Trail, which curves around to Baldy Saddle in another 0.8 mile, then continue 0.9 mile on Old Baldy Trail to the summit.

Elephant Head Mountain-Bike Route

Mountain bikers can follow a very scenic 10 miles one-way on a series of jeep roads and trails between the entrance of Madera Canyon (begin at Proctor Parking Area or two miles down Proctor Road) and a point 0.75 mile past the Whipple Observatory visitor center. Elevations range 3,600-4,600 feet, and the trail is rated "most difficult." It's best done in the cooler months.

Madera Canyon Accommodations and Camping

Santa Rita Lodge in Madera Canyon, 520/625-8746, has 12 rental units with kitchenettes for $83–93 d Feb.–May, $73–93 d Jun–., and discounts for long stays. The lodge also has a gift shop and website www.santaritalodge.com, both handy sources of local information. **Birdwalks** are offered March–Aug. and last about four hours; call the lodge for reservations. **Madera Kubo,** 520/625-2908, rents four cabins for $75 d year-round; it's on the left 0.4 mile past Santa Rita Lodge and on the Web at www.maderakubo.com. **Chuparosa Inn,** 520/393-7370, has three bed and breakfast rooms a bit farther up on the right; website is www.chuparosainn.com.

Bog Springs Campground (elev. 5,600 feet) is open all year for day use or camping; $10 per site. Water is available, and trailers to 22 feet are okay in some sites. Turn left at Madera Picnic Area and go half a mile.

Whipple Observatory

The Smithsonian Institution studies the heavens with a variety of telescopes on Mt. Hopkins in the Santa Ritas. A visitor center at the base of the mountain offers year-round astronomy exhibits and seasonal tours to several telescopes. Inside the visitor center, open Mon.–Fri. 8:30 A.M.–4:30 P.M., you'll see telescope models, video and computer programs, and other exhibits that demonstrate the work done by scientists of the observatory. Photos show some local wildlife.

From March to November, six-hour tours of the observatory depart from the visitor center. The tour starts with a short video presentation at 9 A.M., followed by a narrated bus ride high into the mountains. It's great to let the experienced driver tackle the narrow, winding mountain road, stopping at a 10-meter-diameter reflector designed for gamma ray studies and other telescopes along the way. The famous Multiple Mirror Telescope, one of the world's largest, now has a single giant 6.5-meter mirror using the latest optical and electronic technologies. Its 4.5-story housing weighs 550 tons and the entire structure turns to aim the telescope. At each stop, your guide introduces astronomy and local history and points out distant summits. The outstanding views are almost as good as those from nearby Mt. Wrightson. You may be able to pick out the Guillermo Haro Astrophysical Observatory 56 miles southsoutheast in Mexico. The tour takes a midday break atop Mt. Hopkins for a picnic (bring your own lunch). Be prepared for temperatures 15–20° F cooler than in the valley, possible summer showers, and the thin air at Mt. Hopkins' 8,550-foot summit. Call up to four weeks in advance—especially early in the season—for the schedule (generally Monday, Wednesday, and Friday), directions, and required reservations; 520/670-5707; http://linmax.sao.arizona.edu/help/FLWO/whipple.html. Tours cost $7 adults, $2.50 children 6–12; children under six are not permitted.

The visitor center is 43 miles south from Tucson or 38 miles north from Nogales. From Tucson, head south on I-19 to Canoa Exit 56, then follow signs 11 miles. From the I-19 Exit, you'll go south 3 miles along the east frontage road, east 1.5 miles on Elephant Head Road, then southeast 6.5 miles on Mt. Hopkins Road; all these are paved. From Nogales, you can take I-19 Amado Exit 48, go north 2 miles on the east frontage road, then turn east on Elephant Head Road.

Whipple Picnic Area near the visitor center is open daily all year with a little nature trail, picnic tables, grills, and restrooms. Mountain bikers looking for a challenge can head down the **Elephant Head Mountain Bike Route,** a rugged 10 miles one way, from a trailhead 0.75 mile past the visitor center on the Mt. Hopkins Road. You can drive up the Mt. Hopkins Road on your own for views and a few undeveloped spots for picnicking or camping; a gate 7.5 miles past the visitor center blocks the re-

© BILL WEIR

the Cosmic Ray telescope, Whipple Observatory

maining 5 miles to the top, though you can walk on this road.

Northern Areas

Though little visited, the north end of the Santa Ritas has ghost towns, shady canyons, and towering rocky summits. Back-road enthusiasts can seek out the adobe ruin, mine workings, and cemetery of Helvetia, a copper mining center that came to life in the 1890s and died in the 1920s. It's easily reached from Sahuarita or Green Valley, but you'll need a good map, as there are no signs for the ruin or cemetery. Scenic drives across the Santa Ritas include the fairly easy Box Canyon Road (Forest Road 62) and the challenging Lopez Pass road (4WD needed). You can reach this region from I-19 on the west or AZ 83 on the east.

Eastern Areas

The back roads on the eastern side of the Santa Ritas offer scenic drives and mountain biking too. Hikers can access the Arizona Trail or head off on other trails into the heights of the range. **Kentucky Camp,** a well-preserved ghost town, not only has easy access, but you can stay here! The buildings date from 1904 when the Santa Rita Water and Mining Company started construction of a placer gold mine; financial woes the following year ended the dreams. Volunteers have restored the adobe hotel/office, assay office, and two cabins, but the barn is just a ruin. One of the cabins has opened as a rental unit at $50/day; contact the Nogales Ranger Station for reservations, 520/281-2296. To get here, take AZ 83 south 21 miles from I-10 or north 4 miles from Sonoita to unpaved Gardner Canyon Road (Forest Road 92); follow it west 0.75 mile, turn right on Forest Road 163 and continue 4.25 miles to the gate, then walk a quarter-mile to Kentucky Camp. Cautiously driven cars may be able to do the trip. The gate is often open on Sat. and can be opened on request (call the Nogales Ranger Station) for people who have difficulty walking.

SOUTHERN ARIZONA

AMADO TO ARIVACA AND THE BUENOS AIRES NATIONAL WILDLIFE REFUGE

Amado and Vicinity

Rex Ranch, east from I-19 Exit 48 or 42, 520/398-2914, 888/REX-RANCH, www.rexranch.com, enjoys a quiet and scenic location ideal for relaxation. Guests can use the full-service spa facilities, go horseback riding, mountain biking, or birdwatching, and play golf at a nearby course. A fine-dining restaurant serves European and Southwestern cuisine. Premium-category rates start at $125 d Oct.–May, plus tax and gratuities; slightly less off season.

Amado Territory Inn Bed & Breakfast, just east off I-19 Exit 48, 520/398-8684 or 888/398-8684, offers rooms with views of the Santa Ritas; $120–135 d Nov. –June, $95–105 d July–October. Like many places in the area, it provides a restful atmosphere; rooms have no TVs or telephones, and children under 12 are not permitted; www.amado-territory-inn.com. **Amado Café,** 520/398-9211, next door prepares Southwestern and Mediterranean food Tues. –Sun. for lunch and dinner. Two RV parks offer overnight and long-term spaces about two miles south on the east frontage road (take either I-19 Exits 46 or 42), **Mountain View RV Park** and **De Anza RV Park.**

Two atmospheric restaurants lie just west of I-19 Exit 48. You'll see how the **Longhorn Grill** got its name! The horns originally served as a movie set. Inside, the menu offers meat, fish, pasta, and pizza dishes daily for lunch and dinner; 520/398-3955. Across the street, the **Cow Palace** serves up cowboy, Mexican, and Italian food in a Western setting. It's open daily for breakfast, lunch, and dinner; 520/398-2201.

Arivaca

A paved road winds southwest 20 miles across the desert hills from I-19 Exit 48 to this little village of about 1,500 people. Birders and other nature lovers come to see wildlife at the nearby springs of the Buenos Aires National Wildlife Refuge. You can also get here on paved roads via AZ 286 from the west or on the very scenic but twisting 36-mile Ruby Road (AZ 289/Forest Road 39, part paved, part dirt) through the Coronado National Forest.

Downtown Arivaca has a store/gas station, post office, library, and a small information center for Buenos Aires NWR, all on the main road.

Arivaca Lake

This 90-acre reservoir with its cottonwood- and willow-lined shoreline attracts fishermen, who catch largemouth bass, bluegill, and catfish while enjoying the solitude here. Facilities are minimal—just parking areas, a boat ramp, and outhouses. Single electric motors can be used.

The better road in is from Amado (I-19 Exit 48, 37 miles south of Tucson) to the village of Arivaca, 20 miles (paved). From Arivaca head southeast five miles on Forest Road 39 (paved), then turn left 2.3 unpaved miles to the lake.

The other route follows the Ruby Road; head west 10 miles from I-19 Exit 12 on paved AZ 289 to just before Peña Blanca Lake, then continue west 21 miles on unpaved Forest Road 39, turning right after 2.3 miles. This slow but scenic route winds through the Atascosa Mountains on dirt roads—usually passable by cautiously driven cars—past the ghost towns of Ruby (fenced off; call 520/744-4471 to arrange a visit) and Oro Blanco.

Buenos Aires National Wildlife Refuge

A former ranch purchased by the U.S. Fish and Wildlife Service in 1985, the refuge provides a habitat for over 300 species of birds, including the masked bobwhite that was reintroduced here. You have a good chance of seeing pronghorn, mule deer, coyote, and javelina along refuge roads. With luck, you might spot a mountain lion, coatimundi, ring-tailed cat, badger, desert tortoise, or Gila monster. Grazing over the past 100-plus years damaged the grasslands, which are now being restored with controlled burns. Riparian lands, added later to the refuge, attract both wildlife and visitors. The refuge brochure contains a map, an introduction to the resident wildlife, and advice on visits; it's available at the small visitor center (open weekdays and some weekends next to the Arivaca Mercantile in Arivaca) and at the refuge headquarters north of Sasabe. You can also request one by mail. And while you're at it, ask for a schedule of tours and workshops offered by the refuge.

Most roads in the refuge require 4WD, especially after rains. These back roads are also good for mountain biking, and many loop-trips are possible. You can camp at any of the more than 100 primitive sites along the back roads; no permit is needed, but you must stay at a designated site. The refuge, about 60 miles southwest of Tucson, can be reached from Tucson either via Arivaca or the faster route via Robles Junction.

Seven springs rise from the desert valley at **Arivaca Cienega,** then feed Willow Pond and marshlands just east of Arivaca. A boardwalk trail leads out to the pond, popular for birdwatching, in a 1.36-mile loop.

Arivaca Creek pops up above ground two miles west of Arivaca and supports towering Fremont cottonwood trees, lush vegetation, birds, and other wildlife. A trail makes a figure-eight loop of about one mile. For great views of the area, branch off on the **Mustang Trail,** which leads to the top of El Cerro; it's five miles roundtrip, and the last section is rough with loose rock. You'll need a hat, sturdy shoes, and water, as there's no shade.

Refuge headquarters lies east three miles off AZ 286; the turnoff is between Mileposts 7 and 8. The road in and the five-mile Antelope Drive have been graveled; they're passable for cars when dry. Aguirre Lake, just north of the headquarters, has water and birds only after plentiful rain. Groups can arrange to visit Brown Canyon, a sycamore-lined creek in the Baboquivari Mountains in the northwest corner of the refuge; it's too fragile for public access otherwise. The visitor center at the headquarters, P.O. Box 109, Sasabe, AZ 86633, 502/823-4251, has information and a few exhibits. It's open Mon.–Fri. 7 A.M.–3:30 P.M. and possibly later and on weekends when staffed by volunteers.

Sasabe

This sleepy adobe village on the Arizona side of the border has a store and a nearby guest ranch. The larger Mexican town of Sasabe has about 1,000 inhabitants and lies a mile south of the border. It serves as a ranching center but lacks tourist shops. Besides running cattle, local people export mesquite firewood and adobe bricks. The border is open 8 A.M.–8 P.M., but few travelers cross into Mexico here; there's no source for vehicle permits or insurance, and the 60-mile stretch of dirt road heading south from the border is rough. The excellent Rancho de la Osa Guest Ranch makes a great getaway just a few miles from Sasabe. See description under **Tucson Guest Ranches;** visitors should call first.

TUBAC

After the Pima Indian Revolt in 1751, the Spanish decided to protect their missions and settlers in this remote region. To accomplish their goal, in the following year they built Tubac Presidio, the first European settlement in what's now Arizona. When the Spanish departed in 1776, garrisons of Pima Indians and later Mexicans provided some security. Yet Apache raids and political turmoil in following decades often made life unbearable at times, and Tubac's citizens repeatedly had to flee.

When the United States took over after the 1854 Gadsden Purchase, Tubac had decayed into a pile of crumbling adobe ruins. Prospectors and adventure-seekers, fired by tales of old Spanish mines, soon poured in. They hit rich mineral deposits, and by 1859 Tubac had become a boomtown with Arizona's first newspaper, the *Weekly Arizonan*. The Civil War brought the good times to an end when the troops guarding the town headed east to fight the Confederacy. Apache once again raided the settlement, and the inhabitants once again had to seek safer locales. Tubac recovered after the Civil War, but the boom days had ended.

Much later, when an art school opened in 1948, Tubac began a slow transformation into an artists' colony. Today, the village of Tubac features about 100 studios and galleries displaying fine art and crafts. An exploration of this compact little town will turn up modern jewelry, ceramics, fountains, woodcarvings, prints, batiks, paintings, and other works. Its motto is "Where Art and History Meet." During the week-long **Tubac Festival of the Arts** in February, residents and visiting artists celebrate with exhibitions, demonstrations, and food. Tubac lies 45 miles south of Tucson; take I-19 Exit 34.

Tubac Center of the Arts

This gallery, on Plaza Road near the entrance to Tubac, 520/398-2371, displays excellent work by local, regional, and national artists. Most works are for sale and there's a gift shop. A Performing Arts program offers a variety of presentations. Both adults and children can attend workshops; kids also have a summer program. The Center is open Tues.–Sat. 10 A.M.–4:30 P.M. and Sunday 1–4:30 P.M. from early September to mid-May; $2 suggested donation; www.tubacarts.org.

Tubac Presidio State Historic Park

This park, on the site of the Spanish presidio, recounts Tubac's history since its founding in 1752. A short video provides an introduction. Behind the visitor center, stairs lead underground to excavations of the original foundation and wall. Next, in the museum, models illustrate how the presidio appeared in the early years. Exhibits tell the stories of the people who've lived here during the Spanish, Mexican, and American periods. You can see the printing press used for Arizona's first newspaper and buy a reproduction of the first issue, dated March 3, 1859. The schoolhouse adjacent to the visitor center dates from 1885. It's a successor to Arizona's first school, which was built in 1789.

You can also visit St. Ann's Church, just outside the park; it was rebuilt in the 1920s as the latest in a series of churches built on the site since the early 1700s. The state park itself is historic because it's Arizona's first, established in 1959. Hours are daily 8 A.M.–5 P.M.; admission is $2 ages 14 and over, $1 ages 7–13; 520/398-2252. Just after entering the gateway to Tubac, turn right 0.3 mile on Tubac Road to the park en-

trance. A mesquite-shaded picnic area lies south across the street from the park; no camping.

A **Living History Program** on Sunday afternoons 1–4 P.M. from October to March portrays the Spanish colonial period's crafts, food, traditional medicine, and religion. In October on the weekend closest to the 23rd, the park hosts **Anza Days Cultural Celebration.** This event commemorates the 1775 departure from Tubac of the de Anza expedition (see below) and features entertainers, historic craft demonstrations, food vendors, and re-enactments.

Juan Bautista de Anza National Historic Trail

You can walk along a historic 4.5-mile trail from Tubac Presidio State Park to Tumacacori National Historical Park. This trail is part of a planned 600-mile-long historic trail from Culiacán, Sinaloa, Mexico, to San Francisco, California, along the route followed in 1775-76 by Tubac Presidio captain Juan Bautista de Anza. De Anza led 240 colonists north to start a settlement (today's city of San Francisco) in northern California. The only other section of the trail currently open is a short section in California's Anza-Borrego State Park.

You can start at either Tubac (at the picnic area across the road) or Tumacacori; from either trailhead, you will cross the Santa Cruz River after 1.25 miles. The river may be too high to cross safely or it may be dry. Carry plenty of water, especially in hot weather. There's excellent birding; the state park visitor center has a birdlist. Do not stray from the trail as it crosses private land.

Accommodations

Tubac Country Inn, at the corner of Plaza and Burruel, 520/398-3178, has five suites with continental breakfast; $85–95 d. **Secret Garden Inn Bed & Breakfast,** 520/398-9371, is down a little lane north of the state park; it has two rooms and continental breakfast; $89 d.

Mí Sueño B&B ("my dream"), 520/398-0775, offers Southwest-style rooms in a ranch with an idyllic setting atop a small hill from September to May. A full breakfast is included; only the largest of the three rooms has a private bath; costs run $90–125 d and your horse can stay in the nearby stable. From Tubac, cross over 1-19 to the west frontage road, then turn left 1.2 miles; www.misuenobandb.com.

Tubac Golf Resort, one mile north of Tubac, offers rooms ($140 d), casitas ($170 and $185 d), and suites ($225 d) in winter; add $10 for Fri.-Sat.; prices are lower the rest of the year. The dining room serves American and continental food daily for breakfast, lunch, and dinner. The resort also has an 18-hole golf course, tennis court, pool, and hot tub. It's off the I-19 east frontage road between Exit 40 and Tubac; 520/398-2211 or 800/848-7893. **Burro Inn,** a mile west of I-19 Exit 40, 520/3982281, has rooms starting at $124 d (less in warmer months) and a restaurant serving American and Mexican food, including mesquite-cooked selections.

Campgrounds
Tubac Trailer Tether, on Burruel St., 520/398-2111, offers RV spaces with hookups for $18. **Mountain View RV R,** north on the I-19 frontage road between Exits 42 and 48, 520/398-9401, has basic sites for tents and RVs along with a pool and showers. Rates are $15 without hookups; $21.33 with hookups. **Tumacácori Mini Market,** south of Tubac, has spaces for self-contained rigs.

Food
Tosh's Hacienda de Tubac, at the corner of Camino Otero and Burruel St., 520/398-3008, serves Southwestern and Mexican cuisine indoors or on the patio for lunch and dinner daily (closes Mon.–Tues. in summer). **Melio's Trattoria,** across from the Center of the Arts, 520/398-8494, serves Italian cuisine Fri.–Sun. for lunch and Thurs.–Sun. for dinner, when reservations are recommended. Cross the footbridge in the Mercado for the sandwiches and salads at **Café Fiesta,** 520/398-2332, open daily for lunch. The nearby **Shelby's Bistro,** 520) 520/398-8075 offers a lunch menu of sandwiches, salads, pasta, and pizza plus additional meat and seafood dishes for dinner; closed

Sun.–Tuesday. Both places have patio and indoor seating.

Shopping
Tubac's many galleries sell outstanding art and crafts. You can pick up a map at many businesses or just wander down the lanes. **La Paloma de Tubac,** just east of the state park, 520/398-9231, offers a huge selection of folk art and crafts from Mexico, Central America, and South America; open daily. **Tortuga Books** has a great regional and general offering in front of the Mercado.

Information
Tubac Chamber of Commerce can be reached at P.O. Box 1866, Tubac, AZ 85646; 520/398-2704; www.tubacaz.com. The **Tubac Historical Society** has a library and gift shop north of the state park, but it's open only Thurs.–Sun. from October to May.

TUMACACORI NATIONAL HISTORICAL PARK

This massive adobe ruin evokes visions of Spanish missionaries and devout Indian followers. Father Kino first visited the Pima village of Tumacacori in 1691, saying Mass under a brush shelter. Kino's successors continued their mission work, teaching, converting, and farming, but work didn't begin on the present church until 1800.

Franciscan Father Narciso Gutierrez, determined to build a church as splendid as San Xavier del Bac, supervised the construction by Indian laborers. Work went slowly, and although never quite finished, the building was in use by 1822. Then the fledgling Mexican government restricted funds for mission work and began to evict all foreign missionaries. Tumacacori's last resident priest, Father Ramon Liberos of Spain, had to leave in 1828.

Indians continued to care for the church and received occasional visits by missionaries from Mexico, but raiding Apache made life hard. The last devout Indians finally gave up in 1848, packing the church furnishings and moving to San Xavier del Bac.

Tumacacori fell into ruins before receiving protection as a national monument in 1908, then as a national historical park in 1990. Today, a museum recalls the mission life of the Indians and Spanish with an introductory video, historical and architectural exhibits, and some of the mission's original "santos" (wooden statues). An interpretive booklet for the self-guided tour describes details of the church, circular mortuary chapel, graveyard, storeroom, and other structures. Scheduled tours are conducted Sept.–June and on request by groups. The grounds feature picnic tables, but no camping is permitted. The Patio Garden has herbs, shade trees, and flowers and other plants. Mexican or Indian craft demonstrations take place weekends Sept.–June. **Tumacacori Fiesta** features Indian dances, crafts, and food on the first weekend in December. The visitor center offers books and postcards. Tumacacori is 48 miles south of Tucson near I-19 Exit 29, or just three miles south of Tubac on the east frontage road; 520/398-2341; www.nps.gov/tuma. It's open daily 8 A.M.–5 P.M.; admission is $3/person age 17 and up.

Tumacacori Restaurant, across the street from the mission, serves Greek and Mexican food for lunch and dinner, closed Mon.; 520/398-9038. **Wisdom's Café,** 0.3 mile north, offers Mexican and American food; 520/398-2397.

PEÑA BLANCA LAKE AND VICINITY

The light-colored bluffs overlooking this 52-acre lake inspired the name Peña Blanca (Spanish for "White Rock"). It's at an elevation of 4,000 feet in scenic hills 16 miles northwest of Nogales. Anglers come to catch bass, bluegill, crappie, catfish, and, from November to March, rainbow trout. Mercury in the lake may require catch and release for the warm-water fish, but trout might be okay. The lake has a boat ramp and a trail around the shore. To reach the lake, take I-19 Ruby Road Exit 12 and drive west 11 miles on paved AZ 289. Upper and Lower Thumb Rock Picnic Areas lie just before road's end.

White Rock Campground is in Peña Blanca Canyon upstream from the lake; sites are open year-round and have room for trailers to 22 feet; $5; water may or may not be available. Turn left 0.1 mile onto Forest Road 39 at Milepost 10, one mile before the lake; a smaller section of the campground is 0.1 mile down the road to the lake from the junction.

Forest Road 39 continues west from the lake area through canyons and mountains with some great scenery. The road is slow, bumpy, and unpaved within the national forest, so allow plenty of time. Trails and back roads branch off for further exploration. It's about 21 miles from the AZ 289 turnoff to the Arivaca Lake turnoff, where pavement begins, then another five miles to the town of Arivaca. The Nogales Ranger District office north of Nogales has maps and recreation information.

Atascosa Lookout Trail #100

The path climbs steeply from 4,700 feet through desert vegetation, oaks, juniper, and pinyon pine to the summit at 6,255 feet. Allow a half day for the six-mile roundtrip. See the 7.5-minute Ruby topo map. The trailhead is five miles west of Peña Blanca Lake on Forest Road 39, a dirt road. Look for a parking area on the south side of the road; the unsigned trailhead is on the north side.

From the top, you can see mountain ranges in Mexico to the south, Peña Blanca Lake and Nogales to the east, the Santa Ritas and Rincons to the northeast, the Santa Catalinas to the north, and the Baboquivaris to the west. You can hike year-round except after snowstorms.

Sycamore Canyon Trail #40

The trail is rough in spots but you can follow it downstream all the way to the Mexican border, a distance of 5.3 miles one-way. Plants and wildlife rarely found elsewhere in the United States live in the scenic canyon. The trail crosses both the **Goodding Research Natural Area,** named for a prominent Arizona botanist, and the **Pajarita Wilderness.** The first 1.3 miles is easy walking; after that, boulder-hopping and wading are necessary. Toward the end, the canyon opens up and you'll see saguaro on the slopes. A barbed-wire fence marks the Mexican border. No camping is allowed along the trail.

The trailhead is about 10 miles west of Peña Blanca Lake on Forest Road 39, then left a quarter mile on Forest Road 218 to Hank and Yank Historical Site. These adobe ruins were part of a ranch started in the 1880s by two former army scouts.

Hiking in Sycamore Canyon is good all year. Elevation ranges from 4,000 feet at the trailhead to 3,500 feet at the border. Depending on how far you go, the hike can be an easy two-hour stroll for the first mile or so, or a long (10-hour) 10.6-mile roundtrip day-hike all the way to Mexico; see the Ruby topo map. At the border, you have the options of retracing your steps or heading east four miles along Border Trail #45 to a trailhead on Forest Road 39A.

NOGALES

Nogales, astride the U.S. and Mexican border, is a truly international city. Many visitors to Mexico have shopping on their minds, and Nogales offers a huge selection of handicrafts. You'll also find fine restaurants and serenading mariachi bands. Mexicans too like to cross the border to shop and sample foreign culture.

History

Indians used Nogales Pass for at least 2,000 years on migration and trade routes. The Hohokam came through on their way to the Gulf of California to collect shells prized as bracelet and necklace material. Pima, possibly descended from the Hohokam, settled and traveled in the Santa Cruz River Valley and Nogales area after A.D. 1500. During the Spanish era, missionaries, soldiers, ranchers, and prospectors also passed through. Apache used the pass on raiding forays well into the 1800s. Traders on the Guaymas-Tucson route knew the spot as Los Nogales (Spanish for "The Walnuts"). A survey team marked the international boundary line here in 1855, one year after the Gadsden Purchase.

Two men started what grew into the modern bustling cities of Nogales. In 1880, Juan José

Vásquez established a roadhouse on the Mexican side, and some months later Jacob Isaacson set up a trading post on the American side. The first railroad line to cross the border between the U.S. and Mexico came through Nogales in October 1882. Trade, silver mining, and ranching contributed to the growth of the twin towns. In 1898 the population of 1,500 on the U.S. side made it the fifth largest city in Arizona.

When Pancho Villa threatened Nogales in 1916, the worried U.S. Army established Camp Little on the edge of town. Relations between the two halves of Nogales remained good despite the political turmoil in Mexico, and Camp Little closed in 1933. Tourists discovered Nogales in the 1940s, and tourism, along with trade, keeps the border busy today.

Sights

The **Pimeria Alta Historical Society Museum** provides a good introduction to Nogales. Artifacts and old photos illustrate the long and colorful history of southern Arizona and northern Sonora. An attraction in itself, the building dates to 1914 and housed the Nogales City Hall and police and fire departments. You can see the old jail, hand-powered water pump, law office, and other exhibits. The society's research library and archives offer a wealth of books on regional history as well as an extensive collection of historic photographs; it's open to the public. The museum and library are usually open Thurs.–Sat. 10 A.M.–4 P.M.; call 520/287-4621 for hours; dakotacom.net/~museum. You'll find the distinctive mission-style building on the corner of Grand Ave. and Crawford St., a quarter mile north of the border.

The square granite structure with a shiny aluminum dome, on the hillside to the northeast, is the former **Santa Cruz County Courthouse,** built in 1904; it may be open to the public on Saturdays. Local artists display their work in the **Hilltop Art Gallery** on Hilltop Dr.; 520/287-5515. To get there from Grand Avenue, turn west on Ellis Street, right on Marina Street, then right following signs. It's open Sept.–May, daily noon–4:30 P.M.; free admission.

Accommodations

The winter rates listed here tend to go down in summer.

Under $50: Motel 6, 141 W. Mariposa Rd. (at Grand Ave.), 520/281-2951 or 800/4MOTEL6, has a pool; $40–44 s, $46–50 d.

$50–100: Super 8 Motel, 547 W. Mariposa Rd. (west of I19 Exit 4), 520/281-2242 or 800/800-8000, $50 s, $55 d; **Holiday Inn Express,** 850 W. Shell and Mariposa Rds., 520/281-0123 or 877/232-3630, $70 s, $80 d; **Americana Motor Hotel,** 639 N. Grand Ave., 520/287-7211 or 800/874-8079, $50–55 s, $55–60 d; **Best Western Siesta Motel,** 673 N. Grand Ave., 520/287-4671 or 800/528-1234, $50–52 d; and **Days Inn,** 884 N. Grand Ave., 520/287-4611 or 800/329-7466, $55 d.

Over $100: Rio Rico Resort and Country Club, 12 miles north of town near I-19 Exit 17, 520/281-1901 or 800/288-4746, features an 18-hole golf course, tennis, pool, and horseback riding; Jan.–April rates run $170 d for a room, $235 d for a suite.

About a dozen hotels lie on the Mexican side of the border; check with tourist offices for a map and suggestions.

Campgrounds

Mi Casa RV Park is 4.5 miles north of the border at 2901 N. Grand Ave., 520/281-1150. Overnights cost $15.40 for an RV with hookups and showers.

Food

Most of the restaurants on the Arizona side lie along Grand Avenue. They include **China Star Restaurant,** 272 W. Mariposa Rd. in Mariposa Shopping Mall, 520/281-0633; **Pizza Hut,** 589 N. Grand Ave., 520/287-9257; **Americana,** 639 N. Grand Ave., 520/287-7211; **Denny's** (24 hours), 683 N. Grand Ave., 520/287-4572; **Zutas Papachoris',** with steak, seafood, Mexican, and Greek food at 982 N. Grand Ave., 520/287-2892; and **Las Vigas Steak Ranch** (closed Mon.), 180 Loma St. at Fiesta Market (turn off Arroyo Blvd.), 520/287-6641.

Molina's PK Outpost has historical artifacts on display and a full Mexican menu in the historic Pete Kitchen Ranch, three miles north of Nogales on the I-19 east frontage road, 520/281-1852.

San Cayetano Dining Room at Rio Rico Resort, 12 miles north of downtown at I-19 Exit 17, offers Southwestern and seafood choices; open daily for breakfast, lunch, and dinner; 520/281-1901. You'll find additional restaurants in Mexico; many have English menus and all accept U.S. dollars.

Events

Both sides of the border celebrate **Cinco de Mayo** with a big parade, street fair, and music; most activities take place on the weekends before and after May 5. The Mexican side celebrates **Independence Day** on September 16 and **Revolution Day** on November 20 with parades and other festivities.

The major event on the U.S. side is the **Santa Cruz County Fair** held in Sonoita on the last weekend in September. The fair includes a cow-chip-chucking contest, fiddlers' competition, rooster-crowing contest, and agricultural exhibits. Nogales on the Arizona side sponsors a **Christmas Parade** on the first Saturday in December.

Shopping

Most visitors to Ambos Nogales ("Both Nogales") find it easier to park on the American side near the border ($4 all day) and set off on foot. This saves delays in crossing the border by car and finding parking spots in Mexico. A pedestrian crossing lies at the south end of Morley Avenue.

Mexican craftspeople turn out an astonishing array of products, from Tiffany-style lampshades to saddles. Because a day's wages in Mexico come close to an hour's wages in the U.S., most crafts are real bargains. Be sure to shop around and haggle before laying out any cash. Even in the large fixed-price stores, try asking for a discount. Most salespeople speak English, and you don't need pesos; dollars and major credit cards are happily accepted. There's good shopping near the border in Nogales, Arizona, as well.

Popular buys include chess sets of carved onyx, clay reproductions of Mayan art, painted vases, embroidered clothing, glassware, hand-tooled leather pieces, wool blankets, and woodcarvings. A few items are very unpopular with U.S. Customs and are subject to confiscation: guns and ammunition, fireworks, illegal drugs, switchblades, most meat products, and sea-turtle products. Adults can bring back other goods totaling US$400, including one quart of liquor every 31 days. Also be careful not to bring guns into Mexico.

Crossing the Border

No permit is needed to walk or drive across the border for visits in Nogales of 72 hours or less. To go beyond Nogales, U.S. citizens need proof of citizenship to secure a tourist permit—good for 180 days—at the border. Visitors from other countries should check with a Mexican consulate for entry requirements; they should also see U.S. Immigration about re-entry before stepping across. In Nogales, Arizona, the Consulado de Mexico is at 571 N. Grand Ave.; 520/287-2521.

A separate permit is needed for driving a car in Mexico beyond Nogales. Pick it up at the border or any Mexican consulate by showing proof of car ownership. Large vehicles and trailers can cross more easily at the commercial crossing west of the main crossing; take Mariposa Road (AZ 189).

You also need to buy Mexican auto insurance. Numerous agencies in Nogales, Arizona, advertise Mexican insurance, with daily and longer rates.

You don't need to change money in Nogales; dollars or pesos are welcomed on both sides of the border. For longer trips into Mexico, local currency is essential. Shop for pesos at money-changers near the border on the U.S. side; American stores near the border almost always have a surplus of Mexican currency and will sell it at a good rate.

Recreation

You'll find a public **swimming pool** and **tennis courts** near the War Memorial Park on Madison Street. Another pool is in Fleisher Park farther north on Hohokam Drive.

Golfers can play at three 18-hole courses in the area. **Palo Duro Creek Golf Club** is in the northwest part of town at 2690 N. Country Club Dr.; 520/761-4394. **Rio Rico Golf Course** is 12 miles north of downtown at 1410 Rio Rico Dr., near I-19 Exit 17; 520/281-8567. **Kino Springs Country Club** lies six miles northeast on AZ 82, then right on Kino Springs Dr., 520/287-8701.

Information and Services

The **Nogales-Santa Cruz Chamber of Commerce** is very helpful with information on both the local area and travel in Mexico. A video program presents a visual tour of Santa Cruz County sights, plus information on crossing the border and visiting Mexico. It's open Mon.–Fri. 8 A.M.–5 P.M.; write Kino Park, Nogales, AZ 85621; 520/287-3685. When entering Nogales from the north on Grand Avenue (US 89), turn right on the street just past the Patagonia Road interchange (AZ 82). The Mexicans also have a **tourist office** just south of the Grand Avenue border crossing.

The **Nogales Ranger District** office has recreation information and a forest map for the Santa Ritas and Peña Blanca areas. The office is about five miles north of downtown at 303 Old Tucson Rd. (Nogales, AZ 85621); 520/281-2296. To get there take the I-19 Ruby Road Exit 12, turn south 0.4 mile on the east frontage road, then left 0.1 mile on Old Tucson Road. It's open Mon.–Fri. 8 A.M.–4:30 P.M.

Nogales, Arizona, has a **public library** at 748 Grand Ave.; 520/287-3343. The **post office** lies just east of the border station. **Carondelet Holy Cross Hospital** is west of town at 1171 W. Target Range Rd.; 520/287-2771.

Tours and Transportation

Autobuses Crucero goes hourly to Tucson, taking one hour 45 minutes with stops at Green Valley and other locations along the way. Crucero also goes four times daily south to Hermosillo, Ciudad Obregón, and other cities in Mexico. The bus station is two blocks from the border at 35 N. Terrace Ave.; 520/287-5628. On the Mexican side, buses offer extensive routes at low cost.

The nearest major **airports** are at Tucson (64 miles north) and Hermosillo (280 km/174 miles south). Nogales has a small international airport on Patagonia Road.

PATAGONIA AND VICINITY

The rolling hills of grass and woodlands surrounding Patagonia make up some of the state's finest cattle and horse land. Patagonia, 19 miles northeast of Nogales, lies on the alternate route to Tucson. Many people like to make a loop between the two cities by driving through Sonoita and Patagonia in one direction (I-10, AZ Hwys. 83 and 82) and the Santa Cruz Valley (I-19) in the other.

Patagonia-Sonoita Creek Preserve

The Nature Conservancy maintains over 750 acres along Sonoita Creek as a wildlife preserve. Year-round water and a variety of habitats attract a number of birds; about 300 species have been identified. White-tailed deer, coatimundi, javelina, bobcat, and other animals live in the thickets and woods. Four native fish species, including the endangered Gila top minnow, swim in the creek. The splendid cottonwood-willow riparian forest contains Fremont cottonwoods that tower more than 100 feet. About 2.5 miles of trails make loops through a variety of habitats near the creek; wheelchairs can follow one loop. A new 3-mile loop climbs into the juniper and oak country in uplands on the other side of the road; the trailhead is about half a mile before the visitor center.

The public is welcome to visit, but no picnicking, camping, or pets are allowed; a $5 donation is suggested for those not a member of the Nature Conservancy. It's open year-round, Wed.–Sun. 7:30 A.M.–4 P.M. The visitor center isn't always staffed, but you can see the outdoor exhibits and pick up a trail map and birdlist. Nature walks begin here at 9 A.M. on Wednesday (8 A.M. April–Sept.) and 9 A.M. Saturday year-round; no reservation needed. Check with the preserve for other walks and programs. Visitors during the summer monsoon season should apply insect repellent to keep off chiggers.

To reach the preserve from AZ 82 in Patagonia, turn northwest two blocks on Fourth Avenue, then turn left 1.4 miles on Pennsylvania Avenue. The pavement ends and you'll

have to drive across the creekbed—don't cross if you can't see the bottom. Continue to the visitor center for parking and trailheads. You can also take the back way by continuing on the dirt road 1.8 miles to AZ 82 at an unsigned junction between Mileposts 16 and 17, but the creek ford is likely to be deeper here. For more information, contact the preserve at P.O. Box 815, Patagonia, AZ 85624; 520/394-2400; nature.org.

Hummingbird feeders attract up to 11 species of hummers at a private residence adjacent to the preserve. **Paton's Birder's Haven** is the first house on the left just past the creekbed crossing; park outside the gate (handicapped drivers can park inside).

Parks in Town

The long, grassy park in the middle of town has some tables and the yellow, ca. 1900 Patagonia Depot of the New Mexico and Arizona Railroad; trains stopped running here in 1962 and the depot now contains city offices. Also in the park, the **Patagonia Butterfly Garden** attracts resident and migrant butterflies from May to early October). Nearby **Richardson Park** has a playground.

Accommodations and Camping

The **Stage Stop Inn,** 520/394-2211 or 800/923-2211, has a restaurant and pool in the middle of Patagonia at 303 W. McKeown. Rates are $55 s, $69 d, $79 d kitchenette, and $99 or $125 for a suite.

Two short blocks to the south, **Duquesne Uouse,** 520/394-2732, offers bed and breakfast in a circa 1900 adobe former miners' boarding house at 357 Duquesne Ave.; $75 d.

Dos Palmas offers a 1958 Spartan travel trailer across the street at 362 Duquesne Ave.; it has two bedrooms and costs $75 d ($60 d if staying two nights or more); 520/394-0056 or 866/394-0056.

Circle Z Ranch, 520/394-2525 or 888/854-2525, is four miles southwest of Patagonia,. This working cattle ranch features horseback riding, swimming, hiking, birding, and tennis during its Nov. 1 –May 15 season. Daily rates, including lodging, food, and activities, run $130–145 per person ($160–185 holidays and mid-Feb.–April 30); three-day minimum. Weekly rates are $850–910 per person ($990–1,010 holidays and mid-Feb.–April 30); www.circlez.com.

Patagonia RV Park, 0.7 mile south on the road to Harshaw, 520/394-2491, has showers and offers sites for tents ($10) and RVs ($20 w/hookups).

Food
The restaurant next door to the Stage Stop Inn serves Mexican and American food with a choice of indoor or patio seating. It's open daily for breakfast, lunch, and dinner. Nearby, the **Gathering Grounds,** 520/394-2097, bakes tempting breads and pastries as well as serving sandwiches, quiches, ice cream, and coffees; open daily except Tues.– Wed. for breakfast and lunch at 319 McKeown Avenue.

Velvet Elvis Pizza Company, 292 Naugle Ave. (Hwy. 82), 520/394-2102, offers creative pizza; open Sat.-Sun. for lunch and dinner, then evenings on Mon. (except in summer), Thurs., and Friday. **Cose Buone,** 436 Naugle Ave., 520/394-2366, prepares Italian dinners; call for hours.

Santo's Mexican Cafe on Naugle and the Home Plate Restaurant on McKeown can be smoky, but you could order take-out. **The Wagon Wheel Saloon** (est. 1937) at Naugle and 4th Ayes, calls itself "Patagonia's Original Cowboy Bar"; many antiques and hunting trophies grace the interior.

Information and Services
A **Mariposa Books** offers both a bookstore and a **tourist information desk** with area activities and services at 307 McKeown Ave. (next door to the Stage Stop Inn); closed Tues.; 520/394-0060, 888/794-0060 or visit their website at www.patagoniaaz.com. Events include the **Santa Cruz County Fair** on the last weekend of September. Patagonia also has art galleries, mostly along Naugle and McKeown Avenues. **Kazzam Nature Center,** 348 Naugle Ave. (AZ 82), 520/394-2823, sells regional books and birding

and gardening supplies which are also at www.kazzam.com.

Ghost Towns
Decaying houses, piles of rubble, cemeteries, and old mine shafts mark deserted mining camps in the Patagonia Mountains to the south. You'll need the topo or Forest Service maps to find these old sites. In a 45-mile loop drive, you can visit Harshaw, Mowry, Washington Camp, and Duquesne. You can also drive east to the Huachuca Mountains, Parker Lake, or Coronado National Memorial on back roads. Most are dirt and should be avoided if it has recently rained or snowed.

Patagonia is a good place to start a drive to these sites. Turn beside the post office at the sign for Harshaw (or head east on McKeown Ave.) on the Harshaw Road. You'll pass a trailhead for the Arizona Trail in 2.7 miles. After 5.8 miles from Patagonia, turn right (pavement ends) and continue 1.8 miles to Harshaw, marked by a sign, a decaying house on the left, and the cemetery—worth seeing for its pioneer history—to the right. The road continues to the other sites. Mountain bikers also enjoy touring these scenic backroads.

Patagonia Lake State Park
Head here for a pleasant place to picnic, camp, boat, and fish. The 265-acre reservoir offers largemouth bass, crappie, sunfish, bluegill, catfish, and, in winter, rainbow trout. Mesquite trees and some pines provide shade. Facilities include day-use areas, two handicap-accessible fishing docks, campground loops with and without hookups, showers, two boat ramps, a dump station, and a fish-cleaning station. There's a store with groceries. A nearby marina sells camping and fishing supplies and rents canoes, pedal boats, and fishing boats (you can row or bring your own motor); it's open daily.

The west half of the lake is open for waterskiing and personal watercraft Mon.–Fri. from May 1 to Sept. 30 and daily the rest of the year; the east half of the lake is a no-wake area. Swim at Boulder Beach (no lifeguard).

The **visitor center** has natural history exhibits, videos, a tiny library, and kids projects; you can pick up a birdlist and find out about recent sightings. Birdwatching tours on pontoon boats some days; call for the schedule or drop by the visitor center to sign up. Slide show programs run on Sat. and Sunday.

Sonoita Creek Trail begins at the east end of the hookup campground and winds to the mouth of Sonoita Creek, 1.2 miles roundtrip.

Sonoita Creek State Natural Area, northwest of the state park, holds about 5,000 acres of riparian, grassland, and woodland habitats; trails here are being planned.

At an elevation of 3,750 feet, the park stays open all year; March through October tends to get busy, when the campground (first-come, first-served) often fills by Friday afternoon; it's a good idea to call ahead. Picnic areas also fill up on summer weekends. Groups can reserve a ramada for day use. Boaters may camp at primitive sites around the lake and on islands. Entry fees are $5/vehicle for day use, $10/vehicle for camping, and $15/vehicle camping with water and electric hookups; 520/287-6965. From Nogales, go 12 miles northeast on AZ 82, then turn left four miles on a paved road; from Patagonia, head southwest seven miles on AZ 82, then turn right four miles. The park gate is closed 10 P.M.–4 A.M.

SONOITA AND VICINITY

This little crossroads town is at the junction of AZ 82 and AZ 83 in gently rolling grasslands. Parker Canyon Lake lies 30 miles to the south and east on AZ 83; the first 24.5 miles are paved. Near the junction, you'll find restaurants, shops, gas stations, and a post office.

Accommodations and Food

The **Sonoita Inn,** 520/455-5935, offers spacious rooms—each named for a local ranch—with views of rolling hills. The rustic, yet elegant Western décor and the high-ceilinged common area with a fireplace make this an exceptionally pleasant place to stay; it's expensive, however, at $125 d downstairs and $140 d upstairs, but all rooms drop to $89 d mid-June

to mid-August; you can learn more on the Internet at www.sonoitainn.com.

For a tiny town, Sonoita offers a surprisingly number of fine restaurants. At the highway junction, **The Steak Out Restaurant & Saloon,** 520/455-5205, has a great selection of steaks along with chicken, ribs, and fish; it's open Sat.–Sun. for lunch and daily for dinner. **Grasslands, A Natural Foods Café,** south on AZ 83, around the corner from the highway junction, 520/455-4770, provides a pleasant alternative to the usual café scene. It's open Wed.–Sun. for breakfast and lunch, and Saturdays for German and vegetarian dinners (dinner reservations recommended). You can also buy baked goods, preserves, and local wines here.

Two restaurants just east of the highway junction feature American food with a Southwest flair; both offer a long wine list including some local labels. **Karen's Wine Country Café,** 520/455-5282, prepares meat, vegetable, and pasta dishes and is known for its salads; open Sun. for breakfast, daily for lunch, and Fri.–Sat. for dinner at 3266 Hwy. 82, (one third of a mile east of the highway junction). **Café Sonoita,** 520/455-5278, may have beef, quail, chicken, seafood, and pasta on its chalkboard menu; open Fri.–Sun. for lunch and Wed.–Sat. for dinner at 3280 Hwy. 82 (half a mile east of the highway junction).

Las Cienegas National Conservation Area

The landscape of much of Arizona has changed drastically from the late 1800s, when extensive grazing by domestic cattle severely depleted native grasses. Livestock animals still graze in this area—as they have for 300 years—but they're now controlled. As a result, the grass has recovered and stands as high as six feet. Fifteen inches of annual rainfall support some of the best examples of native grassland in the state. Within the 45,000 acres of the conservation area you'll find large cottonwood trees lining the banks of perennial Cienega Creek, oaks and junipers clinging to the hills, and mesquite trees scattered throughout the range.

The public lands in the conservation area,

previously known as the Empire-Cienega Resource Conservation Area, are open to individual visitors and campers without permits, but group activities do require one. There are no paved roads, campgrounds, or picnic areas within the conservation area. Visitors enjoy bird watching, wildlife (keep an eye out for pronghorn), hiking, horseback riding, bicycling, hunting, and no-facility camping (limited to 14 days). Campfires are allowed, but only dead wood lying on the ground may be collected. For more information and road conditions, call the office in Tucson, 520/722-4289.

You can enter the conservation area on the west from AZ 83 between Mileposts 39 and 40, 6.4 miles north of Sonoita; Empire Ranch Road passes Empire Ranch on the left three miles in from the highway and continues to Cienega Creek and other destinations. From the south, you can enter on South Road off AZ 82 between Mileposts 36 and 37, about four miles east of Sonoita; this road ends at some corrals just east of Empire Ranch. Together, these roads make a scenic 11-mile loop that may be passable to cars in dry weather; both are signed as EC-900.

Cave of the Bells

A variety of minerals and an underground lake attract experienced spelunkers to this undeveloped "wild" cave in the Santa Rita Mountains to the north. Obtain gate key and directions from the Forest Service office north of Nogales or the supervisor's office in Tucson.

Parker Canyon Lake

This 130-acre fishing lake west of the Huachucas is a rarity in a land of little surface water. Trout are stocked in the cooler months to join the year-round population of bass, bluegill, sunfish, and catfish. The water also attracts many birds and other wildlife. The **Arizona Trail** reaches mile 20 from the Mexican border here.

Lakeview Campground (elev. 5,400 feet) is open all year with drinking water but no showers or hookups; $5 day use, $10 camping. A **marina** provides groceries, fishing supplies, licenses, boat ramp, and boat rentals. You can rent a rowboat or a boat with electric motor, but you need to bring your own battery or gas motor (eight hp limit); 520/455-5847. A 4.5-mile hiking trail goes around the lake. Groups can reserve **Rock Bluff** for day use; 520/458-0761 (Lakeview Outdoor Adventures). Parker Canyon Lake lies 30 miles south of Sonoita on AZ 83, 23 miles southwest of Sierra Vista, and 15 miles northwest of Coronado National Memorial; these roads are largely graded gravel.

SOUTHERN ARIZONA

The Cochise Trail

Chief of the Chiricahua Apache, Cochise earned great respect from whites and Indians alike for his integrity and leadership skills. He never lost a battle. The southeast corner of Arizona was named Cochise County in his honor in 1881, despite his having waged war against Anglo troops and settlers from 1861 to 1872. Many historic sites of the Old West lie along a 206-mile loop through this varied country. Tourist offices call this drive the Cochise Trail.

FORT HUACHUCA

When raiding Apache threatened settlers and travelers in the San Pedro Valley in 1877, the army set up a temporary camp near the Huachuca (wa-CHOO-ka) Mountains. In 1886, Fort Huachuca became the advance headquarters for the campaign against Geronimo. Although the army later closed more than 50 forts and camps in the territory, it retained Huachuca to deal with outlaws and renegade Indians near the Mexican border. World Wars I and II and the Korean War saw new duties for the fort; finally, in 1954, it converted to its current task of testing electronics and communications gear and serving as an information center and intelligence school. The website http://huachuca-www.army.mil tells of some of the projects at the base.

Fort Huachuca Museum

As you stroll past the exhibits, the old days come back to life as you read accounts by the men and women who served here. Life could be very tough out on the trail, but Army people enjoyed many aspects of their stay at the fort. Dioramas have life-size figures to show how the officers, soldiers, scouts, and women dressed. Period rooms and a large collection of photos, Indian artifacts, and memorabilia also help tell Fort Huachuca's long history from Apache-fighting days to the present. You'll also learn about the Blacks, nicknamed the "Buffalo Soldiers," Indians, who served

© BISBEE MINING AND HISTORICAL MUSEUM

Cowboy Romancin' at the Parker Ranch in San Rafael Valley, ca. 1910. Except for George Parker, seated in center, all these cowboys were bachelors. When they heard that George's wife was to bring her cousin, a city girl from Chicago, out to the ranch for a visit, they decided to put on some entertainment. The men dressed up like outlaws, pulled their handkerchiefs over their faces, and shot into the air to meet the girl. She reportedly turned back to Chicago and stayed there.

with distinction during the Indian Wars. A gift shop sells history, hiking, and regional books as well as souvenirs. The Annex displays additional exhibits, arranged chronologically around a large hall; wagons and a campfire scene stand in the center.

Barracks and administrative buildings from the 1880s line the parade ground outside. A sign on the south side of the main museum building gives the dates and functions of the old buildings.

The two museum buildings, 520/533-5736, lie on either side of Hungerford (at Grierson), are about 2.5 miles in from the main gate in Sierra Vista; you'll need to follow signs carefully. Open Mon.–Fri. 10 a.m.–2 p.m.; 520-533-1107.

Army Intelligence Museum

Follow signs from the nearby Fort Huachuca Museum to see exhibits on intelligence history and the equipment used to crack the other side's secrets. Life-size figures show intelligence pioneers and personnel at work. The collection even has some aircraft used for spying, as well as radios and cryptography gear. Videos can be seen on request. There's a small gift shop, too. Call 520/533-1127 for hours, or ask at the Fort Huachuca Museum.

Huachuca and Garden Canyons
Each of these canyons offers good birding, picnic areas, and trailheads from which you can hike into the Huachuca Mountains and south into the Miller Peak Wilderness. Huachuca Canyon, reached by a two-mile graded dirt road, lies on the west side of the military reservation. Garden Canyon is on the south side, reached by a paved road; rough dirt roads continue up the canyon past the picnic areas to higher country. For maps and information, you might try the gate where you enter, the Fort Huachuca Museum, or the Forestry Section.

SIERRA VISTA
The town of Sierra Vista grew up outside the gates of Fort Huachuca as a service center. Many army retirees have settled here; they like the climate and social and recreational opportunities, and they can continue to use post facilities. Sierra Vista (pop. 30,000) includes Fort Huachuca (pop. 10,000) and makes up the largest and fastest growing community in Cochise County. The town makes a handy and good-value base for exploring the surrounding region.

When driving toward Sierra Vista, you have a choice of taking the bypass route or going downtown on Fry Boulevard. Fry Blvd. begins at the fort's main gate and heads east through the center of town. You'll find nearly all motels, restaurants, shopping, and other visitor services on or near this busy street. RV parks lie scattered around town.

Arizona Folklore Preserve
Dolan Ellis, Arizona's Official Balladeer and an original member of the New Christy Minstrels, organizes highly enjoyable programs of music, cowboy poetry, and other entertainment. The shows run on Sat. and Sun. and are very popular—you'll need to make reservations; 520/378-6165. A beautiful setting along Ramsey Creek adds to the enjoyment; head 3.5 miles up Ramsey Canyon Road from AZ 92; the turnoff is six miles south of Sierra Vista.

Accommodations
Under $50: Western Motel, 43 W. Fry Blvd., 520/458-4303, has some kitchenettes; $35 s, $40 d. **Bella Vista Motel,** 1101 E. Fry Blvd., 520/458-6737, offers a pool and many kitchenettes; $33.41 s, $40.10 d with tax. **Motel 6,** 1551 E. Fry Blvd., 520/459-5035 or 800/466-8356, has a pool; $35 s, $41 d. **Village Inn Motel,** 2440 E. Fry Blvd., 520/458-4315, features a pool, and many rooms with fridges and microwaves; $30 s, $36 d. **Blue Horizon Motel,** 5150 E. Hwy. 90, 520/458-7820, offers a pool and kitchenettes; $26 s, $30 with tax.

$50–100: Gateway Studio Suites, 203 5. Garden Ave. (near the fort's main gate), 520/458-5555 or 877/443-6200, includes kitchenettes, pool, and a hot tub; $65 s, $75 d. The nearby **Sun Canyon Inn,** 260 N. Garden Ave., 520/459-0610 or 800/822-6966, features a pool, hot tub, and rooms with fridges and microwaves; $66 s, $71 d. **Super 8 Motel,** 100 Fab Ave., 520/459-5380 or 800/800-8000, has a pool; $43 s, $53 d. **Sierra Suites,** 391 E. Fry. Blvd., 520/459-4221 or 800/852-2430, offers a pool and hot tub; $69–99 d. **Best Western Mission Inn,** 3460 E. Fry Blvd., 520/458-8500 or 877/937-8386, features a pool and rooms with fridges and microwaves; $66 s, $70 d. **Comfort Inn & Suites,** 3500 E3. Fry Blvd., 520/459-0515 or 800/228-5150, has a pool, hot tub, and exercise room; $65–125 d. **Thunder Mountain Inn** 1631 5. Hwy. 92, 520/458-7900, has a pool, hot tub, and rooms with refrigerators; $55 s, $60 d, $85–150 d suites. At **Windemere Hotel & Conference Center,** 2047 5. Hwy. 92, 520/459-5900 or 800/825-4656, amenities include a pool, hot tub, fitness-center privileges, and full breakfast; $70 s, 80 d.

Seventeen miles southeast of town near the San Pedro Riparian National Conservation Area, you can stay at **San Pedro River Inn,** 8326 Here-

ford Rd. (Hereford), 520/366-5532; www
.sanpedroriverinn.com. The four adobe houses
have kitchens and cost $105 d with a continental
breakfast. Two ponds attract waterfowl, and the
San Pedro River is just a short stroll away. Your
horse can stay in the stables.

Campgrounds
Pueblo del Sol RV Resort, 3400 Resort Dr. (S.
Hwy 92), 520/378-0213 or 888/551-1432, offers
activities for seniors; $19 RV w/hookups. **Los
Arcos Mobile Home Park,** 650 Busby Dr.,
520/458-6870, has RV spaces for $12.50. **Sierra
Vista Mobile Home Village,** 733 S. Deer Creek
Lane (two miles east on AZ 90/Bisbee Rd.),
520/459-1690 or 800/955-7606, provides RV
spots for $25.50. **Mountain View RV Park,** 99
W. Vista Lane in Huachuca City (about nine
miles north), 520/456-2860 or 800/772-4103,
costs $16.50 for an RV w/hookups. **Tombstone
Territories RV Park,** 2111 E. Hwy. 82 (Huachuca City), 520/457-2584 or 877/316-6714, runs
$22.50.

Food
You'll find a platoon of eateries on Fry Boulevard in front of Fort Huachuca's main gate;
they're listed here from west to east. For American
food, try **Beef Baron** at the corner of 21 Fab
Ave. and Fry Blvd., 520/459-2715; **Golden Corral,** 590 E. Fry Blvd., 520/458-7054; and
Denny's (24 hours), 2397 E. Fry Blvd., 520/458-
1900. **La Casita Mexican Restaurant & Cantina** offers south-of-the-border tastes at 465 E.
Fry Blvd., 520/458-2376. For pizza, choices include **Pizza I-Iut,** at 1297 E. Fry Blvd., 520/458-
8900, and at 3680 E. Fry Blvd., 520/459-8227;
and **Domino's Pizza,** at 209 W. Fry Blvd.,
520/458-3030, and at 3670 E. Fry Blvd.,
520/458-5000.

Sierra Vista's many Asian restaurants have been
credited in part to wives from overseas who married army personnel. Try **Golden China Restaurant,** 220 W. Fry Blvd., 520/458-8588; **Peacock**
(Vietnamese; closed Mon.), 80 S. Carmichael
Ave. (across from the Visitors Bureau), 520/459-
0095; **Toy's Egg Roll Buffet** (closed Sun.–Mon.),
100 E. Fry Blvd., 520/459-7648; **Shanghai Chi-**

nese Restaurant, 1173 E. Fry Blvd., 520/459-
4717; and **Tanuki Sushi Bar & Garden** (Japanese; closed Sunday), 1221 E. Fry Blvd.,
520/459-6853. Sierra Vista offers many other
restaurants, including south on AZ 92. You'll
find supermarkets in the shopping centers on E.
Fry Boulevard, which becomes AZ 90/Bisbee
Road.

Events
The local chamber of commerce maintains a list-
ing of area happenings; you can call the Special
Events Hotline at 520/459-3868.

Athletes age 50 and up compete in the **Senior Games** in January. Artists portray the West
during the **Cochise Cowboy Poetry & Music
Gathering** in early February. **Festival of the
Southwest,** in early May, features music, arts,
and crafts of the Southwest. Fireworks light the
sky during the **Fourth of July** celebration.

Oktoberfest, in September, creates a German
atmosphere with oompah bands, food, crafts,
dancing, and song. **Huachuca Heritage Days,** in
September, brings a big carnival, concerts, food,
and crafts to Fort Huachuca. **Art in the Park,** on
the first weekend of October, attracts artists and
craftspeople from all over the Southwest. Custom
and antique cars shine for **Cars in the Park** on
the second weekend of October. Balloons take to
the air for the **Festival of Color** on the third
weekend of October. **Festival of the Trees** takes
place in the Mall at Sierra Vista at the end of
November and beginning of December. The
Christmas Parade marches on the first Saturday of December. You can enjoy holiday decorations and history in the **Tour of Officers'
Homes** at Fort Huachuca on the first Sunday
of December.

Recreation
Veterans Memorial Park, 3105 F. Fry Blvd.,
520/458-7922, offers picnic tables, a playground,
aquatic center, basketball court, and horseshoe
pits. **Buffalo Corral Riding Stables,** 520/533-
5220, has rides and instruction at Fort Huachuca; closed Mon.–Tuesday. Play golf year-round at
the 18-hole **Pueblo del Sot Golf Course,** 2770
Saint Andrews Dr., off S. Hwy. 92; 520/378-

6444; and Fort Huachuca's 18-hole **Mountain View Golf Course,** 520/533-7092. Catch a movie at **Uptown 3 Theatre** (4341 S. Hwy. 92, 520/378-2858); and **Cinemark Theatres (Mall at Sierra Vista, 520/458-1980.**

Information and Services
Sierra Vista Convention & Visitors Bureau, 520/417-6960 or 800/288-3861, offers information about the sights and services of the region; www.visitsierravista.com. It's at 21 E. Wilcox Dr. (Sierra Vista, AZ 85635), turn south one block on Carmichael Ave. from Fry Boulevard. Hours are Mon.–Fri. 8 a.m.–5 p.m. and Saturday 9 a.m.–4 p.m.

Sierra Vista Ranger Station provides recreation information for national forest lands in the Huachuca and Whetstone Mountains; you can purchase maps and books. The station is seven miles south of Sierra Vista at 5990 S. Hwy. 92 (Hereford, AZ 85615); 520/378-0311; www.fs.fed.us/r3/coronado. It's open Mon.–Fri. 8 a.m.–4:30 p.m.

The BLM San Pedro Project Office, 1763 Paseo San Luis (Sierra Vista, AZ 85635), 520/458-3559, has information on the San Pedro Riparian National Conservation Area. The office is on the east side of town; from Fry Blvd., turn south one mile on AZ 92, left one block on Snyder Blvd., then right about a block on Paseo San Luis. It's open Mon.–Fri. 8 a.m.–4 p.m.; www.az.blm.gov.

Sierra Vista Public Library, 2600 E. Tacoma St., 520/458-4225, is open daily; it's in the northeastern part of town—turn north on Coronado Dr. from Fry Blvd., then right on Tacoma. **Bookman's,** 100 W. Fry Blvd., 520/458-9702, sells new and used books. Hastings Books, Music, and Video, 3758 E. Fry Blvd., 520/4598130, offers regional books.

The **post office** is at 2300 E. Fry Blvd.; 520/458-2540. **Sierra Vista Regional Health Center** is at 300 El Camino Real, south off E. Fry Blvd.; 520/4584641 or 800/880-0088.

Transportation
Sierra Vista Public Transit System runs a bus service in Sierra Vista; 520/4590595. **Golden State** offers bus service to Tucson, Bisbee, Douglas, and Mexico from the station at 28 Fab Ave., south off W. Fry Blvd.; 520/458-3471.

HUACHUCA MOUNTAINS

The Huachucas, south of Sierra Vista, present many hiking possibilities and some very scenic drives. Trails climb from all sides of the range to Miller Peak Wilderness, which contains much of the high country between Coronado National Memorial and Fort Huachuca.

Carr Canyon Road
This scenic road ascends 7.8 miles on the eastern slopes of the range to the cool pine forests at over 7,000 feet. Spectacular views over the San Pedro Valley and distant mountains can be enjoyed at many overlooks along the way. Local people sometimes drive up to a viewpoint to watch the changing colors and lengthening shadows at sunset. The turnoff from AZ 92 is 7.5 miles south of Sierra Vista between Mileposts 328 and 329; the turn is also marked by the Mesquite Tree Restaurant. Pavement ends after 0.9 mile where Forest Road 368 continues to the heights. Cautiously driven cars can do the trip if the road is dry; no vehicles over 20 feet or trailers over 12 feet long are allowed. Snow may close the road in winter. About two miles up, look for the Carr House, which has exhibits and a three-quarter-mile nature trail; it's run by Friends of the Huachuca Mountains.

About 6.5 miles in on Carr Canyon Road, **Reef Townsite Campground** (7,150 feet) lies at the site of a former mining camp. It has water and a $10 picnicking/camping fee. The nearby Reef Group Area can be reserved for day use. **Reef Historic Trail** makes a 0.7-mile loop from the far end of the campground; signs point out mine and mill sites and relate the history. Prospectors filed claims here in 1893, then mined gold and silver until about WW I. Large mills processed the ore, but operations never proved very profitable. Some tungsten and quartz were later mined, but all operations ceased by the end of the 1950s. The trail descends several hundred feet and features fine views of the Huachuca

Mountains and its canyons. For longer hikes, start at the trailhead opposite the entrance to the campground. From here, **Old Sawmill Trail** climbs to Carr Peak Trail, which in turn leads to Carr Peak (three miles), Crest Trail #103 (3.5 miles), and Miller Peak (6.5 miles).

Ramsey Vista Campground (7,200 feet), 1.3 miles farther at the end of the road and near the wilderness boundary, has a $10 picnicking/camping fee but no water. From the trailhead just before the campground, Carr Peak Trail #107 heads up to Carr Peak (2.75 miles), Comfort Spring Trail #109 (0.25 mile), and other destinations; another trailhead lies at the far end of the campground. There's no charge for trailhead parking outside the campgrounds, though donations are accepted. Contact the **Sierra Vista Ranger Station** of the Coronado National Forest for information on exploring the Huachucas; the office is on AZ 92 just half a mile north of the Carr Canyon Road turnoff.

Miller Peak Wilderness

High summits surrounded by sheer cliffs and deep canyons distinguish this rugged area of 20,190 acres in the Huachuca Mountains. Elevations range from 5,200 to 9,466 feet at the top of Miller Peak. Trails wind up the slopes from the east off Ash Canyon, Miller Canyon, Carr Canyon, and Ramsey Canyon Rds., from the south at Montezuma Pass in Coronado National Memorial, and from the west via Oversite, Ida, Bear, and Sunnyside Canyons. The 11.5-mile Crest Trail between Montezuma Pass and Fort Huachuca ties all of the other trails together. Although the long climb is challenging, the mountains offer outstanding views and chances to see birds and other wildlife. The Sierra Vista Ranger Station has descriptions of trails and sells maps and a hiking book for the Huachucas.

Fort Huachuca Military Reservation

The army controls the northern part of the range—secret electronic installations cap some of the mountaintops. The road through the fort between Sierra Vista and Canelo passes over the northern foothills and offers some fine views. Huachuca Canyon in the western part and Gar-

den Canyon in the southern part of the military reservation each have good scenery, picnic areas, and hiking. Upon entering the post, pick up a pass; drop it off at the other end when leaving. See **Fort Huachuca,** above.

Ramsey Canyon Preserve

The Nature Conservancy operates this 300-acre sanctuary for hummingbirds and other wildlife. Up to 14 species of hummers congregate here from spring to early autumn. Butterflies also appear in the warmer months. A year-round stream and a wide elevation range provide habitats for many other kinds of creatures as well, including white-tailed deer, coati, javelina, black bear, and turkey. The endangered Ramsey Canyon leopard frog, which can sound its mating call underwater, lives only here. The Hamburg Trail goes through the preserve one mile, then continues a short way to an overlook (6,380 feet) in the Coronado National Forest. Guided nature walks depart at 9 A.M. on Tues., Thurs., and Sat. from March to October. The Ramsey Canyon bird observation area, Hamburg Trail, and a visitor center are open to the public daily 8 A.M.–5 P.M. March to October, then 9 A.M.–5 P.M. the rest of the year; an entry fee of $5 ($3 for members and Cochise County residents) helps support research here; entry is free for ages under 16 and for everyone on the first Saturday of the month.

Visitors should first register at the visitor center, where a gift shop sells hiking maps and an excellent selection of natural history and regional books. The Preserve can be crowded mid-March through September and the first-come, first-served parking spots may fill; groups should call ahead. The small parking area has an 18-foot vehicle-length limit and cannot accommodate RVs or trailers. No pets, picnicking, or camping.

The preserve is four miles up Ramsey Canyon Road from AZ 92; the turnoff is six miles south of Sierra Vista. For more information on the preserve, call 520/378-2785 or check out The Nature Conservancy's website, www.tncarizona.org.

Just outside the preserve, **Ramsey Canyon Inn Bed & Breakfast,** 520/378-3010, is managed by the Nature Conservancy and offers rooms at

$121–145 d with breakfast and private bath; apartment units have kitchens but no breakfast and cost $145 d or $158 four people. Guests enjoy homemade pie in the afternoon.

Ramsey Canyon RV Park is an adult-oriented place on Ramsey Canyon Road, one-half mile before the preserve, 520/378-0549. Sites cost $16 with hookups (self-contained only) and are usually full.

Arizona Folklore Museum

Dolan Ellis, Arizona's official balladeer, presents musical programs on Sat.–Sun.; they're very popular, so you should call ahead at 520/378-6165. The hall and gift shop are beside Ramsey Creek just before Ramsey Canyon Preserve.

CORONADO NATIONAL MEMORIAL

Francisco Vásquez de Coronado marched through this area in 1540 in search of the mythical Seven Cities of Cíbola. Although his backers judged the quest a failure, Coronado's was the first major European expedition into the American Southwest and the names of both this park and the adjacent national forest honor him.

Coronado National Memorial offers hiking and a scenic drive in the Huachuca Mountains just north of the Mexican border. The visitor center, 520/366-5515, is staffed by National Park Service rangers and features exhibits on the area's history, plants, and wildlife. A video introduces Coronado and the memorial; other videos can be seen on request. You can also purchase regional books and maps. The center is open daily 8 A.M.–5 P.M. except Thanksgiving and Christmas; www.nps.gov/coro.

Outside, a nature walk identifies local flora. There's a picnic area in an oak grove across the road but no campground. The turnoff for Coronado National Memorial lies about midway between Sierra Vista and Bisbee on AZ 92. Turn west 4.7 miles on Coronado Memorial Dr. to the visitor center and another 3.2 miles and 1,345 feet higher for Montezuma Pass; the last 2 miles are unpaved and not suited for vehicles or trailers over 24 feet. You can also take scenic back roads—mostly dirt or gravel—from Patagonia or Nogales. Snowstorms occasionally close the pass in winter. Although the memorial closes at night, the road remains open 24 hours.

Coronado Cave Trail

This 1.5-mile-roundtrip trail winds up the hillside behind the visitor center to a limestone cave with some formations; the first quarter mile is gentle, followed by a steep half mile with some stone steps to the cave entrance. Elevation gain is 470 feet. The cave is about 600 feet long, 70 feet wide, and up to 20 feet high, with some short crawlways. All cave visitors must obtain the required free permit first and carry a flashlight (sold at the visitor center). A spare flashlight is recommended and essential for solo travelers. To preserve the cave's environment, no food, candles, flares, or lanterns should be brought in. Visitors are asked not to disturb wildlife, such as the several species of bats that inhabit the cave at times.

Montezuma Pass and Hiking

Outstanding views of Arizona and Mexico stretch to the horizon from the top of 6,864-foot Coronado Peak, reached by the **Coronado Peak Trail** south from Montezuma Pass in 0.8 mile roundtrip. The path ascends 290 feet with many shaded benches for resting. Signs along the way describe Coronado's expedition in his own words along with accounts by his men and later historians. In one-tenth of a mile, you'll reach the turn for **Joe's Canyon Trail**, 3.1 miles one-way, which connects Montezuma Pass with the visitor center in the valley below; elevation change is 1,345 feet.

Arizona Trail

The southernmost section of this trail begins in the southwest corner of the memorial at the Mexican border. There's no access from the Mexican side, so hikers begin by taking Joe's Canyon Trail southwest 2.1 miles from the visitor center or southeast one mile from Montezuma Pass, then following Yaqui Ridge Trail south one mile to International Border Monument #102. From here the Arizona Trail leads generally northward across the state to Utah.

You can reach Miller Peak (9,466 feet), the highest point in the Huachuca Mountains, on the 5.3-mile **Crest/Arizona Trail** north from Montezuma Pass. Mountain bikers may not ride trails in the memorial or wilderness, but they have many options in the Coronado National Forest to the west.

SAN PEDRO RIPARIAN NATIONAL CONSERVATION AREA

The San Pedro River, though only a trickle at times, nourishes willows, cottonwoods, and other streamside vegetation. Residents of this choice wildlife habitat—one of the richest in the United States—include 350 bird species, 82 mammal species, and 45 reptile and amphibian species. From its beginning in the grasslands of Sonora, Mexico, the river flows north 140 miles to join the Gila River near Winkelman.

The San Pedro Riparian National Conservation Area, run by the Bureau of Land Management, is 1–3 miles wide and stretches for 36 miles from the Mexican border to near St. David. Visitors enjoy birdwatching, nature walks, and historic sites. Hikers, horseback riders, and mountain bikers may use the backcountry trails, but motorized vehicles are prohibited.

Information

You can usually find volunteers daily at Fairbank or San Pedro House, though the people here may know only their immediate area. For more information, contact the BLM's San Pedro Project Office, 1763 Paseo San Luis, Sierra Vista, AZ 85635, 520/458-3559. It's open Mon.–Fri. 8 A.M.–4 P.M. and on the Web at www.az.blm.gov.

Fairbank

This ghost town beside the San Pedro River began its life in 1881 with construction of a railroad. Nearby mines, mills, and booming

Tombstone generated a lot of freight and passenger traffic for the depot. An adobe commercial building (1883), house (1885), schoolhouse (1920), and other structures still stand; interpretive panels tell their histories. Volunteers and the BLM look after the site; there's usually someone here to answer your questions. Fairbank is on the north side of AZ 82, just east of the San Pedro River bridge.

Birders find good opportunities near the river. Hikers and mountain bikers can set off on abandoned roads to the north and south. The site of Grand Central Mill lies an easy 1.5 miles north; foundations display excellent stonework. Contention Mill site and townsite are four miles north of Fairbank, but you'll need a map as the way isn't marked. One could also detour across the river to Terranate.

Presidio Santa Cruz de Terranate

Hikers can experience some of the isolation of this unsuccessful outpost of Spain. In 1775, the Irish mercenary Col. Hugo O'Conor led construction of the fort to extend and protect the northern reaches of New Spain. Apache raids, however, prevented the raising of crops, robbed supply parties, and killed two captains and over 80 soldiers. By 1780, after less than five years of use, the Spanish abandoned the site. A few weathered adobe walls of the chapel and commandant's quarters still stand, along with stone foundations of the walls and other structures. An interpretive trail within the presidio tells of the fortifications and what life may have been like here.

Visitors must hike in. To reach the trailhead, take AZ 82 to Milepost 60, 1.2 miles west of Fairbank, then turn north 1.8 miles on Ironhorse (Kellar) Road (gravel). An easy, well-marked trail winds 1.2 miles across the desert to the site overlooking the San Pedro River. Hikers could extend their trip by continuing north along and across the river to Contention; it's also possible to reach this area from Fairbank via Grand Central Mill. A map, available free from the BLM, will be needed for explorations beyond Terranate.

San Pedro House and Trails

Birdwatchers come here to take advantage of the excellent sighting possibilities. The Friends of the San Pedro River organization runs a bookstore/gift shop in San Pedro House with a large selection of regional and natural-history books; you can also pick up BLM handouts on the San Pedro National Conservation Area. It's open daily 9:30 A.M.–4:30 P.M. Short trails make several loops to the river and ponds southeast of San Pedro House. San Pedro Trail offers longer hikes; it's planned to be 30 miles long, but currently you can follow it south eight miles to Hereford Road and north 3.6 miles to Escapule Road.

Murray Springs Clovis Site

Scientists have unearthed bones of extinct mammoths, bison, horses, camels, and dire wolf here along with stone weapons and tools used by the Clovis Culture to kill and butcher the animals 8,000-11,000 years ago. A one-third-mile interpretive trail loops through the site; interpretive panels have photos of bones and tools found and illustrations of how the Clovis people may have hunted. Signs identify desert plants along the trail and describe their medicinal uses. From Sierra Vista head east 3.8 miles on AZ 90, turn left 1.2 miles on Moson Road, then right 0.4 mile at the sign; or you can take Charleston Road from Sierra Vista or Tombstone and turn south 1.8 miles on Moson Road, then left to the site. Lehner Mammoth Kill Site, farther south in the National Conservation Area, has also yielded bone and Clovis projectile points; sights there are nil and access is difficult.

Camping

Primitive camping (no facilities) is permitted one mile or more from trailheads; parking at some trailheads closes in evenings, so an earlier start is recommended. No car camping is allowed in the National Conservation Area.

TOMBSTONE AND VICINITY

When prospector Ed Schieffelin headed out this way in March of 1877, friends told him the only thing he'd find among the Apache and rattlesnakes would be his own tombstone. But he set out anyway, alone, and staked a silver claim, proclaiming it Tombstone. When Ed struck it rich at an adjacent site, his brother Al said, "You're a lucky cuss." And the Lucky Cuss Mine became one of Arizona's richest. Other claims bore such descriptive names as Contention, Tough Nut, and Goodenough.

The town incorporated in 1879 and contained as many as 10,000 souls just five years later. It was said that saloons and gambling halls made up two of every three buildings in the business district. The famous OK Corral gunfight took place here in 1881—and historians still debate the details. The town's riches attracted many crooks and Apaches, which along with political corruption, gave the region notoriety. Shootings and hangings in the 1880s kept Boothill Graveyard busy. Fires nearly wiped out Tombstone on two occasions, but flooding of the mines by 1886 nearly drove the final nail in the town's coffin. Still, Tombstone, "the town too tough to die," managed to survive, and now attracts throngs of visitors seeking a peek into the old Wild West. You'll experience both the authentic history of Tombstone and pistol-packing entertainment!

Tombstone Courthouse State Historic Park

Drop by the 1882 red-brick courthouse to find out what life was like for the people of early Tombstone. The venerable building, abandoned in 1931 when the county seat moved to Bisbee, has been restored and now houses a museum of artifacts and photos of the old days. The courtroom, lawyer's office, and assay office look ready for business. Exhibits introduce the Indians, prospectors, sheriffs, ranchers, and the famous October 26th, 1881 gunfight. Mining exhibits show how miners dug and assayed their ore. An old bar, faro table, and roulette wheel illustrate how many miners lost their underground riches. Women probably did more to tame the town than the marshals and sheriffs; you'll learn about some of them and see exhibits on family life.

A gift shop offers books and videos about Tombstone's history. Researchers can make an appointment to delve into the extensive historic archives. The courthouse is at Third and Toughnut Sts., 520/457-3311. It's open daily 8 A.M.–5 P.M.; admission is $5 adults, $4 seniors 55+, and $3 ages 4–15.

Gunfights

Guns still blaze and bodies hit the dust in staged gunfights and barroom brawls. The Visitor Information Center has the day's schedule. The action takes place most days at three sites. The **Boothill Gunslingers** re-enact the OK Corral gunfight and other events off Allen Street between Third and Fourth. **Six Gun City,** at Fifth and Toughnut, presents a lively musical show in a series of acts depicting actual Tombstone events; 520/457-3827. **Tombstone Cowboys** promise "hysterically correct" entertainment in a series of action-packed gunfights at the Helldorado, Fourth and Toughnut. Additionally, the **Tombstone Vigilantes** or the **Wild Bunch** put on a show on 2nd, 4th, and 5th Sunday afternoons of each month. All events require a small admission fee.

The OK Corral

The Earps and Doc Holliday shot it out with the Clanton cowboys on this site in October 1881. Markers and life-size figures show how it all happened—or at least one version of the story. Other sights to see include the studio (reconstructed) and photos of Camilius S. Fly, old stables, carriages, a hearse, and even a red-light district shack. Visitors can "walk where they fell" daily 9 A.M.–5 P.M. for $2.50 admission, children under six free; 520/457-3456. Package tickets for $6.50 include the OK Corral, the 2 P.M. gunfight show, Historama, and a copy of the *Epitaph*. Located on Allen St. between Third and Fourth Streets.

Historama

This 30-minute show re-creates the major events of Tombstone with movies and animated figures. Presentations take place on the hour 9 A.M.–

4 P.M.; $2.50, under six free. It's next door to the OK Corral entrance.

Crystal Palace Saloon

Built in 1879, this watering hole and gambling house offered an elegant setting for patrons in early Tombstone. As many as five bartenders stood on duty to serve thirsty customers round the clock. The clientele has changed over the years, but the saloon still serves up drinks and hosts live music. The interior has been accurately restored. In the center of town at Fifth and Allen Streets.

Big Nose Kate's Saloon

This large and colorful cowboy bar began life as the Grand Hotel in 1881. There's lots of stuff to see on the walls in the bar room, but perhaps the most unusual feature is the downstairs "Shaft." Working in the hotel by day, an employee dug in secret at night from his room to prospect in the mineshafts under Tombstone. It's on Allen St. between Fifth and Sixth Streets.

Stagecoach and Wagon Rides

Hop on a stage or wagon for a narrated tour of Tombstone's colorful past. The horse-drawn vehicles depart frequently from near Big Nose Kate's Saloon on Allen Street downtown. Rides last about 15 minutes and cost $5 adult, $4 senior 55+, and $3 children 4–15.

Tombstone *Epitaph*

As one story goes, the town's newspaper got its name when its founder, John P. Clum, took the stagecoach home from Tucson and asked passengers for appropriate suggestions. Ed Schieffelin happened to be on board, and he replied, "Well, I christened the district Tombstone; you should have no trouble furnishing the *Epitaph*." Clum started the *Epitaph* in 1880 and it's still in business. You can visit the office to see the original press and other printing exhibits and to pick up your own *Epitaph*. It's on Fifth Street around the corner from the Crystal Palace Saloon. Open daily 9:30 A.M.–5 P.M.; free admission.

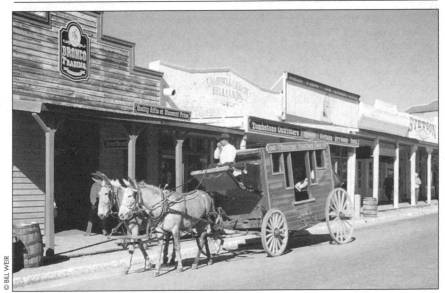

stagecoach tour on Allen Street, Tombstone

© BILL WEIR

SOUTHERN ARIZONA

Bird Cage Theatre

This 1881 dance hall, gambling house, saloon, brothel, and theater provided the finest and most expensive entertainment of the day. During its first eight years, the doors never closed. Prostitutes scouted for customers from the 14 cribs overlooking the hall. A hit song titled "A Bird in a Gilded Cage" written here about the ladies of the night may have given the place its name. Or, perhaps it was because there were so many doves in it, as reported by the *Arizona Star* of August 18, 1882. See if you can find some of the estimated 140 bullet holes in the walls and ceiling. A self-guided tour winds through the theater, below the cribs, past rare circus posters, and gambling tables. A back room has the hearse that carried all but six people on their last ride to Boot Hill. Downstairs, you can imagine life at the bar, gambling tables, and bordello rooms. An 1881 City License here signed by Wyatt Earp allows the Bird Cage to operate a "House of Ill Fame." Many old photos and prints—copies of some of which are for sale in the gift shop—show notable prostitutes and other characters. The exceptionally well-preserved building closed in late 1889 and remained boarded up for 45 years; when it re-opened as a museum, everything inside was still there. It's at Allen and Sixth Sts., 520/457-3421. Open daily 8 A.M.–6 P.M.; admission costs $4.50 adults, $4 seniors 60 and over, and $3 children 8–18; families get in for $12.50.

Pioneer Home Museum

While most of the early houses of miners and their families have been remodeled over the years, this one has been remarkably preserved. It's little changed since Cornish miner Frank Garland and his wife Julia moved in during the late 1800s. Inside you can see the furnished parlor, bedroom, and kitchen. The former dining room has photos of Tombstone's distinguished citizens along with a band uniform and other belongings of the Garlands. A blacksmith shop and a Chevy 1921 delivery truck lie in the backyard. It's open daily 9 A.M.–5 P.M., depending on staffing, at 804 E. Fremont St.; donations appreciated.

Rose Tree Museum

A rose root sent from Scotland to comfort a

homesick bride in the spring of 1885 has grown to cover an amazing 8,700 square feet. The rose tree, believed to be the world's largest, and listed in the *Guinness Book of Records,* is a Lady Banksia. Its sweet-scented white blossoms usually appear in early April. Rooms exhibit many historic photos and a collection of antique furnishings belonging to a pioneer who arrived by wagon in 1880. A gift shop sells new and used books. The museum is at Fourth and Toughnut Streets. It's open daily 9 A.M.–5 P.M.; $2 adults (under 14 free).

Schieffelin Hall

Major theatrical companies of the day performed in this 1881 adobe building, claimed to be the largest adobe in the United States. John Sullivan and a company of boxers gave exhibitions here. Now restored, the hall once again hosts theater companies; upcoming events will be posted here and at the Visitor Information Center. Otherwise, it's usually closed to the public. It's on the corner of Fremont and Fourth Streets.

St. Paul's Episcopal Church

Completed in 1882, St. Paul's is the oldest standing Protestant church in Arizona. Inside you can admire the original stained glass, two ship's lamps, and the sturdy adobe walls. It's open daily at the corner of Third and Safford.

Boothill Graveyard

Here lie the losers of the OK Corral shootout, hanging/lynching victims, assorted gunslingers, and Dutch Annie, a widely admired prostitute. As the graveyard's name suggests, many of those who ended up here died violent deaths. Many of the estimated 300 graves are marked and have much to say about life in old Tombstone. A self-guided tour booklet, available at the gift shop, tells more about many of the people here. Boothill lies just off AZ 80 on the north edge of town; enter free of charge through the Boot Hill Gift Shop. It's open daily 7:30 A.M.–6 P.M.; donations welcome.

Schieffelin Monument

The old prospector's last request was to be buried on top of the granite hills three miles west of town. He specified that "a monument such as prospectors build when locating a mining claim be built over my grave… under no circumstances do I want to be buried in a graveyard or cemetery." Head west 2.3 miles on Allen Street to see this lonesome spot.

Nearby Ghost Towns

Ghost-town enthusiasts may want to explore remnants of former mining towns in the area. **Gleeson,** 18 miles east of Tombstone on a graded gravel road, flourished around a copper mine from 1909 until the 1930s. Operations ended in 1955. You can see ruins of the jail, cemetery, school, adobe hospital, and other buildings. Mine tailings and machinery rest on the hillside.

Courtland, now occupied solely by ghosts, lies one mile east and three miles north of Gleeson on good gravel roads. A jail and numerous foundations remain. Watch out for open mine shafts in the area.

Jimmie Pearce found gold in 1894 at the site of **Pearce,** nine miles north of Courtland. The Commonwealth Mine here was a success, and the town's population reached 1,500 before the mine closed in the 1930s. Reminders of the past include the old store, cemetery, post office, Pearce Church, abandoned houses, and Commonwealth Mine ruins. You can also reach Pearce from I-10; take Exit 331 and head south 22 miles on US 191.

Motels

Under $50: Trail Riders Motel and Mini-RV Park sits on the corner of Fremont and Seventh; 520/457-3573, 800/574-0417; $35 s, $45 d including tax, RV sites for $10 with hookups. **Larian Motel** is at 410 E. Fremont St. (AZ 80), 520/457-2272, www.tombstonemotels.com; $39–49 s, $42–52 d. **Tombstone Sagebrush Inn** has a quiet location and a pool two blocks north of Fremont Street; 520/457-2311; rooms run $39–114 d, with the more expensive having spas and kitchens; weekly and monthly rates are also available.

$50–100: Adobe Lodge occupies the corner of Fifth and Fremont Sts., 520/457-2241, 888/457-2241; $50 d and up, suites available. **Tombstone**

Motel is at 502 E. Fremont St., 520/457-3478, 888/455-3478; from $62 d. The **Best Western Lookout Lodge** has a great view, free breakfasts, and a pool 0.7 mile north on AZ 80, 520/457-2223, 800/528-1234; $75–86 d.

Bed and Breakfasts

All offer guests a chance to spend the night in a piece of history.

$50–100: The **Tombstone Boarding House** has an old-fashioned ambiance with modern comforts in two 1880 adobe houses at 108 N. 4th St., 520/457-3716, 877/225-1319, email tombstonebandb@theriver.com; $50–70 s, $60–80 d. The owner offers a fine-dining restaurant, too. Nearby, **Marie's Engaging Bed & Breakfast** is in a 1906 adobe at Fourth and Safford Sts., 520/457-3831, email maries@theriver.com; $55–65 d with shared bath. **Priscilla's B&B** is a 1904 country Victorian house at 101 N. Third St., 520/457-3844; $45 s, $59 d ($69 d with private bath). **The Buford House** is an 1880 adobe at 113 E. Safford St., 520/457-3969, email bufordhouse@yahoo.com; the five rooms, two with private bath, each have a different theme and cost $65–95 d.

The **Silver Nugget** puts you right over the action of Allen Street across from the Bird Cage, 520/457-9223; the four rooms, two of which have private bath, share a balcony and cost $60–75 including continental breakfast.

Campgrounds

Wells Fargo RV Park features a central location at Third and Fremont Streets. Amenities include a Laundromat, showers, Internet access, and some of the cleanest restrooms in Arizona; 520/457-3966. All sites cost $21.50 for tent or RV, including hookups. **Stampede RV Ranch** at 201 W. Allen St., 520/457-3738, provides a Laundromat and showers, $20 RV with hookups. **Trail Riders Motel and Mini-RV Park,** mentioned under **Motels,** above, offers sites for just $10.

Tombstone Hills RV Park Campground lies one mile north of downtown on AZ 80, 520/457-3829, 800/348-3829. Amenities include a pool, Laundromat, showers, and store;

$20 tent or RV no hookups, $24 RV with hookups, $32 cabin.

Food

Not surprisingly, most restaurants in town feature Western or Mexican decor and food. For a romantic dining spot, try **Tombstone Boarding House's** dining room for a Sunday Champagne Brunch or nightly except Mon. for dinner at 108 N. 4th St.; the dinner menu has steak, lamb, pork, chicken, fish, and vegetarian options; reservations recommended, 520/457-3716.

Longhorn Restaurant, Fifth and Allen Sts., 520/457-3405, offers Mexican, American, and a few Italian items daily for breakfast, lunch, and dinner. **Nellie Cashman Restaurant,** 520/457-2212, has been going on the corner of Fifth and Toughnut Sts. since 1882; today it offers American and a few pasta dishes daily for breakfast, lunch, and dinner; you can read about the remarkable Irish lass who founded the restaurant and see her photos here. **Don Teodoro's Mexican Restaurant,** 15 N. Fourth St., just north of Fremont, 520/457-3647, serves tasty fare daily for lunch and dinner; try their Sonoran enchilada, a thick, flat corn tortilla with toppings. The **OK Café,** at Allen and Third Sts., 520/457-3980, is popular for breakfast and lunch; open daily. **Big Nose Kate's Saloon** has a patio restaurant out back with American, Mexican, and pizza items daily for lunch and dinner.

Tombstone lacks a supermarket, though you can pick up items at the Circle-K on AZ 80 west of downtown and the Tombstone Pharmacy on Allen Street.

Entertainment and Events

Shootouts take place every day throughout the year when weather permits, see **Gunfights,** above. The Crystal Palace Saloon and Big Nose Kate's Saloon feature live Western music on weekends and some weekdays.

Helldorado Days, Tombstone's biggest celebration, features three days of shootouts, parades, dances, and other lively entertainment on the third full weekend of October. Smaller-scale festivities include **Territorial Days** in March, **Rose Festival** in April, **Wyatt Earp Days** on

Memorial Day weekend, **July Fourth, Vigilante Days** on the second weekend in August, **Rendezvous of the Gunfighters** on Labor Day weekend, **Clanton Gang Reunion** in November, and **Emmet Kelly, Jr. Days,** also in November.

Shopping

Many shops along Allen Street sell Old West souvenirs, rocks and minerals, books, clothing, jewelry, and crafts. Some also feature small museums, usually free, that may be worth a look. Tombstone Association of the Arts offers the **Tombstone Art Gallery** next to the Visitor Information Center on Allen Street.

Information and Services

The **Visitor Information Center,** Fourth and Allen Sts., P.O. Box 1314, Tombstone, AZ 85638, 520/457-3929, 888/457-3929, is open about Sun. 10 A.M.–4 P.M. and Mon.–Sat. 9 A.M.–4 P.M. The **websites** www.tombstoneweb.com, www.tombstone1880.com and www.tombstone.org have info on Tombstone and links to local businesses.

The **post office** is on the west side of town at Safford and Haskell Streets. The **Tombstone City Library,** 520/457-3612, offers many regional books in its Southwestern collection and has Internet computers; open Mon.–Fri. 8 A.M.-noon and 1–5 P.M.; it's in Tombstone's 1903 railway station at Fourth and Toughnut Streets.

BISBEE

Bisbee is in the Mule Mountains, 24 miles south of Tombstone and 95 miles southeast of Tucson. Squeezed into Mule Pass Gulch, the old mining town is one of Arizona's most unusual settlements. A tiny mining camp in 1877, Bisbee grew into a solid and wealthy town by 1910. Brewery Gulch, a side canyon, held more than 50 saloons in the early 1900s, earning a reputation as the best drinking and entertainment venue in the territory. Many of the fine commercial buildings and Victorian houses built in the boom years remain. Bisbee's riches, mostly copper ore, came from underground chambers and giant surface pits.

History

The story of Bisbee began over 100 million years ago, when a giant mass of molten rock deep in the earth's crust expelled great quantities of steam and hot water. These mineral-rich solutions slowly worked their way upward, replacing the overlying limestone rock with rich copper ores. Three hundred different minerals, many very beautiful, have been identified.

While looking for silver in 1875, Hugh Jones became the first person to discover minerals here, but, annoyed to find only copper, he soon left. Two years later, Jack Dunn, an army scout, also found ore. He couldn't leave his army duties to go prospecting, so he and his partners made a deal with George Warren to establish a claim and share the profits. Warren, a tough old prospector and heavy drinker, lost Dunn's grubstake in a saloon while on his way to the Mule Mountains. Warren quickly found new backers—Dunn and his partners not among them—and filed claims. Two years later he recklessly put his share on a wager that claimed he could outrun a man on horseback; he lost everything. Warren died penniless, but the suburb south of downtown Bisbee takes its name from him.

New electrical industries needed copper, and investors took a keen interest in Warren's camp. Judge DeWitt Bisbee and a group of San Francisco businesspeople bought the Copper Queen Mine in 1880, though the judge never did visit the mining community named for him. From the East, Dr. James Douglas of the Phelps Dodge Company came to Arizona, buying property near the Copper Queen. After the two companies discovered that the richest ores lay on the property boundary, they merged rather than fight it out in court.

Soon a smelter filled the valley with smoke and the clatter of machinery. Streets were paved and substantial buildings went up. Labor troubles between newly formed unions and mine management culminated in the infamous Bisbee Deportation. In July 1917, more than 1,000 striking miners were herded at gunpoint into boxcars and shipped out of the state. Working conditions improved in the following years, but Bisbee's economic life rolled with copper prices. The giant

Lavender Pit closed in 1974, and underground mining ended the following year. The district had provided more than eight billion pounds of copper from 40 mines. A huge amount of ore still lies underground, so exploration continues.

The town didn't dry up and blow away when the mines closed, however. People liked it here—the climate (5,300 feet), the scenery, the character. Bisbee has become a popular destination for many visitors, artists, and retired people. The city consists of the historic district and the communities of Lowell, Warren, San Jose, and Naco. Although mining has ended, a small leaching and precipitation operation continues to recover copper from waste ore.

mule pulling an ore wagon in the Copper Queen Mine, circa 1910

© BISBEE MINING AND HISTORICAL MUSEUM

Walking Bisbee

The twisting streets offer some great walking and photography possibilities. Main Street, Brewery Gulch, and other downtown areas have well-preserved commercial buildings. Side streets lead past old residences. Two churches are worth a visit, the 1903 Covenant Presbyterian Church with its slender steeple at 19 Howell Ave. (next to the Copper Queen Hotel) and the 1917 St. Patrick's Roman Catholic Church with its 27 stained-glass windows (turn off Tombstone Canyon at the Iron Man statue). You can learn the history of the many early-1900s' buildings in town with the chamber of commerce's *Bisbee Walking Tour* pamphlet. Chamber staff can also put you in touch with people who lead tours. Parking can be a challenge in town—another good reason to get around on foot—but with a little patience you'll find a space.

Bisbee Mining and Historical Museum

Mining dioramas, old photos, minerals, and artifacts take you through Bisbee's early years in a display, "Bisbee: Urban Outpost on the Frontier." It illustrates how the city's urban environment developed with trolleys and other conveniences considered modern at the time. The former General Manager's Office still has its wood-paneled elegance, also on the main floor. A Hall of Minerals reveals exceptional specimens upstairs. Additional mining and ranch-

ing exhibits are here, too. And the Shattuck Memorial Archival Library offers extensive material on local history.

The museum and library are in the 1897 former Phelps Dodge General Office Building in Copper Queen Plaza downtown, 520/432-7071. The museum, an affiliate of the Smithsonian, is open daily 10 A.M.–4 P.M.; admission $3 adults, $2.50 seniors, free for ages 16 and under.

Queen Mine Tour

Don a hard hat, lamp, and yellow slicker for a ride deep underground on a mine car. A guide—himself a miner—will issue the equipment and lead you through the mine. He'll explain history, drilling tools, blasting methods, ore loading, and other mining features in the stope (work area) and tunnels.

The mine operated for more than 60 years before shutting down in 1943. Its seven levels have 143 miles of passageways; the whole district boasts over 2,000 miles. The tour is highly recommended; bring a sweater or jacket as it's cold inside (47° F). There are some steps to the stope area but the rest of the walking is level. The 60- to 75-minute tour leaves daily at 9 A.M., 10:30 A.M., noon, 2 P.M., and 3:30 P.M.; $10 adults, $3.50 children 7–15, and $2 children 3–6. Reservations are a good idea in the busy Jan.–May season and anytime for groups; 520/432-2071, 866/432-2071. Buy tickets at the Queen Mine Building just south of downtown across AZ 80.

SOUTHERN ARIZONA

Surface Tour

A guide recounts the mining history and stories of the area; stops include the Lavender Open Pit and some areas not normally open to the public. A bit of downtown Bisbee is included, too. Tours last about 60–75 minutes and leave the Queen Mine Building daily at 10:30 A.M., noon, 2 P.M., and 3:30 P.M.; $7.

Lavender Open Pit

A total of 380 million tons of ore and waste has been scooped out of this giant hole, which you can peer into from a parking area off US 80, one mile south of downtown. Surface mining began only in 1951.

Bisbee Restoration Association Museum

Drop in to see old photos, mining gear, clothing, and household items of Bisbee's early residents. The museum is downtown at 37 Main Street. It's generally open 10 A.M.–3 P.M., but may close for lunch and on Sun.–Mon.; admission is free.

Muheim Heritage House

On tours through this restored and furnished 1902 Victorian dwelling at 207 Youngblood Hill, you'll see how a prominent family lived early in the 20th century. The house is usually open daily 10 A.M.–4 P.M., but call to check (groups should make an appointment); 520/432-7698 (house) or 520/438-7071 (museum). Admission is $2 adults, free for children. The house is a pleasant walk up Brewery Gulch; continue past Youngblood Hill to stairs that lead up the hillside to the house. If driving, take either the easier Brewery Avenue or the very narrow OK Street to Youngblood Hill, which is not suitable for RVs or trailers.

Miracle Hill

For views of town and surrounding hills, climb to this pilgrimage site above Brewery Gulch. A man with failing eyesight once asked permission from land owner Joseph Muheim for permission to erect a cross here. When the man's eyesight dramatically improved, people began constructing shrines and continue to do so—you may even see a Tibetan one. At the upper end of OK Street, look for a well-trod path, probably unsigned, and follow it to the 5,850-foot summit, also known as Grotto Hill or Youngblood Hill; generally take the uphill branches where the trail forks. The roundtrip is about an hour with a 450-foot elevation gain. There's no parking at the trailhead, so you'll need to leave your vehicle back in town.

Accommodations

Bisbee has a large selection of accommodations, especially inns and bed and breakfasts. The chamber has a list.

Under $50: Jonquil Motel, 317 Tombstone Canyon, 520/4327371, lies a short stroll from downtown; rooms start at $40 s, $45 d. **$50–100: Le Chêne Hotel & Bistro,** corner of 1 Howell and Brewery Aves., 520/432-1832, features spacious rooms, most with views, and all with private bath, $85–1 10 d; www.lechenebistro.com. (Le Chêne is French for "oak tree".)

The **Copper Queen Hotel** has been the place to stay since its construction in 1902 by the Copper Queen Mining Company. Rooms—not two alike—differ in size and features, but all have old-fashioned decor and private bath. The elegant hotel features a saloon, dining room, and swimming pool. Rooms cost $70–136 d. 520/432-2216 or 800/247-5829 in state. The four-story hotel sits downtown on Howell Avenue, behind the Mining and Historical Museum.

The **Bisbee Grand Hotel,** 61 Main St., 520/432-5900 or 800/421-1909, provides a romantic getaway in a 1906 building restored with a Victorian motif features include a Western saloon and billiard room. Rooms and suites, all with private bath, cost $75– 150 d, including a Southwestern breakfast. **Main Street I nn,** 26 Main St., 520/432-1202 or 800/467-5237, dates back to 1888; rooms go for $45–85, suites for $95– 105; mainstreetinn@theriver.com.

LaMore HOtel, 45 OK St., 520/432-5131, is downtown overlooking Brewery Gulch. Bed and breakfast rooms in the restored 1917 hotel cost $55 d with shared bath, $70–80 d with private bath, and $120– 165 for one- and two bedroom suites with bath and kitchen. The recently restored LaMore Hotel Saloon dates from 1910 and is smoke-free. **High Desert Inn,** 8 Naco Rd., 520/432-1442 or 800/281-0510, offers modern accommodations with European ambience for $75–100 d.

The **Inn at Castle Rock,** 112 Tombstone Canyon, 520/432-4449 or 800/566-4449, has a large hillside garden, fish ponds, and rooms done in different themes; $47–75 s, $59–87 d, including breakfast; www.theinn.org. Farther up, **School House Inn Bed & Breakfast,** 818 Tombstone Canyon, 520/432-2996 or 800/537-4333, has rooms in a 1918 school; $60–90 d. **Mile High Court Travel Lodge,** 901 Tombstone Canyon, 520/432-3866, provides suites with kitchens at $55–65 d.   Southwest of town, **El Rancho Motel,** 1104 Hwy. 92, 520/432-2293, offers kitchenettes for $49–55 d. Six miles southwest of Bisbee, **San Jose Lodge and RV Park,** 1002 Naco Hwy., 520/432-5761, features a swimming pool and MexicanAmerican restaurant; $65–75 d.

Hostels

Stairway Haven Hostel & Hotel, 59-B Subway St., 520/432-6671, offers hostel beds ($15); private rooms ($35 s, $35 d), and a two-bedroom apartment ($65); guests have use of kitchens. **Bisbee Community Y,** 26 Howell Ave., 520/432-3542, is a simpler hostel (no kitchens) that only costs $10 per bed.

Campgrounds

Queen Mine RV Park features great views and is close to downtown; take the road to Copper Queen Mine Tours and continue a short way up the hill, 520/432-5006. RVers can stay for $16 with no hookups, $19 with hookups; tenters can pitch for $14 on the gravel sites; rates include tax. Guests have showers and a laundry.

Shady Dell RV Park, 1 Douglas Rd. (behind the Chevron station near the traffic circle), 520/432-3567, has sites for tents or RVs without hookups ($10) and RVs with hookups ($15) as well as showers and a laundry. Vintage trailers in one section of the park offer a trip back in time; their beautifully restored interiors have

cooking facilities; some trailers have toilets, but showers are in the bathhouse; rates run $35–75 depending on size; weekly rates are offered too; reservations required. The tiny Dot's Diner serves breakfast, lunch, and dinner daily.

Turquoise Valley Golf Course off the Naco Hwy., 4.5 miles south of AZ 92, 520/432-3091, has an RV park; $16 RV, including hookups and showers. If you'd like to be out in the countryside, visit **Double Adobe RV Park** on Double Adobe Rd., 520/364-4000. The park has showers, laundry, Internet jack, and a trap range; tent spaces go for $7.50 s, $10 d, and RV sites are $14; www.theriver.com/doubleadobe. Take AZ 80 east four miles toward Douglas, then turn left four miles.

A couple of motels southwest of town also have RV spaces. **El Rancho Motel,** 1104 Hwy. 92, 520/432-2293, offers RV sites for $15. **San Jose Lodge and RV Park,** 1002 Naco Hwy., 520/432-5761, has a pool, Mexican-American restaurant, and RV sites for $15 with hookups. It's six miles from Bisbee.

Food

Food **Le Chêne Hotel & Bistro,** corner of Howell and Brewery Ayes., 520/4321832, serves traditional French bistro food and has a wine cellar; open for dinner Tues. –Saturday. The **Copper Queen Hotel's** restaurant offers continental and American cuisine daily for breakfast, lunch, and dinner; 520/432-2216. **Café Roka,** 35 Main St., 520/432-5153, serves contemporary Italian cuisine for dinner Wed.–Saturday. **High Desert Inn,** 8 Naco Rd., 520/432-1442, serves international cuisine for dinner Thurs.–Sunday.

Renaissance Café, 9 Naco Rd., 520/432-4020, offers breakfasts, sandwiches, pizza, and other tasty light fare with a selection of coffees; open daily morning to night. **El Zarape Café,** 46 Main St., 520/432-5031, cooks up Mexican/American food Mon.–Sat. for breakfast and lunch, Mon.–Fri. for dinner. The **Garden Café,** at 120 Naco Rd., prepares flavorful vegetarian food for breakfast and lunch Fri.–Tues.; on Sun. it opens at noon.

The **Brewery Steakhouse,** downstairs in the 1905 Muheim Block, 520/4323317, fixes sandwiches and salads for lunch, then steak, ribs, chicken, pasta, and seafood for dinner daily. Check out the original interior of the **Stock Exchange Bar** upstairs, 15 Brewery Ave., 520/432-9924, where the Bisbee Stock Exchange conducted operations from 1919.

Olde Tymers Restaurant & Saloon, 202 Tombstone Canyon, 520/4327304, serves American, Cajun, and Mexican cuisine daily for lunch and dinner.   In the Copper Queen Plaza on Main Street, you'll find the **Bisbee Grille,** 520/432-6788, serving Southwestern cuisine of pasta, steak, fajitas, chicken, and shrimp; open daily except Tues. for breakfast, lunch, and dinner. Nearby in the same building, **Bisbee Coffee Co.,** 520/432-7879, has the javas, sandwiches, baked goods, and ice cream to keep customers energized from morning to evening.

For good American food served in an authentic 1957 Valentine Diner, head south to **Dot's Diner,** in the Shady Dell RV Park at 1 Douglas Rd. (behind the Chevron station near the traffic circle), 520/432-2046, open daily for breakfast, lunch, and dinner; it's a small place where you'll meet the locals and visitors. Pies are a big hit here, especially the Bisbeeberry, a tasty mix of blackberries and raspberries.

Cranberry Mercantile sells groceries at 215 Brewery Avenue. **Bisbee Food Co-op** features a natural-foods grocery, deli, and café open Mon.–Sat. for breakfast and dialy for lunch. It's in Lowell Plaza: head south past the Lavender Pit, then turn right at the sign. **Safeway** supermarket is out of town at the Naco turnoff.

Entertainment

Contact the chamber of commerce to find out what's playing in town. **Bisbee Repertory Theatre** puts on their plays at 94 Main St.; 520/432-3786, www.bisbeenet.com/therep. The **Copper Queen Hotel Saloon** offers live music Fri.–Sat. evenings. **St. Elmo's** at 36 Brewery Ave. also present a variety of bands most Friday and Saturday nights.

picturesque old buildings crowd lower Brewery Gulch

Events

Arizona's oldest **July 4th Celebration and Parade** includes entertainment and mining contests. Participants get a real workout in the **Thousand Step Stair Climb** in October. Also in October rockhounds come to town for the **Bisbee Mineral Show.** The **Bisbee Historic Home Tour** and the **Festival of Lights** mark the start of the holiday season on the weekend after Thanksgiving. Art festivals and other special events take place through the year; check with the Bisbee Chamber of Commerce for dates.

Shopping

Bisbee's mines have also yielded turquoise and other beautiful copper minerals. Several shops downtown sell stones set in silver as well as loose and rough stones. Another shop sits at the Lavender Pit overlook. Art shops downtown offer paintings, ceramics, and other work by local artists.

Golf

Turquoise Valley Golf Course has 18 holes, a restaurant, and an RV park. It's off the Naco Hwy., 4.5 miles south of AZ 92; 520/432-3091.

Information and Services

The **Bisbee Chamber of Commerce & Visitor Center** is at 31 Subway St. (P.O. Box BA, Bisbee, AZ 85603), 520/432-5421, 866/2-BISBEE, www.bisbeearizona.com. It's open Mon.–Fri. 9 A.M.–5 P.M., Sat.–Sun. 10 A.M.–4 P.M. The office offers a self-guided tour booklet and can advise on guided tours. A website with information on Bisbee is **@Bisbee Arizona,** a commercial website with local links at www.bisbeenet.com.

Copper Queen Community Hospital is at Bisbee Rd. and Cole Ave., three miles south in Warren; 520/432-5383. The **post office,** 520/432-2052, and the **city library,** 520/432-4232, are at 6 Main St. in downtown Bisbee. Library facilities include Internet computers, and the library has its own website, www.cochise.lib.az.us/bisbee.htm.

Transportation

A trolley of the **Warren-Bisbee Railway** offers a narrated tour of the Bisbee area from the Copper Queen Plaza; check with the chamber for details. The **Bisbee Bus Line** proclaims itself "the biggest, smallest bus line in the West"; it connects the communities of the Bisbee area Mon.–Saturday. The chamber has a schedule, or call 520/432-2285.

Golden State provides bus service to Tucson, Sierra Vista, Douglas, and Mexico; purchase tickets from One World Travel, on OK St. near the Lyric Building, 520/432-5359. **Douglas Super Shuttle** provides service to Douglas, Tucson, and Phoenix from Lyric Plaza, 520/432-4020.

Vicinity of Bisbee

Arizona Cactus & Succulent Research Center, eight miles south of Bisbee near the Mexico border, welcomes visitors and offers free tours and cuttings. The non-profit center promotes knowledge and landscaping uses of cacti and other desert plants through the tours, a newsletter, and a research library. You can purchase books in the gift shop. Most of the plants you'll see belong to the surrounding Chihuahuan Desert and are well adapted to the cold, dry climate at the center's 4,780-foot elevation. Open daily sunrise to sunset; 520/432-7040, www.arizonacactus.com. Donations are welcome. The Bisbee Visitor Center has a brochure with a map. From downtown Bisbee, head south 1.5 miles on AZ 80 to the traffic circle, continue south on Bisbee Road another 1.5 miles through Warren, turn right 4 miles on Arizona Street and follow signs to the Border Road; turn left 0.7 mile on the Border Road, then turn left on Cactus Lane and right on Mulberry Lane to the center.

Naco is a sleepy Mexican border town just nine miles south of Bisbee. There's little to see or do here; the Mexican side is much like the rural communities of interior Mexico. Buses can take you from Naco to Hermosillo, Juárez, Nogales, Casas Grandes, and other Mexican destinations.

DOUGLAS

In 1900, the Phelps Dodge Company, finding Bisbee's smelter too small and inconvenient to handle ores from recently purchased mines in

Mexico, began looking for a new smelter site in Sulphur Springs Valley. They chose this spot and named the new town for Dr. James Douglas, president of the company.

In the early 20th century, Douglas and its sister town in Mexico, **Agua Prieta,** saw their share of excitement. Mexican government troops battled it out in Agua Prieta with revolutionaries Captain "Red" Lopez in 1911 and Pancho Villa in 1915. Pancho Villa even made threats against the town of Douglas before eventually retreating. An international airport—part of its runway in the United States and part in Mexico—opened here in 1928.

The fortunes of both Douglas and Agua Prieta rose and fell with the price of copper. The prettiest sight in Douglas, some residents used to say, was the billowing steam and smoke from the giant copper smelter just west of town. The busy ore-processing plant meant jobs.

Smokestacks of the Phelps Dodge smelter puffed their last in January 1987, but the two cities have diversified into other industries. American companies operate manufacturing plants in Agua Prieta under the "twin plant" concept, using Mexico's inexpensive labor to assemble American products. With these new opportunities, Agua Prieta's population has mushroomed to about 100,000, eclipsing that of Douglas (around 15,000).

Historic Architecture

Many fine early 20th-century commercial buildings line downtown streets. Church Square, two blocks east of the Gadsden Hotel, earned fame in the 1930 *Ripley's Believe It or Not* as the only city block in the world with a church on each corner; it's between 10th and 11th Sts. and D and E Avenues. These old churches and the buildings in the adjacent Douglas Residential District (Seventh to 12th Sts. and E to Carmelita Aves.) are fine examples of period architecture.

The Beaux Arts Classic Revival-style railroad depot, used from 1913 to the end of passenger service in 1961, has been restored to its former elegance; you're welcome to step inside the rotunda and see the stained-glass ceiling. The depot is a couple of blocks north of the chamber of commerce and now serves as the police station, so it's always open.

Douglas/Williams House Museum

This museum, in a redwood house across from Church Square at 10th St. and D Ave., 520/364-7370, holds exhibits on regional history, including photos showing Douglas in its early days and the old smelter in operation. The house itself has some history; it was built by Jimmy "Rawhide" Douglas in 1908, when he was working for his dad, Dr. James Douglas, at Phelps Dodge Company. This is the same Jimmy Douglas who later built the house that's now a museum for Jerome State Historic Park. You're welcome to take a guided or self-guided tour on Tues., Wed., Thurs., and Sat. 1–4 P.M.; donations welcome.

Douglas Art Association Gallery

"The Gallery," 625 10th St. (near the museum), 520/364-6410, is housed in Douglas's first public building—a 1901 hall that has served as town hall, church, school, and library. Inside you'll find displays of local art and a gift shop with handcrafts; open daily 10 A.M.–4 P.M. (1–4 P.M. June–Aug.) A new show is mounted about every two months.

Accommodations

Under $50: The massive five-story **Gadsden Hotel,** 1046 G Ave., 520/364-4481, dominates downtown Douglas. Built in 1907 and rebuilt in 1928, the hotel calls itself "the last of the grand hotels." The lobby features massive marble columns decorated with 14-karat gold leaf supporting a vaulted ceiling with stained-glass panels. A Tiffany stained-glass mural 42 feet long decorates one wall of the mezzanine, reached by an Italian white marble staircase. Over 200 authentic cattle brands embellish the walls of the Saddle and Spur Tavern, just off the lobby. A restaurant serves American and Mexican food. Rooms cost $40–60 d, $70–85 suites; www.theriver.com/gadsdenhotel.

Other lodgings in town are **Motel 6,** 111 16th St., 520/364-2457 or 800/466-8356, $32 s, $38 d; **Travelodge,** 1030 19th St., 520/364-8434,

$33–35 s, $42–45 d; **Travelers Motel,** 1030 A Ave., 520/364-8434, $33 s, $38 d; and the nearby **Border Motel** at 1725 A Ave., 520/364-8491, $35 s, $40 d.

Valley Lodge is 26 miles north of Douglas in Elfrida, 520/642-9218, $37.28 s, $42.60 d w/tax.

Price Canyon Ranch, a working cattle ranch on the southeastern slopes of the Chiricahuas (5,600 feet), features horseback riding, birding, hiking, fishing, and a swimming pool. Guests stay in cabins, $150 per adult and $75 ages 12–15 including family-style meals and riding. The ranch is 37 miles northeast on AZ 80, then left seven miles on Price Canyon Rd. (P.O. Box 1065, Douglas, AZ 85608); if you're coming from Portal, the ranch is about 25 miles south. It's open year-round; 520/558-2383 or 800/727-0065; www.pricecanyon.com.

Campgrounds

Saddle Gap RV Park, at Hwy. 80 and Washington Ave. on the northeast edge of town, 520/364-5824, has RV sites for $11 with hookups. **Douglas Golf & Social Club,** on the north side of town at Hwy. 80 and Leslie Canyon Rd., 520/364-3722, charges $15 for RV sites with hookups.

Double Adobe RV Park, 520/364-4000, offers grassy sites and shade trees. Head 7.1 miles north on US 191 from the west side of Douglas, then turn left (west) 9.6 miles on Double Adobe Road. (The road makes a jog to the south after the store at Double Adobe; follow signs for Bisbee.) Tent or RV spaces without hookups go for $7.50 s, $10 d; RV sites run $14 w/hookups and TV; guests have showers, laundry, a trap range, and 100 acres to roam; www.theriver.com/doubleadobe.

Food

El Conquistador Dining Room at the **Gadsden Hotel,** 1046 G Ave., 520/3644481, serves Mexican-American food daily for breakfast, lunch, and dinner. **Grand Café,** nearby at 1119 G Ave., 520/364-2344, makes another good choice for Mexican-American food. It's open Mon.–Sat. for lunch and dinner. Several other Mexican restaurants are scattered around town, and Agua Prieta has even more.

Las Nubes Steak House, 515 Pan American Ave., 520/364-4936, prepares steak, seafood, and Mexican dishes. **Lai-Lai Restaurant,** 1341 F Ave., 520/364-8898, offers a variety of Chinese cuisines. **Pizza Hut** is at 300 16th St. (AZ 80) on the west side of town; 520/364-7535.

Safeway supermarket is near the border at 90 5th St. (west from Pan American Dr.). **Bashas' Mercado** is at 1300 San Antonio Drive.

Events

Cinco de Mayo festivities take place on the weekend before May 5. The **July Fourth Celebration** includes entertainment, a parade, car show, games, dances, and fireworks at Veterans Park. The **Labor Day Golf Tournament** in September has been running longer than any other invitational golf tournament in the state. **Douglas Fiestas Celebration** in mid-September honors Mexican independence with ballet folkiorico, mariachis, talent show, games, and food at Veterans Park. **Cochise County Fair** presents intercollegiate rodeo, livestock exhibits, carnival, and other entertainment on the third weekend of September at Cochise County Fairgrounds on Leslie Canyon Road. The **Christmas Light Parade** is an evening event of lighted floats held the last Saturday of November.

Shopping

Shops in the first six blocks across the border in Agua Prieta sell **Mexican crafts,** but on a much smaller scale than in Nogales. U.S. dollars will be welcome at most places. Merchants generally have a competitive fixed price, so bargaining isn't as common as in other border towns. There's a parking lot near the border; drive south on Pan American Avenue, then turn left one block on 1St Avenue (the last street before the border station). The Douglas Chamber of Commerce offers advice and a map for Agua Prieta.

Recreation

Veterans Park features picnic tables, playground, outdoor pool, tennis, basketball, and ball fields at Dolores Ave. and 6th St.; 520/364-7038. **Causey Park** is a smaller area with picnic tables and playground at 15th St. and Carmelita, near a pair of water towers. **Douglas Golf & Social Club** features 18 holes northeast of town off Leslie Canyon Road; 520/364-3722.

Information and Services

Staff at the **Douglas Visitor Center,** 1125 Pan American Ave. at 12th St. (Douglas, AZ 85607), 520/364-2478 or 888/315-9999, stock maps and brochures and are very helpful. They may be able to advise on Mexican touring possibilities too. The office is open Mon.–Fri. 8 A.M.–5 P.M., Saturday 8 A.M.–1 P.M.   **Douglas Ranger Station** is in the Coronado National Forest at 3081 N. Leslie Canyon Rd. (Douglas, AZ 85607), 520/364-3468; www.fs.fed.us/r3/coronado. From AZ 80 just northeast of town, turn north on Leslie Canyon Road, then take the first right. Staff can tell you about camping, hiking, and the back roads of the Chiricahua and Dragoon Mountains. The office is open Mon.–Fri. 7:30 A.M.–4:30 P.M.

The Douglas **public library** is at 560 10th St. (at F Ave.), 520/364-3851. The 1917 Beaux Arts-style **post office** sits on the corner of 10th St. and F Ave. downtown. The **Southeast Arizona Medical Center** is four miles west of town on AZ 80, then north at the sign; 520/364-7931.

No permits are needed to visit Agua Prieta; for longer trips into Mexico, obtain papers at the border station. The **Mexican consulate** is at 5411 0th St. (Douglas, AZ 85607), 520/364-3107 or 520/364-3142; open Mon.–Fri. 8 A.M.–2P.M. **Douglas Insurance Center,** 1340 F Ave. (at 14th St.), 520/364-5409, represents Sanborn's Mexican auto insurance. **Arizona Associated Agencies,** 561 10th St., 520/364-2411, also sells Mexican auto insurance.

Transportation

Golden State runs six times daily to Tucson's Greyhound station with stops en route at Bisbee and Sierra Vista. The station is at 538 14th St. between G and F Ayes., 520/364-2233. **Douglas Super Shuttle** provides service to Bisbee, Tucson, and Phoenix from the station at Pan American Ave. and 1st St., near the port of entry; 520/364-9442. Buses in Agua Prieta head out to Cananea, Nogales, Hermosillo, Ciudad Obregñ, Tijuana, Guadalajara and Mexico City.

VICINITY OF DOUGLAS

Douglas Wildlife Zoo

This collection was originally established for propagation of exotic animals and birds. Drop in to see parrots, peacocks, emus, deer, lemurs, apes, and other creatures from near and distant lands. It's open daily 10 A.M.–5 P.M. (to 4 P.M. on Sun.) except major holidays; $3.75 adults, $2.45 children 3–12; 520/364-2515. From Douglas, head west 2.5 miles on AZ 80 to just past the Ford dealership, then turn north 1.7 miles on Plantation Road.

Slaughter Ranch

John Slaughter (1842-1922), a former Texas Ranger, wandered into southeast Arizona in 1884 and bought a lease to the 73,240-acre San Bernardino Ranch. Today his ranch is the last survivor of Arizona's great 19th-century cattle ranches.

Long before Slaughter developed the vast spread, the springs here had attracted Opata Indian farmers, Apache, Spanish, Mexicans, and Americans. Slaughter shipped 10,000 head of cattle one year and employed up to 500 people, including 200 Chinese vegetable farmers. His 1890s' house and other structures have been restored to show ranch life in territorial Arizona at the turn of the century.

The visitor center has a self-guided tour leaflet. Rooms feature period furniture, photo exhibits of Slaughter's colorful career—including two terms as sheriff at Tombstone—and the land's long history. The pond, containing endangered native fish and surrounded by grass and cottonwoods, offers a pleasant spot for a picnic. A trail near the pond climbs the hill to ruins of a U.S. Army post in use during the time of Mexican civil unrest in 1911-23; the view east takes in the San Bernardino National Wildlife Refuge.

The ranch, owned by a private museum, is open Wed.–Sun. 10 A.M.–3 P.M.; 520/558-2474. Admission is $3 adults, free under age 14. From Douglas, head east on 15th Street to the edge of town, then continue 16 miles on the mostly graded dirt Geronimo Trail to the ranch turnoff, marked by a memorial to the Mormon Battalion.

San Bernardino National Wildlife Refuge

At this 2,330-acre refuge, springs and ponds attract 240 species of birds, as well as mule deer, javelina, mountain lions, bobcats, and other wildlife. The waters support endangered Yaqui chub, Yaqui topminnow, Yaqui catfish, and beautiful shiner. Elevations range 3,720-3,920 feet. Old roads and trails make a loop to ponds and wetlands with excellent birding. The entrance is three-quarters of a mile past the Slaughter Ranch turnoff. The gate is open Mon.–Fri. 8 A.M.–4 P.M. and possibly Saturday (call to check).

Leslie Canyon, on the southwest side of the Chiricahua Mountains, protects endangered fish and frogs; it's not open to the public.

Headquarters for San Bernardino/Leslie Canyon National Wildlife Refuge is 11 miles north of Douglas at 7628 N. Hwy. 191, between Mileposts 11 and 12 (P.O. Box 3509, Douglas, AZ 85607); 520/364-2104. The office is open Mon.–Fri. 8 A.M.–4 P.M.

CHIRICAHUA MOUNTAINS

Rising from dry grasslands, the Chiricahua (chee-ree-KAH-wah) Mountains hold a wonderland of rock formations, spectacular views, diverse plant and animal life, and a variety of hiking trails. The name may come from the Opata Indian word *Chiguicagui,* meaning "Mountain of the wild turkeys." Bears live here, so care must be taken with storing food; forest service signs list the precautions to take.

Volcanic rock, fractured by slow uplift of the region, has eroded into strangely shaped forms. Weathering of softer rock at the base of some columns creates the appearance of giant boulders balanced delicately on pedestals. The Chiricahuas harbor a unique mix of Sierra Madrean and Southwestern flora and fauna. Birders come to view coppery-tailed elegant trogons, hummingbirds, and many other species.

Chiricahua National Monument offers the most spectacular erosional features, a scenic drive, many trails, and a visitor center. Chiricahua Wilderness, to the south, protects the highest summits of the range, including 9,796-foot Chiricahua Peak. A narrow mountain road crosses the range from near the entrance of the national monument on the west side to Portal on the east side; not recommended for trailers and sometimes closed by snow in winter. Fort Bowie National Historic Site lies just north of the Chiricahuas; take Apache Pass Road south from Bowie or northeast from AZ 186. Be sure to fill up with gas before coming out to the Chiricahuas, as there are no supplies here. Douglas Ranger Station has information on the Coronado National Forest lands; contact the staff at 3081 N. Leslie Canyon Rd. (Douglas, AZ 85607), 520/364-3468, www.fs.fed.us/r3/coronado; open Mon.–Fri. 7:30 A.M.–4:30 P.M.

Hiking

Forest trails in the Chiricahua Mountains total about 111 miles, but conditions differ greatly. The Rattlesnake Fire in 1994 burned more than 25,000 acres on the western side of the wilderness and dead trees continue to fall across trails. No permits are needed for backpacking or hiking, but South Fork and Rustler Park have $3 parking fees. Topographic maps, such as the *Chiricahua Mountains Trail and Recreation* (scale 1:62,500), show trail locations and lengths; look for them at Tucson hiking stores, some Forest Service offices, and Chiricahua National Monument. The Coronado National Forest (Douglas Ranger District) map shows trails but lacks contour lines and fine detail.

Rucker Canyon (Southwest Side of Chiricahuas)

Four routes lead to Rucker Creek and its pretty canyon; they're unpaved but usually ok for cautiously driven cars in dry weather. From Douglas you can head north on Leslie Canyon Road from the Douglas Ranger Station and cross the Swisshelm Mountains into Leslie Canyon Natl. Wildlife Refuge (closed to the public); after about 30 miles you'll reach Rucker Canyon Road and continue another seven miles to the canyon. Tex

Canyon Road is another scenic route; it turns off AZ 80 29 miles northeast of Douglas and crosses a gentle pass into Rucker Canyon in another 16 miles. You can also take Rucker Canyon Road from US 191, a 22-mile drive one way, or reach the canyon via the Kukkendall Cut Off from AZ 181 near Chiricahua National Monument, a 20-mile drive one way.

Campgrounds usually stay open all year with water available from April to November; sites have a charge of $7 camping or $3 day use. You'll first come to **Camp Rucker Group Use Area** (5,600 ft.) on the left in a desert grassland with scattered oaks and junipers; you can stay here if no group has reserved it. Groups can make reservations with the Douglas Ranger Station. In another 3.3 miles, **Cypress Campground** (6,000 ft.) on the left sits beside the creek in a forest of Arizona cypress, oaks, and pines. **Bathtub Campground** (6,300 ft.) is 0.4 mile farther on the left on a shelf overlooking the creek. A trail below the dam leads to the "bathtubs," depressions carved in the bedrock by the creek. You have to park at the edge of the campground, so it's suited for tenters only. Rucker Lake nearby has completely filled in with sediment and the campground once here is no longer useable. **Rucker Forest Camp** (6,500 ft.) sits beside the creek at the end of the road, 0.3 mile beyond Bathtub, in a dense forest of oaks, junipers, and pines. Rucker Canyon Trail #222 and Raspberry Ridge Trail #228 climb into the Chiricahua Wilderness from here.

The U.S. Army set up a supply depot in 1878 for Indian scouts who patrolled the region on the lookout for hostile Apache. Originally named Camp Supply, it later became **Camp Rucker** after an officer and the man he was trying to save both drowned during a flash flood. The camp saw use until Geronimo's surrender in 1886, when it became part of a ranch. You can visit this remnant of the Old West and walk an interpretive trail past the adobe bakery, still in good condition, and the large ruin of the commissary with its stone cellar. From the junction of Forest Roads 74 and 74E near Camp Rucker Group Use Area, head east 0.7 mile on Forest Road 74 and look for a gate in the fence on the left; park outside the gate, walk in about 0.1 mile, then turn left past the barn to the site.

Turkey Creek Canyon (West Side of Chiricahuas)

West Turkey Creek Campground (5,900 ft.) and **Sycamore Campground** (6,200 ft.) lie along Turkey Creek in a densely wooded canyon of sycamores, pines, oaks, and junipers. Sites have tables and grills but no drinking water or fee; the season is about March to November. From the 90-degree bend in AZ 181 east of Sunizona and south of the Chiricahua Natl. Mon. turnoff, head east on unpaved Turkey Creek Road. Tall pines appear among the oaks and junipers after seven miles and you'll enter the national forest in another mile; West Turkey Campground is on the left just 0.1 mile farther and Sycamore is 1.5 miles farther up on the left. You'll also pass several trailheads in the national forest that connect to the heights.

Sunglow Guest Ranch, 520/824-3334, provides year-round accommodation, gourmet meals, birding, hiking, horseback riding, a fishing pond, and astronomy programs. The nearly 400 acres stretch across to the Coronado National Forest. One-room units run $69/night or $414/week d, two-room accommodations feature a living room and fireplace for $89/night or $534/week d, and the two-bedroom apartments have kitchens and can take up to 12 people ($149/night or $894/week, four people). Each of the rooms has its own courtyard. The new restaurant serves breakfast, lunch, and dinner and is open to the public by reservation. You can bring your horse too. Visit on the Web at www.sunglowranch.com. The ranch is about 15 miles south of Chiricahua National Monument; follow Turkey Creek Road 4.3 miles from AZ 181, then turn right one mile.

Rustler Park Area (Summit Ridge of Chiricahuas)

A scenic mountain road crosses the range through Pinery Canyon on the west near Chiricahua Natl. Monument to Onion Saddle (7,600 feet) and continues east to Cave Creek Canyon and Portal. The road is narrow, bumpy, and mostly unpaved, but may be passable by car for cautious drivers. Trailers and RVs over 28 feet aren't permitted. Snow and fallen trees can close the road at times from December to April. From the entrance of Chiricahua Natl. Monument, take Pinery Canyon Road, which enters the national forest after 3.8 miles; you see many undeveloped camping spots along the next three miles before the grade steepens. **Pinery Canyon Campground** is tucked under tall pines and Douglas fir on the left, 9.8 miles from the start of the road; it has just four sites (no water or fee) and is very difficult to spot if coming from below. The road tops out at Onion Saddle, 11.5 miles from AZ 181. If you're coming up from Cave Creek Canyon on the east side, the driving distance from Portal to the saddle is 13 miles with some great panoramas along the way.

A side road from Onion Saddle climbs south along a ridge to **Rustler Park Campground** (8,400 feet) in pines and Douglas fir. Sites, which may be closed in winter, usually have water from April to Nov.; fees are $10 camping, $5 day use, or $3 for trailhead parking. Steel boxes protect your food from bears.

Hikers here have the advantage of starting from the highest trailhead in the Chiricahuas. The **Crest Trail #270** winds south over the gently undulating summit ridge to Chiricahua Peak (9,796 feet), the highest point in the range, in 10.5 miles roundtrip. Trees, however block the view from the top. **Centrella Point** (9,320 ft.) has a spectacular vantage point overlooking Cave Creek Canyon and far beyond; follow the Crest Trail south to just inside the wilderness boundary, 2.5 miles one way, then turn left 1.9 miles one way on the Centrella Trail #334. Fly Peak (9,666 ft.) is an easy half-mile one-way jaunt from wilderness boundary and has some views through the trees. Many other trails branch off the Crest Trail along ridges or down into canyons. Springs lie just off the Crest Trail but can dry up in drought years.

Cave Creek Canyon (East Side of Chiricahuas)

Although remote, Cave Creek Canyon's spectacular rock features, excellent birding, and paved road access make it a favorite with visitors. You can get here by taking AZ 80 northeast from Douglas for 51 miles or NM 80 south from I-10 for 28 miles, then turning west to the village of Portal at the mouth of the canyon. The road continues up along Cave Creek beneath vertical rock walls past campgrounds, vista points, and hiking trails. The Forest Service operates **Cave Creek Visitor Information Center** 1.9 miles upcanyon from Portal; 520/558-2221. It's open about Thurs.–Mon. 9 A.M.–4:30 P.M. from early April to Labor Day. Cave Creek Nature Trail makes a short loop across the road. For a bird's-eye view of the region, determined hikers can ascend **Silver Peak Trail #280,** a strenuous climb of 3,000 feet over 4.6 miles one way to the 7,975-foot summit; the trailhead is just upcanyon from the information center. Bring a hat and lots of water—there's little shade—and avoid the trail if thunderstorms threaten.

Idlewilde Campground (5,000 ft.) lies on the left across a bridge 0.4 mile past the information center; sycamores, oaks, junipers, and pines provide shade. The season runs April to Nov. with water and fees of $10 camping, $5 day use. **Stewart Campground** (5,100 ft.) is another 0.3 mile up on the left and with the same types of trees; it has drinking water from April to Nov. and fees of $10 camping, $5 day use. On the left 0.4 mile farther, look for **Cathedral Vista** parking; an easy 200-yard walk takes you to a stunning 360-degree panorama of the canyon and the Chiricahuas.

Continue 0.2 mile and turn left on unpaved South Fork Road for a pretty drive up this side canyon and creek to **South Fork Picnic Area** and trailhead at road's end, 1.3 miles in; there's a $3 parking fee. **South Fork Trail** leads up the wooded canyon with some creek fords. Maple Camp, 1.6 miles one way, is a popular destination for birders, though the trail continues up into the high country.

Back on the main road and 0.2 mile upcanyon, turn right across a ford for **Sunny Flat Campground** (5,200 ft.), which despite its name is shaded by sycamores, oaks, junipers, and pines. There's year-round drinking water and fees of $10 camping, $5 day use. A trail begins near the end of the campground and follows the creek downstream about a mile to the information center.

Pavement runs out 1.7 miles farther up Cave Creek Canyon at the Southwestern Research Center of the American Museum of Natural History; staff occasionally offer public programs, which the information center should know about. Turn left just past the research center for **John Hands Campground** (5,600 ft.) one mile in, and **Herb Martyr Campground** (5,800 ft.) 2.2 miles up at the end of the unpaved road; oaks and junipers shade these campgrounds near Cave Creek; they're open all year, no drinking water or fee. If you look up on the cliffs above to the west, you may see Winn Falls making a 400-foot plunge; **Greenhouse Trail #248** climbs up for a closer view. Experienced cavers will enjoy a visit to **Crystal Cave.** A key is needed to get inside; contact the Douglas Ranger Station for access details. The cave is closed April 15 to Aug. 31 to protect bats and other life inside.

Portal

This small community lies on the east side of the Chiricahuas just below the mouth of Cave Creek Canyon. **Portal Peak Lodge** offers rooms year-round ($65 s, 75 d), a tiny café with American and Mexican food (open daily for breakfast, lunch, and dinner; ask for a nonsmoking dining area), and a store which also has groceries and some regional books; 520/558-2223. **Cave Creek Ranch,** 520/558-2334, has a gorgeous setting beside the creek in the lower canyon; the owners are bird enthusiasts, as are 95 percent of the guests here. All of the lodge rooms and cabins have kitchens and run $85–120 d; you can see them on the Web at www.cavecreek ranch.com. No meals are served here, nor are there any trail rides.

CHIRICAHUA NATIONAL MONUMENT

In 1924, President Calvin Coolidge signed a bill making the most scenic part of the mountains a national monument. The entrance is 70 miles north of Douglas, 36 miles southeast of Willcox, and 120 miles east of Tucson.

Visitor Center

Exhibits illustrate area geology, ecology, and wildlife, as well as the lifestyles of the Chiricahua Apache, early ranchers, and the Civilian Conservation Corps. A video narrated by Rex Allen, Sr. (see **Willcox,** below) introduces the monument and its sightseeing possibilities. Rangers can answer questions and advise on road and hiking conditions. Campfire programs are held mid-March to mid-September; check for times. Other naturalist programs may be scheduled too. You can purchase books, prints, posters, videos, maps, and other items. It's open daily 8 A.M.–5 P.M.; 520/824-3560; www.nps.gov/chir. A $6/car entry fee is collected at the entrance station.

Bonita Canyon Drive

This six-mile paved mountain road from the visitor center climbs through Bonita Canyon to Massai Point (6,870 feet), where you'll encounter sweeping views of the rock features and distant valleys and mountains. A new wheelchair-accessible path leads up to the little geology exhibit building for the best panorama. Look north for the profile of Cochise Head. On the way back down this path, you can turn off on the quarter-mile (one way) nature trail to learn how this wonderland of rocks formed and about some of the plants found here; the nature trail also passes some great viewpoints before ending at the parking area. Several longer day-hikes start at Massai Point. Winter storms can close the road, but snowplows clear it soon afterwards.

Hiking

The Chiricahuas are best appreciated on foot, whether on short nature trails or extended hikes. Many species of birds can be seen, from grassland inhabitants near the monument entrance, to mountain dwellers at the top. Rangers advise you to pace yourself, allowing for the altitude and rough terrain, and to carry water on longer trips. Thunderstorms often strike in July and August; if caught, stay low and avoid exposed areas. Watch for rattlesnakes, too; summer is their most active season, though they also slither about in spring and autumn.

You can hike any time of year, but conditions

are usually ideal March-May and Oct.–November. Snow sometimes blocks trails Dec.–February. Monument trails are for day-hikes only; no permit needed. Camping is restricted to the campground near the visitor center, but many backpack trips are possible in the nearby Coronado National Forest. Horseback riding is permitted in the monument, but rangers like to be told when horses are brought in; horse trailers should be parked at the Faraway Ranch parking lot. Dogs are not permitted on any trails except the Faraway Trail, and they must be on leashes at all times within the monument.

Maps sold at the visitor center include Chiricahua topo maps with hiking trails, a geologic map, and a Coronado National Forest map. You can ride to the high country on the **hikers' shuttle,** then walk trails downhill back to the visitor center; the shuttle costs $2 and operates once daily at 8:30 A.M.

Trails

The free monument brochure includes a map outlining all trails. **Faraway Meadow Trail** is an easy 1.2-mile walk between Faraway Ranch and the visitor center. The path winds through lush vegetation watered by a small seasonal stream, a good place for bird watching. A short side trail leads to the campground.

The most impressive scenery awaits hikers on the Echo Canyon Loop and Heart of Rocks trails. **Echo Canyon Trail** winds through spectacular rock formations in a 3.5-mile loop; begin from Echo Canyon parking area or Massai Point trailheads, both near the end of Bonita Canyon Drive. **Heart of Rocks Trail** passes famous rock formations—Punch and Judy, Duck on a Rock, Big Balanced Rock, and others—on a seven-mile out-and-back trip from Massai Point. With a half day, you can make a nine-mile loop by returning on the **Sarah Deming** and **Echo Canyon** trails. **Inspiration Point** is a one-mile roundtrip excursion off Heart of Rocks Trail with views over the whole length of Rhyolite Canyon.

You can also hike all the way down to the visitor center via **Rhyolite Canyon Trail,** 4.1 miles one-way from Echo Canyon parking area or six miles one-way from Massai Point trailhead. **Sug-**arloaf **Mountain** (7,310 feet) is the highest peak in the monument, with excellent views of Arizona, New Mexico, and the Chiricahuas, including the eroded remnants of the volcano that was the source of the rock layers. It's a 1.8-mile roundtrip hike to the summit from the Sugarloaf trailhead. **Natural Bridge Trail,** off Bonita Canyon Dr., offers pleasant but less spectacular hiking to a small rock bridge—actually a fallen rock column—2.4 miles from the road.

Faraway Ranch

Members of the Erickson family lived on this ranch for 91 years before its purchase in 1979 by the National Park Service. Rangers lead tours through the old ranch house most days, offering tales of the family, ranch life, and the surrounding region. You're also welcome to visit the grounds on your own during daylight hours; signs and a small exhibit building relate stories about the ranch and the people who lived here. Trails continue another quarter mile to the 1880 Stafford Cabin, one of the oldest in the state.

Faraway Ranch is 1.5 miles west of the visitor center by road, then a quarter mile in on foot, or you can take the 1.2-mile Faraway Meadow Trail from the visitor center or campground.

Campgrounds and Services

Picnic areas lie along the main road at several locations—see your map given at the entry booth. The first one, Bonita Creek Picnic Area, is on the left just 0.3 mile inside the monument; the last one is at Massai Point at the end of the Bonita Canyon Drive.

Bonita Campground, a half mile past the visitor center, is open year-round with water and costs $8 (no hookups or showers); sites can accommodate trailers or RVs to 26 feet. The campground often fills by mid-day from March to early May; only the group site can be reserved. Dispersed camping outside the monument is another possibility; you can drive up Pinery Canyon Road 3.8 miles to the Coronado National Forest, then look for a likely spot in the next three miles; no water, facilities, or

© BILL WEIR

Lillian Riggs accommodated guests at the Faraway Ranch for many years. Now you can go inside on a tour with a Park Service Ranger.

charge. Pinery Canyon Road begins just outside the monument.

Willcox, 36 miles north of the monument, offers the nearest motels as well as restaurants, stores, and RV parks. Sunizona has the nearest gas, RV park, and cafés; it's 27 miles west of the monument. Sunsites, 38 miles west of the monument, has RV parks and cafés; the Pearce-Sunsites Chamber of Commerce is open Mon.–Fri. 9 A.M.–4 P.M. and Saturday 10 A.M.–2 P.M.; 520/826-3535.

FORT BOWIE NATIONAL HISTORIC SITE

When the Butterfield Stagecoach line began to carry mail and passengers from Missouri to California in 1858, the company built a station near a spring below Apache Pass. Although it was in the middle of Indian country, Cochise and his Chiricahua Apache allowed the station and stage to operate unhindered. All this changed two and a half years later when 2d Lt. George Bascom

falsely accused Cochise of kidnapping and theft. Troops used treachery to seize Cochise, but the Indian chief knifed through the tent he was held in and escaped. Both sides executed hostages, and the war was on. Cochise and his band tried to kill or drive all white people from the region. Unfortunately for white settlers, many army troops left Arizona at this time to fight the Civil War in the east.

On July 15, 1862, Brig. Gen. James Carleton and his California Column were on their way to meet the threat posed by the Confederate invasion of New Mexico when Indians attacked an advanced detachment under the command of Capt. Thomas Roberts at Apache Pass. Roberts fended them off but suggested to Carleton the need for a fort. The first Fort Bowie (BOO-ee) went up within a month. Indian raids continued until 1872, when Cochise made peace with the army in exchange for reservation land.

Bad management by the Indian Bureau, followed by the government's taking back much of the reservation, angered many Apache. Also during this time, they lost their leader Cochise, who had died on the reservation. In 1881, Apache such as the wily Geronimo began leading a new series of raids on both sides of the U.S.-Mexico border. Army cavalry and scouts from Fort Bowie and other posts then rode forth to fight the elusive Indians. Geronimo's small band was the last to surrender, five years later, ending Arizona's Indian wars. The army finally abandoned the fort on October 17, 1894.

Visiting the Fort

Only evocative ruins remain of what had once been a major trade route and military post. To preserve the historic setting, a hiking trail brings visitors to the fort. The three-mile roundtrip is easy with an elevation gain of only 180 feet, but one should consider the 5,000-foot elevation and the summer heat. Good walking shoes, a hat, and water will add to the enjoyment of the trip. You could also bring a picnic and use tables near the visitor center. Shaded benches along the trail allow for a rest or some contemplation. You'll see and learn a lot of the area's history on the way, plus enjoy the mountain views and a variety of wildflowers and other plants. Signs tell of historic events in the area and identify sites such as the stage-station ruin, the post cemetery, a ruin believed to have been the Chiricahua Apache Indian Agency, the Battle of Apache Pass site, a reconstructed Apache camp, and Apache Spring. Just before the main fort, you can head up to ruins of the first Fort Bowie on a quarter-mile-roundtrip side trail; this site proved too small and was replaced in 1868-69 by new buildings on a more spacious site to the east. Signs identify the many ruins of the second Fort Bowie, which operated for 26 years. An optional return trail from the visitor center takes you to a ridgetop with a panorama of the fort and surrounding countryside while adding no distance. The trails are open daily sunrise to sunset; no camping is permitted. Dogs may come along if leashed.

The visitor center, overlooking the fort, has many old photos that show how the fort appeared in its heyday. Exhibits also display uniforms, a mountain howitzer, guns, Apache crafts, and excavated artifacts. You can purchase books on the Apache, U.S. Army, and natural history. The visitor center is open daily 8 A.M.–5 P.M. and has a water fountain and restrooms. For more information or for handicapped access, call 520/847-2500; the website is www.nps.gov/fobo.

Modern highways bypass the area. From the town of Bowie (I-10 Exits 362 or 366), drive 12.5 miles south on Apache Pass Road, of which the last 0.8 mile is gravel; parking is on the right, trailhead on the left.

You can also drive over Apache Pass on an unpaved section of Apache Pass Road from AZ 186. Head 22 miles southeast from Willcox or 14 miles northwest from Chiricahua National Monument to between Mileposts 350 and 351 of AZ 186, then turn east 8 miles on Apache Pass Road. In bad weather, Apache Pass Road can become slippery and is not recommended.

WILLCOX

Willcox (pop. 3,825), just off I-10, is a convenient base for visiting the scenic and historic sights of the area. Started in 1880 as a construction camp for the Southern Pacific Railroad, Willcox became a supply and shipping point for local ranchers. Agriculture is still the town's most important industry. Ostriches, apples, peaches, cherries, grapes, pecans, and pistachios now supplement the mainstays of cattle, cotton, and small grains. Many orchards let customers pick their own fruit during the July–Oct. season; the chamber has a list with directions. Most lie 15–20 miles north on Fort Grant Road. The chamber also has a walking tour leaflet of the historic downtown and information on local birding opportunities.

Willcox has three exits off I-10 and they all lead to the historic downtown. The middle one, Exit 340, is close to the Willcox Visitors Center and the newer motels; turn south on Rex Allen Dr., then right on Haskell Avenue to reach downtown.

Exit 336 on the west side of town and Exit 344 on the east lead to Haskell Avenue/I-10 Business Route, where you'll find the older motels. Turn south one block at the light on Maley

Street from Haskell Avenue for the museums and historic buildings.

Rex Allen Arizona Cowboy Museum

Rex Allen (1920–1999) grew up singing and playing the guitar on a homestead near Willcox. His musical skills led him to the recording industry, then into movies. *Arizona Cowboy*, released in 1950, was the first of his many films; he also starred in the TV series *Frontier Doctor.*

Inside the museum, 150 N. Railroad Ave., 520/384-4583, 877/234-4111, you'll see photos and movie posters of Rex Allen, guitars, saddles, sequined cowboy suits, and a buggy used in *Frontier Doctor.* Music by Rex Allen and by his son, Rex Allen, Jr. plays in the background; you can purchase their tapes and CDs. The Willcox Cowboy Hall of Fame in the back portrays local ranchers; photos show life as it really was for the cowboys. The museum is open daily 10 A.M.–4 P.M.; admission is $2/individual, $3/couple, or $5/family. The park across the street has some tables, a statue of Rex Allen and memorials to him and his movie star horse, Koko.

The museum building is adobe and dates from the early 1890s. It housed a saloon from 1897 until Prohibition in 1919, when a grocery store took over. You'll see other historic structures nearby. The 1881 adobe **Willcox Commercial** store on the corner is the oldest commercial building in Arizona still in use in its original location. Geronimo used to shop here for his sugar and you can purchase western wear and other items. The **Willcox Rex Allen Theater** once hosted early performances by Rex Allen and Roy Rogers; today it screens first-run movies.

Chiricahua Regional Museum & Research Center

Drop in to learn about Cochise and his Chiricahua Apache tribe, early mining and ranching, and the history of the town. Staff also work at tracing genealogy of local pioneers. It's at 127 E. Maley St. between Railroad Ave. and Haskell Ave.; open Mon.–Sat. 10 A.M.–4 P.M.; 520/384-3971. Suggested donation is $2 adult, $3 couple, $4 family.

Rex Allen, Sr., statue by Buck McCain

Southern Pacific Depot

Built in 1880 when the railroad first arrived, the busy depot became the town's business and social center for ranchers, miners and traders. It expanded in 1882 and 1915 and has now been beautifully restored. Step into the lobby to see railroad artifacts and exhibits about pioneer life. A video by Rex Allen, Sr. tells how the building was saved. Open Mon.–Fri. 8:30 A.M.–4:30 P.M.; free admission. It's just west of Maley Street on Railroad Avenue—Willcox's main street in the old days.

Cochise Lake

Birders come to view their feathered friends at this wastewater lake on the southeast edge of town, especially when sandhill cranes visit Jan.–March. Head southeast on Maley Street/AZ 186, then turn south 1.1 miles on Rex Allen Jr. Road, at the sign for Twin Lakes Golf Course.

There's a bird list and registry at the parking area, just past the golf course.

Accommodations

Willcox includes a good selection of motels, RV parks, and restaurants along the I-10 business route and off I-10 Exit 340 (AZ 186). The newer motels cluster near I-10 Exit 340, where you'll find: **Best Western Plaza Inn,** 520/384-3556, 800/262-2645, $59–69 d; **Days Inn** 520/384-4222, 800/DAYSINN, $47 s, $52 d; **Motel 6,** 520/384-2201, 800/466-8356, $35 s, $41 d just south of I-10; and **Super 8 Motel,** 520/384-0888, 800/800-8000, $43 s, $47 d just to the north of I-10.

The rest of the motels lie along the old highway/I-10 business route, and include: **Rite Way Motel,** 550 N. Haskell Ave., 520/384-4655, $25 s, $30 d; **Desert Breeze Motel,** 556 N. Haskell Ave., 520/384-4636, $25 s, $29 d; **Motel 8,** 331 N. Haskell Ave., 520/384-3270, $32 s, $38 d; **Arizona Sunset Motel,** 340 S. Haskell Ave., 520/384-4177, $28 d incl. tax; **Sands Motel,** 400 S. Haskell Ave., 520/384-4640, $25 s, $30 d; **Royal Western Lodge,** 590 S. Haskell Ave., 520/384-2266, $25 s, $29 d; and **Desert Inn of Willcox,** 704 S. Haskell Ave., 520/384-3577, $30 s, $35 d.

Campgrounds

Magic Circle RV Park welcomes both RVs and tenters with pool and showers, just north of I-10 Exit 340; 520/384-3212, $18 tent, $24 RV w/hookups incl. tax. **Grande Vista Mobile/RV Park,** 711 N. Prescott, south from I-10 Exit 340, 520/384-4002 also accommodates tents ($11 incl. tax) and RVs ($17 w/hookups incl. tax). **Lifestyle RV Resort,** 622 N. Haskell Ave., 520/384-3303, features a restaurant (closed Sun.), pool, spa, exercise room, and showers; tent sites are $12, RV sites w/hookups run $20. **Sagebrush Mobile/RV Park,** 200 W. Lewis St. off S. Haskell Ave. behind the Desert Rose Café, 520/384-2872, $10 RV w/hookups. **Fort Willcox RV Park** is farther out S. Haskell Avenue between town and I-10 Exit 336 and has showers, 520/384-4986; it caters mainly to seniors, $10 RV w/hookups.

Restaurants

Downtown has good dining at the **Desert Rose Café,** 706 S. Haskell Ave., 520/384-0514, with a long menu of sandwiches, chicken, fish, shrimp, pasta, and steak plus a wine list; open Mon.–Sat. for breakfast, lunch, and dinner; on Sun., there's breakfast and a lunch buffet, but no dinner. Places to eat just south off I-10 Exit 340 include: **Salsa Fiesta Mexican Restaurant,** 520/384-4233; the 24-hour **Plaza Restaurant,** for American and Mexican food, 520/384-3819; **Michael's** for breakfast and dinner at the Best Western Plaza Inn, 520/384-3556; and **Pizza Hut,** 520/384-3586. Just north of Exit 340 you'll find the 24-hour **Rip Griffin's,** 520/384-9415, offering American and some Mexican food and pasta, plus a buffet option; a **Subway** sandwich restaurant is here too.

R&R Pizza Express and **Safeway** are just south of Exit 340, then right a block on Bisbee Avenue. The **IGA** supermarket is a block farther south on Rex Allen Drive.

Events

Wings Over Willcox celebrates the birds with tours and lectures on the third weekend in January. **Rex Allen Days** honors Arizona's "Mr. Cowboy" on the first weekend of October with a rodeo, parade, Western music, street dance, cowboy poetry, Rex Allen movies, and a carnival.

Recreation

Keillor Park has picnic tables, a playground, outdoor pool, and tennis courts; from I-10 Exit 340, take Rex Allen Dr. one block toward downtown, then turn right one block on Bisbee Avenue.

Twin Lakes Golf Course has a nine-hole course south of downtown; 520/384-2720. To get there, head southeast on Maley Street/AZ 186, then turn south on Rex Allen Jr. Road at the sign.

Information and Services

The **Willcox Chamber of Commerce,** in the Cochise Visitor Center, has the scoop on sights, services, and events of the area; open Mon.–Sat. 9 A.M.–5 P.M. and Sunday 10 A.M.–2 P.M.; you can purchase regional books and gift items. Take I-10 Exit 340 (AZ 186) north, then turn right a half mile on Circle I Road; 520/384-2272, 800/200-2272; www .willcoxchamber.com. **Stouts Cider Mill,** near the visitor center, sells products from local apple orchards daily 8 A.M.–6 P.M.

The **post office** is at the corner of 200 S. Curtis Ave. and Grant Street. **Northern Cochise Community Hospital** is at 901 W. Rex Allen Dr.; 520/384-3541. The **public library** is on the corner of 207 W. Maley St. and Curtis Ave.; 520/384-4271, ext. 503; it's open Mon.–Saturday.

VICINITY OF WILLCOX
Frontier Relics

Orville Mickens has packed this small museum with historical artifacts from Fort Bowie and other areas of the Southwest; he'll also show you his big 1950 Cadillac. The museum is in Dos Cabezas, about 14 miles southeast of Willcox on AZ 186, on the way to Chiricahua National Monument. It's usually open Mon.–Sat. 9 A.M.–5 P.M.; look to see if the gate is open or call 520/384-3481.

Willcox Playa

This giant lakebed south of Willcox is visible from I-10 and covers 50–60 square miles. The playa is usually dry, but after heavy rains it becomes a shallow lake. You may see mirages on the surface in summer. As many as 10,000 sandhill cranes and smaller numbers of ducks and geese winter here from October to about late February. You can see the playa from surrounding highways, but private land makes access difficult. Areas open to birders include Cochise Lake, described above, on the northeast side of the playa, the Arizona Fish & Game Reserve on the southwest side near Kansas Settlement Road, and at wetlands of the Apache Station Wildlife Area on the west side just north of the power plant off US 191.

Cochise Stronghold Canyon

This canyon is set in a beautiful wooded area of towering pinnacles and great jumbles of boulders in the Dragoon Mountains, 30 miles south-

west of Willcox. During the 15 years that the great Apache chief Cochise and about 250 warriors hid out here, no white person was safe in the valleys below. Cochise was never defeated in battle; he agreed to peace in 1872 only when land was promised for his tribe. The Dragoon Mountains take their name from the Third U.S. Cavalry Dragoons.

Today the mountains offer picnicking, hiking trails, birding, and a campground; the first-come, first-served campground in an oak grove has year-round water and costs $3 for day use or $10 for an overnight stay; it can fill on weekends in spring and autumn. A 400-foot paved loop trail has interpretive signs about the Chiricahua Apache's culture and history. A bit farther along the campground loop, the self-guided Stronghold Nature Trail crosses a footbridge and identifies some of the many plants found here; the 0.4-mile-loop also has good views of the rock features that overlook the campground. **Cochise Stronghold Trail** turns off the nature trail and continues up the valley past Cochise Spring and Halfmoon Tank to Stronghold Divide, six miles roundtrip. It's also possible to continue down the other side of the range to a trailhead in West Stronghold Canyon, ten miles roundtrip.

Dispersed camping is possible a couple miles before the campground in Cochise Stronghold Canyon; turn in on Forest Roads 84A or 84B, which connect to form a loop. Equestrians must stay here if camping with their animals. You can also find places to camp on backroads in other parts of the Dragoon Mountains.

A rough but scenic 24-mile drive crosses the southern part of the range at Middlemarch Pass, connecting the ghost town of Pearce with Tombstone to the west. For Cochise Stronghold, take I-10 Exit 331, head southeast on US 191 to the north side of Sunsites, and turn west nine miles on Ironwood Road; pavement ends after three-quarters of a mile.

Amerind Foundation

Secluded among the boulders of Texas Canyon, the Foundation's outstanding museum features archaeological and ethnographic exhibits of the native peoples of the Americas. Amateur archaeologist William Fulton started the foundation in 1937 to increase the world's knowledge of American Indian cultures. The name comes from a contraction of American and Indian. Especially active in research of Southwest and Mexican archaeology, the foundation has amassed an amazing artifact collection; some of which you can see here.

The Amerind's art gallery displays paintings and sculptures by Indian and Anglo-American artists of the 19th and 20th centuries. A museum store sells Native American artwork, crafts, and books. A picnic area is nearby.

The foundation, 520/586-3666, www.amerind .org, is housed in Spanish-colonial revival buildings among the rock formations of Texas Canyon, 64 miles east of Tucson between Willcox and Benson. Take I-10 Dragoon Exit 318, go southeast one mile, turn left at the sign and drive three-quarters of a mile. The museum is open daily 10 A.M.–4 P.M., except June–Aug. when it closes Mon.–Tues.; it's also closed on major holidays. Admission is $3 adults, $2 ages 12–18, and seniors 60 and older.

The Thing

This archetypal "tourist trap" features a whimsical museum with wacky woodcarvings, antique wagons and vehicles, as well as The Thing (You can decide for yourself if it's real.). You'll have to fork out one dollar (75 cents children 6–18) to see the exhibits. Yes, there's also a huge gift shop that sells jackalopes and other regional souvenirs. It's open daily 6:30 A.M. and closes between 8 and 10 P.M. depending on the season; it's just off I-10 Exit 322 between Willcox and Benson.

BENSON

Benson lies 36 miles southwest of Willcox and 45 miles southeast of Tucson. The Butterfield Stage crossed the San Pedro River nearby in the early 1860s, but the town didn't really get going until the railroad arrived in 1880, filling its saloons with cowboys, miners, Mexicans, and Chinese. The community is quiet now and offers motels, restaurants, and campgrounds for travelers.

San Pedro Valley Arts and Historical Society Museum

Photos and artifacts show life in the early railroad, mining, and ranching days. Local handmade crafts are sold. It's open Tues.–Fri. 10 A.M.–4 P.M. (until 2 P.M. May–Sept.) and Saturday 10 A.M.–2 P.M.; closed in August. Admission is free. From Fourth Street, the main street through downtown, turn one block south on San Pedro to the museum; 520/586-3070.

Accommodations

Peak season (winter) prices are given here. The newer motels cluster near I-10 Exit 304: **Days Inn,** 621 Commerce Dr. (just north of I-10), 520/586-3000 or 877/586-3303, $53 d; **Super 8 Motel,** 855 N. Ocotillo (just north of I-10), 520/586-1530 or 800/800-8000, $53 s, $61 d; and **Best Western Quail Hollow Inn,** 699 N. Ocotillo (just south of I-10), 520/586-3646 or 800/322-1850, $55 s, $60 d. Downtown choices include **Benson Motel,** 185 W. 4th St., 520/586-3346, $40 d; **Cavern Gardens Motel,** 757 W. 4th St., 520/586-1406, $25 s, $30 d; **Quarter Horse Motel,** 800 W. 4th St., 520/586-3371, $32 d; and **Sahara Motel,** 1150 S. Hwy. 80, 520/586-3611, $35 s, $39 d.

Two miles west of downtown at I-10 Exit 302 (AZ 90) for Kartchner Caverns and Sierra Vista are **Holiday Inn Express,** 520/586-8800 or 888/263-2283, $89–109 s, $99–119 d; and **Motel 6,** 520/586-0066 or 800/466-8356, $40 s, $42 d.

Skywatcher's Inn, 520/586-7906 (Benson) or 520/615-3886 (Tucson), offers bed and breakfast accommodations at the Vega-Bray Observatory on a hill overlooking the San Pedro Valley; rooms cost $75–110 d and the suite is $160 d. Astronomy sessions with a variety of telescopes cost $95–140 (up to five adults). The observatory also has a planetarium, classroom, and exhibits. Reservations for rooms and astronomy should be made as much as three months in advance for the popular Oct.–March season; www.conimuniverse .com/skywatcher.

Campgrounds

KOA Campground, just north of I-10 Exit 304,

SOUTHERN ARIZONA

520/586-3977 or 800/562-6823, runs $19–22 tent, $22–25 RV w/hookups. **Red Barn RV Park** is also just north of I-10 Exit 304; 520/586-2035; $12.50 tent or RV w/hookups. **Benson 1-10 RV Park,** north of I-10 Exit 304, then right, 520/586-4252 or 800/599-0081, costs $12.50 tent or RV no hookups and $19 RV w/bookups. **Quarter Horse Motel** has an RV park at 800 W. 4th St., 520/586-3371; $15.50 RV w/hookups. **Pardner's RV Park** is on the west end of town at 950 W. 4th St.; 520/586-7887. **Mesquite Valley Golf Course** has an RV park at 800 E. Country Club Dr. off Hwy. 80, about half a mile south of downtown; 520/586-2585; $10.

Restaurants

Galleano's, 601 W. 4th St., 520/586-3523, features both American and Italian cuisine daily for breakfast, lunch, and dinner. **Beijing Palace,** 577 W. 4th St. (Safeway Shopping Center), 520/586-7140, prepares Chinese food daily for lunch and dinner. At the other end of town, **86 Café,** 700 E. 4th St., 520/586-3169, cooks bargain priced American and Mexican food for lunch and dinner daily. Near 1-10 Exit 304 you'll find American favorites at **Denny's** and **Country Folks Restaurant.**

Golf

Mesquite Valley Golf Course offers nine holes, a restaurant, and an RV park at 800 E. Country Club Dr. off Hwy. 80, about half a mile south of downtown; 520/5862585.

Information

Benson-San Pedro Valley Chamber of Commerce, 249 E. 4th St. (P.O. Box 2255, Benson, AZ 85602), 520/586-2842, has information about the town and area. Stop by Mon.–Sat. 9 A.M.–4 P.M. or Sunday 1–4 P.M. (usually) or look them up on the Web at www.theriver.com/bensonspvchamber.

Transportation

Amtrak trains stop downtown three days a week in each direction on their route across southern Arizona; 800/872-7245.

VICINITY OF BENSON

Singing Wind Bookshop

This unique shop, on a ranch near Benson, carries an excellent selection of regional books and other titles. It's usually open daily 9 A.M.–5 P.M., including holidays; 520/586-2425. Go north three miles on Ocotillo from downtown (or 2.5 miles north from I-10 Exit 304), then turn right at the sign and drive a half mile. There's a gate halfway in.

Gammons' Gulch

Jay Gammons loves old towns so much that when he couldn't buy one, he built his own. He carefully assembled the buildings with parts of old ones along with many antiques to create a ghost town that appears to come straight out of the Old West. Jay has also been in the movie business—his dad worked as a bodyguard for John Wayne—and the town and props have been used in films. Every item has a story as Jay or an assistant enthusiastically takes you around to the saloon with its 1880s bar (you can order a root beer), sheriff's office, mercantile store, wagon shop, blacksmith shop, assay office, hotel, wheelwright shop, telegraph office, barbershop, engine house, undertaker, Chinese laundry, and mine. A nature trail loops through the picturesque desert country nearby.

The Gulch, 520/212-2831, is a 12-mile drive out from Benson; from I-10 Exit 306 at the east end of town, head north 11.8 miles on Pomerene and Cascabel Rds. (watch speed limits), turn left 0.2 mile on Rockspring Road, then left to the entrance. Normally it's open Wed.–Sun. 9 A.M.–5 P.M., but since it's so far from town, you'll want to call ahead to check the hours, especially in summer. Admission runs $5 adults, $4 seniors 62 and older, and $1 children 12 and under.

Kartchner Caverns State Park

Discovered in 1974, Kartchner Caverns became Arizona's 25th state park in 1988, but because exceptional care was taken to preserve the pristine interior formations and environment during trail construction, the cave didn't open to the public until November 1999. Beautiful lime-

Jay Gammon plays a tune for visitors in the saloon at Gammon Gulch.

© BILL WEIR

stone formations, softly tinted yellow and red, decorate the living cave system. You'll see magnificent columns up to 58 feet high, delicate "soda straws" (one is a quarter of an inch in diameter and over 21 feet long, but is too fragile to visit), shields, stalactites, stalagmites, and nearly every other type of formation imaginable.

Begin your visit in the **Discovery Center,** where you can watch a video about the discovery of the cave. Exhibits illustrate local geology, cave features, paleontology, bats, and other wildlife. Highlights include a replica of the long soda straw and a reproduction of the 80,000-year-old Shasta ground sloth, whose bones were found in the cave. There's a gift shop and vending machines, but no restaurant. Outside the Discovery Center, you can wander through the hummingbird garden, go for a hike, or have a picnic.

A tram brings you from the Discovery Center to the cave entrance, which has protective air locks. Cave temperatures run 68°F at 99 percent humidity. Guides ask that you not take photos or videos inside the cave. Your guide leads the way through the colorful passages and rooms on a one-third-mile loop. The paved path has gentle inclines that are wheelchair accessible. The tour lasts about an hour, with 45 minutes in the cave. Tours depart daily every 20 minutes from 8:40 A.M.–4:40 P.M. Reservations for the cave tours are highly recommended. If you don't have one, try for one of the tickets sold first come, first served each morning. If you plan on coming without a cave tour reservation, call ahead and ask advice on what time you should arrive and get in line. The reservation number 520/586-2283 is open Mon.–Fri. 8 A.M.–5 P.M. except state holidays.

Foothills Loop Trail provides an aboveground perspective of the park; the 2.4 miles take two-three hours; a spur trail leads to a viewpoint, adding a mile and 45 minutes to the roundtrip. The 4.2-mile **Guindani Loop Trail** heads deeper into the Whetstone Mountains of the Coronado National Forest. Bring water and wear sturdy shoes for these trails.

The park is open daily 7:30 A.M.–6 P.M.; entry costs $10/vehicle (up to four people) and $1 for each additional person or cyclists. This doesn't include the tour and reservation fees, which run $14 ages 14 up, $6 ages 7–13, and free for kids under 7. The campground offers sites with electric and water hookups for $20. Amenities include showers and a dump station. Both tents and RVs are welcome, but everyone should check-in before 5:30 P.M. For more information, contact staff at P.O. Box 1849, Benson, AZ 85602; 520/586-4100; www.pr.state.az.us. It's in the Whetstone Mountains just west of AZ 90, nine miles south of I-10 Exit 302. The park is 49 miles from Tucson, 28 miles from Tombstone, and 19 miles from Sierra Vista.

St. David

This small town is seven miles south of Benson on the way to Tombstone. Phileman Merrill, an adjutant general of the Mormon Battalion, founded the town of Marcus at springs beside the San Pedro River in 1877; it later took the

SOUTHERN ARIZONA

name of another Mormon (Latter-Day Saint). Holy Trinity Monastery lies just south of town.

Holy Trinity Monastery

This Benedictine monastery on the banks of the San Pedro River welcomes visitors to experience the tranquility and spiritual life here. The monastery began in 1974 and now houses 12 monks, two sisters, and a small group of lay people. You're invited to participate in the daily schedule. The community looks after a pecan orchard, large organic garden, and livestock on their 92 acres, which includes lakes and riparian and desert areas. A 1.3-mile trail to the San Pedro River offers great birding. Gallery Trinitas exhibits religious texts, paintings, sculpture, and other art forms. The Museum features historical, Native American, liturgical, and scripture rooms. There's also a library, bookstore, and thrift shop. Guests may stay in rooms or an RV park.

Holy Trinity Monastery is one mile south of St. David on AZ 80, between Benson and Tombstone; look for the 74-foot Celtic cross on the west side of the highway between Mileposts 302 and 303. For more information, contact the monastery at P.O. Box 298, Saint David, AZ 85630, 520/720-4016; e-mail: trinity libtheriver.com.

Resources

Suggested Reading

DESCRIPTION AND TRAVEL

Annerino, John. *Adventuring in Arizona.* San Francisco: Sierra Club Books, 1996. True to its name, this excellent guide lists back-road driving tours, hiking trails, river trips, and climbing routes through the state's most spectacular country. Includes history and travel tips.

Arizona Highways. 2039 W. Lewis Ave., Phoenix, AZ 85009; 602/258-1000, 800/543-5432; www.arizonahighways.com. Published monthly, this outstanding magazine features superb color photography with articles on the state's history, people, places, wildlife, back roads, hiking, and humor.

Babbitt, Bruce, ed. *Grand Canyon: An Anthology.* Flagstaff: Northland Publishing, 1978. Twenty-three authors from the days of the Spanish to the present relate their experiences of the Grand Canyon.

Casey, Robert L. *Journey to the High Southwest.* Chester, CT: Globe Pequot Press, 1997. The author presents travel experiences and advice for southern Utah and adjacent Arizona, New Mexico, and Colorado.

Cook, James E. *Arizona Landmarks.* Phoenix: Arizona Highways, 1985. Recent color photos combine with historic illustrations to illustrate Arizona's natural beauty and human history.

Cook, James E. *Travel Arizona: The Back Roads.* Phoenix: Arizona Highways, 1989. Twenty routes—on and off pavement—have descriptions with brilliant photography.

Fishbein, Seymour L. *Grand Canyon Country: Its Majesty and Its Lore.* (National Geographic Park Profiles) Random House, 1997. Incredible color photography illustrates fine text.

Greater PHXplorer; Official Visitors Guide. Greater Phoenix Convention & Visitors Bureau, One Arizona Center, 400 E. Van Buren St., Suite 600, Phoenix, AZ 85004; 602/254-6500; www.phoenixcvb.com. Free informative magazine revised twice annually.

Green, Stewart. *Arizona Scenic Drives.* Helena, MT: Falcon Press, 1992. Twenty-nine scenic drives are described with maps and camping information.

Halper, Evan, and Paul Karr. *Hostels U.S.A.* Old Saybrook, CT: The Globe Pequot Press, 1998. A comprehensive guide to hostelling with an introduction and listings; it also covers some of Canada. Descriptions give a feel for the atmosphere of each place.

Houk, Rose. *The Peaks.* Phoenix: Arizona Highways, 1994. Text and photos capture the beauty and character of the San Francisco Peaks and the land and towns that surround them.

Klinck, Richard E. *Land of Room Enough and Time Enough.* Peregrine Smith Books, 1958, 1984. The geography, legends, and people of Monument Valley.

Kosik, Fran. *Native Roads: The Complete Motoring Guide to the Navajo and Hopi Nations.* Flagstaff: Creative Solutions Publishing, 1996. Many historic photos illustrate this guide to the Navajo and Hopi lands and surrounding area.

Leydet, Francois. *Time and the River Flowing: Grand Canyon.* New York: Sierra Club-Ballantine Books, 1968. Essays on and color photos of the Grand Canyon.

Martin, Don, and Betty Woo. *Arizona in Your Future: The Complete Relocation Guide for Job-Seekers, Retirees and Snowbirds.* Columbia, CA:

Pinecone Press, 1998. This guide provides "essential data" on many of the state's cities.

Muench, David, and Lawrence W. Cheek. *David Muench's Arizona; Cherish the Land, Walk in Beauty.* Phoenix: Arizona Highways, 1997. More than 120 color photos reveal light, form, life, and ecology in a large-format book.

Muench, David, Frank Waters, and John C. Van Updyke. *Eternal Desert.* Phoenix: Arizona Highways, 1990. Color photography and text interpret the stone, wind, water, life, and tracings of ancient man on the desert; includes advice for travelers.

Mulford, Karen Surina. *Arizona's Historic Escapes.* Winston-Salem, NC: John F. Blair, 1997. The author has searched out 94 memorable places to stay throughout the state that have exceptional atmosphere and history. They include bed and breakfasts, historic hotels, inns, guest ranches, and resorts.

Plate, Harry and Trudy Plate. *100 Best Restaurants in Arizona.* Kelton Publishing Co., revised biennially. Handy guide to many of the best restaurants in the Phoenix area, Tucson, Sedona, and other cities.

Rees, Lucy. *The Maze, A Desert Journey.* Tucson: The University of Arizona Press, 1996. A contemporary Welsh woman explores the wilderness of Arizona on horseback from the Verde Valley to the Hopi mesas.

Searcy, Paula. *Travel Arizona: The Scenic Byways.* Phoenix: Arizona Highways, 1997. Spectacular color photos entice readers on 22 drives through the state's history and scenery.

Stocker, Joseph, and others. *Travel Arizona* Phoenix: Arizona Highways, 1983. Amazing color photos illustrate 16 driving tours of Arizona.

Story Behind the Scenery series: *Grand Canyon; Grand Canyon-North Rim; Glen Canyon-Lake Powell; Rainbow Bridge; Canyon de Chelly; Petrified Forest; Lake Mead & Hoover Dam.* Las Vegas: KC Publications (various pub. dates). Beautiful color photos highlight the descriptions.

Tegler, Dorothy. *Retiring in Arizona: Your One-Stop Guide to Living, Loving and Lounging Under the Sun.* Fiesta Books, 1996. Full of facts to help you choose your area, then settle in.

Tucson Official Visitors Guide. Metropolitan Tucson Convention and Visitors Bureau, 110 S. Church Ave., Suite 9100, Tucson, AZ 85701; 520/624-1817, 800/638-8350; www.visit tucson.org. An informative magazine updated twice yearly; free.

Varney, Philip. *Arizona Ghost Towns and Mining Camps; A Travel Guide to History.* Phoenix: Arizona Highways, 1995. Explore the ruins of Arizona's boom-and-bust towns with this well-illustrated guide.

Wallace, Robert. *The Grand Canyon.* The American Wilderness Series. New York: Time-Life Books. A well-illustrated book covering the Canyon with excellent photography by Ernst Haas.

Writers' Program of the WPA. *Arizona: A State Guide.* Tucson: Hastings House, 1940, 1956. Reprinted in 1991 under the title *The WPA Guide to 1930's Arizona* by the University of Arizona Press. A classic guidebook that still makes good reading.

HIKING, BICYCLING, AND EQUESTRIAN

Adkison, Ron. *Hiking the Grand Canyon National Park.* Helena, MT: Falcon Press, 1997. Following a good introduction, the state's most popular trails are covered, with maps, detailed descriptions, and elevation profiles.

Aitchison, Stewart. *A Naturalist's Guide to Hiking the Grand Canyon.* New York: Prentice Hall, 1985. The author introduces you to Canyon climate, geology, "critters," and plants, then guides you on 30 hikes. Good maps.

Aitchison, Stewart, and Bruce Grubbs. *Hiking Arizona.* Helena, MT: Falcon Press, 1996. One of the best all-around hiking guides to the state; the 102 hikes cover a wide variety of regions and terrain.

Annerino, John. *Hiking the Grand Canyon.* A Sierra Club Totebook. San Francisco: Sierra Club Books, 1993. Easily the most comprehensive guide to trails and routes within the Canyon. A long introduction provides background on geology, natural history, Indians, and hike planning. The large fold-out topo map clearly shows trails and routes. Riverrunners will be pleased to find a section of trail descriptions beginning at the water's edge.

Annerino, John. *Outdoors in Arizona: A Guide to Hiking and Backpacking.* Phoenix: Arizona Highways, 1995. Spectacular color photos and detailed maps illustrate descriptions of 48 hikes.

Bennett, Sarah. *Mountain Biking Arizona.* Helena, MT: Falcon Press, 1996. This handy guide, illustrated with maps and photographs, describes many classic rides.

Blair, Gerry. *Rockhounding Arizona.* Helena, MT: Falcon Press, 1998. A guide to Arizona's natural wealth with descriptions, maps, and photographs of more than 70 of the state's best hunting sites for turquoise, gold, agates, garnet, crystals, and fossils.

Butchart, Harvey. *Grand Canyon Treks.* Spotted Dog Press, 1998. This book combines the text of legendary Grand Canyon hiker and explorer Harvey Butchart's three earlier guides, originally published in the 1970s and 1980s by La Siesta Press. It's a great source of ideas for off-trail hikes and climbs.

Carlson, Jack and Elizabeth Stewart. *Hiking Guide to the Superstition Wilderness.* Tempe:

Clear Creek Publishing, 1995. More than 50 hikes in the Superstition Wilderness are described with trail maps, difficulty rating, and history and legends of the Superstitions including the Lost Dutchman Mine.

Cowgill, Pete, and Eber Glendening. *Trail Guide to the Santa Catalina Mountains.* Tucson: Rainbow Expeditions, 1998. Handy guide to trails and routes of this range north of Tucson.

Fletcher, Colin. *The Man Who Walked through Time.* New York: Random House, 1989. Well-written adventure tale of Fletcher's two-month solo hike through the Grand Canyon. Fletcher was the first to travel its length within the park on foot.

Freeman, Roger, and Ethel Freeman. *Day Hikes and Trail Rides in and around Phoenix.* Phoenix: Gem Guide Books, 1991. Detailed trail descriptions of the excellent hiking and horseback riding in the rugged Sonoran Desert surrounding Arizona's biggest city.

Ganci, Dave. *Hiking the Southwest: Arizona, New Mexico, and West Texas.* San Francisco: Sierra Club Books, 1983. A handy guide with a good introduction, practical hints, and information on a variety of trails.

Hancock, Jan. *Horse Trails in Arizona.* Phoenix: Golden West Publishers, 1994. Descriptions of 42 trails include location, length, elevations, water sources, corrals, and trailer parking.

Kals, W.S. *Land Navigation Handbook.* San Francisco: Sierra Club Books, 1983. After reading this book you'll be able to explore Arizona's vast backcountry with confidence. This handy pocket-guide not only offers details on using map and compass, but tells how to navigate using the sun, the stars, and an altimeter.

Kelsey, Michael R. *Canyon Hiking Guide to the Colorado Plateau.* Treasure Chest Publications, 1995. One of the best guides to hiking in the canyon country, with descriptions and maps for destinations in Arizona, Utah, and Colorado. Geologic cross-sections show the formations you'll walk through. The author uses the metric system, but the book is otherwise easy to follow.

Kelsey, Michael R. *Hiking and Exploring the Paria River.* Treasure Chest Publications, 1997. The classic Paria Canyon hike, with information on nearby Bryce Canyon and other geologically colorful areas. Includes histories of John D. Lee, ghost towns, ranches, and mining.

Kiefer, Don R. *Hiking Arizona.* San Marino, CA: Golden West Publishers, 1991. Fifty hikes, many little known, with tips for safe and enjoyable hiking. The author has also written *Hiking Arizona II* (1993), *Hiking Central Arizona* (1996), *Hiking Northern Arizona* (1996), and *Hiking Southern Arizona* (1996).

Leavengood, Betty. *Tucson Hiking Guide.* Boulder: Pruett Publishing Co., 1997. A comprehensive guide to the hiking trails of the Tucson area.

Mangum, Richard K., and Sherry G. Mangum. *Flagstaff Hikes.* Flagstaff: Hexagon Press, 1998. This comprehensive guide, now in its fourth edition, describes hiking trails surrounding Flagstaff.

Mangum, Richard K., and Sherry G. Mangum. *Sedona Hikes.* Flagstaff: Hexagon Press, 1998. A guide to 135 day-hikes and five vortex sites, with maps and directions.

Mangum, Richard K., and Sherry G. Mangum. *Williams Guidebook.* Flagstaff: Hexagon Press, 1998. Not many people know about the beautiful country surrounding this town south of the Grand Canyon. Most of the book has been devoted to hikes, but you'll also find local history and visitors' information.

Martin, Bob, and Dotty Martin. *Arizona's Mountains: A Hiking & Climbing Guide.*

Boulder: Pruett Publishing Co., 1991. A guide to hiking and climbing in Arizona; includes maps and charts.

Martin, Bob, and Dotty Martin. *Hiking Guide to the Santa Rita Mountains of Arizona.* Boulder: Pruett Publishing Co., 1986. This guide covers mountains and canyons south of Tucson with topo maps, charts, and 52 hike descriptions.

Mazel, David, and Robert Blake. *Southern Arizona Trails.* Berkeley: Wilderness Press, 1997. An excellent hiking guide to many of the designated wilderness areas in the central and southern parts of the state.

Ray, Cosmic. *Fat Tire Tales and Trails.* Flagstaff: self-published, 1998. "Lots of way cool mountain-bike rides around Arizona . . . both summer and winter fun."

Sagi, G. J. *Fishing Arizona.* Phoenix: Golden West Publishers, 1992. Travel directions lead to 50 good fishing lakes with maps of the shorelines plus information about the types of fish found in each lake. The state record for each species is listed.

Steck, George. *Grand Canyon Loop Hikes I.* Chockstone Press, 1989. These long trips all involve extensive off-trail hiking with difficult route finding, cliffs, and major changes in elevation. Experienced Grand Canyon hikers who are well-conditioned and mentally prepared can plan adventurous outings with the detailed descriptions.

Steck, George. *Grand Canyon Loop Hikes II.* Chockstone Press, 1997. This newer and larger book offers additional challenging loops.

Stevenson, Jeffrey L. *Rim Country Mountain Biking.* Boulder, CO: Pruett Publishing, 1995. The 63 rides on the Mogollon Rim range from easy to technical; maps and elevation profiles show the way.

Thybony, Scott. *Official Guide to Hiking the Grand Canyon.* Grand Canyon Assoc., 1994. Introduction and guide to the best-known trails of the Grand Canyon.

Tighe, Kelly and Susan Moran. *On the Arizona Trail: A Guide for Hikers, Cyclists, & Equestrians.* Boulder, CO: Pruett Publishing, 1998. The first guidebook to the Arizona Trail takes you all the way from Mexico to Utah with detailed descriptions. New trail sections continue to be constructed, so you'll need to check for the latest conditions, yet this book makes a great place to start planning your trip.

Warren, Scott S. *Exploring Arizona's Wild Areas; A Guide for Hikers, Backpackers, Climbers, X-C Skiers, & Paddlers.* Seattle: The Mountaineers, 1996. Although the author covers only the designated wildernesses, the 87 described will keep you busy for a long time.

Waterman, Laura, and Guy Waterman. *Backwoods Ethics: Environmental Issues for Hikers and Campers.* Stone Wall Press, 1994. Thoughtful commentaries on how hikers can explore the wilderness with minimal impact. Case histories dramatize the need to protect the environment.

RIVER-RUNNING AND BOATING

Abbey, Edward. *Down the River.* New York: E.P. Dutton, 1991. Abbey expresses joy and concern in a series of thoughtful, witty, and wide-ranging essays on the American West.

Belknap, Buzz. *Grand Canyon River Guide.* Westwater Books, 1990. Covers the 288 miles of Colorado River through Marble and Grand Canyons between Lees Ferry and Lake Mead.

Crumbo, Kim. *A River Runner's Guide to the History of the Grand Canyon.* Boulder: Johnson Books, 1981. Highly readable guide with a foreword by Edward Abbey.

Kelsey, Michael R. *Boater's Guide to Lake Powell.* Treasure Chest Publications, 1991. This comprehensive guide will help you explore the lake, whether traveling in a small inflatable raft, as the author did, or a more luxurious craft. Includes many maps, photos, and hiking descriptions.

Ryan, Kathleen Jo (photographer and producer). *Writing Down the River: Into the Heart of the Grand Canyon.* Flagstaff: Northland Publishing, 1998. Fifteen of today's best female writers tell of their experiences in the Grand Canyon. Impressive color photos illustrate the pages.

Simmons, George C., and David L. Gaskill. *River Runner's Guide to the Canyons of the Green and Colorado Rivers: With Emphasis on Geologic Features, Vol. III.* Flagstaff: Northland Publishing, 1969. This volume covers Marble Canyon and Grand Canyon. It's the only river guidebook to describe the fascinating geology mile by mile through the Grand Canyon National Park.

Slingluff, Jim. *Verde River Recreation Guide.* San Marino, CA: Golden West Publishers, 1990. This guide covers river-running on the Verde and its tributaries with boating tips and natural history.

Stephens, Hal G., and Eugene M. Shoemaker. *In the Footsteps of John Wesley Powell: An Album of Comparative Photographs of the Green and Colorado Rivers, 1871–72 and 1968.* Boulder: Johnson Books and The Powell Society, 1987. Fascinating photo album of identical river views snapped nearly 100 years apart. Photos show how little—and how much—the forces of erosion, plants, and human beings have changed the Green and Colorado River Canyons. The text describes geologic features of each of the 110 pairs of photos. Maps show locations of camera stations.

Stevens, Larry. *The Colorado River in Grand Canyon: A Comprehensive Guide to Its Natural and Human History.* Flagstaff: Red Lake Books, 1998. The introduction and maps guide you from Lees Ferry to Lake Mead with descriptions of geology, Indian history, exploration, flora, and fauna.

HISTORY

Albano, Bob, ed. *Days of Destiny.* Phoenix: Arizona Highways Wild West Series, 1996. Twenty stories about lawmen and desperados and the twisting fates they met.

Chaput, Don. *Dr. Goodfellow, Physician to the Gunfighters, Scholar, and Bon Vivant.* Westernlore Press, 1996. The life of the doctor who lived in Tombstone during its wildest years and patched up Virgil Earp and other shooting victims.

Cline, Platt. *They Came to the Mountain: The Story of Flagstaff's Beginnings.* Flagstaff: Northern Arizona University with Northland Publishing, 1976. Highly readable account of Flagstaff's founding and early years. The author has completed his trilogy on the area with *Mountain Town: Flagstaff's First Century* (1994) and *Mountain Campus: The Story of Northern Arizona University* (1983).

Coolidge, Dane. *Arizona Cowboys.* Tucson: University of Arizona Press, 1984. Working the range in the early 1900s.

Crampton, C. Gregory. *Land of Living Rock.* New York: Alfred A. Knopf, Inc., 1972, 1985. Story of the geology, Indians, early explorers, and settlers of the high plateaus in Arizona, Utah, and Nevada. Well-illustrated with color and black-and-white photos, maps, and diagrams.

Crampton, C. Gregory. *Standing Up Country.* New York: Alfred A. Knopf, Inc., 1964, 1983. Illustrated historical account of the people who came to the canyon lands of Arizona and Utah—Indians, explorers, outlaws, miners, settlers, and scientists.

Dellenbaugh, Frederick S. *A Canyon Voyage: A Narrative of the Second Powell Expedition Down the Green-Colorado River from Wyoming, and the Expeditions on Land, in the Years 1871 and 1872.* Tucson: University of Arizona Press, reprinted 1984. Dellenbaugh served as artist and assistant topographer on the expedition.

Erwin, Allen A. *The Southwest of John Horton Slaughter.* The Arthur H. Clark Co., 1965, 1997. Slaughter's amazing life as a Civil War soldier, Texas Ranger, Indian campaign scout, and cattleman spanned the taming of the West.

Farrell, Robert J., ed. *Manhunts & Massacres.* Phoenix: Arizona Highways Wild West Series, 1997. Eighteen true stories relate some of Arizona's most notorious holdups and massacres.

Farrell, Robert J., ed. *They Left Their Mark.* Phoenix: Arizona Highways Wild West Series, 1997. Sixteen stories of exceptional heroes and characters from Spanish explorer Juan Bautista de Anza to the quiet Pima soldier who helped raise the flag over Iwo Jima.

Faulk, Odie B. *Arizona: A Short History.* Norman, OK: University of Oklahoma Press, 1979. Popular account of Arizona from the first days of European exploration through the territorial years and statehood.

Fontana, Bernard L. *Entrada: The Legacy of Spain & Mexico in the United States.* Tucson: Southwest Parks and Monuments Assoc., 1994 The author guides the reader in text and photos to parks across the country where this legacy has been preserved.

Forrest, Earle R. *Arizona's Dark and Bloody Ground.* Tucson: University of Arizona Press, 1936, 1984. An account of the ruthless Pleasant Valley War between cattle and sheep ranchers.

"The Heart of Ambos Nogales." *The Journal of Arizona History.* Vol. 17, No. 2 (Summer 1976): page 161. The story of Nogales.

Hinton, Richard J. *The Handbook to Arizona: Its Resources, History, Towns, Mines, Ruins, and Scenery.* First published by Payot, Upham and Co. in 1878; reprinted by Arizona Silhouettes in 1954. This volume gives a clear picture of Arizona's early years.

Howard, Kathleen L., and Diana F. Pardu. *Inventing the Southwest: The Fred Harvey Company and Native American Art.* Flagstaff: Northland Publishing, 1996. Illustrated history of how the partnership of the Santa Fe Railroad and Fred Harvey Company brought America and the Southwest Indians together.

Hughes, J. Donald. *In the House of Stone and Light.* Grand Canyon Assoc., 1978. A well-illustrated history of the Grand Canyon from the early Indians to the modern park.

Iverson, Peter J. *Barry Goldwater.* Norman, OK: University of Oklahoma Press, 1997. This biography focuses on the famous senator's influence on Arizona politics—still felt today—and how he can be understood as a man of his time and place.

Johnson, G. Wesley, Jr. *Phoenix: Valley of the Sun.* Continental Heritage Press, 1982. Excellent text and photos trace the development of Phoenix from the ancient Hohokam to the modern metropolis.

Lavender, David. *River Runners of the Grand Canyon.* Tucson: University of Arizona Press, 1985. Descriptions of action-packed adventures on the river, beginning with Powell's trip in 1869 through the closing of Glen Canyon Dam in the early 1960s.

Lummis, Charles F. *Some Strange Corners of Our Country.* Tucson: University of Arizona Press, 1891, 1892, reprinted in 1989. Step back a century to visit the Southwest's Indian country, Grand Canyon, Petrified Forest, and Montezuma Castle.

Mitchell, John D. *Lost Mines of the Great Southwest.* Glorieta, NM: Rio Grande Press, 1933, 1984. Who isn't enthralled by legends of lost treasure? You'll reach for a pick and shovel after reading these.

Pattie, James Ohio. *The Personal Narrative of James O. Pattie.* Missoula: Mountain Press Publishing Co., 1988. Reprint of 1831 edition. An early fur trapper, who claimed to be the first white American to see the Grand Canyon, tells of his experiences in the wild lands of the West during the 1820s.

Powell, J.W. *The Exploration of the Colorado River and Its Canyons.* Mineola, NY: Dover Publications, reprinted 1961 and Penguin USA, reprinted 1997. Powell relates the story of his epic 1869 expedition—the first running of the Colorado River through the Grand Canyon—along with a description of the Grand Canyon and travels in the region. His encounters with Indian cultures provide a glimpse of their traditional ways.

Rusho, W.L., and C. Gregory Crampton. *Lees Ferry: Desert River Crossing.* Salt Lake City: Cricket Productions, 1992. A historical study of Lees Ferry, with over 135 rare and unusual photographs.

Sheridan, Thomas E. *Arizona: A History.* Tucson: University of Arizona Press, 1995. This volume takes the reader from paleolithic times to the 1990s.

Sikorsky, Robert. *Quest for the Dutchman's Gold: The 100-Year Mystery; The Facts, Myths and Legends of the Lost Dutchman Mine and the Superstition Mountains.* San Marino, CA: Golden West, 1991. The history of the most famous lost mine of all.

Smith, Dean, and others. *Arizona Album; The Road to Statehood.* Phoenix: Arizona Highways, 1987. Meet Indians, politicians, lawmen, miners, women, gamblers, and sports enthusiasts in the years leading to statehood.

Summerhayes, Martha. *Vanished Arizona*. Lincoln: University of Nebraska Press, 1979. Reprint of 1911 Salem Press second edition. In 1874 a young New England woman marries an army officer, then they set off together for some of the wildest corners of the West. Her accounts bring frontier Arizona life into sharp focus.

Trimble, Marshall. *Arizona Adventure: Action-Packed True Tales of Early Arizona*. San Marino, CA: Golden West, 1994. Nineteen stories from Arizona's Old West.

Trimble, Marshall. *The Law of the Gun*. Phoenix: Arizona Highways Wild West Series, 1997. Trimble sets the record straight about gunfighters in the Old West, then relates stories about famous lawmen and villains.

Trimble, Marshall. *Roadside History of Arizona*. Missoula: Mountain Press Publishing Co., 1986. These fascinating tales, with many historic photos, have been organized by region and highway.

Wagoner, Jay J. *Arizona Territory 1863–1912: A Political History*. Tucson: University of Arizona Press, 1970. Excellent history of the territorial years.

Woody, Clara T., and Milton L. Schwartz. *Globe, Arizona*. Tucson: The Arizona Historical Society, 1977. Stories of early miners, pioneers, Indian battles, and the Graham-Tewksbury feud, also known as the Pleasant Valley War.

ARCHAEOLOGY

Ambler, J. Richard. *The Anasazi: Prehistoric Peoples of the Four Corners Region*. Flagstaff: Museum of Northern Arizona, 1977, 1983. One of the best overviews of the ancestral pueblo people's history.

Andrews, John P., and Todd W. Bostwick. *Desert Farmers at the River's Edge: The Hohokam and Pueblo Grande*. Phoenix: Pueblo Grande Museum and Cultural Park, 1997. The authors trace this sophisticated prehistoric people from their origins, through their daily life in the Sonoran Desert, to the end of their civilization. The fine text has many illustrations.

Grant, Campbell. *Canyon de Chelly: Its People and Rock Art*. Tucson: University of Arizona Press, 1978. The author describes the geology, archaeology, and history of the canyons. Nearly half the well-illustrated text is devoted to a discussion of the wealth of petroglyphs and pictographs left by the ancestral pueblo people, Hopi, and Navajo.

Gregonis, Linda, and Karl Reinhard. *Hohokam Indians of the Tucson Basin*. Tucson: University of Arizona Press, 1979. Introduction to the prehistoric Hohokam Indians.

Lister, Robert, and Florence Lister. *Those Who Came Before: Southwestern Archaeology in the National Park System*. Tucson: University of Arizona Press, 1983 and Albuquerque: University of New Mexico Press, 1994. A well-illustrated guide to the history, artifacts, and ruins of prehistoric Indian cultures in the Southwest. Includes descriptions of the parks and monuments that contain these sites today.

McGregor, John C. *Southwestern Archaeology*. Champaign: University of Illinois Press, 1982. If you're curious why archaeologists like their work and how they do it, this book presents the motivations and techniques of this special group of scientists. It also describes cultures and artifacts from the earliest known peoples to the present.

Noble, David Grant. *Ancient Ruins of the Southwest*. Flagstaff: Northland Publishing, 2000. A well-illustrated guide to the prehistoric ruins of Arizona, New Mexico, Colorado, and Utah.

Oppelt, Norman T. *Guide to Prehistoric Ruins of the Southwest.* Boulder: Pruett Publishing Co., 1989. An introduction to ancient cultures with descriptions of more than 200 sites in Arizona, New Mexico, Colorado, and Utah.

Patterson, Alex. *A Field Guide to Rock Art Symbols of the Greater Southwest.* Boulder: Johnson Books, 1992. A dictionary-style guide to petroglyphs and pictographs grouped by subject with many illustrations.

Viele, Catherine. *Voices in the Canyon.* Tucson: Southwest Parks and Monuments Assoc., 1980. Highly readable and well-illustrated book about the ancestral pueblo people and their villages of Betatakin, Keet Seel, and Inscription House.

ARIZONA INDIANS OF TODAY

Courlander, Harold. *The Fourth World of the Hopis: The Epic Story of the Hopi Indians as Preserved in Their Legends & Traditions.* Albuquerque: University of New Mexico Press, 1987.

Courlander, Harold. *Hopi Voices: Recollections, Traditions, and Narratives of the Hopi Indians.* Albuquerque: University of New Mexico Press, 1982. A selection of 74 Hopi narrations explaining their mythology, history, exploits, games, and animal stories. One of the best books on Hopi culture.

Dedera, Don. *Navajo Rugs: How to Find, Evaluate, Buy and Care for Them.* Flagstaff: Northland Publishing, 1996. A history of Navajo weaving, including regional styles and practical advice.

Dittert, Alfred, Jr., and Fred Plog. *Generations in Clay: Pueblo Pottery of the American Southwest.* Flagstaff: Northland Publishing, 1980. An introduction to the pottery of the Pueblo Indians, both prehistoric and modern. Well-illustrated with black-and-white and color photos.

Dozier, Edward P. *Hano, A Tewa Indian Com-munity in Arizona.* Orlando: Holt, Rinehart and Winston, 1966. A study of Tewa history, society, religion, and livelihood.

Dyk, Walter (recorded by). *Left Handed Son of Old Man Hat: A Navajo Autobiography.* Lincoln: University of Nebraska Press, 1995, original copyright 1938. This Navajo relates his story of growing up in the late 1800s.

Evers, Larry, ed. *The South Corner of Time.* Tucson: University of Arizona Press, 1980. Stories and poetry by contemporary Indians of the Hopi, Navajo, Tohono O'odham, and Yaqui tribes.

Fontana, Bernard. *Of Earth and Little Rain.* Tucson: University of Arizona Press, 1990. Essays and photos on life of the Tohono O'odham Indians.

Gillmore, Frances, and Louisa Wetherill. *Traders to the Navajos.* Albuquerque: University of New Mexico Press, 1934, 1983. The Wetherills lived in and explored the Monument Valley region, trading with the Navajo. The authors tell stories about lost mines, early travelers, and the Navajo people.

Gilpin, Laura. *The Enduring Navajo.* Austin: University of Texas Press, 1994. An excellent book of photographs of the Navajo people, their homes, land, ceremonies, crafts, tribal government, and trading posts.

Jacka, Lois Essary, and Jerry Jacka. *Art of the Hopi, Contemporary Journeys on Ancient Pathways.* Flagstaff: Northland Publishing, 1998. Beautiful color photos on almost every page of this large-format book show the skills, versatility, and variety of Hopi artists.

James, Harry C. *Pages from Hopi History.* Tucson: University of Arizona Press, 1974. Beginning with the tribe's mythical entrance into this world, the author traces Hopi history through early migrations, encounters with the Spanish, difficulties with Mexicans and Navajo, and resistance to U.S. authority, to their life today.

Locke, Raymond F. *The Book of the Navajo.* Holloway House Publishing, 1992. Navajo legends, art, culture, and history, from early to modern times.

Luckert, Karl W. *Coyoteway: A Navajo Holyway Healing Ceremonial.* Tucson: The University of Arizona Press and Flagstaff: Museum of Northern Arizona Press, 1979. A rare look at an important Navajo ceremony. It requires nine days and involves chanting, fire-making, sand painting, and other rituals. Photos and chant translations provide a peek into intricate Navajo beliefs.

Page, Susanne, and Jake Page. *Hopi.* New York: Harry N. Abrams, Inc., 1982 and Abradale Press, 1994. The authors record Hopi spiritual life in text and large color photos, revealing aspects of everyday living, ceremonies, and sacred places rarely seen by outsiders.

Simmons, Leo, ed. *Sun Chief: The Autobiography of a Hopi Indian.* New Haven: Yale University Press, 1963. A Hopi tells of his experiences growing up in both the Hopi and Anglo worlds, then returning to traditional ways.

Suntracks, Larry Evers. *Hopi Photographers/Hopi Images.* Tucson: University of Arizona Press, 1983. The pages feature photography of the Hopi from 1880 to 1980, including historic photos by Anglos and modern work by Hopi photographers; photos appear in black-and-white and color.

Titiev, Mischa. *Old Oraibi: A Study of the Hopi Indians of Third Mesa.* Albuquerque: University of New Mexico Native American Studies, 1992. Detailed account of Hopi society and ceremonies.

Webb, George. *A Pima Remembers.* Tucson: University of Arizona Press, 1959 (reprinted 1982). Traditional stories of the Pima Indians.

Wright, Barton. *Clowns of the Hopi.* Flagstaff: Northland Publishing, 1994. These characters amuse audiences while protecting traditions. The book couples explanations about their antics—which often have a deeper meaning—with drawings and historic and modern photos.

Wright, Barton. *Hopi Kachinas: The Complete Guide to Collecting Kachina Dolls.* Flagstaff: Northland Publishing, 1985. The author explains and illustrates the wide variety of dolls—from clowns to ogres.

Wright, Margaret. *Hopi Silver.* Flagstaff: Northland Publishing, 1998. History and examples of Hopi silversmithing.

Yava, Albert. *Big Falling Snow.* Albuquerque: University of New Mexico Press, 1992. A Tewa-Hopi discusses the history and traditions of the Tewa and Hopi, including conflicts with missionaries and government officials who tried to Americanize the tribes.

Zolbrod, Paul G. *Diné bahané: The Navajo Creation Story.* Albuquerque: University of New Mexico Press, 1988. Deities, people, and animals come to life in this translation of Navajo mythology.

NATURAL SCIENCES

Alcock, John. *In a Desert Garden: Love & Death Among the Insects.* W.W. Norton, 1997. The author brings both the keen eye of a scientist and the light-hearted view of a gardener as he relates observations of the insect world at his home in the Sonoran Desert.

Arnberger, Leslie P., and Jeanne R. Janish. *Flowers of the Southwest Mountains.* Tucson: Southwest Parks and Monuments Assoc., 1982.

Descriptions and illustrations of flowers and common trees found above 7,000 feet.

Barnes, F.A. *Canyon Country Geology for the Layman and Rockhound.* Treasure Chest Publications, 1978. Geologic history and guide to rockhounding with an emphasis on southeastern Utah and adjacent Arizona.

Bowers, Janice Emily. *Fear Falls Away; And Other Essays from Hard and Rocky Places.* Tucson: University of Arizona Press, 1997. The author invites us along to enjoy nature, whether rambling through the forest or climbing the face of Baboquivari.

Bowers, Janice Emily. *100 Desert Wildflowers of the Southwest.* Tucson: Southwest Parks and Monuments Assoc., 1989. A general introduction with brief descriptions, including a color photo of each flower.

Bowers, Janice Emily. *100 Roadside Wildflowers of Southwest Woodlands.* Tucson: Southwest Parks and Monuments Assoc., 1989. Brief descriptions and color photos of 100 flowers found above 4,500 feet.

Chronic, Halka. *Roadside Geology of Arizona.* Missoula: Mountain Press Publishing Co., 1986. This book—well-illustrated with photos, maps, and diagrams—has been organized along major highway routes. It also covers some national parks and national monuments.

Cunningham, Richard L. *50 Common Birds of the Southwest.* Tucson: Southwest Parks and Monuments Assoc., 1990. Each bird is represented by a color photo and description of migration, feeding, and nesting habits; the text includes Spanish and Latin names.

Desert Botanical Garden staff, and others. *Desert Wildflowers; A Guide for Identifying, Locating, and Enjoying Arizona Wildflowers and Cactus Blossoms.* Phoenix: Arizona Highways, 1997. Text and color photos take you through the seasons in the different desert regions of the state and provide practical advice for growing your own native plants at home.

Dodge, Natt N., and Jeanne R. Janish. *Flowers of the Southwest Deserts.* Tucson: Southwest Parks and Monuments Assoc., 1985. Desert plant and flower guide for elevations under 4,500 feet.

Doolittle, Jerome. *Canyons and Mesas.* The American Wilderness Series. New York: Time-Life Books, 1974. Text and photos give a feel for the ruggedly beautiful country of northern Arizona and adjacent Utah and Colorado.

Earle, W. Hubert. *Cacti of the Southwest.* Phoenix: Desert Botanical Garden, 1980. Lists the 152 known species of cacti in the Southwest, with black-and-white and color photos.

Elmore, Francis H., and Jeanne R. Janish. *Shrubs and Trees of the Southwest Uplands.* Tucson: Southwest Parks and Monuments Assoc., 1976. Color-coded pages help locate plants and trees found above 4,500 feet.

Fischer, Pierre C. *70 Common Cacti of the Southwest.* Tucson: Southwest Parks and Monuments Assoc., 1989. Each cactus is represented by a color photo and description.

Gray, Mary Taylor. *Watchable Birds of the Southwest.* Missoula, MT: Mountain Press Publishing, 1995. Color pictures reveal 68 species in wetlands, open-country, and high-country habitats.

Halfpenny, James, and Elizabeth Biesiot. *A Field Guide: Mammal Tracking in North America.* Boulder: Johnson Books, 1988. No need to guess what animal passed by. This well-illustrated guide shows how to read the prints of creatures large and small. More determined detectives can peruse the intriguing scatology chapter.

Hare, Trevor. *Poisonous Dwellers of the Desert.* Tucson: Southwest Parks and Monuments

Assoc., 1995. The text describes creatures to watch out for—poisonous insects, snakes, and the Gila monster—with advice on insecticides and bite treatment. Also listed are some nonvenomous animals often mistakenly believed to be poisonous.

Hodge, Carle. *All About Saguaros.* Phoenix: Arizona Highways, 1997. Text and color photos take you through the life of this huge cactus and relate how important it is to the Tohono O'odham Indians and to wildlife.

McKee, Edwin D. *Ancient Landscapes of the Grand Canyon Region.* Flagstaff: Northland Publishing, 1982. Brief account of the geologic history of the Grand Canyon.

Nations, Dale, and Edmund Stump. *Geology of Arizona.* Dubuque: Kendall/Hunt Publishing Co., 1997. Learn how time and geologic processes have formed the state's remarkable natural features. The book provides a comprehensive introduction to geology with good photos and illustrations.

Olin, George. *House in the Sun: A Natural History of the Sonoran Desert.* Tucson: Southwest Parks and Monuments Assoc., 1994. This guide, illustrated with many color photos, portrays the Sonoran Desert—why it exists and how life has adapted to it. The text also tells how *you* can adapt to the sometimes harsh conditions there, enjoying the desert in safety.

Olin, George, and Dale Thompson. *Mammals of the Southwest Deserts.* Tucson: Southwest Parks and Monuments Assoc., 1982. Well-illustrated with black-and-white and color drawings.

Peterson, Roger Tory. *A Field Guide to Western Birds.* Chapters Publishing, 1998. Well-illustrated with drawings.

Phillips, Steven J. and Patricia Wentworth Comus. *A Natural History of the Sonoran Desert.* Tucson: Arizona-Sonora Desert Museum, Berkeley: University of California Press, 2000. This one-stop 628-page guide tells of the wonders of the Sonoran desert. Illustrated pages describe the geological setting and climate and provide a guide to the plants and wildlife that make their homes here.

Powell, Lawrence Clark, and Michael Collier. *Where Water Flows: The Rivers of Arizona.* Flagstaff: Northland Publishing, 1980. Essays and beautiful color photos covering seven of Arizona's rivers.

Smith, Robert L. *Venomous Animals of Arizona.* Tucson: University of Arizona Press, 1982. Ever wonder about a scorpion's love life? Good descriptions of poisonous insects and animals, with medical notes.

Sweet, Muriel. *Common Edible and Useful Plants of the West.* Happy Camp, CA: Naturegraph Publishers, 1976. Nontechnical descriptions of plants and trees giving their importance as food, medicines, and other uses. Most of these helpful plants were first discovered by Native Americans and later used by pioneer settlers.

Whitney, Stephen. *A Field Guide to the Grand Canyon.* Mountaineers Books, 1996. Excellent, well-illustrated guide to the Canyon's geology, early Indians, flowers, trees, birds, and animals. Most of the information also applies to other canyons on the Colorado Plateau. Includes practical advice for visiting and hiking in the Grand Canyon.

SELECTED FICTION

Coleman, Jane Candia. *Doc Holliday's Woman.* Warner Books, 1995. Based on a true story of Kate Elder who rescued Doc from a hanging and saw him fight at the OK Corral. The author has also published books of Western poetry.

Coleman, Jane Candia. *Stories from Mesa Country.* Swallow Press/Ohio University Press,

1991. Fourteen short stories illustrate how people—especially women—of the old West dealt with their difficulties.

Grey, Zane. This prolific writer produced 131 novels, including many about Arizona. He built a cabin in the woods below the Mogollon Rim, then made frequent visits during the 1920s. He enjoyed setting off on hunting trips to gather both trophies for his walls and stories for new books.

Ríos, Alberto Alvaro. *Pig Cookies and Other Stories*. Thirteen short stories bring a northern Mexican village to life; the author was born in Nogales, Arizona.

Taylor, Lawrence J., and Maeve Hickey. *The Road to Mexico*. Tucson: University of Arizona Press, 1997. An amusing account of a strange journey, with many cultural insights, from Tucson to Nogales and into Mexico.

Turner, Nancy E. *These is My Words, The Diary of Sarah Agnes Prine 1881–1901 Arizona Territories*. ReganBooks, 1998. A novel about a woman growing up on the rough frontier.

Urrea, Luis Alberto. *In Search of Snow*. HarperCollins, 1994. A novel of a Don Quixote-like character and his pal who search for life and love in the Arizona desert in the mid-1950s.

Williams, Jeanne. *Home Mountain*. St. Martin's Paperbacks, 1990. A love story set on the east side of the Chiricahuas about a woman who followed her dreams to Arizona and met a fearless outlaw and a powerful ranger in the 1880s.

CHILDREN'S BOOKS

Lowell, Susan, and Jim Harris. *The Three Little Javelinas*. Rising Moon, 1992. A Southwest version of the three little pigs story with wonderful illustrations. It's also available as a bilingual Spanish-English edition.

Moreillon, Judi, and Michael Chiago. *Sing Down the Rain*. Kiva Publishing, 1997. Poetic account of the Tohono O'odham Indians' traditional life in the desert; with illustrations.

Skrepcinski, Denice, and others. *Cody Coyote Cooks*. Tricycle Press, 1996. A Southwest cookbook for kids with coyote tales and recipes that kids can follow.

REFERENCE

Arizona Atlas & Gazetteer. Freeport, ME: Delorme, 1996. Topographic maps at 1:250,000 scale show great detail along with grids for G.P.S. use, but they are difficult to read.

Arizona Road & Recreation Atlas. Berkeley, CA: Benchmark Maps, 1996. Exceptionally accurate and easy to read maps available in either atlas or sheet form at 1:400,000 scale. Both versions include shaded landscape and color-coded land-ownership maps.

Cheek, Lawrence W., and others. *Photographing Arizona; Practical Techniques to Improve Your Pictures*. Phoenix: Arizona Highways, 1992. So how do the Arizona Highways photographers get such spectacular results? Find out in this well-illustrated book.

Comeaux, Malcolm L. *Arizona: A Geography*. Geographies of the United States series. Boulder: Westview Press, 1981. A 336-page volume full of information on Arizona geography, settlement, population, resources, and agriculture.

Walker, Henry P., and Don Bufkin. *Historical Atlas of Arizona*. Norman, OK: University of Oklahoma Press, 1986. Clear maps and concise text cover the geography, Indian tribes, exploration, and development of Arizona.

CUISINE

Fischer, Al, and Mildred Fischer. *Arizona Cook Book*. San Marino, CA: Golden West, 1983. A culinary guide to the state, including Indian, Western, and barbecue cuisine. Prepare your own cactus jelly and other delicacies.

Kavena, Juanita Tiger. *Hopi Cookery*. Tucson: University of Arizona Press, 1980. Learn how to make piki bread, fashion a yucca pie, fix squash and fresh corn casserole, and bake a prairie dog.

Mann, Betsey. *By Request: Most Wanted Recipes from Arizona's Favorite Restaurants*. Flagstaff: Northland Publishing, 1998. You can cook up some of the most popular dishes from the menus of neighborhood to five-star restaurants.

Hiking Trails Index

Index

ARCHITECTURE

BIKING

BIRDWATCHING

CASINOS

PANORAMAS

RODEOS

WATERFALLS

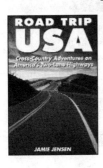

see the USA your way

Hostelling is a special kind of travel that exposes us to new people and cultures, and changes us in ways that impact us for the rest of our lives.

Hostelling International-American Youth Hostels has over 125 unique hostels throughout the U.S. Our hostels are designed to promote interaction among guests. We're on and off the beaten path in high-rise buildings, log cabins, lighthouses and tepees.

Experience our people and culture in an affordable way. Experience hostelling. Experience America!

To become a member,
visit our Web site at **www.hiayh.org**.

U.S.~METRIC CONVERSION

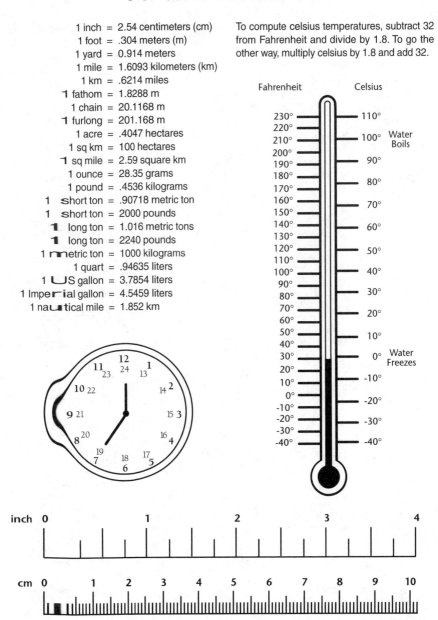

1 inch	=	2.54 centimeters (cm)
1 foot	=	.304 meters (m)
1 yard	=	0.914 meters
1 mile	=	1.6093 kilometers (km)
1 km	=	.6214 miles
1 fathom	=	1.8288 m
1 chain	=	20.1168 m
1 furlong	=	201.168 m
1 acre	=	.4047 hectares
1 sq km	=	100 hectares
1 sq mile	=	2.59 square km
1 ounce	=	28.35 grams
1 pound	=	.4536 kilograms
1 short ton	=	.90718 metric ton
1 short ton	=	2000 pounds
1 long ton	=	1.016 metric tons
1 long ton	=	2240 pounds
1 metric ton	=	1000 kilograms
1 quart	=	.94635 liters
1 US gallon	=	3.7854 liters
1 Imperial gallon	=	4.5459 liters
1 nautical mile	=	1.852 km

To compute celsius temperatures, subtract 32 from Fahrenheit and divide by 1.8. To go the other way, multiply celsius by 1.8 and add 32.

Fahrenheit   Celsius

230° — 110°
220°
210° — 100° Water Boils
200°
190° — 90°
180°
170° — 80°
160° — 70°
150°
140° — 60°
130°
120° — 50°
110°
100° — 40°
90°
80° — 30°
70°
60° — 20°
50°
40° — 10°
30°
20° — 0° Water Freezes
10° — -10°
0°
-10° — -20°
-20° — -30°
-30°
-40° — -40°

inch 0   1   2   3   4

cm 0 1 2 3 4 5 6 7 8 9 10